Contemporary Literary Criticism

Volume 14

Contemporary Literary Criticism

Excerpts from Criticism
of the Works of Today's
Novelists, Poets, Playwrights,
and Other Creative Writers

Dedria Bryfonski
Laurie Lanzen Harris
Editors

Gale Research Company
Book Tower
Detroit, Michigan 48226

STAFF

Dedria Bryfonski, Laurie Lanzen Harris, *Editors*

Emily W. Barrett, Laura A. Buch, Jean C. Stine,
Carolyn Voldrich, *Assistant Editors*

Phyllis Carmel Mendelson, *Contributing Editor*

Carolyn Voldrich, *Production Editor*

Linda M. Pugliese, *Manuscript Coordinator*
Thomas E. Gunton, *Research Coordinator*
Anna H. Crabtree, Catherine E. Daligga, Jeanne A. Gough,
Marsha R. Mackenzie, Nancy C. Mazzara, Lizbeth A. Purdy, *Editorial Assistants*

L. Elizabeth Hardin, *Permissions Coordinator*
Dawn L. McGinty, Filomena Sgambati, *Permissions Assistants*

Library of Congress Catalog Card Number 76-38938
ISBN 0-8103-0101-6

Contents

Authors in this volume:

Preface

Literary criticism is indispensable to the layman or scholar attempting to evaluate and understand creative writing—whether his subject is one poem, one writer, one idea, one school, or a general trend in contemporary writing. Literary criticism is itself a collective term for several kinds of critical writing: criticism may be normative, descriptive, interpretive, textual, appreciative, generic. Conscientious students must consult numerous sources in order to become familiar with the criticism pertinent to their subjects.

Until now, there has been nothing resembling an ongoing encyclopedia of current literary criticism, bringing together in one series criticism of all the various kinds from widely diverse sources. *Contemporary Literary Criticism* is intended to be such a comprehensive reference work.

The Plan of the Work

Contemporary Literary Criticism presents significant passages from the published criticism of work by well-known creative writers—novelists and short story writers, poets and playwrights. Some creative writers, like James Baldwin and Paul Goodman, are probably better known for their expository work than for their fiction, and so discussion of their nonfiction is included.

Contemporary Literary Criticism is not limited to material concerning long-established authors like Eliot, Faulkner, Hemingway, and Auden, although these and other writers of similar stature are included. Attention is also given to two other groups of writers—writers of considerable public interest—about whose work criticism is hard to locate. These are the newest writers (like Bernard Pomerance, John Irving, and Fran Lebowitz) and the contributors to the well-loved but nonscholarly genres of mystery and science fiction (like Georges Simenon, Agatha Christie, Robert Heinlein, and Arthur C. Clarke).

The definition of *contemporary* is necessarily arbitrary. For purposes of selection for *CLC,* contemporary writers are those who are either now living or who have died since January 1, 1960. Contemporary criticism is more loosely defined as that written any time during the past twenty-five years or so and currently relevant to the evaluation of the writer under discussion.

Each volume of *CLC* lists about 150 authors, with an average of about five excerpts from critical articles or reviews being given for the works of each author. Altogether, there are about 750 individual excerpts in each volume taken from about 100 books and several hundred issues of some one hundred general magazines, literary reviews, and scholarly journals. Each excerpt is fully identified for the convenience of readers who may wish to consult the entire chapter, article, or review excerpted. Each volume covers writers not previously included and also provides significant new criticism pertaining to authors included in earlier volumes.

Beginning with Volume 10, *CLC* contains an appendix which lists the sources from which material has been reprinted in that volume. It does not, however, list books or periodicals merely consulted during the preparation of the volume.

A Note on Bio-Bibliographical References and Page Citations

Notes in many entries directing the user to consult *Contemporary Authors* for detailed biographical and bibliographical information refer to a series of biographical reference books published by the Gale Research Company since 1962, which now includes detailed biographical sketches of more than 57,000 authors who have lived since 1960, many of whose careers began during the post-World War II period, or earlier.

Beginning with *CLC,* Volume 5, the method for referring to pages in the original sources was standardized. Page numbers appear after each fragment (unless the entire essay was contained on one page). To make *CLC* even more helpful to students and scholars, the editors have standardized the format for the credit line following each entry. Beginning with Volume 14, all credit lines include a complete essay title, volume and issue number for all journal entries, inclusive pagination for all essays, and total pagination for all books. An asterisk following a credit line indicates that the essay or book contains information on more than one author.

Acknowledgments

The editors wish to thank the copyright holders of the excerpts included in this volume for their permission to use the material, and the staffs of the Detroit Public Library, Wayne State University Library, and the libraries of the University of Michigan for making their resources available to us.

Authors Forthcoming in *CLC*

With the publication of *Contemporary Literary Criticism,* Volume 12, the series has expanded its scope to encompass songwriters, filmmakers, cartoonists, screenwriters, producers, and other creative writers whose work is often evaluated from a literary perspective. These writers take their place with the novelists, poets, dramatists, and short story writers who will continue to be the primary focus of *CLC.* Volume 15 will include criticism on a number of authors not previously listed, and will also feature criticism of newer works of authors included in earlier volumes. Volume 16 will focus on filmmakers and their works.

To Be Included in Volume 15

John Ashbery (American poet)--Will feature criticism on new collection, *As We Know*

Margaret Atwood (Canadian poet, novelist, and critic)--Will feature criticism on new novel, *Life Before Man*

James Baldwin (American novelist, short story writer, and essayist)--Will feature criticism on new novel, *Just Above My Head*

Elizabeth Bishop (American poet, essayist, and critic)

Gwendolyn Brooks (American poet and novelist)

Robert Francis (American poet)

Gabriel Garcia Márquez (Colombian novelist--Will feature criticism on new novel, *In Evil Hour*

Peter Handke (German dramatist)--Will feature criticism on new play, *They Are Dying Out*

Chester Himes (American novelist, short story writer, essayist)

Irving Layton (Canadian poet)

John Le Carré (British novelist)--Will feature criticism on new novel, *Smiley's People*

Doris Lessing (British novelist, short story writer)--Will feature criticism on new novels, *Shikasta* and *The Marriages Between Zones Three, Four, and Five*

Robert Lowell (American poet)

Eugenio Montale (Italian poet, journalist, and critic)

A.G. Mojtabai (American novelist)--Will feature criticism on new novel, *A Stopping Place*

Dorothy Parker (American poet, short story writer, dramatist, and essayist)

Jacques Prévert (French poet, dramatist, and essayist)

Philip Roth (American novelist, short story writer)--Will feature criticism on new novel, *The Ghost Writer*

Mikhail Sholokov (Russian novelist and short story writer)

John Updike (American novelist, poet, short story writer, essayist)--Will feature criticism on new short story collection, *Problems*

To Be Included in Volume 16

Woody Allen (American Academy Award-winning filmmaker)

Bernardo Bertolucci (Italian poet and filmmaker)--Best known for the controversial film, *Last Tango in Paris*

Tod Browning (American filmmaker)--His credits include both silent and sound films, most notably horror films such as *Dracula* and *Freaks*

Luis Buñuel (Spanish filmmaker of surrealistic films)

Michael Cimino (American filmmaker)--Established himself as a director with the Academy Award-winning film, *The Deer Hunter*

Jean Cocteau (French filmmaker)--His technical expertise with special effects is evident in *Orphée*

Maya Deren (American filmmaker)--An important figure in the avant-garde cinema

Carl Dreyer (Danish filmmaker)--Emotional impact and visual beauty characterize films such as *La Passion de Jeanne d'Arc*

Federico Fellini (Italian filmmaker)--Blends elements of fantasy and autobiography in films, most notably, *8 1/2*

John Ford (American filmmaker)--Has made several classic westerns including *Stagecoach* and *The Searchers*

Alfred Hitchcock (British-born filmmaker)--Director of many classic thrillers

Elia Kazan (Turkish-born American filmmaker)--Director of *East of Eden* and the Academy Award-winning *On the Waterfront*

Stanley Kubrick (American filmmaker)--A pioneer in spectacular special effects

Akira Kurosawa (Japanese filmmaker)--When his *Rashomon* won the Grand Prix in Venice in 1951, the West first became aware of the Japanese film industry

George Lucas (American filmmaker)--Director of the immensely popular films *Star Wars* and *American Graffiti*

David and Albert Maysles (American documentary filmmakers)--Their credits include clear examples of cinéma verité, such as *Grey Gardens* and *Salesman*

Ken Russell (British filmmaker)--His films are flamboyant spectaculars; *Tommy* is an example

François Truffaut (French filmmaker)--A leading New Wave filmmaker, Truffaut has become the prototype of the auteur by writing, directing, and sometimes acting in his own films

Lina Wertmüller (Italian filmmaker)--Her films, for example, *Swept Away,* often involve themes of sexual stereotyping and struggles for supremacy.

A

AGNON, S(hmuel) Y(osef) 1888-1970

Born Shmuel Yosef Tchatsky in Buczacz, Galicia (formerly Austria-Hungary; now Poland), Agnon settled in Palestine (later Israel) in 1924 and remained there until his death. Agnon found the material for his fiction, which possesses an ironic, lyrical quality, in ancient Hebrew folklore. He was the recipient of the Nobel Prize for Literature in 1966, the first Israeli and the first author writing in Hebrew to receive this award. (See also *CLC*, Vols. 4, 8, and *Contemporary Authors*, Vols. 17-18; obituary, Vols. 25-28, rev. ed.; *Contemporary Authors Permanent Series*, Vol. 2.)

DAN JACOBSON

["Betrothed"] has some moments of lyrical description and of direct psychological notation which are immediately successful. Yet we are absolutely compelled—by the deliberate insubstantiality of its central events and characters, by its studied narrative disjunctions, and by the author's own interpolated comments—to take it allegorically. . . .

[Reading] Agnon's tales one feels that anything can happen next; and that the author fully intends that the secret of why one thing happens rather than another should remain his own. . . .

Confronted with a series of riddles to which I have no key, I am bound to suspect that my not having the key is the very point of the stories: that they are essentially fables about the universal failures in communication between God and man, and among men. This interpretation would perhaps be confirmed by what one knows of Agnon's passionate attachment to the Talmudic tradition, to the many centuries of devotional writing and study which came to a catastrophic end with the destruction of East European Jewry. In English his work hardly has the power to make us realise anew what that destruction must have meant to the author. But his Hebrew is, I believe, closely packed with evocations of the past; and it may well be that these constant echoes go a long way towards providing the ballast of common experience, the burden of necessity, for which the reader of his fantasies in any other language looks in vain.

Dan Jacobson, "Two Views of Agnon: 1. Dan Jacobson," in New Statesman *(© 1966 The Statesman & Nation Publishing Co. Ltd.), Vol. 72, No. 1865, December 9, 1966, p. 877.*

NAOMI SHEPHERD

[Agnon] is a writer of startling and total originality, resembling other Hebrew writers of the century almost as faintly as he does his European contemporaries.

He draws on vast knowledge of Jewish tradition—that of the commentaries and homilies of the Talmud and the folklore of the Hasidim. His use of their language, their dialectic, their rhetoric, is deliberately imitative, but the ends to which he turns this tradition are entirely his own. Though highly allusive, his prose style is simplicity itself. His range is enormous. . . .

Agnon is not a historical novelist in the accepted European sense: he writes of the last century partly from hearsay, from a kind of folk knowledge passed down from one generation of Jews to another. Nor is he entirely an elegist of a past age, for he can subject the past to satiric appraisal. Nor is he a moralist, though he uses the moralist's voice as a stylistic device. Much of his subject-matter would seem to indicate that he is a religious writer: but his intensely distinctive tone—a combination of the false-naive and the ironical—immediately sets him apart from the writer whose view of the world is dictated by his religious beliefs. His is certainly that recognisable Jewish irony which meets disaster with argument, seeking to reconcile the glories of the divine promise with the realities of the Jewish predicament.

No European writer has expressed more powerfully than Agnon the catastrophic break with the past marked by the First World War. His three great novels describe the culture of Diaspora Jewry at its peak (*The Bridal Canopy* 1931), the wasteland of that culture in Galicia after 1918 (*A Guest for the Night*—untranslated, 1939), and the unsuccessful struggle to reconcile the old world and the new, as seen in the adventures of a simple-minded, orthodox pioneer in Palestine (*Days Gone By*—untranslated, 1945). (p. 877)

In Agnon's stories, as in his novels, the recurring themes are those of perplexity, of wandering, of the chaos that prefigures death. In his secular stories, the family and the home compose a value like that of true faith, and just as obscure and difficult to achieve. Instead of the psychological determinism that runs through modern European writing, we have a kind of fatalism about relations between men and women. Agnon writes quietly, almost pedantically, about violent passions. . . .

The problem of translating Agnon is a very serious one. The fallacy of his translators is to believe that Agnon is writing in an archaic style. . . . Agnon does not write in deliberate archaisms, though his simplicity of style probably began as an attempt to avoid anachronisms. Echoes of the Bible and the Talmud make it difficult for young Hebrew writers to use the language for the purposes of the modern novel. But Agnon welcomes such echoes. Rendered into English, however, as in 'Betrothed', the Biblical phrases and references to Talmudic lore jar violently with the precise social observation of the Jaffa of 50 years ago. (p. 878)

Naomi Shepherd, "Two Views of Agnon: 2. Naomi Shepherd," in New Statesman *(© 1966 The Statesman & Nation Publishing Co. Ltd.), Vol. 72, No. 1865, December 9, 1966, pp. 877-78.*

ARNOLD J. BAND

When we assemble the major motifs found in [Agnon's early] Yiddish poems, we are struck by the similarity between them and the major motifs of Agnon's mature works: the struggle with the devil; violent deaths; the failure of religious ritual to inspire the worshiper; the pervasive sensation of decay in the buildings as opposed to the vitality of the natural world outside; the self-consciousness of the creative artist; the love poems; the deep concern with the destiny of the Jewish people. The inescapable fact is that the kernel of much of Agnon's thematic preoccupation is found in these Yiddish poems. (p. 35)

Not all young Agnon's attempts at prose narrative were successful. At times the didactic message is too obvious, and at times the end of the sketch is painfully artificial. And yet, he already knew how to vary his narrative technique, at times with a "philosophic" preface . . . , at times with a monologue . . . , at times by a situation that becomes intelligible only via flashback, and so on. His forte is neither the description of landscape, nor the external features of his characters, nor psychological detail, but rather human actions, comic or tragic, sublime or ridiculous.

Here already are the ironic tone and structured situation that are salient characteristics of the mature writer. (p. 43)

The Hebrew version [of Agnon's stories] is invariably shorter and presents the plot action in balder form than the Yiddish. He obviously possessed much greater mastery over the Yiddish, which flows effortlessly and melodiously. The Yiddish always conveys a sensuous delight in language for its own sake, which is absent from the Hebrew; in Yiddish the imagery is richer, the verbs more intense, the adjectives more varied than in the Hebrew version. The achievement in prose composition evident in the Yiddish is so superior to that in the Hebrew that one wonders why [Agnon] ceased writing in Yiddish, but continued in Hebrew. Surely only a sentimental or idealistic attachment to Hebrew, the language of the national revival, is the explanation. (p. 49)

Following the Yiddish stories chronologically it is possible to discern a steady growth in mastery of narrative technique from story to story, culminating in the most fascinating of all [Agnon's] literary creations in Buczacz, "Toitentants" ("Dance of Death"). The story really does not comprise a narrative unit (it falls into three distinct sections) but more than makes up for its structural flaw by the force and virtuosity of each part. In addition to pure literary interest, the story is an invaluable historical document for charting the writer's development. (p. 52)

[The opening of "'Agunot" ("Agunot"), 1908] is one of the most famous in Agnon's works, not only because of its historical interest as the first paragraphs printed under the name 'Agnon,' but also because it presents the central cluster of themes in the artist's imagination. The deeds of the Jewish people are a lovely thread that the Lord weaves into a resplendent prayer shawl of grace in which the congregation of Israel wraps itself. This prayer shawl shines even in the lands of exile as it did in the house of the Lord in the royal city of Jerusalem, and when He notices that it has not been sullied or befouled, He nods His head approvingly: Thou art beautiful, my beloved, thou art beautiful. "And this is the secret of the greatness and the might and the exaltation and the true love that every Jew feels." But when the thread breaks, the shawl is blemished and evil winds penetrate within, tearing it; immediately all are ashamed, realizing that they are naked. Then the congregation of Israel wanders grieving and moaning, love-sick like the Shulamite of the Song of Songs. This love sickness for the Lord can be cured only if a spirit descends from on high stirring men to good deeds that repair the lovely thread of grace.

Drawing its metaphorical relationship from the allegorical interpretation of the Song of Songs, wherein Solomon becomes the Lord and the Shulamite becomes the congregation of Israel, the midrash adds substance to the abstract relationship of love by injecting the image of the thread and the prayer shawl. Agnon, in turn, carries the process one step further by spinning an attractive tale around the midrash, which immediately gives his tale a cosmic dimension by establishing a meaningful correlation between human action and human destiny and by raising a simple love story to a commentary on the human condition. It is crucial to concentrate upon this point, whether we call it a technique of composition or an intuitive imaginative grasp of reality, since the midrashic resonance gives body to so many of Agnon's stories and the midrashic method of homiletical expansion automatically induces him to think symbolically, to grasp abstracts through realistic objects and situations and, conversely, to infuse the tangible with transcendental meaning.

Inasmuch as the implication of the cited midrash is general and universal, that is, human strength, happiness, and love are predicated upon divine grace which is predicated, in turn, upon human deeds, the narrative possibilities are virtually infinite; secondary themes can be added and the initial theme of "the broken thread" can also be subordinated to other themes. In "'Agunot" the midrashic theme is injected into a love situation and is itself suffused with religious mystery. (pp. 58-9)

["'Agunot"] is a tale of disembodied souls doomed to be tragically anchored to that which they desire but apparently cannot obtain. That this romantic theme pulsates through a traditional, religious world that theoretically and historically held human experience together in a meaningful fabric, only serves to intensify the sense of alienation and to rend asunder the fabric, the "prayer shawl," of religious life. The void in the human soul immediately transcends the specifically Jewish situation in that it concerns first and last the human soul, which we accept as universal. (p. 60)

To many of Agnon's most devoted readers the stories that appeal the most are those called folktales or legends. It is statistically true that a major portion of Agnon's literary output is usually classified under the generic rubric Folktale, yet, the term folktale is by no means clear or precise and often signifies only external qualities. Broadly speaking, Agnon's folktales have as their milieu the community of pious Jews of either Eastern Europe (mostly Galicia) or the old yishuv in Palestine; the frame of reference is understood to be the world of traditional Jewish life, overseen by an almighty divinity identified as the God of Jewish history, and governed by talmudic law and accepted norms of behavior. The folktale we usually encounter in Hebrew literature since the 1880's is not the creation of naïve pious Jews, but rather of sophisticated urban writers who had experienced the milieu of the folktale as children, but had left that milieu for the city. The folktale therefore becomes a framework for various types of tales; its generic implication is often only external. (pp. 78-9)

[To this day the novelette "Vehaya he'akov lemishor" ("And the Crooked Shall Become Straight"), 1912] stands out as one of Agnon's greatest successes, a work that required but minor editing in later years. . . . If the story was written in four days, as Agnon claims it was, it was a prodigious literary feat. This is the first of Agnon's stories that evoke that "shock of recognition" the reader must feel as he stands in the presence of a great work of art. (p. 83)

More than any other story of this period, "Vehaya he'akov lemishor" utilizes the "new wine in old bottles" technique first tried successfully in "'Agunot"; within the framework of what seems to be a traditional folktale with conventional characteristics, Agnon tells a story that implies values and sentiments utterly different from those ordinarily conveyed by the folktale. An inner tension is therefore created between the plot and the genre in which it is contained. (p. 86)

The narrative technique displayed in the description of the decline of Menashe Hayim at the fair at Lashkovits, and in the moving passage leading up to the discovery that his wife had remarried, is remarkable and has rarely been equaled in Hebrew prose. The significant details are so deftly arranged and controlled that the reader is beguiled into the acceptance of an artistic illusion so convincing that even the constant deliberate intrusions of the writer with deliberately naïve remarks reminiscent of the Hebrew and Yiddish folktale cannot destroy the artistic illusion. The raconteur's ability to charm his audience into the acceptance of the reality of the tale he tells, be it near to or far from the experience of the listener, is unquestionably Agnon's talent and it first manifests itself in overpowering force in this story. (p. 89)

Within the genre of the Agnonic folktale, ["haNidah" ("The Banished One"), 1919] is almost archetypal in that it includes most of the thematic and compositional elements of the other stories of the genre. Great pains are taken to present the folkloristic milieu through which the plot moves; situations rely for their color and causation on the mores of the pious Eastern European community, here called Shibush as it often is in Agnon's stories. Indeed, the plot itself is motivated by the opposition between two distinctly different points of view as to the very nature of life in this milieu. (p. 97)

The suspense of the story is created by the deliberately slow pace in which Agnon works his way to the inevitable tragic ending. Situation by situation we learn more about Gershom, begin to understand him as a person, and consequently watch his steady progress to his doom in sympathy and horror. . . . The drama of Gershom is played out on two levels. On the metaphysical plane he is doomed because of the curse of Reb Uriel, hence the innocent victim of an ideological clash; on the psychological plane he is victimized by his own hypersensitivity. Both tensions, the metaphysical-ideological and the purely psychological convulse the tranquil folkloristic milieu resulting in the inevitable death. . . .

The cycle of stories published under the rubric ["Polin: Sipure agadot" ("Poland: Legends")] constitutes a representative sample of Agnon's creative activity in the [Berlin period]. (p. 99)

These fourteen stories deal with Jewish life in Eastern Europe in past generations. . . . (p. 100)

By positing an expanse of historical experience and referring to local customs and places, Agnon succeeds in creating the image of a distinctive community, an image that becomes more and more central to the writer's imagination as the years pass. Indeed, it is important to note that Galicia and its peculiar Jewish folkways became the main focal point of Agnon's imagination precisely when he was living in the metropolitan centers of Germany and when Buczacz was no longer his home. The Jewish community is unquestioningly God-fearing, a basic fact that provides the writer with a ready-made world of mores and values and allows him to slip naturally into a world of fantasy and mystery. (p. 101)

["Bin'arenu uvizkenenu" ("With Our Youth and with Our Aged"), 1920, one of Agnon's most neglected works,] lacks the coherence and universality that make for great satire. Individual chapters, however, are terribly amusing as they shrewdly expose the foibles of life in Buczacz. The point of view, however, is not sustained for the twenty-seven chapters of the satire and too many autobiographical remarks and passages are strewn among the satiric sections, thereby creating a mixed effect. The writer's attitude toward his youthful persona in the story is not consistent. Only rarely does he include himself in the group to be satirized; frequently he is the outsider who is somewhat wiser than his contemporaries but who never has a personality of his own. And finally, even the satiric material is not related to one theme, which would produce a unified effect. The central object of ridicule, the activities of the young Zionists in Shibush (the literary correlative of Buczacz), is often lost amidst tangential matters and does not add up to the comic comment upon ineffectual political action that it purports to be. (p. 121)

Paradoxically, [*Hakhnasat kala (The Bridal Canopy)*], the first Agnon novel translated into English, is the most alien in atmosphere and style to forms of the novel known to the general reader, and presents the most problems. To one unfamiliar with the Hebrew or Yiddish folktale popular for centuries in Eastern Europe, this novel must seem bizarre; to the Hebrew reader or literary scholar, the novel-like structuring of diverse folktales around several interrelated folk motifs creates numerous questions of interpretation. The internal contradiction is inescapable: the folktale breathes the air of naïveté and ingenuousness while the structuring of a novel implies sophistication and artistic subtlety. (p. 126)

A close reading of the text and a perusal of the critical literature on the novel are more than enough to convince the scholar that the book must be dealt with in terms of ambiguity, parody, and oscillating reality. Unquestionably, the archetype of *Don Quixote* must be invoked, not for its superficial resemblances to *Hakhnasat kala* . . . , but for the narrative modes through which Cervantes set out to parody the chivalric tale. To be successful, a parodist must pay his price to the object of his parody; in entering the spirit of the object, he inevitably adopts some of the characteristics he intends to parody. The closer the parodist is to the object of parody either in temperament, background, or artistic imagination, the more ambivalent will be his attitude toward his object and the more ambiguous his style. Many of the critical problems raised by *Hakhnasat kala* can be solved if we understand that in this work Agnon identifies with the object of his parody to such a degree that there emerges a remarkably sustained ambiguity that is aesthetically independent and ultimately the most fascinating feature of the book.

Its very name, *Hakhnasat kala,* is indicative of many of the problems presented by the novel. The English title, *The Bridal Canopy,* is neither precise nor does it signify the main theme as does the Hebrew; literally, *Hakhnasat kala* means "bringing the bride under (the bridal canopy)," or, more loosely, "marrying her off according to traditional Jewish practices." (pp. 126-27)

No small part of Agnon's success in this novel and in his other works can be ascribed to his felicitous selection of the family as his dominant metaphor for it was both a living unit suitable for novelistic manipulation and the basic cell of the social and religious organism he was describing. . . . (pp. 127-28)

The subtitle, too, is significant: in an obviously archaizing method Agnon follows the convention of certain collections of Jewish folktales by adding an amplification of his title: "The wonders of the Hasid Reb Yudel of Brody (Brod, in Hebrew) and his three modest daughters and the account of the greatness of our brethren the children of Israel who reside in the country of his Majesty The Kaiser." The information given is comprehensive and essential. This is a tale of wonders in which the hero believes in miracles and expects them to happen in his life, in which the very climax of the plot is a miracle. (p. 128)

[The] plot presents a challenge to the critic for once one places it within its literary tradition or questions the simplicity and unity of its point of view, the entire plot appears deliberately incredible. As usual in the Agnon story, the plot line is deceptively simple. (p. 129)

Because the work abounds in parodies and ambiguities, the author stands not outside his work but within every sentence; and since he is demonstrably writing tongue in cheek, the naïve atmosphere of the folktale and the plausibility of the plot itself requires reconsideration. (p. 130)

The initial presentation of Reb Yudel is indicative of the tone of the entire novel. The style is obviously patterned after early hasidic tales with their naïveté, piety, and frequent reference to Scriptures. Reb Yudel himself has the basic characteristics of the literary type of the Hasid: he is poor; he is dedicated to God and His Tora; he is removed from worldly affairs. It is hardly coincidental that his name is mentioned only after two pages of general description of his living habits and even then by his wife who is far more realistic and worldly than he. One feels at the outset that here is a deliberate parody of the traditional hasidic tale. . . . (p. 138)

The endearing simplicity and honesty of the Hasid are conveyed tenderly and attractively; but the reader cannot escape the consuming effect of the parody. The pervasive denigration of the flesh, the relentless remorse that plagues any decision, the reliance on traditional texts rather than empirical experience for corroboration of fact, all dissolve in the acid of satire. Obviously, the exaggerated compunctions coupled with the spirit/flesh antithesis brought out in its most naked terms, tend to corrode the validity of this antithesis as a basic guide or framework to life.

Confronted by these two forces, the winning naïveté and the corrosive parody, which are almost always concomitantly operative in this novel, the reader must take the pains to prevent predispositions from dulling his sensitivity to either aspect. Both should be received in equilibrium until preponderance of one in a specific passage convinces the reader that the impact of that passage is more to one side than the other. The style of *Hakhnasat kala* is best studied under the rubric "ambiguity." . . . (p. 142)

In this novel, the logical, triumphal scene must be the wedding in which all the aspirations of the hero are fulfilled and all the major themes of the novel summed up: the wondrous change of fortune; the actual union of two families with promise of offspring; the acquaintances Yudel made on the road; man's fate and divine providence; the love and study of the Tora; the mistaken identity; the yearning for Erets Yisrael. All these themes are fused and illuminated by the elaborate description of the wedding ritual and celebration. (p. 176)

In *Hakhnasat kala* we see Agnon at the peak of his mythopoetic powers, creating a complete imaginative world at once self-contained and central in the writer's development. . . . The ironies engendered by the disparity between the writer's mentality and that of the mythic world he has created so meticulously are conclusive proof of the psychological distance between him and that world. For any student of literature, this novel offers a rare example of the narrative and spiritual problems involved in a modern attempt at myth-making. (p. 184)

When the first stories of the ["Sefer hama'asim" ("Book of Deeds")] cycle appeared in periodicals during the early thirties, both the critics and the general readers were shocked: the master of the pious tale seemed to be indulging in modernistic, Europeanized mannerisms. The outrage was compounded because the implications of this new mode ran against the grain of current ideology and sentiment. The Hebrew folktale is, in a sense, a literary expression of Jewish nationalist sentiments, of Zionism; in adopting obviously European or "Western" modes, Agnon was clearly exercising an independence of one of the conventions of his audience. And though he continued to write stories of the "Sefer hama'asim" cycle or type throughout the 1930's and 1940's, it was not until the late 1940's . . . that these stories found an appreciative audience. At that point, a new image of Agnon began to form in the reader's imagination, not that of a simple reconteur, but rather of a highly complex "modern" writer with a discernible affinity to the figures of the "existentialist" tradition, to Kafka, in particular. Gradually, more and more readers . . . began to penetrate the bright classical composure of Agnon's prose style to glimpse the murky spiritual anguish below, a veritable "dark night of the soul" that had persisted unnoticed for a quarter of a century. Agnon, of course, had employed dreams, allegories, and symbols before, but had always scattered them among pages of tales and folkloristic detail. In "Sefer hama'asim," however, he developed a highly compressed and suggestive narrative technique, not unlike Kafka's, which was obviously more suited to convey the doubt and confusion of the pious, traditional Jew who is also intellectually a citizen of Western Europe with its broad humanistic tradition. The agonized, ironical imagination was no longer hidden behind a mythic ethos, but instead paraded before the reader nakedly, often a trifle theatrically. The action always takes place in the mind of a hypersensitive, often neurotic, narrator who tells his story in the first person, naturally mixing memory, dream, fantasy, and reality, as the human imagination often does, particularly under psychic stress. Each story has its own structure, carefully contrived to involve the sensitive reader in the spiritual plight of the narrator, a plight that is moving because it can be shared by the reader who recognizes it as his own.

Once apprised so shockingly of the power of blackness in these nonrealistic short stories, critics returned to Agnon's earlier collected works and found there what they had previously overlooked. (pp. 187-88)

[*Ore'ah nata lalun (A Wayfarer Who Tarried for a Night),* 1939] presents few problems in interpretation. The meaning and tone of the novel, sustained from beginning to end by a simple plot outline and a series of homogeneous episodes, is all but inescapable. For here is a relentless panorama of physical and spiritual desolation which seizes the reader with the force of Picasso's "Guernica" with which it is, not too coincidentally, almost contemporary. . . . The unmitigated pain that pervades the book is the pain of a double disappointment. First the visitor discovers that the formerly flourishing Jewish community of Shibush, which always glowed in his imagination as a symbol of the best in traditional Jewish life, was crumbling into despondent ruin, and then the mature man returns to find that the dreamworld of childhood, of innocence, is forever lost. The man who does "come home again" finds that "home" is no more, that "home" is a shockingly hideous panorama of decay. The nostalgia that inspired the visit dissolves, when confronted with reality, into nightmare. (pp. 283-84)

The meaning of the novel is unambiguous, but one crucial misunderstanding common in studies of the book should be clarified at this point. The novel purports to be an autobiographical account of a deeply felt personal experience. True, Agnon did visit Buczacz, the real city that Agnon calls Shibush in the novel, in 1930; true, the story is narrated in the first person and the narrator himself is a character in the story. But narrative technique should not be confused with autobiography, for this leads one to take the novel as a literal, historical statement to be judged on these grounds rather than on those of a work of the imagination. And a work of the imagination it is, as the facts will prove. Agnon did not spend the better part of a year in Buczacz in 1930; he was there for only five days. Buczacz in 1930 was not Buczacz of 1907 when Agnon left it, but it was far from the symbol of desolation which Agnon presents to us as Shibush in his novel. On this point there is abundant documentation. Many critics, moreover, unfortunately tend to inject into their consideration the inescapable fact that the Jewish community of Buczacz was liquidated by the Nazis in the spring of 1943, a fact totally extraneous to the author's artistic vision in this novel. Whatever historical information there is here has been transfigured by the author's artistic vision. Any contention that in future generations Buczacz can be reconstructed from Agnon's excellent description of Shibush is sheer nonsense.

While it is impossible to attribute to Agnon prophetic foreknowledge of the holocaust of World War II, one cannot neglect the *Sitz im Leben* of *Ore'ah nata lalun.* (pp. 284-85)

Throughout the story, situations, people and objects not only call attention to themselves but also refer to a coherent and readily comprehensible world of values which envelops them. While Agnon takes great pains to render the precise form of a statement, the exact implication of a gesture, or the true motive behind a human action, his vision of reality is always expanded by another dimension. Reality is *also* a manifestation or epiphany of a set of attitudes toward the condition of man in the modern world and particularly those modern men whose heritage is specifically Jewish and inexorably challenging in that it is still an integral part of their being. Even the reader who is wary of symbol searching and message hunting cannot deny the factual evidence of this technique: recurrent motifs and images that emerge as symbols, obvious, repeated juxtapositions and contrasts in situations, and the insightful commentary of the narrator himself. The novel does not move on two distinct planes, the realistic and the suggested ideational, like allegory, but on one, the realistic, which is animated and ordered by an inner meaning that in turn is conceived only in terms of the specific situation described. In allegory, the suggested idea can exist without the narrative material that seems to be presented only to concretize, often didactically, the moral to be taught; here, however, values are envisaged artistically only in terms of a specific existential situation. (pp. 285-86)

Usually considered the most tragic of Agnon's three major novels, *Ore'ah nata lalun* is really his most affirmative novelistic statement of belief. Both *Hakhnasat kala* and *Temol shilshom* reject the basic values rendered in them, the former by its unrelieved ironic tone, the latter by its plot action leading to the violent doglike death of its hero. But *Ore'ah nata lalun,* reaches a positive ending in spite of the mood of decay which pervades it. The narrator does rejoin his family in Jerusalem to live the life of the Tora there. Though he has had his childhood obliterated from his consciousness as a possible psychological refuge from reality, in his loss of innocence he gains a new childhood in the figure of the child of Rahel and Yeruham. Their child is given his name, a strange practice for Ashkenazic Jews who usually name the child after a dead person. I suggest that this strange act means that the narrator who entered the story has died as a personality: he has discovered his Shibush is no more, and he therefore undergoes a rebirth signified in the birth and circumcision of the child who will bear his name. (pp. 326-27)

[Agnon, responding to the stirring historical events of 1942-1953,] created many of his most impassioned artistic works, which attempt to cope, however indirectly, with the impulses of the period. . . . The very fact that Agnon did not succumb to the temptation to render superficial, reportorial accounts of major contemporary events sheds much light on his artistic imagination. One does not find concentration camps or heroic battle scenes in his writing; the specific upheavals are rarely mentioned and then only in veiled allusion. What one does encounter, however, is a turbulence of spirit greater than that in any other period of his long literary career, and a tortured grappling with some of the fundamental human questions raised by the actions and passions of those apocalyptic days. "Apocalyptic" is probably the most accurate word for the moral situation that characterizes the *Sitz im Leben* of many of these works, for it is clear that the writer is struggling here, more than ever before, with the moral suppositions of his life. This struggle, common to the major writers of this century, constitutes what Joyce has aptly called "the conscience of the race."

The dialectical moods of nostalgia and nightmare . . . reach their peaks in *Ore'ah nata lalun* . . . , and take new directions in the years between 1942 and 1953. *Ore'ah nata lalun* assumed that throughout this world of crumbling institutions and values, two focuses of faith and behavior still abide: Erets Yisrael and the Tora. . . . [Later] the redemptive power of these two focuses are severely questioned. Certainly, in Agnon's major work of this period, the novel [*Temol shilshom (Only Yesterday),* 1945], . . . all basic assumptions are challenged. (pp. 328-29)

Though not written as a trilogy, Agnon's three major novels, *Hakhnasat kala, Ore'ah nata lalun,* and *Temol shilshom* are related in several crucial aspects. All have their roots in Galicia and extend, in varying degrees, to Erets Yisrael; the degree of extension toward Erets Yisrael increases from novel to novel. The articulation of the relationship between Galicia . . . and Erets Yisrael is one of the central concerns of the writer. The relationship between the heroes is striking. Reb Yudel Hasid of *Hakhnasat kala* is an ancestor, five generations removed, of Yitshak Kummer of *Temol shilshom;* both the narrative "I" of *Ore'ah nata lalum* and Yitshak Kummer of *Temol shilshom* go from Galicia to Erets Yisrael. Hemdat, the young writer in *Temol shilshom,* is as much a projection of the writer's own personality as the narrator of *Ore'ah nata lalum,* but in a more removed and objective sense. And finally, all three novels display an unrelenting obsession with the broader problems of faith, identity, and home which beset many writers in this century. Consequently, . . . the three novels do form a cycle in which each member is illuminated by the other two. . . . [*Temol shilshom*] is doubtless the most successfully realized of the three novels, the richest in connotation, and the most universal in import.

In this novel, Agnon adopts a more straightforward narrative method in which a central figure, Yitshak Kummer, is observed moving through a series of episodes that affect him directly. . . . The book is a *Bildungsroman* that does not follow the conventional passage from innocence to experience but progresses from innocence to a feeble state of experience marked by its periods of bliss and composure often ruffled by the irrepressible consciousness of guilt and failure, and finally moves back to a state of innocence which our hero is not allowed to enjoy for he must pay with his life for his failure. (pp. 414-15)

Like the two preceding novels, *Temol shilshom* has its specific milieu, mostly Palestine of the central years of the Second Aliya. . . . [This milieu] is treated by Agnon as a means and not as an end, as material that he can manipulate for artistic purposes and not as material presented for its own sake. Agnon is not fundamentally a realistic writer and his use of detail peculiar to a period or a milieu should be termed quasi-realism. Were we to treat the book as a work of realism how, then, integrate into it the more than one hundred pages in which the dog, Balak, wends his way through the streets of Jerusalem?

It is the presence of Balak, who ultimately bites Yitshak Kummer, which has distorted much of the critical reading of the novel. . . . The explications have ranged rather amusingly from the inevitable hypothesis that the dog symbolizes the Jewish people, to more ingenious exercises that characterize the dog as a detailed articulation of the psyche of Yitshak Kummer which is presented in the simplest terms. Agnon, himself, has anticipated these critical gymnastics by including in the novel . . . a riotous satire of the many possible ways of interpreting this symbol, and he pokes fun at his critics: "The people of Jaffa who are all opinionated turned their attention to these matters, but did not know to whom they referred. One says 'there's something to it' and another says, 'we should learn the implicit from the explicit.' Meanwhile opinions were split, and there were as many opinions as people in the city." . . . Agnon's satire of his explicators actually reveals part of the truth. . . . [Actually] the dog is a many-faceted symbol alluding to different things in different places. The total meaning of the dog symbol is the sum total of all these facets, the core of which is the ambiguous, bold statement of the preacher Rabbi Gronam Yekum Purkan, "I consider the face of this generation to be like the face of a dog." . . . (pp. 415-17)

[The] agonized conclusion that the face of the generation is like the face of a mad dog is the result of the writer's disillusionment with certain ideals that give life meaning, and of his horrified witnessing of the disintegration of human values in Europe as the twentieth century progressed. (p. 418)

Temol shilshom, because of its density of varied episodes and recurring motifs, requires emphasis on the patterns of motifs and their significance. Neither the plot nor the character of Yitshak is responsible for the excitement of the novel. The plot takes us back and forth from Jaffa to Jerusalem with many digressions that, on first reading, seem to have little to do with the main story line. Yitshak Kummer is a deliberately flat character. Why would a writer choose to bother with him? As we shall see, both the meandering, seemingly suspenseless plot and the lackluster hero grow enormously in interest and significance when we begin to respond to the novel's patterns of motifs. They run throughout the entire novel and relate one episode to another, one attitude to another, even though a particular motif may imply different things in different contexts. And when we note the complex interrelationships of the major motifs, we begin to appreciate the fertility of the writer's imagination and his masterly control over the nagging anxieties of his life during the trying years of the novel's composition, mostly during World War II.

The disintegration of traditional religious practice and belief is the central motif to which all other motifs are organically related. This is why Yitshak must be portrayed as a flat personality. His gradual neglect of religious practices and his family, his assimilation of the behavior patterns of the ordinary haluts, his vague sensation of the tastelessness of life are certainly not due to the specific complexities of his personality, but rather are symptomatic of a generation. As a result, the religious motifs stand out more vividly than the personality of the hero himself. (p. 421)

Yitshak's behavior was, on the whole, nonoffensive and, at times, nondescript. Though a flat character, he arouses sympathy by his sincerity, his naïveté, his fundamental innocence. Why, then, was Yitshak struck down at the moment of his return to the religious way of life? . . . The universe of *Temol shilshom*, the world of Yitshak Kummer, can have shape and meaning only if it is governed by a just divinity. But this does not seem to be the case. Yitshak dies a dog's death, bound to a foul bed in a dark room; that is, he is bound on a meaningless altar, unlike the biblical Isaac whose binding was an act of enormous import for all humanity, and who was not killed in the end, but lived on to bear the message of Moriah to the world through his descendants. There is nothing Yitshak Kummer has done to warrant such punishment. . . . It is therefore necessary to probe the problem of causation to arrive at some concept of the writer's point of view regarding divine justice. (pp. 425-26)

Yitshak's death is . . . ironic because he is bitten and infected by the dog just when he has finally returned to his point of departure: he has returned to the religious practices of the traditional Jew, is married to a pious girl, and therefore theoretically beyond the reach of further temptation. It is absurd to posit Yitshak's death as the just punishment for his waywardness: his sins were minor and he did repent, actually returning to the path of piety. Throughout the book, he seems to be on a quest, however feeble and inarticulate. . . . The quest has two geographical and behavioral focuses: Jaffa and Jerusalem. . . . The novel is, in effect, a literary statement that redemption can be found in neither place, in neither way of life. Jaffa is unsatisfying; the satisfaction that Jerusalem offers is only a brief prelude to a brutal, meaningless death. The total impact of *Temol shilshom* can only be a confession of the writer's nihilism. (p. 444)

Agnon himself seems to be disturbed by the nihilistic implications of Yitshak's death, for he asks in [a] moving passage . . . : "Why was this Yitshak, who was no worse than other men, punished so much?" A possible answer to this question is suggested by the *Sitz im Leben* of the novel, most of which, we should recall, was written in the dark days of World War II when news of the meaningless slaughter of millions of Yitshaks in Europe reached Jerusalem. The correspondence between the central metaphor of the novel and the historical situation is too striking to be disregarded, particularly in a writer so steeped in Jewish literary sources as Agnon. In that the novel implies that there is no satisfying answer to this question, it is an honest, literary confrontation with one of the hard facts of our existence in the twentieth century. (p. 447)

[Nightmare] is one of two main focuses of Agnon's sentiment; the second focus, which is antithetical but complementary to the first, is nostalgia, an almost Proustian struggle to recapture *temps perdu*. But while Proust, in his reconstruction and preservation of the past, begins with the personal experiences of his fictional Marcel and includes through them a panorama of an entire segment of society, Agnon devotes hundreds of pages to the world of pious Jews, mostly of the past century or two, which is presented objectively and in the third person. Usually, neither the writer nor a literary projection of his psyche are characters in the story being told. Indeed, the writer is present only as the mythopoetic creator who consciously reconstructs an entire civilization which he yearns for nostalgically. At times he might entertain the rather fanciful notion that this tranquil world of piety and wholeness *was* the world of his childhood and that he could possibly return to it. But when nostalgic yearnings cannot be fulfilled and the writer realizes that the golden world of his fiction is nothing but fantasy, the nostalgia may very well turn into nightmare as it does in *Ore'ah nata lalun*. Nightmare and nostalgia, then, are two allied moods, both forms of the fictional "romance" that repeatedly endeavors to recapture an ideal world that can never be recaptured. (pp. 449-50)

Though astoundingly erudite in Jewish sources and an observant Jew, Agnon excels all other modern Hebrew prose writers in his devotion to his craft, to aesthetic form—a fact that has led some critics to doubt the sincerity of his attachment to traditional Jewish values or his concern with the vital issues of Jewish life in this century. But the truth is that Agnon intuitively grasps reality and human situations as a writer of fiction and not as an essayist or polemicist. . . . The agonizing spiritual problems that confront serious men of many countries in this century are all present in Agnon's writings, refracted through the artistic prism. (p. 450)

Arnold J. Band, in his Nostalgia and Nightmare: A Study in the Fiction of S. Y. Agnon *(copyright © 1968 by the Regents of the University of California; reprinted by permission of the University of California Press), University of California Press, 1968, 553 p.*

* * *

AI (pseudonym of Florence Anthony, also Pelorhanke Ai Ogawa) 1947-

Ai is an American poet. Describing herself as "one-half Japanese, one-eighth Choctaw, one-fourth black, and one-sixteenth Irish," she creates a racial perspective in her work that is unique and unsentimental. Women are vividly portrayed, and images are powerful and often violent. Critics have praised Ai's poetry for its clear design and skillful craftsmanship. (See also *CLC*, Vol. 4, and *Contemporary Authors*, Vols. 85-88.)

JOHN N. MORRIS

To be very solemn, the difficulty [of Ai's *Cruelty*] has to do with the problem addressed but not resolved by Aristotle, the question of the moral standing of the pleasure we take in the pain in which art often and properly deals. But of course, if I am not much mistaken, art, in any of the usual acceptances of the term, is not very high on the list of this author's intentions. If I inquire why then these utterances arrogate to themselves the honorable name of poetry, the modest answer may be (in such cases it usually is) that they mean to modify or transform our sense of what poetry is. At this point the argument is, as far as I am concerned, at an end. It seems to me that the claims or justifications one might advance for *Cruelty* resemble those one might advance for pornography; and that *Cruelty* is in fact a species of pornography, the pornography of pain. That these pieces exhibit a certain skill, a certain horrible energy, is undeniable; the question is whether that skill and energy are here licitly employed. (p. 108)

John N. Morris, "Making More Sense Than Omaha," in The Hudson Review *(copyright © 1974 by The Hudson Review, Inc.; reprinted by* *permission), Vol. XXVII, No. 1, Spring, 1974, pp. 107-08.**

CAROLYN FORCHE

From Russia, Mexico, Buchenwald and Minnesota, the voices [in *Killing Floor*] speak of patricide, necrophilia, self-immolation, cannibalism and torture, converging in the single voice of an old soul, androgynous and driving, a ghost ranging space and time, drawn to moments in which the oppressed one is moved to act. Ai is concerned with that single moment, revelatory and disassociated, which is the hinge of human history, facilitating radical change, allowing the heart to open to a new order.

She discovers that it is possible to enter a psychological state of anarchy (symbolic always of social anarchy) without becoming hysterical. These poems are cold-blooded, tender and defiant narratives, concerning themselves with the survival of the human will, and a deferential celebration of death as the magnifier of life.

In many of her poems, there are knives, axes, blades or pitchforks, splitting skulls, slicing off pieces of flesh, jabbing the sun. Their cutting edges become, in this poet's hands, instruments for penetrating a social order which has become anesthetized to human agony. . . .

[Because] of the belief in both death and life, there are no senseless acts. In the human spirit's endurance, revolution is possible and transformation, inevitable. . . .

There aren't many poets whose language so precisely resonates with the pervasive concerns of the contemporary human condition.

Carolyn Forche, "Sentenced to Despair," in Book World—The Washington Post *(© 1979,* The Washington Post*), March 11, 1979, p. F2.*

RANDALL ALBERS

There is a poetry of sweetness and light, a poetry that cloaks the viscera and makes of them a human form divine. And then there is the poetry of Ai.

In *Killing Floor,* her long-awaited second book of poetry, Ai fulfills the considerable promise of her first collection, *Cruelty* . . . , where she had written,

> I've never once felt anything
> that might get close. Can't you see?
> The thing I want most is hard,
> running toward my own teeth
> and it bites back.

Ai's whole attempt in *Cruelty* was to open her eyes wide and to see the essentials strongly, clearly, and honestly. The essentials, for Ai, are that we are born and die, and that we love and hate and struggle with each other on a lighted path between those two doors to darkness. This is a theme often obscured by complication, a theme most of us are hard-pressed to face directly. Interruption and amnesia are the order of the day; they breed mistrust, neglect, violence, fear. Ai allows us neither distraction nor forgetfulness, for they are, she sees, the real enemies of human potential. We would rather succumb than survive. Ai will not permit abdication. As she quotes Charles Simic, "He who cannot / Grow teeth, will not survive."

Killing Floor, then, is characterized by the same striking images and strong sense of voice as *Cruelty,* but the vision has widened. In *Cruelty,* Ai adopts a variety of voices which gain their force not from idiosyncrasy but rather from what they share in common, the pain of living under the threat of death. That much of the pain in *Cruelty* is woman's pain should be no surprise. The interrelatedness of life and death leads Ai to the importance of woman as life-giver in a world intent on avoiding the knowledge of death, and some of Ai's most effective images arise out of the stark contrast of birth, or potential birth, and death.

In *Killing Floor,* Ai builds on these strong individual voices and striking images, but she pushes herself much more strongly toward exposing the universal tendencies and effects of this process of living and dying. The push results in two important changes.

First, the personal voice reaches further toward the public struggle to understand and deal with life and death. In addition to the voices of unknown types, a series of public figures appear and speak for their own attempts to understand. . . . The public figures firmly locate private struggles in a larger historical process. If *Cruelty* was the chronicle of little, nameless, unremembered acts of inhumanity, *Killing Floor* is the chronicle of those actions played out with the full force of history's monstrous acts of cruelty resonating in the background. (pp. 119-20)

The best poems in the collection, "Killing Floor," "Nothing But Color," "Ice," "The Ravine," "Sleep Like a Hammer," "Pentecost," and "The Gilded Man" all reveal [Ai's] strong moral stance based on seeing oneself and one's environment clearly, and on the struggle to discover a personal myth.

The second change in Ai's poetry is at first surprising and probably results from the movement toward the universal and the public: of twenty-four poems in *Killing Floor,* sixteen are told in the voices of men. Fathers, fathers to be, young men, sons, male lovers all have their own struggles with living and dying, and Ai's ability to render the male as well as the female fills in further perspectives on these struggles. . . . Relationships are full of pulling and tugging, and just as we cannot obliterate the growing awareness of death, we cannot begin to live until we face it squarely. Until then, we are condemned to acts of cruelty and rage. The antidotes to despair, distraction, and amnesia function only when they emanate directly from a sense of the essentials. (pp. 121-22)

Killing Floor, then, represents a movement from seeing to real vision, vision that looks directly, unflinchingly, at the viscera of existence and tries to communicate their meanings nakedly. The collection represents a movement from depicting personal myths united simply by their shared pain to locating personal myth in historic and public mythic process. It looks at failure and tries to create not heroes but survivors, persons willing to see through the illusion, the distraction, the interruption. With this book, Ai has moved from being a very good poet to being an excellent poet, and, like the narrator of "Ice" (Ai's own great-grandmother?), we should give ourselves over to the lessons of this vision:

> Tonight, wake me like always.
> Talk and I'll listen,
> while you lie on the pallet
> resting your arms behind your head,
> telling me about the wild rice in the marshes

and the empty .45 you call *Grace of God* that keeps you alive
as we slide forward, without bitterness, decade by decade,
becoming transparent. Everlasting.

(p. 122)

Randall Albers, "Ai's 'Killing Floor'," in Chicago Review *(reprinted by permission of* Chicago Review; *copyright © 1979 by* Chicago Review), *Vol. 30, No. 4, Spring, 1979, pp. 119-22.*

HAYDEN CARRUTH

[Certainly] the poet who calls herself Ai ("love" in Japanese, which is part of her ancestry) is among the best [of the Afro-American poets]; this much can be proved already in *Killing Floor,* though it is only her second book and a slim one at that. Many of her poems are in the voices of others, *personae* in the true sense, masks behind which not only she but all of us stand and peer out. This by itself indicates Ai's literary intelligence. Her passion is the thing that counts, however, and it throbs—the word is just—in every rhythm, image, and phrasing. . . . [Ai's] book is a joyous shock. (pp. 89-90)

Hayden Carruth, "Impetus and Invention: Poetic Tradition and the Individual Talent," in Harper's *(copyright © 1979 by* Harper's Magazine; *all rights reserved; reprinted from the May, 1979 issue by special permission), Vol. 258, No. 1548, May, 1979, pp. 88-90.**

G. E. MURRAY

[Ai's second book, *Killing Floor,*] again displays a range of tough-minded images, but these latest poems are further enriched by a framework of quasi-historical vignettes described in the voices of Trotsky, Zapata, Yukio Mishima, Marilyn Monroe and Ira Hayes (an Iwo Jima hero turned skid-row unfortunate). It is Hayes who typifies the poet's reflections on social decay and emotional disaster, admitting: "I'm the one dirty habit / I just can't break."

Dark as this view may be, and however squeamish about themes of mass murder, assassination and infanticide one may be, this poet's authority is uncompromising. She encounters the mirror unshaken, adding ironic emphasis to what is, finally, a motto for her ravishments: "I mean to live."

G. E. Murray, "Book Notes: 'Killing Floor'," in The Nation *(copyright 1979 by the Nation Associates, Inc.), Vol. 228, No. 19, May 19, 1979, p. 578.*

STEPHEN YENSER

[The poems in *Killing Floor*] are obsessed with the human capacity for violence. Deaths by axing, shooting, bludgeoning, strangulation, and *hara-kiri* occur in piece after piece. When the situation lacks overt violence, Ai's metaphors leap into the breach. . . . Touches of perversion here and there heighten the air of Grand Guignol.

A little of the lurid goes a long way, and even though Ai's volume is less than fifty pages few will wish it longer than it is. Yet this book is as easy to respect in part as it is hard to enjoy on the whole. At her best Ai writes a highly disciplined, cleanly organized, fastidiously punctuated free verse that somewhat chastens her subject matter. Her characteristic mode is the short dramatic monologue, and her personae are diverse and sometimes intriguingly complex. Trotsky, Marilyn Monroe, a Nazi homosexual, a Choctaw woman living in the nineteenth century, one of the marines who raised the flag on Iwo Jima—these and others speak in poems that vary little in diction and syntax but greatly in tone and structure. They are rich in both sympathy and implication. (p. 566)

[The] more outrageous the act, the harder to extenuate it—and the less Ai tries to do so. . . . No doubt sympathetic comprehension must wither in the face of atrocity, but when it does we are left with a dramatization of a grisly news item—and perhaps some awe at Ai's negative capability.

[Many of the poems] rely on the sensational for their effects. . . . "Nothing but Color" attributes to Yukio Mishima the broiling and eating of bits of a lover's flesh. One supposes the persona to be Mishima, that is, because the poem is dedicated to him, its speaker claims to be the creator of Etsuko (central character in *Thirst for Love*), and its last line echoes Mishima's suicide note. Someone better acquainted with Mishima's life might pronounce on the cannibalism, but anyone will be puzzled to find that the *hara-kiri* in this poem occurs in the speaker's garden, whereas Mishima's took place in the office of a general at an armed forces base. Ai's reasons for fiddling with fact, or alternatively for encouraging us to think that a fictional persona is Mishima, are obscure. A similar confusion plagues "Killing Floor." In the first section she seems to have Trotsky plead for exile . . . and in the third she has him sitting in a bedroom at a "mirrored vanity" and putting on his wife's maquillage when he is struck from behind (he was in his study, not in front of a mirror, reading an essay the killer had just given him). Are the facts not bizarre enough? Or is Ai ignoring them for some interpretative but inscrutable purpose? In any case, one has to question the propriety of such distortions. . . . (pp. 567-68)

Her treatment of Zapata's murder in "Pentecost," by contrast, turns a scene compatible with fact into a powerful vision. . . . Ai's intensity fuses the agrarian roots of Zapata's revolt, his tremendous will, and his enduring inspirational force, and the metamorphoses make their own little myth. Like imagination and truth, craft and passion are inseparable here—as they are also in "Ice" and "The Ravine," two poems with elegant structures that summary cannot do justice to. . . . Each of these affecting poems tells us in its own way that "Dying doesn't end anything." Together with poems like "Pentecost" and "Jericho" they also tell us that Ai, her depressingly limited vision notwithstanding, is a forceful and gifted young poet. (pp. 568-69)

Stephen Yenser, "New Books in Review: 'Killing Floor'," in The Yale Review *(© 1979 by Yale University; reprinted by permission of the editors), Vol. LXVIII, No. 4, Summer, 1979, pp. 566-69.*

* * *

ALDISS, Brian 1925-

Aldiss is a British science fiction writer, novelist, critic, short story writer, essayist, and editor. His *Billion Year Spree*, a critical history of science fiction, confirmed his continuing efforts to present science fiction as a serious literary genre. He received the Hugo Award in 1962 for *Hothouse* and a

Nebula in 1966 for *The Saliva Tree*. A non-science fiction portrayal of English middle-class life is presented in the first two novels of a planned series: *The Hand-Reared Boy* and *A Soldier Erect*. (See also *CLC*, Vol. 5, and *Contemporary Authors*, Vols. 5-8, rev. ed.)

DAMON KNIGHT

The failure of most recent s.f. novels to say anything new and important, or even very interesting, makes a novel like Brian W. Aldiss's *Vanguard from Alpha,* flawed as it is, worthy of note.

Aldiss writes pointed, dry, highly stylized short stories that pack a great deal into a small space. His novels, those we have seen so far, are pot-boilers. (p. 243)

But even in his comic-book writing, Aldiss is more perceptive than most. The final solution of his puzzle is ingenious and reasonably satisfying; his future world has at least touches of reality, because it's as idiotically patched-together and complicated as our own. . . .

If this writer ever does a novel with his right hand, it will be something worth waiting for. (p. 244)

Damon Knight, "Decadent," in his In Search of Wonder: Essays on Modern Science Fiction *(copyright © 1956, 1967, by Damon Knight; reprinted by courtesy of Advent: Publishers, Inc.), revised edition, Advent, 1967, pp. 241-47.**

RICHARD MATHEWS

[Aldiss] finds the boundaries of simple popularity a limitation, and clearly wishes to venture beyond these limits into the uncharted waters of the experimental and esoteric. Like any prophet, or any writer, he is concerned with the language he uses to communicate—with words that shift and play games, with words that challenge and reveal. Committed to growth and change, he also steadfastly and painfully insists on examining his own nature, his moral stature, and his place in the universe. (p. 4)

[In his remarkable first collection of short stories, *Space, Time and Nathaniel* (1957),] we recognize the unique and challenging imagination which unwinds through countless Aldiss plots. Space and time are of paramount concern. He begins with the abstract theoretical foundations which are the assumptions behind our perceptions of reality. Added to this conceptual frame of reference is the individual perspective which gives it meaning—Nathaniel. Aldiss's world constantly stresses the limits and implications of relativity. The individual is more clearly revealed when set against the boundless perspectives of space. Science fiction was the ideal form for Aldiss, who later observes in the same introduction, "The corsets of conformity pinch on all sides." Aldiss *needs* the infinite space that science fiction allows him, and yet he continually brings us back to ponder the dignity and worthiness of a single human being.

His fascination with personal insight and character quirks adds liveliness to even the most abstract tale, and one of the strengths of these early stories is their characterizations, which are far richer than those usually encountered in the pulp fiction of those days.

Coupled with his theoretical framework of space-time continuum, and the creation of believable and rounded human characters, is Aldiss's delight and skill with literary style, with the words themselves. He purposefully enriched his writing with stylistic techniques capable of adding depth to his fiction. For example, as a gesture to the poetic career he had imagined for himself, he arranged the contents page of this first collection so that the titles of the three types of story are laid out in octet and sextet form, like a sonnet. There are fourteen titles. (pp. 5-6)

Aldiss's concern for structure includes both the macrocosm and microcosm, and in this group of stories he manifests his structural skill in small details (like the arrangement of the contents page) as well as in the overall progression of the stories themselves and their organization into a larger whole. . . . Among the best stories are "Dumb Show" and "The Failed Men" (also called "Ahead"). Both of these demonstrate quite clearly a multi-level awareness of structure which was part of Aldiss's science fiction from the first. (p. 6)

In the skillfully enigmatic stories of *Space, Time and Nathaniel,* Aldiss establishes the terrain he will explore. His concerns with space, time, individual character, growth (change), and language remain prominent throughout the rest of his writing. . . . [The collection] demonstrates a remarkable mastery of form, and an original discovery of worthy subjects. (p. 7)

Most of Aldiss's earliest work was written in shorter forms. . . . All of the most exciting developments in the short story during the late '50s and throughout the '60s took place in science fiction, and Aldiss was among the groundbreakers. . . . Even in the years 1964-67, though he had mastered an original novel technique quite unlike the structure of his short stories, he continued to exercise his talents in abbreviated and concise narratives. . . . It is important to recognize Aldiss's complete mastery of the short story and novella forms. When he first discovered the French anti-novel, and fully developed his own complex novelistic structures in *Report on Probability A* (written in 1962), the book from which one can date his full emergence as a novelist, Aldiss found that the linked stories of *Hothouse* had already begun to evolve in that direction. He recognized in the French *New Novel,* particularly Robbe-Grillet's *Jealousy* and Michel Butor's *Passing Time,* the perfect direction for his own next step. His publishers didn't agree, however, and his novel didn't see print until 1968. (p. 8)

Satire in [*The Primal Urge* (1961) is] indicative of an evolution in Aldiss's writing techniques and thematic material. Initially approaching his themes from a serious perspective, he now probes and crossexamines the motifs until he begins to develop a self-consciously ironic appreciation for his own intensity; suddenly he turns what were serious stylistic questions into humorous entertainment. (p. 11)

In his continuing explorations of the powers and functions of language, Aldiss treats both the external effects of communication—as evident, for instance in "Dumb Show," or the circumstances of *Non-Stop*—and the internal basis for communication: "Thought. Thought: that field of force still to be analysed. Thought: as inseparable from a higher being as gravity from a planet." It is not as if he has divorced language and communication from thought in his earlier published books, but here he specifically moves to explore the internal mental landscape from the very first sentence. The first-person narrator—the Nul Wattol Forlie—speaks in the opening pages, putting us close to the individual consciousness, and revealing the interior distances between characters. Thought is as necessary to proper performance of a translator's functions as idea or theme is necessary to successful fiction. The thoughtful, problem-ridden translator of "The Failed Men" is fleshed out in another guise in "The Interpreter," and one can almost hear Aldiss himself in the "I" of the book: "Thought. . . . It wraps around me, as my senses go about their endless job of turning all the external world into symbols." The issue is clear from the start: "I can know no external thing without its being touched—perhaps in some unguessable way transmuted—by my thought . . . was it real, or a misinterpretation in my mind." Even the physical perspective of this Nul reminds us of Aldiss's technique as a writer: "I lie flat on the wide wall by the old harbour, gazing up at the universe." Like the best authors of fantastic fiction, Aldiss succeeds in treating convincing action in a vast universe by making the familiar objects—single characters, or a comfortably recognizable old wall by a harbor—reassuringly present to lend an air of authenticity and reality to the fiction. (pp. 11-12)

More strongly than any of the earlier novels, *Urge* juxtaposes the primal and futuristic, using irony and humor to make a delightful game of the whole situation. Aldiss's light-handed "Author's Note" is an apology for using real people (like Aldous Huxley) and real brand-names . . . in what is obviously a piece of fiction, one not "really" about modern-day Britain ("Even the weather is too good to be true"). The settings for most of his earlier fiction are far from home, but this location is at "once unreal and typically English." Why has this reality suddenly moved so close to what we recognize?

We can know little of what Aldiss *intended* to accomplish in the shift, but we can discuss the effects. In the first place, he was attempting something new in style and tone, something fresh in science fiction. Behind this novel is the special tradition of English satire. It is part of a widely shared pleasure in tongue-in-cheek extravagance which runs from Jonathan Swift through Evelyn Waugh (*The Loved One*) to Anthony Burgess and Brian Aldiss. The closest parallels to this mode of science fiction are Orwell's *Animal Farm,* and Burgess's *The Eve of St. Venus*—in fact, Burgess and Aldiss have many things in common as contemporary writers of English science fiction, including the British touch for satire, and a passionate influence from James Joyce. There are similar elements in Orwell's *1984* or Huxley's *Brave New World,* but Aldiss hits closer to home with this double satire touching Britain's economic doldrums, the new permissiveness and the functions of power in the welfare state's relations with its public and foreign nations. In the ironic frame of mind, it is difficult to see clearly just what the primal urge is: sex or power, passion or reason, body or soul. (pp. 13-14)

[*No Time Like Tomorrow* (1959) and *Who Can Replace a Man?* (1966)] are collections of multi-faceted stories with common thematic motifs, each maintaining its own integrity. In both *Starswarm* and *Galaxies Like Grains of Sand,* Aldiss . . . has bound [his stories] together with a linked narrative commentary which is distracting and artificial. The running narration of the bridge material spoils the individual character of the stories, and by trying to unify them artificially, Aldiss has only placed them like fine diamonds in overly ornate settings: the conspicuous surrounding prevents a clear view of the stones.

The best practitioners of SF short story construction have created innovations in two directions: they have developed forms in which traditional demands of characterization can be flagrantly violated in favor of strong imaginative action and theme, with thematic material often incorporated in a manner which earlier would have been found more appropriate to the essay than to fiction; and, they have enlarged the conception of setting and space to include interior space, exploring psychological space in geographical narrative terms which unite what might be called "stream of consciousness" techniques with intensely involving narrative story lines to create curious crossbreeds and hybrids.

Though Aldiss has stories which explore both terrains, he has made particular contributions to expanding SF possibilities interiorly. When these efforts first reached public attention in the mid-1960's, along with those of other British SF writers, the movement came to be known collectively as the "New Wave." Although this term has been overworked, it is still useful as a designation of the new narrative approach to stream-of-consciousness fiction, an approach which makes an interior wave in Aldiss's best short stories. The wave comes in on the tide of a new sea discovered by the three authors of short fiction who seem to be obvious influences on Aldiss: Poe, Kafka and Joyce. From Poe he inherits the ability to center fiction on mystery, particularly on abnormal perspectives and situations, containing the whole within an ironically rational point of view. From Kafka, Aldiss has adopted the habit of writing in realistic universals. Often, the realities of Aldiss's fiction are achieved not through details of setting or character, but through the contact with convincing universals: a form of symbolic writing, close to allegory, in which characters and incidents seem to take on the quality of symbols for less tangible forces and principles. While Kafka explored the similarity between man and animals or insects, Aldiss carries this a step forward by comparing man to vegetables and machines. Like Kafka, he is concerned with individual man's relationship to large and intricate systems—governments, bureaucracies, armies, and so forth. From Joyce he adopts a great sensitivity to, and playfulness with, language and sound, the interior monologue (which Aldiss blends with active narration and dialogue), and the story moment referred to in Joyce's works as "epiphany," a sudden, central flash of understanding that bursts upon a reader, not in a climax of action, but of consciousness. In addition, he provides from book to book an evolving portrait of an artist, and attempts to unify morality, theology, and art.

In 1962 Aldiss published what some critics still regard as his most important work, *Hothouse*. Sections of the book had already appeared in various periodicals, but the finished novel achieves a whole much greater than any of the parts. The successful wedding of these smaller units into a unified creation shows great structural skill, and a significant advance over his thematically-assembled short story collections. *Hothouse* documents a progression from Blakean innocence through experience to a higher experience. By turns, it denies and then affirms individual experience; but it remains primarily a novel of opposing cosmic forces rather than a story of an individual character. In fact, Aldiss makes a point of this, particularly in the earlier parts of the novel, where he builds sympathy for a string of individual characters, only to kill them off immediately. This repeated plot device gradually brings home both the distinct individuality of life, and the universal principle of arbitrary death. Exercising his ironic sense of time, Aldiss begins the novel in the far future, with a primitive race of tiny humans in a vegetable world which seems at first more primeval than modern. The thrust of the tale, with its quest-structure, is to delineate a world of dichotomies taking the form of numerous either/or choices: life vs. death, good vs. evil, mind vs. body, animal vs. vegetable, heat vs. cold, light vs. dark; and, having established these dichotomies, to explore the middle ground, the area where one becomes the other, where life becomes death or the past becomes the future. It is no accident that so much of the crucial action near the end of the novel takes place in that no man's land of gray between the unfailingly dark and the eternally light parts of this futuristic world. Nor is it an accident that [the central character] Gren opts at the end of the book to remain where he was born, having come through his learning process to know it more fully and love it more deeply. (pp. 17-19)

Stylistically, Aldiss uses a beautifully shifting form, imitating the shifting realities of the novel, and the gradually maturing consciousness of Gren. The book begins simply, almost as a child's story, with uncomplicated thoughts and direct action. By the end of the book, we have moved through two very complex cerebral organisms, the morel and Sodal Ye. Form imitates content in an altogether pleasing manner. (p. 19)

Gren experiences something like an acid trip, an uncanny piece of writing that closely evokes mystical experience, overwhelming even the rationality of the morel. Aldiss links abstract and concrete impressions in such a way that the words constantly seem to mean more than they say, implying something just beyond our grasp. It is characteristic of Aldiss to include not only mind-boggling visions of space and time, but also an unparaphrastic dimension of experience which can only be labeled mystical. This vision is yet another reality, a true and intense one, and comprises one of the most glorious of human capabilities, a brief glimpse of universal unity and eternity. Aldiss may have attempted a paraphrase of this mystical perception through his awareness of the drug experience—hallucination was another dimension associated with the New Wave—but it remains for Aldiss, more than any of the other writers of the '60s and '70s, to make the profound connections between such experience, the scientific understanding of Heisenberg and Einstein, and the traditional religious and mythical frameworks which have striven to reveal something of this same transcendent human potential. The interior monolog provided here is close to the experience of ecstasy recorded by Christian saints in their union with God. It reaches its absurd extreme in the later hallucinatory novel, *Barefoot in the Head*.

In this instance, Gren returns to normal reality because the transformation he nearly undergoes is reserved for the mindless vegetal forms which fill the *Hothouse* Earth. Nonetheless, the experience makes a deep and abiding impression and colors the rest of the book. . . . Head and tail, beginning and end, past and future: the extremes are shown not as opposites, but as identities in the cyclical process of creative change, a process which is Aldiss's bedrock of belief. It is a faith which affirms the Christian paradox that "in my end is my beginning."

The identity of beginning and end is a part of the heat and cold imagery running through the novel. Temperature is, of course, a natural function of setting and environment, and something one could expect to find in practically any story by Aldiss; from *Equator* onward, however, temperature becomes a particularly important factor. Even the title, *Hothouse,* proclaims the importance to Aldiss of this imagery. (pp. 21-2)

Is *Hothouse* science fiction? The novel is short on outright scientific explanations, and there are mystical realms left totally unexplained. The appearance of the philosophical and priestly Sodal Ye at the book's end moves the fiction further outside the boundaries of science. Sodal Ye is more a prophet than a scientist, despite his considerable practical and scientific knowledge. (p. 22)

The threat of extinction looms over the entire human race, rather than any alien population, in Aldiss's *Greybeard*. Here, as in much of Aldiss's fiction, the men of the future have suffered the effects of globally devastating radiation. Though published in 1964, this novel is still valid as a commentary upon continued flirtation with nuclear weapons. . . . The world of Aldiss's novel depicts a future inhabited by senior citizens, who as a result of radiation have lost the ability to reproduce. There are no children. In addition, civilization has moved rapidly backward. . . . Man has entered a second period of superstition and conflict in Aldiss's world, similar in many respects to the Dark Ages. (p. 26)

Hothouse deals with a vegetal profusion of growth, and with human efforts to survive the overwhelming force of nature; *Greybeard* presents a strongly cyclical view of nature, a picture of secession, of changing domination, and a grand parade of dominant forms alternating with one another. Although the central problem in the narrative is that there will be no new human generation, the repeated images of life's revolving cycles suggest a force at work throughout the universe for renewing existence, one more powerful than whatever man-made forces may oppose the continuation of life. (p. 27)

Based on a short story with a macabre pun-title, "Skeleton Crew," *Earthworks* [1965] begins with the strongest death images and feelings of alienation yet to appear in [Aldiss's] published work. Cut off from any link with the land and nearly alone on an automated ship, the characters are hostile to one another as well as out of touch with their environment. . . . The first scene of the novel is unforgettable, as a dead man slowly comes toward the ship, apparently walking across the water. Religious implications are clearly mixed with the heritage of technology which forms part of the futuristic environment. Here is an apparent miracle which echoes Christ, but in Aldiss's tale, there is no resurrection; the dead man is horribly dead, and offers no hope of salvation. The book begins "on the day of this new dead man," and the personal associations of the book are reinforced by the fact that it is told in first person, making it quite close to the individual consciousness of its narrator, Knowle Noland. The name suggests uprooted and alienated knowledge: knowing, with no land to connect it or oneself to. The narrative style is full of pain and alienation. The voice is excruciatingly self-conscious, and aware of "the imprisonment words bring." The narrator is bound by his name, his knowledge, his head. He is imprisoned by his job—as narrator and crew member—on a vessel with a skeleton crew to look after the automatic machinery which does all the work, adrift on one of those "great grey ships sailing the seas and rarely touching land."

Through a kind of hallucination, we are brought to the central focus of the book. "The Travellers," we are told, "represented some sort of initiative for the future in a continent full of *dead* ends" (my italics).

It is in this section that we begin to witness the resurrection of the book, a life-restoring creative practice of an ancient art: "You need courage because writing is confessing, and my biggest confession of all must come in this section. I love the Travellers, yet I betrayed Jess! . . . I have performed a sort of resurrection of this ancient art form." The narrator becomes a vehicle for Aldiss to confess his inner instincts as a serious writer, attempting to build a vital literature in the 20th century, when the book has already become old-fashioned. (pp. 30-1)

In his selection of a literary approach, Noland picked as his primary one the journey archetype which has run from Odysseus to the Time Traveller. But one cannot actually become a Traveller until one has been sterilized; "A pregnancy was as good as a death sentence to a travelling woman." To be merely a traditional Traveller for Aldiss (the writer) would be sterile and uncreative. *Earthworks* is a prelude to a period of new stylistic fertility in both form and narrative structure. Even its self-conscious narrator-without-a-country, subject to hallucinations which cripple and reveal his life, prefigures the hallucinogenic prose of *Probability A* and *Barefoot in the Head.* (p. 31)

The narrative is a type of picaresque, a series of linked occurrences held together by common thematic concerns, common images, and the personality of the narrator. Highly episodic, it uses cinematic techniques in "fading out," and making associational "cuts" from one scene to the next. As the narrator struggles in the verbal medium, he feels the enormous difficulty of communication. . . . Increasingly, imagistic and thematic materials are thrown together into a context of hallucination, an uncertain sense of reality, an awareness of scale so immense that it is impossible to obtain a comfortable perspective; clear antipathies are difficult to discern. The infinity of exterior space is mirrored by an equally unpredictable and infinite interior space.

Illusion and reality struggle throughout the novel, perhaps personified by the mysterious "Figure" which haunts the narrator from the very first pages, and increases in impact as the book progresses. . . . Aldiss at his most alienated, at his most death-preoccupied, has created a narrator philosophically and emotionally at sea, who desperately grounds his ship. . . . (p. 32)

Earthworks succeeds in wedding the psychological and metaphysical realities in a convincing and compelling narrative structure which sets in motion new direction for Aldiss's SF. It faces the difficulties of language, psychology, and metaphysics, insisting that they should be a serious part of the science fiction writer's explorations. The voice of the narrator reads convincingly as a voice for Aldiss himself: "Philosophy is not my strong point, though I have tried many a time to make sense of my life, and of the killing drag of history, but I tried then to review the phantasies that my sickness had inflicted on me. Some I have set down in this narrative. At the time, they held as firm a place in my understanding as parts of the real world, and the continents of delusion which I had been forced to march were no more fantastic than Africa or England." As Noland waits with the rifle to kill the only leader able to preserve a precarious political order in the world, he is about to unleash the irrational forces of war; as Aldiss seeks to explore human significance amidst alienation, he is about to unleash the psychedelic forces of creative madness. (p. 34)

Time-warps and folds enhance the narrative pleasures of [*An Age* (1967), also published as *Cryptozoic* (1968)]. Bush, a master mind-traveller, is coerced into the service of the Mind Travel Police Patrol, and then turns counter-agent when he is persuaded to serve with subversives and revolutionaries. The twists of the adventure mirror the intricacies of time, and rational understanding assumes the aspect of theoretical gamesmanship, in which Aldiss shows himself a master, spinning and unspinning whole theoretical constructions of the temporal universe. It is interesting and appropriate to note the lack of technological hardware in this tale. *An Age* explores the abstract in concrete terms, and echoes the concern for a metaphysical dimension expressed in *Earthworks.* Essentially a theoretical and conceptual book, the novel presents a future society in 2093 becoming increasingly non-material, in both literal and figurative terms, as more and more people escape into the realm of mind-travel. . . . The problem is largely a question of escapism versus purpose and intent, and like the artist-hero, this aspect reflects a critical awareness of struggle over the purposes of SF. . . . Aldiss comes down clearly on the side of those who [are concerned with] purposeful creative and intellectual growth. (p. 36)

[With *Report on Probability A* (1968)] Aldiss has succeeded in creating an English novel as fresh in both style and conception as anything produced by the flurry of activity surrounding the much-touted anti-novel. His book is distinctly English, with dialog which approaches the fine ear of his gifted contemporary Harold Pinter. And the careful rendering of detail, which has so long been an effective device for lending reality to science fiction, is perfectly at home in this slice into parallel worlds. We confront a hall of mirrors, a corridor not of time (as in *An Age*) but of probability.

Halfway through the novel, the perspective is still not clear. One has encountered innumerable reflections, but has yet to distinguish the mirror from the image being reflected. One is led to conclude that certainty in these matters is not to be found. (p. 40)

Again and again through both the form and the style of [*Report*], Aldiss involves his readers in experience which is not smooth and continuous. The flow of time and the build-up of sequential observations are never allowed to create the illusion of coherence. Coherence would be an assumption of meaning, or absolute truth, and this assumption can never be allowed to come from the author here. It is left to the reader to supply it for himself, if he can.

There is one sense in which experience is continuous, however. Whatever verb tense is used, the consciousness Aldiss imposes on his readers gives the impression of continuous present-time. Every event, character and detail must be recorded, often with identical description, each time it is encountered. People move from one room to the next, and as they emerge into different space they must be described anew. They may or may not be the same people. In any case, we are rarely allowed easy assumptions of knowledge built up from past experience. (p. 41)

What does a science fiction writer do when he finds he has written himself out of science fiction [as Aldiss said he had after completing *Barefoot in the Head*]? The answer in Aldiss's case was to go back to where he had started. "I wrote ordinary novels instead," Aldiss explains. Returning to where he started, in "ordinary" fiction like *The Brightfount Diaries,* Aldiss produced two books which became instant best-sellers in England. He also completed a personal reminiscence, *The Shape of Further Things,* assembled the most comprehensive critical history of science fiction yet to be published (*Billion Year Spree*), and issued several collections of short stories. The period 1969-73 was a time for looking back to his roots, for reflecting upon the history and evolution of the science fiction genre, and constructing a personal memoir which helped put his own past in perspective. He had pushed himself beyond the boundaries of language, history, and genre, and it was time to retrench.

"Ordinary" is a word to be used in its best sense when applied to *The Hand-Reared Boy* (1970); its recording of male rites of passage before the war is one with which any man can identify. The hero is Horatio Stubbs—a name which combines the sublime with the ridiculous—and in this readable and amusing novel, Stubbs comes convincingly to life. His history is continued in *A Soldier Erect* (1971), which follows Stubbs into the early 1940s as he joins the Royal Mendip Borderers, and is dispatched overseas to India. Stubb's battles are mainly for women, and the barracks humor is broader and more genial than anything Aldiss had written earlier. Neither of these novels has been widely read in America, probably because, as Aldiss says, "They embodied too British an experience." But Aldiss also believes "*A Soldier Erect* is probably the best of all my novels, shot through with pain and humour." Whether or not the assessment is accurate, these novels are significant in marking his return to standard fiction devices, without the aid of stylistic inventions or SF gimmicks. The author has thoroughly mastered the fundamentals of writing and the interlude in which these novels were written strengthened his mastery of the form. Horatio Stubbs is one of his most human characters. (pp. 48-9)

Aldiss joyously resurrects old SF stereotypes in *The Eighty Minute Hour* (1975). . . . By reducing the genre of his serious writing to convention format, Aldiss shows himself the detached observer of his own fiction. His own contribution to Space Opera has about it an amused self-consciousness, stylistic flair and dexterity, and a double-edged humor based in the comic multiple meanings of language. These techniques stretch the limits of style and genre with the same exaggeration and audacity as the cramming of 80 minutes into an hour. (p. 54)

Perhaps the ultimate of his landscape novels, *The Malacia Tapestry* [1976] concludes with a human landscape, imperfect and ordinary, but flawlessly beautiful nonetheless. . . .

Whether or not it is his best is difficult to say, but this refreshingly different and masterfully-written book restates once more the depth and breadth of literary scope practiced by Aldiss, and is undoubtedly his best work since *Frankenstein Unbound.* (p. 59)

As he returns again and again to the themes, images, and symbols which occupy his mind, [Aldiss's] Protean changes in form and style catch the reader constantly by surprise. It was change which attracted him to science fiction in the first place—a fiction with more space for change. His later novels are difficult to classify within SF as a narrow genre; Aldiss will not stay within neat boundaries. (pp. 60-1)

Richard Mathews, in his Aldiss Unbound: The Science Fiction of Brian W. Aldiss *(copyright © 1977 by Richard Mathews), The Borgo Press, 1977, 64 p.*

PAUL ABLEMAN

Enemies of the System is essentially derivative, almost a lash-up of elements from Huxley, Wells, Orwell, anthropological accounts of cargo cults and so on. It does not further either the analysis or the resolution of the problem of what happens to an advanced but stagnant culture when it meets a primitive but vital and evolving one. Indeed, Mr Aldiss weakens his central antithesis by revealing that his Utopia includes 'the dreaded reason police.' The System must therefore be in a state of internal revolt, but the matter is never developed. Mr Aldiss seems to have found difficulty in resisting the allure of any theme that has proved its worth in other books, whether relevant to his own or not.

Possibly as a further consequence of the basic lack of purpose, the text is full of inconsistencies. All right, the culture is stagnant but, after a million years which has seen the introduction of interstellar travel, would holiday-makers still drive about in coaches with tyres and squealing brakes? Towards the end of the book it is revealed that much more sophisticated transport systems are available. The coach is thus unmasked as merely a literary device to enable contact with the primitives to be established. Even more unconvincing is the mode of expression of the Biocom citizens. They continually regale each other with rustic saws such as: 'As the teat grows thinner, the kid sucks with greater vehemence'. Hardly what one expects from star-roving gulfhoppers. The truth is that the level of imaginative penetration of an alien, future society achieved by this book is about that of a routine episode of *Star Trek.*

Paul Ableman, "Gulf-hopping," in The Spectator *(© 1978 by* The Spectator; *reprinted by permission of* The Spectator*), Vol. 240, No. 7821, May 27, 1978, p. 25.*

JEREMY TREGLOWN

Enemies of the System has all the easy interest of any cleanly-imagined futurist novel, and effectively juxtaposes its hyper-evolved Biocom tourists with the kangaroo-like, regressed but sporadically dignified human species on the remote planet the tourists visit. Given all this, it's mostly a simple exercise in transposition. Statute-books become computerised statute-banks; fathers are replaced by directors of crèches. All amusing enough, except that the characterisation is rudimentary, the narrative linear, and the dialogue either crudely ideological or absurdly expository. . . . (p. 748)

Jeremy Treglown, "Drunk Dreams," in New Statesman *(© 1978 The Statesman & Nation Publishing Co. Ltd.), Vol. 95, No. 2463, June 2, 1978, pp. 747-48.**

LORNA SAGE

Brian Aldiss is astonishingly prolific, and surprisingly humane and solid. The first characteristic he shares with other science fiction writers . . . , but the other qualities are much more rare. . . .

[*New Arrivals, Old Encounters* and *This World and Nearer Ones*] are very humanly likeable. They are, in other words, without the excesses of mutual abuse and mutual parody SF writers increasingly seem to go in for—the unsavoury consequences of having only partially emerged from their despised but profitable ghetto, their 'small cemeteries on the fringes of a book page' as Mr. Aldiss phrases it. He himself is doing his level best to still the internecine feuds, and to emphasize the creative connections between SF and the ordinary novel.

Of course for him the ordinary novel is a rather tired affair. The stories in *New Arrivals, Old Encounters* with their pared down, if not actually cloned characters, and their plots casually based on superputers and time-defeating communications, make that very clear. From his point of view fictional realism is bound to look like a shortsighted episode between worlds based on total religion or total science. . . .

[The] recurrent theme is the spring-cleaning of men's atavistic fears and hates, and the transformation of metaphysics into a science. The culminating piece, 'Difference,' imagines that process as nearly complete, and injects a further doubt—whether the desired universal theocracy may not always remain a premature solution. 'Men always cheat their gods,' it's said in another story ('Amen and Out'): the future lies in dialogue between the expanding known and the retreating unknown.

These are, as Mr. Aldiss is the first to acknowledge, hoary old ideas. They're rescued by some fetching images, like the dignified characters of 'Amen and Out' . . .—and by—after all—touches of ordinary realism, which enabled him to convey, for example, how it feels to know that 'whatever we are, whoever we are, whether young or old' we're part of the same pattern. It feels rotten, a bit like a bad hangover.

He needs realism to make this stick; he would argue, though, that realism needs fantasy to keep up its side of the dialogue too. The pieces in *This World and Nearer Ones* touch on such arguments. Not, however, as interestingly as the stories do. Mr. Aldiss's tone here is good-natured and relaxed (perhaps too relaxed, unless his reference to 'two great English writers, Henrick Ibsen and Leo Tolstoy' is some sort of specialist joke I've missed). . . .

There are worries about anarchy, and worries about order, and some useful remarks about the commercial and critical standing on SF. It's all a bit desultory, though what does stand out is his contention that the best of British SF is characterised by 'continuing scepticism; above all, scepticism about man's supremacy over nature and the benefits of unremitting technology.'

You could say the same about the best of Brian Aldiss—that while he registers all the glamour of Utopias, orderly and otherwise, he remains humorously, sanely sceptical.

Lorna Sage, "Other Edens," in The Observer *(reprinted by permission of The Observer Limited), No. 9809, August 26, 1979, p. 36.*

JEREMY TAMBLING

[*New Arrivals, Old Encounters*] will appeal to those who like their fantasies given a dressing of Arnoldian high seriousness. My loss, no doubt, but I am left a little cold by such solemnities as 'the universe has a dark corner, the human soul, which is its reflection'—the winning contribution of a five-year-old to a galaxy-wide competition. A bureaucratic nirvana is nicely described in one short story, 'A Spot of Konfrontation': another, 'One Blink of the Moon' is effectively phantasmagoric and spooky; but too often the entertainment is overlaid with vague gestures towards presumed significance. (p. 313)

Jeremy Tambling, "Caged," in New Statesman *(© 1979 The Statesman & Nation Publishing Co. Ltd.), Vol. 98, No. 2527, August 31, 1979, pp. 312-13.**

* * *

ALONSO, Dámaso 1898-

Alonso is considered a pioneer of twentieth-century Spanish poetry and criticism. His early poetry is cool and austere in manner and style, while his later poetry, marked by the terror and tragedy of the Spanish civil war, focuses on more humanistic concerns and is written in free verse. Alonso explores the duality of human nature in his poetry, portraying man's strivings and limitations in a world of ambivalent natural forces. He is acknowledged as Spain's foremost literary critic.

ANDREW P. DEBICKI

Dámaso Alonso is generally recognized as a major literary critic of contemporary Spain, and as the founder of a whole school of stylistic analysis. At the same time he is considered an important poet who, having started his career by writing "pure" and somewhat abstract verse, changes his style after the Spanish Civil War of 1936-1939 and takes the lead in a movement toward a direct and anguished "human" poetry.

This characterization of Alonso as a poet of two styles, though in many respects correct, does not take into account the fundamental cohesiveness of his literary production. If we examine all of his verse, for example, we can see that in spite of certain external differences between his early and his late books of poetry, all of them deal with the same general themes and make use of similar devices. All of them, for example, offer a dual perspective on reality, artistically embodied in certain techniques of imagery and point of view. Likewise, if we study Alonso's criticism, we find certain ideas which pervade and link his stylistic analyses and his more general essays, his earlier works and his later ones. Alonso's views, for example, on the relationship between analysis and intuition, on the ways in which a poem infuses new values into traditional themes and techniques, and on the connections between form and meaning, exemplify such constant points in his criticism. In addition, if we consider Alonso's verse and his criticism in relation to each other, we are able to see some viewpoints and concerns which underlie and shed light on both genres. In both, for instance, Alonso strives to reconcile personal intuitions with objective visions; in both he bases his work on his attitude toward literary form as a unique way of embodying complex essential meanings which cannot be seized in any other way. (p. 7)

[There is] a constant duality in Alonso's work, a shift between the precise and the affective, the learned and the immediate, which can be discerned both in his verse and in his criticism. This seems to be in Alonso's case a particular form of the conflict between the conceptual critic and the poet who seeks meanings intuitively. Alonso, on the one hand, is constantly delving as deeply as possible into the nature and the meaning of phenomena in general and of literature in particular, using his tremendous philological and critical knowledge and acumen to obtain the fullest insights possible. But at the same time he comes to feel the limitations and the imperfections of human intelligence and of humanity, to have an affective awareness of Man's plight and tragedies, and to embody vividly this plight and these tragedies. Alonso's great triumph is that he manages to fuse and combine his two attitudes and his two quests. He does so largely thanks to his sense of what is personally crucial for Man: in his criticism he always asks the question that yields insights as to the works' value for the reader, in his verse he focuses on themes of key import to Man's life. He does this also because of his sense of the creative power of language: in all his writing . . . Alonso combines and orders words so as to pull out of them a wide range of meaning, conceptual as well as affective. (p. 23)

The conflict between an idealized view of life and a harshly realistic one, a conflict which is central to *Poemas puros,* prefigures the clash between a religious outlook and an existential one, and this clash is central to Alonso's later verse. The protagonist who must choose between the poetic and the trivial in *Poemas puros* is an earlier version of the anguished seeker of *Hijos de la ira*. The use of images which combine symbolic and metaphoric values can be seen throughout all of Alonso's poetry: the use of a prosaic vocabulary for poetic effects can be discerned in *Poemas puros* and becomes dominant in *Hijos de la ira*. All this suggests that the poetry of Dámaso Alonso constitutes a single path: his early poems already reveal human, philosophic, and poetic concerns which blossom fully in his later books, and which enable him to become a leader in the poetic renewal which follows the Civil War. (pp. 33-4)

Much of the poetic value of *Poemas puros* is due to the way in which symbols give dramatic precision and concreteness to the otherwise ethereal theme of a common outlook in conflict with an elevated one. At times, indeed, the work might seem too exact in its use of natural and human symbols. But the paradoxical nature of the speaker . . . and the use of detailed tangible images . . . keep the book from falling into an inhuman neatness; while concern with the issue of time relates the work and its theme of a dual reality to a basic question facing Man.

The most successful images that appear in the book seem therefore to possess a dualistic nature. On the one hand they fulfill the traditional role of symbols: that of representing, conceptually and completely, certain meanings outside of themselves. (Thus the speaker embodies the search for ideals, the beloved is an ideal, etc.) In this fashion they pin down exactly the conflict between two points of view. On the other hand, however, these same images add complexity to several poems, and in this fashion operate more like metaphors. (p. 38)

Oscura noticia, like Alonso's earlier poetry, is centered on the conflict between an idealistic attitude and a prosaic one. But now Alonso relates this conflict even more explicitly to the particular issues and problems of human life, to time, death, love. As a result, it becomes less an absolute contrast between the elevated and the ordinary; and more the very immediate struggle which Man faces between his desire to reach various types of perfection (the perfect love, the perfect work of art, timelessness) on the one hand, and the forces which pull him to egoism, which limit him, and which make him susceptible to death on the other. And as the theme of the duality of life is brought closer to our immediate existence, so the techniques of the work place greater stress on the complexities and the shadings to be found in reality. By developing and stressing the role of the protagonist, by using bisemic symbols, and by using details with greater complexity, Alonso incorporates into his poems more of the aspects and the elements related to the dualities actually present in our world.

Possibly the most obvious feature of *Hijos de la ira* is the anguish which it expresses by means of its images of horror, its free verse, its seemingly direct style, and its ordinary and at times prosaic language. . . . [But] this negative picture of the world is balanced by a hopeful view of God, of beauty, and even of certain aspects of Man. . . . *Hijos de la ira* marks the culmination of the conflict between the ordinary and the elevated which we have noted all along in Alonso's creative work. This conflict, however, becomes even more related to the basic problems of immediate human existence. As a result, what was a somewhat abstract contrast between the prosaic and the poetic in *Poemas puros,* and turned into the struggle between the desire for perfection and the limitations of Man in *Oscura noticia,* now becomes an even more vital and individualized conflict between Man's search for religious and personal transcendence on the one hand, and his temptation to egotism, pettiness and destruction on the other. (Now the poet looks at the destructive elements more closely, finding them harder to overcome.)

The book reveals a continued use of the techniques observed in Alonso's earlier verse, but now developed and enriched even further to meet the requirements of the work's more vital nature. Alonso makes use of the protagonist, of a combination of symbol and metaphor, and of a variety of subordinate images and figures; more than in previous books, he forms these elements, and the different poems of the volume, into a tightly knit and unified vision. (pp. 51-2)

The main protagonist of *Hijos de la ira* sees himself negatively more often than not, but this must be interpreted in the context of the book as a whole. Several times we notice that the condemnation which this protagonist heaps on himself becomes, paradoxically, his very means of salvation. . . . [It appears] that it is a confession of his own inadequacy which allows Man to transcend the limitations of the common and the material, and to achieve an elevated attitude. This view becomes, indeed, a major theme of *Hijos de la ira*. (p. 53)

[*Hijos de la ira* takes] us dramatically from acceptance to rejection to renewed acceptance. Thus it has involved us in the path followed by the protagonist, and has embodied forcefully the theme of selflessness as a prerequisite to insight and to a higher outlook.

Although in the context of the book the protagonist symbolizes Man, it is as a particular being who draws shifting attitudes from the reader that he gives the poem its forcefulness. A clear initial identification between this speaker and Everyman would weaken the dramatic effect, and therefore the final paradox: only in renunciation does Man acquire acceptance and dignity. The particular characterization of this man serves, as some of the metaphors seen previously, to give vitality and concreteness to the work, and to prevent us from reducing it to a neat scheme. Yet the symbolic level of the poem is also indispensable. (This level is stressed by allusions in the poem, by the picture of the speaker as a man praying to God, by the context of the book.) Without this symbolic level, the speaker's plight would be trivial—the mere sufferings of an emotionally unstable man. This poem, therefore, reveals a perfect blend of two levels: the descriptive or metaphoric, which focuses on a particular being and makes us feel the immediacy of a particular reality; and the symbolic, which points to a more universal theme. This combination allows the poem to treat its theme both richly and significantly. (pp. 56-7)

The protagonist of *Hijos de la ira* is . . . the cornerstone of the general pattern of the book. Representing Man as he travels through life, he must choose between a selfish, limited outlook on the one hand, and a selfless, wider, and more poetic one on the other. Whatever connections he might have with Dámaso Alonso himself, this protagonist is primarily a literary device embodying a dramatic and complex battle going on within Man. Endowed with both symbolic and metaphoric value, he embodies the basic scheme of the work and is the major factor in its unity. (p. 59)

Without resolving the ultimate problems of religious truth, *Hijos de la ira* [offers] a coherent attitude which Man—be he an orthodox Christian or not—can take in the light of the problems of existence. The protagonist's belief in the order of the universe, his acceptance of a pattern wider than his own whims, and his desire to curb and transcend these whims underlie the whole book. They forcefully represent a way of standing against all that is petty and chaotic in our world, and of asserting the higher dignity and possibilities of Man. They are, indeed, an existential and philosophic attitude which can be asserted by men of widely differing religious creeds. And the dramatic and patterned nature of the book makes it clear that the protagonist's "story" is important as one version, one example of Man's quest for elevation, not as a way of telling us what we should believe.

It is true, of course, that the work accepts the existence of a divine force; and that it leaves the detailed characteristics of this divine force undefined. (God will become more enigmatic in Alonso's later poetry.) Both these attitudes are again, however, quite wide in scope, and could be held by practicing Catholics as well as by skeptics. . . . While operating within his Catholic tradition, Alonso does not limit *Hijos de la ira* to any particular religious view. . . . [He is] constructing a poetic work rather than presenting his own beliefs. (pp. 64-5)

Hijos de la ira, though deeply concerned with basic philosophic questions, treats them in a human and poetic, rather than in a theological or systematic, fashion. The book embodies, vividly and dramatically, Man's struggle for value in his life, his opposition to the chaos and the meaninglessness which surrounds him, and his renunciation of a petty view in favor of a wider one. It offers one version, one compelling example of Man's battle to affirm his dignity; in that it holds meaning for all men of our time—and of all times.

What I have just said about *Hijos de la ira* is also applicable to Alonso's later books, *Hombre y Dios* and *Gozos de la vista*. There too we will find a protagonist struggling against the limitations of his pettiness, of the world, of time, of death. There too we will find the embodiment of a significant human attitude in the face of the philosophic and existential dilemmas facing us. (p. 65)

The choice between viewpoints which [*Hijos de la ira*] presents is a clear outgrowth of the theme of the ordinary versus the elevated which we have been observing since *Poemas puros*. The conflict between Man's search for religious transcendence and his temptation to egotism is but a more personal, more immediate, and at the same time more essentially human version of that constant theme. . . . And the whole theme of a conflict between Man's desire to elevate himself and his awareness of the concrete problems and limitations of existence could perhaps be linked in some way to the duality observable in Dámaso Alonso's own outlook, to the tension between the search for precise and exact insights and the feeling for affective human problems and limitations.

Hijos de la ira also represents a continuation and a development of the techniques already seen in Alonso's earlier work. The book still explores its meanings through symbols which both point beyond themselves to wider issues and retain concrete and metaphoric values. These symbols now reveal greater concreteness, greater wealth of allusion, greater connection with our present era; their metaphoric aspect is more apparent. Most important among these symbols is the protagonist . . . who has constantly helped portray, concretely yet precisely, Alonso's view of the basic conflict faced by Man. All this confirms the feeling that *Hijos de la ira,* for all its directness, is above all an artistic embodiment of its theme. (p. 66)

The central subject of Dámaso Alonso's *Hombre y Dios (Man and God)* is clearly a religious one: the presence of God and Man's relationship to Him. This fact, and the seemingly straightforward and easy-to-understand language in which the book is written, might tempt us into thinking of it as a direct philosophic statement. We might even surmise that Alonso has abandoned the complex art of his earlier poetry to give us a neat vision of a religious creed. Yet such a view would obviously be unsatisfactory; for one thing, it is clear that the overt theses of some poems of *Hombre y Dios* contradict those of others, so that no single philosophic statement could encompass them all.

Hombre y Dios constitutes, in my opinion, a complex poetic inquiry into the question of Man's role in the universe. It does not achieve its complexity by embodying all the different meanings and shadings in each individual poem, but rather by building a carefully constructed whole out of a balance of individual poems, each of which presents a partial (and sometimes simple) view. In this sense *Hombre y Dios* is a tightly-knit dramatic whole, which juxtaposes several opposing views of Man's situation and his relationship with God; on the basis of these views, the book constructs a new synthesis, a new multifacted vision. (p. 67)

Alonso has always achieved some of his most powerful effects by developing his meanings gradually, and by juxtaposing one part of a work to another—rather than by structuring a work as a static architectural unit, to be encompassed all at one time. In *Hijos de la ira* he has in addition made different poems and different characters develop diverse aspects of the central conflict of the book. . . . *Hombre y Dios* [is] a culmination of Alonso's progressive and dramatic technique. . . .

In *Hombre y Dios,* Alonso again presents a contrast between different views of human existence. An easy, God-centered faith shown in the first poems contrasts with a simple, earth-centered outlook revealed in the last one; in between these, the middle section of the book develops an ultimately positive and religious, but at the same time complex and ambiguous, resolution. The very titles of poems and of sections of the book illustrate this dialectical process. (p. 68)

By means of images of Man's role as God's eyes, of Man's free will, and of Man's gift for poetry, [in the middle section Alonso] manages to unite the earlier viewpoints into a new whole—which we may deem paradoxical and logically enigmatic, but which we accept as poetically and humanly valuable. The neat scheme around which the book is organized, its use of philosophic concepts as images, and its stress on absolute questions and on their resolution may make *Hombre y Dios* perhaps a little less immediate, less close to the particular anguish of human beings than *Hijos de la ira*. But thanks to its structure and its use of lyric and dramatic devices it remains a vital embodiment of its theme, an excellent poem; and also one which gives us an even fuller view than Alonso's earlier books of a basic conflict between points of view. (p. 84)

As the title indicates, *Gozos de la vista* treats the subject of human sight, its glories, and its limitations. This subject is, however, also the means of dealing with even wider preoccupations. The values and the perils of human sight evoke the great worth as well as the tragic shortcomings of human beings. The book, as its predecessors, portrays a basic clash between two views. One of these stresses the unique merits of human sight and the consequent dignity of Man, while the other suggests the limitations of his sight and Man's consequent fragility and mortality. The dialectical conflict so important in Alonso's poetry is here renewed; it is focused on a more specific trait and situation than in *Hombre y Dios*—on sight and on the tragedies of blindness. (In this the book resembles more *Hijos de la ira.*) It is related even more explicitly, on the other hand, to basic problems of human existence—to time and to death. *Gozos de la vista* represents an individualized and yet essential treatment of the theme of the dual nature of our existence: its values and its shortcomings.

On the surface, the clash in viewpoints is not as clear-cut here as in *Hombre y Dios;* likewise the work is not so neatly divided into sections representing opposite points of view. Yet the work does reveal a dramatic structure, and much of its meaning does depend on the relations that exist between sections, between poems, and between parts of poems. These relations unfold gradually, however, usually as a result of shifts and reversals within the book. Rather than an "architectural" structure, a single and more static scheme such as the one found in *Hombre y Dios,* we have here a more dynamic one. This structure . . . reveals itself gradually as we follow the path of the protagonist and watch his insights accumulate and modify each other. In this fashion Alonso keeps using dramatic techniques while staying even closer to the predicament of the particular being. (p. 85)

Of the ten sections of *Gozos de la vista,* the first four seem to constitute a unit. Within them the protagonist defines the importance of human sight, climaxing his presentation with a prayer for its survival. In them the tension between the worth and the shortcomings of sight is outlined. The first of these sections is centered on the idea that sight brings man out of a static self-centeredness, permitting him to join together the multiple and changing elements of the world and thus to extend his own existence. . . . (p. 86)

It is important to note that the external reality seen by the protagonist is only defined through its effects on him. Reality is furthermore reduced to a neat scheme, to a series of vertical and horizontal lines which his sight attracts just as an antenna attracts electronic impulses. The focus is then on the man [and] . . . his reception of the outer world's signals. . . . (pp. 86-7)

[Alonso] conveys the idea that Man's sight is a vehicle through which God obtains a human perspective on the world, a perspective otherwise unavailable to Him. In the middle section of *Hombre y Dios,* this idea functioned as an image bringing together a God-centered and a Man-centered view of existence. Here in *Gozos de la vista* the idea plays a somewhat similar role, in that it makes us feel Man's importance as well as his participation in a higher, non-material scheme of things. But in the context of the book, the poem also picks up and stresses an idea already developed in [earlier] sections: that Man's sight is valuable, not because of its physical power, but because it lets Man transcend purely physical nature. By now making sight the instrument of divine perception and a creative force modeled on God, Alonso strengthens greatly the earlier view of Man's transcendence. Therefore, this poem serves now, not so much to merge opposing outlooks, as to stress the unique importance of Man as a superior being, endowed with a perspective both realistic and elevated. (p. 88)

Alonso stresses above all the purely material, base, and unconscious nature of a sightless world. By indicating that such a world cannot be described visually or conceptually, he sets it beneath human thought, human perception, human words. By describing the animals as bubbling, as touching, as gnawing, he accents their base physical characteristics, their lack of intelligence, their inhuman horizontal postures. All this again makes sight the distinguishing trait between a human existence and a lower one: before sight there is no thought, no human dignity. (p. 90)

Glancing back over all of *Gozos de la vista,* we can see that Alonso has used in it something like a large-scale version of a symbol which initially is only suggested, and then gradually becomes defined. . . . After making us feel implicitly that sight alludes to Man's values and blindness to his limitations in sections one through four, Alonso gave us a specific story of a blinding. We could see the wider implications of the story, but did not ignore its particularity; the symbolic level had not yet been defined conceptually, and did not distract us from the specific reality. Now Alonso links blindness and Man's limitations exactly and conceptually, allowing us to see the vast range of his subject. Since this comes only after the concrete level has been established, we do not deem it an excessively abstract presentation. Alonso has used a large-scale version of the "bisemic symbol" again to give his work richness of detail on the one hand, and wider scope and greater precision on the other.

As the symbolic value of sight and blindness is made clear, so is Man's essential tragedy. The human inability to understand God picks up the earlier visions of Man's fragility and mortality, uniting them in a single image of his incapability fully to understand or control his situation. This incapability is stressed in the next two stanzas of the poem, which portray the speaker's unsuccessful efforts to explain colors to a blind man, and his final prayer asking that God should give the blind a new sight. Given the symbolic meaning of blindness just established, these efforts and this prayer represent a desperate (and hopeless) effort to overcome or at least hide Man's shortcomings. The protagonist still requests the concrete and earthly, yet superior and creative, vision which is the unique property and value of Man. But the last sections studied have made clear the impossibility of preserving this vision forever. (pp. 97-8)

Gozos de la vista, like *Hombre y Dios,* reveals a total structure, though one based on a gradual unfolding of parts (I have called it "dramatic"), rather than on the more schematic and static (or "architectural") pattern of the earlier book. The use of general structures in both books seems appropriate, given their combined philosophic and poetic nature. Both of them explore a conflict between opposite views of Man, as did Alonso's earlier verse; but both delve into the more philosophic ramifications and the ultimate implications of this conflict, pointing also to final views or resolutions. Their structures allow these books to move toward these resolutions in a concrete and dramatic manner, making them both full and poetically successful embodiments of their visions.

The use of a structure that unfolds gradually in *Gozos de la vista* forces the reader to follow more closely the path of the protagonist. Certain repeated images, which keep the same general value throughout the work but which also reveal shifts in attitude, support the general structure. . . . (We can remember how colors, windows and a lighthouse repeatedly portrayed Man's outlook; how whiteness alluded to an abstract vision and touch to an animalistic attitude; how eagles portrayed sight and its loss.) All this links diverse parts of the book into a progressive whole. This procedure fits very well the book's increased stress on more immediate predicaments, signalled also by its use of a particular and developing protagonist, its stress on particular happenings, and on the particular image-concept of sight. The wider philosophic view emerges in *Gozos de la vista* from this particularity. In this, we might say that the book combines the greater philosophic stress of *Hombre y Dios* with the greater immediacy and particular intensity of *Hijos de la ira.* (pp. 104-05)

Technical and mechanical terms often undercut any tendency to make Man appear elevated. The scientific terminology also makes us see the protagonist as a painstaking man, curious about scientific detail, and yet also whimsical: he uses scientific terms to comment ironically on Man and his world. . . . All in all, such terms help make the protagonist and the work less pretentious. A work endeavoring to define the value of Man could easily have seemed pompous and hollow, and lost the reader's assent. By making his speaker and his poem aware of the traits of our particular world, Alonso avoids this danger.

Although it deals with the theme of conflicting outlooks on Man with great particularity, *Gozos de la vista* also relates this theme to the basic problems of time and of death. More than Alonso's earlier verse, it rejects any easy confidence in God, and shows anguish at Man's final fate. Yet, in still asserting Man's dignity, the nobility of his belief in higher values and of his trust in an undefinable God, *Gozos de la vista* upholds a positive view. Alonso's concern with the conflict between the high position and the pettiness and shortcomings of human beings has been expressed throughout his poetry; it has received an increasingly existential and immediate, but at the same time more philosophic, treatment; it has led finally to a work less easily optimistic about Man's fate, but one which asserts all the more his value. (p. 105)

[All] of Dámaso Alonso's verse, from *Poemas puros* on down to *Gozos de la vista* and other recent poems, was centered on a conflict between opposing views of Man and his world. At first presented as a rather neat clash between a prosaic and a poetic outlook, it later becomes the conflict between a mundane and a spiritual view in *Hijos de la ira* and *Hombre y Dios;* and the battle between a pessimistic and an elevated attitude to Man and his sight in *Gozos de la vista.* In all these works, Alonso deals with the tension present between Man's awareness of his material nature and his desire to transcend its shortcomings; in all he tries to configure a final outlook which will uphold Man's higher value without depriving him of his own concrete and complex nature. The combined religious and existential perspective embodied in *Hijos de la ira* and in the middle section of *Hombre y Dios,* as well as the final assertion of human dignity in *Gozos de la vista* and the value of poetry presented by several works, are all examples of such a final outlook. (pp. 110-11)

Alonso's constant search for the fullest and most precise knowledge of poetry, as well as his insight into the meanings that can be created by poetic techniques, embody indeed the human quest for order and exact insight. His awareness of affective human problems and his view of the basic existential anguish conveyed by poetry suggest, on the other hand, the realization of Man's tragedies and limitations. Alonso's poetry, like his own career and outlook, strives constantly to bring together in a valuable and enduring vision these two fundamental aspects of human life. Alonso's success in this quest, achieved by means of the techniques and patterns studied, parallels his success in developing a dual yet cohesive outlook on poetry. . . .

In the light of all this, one cannot call Alonso, in my opinion, an initially "pure" and "abstract" poet who later changes his work. Neither can one describe *Hijos de la ira* as a "social" poem: the work transcends immediate social problems, and uses ordinary language to point to wider themes. Nor does *Hombre y Dios* signal a retreat to purely religious statements: we have seen the book's complex outlook, embodied in a dramatic structure. If there is one way of characterizing Alonso's poetry and doing justice to its unity, it is by calling it philosophic. This poetry has constantly portrayed a conflict which is a version of a fundamental problem facing mankind: the tension between the elevated and the common, the abstract and the concrete. Alonso has presented this conflict in increasingly intense and direct ways; he has handled it with greater richness and complexity; and he has made it more and more applicable to particular realities of human life. His poetry, then, is marked by a single but gradually unfolding attempt to uncover a basic reality of our existence. (p. 111)

An awareness of the dramatic nature of Alonso's poetry explains the presence in it of some seemingly redundant statements and some seemingly weak lines (which can be seen most frequently in *Hombre y Dios* and *Gozos de la vista*). Seen in context, these statements and lines of verse dramatize the desperate (and at times petty) speaker, caught in his world, yet trying to rise above it. . . . Alonso does not embody his meanings in tight, static forms; rather he develops them via many progressive or cumulative devices and techniques. These seem most appropriate, of course, to Alonso's basic theme of a conflict in points of view. They turn this conflict into a poetic reality, available to the readers of the future; they allow Alonso's work to remain the best proof of his own view that poetry preserves human values and overcomes human limitations. (p. 112)

Poesí española; ensayo de métodos y límites estilísticos (1950) is probably Alonso's fundamental work of criticism. [It] represents the culmination of his years of thought and work in criticism and critical theory. (p. 117)

[In this work] Alonso tackles a situation faced by many critics: the need to assert simultaneously that a work of art is an independent and irreducible entity, and that it is a means of conveying meaning to a reader. Ignoring the former can make a critic too willing to let anyone read the work as he pleases; ignoring the latter can rob the work of any relevance to Man. By asserting the primacy of the poem's personal value for the reader, and yet pointing out that this value originates in the objective features of the work, Alonso constructs a critical outlook which avoids both an excessive concern with the affective state of the reader, and an unduly cold objectivism. (p. 118)

Always ready to use historical methods for critical ends, Alonso, on the other hand, objects to the grouping of literary works for purely historical or chronological ends, particularly if such a grouping is used as a substitute for criticism. (He does accept cultural history as a discipline independent of criticism.) . . .

It is important to note that for Alonso the "meaning" is not a concept, but a full and complex representation of a reality. It includes multiple conceptual, sensorial, and affective values, organized into a single whole. . . . [The poem is] an irreducible representation of a reality which contains the shadings present in any significant human experience. (p. 119)

If *Lengua poética, Poesía española,* and *Seis calas* [Alonso's primary works of criticism] have mainly characterized Alonso as the founder of a new and precise analytic criticism, his last books accent his stature as a practical critic of extraordinary intuition, who may offer us sensitive insights into every important work of Spanish poetry and prose. Such a division of Alonso's work, of course, reflects a difference in emphasis, not in basic approach. . . . [Alonso's criticism] is always attentive to the literary work as, on the one hand, a precise unique structure, demanding exact intrinsic study; and, on the other, as a vehicle which transmits an irreducible significant vision to the reader. (This double view reflects Alonso's general double perspective, scientific on the one hand and personal on the other. And it relates to the tension between an abstract and an existential outlook . . . in his own poetry.) Alonso merely adapts his cohesive dual view to the needs and circumstances of the times. In earlier books he stresses accurate intrinsic analysis as a necessary vehicle for making the reader see a work as more than a historical example or a collection of data. Having done so, he can in his later works talk more directly about the work's personal value for the reader.

In addition to giving increased emphasis to the poem's impact upon the reader in his later books, Alonso now also pays more attention to the personal situation of the poet. While insisting, as always, that the poet is important for him not as a subject of biography, but as the creator of a unique work, Alonso nevertheless spends time conjuring up a vision of this poet as an individual. . . . In addition, Alonso now writes books based on biography. In *Menéndez Pelayo, crítico literario,* he studies the reversals in outlook and the growth of perspective of this great Spanish critic, and makes his integrity and persistence examples for all critics. In a book on two figures of the Golden Age [*Dos españoles del siglo de oro*], Alonso used biographical materials to shed light on several aspects of poetry, and on certain constant ambiguities of human nature. . . . [In] all these works Alonso does not use his biographical materials to search for the intentions behind literary works. . . . All he is doing is reminding us that the literary work, for all its uniqueness, comes from a human poet and from an era of human history; and that it is directed, in turn, at other human beings. (pp. 129-30)

With his extraordinary insight, his skill in literary, historical, and linguistic analysis, his vast knowledge of all the needed background, and his amazing productivity, Dámaso Alonso emerges as the foremost Spanish critic of our time, and one of the foremost of the world. (p. 131)

Dámaso Alonso makes us both understand and feel how language can be used creatively to embody essential human visions in unique fashion, and thus to overcome the limitations and the chaos facing Man. His criticism shows us these values in the literary works of others; his poetry offers them to us directly. In both genres, by combining exactitude and precision together with a deep personal feeling for literature and for humanity, Alonso shows us how poetry is Man's way of creating and perpetuating meaningful visions. (p. 132)

Andrew P. Debicki, in his Dámaso Alonso *(copyright © 1970 by Twayne Publishers, Inc.; reprinted with the permission of Twayne Publishers, A Division of G. K. Hall & Co, Boston), Twayne, 1970, 167 p.*

GONZALO SOBEJANO

[What] best defines Alonso the critic is precisely his art of definition, his extraordinary ability to see and express the essential features of a literary object. . . .

The principal mission, although not the only one, which he set for himself and which has guided his steps and enabled him to reach goals which no one before had achieved, was, from the historical point of view, a new understanding and evaluation of Spanish lyric poetry of the Golden Age in its embodiment of universal qualities; and from the critical point of view, the study of the literary work as a work of art in language. (p. 255)

[In] no other contemporary Spanish critic . . . have I ever found, to such a high degree and with such revealing fidelity, the desire and gift to define briefly and distinctly, in the way a definition should be made, the nature and essential traits of one literature, period style, literary movement, generation, genre—especially of one writer, one work, and one or another technique of expression. This is what best sets Alonso apart from the critics of his time and country and what best distinguishes him personally, because this exercise of defining is in him principle, constant dedication and major goal. Singularly and repeatedly. And because the arena in which he works unceasingly is language. . . .

Dámaso Alonso's art of definition is not aprioristic, deductive or generalistic, but intuitive, inductive and, in its ultimate form, psychological and physiognomical. (p. 256)

The study of Góngora [one of the outstanding poets of the Golden Age of Spanish poetry] soon brought him to a new interpretation of Spanish literature; not only is it realistic, regionalistic and popular, but also idealistic and universal, constantly straining between opposite extremes which at times confront one another, at times blend in a single text or in a single poet. This definition of the peculiar nature of Spanish literature emerges in opposition to the unilateral definition dominant until that time, not as abstraction or theory but based on his scrupulous examination of the work of Góngora. (p. 257)

Poets such as Garcilaso, Fray Luis de León, Medrano and Jorge Guillén have led him to reflect on classicism and to arrive at a very delicate extraction of its essence: "Classicism is modesty of expression, voluntary limitation," . . . "the classic gift of knowing when to be silent," . . . "a sense of containment, of sobriety, of well-timed silence." Classicism in art is "that which responds to a desire or a permanent longing of Humanity." He uses no fixed notion of classicism to describe such poets: the style of each of them, when studied with penetration, inspires in the interpreter the definition of one or another kind of classicism. . . .

Alonso avoids facile generalizations about periods and cultures with a healthy sense of caution. . . . Each definition [Alonso uses in his work] depends on the perspective from which the critic views different subjects: one does not invalidate the other; they all are similar but each one contributes a different nuance or contains a particular purpose. (p. 258)

There are a few other instances in which Alonso has made fortunate use of classifying concepts: the highly animated revelation, rooted in solid erudition, of a whole area of Mexican and Spanish internal history in the study on "El Fabio de la *Epístola moral*"; the recognition of a sort of neo-mannerism in Calderón, who submitted baroque exuberance to serene order by stylizing, cataloguing and regulating it . . . ; the recognition, in the period between the wars, of a "hyperrealism" or realism raised to the second power, a term applicable both to science and art, and more apt than the overused term of "surrealism" . . . ; or the differentiation between rooted and uprooted poetry, essential for the understanding of postwar Spanish poetry. . . .

Alonso's stylistics finds its most fitting subject in that area where individuality appears as a unitarian whole: in the poet, in the poem. (p. 259)

Alonso has barely concerned himself at all with literary genres abstractly, but when he has done so in relation with this or that concrete commentary, his thought has crystallized with prodigious precision. A poet himself, his preference has been the interpretation of lyrical poetry, from the early ripples of the *jarchas* to the visionary floods of Aleixandre: he is enamored of both learned and traditional poetry, of the well-carved ode and the rustic *villancico*, of the sculptured sonnet and the fluid couplet. The objective of poetry, he has written, "is not beauty, although it often seeks and strives for beauty, but feeling." . . . He has also written, however, "Poetry is nothing more than one of the most effective and rapid ways which man has to rise above the accidental to the absolute." . . . The fundamental theme of poetry in his view is "man in his totality." . . . (p. 260)

Alonso has not turned his back on the theater, which is demonstrated by his thoughtful analysis of the structure of Calderón's comedies and his lucid interpretation of the pure dramatic poetry of Gil Vicente. Pointing to possible methods for dramatizing a non-theatrical work (transposition, germinative development and reductive projection), he has correctly identified the first essential law of the stage: the "law of velocity." . . . But Alonso's greatest brilliance in the art of definition has been achieved in the analysis of the components of expression: structure, rhetoric, syntax, imagery and symbolism, vocabulary, versification.

Today when everything is structure and the earth appears to be inhabited, as they say, by structural man, we may be surprised to see structure defined as "beginning, union, transition, variation, end," . . . i.e., the disposition and articulation of the most wide-ranging signifiers. (pp. 260-61)

The stylistic focusing of syntax is indebted to Alonso for such fertile distinctions as the one made between "progressive and non-progressive" syntagma, the various types of hyperbaton, and the unusual formulas used by Góngora to give an ingenious personal stamp to his learned phraseology. . . .

And finally, he, a great poet, has uncovered and made known the nature and effects of Spanish versification: the brilliance of words placed at the peak of rhythmic intensity in the Gongorine endecasyllable, the ambiguous instability of secondary accents in the modernist alexandrine, the material enrichment of a verse with an emphatic synaloepha and the expressive contraction produced by synaeresis, the different acoustical and symbolic impressions caused by the "soft" and "abrupt" enjambment (a nomenclature coined by Alonso which is in wide use today), the "restless freedom of the assonant," . . . the propensity of the *lira* to "swell at the end," . . . the unfading excellence of the sonnet and many other statements on poetic form which remain imprinted in the memory of the attentive reader.

In a few circumstantial pages, barely five, which Alonso has written in "Praise of the Endecasyllable," his art of defining verses and poets reaches a level of transparent understanding as has rarely or never been found in Spanish criticism. (p. 261)

To define is to explain briefly, clearly and distinctly the essence of something, and it is logical that this be considered basic by someone who has put his greatest effort into the study of style: "Style is everything that individualizes a literary object, be it a work, an epoch, or a whole literature." . . . Like the hen and the egg, the problem of whether Alonso was led to stylistics by his personal gifts for defining individual essence, or whether he owes this ability to his assiduous work on stylistic method, seems to have no solution. I, however, would begin by emphasizing Alonso's dual vocation as mathematician and poet (an innate combination of precision and fervent clarity), keeping in mind the conforming imprint of two simultaneous factors: on the one hand, his spiritual education in a climate of intuitionism, phenomenology, the theory of expectation and perspective, the cubist predominance of abstract figuration, and critical formalism at its height; and, on the other hand, his continuous cultivation of a stylistics of language which began with his own direct dealings with Góngora's commentators and links up maintaining his own personal criteria. . . . (p. 262)

[Synonyms] or related terms, which are symptomatic of Alonso's interpretative language, accompany and modulate his preference for "transparency." It is true that we frequently find in his pages signs of bewilderment (elusive, bitter, sour, tremulous, panting, dart-like, wooded, stormy, confused, wind, mist, passion) and the attributes of darkness (dark, blind, lost, secret, ineffable, magical, astonishment, monster, portent, mystery). But these signs and attributes form the background against which the verbal indices of purity stand out (unripe, bittersweet, slender, silken, lean, narrow, untilled, thin, delicate, subtle, unblemished, virginal, intangible, immutable) and the splendid signs of clarity (neat, clear, exact, mathematical, transparent, crystalline, diaphanous, luminous, radiant, perfect). As forgetfulness makes remembrance memorable, as empty space makes objects visible, as silence makes words audible, so disorder and darkness are the elements in which this desire for integrity and transparency prosper. (p. 264)

Alonso invokes intuition as the point of departure and as the final boundary of his interpretative exercise. Intuition as the beginning of knowledge is necessary for him and for all of us in dealing with men, nature and art. To limit the use of reason in a final act of respect toward the unattainable may serve as a brake on the arrogance of reason and, in any case, is a gesture of quite noble humility. Alonso always pursues clarity through his unique art of definition, determined to limit the difficulty, eliminate confusion and propose a reason of love. He first intuits the essence of the text, allowing the text to inscribe its impression on the "clean slate" of his sensibility as an innocent reader. A detail or two, captured by that purposely unprejudiced sensibility, causes a perception which is opportune and can lead him on from there. Analytical penetration follows at once, from the signifier to the signified or vice-versa; a detailed, minute study of interior and exterior form, which makes a step-by-step delimitation of expressive techniques and groups the main or constant features in provisional synthesis. Just as ripe fruit falls from a tree, so at this moment the definition is born, either in a term, a short sentence, a summarizing conclusion, a title, a subtitle—a definition which expresses the substance of the object without simplifying it, gathering it in the semblance of its concrete and living oneness. After the definition, which has so enriched the pre-critical intuition, the interpreter looks back with excitement to the boundary which he believed impassable. That boundary, however, has been pushed forward considerably, widening the passage of light.

Alonso's art of definition, triumphing over the inertia of pure impressionism, ripping away stereotypes by the rational illumination of unique nuclei, approaching those nuclei with the deep sympathy with which one seeks the truth of a friend's soul, satisfies the intellect, awakens the imagination, nourishes the memory, and moves the will to a love of poetry. If he defined poetry as fervor and clarity, we might well say that his poetical criticism is an eternal witness to a will for unification and intense understanding: a model of fervent clarity. (pp. 264-65)

Gonzalo Sobejano, "On the Interpretative Style of Dámaso Alonso: The Art of Definition," translated by Barbara Huntley, in Books Abroad *(copyright 1974 by the University of Oklahoma Press), Vol. 48, No. 2, Spring, 1974, pp. 255-65.*

PHILIP SILVER

Too much has been made, I think, of the revolutionary quality of *Hijos de la ira*. . . . Instead of an act of revolt it is rather a book that protects itself too well. Like that other milestone of post-Civil War literature, *La familia de Pascual Duarte,* it demands that we accept it on its own terms or not at all. Both the Death of God theology of the one and the criminal insanity of the other provide a literary redoubt with which the authors insulate themselves from the historical moment. In addition, Alonso's poetry, like most modernist Spanish literature is not self-generating but builds on, lives off, previous Spanish literature. It is a high example of the art of literary pastiche, and consciously so. And this too protects it from attack, makes it strangely hermetic and aloof. Also, there is a miscellaneous quality about the way it is arranged, the books are anthologistic, discontinuous and so demand a special kind of indulgence. And finally, the speaker of the poems, that curious and terrifying younger brother of the child-speaker of César Vallejo's poems, is so abject in his self-denigration that we can only wish him better days.

At first glance, *Hijos de la ira* may seem an act of contestation, but when we take a second look from the perspective of thirty years, it seems almost willfully self-indulgent. If this sounds an outrageous, even an irreverent thing to say, recall for a moment the historical reality of Madrid in 1944 and then measure the import of a single religious crisis against that ground. (pp. 286-87)

[In] an earlier article on *Hijos de la ira,* [I stressed] the degree to which that book is permeated with the commonplaces of mystical and ascetic imagery. At the time I attributed the submerged quality of that imagery to a species of ascetic humility. It seemed to me that in doing this I was taking the manifest content of the work as far as it would go. But at the same time the root experience of the work seemed to me to be an overbearing sense of man as the single flawed creature, while the rest of creation was a dense compound with no ontological fissures. And I used this critical perception to justify the religious "content" of the poetry. (God was man's essential Other, his necessary counter-pressure.)

After subsequent readings of the poetry I am still convinced that a variation of what I called the root experience underlies the work, but I can no longer take the religious "content" of the poetry at face value. Instead it now seems to me to be one of several generative systems of motivation—perhaps the most obvious—which disguise and distract us from a more elemental, more concrete, satisfaction that the poet finds in his craft. (p. 288)

Thus, while it is useless to criticize Alonso's poetry because it does not directly reflect the socio-economic realities of Spain in the early 40s, I believe it can be shown that the poetry does in fact reenter the historical post-War world in a special way. . . .

[The] difficulty of the reader-critic—at least this reader-critic—in entering Alonso's creations, as for what I have called the reticence of those creations, is that the basic experience of the poetry is both censored out . . . and at the same time over-determined by succeeding levels of "manifest" content which are themselves incompletely explored by the poet. . . .

To my mind the basic experience underlying the poetry of Alonso, the one that is both masked and over-determined by the various levels in the work, is the creation and the writing of a species of long, flowing, yet controlled verse-line which when exercised brings the poet a sense of gratification that enhances his own feeling of personal integration and continuity. (p. 289)

It will be noticed that although with the assembling of the volumes *Oscura noticia* and *Hijos de la ira* in 1943 and 1944, Alonso's poetry discovers its identity, and this discovery seems to have been triggered by the writing of *La poesía de San Juan de la Cruz* in the spring of 1942, this creative struggle of continuity-discontinuity had already become a subject of thematic concern as early as 1924, the probable date of "Copla" ("La copla quedó partida. / No la pude concluir. / Y era la copla mi vida.") Here as in the later "Dedicatoria final (las alas)" an analogy is made between the continuity of the poetry and the life, as if to speak of the one were to allude to the other. . . . Human life is an anguish because its continuity is illusory. The continuity of the poetry, then, assuages a desire for that "continuity" which humans achieve only in death. . . . [The] preferred term of comparison for . . . life is organic nature, to which the poet attributes the equally desirable qualities of controlled fluidity and density, like the "instress" of which Hopkins spoke. Nature wells up, bursts forth, branches out. It is matched, mated, continuous, like waves breaking on a beach, or frogs jumping into the water, forming "un hilo continuo de ranas verdes." The analogy between this ideal in nature and Alonso's most characteristic verse-line is obvious. It is a long, flowing yet controlled line that generates one metaphor out of another like a budding plant. This species of verse-line is as continuous as poetry itself, described by the poet as perfume, music or light, and it is perfectly designed to convey feeling-states that are also diffuse and continuous like sadness, tenderness, fear or pain. In the fluidity of this verse-line and in the poems it generates the poet is relieved of the burden of discontinuous selfhood which is exchanged for a feeling of plenitude that is coextensive with the poem. (pp. 290-91)

But if Alonso sees an ideal of "instress" in nature, he also sees "inscape," structure and patterning. The impulse to pattern predominates until the explosion of instress in *Hijos de la ira,* it reappears in strength in *Hombre y Dios,* and with "Gozos de la vista" a synthesis of the two principles is achieved, a plenitude possible because the dense instress of *Hijos de la ira* has been clarified, made transparent, in the pattern. A plenitude and a point of rest has been achieved because the long flowing line finds containment in a new form. Thus it seems to me that Alonso's descriptions of his early poetry in "Dedicatoria final (las alas)"—"se quedaba flotando la música, / y flotando, se cuajaba en canción," and "yo vertí mi ternura / en el librito aquel, igual / que en una copa de cristal diáfano"—will also serve to describe the new integration of the two impulses in "Gozos de la vista." In this way the last poems approximate the natural ideal of the dense, clear air in the poet's garden, which he terms "una piscina de amarilla tersura."

On the level of personal style, then, there is a dialectical progression of control and freedom, form and content; the verse-line expands to assimilate the inchoate material of *Hijos de la ira,* to overcome it and to establish a continuous rhythm whose invention and control are perfectly integrated, and a kind of stasis is achieved. In short, the existential discontinuity finds compensation in a controlled, continuous verse-line.

On the next level, that of the thematics of vision, a similar progression can be observed. . . . The core symbolism of the thematics of vision [in Alonso's poetry] seems drawn from a sector of experience that antedates the religious theme. . . . If clarity and innocence of vision are [originally] equated with childhood there comes at a later point a clouding of that vision. The humors that burst forth in *Hijos de la ira* destroy the sense of continuity with the created world and isolate the poet; they are terrors that come from within, but because they darken vision and threaten his existence they are assimilated to a private symbolism of night-terrors and insomnia that can only be exorcised, as in the beginning of "Invisible presencia," by turning on artificial light. Sight then means continuity with creation and darkness means existential anguish at possible destruction. . . . Once however the furor, which in *Hijos de la ira* has a blinding effect, subsides, sight returns. In *Hombre y Dios* human vision becomes the justification of human existence and a species of counter in the struggle between man and God. And in "Gozos de la vista" the glories of sight become the dominant theme altogether. In these last two books it is as though sight had been menaced by blindness, as though a punishment had been averted by some victory in *Hijos de la ira,* so that now with the penalty lifted, in "Gozos de la vista" jubilation, even humor, are possible again. (pp. 291-93)

Thus it seems that on the level of the thematics of vision there is a movement from a childlike candor of vision through darkness and the threat of blindness to a new more complete simplicity and enjoyment of vision, held in such high esteem in the end not because man sees humanly for God, but because by virtue of his eyes man is a participant in the Platonic sea of light that is the world, and which sustains him and nourishes him, reinforcing his sense of self.

The next level, that of the thematics of what I have called the death of God theology of Alonso's poetry cannot, I believe, be said to be important before the composition of his critical study of St. John of the Cross in 1942. . . . [The] intimations of the Godhead that emerge in the course of the book, *Hijos de la ira,* are unclear and even contradictory. . . . What *is* clear in *Hijos de la ira,* however, is that the poet has chosen to hypostatize a terrifying night-vision, to name it God, and to risk destruction by confronting it. This wrathful God is most easily described by what it is not. It belongs to a world, it has the qualities, that are the antithesis of those qualities and that world associated with love and tenderness, with the world of mother and child. In fact the drama that is played out in *Hijos de la ira* takes the form of a struggle in the poet between series of opposing elements, between violence and love, apocalypse and pastoral, hate and tenderness, insomnia and sleep, semen and tears, cold stars and warm sun. As in the case of troubled vision, here too the poet is forced to abandon the maternal world of light and peace, to enter and pass through a dark, threatening foreign area of the self, to discover there within hate and anger, fear and corruption, and ultimately, death. . . . Thus it seems to me that *Hijos de la ira* describes not so much a religious quest in the usual sense as it does a rite of passage cast in a religious mold in which the principal actors within the subject's consciousness are Father, Mother and Child, or in this case, Son. (pp. 293-94)

It is finally necessary to speak, I believe, of a level of psychological motivation in Alonso's work because of the peculiar way in which the three principles mentioned above are weighted in his poetry. The "maternal matrix" and the "pure self" are extremely powerful and vividly portrayed, but the "paternal voice" is never more than a shadowy figure, a frightening *absence,* a true "Invisible presencia," or else, as in *Hombre y Dios,* an intellectualized creation. The Virgin Mary can be vividly described in terms of the earthly mother, but for God there is no earthly model and it is this very imprecision, this freedom, which makes possible the extraordinarily original hypostatization of the poet's own night-terrors. But even here there is progression of a kind, for the poet leaves the domain of the mother, risks blindness, confronts in *Hijos de la ira* the absence of the father (and the father in himself) and in "Gozos de la vista," in "Invisible presencia," integrates paternal and maternal principles so as to be able to write: "Te llamo 'Dios,' oh Padre, oh madre, oh benefactor que me nutres." . . .

Given the peculiar personal resonances of Alonso's religious poetry, it is difficult to speak of the last two as separate thematic levels—theological and psychological—for each seems to shade off into the other. . . . [The] writing of *Hijos de la ira* signaled in the poet's life not necessarily a religious crisis—or not primarily a religious one— but rather a point at which the poet became able to translate psychological material that was always there into poetry. The fact that the same terrors, the same interior demons, are still waiting in the wings to be summoned forth again is attested to in the splendid elegy to Leopoldo Panero, written in 1962, sixteen years after the publication of *Hijos de la ira*. And this fact, it seems to me, confirms the initial hypothesis that, instead of being the central core of the poetry, the religious theme is but another pretext for a stylistic breakthrough, like the thematics of vision and the submerged psychological content. None of these three levels of content seems to me the dominant one, none seems to present a greater coherence than the others. So that we seem justified in viewing each as a manifest content that enables the poet to pursue the expressive possibilities of his characteristic verse-line, as discovered in *Hijos de la ira* and perfected in "Gozos de la vista." This verse-line is a highly mannered, highly literary one, capable of violence and tenderness, imprecation and praise, pure invention and minute description. For the poet it is a necessary appendage inasmuch as its exercise represents a difficult personal integration, a sense of continuous selfhood. (p. 295)

And finally, in closing, we must inquire into the reasons why the exercise of this peculiar, personally integrative style should be so important to Alonso the poet. . . . Alonso is thus very much a member of the Generation of 27, to the extent that the pastoral mode is present in his poetry. But there is one curious note in his depiction of nature that must be mentioned. What I have called its lack of ontological fissures, its continuity can also be a source of fear and disgust. One blue-bottle fly is lovely to observe, but a swarm of insects is a frightening menace. And the same holds true in Alonso's depiction of social relations. There is something horrible about the anonymous sameness of his fellow humans, seen not as individuals but as mass consumers. . . . Human relations, in other words, are characterized by that type of relationship which Sartre calls seriality, according to which a consciousness of the statistical sameness of everyone overshadows and subverts the individual's sense of himself as a center of action. Would it be too far-fetched to suggest that Alonso's sense of radical discontinuity is a magnification of the seriality of modern industrial society, and to suggest, moreover, that the menacing but invisible presence that threatens him with extinction is a hypostatization of this serialized Other? If both these things are true then we should have no trouble seeing that the deepest satisfaction of his style is the practice against all obstacles of a nonalienated kind of work. And to me, at least, this kind of explanation seems as valuable as any other. (pp. 295-96)

Philip Silver, "On Entering Creation: A Second Look at 'Hijos de la ira'," in Books Abroad *(copyright 1974 by the University of Oklahoma Press), Vol. 48, No. 2, Spring, 1974, pp. 286-96.*

GUSTAVO PÉREZ FIRMAT

The Cosmos coheres all right
Even if my notes do not cohere.
Ezra Pound

The epigraph that introduces this paper singles out two terms and establishes their relationship. The terms: cosmos and notes; the relationship: dissimilarity. Pound's notes, unlike the cosmos, do not cohere. I would like to borrow this formula and apply it to the study of the poetry of Dámaso Alonso, but with the following twist: the relationship will remain intact, but the terms will exchange attributes. In Alonso's view of things, it is the cosmos that suffers from incoherence; the cosmological model he adopts is the "exploding universe" of Georges Lemaître, perpetually expanding, perpetually falling apart. His poems, on the other hand, make perfectly coherent use of this hypothesis, incorporating it as one more element in a unified poetic whole. In particular, the two-part poem "Sueño de las dos ciervas" offers a striking illustration of the poetic uses of modern cosmology. (p. 147)

In the poetry of Alonso the motif of the exploding universe achieves its most interesting incarnations when it is used figuratively. By virtue of the kind of universe they depict, relativistic models conform well to the world-view espoused in collections like *Hijos de la ira* and *Oscura noticia* and, therefore, provide a fertile source for metaphor and symbol. . . . Throughout the poetry of Alonso, man is repeatedly situated not only among other men, in a particular city or country, but also in a larger cosmic setting. . . . Technically, this entails a radical distancing of the narrator from the narrated material. (pp. 149-50)

More pertinent to our purposes than the mechanisms of the cosmic perspective are the situations in which it appears. In almost every instance it coincides with passages of high-pitched emotion or acute insight. . . . The intrusion of the cosmic perspective at these privileged moments is significant. From the solemnity of the occasion we can infer the importance of the scenario. Interstellar space becomes the appropriate backdrop for the dramatization of the crucial episodes in an individual's life. (p. 151)

It is not difficult to see why the exploding universe readily lends itself to metaphorization by a poet whose outlook has generally been termed "existential," and who is thus concerned with such questions as alienation, loss of identity, fragmentation of the self, and nothingness. Relativistic cosmologies can be used to represent such an outlook both as it applies to the individual and to society. On the individual scale the disintegration of the primeval nebula images the fragmentation of the individual's identity. . . . In this respect the best gloss for this section is provided by another of Alonso's poems, "En el día de los difuntos":

> Yo me muero, me muero a cada instante,
> perdido de mí mismo,
> ausente de mí mismo,
> lejano de mí mismo,
> cada vez más perdido, más lejano, más ausente. . . .

In these lines discursive language serves to articulate the attitude that is expressed figuratively in [another poem,] "A Pizca"—the agony of aging accompanied by an increasing fracture of the self. Like the galaxies, the fragments of personality drift farther and farther apart with no indication that the pattern can be reversed. At the same time, the dissolution of being can be seen on a larger scale as symbolic of the condition of society. . . . With each of its individual members moving away from each other, the social body also disintegrates. Communication and contact become progressively more precarious as the physical distance is exacerbated by a perceptual distance (the extinction of light). Ultimately, men will not only be separated from each other, they will have become invisible to each other. Moreover, the comparison implies that man has no control over his destiny. He is thrust out into space and cannot arrest his movement or alter its direction.

The Big-Bang metaphor also adds a new twist to the old topic of life as a journey. Traditionally man has travelled from a point of departure, *A*, to a point of arrival, *B*. The nature of *B*, of course, has varied according to the dominant world-view. Until the Enlightenment the kind of afterlife envisioned in Christian eschatology was almost invariably accepted. In the Christian concept of the *homo viator,* the natural culmination of life's journey is union with God. . . . If one adopts the model of the exploding universe as representative of human life, *B* vanishes. Man's itinerary loses its terminus. (pp. 155-56)

["Sueño de las dos ciervas"] picks up and ties together the different threads in Alonso's adaptation of the Big-Bang concept. (p. 161)

Although the poem does not contain any overt allusions to the motif of the exploding universe, we can readily situate several of its images within the Big-Bang complex. . . . The central image of the poem is the familiar one of deer fleeing toward a fountain. Because they are presented as symbols of light and darkness, it is easy to interpret their movement again as imaging the recession of the stars. . . . After having ascertained that the fountain is also fleeing . . . , the speaker asks, "¿Por qué nos huyes, Dios, por qué nos huyes?" His abrupt intromission (the preceding stanzas had been narrated in the third person) as a spokesman for mankind makes evident that just as the fountain represents God, the deer represent man. (p. 162)

In the first part of "Sueño" the dream of the sleeper revolves around three images: the deer running toward the fountain, arrows heading toward a target, and a tree. Considered in isolation, the choice and ordering of images is not without method. By analogy of motion, the arrows are explicitly linked with the deer; since the arrows are probably wooden, we can supply the missing link by associating them synecdochically with the tree. If one then accepts the opinion that the deer symbolize time (light and darkness = day and night) and that the tree symbolizes space, we can conclude that the arrows function as a textual hinge that joins the two in order to form our four-dimensional time-space continuum. (p. 164)

We have in the poem all of the components of a literary topic, but disjointed. It is as if the pieces of a well-known puzzle had been forced together into a novel and strange configuration. Something has upset the traditional coherence and predictability of the scene. I believe that the disorder originates in the fact that the diachronic signification of the images conflicts with their synchronic signification. In other words, the *ciervas,* as symbols, stride in different directions. On the one hand, they are associated with modern cosmology and the world-view it implies; on the other, they participate in a literary tradition whose locus is a previous, completely different, intellectual environment. It is, in fact, the environment of sixteenth-century Spanish mysticism. The central imagery of "Sueño de las dos ciervas" can be directly traced back to the poetry of San Juan, and, in particular, to one of his lesser known poems ["La fonte"]. Alonso's poem derives its meaning from the collision of the diachronic and synchronic planes of symbolism and the subsequent disarticulation of the former. San Juan runs into Lemaître and comes out the worst for wear. (p. 165)

The two poems differ precisely because in San Juan the search is not incessant. From the outset there exists an absolute certainty of reaching the fountain . . . , and the certainty is justified when, in the last stanza, the seeker finds the fountain in Christ, the bread of life ("Aquesta viva fuente que deseo, / en este pan de vida yo la veo"). In "Sueño," on the other hand, the goal is unattainable ("Ay, nunca formas llegarán a esencia, / nunca ciervas a fuente fugitiva"). The poems, starting from the same point, arrive at opposite conclusions. (p. 168)

["Sueño" depicts a] passage from dream to nightmare, from the stable, well-organized cosmos of San Juan to the exploding universe of Big-Bang theories, from illusion to reality. (p. 169)

The complexities of "Sueño de las dos ciervas" in particular and of the motif of the exploding universe in general can be reduced to one unitary thought: man is doomed to incompleteness; he cannot help but live in the imperfective aspect, always yearning for a stasis and never achieving it. The Big-Bang conception and its metamorphoses furnish so many ways of visualizing this condition, whose cause, as "Sueño" makes clear, is theological in nature. Accepting Catholic teaching, Alonso assumes that man is not whole until he rests in the Lord. For this reason the insertion of mystical symbolism in the poem is pertinent and poignant; the writings of San Juan illustrate paradigmatically the feasibility of the union of God and man. With the dismantlement of the world-view that makes possible this union, man is left wandering aimlessly in space. . . . (p. 170)

[In Alonso's poetry] we find the motif of the unanswered question repeatedly imbricated with the Big-Bang. . . . "Sueño" builds toward a series of increasingly strident questions. The interlacing of motifs is logical, for an unanswered question is an abortive attempt at conversation, a mutilated dialogue, and as such, manifests also a kind of incompleteness. This device relates the rhetoric of the poems to their metaphorical and philosophical content. The question is to the answer as the deer are to the fountain as man is to God. And neither God nor the fountain nor the answer is to be had.

The encompassing theme of imperfection (understanding the word in its etymological and grammatical acceptation) explains one last feature of "Sueño," the division into parts. The fact that the poem does not end where it first appears to end, points to the error of thinking that anything comes to a stop. Unexpectedly, as the reader reaches the end of "Oscura noticia," he discovers that the initial poem continues. But one can go further. The "Continuación" also continues. "Oscura noticia" contains an additional poem, "Copla," which states (what else?) that nothing is ever consummated, that conclusions do not exist. . . . (p. 171)

Gustavo Pérez Firmat, "Cosmology and the Poem: Dámaso Alonso's 'Sueño de las dos ciervas'," in Hispanic Review, *Vol. 46, No. 2, Spring, 1978, pp. 147-71.*

* * *

ANTHONY, Florence
See AI

* * *

ANTONINUS, Brother
See EVERSON, William

* * *

AUDEN, W(ystan) H(ugh) 1907-1973

An Anglo-American poet, essayist, playwright, critic, editor, librettist, scriptwriter, and translator, Auden exerted a major influence on the poetry of the twentieth century. His poetry centers around moral issues and evidences Auden's strong political, social, and psychological orientations. The teachings of Marx and Freud weigh heavily in his earlier work, but later give way to religious and spiritual influences. Auden was an antiromantic, a poet of analytical clarity. He sought order, and for universal patterns of human existence. For this reason, some of his work has been criticized as overly detached and facile. Auden's poetry is versatile and inventive, ranging from the tersely epigrammatic to book-length verse, and incorporating his vast scientific knowledge. He collaborated with Christopher Isherwood and Louis MacNeice, and has joined with Chester Kallman to create libretti for works by Benjamin Britten, Stravinsky, and Mozart. He received the Pulitzer Prize in Poetry in 1948, and the National Book Award in 1956. (See also *CLC,* Vols. 1, 2, 3, 4, 6, 9, 11, and *Contemporary Authors,* Vols. 9-12, rev. ed.; obituary, Vols. 45-48.)

DR. NARSINGH SRIVASTAVA

Symbolisation of landscape is one of the major structural patterns in the poetry of W. H. Auden. Aware as he has ever been of the inadequacy of the direct statement for the purposes of poetic art, he has been in search of poetic devices that can fittingly incarnate the ideas about the major situations of the day as well as the universal truths of human psyche and life. Symbolisation of landscape is a method of turning the abstraction into a concrete form and thereby making them take on a new identity. The visual becomes conceptual in the sense that it involves thinking in physical terms of things that are psychic or spiritual. . . . In [Auden's] poetry, city, like island, mountain, valley, frontier and garden, is an important geographical image which he uses as embodiment of psychic and spiritual states.

Auden uses the city image both in terms of the actual and as symbol of some social, moral or spiritual state. . . . We notice in his early poetry that the city image is related, on the one hand, to Auden's symbol of the hero—both false and true—who assumes the role of a prospective saviour of the city, and, on the other, to the image of the island which is embodiment of selfish isolation and escape. Thus, this spatial image signifies the normal social and moral life of a community which, by exercise of human will, may either attain its ideal form—the just city, the good place or the city of God—or may degrade into a ruinous order of a moral and spiritual decadence. (p. 86)

[Auden's] view of the significance of the city symbol is much broader and more concrete than any vague and abstract utopian scheme. The significance of this symbol lies in Auden's emphasis on the relation of the individual to society as well as to his own self; and thus this image like many others that we come across in Auden's poetry, enables him to organise his moral and spiritual experience in a concrete pattern. Except in a few poems of places written on particular cities where focus of emphasis is thrown on the place rather than on its emblematic significance, the city image is used in a symbolic frame of reference. (p. 87)

In Auden's early poetry, the city is generally the actual city which is devoid of the values of the ideal and that is why it is disordered, dirty and immoral. In poem XXII of *Poems,* the images of smokeless chimneys, damaged bridges, locked and deserted power stations picture the industrial ruin, and form a sinister landscape suggestive of moral decadence of the upper classes. . . . [In] Poem XXXI of *Look, Stranger!,* 'As We Like It' . . . , Auden has painted the actual city of our times which is built by the 'conscience-stricken, the weapon-making' and where the 'Wild rumours woo and terrify the crowd'. The poem is highly effective in its description of a world menaced by hatred and fear. It is obvious that a synthesis of Freud and Marx forms Auden's attitude with which he denounces the forces of prejudice, fear and malice. The poem ends on a threatening note of despair which bears echoes of T. S. Eliot's similar depictions of the modern civilization in *The Waste Land* and 'The Hollow Men'. . . . (pp. 87-8)

Thus, Auden's humanistic zeal finds expression through the implicit interaction of the actual and the ideal city. In 'Macao' (*Journey to a War*) Auden paints an ironically realistic picture of the true condition of the immoral city—the city of indulgence. In 'Oxford' (*Another Time,* Part V), we notice that besides the lively picture of the city and its suburb drawn in a reminiscent manner, the emphasis is on the degenerated condition of man; and Oxford as a modern city embodies our civilization of the present age. . . . (p. 88)

It is in 'Paysage Moralise' (*Look, Stranger!*, VII) that the city image is clearly used as a symbol. City is described as an antithesis to islands; and as islands symbolise our isolating and evasive dreams, city is evidently the embodiment of our real life in a society. . . . Auden mentions the ideal of building the 'just city' . . . in his most inspiring poem '*Spain 1937*'. . . . What is significant is the fact that the abstraction associated with the image of the city makes it a purely conceptual image, symbolising the unattained form of an ideal existence. It is obvious that the city is either the goal of a man's quest or the symbol of a social ideal which later on changes into the religious ideal of the City of God. (p. 89)

The development of the city of man through several stages as opposed to the City of God which is attainable by no other effort than our full acceptance of faith, is the central theme of 'In Memorial of a City'. Until the City of God is incarnated within the city of man, life goes on without meaning and purpose. . . . Auden contrasts the condition of the Earthly City belonging to the secular and naturalistic world of the Greeks with the Christian world. The war-torn landscape, which is objectively perceived by the eyes of the crow and the eyes of the camera, and which bears sufficient relevance to the post-war life of our own age, has an implicit double focus; one revealing the misery of the world in time and the other suggesting the 'space where time has no place'. In the naturalistic order of the Greeks, 'gods behave, men die, / Both feel in their own small way'. As opposed to this, the Christian world always adds an eternal significance to the temporal events, and thus composes 'A meaningless moment into an eternal fact'. (pp. 90-1)

Auden saves his description from abstraction [in this poem] by employing mythological and historical figures and literary characters, which, by forces of implicit associations, bring into sharp relief the various forms of weaknesses that brought about their doom. Auden seems to suggest that religious acceptance of our weaknesses, which teaches us humility, can save us from despair; it enables us to wait hopefully for the heavenly city of faith which may redeem the earthly city.

It is worth noting that Auden brings out the significance of the various stages of human civilization by adding precise and appropriate epithets to the central symbol of the city. One can easily discover that what was once an embodiment of a social ideal became very soon a symbol of a juster life and ultimately changed into the city of God. . . . [The] varying use of this symbol points to different stages of transition that occurred in the course of Auden's career. . . . (pp. 91-2)

Auden's symbolic image of a city without walls, which he uses as the title of his last volume of poems, embodies the alienated, disintegrated urban society of today. The urban society, according to Auden, is, 'like the desert, a place without limits' (*The Enchafèd Flood* . . .); and the walls of the city are 'the walls of tradition, mythos and cultures', which 'have crumbled' . . . in modern times, making modern man's life directionless and meaningless. . . . In such a world in which 'the majority lose all genuine taste of their own, and the minority become cultural snobs' (See *The Dyer's Hand* . . .), irony proves to be the best method for depicting the prodigies of such a culture. Auden effectively employs this mode of poetic expression in a number of poems of this volume such as 'Prologue at Sixty', and 'Profile'.

The title poem of *City without Walls* (1969) . . . , relying on the balanced structure of five-line stanzas, depicts the modern urban and highly technological world of 'real structures of steel and glass' . . . in which people have turned compulsorily into hermits. . . . Besides the revealing catalogue of powerful images from the world of today presented in the poem, it is the use of fine irony which characterized the style of the poem, and supports and enlivens its ideational structure. It is largely through the employment of subtle and effective irony that Auden succeeds in exposing the incongruities of the modern world. . . . The pang of cancer [for example] is ironically described as the modern substitute of Crucifixion, and the implied contrast between a purely physical ailment born of some psychic malady and the selfless spiritual sacrifice heightens the effect of the intended irony. (pp. 92-3)

Thus, Auden's use of the city emblem reveals his consistent reliance on the imagistic structure of poetry, instead of the purely sequential one. Although there has been only a partial replacement of the logic of syntax by the logic of metaphor, the use of this image in the fifties and afterwards exhibits an obvious advancement over that of the poems of the thirties. In the later poetry we find a fusion of the reflective and the imagistic styles in place of a style born of the fusion of the discursive and the imagistic which is characteristic of the thirties. Secondly, in poems such as 'In Memorial of a City' and 'City Without Walls', the city image becomes the central symbol in a poem of elaborate meditation on human life. Lastly, Auden's varying use of the city image also reveals his intellectual development from a secular humanist to a religious believer, as [well as] the ideational nature of his poetry. (p. 94)

Dr. Narsingh Srivastava, "The Symbolic Image of the 'City' in Auden's Poetry," in Literary Criterion, *Vol. X, No. 3, Winter, 1974, pp. 86-94.*

TIMOTHY GREEN

In an essay-review of Loren Eiseley's *The Unexpected Universe* in 1970, W. H. Auden identifies genuine laughter with the "spirit of Carnival" and insists that "when we truly laugh, we laugh simultaneously *with* and *at*" [Auden's emphasis]. That is, genuine laughter and the Carnival spirit are both a protest against and an acceptance of human mortality and the contradictions inherent in the human condition. Auden further contends that we feel ambivalent about our mortal limitations and "oscillate between wishing we were unreflective animals and wishing we were disembodied spirits, for in either case we should not be problematic to ourselves." During Carnival, the traditional holidays of license and festivity preceding Lent, laughter resolves this ambivalence, according to Auden, by assuming the dual attitudes of acceptance and protest. The protest element in the traditional Carnival emerges as profanity, mock-aggression, and the inversion of social rank, all of which serve as a cathartic release of repressed discontent. . . . [Yet] the feasting, the revelry, and the general exhibition of human earthiness during Carnival disclose man's comic acceptance of himself as an earthbound creature. (p. 372)

[The] comic temperament of Auden's later poetry [from the 1940s to 1973] shows definite signs of being a thoroughgoing assimilation of the Carnival climate. In fact, while enumerating the poet's responsibilities to mankind in "Epistle to a Godson," Auden avers that poetry's ". . . dominant/mood should be that of a Carnival." Hence, Auden's later poetry essays to be a cogent, verbal embodiment of the spirit of Carnival, a spirit which, at its best, is an anamnesis of man as *Homo Ludens* and an intimation of man as holy fool. Auden's conception of poetry as a game coincides with his notion of the spirit of Carnival; for Auden's later poetry fashions a world of play in which comic frivolity, however irreverent it may seem, is a parabolic indication of the participant's spiritual well-being and a direct affirmation of the goodness of the phenomenal word.

In addition, Auden's appropriation of the Carnival spirit is an acknowledgment of man's status as a fool in the world. This recognition is the equivalent of humility—a good-humored acceptance of the follies and shortcomings of oneself and others. For Auden, worldly imperfection and human suffering do not predicate the inherent depravity of man and the world. On the contrary, Auden's spirit of Carnival is aware of a recourse to a higher realm of consciousness (i.e., faith) from which it is seen that "suffering is an inescapable element in life . . . to be accepted, not as just in itself, as a penalty proportionate to the particular sins of the sufferer, but as an occasion for grace or as a process of purgation." Thus, the Carnival spirit can celebrate man as fool *because* human imperfection is not an occasion for despair but for grace.

Auden's spirit of Carnival, then, arises from an inner reservoir of faith that intuits the pain of human contradictions as both transient and promissory. When introduced into poetry, the Carnival spirit is normally manifested in the personages of beggars, cripples, peasants, servants, or other humble men whose worldly poverty or debility is belied by their joviality, their lack of shame, their comic resilience in spite of apparent misfortune. This "wise fool" is, in fact, the comic hero of literature who glories in what appear to be defeats or defects; for to him they are neither, but rather proofs of his rightness or blessedness.

Auden's poem "The Duet" is significant for its lucid characterization of the comic hero and his Carnival spirit. In "The Duet" Auden contrasts the sorrows of a rich lady in a large estate house to the "happy passion" of a one-legged, one-eyed beggar in the wilds of nature. Whereas the "huge sad lady" bemoans her disappointments in love, the beggar turns his barrel organ in the winter woods and cries "Nonsense to her large repining." . . . The contrast between the lady in "her warm house" and the beggar in the winter wilderness highlights the beggar's Carnival spirit, his ability to resolve his apparent suffering by means of comic celebration. . . . [The] lady despairs in the midst of affluence, and the beggar rejoices in the midst of apparent poverty. The lack of shame, the glorying in apparent misfortune, the praising of the natural world—all signal Auden's characteristic manner of evoking the spirit of Carnival. The beggar testifies to Auden's belief in a religious form of the comic in which one may laugh at his own suffering when he sees this suffering as a sign of his being in truth or as an "occasion for grace." The beggar, then, may be viewed parabolically as a "holy fool" whose celebration in spite of suffering is a comic symbol of faith.

Whereas the Carnival spirit's intimation of sanctity is indirect and parabolic, its celebration of the incidental, the natural, and the right to play is emphatically direct. Furthermore, as Auden notes in "Moon Landing," celebration and delight are serious duties of the poet, especially in a world of impersonal technology, unscrupulous commerce, and subtle regimentation. . . . To Auden, therefore, art should . . . [impart] to man's temporal condition a note of merriment that will liberate him from cybernetic bondage. And this constitutes one aspect of the protest element of Carnival laughter which must thrive, Auden believes, in order to affirm the freedom of individuals and thwart the dehumanizing forces of progress.

The Spirit of Carnival is the salient expression of Auden's belief that frivolity, celebration, and playfulness are as necessary to man's well being as work or worship. . . . Not only is the spirit of Carnival an important reminder that man is *Homo Ludens;* it is also important for the comic hope that it intimates and for the indispensable capacity to persevere amid absurdities and hazards that it symbolizes. (pp. 372-74)

One of Auden's most exuberant encomiums on the Carnival spirit is "Under Which Lyre." The poem elucidates the "dialectical strife" between two modes of life: the pragmatic way, represented by solemn Apollo, and the festive way, represented by playful Hermes. The followers of Hermes are cheerful rogues, the followers of Apollo austere laborers. . . . Auden places his affections under the lyre of Hermes, the god of cunning. . . .

Under the lyre of Apollo, on the other hand, Auden places the rulers of the world, government officials, businessmen, and all who may be generally termed "the management." (p. 375)

The way of Hermes is the way of laughter and the spirit of Carnival. Though delighting in the mischievous, it has the positive function of subverting solemn worldliness and impersonal materialism. . . . As a major part of the spirit of Carnival, Hermetic clownage acts as a gadfly to all those complacencies and inflexibilities of mind which would threaten man's right to and need for frivolity.

Despite its protestations against glumness and dull sobriety, Auden's Carnival spirit regards the world with "*adoration in the eye*." . . . That is to say, the spirit of Carnival is manifested outwardly as "*banter and bawdry*" . . . , but within it repose veneration and charity. The adoring gleam in the eye of the Carnival reveller betokens the secret of genuine laughter—that it is both laughter *at* and laughter *with,* protest but also acceptance. Auden is aware that when the adoration lapses, contempt can intercede to make "The fun turn ugly, / The jokes hurt." . . . But when purged of the demons of spite and stupidity, the Carnival spirit enables the comic man to outwit "hell / With human obviousness." . . . (pp. 375-76)

Another facet of Auden's Carnival spirit is its celebration of the human body, one notable example being "Precious Five," an ode on the five senses. Maintaining the imperative mood throughout, "Precious Five" is an address of the mind to its somewhat capricious body. . . . After the poet surveys the individual responsibilities of each sense organ, his salient command to the "precious five" is to "Be happy." . . . The poet concludes that it is easy to discover reasons "To face the sky and roar / In anger and despair" but that the "singular command" of the heavens is to "*Bless what there is for being*" . . . [Auden's emphasis]—an imperative that is beyond the powers of reason to understand. . . . Auden, accordingly, praises all aspects of the physical world not only because the universe is good but also because he must.

Accepting the tenet, then, that man must "Bless what there is for being," Auden subjects the human body to praise and comic exposure (for even if the world is good, it is not beyond laughter). Praise and exposure are, respectively, the laughter *with* and the laughter *at* of the the Carnival spirit. (pp. 376-77)

Though it is ever a source of anxiety and embarrassment, the body, Auden asserts, must be accepted with good humor. For some it may verge on sacrilege to mention the bowel movements of a Prophet, but Auden risks such impropriety [in "The Geography of the House"] in order to demonstrate that we must laugh at and with our body and its impromptus, not escape into abstract speculation. . . . (p. 377)

Auden's sport with man's biological limitations heralds the unaggressive, celebrative laughter of the Carnival spirit. Without diminishing either the absurdities of existence or the frailties of the body, Carnival laughter signals a healthy acceptance of these contingencies and weaknesses. . . . If laughter is a small consolation in the face of the suffering that men are heir to, laughter affords at least a temporary resolution of the pain. True laughter, however, does not actually displace pain or become unconscious of pain; it accepts the fact of pain and transmutes the experience of it into an occasion for sanctity. Suffering must not lead to despair, as Auden notes in "Memorial for the City":

> . . . as we bury our dead
> We know without knowing there is a reason for what
> we bear,
>
> That our hurt is not a desertion, that we are to pity
> Neither ourselves nor our city:
> Whoever the searchlights catch, whatever the
> loudspeakers blare,
> We are not to despair. . . .

Since man must not despair, the spirit of Carnival is a moral obligation, not merely a fortuitous option. Hence, the human body, that limiting fence of skin within which men struggle for love and meaning, is not to be denied but affirmed in good humor lest men succumb to Manichaeism or some other notion that identifies evil with the natural world.

Another posture of Auden's Carnival spirit that challenges all doctrines proposing the inherent depravity of the phenomenal world is its attitude towards the forms of the natural world. In landscapes and other geographical features of the planet, Auden discerns analogies to the inner world of the individual, analogies which are at once sacred and comical and which affirm the essential goodness of both man and nature. As early as 1941 in "New Year Letter" Auden proposed limestone landscapes as symbols of man, but in "In Praise of Limestone" Auden embroiders and expands the original conception into a more poignant, persuasive image. Monroe K. Spears [in *The Poetry of W. H. Auden: The Disenchanted Island*] suggests that limestone symbolizes "the weakness and individuality of common human nature." . . . In the guise of a monologue spoken to a friend or lover, "In Praise of Limestone" delineates the comic condition of man, focusing on the paradox that man's strength and hope arise from his weakness, his mortal limitations. . . . The speaker concludes his conversation by observing that all he knows is that men must rejoice *with* suffering and weakness, that spiritual harmony is attained only by glorying in imperfection. . . . "In Praise of Limestone" is an intimate, meditative recommendation of the spirit of Carnival, not a direct embodiment of it. Yet, the poem clearly implies, when we do not care what angle we are regarded from, we allow that we are comical creatures and, rather than despairing of that fact, glory in it, having nothing to hide.

Auden's pastoral sequence entitled "Bucolics" also reveals the presence of the spirit of Carnival's discernment of analogies between the human spirit and natural forms. In this, "Bucolics" is similar to many of Auden's later poems which mingle the humorous and the serious. Each of the seven poems of "Bucolics" develops an analogy between natural phenomena and the human realm of values and character. . . . The relationship between playfulness and "holy places" in "Streams" reveals the essence of Auden's notion of the Carnival spirit—namely, that reverent frivolity is man's most appropriate response to the world. (pp. 377-80)

[Only] with Auden's shift to a Christian perspective about 1940 did a comic temperament become, for him, a morally and theologically sanctioned perspective. "Letter to Lord Byron" and "New Year Letter," which were written in the midst of Auden's spiritual transition, both demonstrate and advocate the comic as a mode of vision. In "New Year Letter," for example, Auden asks that men "keep in order . . . a reverent frivolity." Almost thirty years later Auden describes reverent frivolity as the spirit of Carnival, and in the intervening years his poetry strove to embody this spirit of true laughter. Auden's reaffirmation of Christianity in the late 1930s and early 1940s, after a lapse since his childhood, was apparently made with the conviction that faith must not become cranky, too cerebral, or too solemn. . . . [Even] in such explicitly religious poems as "Horae Canonicae," Auden's emphasis is on the ironic-comic duty of man to celebrate the secular world. For the later Auden, the spirit of Carnival is a necessary concomitant of religious faith. If the spirit of Carnival tends toward an earthiness and festivity not normally associated with faith, it does so only to show that religious faith is not the esoteric and staid affair that many have presumed.

When the spirit of Carnival is convincingly embodied in Auden's poetry, it is a revelation of that moment when humor and the sublime merge. Hence Auden's later poetry claims that whenever men are willing to forgo their dignity in order to participate as biological organisms in the rhythms of the physical world, they resolve with Carnival laughter the ambivalence they ordinarily feel towards the human condition and transcend their imperfections by joyfully celebrating them. If the Carnival itself is no longer officially sanctioned in most places, this does not mean that Carnival is the less needed by modern man. On the contrary, it can provide, as Auden demonstrates, a crucial service for the psyche and the spirit even though the modern vestiges of the traditional Carnival are forced to retreat to less public displays and are suggestive, to many, of a pagan orgy. For Auden, the Carnival is a celebration of our common humanity (i.e., our shared biological limitations) and of our global home; and the spirit of this Carnival is expressed as sanctified laughter. (pp. 380-81)

Timothy Green, "The Spirit of Carnival in Auden's Later Poetry," in The Southern Humanities Review *(copyright 1977 by Auburn University), Vol. 11, No. 4, Fall, 1977, pp. 372-82.*

EDWARD CALLAN

The first of Auden's longer works, *Paid on Both Sides: A Charade*, . . . is ostensibly an episode in a continuing feud between two families who live some fifteen miles apart in the Lead Dales of the English north country. . . . (p. 287)

Auden seems to have intended the charade as a vehicle for an ambitious allegory on the life and death instincts—a modern Morality of Eros and Thanatos—that could take its place beside Eliot's *The Waste Land*. . . . *Paid on Both Sides* is a variation on the Orpheus myth that Auden was to employ again with Marxist overtones in his next dramatic work, *The Dance of Death* (1933). . . . (p. 288)

Although it is Freud who supplies the underlying theme of Eros and Thanatos as instinctive energies of the libido, much of the substance of *Paid on Both Sides* is derived from C. G. Jung's *Wandlungen und Symbole der Libido* (1912), a work now best known in English by the title of the revised edition, *Symbols of Transformation*. . . . The *Both Sides* in the title of Auden's charade has reference therefore to Jung's notion of the dual nature, or "ambitendencies," of the libido whereby it energizes not only man's instinctive urges but his creative consciousness also. Jung pointed to archetypal expressions of these ambitendencies in myths of the Hero and of the Primordial Mother. He saw quest Hero myths, particularly those associating the Hero with the Sun, as expressions of man's drive toward consciousness; and recalling Faust's journey to the realm of The Mothers he noted that "the Kingdom of the Mothers is the kingdom of (unconscious) phantasy." . . . Auden embodies these notions and other aspects of the Oedipal theme in *Paid on Both Sides* which, like every "country house charade," has its riddle to be solved. For example, the charade is fairly closely equivalent, in dramatic terms, to Jung's interpretation of the Sphinx as a double being corresponding to "the mother-imago," and representing a force that could not be disposed of by solving a childish riddle. . . . Jung's archetypal Mother, a double being both loving and terrible, who in endowing her children with life also gives death as its end, is a significant figure in a number of Auden's works including the best of the plays with Christopher Isherwood, *The Ascent of F6*. . . . (pp. 289-90)

The map that George and John Nower pour over [in the Charade] is the map of an area Auden chose to mythologize as his symbolic landscape, not only in *Paid on Both Sides* but throughout much of his work. "I could draw its map by heart," he says in "Amor Loci," a poem written forty years after *Paid on Both Sides*. . . .

The landscape's strata and vegetation symbolize both the unconscious and nourishing aspects of the mother; the barns and made objects symbolize the consciousness of her son whose inescapable mother-complex is described in the "Prologue" to *The Orators*. . . . (p. 291)

The moors between Hexham and Brough that are a "symbol for us all" bear traces of continuous human occupation and conscious activity almost since the glaciers retreated. . . . But it is not only the stages of man's historical journey that the moors bring to mind. The strata beneath them bear evidence of the stages of his evolutionary heritage, and, behind that again, of geological time stretching back through the earliest epochs. . . . And since lead occurs in the interstices between the most ancient rock strata, lead-mining symbolizes, for Auden, man's interest in his own psychic depths. (p. 292)

The geography of the Lead Dales does not exhaust the allegorical matter in *Paid on Both Sides*. It gives us the symbolism of the place, but not of time. The action is set at approximately Christmas time, for there is talk of Christmas toys and gifts as well as of the killings in old winters that link it allegorically with winter solstice rituals and vegetation myths. (p. 294)

For the mummers' episodes Auden ransacked Jessie Weston's *From Ritual to Romance* and Frazer's *The Golden Bough* rather more indiscriminately than Eliot did for *The Waste Land;* for where Eliot simmered and salted to taste, Auden serves up raw lumps. Both Frazer and Weston identify a variety of folk customs as survivals of the ritual of the killing and reviving of the vegetation spirit. They find, for example, that mummers' plays reenact a ritual in which a representative of the Tree Spirit is subjected to a mock trial before being killed by an Accuser and subsequently restored by a Doctor. The stock characters are therefore the Accused, the Accuser, a Judge, and Doctor—parts taken in *Paid on Both Sides* by The Spy, John Nower, Father Christmas, and the Doctor. This cast duplicates fairly closely those recorded by Weston for a mummers' play at Newbold. . . . Miss Weston may have also provided a rationale for the elements from Greek tragedy—the Chorus and the pervasive memory of *Oedipus Rex*—that permeate the Charade; for she cites F. E. Cornford on the origins of Attic Comedy in fertility rituals: "They were at first serious, and even awful, figures in the Religious Mystery, the God who every year is born, and dies, and rises again; his Mother and his Bride; the Antagonist who kills him; the Medicine Man who restores him to life." (p. 296)

[In the Charade's trial scene] three manifestations of the unconscious came forward to speak in turn: Bo, Po, and the Man-Woman. The latter represents a primitive life stage before the distinction of sex and therefore speaks from the remote archetypal depths of the unconscious; but Bo and Po are closer to the surface, perhaps in the repressed personal unconscious. (p. 297)

The first of the unconscious manifestations, Bo, is a spokesman for orientation towards the upper world. His cryptic imagery of migrations, mountains, rebirth, and northern ridges resembles that of extroverted seekers in Auden's other poems of the period. . . . In particular his paradoxical phrase:

> By loss of memory we are reborn
> For memory is death,

makes a strong case against the withdrawn or inverted libido which, according to Jung, substitutes "the world of memories" for the upper world. Bo's concluding lines hint at a Quixotic, tomb-conscious quest on northern ridges.

Po, on the other hand, echoes Sancho Panza and seems to favour turning "back to estates / Explored as a child." Po is also womb-conscious, attracted to the regressive road where sorrow sits. . . . Bo and Po are followed by the Man-Woman, who brings associations of war, for this hermaphrodite "appears as a prisoner of war behind barbed wire in the snow" and speaks in verse with slant-rhymes reminiscent of Wilfred Owen's poetry of World War I. This androgynous figure symbolically represents life below consciousness, or at a very early stage of evolution. . . . Jung points to the hermaphrodite as an archetypal figure in dreams, who, like the Atman of the Upanishads, is a "primordial universal being, a concept which in psychological terms coincides with that of the libido."

The Man-Woman as a prisoner of war in winter is an aspect of the libido in need of liberation from regressive forces represented by John Nower's death-wish. . . . The essence of what the Man-Woman says in the trial scene is summed up in Jung's statement: "Whoever introverts the libido—that is to say, whoever takes it away from a real object without putting in its place a real compensation—is overtaken by the inevitable results of introversion." Auden's imagery is eloquent on this point. (pp. 297-98)

[T. S. Eliot] welcomed *Paid on Both Sides:* "This fellow is about the best poet I have discovered in several years"; but except for Auden's close friend Louis MacNeice who contrasted it, to its favor, with Eliot's *The Waste Land,* few others greeted its first appearance with enthusiasm. "It can be very profitably contrasted with *The Waste Land,*" said MacNeice; "It is tragic where *The Waste Land* is defeatist, and realist where *The Waste Land* is literary. *The Waste Land* cancels out and ends in Nirvana; the Charade . . . leaves you with reality as agon." . . . MacNeice, while not quite just to Eliot, may be right about the more positive effect of the charade, for it attempts to explore the unconscious springs of behavior more deeply than Eliot's poetry does, and its acceptance of the double significance of the archetypal loving and terrible Mother is a "yea saying" to the whole of life. But it would take a great deal of generosity to call *Paid on Both Sides* successful. . . . Auden fared much better with the dramatization of Jung's interpretation of the myth of the hero battling the dragon . . . in *The Ascent of F6* where Ransom, on reaching the summit where he dies, encounters his mother as a mysterious veiled "Figure" accompanied by his brother, James, in the form of The Dragon. But this work came six years later.

Auden had, in the meantime, tenuously linked the fate of the archetypal Sun-hero to the death of a class in *The Dance of Death,* in 1933; and it seems likely that his attempts to fit the mythological matter to the more public medium of the stage enabled him to free himself in some degree from introverted concern with private jokes and allusions puzzling to all outside an intimate circle of friends such as Layard and Isherwood. It was for this reason that he partly disowned *The Orators*—"a fair notion fatally injured." But he continued to give prominence to *Paid on Both Sides,* and rightly so; for, whatever its defects, grappling with its riddle offers access to the intellectual motherlode—the Jungian themes that enriched a succession of his more mature works including *The Ascent of F6* and *The Age of Anxiety.*

Auden's dramatization of Jung's notions, so clear in *Paid on Both Sides,* suggests a need for some reassessment of the common assumption among critics that Auden, at the outset, was primarily indebted to Freud. The theory embodied in the charade—the notion of a divided libido energizing both conscious creativity and natural instincts that, in Jung's view, finds archetypal expression in the myths of the questing hero and the loving and terrible mothers—was the fundamental cause of the parting of the ways between Freud and Jung. Auden did not reject Freud. His several essays on Freud's works and his formal elegy "In Memory of Sigmund Freud" are a measure of his admiration and regard. But he found Freud's views on art and artistic creativity less convincing than Jung's accounts of the emergence of creature consciousness—the truly human quality—from the primal core of the libido. (pp. 300-01)

Edward Callan, "W. H. Auden's First Dramatization of Jung: The Charade of the Loving and Terrible Mothers," in Comparative Drama *(© copyright 1978, by the Editors of* Comparative Drama*), Vol. 11, No. 4, Winter, 1977-78, pp. 287-302.*

PETER PORTER

[We should not be tempted] either to believe Auden's own analysis of his creative character, or to divide his output too firmly into the "English" Auden and the "International" one. Of course, his departure for good from England early in 1939 is a very real watershed, but the nature of the change it brought about in Auden's poetry defies simplistic description. I am inclined to follow Edward Lucie-Smith's view, that what Auden learned from America was not how to work but how to be a professional. The 400-odd pages of *The English Auden* are a rich enough testament to his ability to get down to hard work while he lived in these islands. . . . Just as stuffed with aphorisms, brilliant paradoxes and sheer good sense as the later pieces in *The Dyer's Hand* or *Forewords and Afterwords,* [the prose articles and criticism included in this book] are none the less poorly organised, randomly assembled and sorely in need of an editorial pencil. The American Auden was sheerly professional in all his reviews and essays: the English Auden was still the notebook-keeper and amateur healer, tossing off brilliant *aperçus* for readers of *The Daily Herald* on "How to Be Masters of the Machine" or assembling a do-it-yourself-kit for understanding "Psychology and Art To-day." (p. 64)

[Included in *The English Auden* is] an unpublished and unfinished work entitled *The Prolific and the Devourer* which is touching in its rawness. Here are the main ideas which dominated Auden's life right up to his death, but there seems to be no control of their presentation. Had he been able to work them into a properly planned book, the world might well have lost much of the mature poetry he wrote thereafter. These fragments remain like thematic sketches in a composer's notebook: we see the dominating shapes of his imagination, but as yet there is no proper indication of how richly he is going to expand them and counterpoint them in his work. At first sight, these perceptions seem confined to political issues, but the working-out of their consequences can be found in *For the Time Being, The Sea and the Mirror, The Age of Anxiety* and well into the poems of the Fifties and Sixties. Auden always saw politics as an expression of the health of the imagination, and there is a sense in which the later Horatian poetry is quite as politically directed (or as unpolitical if you want to put it that way) as the work of the Thirties. . . . It makes general sense to state that Auden not only wrote well and ill at all stages of his career, but that his abiding interests and characteristics did not change very much over forty years' devotion to poetry. He is an artist who resists the famous three periods of production: his work is like a well-cut gem, it reveals different facets of itself at certain times. It does not get more mature or develop particularly, except in the one sense of literary professionalism. After settling in America, Auden's concern for the technical finish of his poems became more fastidious. (pp. 64-5)

But *The English Auden* leaves the strong impression that this growth of professionalism was not all gain. Mixed up with the rough and ready finish of much of his poetry of the Thirties, there is also a marvellous authority and originality which the later poetry does not possess. . . . *Poems 1930* must be one of the most unexpected books ever to have made its author's reputation. Where, except perhaps in Laura Riding's verbal defoliation and Wilfred Owen's pararhymes, are there any precedents for the first poems of this twenty-three-year-old genius? The material of the poems is not without ancestry—chiefly the sagas, the public school fantasies of himself, Isherwood and friends, and the gnomic marginalia of Blake—but the tone is completely new. And like Byron's tone, which enabled him to wake one morning and find himself famous, Auden's won instant recognition. It is only when we scrutinise these early poems closely that we perceive how far they depart from the canons of poetical propriety which the later Auden set up for himself. For a start, they are *sui generis,* and not fashioned by imitation of some admired model. . . . There are shadows of past structures in them . . . , but they come very close to being unclassifiable formally—uncomfortably so, for the taste of the mature Auden, perhaps, though he always remained fond of the bulk of them and included them, under however many changes of title, in his various collections from the Forties onwards. (p. 65)

After 1930, rhymes, metrical devices, stanza structures, in fact all the traditional armoury of poetry, are applied in full knowledge of their effectiveness and the formal demands they make upon the poet's skill and imagination. But the early poetry is different. It is packed with close rhymes, pararhymes, and cadences out of the nursery, but these are held dissolved in verse of a sleepwalking authority. This is just the way an oracle would speak, we think, as we read such poems as "From the very first coming down", "Taller today", "Love by ambition", "Watch any day his nonchalant pauses", "Will you turn a deaf ear", and "Consider this and in our time." Those first readers in the Thirties who thought they were hearkening to the voice of a new leader, and who interpreted Auden's poems as messages from the battlefront, soon identified with Communism, were not wrong in their impulses, though wholly mistaken in their interpretations. As Edward Mendelson [editor of *The English Auden*] points out, the early poems speak of defeat, of separation, of stories which are not simply incomplete but of which there were probably never any definitive versions. We may wonder how anybody could take *Poems 1930* or even *The Orators* as a call to the collective life. . . . But Auden himself must have been persuaded to think that his talent was amenable to the cause of Communism: for all his brilliance of mind, he was not gifted with total self-knowledge.

His was a most unusual case—a very young poet whose first work was recognised by his contemporaries as new and authoritative. Combined with his didactic bent, this discovery of his authority pushed him towards an explicitness which was sometimes at variance with his talent during the Thirties. After 1930, it seems to me, Auden's work is a sort of development section reworking themes to which the first book of poems gave the exposition. Ideas out of the hauntingly complete early poetry are now subjected to overt elaboration. Except for his remarkable lyrics and songs, many of which were gathered into *Look, Stranger!,* the rest of the Thirties poetry is not as fine as his first published work. Only after he went to America and realigned himself with Christianity did he experience another surge of power of the kind with which he began. . . .

[The] revolutionary art seemingly promised by his earliest work was something he was either unaware of or something he had no intention of providing. The anti-modernist counter-reformation which he led in later years is prefigured as early as *The Orators.* And if in the Thirties he was content to take up forms and influences with an almost games-playing enthusiasm, he quickly turned himself into a virtuoso, whose maturity was accelerated by the more professional air of the United States. . . . The United States is, of course, the home of the academic avant-garde but Auden did not interest himself in this. It was American professionalism which concerned him, and he was more likely to discern it on Broadway than on Black Mountain.

It is hard to read *The English Auden* without wondering equally at the memorable language and the wilful extravagance. The two occur together most frequently in *The Orators* and *The Dog Beneath the Skin.* . . . These live side by side with details of the fifth column of wireless-controlled crows and card packs, and the stink bombs and sanitary-paper sabotage forecast in *Journal of an Airman.* But the extravagance has a point, the amateur versifying has a no-holds-barred exuberance which Auden risked less and less as he got older. . . . (p. 66)

But having praised the exuberance, I can't say I am surprised that Auden quickly outgrew and came to regret the crudity of many of the ideas in the poems of his time of poetical loosening-up. . . . Auden's personality being so strongly didactic, his creative gift had to stand in for the Old Adam in him. He was drawn to the wilder shores of the healers (Homer Lane, Lawrence and "loony Layard"), but also to Freudian orthodoxy and to his mother's Anglicanism. Without the urge to portray the sickness of our species in poetry as exuberant and memorable as anything he wrote in praise of health, he would have been an insufferable prig as an artist. (p. 67)

Not the least of the attractions of *The English Auden* is its reminder that this knowing artist once exhibited character faults like ours, and didn't merely anatomise them. He had not yet put his guard right up. *Poems 1930* is all Old Adam —a wonderful assortment of warnings and battle scenes, not just from ruined industrial landscapes and the haunted pastures of old feuds, but as much concerned with the High Streets and mass culture of an England bleeding to death in the Depression. The one really severe loss suffered by Auden in America was his sense of place. He recaptured it in a touristy sort of way in his poems about the Mezzogiorno and lower Austria, but the real (as distinct from the mythic) America seems never to have entered his imagination at all forcefully. Not even New York is fleshed out in his later poetry. From *New Year Letter* onwards, the landscape of his poems comes from books, and emblematic ones at that. And when he does record more concretely, the scene is usually England again. . . . [He] sets these islands before us like a map. It is much more than a geographical poetry; the vision is of the field of folk itself. . . . "Get there if you can and see the land you once were proud to own" begins one of the poems in Auden's first book. So much of what Auden saw at that time is undated and disturbingly true today. In America Auden moved on to other concerns, but the country he left behind remains very much as he diagnosed it.

The English Auden should enable all those commentators who have been saying for years that he left his gift behind him when he went to America to check on their memories of his work in the Thirties. (pp. 67-8)

It is interesting to note Auden's habit of dropping set-pieces into his plays as with the "Epithalamium" and "The Witnesses"; he had not yet begun to dismember his longer works to provide individual poems for later books—that was to come with his various versions of *Collected Poems*. Therefore, starting with *Paid on Both Sides*, the book is a steady progression forward out of the Twenties up to Auden's departure for the States in January 1939. (p. 68)

There are dozens of masterpieces in [*The English Auden*], some of them the most familiar and loved poems of our century. Has there been a writer of lyrics in English since Rochester who was Auden's equal? That claim can be substantiated on his first decade's production alone—the greater part of it present in this cornucopia of a book. (p. 70)

Peter Porter, "Auden's Cornucopia: The 1930s Texts," in Encounter *(© 1978 by Encounter Ltd.), Vol. L, No. 2, February, 1978, pp. 64-70.*

FRANK KERMODE

Auden came close to a point where he no longer understood his own poetry. . . . [Something] happened that made him close his mind, not to the earliest poetry so much as to that of the middle 'thirties. The *Collected Poems* . . . omits much and alters a good deal of what is retained. This supplementary volume [*The English Auden*], however, contains all the poetry of the specified period, the text being "in the form it reached at the end of 1939." . . . (p. 609)

[*The English Auden*], though it in no way matches the idea people of my age must have as to how an Auden collection should look, is nothing like as hideous as *Collected Poems*, which seems to have been designed as part of a plot to stop people reading Auden. I myself am not quite old enough to have been part of the original audience of *Poems*, but I read *Look, Stranger!* soon after it appeared (and, having heard the word from Cambridge that it demonstrated the collapse of Auden's talent, rushed off to get the early book, wondering what marvels it contained). And it really is a great pleasure to see the poetry of this period decently available once more, unexpurgated, uncorrected, unamended in accordance with a later creed of taste, morals, politics, and religion. (p. 610)

[In the Foreword to the 1966 *Collected Poems*, Auden] describes three categories of poems he is sorry to have written: the dishonest, the bad-mannered and the boring. He does not give examples of the second or the third category. The dishonest poems are those which express feelings or beliefs the author never truly entertained. Because he really disliked modern architecture, he now rejects "Sir, no man's enemy," which ends with a call for "new styles of architecture." The conclusion of *Spain* is immoral:

History to the defeated
May say alas but cannot help nor pardon.

"It would have been bad enough if I had ever held this wicked doctrine, but that I should have stated it simply because it sounded to me rhetorically effective is quite inexcusable." . . . The most famous rejection—of "We must love one another or die" ("September 1, 1939")—is another wanton failure to read a line in its context. Auden had simply decided not to understand. He denies that his revisions and rejections had an ideological motive; but in the dedication to *Collected Poems* (1966) in the Foreword to which these painful remarks appear, he says that "a Christian ought to write in prose, For poetry is magic . . ."

[David] Bromwich justly comments that from the mid-'forties Auden "gave perhaps the most limited description of the aim and use of poetry that has ever come from a major poet; in his ideal world poetry is among the more harmless indoor pastimes." In the Yeats elegy he had written "O all the instruments agree / The day of his death was a dark cold day." This became "What instruments we have agree . . ." "Granted," says Bromwich, "we do not have all the instruments; to say so is perhaps a stroke for moderation and truth. But the poem has stopped singing." But this is, in its turn, too moderate. The original lines have a measure of affectation common enough in the early Auden; they belong to that part of his voice everybody found it too easy to imitate, and that exclamatory "O," often placed where no such ejaculation seems to be called for, is a sort of egotistical announcement or self-advertisement, so that one sees why the new-model Auden of a few years later would cringe at it. Yet it *is* related to an authentic aspect of his earlier poetry; he was always estranging the familiar, and it would not be difficult to cite periphrases, quite as strained as this one, which still somehow succeed. If Auden had bothered to understand the lines he might have dropped them altogether; the worst solution was to change them into something merely silly, as if he were saying that because of his new devotion to the truth he must allow for the possibility that other instruments, not consulted, indicated that the day was in fact unusually warm and bright. The lines have stopped singing, but they have also stopped making sense.

There is a genuine and sad perversity in this failure of Auden to understand himself. It is as if he came to find himself boring, or became unable to connect with himself, as in life he grew less and less able to connect with others. All those schemes and formulas he invented to systematize his views on everything from history to ethics—it was a habit early formed, as we see from some of the prose selections in this new book—served to fence him in, to prevent any real conversation with others, or with his former self. His earlier rhetoric failed later ethical tests, and in acquiring a poetic personality that could live with these faintly schoolboyish standards of truth-telling he lost all sense of the valuable strangeness of the personality it supplanted. (pp. 611-12)

It should be said that many of the changes are of a kind that any poet might make, for example the deft, simple improvements in the poem "Legend." But it still seems to me that much of the early work is travestied. Even the titles, when they are ironical or dismissive ("Venus Will Now Say a Few Words"), tend to put the poems down. The very early work suffers least, perhaps because it is usually gnomic and opaque, not speaking aloud what the later, moralizing poet did not want heard. *Paid on Both Sides*, certainly a work of genius, is spared. The poems which are not are probably lesser works, but they speak out, and in unacceptable tones. Auden's reason for disliking them is hinted at in a casual piece of prose, here reprinted, and dated 1936: "the commonest cause of badness in the arts is being really interested in one subject while pretending to be interested in another. The secret of good art is the same as the secret of a good life: to find out what you are interested in, however strange, or trivial, or ambitious, or shocking, or uplifting, and deal with that, for it is all you can deal with well. 'To each according to his means; from each according to his powers,' in fact." This last quotation would presumably have disappeared had Auden revised the piece for publication later; but one sees what is in process. He decided that some of his poems were only pretending to be interested in what they were saying. And out goes the Prologue to *Look, Stranger!,* "O Love, the interest itself in thoughtless heaven," with its tremendous concluding thirteen-line sentence and its exalted conceits. This poem has an intellectual and technical range quite different from that of *Paid on Both Sides,* but the poet had ceased to be interested in that "possible dream, long coiled in the ammonite's slumber," and now supposed that he never really had been. There is something wrong with a set of rules that excludes so fine a poem from the canon; and there is something wrong with an editorial policy that excludes it from the *Collected Poems* and prints it in a supplementary volume [*The English Auden*], which, however sumptuous, is still only an appendix.

One is glad to have the specimens of early prose. Like other young reviewers, Auden was educating himself in public, and there are passages here that he would certainly have found blush-making in his later years. . . . (pp. 612-13)

The best of the prose has to do with psychoanalysis, for the young Auden had thought seriously about it, and what he had to say is still worth reading for its own sake. The excursions on light verse, though repetitive, are also worth attention, for Auden's doctrine of light verse was soon to become his doctrine of poetry in general. And of course he was always remarkably good at it. . . .

[We] old men who still think of the poems of the 'thirties as part of an almost incomparably good time for modern poetry—when you picked up the literary journals and read a late poem of Yeats, or *East Coker,* or a new Auden—are not going to sit idly by and allow it to be said that he was really in a bad patch of pretending, but eventually got it right; and that people will come to see that he did, abandoning their allegiance to the older texts and the banned poems. At least *The English Auden* will do nothing to strengthen that kind of propaganda. (p. 614)

Frank Kermode, "Another Auden," in The Yale Review *(© 1978 by Yale University; reprinted by permission of the editors), Vol. LXVII, No. 4, Summer, 1978, pp. 609-14.*

B

BACH, Richard 1936-

Bach is an American novelist, screenwriter, and essayist. He is best known for *Jonathan Livingston Seagull,* a novel that Bach claims was inspired by a vision. The novel was a tremendous financial success, although most critics found it banal in theme and simplistic in its ersatz philosophical pretensions. (See also *Contemporary Authors,* Vols. 9-12, rev. ed., and *Something about the Author,* Vol. 13.)

JEAN CAFFEY LYLES

[Some] reviewers have not hesitated to place *Jonathan* alongside Antoine de Saint Exupéry's small classic [*The Little Prince*]. It is true that Saint-Exupéry, like Richard Bach, was an aviator, but—though this may be heresy to *Jonathan*-cultists—that's where the resemblance ends. Bach's heavy-handed allegory is no match for the whimsical charm and gentle wit of *The Little Prince*. . . . (p. 1186)

Jonathan's success in the general book trade is another phenomenon altogether. For example, the *Reader's Digest,* that official organ of Middle Americanism, published a condensation of the book in its May issue. Clearly, here is a work that transcends not only age but culture and politics. Possibly the aspect most responsible for moving *Jonathan* off the shelves is its ambiguity. There's enough symbolism and allegory in the story to delight the most avid symbol hunter. *Moby Dick* it's not; nor am I prepared to class it with *The Old Man and the Sea.* But symbols it's got. And the great virtue of this book is that it means precisely what you want it to mean. . . . No matter what your age, sex, race, annual income, religion or politics, somewhere in the context of your life you can find a use for *Jonathan*'s message that there are "no limits." . . . What Bach has done in essence is to market that panacea of the '50s, the power of positive thinking, in the packaging of the '70s, so that it can be swallowed whole even by those who share the late Adlai Stevenson's sentiments that "I have always found St. Paul appealing and St. Peale appalling." (pp. 1186-87)

Jean Caffey Lyles, "The 'Jonathan' Bonanza," in The Christian Century *(copyright 1972 Christian Century Foundation; reprinted by permission from the November 22, 1972 issue of* The Christian Century*), Vol. LXXXIX, No. 42, November 22, 1972, pp. 1185-87.*

JOHN CAREY

Mr Bach's nice, soggy Christianity [in *Jonathan Livingston Seagull*] could not be expected to fit in unpleasantnesses like the Crucifixion. His book is for those who think the world would be a lovely place if it were full of chummy people and tame animals. Needless to say, such beliefs are for the most part readily divorceable from their owners' actual conduct. It's of interest that Jonathan's spiritual aviation should prove so endearing to a nation currently using its own air power to crush North Vietnam.

John Carey, "The Good in Every Gull," in The Listener *(© British Broadcasting Corp. 1972; reprinted by permission of John Carey), Vol. 88, No. 2280, December 7, 1972, p. 797.**

ARTHUR G. HANSEN

There is no doubt that Bach is passionate about the realm of flight. In fact, flying to Bach is almost a religious experience, and his final essay in [*A Gift of Wings*] comes close to saying just that. . . . If the sky is symbolic of God, the airplane becomes the physical entity coalescing with the human spirit to provide the ritualistic act of worship. The airplane becomes an extension of the flyer. No mere assemblage of nuts and bolts, it is capable of responses (so Bach would claim) that almost transcend physical laws—at least if the aircraft has received tender, loving care. References to airplanes are on an intimate level. . . .

Here are the stories of an unblushing romanticist—a latter-day Icarus with his gift of wings. While a "white-knuckle" air traveler may fail to appreciate Bach's peculiar perspective, his style and enthusiasm will undoubtedly make an impression. But the book does, nevertheless, have some depth to it.

Basically, this is an accounting of one man's feelings about life and the things that make life worth living. Flying is the means for expression rather than an end in itself. Readers of *Jonathan Livingston Seagull* will catch the significance of Bach's remark, "Flying, once again, is overcoming, not the distance from here to Nantucket, but the distance from here to perfection." Flying is aimed at finding life itself and of living it in the present. It is the challenge of independence—"If you wish a world where your destiny rests completely in your own hands, chances are that you are a naturally born pilot." One suspects that the main issue under discussion in *A Gift of Wings* is the never-ending search for transcendence. This was also the core of *Jonathan*—we really can be more than we are if we try hard enough. We all have the means to do so. What we need is the will, an adventuresome spirit, and an idea of what we might eventually become with practice and effort. . . .

Bach has a passion and a pen and he puts the two together with warmth and skill. If one wishes a bit of spirit-lifting along with pleasurable reading, then Richard Bach's *A Gift of Wings* is certainly worth examining.

Arthur G. Hansen, "The Saturday Evening Post Bookshelf: 'A Gift of Wings'," in The Saturday Evening Post *(reprinted with permission from The Saturday Evening Post Company © 1975), Vol. 249, No. 3, April, 1975, p. 72.*

RICHARD R. LINGEMAN

I guess a lot of things that are said in ["Illusions"] are the kind of sentences somebody might want to embroider on a sampler—or bake into a fortune cookie. Bach seems sincere—he even ends up a messiah himself in the book and says there's room at the top for everybody. Maybe there's some truth in this—I can't really tell one way or another. My own inclination after reading it was to think up some sayings of my own like, "If this book helps get you through the night, then it's better than Jack Daniels" and "Ideas are not necessarily true if you can't disprove them" and "Everybody is free to do anything, including ignore this book."

Richard R. Lingeman, "Books: New Wings, Old Seagull," in The New York Times *(© 1977 by The New York Times Company; reprinted by permission), April 1, 1977, p. C27.*

ANDREW M. GREELEY

As serious religion, "Illusions" does not even begin to be anything more than [fantasy literature]. The twin problems of purpose and evil with which religion has traditionally wrestled are not even addressed, but dismissed as illusory. If religion is the modest dogma that God is not mad, then "Illusions" is an irreligious book, because it suggests that it doesn't matter whether He is or not. Nor do the simple ethical imperatives of Shimoda do justice to humankind's agonizing over the implications of its world views of moral behavior. Shimoda and Bach dismiss ethical ambiguities as easily as they dispose of existential anxieties.

It is hardly fair, I suppose, to apply such serious paradigms to a playful exercise of the fantastic imagination; still, one has the impression that Bach wants the book to be taken very seriously indeed. It is fantasy, all right, but fantasy with implications for action. We should all live the way Shimoda did.

Ultimately one's judgment of "Illusions" will depend on one's taste for the fantastic. Some will think it heretical, even blasphemous—if such sins can still be committed. Others will find it cloying and cute. Many readers may decide that it is a charming, light-hearted story with important insights into the meaning of human life.

For whatever it may be worth, my own reaction was underwhelming. . . . I think I'll stick with St. Mark.

Andrew M. Greeley, "Jonathan Livingston Shimoda," in The New York Times Book Review *(© 1977 by The New York Times Company; reprinted by permission), April 10, 1977, p. 11.*

JOSEPH McLELLAN

It would not be quite accurate to say that the material in *Illusions* is shopworn, but it is becoming common currency in the reading offered to American mass audiences: enlightenment, miracles, reincarnation, out-of-body experiences. . . .

There is nothing particularly wrong with [Bach's] anecdotal enlightenment, except that there is nothing particularly right about it either. It leaves the recipient where he was before the process began, except that he may have a dim recognition of the existence of other places. The problem, like the advantage, is that it is too easy; Lao Tzu might have said: "The Tao that is facile is not the true Tao." . . .

Perhaps the ultimate enlightenment—nirvana—comes when you perceive that the self, too, is an illusion, a game, or perhaps merely a temporary ripple on the surface of the continuum. Bach gives no evidence that he has any idea of this level of enlightenment; his book is riddled with the illusion (or the reality; it's all the same) of self. The book is clearly the product of Richard Bach, avid pilot of small aircraft, author of a number of books about flying and of one book—*Jonathan Livingston Seagull*—that captured the popular imagination in a wholly improbable way and dominated the cash registers for an interminable period five years ago. This is, of course, a relatively hard self to escape from and the need for such an escape is probably not evident to its proprietor. So be it; writing best-sellers may be a better game than achieving ultimate oneness with the All.

Illusions has certainly one of the requirements for a best-seller in the field of pop mysticism; that easiness which is both its charm and its danger. Bach climbs the foothills of a Himalayan range, and at the end of this not uninteresting book one feels that he has uttered the first "gu" of guruhood.

Joseph McLellan, "A Wing and a Prayer," in Book World—The Washington Post *(© 1977,* The Washington Post*), April 24, 1977, p. E5.*

* * *

BAINBRIDGE, Beryl 1933-

Bainbridge is an English novelist, playwright, and essayist. Her fictional world is a drab, claustrophobic one, peopled by unhappy, unlucky denizens of the lower-middle class. The dreariness of subject and setting is, however, relieved by her satiric wit and spirited dialogue. (See also *CLC*, Vols. 4, 5, 8, 10, and *Contemporary Authors*, Vols. 21-24, rev. ed.)

OLIVIA MANNING

Nothing in Beryl Bainbridge's previous novels would lead one to expect she could launch out upon a *tour de force* of this nature. *Young Adolf* is a remarkable work. She returns to her funny and keenly observed lower middle class world, but now she presents it merely as a background for a startling portrait: the portrait of Adolf Hitler, a subtle embryo of the man himself. . . .

If I have any complaint to make about a novel I have greatly enjoyed, it is that very little happens in *Young Adolf*. . . .

The main ingredients of the novel are the city of Liverpool itself: grey, wet and cold as charity: and the still unformed character of the future dictator: vain, hyper-sensitive to snubs, temperamental, ambitious beyond his natural talents, with an urge to power, a prevision of some great destiny, but with no idea how it will be realised. It is a brilliant *ébauche* for the later figure that was to become so deeply etched upon the consciousness of his contemporaries. (p. 52)

Olivia Manning, "Beryl Bainbridge's 'Young Adolf'," in Books and Bookmen *(© copyright Olivia Manning 1978, reprinted with permission), Vol. 24, No. 2, November, 1978, pp. 52-3.*

BLAKE MORRISON

Young Adolf is less of a success than its fascinating origins might have led us to suppose. . . .

[By] forcing Adolf to suffer various Chaplinesque indignities, [Bainbridge] works a kind of comic historical revenge. In the course of the novel, Adolf is knocked over the head, bitten by fleas, drenched to the skin, dressed up in women's clothes. The slapstick purges old resentments, and largely frees Bainbridge from the task of 'explaining' Hitler psychologically. It must have been tempting to indulge in the ironies of hindsight, but in this respect the novel is aptly restrained: only as Adolf finally departs is a character allowed to observe: 'Such a strong-willed young man. It is a pity he will never amount to anything.'

For all that, *Young Adolf* is a disappointment—a brilliant idea, but one too sketchily (and perhaps too hastily) carried out. Bainbridge is good, as we'd expect, on Liverpool . . . , but remains a novelist more at home with the 1940s (and the present) than with 1912. Not only are many of the usual narrative tensions absent, but Bainbridge can't quite prevent herself from getting Adolf on the analyst's couch (persecution mania, fits, hallucinations, anti-Semitism and all). And when she does 'analyse'—'School had been rotten, and his father, and Linz and Vienna. Even his beloved mother had died rotten of a cancer. It was a rotten world'—the results can look disconcertingly vapid. (p. 630)

Blake Morrison, "Looking Backwards," in New Statesman *(© 1978 The Statesman & Nation Publishing Co. Ltd.), Vol. 96, No. 2486, November 10, 1978, pp. 630-31.**

DIANE JOHNSON

Beryl Bainbridge's novels are published in the United States but not much known there, which is something to be regretted. Like a family of gifted eccentrics, they are diverse, yet there are strong similarities, as there always must be in the work of an original and accomplished writer—perhaps it is the essence of accomplishment. In any case, Bainbridge's novels seem unlike those of other people, unless perhaps they resemble, in their economy and formal elegance, the novels of Henry Green. They are her own; the plots each with its lurking catastrophe are similar, the characters, each so memorable in his way, are similar too. Four simple distinctions are preserved: they are divided into males and females, and into a type that is large, fleshy and pale—those are the people with power and energy—and other, often more sympathetic people who are small, thin, odd and astounded, like Binny in *Injury Time* or like young Adolf. As in life, things divide men from women. They do not look at the world the same way. The men are imprisoned in conventions, slaves to little rituals to preserve self-respect or comfort. Their lustful impulses are often checked by bourgeois compunctions. The women, more passive, are oddly freer, social reforms just go on over their heads. They long to pass for normal but never to be normal, for they consider that they are normal. All of Bainbridge's books have a way of being about the assumptions of society about normality and people trying to fit in and have what they want too.

For an American reader discovering Beryl Bainbridge, only one complaint mars universal admiration: the complaint concerns the passivity of the characters towards their environment and their fate. Masters of expedience, resilient despite their resignation, practised at making do, at sly deceptions on the givens of their situations, they are capable of *tour de force* contrivance for the sake of comfort, respectability or survival. . . . Perhaps Americans are surprised that the characters do not exert themselves more mightily than [they do] against outrages of poverty and inconvenience; although exigency is certainly a fact of American life, it has little place in American fiction.

Bainbridge's creatures are not disenchanted. Their illusions are so trivial that circumstances do not conspire to deprive them. On the big subjects—who they are and what will happen to them—they have no illusions at all. They never escape. "I knew it would be me", says Binny as the desperadoes carry her off. Bainbridge is wonderful on sex, for each character she seems to have located the exact conjunction of desire and social prudence that controls his sexual behaviour. She knows the point at which people will say to hell with it, in any crisis. Her characters don't have illusions, they have bruises—always bruises of the spirit, often literal bruises, and sometimes lacerations. . . .

Young Adolf gathers up with astonishing success some . . . figures from Bainbridge's other books. An attentive reader might have seen him coming, might have glimpsed his face elsewhere, sensed his attraction for the novelist who had yet to unravel his place in her imaginery scheme. . . .

Young Adolf is not a historical novel in [the] usual sense—that is, a dramatization of known events—it is an invention of another kind, a feat of imagination and craft, without definition.

Whatever the real facts of Hitler's life we believe this account in part because of its manner, detailed and confident, and because it does not insist too stridently in foreshadowing the later reality. Adolf, depressed, hungry, pitiful, driven to expedients, is very like a character in a book by Beryl Bainbridge. That the shirt, the moustache, the uniform, the hairstyle he will later wear, are all acquired during his five-month stay in Liverpool says something, doubtless, about the large consequences of small accidents; and that is characteristic Bainbridge, too. But mostly, when we get a glimpse of the future, the moment veers off into comedy. . . . The novel's time is told so absorbingly, and with such authority, that we lose our power to hold the future in mind. This is the method of all of Bainbridge's novels, each moment rendered vividly in the mind of one character or another, presented to the reader through his thoughts or his vision. . . .

[Often] the interpretative consciousness, in this and in others of Bainbridge's novels, misinterprets, misunderstands what it sees, or sees too little. Human limitation is the basic assumption of this novelistic method. Because all consciousness is limited, a number of minds are needed from whom only the reader gathers all. It is because the characters never grasp the entire picture that the gothic and grotesque touches in the earlier books, and the historical game here, have, none the less, such an authoritative manner of truth.

A mosaic of personal interpretation reveals the disadvantage humans live under. It also makes Bainbridge's novels very funny. And her way of shifting from mind to mind enables her to escape what would otherwise be the great danger of her method, the danger of slipping into caricature or ridicule. No matter how ridiculous or stereotyped—an old maid, a gesticulating Italian—the immediacy and clarity of each person's perceptions remind us that he is unique, not to be sneezed at, things have happened to him. . . . When the characters seem comic to the reader, it is because they seem comic to each other, not to the author, who is virtually invisible in all her work, except for the occasional stage direction. By being only partially perceived, the horror which underlies and threatens in all her narratives seems mere daily horror.

The eventual horror in *Young Adolf* when it is understood cannot be dismissed or forgiven; but none of the characters can foresee it, and we, confined to their minds, can almost forget it. If we refer in our minds to events outside the novel, we perceive Bainbridge's suggestion, no doubt not entirely mischievous, that when the real horror comes, it will have had its origin in the England of 1912.

Bainbridge is never doctrinaire, seldom so explicit; yet political implications develop logically from her recurring interest in the relation of ordinary people to authority. The characters in her novels are always testing it out. They are usually victims, even if only of the tyranny of social convention, or the tyrannical fear of not being respectable or the tyranny of near-relations over one another. . . .

Bainbridge seems fascinated, also, with the conspiracies among powerless people to defeat authority; the Italians at the bottle factory, or, in this novel, when they conspire to . . . get Adolf a job. Alois gets him an interview, and, because he has no shirt, they make him look respectable with "a tray cloth embroidered at the edges with bunches of cherries, which in some fashion he had stuffed into the revers of his black coat". Thus pitiably got up, wet with rain, Adolf waits outside the hotel. "Several times he started to climb the steps towards the Commissionaire who guarded the entrance to the building, and on each occasion he lost courage halfway up and turned back. He couldn't risk a rebuff." Thus we are made to sympathize and pity the monster of the world. It is a complicated exercise in social sympathy that Bainbridge demands of us, and is her most ambitious treatment yet of the serious concern and conviction that underlie her comedy.

Diane Johnson, "The Sufferings of Young Hitler," in The Times Literary Supplement *(© Times Newspapers Ltd. (London) 1978; reproduced from* The Times Literary Supplement *by permission), December 1, 1978, p. 1385.*

Bainbridge's earlier novels for the most part delineate the dingy little lives of those who for one reason or another are not equipped to deal with the ordinary demands of social life, and in Hitler [in *Young Adolph*] she may have found the quintessence of the type. Surprisingly, she has succeeded in the seemingly impossible task of making him interesting and human—one begins to think of him as "young Adolph" rather than as "Hitler"—without giving him any sympathy whatsoever. And astoundingly, despite the predictable ending and occasional stretching of readers' credulity, *Young Adolph* is wildly, broadly funny: gallows humor at its most extreme. (pp. 133-34)

"Life & Letters: 'Young Adolph'," in The Atlantic Monthly *(copyright © 1979 by The Atlantic Monthly Company, Boston, Mass.; reprinted with permission), Vol. 243, No. 3, March, 1979, pp. 133-34.*

NEAL ASCHERSON

Beryl Bainbridge has written a great deal, with compassion and cunning, about the weak. Sometimes they are women, locked into some male-constructed paddock whose grass is growing thin but whose gate is rusted shut. Sometimes, but much less often, they are men. There is something of the pasha in the gaudy display and bulging bellies and bedroom tyranny of most of Bainbridge's men, but a few turn out as pathetic as only an aging pasha jostled by infidels can be. All of her novels, in more or less explicit ways, are about an increasingly bewildered and helpless England, the display gone shabby and the belly sagging and the knack of tyranny lost somewhere, a kindly but uncomprehending old country giving up hope of understanding the younger world, suffering some pain now and feeling the cold more.

But in this new, amazing short novel [*Young Adolf*], she has taken up a helplessness that doesn't finally resign itself. The idea is disconcerting. The young Hitler, escaping from the Vienna doss house, comes to spend a month with his relations in Liverpool. In their grotesque, hand-to-mouth household, he passes a few weeks. Then, as pallid, erratic, and hysterical as he came, he takes the train home again.

Adolf, we know, will triumph in the end, far beyond the close of the novel, in a supremely evil self-assertion. Here in Liverpool, he is almost a sympathetic character as he is engulfed in the mysterious purposes and eccentricities of other people.

At the novel's center is the figure of Mr. Meyer. A Jewish socialist, he turns out to be running an underground organization which attempts to hide poor children from the city welfare department, to prevent them from being taken from their parents and stowed in an orphanage.

[Adolf] witnesses the defeat of the plan, in a slum house off Scotland Road, when "the night men"—the welfare officials—burst in and take the children away. Meyer brandishes a stick, then gives in without resistance. And here we are encountering a plain allusion to the future, a device which in hands less delicate than Bainbridge's could easily go wrong and produce a sentimental discord. The Holocaust is prefigured, as the officials "select" children and take them away to their fate and as Meyer and his helpers surrender without a blow. The humiliated Meyer tells Adolf; "Let the minority act with enough authority, and the majority will walk like lambs to the slaughter."

It's the measure of this highly original, immensely skillful novel that such literary risks are successfully taken.

Neal Ascherson, "The Damned," in The New York Review of Books *(reprinted with permission from* The New York Review of Books; *copyright © 1979 Nyrev, Inc.), Vol. XXVI, No. 5, April 5, 1979, p. 27.**

JUDITH CHERNAIK

Beryl Bainbridge has an extraordinary ear for the speech of drifters, refugees, entrepreneurs of various kinds, Irishwomen; her characters [in *Young Adolf*] probably exist in the seedier back streets of Liverpool and other ports but then again she may just as well have invented them. She has an uncanny knack for capturing place and time; every detail seems exactly right, from the railway carriage to the Liverpool docks in 1912, to the bedrooms, kitchens and basements in which her oddly-assorted characters live out their dreams, plaster cracking, dry rot eating away.

The novel unfolds effortlessly, inventively; it is the writing of a natural. (p. 142)

Judith Chernaik, "Class and Time," in London Magazine *(© London Magazine, 1979), Vol. 19, Nos. 1 & 2, April-May, 1979, pp. 140-43.**

* * *

BALLARD, J(ames) G(raham) 1930-

An English novelist and short story writer born and reared in Shanghai, Ballard, according to Brian Aldiss, represents "one of the few stimulating forces in contemporary sf." (See also *CLC*, Vols. 3, 6, and *Contemporary Authors*, Vols. 5-8, rev. ed.)

MARTIN LEVIN

Mr. Ballard plays two themes in ["Concrete Island"]. The external theme is the Robinson Crusoe gambit—a foolproof narrative ignition. (How can a maimed motorist survive for days on a devil's island rimmed by traffic?) The internal theme is the search-for-self motif. (What is Robert Maitland *really* like?) Mr. Ballard fades in the second when he introduces a couple of surprise tenants of the concrete island: Proctor, a brain-damaged acrobat, and Jane, a social dropout. With these two Beggar's Opera types as companions, the architect's tenure takes on a surrealistic air. What do they want? What does Maitland want—besides Out? Mr. Ballard raises some tantalizing questions, even if he doesn't answer them satisfactorily.

Martin Levin, "Fiction: 'Concrete Island'," in The New York Times Book Review *(© 1974 by The New York Times Company; reprinted by permission), December 1, 1974, p. 78.*

NICK TOTTON

The stories collected in *Low-Flying Aircraft* are as stylish as anything [Ballard] has done, and told with that meticulously apocalyptic sobriety which is scarcely to be characterised as whimsical or sentimental. But Dr Ballard has kissed the Blarney Stone. He *is* whimsical—though admittedly he has a whim of iron; and he has perfected an idiosyncratic literary form which, while not precisely sentimental, might be called the Art of the Neurasthenic. He is a sick man who fondles and caresses his illness into performing the most amazing tricks—but, awkwardly, one of Dr Ballard's major symptoms is repetition compulsion. Like so many of his characters, he endlessly permutates the arid fragments of disaster in an empty gesture of making whole. Buckmaster in 'The Ultimate City,' the longest piece here, creates monuments to vanished high technology in complex pyramids of televisions or automobiles; Dr Ballard shuffles his Tarot pack of hallucinatory images into new patterns, seeking the lost *gestalt* that could reverse the fragmentation process. But this, too, is only a monument, fragments shored uselessly against our ruin; as Dr Ballard fully realises.

A more direct way of putting it is that for some years Dr Ballard has been writing the same stories over and over again. Unable or unwilling to do otherwise, he has made a minor virtue of necessity: he now tells his stories very well indeed. He knows his instrument inside out, and can plumb its every resonance as he repeats the same handful of tunes. He has also extended his research a good deal: . . . he is a synthesist—but one who never attains true synthesis, only suggestive juxtapositions of concepts he cannot fuse.

Nick Totton, "Gems and Ruins," in The Spectator *(© 1976 by* The Spectator; *reprinted by permission of* The Spectator*), Vol. 237, No. 7745, December 4, 1976, p. 26.**

MICHAEL WOOD

There was a time, some ten or fifteen years ago, when the notion of "inner space," usually associated with the writings of J. G. Ballard, threatened to change the direction of science fiction. The mind, it was suggested, was the genre's true subject. Down here in the human head, away from the galaxies, was virgin land, Freud's new frontier. . . .

Science fiction soon settled back into its old tracks and took to the stars again, but fantasy and dream, long outlawed by the more earnest practitioners, had found their way back into the form—at least in some of their more clinical aspects. The word *terminal,* for example, echoes mournfully through Ballard's stories and novels. Visions of endings are everywhere: a world winding down, its inhabitants dropping off one by one into a collective final sleep; an all but abandoned earth, its oceans bleached dry, its surface a desert of sand and salt; a group of dead astronauts circling the planet like satellites, doomed to orbit for decades until their capsules cave in; Eniwetok, a cluster of disused concrete bunkers and runways and weapons ranges, littered with broken B-29s and Superfortresses, natural home of a missed apocalypse, "an ontological Garden of Eden," as one of Ballard's characters ironically says.

It is difficult, in these scenes, to separate the private terror from the public possibility, the personal nightmare from the nightmares of history. In all the stories the stress clearly falls on the mental conditions being shown, the inner spaces of psychosis and the approaches to psychosis. The historical places and imaginable historical disasters are figures; they are shapes and traces the psyche has found for the making of its own portrait. . . .

Ballard is a master of conventional science fiction, and [in *The Best Short Stories of J. G. Ballard*] shares its cherished worries about crowded city life, the domination of time, the encroachments of technology, and the ravening consumer society. . . .

But in spite of the skill and the invention that go into these pieces, Ballard's heart, or his head, is elsewhere. He is not primarily interested in the narrative line of his stories, or in the people caught up in the situations he has devised for them. He is interested mainly in images of the kind I have mentioned, an abandoned Eniwetok, an earth without oceans, a universe of sand or coral or salt or concrete. He hints, in two stories, at the horrors of life without sleep—operations are performed to allow men to stay awake all the time. He has characters collect, again in two different stories, what he calls "terminal documents": Beethoven's final quartets, a transcript of the Nuremberg Trials, the fusing sequences for the Hiroshima and Nagasaki bombs. . . .

[This] is writing which is often obsessive, and frequently in energetic bad taste. It evokes a mind, or a series of minds, haunted by dreams of emptiness and annihilation. We may not share these dreams at all—I don't—but the best of Ballard's remarkable stories—"The Voices of Time," "The Cage of Sand," "The Terminal Beach," "The Atrocity Exhibition"—confront us with landscapes we can neither disown nor forget. Even the most cheerful and least speculative of us will remember moments when this burned and ending world might have been ours. (p. 28)

Michael Wood, "This Is Not the End of the World," in The New York Review of Books *(reprinted with permission from* The New York Review of Books; *copyright © 1979 Nyrev, Inc.), Vol. XXV, Nos. 21 & 22, January 25, 1979, pp. 28-31.**

HERMIONE LEE

J. G. Ballard is well established as a remarkable fantasist, and 'The Unlimited Dream Company,' a rich, seductive and challenging work, confirms his mastery of a very particular idiom. . . .

The emergence [in the novel of a] pagan paradise from the world of motorways and supermarkets (always potent settings for Ballard) is as much a play on wish-fulfilment as an allegory of salvation. The tropical landscape [the protagonist] Blake 'dreams up' enacts Freud's analogy between fantasy and 'nature reservations,' and the novel mysteriously but alluringly describes what might happen if archetypal dreams of eroticism and ambition were to 'come true' in the real world. There's too much decoding to do—every detail needs interpreting, and the hero's name is an irritant—but this nagging potential, common to allegory, is diverted by Ballard's almost Melvillean eloquence ('Already I saw us rising into the air, fathers, mothers, and their children, our ascending flight swaying across the surface of the earth, benign tornadoes hanging from the canopy of the universe'), as lush as the flowering vines he hangs from his multi-storey garages.

Hermione Lee, "The Stuff of Dreams," in The Observer *(reprinted by permission of The Observer Limited), No. 9817, October 21, 1979, p. 39.**

MALCOLM BRADBURY

[More and more J. G. Ballard] looks like a leading figure in a very rich and developing field. His earlier work was usually cast as science fiction, but he has long since worked loose from that pocket. Like many excellent contemporary writers, from Italo Calvino to Thomas Pynchon, he draws on science-fiction methods to create a magical modern fantasy. A writer of enormous inventive powers, an explorer of the displacements produced in modern consciousness by the blank ecology of stark architecture, bare high-rises, dead superhighways and featureless technology, he has, like Calvino, a remarkable gift for filling the empty, deprived spaces of modern life with the invisible cities and the wonder worlds of the imagination.

"The Unlimited Dream Company" is a book of this kind, a remarkable piece of invention, a flight from the world of the familiar and the real into the exotic universe of dream and desire. Indeed, the image of flight dominates the book. (p. 14)

Blake's name, presumably, is no accident. He opens the doors of alternative perception and evokes apocalyptic mirages of heaven and hell. Mr. Ballard invents a superabundant world for him to perform in. . . . It is heady stuff, a dreamy pastoral, but Mr. Ballard sustains it from a well-funded imagination, a prolix style and a great mythical sense. At times, but only at times, the metaphors grow a little too thick, and the pastoral too innocent. But this is above all a book about the fertility of the imagination. It is dense and erotic and magical, a pleasure to read. And it leaves me with no doubt that Mr. Ballard is a very important fantasist. (p. 16)

Malcolm Bradbury, "Fly Away," in The New York Times Book Review *(© 1979 by The New York Times Company; reprinted by permission), December 9, 1979, pp. 14, 16.*

DAVID PRINGLE

"The Violent Noon" [Ballard's first published story] is a story about terrorism and military reprisals, set in Malaya during the Emergency. Although it is not SF, it prefigures many of the concerns of Ballard's writing, with its jungle setting, its element of violence, and, above all, a plot which hinges on a psychological paradox. . . . Ballard needed science fiction: the pressure of his imagination demanded a freer outlet than could be provided by conventional short stories in the mode of Conrad or Somerset Maugham. (p. 5)

Yet the main influences on Ballard's writing were to come from outside the SF field. Romanticism, Symbolism, Surrealism, and the whole "modern movement" in literature and the visual arts have left their marks on Ballard. (p. 6)

[Ballard is] one of the few contemporary writers (in or out of the limited field of science fiction) who has a voice authentically his own. Ballard is an Original but he is not a Sport, which is to say he has his own voice but it is a voice which echoes certain earlier voices, and it is a voice which has much to say to modern readers. Ballard's fiction *connects* with the world of today; it draws strength from a literary and artistic tradition, but it also reflects and comments upon the nonliterary reality which surrounds us all. This amounts to a definition of "originality," in the best sense. There is no other living writer associated with the SF field who is original in quite the same way, or to quite the same extent, as Ballard. . . . He is a writer whose subject matter and imagery are always unerringly *relevant* to the concerns of the *contemporary* world. It is his ability to choose the correct subjects (and the appropriate images to embody those subjects) which gives him his "charismatic" quality as a writer. From the atom bomb to the automobile, from the prison-camps of World War II to the high-rise blocks of today, he has filled his fiction with images of our world, our times. As Ballard said in his essay on William Burroughs in 1964, "science fiction . . . is now failing in precisely those areas where the future has already become the past." His own work has been an impressively consistent attempt to mitigate that failure (and the failure, as he sees it, of the traditional social novel)—in short, to deal with our present environments, both "inner" and "outer," in their own terms. (pp. 7-8)

[His] body of work can be divided into two major "periods," with a third just beginning. The first period, 1956-1965, saw the publication of four novels—*The Wind from Nowhere* . . . , *The Drowned World* . . . , *The Drought* . . . , and *The Crystal World* . . .—and fifty short stories. This was Ballard's early, "romantic" period, a time when he concentrated on inner landscapes rather than outer. . . . The second period, 1966-1975, saw the publication of *The Atrocity Exhibition,* a collection of closely-linked stories and pieces, and three novels—*Crash* (1973), *Concrete Island* (1974) and *High-Rise* (1975)—as well as some twenty unconnected short stories. This was Ballard's middle, "dark" period, a time when he shifted his interest to outer landscapes, eschewed most of the SF conventions, and brought his fiction closer to the present day. . . . There are signs (although they can only be read tentatively) that Ballard is entering a [third and] mellower phase; his stories are tending towards the fantastic again, back to the inner landscapes. (p. 8)

During his first period, Ballard was recognizably an SF writer. His favorite device was the biospheric disaster. . . . [Two stories from this first period] are demonstrations of Ballard's technical mastery of conventional SF forms. "Billennium" is a vivid and blackly humorous treatment of the overpopulation theme, while "The Subliminal Man" is an equally accomplished cautionary tale about the future of advertising and the consumer society. (pp. 8-9)

But in this period Ballard also wrote a large number of psychological horror stories. . . . ["The Drowned Giant" (1964)] is perhaps Ballard's most "perfect" short story—melancholy, ironic, and extraordinarily resonant.

Other excellent stories which belong to this period are the humorous fantasies [set in a luxury resort known as Vermilion Sands.] . . . They are marvellously inventive tales, told with a lightness of touch that is not always characteristic of Ballard's writing. . . . Although they have an amusing surface and are filled with throwaway invention, the Vermilion Sands stories are fundamentally serious in that they deal with the problem of leisure in a rich, highly-automated society. (pp. 9-10)

[The] bulk of Ballard's fiction during [the second] period was present-oriented, and involved little or no scientific extrapolation. It did, however, continue to be a fiction concerned with human beings and their environments—most especially *technological* environments—and hence it could be claimed as SF of a sort. (p. 10)

[In *The Atrocity Exhibition,* stories of this second period,] Ballard used a new form as well as a new subject matter. The narratives are non-linear—that is to say, the elements of the plots are shuffled in order to achieve an associative rather than a sequential relationship. . . . The images are sharp, the language spare. The result is a kind of hard prose poetry—"hard," because so much of the imagery is technical, medical, architectural, or cinematic. The narratives appear to move on a number of different levels, reflecting the actual media landscapes of our present society. An objective, outer environment of motorways, TV screens, advertising hoardings, hospitals, and car-parks becomes "internalized"—a terrain of codes and latent meanings, like that of a dream. (p. 11)

Many regard [*Crash*] as his masterpiece; others see it as an unfortunate aberration. In our synoptic view of Ballard's career, it can be seen as the climax of his central, dark period—a book which deals uncompromisingly with the psychopathology of the everyday environment in a contemporary large city. . . . (p. 12)

In his nascent third period, Ballard has returned to shorter forms. The major work published so far is the novella "The Ultimate City" (in the collection *Low-Flying Aircraft and Other Stories,* 1976). Here Ballard is once more writing SF: set several decades in the future, the story describes a post-technological society and the attempt of one young man to recapture our own high-technology era. It is a relaxed work with a decidedly "romantic" feel (in contrast to the four harsh books which preceded it). (pp. 12-13)

[Ballard] is not a writer to be judged on his novels alone. He is very much at home in shorter lengths, and his talents are often displayed to the full within the compass of, say, 10,000 words. Ballard tends to compression; at one extreme this leads to the remarkable density of the *Atrocity Exhibition* pieces. . . . (p. 13)

Ballard has a painter's eye rather than a poet's tongue, and this goes some way towards mitigating [the charge] . . . that his prose is lacking in elegance. Ballard's is a heavily metaphorical style, dense with subordinate clauses, qualifications, and asides. He prefers the simile and the metaphor to the euphonious phrase, and the result is an often deliberate harshness, a jangling of imagery and idioms which is highly reminiscent of the usages of the Surrealist writers. His passages of description often work by presenting several discrete images in swift succession, each modifying the whole, sometimes to the point of apparent contradiction. . . . Although he has been accused—sometimes justly—of verbal clumsiness and poor syntax, Ballard is in fact a master of his own brand of dense descriptive prose, sown with well-turned throwaway phrases and haunting parentheses. . . . If it is true that he has made his own language [as one critic claimed], then it is hardly surprising that we should experience occasional difficulty in reading it. At its most dense and evocative, Ballard's prose requires the reader to *work* —a demand which is certain to make its author unpopular with some. (pp. 14-15)

Ballard's novels and stories are full of "things seen"—landscapes, objects, creatures. He is an intensely visual writer who deals in images and "properties." For anyone who has read more than a few of Ballard's stories these landscapes and properties are instantly recognizable. They may belong in fact to the everyday world, they may sometimes be used by other writers, but once seen through Ballard's eyes they become unforgettably "Ballardian." (p. 15)

It is my belief that Ballard's use of symbolism has, on the whole, been more conscious, more intelligent, and more innovative than that of any other contemporary SF or fantasy writer (which is not to say that Ballard has "placed" every symbol, with a devious cunning, so that the whole can be unravelled like an explicit code; there may be deep meanings in Ballard's fiction, but there are no Hidden Messages). He has sometimes maintained and sometimes altered the traditional symbolic patterns in order to suit his own sensibility, and in order to mirror the dilemmas and perspectives of the modern mind. Throughout his novels and stories he has built up a structure of symbols which is very much his own, and which is recognizably "contemporary" (reflecting all the *angst* of the post-nuclear period), and yet which can at the same time be approached as a variation on the ancient fourfold pattern of Heaven and Hell, the Garden of Eden and the Fallen World. There are even four "elements" which dominate the landscapes in Ballard's fiction, four primary substances which set the tone of his stories. They are Water, Sand, Concrete, and Crystal.

Water and sand, concrete and crystal are to be found somewhere in virtually all of Ballard's fictions, and each is in fact a symbol with an aggregate of meanings, overtones, associations. Secondary symbols group themselves around these four major ones, and in different stories they combine in different ways. Ballard's work must above all be taken as a *whole* rather than as a number of discrete tales. Viewed as a whole, it will be seen to have a quite profound significance. (pp. 17-18)

Ballard's heroes may be worldly-wise, but they are scarcely men of action (although there is usually a certain amount of "action" required of them: dodging bullets, driving cars, piloting aircraft, or simply being able to endure hostile environments). They are usually haunted by a sense of failure (often the failure of a marriage, or of a career) and are driven by obsessions. Frequently, they are semi-recluses, choosing to strand themselves in some bizarre terrain which reflects their states of mind. . . . In short, Ballard's heroes constitute a typical Ballardian paradox: they are strong men, chiefly notable for their weaknesses. (p. 38)

The other characters in Ballard's stories are usually vividly portrayed, and yet they have an air of unreality about them. The descriptions are normally brief, limited to clothing accouterments, and facial expressions. It does not take us long to realize that these other characters conform to set types, and that these types form a consistent pattern throughout Ballard's fiction. They are, to a certain degree, emblematic—perhaps even figments of the protagonist's imagination. . . . (p. 39)

The "death of affect"—the growth of a ruthlessly emotionless and guiltless form of individualism—is one of the great themes of Ballard's fiction. (p. 41)

Ballard, it would appear, is motivated by a death-wish: he can imagine no fate for the human race other than the negatively apocalyptic. (p. 51)

[There] are a number of other themes—or existential situations—which are commonly delineated in his fiction. For the purposes of this discussion we can limit these to four, divisible into balanced pairs, and call them the themes of Imprisonment and Flight, Time Must Have a Stop and Superannuation. The terminology is not Ballard's, nor are these themes the only ones which can be "extracted" from his work. It is a testament to the thematic richness and variety of Ballard's fiction that it can be placed profitably in many contexts and seen from numerous different angles. (p. 53)

Clearly, these four themes are not all "pessimistic." They seem to balance each other in emotional tone—the apparently gloomy and perverse (imprisonment or self-incarceration) offset by the hopeful and transcendent (flight and "the open transits of the sky"—a phrase from "The Ultimate City"). Yet all four can be seen as aspects of the same basic concern—an exploration of the emotional significance of change, decay, entropy, death. . . . [Death] may be his deeplying theme, but he deals with death as a fact of life: a human fact. His fiction represents a coming to terms with, rather than a revelling in or a flight from, death. (p. 57)

In a society which is human-created but largely out of individual human control, a society which presents us with a myriad technological extensions of our own unconscious impulses . . . , Ballard is one of the last champions of the solitary, rational awareness. One senses that much of Ballard's fiction is about the preservation (and surrender) of individuality in the face of encroaching technological and social change. To this extent, he is a representative of the humanist and liberal tradition, and his purpose is a positive one: by making us more aware of our "desires" he is helping to free us. Like Freud, he strives to bring the unconscious into the open. His stories explore the collective unconscious, the externalized psyche, which is plainly visible around us and which belongs to us all. This is achieved through the manipulation of symbols and themes which are both personal (to Ballard) and highly contemporary. Ballard's world is his own, but it is also recognizably ours: the alien planet Earth. (p. 60)

David Pringle, in his Earth Is the Alien Planet: J. G. Ballard's Four-Dimensional Nightmare *(copyright © 1979 by David Pringle), The Borgo Press, 1979, 63 p.*

* * *

BARAKA, Imamu Amiri 1934-

Baraka, formerly known as LeRoi Jones, is an American poet, playwright, short story writer, essayist, jazz critic, and editor. Baraka's subject is the oppression of blacks in white society and his work is an intense emotional response to this condition. He received acclaim for his first professional production, *Dutchman*. His subsequent work for the theater has provoked both praise and controversy. His poetry and prose are characterized by difficult syntax, often obscuring the logic, but never the purpose, of his thought. Having rejected white values and white society, Baraka strives to create art with a firm didactic purpose: to forge an Afro-American art that reflects the values and sensibilities of the black community. (See also *CLC*, Vols. 1, 2, 3, 5, 10, and *Contemporary Authors*, Vols. 21-24, rev. ed.)

DENISE LEVERTOV

[In *Preface to a Twenty Volume Suicide Note*], where the poems are arranged chronologically, one can see even as the chaff flies that the grain is good. [Jones's] special gift is an emotive music that might have made him predominantly a "lyric poet," but his deeply felt preoccupation with more than personal issues enlarges the scope of his poems beyond what the term is often taken to mean. . . . I feel that sometimes his work is muddled, and that after the event he convinces himself that it had to be that way; in other words, his conception of when a poem is ready to printed differs from mine. But . . . he is developing swiftly and has a rich potential. Certain poems—especially "The Clearing," "The Turncoat," "Notes for a Speech"—show what he can do. They are beautiful poems, and others that are less complete have passages of equal beauty.

Since beauty is one of the least precise words in the language I had better define what I mean by it in this instance: the beauty in Jones's poems is sensuous and incantatory, in contrast to the beauty [found in poetry like Gil Sorrentino's] which is a sensation of exactitude, a hitting of nails on the head with a ringing sound. In his contribution to the notes on poetics at the back of . . . *The New American Poetry,* Jones speaks of Garcia Lorca as one of the poets he has read intensely; and what is incantatory (magical) in his work, while it is natural to him, may well have been first brought to the surface by the discovery of an affinity in the magic of Lorca. (p. 252)

Denise Levertov, "Poets of the Given Ground," in The Nation *(copyright 1961 by the Nation Associates, Inc.), Vol. 193, No. 12, October 14, 1961, pp. 251-53.**

C.W.E. BIGSBY

The fear which pervades LeRoi Jones's work is that of a loss of identity—a fear which becomes socially relevant when extended to the scale of racial assimilation. In this context violence functions . . . as a means of discovering and forging identity. . . . [Jones's] is a sensitivity, created by the extremes of racial guilt and discrimination, which can see no middle ground between man as victim and man as rebel. . . . While the violence which emerges as the strongest mark of Jones's work does at times show something of the ambivalence which Brecht had felt, there is an element of unabashed relish in its presentation, particularly in *The Slave* and *The Toilet,* which constantly threatens to undermine its validity both as drama and polemic. (p. 140)

LeRoi Jones's fierce commitment is such that he has felt himself bound, at times, to attack those who have apparently transcended the immediate concerns of racial injustice. . . . 'A writer' he insists, 'is committed to what is real, and not to the sanctity of his *Feelings.*' While this is a distinction which Kafka or Lawrence, for example, could not have felt to be a real one it is indicative of Jones's refusal to accept a humanistic interpretation of the racial situation. What is real is the economic and political history of the Negro; what is fanciful is the belief that racial friction is a moral failure which can be corrected by individual soul-searching. . . . [While] he has actively supported Civil Rights Jones's plays boast a simple objective, for, unlike Baldwin, his vision is not of a unified society but rather of a world in which the present order is inverted. In this context his attraction to violence becomes little more than an aspect of revenge while his plays are dedicated less to urging a humanistic commitment than a revolutionary separatism. (pp. 141-42)

Jones's insistence on the irrevocability of history, expressed in the bitter poem which had followed Kennedy's death [''Exaugeral Address'' is in *Dutchman*] clearly demonstrated in racial terms. . . . [His] play challenges the whole proposition of integration. The question which he is asking is, 'integration into what?' Western rationalism, 'the great intellectual legacy of the white man', has in his eyes led merely to the rationalisation of repression and violence. (p. 146)

[*The Slave*] is described by Jones as a fable. As such it represents his attempt to circumvent what Pirandello, Artaud and Beckett had seen as the fundamental flaw of the theatre —the arbitrary and imprecise nature of language. . . . [Yet Jones] does not dispense with language or transform it into a ritualised sub-structure of intonation and timbre but relies, like Gelber and Albee, on what he calls a 'meta-language'—the tangental communication of the parable. The parable which he presents here is an apocalyptic vision seen in purely racial terms. *The Slave* is in essence an extension of the conflict of *Dutchman* to what Jones clearly sees as its logical conclusion. 'Discovering racially the funds of the universe. Discovering the last image of the thing. As the sky when the moon is broken.' (pp. 147-48)

Despite a further indulgence in his particular forte for a gratuitous violence inflicted on his white characters *The Slave* does progress considerably beyond the oversimplifications of *Dutchman.* For when Walker Vessels, who in the main body of the play is the leader of a Negro revolt, delivers a prologue dressed as a field-slave, he condemns that which 'passes as whatever thing we feel is too righteous to question, too deeply felt to deny' as 'a deadly filth' . . .—a considerable advance over the dogmatic assumptions of *Dutchman.* For in that play . . . he was content to destroy one cliché but to replace it with another. If he attacked the deep-rooted association between black and evil he did so only to recall that the curse of corruption and death derived from a white Eve. Here, however, he is not merely concerned with the injustice of the racial situation but, ostensibly at least, also with that intellectual slavery which is an aspect of blind dogmatism. . . . For all his calls for objectivity, however, the sheer force of his commitment and even his hatred once again takes possession of his drama and the play fails to realise the potential suggested in the prologue. (pp. 148-49)

Walker himself is the realisation of that potential which had been embodied in the person of Clay, in *Dutchman.* He is no longer a poet, as Clay had been, for in the place of poetry he had discovered the 'sanity' of violence. He shuns both the egocentricity of the artist and the self-justification of the social critic. . . . While Jones's contempt for docile assimilation is complete he does show here an ambivalence in his attitude which he would claim stems directly from the nature of the Negro's dilemma. Walker cannot remain neutral yet he admits to dissatisfaction with a solution which is in essence merely an inversion of the problem. (p. 150)

Jones's plays . . . are, at base, revenge fantasies—public rites of purgation in which the audience is invited to participate. (p. 151)

The alienation of Jones's rebel is in essence spurious. Far from dissociating himself from the corruptions of the dominant society his aim is to join it on his own terms. The change which he would force on that society is not a moral but purely a structural one. Slavery remains intact except that its victim is of a different pigmentation. Where once it had been the black woman who had been violated by the white man and who, in time, had her children taken from her now, in *The Slave,* the situation is reversed. (p. 152)

In the terms of both of his major plays his approbation is reserved for those who remain actively aware of historical truths and the need for racial pride; alert alike to the facts of oppression and the need to maintain a separate culture and identity. Language becomes a sign of membership in this group—a gesture of rejection as powerful but ultimately as self-defeating as the jargon of a fading Beat movement. Nor are these personal biases always entirely integrated into the body of his play. His casual dismissal of all those outside of the inner circle of committed savants is less a significant aspect of either Clay's or Lula's character for example than of Jones's own prejudices. . . . It is clear that the language and indeed the plays themselves are seen as a weapon. They represent a declaration of disaffiliation. . . . Yet with their rigid categorisation, their justification of the stereotype they represent a blunt weapon and an unconvincing declaration. (p. 153)

[The] subject of *Dutchman* and *The Slave* is less the actual plight of the Negro, about which we learn practically nothing, than the difficulties and dilemmas of the Negro writer. The poet, the social critic and the Negro activist are at war with one another. For while on the one hand he demands a literature of commitment, vigorously declaring itself, on the other hand he says that a poem 'can be made out of any feeling' and that a poet—someone, that is, with a 'tempered sensibility'—should be able to write about anything at all and make it into 'something really beautiful'. This same duality is observable in his own work and while the plays, as we have seen, tend to be savagely tied to the Negro/white conflict, his poems frequently attain to an objectivity and universality denied his drama.

In common with most didactic writers Jones is something of an artistic pragmatist. The value of an idea or individual life is governed, he writes, by the extent to which it can be said to be 'specific and useful'. From this it follows that value and effectiveness tend to be associated in his mind and emotional response becomes confused with intellectual assent. Thus while his disturbing revenge fantasies provoke a predictably ecstatic response from Negro audiences it is far from clear if this is indicative of their clear perception of his meaning or rather of their conscious participation in a public purgative rite.

Despite the obsessions which continue to undermine the value of his work LeRoi Jones is one of the few Negro playwrights who has shown an interest in and an understanding of the nature and problems of drama itself. . . . While LeRoi Jones is in no sense an innovator, however, he does demonstrate a mastery of dramatic technique which reveals a genuine potentiality. The technique which he uses is essentially that employed by Albee and before him by Durrenmatt and Brecht. The 'metalanguage' which is his attempt to transcend the barrier between individual perception and artistic intention is his endeavour to express something 'not included here'. . . . Resting in myth and structured on the parable, as is Brecht's *The Caucasian Chalk Circle,* Durrenmatt's *The Visit* . . . and Albee's *The Zoo Story,* his plays, and especially *Dutchman,* attempt to communicate through metaphor and hyperbole. Yet it is precisely his failure to communicate which ironically constitutes the greatest weakness of his work. . . . Jones's is a talent lacking in discipline and controlled by a desperate commitment yet he is clearly aware of the real potentialities of the theatre. For if *Dutchman* lacks both the depth and control of Albee's *The Zoo Story* it does reveal an understanding not only of dramatic technique but also of the need for the modern theatre to examine the roots of its own power. (pp. 154-55)

C.W.E. Bigsby, "LeRoi Jones," in his Confrontation and Commitment: A Study of Contemporary American Drama, 1959-66 *(reprinted by permission of the author; © 1967 and 1968 by C.W.E. Bigsby), University of Missouri Press, 1968, pp. 138-55.*

THEODORE R. HUDSON

Jones has named specific influences on his development as a writer. They include T. S. Eliot (especially on Jones' earlier, "academic" poetry), Ezra Pound (especially for imagery), William Carlos Williams (especially for a sense of speech in poetry), and Federico Garcia Lorca (for, among other things, helping him break from the Eliot influence). [Nathanael West, Mark Twain, and Eugene O'Neill may also be considered influences.] (p. 57)

It is safe to say that all the writers who gravitated to the Village during the late fifties and early sixties affected each other's work, directly and indirectly, and in varying degrees. . . . [Some] of his early contemporaries named by Jones as having influenced him at that time are Gary Snyder, Frank O'Hara, Robert Creeley, and Allen Ginsberg. . . .

[Regardless] of sources and influences, Jones always has been stylistically a distinct writer. It is an understatement to say that the writing of LeRoi Jones is manneristic. There is in it a remarkable absence of mundane, pedestrian expression. Hackneyed language or a cliché is rare in his works, and when it does exist chances are that it originated with Jones and became trite because of his own repetition of it. Indeed, it seems as if he almost perversely determines to create new forms, new ways of structuring content, new phrases for new thoughts. . . . But the very inventiveness of his writing . . . makes for difficult reading. Some of his more individualistic and strangely presented works do seem to be either chaos or mere dross. Sometimes one may wonder if Jones is playing games with his readers—or with himself. (p. 58)

[One] must consider his theory of art as it applies to matters of form, technique and style, for Jones simply must be read on his own artistic terms: "Form is simply *how* a thing exists," he says. "Content is why a thing exists." To him, the two are inseparable. . . .

One must keep in mind, too, Jones' tenet that the essence of art is process rather than artifact. One should examine Jones' writing with the attitude that his style is a record of a creative process, possibly a spontaneous creative process. To look only for rational, conscious, and ordered style in Jones' work is to subvert explication and to beg for a misreading or a nonreading. In connection with . . . the spontaneous element in Jones' writing one must also keep in mind his insistence upon initial reliance upon what is felt rather than upon what is thought. . . . And one must always keep in mind that Jones posits that "feeling predicts intelligence."

LeRoi Jones has written that "words themselves become, even informally, laws." The language that Jones employs to make his own laws, or definitions, comes by choice from his personal, sometimes private, and ethnic frames of reference. Shortly after his first published works, he consciously began to avoid "white" language in favor of "black" idioms, grammar, and syntax. (p. 59)

When one seeks to explicate Jones' language, one should . . . seek to understand his frame of reference. For example, the derogatory term "faggot" must be understood in Jones' ethnic context. If he uses it to describe an American of African descent, he is usually talking about a male who reacts to challenges (often ethnic-oriented challenges) to his manhood by pretending to ignore, by compromising, by capitulating. In this sense NAACP official Roy Wilkins in Jones' eyes is an "Uncle Tom," a compromiser of his innate blackness, and is therefore a "faggot." On the other hand, if Jones uses "faggot" to describe a white American male, he is talking, literally or symbolically, about a physical homosexual, a degenerated man who has perverted his natural physical urges. The white "faggot" is lower than the black "faggot" on Jones' acceptability scale. (pp. 59-60)

Especially in nonfiction prose, Jones is discursive, expansive, given to restatement. He tends to write complex and compound-complex sentences, with frequent appositional, parenthetical, and other subordinate grammatical elements. This is particularly noticeable in his earlier writing. . . . At other times this expansive style is characterized by staccato effects, sentence fragments, sudden grammatical shifts, exclamatory interpolations, and asides. (pp. 61-2)

[He] can be expansively lucid . . . [or] curtly cryptic. When he apparently wants to be, he is direct and explicit; when he apparently wants to be, he is indirect in the sense that his "meaning" is tied up in associational complexes of sound, image, and diction. His more bafflingly dadaistic and surrealistic style is especially apparent in his prose fiction. . . . [Sometimes an] entire piece evokes an impressionistic aura or mood that defies paraphrase into "meaning." (pp. 62-3)

[Punctuation] in his earlier nonfiction prose is generally standard, or conventional, but in his later nonfiction prose the punctuation is frequently unconventional. His prose fiction and poetry are a different case though, due in part to unconventional syntax but more often due to what must be artistic compulsion. It is not unusual for him to insert a comma between a subject and its verb, even when no elements intervene, as in "White, is abstract." He inserts a comma for separation, for pause, for impact. . . . Jones is fond of parentheses, and . . . uses the open parenthesis. He frequently will capitalize all letters in a word or group of words, and he frequently uses all lower case letters, even in titles of works. He has a tendency to use the diagonal, or slash, between words or parts of words, usually where meaning is purposely ambivalent, as in "STATE/MEANT." Sometimes he will write a contraction and omit the apostrophe, as "aint," or he will abbreviate a word, as "cd" for "could" and "blk" for "black." (pp. 63-4)

Jones is an incurable manipulator of words, almost always in an attempt for straight humor or for satire. He makes puns [and portmanteau words]. . . . Only Jones would write, "The undertaker was a stereotype nigger faggunder, taker." Jones also plays with the sounds of words. . . . [He puts words] into contexts that will twist meanings: he speaks of "Mozart's Ornithology" to connote jazzman Charlie "Bird" Parker's works being bastardized by white musicians. (pp. 64-5)

A major technique employed by Jones is humor. . . . [His] is incisive satire, satire informed by a certain "hip," or superior, sensibility, by an urbane sensibility developed in street lore, by a contempt born of too much perception. . . . His humor tends to be broad and farcical in his later works, those works intended to be "less uselessly 'literary'"—works intended to be more practical and more easily grasped by the masses of black people. (pp. 65-6)

Unusual symbolism and imagery, among other things, make difficult the explication of certain of Jones' works. Of course, . . . explication as getting literal "meaning" is fruitless since no "meaning" is intended. Because so much of his symbolism and imagery is abstruse, it is easy to overlook the fact that Jones does employ conventional symbolism and imagery. (p. 66)

Once the reader has a superficial grasp of the facts of Jones' life, some of his symbolism becomes apparent and requires no special study. Social workers and postal workers, for example, are obviously his mother and father, projected as decorous, middle-class oriented, and rather alienated from their inherent blackness. (p. 67)

Jones is not given to the use of abstract terms as symbol-images. There are, however, two which bear mentioning, God (sometimes with a lower case "g") and energy. The first, God, is used for normal denotations as well as for symbolic connotations. God, to LeRoi Jones, is a matter of definitions; he sees God meaning different things to different people. . . . To Jones the Christian God as conceived by Western whites is a God to suit their purposes. . . . It is not surprising . . . to find Jones later proclaiming that "The Black Man is making new Gods," black gods issuing from black spiritual consciousness. . . . In *Black Music* he says, ". . . God is, indeed, energy," . . . and he thinks of "God as evolution. The flow of is." . . . (p. 69)

Energy as Jones uses the term is the divine force for creativity. . . . Blacks, he feels, are the possessors of natural energies, of divine powers of creativity.

A city boy and man, LeRoi Jones does not use much imagery connected with physical nature. He does, however, use sun, wind, flame, water, and forest. At times he will use sun traditionally, to mean enlightenment, happiness, wisdom, or "energy." . . . At times he will use sun to signify divine blackness, speaking at such times of blacks as "sun people" and warning others, in a reversal of meaning, to

> Beware the evil sun . . .
> turn you black
> ("Hymn for Lanie Poo")

Wind as a symbol connotes spiritual essence: "And let us think of soul, as anima: spirit (*spiritus*, breath) as that which carries breath on the living wind." . . . Flame, rather conventionally, means the unerring intellect or realistic perception. He assesses himself, in his preface to *Black Magic*, as "the soothsayer, one flayed by evil as a fountainhead of reality finally glimpses of true airflame." Water, river, ocean, wet and their cognates can often be interpreted as fecundity or creative refreshment of an abstract sort. It is that quality necessary for all life, a quality roughly opposite to T. S. Eliot's desert, cactus, and dry. The quality is a catalytic agent: "You are myself's river." Forest, in much the same manner that Dante used it, is a lost or dangerous or uncharted state. In this sense, Jones will occasionally use forest to represent white Western civilization. . . . Or he might use it to represent the uncertain future or the unknown present. . . . (pp. 70-1)

Symbols derived from urban settings include steel, pavement or concrete, hallways, window. Steel, conventionally, is used to project cold, hard materialism that is devoid of feeling. Pavement and concrete conjure concepts of the impersonality, indifference, and hardness of urban life. Hallways are passageways from phase to phase in life. Window is a frequently employed, important Jonesian symbol-image. It stands for a perspective on life, a frame of reference from which one sees and evaluates experience. Conversely, one's concept of another person's perception is signified by looking into that person's window. . . .

Jones rarely uses color symbolism, except for green and grey. Green, he supposes in "Vice," is "a color of despair and wretchedness." Predictably, grey symbolizes the white life style and, concurrently, the common connotations of ugliness, spoilage, death. (p. 71)

Sometimes he will use a lady (or "bitch" or "dead lady") to represent Western or white American culture.

Another group of Jonesian symbol-images is based upon the body and its functions. Meat or flesh is sometimes used by him to symbolize intuitive urges, noncerebral and transcendentalistic urges. . . .

A subgroup of body-function symbol-images has to do with sex. Masturbation, as Jones uses it, represents an individualism based upon self-love or it represents love which cannot find external connectives and therefore is turned within. . . . Homosexuality and heterosexual perversion may be considered as broadly symbolic of misuse of creative energies, as a deliberate turning from what is natural and good, as a degeneracy, as an avoidance of reality. (p. 72)

[Heterosexual intercourse] indicates the closest possible human interaction. This relationship may be on the physical level, but most of the time it is representative of a spiritual or emotional intimacy in which there is, ideally, a mutually beneficial, intimate giving and getting. (pp. 72-3)

In Jones' works, sterility is often symbolized by urination (he uses the term "pee" and its forms). The opposite symbol would be productive orgasm. Urination implies a useless, wasteful, and unproductive expenditure of creativity. With this in mind, a reading of Jones' *The Toilet* grows richer in symbolism, for he frequently has his characters urinating, flushing urinals, and the like, indicative of the unproductivity and misdirection of their actions in effecting respect and love. . . .

The last symbol-image to be considered here is dance, which he uses to depict the total experiencing of life, for immersion into life. This being so, when Lula entices Clay to dance with her [in *Dutchman*], she is enticing him to engage wholly in her way of life, and on her terms. (p. 73)

[There] are Jonesian passages that defy rational paraphrase or explication. When he writes of "24 elephants" stomping out of the subway "with consecrated hardons" he is enigmatic. But perhaps that is what he intends, an enigma. (p. 74)

[The] study of LeRoi Jones' life reveals a gifted young person who while living a racially integrated life during the late 1950's and early 1960's became a major literary figure in the intellectual and artistic avant-garde; who then turned from this social, intellectual, and artistic ambience to become the leading theoretical and practicing black cultural nationalist, a community leader, and a political organizer and catalyst. . . . Jones' characteristic ways of perceiving and thinking show the following: he conceives of culture as the total of life's activities and of art as process; he anticipates the atrophy of Western culture and a concomitant rise of a black culture; he gives some evidence of being anti-white America, anti-Semitic, and anti-Negro middle-class, or positively stated, he is strongly pro-black (not pro-Negro). He believes in the superiority of separatism and active resistance over assimilation and passive resistance as methods of dealing with America's race problems. He advocates cultural, social, spiritual, economic, and political black populist nationalism. . . . [His] characteristic modes of expression reveal a versatile writer keenly aware of the power of words as laws—that is, as a means of molding public attitudes and ultimately as a means of attaining and maintaining power; highly inventive in the use of language; dadaistic in matters of mechanics and form; humorous both in a general way and satirically; original, occasionally to the point of being cryptic, in style; and highly original and personal in the use of figurative language, particularly in the use of symbol-images.

These three—his experiences, his characteristic ways of thinking, and his characteristic ways of writing—interact in such a way that it is difficult to say what is cause and what is effect in any given situation. The Jones-to-Baraka movement was an evolutionary process, Barakan characteristics always having been present to some degree and in some form.

The examination of Jones' literary works . . . shows: His nonfiction prose, more than any other genre, is revelatory of his ideologies, philosophies, and theories. It is also indicative of his stylistic versatility. His fiction is the most consistent of all genres in terms of style, being essentially of two types, "association complexes" and "fast narratives." He has written practically no fiction since *System* and *Tales*. His poetry has changed in content, form, and style from private and lyrical poetry of the avant-garde type to public and exhortative poetry of the black aesthetic persuasion. As his poetry has changed, it has depended less upon compression and symbol-images, more upon prose-like declarations. His drama has changed drastically in structure and technique but not basically in theme since his early success, *Dutchman*. His later drama tends to be impulsive, pageant-like, and ritualistic, and it has become openly a medium for teaching, evangelizing, and motivating. (pp. 177-78)

Classifying or typing Jones as a writer is not easy, for he is versatile in both genre and style. Within his writing one can find elements of different literary periods, schools, and movements. For example, he is "baroque" in his asymmetrically structured fiction, in his juxtaposition of the unexpected with the expected in poetry, in writing whatever his mind unfolds at the time he is writing. He is "realistic" in his use of actual speech idioms and in, for example, his emotional and physical setting for *The Toilet*. He is "neoclassical" in his use of subway riders as a sort of chorus in *Dutchman*. He is "folk" in his depiction of life in the subculture known as the inner-city and in his use of ethnic language and lore. He is "naturalistic" in his tracing of the social causes of man's experiences, as in his tracing in *Blues People* of the causes of changes in jazz. But more than anything else, categorized according to literary labels he is "romantic."

In a general way, Jones is a romantic in the sense that many literary historians and scholars consider the post-Romantic Period symbolists, imagists, realists, naturalists, dadaists, impressionists, and other modern writers as latter day romantics or as part of a romantic continuum. He is a romantic in more specific ways as well. Like Emerson and certain other romantic writers, in a transcendentalistic way Jones places great faith in intuition, in feelings. As he applies this faith in an ethnocentric way, he would have blacks place faith in what he assumes to be their singular mystical impulses. He is antirational in the way that romantics of Western European literature were opposed to the "cold" rationality of neoclassicism. Moreover, in connection with this reliance upon innate urgings and promptings, Jones inescapably asserts, as Blake and other romantic mystics contended, that man is divine, although, as Baraka, Jones would argue that the white man has perverted his, the white man's, divinity. Also, Jones is . . . romantic in that he is disdainful of the organized and orthodox religion of the majority and in that he has been himself a religious speculator and seeker. Next, Jones is romantic in his concern for the well-being, freedom, and dignity of the economically and politically weak, the dispossessed, the oppressed, and the downtrodden, as were the past century's romantic political and social libertarians and romantic champions of "humble" people. Further, Rousseau-like in his concern for the full development of man's potential, Jones sees his contemporary social, cultural, and political institutions as destructive of (black) man, so he would have man destroy, change, or control these institutions so that they, in his opinion, serve man rather than have man serve them. Further, Jones, like the Shelleys of the Romantic Period, is a visionary who sees creative artists as providers of philosophical and ideological bases for change. Next, in regard to technique, Jones, like many romantics of the past, will have little to do with conventional and prescribed forms and techniques, insists upon using the "language of the people," and constantly strives for new ways of writing, searching for what he calls a "post-American form." And it is obvious that Jones, as have countless romantics, uses his creative imagination to inform and shape his literary work. (pp. 178-80)

[According to commonly recognized Western criteria for all literature] he would rate very high on originality of expression, and he would be credited for creative use of his materials, individualistic thinking, and aptness of expression (figurative language). By conventional standards, he would be found lacking in control of his materials (form), undisciplined as a craftsman, and lacking in the expression of, for want of a better term, what would be called philosophical (in the sense of being commonly agreed upon) truth. As to those inescapable canons, universality and timelessness, he would be scored minus in one sense and plus in another sense. He would be downgraded on these two in that the very ethnocentrism and topicality of his content and method are antithetical to concepts of unlimited time and space. But he would be upgraded on these two in that the essential problem with which he concerns himself—man's inhumanity to man and what this does to all concerned—has existed everywhere, always. (p. 180)

[On] the basis of established and generally accepted Euro-American criteria for great literature, it cannot be said that LeRoi Jones has produced great literature.

Let us now consider Jones as a black aesthetician. It must be stressed that it is not our purpose here to argue if there is or is not a black aesthetic, nor, assuming that there is a black aesthetic, to argue whether or not a Western aesthetic and a black aesthetic are in the final analysis significantly different or mutually exclusive, nor to argue if a black aesthetic is or is not properly a part of a larger Western aesthetic, nor to argue whether the corpus known as black literature in the final analysis is or is not analogous to literary schools, categories, or movements of different times and places.

But let us assume that Jones, as he says, is not trying to write according to generally recognized principles of a Western aesthetic. Let us assume that there is a black aesthetic and that Jones, as he says, is writing according to principles of this black aesthetic as they apply to literature. At this point we are somewhat blocked, for there now exist no codified and commonly recognized criteria for such literature. This being so, what we can do is look at the elements and characteristics of this literature as pronounced by those who speak or write about the black aesthetic and as exemplified by those who profess to be or seek to be creative black aestheticians. These interrelated elements and characteristics include prominently: utilitarianism; strong ethnocentric content; black nationalistic content; identification with the black masses; collective or communal black, as opposed to an individualistic or private, attitude; cynicism about or rejection of Euro-American culture values; disregard for the type of universality which black aestheticians claim the American literary establishment wrongly equates with Westernism (Euro-Americanism) rather than with worldism; usefulness for social, political, and economic change; ethnic pride and celebration of a hitherto sometimes avoided or disdained black culture (life style and value system); urban and rural black folk elements; "black language"; energetic diction; experimentation in search of new, or black, forms and techniques. Jones' writing exhibits all these elements and characteristics, and in high degree.

Jones, especially as Imamu Amiri Baraka, is not in the business of composing poems, constructing plays, or creating fiction for the sake of poetry or drama or fiction. He is in the business of effecting change that will be to the advantage of black people. He is a political organizer and catalyst and a cultural theorist and leader. To the extent that it will aid him in these areas, his writing is, to him, art. An essay, a poem, a story, or a play that will get across a point, convert an unbeliever, destroy an enemy, promote the Jihad, organize a fragmented group, or raise a black's appreciation of himself is an artistic essay, poem, story, or play. In other words, Jones is attempting to practice an important tenet of black aestheticism, that literature be of practical value to black people. (pp. 180-81)

There is no doubt that his intention is to write for black people. But can the masses understand him? Do the masses of black people read his works? Is he communicating with black people on the streets? Is he writing clear "posters"? The answer is, too frequently, no. Baraka has not succeeded in eliminating his early Jonesian inclination to esoteric, academic, metaphysical, and abstruse writing. The majority of his readers still are the white intellectuals, the black college students, and the relatively small "in-group" of black cultural nationalists and other Afro-Americans not identified as being a part of the bulk of the black masses. The average inner-city "dude," the average black man-on-the-street knows little if anything at all about either LeRoi Jones or Imamu Amiri Baraka and his literary works. (pp. 181-82)

By and large, according to the existing principles of black

literary aesthetics, LeRoi Jones is considered to be the supreme writer. Moreover, he is recognized to be the leading theorist and spokesman for the current black cultural movement. . . .

There are those who will say that Jones was the first and most important mover and exponent of his age's black aestheticism and its concomitant black cultural nationalism. . . . (p. 182)

By using his gift with language and his particular sensibilities to explore situations afresh, to challenge existing beliefs, to rage against what he perceives as evil, to provide fresh insights, to propose new directions, in short, to illuminate life and to seek to better the quality of life, our author —Mr. LeRoi Jones, or Imamu Amiri Baraka—is accomplishing a prime function, is fulfilling a prime responsibility of the literary artist. (p. 183)

Theodore R. Hudson, in his From LeRoi Jones to Amiri Baraka *(reprinted by permission of the Publisher; copyright 1973 by Duke University Press, Durham, North Carolina), Duke University Press, 1973, 222 p.*

JAMES ROBERT PAYNE

The inclusion of the 1967 work *Slave Ship* alongside the recent *The Motion of History* (1976) and *S-1* (1976) in [*The Motion of History and Other Plays*] reveals Baraka's movement from the view of what he terms "the petty bourgeois of the oppressed nationality," represented by *Slave Ship*, to a Marxist orientation, represented by *The Motion of History* and *S-1*.

After ten years *Slave Ship* remains a powerful document of mid-1960s Afro-American consciousness. White slavers cannot destroy the African spirit, and indeed unwittingly introduce black culture, especially music, into America via their slave ships. . . .

In short scenes interpreting American historical events ranging from the present to the seventeenth century, *The Motion of History* portrays black and white proletariats learning to unite against their oppressors. Baraka dispenses with black nationalist preoccupations and focuses on the dramatization of the historical roots of unjust American class and black-white relations. Particularly effective are satirical portraits of solipsistic young bohemians, sidetracked by drugs, Eastern religion and other fashionable diversions, and of poor Southern white types, betrayed and played off against the blacks by establishment whites. Although the idea that black and white workers should unite against their common oppressors is of course not new, Baraka's empathetic presentation of the budding insight and growth of common understanding of individual white and black workers is strong and moving.

S-1 presents near-future American political history when the outbreak of war serves as an excuse for fascist repression. . . . In a recent interview Baraka criticized some of his early work "for celebrating the subjective and the idealistic." . . . *S-1* reveals a rather extreme and simplistic idealization of Marxist-Leninism.

James Robert Payne, "World Literature in Review: 'The Motion of History and Other Plays'," in World Literature Today *(copyright 1979 by the University of Oklahoma Press), Vol. 53, No. 2, Spring, 1979, p. 293.*

DARRYL PINCKNEY

Amiri Baraka, formerly LeRoi Jones, has lost none of his fury since the Black Power movement of the 1960's. He has, however, sacrificed artistic vitality on the altar of his political faith. Selected by Baraka, the work gathered in ["Selected Plays and Prose of Amiri Baraka/LeRoi Jones" and "Selected Poetry of Amiri Baraka/LeRoi Jones"] is offered as a summation of his creative life. . . . The change revealed in Baraka's style over the years is dramatic—from Beat non-conformist to militant black nationalist to, lately, self-styled leader of a revolutionary vanguard, one who is fond of quoting Stalin, Mao and The Peking Review.

Baraka's writing is defined by vehement repudiations, littered with discarded identities. Much is swept under the carpet, and the frayed edges are then nailed down with a sledge hammer. (p. 9)

Baraka has always shown a willingness to embrace radical beliefs, and consequently his writing is alive with the political and social issues of race in American life. But his early work is far better than his recent efforts: he now seems content to express his Marxism in the most reductive, shrill propaganda. Increasing ideological self-consciousness and self-congratulation have caused him to write with the heedless fanaticism of a religious convert. Baraka has abandoned his gripping depiction of large, historical questions in favor of the didacticism of proletarian utilitarianism, just as Brecht hoped to create a theater that would inspire militancy in the audience.

There is much exasperation and bitterness in Baraka's artistic vision—and also a complicated ambivalence toward the masses he wishes to liberate. . . . Baraka's inability to reconcile his nihilistic postures—his yearnings for blasphemy —with the frustrations of political reality lessens his authority as a spokesman and as a writer.

Many of the essays in this collection are governed by a punitive, vindictive inclination, which is part of Baraka's rhetorical style as one who has mounted the ramparts. "Newark, Before Black Men Conquered," from "Raise Race Rays Raze" (1969) is ruthlessly honest about the corruption of political life in that city. It also reveals Baraka's angry ambition. He is less self-promoting and a much more interesting, skeptical observer in the essay "Cuba Libre," from "Home," which is about his visit there in July 1960. It is a valuable piece of reportage. Baraka describes his impression of Castro, the changes in the country's institutions, the mood of the people and the exuberant anniversary celebration at the shrine of the Revolution, Sierra Maestra. The essay also marks the beginning of Baraka's political odyssey, his search for the revolution in America.

Now that Baraka identifies himself as a Marxist, he has shrewdly omitted from this collection essays from his nationalist period. . . . Though the essays printed here differ in subject matter—Baraka now cares more for the dictatorship of the proletariat than he does for the glorification of Black Manhood—they exhibit the same lust for doctrine, the joy of jargon. "Capitalism is an economic system, a mode of production, characterized by private ownership of the means of production, the lands, the factories, mineral wealth, transportation, communication, waterways. This means of production is owned privately by a single class in capitalist society called the capitalist class or the bourgeoisie." The novice recites his catechism, and the solemnity is almost comical. The utter lack of sophistication in Baraka's analysis makes these essays—"The Revolutionary Tradition in Afro-American Literature," "National Liberation Movements" and "Black Liberation/Socialist Revolution"—feeble contributions to the Marxist critique. In one of his late poems, Baraka attacks Angela Davis for being a "movie star" and "fronting" for the lies of the Communist Party. A pity, for he could learn something from her application of the materialist methodology to black history, regardless of what he thinks of her party affiliation.

One often wonders to whom these essays are addressed. They exhibit an alarming pedagogical condescension. . . . Baraka is better on the subject of black music and society. One wishes for more of that and less of his political flailings. (pp. 9, 29)

[Only] four of Baraka's plays have been reprinted, and this is unfortunate because he is a highly gifted dramatist. Much of the black protest literature of the 60's now seems diminished in power, even sentimental. But "Dutchman" (1964) immediately seizes the imagination. It is radically economical in structure, striking in the vivacity of its language and rapid shifts of mood. Part of Baraka's brilliance as a dramatist is to transform familiar situations into twisted, inflamed projections of the future, prophecies of what is to come in America's racial struggle. This is true of "The Slave" (1964), in which a domestic crisis is juxtaposed against a race war. . . .

The poetry shows the progression of Baraka's thought, but in a much more intimate and vivid way than the prose or the plays do. Even in the poetry from the nationalist phase, the elements of folk culture are more successfully employed, and perhaps this is the communication with the masses to which Baraka aspires. The poetry also illustrates the change in Baraka's use of his art. His most recent poems, "Poetry for the Advanced," published here for the first time, are written from a drastic loss of openness. Baraka's ear for the vernacular, his wit and the ease of his imagery have been replaced by denunciations, by the repetitive messages of propaganda. . . .

The change in Baraka's work is bewildering: it is almost a parody of revolutionary art. Frankly, it is tiresome. And this is very sad, because Baraka, a prolific and provocative writer, is one of the few blacks to come from a genuinely avant-garde tradition. In his early plays, there is a picture of the black man as complicated, a relief from the pieties of the realistic tradition in black theater. In his early poetry, there was an engaging voice, one outside convention, and an awareness of forms. These things have been lost in the haste and rigidity of Baraka's political journey. (p. 29)

Darryl Pinckney, "The Changes of Amiri Baraka," in The New York Times Book Review *(© 1979 by The New York Times Company; reprinted by permission), December 16, 1979, pp. 9, 29.*

* * *

BARTH, John 1930-

Barth, an American novelist and short story writer, is a skillful parodist, satirizing language and literary style, the tools of his craft, as well as social and moral conventions. Fascinated with literary theory, Barth explores in his novels the complexities of myth and the traditional concept of the hero in literature. (See also *CLC*, Vols. 1, 2, 3, 5, 7, 9, 10, and *Contemporary Authors*, Vols. 1-4, rev. ed.)

BEVERLY GROSS

It is striking . . . to see how much Barth's fiction has been moving toward the fulfillment of an idea—the idea being the repudiation of narrative art. . . . That is the paradox of Barth's novels: they are about paralysis, they seem even to affirm paralysis, yet they have more narrative energy than they know what to do with. (pp. 95-6)

Each [of Barth's four first novels] is generally longer, wilder, more ambitious, more outrageous than its predecessor, and at the core of each is a greater nihilism. . . . Nihilism is merely a quirk of character in *The Floating Opera* and *End of the Road;* it is not much more than a setting for comedy, a device for irony. But nihilism is what *The Sot-Weed Factor* and *Giles Goat-Boy* come to. It is the moral, meaning, and upshot of experience in these novels, and it is embedded in their very form. *The Sot-Weed Factor,* disguised as an eighteenth-century novel, is really a radical definition of the novel of the twentieth century. *Giles Goat-Boy,* disguised as cosmic allegory, keeps undercutting its own allegorical premises by denying the possibility of meaning, identity, and answers in a world in which these things are always shifting, masked, and unattainable. The deeper nihilism of [these] . . . novels comes from their proclaiming not so much the impossibility of life but the impossibility of narrative.

All this talk about nihilism suggests the greatest paradox of all. Barth is most immediately a humorist. . . . The comedy in Barth's novels is the mockery of emotions and moral values: what his characters feel and perceive is only further grist for hilarity. . . . [For example, his *ménage à trois* situations are] a kind of touchstone. The ordinary moral and psychological implications don't count here at all. What immediately counts is, on the level of plot, the entanglements; on the level of meaning, the nuttiness. But what also counts, beyond immediate laughter, is a lingering sorrow, an underlying disgust, and a metaphor for the impossible strain of human attachment and commitment. (pp. 96-7)

Fine black comedy. *End of the Road* seems at first to be much like the other comic monuments of the decade. It has the right ingredients: a psychotic therapist, an identity crisis, a wild *ménage à trois,* ironic views of our crippled society and trivial culture—a groovy corroboration for the disaffected. But something happens to this novel: its ending is appalling. *End of the Road* repudiates itself, or rather it repudiates what would seem to be its glib ability to deal with, and therefore dismiss, ugliness, pain, and despair. Rennie's pregnancy is initially part of the incongruous comedy: the problem is that she doesn't know whose baby she is carrying. . . . Rennie decides to have an abortion. More madcap exasperation for Jacob who has to hunt down an abortionist. But Rennie's butchering on the operating table is the shattering fact of *End of the Road.* The ugliness is sudden, undisguised, unironic. The emotional crisis preceding it . . . was only the game. Rennie's hemorrhaging corpse cannot be transformed into comedy, nor does Barth try. That is the second stage of undercutting: having reduced everything to comedy, the book suddenly reduces its comedy to loathesomeness. (p. 98)

Roles are the motif of all Barth's novels. Todd Andrews' life is a succession of identities—rake, saint, cynic—the search for a character appropriate to his ailing heart. Henry Burlingame reappears in different guises throughout *The Sot-Weed Factor.* . . . George the Goat-Boy, wavering between goat and boy, seeking the proper stance in which to assert his Grand Tutorship, keeps changing his advice to the people around him with each new modification of what he takes to be his gospel. But most of all it is John Barth who emerges as the seeker of self. He is an author in search of a disposition. The novels are not only about roles—they *are* roles. Barth's novels are comic masks for a tragic face. Barth is an inveterate comedian because he depends on the masks, and not only to hide his face but to discover it, and not only his face, but ours.

That doubtlessly is what makes Barth at once so interesting and so irritating. The comedy which seems to be everything is really nothing: it exists to announce its own inadequacy. . . . *Giles Goat-Boy* is Barth's best novel and his worst—a paradox which somehow accords with the tentative theme of the book: that passage and failure are really the same thing.

Giles Goat-Boy is almost impossible to describe, summarize, or account for. Above all, it presents a problem of understanding that is its most unsettling feature. The problem of understanding *Giles Goat-Boy* is the problem of understanding Barth, and more precisely, the extent of Barth's seriousness. In this book Barth wears not one mask but several. Philosophically, the book keeps undermining itself and shatters its own testamentary message in a series of editorial comments at the beginning and postscripts at the end. *Giles Goat-Boy* is a peculiar blending of frivolity and profundity. It often seems to be simultaneously both (a duality we have come to expect from Barth); but at various times one aspect so dominates the other that the reader is made to feel twinges of guilt for having treated as fun so penetrating an exposure of the status of twentieth-century life; at other times he is likely to feel embarrassed for having been so stodgily receiving a book which continually explodes into aimless hilarity. Surprise is one thing, but frustration is another, and *Giles Goat-Boy* is less surprising than it is frustrating. There is something profoundly wrong with *Giles Goat-Boy* and the best explanation I can offer is that the book plays its duality too hard and finally works against itself. This seven hundred page novel is perhaps the world's shaggiest dog story: it comes out meaning nothing at all. Nowadays we don't mind that very much in our art when so much of it is set up to proclaim inanity. The disturbing and perhaps defeating thing about this novel is that it is set up to mean something. The novel leads us to expect a revelation, and at the end there is only a wisecrack.

On the narrative level, *Giles Goat-Boy* is also exasperating. It is enormous, unwieldy, often tedious. . . . Barth's characters have become increasingly eccentric with each new novel. In *Giles Goat-Boy* they are not much more than emblems for their hang-ups. (pp. 98-100)

Giles Goat-Boy is . . . a dialectic without a synthesis, which explains why, on a certain level, the book is so unsatisfying. The dialectical structure makes for a remarkable tediousness and mechanical predictability; the lack of a synthesis makes for frustration. A horrible hoax is what several critics have called *Giles Goat-Boy,* and a horrible hoax is what it is—the book exists to confute expectations. That is its greatest irritation as well as its chief delight, the source of both its meaning and its meaninglessness.

Why there is no synthesis in *Giles Goat-Boy* is because in this book where everyone is looking for the right Answers to insure Passage, the only point is that there are no Answers. If Barth's novels have a message it is that. Each successive novel is an elaboration on that theme. . . . Their nihilistic premises abide.

They abide but they answer nothing. Even . . . where the nihilism is something arrived at it is hardly an answer. Nihilism disqualifies the very possibility of believing in answers, even the answer of nihilism itself. Nevertheless there is something upheld and sanctified in *Giles Goat-Boy* and *The Sot-Weed Factor:* the sheer fact and value of experience. Despite the unreality of these books they are both deeply immersed in life, that is, in life as process. (pp. 101-02)

Nihilistic form—a contradiction in terms, no doubt, but Barth seems to elicit such things. What is nihilistic about the form of *The Sot-Weed Factor* and *Giles Goat-Boy* is that each book becomes an anti-novelistic assault on itself. The books are not anti-novels in the usual sense. . . . The *anti* in "anti-novel" usually conveys the idea of counteraction: such novels are experimental alternatives to what the novel form has conventionally come to mean; the anti-novel widens the expressive possibility of a genre that has been called dead or dying for the last fifty years. Barth's novels may be doing that, but I would like to suggest that with regard to Barth the *anti* could also carry the . . . meaning of hostility. *The Sot-Weed Factor* and *Giles Goat-Boy* are not just experiments—they are attacks. Attacks on themselves. Attacks on the novel genre. Attacks on the narrative impulse. And attacks on the author who perpetrated them. At the end of these novels one sees that their madly complicated structures have led nowhere; one suspects that the point of each book was to expose the fraudulence of narrative art; and one wonders how Barth was able to write them at all. The books contain frequent pronouncements from the narrator against the very enterprise he is engaged in. Concomitant with the ethical nihilism which is thematic to the novels is this aesthetic nihilism in Barth's own voice. (p. 102)

The Sot-Weed Factor is an eighteenth-century novel only in substance; in essence it is an expression of the twentieth-century vision of John Barth. What emerges out of the convoluted action is profoundly at odds with the rationalistic convictions of the Age of Enlightenment. (p. 103)

Dubiety, futility, and finally, self-mockery. *The Sot-Weed Factor* stands as a parody of narrative art with all its assumptions, traditions, prerogatives, and ends. That is its ultimate anti-novelism. The book is a put-on of the very thing it seems most to be cherishing: the narrative impulse itself. Barth has always shown an overwhelming self-consciousness about that impulse. *The Floating Opera,* narrated by Todd Andrews, is filled with asides about the trickeries, contortions, and even distortions involved in getting a story told: "Good heavens! How does one write a novel? I mean, how can anyone possibly stick to the story, if he's at all sensitive to the significances of things?" In one form or another that self-consciousness is always there; in [*Giles Goat-Boy* and *The Sot-Weed Factor*] it takes the particular shape of self-mockery. The concluding section of *The Sot-Weed Factor* is entitled "The Author Apologizes to his Readers," and in it Barth does indeed apologize for playing fast and loose with history, reality, and narrative form.

The self-consciousness of a writer like Henry James is directed toward the exquisiteness of his craft; Barth's self-consciousness is more akin to embarrassment. It is as though Barth wonders how he or anyone could take seriously the novelist's professed aim of giving shape to life. Once the fraudulence of narrative art is assumed, exquisite craftsmanship would only compound the felony. (pp. 104-05)

[The] prefatory matter to *Giles Goat-Boy* epitomizes the rhetorical amorphousness of Barth's novels—the troubling sense he gives of not being altogether there. It is Barth's most elaborate masquerade. (p. 106)

Before the novel proper begins, we encounter a foreword from the author himself. Barth is in his best disguise here—the mask he is wearing is of his own face. Crippled with writer's block, he frets about his inability to get going on his current novel and laments over the shortcomings of his last one. He then tells about the delivery to him of the manuscript of *Giles Goat-Boy,* of which he claims to be only the editor, the real author being either the goat-boy or the computer which sired him. This elaborate prefatory matter challenging the authorship and quality of *Giles Goat-Boy* as well as the worth of anything that Barth has written is a fanciful disclaimer but a symbolic one as well. (pp. 106-07)

Symbolically that is what all the editorial matter of *Giles Goat-Boy* is about. John Barth does not exist. The nihilistic tendencies of contemporary thought which have in one direction led to existentialism. have led Barth to non-existence; non-existence in the sense that these novels are written by an author without a face, a stance, an identity, a commitment. . . .

Barth does not exist because he is merely a welter of contradictions: a moral amoralist, a comic tragedian, an absolute relativist, a nihilistic enthusiast. He writes books whose implications have become more and more gloomy as their shape and quality have become more and more exuberant. And as his books have increasingly taken on the aspect of moral fables, their meaning has become increasingly indecipherable. All that remains clear is their basic nihilism.

> Nothing "works," in the sense we commonly hope for; a certain goat-boy has taught me that; everything only gets worse; our victories are never more than moral, and always pyrrhic; in fact we know only more or less ruinous defeats.

This sentence from the cover-letter of *Giles Goat-Boy* could be pretty fairly appended to the other novels as well. (p. 107)

Beverly Gross, "The Anti-Novels of John Barth," in Chicago Review *(reprinted by permission of* Chicago Review; *copyright © 1968 by* Chicago Review*), Vol. 20, No. 3, November, 1968, pp. 95-109.*

GORE VIDAL

For a dozen years I have been trying to read *The Sot-Weed Factor.* I have never entirely completed this astonishingly dull book but I have read most of John Barth's published work and I feel that I have done him, I hope, justice. There is a black cloth on my head as I write.

First, it should be noted that Barth . . . is a professional schoolteacher. He is a professor of English *and* Creative Writing. He is extremely knowledgeable about what is going on in R and D [Research and Development] land and he is certainly eager to make his contribution. (p. 111)

The Floating Opera (1956) and *The End of the Road* (1958) are two novels of a kind and that kind is strictly R and R [Rest and Recuperation], and fairly superior R and R at that. . . . [*The Floating Opera*] is written in first person demotic (Eastern shore of Maryland, Barth's place of origin). The style is garrulous but not unattractive. . . .

Certainly Barth began as an old-fashioned writer who wanted us to know all about the adulteries, money-hassling, and boozing on what sounded like a very real Eastern Shore of a very real Maryland. . . . (p. 112)

In 1960 Barth published *The Sot-Weed Factor.* . . . I am usually quick, even eager, to respond to the outrageously funny, the villainously slanderous [as *The New York Times Book Review* called his book]. . . . But as I read on and on, I could not so much as summon up a smile at the lazy jokes and the horrendous pastiche of what Barth takes to be eighteenth-century English. . . . I stopped at page 412 with 407 pages yet to go. The sentences would not stop unfurling; as Peter Handke puts it in *Kaspar:* "Every sentence helps you along: you get over every object with a sentence: a sentence helps you get over an object when you can't really get over it, so that you really get over it," etc.

To read Barth on the subject of his own work and then to read the work itself is a puzzling business. He talks a good deal of sense. He is obviously intelligent. Yet he tells us that when he turned from the R and R of his first two novels to the megalo-R and R of *The Sot-Weed Factor,* he moved from "a merely comic mode to a variety of farce, which frees your hands even more than comedy does." Certainly there are comic aspects to the first two books. But the ponderous jocosity of the third book is neither farce nor satire nor much of anything except English-teacher-writing at a pretty low level. I can only assume that the book's admirers are as ignorant of the eighteenth century as the author (or, to be fair, the author's imagination) and that neither author nor admiring reader has a sense of humor, a fact duly noted about Americans in general—and their serious ponderous novelists in particular—by many peoples in other lands. It still takes a lot of civilization gone slightly high to make a wit.

Giles Goat-Boy arrived on the scene in 1966. Another 800 pages of ambitious schoolteacher-writing: a book to be taught rather than read. I shall not try to encapsulate it here, other than to say that the central metaphor is the universe is the university is the universe. I suspect that this will prove to be one of the essential American university novels and to dismiss it is to dismiss those departments of English that have made such a book possible. The writing is more than usually clumsy. (p. 113)

By 1968 Barth was responding to the French New Novel. *Lost in the Funhouse* is the result. A collection (or, as he calls it, a "series") of "Fiction for Print, Tape, Live Voice." Barth is not about to miss a trick now that he has moved into R and D country. The first of the series, "Night-Sea Journey," should—or could—be on tape. This is the first-person narrative of a sperm heading, it would appear, toward an ovum, though some of its eschatological musings suggest that a blow-job may be in progress. Woody Allen has dealt more rigorously with this theme.

The "story" "Lost in the Funhouse" is most writerly and self-conscious; it chats with the author who chats with it and with us. "Description of physical appearance and mannerisms is one of several standard methods of characterization used by writers of fiction." Thus Barth distances the reader from the text. . . . Some of [the] schoolteacherly commentary is amusing. But the ultimate effect is one of an ambitious but somewhat uneasy writer out to do something brand-new in a territory already inhabited by, among other texts that can read and write, the sinister *Locus Solus,* the immor(t)al *Tlooth* and the dexterous *A Nest of Ninnies*.

It is seldom wise for a born R and R writer to make himself over into an R and D writer unless he has something truly formidable and new to show us. Barth just has books. And sentences. And a fairly clear idea of just how far up the creek he is without a paddle. (p. 114)

In 1972 Barth published three long stories in a volume called *Chimera*. Two of the stories are based on Greek myths, for are they not, as admirers of Jung declare, part of the racial memory, the common stock of all our dreams and narratives? Well, no, they are not. The Greek myths are just barely relevant to those Mediterranean people who still live in a landscape where the *anima* of a lost world has not yet been entirely covered with cement. The myths are useful but not essential to those brought up on the classics, the generation to which Dr. Jung (and T. S. Eliot) belonged; and of course they are necessary to anyone who would like to understand those works of literature in which myth plays a part. Otherwise they are of no real use to Americans born in this century. For us Oedipus is not the doomed king of Thebes but Dr. Freud's depressing protagonist, who bears no relation at all to the numinous figure that Sophocles and Euripides portrayed. Thebes is another country, where we may not dwell. (pp. 114-15)

The incorporation of Greek myth into modern narrative has been irresistible to those who have difficulty composing narrative, and no Greek. These ambitious writers simply want to give unearned resonance to their tales of adultery on the Eastern Shore of Maryland, of misbehavior in faculty rooms, of massive occlusions in the heart of the country. But the results are deeply irritating to those who have some sense of the classical world and puzzling, I would think, to those taking English courses where the novel is supposed to have started with Richardson. . . .

The first story [in *Chimera*] is taken from Arabian mythology, a narrative called "Dunyazadiad," as told by the "kid sister of Scheherazade." (p. 115)

The kid sister of Scheherazade is a gabby co-ed who mentions with awe the academic gifts of her sister "Sherry," "an undergraduate arts-and-sciences major at Banu Sasan University." . . . This unbearable cuteness has a sinister side. Since Barth's experience of literature and the world is entirely that of a schoolteacher, he appears to take it for granted that the prevailing metaphor for his own life (and why not all life itself?) is the university. There is also an underlying acceptance of the fact that since no one is ever going to read him except undergraduates in American universities, he had better take into account that their reading skills are somewhat underdeveloped, their knowledge of the way society works vague, and their culture thin.

Barth's *Hamlet* would no doubt begin, "Well, I guess flunking out of Rutgers is no big deal when I got this family up in Wilmington where we make these plastics that, like, kill people but I'm changing all that or I was going to up until my mother went and married this asshole uncle of mine. . . ." Perhaps this is the only way to get the classics into young television-shrunk minds. But the exercise debases both classic and young minds. Of course Barth is no fool. He is often quick to jump in and forestall criticism. Sherry's kid sister remarks: "currently, however, the only readers of artful fiction were critics, other writers, and unwilling students who, left to themselves, preferred music and pictures to words."

Sherry is helped in her literary efforts to think up 1001 stories by a genie who is, like so many of Barth's male protagonists, a *thoroughly good person*. . . . [We are] told that "he was no more tempted to infidelity than to incest or pederasty." I guess this makes him about the best genie on campus. Between Genie and Sherry there is a lot of talk about the nature of fiction, which is of course the only reason for writing university fiction. There is not a glimmer of intelligence in this jaunty tale.

Barth was born and grew up a traditional cracker-barrelly sort of American writer, very much in the mainstream—a stream by no means polluted or at an end. But he chose not to continue in the vein that was most natural to him. Obviously he has read a good deal about Novel Theory. He has the standard American passion not only to be original but to be great, and this means creating one of Richard Poirier's "worlds elsewhere": an alternative imaginative structure to the mess that we have made of our portion of the Western hemisphere. Aware of French theories about literature (but ignorant of the culture that has produced those theories), superficially acquainted with Greek myth, deeply involved in the academic life of the American university, Barth is exactly the sort of writer our departments of English were bound, sooner or later, to produce. Since he is a writer with no great gift for language either demotic or mandarin, Barth's narratives tend to lack energy; and the currently fashionable technique of stopping to take a look at the story as it is being told simply draws attention to the meagerness of what is there.

I am obliged to remark upon the sense of suffocation one experiences reading so much bad writing. As the weary eyes flick from sentence to sentence, one starts *willing* the author to be good. Either I have become shell-shocked by overexposure to the rockets' red glare and bombs bursting in air or Barth has managed a decent narrative in "Perseid." As usual, the language is jangling everyday speech. . . . The gods and demigods are straight from Thorne Smith, who ought to be regarded, in A.H. Harry T. Moore's *galère,* as the American Dante. But the story of the middle-aged Perseus and his problems of erection (and love) with a young girl seems at times authentic, even true . . . despite Barth's unremitting jocosity. . . . (pp. 115-17)

Gore Vidal, "American Plastic: The Matter of Fiction" (1974), in his Matters of Fact and of Fiction: Essays 1973-1976 *(copyright © 1977 by Gore Vidal; reprinted by permission of Random House, Inc.), Random House, 1977, pp. 99-126.**

LINDA A. WESTERVELT

Toward the beginning of his confession, the narrator of

Dostoevsky's *Notes from Underground* writes, "I am firmly convinced not only that a great deal of consciousness, but that any consciousness is a disease." John Barth, among other recent writers who deal with the theme of identity in the tradition of Dostoevsky, takes the inner division that results from self-consciousness and, by metaphoric extension, makes it a resource—namely, the subject of his fiction. Then, he forces the reader to experience self-consciousness by making him as aware of his role as reader as Barth is of his role as writer. The reader engages in a dialogue with a series of narrators, with reader and narrator consciously dependent upon one another. In challenging himself to sport with, to create a "game" out of this situation, Barth on the one hand educates his reader to confront the problem of self-consciousness, at the same time that he challenges himself to play an exemplary game with such a created reader. Writing innovative fiction of artifice, he attempts to create a reader who, if he appreciates the story first, comes also to enjoy the "good clean fun" of the verbal and technical "circus tricks." Thus, he educates a reader capable of engaging in virtuoso reading.

In spite of the Barth-like Genie's claim in *Chimera* that the relationship between "teller" and "told" is a "love-relation, not a rape," Barth does not, as might be expected, always woo the reader. At times he even seems disdainful, as though he resents his dependence upon the reader for the existence of tale and teller. Most notably in *Lost in the Funhouse,* Barth uses extravagant and shocking methods to elicit the reader's response. Although these concerns are present in all of Barth's work, he considers self-consciousness and engages in elaborate sport with the reader most explicitly in "Lost in the Funhouse," "Life-Story," and "Title" in *Lost in the Funhouse* and in "Dunyazadiad" and "Bellerophoniad" in *Chimera*.

"Lost in the Funhouse" . . . contains at least ten versions of Ambrose's adventures in the funhouse. Despite digressions about past trips to Ocean City, factual information, and Ambrose's daydreams, the description of the ride to and from Ocean City provides a "realistic" frame for the multiple versions of what occurs in Ocean City. Inside that frame, however, the plot resembles the ideal plot described in Borges' "The Garden of Forking Paths," one which "had the possibility of continuing indefinitely" because its author never chooses one possibility while eliminating others, but rather "he chooses—simultaneously—all of them." (pp. 42-3)

It is very difficult to ascertain which version of the journey is the "real" one, or even whether or not Ambrose got out of the funhouse. At times the narrator's versions of getting lost in the funhouse merge with Ambrose's fantasies. . . . Like the narrator, who is self-conscious about his techniques in constructing his story, Ambrose watches himself watching himself choose among the diverging paths in the funhouse. . . . Merging fantasy and narrative possibility, Barth increases the reader's participation by making him attempt to determine who is speaking. At the same time, of course, he presents the reader with an unsolvable problem. (pp. 43-4)

Even though he does not always call attention to them, Barth provides the reader with blanks like the empty page in Sterne's *Tristram Shandy* which is to be filled with particular versions of the Widow Wadman. The reader can continue the description with whatever he associates with [the subject]. The narrator's thoughts about technique are also left dangling for the reader to fill in from his knowledge of narrative convention and from the context:

> And [the story is] all too long and rambling, as if the author. Assertions of this sort are not effective; the reader may acknowledge the proposition, but. We should be much farther along than we are. . . .

Of course, by leaving blanks at opportune places, the narrator invites criticism. One possible construction—that the story is "rambling, as if the author" were mad and presumptuous enough to believe that his funhouse is fun—is an angry interpolation the author seems to allow if not invite. The reader is further encouraged to vent his spleen by the narrator's own self-conscious interjections which undercut or mock techniques which he has just used or is about to use in the narrative. . . . The narrator's techniques—the multiple versions of the plot that exist simultaneously, the unfinished sentences, the clever but abusive discussion of technique, as well as the obvious insults—do not prevent our taking an interest in Ambrose, but they do frustrate the reader's attempt to learn more about Ambrose and to become involved in his story. That is, he reads all the technical discussion and manipulation by the narrator because of his interest in Ambrose and his hope that the main expectation "Lost in the Funhouse" sets up, learning what happens to Ambrose, will be fulfilled. It is as though Barth is proving to the reader that despite his choosing *Lost in the Funhouse,* he is, after all, one of those who prefers "rousing good yarns" and the story of initiation to self-conscious discussion of technique. (pp. 44-5)

In sharp contrast with "Lost in the Funhouse," . . . "Autobiography" consists of a voice talking about itself, the irreducible element of narrative. Similarly, in "Title" and in "Life-Story" the narrators try to "skip particulars," meaning both details and words. . . . Both of the narrators and their companions have no names or other characterizing traits except their similar intellectual concerns. They challenge themselves to find out how many particular words they can omit from their stories while still making sense. . . . Relationships between lovers . . . , speakers, and words in sentences are breaking down. Nevertheless, at the same time that the narrator complains that the writer's medium is artificial, without "native appeal" or "first-order reality," but "invented specifically to represent," and argues that "literature's not likely ever to manage abstraction successfully," Barth succeeds in having abstract words arranged in familiar grammatical patterns make sense.

The other implication of Barth's use of abstract rather than particular words is that he is confronting and dramatizing the demise of the word. (pp. 45-6)

The satiric narrator in "Life-Story" mourns that it is no longer possible to write serious realistic literature, "rousing good yarns," with "passion and bravura action in my plot, heroes I can admire, heroines I can love, memorable speeches, colorful accessory characters, poetical language." . . . Like Ambrose, who dreams of constructing funhouses modelled on but grander than those he knows, this narrator wants to write in the medium and genre which are already "moribund" *because* they are such. He implies that he wants to write a story that will be like *France II,* "the grandest sailing vessel ever built, . . . constructed . . . not only when but because the age of sail had passed." . . . Thus, his work would be a kind of anatomy of stories, at once a grand summary statement, making use of all prior techniques, and a tribute to a passing era. As a gesture, its construction is also a protest against change, carried out at a time when change is regarded as inevitable. Building such a sailing vessel (or funhouse or novel) would be a self-conscious exercise, with idea rather than function as its main concern. . . .

The narrator's doubts about his own talent in the face of what he sees as a time of great social upheaval and the task he sets for himself as summarizer of the old and harbinger of the new profoundly affect his characterization of his reader. His desperation makes him bold and somewhat heedless of the reader's feelings. Both in "Title" and "Life-Story," "Barth" the implied author willingly risks alienating the already chary reader in order to convey and evoke the artist's own frustration and terror in the face of the demise of culture and literature. (p. 47)

Tale, teller, and told are confused in the tangle of voices. Despite the fact that he creates first-person artist-narrators who voice concerns similar to his own, Barth also gives the reader signals that his narrators are not to be identified with him in any simple fashion. As he playfully remarked in an interview with Joe David Bellamy in *New American Review,* Barth prefers using a first-person narrator because any technique can then be said to "only reflect the anachronistic presuppositions of that narrator," and cannot "be charged against the author." Similarly, any of his narrators' excesses, extreme attitudes, extravagant claims, or limitations cannot be attributed to Barth. Thus, he "has it both ways:" he creates personas who rage about the inadequacies of their medium and prophesy the impending doom of story and civilization, while he exploits medium and convention within their narratives. (p. 48)

Throughout *Lost in the Funhouse* the reader's response, which consists of a mixture of shock, anger, impatience, and delight, is similar to his reaction to the direct address in "Title" and "Life-Story." Flattering and insulting the reader all at once, "Barth," the implied author, invites him to complete or realize the text and holds him off from doing so. Of necessity, at the same time that he is playfully inducing vertigo in himself by parody, wordplay, repetition of motifs and words, and his use of punctuation, Barth is also forcing that state upon the reader. He points out that "Lost in the Funhouse" is a typical story of an adolescent approaching maturity in order to activate the reader's expectations about character and resolution from his prior reading experience only to frustrate the reader by leading him through a verbal funhouse in which Ambrose and the reader get lost. (pp. 49-50)

Insofar as Barth creates a reader who grants the fiction and the author their existence and who affirms the value of the artistic endeavor, technical virtuosity notwithstanding, Barth observes the traditional author-reader relationship. In sporting with the reader, he introduces another element into that relationship. While there is a pedagogic aspect to his destroying the illusion of the fiction within the work itself, his belittling the art of storytelling and of reading is ultimately abusive of both author and reader. It is as though Barth resents his dependence upon the reader and fears his reader's "possessing," completing, and judging the text, a concern that is reflected in one of Barth's major themes. (p. 50)

Just as in his early work Barth's character Jake Horner comments on the inadequacy of the imagination in dealing with experience, in his latest work his narrators continue to undercut the artistic activity within the artwork itself. There is an important addition to *Chimera,* however. Even though the Genie's appearance in Scheherazade's library may be ironic, it is the Genie's philosophy which informs *Chimera.* That is, while Bellerophon wanders about complaining of his inability to mold life into art and of his failure to find meaning in the process, the Genie, who is closer to Barth, recognizes the limitations of art and still affirms it:

> "Art, . . . if it could not redeem the barbarities of history or spare us the horrors of living and dying, at least sustained, refreshed, expanded, ennobled, and enriched our spirits along the painful way. . . . Some fictions, he asserted, were so much more valuable than fact that in rare instances their beauty made them real."

This acceptance enables Barth to conceive of his relationship with the reader in *Chimera* as a more equal partnership, one in which teller and told both willingly share and participate. (pp. 54-5)

Linda A. Westervelt, "Teller, Tale, Told: Relationships in John Barth's Latest Fiction," in The Journal of Narrative Technique *(copyright © 1978 by* The Journal of Narrative Technique*), Vol. 8, No. 1, Winter, 1978, pp. 42-55.*

JOE WEIXLMANN and SHER WEIXLMANN

[Barth's aesthetic] embodies a conscious attempt to go beyond Joyce—by going backwards. Like the protagonist of his "Perseid," who must return to Joppa, the scene of his youthful heroics, if he is to go forward with his life, Barth roots his strategy in the Shakespearean realization that fiction is "a kind of true representation of the distortion we all make of life." It is crucial, he feels, to attempt to deal with the discrepancy between art and Reality, and he finds that the most effective way to do so is "to acknowledge right off the bat 'this is artifice'—which, of course, is among other things a sly way of getting around the artifice. It's an old gambit, . . . particularly popular in Renaissance drama: life is a play, the world's a theatre, existence is a dream, etc., etc." He reasons that ". . . by continually rubbing the audience's nose in the artificial aspect of what you're doing, you're really deliberately confusing the issue you're pretending to clarify, transcending the artifice by insisting on it." Barth's primary vehicle for putting this strategy into practice is his extremely baroque plotting. (p. 193)

Barth's novella ["Perseid"] is elaborately framed and sports an intricate plot. Relying on various accounts of the Perseus myth, Barth retells the story and extends it by reinterpreting certain actions of the original and by inventing a second quest which Perseus undertakes during middle age and which results in his metamorphosis into the constellation Perseus. At the outset of the novella, Perseus, estellated in the Northern Hemisphere, is telling the reader of telling the New Medusa (in Barth's version of the tale, the girl was reassembled after her beheading by Perseus on his youthful mythic quest) of the time he told an Egyptian girl,

Calyxa, about setting out at age forty to relive the heroic quest of his youth. The complexity of the frame pales in comparison to the way in which the plot unravels itself. Graven scenes depicting key events in Perseus' life spiral around and behind the wall of the chamber in the shrine in which Perseus finds himself. The scenes are represented on two sets of seven panels, the second set being "correspondent to the first in relative proportions, but of grander breadth," and the sixth panel of each set being "septuple in proportions similar to the whole's." One set of seven portrays Perseus' initial quest; the next seven relate his middle-aged journey. Whereas the first set is commissioned from extant myth, the last seven panels are of Barth's imagining. The reader, like Perseus, is exposed to only one panel at a time. (p. 196)

The plot of "Perseid" exemplifies what Barth, in "The Literature of Exhaustion," refers to as a *regressus in infinitum,* a story-within-a-story (framed, in this instance, by third and fourth stories) which keeps reflecting back onto itself. Mirroring other than that associated with plot also occurs: There are repetitions of character types . . . and attributes . . . and of props and furniture in the story which turn back upon themselves—and even upon other writings by Barth. Especially noteworthy in this regard is Barth's use of the number seven, the most important of all the typological numbers and the symbol of completeness, consummation, and unity. Perseus' tale is told on seven-part panels; Calyxa has sent the protagonist seven letters; Perseus exchanges his troubles with the New Medusa at the rate of "'seven to one'" . . . ; the Nile is said to have "seven mouths" . . . ; and the story ends after Perseus and the New Medusa have asked each other seven questions. (p. 199)

The structuring of the persona in Barth's "patterned tale" is likewise intricately effected. Perseus begins the story simply with a "Good evening" . . . and, when the tale is over, closes by saying, "Till tomorrow evening, love. . . . Good night. Good night." . . . By this point the narrative has revealed that nearly all of the major characters in the story have been immortalized as constellations or stars of constellations, that the stars themselves are the tale-bearers, and that, the day having passed from evening to night, the darkness is nearly spent. The stars will be unable to repeat their tale again until after the setting of the next day's sun. Unlike the tripartite "Dunyazadiad" and "Bellerophoniad," "Perseid" has but a single section, labeled 1. Two and 3, as well as 4, 5, 6, etcetera, will be replays, the tale being "nightly rehearsed as long as men and women read the stars." . . . (p. 200)

Barth's prose is smooth and graceful and sounds good to the ear when read aloud. "I like plot in fiction," Barth once remarked, "in the same way that I like melodic music." He thinks of his writing as an exercise in orchestration: By rescoring aging literary conventions, he achieves a contemporary effect. . . . Although Barth has experimented extensively with certain aspects of technique, he is, in one area at least, an admitted conservative. In all of his fiction, he has strived "to preserve the appeal that narrative has always had to the imagination: the simple appeals of suspense, of *story,* with which I've been in love since the beginning." (p. 201)

That Barth often handles his mythic newborn humorously and irreverently should not lead one to think that he is writing without ideological and philosophical commitment. . . . [Whereas] Barth may advance his tale with verbal and situational wit, the humor invariably leads one back to the notion of something serious. When, for example, Perseus is deprived of his carefully filed fan mail as well as the other memorabilia in his brassbound box by Andromeda . . . , we are presented with a foreshadowing of a recurrent failure of the hero in the second heptatich—impotency or the inability to perform.

Barth also uses paradox to deepen the seriousness of "Perseid," much as he does in *Giles Goat-Boy,* and to prevent the tale from becoming maudlin. . . . Echoing the subtitle of Barth's fourth novel, Perseus refers to his immortal mate as "the paradoxic precious New Revised Medusa." . . . The possibility of attaining her means forsaking his "fond dream of rejuvenation" . . . and committing himself to an unsure future, risking his life for love; yet that is the very thing which makes the Medusa "precious." And though the risk appears to have been worth it, several nagging questions persist: Did Athene actually restore the Medusa to her original beauty? Did Perseus kiss the Medusa in bad faith and reGorgonize her? . . . There is, simply, no way to be sure. The reader leaves the tale wiser but unsettled—perhaps imagining alternate endings, further widening and extending the myth. As the New Medusa observes, "'that's another story, another story . . .'." . . . (pp. 205-06)

Joe Weixlmann and Sher Weixlmann, "Barth and Barthelme Recycle the Perseus Myth: A Study in Literary Ecology," in Modern Fiction Studies *(© copyright 1979 by Purdue Research Foundation, West Lafayette, Indiana), Vol. 25, No. 2, Summer, 1979, pp. 191-207.**

TONY TANNER

Much of John Barth's fiction arises out of his scrupulous, exacting, sometimes excruciating, consideration of his own position as a Novelist writing Now. The state of fiction is as much on his mind, if not more, than the state of America or the world; indeed he would probably argue that to be deeply concerned with the former is only another way of being deeply concerned about the latter. (p. 1)

As he writes in *Letters:* "I am by temperament a fabricator, not a drawer-from-life." This, of course, begs all kinds of big questions, and Barth is very adept at teasing and drawing fiction, or fabrication, out of just such begged-questions. But it does pose a problem. If Barth wants to avoid "obscure pretension" and "cynical commercialism" what . . . is he to write about? And in what way?

In *Letters* we have the answer. He will write about all his own novels and the characters therein; he will bring those characters together in bizarre, unexpected and complex—not to say ambiguous—relationships; he will intertwine the plots of their lives with amazing dexterity (and at times almost perverse obliquity); mixed in with those plots he will introduce many of the plots which were involved in the history of the first 40-odd years of the American republic and in turn intertwine those with some of the plots . . . which are active in contemporary America. "Revolution," in every sense, is a theme of the book, along with the question of whether America needs, will have, or even permit, a "second revolution," and what form it might or could take. He will write this in the form of an epistolary novel, with more than one eye on the early years of the English novel when Richardson's epistolary fictions seemed to initiate and then (almost) exhaust the genre. . . . (pp. 1, 8)

But what! let us imagine some churlish non-dreamer exclaiming, is Mr. Barth so low on imagination that he has to bring out of retirement and dust off his old creations (with an aging British broad thrown in to up the sexual ante) and go on about his old obsessions with history, fiction, fabrication, fabulation, narrative, heroic patterns, Lord Raglan and Joseph Campbell, etc.? The answer to that is—no, there is much more to the book than that. And as always John Barth knows exactly what he is doing. . . .

John Barth has taken on his imaginative past (as well as that of America) to see whether the past can be, not just a marsh forever sucking the present backwards into its own entropic determinisms, but a fecundating and fertilizing material that can promote the issue and growth of something new. This is why, I think, there is a recurring preoccupation with all forms of recyclings, re-presentations, computer RESETs, the redreaming and rewriting of history, and reenactment. . . .

The problem is "How transcend mere reenactment?" In other terms, familiar to readers of *Chimera,* it is a matter of breaking out of circles and moving into a spiral motion. "Closed-circuit history is for compulsives; Perseus and I are into spirals, presumably outbound." Thus Ambrose Mensch and, presumably, John Barth who, in one of his letters about his own book, agrees that "the ground theme be not so much revolution or recycling as reenactment"—and how to move beyond it by going through it. . . .

So, what, after all, kind of novel do we have here? Groping for words, let's call it an example of reluctant-sceptical-nostalgic-exuberant realism. Yet, that is the genre that Barth has, waywardly, idiosyncratically, marvellously, made his way back to. "Tranquilly I turned my back on Realism, having perhaps long since turned it on reality," says Ambrose Mensch, who then confesses (is that you, John Barth?) to having become "reenamored" with "that most happily contaminated literary genre: the Novel, *the Novel, with its great galumphing grace, amazing as a whale!*" . . .

The book is full of wonderful things (as well as some longueurs and some hair-tugging complexifications of intrigue and plot). It is a very remarkable work, which not only dramatizes, but analyses, plays and works with, and moves towards moving beyond what Barth himself defines in the following:

"*Conflict:* last-ditch provincial Modernist wishes neither to repeat nor to repudiate career thus far; wants the century under his belt but not upon his back. *Complication:* he becomes infatuated with, enamored of, obsessed by a fancied embodiment . . . of the Great Tradition and puts her—and himself—through sundry more or less degrading trials, which she suffers with imperfect love and patience, she being a far from passive lady, until he loses his cynicism and his heart to her spirited dignity and, at the *climax,* endeavors desperately, hopefully, perhaps vainly, to get her one final time with child."

Well he did, he has. And in language and narrative which "like an icebreaker, like spawning salmon, incoming tide, or wandering hero, springs forward, falls back, gathers strength, springs farther forward, falls less far back, and at length arrives—but does not remain at—its high-water mark." *Letters* is a prodigious and quite remarkable achievement—a landmark, if indeed not a high-water mark. But perhaps it must be the only one of its kind—that "final" fling with Dame Realism.

As you move into your spiral, where next, John Barth? Presumably outbound. We all hope so. (p. 8)

Tony Tanner, "Yours Sincerely, John Barth," in Book World—The Washington Post *(© 1979,* The Washington Post*), September 30, 1979, pp. 1, 8.*

GEOFFREY WOLFF

[John Barth's] first novel since *Giles Goat-Boy* (1966) is, as publishers like to say, an event. *Letters* . . . is a big event, almost half a million words, 864 pages, seven years in its making. . . .

Be forewarned, then: Here is yet another fiction whose principal purpose is to regard itself, to finger (seldom lovingly, often contemptuously) its own artifices, to play the venerable modernist game of Seems and Is. In keeping with his preoccupation with what he has called "exhausted" literary forms, the "used-upness" of, say, the picaresque novel, which he exploited and parodied in *The Sot-Weed Factor,* Barth has chosen to fabricate an epistolary novel.

Barth's *Letters* is nothing if not implausible. Five of its seven correspondents are characters or the descendants of characters from Barth's previous fictions. . . . A sixth character is called "the Author" or "John Barth." . . .

The "John Barth" of *Letters* is an autobiographical fragment, or figment. . . . *Letters* is coyly referential; I cannot imagine a reader ignorant of Barth's previous fictions able to comprehend it or willing to bull through it. Barth's courage and stamina are not in question. . . .

Loyalty to *Letters* demanded a daunting complexity of plot and time. . . .

Barth has been attracted, sometimes harmfully, by the schematic. The Rube Goldberg fictional devices of *Giles Goat-Boy* hobbled that huge novel; they cripple *Letters.* (p. 17)

With the exception of *The End of the Road, Letters* is the only work by Barth for which I feel no affection. Its inventions seem complicated to no surprising end. It lacks the comic gusto that has characterized his fiction since *The Sot-Weed Factor.* The prose, as precise and carefully wrought as you might expect, is also flat, monotonous. Lady Amherst, discussing her carnal circus with Ambrose Mensch, comes most interestingly to life, but the best run of sustained writing belongs to Todd Andrews, in a series of letters to his dead father, describing with love a cruise along the Eastern Shore and up the rivers of Chesapeake Bay before he kills himself, as his father killed himself in *The Floating Opera.*

Barth is the reader least inclined to deny what is arid in his work, what is merely systematic. From "Life-Story," in *Lost in the Funhouse,* comes this direct address to the reader, almost a Barthian signature by now, another exhausted device he dares refresh:

> The reader! You, dogged, uninsultable, print-oriented bastard, it's you I'm addressing, who else, from inside this monstrous fiction. You've read me this far, then? Even this far? For what discreditable motive? How is it you don't go to a movie, stare at a wall, play tennis with a friend, make amorous advances to the person who comes to your mind when I speak of amorous advances? Can nothing surfeit, saturate you, turn you off? Where's your shame?
>
> (pp. 17, 19)

In these passages, audacious risks are redeemed by the only thing that could possibly redeem them: prose of energy and perfect timing. For whatever reason, and with stubborn courage, John Barth has denied the tonal range of his wonderful instruments to his letter writers. Here *they* are merely instruments, their language merely letters. (p. 19)

Geoffrey Wolff, "Long Letters, Lost Liberty, Languid Love: Barth's Mail" (first published in Esquire *magazine; copyright © 1979 by Esquire Publishing, Inc.), in* Esquire, *Vol. 92, No. 4, October, 1979, pp. 17, 19.*

PHILIP STEVICK

In a novel [*Letters*] that takes many risks, the identity of the correspondents is the biggest risk of all. They are all figures from Barth's previous fiction. . . . [Even] though the letters generate their own energy and the correspondents develop their own lives, the choice of the correspondents still retains a coterie effect. . . . The device does, to be sure, expand two conceits which, now and then, enter the minds of all readers of fiction. The first is that playful act in which one rearranges characters, placing Becky Sharp in *Swann's Way* or Huckleberry Finn in *The Wings of the Dove*. Barth's fictions are very different from one another; and thus characters from each of them, placed in the same work, make a collage which is startling and amusing. The second conceit is that equally playful act in which one imagines the lives of characters after the book is finished. . . . And here too, Barth's choice allows him an eccentric excursion into the implicit sequels of his characters' lives. Two more significant effects of such a choice, however, are the exercise they permit Barth with the fictive and the real (characters ingratiate their way into the book, or deny any interest in becoming a part of the book, all of this in letters to Barth, an author then living in Buffalo, the fictional invention of an author, named Barth, then living in Buffalo), and the exercise they permit Barth with history, which is, ultimately, the "subject" of the novel. (p. 341)

[*Letters*] is, in its way, an extraordinary exercise in intersecting perspectives, intersecting rhetorics, intersecting ways of organizing the world. . . . Although I can think of many works, historical and fictional, that treat history encyclopedically, reaching for range, scope and inclusiveness, I can think of no other work that seeks to bring together jingoism and detachment, the eyewitness view and the distant generalization, the computerized, and the humane, the sensuous and the chaste, the compulsively gossipy and the bored, the affectionate and the cynical. It is a book that confirms one's conviction that, for pure talent, the ability to do anything with words, nobody is better than Barth. But the rhythms of *Letters* tend to overwhelm. That old-fashioned epistolary novel immersed us in the continuing lives of its correspondents, like an afternoon soap, and its duration seemed somehow appropriate to the intimacy of its experience. Barth's book, on the other hand, does not invite us to enter a world: there are seven different and incongruent worlds. It does not invite us to enter the chess game of moves and countermoves that the older form provided, because the correspondents rarely interact or, when they do, they generally interact only perfunctorily. . . .

Implicitly concerned with the middle of life—the author's, his characters', everybody's—his novel gathers elements from his brilliant career into a form unlike anything before it. But in the process he gives his drolls and dreamers more weight than they can bear. (p. 342)

Philip Stevick, "Letters from Incongruent Worlds," in The Nation *(copyright 1979 by the Nation Associates, Inc.), Vol. 229, No. 11, October 13, 1979, pp. 341-42.*

FRANK McCONNELL

[In *Letters*, the] subplots, counterplots, and crossplots . . . exfoliate maddeningly and impinge even more maddeningly upon one another. Its language ranges from the disconcertingly flat and factual to the disconcertingly baroque, from drab to lunatic-ornate. And when it is not tracing insane patterns of coincidence and repetition—patterns almost as insane, indeed, as those of "real life"—the story is variously lubricous, violent, and macabre: rape, murder, suicide, arson, pillage, incest, and cancer are among the prominent and structurally supporting gargoyles of Barth's design. . . .

[Everything] is—deliberately—"wrong" with *Letters* that is "wrong" with that most ancient, most shaky, and most cherished of human defenses against the void: fiction itself. Between the bloodless abstractions of reason and the bloody compulsions of passion we live out our single lives and the life of the species, and we make up stories, invent mythologies, to explain and heal the real, the infinitely recapitulated Fall of Man, the fissure of head and heart. Barth has always known this, and has explored its tragicomic implications in six brilliant previous books. . . .

But in *Letters* he rehearses and realizes, more brilliantly than ever before, the essential and humanizing paradoxes of fiction. . . .

[As Barth has] always understood and articulated, you can't begin to think about the future until you have thought about, and assimilated, the past: the structural, timeless past of storytelling and mythmaking themselves, and the murderous, misguided, historical past of the storytelling and mythmaking human race. . . . [We] have discovered more and more how rigorously the patterns of our myths determine the possibilities of our action.

But of course this is the burden of self-consciousness, the bane of fiction for the last hundred years or more: How, after you have learned that a myth is a myth, can you believe in it, live your life within its saving parameters? Conrad, Joyce, Greene, Kafka, and Mann all addressed, in one way or another, this crucial narrative, social, and political problem. And Barth, more than any other American novelist of his era—except, perhaps, Thomas Pynchon—has continued this, the major, tortuous, and brave tradition of modern writing. What, in the most honored and outmoded traditions of storytelling, might yet survive to make our lives not only tolerable but joyful? In *Letters,* by returning to the officially "exhausted" tradition of the 18th-century epistolary novel, Barth is not simply attempting, by a stylistic *tour de force,* to resuscitate a discredited form, but to reexamine the possibilities of the novel itself, and of his own career, his own vocation, as a novelist.

Thus, all of the characters in *Letters* are obsessed, in one way or another, with the Pattern of their previous lives (*i.e.,* the patterns of the novels in which they originally appeared, and the larger, all-encompassing Pattern of heroic legend). Can the Pattern, somehow, be transcended, or are we all, drolls and dreamers, doomed to endless repetitions of the already-said, the already-written? And what if, more terrifyingly, *the pattern itself* includes "transcendence" as one of its terms? (p. 6)

[All the characters] are obsessed with the chances for breaking out of, or the necessity of repeating, pattern: They are trapped in the killing dichotomy of fire and algebra that defines our lives, too. But so is John Barth; or "John Barth," the "Author," who is also one of the characters in *Letters*. He announces that he would like to break out of the trap of self-consciousness that is the heritage of the modern writer, and re-establish the cordial relations once enjoyed between the novel and "reality," whether psychologically, sexually, socially, or politically understood. The book is really about mid-life crisis: the mid-life crisis of literature itself, of Western (particularly American) civilization, and of John Barth, middle-aged novelist.

Indeed, this self-confrontation at mid-career may be the single finest achievement of this exceptionally fine, very important book. . . . Barth, who has always been a writer fond of taking a risk, has risked as much as possible in this book, to the extent that his previous career (the "First Cycle" of his life), his earlier novels, and his hope to continue both as novelist and as man, all depend upon the success of *Letters,* the ability of this involuted, intricately designed epistolary fiction to break past the boundaries of Pattern into something like a perception, an articulation, and even a habitable version, of life itself.

That is to say that Barth has confronted, in *Letters,* the besetting and crucifying condition of contemporary writing as fully as anyone now at work in the arid vineyards of fiction. That he has succeeded splendidly in that confrontation is, I think, beyond question. But what is not beyond at least analysis and comment is the main plot, the central story of *Letters* that dramatizes that success. . . . Ambrose, who for years has been trapped within the uncertainties of self-conscious, self-advertising fiction, becomes the passionate, insatiable lover of Germaine. Their torrid, often obscene affair is, in fact, the main plot of the novel, into which the elaborate sub-plots of the other characters enter. And it is, of course, also the love affair of John Barth, Ambrose's creator and double, with the muse of the novel, the muse of storytelling, the muse of the literary tradition itself. . . .

Germaine herself finally becomes pregnant by her young, involuted lover and husband-to-be. The postmodern poet has begotten, upon the muse of literature herself . . . a new birth. And that new birth is the novel, *Letters,* itself: A pattern that describes the breaking of patterns, a story whose intricate turnings articulate the human depth and pathos underlying all stories, and a fiction that becomes "real" by defining itself, splendidly and with preternatural intelligence, as fiction. (p. 7)

Frank McConnell, "Barth Reviewed," in Books & Arts *(copyright © 1979 by The Chronicle of Higher Education, Inc.), n.s. Vol. I, No. 4, October 26, 1979, pp. 6-7.*

BENJAMIN DeMOTT

[The author of *Letters* manages] to keep a sober promise he makes early on, namely that "the several narratives will become one." He brings it off by framing the individual narratives in a film production, an attempt by a moviemaker to create a screen version not of one of his books but of all of them, including those still unwritten. (p. 91)

Midway in *Letters,* Barth reproduces a patch of his own correspondence in which he asserts that the book "will *not* be obscure, difficult, or dense in the Modernist fashion." And he adds that, while "it will hazard the resurrection of characters from my previous fiction . . . as well as extending the fictions themselves, [it] will not presume, on the reader's part, familiarity with those fictions, which I cannot myself remember in detail." I'm sorry to report that there's some self-deception in these observations. Ambiguities of identity in the chief characters, the irrelevance of whole chapters of historical matter to what the nonspecialist reader must regard as the narrative main line, the author's near obsession with historical and linguistic correspondences, doublings, and layerings—these combine to produce extreme difficulty. And if it is true that Barth doesn't expect his reader to know his previous books, it is no less true that readers ignorant of them are bound to be mystified often. . . .

Is it really worth bothering? Yes and no, leaning yesward. Besides Germaine Pitt, much Rabelaisian humor, and the high-camp theatrics of the filming episodes, *Letters* contains at least two extended and admirable sections of narrative—a carefully detailed history of a family of Eastern Shore stonemasons, and a farewell cruise around the Chesapeake on a skipjack whose captain has a movingly precise appreciation of the joys of pure physicality. In addition, the author's speculative intelligence is rarely out of sight. . . . And while Barth's fascination with the technology of narrative is often wearing, it does stimulate brooding on the meaning, for contemporary life, of the decline of the storytelling craft. . . . John Barth's bemused teasing out and exhibition of the story elements of his fable comes to seem, well before the end, a mode of decent piety—a last touching attempt, in the twilight of yarn-spinning in words, to evoke and objectify the beauty and mystery of the spinner's skills.

More important than any of this is the scrupulousness with which the book's basic theme—call it the fiction of fiction—is explored. Other writers besides Barth—the best of the type is surely Thomas Pynchon—create figures whose lives, like Germaine Pitt's, are dominated by fictional forces or myths beyond their understanding. Few writers work as patiently or as ingeniously as Barth at explaining the derivation of such figures—why they have cropped out all at once in our fiction, what their roots are in contemporary intellection. Time and again in *Letters* the author invites his reader to ponder the present status of the idea of the real and the unreal, present thinking about the arbitrariness of signs, present critiques of naive realisms, scientific and otherwise. Time and again his narrative becomes an instrument for renewing comprehension of the universal human enclosure in fictions novelists never made—the truth, that is, "that our concepts, categories, and classifications are ours, not the World's. . . ."

Whether the novel as hitherto constituted is the proper setting for such instruction can be debated. So too can the wisdom of promoting complex epistemological fiction in a manner suggesting that a swell evening's read lies ahead. And there is something in this late-twentieth-century embrace of the theme of reality as mirage that hints at enfeebled responsiveness—inability to awaken any sense of pain and injustice except that which deals abstractly with them as "clichés." Yet despite all this, *Letters* remains worth wrestling with. It is by turns a brain-buster, a marathon, an exasperation, a frustration, a provocation to earnest thought. Barth is preaching, wittily but with total conviction, on the limits of our kind, on the sanity of doubting that we know where, in our lives, fiction stops. His book intimates that things as they are—the myths of the West, of free enterprise, of the scientific method, of the energy crisis, all those orderings of life shaped in the nightly news—may hold less of a key to the truth of our being than the dream some neighbor is dreaming as we turn the page. A piece of me believes this; therefore I think *Letters* has a future. (p. 92)

Benjamin DeMott, "Six Novels in Search of a Novelist," in The Atlantic Monthly *(copyright © 1979 by The Atlantic Monthly Company, Boston, Mass.; reprinted with permission), Vol. 244, No. 5, November, 1979, pp. 89-92.*

JOSEPHINE HENDIN

John Barth has seen art as the world "elsewhere," the better world where nothing disappears. *Letters* is his *billet doux* to literature and his plea to his own creations to return the gift of life. . . . Barth attempts a kind of self-renewal through retrieving and repossessing his fictional offspring and his youth as a writer. Wading through the plots and people of his past novels, Barth seems to search for some fresh emotion. Although he fails to find it, his search is itself a wily and powerful statement of *Letters*'s best subject: aesthetic ambition.

Of our contemporaries, only Barth has looked to art for the key to life. In the past, his characters have outwitted even suicidal despair by seeing themselves as storytellers, by weaving fictions that conceal their troubles. They seem to find the magic words, the abracadabras, that permit them not to distinguish style from lifestyle. The logic of sentences seems to refute mental chaos, syntax helps collapsing personalities cohere, and parody operates as a force for order for characters who become only witty voices. . . .

In *Letters,* Barth opens up the dark side of formalism. No virtuosity can redeem some of his characters from chaos and collapse. Their obsessional need to pattern life verbally exemplifies and embodies their derangement. The book abounds in "patterns" based on the repetition of numbers, word games, alphabet tricks, and anacrostics which seem to have been reeled out by an overcharged computer. Style is no longer a value to live by but, too often in *Letters,* a control mechanism gone out of control. Unable to resuscitate many of his old friends and plots, Barth produces massive, inert mounts of verbiage lacking emotion or human meaning. But pressed between these are brilliant passages in which Barth confronts the frustrations of art.

Barth's love letter to *belles lettres* contains comic reproaches to the culture that has not shared his veneration of form. His epic of the American sensibility is no *Aeneid,* no embodiment of the ideals of solidity and purpose, but his mock-serious invention, *Anarchaid.* Virtually all of Barth's characters in *Letters* find their fate tied to the fate of American culture. They are mysteriously connected with the aesthetic ideals embodied—and heartily travestied—by a Tower of Truth. (p. 32)

Barth does not always save himself from turning *Letters* into alphabet soup. He succeeds only in the warmest sections where literature is a love affair between a writer and his aesthetic ideal, fleshed out as a woman. . . .

What redeems this love affair from excessive symbolism is Barth's ability to press into it genuine despair for a lost world of energy and emotion. (p. 33)

What Barth has created in *Letters* is the ambitious elaboration of the modernist concern with the derangements of art, sex, and culture. At its best *Letters* can be to his work what *Magister Ludi* was to Hesse's, *Ada* was to Nabokov's, and *Gravity's Rainbow* was to Pynchon's. But *Letters* too often accentuates the narrowness of Barth's vision. In its too frequent constriction and in the incestuous unions of its characters, it has the unintended effect of calling into question the meaning of an art that is so entirely self-referential and self-limiting. And the insularity of Barth's wish only to relive, recapitulate, and retrieve forces us to see again that one of the great human tragedies is self-enclosure. (p. 34)

Josephine Hendin, "Books and the Arts: 'Letters: A Novel'," in The New Republic *(reprinted by permission of* The New Republic; *© 1979 The New Republic, Inc.), Vol. 181, No. 22, December 1, 1979, pp. 32-4.*

* * *

BAXTER, James K. 1926-1972

A New Zealand poet, playwright, and critic, Baxter is generally ranked among the finest authors that country has produced. His work is strongly regional, drawing inspiration from the New Zealand wilderness, its tribal history, and natural cycles. Baxter's rejection of conventional social standards is evidenced by the unorthodoxy of much of his verse. A devout Christian, he has shaped his poetic philosophy to include elements of both religious and classical mythology, creating a viewpoint that is as highly moral as it is individualistic. To Baxter, a poem must be "a cell of good living in a corrupt society." Stylistically, his work is lyrical and metaphorical, and often shows the influence of Lawrence Durrell and Robert Lowell. (See also *Contemporary Authors,* Vols. 77-80.)

E. H. McCORMICK

[James K. Baxter] is, indeed, the central figure in the contemporary scene, mediator among writers of different ages and outlooks, focus of highest hopes for the future. Not that he belongs in the category of the 'promising'; while still in his early thirties, his past as poet and critic is already substantial. . . . Familiar themes—nature's menace, the spiritual strength of the Polynesians, the precariousness of European occupation—reappeared [in *Beyond the Palisade* (1944)], acquiring fresh force through Baxter's matchless gift of phrase and lyric. This indigenous vein, with others exposed by the youthful virtuoso, might have occupied a lesser poet for the rest of his career. But Baxter has repeatedly been compelled to disappoint expectations, to follow not the predictable and approved course but the stonier path dictated by his own *daimon*. His next work, *Blow, Wind of Fruitfulness* (1948), was superficially less attractive than its predecessor, though it contained profounder poetry. It seemed to proceed from a state of spiritual depression, reflected in the images of winter pervading the collection and in the studied avoidance of rhetoric. . . . *Recent Trends in New Zealand Poetry* (1951) was remarkable not merely for the maturity of its judgments but for its strong ethical bias. Poetry, Baxter affirmed, 'should contain moral truth,' every poet 'should be a prophet according to his lights.' . . . The garments of teacher and exemplar are not easily assumed in our times; and in his next collection, *The Fallen House* (1953), Baxter himself could supply no simple message to a distracted world. Instead, like Hart Crane, he mined 'the black gold / Of prophecy' from an experience that was often bitter and sometimes sordid; he praised and in his own person illustrated a 'passionate integrity.' . . . (pp. 141-42)

A critical study, *The Fire and the Anvil* (1955), and the parodies of *The Iron Breadboard* (1957) may be cited as further expressions of an intelligence which has flowed, with vitalizing results, into almost every branch of contemporary letters. Baxter's presence, in fact, goes far to explain why in recent years Wellington has become the most vigorous centre of New Zealand verse. (p. 142)

E. H. McCormick, "The Middle Decades," in his New Zealand Literature: A Survey *(© copyright Oxford University Press, 1959; reprinted by permission of Oxford University Press), Oxford University Press, London, 1959, pp. 136-61.**

ROGER GARFITT

When James K. Baxter, who died far too young in New Zealand last year, began his last book [*Runes*] with a section entitled 'after Catullus', it was anything but an academic exercise. One of the sources of Baxter's power was that when he drew on myth or literature, whether classical or Biblical, it no longer seemed an outside allusion, but became a natural source of reference, immediate and intimate. . . . What he shared with Catullus, and with Rimbaud, whom he translated brilliantly, was a primary intensity of feeling, an apprehension in which the passing detail retained its depth of sensuous texture, yet acquired an almost elemental force. It brings him equally close to the Jacobeans, who experienced afresh, in the tropes of classical rhetoric, the shock of mortality—'I thought, shoving my muscle through black hair, / "What is a man, this glittering dung-fed fly / Who burrows in foul earth?"' ('Henley Pub', from *Selected Poems*)—and gave him an affinity with his Calvinist forebears that was perhaps more formative than his own Roman Catholic belief. . . . [His] urgency and directness are not qualities he has learned from Catullus: they are constant throughout his work.

What he does gain from Catullus is an extra impudence, a greater colloquial freedom, which enables him to bring off the Catullan jokes perfectly. . . . When this freedom is added to his own world-weariness, it produces a voice that is nearly hysterical in its complexity of feeling, almost heroic in its attempt at self-command. . . . This colloquial bite carries over into the directly personal poems that follow, and through them into the landscape poems. . . . In fact, there is a significant difference between these landscapes and those of earlier poems: no longer 'the only world I love, this wilderness', the desolation is interleaved with the warmth of human presence, actual or remembered. In the last section of the book, there is a further, and more mysterious, development: unmistakably, these poems await death, at first as the dawning of new understanding, then as making sense in itself. . . . [His] final glance at the city, in which the vicissitudes of a man's life and career are first shaped into a primeval struggle, and then take on another, quieter meaning, within a scheme at once precise and vast, is characteristic of Baxter's power and subtlety. These poems are distinctive, both in their warmth, and in their disconcerting finality: they complete an achievement whose importance has already been recognized, and must surely grow with time. (pp. 118-20)

Roger Garfitt, "Colloquial Bite," in London Magazine *(© London Magazine 1973), Vol. 13, No. 3, September, 1973, pp. 118-24.**

CHARLES DOYLE

More clearly than with many artists, Baxter's life and work are interdependent. From the first a controversial and complex figure, he apparently contained within himself profound contradictions. Deeply moral, he flaunted the conventions of his society over and over again. . . .

Finding much in New Zealand life to attack, he yet realized that his true personal center was inseparable from his own country. (p. 19)

His four books of poetry . . . were widely recognized as the work of a major talent. Presumably, had he been a British or American poet his name would now be much better known. Yet, although one of the finest poets of his generation writing in English, he made virtually no effort to establish a reputation outside the confines of his own small country. This circumstance derives from one of his great strengths, his rootedness in the land and community in which he lived. (p. 20)

Indications throughout Baxter's writings, at every stage, suggest that he was naturally disposed to a belief in God, and that for him the Christian religion was a matter of serious concern. (pp. 30-1)

Pervaded by spirituality as they are, his last writings continue to manifest such apparent contradictions [as Baxter's lifestyle itself did, combining the spiritual with the crude]. But they may be more apparent than real. Baxter had always been this kind of mixture, and at the end, many would say, his life was an integrated whole, the meeting of *yin* and *yang*. (p. 35)

Many key poems of Baxter's first volume, *Beyond the Palisade,* were written by the time he was seventeen. . . . Work contained in [the notebooks from which Baxter drew this volume] has a greater range both in substance and technique, than is revealed in *Beyond the Palisade*. Available to him was a considerably larger collection, looser and more colloquial in texture; the making of the book was a considerable act of self-criticism and self-shaping.

As it is, *Beyond the Palisade* displays versatility in polished use of short-lined quatrains and longer, more ruminative forms. Its themes include the force of nature ("Eagle"); nature's cruelty and menace . . . ; man's cruelty within nature; . . . the difference between Maori and *pakeha* (white settler) in terms of belonging to the land, the poverty of *pakeha* existence in relation to it, and the consequent poverty of *pakeha* history. Dominating the whole book is a sense of isolated man in the clutch of mortality and cruel, indifferent nature. . . . (pp. 38-9)

[Baxter essentially] chose to continue his selection for his first published book so that it centered on New Zealand. From the notebooks he could have taken work concerned with war in Europe, or containing references to Van Gogh, El Greco, Napoleon, etc.—poems which (leaving aside the question of merit) would have given the book a different aura, a larger and more outward-looking perspective. Absent from *Beyond the Palisade* but present here and there in the notebooks is a certain lack of reverence, an attitude which was to prove so fruitful in Baxter's maturity. In 1944 he might not, perhaps, have made a better book, but he could have produced one equally competent and yet not so pervasively solemn as the one we have. Yet, reading both sets of material, one is convinced that right instinct led to his limiting of focus, refusing the easy light, attaching himself instead to a small group of symbols which grasp, intuitively, a New Zealand still empty of man. . . . To the end of his life and with ever-deepening commitment, Baxter believed in the need for the tribe, attributing the desperate state of society to the destruction of "the stubborn clans" and man's failure to rebuild them. In this respect he anticipated the work and attitudes of Gary Snyder and others. . . . From an early stage his work shows signs of his longing for a positive human community.

Two books, *Blow, Wind of Fruitfulness* (1948) and its successor *The Fallen House* (1953), established Baxter's reputation as a poet. . . . Within a very few years Baxter was to astonish with the lyric elegance and grace of much of his work, so that in later years critics coping with the jagged, spiky poems of the 1960s showed at first a tendency to hark back to the mellifluous sweetness of the early work. (pp. 40-1)

Blow, Wind of Fruitfulness, pervaded by a youthful romanticism, is preoccupied for three-quarters of its length with the idea of death and with man's Promethean struggle amid life's solitariness. . . . Almost every poem deals with death and the grave. . . . From the charnel-house tone a casual reader might gather that here is another poet more than "half in love with easeful death"; but Death is "no barren cycle," rather "A truth as eternal as life is eternal". Sometimes the two attitudes, wallowing in death or incorporating it into the meaning of one's life, seem fused. . . . (pp. 42-3)

"Earth does at length her own sweet brood devour": recognition of this, the struggle to accept and assimilate it, is the chief ground of Baxter's early work. (p. 43)

Blow, Wind of Fruitfulness is, at its center, the locating and clarifying of a personal quest of the soul and, equally, it continues Baxter's discovery of his own voice as poet. . . . As [Allen] Curnow saw it, the older poets [of the country] had turned away from "assertions about New Zealand" in favor of more personal and universal themes. He concludes: "The way in which certain conceptions of his country haunt the background of Mr. Baxter's poetry, having receded from the positive foreground of older poets, encourages the belief that something of continuing effect was achieved by them." For a "tradition" of good poetry not more than a quarter of a century old, this was an important consideration! Baxter more than bore out the implied hope that he would continue to build and strengthen the national poetry. In later years he was to take an antichauvinist position in literary quarrels about New Zealand, but ultimately he was to prove much ampler, as a poet and individual, than both parties to the argument. (pp. 50-1)

The Night Shift (1957) [is] a joint work containing "poems on aspects of love" by Baxter, Charles Doyle, Louis Johnson, and Kendrick Smithyman. . . . Baxter's section, "Songs of the Desert," was described not unfairly by Erik Schwimmer as "a series of loudly intoned approximations," and it does exhibit Baxter's dangerous facility in employing the stock responses of decadent romanticism. Yet, inevitably, even these poems (and it has been said that Baxter's are the weakest in the book) have their moments of powerful perception. . . . (p. 51)

The first phase of Baxter's career may be seen as culminating in the publication of *Poems Unpleasant* (1952), another joint book, this time with Louis Johnson and Anton Vogt. . . .

What Baxter shares with Johnson, here and elsewhere, is a faculty for seeing experience in mythological terms, for perceiving the archetype behind the commonplace. . . .

Baxter's poems, still, are haunted by literary echoes . . . , and he is much preoccupied by, and skillful with, traditional literary forms. More clearly now he perceives the terrifying split between deadening habit and the forgotten "language of the heart." . . . Here again is the lament for the creative energy of the lost, whole, animistic vision. (p. 52)

Baxter was not an intellectually complex poet, but his vision of human experience goes far beyond the merely intellectual, and this is apparent even in his early work. His vision encompasses the child born to darkness, whose fall from innocence is his awakening to death. Without this awareness the child would dwell in the earthly paradise, but it is in his death-discovery that he becomes a man. By definition, man is his own destroyer. In life he can attain a temporary contact with Eden through following his sexual instinct. Through it he creates, but he does so in the knowledge that whatever is created by man must die. However, any one human death is not final and life itself is, in some sense, eternal. With this sense of the eternal, Baxter set out on his later journey, toward eventual fruitfulness. (p. 54)

Throughout *The Fallen House* poem after poem suggests fear of the outside world. For the protagonist entering the world (and the world entering him) becomes more deeply alone. (p. 58)

Poem after poem in *The Fallen House* shows advance on his earlier work, chiefly by increase of what Baxter himself later referred to as "experiential knowledge" which he thought the very basis of poetry. With a few lapses, they are based on detailed recording of concrete experiences. Since Baxter is primarily a maker of parables and perceiver of myths this adherence to the concrete is vitally necessary. He is not a poet of ideas, but of mythologized events. . . . His parable-making and mythologizing methods imply teaching and imply archetypes behind incidents. Concreteness, therefore, is of the essence. Strange and disappointing then that his next work, *Traveller's Litany* (1955), should fall into the twin snares of pastiche and generalization; all the more strange because he had, in the interim, spoken cogently on modern poetry in his MacMillan Brown lectures, published that same year as *The Fire and the Anvil.* (p. 62)

Traveller's Litany expresses Baxter's Marian devotion. . . . In what might well have been a major statement he contrasts Eros . . . and Mary, Mother . . . ; but the sequence rises to no necessary order and, redolent of literary echoes as it is, makes uncomfortable reading as a devotional act. What it does is to bring into somewhat muzzy focus Baxter's sense of the split nature of woman. At the same time he was becoming progressively more conscious of man's split nature. In "Notes Towards an Aesthetic" he sees the split as between Orpheus and Promethus, figure of song and figure of power. . . . "Freedom to do good and evil" worked in Baxter's psyche in those years to make both him and his work appear extremely erratic; but beneath this had begun, it now seems, the slow awakening of an interior harmony. (pp. 62-3)

In Fires of No Return provides a quite coherent and full account of the talents of the young Baxter. Three poems in section 2 collected for the first time are particularly interesting: "Seraphion," "Elegy at the Year's End" and "Lament for Barney Flanagan." Never a proponent of art for its own sake (nor, I believe, of the New Critical dogma that art should be considered without reference to its creator), it is nonetheless possible that as late as 1954 Baxter saw art as the supreme human activity, the artist therefore as privileged. From different angles, in each of the three poems mentioned above is a convergence of life and art. . . . Baxter was much interested in the interconnections between artists' lives and their work. Speaking of Wilde and Villon, he makes the important observation that "their work was a creative recognition of precisely those situations which their vices had helped to create." (p. 66)

For all its brilliant moments, however, the last section of *In Fires of No Return* (the new poems) offers no clear development from earlier work, although a change is astir. Still the engagement with Christianity is not wholly unequivocal; concern for humanity is there, but somehow blurred, and often marginal; also present is continued lament for the lost simplicities of the past. New development is confined largely to the technical level. A new tone is beginning to emerge, which, heard in retrospect, is harsher, stonier, sparser. The rhetorical fullness and richness on display in earlier poems such as "Rocket Show," "The Bay," and even "Elegy at the Year's End" are giving way to a textural spareness evident in the book's title poem, in "Auckland" . . . , and in "At Akitio." Here are the first signs of change which resulted, within a few years, in the gristly directness of *Pig Island Letters,* a directness achieved with no loss of richness. Alongside these signs of what is to come, and making them harder to recognize, are moments of what [J. E.] Weir justly calls baroque rhetoric. The two combined gave some commentators the feeling that Baxter had lost genuine contact with his Muse, but the matter was before too long to become clearer. From this time on, there gradually comes into the foreground Baxter's engagement with . . . his society, which ultimately was to absorb his full attention. (p. 71)

[By the early 1960s] Baxter has arrived at "the middle years" for which are kept the knowledge of man's difficult struggle to find the fragments of his soul and piece them together. Becoming a Catholic convert did not, as he knew it would not, solve that problem but merely brought it more clearly into focus. (pp. 72-3)

Evidence of change begins with the "current" poems of *In Fires of No Return.* If one looks for marked change in the Asian poems of *Howrah Bridge* . . . one will find little obviously new. At first reading, despite their density of local color, they may seem somewhat disappointing, without new preoccupations or particular insights. Baxter's experiences of gruesome poverty in India led him to condemn social systems based on economic values, but for him this is not especially new, as witness such New Zealand pieces as "A Rope for Harry Fat." . . . What is new in the poems is a tone of voice, a sinewy quality which signals the banishment from then on of displays of rhetoric merely for its own sake.

Baxter has been much discussed as a consummate imitator of models. . . . More or less beneficent influences in earlier stages had included Auden and MacNeice, Yeats and Hardy. Even a cursory look at the early work shows that Yeats was on the whole a bad influence, Hardy a good one. . . . All the influences mentioned were formative, but [Lawrence Durrell] a different kind of poet from any of these (and indeed from Baxter himself) now helped him to make a quantum leap in finding his own true voice. (pp. 73-4)

Since Baxter matched a mellifluous and resonant voice with a mental tendency to mellifluence and resonance, [the] astringency learned from Durrell was a great boon and is a likely source of the change, a shift of consciousness toward a sparser, tauter attitude. The better new poems in *Howrah Bridge* . . . manifest the change. . . . (pp. 74-5)

What Baxter felt imprisoned by was man's schizoid condition in our society, that condition which he felt as "Pig Island." . . . [He] speaks of "the great white heart of Pig Island, that wild interior island of the mind," presumably . . . the precious animistic core of experience, which, for him, had ultimate value. . . . Baxter has two "starting-points". One is the remembered childhood paradise, the other that "man is a walking grave." . . . "Pig Island," then, inward and wild, is itself a schizoid conception. First, it is what the *pakeha* has done to Ao-tea-Roa; second, it is both the "tough" life to which man is condemned and the wrestling ground whereon he must fight for salvation, for the transformation of his mirage-laden desert into the green, well-watered garden. (pp. 75-6)

[With *Pig Island Letters,* Baxter] seems to reach an entirely new level of achievement, especially in the title poem. Old faults, shopworn rhetoric and stock response, still linger, but not importantly. Newly evident is a remarkable conjunction of tautness and freedom.

Dominant is the thirteen-part "Pig Island Letters". It must have occurred to Baxter, since he adopted and developed the form, that the sequence is suited to his particular bent of mind, his tendency to return to, and meditate upon, the same few concerns. Technically influenced both by Lawrence Durrell and Robert Lowell, *Pig Island Letters* is distinctively Baxter's and is, besides, free of the formal stiffness and artificiality of his youthful "Cressida" and the pastiche mauve dolors of *Traveller's Litany.* Most eloquently, it is a weighing and judging born of "experiential knowledge." (p. 76)

By the end of his life Baxter clearly felt that there was some special grace (I mean the term, if I may, somewhere between its aesthetic and religious connotations, sharing in both, not fully committed to either)—some special grace in failure and destitution. (p. 80)

Much of the feeling of *Pig Island Letters* centers on lack of love, on frustrated lives. (p. 82)

The sense of inner destitution continues growing. . . . Present also, as it is throughout Baxter's later work, (in this case in "East Coast Journey") is an explicit death-wish, whose primary cause is loss of the youthful vivid sense of nature ("Waipatiki Beach"), so that one has arrived at *Nada,* the cold hub, "The absolute unmoving hub," from which the only refuge is in the hollow listening place. . . . (p. 83)

The Man on the Horse is easy to fault as a single work. Apart from the strong force of its author's personality, it has no unity. Rather is it a source book, full of rich insight and observation, composed typically with a deceptively casual air. Outside his poems, it is our prime firsthand document on "Baxter the poet," its *ad hoc* presentation being characteristic of the man and his sense of the purpose of poetry as expression of "experiential knowledge." (p. 85)

Before publication of the rather odd "selected poems," *The Rock Woman* in 1969, *The Lion Skin,* a group of eleven short poems, was issued. . . . Most of the poems deal with the marital relationship, and do so in a discursive way which has the air of self-parody. Once again, as in the cases of *Traveller's Litany* and *The Night Shift,* Baxter had put together as a single work a highly unsatisfactory batch of poems. Looking over the span of his career one discerns an undulating pattern, with periods which suggest a diminished alertness. Perhaps this accounts for the effect of *The Rock Woman,* a disappointing retrospective selection of the work of a quarter of a century. (p. 87)

From very early in his career, Baxter believed that the link between artist and society is close, and necessary. He suggested that "the analogy between the processes of art and the ritual of tribal magic is an exact one. Both enable catharsis by discovering shape in history, thus relieving the isolation of the individual." . . . He saw the artist as "a cell of good living in a corrupt society." . . . (p. 88)

Much of his work suggests that his human world is experienced as chaos, for which his repeated image is "the lion's den"—thus, in *Pig Island Letters* a poem is "A plank laid over the lion's den." Man's struggle is to reduce chaos to life-giving order, though Baxter does not finally make clear whether, as he sees it, the individual imposes order or simply discovers an order already inherent in nature. Whatever the case, he began by seeing poetry both as the means of individuation and the expression of the journey toward individuation.

A poet of varied moods, modes, and approaches, Baxter by and large is subjective, expressionist; but he is not merely confessional, even though at one stage in his career he admired, and learned from, Robert Lowell. His seminal early reading of Jung confirmed his sense that day-to-day experience has much more than its surface significance, hence his lifelong habit of parable-making and his declaration that consciousness itself can only assimilate "the crises, violations and reconciliations of the spiritual life in mythical form." . . . He is not "confessional" if only because he sees himself as typical or paradigmatic as well as individual. In some part, too, his mythologizing is exploratory, an attempt to locate and clarify his own archetypes.

Another part is his effort to locate himself in the world. When still very young, he concluded that in searching for the true self, the discovery of a home in nature, identification with a place and a past are vitally necessary. (pp. 88-9)

Much of his first book, *Beyond the Palisade,* concerns the natural New Zealand environment, the *pakeha* ancestors failing to make a home there, the land remaining a "cold threshold land" still overshadowed by "the weight of an earlier and prehistoric isolation." Brooding Nature is felt as indifferent or hostile, ground of man's suffering and defeat. This passive, oppressive sense of it continues in *Blow, Wind of Fruitfulness,* but the landscape is more peopled and there are more localized, specifically human experiences. By 1951 Baxter felt clearly that animism is essential to the artist's view of the world, his greatest contribution being the linking of "submerged animism with our immediate affairs." A few years later, in *The Fire and the Anvil,* he declared it the poet's task to lay bare "the animistic pattern which underlies civilized activity." . . .

Animism he took to be characteristic of the child and the primitive, and he believed that poetry's vital force derived from rediscovering and revaluing childhood experience, which was at one with nature in "the paradise of childhood," Eden, the lost garden. In contrast, New Zealand's natural environment was experienced by the *pakeha* intruder as remote, impersonal, indifferent, an obstacle to his material possession of the land. (p. 90)

As Baxter sees it, there are two very different kinds of adult in modern society. These are *natural man* and *bourgeois man,* and each is incomplete. . . .

Natural man and bourgeois man is each a "half-man," and "the poet as family man" experiences a double portion of Original Sin, for he is conscious of his participation in each half and finds himself involved in a hopeless struggle to integrate the two, though he is instinctively nearer to natural man. . . . (p. 91)

Social criticism began to occupy a central place in Baxter's poetry in the mid-1950s; from that time on he employed the poem as a weapon in dealing with a variety of social problems. (p. 93)

Some of the young Baxter's poems evoke the particular characteristics of New Zealand: mobs of sheep, beer-drinking, "the earth-wave breaking / to the plough." . . . Such poems [as "Farmhand" and "Elegy for an Unknown Soldier"] capture neatly enough the innocence of a young man who does not know himself, scion of a land spiritually and historically impoverished and yet obscurely felt to be his, and behind this the double inarticulateness, of the man and of the land itself. Baxter never ceased, in some measure and in some part of himself, to share these pieties; but it was not his, nor his hero's, fate to remain "effortless and strong." . . . What he discovered he began to discover early and it haunted him. At first intermittent, these were early glimpses of the desperate absence of, and desperate need for, *agape*—a lack which he felt was importantly at the center of his own experience and that of his society. (pp. 100-01)

From start to finish Baxter's work is permeated with biblical allusion. Many of the references to Adam tend to portray him as the type-figure of unfallen man, content yet in Eden, to whose company one prays to return. . . . (p. 106)

That curious small collection *The Lion Skin* takes the lion's death as its governing metaphor, with the protagonist as Samson. Although most of the poems here concern marriage, the group opens and closes on the theme of drunkenness, and the lion skin may be seen as the whole urban way of life. (p. 108)

Examining the various facets of the Baxter "hero" is, in a sense, a way of approaching his themes and a way of recognizing that man is at the center of every one of them. As we have seen, he was conscious of the "traditional" New Zealand figure of "man alone" which he discusses at some length in *The Fire and the Anvil.* Typically he sees the figure as hobo or social outcast, who is sensitive to the need for "single vision," unifying love, and who is driven by that sensitivity, his isolation forced upon him by his inability to respond to pressure to conform socially. "Man alone" is the artist *sans* artistic capacities, and the artist, because he has made the same discoveries about the crudity of social stereotypes, will sympathize with the "man alone." (pp. 110-11)

Perhaps the real heroes, the real center, of Baxter's work are the destitute. . . . Contemporary society, he felt, is joined by the mere illusion of togetherness, but the necessary condition for struggle toward truth is solitude without separation. (pp. 111-12)

A tribesman cut off from his tribe by a peculiar and special gap, [Baxter's poet-hero] is the *revealer* of what lies under the surface, or one who discovers in his cage of mirrors facets of the unexpected and lays bare human depths for all to see.

His type of the poet-hero is Burns. . . . Burns, for Baxter, was the poet as natural man, or, rather, in whose consciousness natural man fought hard to hold off the strait-jacket of respectable burgherdom. Not conformity to social mores, not being a "concerned citizen" offering his contribution to maintenance of the status quo, but recognizing the true nature of his own selfhood and the selfhoods of others . . . this spirit governs the whole presentation of "The Man On the Horse," his fine exegesis of "Tam O'Shanter" and apologia for the life and work of Burns.

Nevertheless he came to feel that poets must "learn to live like other men," bridging the gap, waiting for the "moment of art" which "can never stay." . . . (pp. 113-14)

References throughout his work to friends . . . show how great a value Baxter placed on friendship. Eventually this was to grow for him into the central heroic quality *aroha*—the power of love, the capacity to forget self and put all the force of one's being into a concern for "Thou." . . .

A sense of loss . . . is at the core of Baxter, and, in consequence, his hero is a seeker, be it for "The wild lost city of a mother's love," "the bay that never was," or the wholeness all too briefly glimpsed in childhood. From this lost "single vision" the human being is apparently condemned to traverse the "black swamp" of adolescence, to survive the death of "the first Adam" in himself, and to mourn for his "lost estate." Somewhere within himself the hero carries a vision of fullness and this vision is an element in his very destitution. . . . (p. 115)

Whereas in his early work Baxter lamented man's loss of the capacity to float untutored on the waters of Chaos, later an acceptance of that loss and a search for comradeship in loss clearly became his protagonist's goals. Beyond that, in the late work, is the acceptance of, indeed the looking for, death. In Freudian terms the early longing for lost childhood and the late willingness for death derive ultimately from the same source—the tendency of all living things to return to an inorganic state. From *Pig Island Letters* onward Baxter seems to hold that, in his journey, the individual must learn to accept the reality of his own personal death. (p. 116)

Just as Baxter distinguished between natural man and bourgeois man, he perceived a comparable division in woman. The line of division is not as clear, however. . . . [In] addition to his seeming antithesis between Venus (or Delilah) and Mary, there are traces of the idealized Beatrice and her antithesis, living metamorphoses of the "kitchen god." (p. 118)

Baxter's whole view of woman was traditionalist. Sometimes Pauline, more often he held the Augustinian attitude that, "Through a woman we were sent to destruction; through a woman salvation was sent to us." (p. 123)

[For] Baxter both the not-self and the subconscious were female, the first both beguiling and threatening, the second "protective and maternal," both merging in the projected mother-figures of his poems. This digression on the mother, however, would be incomplete were we not to note that the human mother-figure eventually gives way to Gea, the Earth Mother, in whom are the source and order of creation. (p. 125)

Although Baxter's ultimate devotion was professedly to Mary, . . . he recognized the force, the inevitability, and even the positive value of Venus. For full humanity, it seems, both the Baudelairian and Christian levels of love need to be experienced. (p. 133)

Of the twenty-odd [plays Baxter] wrote . . . few, if any, are as accomplished as his best poetry. (p. 134)

James Bertram offers a succinct summary of observations Baxter made to a postperformance discussion group: "He said that his central purpose was psychological, that he had intended to present compulsive characters acting compulsively; that he preferred Strindberg to O'Casey; and that Aristotle was out of date." . . . [He] changed his mind eventually about Aristotle . . . ; but the shift, according to his explanation of it in a lecture, was toward subjectivity: unity of action means "a coherent myth" expressed in terms of local knowledge and experience; unity of time is the lifespan, the "permanent now" of Everyman; unity of place is the stage itself, a little universe whereon the members of the audience project "the communal drama of their own minds." By no means a faithful interpretation of the Aristotelian unities, these definitions offer useful enough guidelines to Baxter's drama.

Very often one has the impression that it is he, the playwright, who is the "projector." The focusing consciousness of his first play, *Jack Winter's Dream,* is an externalized counterpart of himself in the form of a narrator, a mechanism which . . . he developed along lines established by Dylan Thomas in *Under Milkwood.* Thomas' influence combined with that of Synge to produce a Baxter variant of pseudo-Celtic prose-poetry. . . . (p. 135)

Over the years, the use of language in drama continued to be a preoccupation of Baxter's. . . .

[Although he never succeeded in creating fully authentic stage dialogue,] few New Zealanders can have been more conscious of the colloquial speech of their countrymen. Of a piece with his own involvements, he was particularly aware of the idiom of what he sometimes called "pub conversation." . . . In writing dialogue Baxter seemed to feel easiest with an idiom which was basically proletarian, but heightened by a rich sense of poetry. (p. 136)

As a young writer [Baxter] was ridden and carried away by rhetoric, but in [his] late works, at his best, he has more control over the functional use of language. In *The Temptations of Oedipus,* words, language, have become a theme. (p. 137)

[Baxter's] first play was a radio play, and this demanded a specific approach. He told the *Listener,* "In a radio play . . . all those things that would otherwise, on the stage, be visual—gesture, setting and appearance of actors—must find emotional equivalents in the spoken word. That is why the poetic prose method is very suitable." Obviously, it was innately Baxter's notion that the equivalent had to be "emotional." . . . Baxter was well aware of the subjectivity of his plays, the likelihood that many of his characters emerged, horned or hornless, from what he once called his "menagerie of interior selves." . . . [He] believed that the participation of actors, playwright, and audience, all three, is subjective. (pp. 137-38)

All that has been said thus far may suggest some weaknesses of Baxter's technique. One is a tendency (confined largely, but not entirely, to the earlier plays) toward "poeticality"; another is a fault attributable to his central view of literature, that it affects men's conduct, or ideally should do so—he is at times inclined to be discursive. A countervailing tendency is for the action, at times, to be perfunctory. (p. 139)

[Hal] Smith makes a parallel between Baxter's drama and the poetic drama of Lorca, suggesting that both sacrifice possible psychological depth in their characters to the use of characters as symbols. In this respect, the strength Baxter's poetry undoubtedly gained from his mythologizing and from a life-giving consciousness of the "mythical substratum" available in Greek myths and legends proves to be a weakness in the plays, for it leads to a predetermined (and consequently static) structure. (p. 140)

The most important influences on Baxter's playwriting . . . were the two French dramatists Sartre and Giraudoux and the classical Greek dramas. . . . [Sartre's] *The Flies* and Giraudoux's *Tiger at the Gates* were [Baxter's] "springboard" in adapting from the original sources for his Greek plays (*Mr O'Dwyer's Dancing Party, The Sore-Footed Man, The Bureaucrat,* and *The Temptations of Oedipus*), because he had realized the dangers of attempting direct translation. . . . From Giraudoux in particular, a master of parallel and antithetical dialogue, he learned the technique of having characters together onstage, each expressing himself, as it were, in a different key, failing to communicate because each was narcissistically confined in his own world.

When we turn to the substance of Baxter's plays, particularly his themes, we find ourselves on familiar, perhaps richer, ground. A list may make this clear: free will, death, religion, drunkenness, commitment, destitution, words, love, materialism, community, the lost garden, bureaucracy, marriage, existentialism. Perhaps the center of that ground is "the enigma of human freedom". (pp. 142-43)

[The] question of freedom is complex, and the condition is composed of both commitment and detachment. Perhaps for this reason *The Temptation of Oedipus* seems the most resonant of all Baxter's plays, for in it Oedipus is shown as, first, "condemned" to destitution, he has *fallen.* What the play comes down to, though, is an exploration of his discovery of the "freedom" inherent in suffering. (p. 144)

Love and the various forms of lack-love, anti-love and vacuity are also central themes in Baxter's drama, though one of its thematic weaknesses is that the negative seems always much the more dominant. (pp. 144-45)

Human bafflement and inconsistency are integral to *The Temptations of Oedipus,* as also is a critique of materialism. Oedipus is torn between kingship and brotherhood; Ismene confuses *eros* and *agape.* Part of the dire message is that the seekers after wholeness dwell in confusion, whereas the hunters for material power are clearheaded. . . .

[Religion] is a major theme in Baxter's plays. (p. 146)

Having rejected sociological and "realistic" forms of drama, Baxter eventually cleaved to another myth-form, the Christian liturgy. In a beautiful image in his introduction he describes *The Band Rotunda* (a location reminiscent of altar and tabernacle) as formally choral and episodic. (p. 147)

[The] focus of drama, for Baxter, always comes back to the nature of selfhood, which is why he considers all drama "religious," for he felt that all self-projections were manifestations of the gods within, a showing forth from "the incurable pantheism of the human soul," and at the same time from the abyss or the void. . . . It is at the hollow center that the individual must discover himself. Baxter's attempts to project that center onto a theater stage are notable, at their best, for a somber poetry, a probing vigor, and genuine compassion. (p. 148)

[Baxter] had a double view of nature. As he put it in "Literature and Belief": "The whole visible creation, which we are bound to believe is the work of His Hands . . . shows magnificent, delicate and exquisite art in every detail." . . . Alongside this he continued in a fatalistic view of human experience: the world we are presented with (or, at least, perceive) is Chaos manifest, once we have left "the green inn." Amid that chaos Jesus and Mary are consolation. (p. 149)

Christian feeling permeates the texture of the new poems in *Howrah Bridge and Other Poems,* together with the view of human experience implied in the title of "Ballad of Calvary Street." What is endured in Calvary Street now begins to acquire possible positive value, that of personal destitution, of humans enduring the *"fire / Where affliction makes them whole."* . . . Passive resignation is more dangerous than the self-flagellation of a St. Simeon Stylites. The maxim Baxter puts in the peddler's mouth in "The Tempters," *"Thirst, obey, endure,"* speaks for more than mere passivity.

Again we arrive at the crucial *Pig Island Letters,* the whole framework of which is religious, beginning from a sense of human circumscription. The human universe is "God's body blazing on damnation's tree," and the Christian life is seen in each case as taking form from Christ's Passion. (pp. 151-52)

In *Jerusalem Sonnets* (1970) [Baxter] established the serviceable two-line unrhyming stanza which became the chief medium of his Jerusalem poems, the line itself at core a pentameter shaken loose of formal restriction. . . . The work's strength is certainly not in "making it new," and Baxter here further confines (and defines) his scope by adhering to the fourteen-line sonnet length, even though otherwise ignoring the traditional form. If he is not "masturbating his ego" (in a phrase of Simpson's) he is very much at the center of the sequence, what he does and what he suffers. But there is a new kind of integrity. Rhetoric has been burned off, and the simplistic has become simplicity. As Murray Edmond justly says, "by the time of the *Jerusalem Sonnets* Baxter didn't give a damn about his style as he had in the past. The mask of style—the accepted notion of what poetry is—has been dropped to reveal the man himself, guileless." . . .

No peak moments of high rhetoric grace these thirty-nine sonnets. What matters is what Baxter is thinking about and, equally, how: his devotion to the Lord (a Christian Lord, but Maori in His names: *Te Atua*—God, *Te Ariki*—Christ . . .). (p. 155)

The sequence has unobtrusive shape, beginning with the protagonist's sense of his own suffering. . . . His concerns are poverty of self, seeking comfort in God, its elusiveness in this life, but the rare moment always possible of love shared. (p. 156)

The four sonnets which close the sequence rise to a remarkable pitch of eloquence, at once controlled and free. (p. 157)

[An] immensity of judgment, a lifetime's, is in the texture of these poems. Here Baxter's notable rhetoric is completely in service to the conviction of his whole experience; yet he is no propagandist, no proselytizer. Clearly, graced with moments of high simple beauty, the sequence gives an account of his spiritual struggles and his vision of a tribe. For all the suffering which permeates the work, we witness in it the overt beginnings of a profound metamorphosis.

In *Jerusalem Daybook* (1971) Baxter again used his newfound "sonnet" form but in conjunction with other verse-forms and heavily interspersed with prose. (p. 158)

The whole book is pervaded by the spirit of humility, poverty (destitution), and acceptance. If we are to remain within our customary categories, it is perhaps more a religious work than a work of literature. Interspersed with poems, the prose has no rhetorical pretensions and no particular distinction, unless directness and clarity be so regarded. The matter of it derives from Baxter's lifelong concerns, here dealt with in a spirit of culmination. (p. 159)

Two-thirds of *Autumn Testament* (1972) is taken up with the title poem, which otherwise resembles *Jerusalem Daybook* in being a mixture of prose and poetry. (p. 163)

"Autumn Testament" (the title poem) is a rambling poetic and meditative journal, without particularly striking coherence as a piece of writing, but rather held together by the spirit of the man who wrote it. A recurring concern, especially in the early sections, is with the need for food, a perhaps not unconscious parallel with the need for spiritual sustenance. (p. 164)

His ultimate message (and Baxter's late work is undeniably a message) is simple enough, namely, that "Fear is the only enemy" (sonnet 46). Fear of the natural self has, all along, been root cause of the puritanism Baxter fought.

The closing sonnet of this fine sequence (sonnet 48) is intensely interesting in relation to Baxter's whole career. It is a total acceptance of all the negative elements in himself and in life. The spider, tantric goddess, is Spiderwitch, the temptress, in profounder form—a manifestation of the Terrible Mother, or Great Mother. . . . In his concluding lines Baxter seems to merge this creature with the judging God . . . , but the daunting image is offset by the prayer and by the tone of acceptance which pervades the whole latter part of the poem. (pp. 166-67)

Because, taken together, the Jerusalem writings constitute Baxter's greatest literary achievement, it is tempting to see them as climactic. But it is both to misunderstand and undervalue them if we consider them merely as pieces of literature and merely as a culmination. As Murray Edmond noted, the barriers of mode broke down—between prose and poem, between letter and diary, essay and sermon, between mere writing and life itself. Not so much an "adjunct" (Edmond's term), these writings are an integral part of a whole life, one which lived out its early aim, to be "a cell of good living in a corrupt society." (p. 168)

Charles Doyle, in his James K. Baxter *(copyright © 1976 by G. K. Hall & Co.; reprinted with the permission of Twayne Publishers, A Division of G. K. Hall & Co., Boston), Twayne, 1976, 189 p.*

* * *

BEAUVOIR, Simone de 1908-

French novelist, essayist, playwright, autobiographer, and proponent of existentialist philosophy, Beauvoir was a longtime associate of Jean-Paul Sartre. In her novels Beauvoir is concerned with explicating her philosophy, as in, for example, *The Mandarins,* which explores the problem of commitment and action among French intellectuals following the Second World War. She is the author of the immensely influential *The Second Sex.* (See also *CLC,* Vols. 1, 2, 4, 8, and *Contemporary Authors,* Vols. 9-12, rev. ed.)

D. J. ENRIGHT

Scandalized by the neglect into which [the Marquis de Sade] has fallen, yet repudiating the obvious topsy-turvy whereby he has been deified, [Mme de Beauvoir asks in her *The Marquis de Sade*] that he be regarded as a man and a writer. Yet it is not as author nor as sexual pervert that he interests her, but by his efforts to justify his perversions, to 'erect his tastes into principles'. 'He dreamed of an ideal society from which his special tastes would not exclude him.' . . .

Mme de Beauvoir tells us that 'eroticism appears in Sade as a mode of communication, the only valid one' between persons. Since she then admits that 'every time we side with a child whose throat has been slit by a sex-maniac, we take a stand against him', it is possible that she is using the word 'communication' in some highly paradoxical sense reserved to philosophically-trained intellectuals. For the rest of us, Sade's message on this point might seem to come to, F . . . you, Jack (or Jill), I'm all right. . . .

For Mme de Beauvoir, Sade's value, his contemporary importance, lies in the fact that 'he chose cruelty rather than indifference'. His sincerity encourages her to hail him as 'a great moralist'. The aptest comment is M. de Bressac's casual remark to his servant, which I quote from memory: 'Now, Joseph, you b . . . Justine, and then we shall feed her to the dogs.' Mme de Beauvoir shares one of her protégé's characteristics: humourlessness. . . .

'Must we burn Sade?' asks Mme de Beauvoir. Now that you mention it, why not? He teaches us little about human nature which we couldn't gather from a few minutes of honest introspection. But maybe we can learn something more useful from Mme de Beauvoir's solemn excogitations, something about our scornful reluctance to face the realities of our selves and of others' selves, and our preferred contemplation of modish dummies, those highbrow status symbols, ourselves as heroic monsters or grand victims, our inflation or reduction of ourselves and others to ingeniously explicated strip-cartoons, as unreal as the wicked Juliette and as empty of life as the virtuous Justine.

D. J. Enright, "Books in General: 'Le Marquis de Sade'," in New Statesman *(© 1963 The Statesman & Nation Publishing Co. Ltd.), Vol. LXV, No. 1662, January 18, 1963, p. 82.*

NADINE GORDIMER

Entertained, appalled (once or twice), irritated (occasionally), enthralled (often), amused (in places where this was not the author's intention), moved and, above all, compelled to stay with her to the last page, I stand back from [*Force of Circumstance*] and, for me, this life gives purchase most clearly in three aspects and in this order: the experience of being French during the Algerian war; the position of the Leftist outside the Communist Party; woman as intellectual. Here is Simone de Beauvoir.

Being female was a precondition, yet, in order of importance, I put it third in the forces that have shaped her life because she has dealt with it, in the particular context of that life, successfully—even triumphantly—and in this last volume [of Simone de Beauvoir's three-volume autobiography] it crops up more in the light of reflection on these triumphs than in the glare of battle enjoined. (p. 73)

[Simone de Beauvoir] has constantly been accused of wearing [Sartre's] opinions. She gives quite a lot of space to refuting this. If, as she seems to think, the allegation comes from the old anti-feminist guard, why grant it so much attention? They have long since lost the power to 'draw' her when they touch upon other aspects of her life. If, on the other hand, she is accused without prejudice, as an intellectual, of being unduly under the influence of the thought of another, and one takes her refutation in this context, fair enough. We can accept that we cannot know the extent to which these two very different . . . minds have interacted; the trouble is that her autobiography provides circumstantial evidence. . . . Throughout her book, Simone de Beauvoir has an irritating habit of writing 'we thought', when surely, since this is her own story she is telling, her own development, however closely entwined with another's, that she is describing, she ought to be writing 'I thought'. (pp. 74-5)

> It was not of my own free will . . . that I allowed the war in Algeria to invade my thoughts, my sleep, my every mood.

Almost exactly halfway through *Force of Circumstance* this invasion begins. By the time the last page is reached, it has established itself as the definitive experience of the writer's life. It is a destruction, not a culmination; and that is the real reason why this woman, who can say 'when I look back over the past, there is no-one I envy' at the same time ends her book in despair. (p. 75)

'. . . the horror my (the middle) class inspires in me has been brought to white heat by the Algerian war': it was not that her experience of that war went deeper than her politics, but that her political convictions found their depth in her experience of that war.

Other things central to her being were put to the test by the same event—love of country, even lovove of life. The first did not survive; the second seems damaged beyond healing. All through the last half of this volume the record of destruction grows. (p. 76)

As a testament of the shaking of the foundations of individual existence . . . , this autobiography has no rival I have read. Simone de Beauvoir's sorrowful sense of disgust with life is surely not so much the inability to accept an ageing body, as the other kind of self-loathing that comes from having to accept that for years one has no longer been able to bear one's fellow citizens. Let this stand against the judgment of some French critics that the sorrow is the confession of the failure of a philosophy, and against the world's jealous insistence that a woman so brilliant, celebrated, and (by now) even rich, *ought* to arrive at a different reckoning. (p. 77)

Nadine Gordimer, "Taking into Account," in London Magazine *(© London Magazine 1966), Vol. 5, No. 10, January, 1966, pp. 73-7.*

V. S. PRITCHETT

In this short, painful and honest book [*A Very Easy Death*], Simone de Beauvoir describes the death of her mother from cancer, in some clinical detail, and the changing emotions the daughters felt. She also attempts, as a rationalist—who saw with surprise her conventionally pious mother indifferent to the consolations of religion—to think again about a subject that none of us now cares to think about. . . .

It was what is called 'an easy death'; but the death in her mother's face was joined to the violent spirit of rebellion: 'she asserted the value of each instant.' The sight made Simone de Beauvoir hate the clichés by which we defend ourselves against old age and dying. She saw 'the reassuring curtain of everyday triviality' ripped away. Her conclusion was that if we must yield, we cannot be acquiescent:

> There is no such thing as a natural death, nothing that happens to a man is ever natural, since his presence calls the world into question. All men must die; but for every man his death is an accident and, even if he knows and consents to it, an unjustifiable violation.

The literature of resignation is generally more eloquent than Simone de Beauvoir's book is, but her honesty and her observation of feeling and circumstance have their own value, they arrest the evasions of the contemporary conscience.

V. S. Pritchett, "Unholy Dying," in New Statesman (© *1966 The Statesman & Nation Publishing Co. Ltd.), Vol. 71, No. 1831, April 15, 1966, p. 540.*

ERICA HARTH

[One] of the principal questions of *Les Mandarins* is whether or not literature is possible for the politically committed writer. (pp. 177-78)

[It] was Simone de Beauvoir who discovered alienation as the specific anguish of the French writer during the years of the Algerian Revolution. As the number of massacres and tortures mounted in the mid-fifties, she was to experience for the first time the sense of being an exile in one's own land. . . . (p. 178)

The question of what possibilities are open to the writer . . . before the advent of a society in permanent revolution, is . . . explored by Simone de Beauvoir in *Les Mandarins*. Reflecting the increasing sense of loss and isolation felt by the intellectual left as the post-war years slipped into the Cold War era, her novel strikes a note of cynicism. . . . Perhaps the most somber moment of the book occurs when the two writers, Henri and Dubreuilh, confront together the decay of their own intellectual and political integrity in the face of a morally bankrupt society. Henri's surprising confession to Dubreuilh of the false testimony he bore in favor of his girlfriend, who had indulged in sexual fraternization with a German during the war, and Dubreuilh's even more surprising casual acceptance of it leave the reader with a shocked hopelessness: if a society reaches a certain degree of political sloth and corruption, there may no longer exist a "real" much less a "virtual" public, and the writer may indeed have no role to play at all. (p. 179)

We find in *Les Mandarins* . . . a whole spectrum of attitudes toward literature. On one end is Dubreuilh, with his desire to replace literature by politics, whose world had fallen apart at the Liberation, when the political and intellectual realms began to diverge. Not knowing how to deal with the new situation, he has decided that any book he would write would be either "harmful" or "insignificant." On the other end we find the irremediably bourgeois Lambert, who, although he too is having trouble in writing, would ultimately not reject an "insignificant" literature redeemed by style. . . . In the middle is Henri, who oscillates between Dubreuilh's pessimism and his own genuine enthusiasm for the idea of writing another novel. Interestingly enough it is Dubreuilh who encourages Henri to continue writing novels, as if he were attempting vicariously to revive his own interest. He is also concerned with the political consequences of possible paths for literature of the left. On the one hand he cautions Henri against a literature of pure propaganda; on the other, he voices fear that if the left fails to produce, literature of the right will eclipse it. The esthetic he proposes seems to approach Sartre's idea of literature as a "recuperation of the world." The fictional universe is at once alive, rich, and modifiable. . . . (p. 180)

It would seem that Simone de Beauvoir continued this debate with herself, for we find toward the end of the third volume of her memoirs a particularly embittered reflection on the impasse reached by French literature since the end of World War II. Worn out by the political and moral turmoil of the Algerian war, she states that literature—and especially that of her own country—provided her then with nothing. . . . [How] can the novel be saved from "insignificance" without resorting to the stratagems of a Lambert or of the *nouveau roman*?

The answer to a large extent depends on the experience and utilization of alienation by the writer. (pp. 180-81)

Simone de Beauvoir, who came of political age after the war, experienced alienation predominantly as negativity, contestation by a minority, with whom she did feel solidarity, of the power of the collectivity. She may have experienced briefly, at the Liberation, [a] positive sense of being French. But as she was to view the oppressive force during the Algerian war period as coming from *within* the collectivity itself, she was to feel with growing regret how deeply she was *not* French. Because the solidarity of the left began to crumble almost immediately after the Second World War, Sartre's vision of the "public" was progressively undermined, and his and Simone de Beauvoir's increasingly bleak views on literature converged. Sartre's concept of a committed literature is based on the assumption that the real and virtual publics exist. If they are found wanting, does the whole theory collapse? Not necessarily, but the question becomes one of priorities. The public must then be created, and the road to realization of this goal would seem to be political, not literary. The overwhelming vote cast for de Gaulle in the 1958 referendum served only to confirm for Sartre and Simone de Beauvoir the urgent necessity of according priority to political writing and activity. (p. 181)

Erica Harth, "The Creative Alienation of the Writer: Sartre, Camus and Simone de Beauvoir," in MOSAIC: A Journal for the Comparative Study of Literature and Ideas *(copyright © 1975 by the University of Manitoba Press; acknowledgment of previous publication is herewith made), Vol. VIII, No. 3 (Spring, 1975), pp. 177-86.**

IRÈNE M. PAGÈS

Les Belles Images, "The Pretty Pictures": the title is ironic. It tells us that Simone de Beauvoir intends her novel to be a criticism of idealism. Less obviously, it refers to a Sartrian conception of the image which we need to understand if we are to grasp the full significance of the novel. The "pretty pictures" from which it takes its title refer not to the mental images of classical psychology but to an "attitude of absence" or a flight from everyday existence. The narrative technique used in this novel seems particularly adapted to its subject, which is the *séparation* made by the narrator's consciousness between the real and the imaginary. The language plays on metaphors dealing with various forms of pictures: posters, reflections in mirrors, television screens, photographs, films, kaleidoscopes, frescoes. More interesting still is the fact that not only is the narrator's own speech such as to disintegrate the "pretty pictures" which, in her immediate surroundings, take the place of reality, but it also makes what is real insubstantial, it brings about a *désubstantification* of the real.

In this book it is no longer a question, as in the earlier novels of Simone de Beauvoir, *Les Mandarins,* for example, of bringing a heroine to an awareness of the emptiness of her existence and of her separation from the apparently justified existence of others. On the contrary, now it is in the lives of her relatives that the narrator and leading character, Laurence, has to discover emptiness and unauthenticity. More exactly, she is led to realize the "unreality" of the reality around her. This demands of her a sense of the true and the false, a sense which cannot come to her from any rational evidence.

By giving her protagonist a profession which deals in illusion and the bending of the truth, Simone de Beauvoir has solved the problem she has set herself: she makes her heroine a publicity editor in an advertising firm. As a slogan-writer, Laurence at least knows what is meant by deception and falsehood. . . . [By] making her heroine professionally concerned with the pursuit of the false, the author has instilled in her a need for the true, a need which exists in all of us, but which is usually only latent. Thus, what is particular about Laurence is that she feels in a more continuous and intense way what most human beings feel only in rare moments of awareness.

Everything in the novel derives from Laurence's inner experience. She comes to perceive what is "unreal" in the way other people talk and behave around her only because she senses the existence of a reality from which she herself is cut off. The few signs which she perceives of this reality make her aware of it. In existentialist terms, the existence and the monologue of Laurence are filled with an "absent presence". Still, if everything in *Les Belles Images* starts from an inner experience and is summed up by it, nevertheless everything takes place through events and through characters, and a background of historical reality is woven into the novel by means of dialogue. But the literary interest of the book obviously lies in Laurence's inner crisis rather than in the portrayal of the background against which this drama takes place. It is a drama of moral significance, and Simone de Beauvoir has chosen for it a narrative technique—extended monologue—that is perfectly adapted to her purpose. (pp. 133-34)

It is the function of Laurence's monologue to reflect on the words and behaviour of others, and then to strip these words and this behaviour of the meaning they have in the existence of others. Laurence has been assigned a unique experience: that of emptying existence—not her own, exclusively, but also the common existence in which she takes part—of its so-called reality, and, on the other hand, to live in another reality quite remote from her immediate surroundings. (p. 134)

Laurence takes refuge in that distant reality represented for her by the poster of a starving child of the Third World, by reports read in the papers or seen on television. And it is against this background of images of the suffering of the world—war, famine, exile, torture—that she sees for what it is the reality of the lives of those around her. . . . All these existences have something in common. They do nothing but *se vivrè,* live for themselves. All these characters, each in his own way (even the father, ever in pursuit of pictures of the past), have built up for themselves their own picture of the world, in which they find harmony and peace. These are the "refuge worlds" which make Laurence sick, give her *la nausée.* All escape into imaginary worlds. (p. 135)

In the monologue of *Les Belles Images,* as in the "subconversations" which form the monologue of [Nathalie] Sarraute's novels, a verbal alchemy takes place: reality becomes words, words become reality. (p. 136)

No spatial perspective whatsoever unites the entire thing; we are confronted with a construction which makes discourse its organizing principle, i.e., a thought which, in its own way, under our eyes rearranges matters observed: we thus deal with a *pensée en action,* in the present, with an existence which is unravelling and telling itself, and not with the reconstitution of a story, in the past. (pp. 137-38)

As to the punctuation, we note that words of others are given between quotation marks and that the questions, exclamations and thoughts of the narrator herself are separated from her monologue either by hyphens, or else by parentheses.

Why hyphens here, parentheses elsewhere, when we are dealing with the thoughts of one and the same person? Why quotation marks to report the thoughts of others, parentheses and hyphens only for the thoughts of Laurence? It becomes evident that this punctuation has a particular significance. We notice that what is important here is the way in which outside concrete reality can be either negated or affirmed, according to the level to which punctuation assigns it within the story. . . . Generally speaking, the effect of this *séparation* is to make us perceive the moments during which Laurence "empties" the existence of the others of all reality. . . .

Punctuation replaces here the reasoning within the traditional novel. (p. 138)

[The] "objectification" by Laurence of everything that surrounds her, including human beings, makes her, in our eyes and right from the beginning, superior to the others. And, even though we refuse to acknowledge the nuance of irony in Laurence's quotation marks, even though we refuse to see in them the least value judgment, we are forced to admit that Laurence sees in the others what they themselves do not see. . . .

The way in which Laurence looks at the others tends to establish a clear-cut difference between her existence and theirs. The others seem to exist only through a close relationship with objects. They are consumers attached to the material world. To use Sartrian terminology, the protagonists seem to confuse "to be" with "to have", "to appear" with "to exist." Which is to say that their existence can only be defined through the relationships they have with objects as formed by a vision of life that they have borrowed from de luxe magazines such as *Votre Maison* or *Plaisir de France*. . . . (p. 139)

Les Belles Images shows a distinct advance over the earlier novels of Simone de Beauvoir. Shorter and less massive than the others, this apparently banal story is told in a carefully constructed style in which everything is centred on the picture, *l'image.* This technique, incidentally, is in itself a criticism of the materialism of our age, enslaved as it is to pictures and publicity. Here, the political and social reality of the world today is, contrary to appearance, more than ever before our eyes. It is represented in the form of posters or images on a television screen, or it obtrudes itself into conversations in the form of hackneyed phrases. As a matter of fact, reality never appears to the characters of *Les Belles Images* except in the form of pictures or of *clichés*. Laurence, the narrator, gradually becomes aware of the "unreality" of the way in which those around her view the threat of the atom bomb, or famine in the Third World. The world in which she was brought up and in which she still lives gradually appears to her as sheltered, something of a cocoon. Thus, her perception of reality is split, and it is this which sets in motion within her the process of *séparation*. In the end, she will destroy the myths that enwrapped her earlier way of life. (p. 140)

One year after *Les Belles Images* appeared *La Femme Rompue*. This consists of three stories testifying once again to a definite literary aim. It brings together three different types of monologues: a diary in "La Femme Rompue", a subjective monologue in "Monologue", and an extensive monologue very similar to the one in *Les Belles Images* in "L'Age de Discrétion". This book forms a sequel to *Les Belles Images* to the extent that it portrays women asserting their own truth against a background of unauthenticity. Hence, the two latest novels of Simone de Beauvoir could be said to form a trilogy about woman at the three critical ages of her life: the woman of thirty in Laurence of *Les Belles Images;* the woman of forty-five in "Monologue" and "La Femme Rompue"; and finally the woman of sixty in "L'Age de Discrétion". Simone de Beauvoir tells us in the introduction to the three stories that she is concerned to show failed lives. "I feel at one with women who have assumed responsibility for their lives and who struggle to succeed. However, this does not prevent me from being interested in that part of failure that is inherent in every life." (p. 141)

Irène M. Pagès, "Beauvoir's 'Les Belles Images': 'Desubstantification' of Reality through a Narrative" (copyright © by Forum for Modern Language Studies *and Irène M. Pagès), in* Forum for Modern Language Studies, *Vol. XI, No. 2, April, 1975, pp. 133-41.*

* * *

BECKETT, Samuel 1906-

Beckett is an Irish-born playwright, novelist, poet, critic, essayist, short story writer, and translator who now resides in Paris and writes predominantly in French. He is usually grouped with Pinter, Genet, and Ionesco as a member of the Theatre of the Absurd and explores existential, absurdist themes in all of his creative work. His themes are reinforced by a literary style that experiments with formlessness and fragmented language, reflecting the influence of James Joyce, to whom Beckett was both secretary and literary colleague. The recipient of the Nobel Prize for Literature in 1969, Beckett has had a major influence on contemporary drama. (See also *CLC,* Vols. 1, 2, 3, 4, 6, 9, 10, 11, and *Contemporary Authors,* Vols. 5-8, rev. ed.)

EDITH KERN

[No] one has been more felicitous in illustrating black humor than Winnie in Beckett's *Happy Days,* as she asks the rhetorical question: "How can one better magnify the Almighty than by sniggering with him at his little jokes, particularly the poorer ones?" . . . (p. 89)

One usually remembers with glee the scene in *Gulliver's Travels* where he tells about his arrival in the land of the Lilliputians and—frightening monster that he appears to be—has to submit to a minute search of his person by the country's officers. "I took up the two officers in my hands," he reports, "put them first into my coat-pockets, and then into every other pocket about me, except my two fobs, and another secret pocket which I had no mind should be searched, wherein I had some little necessaries that were of no consequence to any but myself. In one of my fobs there was a silver watch, and in the other a small quantity of gold in a purse." (p. 90)

If Swift's humor . . . provides us with a satire of and an insight into the spirit of the eighteenth century by revealing to us the content of Gulliver's pockets, Beckett's humor displays before us a great number of characters provided with or even contained in pockets and redolent of the spirit of our age as well as timelessly pointing beyond it. (p. 95)

It is perhaps because Beckett's protagonists are so often on the go, and carry all their belongings with them, that their pockets and bags are given so much attention in almost every one of his works. The protagonist of *Watt,* for example, as if to emphasize the futility and emptiness of his existence and to symbolize homeless man clinging to useless possessions, usually carries about two small bags. They are preferable to one large bag, he tells us, and he would have preferred to carry none at all. Those bags are three-fourths empty. One of them is carried by Watt as if it were a club, the other as if it were a sandbag. What they contain Watt never divulges, for what counts is that they are cumbersome and yet difficult to abandon; self-imposed yet insignificant—like most of man's burdens. In *Waiting for Godot,* Lucky almost collapses under the weight of a heavy suitcase each time he appears on stage. He seems unable even to put down his load and seems doomed to carry it for eternity.

There are other Beckett characters with pockets full of such futile objects as pieces of string, carrots, and turnips. Among them are Vladimir and Estragon of *Waiting for Godot.* The protagonists of the unpublished novel *Mercier et Camier* ransack the pockets of their only possession, a raincoat, before abandoning it, and find there "a whole life." . . . (p. 97)

[In the novel *How It Is*] the protagonist crawling naked through the mud clutches a sack which is tied around his neck with a cord. It contains cans of tuna which he opens by means of a can opener and whose content he consumes from time to time listlessly. In its sadism and its humor, which is as black as the mud, this novel seems to stress the sack as container even more than its content. The fact that the word *sack* belongs to the few basic words of the Indo-European vocabulary which have maintained themselves in almost unchanged form in all its tongues attests to its fundamental significance. Being capable of an infinite number of sexual and basic biological connotations, the word occurs in innumerable metaphoric and proverbial expressions and can be associated with gestation, birth, and burial. Not only the protagonist is naked here, but his entire world has been reduced and stripped to its essentials.

One does not need a Lilliputian point of view to see reflected in such pockets filled with strings, burnt matches, and dust, such sacks carried by naked protagonists crawling in the mud the reflection of a universe which is far removed from that of Swift. In the black humor of Beckett neither reason nor the inventions of man's fertile mind finds expression. Man seems no longer the master of a universe which he can bend to his desires and from which he can extract useful tools—as long as he adheres to reason. His life is but dust. The objects which surround him encumber him, rather than help him by their purposefulness. If he introduces objects in his writing, Beckett, unlike some contemporary French novelists who have "taken the side of things," reveals a world where "things are in the saddle and ride mankind." This is, above all, the impression conveyed by Winnie, the protagonist of his play *Happy*

Days. . . . Winnie's vanity and adherence to decorum become ludicrous in view of her strangely stationary and totally isolated existence, and we inadvertently join in her "sniggering" and her "laughing wild amid severest woe." (pp. 98-9)

Winnie's world gains a deeper significance because she herself is in a pocket as it were. For she is buried in a mound of earth, at first to her waist and then to her neck. Alone in that deserted plain and in her pocket-like mound, Winnie seems almost a stage rendering of Heidegger's concept of *Dasein,* that is, of human existence. She seems to be that *lumen naturale* that sheds the light of human understanding upon the universe of which man is part, bestowing individuality and temporality on that-which-is-there. Without her presence, the plain wherein she is situated, the clouds in the sky would be the same but would remain undifferentiated. Winnie seems, however, helplessly "thrown," in the Heideggerian sense, into time, place and human-ness, while surrounded by the implements which belong to the everyday existence of man. But she also evokes Kierkegaard's "knight of infinite resignation" as she indulges in the humdrum occupations of Everyman (or Everywoman in her case) and does so with what would seem an inner freedom, the result of her awareness of the absurdity and paradox of existence. She seems to be inspired by the Kierkegaardian belief that the conception of an eternal happiness transforms the individual's entire existence and "is a process of dying away from the immediate." For while she busies herself with the numerous things that are all about her in bag and bodice, her mind desires to be free—even of her body which is imprisoned in the large pocket of the earth. She can call the day a happy day and yet long for the moment "when flesh melts at so many degrees and the night of the moon has so many hundred hours" and when she "would simply float up into the blue."

Yet even the human mind is envisioned by Beckett as something like a pocket, something similar to a sphere or a sack. (pp. 99-100)

[In the novel *Molloy* the] room where Molloy, turned writer, arrives after his wanderings, "his mother's room" or womb, resembles [a] dimly lighted limbo. And similar limbos are inhabited by Malone and the Unnamable: enclosures that are limp and shapeless, permeated by a grayish light—sacks. They evoke the image of the Baudelairean "gouffre interdit à nos sondes," to which Beckett refers in his essay on Proust and wherein he sees "stored the essence of ourselves, the best of our many selves and their concretions that simplicists call the world." This was the source, Beckett claimed, from which "Proust hoisted his world," using "involuntary memory" as his "diver." For Beckett, then, the writer's experience consists above all of descent, and his task is to report of the treasures he has found in that bottomless sack filled with pure forms and commotion.

It is obvious that, unlike that of his literary Irish ancestor, Beckett's *humour noir* no longer implies a belief in man's ultimate salvation to be reached through the use of reason and ingenuity. What is contained in the pockets of his protagonists progressively defies order and purpose. It bespeaks, on the contrary, a universe both adrift and encumbered with meaningless objects, a universe which has lost the conviction that machines are perfect and that man may strive for perfection with their help. In this world, machines—whether human bodies or bicycles—decay and remain as sheer memories. It is as impersonal as the world of Lemuel Gulliver. Not because man is considered here above all a social being but because his individuality is but ephemeral in the perpetual coming together and falling asunder of forms. Thus what man carries in his pockets, bags, or sacks becomes less and less meaningful and is discarded until from the pockets of earth and body there emerges man's mind replete with treasures which no Lilliputian but only the writer can extract and present to our disbelieving and wondering eyes. (pp. 101-02)

Edith Kern, "Black Humor: The Pockets of Lemuel Gulliver and Samuel Beckett," in Samuel Beckett Now, *edited by Melvin J. Friedman (reprinted by permission of The University of Chicago Press; © 1970 by The University of Chicago), University of Chicago Press, 1970, pp. 89-102.*

MARK J. SACHNER

Beckett's novels push the concern of art beyond its visible object, beyond even "the fiction of the artist" in the act of manipulating that object, and deep into the artistic consciousness as it perceives itself in action. Beckett uses the novel and the necessary presence of a narrator to focus on the problems that are inherent in the basic narrative task of telling a story, the act which is the narrative premise of his trilogy—*Molloy, Molone Dies* and *The Unnamable*—and of *How It Is.* But before the Beckettian story can be told, an initial act of perception must occur as the springboard for the narrative. The object perceived by Beckett's characters and narrators can be either external or internal, and the resultant form and content of the novel are largely determined by that object. Viewed chronologically, each of his narratives moves progressively away from plot as its key ingredient and toward a growing concern with the acrobatics of language and consciousness within the narrative act itself. Hence, the initial act of perception in Beckett's novels is usually of the self at work, telling stories, creating fictions: stories and fictions about the self at work, telling stories, creating fictions.

In *Murphy* and *Watt,* his characters are distinguished by the tight, behavorial grip which they compulsively maintain on themselves and on their personal environments. . . . Each man turns the world of experience into one of private games that, once played, replayed, and yet again replayed, eventually cease to look like games and ultimately become the real thing. Each man is consumed by a consciousness turning ever inward and is finally consigned to the quintessentially private world of Beckett's fiction, the insane asylum.

The physical and psychological preoccupation with self in the characters of Murphy and Watt intensifies in the trilogy, in which each of the first-person narrators is a writer. Each narrator seizes experience *qua* experience and refines it into *literary* experience. . . . Not only is the experience written about through the eyes of the narrator, but the experience itself is one of writing. So, too, the consciousness that lies behind the writing is an artistic consciousness, preoccupied not only with self, but with the *artistic* self at work.

For example, in *Molloy,* the first novel in the trilogy, Molloy's and Moran's consciousnesses ostensibly focus on external objects: Molloy is looking for his mother, and Moran is looking for Molloy; but each also focuses his attention on himself in the act of pursuing his external object. . . . Each receives instructions to write, apparently from an outside source, yet each chiefly concerns himself with his own private need to relate his story. The novel's narrative style reflects the tension between the external and internal objects of the narrator's consciousness; the narrative attempts to proceed according to linear plot, but is structurally maintained by its highly self-reflexive quality.

The game that Murphy and Watt make out of life, and which eventually overtakes them, becomes in the trilogy progressively less of a game for Molloy, Moran, Malone, and the Unnamable as each respective narrator becomes progressively immersed in the game that he has chosen as his life style. Each character in the trilogy, as a writer, becomes a successive avatar of the Beckettian consciousness that endures the sufferings and failures of an existence that must be not only lived, but also explained and justified through its artistic recording. (pp. 144-47)

As Poe points out in "The Imp of the Perverse," "It would have been wiser, it would have been safer, to classify [man's behavior] (if classify we must) upon the basis of what man usually or occasionally did, and was always occasionally doing, rather than upon the basis of what we took it for granted the Deity intended him to do." Beckett's characters, like Poe's often anonymous but highly self-conscious first-person narrators, resist our need to judge on the basis of what should or ought to be. Rather, they embody the failings that are more characteristic of human nature than are the triumphs, and they insist on being drawn idiosyncratically. In Beckett's trilogy, they draw *themselves* idiosyncratically, since their metaphor for life is the act of writing itself. Likewise, the attempt by Murphy and Watt to manipulate their lives by subjecting every facet of experience to seemingly endless permutations prefigures the attempts by the trilogy's narrators to gain an aesthetic control over their fictions as they write them.

What is especially revealing about this control of the narrator over his fiction in Beckett is that we are made to see life as Poe saw it—that is, "upon the basis of what man usually or occasionally did, and was always occasionally doing." What man "always occasionally" does is to live a life based largely on lapses and failures. Like Molloy, we base our lives largely on failures that are not always punctuated by triumphs. Like Molloy, we forget more than we remember. In fact, the more we know, the more we have to forget. We see more that repels us or that we are indifferent to than that gives us pleasure. We ingest and then belch, break wind, vomit, snore, sneeze, sweat, secrete mucous or excrement from every opening in our bodies; we spend enormous periods of time flat on our backs; we grow fungus between our toes and collect lint in our navels; lice love us; other humans rarely do. Our bodies age and grow infirm; we die. We also go mad. The psychological disease that characterizes Poe's narrators is handed down through Dostoevsky—whose Underground Man has both a heightened consciousness and a diseased liver—to Beckett, whose narrator's consciousnesses also heighten in response to their ailing bodies. (pp. 147-48)

This coincidence of failure, or of the impossibility of continuing, with the absolute necessity of going on manifests itself through the pain and confusion of Beckett's narrators. Through the confusion, final solutions are impossible to come by; life is often brought to a standstill while the contradictory poles of necessity and impossibility hold each other and the protagonists, who are caught in between. When, at the close of each act of *Waiting for Godot,* each of the tramps suggests to the other, "Well, shall we go?" and the other replies, "Yes, let's go," the stage directions tell us that it is to be otherwise: *"They do not move."* For the four incarnations of the writer who doubles as narrator in the trilogy, the problem becomes progressively more complex and finally crystallizes in the closing lines of each novel as the act of writing becomes more and more the central focus of the work itself. (p. 149)

In Moran's section, the stasis takes on yet an added literary quality and calls into question language itself, along with the situation of Moran as a teller of tales, or as one whose life depends on his ability to write up an accurate report of his search for Molloy: "It told me to write the report. . . . Then I went back into the house and wrote, It is midnight. The rain is beating on the windows. It was not midnight. It was not raining." . . . For Moran, and for the reader who has been dragged along with him, fact and fiction have merged in these closing lines, as have the telling of truth and lies. . . . Moran's failure to establish clearly the narrative distance between the last two sentences and the two preceding sentences in the passage quoted above temporarily throws the reader off balance. The distance between narrator and narrative, or between the subject and his object, has ceased to exist. The writer and that about which he is writing have become, for the moment, one. The confusion of the narrator has been passed on to the reader, and both are held immobile as *Molloy* grinds to a halt. Moran's section of the narrative, which begins with his saying simply, "It is midnight. The rain is beating on the windows," . . . is tantalizingly close to coming around full circle. The last two equivocal sentences, however—"It was not midnight. It was not raining."—defy our urge to tie the narrative up into a neat little package. At the end of his narrative, Moran's verbatim repetition of the opening image of rain falling on the windows informs us of his wish to *cease* writing, while the ambiguous repudiation of the image in the last two sentences leaves the narrative open-ended and informs us of the necessity for keeping on.

The failure that grounds Moran's narrative is two-fold and contains both the failure of a piece of literary art (*i.e.,* Moran's report) fully to resolve itself internally, and the failure of Moran as a teller of stories clearly to distinguish between fact and fiction and thus fully to actualize his own life as a writer. The sum total of all the uncertainties and ambiguities that are present throughout the novel appears in those last four sentences.

The narrative failures that characterize *Molloy* further weave themselves into the fabric of Malone's stories in *Malone Dies.* Malone assumes the role of one who creates fictions in order to reaffirm the importance of the days that remain before he dies. His central failure in relating those fictions is two-fold. First of all, he is unable fully to prevent his private wants from interfering with the stories that he invents about his fictional heroes, Saposcat and Macmann. . . . Secondly, his problem is one of language and the act of finding the right method of fictionalizing. His narrative is punctuated by expressions of frustration that temporarily intrude upon the story itself. . . . (pp. 149-51)

Both problems—that of his personal life intruding upon his fiction, and that of finding the right words with which to express that fiction—are two sides of the same coin. Both have their roots within the consciousness of the narrator, and both converge into a failure within the fiction that jeopardizes the integrity not only of narrative distance between writer, work and audience, but of narrative convention as well. This failure touches on both the subjective writer and the object of his creative energies, and calls into question the ontology of the fictional process, which requires the perception of self as its initial premise, but which cannot remove that initial perception from the finished product. The fictional object emanates from the writer's subjective consciousness, and the moment of crisis for both subject and object occurs when they become one within the work of art. Implicit in the extensive awareness of self in *Malone Dies* is a paradoxical effort on the narrator's part to escape from that self through the fictionalizing process in order to refine the narrative. As the consciousness of Beckett the writer is incarnated through the consciousness of his narrator Malone, so, too, does Malone seek his fictional avatars through his creatures Sapo and Macmann. But when subject and object have a tendency to become fused in Beckett's novels, the narrative has a corresponding tendency to stagnate and freeze up; hence Malone's frequent exclamations of "I can't" and "This is awful." But even as Malone protests his inability to continue, he, like Beckett, finds that he has no choice but *to* continue with the fiction that he has boxed himself into through the workings of his consciousness and of language. As much as he would like to stop writing, speaking or thinking, he cannot, for to deny thinking would be a repudiation of consciousness, that last vestige of life that remains once the body begins to fail; it would inevitably be a repudiation of life itself, and life is that to which Beckett's characters cling most tenaciously, even to the point of death itself, so long as there is a thought in their heads or a word at their lips.

So Beckett's canon of novels is really quite life-oriented, even as it, like the landscape of *Waiting for Godot,* asymptotically reduces itself toward the bottom line of existence without ever actually touching zero. What keeps the curve of his fiction moving on into infinity as it forever approaches, but never meets, its own destruction is the presence of the artistic consciousness that maintains itself through the narrative voice. The failure of a work of art to succeed at resolving the ironic bond that fuses subject and object, or creator and created, is precisely that which impels Beckett and his avatars to explore further that failure by continuing to write and, metaphorically, to live. Thus, the pattern of failure from which there is no escape continues.

This paradoxical problem of reconciling the urge to stop writing with the obligation to go on writing reasserts itself for the final time in the trilogy in *The Unnamable* with the narrator's closing words: ". . . you must go on, I can't go on, I'll go on." . . . Throughout *The Unnamable,* the narrator attempts, as he later does in *How It Is,* to divest himself of responsibility for the work that he is creating by fictionalizing his consciousness through other characters. . . . What results is a confusing and comic transposing of fictional identities from that of the unnamed narrator outward. In the process, the identity not only of the narrator, but also of the narrative, becomes confused and distorted. (pp. 151-53)

In the midst of all this confusion, the "I" nonetheless returns as the narrative voice, only to find at the end that he has become so engrossed in his fictional creatures that the problem which he sought to eliminate by creating those characters—*i.e.,* the problem of self-awareness—has returned to haunt him. The narrator is forced to assume the final responsibility for his fiction. The escape from self has become an exploration of self and has led back to an awareness of self in those final words: ". . . you must go on, I can't go on, I'll go on." *You* becomes *I; You* has always been *I; You* will remain *I.* Likewise, in the narrative context, subject and object become for the first person narrator one, and the novelistic "I" can never claim final autonomy from its milieu. So, too, is the writer irrevocably bound to his fiction, since any fictionalized voice that he assumes as a disguise inevitably becomes but another avatar of the artistic consciousness. All of Beckett's fictionalized avatars thus retain the germ of a common identity. (p. 154)

Although Beckett's characters visibly grow old and suffer from various physical infirmities, ultimately the pain is that of failure—the failure of language to make itself clear and, lying behind that, the failure of the artistic consciousness to come successfully to grips with its integral relationship to the work that it creates. (p. 155)

Mark J. Sachner, "The Artist as Fiction: An Aesthetics of Failure in Samuel Beckett's Trilogy," in The Midwest Quarterly *(copyright, 1977, by* The Midwest Quarterly, *Pittsburg State University), Vol. XVIII, No. 2, January, 1977, pp. 144-55.*

J. D. O'HARA

In English the Irish are the great sentimentalists. The dour Scots, the babbling Welsh, and the destiny-laden English are not in it for sheer heart-wringing sentiment, the chuckle that stops short in a sob, the tear in the sparkling eye. Pause now for an ad hoc definition: sentimentality emphasizes not the racking passions—snarling hatred, implacable resentment, love that makes the heart leap in its bone-cage —no, not those, but the retrospective melancholy of sweet love lost, life's intensity cooled, chances missed and the road not taken, the living backwards with one's wet eye fixed on what might have been, with the absurd conviction that what can never come again was unutterably valuable . . . ah there! and ah then! Paradise lost, in short, with the addition offered by Samuel Beckett, that the *only* true paradise is the paradise that has been lost.

In art, especially in Irish art, as in life, the signs of sentimentality are easy to read: the dying fall and the fragmented speech; the gesture halfhearted and abortive, as when the arms that reached out briefly toward another return to hug the self; the tale set in the past and told with the brevity of a foreknown defeat, reaching no climax, fizzling out. . . . No one recently has chronicled this post-Finnegan fall better than Samuel Beckett.

There is no intention here to sell sentimentality short. Not only is it a valid basis for grasping at life's fleeting feelings while avoiding its traumatizing horrors but, more to the point, it is capable of generating remarkably enjoyable art. For most of his literary life Beckett has performed rigadoons, pavanes, and dances of death over his touching themes. Like Jackson Pollock on canvas, Beckett has overlaid his texts and textures with all the glitter of Irish wit, Celtic theology, European literature, and Catholic philosophy, *interalia.* But the paint thinned to a trickle with the last words of the last novel of his immensely impressive trilogy: "I can't go on, I'll go on." In one more novel, *How It Is,* and in handfuls of smaller texts, Beckett did indeed attempt to go on with his old themes—the isolated self, the mental being in a physical world, the irrelevance of knowledge, the evasiveness of identity, the absence of objective truth, the meaningless patterns of our eternal recurrences—but he stripped his investigation of its previous baroque complexities, whittled it down to the bare bones of immediate experience, and still found himself, and still finds himself, at the threshold, only beginning to end.

Meanwhile a new set of more explicitly emotional themes had begun to orchestrate themselves. In due time scholars will probably fix its official overture by triangulating Beckett's postwar visit to his dying mother in Ireland, his play *Krapp's Last Tape,* and his curious French poem "Mort de A.D." . . . Until all this is clarified we can only note that in the many plays and short fictions of Beckett's later years the dominant themes are regret, remorse, inescapable loneliness, lost love, and wasted life. That voice in the protagonist's head is not now occupied in bullying him or her about identity, meaning, or duty; instead it voices the *agenbite of inwit.* But not gnawing about great sins committed or great deeds botched: Beckett's themes, more obviously than before, are those of sentimentality, of paradise lost or missed out on. The Beckett who once performed such mental gymnastics to prove that happiness is impossible now creates character after character who regrets what might after all have been, or who is inconsolable about a life to which no lasting happiness has come. The essence of this new complex is evoked in one of his present fizzles, a short piece entitled "Still." It consists basically of one described movement in which a character seated and staring fixedly out a window at the dying day raises one hand and rests his face in it. But Beckett's dry, minimally concerned narrative voice describes this gesture with preternatural concern, breaking it down into split-second sequences as a moving-picture film would do; and this intense focus on the emotional significance of a detached, momentary gesture evokes sentimentality at its finest—the quintessence, one suspects, of dozens of Victorian engravings. (pp. 216-17)

Like most writers who concentrate on the essence of a theme rather than its complexity, Beckett has found himself writing increasingly briefer and more condensed works in recent years. He is concerned with situations, not with the problems and resolutions that constitute plot. As a result his fictions have come to resemble prose poems, and his plays approach *tableaux vivants.* In both forms motion takes on the character of musical theme rather than goal-oriented action; repetition is basic to it, a repetition characteristically stopped short in favor of the final silence to which Beckett so often calls our attention. His two present collections, the theatre pieces of *Ends and Odds* and the abandoned prose *Fizzles,* demonstrate all these qualities, though some of them remind us also of the drawn out dying of his earlier concerns.

Most of the fizzles were written first in French and published first as *Foirades.* For the most part they are abortive attempts, stories that never got off the ground (Beckett's harsher unofficial title was "Shit"), and they show him attempting to get plots underway, to find a satisfactory third-person narrative voice, to develop obstinately static situations. (p. 217)

Since they really are what they claim to be, the publication of the fizzles is puzzling, but the eight stage and radio plays of *Ends and Odds* need little excuse. The Odds, described as "Roughs for Theatre and Radio," are untitled and on the whole unsatisfactory, and they include some curious revivals of Beckett's strange interest in those vaguely official scribes, detectives, and enforcers . . . who from time to time lend a depressing air of Chesterton or Graham Greene to his writing. But in three of the Ends, *Not I, That Time,* and *Footfalls,* the collection offers some of Beckett's finest dramatic work. In each, the mind divided against itself expresses life at a dead end, existence aborted, the sense—to which Beckett has turned so often in his later works—that one has never really been born. "Never the time and the place and the loved one all together," Browning wrote; never a consummation of life. Beckett is quick to add that even if the occasion should offer, we are likely to be looking away, and that even if the consummation should improbably occur, we should still be obliged to live beyond it for many an endless year. Such stipulations lie at the melancholy heart of the sentimental experience, and these plays, brief and even dry as they appear on the page, can wring that heart painfully, as many theatregoers have already testified. (pp. 217, 219)

These plays are not tragic, though they have been called so; tragedies deal with a much wider compass of significance, much deeper confrontations with existence. But these are marvelous sentimentality, worth any theatregoer's hushed attention. (p. 219)

J. D. O'Hara, "Beckett Piece by Piece," in The Nation *(copyright 1977 by the Nation Associates, Inc.), Vol. 224, No. 7, February 19, 1977, pp. 216-17, 219.*

ROBERT MARTIN ADAMS

Beckett is Irish as was Joyce; but there is no sign that the politics of Irish independence ever disturbed Beckett as they did the writer who was eighteen years his senior. . . . Beckett makes only vague, distant, and occasional allusions to Ireland in his fiction. Names of characters apart, a couple of hundred words deleted from his four-hundred-page trilogy would efface every recognizable vestige of Ireland and the Irish. Irish folklore and Irish humor hardly exist in Beckett's world, even for purposes of parody or sardonic comment. . . . Beckett could much more properly be described as a Parisian who was born in Ireland. . . . (pp. 90-1)

Beckett is . . . [close] to wholly mythless man; the philosophical problem which preoccupies him is the relation or non-relation between the mind and exterior reality, and to this problem ecclesiasticism, with all its trappings, is wholly irrelevant. Joyce sees through the exterior tegument of the world to a meaning hidden behind its physical texture; Beckett, in traditional Protestant fashion, hears inner voices. They do not seem to say the traditional things to him or to his characters, but they guide both along that quest or pilgrimage which is the oldest and most traditional of Protestant metaphors for the spiritual life. In their different unbelieving ways, both Joyce and Beckett are haunted by the doubt that the God in whom they disbelieve may exist, probably as a secret, malignant force concerned chiefly with tormenting His creatures. (p. 91)

In his early prose particularly, [Beckett] is not above using an occasional exotic reference like William of Champeaux, very much as Joyce makes use of Joachim Abbas; but the later style of Beckett is harder, dryer, flatter, more stripped than anything in Joyce. Along with the specifics of time, place, and particular reference, circumlocutions and metaphors drop away; the later art of Beckett depends on utter simplicity of diction and grammar, frequent repetition, carefully controlled rhythm. (p. 92)

So far as Beckett concerns himself with pattern at all, it is with incomplete pattern; his circles are never closed, his lists are always bogus, when he plays games they cry aloud in advance their own meaninglessness. The depth of Beckett's morbidity is sometimes obscured by his extraordinary comic touch; the comic inspiration of Joyce is sometimes swamped by the gigantic structural complexity of his books.

Joyce . . . was a man who aspired by a process of addition to put everything into his volumes; Beckett, working by a contrary arithmetic, has steadily subtracted more and more from his books, emptying them of substance, and working toward the cold and dark of a naked consciousness, aware only of itself, confronting the absolute zero of non-experience. Every one of Joyce's books is in its own way a *summa*—[*Finnegans Wake*] most of all; Beckett's writings all aspire to the condition of *nullas*—questioning, thus, the nature of their own existence in a manner more radical than Joyce ever attempted. Joyce's undertaking may have been megalomaniac, but it was not absurd, did not involve a contradiction in terms. (p. 93)

The core of [Beckett's] problematic has always been the extravagant, almost vindictive isolation of [his] characters from one another, from the resources of history, society, and their own past—even from their own minds. In fact, we wrong them even to talk of them as "characters"; for though there are in the various books entities called "Murphy," "Watt," and so forth, these are mere verbal parcels of convenience; their ingredients are jumbled together as provisionally and insecurely as the contents of a grocery bag. It is their disintegration, continuous from work to work and continuous in that context as nothing is within the individual fictions, that makes for the fascination of Beckett's *oeuvre*.

The first of the major books, *Murphy*, seems closest to being a "normal" fiction, having a sort of intrigue, a distinct locale, and several personages who surround the central enigma and try with comic ineptitude to interact with him. But Murphy himself, with his icy eyes and utter indifference to all others and everything other than his own mind, is one of the coldest and least human of Beckett's isolatos. . . . The highest and most satisfying level of his mental activity is described as that which involves most complete autonomy for the mind—the achievement of a dark containing

> neither elements nor states, nothing but forms becoming and crumbling into the fragments of a new becoming, without love or hate or any intelligible principle of change. Here there was nothing but commotion or the pure forms of commotion. Here he was not free but a mote in the dark of absolute freedom. He did not move, he was a point in the ceaseless unconditioned generation and passing away of line. Matrix of surds. . . .

Behind this complex panoply of metaphorical disguises lies the concept of chaos, perhaps as figured in the concept of Brownian motion; as a "matrix of surds," or womb of irrationals, Murphy instinctively moves toward madness as a state of ultimate satisfaction. (pp. 95-6)

A plot which runs the protagonist so directly and eagerly toward the large black hole which awaits us all, and which most of us would take some pains to avoid, needs no motive energy to move it forward, but rather brakes to hold it back. *Murphy* is the best example prior to *Godot* of a literary action used to postpone rather than advance the movement of a development possessing its own inertia. Since he has no real function in moving forward the story (it gets where it is inevitably going without any of his efforts), the author is free to embroider intellectual and stylistic curlicues on the margins of the tale—which he does with the owlish solemnity of an insane scholar. . . .

The subzero temperature of *Murphy*'s major theme is partly mitigated by the drollery of its manner, and many readers have found it the most accessible of Beckett's fictions—partly, perhaps, because they take it at about three-quarters of its basic potency. (p. 97)

Like Murphy, [Watt] is a matrix of surds; and, as with Murphy, all his intellectual defeats and impasses seem to flow from a central incapacity to define what (Watt) is man. In *Watt* we have a first manifestation of that clown-in-waiting around whom *Godot* is built; we have the further pathos of an irrelevant vocation and a mind alienated among its own games. There is the pedantry-*shtik* in the form of a hilarious mock-examination; there are the pratfalls interspersed with metaphysics, the robot-mannerisms interrupted by Pascalian shivers at the silence of infinite space. Yet by and large the book is static, and its disparate parts do not successfully interact with one another. Some people have suggested that the impasse which the book represents derives from its relation to Joyce, its over-dependence on a baroque style. Apart from the absurdity of identifying the baroque style with Joyce, this doesn't seem right in itself. What *Watt* lacked was precisely the kind of inward and unifying passion, the sense of seeing into something and making a felt whole of it, the immediately present example of which was *Finnegans Wake*. Evidently, abandoning English helped Beckett toward a new sort of book by cutting off certain sorts of verbal vaudeville. No doubt the loneliness and the danger of the war years, and the gigantic questions they posed about the nature and the future of man, also pushed him toward the stripped and inward vision. But I do not think the great breakthrough of the immediate post-war years was for Beckett an escape from Joyce so much as a fulfilling of himself through a part of Joyce that he had not previously tapped, at least not very successfully. He could no longer stand outside his characters and watch them perform; he had to get in them and through them. And they were, because of their alien, alienated disposition, and the nothingness immediately beyond them, far harder to get into than any figures in the Joycean *oeuvre*. (pp. 98-9)

By abandoning Joyce in order to pursue himself, Beckett rediscovered Joyce. He did so not through the use of Joycean techniques—out of the entire panoply of Joycean techniques, Beckett took over only the interior monologue—but in a much less specific way. . . . [In the mature work of

Beckett, Joyce] is nowhere overtly, but everywhere tacitly and by implication. Classical analogues, Viconian cycles, macaronic speech-distortions, mosaic composition, archetypes of all sorts—the great clanking machinery of Joycean fiction drops away. There remains the unbroken murmur of a confession made without a priest, a sifting and straining of the consciousness, a casting aside of everything which is not the quicksilver moment of self-awareness. This is not Joycean, it is Joyce.

The first novel of the trilogy, *Molloy,* is on the whole the most classical and humane, even hopeful, of Beckett's books. It is the story of two interlocked, middle-aged, vaguely Irish males; Molloy is on a pilgrimage to his mother's house, Moran is under a mysterious injunction . . . to seek Molloy. (pp. 99-100)

The two stories, which are largely separate and particularly hazy at the moment when they coincide (if they do), must be joined by the reader through counter-poised judgments of Molloy and Moran. The former is ascetic, unworldly, a physical wreck but somehow marked with the almost visible trait of nobility. With policemen and churches he has nothing whatever in common. Moran, on the other hand, is mean, prudent, spiteful, and legalistic—a rate-payer, a church-goer, a model of minor officialdom; his treatment of his son is a nightmare of petty tyranny. The pair might be variously considered as open and closed, as ethical and acquisitive, as libido and superego, as artist and functionary —Beckett leaves them plastic to all these dualisms, and to many others. (p. 100)

Molloy is . . . a novel which reaches its climax in a desert flowering—a triumph of the liberated imagination, as in 19th-century novels. It is able to do this because it starts Moran in an almost Dickensian far-back. Molloy, who starts much farther out, does not get so far. . . . The two pieces of the novel, which are easily separable, would make a wholly different book if their order were reversed; thinking of it that way may make us feel that Moran's victory is only the Pyrrhic one of having fitted himself to advance faster and with fewer impediments toward the grisly end which stares Molloy in the face. (p. 102)

The novelty of *Malone Dies* lies, I think, in a systematic derangement of the narrative for which there doesn't seem to be much precedent, in Joyce or elsewhere. Malone, for example, begins his narration in a hospital bed from which he is scarcely capable of stirring; when he drops his pencil and notebook, he has to spend several days groping with a stick to recover them. Yet "much later" he comes to again "in a kind of asylum," and registers the kind of surprise at this development which implies that he hasn't been in asylum all along. . . . These and other absurdities of similar nature are cracks and incongruities in the physical texture of the story, designed, one supposes, to discredit the story as a mock-reality. They are not the product of a hallucinated vision (psychological, that is), nor are they puzzles planted in the fiction for the reader to decipher like a docile, clever schoolboy. They are not, in that sense, structural. They are a product of the history of the English novel, a history which Beckett was in process of shedding—as inevitable a product as that superb sentence of Malone's, at the climax of his description of the asylum: "A stream at long intervals bestrid—but to hell with all this fucking scenery." All the way through *Malone Dies* one can feel the impatience of an author itching to discard the simulacra of fiction, to be rid of that code of meaning and artifice of economy by which fictions are bound to regulate themselves.

The Unnamable takes the full plunge, sweeping aside the whole gallery of Beckett "characters" and their stories, as mere "mannikins" and "a ponderous chronicle of moribunds." Not without some disgust, the author must push these away to replace them, as fictional characters, with himself, who in addition to being Samuel Beckett in person is noman and everyman, nowhere and everywhere, timeless and yet submerged in the stream of time. . . . Though he may be unnamable now (we cannot be sure the title applies to him, it may also apply to the process he is trying to define, conventionally and corruptly known as human life), the speaker of the book has had various names, Mahood most recently, perhaps Basil before that, and Worm even before that; he obviously faces a serious prospect of being Worm again very shortly. His meditation is on first and last things in an effort to define what is or should be the quality of his existence as Mahood; the pun on "manhood" is not very remote, and is surely intended to be felt. It is a meditation, remorselessly monotonous and persistent, on a single aspect of the human condition; it proceeds on the unspoken assumption that to define self it is necessary to strip away externals and accidents. . . . Beckett's working out of this paradox has few of the characteristics of fiction. There is no action, no contrast of motives, no manipulation of sympathy, no "rendering" in the Jamesian sense. Though it implies sustained and serious thought, and imitates the processes of thought, the stream of monologue is more like worry than thought, a ceaseless shaking and gnawing and teasing of the question, what is it to be a man?

Like the *Wake, The Unnamable* has to be read slowly and with painful concentration on each sentence; skimmed across, it yields chiefly a sense of endlessly reiterated, musclebound depression. But read slowly and questioningly —preferably with the French original close to hand—it yields an enormous sense of imaginative vitality struggling under crushing pressure. (pp. 103-05)

Beckett *in propria persona* claims to hear voices and to recite in his books words spoken by outside agents. Within *The Unnamable* these voices make some sense as the voices of the past, of history, or of conventional moralizing. In one very moving series of metaphors they are teachers, badgering the backward student Mahood to recite a rote definition of man that he cannot get through his head. Indeed, it wouldn't be hard to see them as the structure, not only of society but of "systematic" thought and "formal" language, such as the narrator is struggling to use against itself, in the forlorn hope of cutting it short. They are the rags, not only of respectability but of conventional categories, all of which must be stripped off if we are to see unaccommodated man (the allusion is trite but inescapable) as the poor bare forked animal he is.

By contrast with the vaudeville turns of *Murphy* and *Watt,* the language of *The Unnamable* is taut, stripped, and very limited in vocabulary. There is an occasional freaky bit of theological pedantry or anatomical specificity; in his Ali Baba incarnation, the narrator blurs the proprietress of his bistro by calling her now Marguerite and now Madeleine; but his uncertainties lie deeper than those of perception, and he focuses on them myopically, monomaniacally, struggling to the end of the book to say himself, to be said. In these closing passages the counters get fewer and more familiar, the moves are shorter and bump more abruptly into their own contradictions, the transitions blur, and the pace quickens, as the prose seems to slide irresistibly under its own momentum toward the last, utterly simple, impasse. It is a supreme imaginative achievement. (p. 106)

The given from which Beckett scarcely wavers is the dilemma of post-Cartesian philosophy; if the only evidence of being is thinking, and thinking is largely conditioned, no man can know who he is or that he is, save by a ruthless process of pulling down and putting off. . . . [The] path of approach—indirect, hesitant, and beset with false steps—suggests how hard Beckett found it to reach the center of his subject. In this sense, *The Unnamable* validates the entire previous career; if it is not a supremely difficult achievement superbly accomplished, then the entire discussion of Beckett as a literary artist moves down several pegs. I think that step will not be necessary.

A narrower vision, a different focus, a much more limited and less symphonic art, were first conditions of Beckett's liberation from Joyce. One consequence of these choices . . . is a kind of instability of tone and uncertainty of taste that draws him, from time to time, into two different eccentricities where it's neither easy nor rewarding to follow him. One is self-pity and self-dramatization, the other a kind of mechanical testing of the written language by depriving it progressively, and arbitrarily, of its resources. (p. 107)

[A] second fault is illustrated by Beckett's one major fiction since the trilogy, *How It Is*. . . . The problems which this narrative poses itself, in the form of deliberate deprivations, are so massive that they overwhelm anything that can be achieved within their limits. Throughout the book the unnamed speaker grovels and gropes aimlessly, face down in icy mud; he speaks only in gasps and broken ejaculations, dispensing entirely with punctuation and often with syntax. . . . A monotony of pain has seldom been rendered so monotonously or so painfully. The language of *How It Is*, like the landscapes inner and outer, is scrupulously drab—literal, flat, and repetitious, with only a rare indulgence in nuance or rhythmic subtlety. One can't fail to stand in awe of the artistic integrity that brought Beckett to this dark, dead pocket of imaginative prose, while still feeling that in the course of assassinating the novel—an avowed aim—he has killed a good deal else. (pp. 108-09)

It's the irregular in-and-out of this motion, the alternation of anguish with a vacancy which is particularly effective and possible onstage, that gives Beckett's plays their agonizing rhythm. . . . As a writer for the stage, Beckett not only owes little that is distinctive to Joyce, he is far and away superior, primarily because of his extraordinary gift for interweaving the rhythms of speech and action. . . . The schism that Beckett underwent when he divided himself into dramatist and narrator must have been quite as important to his development as his passage from French to English.

Underlying all these formal considerations is a matter which is not very easy to talk about, but which any reader of Beckett's *oeuvre* can hardly avoid sensing—I mean the presence of a quality which, for lack of a better word, can be called the sacred. Beckett himself does not try to represent directly this condition. (In *Molloy*, there is a use or two of "azur," Mallarmé's sacred word; but it disappears in the translation, and is never used, systematically or otherwise, thereafter.) His nasty, disintegrating, foul-mouthed old men do not appear likely candidates for canonization, and in fact they do not so much contain the sacred as stand (or crawl or creep) in its presence. Through their rage, their impatience, their compulsion to make and destroy formulas, we sense something that moves them far beyond the prudent accommodations of the here and now. They are willing to shred the world and themselves into little pieces if only they can understand before they die what it has meant to be a human being. This quality, at which one can only gesture inadequately with words like "sacred," is wholly unrelated to ecclesiasticism or any sense of reverence for the divinity—who, to the Beckett spokesmen, often seems like the cruel perpetrator of a set of inhuman practical jokes. There is no sense of awe or hush in Beckett's approach to the sacred, no strained spiritual effort, no talk of the soul or patter about its dark night, *via negativa*, and so forth and so on. Beckett's saints are do-it-yourselfers. They have a healthy sense of reluctance about the saintly vocation; they spit and snarl, they try to shirk and evade their responsibilities. But by incessantly adding, subtracting, multiplying, and dividing the meager quantum of their thoughts, they bring themselves into the presence of, or at least very close to, the pure, informulable, minimal essence of being—close enough so that its radiance is felt. Admittedly, this is not "the sacred" in the sense of "the otherworldly," but it is quite as remote from the easy quotidian as the old "sacred" used to be; and alongside its pains, palaver like Joyce's youthful talk of "epiphanies," and the Shelleyan ecstasies of Stephen Dedalus, start to sound pretentious and inauthentic. I speak here only of the youthful Joyce. At the height of their achievement both Joyce and Beckett bring us into the presence of a direct vision, beyond the genres of tragedy and comedy, from which most of the screen elements of traditional fiction, such as "action," "characterization," and "rendering," have dropped away. They are replaced by a silent mutual enfolding, a perception of, if not contact with, oneness of being—congruent structures of mind, mood, and cosmos effortlessly flowing into one another. Probably Beckett does not carry this vision further than Joyce; but he pursues its traces more single-mindedly, perhaps because he doubts it more deeply.

Seen as a spiritual activity which reaches through art to some sort of ultimate, however defined, Beckett's writing is inevitably self-destructive—that is, it uses literature, and uses it up, in the service of an imperative which lies beyond words arranged to produce effects. Having found, essentially in the trilogy, the path to his end, Beckett in his later writings has been chiefly concerned with shortening it. (pp. 109-12)

Beckett's vision is the last step this side of Zen, and his absurdity serves the same end as Zen-absurdity, to open cracks in the texture of things for the vision to shine through. Joyce is an artist of transparency, Beckett of these cracks and grotesque disparities. But the fact of vision, hard as that concept is to define or illustrate, is the main element uniting Beckett with Joyce. Beckett is the chief post-Joycean novelist to throw away his predecessor's machinery and concentrate on the attempt at vision. . . . Quietism is Beckett's end, and his vision flowers out of a deep, contemplative quiet.

The concepts of ending and finality fascinate Beckett; his books are all studies of terminal cases under indefinite reprieve; and anyone who cites him as a special instance of Joycean influence has to face the possibility that he represents the last closed doorway in that cul-de-sac down which Joyce is said to have led the English novel. He is, in effect, the promised end. . . . He works only at the very highest pitch, using minimal materials and aiming at a very narrow range of effects; the sense that he is squeezing the last meager drops from a very dry sponge is the consequence of a deliberate artistic decision, not of The Decline of the West. His endings, long threatened and desperately struggled against, are generally equivocal when they arrive, because to say the last word on man is impossible, however grim his condition. (Zeno's paradox has a special application here: if the last word can be said, somebody must exist to say it, about whom at least one further thing can be said.) As he passionately refuses formulas for himself, so it seems misleading or worse to encapsulate Beckett in a formula. He has kept open the possibilities of humanity by cutting the throat of literature and forcing his readers to confront naked conditions of mere existence—without sham exhilaration or despair, but coldly, very coldly. (pp. 112-13)

Robert Martin Adams, "Samuel Beckett," in his AfterJoyce: Studies in Fiction After "Ulysses" *(copyright © 1977 by Robert Martin Adams; used by permission of Oxford University Press, Inc.), Oxford University Press, New York, 1977, pp. 90-113.*

ENOCH BRATER

Though the originality and durability of Beckett's novels and plays assure his reputation as a major writer of our time, his work as poet has attracted far less sympathetic attention. All the while expanding that "gallery of moribunds" he has made so authentically his own, Beckett has been writing poems on the sly. . . . Distilled from the hardy irregularities of Joycean rhetoric, Beckett's voice in verse has the same haunting cadence, the same "dour questing," the same "dread nay" we recognize from his drama and prose. Like some "death-mask of unrivalled beauty," Beckett's poetry offers us a very unexpected detour into the formalities of lyrical structure.

Beckett's lyricism will come as no surprise to audiences accustomed to his skillful transformation of the prosaic into the poetic. Even in *Waiting for Godot,* where two tramps mark time in an almost empty eternity where all certainty is provisional, the playwright presents us with a drama of indirect action reminiscent of Chekhov's stage lyricism. . . .

Beckett's voice can be most vigorously poetic when he is not writing specifically in poetry. Some of his most lyrical statements take place when we are least likely to expect them. Crawling in the mud, buried up to the waist in a mound of earth, listening all alone to a tape recorder roll on to silence, or making "immaculate" love in a garbage dump, Beckett's dramatic and fictional characters forever impress us through the poetic vitality that shines through their despair. The lyricism catches us off-guard, for the landscape leads us to expect nothingness but delivers romanticism instead. Hope springs eternal: there is splendor, suddenly, in the trash.

Ironically, Beckett can be far less lyrical in his poems. In "Whoroscope," his first professionally published piece, Descartes is a finicky eater who likes his omelette made of eggs hatched from eight to 10 days before. "Shorter or longer under the hen and the result," a note assures us, "is disgusting." Even lowly albumen cannot escape the philosopher's wrath: "What's that? / A little green fry or a mushroomy one? / Two lashed ovaries with prostisciutto?" Heavily allusive, the poem's circumlocution and discontinuous form are strictly "Ex Cathedra": Pound's advanced techniques ("very dissociated and recombined") take it on the chin within the confines of Beckett's Cartesian railing. . . .

Not all of the poems in English and French incarnate in this same youthful exuberance. In this respect "Whoroscope" is unique, for the poems which follow in this collection trace far more somber tones. Sometimes based on Provençal forms, the 13 poems originally published as *Echo's Bones and Other Precipitates* reflect the uneasy consciousness of the writer's developing sensibility. An index of the poet's own wandering, the scene shifts from place to place, now Dublin, now Paris, now London, but the plaintive voice is always the same. (p. 33)

The poetry of the '70s bears an inflection characteristic of Beckett's current preoccupation with minimalism in drama and prose. The "hellice eyes" of "dread nay" are apparitions which materialize everywhere in the enigmatic residua, those short prose-poems of recent vintage Ruby Cohn describes as "lyrics of fiction." As in *Ping* and *Imagination Dead Imagine,* "the subject falls far from the verb and the object lands somewhere in the void." We have heard this "far cry" before, but the actual manifestation in verse serves to remind us once again how close Beckett's later work in prose comes to poetry. There are correlations with dramatic values too. The "something there" in the poem of the same name ("not life / necessarily") might accurately delineate the "semblance" so fearful in *Footfalls,* while the "steps sole sound / long sole sound" of "Roundelay" defines the refrain of May's obsessive pacing in the play. Despite the minuscule dimensions of this recent work, the "stiff interconnectiveness" of Beckett's world remains as strong as ever.

The translations from Eluard . . . , Rimbaud . . . and Apollinaire . . . are remarkable examples of Beckett's skill in rendering the sound and sense of one language into another. Here is the same discipline in adaptation Beckett has effected in his own English to French/French to English material. Of very special interest in this volume are the eight maxims translated "long after" Sebastien Chamfort, where Beckett makes an unusual departure from the text to render a neo-classicism all his own: "Better on your arse than on your feet, / Flat on your back than either, dead than the lot."

If Beckett offers us no major breakthrough in modern poetry, it is largely because he directs his talents as "homo logos" to the other genre he has consistently reshaped to meet his own literary needs. In love with the aside, the tangential comment, the footnote and the mathematical calculation ("Not count? One of the few pleasures left?") Beckett has fashioned a vehicle for himself in drama and prose which allows him to be romantic and irreverent at one and the same instant. Yet the simultaneity of voices speaks with conscientious regularity throughout his verse in a "mixed choir" of laughter and tears. Even though the important poetry is to be found in his prose and the essential lyricism in his drama, the collected poems in French and English present us with nothing less than the minor work of an acknowledged modern master. Here is the "mixed declension," "a permanent abode" in verse for Beckett's continuing fascination with "the blue celeste of poesy." (pp. 34-5)

Enoch Brater, "Books Considered: 'Collected Poems in English and French'," in The New Republic *(reprinted by permission of* The New Republic; *© 1978 The New Republic, Inc.), Vol. 178, No. 7, February 18, 1978, pp. 33-5.*

VIVIAN MERCIER

Perhaps because his father was not religious, Beckett seems to have felt no anguish in turning away from the Anglican beliefs of his youth; his mother, on the other hand, was deeply religious in a rather narrow evangelical way. Loss of faith, however, clearly has not prevented him from exploiting his Protestant heritage, any more than it prevented James Joyce from exploiting his Catholic one. . . .

A Portrait of the Artist As a Young Man has made millions of readers aware of the thoroughness of Joyce's Catholic education under the Jesuits. It is not generally known, however, that Beckett's Anglican training was almost as thorough. The religious education he received at his mother's knee is vividly dramatized by the famous photograph of him kneeling to pray there at an early age. His years from four to nearly fourteen doubtless saw little slackening in that training, and the ensuing three-and-a-half years as a boarder at Portora Royal School, Enniskillen, Northern Ireland, unquestionably subjected him to a sternly evangelical regime. Founded by none other than the King James I of England who gave his "special command" for the famous Bible translation, Portora has usually had a Church of Ireland clergyman as Headmaster. (p. 266)

One could argue that all his Portora religious training was wasted on Beckett because he lost his faith soon after leaving the school. I believe, on the contrary, that it reinforced his earlier upbringing in certain ways and helps to explain why, at different stages of his literary development, different aspects of his religious heritage come to the fore. One thing at least is certain: there is *no* stage of that development which does not possess a religious dimension. Much has been written by critics about the influence of Dante on Beckett's writing, but surely it is most unlikely that he would have become susceptible to that influence at Trinity if he had not first received such a thorough grounding in the Bible?

It was natural, given his loss of faith, that Beckett's early works should treat his religious heritage with self-conscious irony. We have seen something of this already in *More Pricks Than Kicks*. His next important work, *Murphy*, . . . is positively sly in its biblical allusions. Take this passage, for example:

> "I greatly fear," said Wylie, "that the syndrome known as life is too diffuse to admit of palliation. For every symptom that is eased, another is made worse. The horse leech's daughter is a closed system. Her quantum of wantum cannot vary."

The idea of life as a syndrome made up of innumerable symptoms is clear enough, but who is "the horse leech's daughter"? In Proverbs (30:15), we read, "The horseleech hath two daughters, crying, Give, Give." Although "horseleech" could mean "veterinarian" when the King James was written, the horseleech referred to is a large bloodsucker. Clearly the proverb stuck in Beckett's mind because of the oddity of its expression and its quaint image of insatiable desire.

In the same chapter of *Murphy* he uses a more familiar quotation in the same disrespectful style. On learning that all the bars in Dublin are closed for the "holy hour" between 2:30 and 3:30 p.m., Wylie's friend Neary "leaned against the . . . railings and cursed, first the day in which he was born, then—in a bold flash-back—the night in which he was conceived." No hint is given that these were not original remarks, but I need hardly refer readers to the Book of Job (3:3) "Let the day perish wherein I was born, and the night in which it was said, there is a man child conceived."

Obviously quotations like these do not take the Bible or its message very seriously: Job's cry of utter despair has nothing in common with the temporary inconvenience being undergone by Neary. It is not until after World War II that Beckett confronts the basic teachings of Christianity in his work. At first sight, this confrontation may be mistaken for a total denial and rejection. One could quote, for example, the notorious line from *Endgame*. Hamm, Clov and Nagg pray silently to God; they are disappointed when they get no response; Hamm shouts, "The bastard! He doesn't exist!" (Clov answers, "Not yet.") This blasphemy affirms God's existence even in denying it: how can He be a bastard (or *un salaud,* as the French put it) if He doesn't exist? *All That Fall* takes a bleaker view: after Mrs. Rooney quotes "The Lord upholdeth all that fall . . . ," (Psalm 145 in the King James—144 in the Vulgate) she and her husband "*join in wild laughter.*" God does exist, they imply, but He never intervenes in the workings of His universe.

Yet the meaning of Beckett's first play, *Waiting for Godot,* is deeply ambiguous. Beckett has remarked that if he knew who or what Godot is, he would have said so in the play, but it certainly can be read as a play about waiting for God, or the Revolution, or the Millennium: although Godot seems not to come, who is to say that he won't turn up tomorrow? I myself have suggested more than once that Pozzo is in fact Godot, and therefore Godot arrives in both acts without being recognized. The first time, he is rather cruel, like the God of the Old Testament. In the second act, he is blind and long-suffering, almost Christlike. At the end of Act Two and of the play, Didi and Gogo are still waiting, like Jews expecting the Messiah, or Christians awaiting the Second Coming. One of the great ironies of the New Testament, from the Christian point of view, is that Jesus was not recognized as the Messiah by most of the Jews he came to save. Christians are also warned that the Second Coming of Christ may be as stealthy as "a thief in the night." *Waiting for Godot* suggests that when the Savior comes he is never recognized, but this is perhaps less depressing than the idea that he does not care enough for us to come at all.

After mockery and serious confrontation there comes the third stage of religious influence upon Beckett's literary development, dating from the publication of *Comment c'est* in 1961. . . . Beckett has given up wrestling with the angel: instead of continuing his love/hate relationship with Christianity, he is now writing a sort of Scripture of his own. . . . *How It Is,* itself a text of barely 150 pages, has been followed only by very much shorter prose works: all of them are described by their author as fragmentary, as *Residua* or *Fizzles*. Among these shorter works, several seem to offer a prophetic vision of the end of a world that has not yet quite ended, or (to put it another way) the moments before entropy, or (to put it yet another way) time just before it stops.

I am deliberately mixing religious and scientific terms to convey the paradoxical style of these late works. Stretches of them are written without verbs and read like notes for a coldly precise scientific report, but suddenly we find a turn of phrase that reminds of the King James Bible, without being in any way a quotation. These phrases would not be out of place among the Minor Prophets or in the Book of Revelation. My favorite, both for its rhythm and for its ironic message of hope, comes from *Lessness:* "He will curse God as in the blessed days face to the open sky the passing deluge." Roll *that* on your tongue while you consider its implications: God and Man together again, believing in each other, blaming each other, afflicting each other. Not "happy days" exactly, but blessed days, and certainly happier than those after the recent greatly exaggerated death of God, when Man suddenly found it hard to believe in his own existence. (pp. 267-68)

Vivian Mercier, "Samuel Beckett: Bible Reader," in Commonweal *(copyright © 1978 Commonweal Publishing Co., Inc.; reprinted by permission of Commonweal Publishing Co., Inc.), Vol. CV, No. 9, April 28, 1978, pp. 266-68.*

ANTHONY S. BRENNAN

Most of Beckett's characters have, to put it mildly, come down in the world. From the heroic heights of freewheeling movement that some of them achieve on bicycles, they journey backwards down the evolutionary ladder to a reptilian crawling in mud, or even to the vegetable condition of Winnie in *Happy Days*. . . . Virtually all of the quotations Winnie uses come from literature that is concerned with confronting death or with despair at the limited amount of time we have on earth. Beckett knows how many writers have charted this territory before him. But Winnie tosses off these deeply troubled moments as though they were jingles. . . . Beckett chooses his quotations with great care and they are all more deeply relevant to Winnie's condition than she realizes. (pp. 205-06)

Beckett is not the kind of writer who could say with Eliot of his literary allusions "These fragments I have shored against my ruins." His use of great literature is as self-consciously deliberate and as ironical as Eliot's, but it is not shaped by nostalgia nor directed by a conservative temper. Eliot wishes to remind us how far we have fallen away from the standards of the earlier aristocratic cultures of the western tradition. He offers literary allusions and parodies as touchstones by which we may recognize the hideous banality of the modern world and thereby return to higher spiritual values. Beckett's purpose is entirely opposite, for he relentlessly asserts that we are stuck with the hideous banality and can never return to a time in which tragedy and epic flourished, where man, ennobled by suffering or transfigured by passion, could achieve self-knowledge and a dignity that could awe an audience.

It is important to recognize how deliberately literary Beckett is. I would argue that Beckett sees himself as writing a kind of coda to the whole western tradition. (pp. 223-24)

Winnie's use of quotation is one of the many devices she has resorted to in brightening up her life, and it involves rich and complex ironies. As the jewels of poetry that she recovers sparkle through the drossy collection of clichés which constitute her own speech, we realize how banal her education has been. The passages she abuses so cheerfully remind the audience of earlier ages, principally the Renaissance, when men had different concepts of order. . . . In enduring her fate she relies on the detritus in her handbag and on her classics. Beckett never allows the fact to escape our attention that she draws as much comfort from toothbrush, mirror, and lipstick as she does from Shakespeare, Milton, and Keats.

Many critics have noted the frequency of literary allusion in Beckett's work but no systematic study of this aspect of his art has been undertaken. His work up to and including *Murphy* is full of the brittle, mocking, self-consciously clever techniques so characteristic of those who need to display the habits of academic thinking to demonstrate their superiority to them. The most obvious explanation of Beckett's switch to writing in French, as he indicated himself indirectly, is that it imposed a restriction on his propensity to be seduced into supplying the learned verbal tricks and literary echoes that so clearly determine much of the tone of his early work. His work, however, continued to be directly shaped by the European literary tradition, a fact which can hardly surprise us in a man who regarded James Joyce as a kind of mentor. It would not be too much to claim that his work is directed to, and can only be fully understood by, people who are familiar with the literary frame of reference.

Every scene in Beckett evokes a host of literary associations. In the language and tone we are so often reminded of Swift, in landscape and character we uncover echoes of Synge and Yeats, in the juxtaposition of moods we recognize a facility akin to that of Shakespeare, in the atmosphere we are obliged to recall Dante, Milton's Hell, and *King Lear*. But above all, of course, we are aware of relentless parodic references to the Bible. . . . The constant interplay of . . . shadowy parallels serves to reinforce Beckett's bitter ironies as he inverts the message of the Bible and portrays a godless world. His heroes cannot walk on water nor can they take up their beds and walk; they limp along with stiffening joints and fall into a reptilian crawling that Beckett, with the dianoetic laugh he defines so well in *Watt*, means us to relate to Milton's Satan. (pp. 224-26)

Beckett often presents the development of his characters as a backward climb down an evolutionary ladder, for *homo erectus* seems to drift inevitably towards the floundering and wriggling in primeval slime that is so mercilessly imaged in *How It Is*. On that journey the writer-hero tries to unload his excess baggage—the comfort of objects, of pieces of clothing, the distraction of companionship and sexual endeavor, the need of shelter. This shedding of habits is attended by the most urgent need, the impossible task of dispensing finally with words and achieving silence. In the trilogy and the plays the writer endeavors to exfoliate a series of characters who, in telling their stories, try to observe a measurable progress towards the desired end, but even the Unnamable cannot spiral into the void. Wound inextricably into this task of coping with the burden of existence is Beckett's preoccupation with making us aware of the considerable baggage of the western cultural tradition that we trundle along with. We are inheritors of a treasure house of literary masterpieces. But the values and beliefs which made those works moving, meaningful, and instructive in earlier societies are now inaccessible to us as ways of organizing our behavior and making sense of the world. These fragments of the past cling to us and cannot be sloughed off or silenced any more easily than the fictional selves that torment his characters. They may use the fragments, as Winnie does, to distract themselves, or they may be unconscious of them. But Beckett does not mean the reader to be unconscious of them. By forcing us to relate his world in ironic contrast to a larger framework, he underlines the inescapable bleakness of that world. The literary fragments reinforce our awareness of how isolated we are, how bereft of all aid. In his guerrilla warfare with literature Beckett presents characters who can escape neither into nor from their own fictions, and by constant allusion he reminds us, in the very process of reading him, that we cannot escape our essential condition in the fiction of other writers. (pp. 226-27)

Anthony S. Brennan, "Winnie's Golden Treasury: The Use of Quotation in 'Happy Days'," in Arizona Quarterly *(copyright © 1979 by Arizona Board of Regents), Vol. 35, No. 3, Autumn, 1979, pp. 205-27.*

* * *

BELSER, Reimond Karel Maria de
See RUYSLINCK, Ward

* * *

BENEDIKT, Michael 1935-

Benedikt is an American editor, poet, critic, translator, playwright, and song composer. His poetry, with its surprising shifts in subject and logic, reflects his interest in surrealist art and theater. He has also experimented with prose poems. (See also *CLC*, Vol. 4, and *Contemporary Authors*, Vols. 13-16, rev. ed.)

JEROME J. McGANN

The purpose of Michael Benedikt's collection of prose poems, *Night Cries,* is straightforward enough: to see the world lying about us in a new way, to strip off the veils of familiarity (Shelley), to open the doors of perception (Blake, Huxley). It is one of the oldest and most resilient of Romantic subjects, and Benedikt re-presents it out of its modern Romantic traditions of symbolist and surrealist literature.

Mr Benedikt's project, like that of his forebears, lays down one fundamental imperative. If the world is to be seen in a new way *forever* . . . , then the source of vision and understanding has to be broken in upon and cleansed. Tradition has always dictated that such a cleansing is an inward affair, a matter (literally) of insight. Mr Benedikt is a very traditional poet, and his Nietzschean parable "The Doorway of Perception" states the programme in no uncertain terms. . . .

[Mr Benedikt] is a selfconscious manipulator of the form. Many of the poems here are parables about the virtues of prose poetry and the vices of verse. . . . "The Muse in Armor" brings the obvious charge that verse is stuffy and insincere. . . .

The second charge against verse is related to the first: that to write in verse one must calculate. Verse entails deliberations, and ends in craftiness. . . .

Mr Benedikt's book interests me precisely because it is so selfconscious about itself, so well *made,* that the conventions of its art—the art of the prose poem—are easily visible. . . .

The final argument suggests that verse encourages "poetical" inflation of the ordinary and the human. . . . *Night Cries* parodies many standard poetical *topoi,* and brings them down to earth. . . .

The prose poem offers an alternative in all three areas. What interests me most above these alternatives is that they make up a set of poetic conventions in terms of which the prose poem carries out its manoeuvres. . . .

Mr Benedikt has mastered these general conventions, as he has mastered the many stylistic devices which they call forth. . . . His book is important—it is also enjoyable—because it offers a fine, a clear opportunity to understand the craftsmanship of poetry, and particularly the craftsmanship of a poetic form whose general ideology, Romanticism, has so far succeeded in its programmes that many still find it difficult willingly to suspend their disbelief while reading it. Like all poetry, this sort of work is neither to be believed (romantically) nor disbelieved (critically). One must either respond to it selfconsciously (if one is inclined to the Romantic), or follow one's understanding of its forms until one appreciates the grace of its art. . . .

Jerome J. McGann, "The Virtues of Prose," in The Times Literary Supplement *(© Times Newspapers Ltd. (London) 1976; reproduced from* The Times Literary Supplement *by permission), No. 3880, July 23, 1976, p. 911.*

BEN HOWARD

Coming upon Michael Benedikt's collection of brief prose pieces [*Night Cries*], one should perhaps be reminded of the traditions of the prose poem and of French surrealism, from which these pieces appear to be derived. But what comes to mind instead is Gertrude Stein's dictum that "remarks are not literature". . . . For the apparent purpose of these pieces is to pose novel hypotheses and situations and to make amusing, unexpected remarks. . . .

[Characteristically an] arbitrary relationship will be premised, usually in the title. A dramatic situation involving the speaker and a personified physical object will then be established, and a linear narrative or conceit will be developed, employing explicit physical imagery. The theme will often be sexual or scatological. The tone will be detached, bemused, sarcastic.

The weakness of the method should be evident from the description. It is deductive, and it is very often predictable. The imagery and episodes, however shocking or clever, vivid or violent, become so many supporting instances of a proposition stated at the outset. The speaker sees a face in the trash; and since we know from previous anecdotes that he is given to personification and to establishing relationships with inanimate objects, we can pretty much predict what will follow. The result is that, although these pieces present many instances of sudden violent action . . . they present few surprises. From the first sentence, if not from the titles alone—*The Sarcophagus of the Esophagus, The Nipplewhip, How to Disembark from a Lark*—one can usually guess the outcome.

The predictability of the pieces is in direct conflict with

their apparent purpose, which is to subvert the reader's conventional perceptions. Judging from their many obscenities, these narratives have been designed to offend the reader; and at their more vulgar moments . . . they succeed in doing just that. But if their larger purpose is to jar the reader's established modes of perception, they must be deemed a failure, because their lack of any evident conviction allows them to be relegated rather easily to the shelves of the novelty shop. Benedikt's methods do result in fresh perceptions, as when he invites us to view sleep as a place to which one drives "down the highways of staying awake", or when he suggests that "passing through" the eyes of his "detective wife" is like "clearing Cuban-American customs!" But the bulk of the statements in his book seem based on nothing more compelling than a pun or a rhyme or a roll of the dice. And though they provide many new perspectives on ordinary experience, they make no case for adopting any of those perspectives. Indeed, the author seems to dare us to believe in his fictions. (pp. 289-90)

Ben Howard, "Four Voices," in Poetry *(© 1977 by The Modern Poetry Association; reprinted by permission of the Editor of* Poetry*), Vol. CXXX, No. 5, August, 1977, pp. 285-92.**

KATHLEEN WIEGNER

Michael Benedikt . . . seems to have given up on mankind altogether and makes his work a series of jokes at its expense. To write a Benedikt poem (or prose poem in the case of *Night Cries* . . .) you begin with something obvious and expand until it becomes absurd. Anyone with any wit at all can do it. The language is filled with clichés, figures of speech, puns, morals that cannot be subjected to any scrutiny at all before they begin to break down. (p. 45)

I also have an argument with the concept of the prose poem. . . .

From a jaundiced perspective it appears that a prose poem writer throws out the craft of poetry and the bother of inventing a story with plot and character for an easier alternative. (p. 46)

Finally I admit to being alienated by Benedikt's surrealism. One of the things that people like about surrealism is that it only confirms their own worst suspicions about the world—that people are dead and all life has passed to inanimate objects. People in these poems are so dead, in fact, that they are menaced by their own clothes or furniture which are now much more alive. There must be an incredible amount of cultural masochism at work to permit people to go on believing this nonsense, or depths of self-hatred which are bottomless. People and objects are *not* "interchangeable " (as one of Benedikt's admirers so glowingly says they are). Is it any more profound to endow a garbage pail with the personality of a tart ("A Face in the Trash") than for Joyce Kilmer to give a tree the personality of a loving mother? Benedikt's poem is certainly more in tune with modern sensibility not only in its imagery but in the note of hysteria on which the poem ends. His poems hover lovingly over the worst that can happen in any situation. . . . When Benedikt cuts close to the accident-prone nature of existence free of the bad puns and corny jokes, as he does in this poem, his vision is quite convincingly real. Too often there is no more grace and wit in his anger than the man in a barroom argument who, when baited beyond endurance can only respond "shove it. . . ." (pp. 46-7)

Kathleen Wiegner, "Heroes and Heroines of Private Life," in The American Poetry Review *(copyright © 1977 by World Poetry, Inc.; reprinted by permission of Kathleen Wiegner), Vol. 6, No. 5, September-October, 1977, pp. 45-7.*

* * *

BLISH, James 1921-1975

Blish, an American science fiction novelist, poet, critic, short story writer, playwright, screenwriter, and author of young adult novels, was considered a master of science fiction. He avoided popular fantastical ideas, creating instead realistic dramas based on feasible technological innovations. He was best known for *A Case of Conscience*, a novel that earned him the Hugo Award in 1959. Blish also wrote criticism under the pseudonym of William Atheling, Jr., and adapted several of the "Star-Trek" television shows into novels. (See also *Contemporary Authors*, Vols. 1-4, rev. ed.; obituary, Vols. 57-60.)

RICHARD D. MULLEN

Although some of the contradictions [in Blish's *Cities in Flight* tetralogy] surely result from authorial carelessness, forgetfulness, or indifference, they are too numerous and too prominent to be regarded as anything other than an essential feature of the overall story. Since point of view is rigidly controlled throughout the work, every statement can be attributed to one or another of the various characters. Given this fact, we can make sense of the tetralogy by regarding it, not as a fiction in which a universe has been created by an omniscient, omnipotent author, but as historical narrative with a large admixture of myth; that is, by assuming that behind the sometimes accurate, sometimes erroneous, sometimes mythical narrative there is an actual history. . . .

[The] explicit Spenglerianism of *Cities in Flight* is erroneous in one of its details, highly dubious in others . . . and rather absurd overall. The flat error is in the statement by Robert Helmuth that the building of the pyramids (which occurred in what Spengler considers the Egyptian springtime) was "the last act of an already dead culture." . . . The overall absurdity lies in . . . the idea of the "cultural morphologist":

> Chris recognized the term from his force-feeding in Spengler. It denoted a scholar who could look at any culture at any stage of its development, relate it to all other cultures at similar stages, and produce specific predictions of how these people would react to a given proposal or event. . . .
>
> (pp. 177-78)

Spengler never uses the term "cultural morphologist," and he would surely never have imagined that his work could be put to any such narrow uses. If cultures are organisms, you can make for a culture predictions of the kind that can be made for any organism. . . . As a matter of fact, the cultural morphologists of *Cities in Flight* never actually practice their trade: the various "cultures" with which the heroes deal are never presented with enough fullness to allow for any kind of Spenglerian assessment; the various stories turn on coincidence or on individual psychology of a rudimentary sort and would not be essentially different if explicit references to cultural morphology were entirely eliminated —which could be done by deleting a handful of sentences.

But to say all this is not to say that *Cities in Flight* is of no interest to the student of Spengler. The first volume gives us an intelligently Spenglerian view of the near future, and the other three, albeit very sketchily, the life story of a Spenglerian culture. In comparison with most science-fiction novels and series, *Cities in Flight* is a very rich work indeed. (p. 178)

Richard D. Mullen, "Blish, van Vogt, and the Uses of Spengler," in Riverside Quarterly *(copyright 1968 by Leland Sapiro), Vol. 3, No. 3, August, 1968, pp. 172-86.**

THOMAS D. CLARESON

James Blish leads a double role. As Blish he is one of the most accomplished sf novelists now writing, as attested by such titles as *Black Easter, Cities in Flight,* and the recently published *And All the Stars a Stage.* As William Atheling, he has equal importance as one of the most provocative critics now writing of the genre.

More Issues at Hand confirms this importance. He is one of the few popular critics who has always measured sf by its artistic merit and who explicitly shows himself aware of its relationship to a literary tradition that stretches back beyond Wells and Verne. In his first essay, dated 1965-1966, "Science Fiction as a Movement," he sets forth a basic theme: "The process of gradual re-assimilation of science fiction into the mainstream of literature . . . is bound to be painful for fans who want to claim some special superiority for the genre (as well as writers who would much prefer *not* to have the usual standards of criticism applied to what they do). . . ." In his introduction he calls for "a technical critic" whose work "usually takes the form of *explication du texte,* or what used to be called New Criticism."

If the academic critic who has weathered the tornado of the New Criticism smiles at this, he betrays his own naivete as to the history and present state of sf criticism and fails to recognize that to have a popular critic call for such criticism is indeed an indication of how far the genre has swung from its earlier interest in "probable/plausible" prophecy and gadgetry to its present concern with the genre as a framework for symbolic statement. This concern, with its emphasis upon literary technique, is the trademark of many of the present sf writers; among them Blish is one of the principal voices insisting upon a high standard of literary quality for the whole genre.

If at times he seems to be lured from his central view by an emphasis upon personalities, one must realize that this is, first and foremost, a result of the isolation thrust upon the genre by academic and general criticism over the years, and second that it is the result of him addressing himself in many of his essays and reviews to that isolated in-group through the specialist magazines. This in itself proves important to an understanding of criticism of the genre, and it occurs in Blish's criticism most when he accesses what he regards as the inadequacies of "New Maps and Old Saws: The Critical Literature." (pp. 247-48)

Here, then, is much of the central issue in sf generally and sf criticism specifically. Is the genre to be judged in terms of its ideas, or is it to be judged by those standards by which all fiction is judged? The answers are legion; the quarrel between the polar views continues, most recently focusing upon the movement known as the "New Wave." . . .

Be that as it may, in *More Issues at Hand* Blish insists that sf writers maintain the literary merit of the genre, berating them when they do not. . . . (p. 248)

Throughout these essays, gathered from his writings during the 1960's, Blish remains his own man, refusing to follow the momentary fads of that specialized in-group audience, always holding firmly to the vision of a science fiction that can at the same time be a literature of ideas deserving the highest praise that can be given any fiction. That is why he is one of the foremost, indispensible popular critics now writing; that is why *More Issues at Hand* should be read closely by anyone interested in the genre. (p. 249)

Thomas D. Clareson, "Book Reviews: 'More Issues at Hand: Critical Studies in Contemporary Science Fiction'," in Journal of Popular Culture *(copyright © 1971 by Ray B. Browne), Vol. V, No. 1, Summer, 1971, pp. 247-49.*

EDWIN MORGAN

The Day after Judgment is an exhilarating and hair-raising sequel to Mr. Blish's *Black Easter,* the two connected books now forming the centre-piece of a trilogy, flanked by *Doctor Mirabilis* and (still the best) *A Case of Conscience,* in which the author has aimed to dramatise, in terms of Science Fiction and black and white magic, some of the questions already posed by Milton and Marlowe concerning the powers of God and Satan, the nature of the demonic and the reach of human knowledge. In the present book, Armageddon appears to have arrived, God to have died and Hell to have pushed through to the Earth's surface in Death Valley, California. Can demons be destroyed by material weapons of ultimate sophistication? If so, should they be? Or would the result of that be even worse, since spiritual good and evil are interdependent? The Strategic Air Command, introduced with some satire, has no inhibitions, but the climax is very exciting. A perilous pastiche of Miltonic blank verse makes the end wobble a bit.

Edwin Morgan, "Psophie," in The Listener *(© British Broadcasting Corp. 1972; reprinted by permission of Edwin Morgan), Vol. 87, No. 2247, April 20, 1972, p. 524.**

ROGER BAKER

James Blish commands considerable respect as a science-fiction writer and his novels generally have a narrative directness and a thematic credibility that confounds sceptics. [*And All the Stars a Stage*], though written as usual with simplicity and a lack of pseudo scientific mystification, seems to contain too many themes for comfort. . . .

[Blish makes up for some of the disappointments in this work] through the excitement of his space flight, of two abortive attempts to land (one of which would make an adventure novel alone) and his big finish which has a neat twist, though again a not unfamiliar one and one which experienced sci-fi readers will predict. For once Mr Blish has failed to balance the science with the human interest and I for one, feel cheated.

Roger Baker, "Fiction: 'And All the Stars a Stage'" (© copyright Roger Baker 1973; reprinted with permission), in Books and Bookmen, *Vol. 18, No. 6, March, 1973, p. 80.*

In both style and content [*Midsummer Century*] has its

roots firmly in the SF of the American 1950s, and is in fact an expanded magazine story. The scientist hero, Martels, is displaced in time by the weary old expedient of falling into his new radio telescope. Arriving in AD 25000, he finds himself a disembodied mind sharing the perspex cranium of an electronic brain which is periodically consulted as an oracle by pilgrim tribesmen. . . .

Machines with minds is a stock SF theme, just as the device for getting Martels to AD 25000 is a traditional one. That heavy facetiousness of style is characteristic also: "In all the ointment which the world had provided for the anointing of John Martels, DSc. FRAS, etc., there was only one fly: there was something wrong with his telescope." Thus the first paragraph in a book which, stripped of its conventions, is a slender little adventure story of nowhen. Perfectly agreeable genre stuff, were it not that Mr Blish becomes wantonly pretentious by exploring an alleged hinterland where mysticism and pure maths meet deep in the heart of a transistor. Bad luck for him that algebra + Zen = claptrap.

"News from Nowhen," in The Times Literary Supplement *(© Times Newspapers Ltd. (London) 1973; reproduced from* The Times Literary Supplement *by permission), No. 3740, November 9, 1973, p. 1377.**

BRIAN M. STABLEFORD

When a number of writers, including Kurt Vonnegut, expressed resentment at the fact that their work was thought of as "science fiction," and did everything in their power to avoid the label, Blish campaigned for all "loyal" science fiction writers to insist that their works should be clearly labelled, and for they themselves to wear the title of "SF writer" with pride. He was always an earnest advocate of . . . [specifying] that known scientific facts should never be violated by science fiction, which must work only within the realms of the possible. He also wanted science fiction to be *good*—to be literate as well as logically competent. As a critic he was merciless when attacking on either front. (p. 4)

There is a great deal of labelled science fiction [in which] . . . the establishment of the basic hypothesis [is] little more than a ritual process involving the deployment of conventional key phrases ("mutation," "space warp," "hyperspace," etc.) rather than the extension of connecting threads to real scientific knowledge and theory. The priority in such fiction is on reasoning forward from the idea to its possible consequences. In Blish's fiction a much heavier emphasis is placed on reasoning *backward* in search of firmer foundations for ideas, and it is in the corollaries generated by the formation of elaborate supportive structures that he characteristically finds the impetus to go forward again. It is to a very large extent this essential thoughtfulness, and the more analytical approach to science fiction that it generates, which gives the work of James Blish its unique qualities. All of his major endeavors follow the pattern of first going back in search of a historical and rational background to set his ideas in perspective, then going on ahead to take them to their logical conclusion.

Other hallmarks of Blish's work can be seen in embryonic form in "There Shall Be No Darkness." One is the ability of the characters to adapt to the situation in which they unexpectedly find themselves. There is an *orderliness* in their reactions which reveals them to be sensible, open-minded, and capable people. Sometimes this revelation is unconvincing, in that we know that most people are not like that. . . . Readers have occasionally taken this to be evidence of a lack of emotion [on] the part of the characters concerned—they often seem callous and calculating despite the author's careful reference to their emotional states. This commitment to the scientific method, apparently strong enough to make it difficult for Blish to model characters not similarly possessed of it, is one of the principal shaping forces in the author's literary philosophy. (pp. 9-10)

Blish's concentration on the *method* of science rather than its apparatus results in the fact that in many of his stories resolution is sought by analysis and redeployment of the material of the hypotheses rather than by further innovation. A great deal of science fiction takes advantage of the genre's tremendous potential for *deus ex machina* resolutions. The world is menaced by aliens or mad scientists whose threat is embodied in their miraculous *gizmos*. The hero is harried and persecuted for the requisite number of chapters, then disappears into his laboratory to emerge with an equally miraculous *anti-gizmo* which saves the status quo. One imaginary invention is cancelled by another, conveniently and economically. It is possible to read science fiction for many years without noticing this pattern or realizing how easy it is to manipulate. Over the last ten or twenty years such formularistic solutions have declined largely because conscientious writers have rejected them as unsatisfactory, but they were a godsend to pulp hacks. Blish became conscious of the essential falsity of the device early in his career, and none of his good work makes use of it. (p. 10)

[Blish] is committed to the point of view which insists that if the phenomena are real then the scientific method must be adequate to the problem of systematizing them and revealing the techniques of their manipulation. It is always possible, in the literary cosmos to which Blish's fiction belongs, to gain knowledge *and to apply it*. (p. 12)

Blish's works give the impression that he never found writing easy, and that even his poorer stories were far from effortless. His prose is always *constructed*—often carefully so, sometimes with a high degree of artistry, but nevertheless artificial. His writing was not blessed with any innate elegance, and such grace as is manifest in his stories had to be incorporated by design and hard work. He was primarily a *skillful* writer rather than a naturally talented one, but there are advantages in having to work hard at the business of prose construction, and one is a heightened awareness of literary architecture. This is what equipped him to be a good critic, for he had more insight into the methodology of writing than any of his contemporaries. The points made in the essay "Some Propositions", which opens *The Issue at Hand* . . . demonstrate this preoccupation with methodology, as does his famous crusade against "said book-isms." His best fiction, too, is exceedingly well-planned, carefully balanced, and scrupulously precise in its prose and narrative structure.

In his poorer work, therefore, Blish's presentation is often lifeless and mechanical. In many stories, as in *The Warriors of Day*, he failed to capture the essential *esprit* that was more necessary to their function than the elimination of bad writing-habits. The cause that underlies this failing, however, also underlies the values in his successful work: the elaborate supportive structures which add weight to his ideative adventures, and the meticulousness with which he develops the psychology of his characters and guides their intellectual pilgrimages. (pp. 14-15)

There is a certain irony in the fact that Blish—the most careful and self-conscious of science fiction writers—should *accidentally* incorporate into a story [''Surface Tension''] the qualities necessary to make it into a classic, and then find himself unable to figure out how he had worked the trick. His diagnosis—that he ''touched a nerve more mythological than molecular''—is surely correct, and his failure to discover how is probably a case of being unable to see the wood for the trees. (pp. 16-17)

[In] ''Surface Tension'' we find a group of inquiring minds, opposed—inevitably—by the forces of cautionary conservatism. They are all set to challenge issues of dogmatic faith, and (though they cannot know it) are on the threshold of the discovery that there lies beyond the horizons of their perceived world a vastly greater and more wonderful cosmos. . . . [The story succeeds because it espouses] the world-view of [its] characters, which is intrinsically more limited than that possessed by the reader, so that the reader can anticipate their moment of revelation and know its ''true'' significance. (pp. 17-18)

The significance of this particular myth within science fiction is that it reflects the actual ambition of the medium itself, which is to demonstrate to the reader that he lives in a world pregnant with hitherto-unimagined possibilities, and to provide a new context for the events of the mundane present. . . .

The crucial lines of ''Surface Tension,'' however, are those which link the mythical quality of the story to the particular concerns of the author, presenting once again the insistence that the key to achievement is *knowledge*. (p. 18)

Blish's future history is more than ''just'' history. It is the working out of what we could only call a divine plan if we were not dealing with a godless universe. The apocalyptic conclusion of *The Triumph of Time* owes nothing in the literal sense to Spengler, but it is entirely in keeping with the nature of the exercise. It gives the whole tetralogy [*Cities in Flight*] an imaginative sweep which is quite unparallelled in science fiction. Nor does it do what Blish, in his ''profoundly religious opinion,'' believed that the science fiction writer should not do—. . . it does not rest on assumptions generally believed to be false, but instead *adds to* its quasi-scientific hypotheses certain metaphysical hypotheses. (p. 26)

They Shall Have Stars is part political melodrama and part psychological melodrama. The Western world has entered the final phase of the decline specified by Spengler, which is called ''Caesarism.'' . . . The novel is densely written, packed with long dialogues containing abstruse exchanges of social philosophy. It is very difficult for the reader who comes to it for the first time to identify with the world-view of the story and appreciate the significance which the author is attempting to attribute to its events. It is yet another story of conceptual breakthrough, but it is not easy for the reader to perceive the magnitude of the breakthrough. In many ways, though, this is the strongest element in the whole structure—it was in the assembly of supportive structures for his main premises that Blish was always at his best.

A Life for the Stars introduces a complete change of pace. It is an easy-going novel, and its commentary—as would be expected in a juvenile work—is much simpler. The hero begins the book by knowing nothing, and for the first few chapters his is a worm's-eye view of life in the flying city of Scranton. As he learns more about the historical context to which he belongs, so does the reader. The reader who comes to it as the second part of the tetralogy has the added advantage of having read *They Shall Have Stars,* and has the perspective inherited from that volume to balance against the hero's slow accumulation of wisdom.

Earthman, Come Home remains slightly awkward against the setting of the tetralogy (despite the fact that the tetralogy is really a series of afterthoughts expanding out from it). The opening sections retain many of the trappings of traditional space opera, including the invocation of super-scientific devices more or less *ad hoc*. . . . The pieces, however, never quite fit together well enough to be an integrated novel in their own right, and there are aspects of them which seem to be at odds with the greater whole of the tetralogy. (pp. 26-8)

[*The Triumph of Time*] is basically a conversation-piece, most of its ideas remaining no more than ideas, confined in the heads of the characters. (p. 28)

The determination to probe a little more deeply into the implications of commonplace science-fictional notions is the seed of many Blish stories, and even when the stories were unsuccessful they could often strike a disturbing note in bringing to the surface something that lay concealed within common patterns of thought. Many of these moments of revelation are unpleasant or horrific, and there is a persistent bitterness in Blish's disenchantment with certain aspects of the real world . . . ; sometimes there is a colder breath of hostility which amounts almost to disgust. This hostility is usually momentary, though there are one or two stories which are built around such moments, and is almost invariably the result of a penetrating insight into the implications of some of the darker possibilities opened up by the science-fictional imagination. (pp. 32-3)

It is a little strange . . . that Blish should be so widely considered to be an emotionless writer. The truth is that the intense emotional experiences which are suffered by the characters in these stories are of a kind which many readers simply do not recognize. The pain suffered by virtually all of Blish's characters who *do* suffer is a species of anguish characteristic of alienated intellectuals: it is an anguish which arises out of unusual insight and special intelligence. . . .

Perhaps the boldest of all Blish's fictional experiments in thought is the novel which he wrote in collaboration with Norman L. Knight, *A Torrent of Faces* (1967). (p. 35)

The ambitiousness of *A Torrent of Faces* is made clear by the preface, in which its premises are stated. In the year 2794 the world's population is one thousand billion. In order to support such a population nothing less than a worldwide Utopian society can be envisaged. The economic system of this Utopia is fascism. The main theme of the book is the vulnerability of such a world to disaster, and its climax is a kind of apocalypse.

A Torrent of Faces never quite works. . . . [The] biological speculations in the story are entirely subverted by the convenient miracle which gives hybrid humans all kinds of wild talents—it is disappointing to find Blish accepting such a commonplace fantasy for the sake of convenience. The prospect of new evolutionary horizons for the human race allows a note of optimism to be introduced at the end of the book, but it is without sensible foundation and rings very hollow. Nevertheless, the book features some beautiful imagery and some fine ideative flourishes, and is one of the key works of the brief period of Malthusian panic which science fiction suffered at the end of the Sixties.

The same themes that are featured in *A Torrent of Faces* recur in the novella "We All Die Naked" (1969). . . . (p. 36)

In "We All Die Naked" the bitterness of such stories as "Tomb Tapper" and "A Dusk of Idols" bursts its bounds, and the novella becomes a virtual tirade against human folly. Its moral is that we deserve what we will get for being what we are, and Blish seems to take a savage delight in making the point as brutally as possible. It is a story which contrasts sharply with his more sensitive and more carefully-considered pieces, and is perhaps the darkest of all of Blish's moments of dark vision: the moments when he perceives Hell on Earth. After "We All Die Naked," Blish wrote only two significant works of science fiction, the first being *The Day After Judgment,* in which the classical Hell of Medieval Christianity is *literally* raised on the surface of Earth; and that story not only concludes the series of investigations begun in "A Case of Conscience," but also shows something of the relationship between that series—which is predominantly an intellectual inquiry—and the particular kind of horror which haunts so many of the author's emotively powerful pieces.

While Blish was undoubtedly attracted to science fiction largely because of its potential as a medium for experiments in thought, this was not his sole reason for writing it. He was interested in writing as an art, as a craft, and as a business, and he was never ashamed of this triple priority. Many of his experiments were not experiments in thought but experiments in writing technique, and these experiments ran the entire gamut from *avant garde* surrealism to flamboyant space opera. He was invariably a *calculating* writer, and this is shown no less by *The Warriors of Day* than by "A Case of Conscience." Many of his literary experiments are pure adventure stories, some are rather bizarre curiosities. Barely a handful can be accounted genuinely successful, but many more of them have some features of interest. (p. 37)

Though this period of Blish's career also produced the full-length version of *A Case of Conscience* and *The Triumph of Time,* it cannot really be said that Blish's attempt to establish himself as a novelist rather than a short story writer was immediately successful. It is arguable, in fact, that he only ever produced one novel of note that did not emerge from a substantial novelette or group of stories written previously, and that that was the only one of his novels where he forsook entirely the apparatus of science fiction. He did write three successful novels later in his career—*Black Easter, The Day After Judgment,* and *Midsummer Century* —but all were short and might better be regarded as novellas than as full-length works. All in all, with the one striking exception of *Doctor Mirabilis,* it must be said that all his experiments in novel-writing were failures, when measured against his own high standards of assessment. The determination to experiment, however, never left him, and it continued to produce some rather bizarre results. (p. 42)

Within the space of a decade Blish wrote six novels intended for juvenile readers: *The Star Dwellers* (1961), *A Life for the Stars* (1962), *Mission to the Heart Stars* (1965), *Welcome to Mars . . .* (1968), *The Vanished Jet* (1968), and *Spock Must Die!* (1970). Although these books belong to the later phase of his career they constitute the weakest section of his output. (p. 46)

[*Spock Must Die!*] represents Blish's original contribution to the mythology of the TV series *Star Trek*. . . . It is a combination of space opera and whimsy, quite typical of the *Star Trek* mythos, though much more lavish with the special effects than the limitations of TV (especially the budget) would have allowed in a script. It is a glib story, and even has sub-climaxes which one can easily imagine bracketing commercial breaks. Playful self-indulgence extends far enough to allow the introduction of *Finnegans Wake* and its syncretic language into the plot. . . . (p. 49)

The *Star Trek* books brought Blish a financial security which he had not previously enjoyed, and also a very considerable juvenile audience. The relaxed attitude which is evident in "Getting Along" and *Midsummer Century* is almost certainly the result of this change in his professional fortunes. The same relaxation is obvious in *Spock Must Die!,* and there is a certain propriety about its presence there. Its very existence is an ironic comment on the unpredictabilities of a career in postwar science fiction, and the compromises that were necessary in order to contend with the vagaries of the marketplace. It would be wrong to imply that it was a cynical book, any more than *The Warriors of Day* or *The Night Shapes* was a cynical book, but it is one that carries with it a consciousness of a special irony and an awareness of the disjunction between what Blish found in science fiction that made it into his vocation, and the kind of demand which sustained the *genre* in the marketplace of literary mass-production.

The juvenile novels, assessed as a group, show up rather starkly all of Blish's limitations as a writer, while only rarely allowing his virtues to show through. His own interests were intellectual; his best writing concerned itself with the development of sophisticated, many-faceted arguments giving elaborate treatment to abstruse questions of metaphysical and moral philosophy. When his imaginative explorations were held back—as they were by the demands of standardized pulp writing and the demands of the juvenile market—his artistry was lost, and he became a mediocre writer, at best no more than competent. . . . In order to assess in any meaningful way his contribution to twentieth-century science fiction, it is necessary to focus on that work which owed least to the pulp heritage of the *genre*. He was, above all else, a methodical and meticulous writer, and he showed up to best advantage in projects which could not have been undertaken by any other kind of approach. The questions to which he addressed himself in such projects are peculiar enough to warrant description as "esoteric," and perhaps the books which emerged from them are esoteric, too. Nevertheless, they can be read and appreciated by any reader who has a degree of interest in their subject matter, simply because he took such pains to lay out his work in a careful and orderly manner. (pp. 49-50)

The premise of ["Cathedrals in Space"] is deceptively simple. An expedition to an alien world includes a member of the Society of Jesus. In collaboration with his fellows he must decide whether Earth is to establish interplanetary relations with the inhabitants of this world with a view to exploiting its mineral wealth—specifically lithium, useful for making atomic weapons. His companions, of course, approach this issue in strictly secular terms—where they touch moral questions their attitude is utilitarian. Blish's interest, however, lies with the Jesuit, for he has a rather different attitude to Lithia and its inhabitants, determined by the context of the *theological* problem of the plurality of worlds. He has to decide where the Lithians stand not only relative to man but also relative to God, and in the story he is driven to the inescapable conclusion that the Lithians are creations of the devil, set as a snare for mankind. (pp. 52-3)

Blish ably preserves the ambiguous perspective necessary to the story by concentrating on the *subjective* meaning which the question has for his main character.

Doctor Mirabilis (1964), which continued the line of inquiry, is also a story about a man and his subjective experience of the dilemma generated by a dual commitment to empirical inquiry and religious Authority. It is an intellectual biography of Roger Bacon, the thirteenth century friar who was the key character in an abortive Medieval movement to incorporate the methods of experimental science into contemporary philosophy. The book deals directly with the question which faced Bacon—the question of whether his search for truth by such means was justified, or whether it represented the snare of heresy. It is primarily a story of discovery, but it is about discovery in a context of thought very different from that which controls our attitude to discovery.

Only in the third part of the trilogy, made up of *Black Easter* (1968 . . .) and *The Day After Judgment* (. . . 1972) do we move away from subjective experience to the embodiment of the problem as a display of events, when the devils that may have set traps for Father Ruiz-Sanchez and Roger Bacon appear on the literary stage in person to claim their reward. Here—to begin with, at least—there is no manifest ambiguity, but simply a straightforward account of the consequence which might follow if the initial premise were true. Here, the quest for knowledge (pursued for the sake of curiosity) leads to the ultimate experiment: the release of the fallen angels from Hell. Once released they reveal that God is dead and that they are free forever. Lucifer is the new master of Creation, and the human race has been delivered into his hands.

Once again, this three-stage development follows Blish's customary pattern—the second novel goes back to establish the foundations of the whole project (and represents the work most competently, comprehensively, and artfully done), while the third part pushes on to the ultimate conclusion. (pp. 53-4)

Blish's meticulous attention to detail and his careful stylistic contrivance were ideally suited to the re-creation of a distant historical period—not only its environment and its social habits, but, crucially, its intellectual climate and ways of thought. The historical novel as a *genre* has mostly been concerned with mere costume drama (as, of course, has science fiction), but Blish was working well outside normal *genre* priorities, aiming for a special kind of realism. The context provided for the book by the line of thought extending out of *A Case of Conscience* was ideal for a life of Roger Bacon, whose actions did not divert the course of eventful history, and who was more-or-less forgotten by the intellectual tradition of Europe, but whose philosophy was a striking anticipation of the rebirth of empiricism in the seventeenth century.

[*Doctor Mirabilis*] is, of course, a tragedy, not of lost love but of lost intelligence. Not many writers would have been capable of appreciating or expressing that particular tragedy, but Blish was ideally fitted for the task, and he carried it off brilliantly. It is a work which deserves to be far better known than it is, and a work which invites wholehearted admiration from anyone interested in the history of ideas.

Given the status of the first two parts of the *After Such Knowledge* trilogy, *Black Easter* and *The Day After Judgment* are somewhat disappointing. They are outstanding if only for their basic hypothesis, which is startling in its boldness, and for their flamboyant development of it. . . . The parodic element of the novels occasionally expresses itself in terms of a whimsical levity which—to my mind—strikes a jarring note. . . . This is, however, only a minor cavil—the real failure of these works to live up to expectations is their rather stumbling progress from one stage-set to the next. They move gracelessly, in a series of fits and starts, knowing where they are going but never quite sure of the best route. (pp. 57-8)

All in all, the *After Such Knowledge* trilogy, taken as a whole, is an uneven work, but nevertheless a coherent one. It is unique in combining three different *genres* into one intellectual enterprise, and by doing so it helps to point out some of the utilitarian merits of all three as vehicles for experiments in thought. It is a fascinating endeavor, and there is nothing else like it in modern fiction. At least in part, it also represents a considerable literary achievement. (p. 58)

All of [Blish's] significant works are attempts to make readers emerge from the reader-experience with the feeling "'I never thought about it that way before.'" Blish was a pioneer within American *genre* SF in forsaking the almost-exhausted physical horizons for the infinite moral and philosophical horizons. He was not alone in this, nor was he the first such pioneer, but he made his own way, and broke new ground where others have followed. (p. 59)

Brian M. Stableford, in his A Clash of Symbols: The Triumph of James Blish *(copyright © 1979 by Brian M. Stableford), The Borgo Press, 1979, 62 p.*

* * *

BOLT, Robert 1924-

Bolt is a British playwright and screenplay writer. He is perhaps best known for his play *A Man for All Seasons,* which also became a successful film. While not considered innovative stylistically, his work is characterized by well-constructed plots and a brilliant use of dialogue. (See also *Contemporary Authors,* Vols. 17-20, rev. ed.)

MARTIN PRICE

[The appearance of Robert Bolt's *Flowering Cherry*] has raised the usual question of whether here is at last a new writer of importance. (pp. 54-5)

There are overtones in Bolt's play which recall Osborne's *The Entertainer*. . . . What strikes one in the two plays is the attempt to imply something about contemporary England through a study of the middle generation. . . . Jim Cherry's empty job is set against the nostalgic recollection of life on the land. [The] lost middle generation is brought to crisis and self-destruction by the demand of its children for candor and clarity. In Bolt's play, where neither parents nor children quite come to understanding of their plight, it is a cruel adolescent girl who destroys illusions. . . . [There] is a kind of maudlin egocentricity growing into ruthlessly irresponsible use of others. The neurotic middle-aged man becomes . . . a symbol of that generation that stands between the old convictions which once fertilized life and a new ordering that will clear away their vestiges. It is a generation living on the patterns of the past without either believing in them or rejecting them—the generation, one might say, of the Suez crisis rather than the Battle of Britain. (p. 55)

Martin Price, "The London Season," in Modern Drama *(copyright © 1958, University of Toronto, Graduate Centre for Study of Drama; with the permission of* Modern Drama*), Vol. 1, No. 1, May, 1958, pp. 53-9.**

JOHN McCARTEN

A drama based on the political confusions of sixteenth-century England might readily succumb to turgidity and bombast, but Mr. Bolt [in "A Man for All Seasons"] has avoided extraneous historical detail to give us a sharp and brilliant portrait of a man who might just as easily be of our day as of King Henry's. The stuff More is made of doesn't lack its heroic element, but he is never obtrusively larger than life; indeed, the limit of his daring consists in saying nothing when he is asked to swear allegiance to Henry as head of the Church of England, on the ground that silence may or may not mean an affirmation—a quibble that he hopes will save him and his family from the consequences of disloyalty to the throne. He is wise, witty, gentle, affectionate, and often perplexed, and in his efforts to abide by the letter of the law—something he understands and cherishes—as he drowns in a sea of intrigue, he is a pathetic but never an ignoble figure. (p. 117)

John McCarten, "The Reluctant Martyr," in The New Yorker *(© 1961 by The New Yorker Magazine, Inc.), Vol. XXXVII, No. 42, December 2, 1961, pp. 117-18.**

ROBERT BRUSTEIN

After some years of neglect, the chronicle history play has been enjoying a rebirth among the more literary English and French dramatists. Up till now, the results have been rather indifferent, but in Robert Bolt's *A Man For All Seasons* we finally have an effective example of the genre. A faithful account of the martyrdom of Sir Thomas More, this work is too diffuse to be completely successful, yet, compared with more vulgar dramatic biographies like Anouilh's *Becket* and Osborne's *Luther,* it shows remarkable intelligence, historicity, theatrical ingenuity, and good taste. I confess that the work took me by surprise, for nothing in Bolt's last entry, an inept piece of contemporary realism called *Flowering Cherry,* prepared me for the kind of form and substance he handles with such authority here. Yet, I can think of at least two reasons why he and his contemporaries are now turning to history for their subject matter. As Bolt unwittingly demonstrated in *Flowering Cherry,* modern man has become so trivial and uninteresting that he has lost his power to involve us, while modern mass society has inhibited even the superior spirits from expressing themselves through significant action. (p. 28)

A second reason for the growing popularity of the history play has to do with the influence of Brecht who brought new eyes to the past and new techniques for putting it on the stage. It is Brecht's spirit, tempered by the spirit of Elizabethan drama and of More himself (whose writings, transcripts, and sayings appear as dialogue in the play), that hovers over Bolt's new work. . . . For the purpose of setting the stage, bridging transitions, and commenting on the action, Bolt has supplied a Brechtian Chorus, who also plays all the lower class characters—a greedy, ironic, calculating opportunist called . . . The Common Man. And just as Bolt's Chorus assumes some of the functions of the Story Teller in *The Caucasian Chalk Circle,* so Bolt's interpretation of More . . . recalls Brecht's concept of Galileo, another historical figure hounded by authorities. (p. 29)

Without scanting More's wit, Bolt interprets him more as a melancholy intellectual aristocrat, desperately trying to preserve some private corner of conscience, while preserving his life at the same time. . . . More's death, the wages of integrity, is for the ages; but the moral is for our own time, when the common man . . . preserves his skin through compromise and accommodation. (pp. 29-30)

Robert Brustein, "Chronicle of a Reluctant Hero," in The New Republic *(reprinted by permission of* The New Republic; *(© 1961 The New Republic, Inc.), Vol. 145, No. 24, December 11, 1961, pp. 28-30.*

JOHN SIMON

Bolt's Sir Thomas More [in *A Man for All Seasons*] is an intellectual blessed with common sense and cursed with a conscience. He is witty, charming, and wise, and not especially eager to add to these the supererogatory virtue of heroism. His unshakable belief in Catholicism is coupled with an almost equal faith in the law . . . , which will protect his conscience provided it has the good sense of not going naked to its enemy. He is as loyal a minister to Henry as superior intelligence will permit, as good a husband and father as a man who lives most warmly with ideas can be, and surely the unworldliest man of the world. The play shows how this upright and religiously orthodox man, who cannot agree to Henry's remarriage and England's consequent divorce from the Church of Rome, is hounded into heroism. When no amount of prudence and legal ingenuity can shelter him from the ever fouler machinations of his enemies, he finally meets the tragic greatness thrust upon him with the spiritual and verbal grandeur of a Socrates. It must be admitted that Mr. Bolt, though relying scrupulously on documentation and even quotation from More's own words, has somewhat idealized his hero—the acrimonious religious polemist who helped bring about the death sentence of a mere translator of the Bible into English is certainly not present—but he has given us a believable, unwhittled-down Sir Thomas, and who could ask for More?

The play does have its limitations. It is, by the very nature of being a "history," forced to look at things a little more panoramically than profoundly. Bolt does his best to compress the variousness and proliferation of history into a few typical, clearly defined figures and situations, but he is still not quite successful in making most of his characters anything but accessories before the fact of the protagonist. Nor is this protagonist all that one might desire. Heroism, indeed martyrdom, out of doctrinal differences in religion may still be moving from our point of view, but it does not carry the urgency of self-sacrifice for some other, socially more compelling, cause. True, we can translate, and are encouraged to do so, More's struggle into certain contests of our time, but it is like translating out of the Chinese into English: the gap between the cultures and languages is too great to permit more than estimable approximation. Added to this is the fact that More had no adversary worthy of his talents: Henry VIII had nothing but his despotism, Cromwell only his low cunning and unscrupulousness, and the others not even that. There is no good chance, therefore, for a clash with real dramatic thunder and blazing intellectual lightning. There are, in fact, the very limitations of the hero's unfleshly, cerebral middle age.

But all this can prevent the play only from being great—not from being very good indeed: intelligent, pungent and absorbing. Even the slight preponderance of the intellect is nicely mitigated by sufficient action and by the presence, or, rather, omnipresence, of a chorus labeled "The Common Man." This fellow, whether he comments on the happenings or actually participates in them in various roles, is always considerably lower than the angels—say, roughly, audience-high. He is everything from Shakespearean clown to Brechtian opportunist, he reeks of bonhomie and bestiality, and earns his bread by the sweat under his collar. (pp. 10-11)

John Simon, "Play Reviews: 'A Man for All Seasons'," in Theatre Arts *(© 1962 by John Simon), Vol. XLVI, No. 2, February, 1962, pp. 10-11.*

ROBERT W. CORRIGAN

[*A Man for All Seasons*] is one of the finest achievements of the modern theatre, and one of the great dramas of selfhood of all time. (pp. 27-8)

Bolt sees all too clearly the effects collectivism have had upon the individual. In his preface he describes how in our time we have lost all conception of ourselves as individual men, and as a result we have increasingly come to see ourselves in the third person. As this happens we are less and less able to deal with life's psychic, social, and spiritual collisions. Thomas More does not see himself in this way; he is "a man with an adamantine sense of his own self. He knew where he began and left off," and the action of the play is best described as a series of collisions between More and a group of powerful and able men who would have him deny his selfhood to serve the wishes of his king. (p. 28)

The matter of the oath [which King Henry VIII required of More, stating that the King was right in divorcing his first wife to marry Anne Boleyn] is the crucial issue of the play. In a collective society the individual tends to become an equivocal commodity, and when we think of ourselves in this way we lose all sense of our own identity. More's refusal to take the oath is Bolt's way of asserting that even under the greatest of pressures man can exist unequivocally; that it is possible to live in the modern world without "selling out." . . . Because of his inviolable sense of himself, Sir Thomas More cannot take an oath that would in effect deny his whole being. (pp. 28-9)

For Bolt, . . . only those conflicts between real alternatives are meaningful; and, therefore, More's antagonists are not straw men. King Henry is a giant of a man; he has a keen intellect, a sharp wit, a pleasing disposition (except when he is crossed), taste and sensitivity, and a gluttonous thirst for life. Only in the realm of ethics is this mercurial personality deficient. Cromwell, too, is a man of great power. . . . Norfolk, too, has significance as an antagonist. He lacked moral and intellectual strength, but he was a good friend. And the claims of friendship can sometimes be a more dangerous foe to integrity than open opposition. But if the claims of friendship are difficult to withstand, those of love are almost impossible. In this regard, More's faithful wife and family must also be considered powerful threats to his selfhood. . . . And, finally, there is More's strongest antagonist: the Common Man, that "plain simple man" who just wants "to keep out of trouble." Quite rightly, More cries out passionately "Oh, Sweet Jesus! These plain, simple men!" For it is the Common Man—sentimental, faithless, and concerned only for his own safety and welfare—who, out of his own sense of inadequacy, ultimately judges and executes the heroes of selfhood. (pp. 29-30)

Bolt has no illusions about the sufficiency of human law, but he sees it as the only defense man can create to fight against the forces of evil. . . . Ultimately, because men and their laws are corruptible, More cannot escape that fatal web that has ensnared him; but he dies knowing that his soul is his own, and "a man's soul is his self." . . .

In a time when social and economic forces tend to destroy individual integrity and the courage to accept the Destiny of our own identity, many people have lost faith in the power and the possibility of heroism. Robert Bolt has not! (p. 30)

Robert W. Corrigan, "Five Dramas of Selfhood," in The New Theatre of Europe, *edited by Robert W. Corrigan (copyright © 1962, by Dell Publishing Co., Inc.; reprinted by permission of Dell Publishing Co., Inc.), Dell, 1962, pp. 9-31.**

J. C. TREWIN

Robert Bolt [is] concerned fiercely with the problems of the individual and his social conscience. . . . [*Flowering Cherry*] proved to be the portrait of a failure, a study of futility, frustration, and self-deception (today a continuing theme).

Jim Cherry is an insurance agent. He is also an abject failure in life, a dreamer who uses his rhapsodies and reveries as a kingdom of escape. . . . Throughout [the play we observe] the affinity with *Death of a Salesman.* [At the denouement] there is a symbolic vision—it might be called *Death of an Insurance Agent*—when, as he sinks to the floor of his kitchen, blossoming trees rise suddenly all round him and we turn from harsh reality to the method of Miller and Kazan. Until this it has been an uncommon play, uncommon because the man, his wife who goes as far in loyalty as any woman could, and the son and daughter so critical of their parents, have clearly formed one household through the dismal years. Many stage families are assembled roughly and implausibly. We can believe in Bolt's, and it means a good deal to such a play as *Flowering Cherry.*

For a while the dramatist's achievement here was suspect. . . . [The] play appeared to be dangerously lucid, a straight, sharp narrative. Surprisingly, Bolt proceeded to a chronicle of Sir Thomas More, called *A Man for All Seasons*. . . . (pp. 119-21)

Robert Bolt tells the story with ingenuity and a controlled passion. (pp. 121-22)

[The figure of the Common Man binds] together the plot and [gets] it to work swiftly. . . . I like Bolt's technical devices in this play. My regret is that he complicates things so much in the published Preface where he seeks to clarify. (p. 123)

Robert Bolt has written one of the few contemporary portrait-plays likely to last; we can see this in performance, and we do not want too many aids and footnotes later.

Bolt's next play (earlier in order of writing) was his fiercest, *The Tiger and the Horse,* taking its title from some words of Blake, 'The Tygers of wrath are wiser than the horses of instruction'. . . . [This play]—even if, as Bolt admits, its people are unnaturally articulate—[presents] an urgent conflict in which the man who has held himself apart can no longer (in the stock modern phrase) remain uncommitted. Again, if you like, a form of self-destruction. (p. 124)

Most of Robert Bolt's people are real, though in ill-judged performance the subordinate characters of *A Man for All Seasons* can stiffen. Watching and thinking with the half-dozen in *The Tiger and the Horse,* we never lose valuable minutes asking what the clue is: we are at once involved. Without this no play can truly succeed. If we stand outside, staring incredulously, the dramatist has failed. It can be said of . . . [Robert Bolt that he calls] us immediately to the stage. Bolt has a developing eloquence. (p. 125)

[His] work (with an added personal force and authority) has the textbook requirements, character, conflict, ideas, narrative, and so forth—though when we are actually sitting at a play, how many of us docket these things and slip them into pigeon-holes? It is enough that a play compels, that it lingers, that it has been experienced, not listened to frigidly. There have always been 'waves'. Bolt . . . should endure through the next few. (p. 126)

J. C. Trewin, "Two Morality Playwrights: Robert Bolt and John Whiting," in Experimental Drama, *edited by William A. Armstrong (copyright © 1963 by G. Bell and Sons, Ltd), Bell and Sons, 1963, pp. 103-27.**

ANSELM ATKINS

A striking example of the coincidence of opposites has been created by Robert Bolt in his play, *A Man For All Seasons.* The crude stagehand dressed in satanic black and called the "Common Man" is an exact shadow of Thomas More, the saint-protagonist. More and the Common Man, who at first sight seem so irreconcilable, are two sides of an equation. . . .

Bolt, who is not a Christian in "the meaningful sense of the word" . . . , makes abundantly clear in the Preface that More's most praiseworthy virtue is his tenacious hold on his self. (p. 182)

Bolt has a good reason for saying that the Common Man is "harder to find than a unicorn." . . . This statement cannot be put aside, for it has two meanings which, taken together, locate the playwright's central idea. One meaning is that the Common Man is no easier to find than More the saint. Here we get an inkling of the More-Common Man identification. A second meaning implies that we do not recognize the Common Man in ourselves because we fail to acknowledge our innate capability—and responsibility—of achieving a self-based "sanctity" like that of Bolt's More. The last lines of the play are the Common Man's "recognize me." What we are asked to see is that the Common Man is Everyman—and also—More. Logic then invites the inference that every man is More. We each have a self and the theoretical ability to be true to it. The concealed middle term—that the Common Man *is* More—is the secret of the play. Without knowledge of that key we are unable to avail ourselves of Bolt's conclusion. . . .

More and the Common Man are eminently rational, in an earthy reptillian way. The former says man's task on earth is to serve his master "wittily, in the tangle of his mind." . . . Now the Common Man in the role of "Publican" (the Common Man takes several parts in the play) is called by Cromwell the "master statesman of us all." . . . The sequence in question has him playing dumb, repeatedly protesting that he just doesn't understand Cromwell's drift. But this is precisely More's tactic, too. (p. 183)

Another minor but clearcut case of mimicry occurs in the Tower scene. More frantically tries to make Alice "understand" the reasons behind his refusal to take the oath. . . . He no sooner succeeds than the Common Man, as "Jailor," comes to rigidly enforce the family's scheduled departure from the Tower. He thereupon finds himself in More's own position: he cannot get through to the More family. Even More himself cannot "understand" him. The two are thus identified in their frustrated effort to have someone else understand the inviolability of their conscientious commitments.

The same scene illustrates yet another characteristic, important beyond the level of mere mimicry, of More and the Common Man. Each has the ability to take an unshakable stand on some issue, even though the issues in question differ comically. Usually the Common Man takes bribes, tells lies, tipples, and is as Machiavellian in his petty way as More is worldly wise on the grand scale. The Common Man is as lax morally as More is flexible in ordinary dealings. But there is a certain point beyond which neither will go, and one is as adamant there as the other. . . . [If] we compare the two on the level of Bolt's theme of virtue as adhesion to the self, we begin to suspect that their similarities are more basic than their differences.

In conversation with Chapuys, the Common Man boasts of serving only one master, and displays a large cross to show what he means. This involves a double deception, for he attaches no religious meaning to the cross, nor is he really being faithful to his master-of-the-moment, Chapuys. But he certainly is true to another master: himself. His statement is, then, ironical. It is precisely the ironical content that aligns him with More. For while More makes God his sole Master, he does so *by* serving his own conscience; that is, by keeping himself inwardly inviolable. (pp. 184-85)

Fate will indeed bend More this way and that, wresting from him all but his last possession. Deep irony lies in the fact that the Common Man's career brings him to bay also, forcing him to choose between the preservation or loss of his self. (p. 185)

That differences exist between More and the Common Man is, of course, clear enough. The self More wants to preserve is his soul: "a man's soul is his self!" . . . The Common Man's self is his earthly, bodily, pot-bellied life. He does not say explicitly that he has no soul, but his amoral outlook suggests that at best he gives his "immortal soul" little thought. However, this contrast between the two does not really create a difficulty for the identity thesis advanced in this paper. Bolt, after all, never praises More for equating the self with soul (in the Christian sense), nor is it likely that he agrees with More on that doctrine. It is not More the Christian believer whom Bolt lauds, but More the guardian of the *self*. . . . The only factor of interest to Bolt and to us is the outlook which More and the Common Man share. And here the play's evidence is incontrovertible: each has something called a "self," and means to keep it.

A further difficulty can be posed, but in the end it only strengthens my thesis. The Common Man is a great clothes changer. Does not his role-wizardry make him a symbol of the man who has no self at all, the man laminated out of endless external layers, an Anyface with no abiding self-core? I think not. Rather, it makes the distinction between the Common Man's outer skin and inner self more vivid. His character is consistent throughout the play; he is no polyschizoid. Whatever his costume, he is the same canny, conniving, *self-interested* man. . . . Surely the ardent Carlyleian or Swiftian could find clothes-philosophy operating with More as well: when he appears in cassock, and is stripped of it . . . ; when he assumes the Chancellor's chain of office, and relinquishes it . . . ; when he ends in prisoner's rags in the Tower; when he takes off his hat at the scaffold. Even the circumstances of his living quarters change: rich house, poor house, prison. In all these fluctuations of fortune, More remains as constant as Job. (pp. 186-87)

Bolt has used every artistic device feasible within the limits of a two-act play to model the features of a (supposedly) minor character on those of its central figure. The Preface, by refraining from overt reference to this fact, establishes itself as a quasi-integral part of the artist's work. Had it revealed his intentions completely, it would have descended to the level of literary self-criticism. Indeed, any hint of the More-Common Man identification coming from outside the play proper would have nullified one of the play's essential features: the demand for audience recognition. For Bolt intends to evoke a triple recognition: of ourselves as the Common Man, of the Common Man as More, and (therefore) of ourselves as More.

The theme of recognition in *A Man For All Seasons* has further implications if we consider Bolt's acknowledged debt to Bertolt Brecht's theater of alienation. . . . In this genre the audience is reminded by startling contrivances of its distance from the action. It watches from the outside, deprived of involvement with the players. The use of an actor like the Common Man, who addresses the audience and comments on the action, is a typical alienation device. But Bolt says quite plainly in the Preface . . . that the Common Man is meant to draw the audience *into* the play by addressing it "in character." What Bolt is preferring to alienation is *recognition*. He challenges the audience with the ancient "know thyself." (p. 187)

If a man truly knows himself—and Bolt thinks the "rueful notes of recognition" . . . were few—he will discover himself in the Common Man. And if he is able to see that the Common Man and More actually exemplify the same attitude, he will see himself in More, and More in himself. If, happily, this occurs, he may have taken another step toward the Receding God. (p. 188)

Anselm Atkins, "Robert Bolt: Self, Shadow, and the Theater of Recognition," in Modern Drama *(copyright © 1967, University of Toronto, Graduate Centre for Study of Drama; with the permission of* Modern Drama*), Vol. 10, No. 2, September, 1967, pp. 182-88.*

MOLLIE PANTER-DOWNES

[Another] play about Mary Queen of Scots and Queen Elizabeth may not have struck anyone as an exhilarating prospect, but Mr. Bolt has succeeded in bringing off [in "Vivat! Vivat Regina!"] a double portrait that is extremely distinguished, convincing, and as brilliantly fresh as though he and we were looking at his sitters for the first time. . . . The curious love-hate relationship between Mary and Elizabeth is well brought out—scornful on Mary's side, half wistful on Elizabeth's. (pp. 160-61)

Mollie Panter-Downes, "Letter from London," in The New Yorker *(© 1970 by The New Yorker Magazine, Inc.), Vol. XLVI, No. 39, November 14, 1970, pp. 158, 160-63.**

HENRY HEWES

[*Vivat! Vivat Regina!*] sets out to demonstrate Bolt's reasonable contention that Queen Elizabeth I gradually abandoned vivaciousness to become a marvelously skillful head of state, while her rival, Mary, Queen of Scots, turned into a richly human woman as she lost her political battle. . . .

The character transformation works better for Elizabeth than for Mary. Although the "Virgin Queen" is predisposed toward coldness by her unhappy childhood with no mother and a father who disowned her, in her early scenes with Robert Dudley we nevertheless feel that she might have bloomed more fully if that romance had not been blighted by his fickleness and her royal obligations. . . .

Mary, on the other hand, appears a carnal woman from the start, and the episodes of the play prove this point repeatedly. . . . It is a defect of the play that it remains unclear as to whether a less amorous Mary might not have been able to outmaneuver Elizabeth.

But *Vivat!* has a number of theatrical virtues. First of all, there is Bolt's way of making history seem modern by introducing realistic details not found in some history books. . . .

Then there is Bolt's wit. When Cecil asks Elizabeth if she wants him to say what he thinks or what she wants to hear, she replies capriciously, "Oh, Cecil, can they never be the same?" . . .

And finally, there is Bolt's dramatic sense. He can, for instance, get great fun out of having Elizabeth dictate instantly a decision that she claims to have arrived at through "long thought and anxious prayer." He knows how to make startling a deliberate understatement at the climax of a scene. He has found an ingenious way to bring home the truth to Elizabeth by the indirect device of having Cecil tell her all the things Mary was not ("worthy, thoughtful, self-denying, diligent, prepared"). And one admires his nerve when he has Mary discard her black cloak and go to her death in a red nightie. (p. 62)

That we tend to be intrigued and amused more than we are moved by *Vivat!*'s unabashed use of theatricality suggests that Bolt's storytelling scheme here is less effective than the one he used in *A Man for All Seasons*. But his insight into both stories may be equally profound, and his behind-the-throne glimpses make spiffy theater. (p. 63)

Henry Hewes, "Queensmanship," in Saturday Review *(© 1972 Saturday Review Inc.; reprinted with permission), Vol. LV, No. 7, February 12, 1972, pp. 62-3.**

C

CALDWELL, Erskine 1903-

A novelist and short story writer of the Deep South, Caldwell is best known for his novels *Tobacco Road* and *God's Little Acre*. Caldwell blends comic pathos and broad humor, often suggesting serious themes in a seemingly naïve manner. The family, race relations, and traditional moral values are confronted by ideological and social conflicts in many of Caldwell's finest works. (See also *CLC*, Vol. 1, 8, and *Contemporary Authors*, Vols. 1-4, rev. ed.)

T. K. WHIPPLE

Mr. Erskine Caldwell's collection of stories "American Earth," is closer to [representing the simple American folk narrative] than any other book I know. To be sure, his field is limited—his first dozen sketches and incidents are entitled "Far South," his second twelve "Farthest East"—and he is so good a writer that the flavor of locality is strong in his work; but there is nothing necessarily local about the genre which he has chosen. It could be used equally well for all other parts of the Union.

While presumably one must not suppose that Mr. Caldwell's stories are autobiographical, it is as if he were telling offhand of things that had happened to him or that he had run into—insignificant in themselves perhaps, but somehow, though one could not say why, memorable. Always he is, or pretends to be, the unsophisticated raconteur. Character, emotion, significance, are secondary, at most implied; plot is nonexistent; he deals in sheer incident, the primal germ plasm of narrative. Of the many contemporary efforts to get back, in revolt against the overelaborate and artificial productions of recent art, to some unexhausted original rootstock, Mr. Caldwell's is one of the most successful.

Mr. Caldwell goes back even farther than the folk for his fresh start; he reverts to boyhood. Much of his best work shows that bright, wide-eyed innocent fascination with everything dirty, nasty, horrible or gruesome which is one of the strangest and most unfailing traits of small boys. Even Mr. Caldwell's treatment of sex seems somehow pre-adolescent. His writing has a fresh, direct immediacy of juvenility which is extremely rare—and since his folk, even his adults, are the sort who stay juvenile all their lives, there is no incongruity. (pp. 130-31)

Since this is his first book—with the exception of "The Bastard," which was privately printed—one expects the unevenness and uncertainty which one finds; the serious peril is not his occasional fumbling, but his too frequent affectation. His naïveté too often is plainly a self-conscious pose. He is not free from preciosity—and of all kinds of stories, preciosity is most fatal to his kind. In part, this quality springs from a too devoted imitation of Sherwood Anderson; in part from a deference, perhaps, to the [occult magazines] which have printed Mr. Caldwell's stories but with which, one suspects and hopes, Mr. Caldwell has little really in common. Especially are these effects evident in the third part of "American Earth," which contains only one long piece consisting of numerous tiny disconnected bits of fact and phantasy—a type of thing which seems, now at least, not to be the writer's forte.

Mr. Caldwell's unmistakable ability, his out-of-the-ordinary and interesting talent, and his very remarkable achievement justify us in having great hopes of him. Let us pray, however, that he may be delivered from the highbrows. (p. 131)

T. K. Whipple, "Two Judgments of 'American Earth': Part I," in The New Republic *(reprinted by permission of* The New Republic; *© 1931 The New Republic, Inc.), Vol. LXVII, No. 863, June 17, 1931, pp. 130-31.*

MALCOLM COWLEY

Mr. Caldwell is a literary child of the "occult" magazines. . . . What I dissent from in Mr. Whipple's review [see excerpt above] is that he attacks precisely the portion of "American Earth" in which the author's original qualities are most evident.

I refer, of course, to the "disconnected bits of fact and phantasy" which compose the third section of the book. Here Mr. Caldwell achieves a sort of violent poetry, simple, romantic, arbitrary and effective; it is a mood unique in American prose. . . . His figures of speech are expressed in terms of hyperbolic action. (p. 131)

I don't mean to imply that the whole third section of the book is on the same high level. There are trite and sentimental passages which move one to personal fury against the author; there is also, as Mr. Whipple says, a good deal of preciousness and affectation. But for [certain] figures of speech . . . , and for the episodes which surround them, one could forgive any amount of faulty writing. Erskine Caldwell brings a new quality into American fiction: may due credit be given to the little magazines which recognized his talent. (p. 132)

Malcolm Cowley, "Two Judgements of 'American Earth': Part II," in The New Republic *(reprinted by permission of* The New Republic; *© 1931 The New Republic, Inc.), Vol. LXVII, No. 863, June 17, 1931, pp. 131-32.*

ROBERT CANTWELL

[*Tobacco Road* was] a potent influence in the transition of popular fiction from the sentimental romance to the sexual shocker. Before *Tobacco Road* the sort of explicit erotic scenes that appeared in the novel were found in works of limited circulation, sanctioned by claims of artistic integrity; after attempts to suppress *Tobacco Road* were successfully resisted, such material became a staple product of commercial fiction designed for mass consumption.

As a social document, *Tobacco Road* was a highly effective instrument in the various projects of soil conservation and social welfare of the time. The intellectual climate was favorable to a view of the underprivileged South that Caldwell had dramatized so powerfully. His picture of Tobacco Road was one that inclined urban intellectual society to take a tolerant view of its own shortcomings. It was particularly congenial to a society that was undertaking, in the New Deal, large-scale ventures in state control, for the people he wrote about were plainly in no condition to help themselves. And on literary grounds Jeeter Lester is a monumental figure. He is a joke, a comic-strip character, but also a genuine imaginative creation, like something out of folklore and legend—a comic King Lear in his elemental dignity and his tattered regal composure as he struggles with flat tires, or steals turnips and philosophizes quietly on the relations of God and man—a slapstick burlesque, and yet a really great preacher, with a marvelous flow of natural and spontaneous eloquence, and simultaneously an enduring image of American rural poverty. Had the characters of Tobacco Road been drawn sympathetically, the tragedy they embody would have been at best an echo in prose of the elegy in a country graveyard; as comic characters, they make that poverty unforgettable.

There is a consistent element in all of Caldwell's novels, a concept of the people on the land as a persisting human reality, constantly compared with transient, grotesque or violent aspects of contemporary civilization. (pp. 252-53)

Caldwell's early novels were written in an ardent and crusading spirit, and their message was the human cost of the depletion of the soil, and the dehumanization of people for whom an industrialized society had no place. He wrote with passionate conviction of people who were doomed to live on Tobacco Road. . . . [There is] a flat oppressive atmosphere of opaque heartlessness pervading the books, the result of the dehumanization of people who no longer had any real relation to the life around them. (pp. 253-54)

Caldwell's later novels adapted the pattern to different Southern settings. . . . (p. 254)

As Caldwell's novels settled into a pattern, the theme of depletion became increasingly important in them. It served to account for the rigid and inflexible psychology or the malignant purposes of people who lacked the immediate economic drive of the dwellers on Tobacco Road, but who nevertheless behaved in the same fashion at a different social level. . . .

The complete hopelessness of his characters, however, had unexpected consequences. Their dehumanization left them morally disembodied. They floated away from the world of normal reactions as if they had conquered some moral gravitational force. They were starving, certainly, and their hunger was described with bleak power, but they starved in an intermittent fashion, able to act with vigor and determination whenever the action required it. The erotic incidents were more detailed than was customary in the popular fiction of the thirties but they were relatively light-headed, or light-hearted, and touched with the same air of inconsequence. (p. 255)

However unreal or grotesque the sequences in Caldwell's novels, the one absolute is the tragedy caused by the depletion of the soil, or the deadening and hopeless routine that is followed because it was once necessary to follow it. In his fiction the psychological consequences of soil erosion and kindred evils are the central matter, and this is a side of the subject that the agricultural bulletins did not deal with. In Caldwell's world when the soil ceases to produce, something unreal and irrational saps all experience of its meaning. His farmers are spiritually dispossessed when they cling physically to land that can no longer support them, cut off from their rightful place by something they do not understand. The consequences are not only economic. The intelligence that was geared to a productive cycle does not continue to operate effectively when the cycle is broken. The reason for their customs and codes has vanished, and as a result all their doings become misplaced and untimed, unguided by necessity, or guided by the ghosts of former necessities. They seem to act out experience, rather than to experience anything, and go through the motions of something that once had significance. . . . (p. 256)

In Caldwell's early books there was an element of mystery about the farmers who clung to the land that could no longer support them. Why didn't they leave? There was nothing whatsoever in the sullen backwaters and crossroads that Caldwell pictured to keep anyone there. There was no love of the region or the people, no comfort, hope of gain, or fear of encountering elsewhere something worse than what they endured where they were. They were starving, and it was essential to Caldwell's view of them that they would continue to starve as long as they remained there. In *Tobacco Road,* it is true, Jeeter Lester has a buried affection for the country, the odor of freshly plowed ground and the smell of broomsedge smoke, mixed up with his memories of its past productivity and his determination to make it produce again. In Caldwell's later novels the situations sometimes made it necessary that at least the possibility of flight should be considered. The characters weigh the idea, sometimes even discuss it, and occasionally try, though never with hope or the vision of a different and happier existence. For the most part it seems impossible to them even to get anywhere else, a project beyond their powers, though they are not clear as to why, nor does Caldwell give a clear explanation of their sense of imprisonment. . . .

The farmers doomed to starve on Tobacco Road, the Negroes in their cabins, and the children whose wills are crushed by domineering parents are involved in a mystery that seems increasingly sinister, characters in a horror story that is over before Caldwell begins his tale. (p. 257)

Usually . . . physical escape for Caldwell's characters is impossible because they make whatever environment they enter like the one they left, or because somebody manages to get the money that was supposed to be used for their fare. But occasionally, also, the grotesque and melodramatic incidents that follow their attempts to get out of Tobacco Road fit into a vaguely-outlined pattern of half-pursuit or punishment. Humor, and their utter bewilderment, obscures a sense of something malignant and relentless at work when they are away from home, and it is only in retrospect, or in view of Caldwell's novels as a whole, that the high proportion of violence in them . . . becomes related to their fear of the great world beyond their own barren acres. (p. 258)

The threefold destiny of Caldwell's characters hinges on their certain doom if they remain where they are, the numbed sense of helplessness that prevents their getting away, and a third element, a real or imaginary semi-organized force, perhaps merely the community of individuals with common predatory experience, perhaps a genuine underworld or underground organization, which harries them implacably through the third rails and live wires of an industrialized society if they do attempt flight. (p. 259)

In his introduction to *Tobacco Road,* Caldwell noted that first tobacco, and then cotton, had flourished in the Georgia farmlands; both had come and gone; "but the people, and their faith, remained." That concept of the people on the land contributed a saving simplicity to his work. . . . Even when his stories are hackneyed melodramas, imitations of his own successes, or labored shockers, the sense of the permanence of working the soil brings them back to earth; they are never only shockers and thrillers, and their dishonesties are the obvious fabrications of a transparently honest man. Caldwell is often critically appraised as a literary subject of the sort of doom he pictures in his novels, as a writer whose very great natural ability has been exhausted by the constant reworking of the same material. But I venture to believe that a reason both for the first impact of his books, and for the subsequent decline in his critical standing, is more directly related to something within the intellectual world itself.

We are in a creative environment not so different from the world that he pictured in *Tobacco Road.* Comparable scraggly and stunted blossoms are all around us. (p. 262)

No doubt every age produces its share of works that appear in their own time as the literary equivalent of stunted cotton plants on Tobacco Road. It is merely that the present state of letters is not so flourishing as to permit among literary men too superior a view of Jeeter Lester's failure to make his land produce. (pp. 263-64)

Robert Cantwell, "Caldwell's Characters: Why Don't They Leave?" in The Georgia Review *(copyright, 1957, by the University of Georgia), Vol. XI, No. 3, Fall, 1957, pp. 252-64.*

SYLVIA MILLAR

Thirty years divide *Tobacco Road* from *Annette:* Mr Caldwell's obsession with stunted sexuality remains. The sharecropping paupers of Georgia might seem a far cry from middle-class life in the suburban South, but the differences between Tobacco Road and Flower Street, Zephyrfield, are superficial. The clash continues between baffled male brutality and traumatized female innocence. . . .

[Annette's] glibly appropriate fate reflects on Mr Caldwell's glum view that all girls are innately concupiscent and get their just deserts.

Sylvia Millar, "Deflower Street," in The Times Literary Supplement *(© Times Newspapers Ltd. (London) 1974; reproduced from* The Times Literary Supplement *by permission), No. 3793, November 15, 1974, p. 1277.*

EVE OTTENBERG

Like many travel books, Erskine Caldwell's "Afternoons In Mid-America" is fragmentary. Since neither plots nor characters generally hold travel books together, the point of unity is usually the author's observing eye. But Caldwell's eyes never stay on one thing long enough to connect it with anything else. "Afternoons In Mid-America" rushes off in all directions at once, leaving the reader dizzy and, depending on temperament, annoyed or amused.

"Afternoons In Mid-America" skips from the banks of the Mississippi, up to the Dakota Badlands, back to the town of Ogallala, Nebraska, then down into cowboy country and what used to be the dustbowl. With periodic leaps of the imagination to just about anywhere from the mountains of Tibet to the streets of Budapest, Caldwell devotes each chapter to a different mid-American town. . . .

Caldwell fights his own centrifugal force by focusing on similarities among the inhabitants west of the Mississippi; the people interviewed repeatedly express love of the land and a sense of roots deeply embedded in a particular locale. . . . These people enjoy their quiet, predictable routines, appreciate the simple way of life and do not yearn for great wealth or power.

Such attitudes appear in many of Caldwell's 40-odd books, especially in those classics of his fiction, "Tobacco Road" and "God's Little Acre." In his new book Caldwell generalizes about these attitudes and often seems to be talking more about his idea of these people than about the individuals themselves.

Ultimately, when generalizations—about the simple life, or the evils of East Coast capitalism versus Midwest populism, or whatever—take over to this extent, they stunt the development of a true unity of ideas, themes, impressions.

Generalization . . . was the great strength of Caldwell's early novels. His work epitomizes the slice-of-life school of fiction, so popular in the middle decades of this century. By portraying social settings, poverty, or the effects of ignorance, Caldwell conveyed powerful "messages." But such novels become static and self-conscious if they *tell* the reader what to think instead of demonstrating or convincing by means of the story. Caldwell's late novel about racism, "Summertime Island" slipped a little into that didactic pitfall as does "Afternoons In Mid-America."

Despite flaws, an honesty and a clear morality thread through "Afternoons In Mid-America," Caldwell's heart still goes out to the underdog and he doesn't lose track of the differences between rich and poor. An old-style internationalism emerges in his frequent remarks about the similarities between people from all parts of the globe. . . . So in a time when the distance between popular and academic writing continues to widen to the damage of both groups, a book neither snobbish nor sensationalistic has a point of view which is rare indeed.

Eve Ottenberg, "Caldwell Skips About Midwest," in The Christian Science Monitor *(reprinted by permission from* The Christian Science Monitor; *© 1977 The Christian Science Publishing Society; all rights reserved), January 21, 1977, p. 19.*

SCOTT MacDONALD

In many of his stories Caldwell's style is so spare and so completely unadorned that the reader learns just how few of the traditional literary devices a writer can use and still create stories which are meaningful and effective. While the hallmark of Caldwell's prose style is simplicity, however, a careful investigation of the stories in such collections as *American Earth, We are the Living, Kneel to the Rising Sun, Southways, Jackpot, The Complete Stories,* and *Georgia Boy* shows that Caldwell has worked successfully with a variety of technical devices. Particularly impressive is his extensive experimentation with repetition. (p. 213)

Some of the repetition in his stories is a reflection of the Steinesque idea that people continually repeat themselves in conversation, that, in fact, repetition is one of the most fundamental qualities of speech. Nearly every character in Caldwell's fiction habitually repeats seemingly offhand phrases and sentences which often serve as indices to aspects of the character's personality. Further, instead of purposely avoiding repetitive detail in descriptive passages, Caldwell normally presents the reader with a few well-chosen aspects of a scene and then repeats them whenever the setting needs comment. The result is simple but vivid description often made memorable by the degree to which the simplicity reflects the unsophisticated lives of the characters.

In much of Caldwell's short fiction repetition also functions in more complex and unusual ways. In many stories a limited number of repeated phrases and sentences are used to emphasize various types of structure. In "The Automobile That Wouldn't Run" and "Saturday Afternoon," for example, action begins at a certain place, moves to a second location, and then returns to the starting point. In both stories the style reflects this movement. . . . By using repetition in this manner Caldwell gains two results. First, he brings the stories to a decisive conclusion, and second, he creates a strong final emphasis on the basic immovability of the central characters. (pp. 213-14)

In some of Caldwell's best stories repetitious style is used far more emphatically and results in three different general effects. First, in such stories as "The Medicine Man," "Where the Girls Were Different," and "August Afternoon" heavy repetition emphasizes erotic excitement. In other stories a consistent barrage of repeated lines creates a feeling of almost insane frenzy. Finally, in some stories heavy repetition causes conversations to take on symbolic implications. (p. 214)

Another general aspect of Caldwell's experimentation with repetition is his blending of repeated statements with colloquial diction, rhyme and rhythm to create stories which might be called prose folk ballads. The most successful of these stories are "Candy-Man Beechum" and "The Fly in the Coffin," both of which are attempts to portray aspects of black life in the South.

Caldwell uses colloquial diction in "Candy-Man Beechum" and "The Fly in the Coffin" in an unusual way. Most stories about blacks written by both whites and blacks are presented by narrators who use standard white American English. In "Candy-Man Beechum" and "The Fly in the Coffin," however, Caldwell uses third-person narrators who present events in a convincing rendition of black English. (pp. 220-21)

[This creates] a feeling that the reader is not simply observing events involving black people but that he is listening to tales which are products of black folk culture.

Caldwell uses repetition to develop a prose chorus in each story, and he carefully controls its appearance to emphasize aspects of the action. (p. 221)

In "The Fly in the Coffin," a yarn in which a dead man interrupts the joyous celebration of his funeral to demand a fly-swatter so he can kill a fly which has gotten trapped in his coffin, the chorus is a three-statement conversation between Aunt Marty and Woodrow. Three times Aunt Marty says, "You, Woodrow, you! Go look in that corncrib and take a look if any old flies worrying Dose" or a slight variation; three times Woodrow hesitates to obey her; and three times Aunt Marty assures Woodrow that he must protect Dose from the flies. . . .

The ballad-like feeling created in the two stories by Caldwell's combination of colloquial diction and repetition is enhanced by his unusual use of rhyme and rhythm in specific sentences. When Candy-Man is unjustly stopped by the "white boss," for example, he says, "I never bothered whitefolks, and they sure oughtn't bother me. But there ain't much use in living if that's the way it's going to be." The rhyme of "me" and "be" is made particularly emphatic by the rhythmic similarity of the two sentences. (p. 222)

Caldwell controls both the number of repeated words, phrases, and sentences and their distribution to create a wide range of effects, many of which are exciting and unusual. He also experiments with colloquial diction and with rhyme and rhythm and blends these aspects of style with repetition to create vibrantly musical folk ballads, prose pieces which may be unique in English. (p. 223)

Scott MacDonald, "Repetition as Technique in the Short Stories of Erskine Caldwell," in Studies in American Fiction *(copyright © 1977 Northeastern University), Vol. 5, No. 2, Autumn, 1977, pp. 213-25.*

RICHARD GRAY

[Caldwell's theme] is one of degeneracy—the reduction of the human being to the lowest possible levels of his experience. In appearance, at least, his rural characters bear no resemblance to the Jeffersonian yeoman whatsoever. Grotesques responding only to a basic physical urge, they represent an abstraction not merely from the human to the animal but from the complete animal to a single instinct. . . . Caldwell insists upon keeping his readers at a distance—on presenting his [characters] entirely in terms of externals and, in the process, dehumanizing [them]. (p. 112)

Nearly all of his country folk (the title seems a much more appropriate one than "farmer") operate between the poles of greed and sexual desire, and such comedy as his novels possess is generally the result of the violence that either or both of these instincts tend to provoke. In fact, the comic note is at its wildest in his fiction when the two instincts actually clash, throwing the victim of the subsequent cross fire into confusion. (pp. 112-13)

Caldwell owes a profound debt to the Southwestern humorists, and to George Washington Harris in particular—a debt that is betrayed among other things by their common dependence on a broad and grotesque type of comedy. The specific borrowings from Harris are at their most obvious in *Georgia Boy,* . . . in which the boy of the title recounts the antics of his "old man," and in the process draws us the portrait of a delightful and impoverished scapegrace not unlike Sut Lovingood [Harris's major character] himself. But these are less interesting, I believe, than the kind of understanding of Harris and his methods that can be inferred from Caldwell's more important fiction—by which I mean from *Tobacco Road, God's Little Acre,* and perhaps *Tragic Ground* as well. In such cases it is not merely the surface structure of Southwestern humor that is recovered but the relationship obtaining between that structure and the ulterior purposes of the writer. Comic these books may be, but the comedy is all the sharper, the wit all the more pungent and the characters that much more striking, because (just as in *Sut Lovingood*) everything is unambiguously attached to an underlying and genuinely serious series of intentions.

Exactly how these intentions manifest themselves is (again as in *Sut Lovingood*) as much a matter of context as anything else, the total situation in which the humorous moments are played out. The comedy is still a comedy of waste, of human potential denied and frustrated, and that fact is communicated to the reader in part by Caldwell's barren landscapes—whether it be the decayed rural landscape where his farmers are described living in reluctant exile or the urban scene, to which they may retreat occasionally in pursuit of an illusory alternative. . . . Caldwell sees the hopelessness of the rural landscape penetrating the town, to make it unavailable as a resource for impoverished farmers. A common dust . . . settles over city and adjacent countryside alike, so creating a pervasive sense of fruitlessness. And this is the stage on which the Lesters, the Waldens in *God's Little Acre* and all their kind must act out their comedies of frustration; or, to be more accurate, this is the environment that prescribes their frustrated lives.

That it *is* a comedy of frustration we are concerned with here, a series of appropriate responses to a thwarting environment, is witnessed by the habitual activity of Caldwell's characters. For the gestures that make them comic have nothing at all to do with intrinsic evil, however violent and grotesque they may appear to be. On the contrary, Jeeter Lester and Ty Ty Walden (in *God's Little Acre*) are exactly like Sut Lovingood in that they are presented as the *victims* of evil, whose strange behavior demonstrates the response of the innocent to circumstances he cannot control. The whole trouble with Caldwell's characters, as with Harris's, is that they have no relevant connection with the emergent social structure, and so are at best anomalies in that structure and at worst encumbrances to it. And Caldwell, unlike Harris, makes sure that the reader is aware of this by explaining, very early on in most of his novels, how people like the Lester family and the Waldens have become the way they are. Both the Lesters and the Waldens were, we learn, once well-to-do landowners. But they fell upon hard times—partly as a result of natural fluctuations in the cotton and tobacco markets, and partly thanks to the machinations of the financiers, the bankers, and the Wall Street brokers. . . . In effect, big business has assumed *direct* control of farming, rather than working through the power of its credit, and in doing so has created a new, large-scale agricultural system in which the Jeeter Lesters and Ty Ty Waldens of this world have no place. Jeeter, Ty Ty, and their kind have been turned into anachronisms, an irrelevant nuisance to the present owners of the land; and the most they can hope for, really, is that they will be left alone on the farms they occupy, to eke a meager existence out of them.

This, more or less, is the starting point for nearly all of Caldwell's fiction, and certainly the basis of his finest novels. The farmer, he argues, has been "robbed of his livelihood by the downfall of the old systems of agriculture," and this in turn has led to the physical deterioration we now see and to his moral collapse. Treated like an animal he has become an animal; excluded from the human community in an economic sense he has degenerated into a kind of moral leper as well, whose humanity is more a matter of biology than of character. The argument is an utterly deterministic one, of course. But, then, so also is the argument implicit in most stories of the old Southwest. More to the point, the determinism is not, I think, objectionable because it can be seen as part of a total strategy of caricature. Life is simplified and character is distorted in Caldwell's fiction, it may be true, but this is done in a conscious and valuable way—so as to isolate certain specific aspects of the author's given experience and, in isolating them, to explain them.

Given this self-conscious determinism of approach, and the tendencies toward caricature and generalization that accompany it, it becomes less surprising, I think, that Caldwell should impose the status of a demonstration on every aspect of his characters' behavior; the reader is, after all, being summoned to witness what is likely to happen when a certain type of social and historical situation exists. There is a profoundly illustrative quality, for instance, not just about particular scenes in *Tobacco Road* but about its major source of comedy. This is Jeeter Lester's belief that one year, next year perhaps, he will be able to plant a tobacco crop. Under the influence of this belief, he is forever burning the ground in preparation for the planting until eventually, at the end of the novel, he sets fire to his own house, killing himself and his wife in the process. The belief is an idiosyncratic one, certainly, leading to situations that range from the ludicrous to the macabre, but not so idiosyncratic that it cannot act as a gauge of Jeeter's innocence, and the desperate nature of a situation that imposes such desperate remedies on its victims. Similarly, Ty Ty Walden's habitual activity of digging up his land in search of gold, absurd though it may appear to be, is founded on the supremely illogical and revealing logic of the helpless naïf. He cannot live on what he gets *out* of the land, Ty Ty reasons, so why not try to live on what he finds in it? There is perhaps a hint of blasphemy in his behavior too . . .—the idea that rooting about in the land for gold, oil, or whatever represents a despoliation, an act of rape that is the very opposite of the enrichment offered to the soil by the agricultural activity. But whether this is part of Caldwell's intention or not, there can be little doubt, I think, that he does intend Ty Ty's behavior, like Jeeter's, to achieve the apparently paradoxical feat of being representative by virtue of its idiosyncrasy. Its illustrative quality, that is—as an indication of rural decline and the despair to which this decline leads—is made to depend for its impact on the comic absurdity of the illustration.

The humor is not left in isolation, though, to carry the entire freight of meaning of the book unaided. As in *Sut Lovingood,* the dominant strain of comedy is punctuated by an occasional lyric note that reminds us of what might have been in more favorable circumstances—of how people like Jeeter Lester and Ty Ty Walden could have developed given the proper opportunity. The few times that Jeeter is allowed to express his "inherited love of the land" offer us some beautiful instances of this. . . . [Such lyric passages help] us to recognize and to accept the latent dignity of the speaker. . . . [They also] contribute a new dimension of feeling to the narrative, a sense of pathos that depends upon seeing that, within the limits established by the comedy, the desires expressed here are destined to remain unconsummated. (pp. 118-122)

It is only a step beyond this strategy of contrast between the comic episode and the lyric moment to that of placing active commentary in the mouths of the characters—commentary, that is, that does not simply imply a criticism of the given situation but insists upon it. Needless to say, Caldwell frequently takes this step. His characters suddenly pause, as Jeeter does when he is stealing the bag of turnips, and turn upon their own grotesque attitudes in order to explain them. . . . [Caldwell] makes his characters articulate their own sufferings, so that we are never left in any doubt as to where to place the blame. (p. 122)

Caldwell has complicated the function of reporter by adding to it that of the caricaturist, a creator of the grotesque. On top of that, he has forced on the reader an attitude of radical detachment. . . . [Characters] as well as the audience seem to be made aware of the illustrative quality of the action. As a resource this attitude of detachment is, of course, just as much of an inheritance from Southwestern humor as the strategy of caricature is. But Caldwell develops it much further than any previous humorist ever did. . . . [The] distance placed between reader and character in Caldwell's best fiction is, I think, significantly related—both in its purposes and its effects—to Brecht's core idea of *Vermfremdung,* or audience alienation. The idea, stated simply, is this: that in an "epic" play the audience, instead of being invited to involve themselves in the action, should be forced to adopt an attitude of clinical detachment toward it. Consequently, what happens on stage will be witnessed as an explicable social phenomenon with its own definite causes and room for subsequent maneuver. The sense of an experience participated in is forfeited, according to this theory, but what (ideally) is gained in its stead is a new certainty—the knowledge that comes from having located the dramatic action firmly in its historical time and social place. The events the writer describes become part of an explicable series—their origins understood, the problems they pose carefully defined, and solutions to these problems offered, ready and waiting, for the audience to act upon. This is very much the notion of playwright—or novelist or poet—as scientific historian, and committed scientific historian at that. (p. 123)

The sense of problem solving—the feeling that we are being asked to look at the action in very much the same spirit as a scientist looks at an experiment—is in fact as pronounced in books like *Tobacco Road* as it could be in any "epic" play—more pronounced, even, since Caldwell likes to add his own comments to those he puts in the mouths of his characters. Asides from the author occasionally supplement asides from his creations, so as to make the didactic intention of the story perfectly clear. This, admittedly, has some use simply because it helps to settle any doubts that may be left in the reader's mind—both about what Caldwell is trying to do, and what he is trying to say. But, on the whole, I think it is a mistake. At such moments, it is very difficult for him not to sound like a schoolmaster talking to an exceptionally dull pupil. . . . [The] specific proposals he makes are pretty various—ranging as they do from pleas for more government aid to the occasional invocation of the principle of self-help, and taking in agricultural schools, crop rotation, and land recovery along the way. The variety of his proposals, however, should not prevent us from seeing that everything he says stems ultimately from one core belief, a single premise. This is how Caldwell states that premise in one of his books.

> Until the agricultural worker commands his own farm, either as an individual or as a member of a state-allotted farm group, the Southern tenant farmer will continue to be bound hand and foot in economic slavery.

Caldwell, as I think this brief passage indicates, is finally a traditional writer. His characters are traditional; his humor is traditional (although, certainly, it is broader and wilder than the Southwestern humorists' ever was); above all, the social and political program implicit in his work is traditional. For what that program boils down to is a belief in the pieties of the small farm. The dream of a chosen people tilling their own fields in perfect freedom: that is the dream Caldwell expresses here—and that also is the dream which dictates nearly all of his problem solving. No matter how little we may realize it while we are enjoying some of the surface details of his comedy, Caldwell—in every one of his finest stories—is trying to draw us back steadily into the world of Jeffersonian myth.

Once we realize this—that the ideal of the good farmer hovers as an admonitory image at the back of Caldwell's best novels and tales—then, I think, the principal reason for the almost apocalyptic violence of his work becomes clear. All the events that occur in books like *Tobacco Road* and *God's Little Acre* are wild and grotesque, ultimately, because they represent for their creator such a radical departure from the Jeffersonian norm. Jeeter Lester and Ty Ty Walden are not the noble farmers of regional legend and the fact that they are not, the fact that they stand for *a dream or an ideal betrayed,* is, I believe, meant to be the real measure of their absurdity. No blame attaches to Jeeter or Ty Ty for their plight, far from it, but that only makes it the more difficult to bear—the more difficult for them to bear, that is, for their author to bear and, most important of all, for us to bear as well. For it would be putting matters in their right perspective, I think, to say that Caldwell insists on the difference between Jefferson's tillers of the earth and his own Georgia crackers, and then imposes full responsibility for this difference upon a corrupt social machine, precisely so as to arouse *our* anger and encourage *our* demands for change. (pp. 124-25)

[In] some of the stories that he wrote after *Tobacco Road* and *God's Little Acre,* these beginnings are carried through to a detailed portrait of that alternative. Caldwell then shows us the reorganization of farm management and the restructuring of rural society actually taking place, and being succeeded in turn by a revival of spirit among his characters. Obviously, the intended effect of these stories is one of uplift; the author wants us to experience a sense of release because the oppressive circumstances, and with them the claustrophobic atmosphere, of the earlier narratives have been dissolved. Their actual effect is a lot less exhilarating than that, however, and the reasons for this take us right back to the virtues of that earlier work: we can define why Caldwell succeeded in *Tobacco Road* and *God's Little Acre* by understanding why he is failing now. For what Caldwell does as a preliminary to drawing his portrait of a better life is to take his rural folk out of the grotesque, comic world of the Lesters and the Waldens—which is a necessary step, certainly, but one that deprives him of his previous excuses for the simplifications and determinism of his argument. The one-sided portrait can no longer be defended as part of a satirical strategy. And having done this he does not really know what to do with his people, because he does not have any other satisfactory approach available to him—one which would make them meaningful and at the same time vivid and believable too. His characters have lost the power of a Jeeter Lester—the power, that is, deriving from the deliberately isolating and exaggerating tendencies of the comic method—without acquiring any of the more complicated interest, or more sophisticated contact with their time and place, that the participants in a more strictly "realistic" fiction should possess. . . . [They] have no imaginative life of their own. . . . They are merely mouthpieces for utopian attitudes. . . . The values, previously implied, have been allowed to occupy center stage; and—unfortunately for Caldwell—they have not benefited in the process either from an involvement in credible experience, or from contact with the sort of vivifying literary medium that the comic tradition of the old Southwest represents. (pp. 126-27)

As in all the best Southern literature, . . . idea and event are made to interact so as to produce a thoroughly traditional reading of the environment—a reading, that is to say, that depends on the earlier history of that environment without being circumscribed by it. But in later novels like *A House in the Uplands* this interaction more or less ceases. The idea remains unenlivened by any contact with experience; or, on those occasions when Caldwell does return to journalism—a comic account of things as they are—that journalism does not seem to have an ulterior motive any more. It no longer radiates the kind of significance that would come from its being placed within the framework of a controlling idea. Idea *or* event, dream *or* journalistic report: the two things exist separately, even if they both occur within the covers of one book. And what we are left with, consequently, is either heroic posturing . . . or a descent into episodes of comic violence and degeneracy that have no purpose beyond themselves, that are, in a word, sensationalistic. We are not being asked to register the gap between fact and potential any longer; only to indulge in daydreaming about what might happen in the best of all possible worlds, or to enjoy the cheaper thrills offered by a random and meaningless enumeration of some of the more sordid facts of life. The strategy of detachment is, in sum, replaced by one of vicarious excitement. This is a sad end for somebody like Caldwell, who started off so well. . . . [This is] what happens when the functions of reporter and mythologizer are separated for a writer—and history is then translated by him into a refuge for some dormant principle or, alternatively, into a series of disconnected happenings. (pp. 127-28)

Richard Gray, "The Good Farmer: Some Variations on a Historical Theme," in his The Literature of Memory: Modern Writers of the American South *(copyright © 1977 by Richard Gray), The Johns Hopkins University Press, 1977, pp. 106-49.**

* * *

CALLAGHAN, Morley 1903-

Callaghan, the Canadian novelist, short story writer, and playwright whom Edmund Wilson once described as "perhaps the most unjustly neglected novelist in the English-speaking world," has been active in the literary world for more than fifty years. Throughout his career his work has been characterized by its clean, journalistic style, ironic tone, and strongly moralistic themes. (See also *CLC*, Vol. 3, and *Contemporary Authors*, Vols. 9-12, rev. ed.)

HORACE GREGORY

In some respects Morley Callaghan is by far the most interesting member of the contemporary hard-boiled school of fiction. Under the surfaces of a prose style that runs in deadly parallel to the familiar technique of Ernest Hemingway, he uncovers a warm, vibrant, boyish personality. He exhibits a curiosity about human behavior that seems to be at war with the very method he has chosen as his medium. His short stories and novels are actually concerned with the subtle, often tender, sometimes downright sentimental phases of human relationship. As evidence of his vitality he displays a wholesome sense of humor in his very short story about a young priest facing a problem in practical theology as he tries to expel a drunkard from a confessional. Even in the hands of Ernest Hemingway, the hard-boiled manner is suspect—behind a brightly polished exterior you discern a soft, almost tearful admission that the world is no place for sweet young lovers—and in the case of Morley Callaghan you half expect the apparition of another Booth Tarkington, gifted with the naive curiosity of a Sherwood Anderson. (p. 45)

Horace Gregory, "Mr. Callaghan's Medium," in The Nation *(copyright 1930 by the Nation Associates, Inc.), Vol. CXXX, No. 3378, April 2, 1930 (and reprinted in* Morley Callaghan, *edited by Brandon Conron, McGraw-Hill Ryerson Limited, 1975, pp. 45-6).*

HUGO McPHERSON

Callaghan's importance has nothing to do with style. His control of language, despite the triumphs of a dozen short stories and numerous passages in the novels, was for many years uncertain; and his tendency to synopsize rather than dramatize led him to substitute hazy case histories for living patients. Having learned the fashionably flat accent of James T. Farrell and Sherwood Anderson, the youthful Callaghan was content to present people who dressed "nicely" or "neatly"; who looked "lovely" or "handsome"; who felt "sad" or "jolly" or "simply splendid"; and who spent interminable hours chatting "easily", just out of earshot. But where Farrell's mannerism was relentlessly consistent, Callaghan's was erratic. He could rise to moments of brilliant description when he remembered his native Toronto sharply, and he could recreate a fight or a lunch-counter conversation with the authority of a good documentary film. Too often, however, his interest in *theme* led him to abuse the expectations that he had established in his reader. He had not learned, and did not learn until 1937 (*More Joy in Heaven*), that each scene could simultaneously delineate character, forward the action and develop meaning; or that the illusion created by fiction, whatever the convention adopted, must be fully coherent. It is an evasion, moreover, to say that Callaghan creates "thin" characters because he wants us to see them as symbols. . . . [The] whole success of his fiction depends on our willingness to accept his characters as *living* men.

Callaghan, then, is not primarily a stylist. The critics of the 'twenties who enthusiastically and mistakenly compared him with Hemingway were soon stricken with amnesia. Their young discovery, careless of the fashionable idiom as well as the *dernier cri* of socialism, wrote as badly as Melville.

But Callaghan, like Melville, had something to say, and he has learned to say it with increasing richness and power. He has given us a modern vision of the human condition which has no parallel in Canadian fiction. It is this that makes him an important writer. Beginning, like the other writers of the 'twenties, with the ruins of a world just "saved" by a War to End War, he reacted to its confusion and despair with complete originality. . . . [He] faced the facts of his generation and probed through and *beyond* them to find a secure ground for action and belief. He became, in short, a religious writer—not one of the apologists who defends traditional religion by contriving convenient modern *exampla,* but an artist who looked searchingly at his experience (including the potent -isms and -ologies of the day) and concluded that the temporal world cannot be self-redeemed; that human frailty is bearable only in the light of divine perfection.

In this sense, Callaghan's vision is closer to the art of T. S. Eliot than to any of the novelists whom he resembles superficially. But his consuming interest in the life of the ordinary, inarticulate man and his compassion for human suffering has given his work a unique character. Confining himself largely to people who "feel"—people who are barren of "ideas" in any sophisticated sense—he has had to discover a means of revealing dramatically the nature of their quest for significance in the terrifying flux of the modern world.

At length (and this takes us to the story of his development as a novelist) he has wrought out a fictional form in which the surface events function simultaneously as realistic action and symbolic action, revealing both the empirical and the spiritual conflicts of his protagonists. This duality, moreover, is never merely a tricky fictional device calculated to entertain both the naïve and the knowing; it is fundamental to Callaghan's perception of the interdependence of the spiritual and empirical realms. Man's career occurs in the imperfect world of time, but its meaning (man's dignity or "place") depends finally on a larger reality *out of time*. To escape the first world is physical death; to ignore the second is to embrace the condition of the Wasteland—life-in-death. This tension, to which Callaghan's best fiction gives dramatic form, is the fundamental tension of life. By exploring the relation of these two worlds—empirical and spiritual—Callaghan has written the "little man's" *Ash Wednesday* and *Burnt Norton*. (pp. 60-2)

Undoubtedly [*Strange Fugitive*], with its jazz-age atmosphere of speakeasies and available women, and its dramatic testimonial that crime does not pay, said what a conventional reader wanted to hear. Harry Trotter, after all, was a weak-witted, dangerous little rat who got what he deserved. Society maintains its health by exterminating such unscrupulous rodents, or by allowing them to exterminate each other.

But the book is crowded with a host of things which suggest that Callaghan wished to communicate something quite different than this conventional platitude; that he was interested not in the feelings of an outraged community but in the plight of an inarticulate and confused soul such as Harry Trotter. (p. 63)

[The] fabric of the novel is so full of untied threads and accidental knots that no reader could be expected to see its pattern clearly, or to be convinced by its statement. For all its surface "freshness", what we see in *Strange Fugitive* is the uncertain attempt of a young artist to say something that he has felt profoundly.

It is worth dwelling on the defects of this book for a moment more so that we may see clearly the artistic problems that Callaghan had to overcome. On the realistic level, he failed to give all of his *dramatis personae* an organic function in the action. In real life, perhaps, every person with whom we have more than casual contact adds his pebble or sliver to the developing structure of our identity. But in fiction, where the artist strives to create an illusion of completeness within limited space, there is no room for passing minutiae; these things must be distilled to produce the maximum effect with the minimum of means. *Strange Fugitive* distracts the reader with characters and motifs that have only a momentary importance in the tale. (p. 64)

In *Strange Fugitive* . . . we have a first definition of Callaghan's two worlds, and an illustration of the failure of one individual to rise above the mechanical, cause-and-effect morality of the empirical realm. At the same time, we see that Callaghan's statement has failed artistically, in part because of the facility of its style, but more seriously because of its failure to make surface incident and implicit meaning fully resonant and coherent.

In the two novels which follow *Strange Fugitive,* Callaghan moves deeper and deeper into his exploration of the two worlds with which man must come to terms if he is to realize his humanity fully, but his mastery of both style and form are still uncertain. If theme and plot are married, they maintain separate establishments. Thus *It's Never Over* and *A Broken Journey* both develop in a series of episodes which, whatever their symbolic significance, fail to cohere as plausible action. (pp. 65-6)

Symbolically, [*A Broken Journey*] is meaningful, but at the level of fact it is incredible. By failing to create a believable empirical world, Callaghan has failed himself and his reader. His statement possesses only a theoretical validity. (p. 66)

[Through] the narrow discipline of the short story, he learned to achieve a completeness of effect that eluded him in the novel. A good dozen of the stories collected in *Now That April's Here* (1936) treated one aspect or another of the grand theme with a luminous sureness and economy. He was able, moreover, to shift the emphasis of his exploration from negative to positive: instead of showing how people . . . failed in their quest to find their secure "place" in the universal scheme, he learned to create characters who *achieved* the quest.

The shift from negative to positive begins with *Such Is My Beloved* (1934), a remarkable novel whose hero is a priest—a "little man" like Callaghan's other heroes—but one who has made an overt spiritual affirmation. It is significant, I think, that Callaghan should now turn to an explicitly Christian pattern. Since many of the protagonists of his earlier work were led to "feel" the religious position as the only workable answer to the human predicament, it is appropriate that he should examine this conclusion in terms of a hero who has bound himself fully to the religious way of life. (pp. 66-7)

In *Such Is My Beloved* Callaghan has created his first coherent parable of the nature of man's earthly quest. The symbolism is traditionally Christian, but it is never *imposed* upon the materials. The novel is a "test" so to speak, of the conviction towards which Callaghan's heroes move, and though the temporal church does not come off unscathed, the test is nonetheless valid; for love—a *transcendent* love such as Father Dowling's—is the only response which gives meaning to the inescapable facts of human weakness and pain.

Yet *Such Is My Beloved,* significant as it is in Callaghan's developments as an artist, is not fully satisfactory as a novel. The Robisons, the powerful parish do-gooders, are too thinly realized to be convincing as Father Dowling's opponents, and the sad Italian family, burdened with twelve children, plays an exemplary rather than organic part in the novel. Nevertheless, Father Dowling's story clinches Callaghan's confidence in his perception of *two* worlds which are indispensable to man. His subsequent work will proceed to show that Love is a possible attainment in the life of Everyman.

They Shall Inherit the Earth (1935) though still unsuccessful in creating a coherent world, gives us a hero who learns through pain and suffering that love is as much a renouncing of the self as a triumph of the ego. The most interesting thing about this work is the new meaning which Callaghan attaches to the figure of his heroine. In the first novels there had been a clear-cut distinction between the luscious mistress and the loved one who (whatever her beauty) filled the hero with an oppressive sense of mingled duty and longing. Now, in the figure of Anna, we discover that physical love can become a blessing and a fulfilment if the lover will only give himself unreservedly. Real love teaches a vast tolerance and a willingness to submit the selfish needs of the self to a larger unity. . . . True love is, finally, a recognition of divine love which lifts us above the particularity of the temporal order into the timeless permanence of the One.

Having thus defined the nature of his two worlds and tested his conviction that man can realize his humanity only by applying the values of the second to the circumstances of the first, Callaghan devoted himself in the novels which followed to deepening and sharpening the expression which he gave to his vision. *More Joy in Heaven* and *The Loved and the Lost* are good novels by any standard. In style they are firm and direct. The stereotyped diction has given place to a much more concrete, precise vocabulary: sentences which habitually tapered away in spineless participial constructions have been eliminated; and the narrative manner has moved more and more towards carefully dramatized scenes. Still better, image-symbol motifs are no longer used episodically, but are maintained skilfully throughout the entire action. Callaghan, in short, has gone far towards giving his fictional structures the coherence and richness that is fundamental to art.

In this process one other important development has taken place. Callaghan now knows . . . that the hero who achieves his quest will be, in worldly terms, a baffling, implausible figure. (pp. 67-9)

More Joy in Heaven is one of the most piercingly ironic books in modern literature—a relentless document of the fate of a Saviour. (p. 69)

Here there is scarcely a character or an image which does not function organically in the devastating spectacle of [the martyrdom of the Savior-figure]—Mankind's terrifying habit of making and breaking plaster saints without grasping the meaning of *real* saintliness. This is indeed a work calculated to make mad the guilty, appall the free and confound the ignorant. (p. 70)

The body of image and incident with which Callaghan fills out [the] beautifully conceived structure [of *The Loved and the Lost*] adds a dimension that was at best inchoate in the first novels. It is probably true, as Malcolm Ross has suggested, that Callaghan "plays by ear" in constructing such harmonies. His avowed anti-intellectualism would seem to argue against a high degree of self-consciousness. But whether self-conscious or "natural", his mature control of form cannot be gainsaid. The examination of two image patterns in *The Loved and the Lost* must suffice as illustration. In his opening description of the geography of Montreal, Callaghan tells us that "Those who wanted to remain as they were liked the mountain. Those who wanted a change preferred the broad flowing river. But no one could forget either of them." As this basic dichotomy develops, it defines pictorially the complex limits of the action. The mountain, the home of the rich and powerful *whites* appears as a menacing barrier of *black* stone to Jim McAlpine. The lower town, home of the negro population, on the other hand, appears as a dazzlingly *white* blanket of snow. White and black, then, light and darkness, sight and blindness, are characteristic of *both* parts of the human city. The weak and despised, living near the river, want change; the rich and the powerful, living on the mountain, prefer things as they are. But neither group is blameless. The meeting place of the two groups is the secular temple of an arena where they witness the legal ritual of a hockey game.

This, then, is the mixed community of mankind in which Jim and Peggy must test the validity of their respective views of the *meaning* of man's quest. Again the white-black imagery helps the reader. Jim, as a child, had been excluded from the garden of his wealthy friends by a high black hedge. As an adult, this hedge is translated for him into the black barrier of the mountain. And it is this barrier which he is determined to conquer. He will climb his mountain or hedge, and guard his position jealously. Peggy, on the other hand, found her sanctimonious "socially acceptable" home an intolerable cage of man-made rules. She discovered pleasure in simple communion with a negro family—the outcasts of the community. Peggy's course, in short, led her to recognize the value of *love*—quite uncompromised by worldly considerations. Jim's course led him to value the worldly rewards of money and power above all else. For him, black has become the symbol of hate and exclusion; for her it is the sign of love and community. (pp. 72-3)

The Loved and the Lost . . . sees Morley Callaghan's art reach a distinguished fulfilment. It is a parable as old as faith, as relevant as man's apparently undying need to realize his best self, and as durable as language. (p. 73)

Hugo McPherson, "The Two Worlds of Morley Callaghan," in Queen's Quarterly, *Vol. LXIV, No. 3, Autumn, 1957 (and reprinted in* Morley Callaghan, *edited by Brandon Conron, McGraw-Hill Ryerson Limited, 1975, pp. 60-73).*

HOWARD ENGEL

In . . . *A Fine and Private Place,* Morley Callaghan writes in the familiar parables that have marked his work since his first published novel came out in 1928. He is concerned with the conscience, the moral part of humanity, the part that makes man different from the animals and more interesting to watch. Yet throughout his long career he has observed people as though they were beasts at play. He records our battles, our coupling, our struggles for supremacy, our defeats. He is delighted to show how men behave badly in a social world of their own creation. He does this with tightly organized stories that are almost Biblical in their spare directness. From *Strange Fugitive,* a working class *Decline and Fall,* through novels like the gallows-obsessed *It's Never Over* and *They Shall Inherit the Earth* to the more familiar *The Loved and the Lost,* Callaghan marshals his people in tightly controlled moral tales that betray the masterful short story writer he is.

A Fine and Private Place works like a short story, or . . . a *novella.* There are no extra characters or incidents. It is pared to the bone, as you would expect from Callaghan; there is no fat. As in all of Callaghan's novels, the city in which he places the story plays a part as important as the leading players. Here the city is Toronto. (p. 63)

Callaghan is one of the few writers of his time to produce a body of work. In a country of one-book writers, he stands out. His books have been criticized as being uneven and over-disciplined, but they always have a concentration and rough-hewn energy that transcends the tight style he picked up so long ago.

In *A Fine and Private Place,* a title borrowed from Andrew Marvell's "To His Coy Mistress," we are invited to look at the dark side of life. The fine and private place of the title is the grave. As a title it has its problems. Over the book may fall the shadow of death, but it is not about death. . . .

A Fine and Private Place has the compactness of Callaghan's early work. It is a short book, lacking the wider focus of *A Passion in Rome* and *The Many-Colored Coat.* . . .

In the main, none of the characters is compelling or interesting enough to demand a commitment from the reader. . . .

At its worst the book seems a simplistic manoeuvring of people and events to fit a preordained pattern. At its best you forget all that and just read and enjoy. There are hundreds of tiny observations of human behaviour that make up the difference. . . .

While I am not calling this book a success, I would say that it is a welcome addition to the Callaghan canon. Callaghan is a peculiar writer. In the details he often falls apart before your eyes, but when you look at him, head on, see what he has created in more than fifty years in more than seventeen books, you sink in amazement. He sits across the path of Canadian literature like an old Labrador, you're not quite sure how to approach him, but you can't ignore him. (p. 64)

Howard Engel, "Callaghan's World of Criminals and Saints," in Saturday Night *(copyright © 1975 by* Saturday Night*), Vol. 90, No. 3, July/August, 1975, pp. 63-4.*

JUDITH KENDLE

Content with the assumption that [Morley Callaghan] is a Roman Catholic novelist, most criticism simply ignores the seriousness of his quarrel with the Church, and to date there has been no acknowledgment of the aesthetic nature of his views. It is possible, at least, given the importance Callaghan attaches to his vocation as an artist, that his moral philosophy owes as much to aesthetic considerations as it does to Roman Catholic doctrine. Such, indeed, has proved the case. Whether or not Callaghan's criticism of Christianity arises out of his youthful determination as an artist to look at the world freshly for himself, it is clear that he plumps for individual insight and imagination in preference to doctrinal approaches to truth. He tends, in fact, to equate superior insight with artistic talent or appreciation and to delegate to the Artist the moral grandeur and the sympathy more commonly reserved for the Priest. Confidence in art, moreover, virtually replaces his faith in orthodox dogma or creed; wherever traditional belief survives it has undergone significant change. Thus, while his belief in the transcendent power of love and concern for the spiritual life of the individual are derived from the Christian tradition, Callaghan means something very different from *caritas* by love and is, for the most part, resolutely critical of orthodox, doctrinal, and institutional forms of Christianity. Not enough attention has been paid to the author's own disclaimer: "The last thing that's in my mind is to write religious books." (p. 13)

Callaghan often finds himself in violent disagreement with major tenets of the Christian faith. He is particularly distressed by Christian pessimism about human nature and theological conceptions about the nature of love and inveighs loudly against their survival in the works of Roman Catholic and secular writers alike.

He disagrees, for example, with the dualism he discerns at the heart of Western Christianity. Indeed, he identifies it in *That Summer in Paris* with "that fantasy running through modern letters and thought that man is alien in this universe" and regards writers as various as Pascal and Henry Miller to be equally heir to that tradition. . . . In the same work, he is distressed by Christian fears of human sexuality and attacks an otherwise "beautiful writer" like Mauriac's evident "disgust with the flesh." Callaghan feels positively "pagan" in comparison and even views the "correct copulations" of D. H. Lawrence as an Anglo-Saxon over-reaction.

Hierarchical conceptions of love are thus mocked in *Such is My Beloved,* and the entire Christian vision of life as sorrowful rejected in *A Passion in Rome* (1961). Orthodox theological opinion which considers man's spiritual love for his fellow man to be but a pale imitation of Divine *caritas,* and where sexual passion does not rate at all, accords ill with Father Dowling's own experience in the first novel as evidenced by his reading of the "Song of Songs," while Sam Raymond contends in the second that "any fool could see" for himself that, far from being a miserable existence compounded of sex, sin and suffering wherein the only escape from "desire" was death, the human condition is frequently enjoyed by men and women, whose only sin, if any, is their obvious delight in sensual pleasure.

Callaghan is also critical of Christian conceptions of human nature as fallen and of Redemption only through Grace, regarding them as destructive of human dignity, responsibility, and free will. The idea of "original sin" does not appeal to him, nor to *Strange Fugitive*'s hero, Harry Trotter; speculation about innate depravity bores and irritates Callaghan; and he regards Christianity's "awareness of evil" as "a hopeless spiritual trap." (pp. 14-15)

[The] whole burden of Callaghan's moral philosophy, with its emphasis upon the fullest self-realization possible and upon life as it is lived upon this earth, is often inimical to the other worldly and self-sacrificial Christian tradition of Redemption through Grace and out of Time. Regarding mortality as "a gloomy inevitable experience," Callaghan explains in his memoirs how he himself avoided morbid preoccupation with death (as well as futile speculation about the meaning of life) by immersing himself as fully as possible in the day to day business of living in order to realize . . . all his "potentialities" and "possibilities" as a man. (p. 15)

Despite quarrels with authority and Christian doctrine, Callaghan retains affectionate respect for Mother Church. A variety of churches file across his pages as inescapable physical facts and spiritual signs of man's loftiest aspirations; priests do, upon occasion, tender perfectly good advice, and many of his characters, notably his women, draw strength and comfort still from their faith and from traditional ritual and dogma. There is, on the other hand, neither hesitation to expose imperfections, nor compunction to mute condemnation of the Church's palpable failures. The work witnesses, in fact, to the demise of Church influence in society, and to the disaffection of contemporary man.

It would seem that Callaghan hopes to fill the gap. Readily admitting "there is no doubt I'm hopelessly corrupt theologically," while aiming, nevertheless, as he explains in *That Summer in Paris,* to "relate a Christian enlightenment to some timeless process of becoming," Callaghan proceeds by way of intuition to a set of personal convictions which owes more to his own aesthetic philosophy and the creative process than to orthodox Christian belief, and whose expression in terms of religious symbol or jargon betrays ironic distance as much as their source. (p. 16)

On the one hand, a Biblical text is used in *They Shall Inherit the Earth* to refute Christian otherworldliness with irony, while on the other "the bold sensual phrases" of religious poetry stand in direct opposition to theological commentary. Far from religious exhortation to transcend the sensual self through spiritual striving, Callaghan interprets "The Beatitudes" as a call for self-realization and wholehearted commitment to the world. Similarly his reading of the "Song of Songs" in *Such is My Beloved* contradicts orthodox opinion. (p. 17)

[One could argue] that Callaghan's sense of metaphor, particularly his attempt as he explains it in his memoirs to reunite the "flesh" and the "word" in his work, is Catholic in a fundamental way. . . . Whether or not Callaghan achieves reconciliation in his work, it is likely that he has some such theory in mind in view of his distaste for separations and duality. It is possible, in fact, that what he is arguing for in novels like *Such is My Beloved* is a renewed sense of the sacredness of ordinary human experience, which the Church, in his view, has forgotten. One misses, however, in Callaghan "that sense of commitment and obligation, which," it has been suggested, "is the essence of religion." Callaghan's allegiance is all to himself. . . . Resisting the authority of Christian dogma by treating the Bible as a piece of literature, Callaghan effects a transformation of belief. Traditional religious concepts are reinterpreted in the light of his experience as an artist, and the Christian faith is ultimately replaced with what amounts to a theology of the creative imagination. Resurrection in terms of metaphysics is dismissed; innocence born of ignorance is a sin; and salvation is achieved through awareness. (p. 18)

[Callaghan makes] an unusual connection in his work between innocence and evil. He suggests, moreover, that innocence that is not knowing is a sin. Three of his novels in particular, *Such is My Beloved, More Joy in Heaven,* and *The Many Colored Coat,* illuminate the relationship between the two. (p. 19)

It is tempting to read Callaghan's work as an exercise in rationalization. If the sudden finality of revealed truth is rejected, then the artist is obviously free to choose his own. Certainly he insists upon his own insights. Whether or not, or how serious the author is in his equation of the Artist with an All-seeing God, it is clear that he usurps "the old authoritarian priest." Indeed, Callaghan's treatment of the Roman Catholic Church is related to an essentially aesthetic philosophy of life, and the effect of this upon the work is crucial. Not only are efforts made in the novels to combat traditional concepts of innocence and the fatal fall to knowledge with complementary myth, with a kind of redemptive quest for awareness and the approach of the Artist to God, but orthodox ritual and symbol are put to literary as opposed to devotional use. . . . If God has not quite disappeared from Callaghan's pages, His Church has become historical fact, and as the Bible fades more and more into myth and literature, it is clear that it is imaginative approaches that are redemptive. . . . (pp. 21-2)

Judith Kendle, "Callaghan and the Church," in Canadian Literature, *No. 80, Spring, 1979, pp. 13-22.*

* * *

CAMUS, Albert 1913-1960

Camus, an Algerian-born novelist, dramatist, and essayist, had a profound influence on modern philosophy, particularly on existential thought. Camus's conception of the human condition is predicated upon the constants of evil and death. Rejecting religion for reason, Camus concluded that the universe is itself irrational. It was individual action and the power of the individual will that provided life with value and purpose for Camus. He received the Nobel Prize for Literature in 1957. (See also *CLC*, Vols. 1, 2, 4, 9, 11, and *Contemporary Authors,* Vols. 89-92.)

JEAN-PAUL SARTRE

In *The Myth of Sisyphus,* . . . Camus provided us with a precise commentary upon [*The Stranger*]. His hero was neither good nor bad, neither moral nor immoral. These categories do not apply to him. He belongs to a very particular species for which the author reserves the word "absurd." But in Camus's work this word takes on two very different meanings. The absurd is both a state of fact and the lucid awareness which certain people acquire of this state of fact. The "absurd" man is the man who does not hesitate to draw the inevitable conclusions from a fundamental absurdity. (pp. 108-09)

Primary absurdity manifests a cleavage, the cleavage between man's aspirations to unity and the insurmountable dualism of mind and nature, between man's drive toward the eternal and the *finite* character of his existence, between the "concern" which constitutes his very essence and the vanity of his efforts. Chance, death, the irreducible pluralism of life and of truth, the unintelligibility of the real —all these are extremes of the absurd.

These are not really very new themes, and Camus does not present them as such. They had been sounded as early as the seventeenth century by a certain kind of dry, plain, contemplative rationalism, which is typically French and they served as the commonplaces of classical pessimism. (p. 109)

By virtue of the cool style of *The Myth of Sisyphus* and the subject of his essays, Albert Camus takes his place in the great tradition of those French moralists whom Andler has rightly termed the precursors of Nietzsche.

As to the doubts raised by Camus about the scope of our reasoning powers, these are in the most recent tradition of French epistemology. . . . Camus shows off a bit by quoting passages from Jaspers, Heidegger and Kierkegaard, whom, by the way, he does not always seem to have quite understood. But his real masters are to be found elsewhere.

The turn of his reasoning, the clarity of his ideas, the cut of his expository style and a certain kind of solar, ceremonious, and sad sombreness, all indicate a classic temperament, a man of the Mediterranean. His very method ("only through a balance of evidence and lyricism shall we attain a combination of emotion and lucidity.") recalls the old "passionate geometries" of Pascal and Rousseau and relate him, for example, not to a German phenomenologist or a Danish existentialist, but rather to Maurras, that other Mediterranean from whom, however, he differs in many respects.

But Camus would probably be willing to grant all this. To him, originality means pursuing one's ideas to the limit; it certainly does not mean making a collection of pessimistic maxims. The absurd, to be sure, resides neither in man nor in the world, if you consider each separately. But since man's dominant characteristic is "being-in-the-world," the absurd is, in the end, an inseparable part of the human condition. Thus, the absurd is not, to begin with, *the object of a mere idea; it is revealed to us in a doleful illumination.* "Getting up, tram, four hours of work, meal, sleep, and Monday, Tuesday, Wednesday, Thursday, Friday, Saturday, in the same routine" (*Sisyphus*), and then, suddenly, "the setting collapses," and we find ourselves in a state of hopeless lucidity.

If we are able to refuse the misleading aid of religion or of existential philosophies, we then possess certain basic, obvious facts: the world is chaos, a "divine equivalence born of anarchy"; tomorrow does not exist, since we all die. "In a universe suddenly deprived of light and illusions, man feels himself a stranger. This exile is irrevocable, since he has no memories of a lost homeland and no hope of a promised land." The reason is that man is *not* the world. . . . This explains, in part, the title of our novel; the stranger is man confronting the world. Camus might as well have chosen the title of one of George Gissing's works, *Born in Exile*. The stranger is also man among men. "There are days when . . . you find that the person you've loved has become a stranger." The stranger is, finally, myself in relation to myself, that is, natural man in relation to mind: "The stranger who, at certain moments, confronts us in a mirror" (*The Myth of Sisyphus*).

But that is not all; there is a *passion* of the absurd. The absurd man will not commit suicide; he wants to live, without relinquishing any of his certainty, without a future, without hope, without illusion, and without resignation either. He stares at death with passionate attention and this fascination liberates him. He experiences the "divine irresponsibility" of the condemned man.

Since God does not exist and man dies, everything is permissible. . . . [The] absurd man, rebellious and irresponsible, has "nothing to justify." He is *innocent,* innocent as Somerset Maugham's savages before the arrival of the clergyman who teaches them Good and Evil, what is lawful and what is forbidden. (pp. 109-11)

And now we fully understand the title of Camus's novel. The stranger he wants to portray is precisely one of those terrible innocents who shock society by not accepting the rules of its game. He lives among outsiders, but to them, too, he is a stranger. . . . And we ourselves, who, on opening the book are not yet familiar with the feeling of the absurd, vainly try to judge him according to our usual standards. For us, too, he is a stranger. . . .

[You] probably hoped that as you progressed your uneasiness would fade, that everything would be slowly clarified, would be given a reasonable justification and explained. Your hopes were disappointed. *The Stranger* is not an explanatory book. The absurd man does not explain; he describes. Nor is it a book which proves anything.

Camus is simply presenting something and is not concerned with a justification of what is fundamentally unjustifiable. (p. 111)

Camus does not require that attentive solicitude that writers who "have sacrificed their lives to art" demand of the reader, *The Stranger* is a leaf from his life. And since the most absurd life is that which is most sterile, his novel aims at being magnificently sterile. Art is an act of unnecessary generosity. We need not be over-disturbed by this; I find, hidden beneath Camus's paradoxes, some of Kant's wise observations on the "endless end" of the beautiful. Such, in any case, is *The Stranger,* a work detached from a life, unjustified and unjustifiable, sterile, momentary, already forsaken by its author, abandoned for other present things. And that is how we must accept it, as a brief communion between two men, the author and the reader, beyond reason, in the realm of the absurd.

This will give us some idea as to how we are to regard the hero of *The Stranger*. If Camus had wanted to write a novel with a purpose, he would have had no difficulty in showing a civil servant lording it over his family, and then suddenly struck with the intuition of the absurd, struggling against it for a while and finally resolving to live out the fundamental absurdity of his condition. The reader would have been convinced along with the character, and for the same reasons.

Or else, he might have related the life of one of those saints of the Absurd, so dear to his heart, of whom he speaks in *The Myth of Sisyphus:* Don Juan, the Actor, the Conqueror, the Creator. But he has not done so, and Meursault, the hero of *The Stranger,* remains ambiguous, even to the reader who is familiar with theories of the absurd. We are, of course, assured that he is absurd, and his dominant characteristic is a pitiless clarity. Besides, he is, in more ways than one, constructed so as to furnish a concerted illustration of the theories expounded in *The Myth of Sisyphus.* For example, in the latter work, Camus writes, "A man's virility lies more in what he keeps to himself than in what he says." And Meursault [is] an example of this virile silence, of this refusal to indulge in words. . . . (pp. 112-13)

[Meursault] has always lived according to Camus's standards. If there were a grace of absurdity, we would have to say that he has grace. He does not seem to pose himself any of the questions explored in *The Myth of Sisyphus.* . . . The character thus retains a real opacity, even to the absurd-conscious observer. He is no Don Juan, no Don Quixote of the absurd; he often even seems like its Sancho Panza. He is there before us, he exists, and we can neither understand nor quite judge him. In a word, he is alive, and all that can justify him to us is his fictional density.

The Stranger is not, however, to be regarded as a completely gratuitous work. Camus distinguishes, as we have mentioned, between the *notion* and the *feeling* of the absurd. He says, in this connection, "Deep feelings, like great works, are always more meaningful than they are aware of being. . . . An intense feeling carries with it its own universe, magnificent or wretched, as the case may be" (*The Myth of Sisyphus*). And he adds, a bit further on, "The feeling of the absurd is not the same as the *idea* of the absurd. The idea is grounded in the feeling, that is all. It does not exhaust it." *The Myth of Sisyphus* might be said to aim at giving us this *idea,* and *The Stranger* at giving us the feeling. (p. 114)

Camus talks a great deal; in *The Myth of Sisyphus* he is even garrulous. And yet, he reveals his love of silence. . . . [In] *The Stranger,* he has attempted *to be silent.* But how is one to be silent with words? How is one to convey through concepts the unthinkable and disorderly succession of present instants? This problem involves resorting to a new technique.

What is this new technique? "It's Kafka written by Hemingway," I was told. I confess that I have found no trace of Kafka in it. Camus's views are entirely of this earth, and Kafka is the novelist of impossible transcendence; for him, the universe is full of signs that we cannot understand; there is a reverse side to the décor. For Camus, on the contrary, the tragedy of human existence lies in the absence of any transcendence. . . . (pp. 115-16)

He is not concerned, then, with so ordering words as to suggest an inhuman, undecipherable order; the inhuman is merely the disorderly, the mechanical. There is nothing ambiguous in his work, nothing disquieting, nothing hinted at. *The Stranger* gives us a succession of luminously clear views. If they bewilder us, it is only because of their number and the absence of any link between them. Camus likes bright mornings, clear evenings, and relentless afternoons. His favorite season is Algiers' eternal summer. Night has hardly any place in his universe.

When he does talk of it, it is in the following terms: "I awakened with stars about my face. Country noises reached my ears. My temples were soothed by odors of night, earth, and salt. The wonderful peace of that sleepy summer invaded me like a tide" (*The Stranger*). The man who wrote these lines is as far removed as possible from the anguish of a Kafka. He is very much at peace within disorder. Nature's obstinate blindness probably irritates him, but it comforts him as well. Its irrationality is only a negative thing. The absurd man is a humanist; he knows only the good things of this world.

The comparison with Hemingway seems more fruitful. The relationship between the two styles is obvious. Both men write in the same short sentences. Each sentence refuses to exploit the momentum accumulated by preceding ones. Each is a new beginning. Each is like a snapshot of a gesture or object. For each new gesture and word there is a new and corresponding sentence. Nevertheless, I am not quite satisfied. The existence of an "American" narrative technique has certainly been of help to Camus. I doubt whether it has, strictly speaking, influenced him. (p. 116)

I catch a glimpse of a poetic prose underneath, which is probably Camus's personal mode of expression. If *The Stranger* exhibits . . . visible traces of the American technique, it was deliberate on Camus's part. He has chosen from among all the instruments at his disposal the one which seemed to serve his purpose best. I doubt whether he will use it again in future works. (p. 117)

Camus's story is analytic and humorous. Like all artists, he *invents,* because he pretends to be reconstituting raw experience and because he slyly eliminates all the significant links which are also part of the experience.

That is what Hume did when he stated that he could find nothing in experience but isolated impressions. That is what the American neo-realists still do when they deny the existence of any but external relations between phenomena. Contemporary philosophy has, however, established the fact that meanings are also part of the immediate data. But this would carry us too far afield. We shall simply indicate that the universe of the absurd man is the analytic world of the neo-realists. In literature, this method has proved its worth. It was Voltaire's method in *L'Ingénu* and *Micromégas,* and Swift's in *Gulliver's Travels.* For the eighteenth century also had its own outsiders, "noble savages," usually, who, transported to a strange civilization, perceived facts before being able to grasp their meaning. The effect of this discrepancy was to arouse in the reader the feeling of the absurd. Camus seems to have this in mind on several occasions, particularly when he shows his hero reflecting on the reasons for his imprisonment. (p. 118)

Where Bergson saw an indestructible organization, [Camus] sees only a series of instants. It is the plurality of incommunicable moments that will finally account for the plurality of beings. What our author borrows from Hemingway is thus the discontinuity between the clipped phrases that imitate the discontinuity of time.

We are now in a better position to understand the form of his narrative. Each sentence is a present instant, but not an indecisive one that spreads like a stain to the following one. The sentence is sharp, distinct, and self-contained. It is separated by a void from the following one, just as Descartes's instant is separated from the one that follows it. The world is destroyed and reborn from sentence to sentence. When the word makes its appearance it is a creation *ex nihilo*. The sentences in *The Stranger* are islands. We bounce from sentence to sentence, from void to void. (pp. 118-19)

The sentences are not, of course, arranged in relation to each other; they are simply juxtaposed. In particular, all causal links are avoided lest they introduce the germ of an explanation and an order other than that of pure succession. (p. 119)

This is what enables Camus to think that in writing *The Stranger* he remains silent. His sentence does not belong to the universe of discourse. It has neither ramifications nor extensions nor internal structure. (p. 120)

[Can] we speak of Camus's novel as something whole? All the sentences of his book are equal to each other, just as all the absurd man's experiences are equal. Each one sets up for itself and sweeps the others into the void. But, as a result, no single one of them detaches itself from the background of the others, except for the rare moments in which the author, abandoning these principles, becomes poetic.

The very dialogues are integrated into the narrative. Dialogue is the moment of explanation, of meaning, and to give it a place of honor would be to admit that meanings exist. Camus irons out the dialogue, summarizes it. renders it frequently as indirect discourse. He denies it any typographic privileges, so that a spoken phrase seems like any other happening. It flashes for an instant and then disappears, like heat lightning. Thus, when you start reading the book you feel as if you were listening to a monotonous, nasal, Arab chant rather than reading a novel. You may think that the novel is going to be like one of those tunes of which Courteline remarked that "they disappear, never to return" and stop all of a sudden. But the work gradually organizes itself before the reader's eyes and reveals its solid substructure.

There is not a single unnecessary detail, not one that is not returned to later on and used in the argument. And when we close the book, we realize that it could not have had any other ending. In this world that has been stripped of its causality and presented as absurd, the smallest incident has weight. There is no single one which does not help to lead the hero to crime and capital punishment. *The Stranger* is a classical work, an orderly work, composed about the absurd and against the absurd. Is this quite what the author was aiming at? I do not know. I am simply presenting the reader's opinion.

How are we to classify this clear, dry work, so carefully composed beneath its seeming disorder, so "human," so open, too, once you have the key? It cannot be called a *récit,* for a *récit* explains and co-ordinates as it narrates. It substitutes the order of causality for chronological sequence. Camus calls it a "novel." The novel, however, requires continuous duration, development and the manifest presence of the irreversibility of time. I would hesitate somewhat to use the term "novel" for this succession of inert present moments which allows us to see, from underneath, the mechanical economy of something deliberately staged. Or, if it is a novel, it is so in the sense that *Zadig* and *Candide* are novels. It might be regarded as a moralist's short novel, one with a discreet touch of satire and a series of ironic portraits (those of the pimp, the judge, the prosecuting attorney, etc.), a novel that, for all the influence of the German existentialists and the American novelists, remains, at bottom, very close to the tales of Voltaire. (pp. 120-21)

Jean-Paul Sartre, "Camus's 'The Outsider'" (1943), in his Literary and Philosophical Essays of Jean-Paul Sartre, *translated by Annette Michelson (copyright 1955 by S. G. Phillips, Inc.; reprinted by permission of S. G. Phillips, Inc., in Canada by Hutchinson Publishing Group Ltd), Criterion Books, 1955 (and reprinted as "An Explication of 'The Stranger,'" in* Camus: A Collection of Critical Essays, *edited by Germaine Brée, Prentice-Hall, Inc., 1962, pp. 108-21).*

HENRI PEYRE

The works of Camus, as they stand interrupted by fate, utter a pagan message which is to be set beside that of the great pagans of antiquity and that of some of the modern pagans to whom Christianity owes an immense debt of gratitude—for they have asked the right questions and constrained Christians to evolve ever more satisfactory answers to them. "Neo-paganism is the great spiritual phenomenon of our age"—thus wrote, in *The Drama of Atheistic Humanism* (1944), the eminent Jesuit thinker, Father Henri de Lubac, who deplores it, but courageously concedes that many noble souls, indeed many "blinded Christian souls" are attracted to the renovated paganism of today.

Instinct and doctrine blend in Camus's pagan assertions. His early series of essays, *Noces* (Nuptials), sings a paean to the wedding-feast of sky, sea, and the Algerian earth, supplemented by several equally rapturous prose canticles in honor of his "invincible summer" burning through the hours of distress and squalor in his youth. Their motto is a vehement denial of any longing for another life. Four pages before the volume closes, he propounds the conclusion: "The world is beautiful and, outside it, there is no salvation." The opening lines of the book are a disclaimer of all myths and intellectual structures erected to frustrate or to justify man's naïve desire for earthly happiness. "There is but one love in this world. To embrace a woman's body is also to retain, close to one, that strange joy which descends from the sky to the sea . . . I love this life with abandon and I want to speak of it freely; it fills me with pride at my human fate." *Hic et nunc:* here and now Camus, the young Pagan, like his three immediate predecessors in French literature, the Gide of *Fruits of the Earth,* Montherlant, and Giono, wants to savor the delights of life. The notion of hell appears, but as a pleasant joke, conceived by the imagination of most virtuous persons. Immortality, and any ultimate rewards promised to those who elect the Pascalian wager, are spurned. "I do not choose to believe," states the worshipper of the wind at Djemila, in *Noces,* "that death opens onto another life. To me it is a closed door." Those delusions are but an attempt to unburden man of the weight of his own life. And Camus prefers to carry his burden himself. (p. 66)

The name of Pascal has been invoked in connection with that of Camus, perhaps too lightly. A writer in the Christian monthly *Esprit,* Simone Fraisse, rightly argued, in March 1959, that much deeper affinities linked Camus to Lucretius. To the Latin poet, Epicurus was already a man in revolt, spurning the concept of Providence, haughtily consenting to his role of Sisyphus: he did not deign to indict the gods, for they had no share in the evil of the world. They passively watched it. Camus read his own mood as a rebel, intoxicated with the absurd, in the "prodigious image of divine sanctuaries swollen with the accusing corpses of the plague" which closes Lucretius's sixth and last book. But he added to Lucretius's resigned pessimism the modern concept of men's solidarity. After writing in *Noces* that "there is no shame in being happy," he had a character in *The Plague,* Rambert, remark, when faced with the omnipresence of evil: "There is shame in being happy all alone."

Much wishful thinking has been lavished over *The Fall*. . . . [Readers] of misguided good-will, lured by the title, thought they could descry anticipatory signs of a Christian attitude in *The Fall.* Meursault [in *The Stranger*] was in a sense an innocent sentenced for a crime which he had committed but not willed, and could be viewed, as Camus owned ("paradoxically," he underlined) as "the only Christ that we deserve." To searchers for allusions, Meursault's last wish for a large crowd to witness his execution, "so that all be consummated" might even recall the "consummatum est" whispered by the crucified Christ in the nineteenth chapter of St. John. But the hero of *The Fall* is an embittered, sarcastic nihilist, a garrulous talker merging his own guilt in the guilt which he instills in all those whom he forces to listen to him. If anything, that baffling tale should be read as a satire of the self-indictment practised by Christians and atheistic Existentialists alike, by Dostoevsky's "buffoons" as Camus called them in his "Exil d'Hélène," and by the advocates of universal and unlimited responsibility. After Tarrou and Rieux [in *The Plague*], the mouthpieces of a lofty ethics which did without God so that nothing be ravished from man's prerogatives, those idealists dreaming of being saints without God and pure of all expectation of any reward, Clamence [in *The Rebel*] strikes us as a totally desperate and sneering cynic. The book, unlike *The Plague,* truly has "no exit." Clamence's hell is, as in Sartre's play, the judgment of men, the glaring presence of the others.

Camus is profoundly opposed to all Christianity stands for: first the notions of incarnation, of grace, of redemption, of repentance, and of collective guilt for some sin committed, unbeknown to us. In that sense, as Camus himself remarked . . . and as J. P. Sartre had shrewdly explained as early as February 1943 ("Explication de *L'Etranger*" in *Les Cahiers du Sud*) [see excerpt above], Camus stands at the opposite pole from Kafka, "the novelist of impossible transcendence": for Kafka, enigmatic signs appear to point to an inhuman and undecipherable order; for Camus, there is no transcendence whatever. The very notion of sin, he avers, is meaningless to him. (pp. 67-8)

But Camus's most original revolt is against hope. . . . Camus indicts hope as a form of resignation, robbing man of energies which he needs, in order to enrich a God who "hardly needs them." . . . (p. 68)

Camus's world is one of universal condemnation to death, as Pascal's world was. But to the stranger, to the unfortunate men of good will in Oran harassed by the plague, to his companions in the Resistance, to the unbelievers of today who spurn the use of those small screens which Camus declared he had seen in Italian museums, through which the scaffold was concealed from men sentenced to death, to the bitter characters sketched in *The Fall* and in *Exile and the Kingdom,* the issue seems to require an anti-Pascalian answer: what are the positive values which persist in this world of mortals sentenced to death? Such paganism or disbelief in Christian values is a novel phenomenon of the twentieth century. Camus noted it in a curious footnote to his article, "Portrait d'un élu," in *Cahiers du Sud,* April 1943: "Contemporary unbelief does not rest on science as it did toward the close of the last century. It denies both science and religion. It is no longer the skepticism of reason in the presence of miracle. It is a passionate unbelief." (p. 70)

Henri Peyre, "Camus the Pagan," in Yale French Studies *25 (copyright © Yale French Studies 1960), 1960 (and reprinted in* Camus: A Collection of Critical Essays, *edited by Germaine Brée, Prentice-Hall, Inc., 1962, pp. 65-70).*

DONALD LAZERE

To appreciate Camus fully . . . it is necessary to encounter as an ensemble his novels, stories, plays, philosophical and lyrical essays, journalistic political criticism, speeches, interviews, and notebooks, as though they formed a single, multivolumed creation like Proust's *Remembrance of Things Past* or Durrell's *Alexandria Quartet*. (p. 4)

The reader is likely to get his first concrete indication of Camus's dialectical method from his unorthodox custom of making explicit cross-references between his fictitious works. (p. 5)

A second unifying technique is certain key images that Camus uses repeatedly, from his first to last writings, as titles and motifs: the stranger, the plague, the fall, the judge, the condemned man, the sun and sea, the two sides of the coin, exile and kingdom, lucidity and indifference, speech and silence, solitude and solidarity. His thematic associations with these images are usually fairly constant, so that they become a kind of shorthand for his continuing preoccupations. Sometimes, however, he works ironic variations on them or gives them multiple meanings, thereby creating tension between their appearances in different contexts. (pp. 5-6)

[Camus's] method was to fragment in each work one facet of his personality, one line of argument, one of several possible responses to a common condition such as the absurd, in such a way that only assembled in their totality would they reveal his full intention. This method enabled him to temper the intense emotionality that most readers associate with his writing with an equal measure of ironic detachment that he is not usually credited with. (p. 8)

L'Envers et l'endroit and *Nuptials* are concerned primarily with the necessity to detach oneself periodically from both legitimate social commitments and the flux of habitual social routine, with its illusions of immortality, stability, and self-importance, in order to establish an identity in solitary relation to the indifferent natural world and thereby to confront one's own mortality as a part of nature and to heighten appreciation of being alive. The sense of solitude and personal insignificance resulting from this dislocation of everyday routine in face of death, which is regarded as valuable in his first two books, regresses at the beginning of *The Myth* into a source of anxiety as one aspect of "the absurd," along with other aspects including the apparent nonexistence of God, the lack of unity, purpose, or rationale in the natural universe, and the frustrating restrictions of human understanding. Camus ends up accepting absurd alienation in *The Myth,* concluding that the insignificance and ephemerality of the individual's existence actually constitute its unique, irreplaceable value. He introduces the theme of metaphysical revolt in calling for the man of absurd awareness to rise above his overwhelming, lonely fate by bearing it defiantly rather than killing himself, to stave off death through prolonging and savoring every moment of life, and to combat the limitations of reason by maintaining constant lucidity.

The Stranger and *The Misunderstanding* dramatize more fully than *The Myth* that aspect of the absurd concerning the capricious twists of fate, while *The Stranger* and *Caligula* add to metaphysical absurdity and revolt the parallel dimension of revolt against the social absurdity of conventional morality and arbitrary legal authority, especially in the extreme form of capital punishment. *The Stranger,* like *The Myth,* asserts the primacy of individual, flesh-and-blood reality against any abstract notion that claims to supersede it. (pp. 9-10)

The absurd takes a political form in *The Rebel* and other writings after World War II about the capricious course of modern history, particularly in revolutions that have miscarried and ended up reinstitutionalizing murder as a political policy in both bourgeois and communist states. A total commitment to nonviolent resistance expressed in *Neither Victims nor Executioners* and by Tarrou in *The Plague* is modified in *The Rebel* and *The Just Assassins* to a doctrine of "limited guilt" whereby the rebel recognizes that he may have to kill in a just revolution or war, but only as a last resort and on the condition that he be willing to sacrifice his life in return so as to avert a cycle of revenge-killings or the political legitimization of murder. (p. 10)

This thematic line is elaborated through Camus's underlying vision of life's ambiguity and its reflection in his literary style through his frequent use of parallelism, antithesis, paradox, and ironic reversal. . . . In his world view the natural universe and man's fate are enigmatic, capriciously fluctuating forces, and our experiences are charged with many levels of possible meanings and implications that are sometimes complementary or parallel to one another, sometimes antithetical. His fascination with ambiguity shows in his titles . . . and in his frequent use of dualistic phrases like "solitary/solidary," "judge-penitent," "ambivalence" "equilibrium," "duplicity," and "equivocation." (pp. 10-11)

For Camus this pluralism pervading every area of life is sometimes a cause for anxiety . . . but it is also the source of a benign, Montaignian skepticism and tolerance, a distaste for absolutism, whether in politics, philosophy, morality, or aesthetics. . . . This pluralism provides, above all, an ennobling challenge to encompass and hold in dynamic balance the whole range of complex, self-contradictory possibilities that life offers. (p. 11)

Among Camus's array of balanced antitheses, the less complicated include unity and diversity . . . , pessimism and optimism, sensuality and intellectuality, and the life-giving and destructive sides of nature. Disillusioned recognition of life's limitations is offset by its intensification of the values remaining within those limitations. . . . (p. 12)

A more complex series of antitheses stems from possible alternative attitudes toward death. First there is terror in facing it, balanced by the pride of acknowledging it honestly: "I want to keep my lucidity to the last, and gaze upon my death with all the fullness of my jealousy and horror" [as Camus states in *Lyrical and Critical Essays*]. He also finds this lucidity toward death to be a means of intensifying life's joys, in the *carpe diem* tradition. . . . (p. 13)

[Camus's] attitudes toward death becomes subsumed in the first half of a larger antithesis in which the solitary egocentricity of Camus contemplating nature and natural death is balanced against his social conscience. . . . (p. 16)

Camus's theoretical writings about the literary artist's vocation incorporate the same balance between egocentricity and social responsibility. . . . He significantly modified the theory of art for art's sake . . . along much the same lines as André Malraux—to begin with, infusing it with a heterosexual sensibility in contrast to its previous frequent association with homosexuality. Furthermore, *The Rebel* and later expressions of literary theory develop his conviction that no artist, no matter how egocentric, can work in isolation. . . . (p. 18)

Finally, the writer must always draw from his time for material, and only the most effete author can remain uncommitted when faced with the urgency of our present crises. The challenge is to assimilate the present temper into works that are both significant socially and substantial aesthetically. (p. 19)

His most widely inclusive antithesis is that between romantic and classical values and stylistic traits, the reconciliation of which is a rare, admirable achievement in the twentieth century. . . . [In Camus's view, romantic and classical values] are not entirely antithetical; classicism, rather, encompasses romanticism, since the balancing of opposites itself is a central classical and neoclassical doctrine. . . . (pp. 19-20)

But the classical spirit is subject to abuses too. Camus's exhortations to emotional and intellectual intensity are in the tradition of the romantic movement's reaction against the rigidified neoclassicism of the late eighteenth century, a reaction that has been repeated in the twentieth century by French surrealism and existentialism, and later the American beat and hippie movements, against the atrophy of the classical virtue of decorum into academic stuffiness or bourgeois insipidity and priggishness. Thus, if classicism can be seen as a controlled romanticism, controlled romanticism can also be seen, in an author like Camus, as a regenerated classicism.

A final way he combines the two traditions is to enclose his romantic subjects or heroes in a classical style and structure. Classical stylistic convention as well as ideology can be seen in his constant use of antithetical devices like parallelism, balanced sentences, chiasmus, and oxymoron. In contrast to romantic verbal effusion, involution, and rejection of set forms, his prose is typically concise and clear (aside from some lapses in *The Myth* and lyrical essays), his literary forms tightly, symmetrically structured. (pp. 20-1)

Camus blends still more antithetical attitudes into the paradoxes that mark almost every page of his writing. The paradoxes inherent in the absurd condition provide the dramatic reversals of *The Myth:* The absence of a God or transcendent meaning in life, which he begins by postulating as a justification for suicide, ends up making life *more* worth living; reason is incapable of making sense out of life, yet it is valuable insofar as it gives us a concept of what sense is and a rational articulation of its own limitations. The crucial shift in emphasis in his writing after *The Myth* from the phase of the absurd to that of rebellion pivots on a paradox that he expresses in the introduction to *The Rebel:* If I conclude that the value of my freedom and egocentric pleasure make my own life worth living, I must through simple empathy say the same about everyone else's life. Therefore, murder as well as suicide is proscribed, my freedom must be limited where it interferes with others', and in order to defend the principle of the value of life, freedom, and pleasure, I may have to sacrifice my own when others' are threatened. Thus Camus in his personal dialectical development recapitulates the ambivalence from total irresponsibility to total responsibility that is central to existentialist thought from Dostoevsky to Sartre. (pp. 21-2)

Similarly, in his literary theory he transmutes the narcissism and political escapism or elitism usually identified with art for art's sake into a politically committed, democratic aesthetic. . . .

Another form of paradox is the ironic reversal by which a line of action carried too far merges with its opposite or the condition against which it was intended to rebel. An excess in one's assertion of freedom destroys others' freedom and eventually his own, as in the case of Caligula. Rebellion against a murderous universe (Caligula) or society (Meursault) can make the rebel a competitor in murder. The romantic quest for apocalyptic transcendence of bourgeois banality can end in intellectual or physical self-annihilation that is equally banal. (p. 23)

A full recognition of the protean, unpredictable side of Camus's writing that emerges from these patterns of ambiguity, antithesis, ambivalence, paradox, and ironic reversal shows how far off the mark are those readers and critics who regard him as somber, monolithic, or unremittingly tendentious. . . . In fact, his flair for playing riddle games and for shifting roles was so strong that he must have come to feel misgivings about its tendency to undercut his more serious, straightforward intentions. (p. 24)

The monumental artistic plan and ideological comprehensiveness of Camus's total work approach a complete world system, a synthesis of metaphysics, ethics, history, political theory, social psychology, aesthetics, and semantics into a single, consistent viewpoint. Part of his fascination is the same as that of other philosophical or literary system builders. . . . And he is open to the same criticism, on philosophical if not on artistic grounds, that he sometimes oversimplifies or bends reality in trying to make everything fit his system. (pp. 24-5)

All of the foregoing indicates why he is a difficult author. It is not that he is prone toward obscure, scholarly allusions in the manner of T. S. Eliot, or toward the occultism and private fantasies of symbolist and surrealist poets, or even the rigorous formal philosophy of Sartre. It is, rather, that assimilating the magnitude, complexity, and kaleidoscopic dynamics of all his major works combined presents the reader with an aesthetic challenge. . . . (p. 25)

In the end, it is ironic that Camus, who has generally been underestimated by both Marxist and formalist critics—two schools that he considered to be at equally excessive poles in their exclusivity—actually provides an exemplary subject of study for the combination of aesthetic and political concerns valued by the former and for the literary complexity valued by the latter. (pp. 25-6)

Camus's aesthetic is closer to that of Coleridge, who is often cited as a forerunner of the New Critics; in contrast to the latter, though, for Coleridge as for Camus the internal dynamics of the literary work are not constrictingly divorced from the external world but are enriched all the more by being viewed as a microcosm of the artist's organically unified world view. Part of Camus's unique accomplishment in our time is that his stylistic and formal elaborateness is not an aesthete's affectation or attempt to flee reality into an artificial paradise but an integral extension of and key to his total vision of reality. (p. 26)

The most prominent motif unifying Camus's writing is the problem of judgment, to whose multiple forms he attributes the crucial spiritual and social ills of the twentieth century. He develops some aspects of this theme in expository order in the essays, while in the fiction and drama he reveals other aspects through a variety of literary techniques: images of the judge, jury, prosecuting and defense attorneys, witness, guilty verdict, prison, and death sentence run all through these works on the level of literal action and as metaphor, symbol, and allegory. His system here involves four parallel elements: metaphysical and human judgment and the rational and irrational forms they both take. . . .

The imagery of rational metaphysical judgment derives from the Christian conception of God as the final judge, who omnisciently dictates standards of innocence and guilt and accordingly rewards or punishes men after death. Camus sees rational human judgment as society's appropriation of God's judicial powers. (p. 28)

Governmental absolutism reveals itself not only in war but in capital punishment, which Camus repeatedly attacks as legalized, rationalized murder. (p. 29)

In opposition to "rational" religious and social judgment, Camus expresses his themes of metaphysical absurdity and social nihilism in images of irrational judgment. Neither Camus nor any of his fictional heroes believes in God, an afterlife, or any rationale in the workings of the universe. . . . Death obliterates all of society's distinctions between innocence and guilt, and a premonition of his death exposes to a man the artificiality of society's rules, freeing him to rise above them and live any way he pleases.

If freedom from religious and social judgment is pushed to its extremes, however, it in turn becomes another form of judgment; unlimited freedom legitimizes nihilistic murder, by which man becomes the accomplice of the universe as capricious killer. . . . (pp. 29-30)

[Murderous] forms of metaphysical and human judgment figure centrally in Camus's fiction and drama as well as in the philosophical and journalistic essays. The novels, stories, plays, and earlier lyric essays also extend the theme of social judgment dramatically into more mundane areas—such as the everyday, arbitrary rituals of conventional morality, the officiousness of clergymen, judges, and bureaucrats, the petty vanity of individuals who need to give an air of importance to their banal daily routines or to consider themselves morally superior to their neighbors. (p. 30)

The complexity of the judgment theme can be confusing, and failure to distinguish between its multiple aspects has caused many readers and critics to miss the ironies and structural dynamics that Camus gets out of paralleling metaphysical and human, rational and irrational judgment. In *The Fall* preeminently, all four forms of judgment are closely intertwined in Clamence's fevered, devious discourse on guilt; here, and to nearly an equal degree in each of the other works, it is necessary to distinguish carefully which forms of judgment Camus is dealing with and on what literary levels they are functioning at different stages of the story. (p. 31)

Out of the values of *The Stranger* and *The Plague* Camus synthesized a humanitarian ethic for our time. From *The Stranger* he retained Meursault's simple, pagan sensuality free from illusions of immortality or a God to justify one's values, as well as his freedom from society's arbitrary laws and self-righteousness. However, Meursault's is "a still-negative truth," as Camus says in a 1955 foreword to *The Stranger* . . . , because Meursault ultimately denies life's value and because he kills, albeit accidentally, without contrition. In *The Plague* Rieux and Tarrou make Meursault's negative truth positive. By battling against the plague—and, allegorically, against natural death and nihilism—Rieux attests to the value in every man's life that justifies fighting to stay its inevitable execution. Tarrou makes explicit Meursault's instinctive rebellion against social judgment in its everyday forms and especially in its most severe form, rational murder committed under the authorization of capital punishment or militant "Justice." In defending human happiness against any life-threatening force—metaphysical or human, irrational or rational—Rieux and Tarrou define the boundary of individual freedom at the point where it destroys one's own or another's life. (p. 43)

However, the theme of Camus's last novel, *The Fall,* is that most men today are, unfortunately, incapable of gaining this humanitarian salvation because they have been conditioned by centuries of Christianity to need a belief in the transcendent authority of God and further conditioned by recent decades of totalitarianism to need absolute social authority. (pp. 43-4)

Camus follows the . . . general theme of men's flight from rebellion and freedom in several of the stories in his final work of fiction, *Exile and the Kingdom.* The multiple levels of the theme are most effectively embodied in "The Guest," which is primarily a dramatization of the French colonial intellectual's divided sympathies in the Algerian conflict but which also has a symbolic dimension in which Camus explores the idea of a humanitarian Christ who comes to free men from religious and social judgment.

Christian critics who have claimed to see indications of an impending conversion by Camus in *The Fall* and other late works have missed the irony in his use of Christian imagery against orthodox Christian doctrine. (pp. 48-9)

One of the central, and typically ambiguous, words throughout Camus's writing is "meaning." He uses the noun *le sens* and the verbs *signifier* and *vouloir dire* to refer both to a metaphysical purpose, justification, or scale of moral values in life and to epistemological "sense"—semantic signification and the rational unification and explanation of sense experience. . . .

Camus divides the multiple aspects of the absurd that he enumerates in *The Myth* into what can be termed metaphysical and epistemological absurdities. The former include the brevity of life and inevitability of death, the indifference of the natural universe to human existence and of men to one another's existence, and the absence of a God and an afterlife that would give this life a transcendent purpose or universal system of moral values (although Camus approaches the existence of God more as an epistemological problem than as a metaphysical one; he does not deny God's existence but our ability to ascertain it rationally). Epistemological absurdity further entails the limitations of human understanding in general—the foundering of reason in logical dilemmas, the mind's failure to explain or unify experience totally, the frustration of our "nostalgia for unity, that appetite for the absolute . . .". . . . (p. 52)

Camus summarizes all of these metaphysical and epistemological aspects of the absurd in the formulation "life has no meaning"; the central question of the book then becomes whether "refusing to grant a meaning to life necessarily leads to declaring that it is not worth living." . . . He assumes that it is the belief life has a meaning, in all of the above senses, that makes most men feel it is worth living. But, he asks, is the absence of metaphysical and epistemological *meaning* in fact equivalent to the absence of all *value* in life, or can values be found that make life worth living even under the conditions of absurd meaninglessness? His answer from the beginning is, "In truth, there is no necessary common measure between these judgments." . . . Indeed, he later concludes, "It was previously a question of finding out whether or not life had to have a meaning to be lived. It now becomes clear, on the contrary, that it will be lived all the better if it has no meaning." . . . (pp. 52-3)

On the metaphysical level, he explains, the absense of God—or more precisely our absence of knowledge that there is a God—dictates existential freedom . . . ; recognizing the brevity of life and denying an afterlife provide an imperative to savor every minute of this life; the lack of any preordained purpose or moral value system is an invitation to create one's own life style and to substitute "the quantity of experiences for the quality." . . . (p. 53)

On the epistemological level, reason is valuable within its limitations for two reasons. To begin with, its failure to explain and unify experience is not total. . . . And reason provides the source not only of a minimal sense of coherence but of another form of revolt, that of the human mind defying the mindlessness of the rest of the universe and grappling with its own limitations: "To a man devoid of blinkers, there is no finer sight than that of the intelligence at grips with a reality that transcends it." . . . To deny the value of reason altogether, through irrationalism, mysticism, or the religious-existentialist leap to faith in God, is to commit "philosophical suicide," the intellectual equivalent to literal suicide as a response to metaphysical absurdity. (pp. 53-4)

One more dimension of meaning and value remains to be integrated into Camus's overall pattern—that dealing with language and literature as communication. One of the set of paradoxes providing the transition from the period of *the Stranger* and *The Myth* to that of *The Plague,* "The Enigma," and *The Rebel* is that, although part of the absurd condition is man's solitude in the natural universe and in society, this very solitude can become a source of solidarity between men recognizing their common condition. In the later works Camus accordingly comes to emphasize the communicative function of language and literature along with their life-affirming and unifying functions. In *The Myth* language and literature are already forms of rebellion against total meaninglessness, and in *The Rebel* Camus defines all rebellion as communal. In *The Stranger* part of Meursault's "negative truth" is his minimal linguistic communication and compassion with the other characters—although he thinks of the latter primarily in terms of the fellowship of men condemned to death. In the subsequent works Camus moves toward a more life-oriented concept of compassion between men, which he expresses in the image of "dialogue," as opposed on one hand to the silence associated with accepting the absurd and on the other hand to the verbose monologues of those who use language to set themselves above others. To the metaphysical and social ills he has been concerned with previously are added those resulting from faulty communication. (pp. 67-8)

[The] communicative value of literature becomes obvious: "If he speaks, if he reasons, *above all if he writes,* immediately the brother reaches out his hand." "Even if the novel describes only nostalgia, despair, frustration, it still creates form and salvation"—salvation through compassion between men in their common nostalgia, despair, and frustration. Camus's entire development of the theme of meaning and value can be seen as culminating in his final ideal of the vocation of the writer, whose challenge is double: first, to strike a balance between negating false hopes of total metaphysical or epistemological meaning and affirming the validity and value in life's limited level of meaning; and second, to be "the artist [who] fashions himself in that ceaseless oscillation from himself to others," again striking a balance between that degree of solitude inherent in the absurd condition as well as in the artistic temperament, and that degree of solidarity attainable through literary creation. (p. 70)

Camus's essays on the social responsibility of artists and intellectuals are of special importance today because this subject has provoked increasingly intense debate in France and the United states since the time of his death and was a crucial point on which he was opposed to Sartre and subsequent revolutionary ideologists. . . .

[His] literary theory is most distinctive as a middle path between two opposite extremes prevalent in twentieth-century aesthetics. On the one hand, in Camus's analysis, nineteenth-century notions of pure art for art's sake have led to ahistorical formalism and social isolation or dandyism in the artist, who by abdicating public responsibility leaves mass culture the exclusive realm of trivial entertainers and mass politics that of unscrupulous professionals. (p. 101)

On the other hand, he asserts, the realistic tradition has also had its excessive offshoots. Naturalism, as for example in Hemingway or the "tough" American detective that was an intellectual fad in France during the 1940's, claims to record life impassively, in its totality, without the artist interposing selection, arrangement, or judgment—an impossible claim to begin with, in Camus's view. It binds the writer, at least in theory, to an isolated historical moment and impersonal themes and style. Because these two extremes either totally ignore or accept the world as it is, neither serves rebellious art's purpose of "correcting creation." . . . (pp. 101-02)

If Camus had never written any fiction or drama he would still be likely to rank among the outstanding authors of the twentieth century solely as a literary essayist. . . . [The exemplary quality of his prose] is distilled in its purest, most autonomous form in the essays.

Because of their individual brevity and occasionality, the essays in *L'Envers et l'endroit, Nuptials,* and *Summer* are too often regarded as minor works, thematic corollaries to *The Myth* and *The Rebel.* . . . Artistically, however, both individually and as a collective unit, the lyrical essays often surpass the "major" essays and stand among his very finest works. Here Camus is most fully, comprehensively himself, in contrast to the ironic personae of his fictional narrators and to the single lines of formal argument that he isolates in *The Myth, The Rebel,* and the political journalism. The personal essay is the medium in which he is most at home—that is to say, in the world of immediate, concrete experience. Here he relaxes and speaks in his own voice of the actual settings and personal relationships of his life, the flesh-and-blood inspirations of the abstract themes of *The Myth* and *The Rebel.* Here too he reveals the compassion, the warmth of personality and zest for living, the amused affection for the details of everyday life that he subordinates in his fiction and plays—perhaps regrettably—to the creation of mythic settings and characters and crisis-pitched action. (pp. 117-18)

Dominating all else is his rhapsodic love affair with the Mediterranean sun, sea, and flower-covered landscape. He succeeds in elevating intensity of sense experience into a rationalist metaphysic and in exalting the communion of man with nature in overtly sexual imagery without ever lapsing into mysticism, pantheism, or the pathetic fallacy. . . .

Thematically and stylistically, the individual lyrical essays —even the earliest ones in *L'Envers et l'endroit*—contain his most concise, integrated expressions of his ideal of keeping life's paradoxes and antithetical possibilities in balance. . . . (p. 118)

Structurally, the essays follow a typical pattern of a passage of straight narration or description that evokes a meditation that is in turn elaborated into a paradoxical metaphor or aphorism. . . . They are further characterized by a rise to poetic diction in the closing paragraphs. . . . (p. 120)

The lyrical essays have the expository form of tightly knotted prose poems, challenging the reader with complex extended figures of speech, obliquely expressed themes, elliptical jumps in narration and thought, and cryptic motifs that reveal their meaning bit by bit as they recur with variations from essay to essay—such as silence, indifference, black sun and dark flame, or the seaside cemetery near Algiers. (pp. 120-21)

As a journalist Camus was one of the few in the midcentury to produce a substantial body of daily and weekly articles of lasting literary value, only a small number of which have been translated into English. (p. 123)

His own journalistic ideals and practice exemplified what the periodical press can and should be: the application to daily events of a refined humanistic sensibility, long-range historical perspective, and a radical integrity. . . . (p. 124)

It is important to note . . . that, while on international affairs his reasoning was becoming strained and his rhetoric hollow by the late fifties, on a domestic issue he could still, in 1957, write his most radically incisive political statement, "Reflections on the Guillotine." . . . [This essay] best epitomizes Camus's journalistic style, and indeed his entire art and thought. Here Camus marshals all his powers of novelistic and dramatic description and of straightforward journalistic exposition, heightened literarily by bristling irony, paradox, and aphorism and supported philosophically by his most maturely refined and concisely articulated metaphysical, political, and moral principles. The result is one of the most devastating polemics against capital punishment ever written. (pp. 126-27)

The Myth of Sisyphus is Camus's most difficult work, particularly in the first . . . sequence, "An Absurd Reasoning," which presents stylistic challenges similar to the lyrical essays—dense construction, digressive asides, elliptical jumps between sentences, cryptic aphorisms—and compounds them with a lengthily sustained, involved line of argument in a combination of philosophy and literary essay reminiscent of Kierkegaard or Nietzsche. The book is filled with nearly as many points of ambiguity as *The Stranger,* which would undoubtedly be a defect from a purely philosophical point of view but which makes it all the more engrossing as an aesthetic creation, embodying in its own structure the epistemological pluralism that comprises one aspect of the absurd. (p. 130)

[A] factor contributing to the book's emotional power is its dramatic techniques like the buildup of narrative tension and dynamic modulations in tone. Camus displays his flair for drama in the startling opening—"There is but one truly serious philosophical problem, and that is suicide" . . . — and in the way he systematically demolishes all the illusory values that sustain conventional life, then amid this seeming wasteland builds a new scale of values consistent with the absurd in which "everything resumes its place and the absurd world is reborn in all its splendor and diversity." . . . *The Myth* shares with the fiction and lyrical essays Camus's characteristic of rising in climactic paragraphs to a rhapsodic tone and intensely poetic diction. . . . (p. 131)

The Myth's ambiguities begin with the central term itself, "the absurd," partly because Camus isn't entirely consistent in its usage, partly because he considers it essentially an indefinable, emotional quality, such as beauty. . . .

The book's expository structure also contributes to several ambiguities, some doubtlessly intentional, some probably not, that tend to mislead unwary readers. The shock opening leads one to expect a discourse on suicide in general, despite Camus's subsequent qualification that he is only dealing with suicide as a response to the absurd. (p. 132)

As his aesthetic theory has indicated, Camus's writing generally does not convey a highly developed sense of specific social or historical situation. Although in his reportage he did criticize the inequities of class society, in his fiction, drama, and literary and philosophical essays he purposely strove for universal truths even when he located them in recognizable social settings. The price he paid was a certain loss of fidelity to those specifics of existence that vary enormously between different social strata and historical moments. (p. 137)

Camus [maintains] the customary ambiguity of his titles in *L'Homme révolté,* which translates either as "Man in Revolt" or "The Revolted [or 'disgusted'] Man." The essay's artistic complexity is mainly contained in its monumental structure and a world view synthesizing metaphysics, political and literary history and theory. In lieu of his projected 1500-page "The System," it is the closest approximation to his *summa,* encompassing virtually all aspects of his formal thought and all the stages in the dialectical development of his themes. (p. 139)

Whatever the drawbacks of *The Rebel*'s massively symmetrical structure, it effectively underscores the theme of man's perpetual passion for unity, forming an organizational counterpart to the reflection of absurd pluralism in *The Myth*'s fragmented exposition.

The introduction is one of the key passages of his entire works, encapsulating the transition between the phase of the absurd and that of rebellion. Picking up from where *The Myth* leaves off, Camus moves from the problem of suicide to that of murder. Although he does not mention the titles of his earlier works, he implicitly contrasts the nihilistic implications of the absurd, those followed by Meursault and Caligula, with the affirmative implications in *The Myth,* whose line of argument, if followed accurately and to its end, rejects nihilistic suicide and now by extension rejects nihilistic murder as well: "To say that life is absurd, the conscience must be alive. How is it possible, without making remarkable concessions to one's desire for comfort, to preserve exclusively for oneself the benefits of such a process of reasoning? From the moment that life is recognized as good, it becomes good for all men." . . . (p. 141)

In the end, Camus's exhortations are only fully applicable to volunteer rebels, especially intellectuals, within the bourgeoisie—one of whom, as Sartre reminded him, Camus himself had become. Camus's political theory in general is most meaningful as a program for middle-class intellectuals and artists involving themselves and their distinctive sensibility in historical struggle. These men, however, are apt to play only a marginal political role at best. Camus recognized this and at times gives the impression in *The Rebel* that he is trying mainly to formulate an ethic of minimal nonviolence for himself while conceding, like Tarrou, that other men must go on murderously making history. In this light, *The Rebel* stops short of proposing a universal political program, which is undoubtedly a grave limitation. On the other hand, perhaps the reader can best do it justice by approaching it with the understanding that its title applies mainly to the intellectual *engagé* and perhaps even more specifically to Camus himself. (pp. 149-50)

Dualities pervade [*The Stranger*] in theme and structure. . . . [There are] the parallels between God's and society's judgment and between natural death and capital punishment. There is another important thematic parallel between the absurdity of nature or fate and that of society. (p. 160)

Society as Camus portrays it is as duplicitous, capricious, and lethal as fate, with one vital difference: fate makes no claim to rationality, while society does make one. (p. 161)

[Fate] ironically links incidents that would seem to have no logical connection (e.g., Meursault's behavior at his mother's funeral and his trial for murder), and a foresight of death, by reducing all actions to the same level of importance, creates an identity between the most disparate events. Instead of mystical doctrines in which all objects and events are identified with one another in their equal significance, Camus presents the reverse: all are identified in their equal *in*significance. . . .

Camus's observations on the duality of nature, society, fate, and the ironic identification that death effects between diverse events mold the novel into a highly symmetrical structure. (p. 163)

The most disputable issue in *The Stranger* is whether its final implication is really that "life isn't worth living." Meursault's meditation shortly before being executed, "From the moment one dies, how and when has no importance," can be regarded as the key to his whole character. Camus may be asking us to consider the startling hypothesis of a man who in the midst of life is as indifferent to his fate as he will be after death. (p. 166)

[It] is likely that Camus intended to leave open the possibility of at least two contradictory conclusions to make the book illustrate that "this world is nothing and this world is everything—there is the contradictory and tireless cry of every true artist." The only unequivocally affirmative theme is to be found, not explicitly in Meursault's narrative but in the novel's literary structure and in the author's having remained alive and choosing to write that novel. . . . (p. 169)

Of all Camus's works *The Stranger* is undoubtedly filled with the most paradoxes, both internally and in relation to his life and other works. The ending ironically reverses conventional notions of innocence and guilt. (pp. 169-70)

By conceiving a story and a novelistic structure that epitomize the pluralistic nature and internal contradictions of the absurd, by enriching the novel with multiple meanings and paradoxes on every level, Camus infused *The Stranger* with a distinctive vitality that makes this slim *récit* unique among his works and those of any other author. He was never again to attain its richness in any of his later works, although this is not to deny their own distinctive virtues or justification for being less complex. *The Stranger* is one of those rare, fertile inventions like *Hamlet, Moby Dick, The Brothers Karamazov, Ulysses,* or *The Great Gatsby* that even the greatest of writers are seldom fortunate enough to create more than once in a lifetime: a combination of will, in the author's felicitous original conception, and of good fortune in the way this conception quickens and expands to take on a life of its own. All the elements coalesce to form a simple, yet infinitely intricate pattern, and the levels of meaning proliferate to produce an artistic organism that is as protean, enigmatic, and endlessly tantalizing as the human condition itself. (pp. 171-72)

In *The Plague* Camus audaciously synthesized the ultimate extension of [realism and symbolism] into an allegorical naturalism. He had previously demonstrated his native mastery of the metaphysical plane in fiction and drama, on which plane the plague allegorizes the absurd, natural death, the problem of evil. . . . He is an incisive social psychologist in his portrayal of a trapped community, a portrayal that reveals universal truths about any group of humans in crisis. . . . (p. 173)

To sum up *The Plague*'s strong points, it is on first reading as gripping and moving as anything in world literature. Only on subsequent, closer rereadings do its limitations become troublesome. Stylistically it lacks the enduring fascination of *The Stranger*'s verbal complexities and *The Fall*'s epigrammatic incisiveness. . . . The various symbolic levels and Rieux's doctor-artist dual role are rather static techniques of structural ambiguity compared to the dynamic interaction between Parts One and Two of *The Stranger* or the innumerable possible interpretations of individual passages and of that novel as a whole. It should be remembered, however, that by the time of *The Plague* Camus has become committed to a more straightforward literature, having developed an antipathy toward the abuses of linguistic ambiguity that he expresses through Tarrou: "All our troubles spring from our failure to use plain, clean-cut language." . . . (pp. 175-76)

The philosophical dialogues between Rieux, Tarrou, Paneloux, and Rambert, although substantial thematically, tend to make stilted, bombastic fiction. . . .

After the first reading, without the suspense and emotional involvement in the characters' fates, Rieux, Tarrou, Cottard, and Paneloux do not retain enough individual complexity or appeal to become much more than the abstract voices of philosophical positions. . . . (p. 176)

Furthermore, weak points in the book's elaborate symbolic system lead to problems in structure and interaction between characters. Camus situates his fictional Oran outside of a specific historical and political context. Consequently, he can only bring in politics through Tarrou's flashback monologue, which, though one of the outstanding parts of the novel in itself, is dramatically and thematically an artificial interpolation. (p. 177)

Moreover, on the naturalistic level *The Plague* conveys little consciousness of social class in Oran. We do not see enough of the difference in the effects a plague—or a military occupation—would have on the rich and the poor. (p. 181)

A different critical perspective from that applicable to *The Stranger* and *The Plague* needs to be brought to bear on evaluating *The Fall*. To begin with, it contains fewer conventional novelistic elements. There is really only one character and not much of a plot; the technique derives almost exclusively from the resourceful use of first-person narrative point of view. (p. 183)

The Fall marks a culmination of nearly all of Camus's main themes: metaphysical and human judgment, dandyish egoism vs. altruism, monologue vs. dialogue, Europe vs. the Mediterranean and tropics, communist and Christian authoritarianism, an antireligious, secularized Christian ethic, and conflicting loyalties and fears between maternal and paternal forces. The fullest appreciation will result from recognizing its climactic significance in the overall pattern.

Although it is his least conventional novel in plot and characterization, it is all in all his most literary fictional work. In its genre it owes much to the tradition of spiritual autobiography and confessional literature. . . . (p. 184)

The Fall . . . marks a successful change of form for Camus to an overtly traditional literary style and allusiveness. He obviously did not choose this style, however, simply to show that he could master it. In the unsavory character of Clamence, who represents the humanistically educated, cultivated European, he is calling into question the whole cultural tradition of Western civilization. (p. 186)

Another extratextual dimension contributing to the complexity of *The Fall* is its elements of autobiography. . . . Clamence's occupation as a lawyer for noble causes is an obvious analogue for Camus's public image as humanitarian author, an image he bridled at and is satirizing here. (p. 188)

The main limitation in *The Fall* is not any weakness on its own terms, within which it is difficult to find fault, but a general one in Camus's fiction that becomes most acute here. There is a paucity throughout his work of long-term, gradually developed characterization and relationships between people in more or less normal life situations. . . .

The dimension lacking in his fiction can be pointed up by comparing him to a master of characterization like Proust, the one twentieth-century French novelist who most clearly surpasses Camus in scope. (p. 194)

Camus did have a surprising capacity for dialectical reversals, and it is quite possible that he would have mastered the traditional techniques of interpersonal characterization and naturalistic, historically situated exposition in [''The First Man,'' the novel he was writing at the time of his death]. (p. 197)

In the six stories of *Exile and the Kingdom* Camus is trying out new techniques: a relatively objective third-person narration in all of them but ''The Renegade,'' which is his only attempt at interior monologue; a light, urbane tone in the satire on upper-bohemian Paris social life in ''The Artist at Work''; a feminine point of view in ''The Adulterous Woman''; extensive stretches of detailed realistic narration and description with few symbolic overtones in the early parts of ''The Adulterous Woman'' and ''The Growing Stone'' and throughout ''The Silent Men.'' He is also trying to fill some gaps in the subject matter of his previous works: sustained accounts of marital relationships in ''The Adulterous Woman'' and ''The Artist at Work''; mundane central characters and workaday settings in ''The Adulterous Woman'' and ''The Silent Men''; a Parisian locale in ''The Artist at Work''; most strikingly, the less attractive side of the coin of Algeria's landscape and life—''The Renegade'' takes place under inhumanly hot sunlight, ''The Adulterous Woman,'' ''The Silent Men,'' and ''The Guest'' in wintry cold. The stories are woven together thematically by various paradoxical mixtures of familiar antitheses: exile and kingdom, solitude and solidarity, freedom and servitude, silence and noise or speech. Each of the central characters suffers from divided loyalties, each is literally or figuratively a foreigner, isolated in the midst of society. (p. 199)

Exile and the Kingdom's most striking technical feat is the style of the interior monologue in ''The Renegade,'' much of which is unfortunately lost in translation. . . . The tortuously elongated sentences, ungrammatically linked without punctuation or by commas, are the antithesis of *The Stranger's* curt, disparate sentence structure. Clamence's verbose quasidialogue, verging toward the end of *The Fall* on delirium, is reduced here to a man without a tongue raving interminably to himself—the ultimate image of everything Camus has said about the perversion of language to isolate and enslave men. A litany of anguish is created by the rhythms of three, six and twelve-syllable syntactic units that suggest the French alexandrine poetic line, reinforced by internal near rhymes. . . . (p. 202)

''The Growing Stone'' is the most obvious instance of the impression the whole book gives that Camus had not fully mastered the short-story form. ''The Guest'' is the only story that ranks with the three novels in successful cohesion of theme, structure, expository technique, characterization, and realistic and symbolic elements. ''The Renegade'' is perhaps equally well written but is emotionally unmoving, perhaps because its narrator is the only one of Camus's central characters who is totally unsympathetic. ''The Adulterous Woman'' is too obviously written around the tour de force ending; like ''The Growing Stone,'' the realistic scene setting of its first half is somewhat listless and unnecessarily long. ''The Artist at Work,'' on the other hand, is a moderately effective study in satirical realism up to the ending where, as in ''The Growing Stone,'' the sudden shift to highly contrived symbolism disrupts the previous development and tone. ''The Silent Men'' is successful as far as it attempts to go but is too short for us to become fully absorbed in its characters or situation. It and ''The Growing Stone'' might have served better as points of departure for longer fictional works; in fact, ''The Silent Men'' may provide us with a hint of the direction Camus would have taken in the work based on his youth in Algiers that he projected in the 1958 preface to *L'Envers et l'endroit*. But the subjects of these and several of the other stories are also precisely those he had had the least success dealing with in depth: realistically portrayed working-class an colonial situations, marital relationships, the feminine viewpoint. Perhaps his very choice of the short-story medium, which is a constricted one to begin with and which by the 1950s was becoming even more obsolescent than the novel, was a tacit admission of his inability to treat these subjects with the fullness they require. (pp. 209-10)

In spite of his lifelong passion for the theater, Camus never attained full mastery as a playwright. All four of his plays make better reading than stage pieces, although each has its moments of theatrical power. *Caligula* and to a lesser degree *The Just Assassins* were successful in their original productions and revivals in France, but neither received as much acclaim as his adaptations of Faulkner's *Requiem for a Nun* and Dostoevsky's *The Possessed*. . . .

Camus was preoccupied with the challenge of finding a contemporary dramatic form equivalent to Greek tragedy. . . . (p. 211)

[It can readily be seen] that Camus is writing, not in the Shakespearean tradition we are attuned to, but in that of Racine and Corneille, who have never been popular in England or America, and of Greek tragedy, which we tend to regard more as a subject for literary study than as viable stagecraft.

Even when his theater is considered on its own terms, though, it has serious limitations. There is too much talk, too little action, too little modulation in pace and mood; the unrelenting stage of siege on the audience's emotions is overly demanding, more so in the theater than in a private reading that can be broken up at will. The characters are too often stiff, their dialogue pompous and stilted. Dialogue is not one of the strong points of his fiction, and his restriction to it here, with only the truncated narration and description that can be put into the characters' mouths, precludes the features that most enliven his fictional language: lyricism, ambiguities in diction and viewpoint, multiple levels of significance. Another of his general weaknesses, the portrayal of lovers, is preeminent in *State of Siege* and *The Just Assassins*. (pp. 212-13)

Caligula has with justice been widely recognized as the one play that ranks among his best works. Theatrically, it provides an acting tour de force in the title role. . . . It is the only play that fully achieves Camus's distinctive resonance and complex of meanings. . . .

Caligula has the grandeur of a classical tragic hero. He is never simply a tyrant, never impelled by pragmatically self-advancing motives, mere lust for power or sadism. He is, rather, the disillusioned romantic hero of *The Rebel,* compelled to do evil out of nostalgia for an unrealizable good. (p. 213)

Caligula's assertion of egoistic freedom, then, is not self-serving so much as it is exemplary. His tragic flaw lies in not recognizing that "no one can save himself all alone and that one cannot be free at the expense of others." . . . (p. 214)

The main weakness in *Caligula* as a stage piece is its pacing. . . . Nihilism is a difficult subject to dramatize without monotony: when you have wiped out all human values in the play's first ten minutes, where do you go from there? Rather than having Caligula start to pass death sentences in the first act, Camus might have better modulated the tone and built up suspense by restricting Caligula's actions at first to disrupting social and legal rituals, thereby allowing for more satirical social criticism, and only later having him escalate his caprices to killing.

The Misunderstanding is the play that most closely approximates Greek tragedy in its concentrated, inexorable movement toward a fatal resolution that the audience already knows. . . . It is also his most Sartrean work in portraying the subjective existences of a set of individuals at cross-purposes with one another as an aspect of the absurd. . . . Camus's darkest work, its considerable theatrical power lies in the sheer, stark anguish of human beings undone by the caprices of fate. This dramatic strength, however, is also a drawback; the sustained agony is perhaps too much to expect a modern audience to sit through for three full acts—although it must be granted that the same criticism can be directed at *Oedipus Rex.* In any case, the brief plot is somewhat padded out, and the play would probably work better on stage reduced to one act. (pp. 214-15)

In his 1957 preface Camus emphasized that *State of Siege* was in no sense an adaptation of *The Plague;* still, it is clearly a companion piece, a variation on many of the same themes. (p. 217)

In this kind of experiment it is nearly impossible to predict ahead of time whether the play is going to work on stage or not. In this case it emphatically did not. The various styles fail to work individually and disastrously fight against each other collectively. . . . Nevertheless, the play has its appealing points, mainly in the love-duty conflict and the political satire, and if he had lived to revise it, as he likely would have, by pruning out some of the cumbersome elements like the choruses and symbolic machinery he might have salvaged it. . . .

[*The Just Assassins*] provides a striking contrast in its straightforwardly realistic structure and dialogue, controlled tone, and the sublety of its political thought. It is much the better play and one of Camus's most mature works, even though its theatrical effectiveness is limited by an excess of talk and deficiency of onstage action, the latter perhaps partly a conscious effort toward French neoclassical decorum. (p. 219)

After more than a decade, it is still difficult to talk about Camus's death without giving in to the temptation toward excessive poetic license. The unavoidable literary interpretation, that the fatal auto wreck seemed preordained as the ultimate dramatization of Camusian absurdity, tends to depersonalize the human body and mind that were crushed therein—as Camus would have been the first to point out. (p. 253)

Nevertheless, in spite of Camus's own early acknowledgment that a creative career usually ends not in definitive resolution but in "the death of the creator which closes his experience and the book of his genius," it remains an inconsolable outrage that a senseless accident should have cut short a life of such youthful vitality and an artistic and ideological creation of the utmost importance for our time while it was still in full evolution. (p. 254)

Donald Lazere, in his The Unique Creation of Albert Camus *(copyright © 1973 by Yale University), Yale University Press, 1973, 271 p.*

PHILIP MOONEY

For Albert Camus the struggle to achieve meaning in human life must always be an affirmation of the love that engendered it. This conviction is the key thematic in Camus' novel, *The Plague* and finds expression in the character Tarrou. Tarrou's is a quest for total meaning in life: "What interests me is learning how to become a saint." Tarrou is definite about the path he must follow to reach the peace assuring meaning to life. It is the "path of sympathy," the way of charity. "But you don't believe in God," his friend, Dr. Rieux charges. Tarrou's rejoinder is to the point: "Exactly! Can one be a saint without God?—that's the problem, in fact, the only problem, I'm up against today." . . .

Camus' ethic of fraternal charity bestowing meaning and securing sanctity in human living is, in reality, a theistic ethic—the Gospel law of charity. . . . Camus, in refusing the pseudo-God of an unkind Christianity is in reality opting for the true God of authentic Christianity and . . . his indorsement of fraternal charity as man's way to peace and meaning in life is radically, though unwittingly, a call for man to love the God who has identified himself with the least of his brethren. (p. 76)

From his earliest appearance in print, Camus was haunted with the notion that our world is a universe which has no place for us, in which our life makes no sense. . . . His early experience told Camus of man's isolation:

> In a universe suddenly divested of illusions and lights, man feels an alien, a stranger. His exile is without remedy since he is deprived of the memory of a lost home or the hope of a promised land. This divorce between man and his life, the actor and his setting, is properly the feeling of absurdity.
>
> (p. 77)

The absurdity of death, reducing man's activity to a matter of indifference, becomes the basis of man's "inner freedom" from all restraints. (p. 78)

[However, there is a certainty] that there are values in life, even in the face of the absurd. Consequently, there are corresponding limits to the exercise of human freedom. . . .

The limits to his freedom in man's rebellion against the absurd situation in life are set by the "value" revealed in the "movement of revolt."

> In the absurd experience, the tragedy is individual; with the movement of revolt it is conscious of being collective. It is the adventure of all. The first progress of a mind struck by this estrangement is to recognize that he shares this estranged condition with all men and that human reality in its totality suffers from this distance in the relation of oneself and the world.
>
> (p. 79)

This solidarity with all men is the *value*—so important for Camus—that is revealed by the movement of revolt and that forms the basis of his ethic of fraternal charity. . . .

> We have, then, the right to say that any revolt that claims the right to deny or destroy this solidarity loses simultaneously its right to be called revolt and in reality becomes an acquiescence in murder. In the same way, this solidarity, except in so far as religion is concerned, comes to life only on the level of revolt. And so the real drama of revolutionary thought is announced. In order to exist, man must rebel, but revolt must respect the limit it discovers in itself—a limit where minds meet and, in meeting, begin to exist.
>
> (pp. 79-80)

Paradoxically, Camus' ethic of revolt implies the ethic of fraternal charity that came to be dominant in his later drama and fiction. (p. 80)

But the deeds of charity must flow from a kind heart. When Camus acknowledges in *L'Envers et L'Endroit,* "I am linked to the world by all my acts, to men by all my pity and gratitude," he is emphasizing the interior, the affective side of charity. It is the kindness that refuses to pass the absolute judgment that excludes man from the company of his fellows; it is the merciful kindness that, upon seeing a stranger, takes him to heart.

Two of Camus' most impressive characters were "strangers"—Meursault in *The Stranger* and Tarrou in *The Plague,* the former the stranger-victim of man's unkind judgment, the latter the stranger-saint with the kind heart. . . . Neither jury nor prosecutor had the resources in kindness of heart to reach the person of Meursault as he was in himself. Camus draws "the absurd contrast between what we know Meursault to be and what the court decides he is." (pp. 82-3)

In contrast with Meursault, Tarrou had experienced family affection. . . . Having known kindness, Tarrou had the power to show kindness. Furthermore, seeing a man sentenced to execution had worked upon his heart in such a way that he could never acquiesce in any man's being sent to his death and led him to "take, in every predicament, the victim's side," as he followed his "path of sympathy" to the end. (p. 83)

For Camus charity shows itself effectively as completely generous and all-embracing only because it springs from a kind heart, a merciful heart that will not judge the brother nor treat any man as a stranger, a sincere heart from which all selfishness has been purged. Tarrou had realized that man's "inhumanity to man" had come from unpurged hearts, "that each of us has the plague within him." For Tarrou purgation released the power of sympathy; it involved *metanoia,* the change of heart from *"être solitaire"* to *"être solidaire,"* to invoke Camus's favorite catchwords. (p. 84)

What Camus has portrayed as the ultimate human quality throughout his writing is in essence the *agape* of the Gospels: "*Agape* will be able to minister openly and unreservedly to a neighbor, but only from an utterly selfless heart." . . .

Camus sharply diverges from the Christian position when he refuses to set the roots of neighborly love in any love for God. Camus' is the conviction that the charity wherein man finds his perfection as man is not consistent with belief in the Christian God. . . . (p. 87)

The scandal of indifference to a brother in need is overshadowed by an even greater scandal in Camus's eyes: "C'est toujours l'Eglise en tant que compromise par l'Inquisition et ses variantes, passées et présentes, qui constitue la pierre d'achoppement de Camus devant le christianisme." ["It is always the Church as compromised by the Inquisition and its variants, past and present, that constitutes the stumbling-block of Camus before Christianity."] Camus is turned away by Christianity's being, in any way, a party to a judicial process that commits the supreme unkindness of turning a man out of society in rendering absolute judgment against him. Camus sees the court that condemned Meursault, with its Christian prosecutor and its Christian jury, as a modern counterpart to the Inquisition in its harshness. In the name of Christianity, this court severs the last, weak tie to community that the unfortunate Meursault has with his fellow man. . . . (p. 88)

[The scandal of the] unkind Christianity that Camus rejects is equally disavowed by Christ and His late vicar. The Christianity, then, that Camus dismisses is a pseudo-Christianity; the God he refuses a pseudo-God. . . .

Camus has averred that "if a rebel blasphemes, it is in the hope of finding a new God." Camus' search for meaning, for some principle by which the happiness and misery of man can be explained is a quest for the good who is in reality the hidden God. (p. 89)

Philip Mooney, "The Theistic Basis for Camus' Ethic of Charity," in THOUGHT *(copyright © 1977 by Fordham University Press; reprinted by permission of the publisher), Vol. 52, No. 204, March, 1977, pp. 75-94.*

PHILIP THODY

It was not until 1961, almost nineteen years after its first publication, that any critic suggested in print that Camus's *L'Etranger* could be read as a 'racialist' novel. (p. 61)

Camus himself insisted that he saw *L'Etranger* first and foremost as a book about a man who is a martyr to truth. . . . Throughout the novel, the reader is invited to sympathise with Meursault and see his cult of physical sensation—his delight at the crisp dryness of a hand-towel at midday, his love of swimming and making love, his appreciation of the sights and sounds of Algiers—as infinitely superior to the conventional values which are always being offered to him. Meursault, we feel, is right not to exchange the sun-drenched beaches of Algiers for the cold courtyards of Paris, right to prefer straightforward sensuality to Marie's sentimentalised idea of 'love', right to place the reality of this life higher than the hypothetical consolations of eternity, right to persist in his vision of the truth as he sees it even if this does lead him to the guillotine. How, then, can a novel with so attractive and honest a hero be seriously interpreted as embodying so unpleasant and life-denying an ideology as racialism? How, moreover, can so conscientious and self-conscious an artist as Camus have written a book which so contradicts the values which he officially defended in his lifetime? For he was not only the first French writer seriously to concern himself with the Algeria problem, campaigning as early as the 1930s in favour of equal treatment for Arab and European alike. He was, in 1945, virtually the only French journalist to warn of what was going to happen in Algeria if France did nothing to change its basically colonial status.

Once the book is isolated from Camus's life, however, the racialist undertones of *L'Etranger* becomes so easy to detect that one wonders why critics should have taken so long to point them out. The action of the book takes place in Algeria, sometime in the 1930s, at a period when there were some nine Arabs to each European. But only the Europeans have names: Meursault, Pérez, Masson, Sintès, Salamano, Cardona. The Arabs, in contrast, are a nameless, undifferentiated mass. When Marie comes to visit Meursault in prison, both she and the old woman—a European—who sits next to her are described with that attention to physical detail which is so agreeable a feature of the novel. . . . Camus either ignores the indigenous population of Algeria completely or treats it merely as a convenient backcloth against which the really interesting dramas, those involving Europeans, can be acted out.

Moreover, it can be argued that the Camus of *L'Etranger* does more than merely ignore the Arabs. . . . He tells a story in which the interests and point of view of the non-European characters are so totally sacrificed to the concerns of the 'whites' that one begins to wonder just exactly what his own subconscious attitude towards the two races was. For what actually happens in *L'Etranger,* when seen from the standpoint of the Arabs, is a peculiarly unpleasant example of both racialist and sexual exploitation. (pp. 61-2)

Camus wrote [the novel] at a time when he was working on *Le Mythe de Sisyphe,* his essay on the absurd, and wished to illustrate the idea that 'a supernumerary employee in the post office is equal to a conqueror if they have the same degree of awareness'. . . . Meursault, at least in Camus's conception of him, is a man who has gone through the experience of the absurd before the novel begins. He has had the overwhelming sense of his own mortality and consequently become aware of the 'blood-stained mathematics which command our lives'. . . . He is therefore living out the rest of his life in that 'weariness mingled with surprise' . . . which characterises the 'absurd man', consciously refusing the consolations of religion or any other form of reconciliation with the world. He knows that he is going to die and this knowledge, as he tells the priest, has taken all meaning from such normally all-important experiences as the death of his mother or the love which other human beings have for him. Drying his hands on a crisp towel at midday is just as important as being promoted to a better job. Indeed, insofar as physical sensations are the only reality in an absurd and valueless world, such an activity is more important than the worship of the bitch goddess success which would be implied by accepting his boss's offer of a new job in Paris, and Meursault needs to make only one more discovery about life to become one of the heroes of the absurd celebrated in *Le Mythe de Sisyphe.* He needs to find out that 'no depth, no emotion, no passion and no sacrifice could give the same value in the eyes of the absurd man to a conscious life lasting for forty years and a full awareness extending over sixty'. . . . He does this when, lying in his prison cell thinking about the possibility of being reprieved, he feels his eyes tingle with delight at the thought of 'twenty years of life to come'. . . .

But in order to bring his hero to this point of awareness, Camus has to have him sentenced to death. . . . Such an ending also has the advantage of enabling Camus, early in his career, to give vent to the hatred of capital punishment which dominates *La Peste, L'Homme révolté* and the *Réflexions sur la guillotine,* as well as to express his mistrust of a legal system in which it is often more the skill of his lawyer than his own guilt or innocence which decides whether someone accused of murder is executed or acquitted. Neither were these the only considerations which led Camus to organise the plot of *L'Etranger* around a murder trial and a legal execution. He always thought of himself primarily as an artist, and clearly derived great satisfaction from constructing a narrative in which, as in *L'Etranger,* the completely innocent experience of events in the first half of the novel is interpreted as overwhelming evidence of guilt in the second.

All the different and overlapping intentions that Camus had in mind when writing *L'Etranger* thus involve a novel in which the central character is sentenced to death. All Camus therefore had to find was a convenient anecdote. The story of Sintès, Meursault and the Arabs eminently satisfied this condition. It nevertheless involved—and this is the central plank upon which a 'racialist' interpretation of *L'Etranger* is based—the total subordination of Arab to European concerns. (pp. 63-4)

[It is argued, however, that] a 'racialist' reading of *L'Etranger* completely distorts the novel and prevents us from seeing it as the masterpiece of irony, lyricism, humour and tragedy that it is. . . . It is consequently yet another example of the way in which contemporary considerations can completely distort our understanding of a work of art by preventing us from seeing it either objectively or in relationship to its time or the terms in which the author originally conceived it. It is, moreover, totally unsound because it makes the very elementary mistake of failing to distinguish between the author of a book and the fictional character whom he invents to tell the story. (pp. 65-6)

[It] is Meursault who is the racialist, not Camus himself. Indeed, by presenting events to the reader through the eyes of a 'Poor White', Camus is himself condemning both Meursault and the male-dominated, colonialist society which he represents. It is not Camus but Meursault who tells the story in which Arabs figure only as small part players and in which the murder of an Arab deserves only the most superficial of passing comments. Camus, in contrast to his fictional creation, is actually using both the events of *L'Etranger* and Meursault's own attitude towards them in order to underline how prejudiced and unbalanced he finds the colonial system which existed in Algeria in the 1930s.

This could well be a fruitful and defensible way of reading *L'Etranger* if it were not for one thing: The comments which Camus himself made about Meursault's character. For it is very clear, from the entries he made in his Notebooks when the novel was published, from an interview which he gave in 1946 and from the preface he wrote in 1955, that he did not have this kind of critical attitude towards the narrator in *L'Etranger*. The character of Meursault, he noted in 1942, was based partly upon two other people—one a man, one a woman—and partly upon himself. But he did not suggest that he rejected those aspects of his own personality which had gone to form his fictional hero. When the Catholic critic André Rousseaux attacked the novel for presenting a character 'without humanity, without human value, and even . . . without any kind of human truth', Camus drafted a long letter of reply—which he never in fact sent—but in which he summed up the meaning of the book as being either that 'society needs people who weep at their mother's funeral' or that 'you are never executed for the crime you think'. But although he mentioned 'ten other possible' ways of looking at the book, [Camus] gave no indication that he saw either Meursault or the attitude he represented as defective or inadequate. In 1946 he went even further when he told Gaëtan Picon that 'men in Algeria live like my hero, in an absolutely simple manner', and implied that their attitude towards life was, in many respects, preferable to that of the average Northern European. But he again abstained from any unfavourable comment on Meursault, and carried his enthusiasm for the main character of *L'Etranger* even further in 1955 when he described him as being 'inspired by a passion which is profound because unspoken, the passion for the absolute and for truth' and said he was 'the only Christ whom we deserve'.

It is in many ways unfortunate that Camus made these remarks about *L'Etranger*. Had he not yielded to the pressure which literary journalists and enterprising scholars so frequently put upon French writers to say what they 'really intended to do' in their books, *L'Etranger* would be far less vulnerable to the type of criticism put forward in the first part of this article. For it is only when we follow out the implications of Camus's remarks and begin to look at it as a novel about moral values that its flaws and inconsistencies appear. So long as it is seen as the study of a man who is genuinely 'an outsider' in the sense of someone who lives in his own private world and is simply not at all interested in what anybody else thinks about him, *L'Etranger* is . . . invulnerable to criticism on moral grounds. . . . Indeed, the remarks which [Camus] made about the novel after 1943 nowadays have the curious and wholly unintentional effect of making it seem a much less satisfying and intriguing book than it is when we read it in isolation from its author's proclaimed intentions. For they also have the effect of underlining, by contrast, what a poor fool Meursault is in his relationship with Raymond and how insensitive he is in his attitude to Marie. (pp. 66-8)

To revisit Camus's *L'Etranger* is thus, for me, first of all to realise how unwise creative artists are when they yield to the temptation of telling us what the meaning of their works 'really is'. . . . [The] impression which a book makes on its readers can change with the passage of time. In the 1940s, when writers, critics and readers were obsessed with the idea of the absurdity of the world, *L'Etranger* seemed an almost perfect illustration not only of this absurdity but of a valid reply which men could make to it through their personal attitudes and private experience. . . . It was only when the happy pagans celebrated in the pages of *Noces* became the shock troops of the Organisation de l'Armée Secrète, a violently racialist body devoted to keeping Algeria French at all costs, that critics inspired by an equal and opposite intolerance pointed out features of Camus's work which nobody had notice before. Henri Kréa, Pierre Nora and Conor Cruise O'Brien [who originally pointed out the racialism in *L'Etranger*] thus gave an excellent illustration of how right Baudelaire was when he said that literary criticism should be 'partial, passionate and political'. (p. 68)

Philip Thody, "Camus's 'L'Etranger' Revisited," in Critical Quarterly *(© Manchester University Press 1979), Vol. 21, No. 2, Summer, 1979, pp. 61-9.*

* * *

CANETTI, Elias 1905-

Canetti is a Jewish-Austrian novelist, dramatist, and essayist currently residing in England. Writing only in German, he is best known for his award-winning novel, *Auto-da-fé*. Deeply disturbed by the social climate of twentieth-century Europe, Canetti is obsessed with the effect of mob psychology on the alienated individual. His satirical works are concerned with the absurdity and chaos of modern life. (See also *CLC*, Vol. 3, and *Contemporary Authors*, Vols. 21-24, rev. ed.)

KATE O'BRIEN

[An] appalling noise of evil . . . roars through *Auto-Da-Fé*, and breaks the fabulous, symbolical intellect of [the protagonist] Pieter Kien.

The book is practically indescribable. It can only be read as a gigantic fable—of topical application, if you like, for never surely was it easier to find parallel in general, current life for the overthrow of reason in man by the forces of beastliness? Canetti wrote his books in Vienna about ten years ago, and it was published just before Vienna was overthrown by the *Anschluss*. It cannot be doubted that he was pressed to his particular theme by the universal doom being played out within hearing of us all; but he holds his frenzy down to one awful, legendary case. He simply shows us, in agonisingly slow detail, the destruction of the mad, pure mind of one man, a kind of genius, by one or two mindless, sub-brutal fellow-creatures. Did I say "simply"? The method is not simple. With desiccated, pedantic caution he reflects fantasy against fact, merges nightmare with routine, cupidity with fanatical innocence, and so establishes all his forces as one great hell that the exhausted reader cannot after a few pages tell light from dark, or hell from hope. All in a curiously dry writing, where no detail is spared, and while asking the most detached patience for phantasmagoria beyond comparable echo.

The author asks too much of us; we are too tired for this. Swift and Joyce had more mercy, and each also had the weakness, if you like, of spiritual reference which they could not evade. There is none of that here. There is no God, from any theology; there is no light. Only vileness enthroned, and reason nobly flying to its own obliteration. A mad, magnificent work which we are not able to endure, which perhaps we are right not to accept, but of which we dare not deny the genius or the justification.

Kate O'Brien, "Fiction: 'Auto-Da-Fé', in The Spectator *(© 1946 by* The Spectator; *reprinted by permission of* The Spectator*), Vol. 176, No. 6152, May 24, 1946, p. 540.*

IAN WATSON

[Canetti's] work consists—apart from a small number of plays—of two very large books: the novel *Auto da Fé* (first published . . . in 1935 as *Die Blendung*), and the treatise *Crowds and Power* (*Masse und Macht*, . . . 1960). They are "large" books not simply in length, but equally in scope and conception. The single novel is a most unusual novel and the single treatise a most unusual treatise. The dialogue in *Auto da Fé*, for instance, is hardly dialogue in the normal sense: rather, it alternates between vast diatribes reminiscent of the legalistic speeches in Kafka's *Castle*, and what can only be described as the cut-and-thrust of misunderstanding, anticipating Ionesco. *Crowds and Power*, while nominally a scientific study in social psychology, is shot through with all the imaginative panache and visionary mania of the novel, and might almost have been written by Dr. Peter Kien himself, midway as it were between his scholarly theses on Chinese Philosophy and his later demented Swiftian project for a Psychology of Trousers. The two books, the fictional and the non-fictional, impinge upon one another constantly; the madness of the one provides the method of the other.

If at first glance Canetti appears to be concentrating in *Auto da Fé* upon the isolation and alienation of the Individual, and in *Crowds and Power* upon the psychology of the Masses, this distinction is not an absolute one by any means. Kien finds himself constantly threatened by the Crowd; and the madness of the Individual is interpreted as a surrender on his part to the Mass-Mind present within everybody. . . . *Crowds and Power* concludes with a study of the individual paranoiac, returning full circle back to Kien. The One and the Many are not separate phenomena but rather polar opposites, which—like the Poles themselves—depend upon one another for their existence. A similar relationship exists between these two books. *Crowds and Power* is quite as remarkable a work of the imagination as *Auto da Fé*, and to distinguish between the two books by saying that one is non-fiction and the other fiction would be a mistake, since the idiom and methods of Canetti the social psychologist do not differ radically from those of Canetti the novelist. The same vision animates both books.

Bergson suggested that Comedy occurs when men cease to act with the elasticity which we expect of them as living human beings, and begin to behave like machines. . . . Yet machine-like though many of the actions of Canetti's characters are, it is in their dialogue that this inelasticity is particularly apparent. Canetti's method is here very close to Ionesco's (although there is not that element of sheer nonsense which we find in Ionesco, since Canetti is not concerned with the ultimate breakdown of language as such). . . . The dialogues which take place in *Auto da Fé* are far from conversations in the normal sense—where one remark inspires a second appropriate remark; nor are they even the kind of phatic babble which Ionesco gives us in *The Chairs* where, though the elderly couple can hardly be said to be communicating, since they flatly contradict one another's statements from time to time, at least the noise of talking provides companionship. The dialogue in *Auto da Fé* is more like a mutual Pavlovian slavering as bells are rung. And the bell to which each character responds is an entirely different and private one—a bell located inside the character's own skull, ringing the changes on his or her personal obsession. (pp. 185-88)

[Canetti's characters display] the obsessions and fantasies of everyday life, raised to a new pitch of intensity, where they possess the exaggerated savagery of a cartoon strip. . . . (p. 188)

The central theme of *Auto da Fé* is Obsession as a necessary consequence of Egotism: the concentration upon the One to the detriment of the Many. Clichés are the obsessions of commonplace individuals. It is ironic that we should meet Kien in the first chapter of *Auto da Fé* busying himself noting down *idées* and *sottiseries* in his pocketbook, like some latterday Flaubert compiling a new *Dictionnaire des Idées Reçues*, since one of his own characteristics is unquestioningly to accept the clichés of the world-at-large upon all topics outside of his own narrow specialist field. . . . The examples which Kien gives of ideas that ought to be unquestioningly accepted are admittedly acceptable enough: that the earth revolves round the sun, and the moon round the earth. Still the principle is a dangerous one, reflecting not only the compartmentalisation of Knowledge from which Mankind suffers today, but also a simple inability to apply one's intellectual equipment to Life: thus it never occurs to Kien that normal experiences are happening to him. . . . Intellect and life have failed to mesh, resulting in self-delusion. (pp. 188-89)

The terrifying thing about Canetti's novel is not that one intellectual superman is alienated from Life, Society, the People, but that Kien is by no means unique in his alienation from Reality. There is possibly only one "sane" character in the whole book and this is Kien's brother George, who is an alienist, perhaps therefore the only person whom we might paradoxically expect to be sane. The rest of the world, from intellectual right down to charwoman, is mad. No one can see what is going on objectively. Everyone distorts it to fit his own grotesque private mythology. . . . It is only by good luck that truth and justice survive. How can they survive at all, if this is the nature of society—a society of madmen? Arguably they simply survive because society's members, although obsessed and egotistical, are essentially cliché-ridden and as such not only tolerate but encourage each other *en masse*. Clichés are, as I said, commonplace obsessions. The dichotomy between intellect and experience, though perfectly apparent in the case of Kien, does not strike me as nearly so important as its *function* as an obsession. . . . Canetti himself regards the form of the delusion as being more important than the content. *Auto da Fé* is not a cautionary tale about the dangers of Dissociated Sensibility, but a ghastly parable about the egotistical obsessions present in every one of us—whether he is an intellectual or a caretaker does not matter. (pp. 190-91)

Crowds and Power rivals in ingenious interpretation and daring analogy anything that Kien could figure in his madness, being not so much a work of Science as a work of Vision, of Imagination. Skimming through *Crowds and Power* the first thing to notice is the *absolute* character of the book; there is next to nothing in the way of reference to other sociologists, psychologists or political scientists. Where have Freud, Fromm and Adler disappeared to?

Where are Mannheim, Malinowski and Frazier? . . . When Canetti quotes, it is not from other theorists, but simply from source materials as diverse as Josephus, Primitive Folklore, and Travellers' Tales. His theories are pure of other men's theories, or at least give the impression of being pure. He possesses the Truth and needs no "names" to brace it. His Truth is an *a priori* World System, a creation *ab ovo*. What "Truth" can be anything *less* than a World System? But in order that this system may effectively embrace the world, many ingenious analogies and interpretations will be necessary. Thus it happens that Canetti's system has close affinities with the paranoia which he so tellingly ascribes to Kien. This is how Canetti defines paranoia:

> The paranoiac exhibits a mania for finding causal relations, which finally becomes an end in itself. Nothing that happens to him is chance or coincidence; there is always a reason, which can be found if searched for. Everything unknown can be traced back to something known. . . .

Except for the fact that this search for hidden meanings does not quite become an end in itself but remains controlled by a formidable intellect, why shouldn't this definition of paranoia also serve very well as a definition of Canetti's scientific methods?

He is disconcertingly ingenious. Take his analysis of "National Crowd Symbols." The crowd symbol of the Germans is the army. Fair enough. But the army is more than simply an army: it is also a marching forest. The trees in a forest are tall, innumerable, densely packed, relatively uniform. . . . In Germany . . . forest and army interpenetrate one another in the mass mind. The dreariness of the army is mitigated by the life and vigour of the forest, while the German recruit takes for his law the straightness and rigidity of his well-beloved trees. This too is acceptable. But now Canetti displays his essential ingenuity—for the solitude of the wandering youth alone in the wild forest, which is such an emotive symbol in German Romanticism, is not the escapism that it appears to be on the surface: on the contrary it is an encounter with destiny, since the solitary wanderer among the trees is actually anticipating his entry into the army. And thus paradoxically self-love and social are the same. (pp. 194-95)

For Canetti, essence firmly precedes existence. Certainly Kien is a perverted Platonist: for him, Reality merely bears out the *printed* original—thus he is interested to confirm his knowledge (culled from Persian love poetry) that flowers smell sweet, by actually smelling some one day, although he considers the experiment of smelling them to be rather a gratuitous exercise. This mythical-symbolic method can even be extended to explain the facts of science, which we might have considered to be reasonably inviolable and objective. . . . Whatever the "scientific" weaknesses of . . . [such arguments] may be is largely irrelevant since [their] success is not as social science but instead as myth. . . . Myth retains its power even when the facts which once appeared to buttress it are overturned. Written as science, the works of Freud and Jung become myth due to the vision that inspired them; but Canetti's work, though written in the guise of Social Science, is myth at once.

Myth demands a novel and unremitting viewpoint. Hence Canetti's technique often consists of a scrupulous, almost childish realism, and the relentless documentation of familiar things from a peculiar and partial angle. . . . [A] slightly zany singleness of focus contributes much to the impact of Kien's obsessions, not to mention those of Therese, Fischerle, and all the other population of *Auto da Fé*.

Canetti's originality is inseparable from his idiosyncracy. The lack of documentation in *Crowds and Power*—for a scholarly work, that is—we can account for by the book's real function as Myth: but also by Canetti's independence of other authorities. Malthus and the Malthusians he rejects, for in his opinion the birth-rate has nothing to do with the true mechanisms of increase at work in the human race. . . . Freud with his personalist psychology he also rejects. He even dismisses, with characteristic panache, the very concept of self-preservation. . . . (pp. 196-98)

Everything is created afresh. Canetti develops his own terminology, which has not been heard before: the "increase pack," the "sting of command," the "crowd crystal," the "reversal crowd," the "discharge." Myth, like paranoia, mobilises the whole world round one idea or cluster of ideas. For this reason we might describe *Auto da Fé* as a totalitarian fantasy, even though the Vienna which it describes has not heard of Nazi politics and has only a leaven of anti-semitism (this despite the date when the book was published—1935—and the fact that Canetti is Jewish). The obsessions which dominate Canetti's characters are ruthless, thoroughgoing and universal. The savage world of George Grosz is their pictorial equivalent. The success of Canetti's mythmaking in *Auto da Fé* lies in this totalitarianism, in achieving which he overcomes one of the main hurdles of the fantasy-writer—diversification; which is when, given the initial fantasy situation together with an awareness of its all-embracing potential for a large-scale commentary on the world from a ruthlessly narrow angle, the fantastic persona has to venture out from his keep into the wide world. The writer will have to offend the sequel-loving *lecteur moyen sensual* who would like nothing better than a picaresque reduplication of the same adventures, and forge a new fantasy world as fascinating as his first. (pp. 198-99)

Finally, what is the position of Canetti's readers? We have followed the downfall of the obsessed Kien for five hundred and twenty-two pages with pity, terror and black humour. But we have picked up this long, densely-packed book, with its meagre amount of conversation, in the first place. . . . We are by no means innocent of his obsession.

But then, no *single* person is innocent in Canetti's world, whether he is a doorkeeper or a doctor of philosophy. "Man petrifies and darkens in the distances he has created," Canetti avows in *Crowds and Power*. . . . It is only in crowds that we are innocent; but it is a savage kind of innocence. (p. 200)

Ian Watson, "Elias Canetti: The One and the Many," in Chicago Review *(reprinted by permission of* Chicago Review; *copyright © 1969 by* Chicago Review*), Vol. 20. No. 4, & Vol. 21, No. 1, May, 1969, pp. 184-200.*

DAGMAR BARNOUW

[Canetti's] precise and intense involvement with three languages, most intimately with German, corresponds to the *locus* of his writing: between the conventional literary genres as well as between different fields in the social sciences. . . . The thoroughness with which the novel [*Die Blendung (Auto-da-fé)*] and the two early dramas, *Die Hochzeit* (*The Wedding*, 1932) and *Komödie der Eitelkeit* (*Comedy of Vanity*, 1934) record a confusing variety of "acoustic masks,"—a character's speech habits that outline his individual functions and interactions in a group as definitely as would a visual mask—is indeed exhausting and requires intense concentration from the reader/listener/spectator. Canetti has always demonstrated his respect for his audience by demanding that kind of concentration and justifying it with the precision of his language.

Canetti, who considers himself to be essentially a dramatist in all his writings, developed the concept of the "acoustic mask" under the influence of Karl Kraus, the Viennese social and literary critic, writer of aphorisms, philosopher of language, poet and journalist. . . . Above all [Kraus] wanted to make his readers doubt the "official" interpretation of their social reality, the conventions of language. He asked them to read and listen precisely, to take language "at its word"; doing exactly this, his judgments implicit in the "acoustic quotations," as Canetti calls them, . . . were irresistibly right: the world in which we live is seething with stupidity and cruelty and so is its medium, the corrupted language of daily life. (pp. 1-2)

He learned from Kraus, Canetti says, the feeling of an absolute social responsibility, bordering on obsession, and he learnt to listen; from now on the voices of reality would pursue him, would never set him free again. . . . The novel *Die Blendung* brings them to full expression, a virtuoso performance, frightening in its perfection that subjects also the reader to relentless persecution by the monotonous, powerfully inarticulate acoustic masks of the housekeeper Therese and the janitor Pfaff. The novel and the two early dramas are satirical, emphasizing the need to expose human folly, greed, cruelty by recording speech-habits; they are most persuasive witnesses to Kraus's method of "Wörtlichkeit" [literature]—they also show Canetti's growing reservations about his teacher. He sees Kraus's grandiose limitation precisely in his lucid, aggressive concentration on the sentence: the exposed subhuman imperfection of the quote, the inhuman perfection of the comment. Canetti explains the ultimately dangerous exclusiveness of Kraus's method in putting language on trial, by describing how his sentences are forming a "Chinese Wall" . . . a perfectly closed structure, that has, by its very perfection, sapped the empire it had been meant to defend. (p. 4)

Recognition of the essential insufficiency of any judgment had far-reaching structural and verbal consequences for Canetti's writing. Kafka's influence—he is, together with Kraus, the most important writer for Canetti—asserts itself, his gentle precision sustaining the full horror of social cruelty but making it more gradually accessible through the deeper willingness to interact verbally with the "other," the hateful, the one that is "outside" the world created by and familiar to the self. (pp. 4-5)

[The] experience of total destruction drives [Canetti] to understand why man is capable of doing to man what he did: "My uncanny power was in chaos," Canetti notes in 1945; "I was certain of it as of the whole world. Today even chaos has exploded. No structure was senseless enough but that it could have disintegrated into something even more senseless, and wherever I sniff, all is heavy with the smell of extinguished fires."

Chaos had been safe in its brilliantly perfected presentation in *Die Blendung* and the early dramas. *Masse und Macht*, the drama *Die Befristeten (The Deadlined)* which grew out of this study, are set against chaos. Accordingly, Canetti's poetic language has simplified and purified its imagery, concentrating on the complexities of relations between images, abandoning the earlier works' powerful mimic fascinations, their ultimately isolating mock surrender to the real. He wanted his writing to be perfectly accessible; the growing simplicity of his language is one of richness and ever greater precision. The differences between various voices have become more subtle, the nuances of the play with idioms and intonations much more delicate. From recording the reality of twentieth-century Vienna he went on to record the reality of many very different places in very different periods of history through their myths. Yet the preserved individual voices from so many different civilizations are closer together than those that share Vienna as their origin. They have in common distinct perceptions of crowds, visions, speculations about them and their relationship to power, perceptions of the annihilation of all existence in death, of the attempts of powerful rulers to become as absolute as death, always to be the survivor, to be the only survivor. (p. 6)

The presence of many . . . voices restrained by their mythical modes, finally enable Canetti to find meaning in speaking about contemporary totalitarian execution of power. (p. 7)

[In the wake of destruction and extermination, Canetti] entered the life-long process of "understanding what had happened, what was happening." In the preface to the first collection of his notes, *Aufzeichnungen 1942-48*, he writes that in order not to be able to turn away from "the naked world" for even one moment . . . he had to collect as much information as he possibly could about the ways in which men had lived together and had understood their attempts at coexistence. The very wide and flexible concept of history included a great variety of such attempts. The *Aufzeichnungen*, in addition, recorded projections of social possibilities that history had suppressed. They are sketches of Utopian societies in which many of the problems that are taken for granted in our society are taken literally, above all the social problem of death. . . . It is always the problem of human time against numerical time, against the acceptance of the fact that the individual is defined by the number of years he has lived already and still has to live; it is, in so many different forms, the problem of the deadlined.

Crowds form in various ways—described with concrete precision in *Masse und Macht*—for killing, for fear of being killed, under orders of killing and getting killed. . . . [Living in a room in Vienna, suspended between the crowds on an adjacent soccer field and an insane asylum, Canetti had] formed a "disquieting" image of the monstrous extremes of its various forms of existence. The mystery of the crowd that he heard and the closed world of the mad became interwoven and were to be the basis for his understanding of the paranoic ruler who wants to incorporate crowds—more than just symbolically so—, to make them his own completely so that he can survive them. (pp. 8-9)

Canetti does not judge crowds directly like Ortega y Gasset who argues from a particularly limited "elitist" position, or indirectly like the stoical Freud who finds them frighteningly alien and therefore keeps them at bay. He demonstrates their destructive potential, their deadly interaction with systems of power whose operators know, as Hitler for instance showed very clearly, that the member of a mass-society which is, of course, a hierarchically structured group of a great number of individuals, is willing to forget the sting of death . . . if he can rid himself, through temporary immersion in the crowd, of the sting of isolation.

The more intensely Canetti experienced death during the war, the more his hatred grew; he began to doubt the "natural law" of death. . . . [Through] his very pain and hatred of death, [Canetti] came to realize that the concept of life without death, or at least of life not accepting itself as being defined by death, would be the most natural, self-evident human reaction, and made it his own. . . . Canetti holds that death is the oldest fact, "older and more incisive than any language"; the human sciences, on the other hand, have abstracted the concrete social problem of death into a natural law because of the difficulties it poses. The drama *Die Befristeten* demonstrates in detail what tolerance of this kind does to the relations between men, by simply converting the private taboo of death that we are forced to live with to the public taboo of the "deadlined," who know how long they have lived but must not share that knowledge. In their society each person has been given his exact limited lifetime by some Higher Being: that is, the controlling power system; he has, in fact, been given death. Taken so literally, acceptance of death emphasizes the fallacy of autonomy, the isolation of man through the tenacious illusion that his life, as it is given to him, can ever be his, as long as there is death, and the moral effect this illusion has on him and on his social relations. (pp. 9-10)

The deadlined know [when they shall die]; and they are, for this very reason, more evil, more distorted than the most grotesque characters from the early dramas or *Die Blendung*. Their surface normalcy, their calm dulled voices are functionally deceptive. The author's intention is that we recognize them as close to us and therefore decide that we shall be different.

The drama's prologue defines its Utopian location: "nowhere" in our time, but possibly swept up against us with the flux of time to come. *Einer* and *der Andere* talk about the prehistoric time when people bore names that were not indicative of the "Moment"—"Augenblick," that is, the moment of their death; when, in fact, people were left in uncertainty about their deaths and therefore unable to decide about the arrangements of their lives in autonomy. The autonomy that the speakers claim to possess is distinctly though subtly questioned by their author: their conversation is nothing but a rehearsal of programmed ideas and clearly shows the limited rational capabilities of the speakers. Talking about the monstrous insecurity "those people" had had to live with, they agree that they lived like animals. They are unable to make the connection between their own "freedom" from thinking about possibilities of disaster—because they know precisely when to expect it—and the animals' apparent unconcern: that indeed they are much more like animals in this crucial respect than their pitied predecessors. . . . The prologue warns that something very sinister has happened to man between the time of the audience and the time of the speakers; and the climax of the rehearsed introduction: "I see the publication of the *Moment* as the greatest progress in the history of mankind," is the final thrust of that warning. Acquainted with Canetti's studies of crowds and power, and his *Aufzeichnungen,* one will immediately detect the direction of the attack in the prologue: the most important human faculty, spontaneity, is petrified in this programmed arrangement of life that is one's arrangement with death. (pp. 10-11)

[Canetti introduces] a person who actually allows himself to doubt. His name is *Fifty,* and, being about that age, his "Moment" is very close. His doubting the certainty of his death undermines, as we are shown, the very basis of the society he lives in and thus serves both as the main impetus for the dramatic action and as its structural control. Each unit, one or two short scenes of presentation—men, women and children talking about the problems connected with "der Augenblick"—is followed by a unit of comment: *Fifty* trying to guide whomever he talks to towards doubt. (p. 12)

Fifty is [inexperienced in the ways of the world] because he does not know the phenomenal aspects of the taboo that rules the society he lives in: the opening of the capsule by the *Kapselan* at death, the birth- and death-ceremonies. Thus he does not know the forces that rule this society, and he might as well have come to visit from another planet. It is true, this is not very consistent with the slowly emerging power-system of this Utopian society; but Canetti, in order to make the problem clear, needed an observer of horror who was himself guilty of its existence. *Fifty's* tolerance of . . . [the taboo] in which his [naïveté and piousness] meet is what Canetti thinks most destructive in men, because it causes them to accept the certainty of death without being certain of it, as they have never consistently tried to prove the opposite. The people living in the society of *Die Befristeten* have only been pushed one step further to the point where doubting that certainty is punished with mechanical immediacy by external forces; but they are by no means essentially different from *Fifty,* before he starts doubting, or us. Our relationships are as much deformed by the tolerance of the certainty of death as theirs; it is only a question of surfacing. We, too, unresisting, accept ageing as a devaluation of the individual, expecting as "natural" a waning of the joy and will to live and of the faculty for spontaneity. Their labelling that "value" by names is only a bolder metaphor for the same thing, pressed out of a more perfected control system.

Canetti does not oppose the fact of death; he opposes the acceptance of death as a fact, and asks to be joined in this opposition. . . . [Canetti's voice is] puzzled; it questions, analyzes, uses . . . extensive looser metaphors. But the rage is unrepressable even by the sadness of the subjunctive mode. . . . The last two scenes in the first part of the drama present the conclusion we have been led toward: a demonstration how all human certainty, especially that of death, has to be premature and is therefore vulnerable to manipulation. *Fifty,* now in the presence of the *Kapselan* and the assembled *Volk,* a large group of the *Unequal (die Ungleichen),* is informed that his "Augenblick" has come. However, this information is, as *Fifty* points out quite calmly, a verdict based on a fraud. All of *Fifty*'s encounters in the first part of the drama served to confirm his—and the audience's—suspicion of the institution of "der Augenblick." Now, as his own "Moment" is at stake, he denies its validity, claiming he is not yet fifty years old. (pp. 13-14)

The *Kapselan,* disturbed about the unexpected resistance, reveals the fraud even more clearly by giving *Fifty* another reason for why he has to die: he has disturbed a funeral . . . and for this crime he is condemned to die publicly. . . . If, however, the "Moment," allegedly the most private affair, can become public simply by decree, then it has never been the person's. Death, then, as *Fifty* suspected, is always inflicted, an execution, based on wilful decisions removed from human logic. (pp. 14-15)

It is demonstrated here how the extreme autonomy of the individual, based on the "exact" knowledge of the "amount" of time allotted to him, is a responsibility that isolates him irreparably and thereby creates the premise for his perfected availability. . . .

In this vacuum freedom, autonomy is an entirely negative concept. . . . There is no freedom to arrange one's life in the allotted time, because human time, even if it "contains" work to the exclusion of human relationships . . . , cannot be measured in numerical terms. If it is, human time must become a taboo, something to be afraid of. (p. 15)

In many of his *Aufzeichnungen,* Canetti objects to religion in any form as the illegitimate attempt to ease the sting of death: "The boldest element in life is that it hates death, and despicable and desperate are the religions that blur out this hatred." He points to profound psychological inconsistencies that must have been very carefully nourished by external forces: "The behavior of martyrs does not seem contemptible to anyone even though they did everything with regard to an *eternal life*. How contemptible these same martyrs would seem to the adherents of Christianity, had they been concerned about eternal life *here,* instead of somewhere beyond." Against the imposed closed belief of established religions depriving man of the possibility to develop his own belief out of his own experience, Canetti insists: "There is no foretelling what men will be capable of believing as soon as they have driven death out of the world." (pp. 16-17)

Fifty with perfectly human logic appeals to *Volk,* the hierarchically structured gathering of believers, to take his case as a negative proof for their belief: "My passion is to mistrust the *Moment*. My passion, by accident, differs from yours. But it may be useful to you. It will be an opportunity to test if one has to die at one's *Moment, even if he does not believe in it*. I do not believe in it!" . . . (p. 18)

[However, seeing a way out, *Fifty*] promises repentance and recants. The *Kapselan*'s repeated promise, in turn, is to let *Fifty* die peacefully whenever his "Moment" has come. This way the "super-natural" "Moment" has been exposed as a fraud twice; it is really an execution that can be carried out sooner than promised, but also later than threatened, whenever expedient. It should, in any case, now be clear to all the subjects of death that they have sold out to a fraud, forfeiting their right to doubt death. . . . [A] litany-like exchange between the "Chorus of the Unequal" ("Chor der Ungleichen") and the *Kapselan* presents the dogma of the hagiocracy of death under which the dead-lined live, and its paralyzing influence on the human mind. . . . (pp. 18-19)

[Here, it is dramatically] shown that "knowing" time means limiting it to its numerical dimension: waiting for the "Moment" is nothing but a mechanically reliable motion toward it. The human dimension of time that is dependent on coexistence with others is obliterated. Significantly the Chorus does not think it necessary to explain why man does not enjoy being together with man. No sadness about separation, no resistance against isolation is permitted. Life has indeed been robbed completely of its most important sustenance: the recognition of death as *the* enemy. This large group of believers cannot become a crowd anymore, unless for a short moment, closing in on a new believer. The stimulus of the fear of death could make a true crowd form and increase that would grant immeasurable moments of togetherness to the isolated "Unequal" and might even be strong enough to reverse the direction, against death. To have been robbed of the sting of death means to have been robbed of the strength of equality at least in the face of death. (pp. 19-20)

[Many] of Canetti's *Aufzeichnungen* express the melancholy surprise that he appears to be so alone in his argument that it is of the utmost importance for the quality of human relationships to understand the necessity to doubt the certainty of death. His expression of surprise is not a comment on the insensitivity of everybody else beside him, but rather a question put to himself about what it is that makes him wonder. It is his hatred of power which always aims at selective survival, his fierce compassion with the weakest, the most impotent, the dead. . . . Not the fight against the "natural law" of death, then, is the impossible task, but how to preserve one's humanity in the position of the survivor, in the position of power. . . . *Fifty,* very much an extension of Canetti himself who wrote the drama approaching his fiftieth year, proceeds from this position. Not having treated his years as capital, as numerical time—"I have enjoyed living too much to think of years" he says—he suddenly realizes the preciousness of his time by filling it with the other person's desire for life, joy in life that he himself has so deeply experienced. (pp. 20-1)

Including the others in the preciousness of his own time, *Fifty* gains the freedom to act against its destruction. Applying force, he takes possession of some capsules and, opening them and his own, sees that they and indeed all capsules are empty. . . . Accordingly, the *Kapselan*'s punishment for *Fifty* is to leave him to his own anxiety now that he is certain of the uncertainty of his death. *Fifty,* however, rejoices in this uncertainty. Fear is a quality of the living; it may mean openness to potentiality and change. . . . The equation between contentment, the absence of fear, and death is evident.

The drama demonstrates not only that anything is better than death, even anxiety; but rather, that the acceptance of anxiety, its effect on daily life, is necessary to combat death. (p. 22)

For *Friend,* liberation has come too late; his new uncertainty reactivates his grief and exposes the possessive quality of his love for his sister. The drama ends with *Fifty* trying—in vain—to convince *Friend* to set his sister free, not to force her back to the past of the child, of *his* little sister, to grant her her own life, should she be still alive, to grant her her own potential. *Friend* has the last word, asserting his intention not to give up the search for his sister: this is the last line of the drama, the last and most convincing example it offers of how the certainty of death destroys the delicate balance of human relationships, gives one man power over the other, finally gives one man power over many men.

We are not offered hope—other than that *Fifty* has survived his experiment—but a very precise and detailed documentation of how the acceptance of death destroys all life that is worth living. It is a terrifying documentation, because it is, contrary to the documentation of the great wars Canetti and his readers have been living with since the beginning of this century, so perfectly accessible to the imagination. War, of course, is most crucially sustained by that hated attitude toward death that destroys relations between individuals as well as between peoples. War, mass execution, should be the most powerful reminder that all death is execution—always inflicted, never one's own—and therefore we ought to be able to stop it or at least restrain it. "Is everybody too good to die?" Canetti asks; and he answers: "One could not tell. First everybody would have to live longer." More time, both numerical and human, is needed to enable men to make their own lives—that is, to make them worth living. "The notion that life is a gift seems monstrous to me." It is one's own from the beginning, especially one's own potential. Precisely this insight means not accepting the death penalty for another human being or oneself, but to question the judgement behind it and the evidence behind the judgement which is the quality of human relationships: "Whoever knew what it is that brings men together would be able to save them from death. The mystery of life is a social mystery. Nobody is on its track." Thus Canetti writes, as if despairing of his fight against death and the validity of his case against the Deadlined. His whole work, however, is sustained by an eminently persuasive determination to move toward the solution of that riddle. (p. 23)

Dagmar Barnouw, "Doubting Death: On Elias Canetti's Drama 'The Deadlined'," in MOSAIC: A Journal for the Comparative Study of Literature and Ideas *(copyright © 1974 by the University of Manitoba Press; acknowledgment of previous publication is herewith made), Vol. VII, No. 2 (Winter, 1974), pp. 1-23.*

SIDNEY ROSENFELD

[Elias Canetti] is a profoundly and fruitfully introspective writer. . . . This quality is witnessed by the hundreds of aphoristic and diary-like "jottings" from the years 1942 to 1972 that constitute *The Human Province*. . . . At the same time, he is a writer whose sensibilities are keenly attuned to the most critical problems of the modern epoch. *Crowds and Power,* with all its indebtedness to cultural anthropology and the literature of myth, was intended at bottom to be a sociopsychological investigation of fascism in its deepest origins and broadest ramifications. *The Voices of Marrakesh* offers yet another view of this versatile writer. It is a travel book, but such as only Canetti could write. It reveals his intense inquisitiveness in productive alliance with an equally individual respect for the uniqueness of individual fate. Through poetically heightened observation he illuminates and yet preserves the secrets of his exotic encounters in Morocco. . . .

Canetti translates into English well. Possibly because he is so markedly *original,* he cannot be falsified . . . . [This originality] emerges forcefully in these three works, which are vastly distinct from each other and yet finely linked as artistic testimonies of a rare spirit to the life of our times.

Sidney Rosenfeld, "World Literature in Review: 'The Voices of Marrakesh: A Record of a Visit', 'The Human Province', 'Crowds and Power'," in World Literature Today *(copyright 1979 by the University of Oklahoma Press), Vol. 53, No. 2, Spring, 1979, p. 290.*

* * *

CHAR, René 1907-

Considered by many to be France's greatest living poet, Char celebrates life while acknowledging its pain and chaos. Involvement with World War II shaped his major themes, and his early association with the surrealists fed his imagination and colored his imagery. Char's poetry has been labeled "hermetic," for it often suggests the poet as prophet and poetry as a kind of religion. His work has been illustrated by such notable contemporaries as Braque and Picasso, and set to music by Pierre Boulez. (See also *CLC,* Vols. 9, 11, and *Contemporary Authors,* Vols. 13-16, rev. ed.)

ROBERT W. GREENE

With few exceptions, René Char's poems start out at a high pitch of intensity, which they rarely relax and in fact usually increase. Char, moreover, maintains his extremely tense, vigorous style at least as consistently in his prose poetry as he does in his verse poems. That this should be so is quite remarkable given the inherently discursive, muting tendency of prose as compared with the more paratactic possibilities of verse, hence its greater potential for dramatic, polarized juxtaposition. Because of the tension that obtains between the eruptive texture of his poems and the smooth prose vehicle that he often elects to use, Char seems both more impressive and more authentically himself as a prose poet than as a poet in verse. In either form, however, his unfailing capacity to energize to the utmost degree the individual words and phrases of what are in the end thoroughly organized structures suggests that a convulsive paradox throbs at the heart of his poetry, that in Char the forces of total anarchy, if not utter destruction, are constantly at war with those of complete control, absolute order.

The striking incongruity between texture and structure in Char, while it is doubtless responsible for the almost palpable vitality that his texts possess, also reflects the poet's abiding commitment to the principle of contradiction. Char rejects one of the fundamental premises of Western thought, Aristotle's principle of identity (a thing cannot at the same time be itself and something else), in favour of the belief in the identity of opposites espoused by Heraclitus, whom Char admires enormously. Nevertheless, despite the convergence of views between the two men in this basic area and despite Char's growing predilection over the years for a Sibylline, Heraclitus-like aphorism, the unique qualities of his poetry, especially his prose poetry, would scarcely emerge from a comparison of that poetry with the pre-Socratic's fragments. On the other hand, because of their philosophical affinity, linking the two men's names does constitute a useful point of departure.

Char's adherence to Heraclitean contradiction is felt throughout his *oeuvre,* from titles of collections through poetic technique to the deepest level of vision. The title of one of his recent plaquettes, for example, joins two semantically opposed but phonically similar nouns, *L'Effroi la joie* . . . , a coupling that sums up Char's whole quickened, apparently ambivalent and yet ultimately affirmative response to life. 'Commune présence', a poem of major importance for Char and a relatively early text (1936), comprises a number of paired contraries that shed light on both his technique and his vision. Its last eight lines are particularly significant in this regard:

Tu as été créé pour des moments peu communs
Modifie-toi disparais sans regret
Au gré de la rigueur suave
Quartier suivant quartier la liquidation du monde se poúrsuit

Sans interruption
Sans égarement

Essaime la poussière
Nul ne décèlera votre union.

In tone and substance the first two lines contradict each other. After a gentle exhortation in which the poet informs someone, doubtless himself, that he must be ready to rise to exceptional occasions, he then says, in effect, 'Adjust and fade away without a murmur'. Line three completes the sense of line two and resolves or at least recognizes the conflict between that line and the first. The key phrase here, virtually a contradiction in terms, is 'rigueur suave', ['harsh softness'] whose first word captures the essence of line one, while 'suave' picks up line two. Like the title *L'Effroi la joie,* the phrase 'rigueur suave' exemplifies one of Char's basic techniques, that of juxtaposing semantically incompatible words for a specific effect. The phrase also conveys, in its context, Char's attitude towards life, which seems to be an unsynthesized combination of total resistance and total acceptance. The surface tension he creates by lining up mutually exclusive terms is thus mirrored at the poem's depth, where Char's fundamental, paradoxical stance is adumbrated.

The next three lines also contain a contradiction, if in a slightly less obvious way than the first three lines. The fourth and fifth lines quickly present the entropic view of the world's destiny that haunts so many twentieth-century writers (Beckett being perhaps the most overtly obsessed by it). But Char's variation on this deeply pessimistic theme comes with line six, which both parallels line five and diverges from it drastically. The final decline of all and everything into formlessness is already in progress and it is relentless, but that does not or at least should not create *égarement,* inner disorder. The inevitability of cosmic chaos need not undo spiritual order. The lines 'Sans interruption / Sans égarement' [without interruption / without mistake] thus embody a contradiction that is not unlike those contained in the phrases 'rigueur suave' and 'fright joy'.

The last two lines of 'Commune présence' are set off from the rest, and rightly so because they contain a climactic command—'Essaime la poussière' ['Swarm the dust']—and its reward if heeded—'Nul ne décelera votre union' ['No one will decelerate your union']. With the first of these lines we have yet another contradiction in terms; a swarm of bees and a cloud of dust are only visually analogous (just as *l'effroi* and *la joie* are only phonically similar). In essence they are contraries, the one suggesting fragments vitalized, unified, about to move up and away, and the other connoting destructive explosion followed by drift into ever greater dispersion and eventual nothingness. The injunction and its promise assert that the final, centreless settling of the particles is not to be denied but seized and turned into a swarm, and that if this is accomplished a state of at-oneness with the world will be attained. Once again by establishing a verbal polarity the poet reveals his moral vision. In terse, elliptical and imperious language he enjoins his listener (himself and now his reader too?) to accept the fact of entropy but to resist the inner paralysis that can accompany such lucidity.

'Les premiers instants', a prose poem belonging to a group entitled, significantly *La Fontaine narrative* (1947), typifies Char's poetry in ways that take us beyond Heraclitus and 'l'exaltante alliance des contraires'. But even before we read the poem, we see in the group title an internal contradiction. For a fountain, even as it arcs into being, also and at every instant disappears, its myriad droplets resembling so many scattering specks of dust. But the adjective 'narrative' gives this fountain's perpetual disintegration a form that saves it, that of duration and continuity. The bead-droplets are as strung out on a rosary and told, narrated. Here, as in the case of the rising swarm, a violent burst or explosion is held together, a split second of perception prolonged. What at first seemed the inappropriate union of discordant terms ('fontaine' and 'narrative') now appears as a truly exalting alliance of contraries.

The text of 'Les premiers instants' offers similar harmonious discords. (pp. 802-04)

In a sense the entire text is devoted to defining its first word, 'Nous'. Paradoxically, it accomplishes this task not through delimitation or exclusion, the usual methods of definition, but by a gesture of opening up, of inclusion. The self (already expanded somewhat by the choice of 'Nous' over 'Je') is rapidly and thoroughly effaced as a subject that stands apart from and gazes upon a scene as object. Rather, it is invaded and given identity by a series of ineffable perceptions, which it nonetheless formulates and in so doing endows with existence. Subject and object thus create each other through a fruitful dialectic. (p. 804)

As it moves from its first word to its last, Char's poem dramatizes phenomenology's notion of intentionality. Perceiver and perceived fit into an overarching scheme that both exceeds them and permits the experience of *dévoilement,* the unveiling of being, to occur. For the 'subject' in this case ('Nous') exists only to the extent that it is annihilated as a private, closed entity and reborn in each and every one of its 'objects', where it finds its only real delineation. Furthermore, for Char poetry and truth are synonymous, while an individual poem is 'lumière, apport de l'être à la vie' ['light bringing being to life']. What 'Les premiers instants' shows us is that poetry can be the means by which we lose our separate selves and accede to the fullness of being, to truth. . . .

[In the poem 'Front de la rose'] time, in a way peculiar to Char alone perhaps, is suspended, the present instant isolated. What is specifically lopped off is the past, and we are totally at one with our immediate perception of the rose. But present time in Char, if it obliterates past time, always implies future time, or, more precisely, a leaning or a straining toward the unexpected not yet ordered gift of the unknown, toward 'l'inespéré' ['the unexpected']. Also, Char's present is not stillness but movement, not concentration of the self in frozen recollection, but headlong dispersion of the self throughout the endless pathways of experience, be they rosy or thorny, wild or tamed. (p. 805)

In Char's poetic universe the true opposite of light, especially sunlight, is rain. But here too the polarity is slippery. In 'Front de la rose', for example, the walking figure at the beginning of paragraph two, a positive presence in Char, goes far toward neutralizing the menacing associations of 'sur la terre des pluies' ['on the ground of the rains']. The title of a recent collection by Char offers an even more striking case of harmonious discord involving rain: *Dans la pluie giboyeuse*. . . . A cloud bursts and then rain falls, thereby losing its once great height and unity. Rainfall as centreless settling toward formlessness diametrically opposes the image of the rising swarm that is central to Char's poetry. But by modifying his noun with 'giboyeuse' ['full of game'] the poet counterbalances the negative weight of 'pluie'. To be in the game-rich rain is perhaps not such an unhappy fate after all.

One prose poem in *Dans la pluie giboyeuse* ['Bienvenue'] has an exceptionally high density of subtly interwoven and revelatory contradictions. The poem's title alone, 'Bienvenue', strongly hints that a heightened, future-oriented moment has been reached, the importance of which eclipses all past time or at least relegates it to a purely waiting or prefatory status. As in the case of 'Les premiers instants' and 'Front de la rose', the present instant, cut off from what has been and turned toward what is to come, will in all likelihood focus on itself. (pp. 806-07)

The poem's basic conflict involves order and disorder, with Char clearly favouring the latter. Under the rubric disorder we find lack of symmetry, youth, future orientation, rising flight, joy, a fervent ode, forgetfulness, and the sun; while under order we see hatred, gigantic rot, hard fixity, reductive shaping, descent into the abyss of hell, and, by implication, the past. Though totally schematic, this two-way breakdown does not fundamentally misrepresent 'Bienvenue', which seems to dramatize Char's own admission that 'l'obsession de la moisson et l'indifférence à l'Histoire sont les deux estrémités de mon arc' ['the obsession of the harvest and the indifference to history are the two extremities of my bow']. The poet would rather harvest the peak of the here and now than mould what has gone by into History.

'Bienvenue' ends as it begins, with a hortatory command. But now it is wished that concrete and abstract, material and moral, merge, that written immortality (the fervent ode?) be both the stone in which it is inscribed and the lesson it conveys. Yet leading into and undermining whatever optimism the wish may generate is the implicit avowal of a total context of falsehood, a global war of lies: 'Mentons en espoir à ceux qui nous mentent' ['We lie hoping to those who lie to us']. On examining these words closely, however, we note that the symmetry between liar and liar is not perfect. The phrase 'en espoir' ['hoping'] destroys the statement's balance and dilutes its pessimism by introducing, literally, the element of hope, hope that a lie will become a truth, that contradictions will cease to exist as such, that order and disorder will become one and the same.

The vitalizing imbalance that the phrase 'en espoir' injects into an otherwise perfectly balanced statement actualizes the poem's second sentence: 'L'asymétrie est jouvence' ['asymmetry is youth']. This brief remark, moreover, provides us with a major key to Char's poetry. His contradictions, never balanced, always gravitating toward identity, have a dynamism, an electric élan, as if they did indeed spring from 'la fontaine de jouvence' ['the fountain of youth']. Char's present, for example, stands between past and future, but it pulsates precisely because it lists in the direction of the future, because of an imbalance without which there would be only stasis, paralysis.

The first sentence in 'Bienvenue' also resonates far beyond its immediate context: 'Ah! que tu retournes à ton désordre, et le monde au sien' ['Ah, that you return to your disorder, and the world to its own']. Char, we now see, begins this poem the way he ends 'Commune présence', accepting entropy as the inevitable fate of all and everything. At the same time, however, and again as he does in the closing lines of 'Commune présence', the poet transforms that dreadful knowledge into something positive. (pp. 807-08)

In 'Commune présence', and in one way or another throughout all of Char, poetry and life are not distinct but coextensive, the former being simply the tragic, contradictory sense of the latter. If in this poem Char expresses both disgust with the idea of submission . . . and commitment to it . . . , he does so because the two responses co-exist in him. Such contradictions abound in his work, giving it a steady pulse beat and an immense tensile strength, just as they abound in life, causing it to breathe and making it impregnable to any sure penetration, impossible of any definitive sorting out. His poetry creates not symbols which distance us from life but contradictions which draw us ever closer to life's mysterious core, to that leap, that contact and that spark which, paradox of paradoxes, form the vital centre of cosmic disintegration:

> Dans le chaos d'une avalanche, deux pierres s'épousant au bond purent s'aimer nues dans l'espace. L'eau de neige qui les engloutit s'étonna de leur mousse ardente.

(p. 808)

Robert W. Greene, "René Char, Poet of Contradiction," in The Modern Language Review *(© Modern Humanities Research Association 1971), Vol. 66, No. 4, October, 1971, pp. 802-09.*

MECHTHILD CRANSTON

Though it never took the form of a whole-hearted commitment, René Char's participation in the surrealist movement is, nevertheless, a fact of literary history, a fact which, furthermore, played a decisive role in the development of the poet and the man. (p. 2)

During his brief surrealist apprenticeship, Char gained, I believe, two important insights: (1) the realization that the existing socio-political order was in need of re-examination and with it the consecrated canons of art, and (2) the certainty that violence and destruction would not solve the problems faced by his generation. . . . The investigation of the outer world had to lead [the] poet back to a re-examination of his inner universe. There René Char sought the answer to the apparent contradictions of a world shared by partisan and poet, violence and magic. (pp. 2-3)

The key-notes of Char's poetry of 1930-1934 are given by words such as *attentat, barbare, brutal, cadavre, carvan, cataclysme, catastrophe, coup, couteau, crasse, crénau, crever, crime, cruel, égorger, fer, gratter, matraque, meutre, offensant, pourriture, rage, résistance, révolution, rude, saigner, sang, sauvage, scandale, sévère, suicide, tomber, trancher, tuer, viol, violence, violent*. . . .

A poem from *L'Action de la Justice est éteinte* [a volume

dedicated to Breton], "Les soleils chanteurs", mentions the kinds of violence—natural catastrophies, accidents, suicide, sickness, crime—which, to the mind of the young surrealist poet, must be called upon to revitalize poetry. . . . (p. 3)

Another text from the same collection, titled simply "Poème" . . . adds to the previous list "le crime passionnel, le viol, l'attentat à la pudeur, sources authentiques de la poésie" ["the passionate crime, rape, outrage on decency, authentic sources of poetry"]. . . . It is believed, at this time, that poetry may best be accomplished in a "climat de chasse" ["climate of the hunt"] that will favor the "Meurtres productifs" ["productive murders"] of the poet. . . . Crime is not only honorable, but desirable, if it can lead to new conceptions of art. . . .

This new poetry requires a new language. Gone is the melancholy tone of "Ce Soir" (Char's first published poem, written at school), gone the hesitant efforts of the young Char to establish a dialogue with the world around him. Words now are like hammers that can kill. . . . (p. 4)

In the best surrealist tradition (and following Lautréamont, whom he read at this time), Char speaks of revolt against the order of nature, against the established order of society, and against the ethic and aesthetic codes imposed by man upon both. Hence references to sickness, suicide, fratricide, matricide, regicide, and to the generally unaccepted forms of love. . . .

Char finds his most suitable metaphors for the alliance of violence and magic in the world of the mineral. (p. 5)

References to chemicals, metal and machinery are . . . "in the air" during the early years of surrealism, used by the surrealists and *modernistas* in their praise or condemnation of our 20th-century environment. In the poetry of René Char, they represent a farewell to romantic verse and its endless hymns to nature. . . . (pp. 5-6)

In Char's post-surrealist poetry, references to metals and chemicals are rare. There are the notable exceptions of the "coq de fer" in *La Parole en archipel* . . . , and the "abeille de fer" of "Apparition d'Aerea", first published in 1962. Both of these are symbols of war. However, evocations—or rather, provocations—of violence of any type diminish in Char's poetry after 1938. At least, violence and aggression are no longer seen in the same light. It is no longer the poem or the poet that is "offensant d'agression", but the world around them. (p. 6)

The songs and fables of *Placard pour un chemin des écoliers* are among the most haunting poetry Char ever wrote, and one would have to go back all the way to the Spanish *romances* of the 15th and 16th centuries to find a poem that would equal the mysterious beauty of such poems as, for example, "Compagnie de l'écolière". . . .

Where once the natural world was condemned to death through calcification, [in the poems of 1934-1936] we now see even the mineral world come to life. . . .

The poet achieves an extraordinary swiftness in these poems which show all matter in perpetual motion. The roads run along more quickly than the children on their way to school; autumn loses its breath. . . .

Preference is now given to vegetable matter. The stars have a "tige émoussée" ["blunt stem"]; even metal grows like a flower. . . . The human body itself is made to partake of the vegetable world. All heaviness is taken from it. . . . (p. 7)

In these poems of 1934-1938, the poet—"apprenti de la combustion" ["apprentice of combustion"]—is concerned with the breaking up of dead matter, with the revitalization of poetry no longer through outward violence and arbitary aggression upon nature (practiced by the sorcerer's apprentice of *Le Marteau sans maître*), but by means of critical reexamination of his own inner universe, his own past. . . . Man cannot relate to nature by destroying it. Rather, he must adjust his vision so as to bring the apparent chaos of the universe into proper focus. . . . Stars become flowers painted on a child's bedroom wall. The machine, like a dog, lies down at the feet of man. Nature is no longer the enemy, above and beyond man. It has come down to his level and accepted man as its master. . . . Though once a hostile element, [Nature] now partakes of the healing power of sage and comes to the aid of poet and partisan. In *Feuillets d'Hypnos* all of nature participates in the quest for harmony. . . .

Everything heavy and destructive now becomes light and life-bearing. In *Poèmes militants,* even the grass was made of lead and stone. Now lead is melted, it flows like oil and is ultimately transformed into the alchemist's gold. . . . (p. 8)

As the body takes on the properties of vegetable matter, so the mineral assumes human form. Char now sees in the rock the protective form of an eyelid . . . ; the forge becomes "la forge des reins". . . . Everything is taken down one step (judged by Char's original scale of values), so that the mineral world completely disappears or else is subjugated to the animal will. (p. 9)

Then came World War II. Violence and aggression, once the intellectual prerogatives of an artistic élite, now became the ugly reality of everyday and every common life. (p. 13)

Though Char continues to write, he publishes nothing during the difficult years of the Resistance (1940-1943). When *Fureur et Mystère* comes out in 1948, it contains no hymns to victory. There is not in all of Char's poetry or prose of this time any of the joy and exuberance of Apollinaire's *Calligrammes.* To this day, what Char admires most in "Guy au galop" is precisely this seemingly carefree poetry written by Apollinaire during his service at the front, where his sense of wonder was not troubled by the fear of annihilation. Char is of a very different nature, and he is fighting a different kind of war. The notations in his war-journal, *Feuillets d' Hypnos,* "écrites dans la tension, la colère, la peur" (Preface), consist of cold tactical calculations, philosophic meditations, short lyrical intermezzi and angry outcries against the senseless violence of war. (pp. 13-14)

In the midst of death and destruction, caught up by the machinery of war, Char forgets the lessons of surrealism and the songs of Maldoror. He denounces the murderous world of the machine. . . . The poet now rebels against his intellectual heritage, against the easy and comfortable superiority of the pessimist whom he had once imitated. . . .

Violence and aggression are no longer gratuitous, sickness and death no longer the subject matter of sophisticated poetry. Face to face with the reality of war, Char seeks to return to childhood innocence and peace, to the world of health to which his first post-war aphorisms, gathered under the title of *A la Santé du Serpent* (1945-1947) are dedicated. The collection opens with the cry: "Je chante la chaleur à visage de nouveau-né, la chaleur désespérée". . . . (p. 14)

Humility is not only a new word, but a new attitude in Char's poetry. The aggressiveness, the revolt, the violence of *Le Marteau sans maître* do not recur in his post-war verse. Though Char will never again recreate the carefree atmosphere of the "Cylindre à vapeur" and never again write with that lightness of touch, some of the texts he publishes in *Les Matinaux* (1950) recapture—if in a more subdued key—themes of the *Placard pour un chemin des écoliers*. (pp. 14-15)

By means of the "glorieux mensonge" ["glorious lie"] poetry, René Char has come to terms with the inner and outer chaos of his world, with the contradictory existences of partisan and poet. Magic has taken from violence the sting of destruction and death. The *phosphore meurtrier* gives way to the *ignis fatuus*. The eyes of the dying man are sealed by amber, "ayant l'expansion des choses infinies" ["having the unreservedness of infinite things"]. As he dies, man is magically transformed. All earthly heaviness is taken from him. He is made light as a ray of sunshine, he is lifted from the earth and rejoins the . . . *mythe millénaire* [myth of the millennium]. (p. 16)

The poet has lifted the laws of man and burst the narrow confines of a man-made reality, for which he has substituted the "glorieux mensonge". Not through violence . . . , but through the magic of poetry he has changed the established order of things, solved the apparent contradictions of nature. He has recaptured the original harmony of the Heraclitean universe, has recreated "Les premiers instants" where shark and seagull could live together as *loyaux adversaires*, where earth and sky were united and man still believed in the promise of the rainbow. . . . (pp. 17-18)

The destructive forces of nature have been put to creative use. They have torn man away from his house of low doors, lifted him beyond the *modicité quotidienne*, forced him into the open, where he will join the *bête ineffable* whose victory shall have no end. . . .

In his new humility, René Char has found the poem for which Lautréamont—and the surrealists—looked in vain. (p. 18)

Mechthild Cranston, "Violence and Magic: Aspects of René Char's Surrealist Apprenticeship" (copyright © by Forum for Modern Language Studies *and Mechthild Cranston), in* Forum for Modern Language Studies, *Vol. X, No. 1, January, 1974, pp. 1-18.*

VIRGINIA A. La CHARITÉ

Any examination of the whole body of Char's work reveals a variety of written modes: regular verse poems (sonnet, ballade), free verse texts, prose poems, aphorisms, diary notations, prefaces, essays, introductions to art catalogues, radio scenarios, theater, and ballet. One aspect which these multiple forms of written expression have in common is Char's interest in the plastic arts, for some mention of an artist is found in all of his writings. In fact, in his aphorisms and poems Char acclaims Georges de La Tour as one of his major sources. Moreover, besides the many contemporary artists mentioned in his work, Char has written numerous verse and prose poems on Georges Braque as well as a lengthy essay, *Flux de l'aimant* (1965), on Joan Miró. . . .

Because of his writings on artists and, more important, because of his constant references to La Tour and homages to Braque, Char seems to fall into that general category of modern poets who collaborate with painters because of the affinities between the poem and the painting. (p. 14)

However, René Char is more than vitally interested in painting and its adjuncts. He is himself a practicing painter who has illustrated some of his own poems. . . . But these "minuscules" with sketches by the author are not readily available, and, until the publication of *La Nuit talismanique* in 1972, Char as a practicing artist was relatively unknown. And, simultaneously, *La Nuit talismanique* brings to a head a fundamental critical question: is there a difference between Char the poet and Char the painter? An analysis of the mechanics of meaning in his latest venture into plastic creative activity indicates a previously undetected non-verbal poetics; with *La Nuit talismanique,* the Char of day and expression in word forms gives way to Char as a poet of night and silence, for Char the painter not only complements the poet but also brings to his multiple poetic forms a new dimension beyond the poem.

The format of *La Nuit talismanique* is curious. In one sense there are three parts: an introduction and two main divisions: *Faute de sommeil, l'écorce* . . . and *La Nuit talismanique qui brillait dans son cercle* . . . which is subdivided into two parts. Moreover, thirty-seven drawings (a count which includes the picture on the cover) accompany these texts. (pp. 14-15)

The section, *Faute de sommeil, l'écorce* . . . can be viewed in several ways. The simplest one is to say that the section consists of 25 drawings and 4 previously published poems: "L'Inoffensif," "L'Issue," "Nous tombons," and "Éros suspendu" (*La Parole en archipel*). Moreover, four other poems are also reproduced in their entirety but superimposed on drawings; there are a total of twenty-three aphorisms, of which four are reproduced in longhand (just as all eight poems), twelve are in italics, and seven are superimposed on drawings. Hence, there seem to be three forms in this section: poem, aphorism, and drawing, as well as an obvious interrelationship between the written word and the illustration. The most striking text in this respect is perhaps "L'Oiseau spirituel," originally published in *Hommage à Georges Braque*. . . . The black and light-grey sketch depicts a chain of mountains at the bottom; to the right, and going up the entire side, is an impressionistic rocky crag, cliff, or bush; fully three-fourths of the drawing is cloudy sky on which is superimposed in black ink in Char's hand the text—the text becomes the bird and completes the sketch. It is neither the poem nor the picture but the conjunction of the two, wherein the poem receives its actual significance and takes on meaning before it is read. Like a painting, the poem first is grasped as a whole and the details follow this initial experience. The picture is a poem, and the poem a picture.

The same is true of the other three poems superimposed on drawings: "Obéissez à vos porcs qui existent . . ." . . . , "Aubépine," and "Je ne suis pas seul . . .". . . . But the omission of the titles of two of these short poems, "Contrevenir" and "La Grille," gives them the appearance and quality of the aphorism. Instead of maintenance of the usual

Char distinction between two formal modes, namely the poem as application of the general truth of theory which is expressed by the aphorism, we find that all previous differentiation between poem and aphorism disappears. Conversely, the same applies to the seven aphorisms which are superimposed on drawings: they emerge as poems. (pp. 15-16)

With the effacement of the stylistic distinction between poem and aphorism, attention to the drawings in *Faute de sommeil, l'écorce* . . . reveals that not one of the sketches is free from the written word; all of the remaining drawings which do not have writing superimposed on them are accompanied either by an aphoristic statement or a title. The drawing attracts attention first, then the words of the title or accompanying statement come into view. The first sketch in *Faute de sommeil, l'écorce* . . . is a red and black criss-crossing of lines; it portrays a dense thicket from which there is no relief except for a rosy globule on the left side. The accompanying statement is: "Sortir de l'Histoire se peut. En dynamitant ses souterrains. En ne lui laissant qu'un sentier pour aller." The explanation of the drawing suddenly seems evident: the dark confusion created by plurality and contradiction can be cleared up through a refusal of historical linearity and a revolt against the condition of determinism through art. . . . The drawing is not a thicket, but a pond, and the dominant red and black coloration fades before the rosiness (hope and trace) of the poem—but this poem is not a poem in that it is not limited to verbal composition. On the contrary, it is the visual experience of the drawing in interaction with the written word which creates the poem. And, what is more, it is formless—beyond both the written word and its plastic representation. (pp. 16-17)

The section entitled *La Nuit talismanique qui brillait dans son cercle* offers several striking contrasts to *Faute de sommeil, l'écorce*. . . . In the first place, the number of drawings greatly diminishes; there are a total of nine, seven in the first subsection and only two in the second. Moreover, only three of the nine are in color, as compared to 19 in color in *Faute de sommeil, l'écorce*. . . . Although each subsection begins and ends with an illustration, an arrangement which emphasizes somewhat the position of the drawings and underscores their importance, one is struck by the dominance of the printed word.

The first subsection contains one introductory prose text, "Dévalant la rocaille aux plantes écarlates," and six additional texts, whose form is closer to the aphorism than to the prose poem composed in separate paragraphs. There is inner cohesion from one paragraph or entry to the next, just as there is in *Moulin premier, Partage formel,* and *Rougeur des Matinaux*. But unlike previous aphoristic groupings, the six texts of *La Nuit I* can be read without any point of reference, for even the titles are autonomous entities. To enter these texts is comparable to entering an art gallery; it does not matter which way one begins the tour, in which room or along which side of the wall; any direction will eventually yield the artistic experience. (p. 17)

The only statement which accompanies a drawing in either subsection is found in *La Nuit I,* and it succintly summarizes the esthetic operation of these texts: "Entre l'exprimé et le décrit, j'offre la fleur de sauge." . . . The illustration, "La Sauge des villages," is a wax bas-relief of a salvia plant; each of the component parts of the flower is isolated as though it had been taken apart and laid out on a board or table in order to show its actual plurivalent nature. It is not a salvia plant in its usual state and is neither expressed nor described as such. It is evoked, and in its evocation it provokes the viewer into expression and description. The viewer even supplies the color, scarlet, for the bas-relief is reproduced in black and white. In this case, the illustration betrays the usual nature of painting; it does not give the whole first and then the details; rather, it presents the various parts and the whole comes afterwards, just as the printed text functions. (p. 18)

La Nuit II consists quite simply of 13 poems in free verse and prose and only two drawings. Here we seem to return in both texts and illustrations to the original distinctions between written and plastic art that precede the publication of *La Nuit talismanique*. It seems that Char has elected the printed word over plastic form; in a sense he has, in another sense there never was any "choice" to be made; but in his plastic venture, primarily in *Faute de sommeil, l'écorce* . . . , he retains the plastic experience that projects the printed form beyond the confines of the page. . . . Char abolishes all formal distinctions of expression by showing that cause and effect are synonyms—the effect of a painting or text on its viewer is the cause. As the talismanic night prepares for the morning experience of sunlight, the effect of dark is the cause of light and the cause of dark has the effect of light. In the same way, the final illustration in *La Nuit II* . . . is a talisman [a pebble] which concretely demonstrates the convergence of plastic and written expression. (pp. 18-19)

The mute stone in the first and last illustrations of *La Nuit talismanique* initiates the poetic dialogue which begins and ends in silence. It may indeed be seen as a talisman whose effect is its cause, whose magical powers enable man to become a poet and intervene in his world.

The pebble as illustration or text acts "comme un filtre qui s'interpose entre nous et la conscience rigide que nous avons du réel, pour que, la magie aboutie, nous soyons la Source aux yeux ouverts." The return to the source of origin, silent matter, is a return to night. In the conversation between a painter (Braque) and a poet (Char), the role of night alone binds together the plastic and written approaches. . . . Night is the cradle of light, and without night light has no meaning. Light is dependent upon contrast with shadows, but night, unlike light, is autonomous: "La nuit ne succède qu'à elle." . . . In contrast to day or light, night is endless, for it is neither limited by horizon, "toute lumière, comme toute limite," . . . nor subject to time: "La lumière a un âge. La nuit n'en a pas." . . . Hence, while light may take the form of a poem, night is beyond form and is poetry. (pp. 19-20)

The unspoken (and unwritten) words are the ones which the poet hears: "des mots essentiels, des mots qui portent immédiatement secours." Silence, "la signification qui ne s'évalue pas," initiates dialogue, just as night goes towards action: "La couleur noire renferme l'*impossible* vivant. Son champ mental est le siège de tous les attendus, de tous les paroxysmes. Son prestige escorte les poètes et prépare les hommes d'action."

The unspoken dialogue of painting becomes a poetic structure which maintains the beneficence of night. As in the case of two earlier volumes, a personal crisis reverses the prestige of night and the poet turns to plastic expression. . . . Not unlike the primitive man of the Lascaux grotto wall drawings, Char uses unsophisticated materials for plastic expression; he picks up what is more or less on hand, not an easel and palette, but ink, sealing wax, birch bark, feathers, knives, nails, blotters, and his drawings in appearance and texture reflect a primal quality. The dominant color is black—"couleur noire qui renferme *l'impossible* vivant"—black lends depth and solidarity to the illustrations, and the black script of texts in longhand, either superimposed on illustrations or set apart from them, commands the eye from page to page.

Hence, Char is not the poet of white space, but of black traces across the void. . . . By the end of *Faute de sommeil, l'écorce* . . . , the restorative powers of night have been reconquered through the silent medium of plastic art.

Thus, in the second half of the volume, *La Nuit I* and *II*, the number of illustrations dramatically decreases, as the poet sets aside his "précaires outils" and returns to the text. This return to the medium of the written word remains within the dual referentials of silence and beneficent night. Although the title of this section is *La Nuit talismanique qui brillait dans son cercle,* which reverses *Faute de sommeil, l'écorce* . . . , the title of the volume and of the first illustration (the cover) is *La Nuit talismanique,* a title which significantly contains no modifying clause which refers to light. Light is known only through night. (pp. 20-2)

Char's election of silence and night is a recurrent pattern of esthetic practice with regard to his poetry as well as to the plastic arts. As he inverts form, dialogue, and light, he returns to "le coeur de l'éternel"; it is not a matter of looking upward, of aspiring to the stars, but of looking downward, to earth, in order to negate space and time. . . .

Char does not pretend to raise man to the celestial through some mythological celebration; on the contrary, he seeks our self-sufficiency. The last printed text in *La Nuit talismanique* is entitled "Sommeil aux Lupercales." This Roman fertility rite in honor of the rural deity, Lupercus, was a rather licentious celebration, but the key word in the title of the poem, *sommeil,* indicates that man has no need to honor the gods, for he has the same powers over himself and his world as they are assumed to have. The final strength of the talismanic night is its conquest of determinism in all forms; creative power, the "divine" ability to intervene in the world, is the human privilege of art. (p. 22)

In one sense, *La Nuit talismanique* may be considered linear; there is a definite progression from *je* to *nous,* insomnia to sleep, isolation to fraternity, reprinted texts to original texts, night to day, artificial to natural light, predominance of illustration to predominance of printed text. However, such a point of view denies the inherent circularity of the volume. The geometrical figure of the circle is the primary shape in the illustrations as well as in the texts. It is to the round pebble of the cover that the reader-viewer returns at the end, and only by this return to the beginning do the illustration on the cover and the volume as a whole gain their full significance. Secondly, Char begins this work encircled by night which has lost its restorative power and is countered only by the small circular light of the "électricité haïssable," . . . he moves to the circle of flame cast by a candle to the full circle of the sun at noon, "feu de midi," . . . which is possible because night reasserts itself as a talisman whose primary attribute is to bring happiness. (pp. 22-3)

Yet, implicit in the circularity of *La Nuit talismanique* is its quality of solidity. Char is often described in terms of aerianness, fugacity, and ephemeralness, but these characteristics of his work are structurally contingent upon his usage of terms of hardness, weight, and density, such as rock, mountain, earth, almond, coral, tree. These objects of opaque solidity are actually the base of his poetry, while the ephemeral ones are the summit, just as the efficaciousness of day and light is inextricably dependent upon the beneficence of night. In *La Nuit talismanique,* circle, opacity, and hardness come together and are visually objectified by the round, hard, dense stone. It might perhaps be argued that the Char image which fuses this *base et sommet* is dust: "Fils, cette nuit nos travaux de poussière / Seront visibles dans le ciel." (p. 23)

The flash (*éclair*) which lights up the poet's traces endures through his magical talisman, the poem. These are the traces which "font rêver" in the same way as Hierle's portrait of Char's father transmits "dans le présent de son regard un rêve qui ne lui appartient pas mais dont nous sommes ensemble l'Écoutant." . . . It is not a Proustian "lanterne magique" which lights up the fundamental unity of our reality, but a "buvard magique," . . . which obscures in order that the viewer may listen to the unity he sees. Hence, "Le Serpent" . . . becomes on the blotter a bird in flight. The portrait on the small hard stone on the cover of *La Nuit talismanique* immediately expresses the durable and solid fusion of man and nature, yet it is undeniably a work of art, a poem. But a poem which must go beyond its own form, just as the mysterious pebble of "Signe sur caillou" leads from earth to sky. To bring the poem and the painting into opposition is to pose the unity of poetry. (pp. 23-4)

Virginia A. La Charité, "Beyond the Poem: René Char's 'La Nuit Talismanique'," in Symposium *(copyright © 1976 by Syracuse University Press), Vol. XXX, No. 1, Spring, 1976, pp. 14-26.*

MICHAEL EDWARDS

René Char's poetry arises from pain, and exists because of it. His creativity confronts it, opposing to the pain of *Chants de la Balandrane,* which is often the thought of death, things that, if they cannot remove it, can harden it, and transform it into an energy. He takes a purchase on places around where he lives in southern France, like the farm of the title, situated on a wooded plateau "where the ruins of numerous abandoned wells still stand" He celebrates hard things in nature, especially the enduring earth, like certain naked winter fields that, in a typically dense cluster of metaphors, are seen as "daughters of the hoarfrost" and "stars" that "finish the crumbs of their nocturnal food on the table of the sun".

He also confronts pain with analogy, with the metaphors of the imagination that relate him to the processes of nature. In particular, the potent ambiguities of fire and cold are made to act in his life as they act in the seasons, in the life of the planet and even beyond. Analogy is a placing of his own "destiny", a word he uses, and also a triumph of poetry.

For the project of Char's poetry is to be just that: a triumph. The poems are concentrations of force produced from painful emotions toughening into vision and into phrases. . . . Char concentrates the mind by his compression of thought and feeling and at the same time concentrates the body by pressing into sentences strong sounds and compacted rhythms. He makes French an unexpectedly adamant language, in the ear and in the mouth.

In taking on life, as it were, in each poem, Char is aided by a tradition of rhetoric, in both the strict and looser senses of the word, and by a tradition of how to conceive the task of the poet. It is difficult to imagine an Englishman writing like this. Yeats was probably the last English poet to feel at home in both traditions, and his extremism has made them suspect. . . .

It is because Char's poetry bursts up from a vital centre, and homes on to fundamental images of fire, cold, water, night, that it can afford, against all odds, not to develop. . . . The urgency of the writing and its continuing discovery of brilliant and moving new metaphors from its own hoard allay any disappointment that, at seventy, Char is not surprising us by advancing into an unforeseeable "last period".

Michael Edwards, "Confrontations with Pain," in The Times Literary Supplement *(© Times Newspapers Ltd. (London) 1978; reproduced from* The Times Literary Supplement *by permission), No. 3975, June 9, 1978, p. 643.**

* * *

COOK, Robin 1940-

Cook is an American novelist. A practicing physician, he has based much of his suspenseful fiction on personal experience.

CHARLES J. KEFFER

[*Coma*] is an absolutely fascinating story! . . .

Robin Cook is a doctor and an excellent writer of suspense fiction. I was on the edge of my seat through most of it. All of the technical terms and procedures are here and they add to the reader's involvement in the story even though he or she may not know the difference between halothane and succinylcholine. Having a woman as the protagonist allows the author to provide an interesting perspective on women and careers. Finally, I do not think anyone can beat the suspense and the story line developed throughout this novel. It is so close to the truth that one has to reinvestigate the title page to be sure that it really did say "A novel by Robin Cook."

Charles J. Keffer, "Fiction: 'Coma'," in Best Sellers *(copyright © 1977 Helen Dwight Reid Educational Foundation), Vol. 37, No. 3, June, 1977, p. 67.*

DAVID BRUDNOY

[Dr. Robin Cook in *Coma*] writes convincingly, compellingly, of a black market in human organs. Having concluded that he could turn out a best-seller by "dissecting" dozens of suspense and mystery novels, Cook has quite methodically packed his own novel with other authors' tricks, and sometimes the formulaic quality detracts from the book's quickening excitement. But by and large this is a horror story of the first order . . . , and it strikes to the core of many people's queasiness about the current debate as to when death occurs. . . . In his final "Author's Note," Dr. Cook makes plain his own antagonism to what he calls the legal-medical "mumbo-jumbo whose origins lie in the dark ages of English law" and his preference for the "noble use" of healthy organs. But *Coma,* a corker of a novel, will do little to advance that cause; it will rather—in addition to giving anyone who picks it up a splendid read—make a lot of jittery folks more than a little more apprehensive about the medical profession in general, and surgical procedures in particular.

David Brudnoy, "Books in Brief: 'Coma'," in National Review *(© National Review, Inc., 1977; 150 East 35th St., New York, NY 10016), Vol. XXIX, No. 30, August 5, 1977, p. 899.*

TOM PAULIN

Inevitably, perhaps, there are no emotions in *Coma,* a brash, oddly fascinating and unintentionally hilarious fantasy about black market tissue-transplants. Its author is a scuba-diving medical instructor at Harvard who admits in an admonitory epilogue to having recently acquired 'a heightened regard for female physicians and female medical students'. And so, out of a formula of medical jargon and behaviourist psychology, he has created a female character of the purest plastic. . . . As a story, *Coma* has a fairly high rating on the hedonic calculus, often inducing that sudden tightening of the throat muscles which is a sure indication that the patient is about to laugh.

Tom Paulin, "Head-Knowledge," in New Statesman *(© 1977 The Statesman & Nation Publishing Co. Ltd.), Vol. 94, No. 2422, August 19, 1977, p. 251.**

JACK SULLIVAN

"Sphinx," a wordy thriller about black-market intrigue in Egypt, is as inert as its many mummies. For a few chapters, the reader wonders whether they are inert at all. The references to the "Curse of the Pharaohs," the ominous flashbacks to ancient Egypt, and the mysterious deaths of tomb-violators all suggest that an avenging mummy will soon emerge. Mr. Cook, however, exploits the mummy-tale formula for other purposes. Coinciding neatly with the King Tut craze, his interest is in the material glitter of Egyptian artifacts. These he describes in intricate detail, as if to deflect attention from the tedious plot. . . .

Even Mr. Cook's sense of place and history, the novel's one strength, is compromised by triteness: "It must have been a fascinating era, full of turmoil, upheaval, and emotion." Making adventure-story clichés work requires at least a modicum of self-awareness and humor. . . . But when Mr. Cook writes of "Stygian darkness" or tells us "The silence was deafening, the blackness impenetrable," he does so with a straight face, with a sense of discovery—with "renewed enthusiasm" every time.

Jack Sullivan, "Thrillers and Killers: 'Sphinx'," in The New York Times Book Review *(© 1979 by The New York Times Company; reprinted by permission), May 13, 1979, p. 23.*

GEORGE COHEN

[Cook] can't miss with [*Sphinx*]. There is adventure, sex, torture, murder, and a feminist heroine, Harvard Egyptologist Erica Baron, who discovers a pharaoh's tomb full of priceless treasures. There's also a diverse assortment of characters, some of whom seek to kill her. King Tut, move over.

George Cohen, "Fiction: 'Sphinx'," in Booklist *(reprinted by permission of the American Library Association; copyright 1979 by the American Library Association), Vol. 75, No. 18, May 15, 1979, p. 1419.*

* * *

ĆOSIĆ, Dobrica 1921-

Ćosić is a Yugoslav novelist and essayist. His war novels, noted for both their psychological depth and their historical understanding, depict the plight of Serbian peasants victimized by world war. His first novel, *Far Away Is the Sun,* is considered a classic of resistance literature.

ZORAN GAURILOVIĆ

Vreme smrti (Time of Death) strikes a new path in the development of the Serbian novel because it opens many hitherto unknown areas, offers new esthetic values and demands new answers to the old questions. . . .

It is not easy to say what the basic virtues of the novel are, simply because there are so many. The book has many layers and meanings; it is closed inwardly and yet open to ideas, so it is hard to make more definite judgments. For, to take for a subject an entire country under extremely dramatic historical conditions, to compress its fate into a novel, to place that fate and drama firmly within the European framework and within even larger questions of the meaning of national sacrifice and resistance—all that represents much more than what we are accustomed to in our fiction. *Vreme smrti* belongs to those exceptional works in which time distances are artistically bridged.

Vreme smrti is not a chronicle nor is it a pathetic description of great events. It is a work of art through which these events are presented as fateful moral and intellectual decisions which at that time were not yet quite clear. For everything is here: the actors of the drama, the question of Serbia's place in Europe, the problem and vision of Yugoslavism, the relations with the Allies and also the moral sense of the sacrifice and endless meanings of the victory. Therefore *Vreme smrti* offers a singular truth about events that are strongly felt even in our day. At the same time the work contains ideas, strong antiwar accusation, problems, doubts, love and dilemmas. Passionately immersed in the very being of the nation, the novel brings that being to light and to a wider and more universal level. Through this the narrow framework of time, so prevalent in the Yugoslav novel, is widened. The randomness and coldness of real facts are formed into a dialogue with the meaning of historical existence.

Zoran Gaurilović, "World Literature in Review: 'Vreme Smrti'," in World Literature Today *(copyright 1977 by the University of Oklahoma Press), Vol. 51, No. 1, Winter, 1977, p. 126.**

NJEGOŠ M. PEIROVIĆ

A major literary work of our century, *A Time of Death* is a colossal novel in the best classical tradition of Dostoyevsky and Thomas Mann. It is the story of the survival of the Serbian people in one of the most tragic periods of their history—the First World War. . . .

Set in the midst of this senseless destruction and rage, when death was so common that it went almost unnoticed, Dobrica Ćosić's masterful plot rises to the grandeur of his people's dignity and aspirations. With great compassion and humanistic perception, Ćosić portrays the soul-searching anguish of Vukašin Katić, leader of the Serbian Parliamentary Opposition, who must see his only son, Ivan, sent to the battlefield. Katić queries whether liberty and independence are worth the ultimate sacrifice of the country's young.

Njegoš M. Petrović, "Fiction: 'A Time of Death'," in Best Sellers *(copyright © 1978 Helen Dwight Reid Educational Foundation), Vol. 38, No. 1, April, 1978, p. 4.*

IVAN SANDERS

[Measured] against classic war novels Dobrica Ćosić's massive work [*A Time of Death*], a shortened version of an even vaster cycle of novels about Serbia's struggle for survival during World War One, hardly qualifies as a masterpiece.

The author may have had *War and Peace* in mind all along; he may have wanted to communicate the reality of war even more graphically than Tolstoy did—in one battle scene a student soldier hears the screams of men hit by shrapnel, and exclaims: "I don't remember anything like that from *War and Peace.*"—but the novel lacks Tolstoy's luminous and urgent realism. It, too, paints a broad canvas and fills it with a host of representative types, but Tolstoy's willed randomness is missing. There is too much crucial dialogue and revealing interior monologue here; too many neatly described scenes. Of course, it may be unfair to compare every realist war novel to *War and Peace,* though Ćosić invites comparison, not only by making pointed references to the Russian masterpiece, but by reaching conclusions about war that are remarkably close to Tolstoy's views. For Ćosić, as for Tolstoy, war becomes a metaphor for the human condition. (p. 412)

Perhaps it is because *A Time of Death* is such a perfect example of national literature that its significance wanes when read in translation, in a different cultural milieu. Even though Ćosić is too sophisticated an artist to exploit nationalist feelings—the book is not so much a paean to Serbian fortitude as a study of a people in mortal danger—there are a great many names, places, dates in the novel that resonate with meaning only for the Serbian reader. The outsider may vaguely sense the reverberations, but he can not be moved by them.

Nevertheless, as a historical novel *A Time of Death* documents convincingly the ordeal of a small nation overrun by a powerful neighbor and abandoned by her allies. (pp. 412-13)

When the peasants are made to talk too much like peasants; when too many students are portrayed as disillusioned idealists; when conversations between generals and junior officers are interlarded with clichés and stock responses, the reader wearies of the novel, and of the author's compulsion to tell all. But when the immense destruction and dislocation of war are concentrated in comprehensible tragedies—a father mourning his son, a soldier desperately searching for his horse, a student rushing to his death to prove he is not a coward—then *A Time of Death* becomes a poignant tribute to human dignity and perseverence. (pp. 413-14)

Ivan Sanders, "Tolstoy in Serbia," in Commonweal *(copyright © 1979 Commonweal Publishing*

Co., Inc.; reprinted by permission of Commonweal Publishing Co., Inc.), Vol. CVI, No. 13, July 6, 1979, pp. 412-14.

* * *

COX, William Trevor
See TREVOR, William

* * *

D

DAHLBERG, Edward 1900-1977

Dahlberg, an American novelist, poet, and critic, was predominantly known for his idiosyncratic style and literary opinions. (See also *CLC*, Vols. 1, 7, and *Contemporary Authors*, Vols. 9-12, rev. ed.)

ALLEN TATE

Mr. Edward Dahlberg's *Can These Bones Live* is an American classic, even if only a few people know it; but what kind of classic, it is difficult to say. Criticism as we write it at present has no place for it, and this means that I shall probably not be able to do justice to my own admiration. Mr. Dahlberg, like Thoreau whom he admires more than any other nineteenth-century American, eludes his contemporaries; he may have to wait for understanding until the historians of ideas of the next generation can place him historically. For we have at present neither literary nor historical standards which can guide us into Mr. Dahlberg's books written since *Bottom Dogs*, which was published more than thirty years ago. It is significant that he has repudiated this early, naturalistic novel, in spite of the considerable admiration that it won and still retains among a few persons. *Can These Bones Live* may be seen as the summation of a three-part visionary and prophetic work which includes *The Flea of Sodom* and *The Sorrows of Priapus*.

We shall get nowhere with Mr. Dahlberg if we begin with an enquiry into his influences and his philosophy; this kind of thinking would inevitably be reductive. We must return repeatedly to the text to ponder hundreds of aphorisms, epigrams, and paradoxes which add up to an intuitive synthesis of insight which defies logical exposition. The immediate tradition in which Mr. Dahlberg finds himself (*he* did not find *it* or deliberately construct it) is American, and it has a span of more than a century: his mind plays back and forth between Henry David Thoreau and Randolph Bourne, but that the vision has this American stance is only the accident of Mr. Dahlberg's being an American; for the range of allusion and insight is universal and unhistorical and would probably be what it is had the author been born in Rumania and never left there.

It could be said that Mr. Dahlberg is anti-historical, history being the temporal account of man as he exists in and for the state. Mr. Dahlberg, in the line of Thoreau and Bourne, rejects the state. . . . Although the enormous vitality of the style has sources in Hebraic and Classical cultures, this book is a brilliant and profound survey of American literature. . . . I do not know any formal critic whose "method" would allow him the sudden collocations and analogies which Mr. Dahlberg can call upon at will to extend and deepen his insights. (pp. 314-15)

Mr. Dahlberg's gift for comparative insight . . . permits him to see American writers against the background of the past. [For example, in] talking about Whitman and Poe, . . . he reaches casually into the past, putting his finger upon Dante, and *illustrates* with great precision (there is no *definition*) the limitations of the Americans. . . . This looks like a rejection of Poe and Whitman, but it is rather the awareness of an historical perspective. (pp. 315-16)

In the last chapter Mr. Dahlberg returns to the relation of man to the state. He says: "Each generation must drink deeply its own tragic life." His tragic vision of the human condition redeems what might otherwise appear to be a kind of romantic anarchism, a total rejection of man *in* society, or of men *as* society.

He does not know what kind of society men should have; but he knows what the complete man should be; and he knows that the complete man cannot develop under the State. . . . Does he see all societies as forms of Statism? I suspect that he does; and to the extent that he does he tends to see the poet as the perpetual dissenter and outcast. . . . When it was first published, more than twenty years ago, the late Ford Madox Ford called [*Can These Bones Live*] a "work of genius," an opinion with which I whole-heartedly agree. . . . I submit that one may learn more about the human condition in our time from this book than from a dozen labored sociological tracts. (pp. 316-17)

Allen Tate, "A Great Stylist: The Prophet as Critic," in The Sewanee Review *(reprinted by permission of the editor; © 1961 by The University of the South), Vol. LXIX, No. 2, Spring, 1961, pp. 314-17.*

JULES CHAMETZKY

It is time to stop thinking of Edward Dahlberg as a sport in American letters, whose principal achievement would appear to be his unique style. When critics today talk about Dahlberg's style, they are usually referring to his late work; his early work of the Thirties is usually regarded as a stylistic phase that Dahlberg had to outgrow in order to achieve his maturity. The mature style reveals itself to best effect in *Because I Was Flesh* . . . in a prose a-dazzle with rich metaphor, erudite allusions to religious and pagan mythologies, passionate attention to the rhythms and music of the periods. . . . Dahlberg's mature style is a strategy for distancing himself from and yet, paradoxically, possessing the myth of his life; and that this purposeful use of an ornate, idiosyncratic style is one characteristic he shares with, say, Walt Whitman, Augie March, and scores of other American writers and Ishmaels. (p. 64)

Much of the slang in *Bottom Dogs* dates the book ("Those micks were sure-fire slingers, no spiffin"), threatens to trivialize it, but finally can be endured by a sympathetic reader. More significantly, much of the book is written, as Dahlberg says . . . , in a "rough, bleak idiom." . . . We can recognize at once that the loathsomeness of the observed world is in the naturalistic tradition everywhere evident in American letters between *Maggie* and *Last Exit to Brooklyn*. . . . The naturalistic impulse, so strong in the Thirties, was by no means the exclusive possession of that period. Nor was the use of "the rude American vernacular," so much favored by early proletarian realists. . . . Dahlberg's free use of this vernacular, combined with his predilection for the harsh bottom-dog world of America that he had experienced at first hand, suggests immediately his important position on the eve of the Depression with its subsequent vogue of proletarian realism and naturalism. . . . Dahlberg's language of disgust, his imagery of rot and decay—and most importantly—his pioneering exploration of the bottom-dog milieux of flophouses, hobo jungles, and freight cars certainly places him in the vanguard of that school. In his first two novels [*Bottom Dogs* and *From Flushing to Calvary*] Dahlberg charted in original fashion the territory that was to become painfully familiar in so much of the radical literature of the Thirties. (pp. 65-6)

What may strike a contemporary reader at once is the uncertainty of the narrative voice in *Bottom Dogs*. There is much inconsistency, e.g., in the spelling and use of the slang, and the narrator falls in and out of his bottom-dog idiom rather erratically—a reflection, surely, of the author's uncertainty about his point of view toward the material at hand. And that, of course, is the crucial issue; what is Dahlberg to make of the lives of his chief protagonists, Lorry and Lizzie Lewis?

These lives, so intertwined that we may call it *this* life, is the subject of Dahlberg's early fictions—and of *Because I Was Flesh,* which he calls an autobiography—and this life, even in outline, is an eccentric one. (p. 66)

The elements of the life [portrayed in *Bottom Dogs*] are bizarre, marginal: a calculated study in alienation and displacement. A lady barber? A Jewish lady barber in the heartland of America in the "Teddy Roosevelt Days" (as the first chapter in the saga is called)? A Jewish illegitimate non-orphan orphan? What indeed to make of this matter, and how to come to terms with it? That is Dahlberg's subject in the early days, and if the voice is occasionally uncertain, we should remember that the territory he pioneered was only fully claimed in the Fifties—in the wake of Saul Bellow's Augie March, that other Jewish illegitimate non-orphan orphan from the American heartland. A measure of the distance we have come is that Augie could unself-consciously proclaim his America identity in his opening words, and what to Dahlberg must have seemed eccentric would very likely seem to a contemporary only a walk somewhat on the wild side, and probably quintessentially American. (p. 67)

In his introduction to the first edition [see *CLC,* Vol. 7] Lawrence distinguishes Dahlberg from the true tragedian, who "dramatizes his defeat and is in love with himself in his defeated role . . . Lorry Lewis is in too deep a state of revulsion to dramatize himself." . . . Certainly the rats, mud, and grease imagery, the sordid image of a world of sleazy rooms in which someone's hand is always up a woman's dress, records the deep revulsion of the narrator toward much of Lorry's milieu. Yet much of the book reveals a narrator as elegiac as he is repulsed. . . . [In] the orphanage sections, in the section on Los Angeles, and under the 8th Street viaduct in Kansas City, one is struck by the narrator's effort simply to name, and perhaps thereby to claim, the elements of his experience. By the act of recording, he hopes to invest them with a kind of epic dignity, conscious always of a pathos and continuous irony because of their commonplace and unheroic nature. But the effort to include, legitimize, and even celebrate, these ingredients of what we are now less embarrassed than formerly to call "an American life" seems to me to require recognition. (pp. 67-8)

The struggle central to and constant in *Bottom Dogs, From Flushing to Calvary,* and *Because I Was Flesh* is between rejection and acceptance, repulsion and love, of the mother. In *Bottom Dogs* the issue is not as clearly in focus as it will be in the later books: the narrator is so close to an experience that seemed unique, eccentric, and painful, that the best he can achieve is an act of naming.

In *From Flushing to Calvary* Dahlberg closes upon his subject with more assurance. The structure is very much tighter, the action complete, the scene more unified, the problem of mother-son-identity more definitely at the center. (p. 69)

If the vernacular and the literary tend to jostle one another uneasily in *Bottom Dogs,* they are more clearly defined and separated in *Flushing*. The narrator commits no "errors" in diction and spelling, and he divides the literary and the vernacular worlds between Lorry and Lizzie. . . .

Flushing is Dahlberg's portrait of the artist as a young man. Unlike Joyce's young man, however, who had been to school to the Jesuits and could soar above the nets of religion, country, and family by committing himself wholly to his mythic father, Dedalus the fabulous artificer, to art, Dahlberg's artist is an auto-didact American, uncertain about even locating his country, family, religion. At the end, he can only commit himself to the road. Lorry's final snatch of a Maccabean stanza, "triumph, triumph crowns our glorious way" is therefore a bitterly ironic commentary on his sense of defeat rather than his exaltation. The road from Flushing—the dreary wasteland of Brooklyn and Long Island flats, his America—to Calvary produces a crucifixion but no apotheosis. The death of his mother follows upon the death of his hopes for a spiritual father, so the artist is completely orphaned.

Opposed to Lorry's life and its crises are the long sections devoted to the rhythm and pattern of Lizzie's days. They are the book's triumph; her voice and the vernacular tradition it embodies are the real strength of *Flushing*. In a language authentically her own—and recognizably the product of an American experience—she reveals herself in all her shabbiness and glory. (p. 70)

So the ambivalent relation to the mother is at the heart of this book. Besides the obvious Oedipal overtones, what I am trying to suggest is the cultural significance of the relationship. Dahlberg's love-hate relationship must perforce include Lizzie Lewis's America. *Flushing* reveals a perfect tension between exorcism and celebration, an achieved dramatization of this problem. It is unjustly neglected as such, and as another document in the long tradition of American writers struggling to accommodate themselves to their complex fate.

Dahlberg has presumably repudiated these works of his suffering youth. A wholly different man appears in the later work—especially those books and essays concerned with "the dialogue with the body"—in a voice that is prophetic when it is not crotchety. Yet the subject of *Because I Was Flesh* is obsessively, it would seem, the same as in the two early works discussed, and in them elements of the new voice are present in one way or another. There are important differences, of course—among them, two are especially noteworthy. First of all, Dahlberg can accommodate without a feeling of strain his acute sense of the observed world and its "rude vernacular" with his vast learning and his penchant for high style, to the enrichment of both. It would seem that after thirty years, in this respect at least, Dahlberg and America may have come of age. That is, despite the rage and thundering of his prophetic works, Dahlberg's pain in accommodating himself to his two worlds has abated: so long, that is, as he removes it from the sphere of action demanded by the novel form, he can come to terms, at least verbally, with his mother's life and his own. The chief difference, and it probably makes all the difference, is Dahlberg's process of mythicizing and so both distancing himself from and possessing his past.

By placing his mother and his America within a context of timeless literature, religion, and mythology, the pain and misery of his own time is transcended, singularity is transformed to universality. (pp. 71-2)

Jules Chametzky, "Edward Dahlberg, Early and Late," in Proletarian Writers of the Thirties, *edited by David Madden (copyright © 1968 by Southern Illinois University Press; reprinted by permission of Southern Illinois University Press), Southern Illinois University Press, 1968, pp. 64-73.*

HERBERT LEIBOWITZ

"Autobiographical books are plain, honest perjury," [Dahlberg] remarks in *Alms for Oblivion*. The present is an absolute sphinx and the past an equally grim riddle: "We never learn anything, but simply call old errors by new names." Doomed to repetition, "we only do what we are," and what we are is hopelessly duplicitous. Man's nature is vicious, "politics mutilates the individual," and knowledge is intellectual pride, a deluded comfort, since it does not influence our behavior. Above all, we are the miserable prey of our erotic furies.

Character, Dahlberg insists like a hanging judge, is intransigently fixed; devious, murderous, guilty of eating his own nature, a Cain bearing the stigma of his separation, man seeks atonement in vain. This blunt determinism, gleefully condemning all explanations of motive as corrupt self-interest, is hardly an inducement for composing a memoir. Not surprisingly, Dahlberg calls *Because I Was Flesh* "an autobiography of my faults" and, like a Missouri Rousseau, confesses his vices, defects, and "flinty heart," thus validating to himself that the self is an emotional Mojave Desert.

Dahlberg, reluctant to admit that he has much of a central consciousness ruling over the sequences of memories that could comprehend his life, chooses a flexible structure. *Because I Was Flesh,* he announces, is a "memoir of my mother's body." Lizzie Dahlberg is perceived from the outside, with Edward Dahlberg's suffering shifted to the charged prose style. Strict chronology has nothing to do with the psychological poetry of the mother-son relationship; *that* exists in the timeless realm of myth and dream.

Finally, *Because I Was Flesh* is also a portrait of the American artist as Proteus: porcupine, vagabond, fox, saintly fool, and "crazy waif of the Muse." By reviling himself for his shameful failings—inconstancy, unruly will, impotence of feeling—Dahlberg licenses his performance as the prophetic scourge of the world's follies. As he tells, ruefully and comically, the story of his (and his mother's) endless humiliations, he embroiders fact with fiction. He becomes the dervish of words, an author of wisdom literature for a world in which such wisdom is useless. . . . *Because I Was Flesh* is thus a calculated leveling of our individual and collective self-esteem; heroism or a scrap of self-knowledge enters our consciousness only through the occasional windfalls of art. The morally examined life is a necessary fraud. (pp. 473-74)

Because I Was Flesh is a masterpiece of Oedipal obsession, a poetic memoir of primal sunderings and rages. At its heart, as at the heart of all Dahlberg's writings, lies his exasperated love for his mother Lizzie and his quest for knowledge of his father Saul, a feckless womanizer, whose desertion is the other unappeasable demon of his childhood. . . .

Where Oedipus at Colonus achieved a mysterious grace, Dahlberg's nomadic spirit remains bruised, defiant, wise in the lore of antiquity yet without that fundamental self-awareness that might reconcile him to his bereaved past. Yet paradoxically *Because I Was Flesh* converts Dahlberg's long internal exile into the consoling power of myth. A Book of Lamentations, it moves in a shower of aphorisms between comedy and prayer. . . .

In the rich iconography of the autobiography, Lizzie acts Mary Magdalene and Mater Dolorosa to Dahlberg's Jesus, Hagar to his Ishmael, and Delilah to his Samson. She dominates the book as effortlessly as she does her son's emotions. (p. 474)

[Dahlberg's] paralyzed will demonstrates for him the finality of our stricken, fallen natures: character is genetic fate. Our incestuous desires and guilt, our original trauma, like shrapnel in the soul, fester to the end of our days. The myth of recurrence triumphs. "Eros goes as far back as Chaos," Dahlberg tells us. Sex is force, not sentiment, as amorally destructive as Henry Adams's dynamo. (p. 479)

If "the miracle of perception is bound up with the miracle of love," as Dahlberg claims, he is self-condemned to dwell in the "dungy caves of the Cyclops." And, indeed, Dahlberg's artistic career has drawn sustenance from an absolutist's dogma of impossibilism. Loathing separation, he destroys the intimacy he craves with a violent compulsiveness and lives in "boreal solitude." . . . "Nobody ever overcomes the phantasms of his childhood. The man is the corrupt dream of the child." This self-fulfilling prophecy universalizes his destitution. It is the moralist's meager solace. The rhetoric is magnificent, but is it true?

Our reason may be deformed and our will enfeebled, and we may be estranged from ourselves as from others, but, as Edwin Muir has remarked, "Without forgiveness our lives would be unimaginable." Fortunately, Dahlberg's art is wiser than his philosophy. For like Muir, he has understood that the imagination is potentially an instrument of immortality. In the twined life of mother and son, he has woven a web as subtle and intricate as the fatal pattern that tied Hippolytus and Phaedra. When "gibing Pilate," the spokesman for the moral average, counters Lizzie's angry question, "Why am I miserable, while others who are pitiless and contemptible are so fortunate?" with the retort, "What is Truth?" and she replies quietly, "My life," the moment is one of the most heartbreaking in all the literature of autobiography.

Through the eloquence of his art, Dahlberg can set aside blame, self-laceration, and misanthropic humor and sing an anthem that bestows upon his mother the blessing of a conciliating grace:

> When the image of her comes up on a sudden—just as my bad demons do—and I see again her dyed henna hair, the eyes dwarfed by the electric lights in the Star Lady Barbershop, and the dear, broken wing of her mouth, and when I regard her wild tatters, I know that not even Solomon in his lilied raiment was so glorious as my mother in her rags. *Selah.*

This rapturous prose, the rise and fall and swelling of ecstatic revelation, and the intoning of the Psalmist's mysterious cadence bring aesthetic concord and a measure of peace to his wounded ego. His Oedipal obsessions have been subdued in the grandeur of reattachment, for he has finally been able to reassemble the image of his mother, which eluded him in the orphanage, in his wanderings, and in most of his books. *Because I Was Flesh* is Dahlberg's greatest act of expiation. . . .

"Aesthetics is a style of living, enunciation—and affectation," Dahlberg has said. The sheer flaunting artifice, the deliberate archaizing of his style, have stirred controversy and antipathy. Critics have derided him as an American Euphues, a poseur given to rodomontade. There is truth in these charges, but they miss the point because his style is consonant with his moral vision. Despising the pedants, he became a ferocious compiler of literary texts, fables, and aphorisms. An autodidact, he offers lessons in the anthropological customs of primitive men, usually deemed superior to "civilized" men—a small group of savants is exempt from Dahlberg's strictures against the modern world—because they are not separated from nature and their testicles do not drive them mad—or at least much less so. (p. 480)

Dahlberg's style, though willfully invented, is a necessary outgrowth of his sense of self. . . . His style is a flamboyant procession of words, the verbal equivalent, say, of one of Montezuma's rituals. It is expensive but clear even when he succumbs to a bout of tedious harangue. Dahlberg's defense is characteristic: "Long ago I resolved to be, like Crates, a jocose iconoclast, to see whatever my eyes compelled me to regard without blinking the worst by calling it the best, and to accept my hindrances as the founts of any perceptions I may be lucky enough to discover."

But this rationale and its dependence on random inspirations cannot cancel the fact that Dahlberg often wears blinkers. His petty side is not pretty to watch. His vigilance to expose and correct error turns him into a vigilante. . . . Spiteful and jealous, he has cultivated the art of denigration, as if by fiat he could demolish the truths of his artistic siblings and thus remove the threat to his aesthetic identity. His stylistic excesses are the orphan's pugnacious defense.

All of Dahlberg's writings have been autobiographical. In his apprentice days, he followed uncritically the conventions of the naturalistic novel. The narratives of *Bottom Dogs* (1930), *From Flushing to Calvary* (1932), and *Those Who Perish* (1934) are oppressively literal, dazed transcripts of brutalized experiences. . . . The language of [*Bottom Dogs*] is bare of mythical adornments, a flat morose voice moving over the terrain of memory, never straying from its tone of inert defeat, as the hero, Lorry Lewis, wanders across America. There is no connection among characters, just a drab amnesia, the stylistic counterpart of the Great Depression. (p. 481)

The prose of *Bottom Dogs* has a "sapless complexion." It is as riveting as one of Mary Baker Eddy's Christian Science tracts. . . . The author parcels out information as if he were giving street directions to a stranger, betraying no feeling. He cannot carry a tune. The rhythm is slack, the rhetoric minimal, neutered, reductive, its dullness the "sign of a weak and stingy imagination." In contrast, the prose of the autobiography is expansive, droll, animated, physical. . . . Dahlberg's style has body and a robust flavor spiked with wormwood.

Dahlberg himself came to consider his early novels as mediocre manipulations of his childhood and young manhood, disfigured by self-pity—in short, dreary imitations of proletarian naturalism. He has repudiated them and refuses to reread them. In *The Flea of Sodom* (1950), Dahlberg describes his radical shift away from the linguistic void and gibbering of robots that he says marked much of the fiction and discourse of the thirties. He drastically revamped his style. (p. 482)

[For Dahlberg, the artist] is a centaur guarding and adding to the stock of a nation's myths by which it learns who and what it is. This task was particularly crucial for America, whose myths and legends had been neglected, or forgotten, or never acquired. Dahlberg thus recast himself as La Salle, Cabeza de Vaca, and William Bartram, solitary explorers willing to track the headwaters for samples of our autochthonous roots. In renouncing history, that cluttered record of bloody and wasteful events, in favor of fable and prehistory, whose revivifying waters are "a surety of man's sanity," he converted his isolation into a virtue. In other words, he started making "a marvelous mask" and found a style manufactured half from the honey of books and half from his own venomous wit.

The new style emerged fully caparisoned in *Can These Bones Live* (1940). The title is exemplary: in a series of acrid, biblical, Brownean essays, he examines the American tradition and selects his own (narrow) usable past: Bartram, Thoreau, Melville, Sherwood Anderson, Dreiser. For the first time, he plays the *enfant terrible,* smashing idols with exhilarating swipes of the pen—and he indulges his love of pithy and provoking opinions. In the books that came out in the years before he began writing *Because I Was Flesh* in 1959—*The Flea of Sodom, The Sorrows of Priapus* (1957)—he refined his style and continued his didactic buccaneering. . . . *The Flea of Sodom* is so violently turgid in its debunking of left wing attitudes—it is a private exorcism of old political demons and a purge of thirties' apparatchiks—that it verges in incoherence.

Yet for all its superfluities, Dahlberg's baroque style has extraordinary energy, its bookishness balanced by a racy humor, its erudition as beautiful as carved lithic objects. And it suits the inner man, whose planetary influences were so extreme. After all, he has had only one story to tell, so that one should not seek any more variety in his moral injunctions or his stiff-necked cries against the stiff necked—he packs the modern world off to hell with as much skill as Dante's Cerberus—than in a hammer striking an anvil.

Dahlberg's style achieves consummate greatness in *Because I Was Flesh.* And his imagination flourishes with a chaste ornateness. Sublimation and the sublime are cognates. (pp. 482-83)

Dahlberg tries to repair his broken world with mythic plumbing. He extends the boundaries of his purview from Kansas City to the heights of Lake Titicaca, as if his long pilgrimage in search of his origins forced him back against the stream of time to the child's dreams and the troglodytic world of the unconscious. . . .

The Word is Dahlberg's redeemer. In becoming flesh, it grants self-mastery. He no longer need "Be on guard against the world" all the time; words guide his feelings to a taut harmony. Language may be "as unreasonable as life," but in *Because I Was Flesh,* Dahlberg imbues it with heroic assurance—it is often all that stands between him and a dour capitulation to nihilism, that "ineradicable infamy." The profligacy of language, unlike that of sex, sustains him and enables him to overcome the vehement, coercive ideology he nursed from childhood. Words become his loving, nurturing parents, and *Because I Was Flesh* the wanted "song of desire." (p. 483)

Herbert Leibowitz, "Stoking the Oedipal Furnace: Edward Dahlberg's 'Because I Was Flesh'," in The American Scholar *(copyright © 1975 by the United Chapters of Phi Beta Kappa; reprinted by permission of the publishers), Vol. 44, No. 3, Summer, 1975, pp. 473-83.*

FRANK MacSHANE

Like *Bottom Dogs,* [Dahlberg's] early novels, *From Flushing to Calvary* and *Those Who Perish,* were socially committed. They arose from his own political experience of the opposed extremities of Stalinism and Nazism. More deeply, they were fed by his own anger at injustice. They were written in a colloquial style suited, as was thought, to the proletariat that was supposed to be reading *New Masses.* These novels received critical attention but they showed no artistic growth, so Dahlberg, who meanwhile had fallen out with the Communists and who had genuine literary ambitions, ceased writing and began to read. Repudiating writing that had an immediate social purpose, he entered a period of silence that was so prolonged he published only three new books in the quarter-century that preceded 1960. Thereafter, he published an average of a book a year—an astonishing burst of activity for a man of his age. (pp. 57-8)

[In] *Because I Was Flesh* [the] bare narrative was given substance by the rich prose in which it was written—a prose that incorporated literary, historical and mythical references so as to give the story greater resonance than was possible when accepting the limitations of colloquial English. The danger of the method is that it can be artificially literary and therefore pretentious; but *Because I Was Flesh* is grounded in observed reality. (p. 58)

Edward's iconoclasm was useful . . . in the way he assessed authors—especially American writers, for he was always conscious of his own roots. He venerated those writers—Dreiser, Anderson, Thoreau—who were close to nature and who celebrated the woes and pleasures of unsophisticated "front-porch America." He was violently opposed to the modernists—Pound, Eliot, Joyce—because he thought they debased the classics they pirated and because he considered them to be cold Narcissists with no feeling for others. He detested their destruction of syntax which he credited to their lack of feeling. (p. 60)

[Above all, Dahlberg] was a moralist. In his correspondence with Herbert Read in preparation for the book *Truth Is More Sacred,* Dahlberg outlined some of the points he wanted to raise, and among the first were "the disappearance of morality in modern letters" and "the emphasis on words rather than ideas which should take care of the form." In his best art, as in *Because I Was Flesh,* he was able to balance moral judgment with loving observation—the direct rendering of experience—so that there was both instruction and delight. But often morality got the upper hand, and in life as in some of his work, it became intolerable.

In the end, Dahlberg may emerge mainly as an aphorist. In this mode his literary skills are wonderfully effective in commenting on the contradictions of ordinary life. "The older one grows the more he doubts that he was ever alive," he observes in one book; in another, "The longer you know a person, the more nebulous he becomes; by the time you are friends, you may be strangers to one another." All of Dahlberg's work tends towards observations such as these or, put another way, his disparate works—essays, novels, letters—may be seen on the whole as a vast collection of maxims. We may forget the drift of literary argument or we may grow deaf to the insistent tone of his judgments, but we are always captivated by the almost casual epigram that reveals both feeling and intellect. In the literature of our time, Edward Dahlberg may occupy a position analagous to Thoreau's in the nineteenth century—that of a man known mainly for one book and for memorable sentences from his other writings. (pp. 67-8)

Frank MacShane, "Edward Dahlberg: 1900-1977," in The Massachusetts Review *(reprinted from* The Massachusetts Review; *© 1978 The Massachusetts Review, Inc.), Vol. XIX, No. 1, Spring, 1978, pp. 55-68.*

* * *

DAVENPORT, Guy, Jr. 1927-

Davenport is a short story writer, essayist, poet, editor, illus-

trator, and translator of classical Greek. (See also *CLC*, Vol. 6, and *Contemporary Authors*, Vols. 33-36, rev. ed.)

RICHARD PEVEAR

The highly developed critical sensibility of the modern era is a product of fiction. The *Tatlin!* stories are, in part, essays in a criticism by mimesis. The most difficult thing for an article to convey about the writing in *Tatlin!* is its subtle use of known voices and styles of prose. . . . The book is, simply, superbly written, and I know of no one in our language who can equal its accomplishment.

In method the stories are comparative, analogical; they develop through parallels and oppositions, through contrasts built around the same motif—for instance, the motif of the flying machine, which Tatlin attempts to humanize in his glider or "air bicycle," which appears in the Kafka story as an awkward bit of flying junk, but reappears in "Robot" as the Messerschmidt, and in "The Dawn in Erewhon" finally as the craft that takes Neil Armstrong to the moon. It is a historical-critical method, aware of evolutions, affinities, echoes, recurrences; a method that will join together the German planes flying reconnaissance over southern France with the discovery of Aurignacian paintings at Lascaux.

But it is above all a fictional method. The stories are described in the book as "assemblages of history and necessary fiction." . . . But the stories function least as assemblages, more as essays in criticism, most as fictions. (pp. 143-44)

The ruling spirit of *Tatlin!* is not constructivism, it is the spirit of reverie. And it seems to me that the origin of the stories must have been more in reverie than in thought: dreams of an educated mind, the sort of thing that comes into your head as you sit among the books and objects in your study. . . .

Reverie attaches to ideas as well. "The Dawn in Erewhon" is a tissue of ideas that are elegantly formed, savored for their resonance, made fragrant with strong coffee and the honey and tar of tobacco, and never really thought. They are ideas as beautiful objects, ideas as tokens of an ingenious mind; what counts is not the ideas themselves but the feeling of having them. (p. 144)

Dreams of the wise man are an important part of *Tatlin!* These figures are represented as having wisdom, though what they think remains unthought in the stories. Fiction is a medium for reverie, for the romance of reality, for synthetic portraiture; it is not a medium for thought. But the preponderance of thematic ideas in these stories seems to call for thought. Ideas are not presented as traits of character; on the contrary, characters are chosen because they represent ideas. But the repetition of the same cluster of ideas throughout the book makes one feel, after a while, that the characters are trapped in them and limited by them, that they are tired of speaking these incantations that have frozen them into attitudes. The end of "Tatlin!" and the end of "The Dawn in Erewhon" have the same melancholy; it is like a sudden aging. Fiction encourages us to see the characters in *Tatlin!* as living human beings, but the author's hand pushes them toward abstraction and caricature. Yet the author is forbidden by the techniques of fiction to let his hand show. (p. 145)

The story ["The Dawn in Erewhon"], which draws together the other five and at the same time reflects back on them, is itself polymorphous; it maintains the spell of fiction, yet is also a fantasia on the writing of fictions; its ideas, particularly its Utopian theme, are presented seriously in one place but travestied in another; its ideal man, both thinker and gymnast, rebirth of the archaic in the modern, is shown at the same time to be narcissistic, epicurean, vague, pretentious, and ill-at-ease. Why is it all so curiously two-sided? I think that is the right question to ask of the story, provided it is asked inquiringly. Reverie and critical intelligence mingle in various ways in *Tatlin!;* here they are in complex opposition. If the story were resolved either into consistent fiction or into satire, it would lose its peculiar rightness.

The puzzle of Adriaan van Hovendaal holds the materials of the story together. He is presented rather simply, as a light-hearted visual thinker, an orderly sensualist, a dreamer of worlds. . . . Adriaan van Hovendaal is a man of leisure. He thinks analogically, brilliantly, easily; he has an appetite for thinking. But his thought meets no opposition, and therefore it has no conception of necessity and is devoid of will. In this contradictory condition there is a real and disturbing truth, a truth of character that is also a truth of history. It seems almost to have taken the story by surprise.

Pathless on all paths: something of this realization comes over Adriaan van Hovendaal in the next to last chapter of the story, though its tragic poetry is colored by epicurean melancholy and a stoic resolution. His pathlessness is the impasse of fiction, the inner condition of our time, and if it has been recognized critically before, it has rarely been given such familiar likeness. It is a portrait relieved of gravity but not of seriousness, at once a self-confession and a self-satire, a study in the problematics of the modern neopagan, city-dwelling intellect. (pp. 145-46)

Richard Pevear, "'Tatlin!', or the Limits of Fiction," in The Hudson Review *(copyright © 1975 by The Hudson Review, Inc.; reprinted by permission), Vol. XXVIII, No. 1, Spring, 1975, pp. 141-46.*

RICHARD WERTIME

[The six stories in *Tatlin!*] have a maturity, a philosophic depth, and a richness of effect beyond the reach of the younger writer, even one like Thomas Pynchon, whose artistic ambitions and temperament are not so different from Davenport's. What distinguishes these two, mainly, is a difference in orientation: Davenport is an erstwhile friend and devoted student of Ezra Pound's; and in its intense, eclectic and well-nigh overbearing erudition, *Tatlin!* is offered to us as a fit companion to, if not a worthy competitor of, *The Cantos, Ulysses, Finnegans Wake,* and Eliot's major works. This is no small self-assertion; but then, Davenport's fiction asks to be weighed on such scales. And if I have reservations, they pertain to the problems of esoteric fiction in general, and are couched within an admiration that I hope will become self-evident. (p. 948)

Tatlin! is, to begin with, more than an aggregate of stories. As much as Welty's *Golden Apples,* or Anderson's *Winesburg, Ohio,* or Selby's *Last Exit to Brooklyn*—all so very different—it is a cohesive, total work. Two longer pieces, both novella-like in their scope, frame four shorter tales. In subject and effect these middle pieces are lighter than the two flanking stories. As other reviewers have pointed out, this is not "short fiction" in the customary sense. These are tales full of essaying, imaginative renditions of historical facts, revolving meditations on the philosophic problems that have most vexed our century. Davenport has virtually contrived a new genre to house the breadth of his interests. Happily, to my mind, his work is still fictive in essence. In fact, its most striking attribute is not the intelligent commentary on the human condition—and there is plenty of that—nor yet the dazzle of its language, about which I shall have a good deal more to say later; it is, rather, the keenness of the eye which observes. It is a funny, often hilarious book, one packed with the drama of the mundane, the minor. It also jolts us by rehumanizing historical figures who have grown remote and unreal with the passage of time. Franz Kafka appears implausibly as a tourist off in Italy, and Edgar Allan Poe appears in a parallel tale, in St. Petersburg. We watch the philosopher Herakleitos take his morning exercises with slave, student, and servant-girl. Like the humor, such characterization is didactic in its intent: we are forced to be sceptical of overly lofty notions and encouraged to see the unity in the diversity of the world. Davenport's Herakleitos says that "the most beautiful order of the world is still a random gathering of things insignificant in themselves." This "in themselves" is tricky. For the artist both does and does not "give" his subjects beauty. As another character says, in rather more impacted language, "It is elective affinities that knit the discrete particulars of the world into that artificial fabric whose essence we perceive as beauty." Kierkegaard provides the means of reconciling these statements in his definition of admiration as happy self-surrender. *Tatlin!* is a work informed, indeed, suffused with admiration.

The first story, "Tatlin!", is an epic of sorts in miniature—though I suspect that such a description of it will strike some readers as odd. It concerns one Vladimir Tatlin, versatile Russian of this century, who . . . was a victim of the Soviets' brutal and stifling ideology. What the story does, essentially, is to weave together pieces of this man's personal life with pastiche glimpses of the restless Western world during the years that Communist Russia was promoting, then reneging on, its political promise. The final effect is panoramic: art, aviation (both enduring themes in all these stories), engineering, modern philosophy, world travel, childhood dabblings; all of these collect to express the "spirit of the age," which, though less grim for Davenport than it was for Joyce and Pound, is nevertheless bewildering and awesome in its complexity. (pp. 949-50)

["Tatlin!"] acts as an induction to the rest of the book in both its presentation of character and its technical brilliance. The utilization of counterpoint; the sprinkling of aphorisms; the energizing use of names of everything imaginable; the *entrelacement* lifted, perhaps, from medieval narrative; the devotion to quaint tidbits that light up suddenly—these typify, like the character of Tatlin himself, much of what follows. (p. 950)

In "The Aeroplanes at Brescia," the second story in the collection, we find Franz Kafka off in Italy with friends, a reminder of the fact that Kafka is not, indeed, a character in a fiction by Kafka. The story is set at an aerial show. . . . At the end of the story, while the show is winding up, Kafka's eyes mist over suddenly with an undefinable emotion. Does he feel the odd joy of watching a new era open? Or are there darker intimations, a vague prophetic sense of what this new era will bring?

The next story, "Robot," extends the theme of ambiguity as well as the kindly, whimsical tone. It chronicles the discovery of the Lascaux cave-paintings by a dog and a group of boys out playing in the woods. . . . Random accident, here, shades over into serendipity, into epiphany, and the implication is that the same is true of most of man's great discoveries.

The next story in the book, "Herakleitos," is about celebration, and is itself a celebration. A young man, Knaps, has come from his rocky Arkadian homeland to listen to the wisdom of Herakleitos. The story spoofs beautifully the life of a college teacher; of all the characters assembled between the covers of *Tatlin!,* Herakleitos is most conspicuously a *persona* for Guy Davenport. . . . At the story's conclusion, Herakleitos and his "family" naue eir offerings in the temple of an unnamed female deity, who is probably Artemis, Mother of Lions; and the book Herakleitos lays at her black basalt feet, in announced fulfillment of his promise, is also this one, *Tatlin!,* Davenport's own.

Tatlin! may be properly said to crest with "Herakleitos." The two stories following it, the one very short and the other very long, are, if not darker, at least more complicated and troubled by perplexity. But the figure of Herakleitos persists; and he has emerged by the work's end as one of the two presiding geniuses of the author's philosophy. The other is Pythagoras, inventor of abstract order, lover of pure numerical harmony. These two exist in absolute complementarity and paradoxical otherness; together they unite the worlds of mind and random matter. Blake figures heavily in this synthesis too. . . .

I must scant the penultimate story (the one about Poe in Russia) in order to get to "The Dawn in Erewhon," which occupies fully half the collection under consideration, and which is the story that best exemplifies the peculiar strengths and limitations of Davenport's writing. The reader of *Tatlin!* will know, almost as soon as he opens the book, that it is a man of staggering erudition whose company he is sharing. And he will be impressed rightly. This is a writer, in addition, who knows the risks which he has taken, and who feels up to whatever quarrel he may have with our sensibilities. . . . [The] verbal diet, already rich in the first five stories, becomes in "The Dawn in Erewhon" so heavily virtuosic as to be, at times, cloying. One begins to wonder if Davenport isn't waging war against *Finnegans Wake,* isn't out to capture the record for the number of different vocables used. This is, let me emphasize, a first and not, possibly, a lasting impression; I would demean the author wrongly if I portrayed him here as having trundled out his knowledge for the paltry purpose of leaving his readers stunned. (pp. 951-53)

Davenport is a "layerer." Yet hearty banqueting has its limits; and these are limits that will fix themselves, like a kind of floating boundary, between the tolerance of the reader and the economy, the utility, of the author's style. *Tatlin!* enters a world not overly tolerant of opulence, especially verbal opulence of the traditional and allusive sort. In prose, as in poetry, the contemporary writer fears the charge of dandyism a great deal more than that of flatness. And this is, in many ways, unfortunate.

But I must still take up the quarrel. And to do so, I will

have to turn to plot and structure. What actually happens in "The Dawn in Erewhon"? Although the story doesn't lend itself to easy summarizing, it does have distinct narrative strands which interweave. The most conventional and accessible of these concerns Adriaan Floris van Hovendaal, a contemporary Dutch philosopher. Adriaan teaches at a university and writes on odd subjects. . . . He also, and this is of equal importance, is building his own utopia, a private kingdom of freedom whose principal liberty is sex. In a sense, "The Dawn in Erewhon" is "Herakleitos" much extended; and if Herakleitos looks like a *persona* for Guy Davenport, Adriaan might well be his chosen alter ego. . . . [He has] a relationship with a girl named Kaatje. . . . They make love prodigiously, take sun in the buff almost as often, and blend their rapt sensuality with a daily fare of study and thought. (pp. 953-54)

[There] is a pleasantly unworldly quality to the plot's erotic aspect. And Davenport chooses to play it good-naturedly. While this strand of action works its way toward its conclusion, a conclusion not very surprising but nonetheless a little disquieting, the other strands—so different, it seems—are gradually revealing their relation to, their oneness with, the more evident doings. Out of antithesis comes synthesis. The moon is used to symbolize this synthesizing motion. . . . [By] the final page of *Tatlin!* the staggering distance separating moon and earth is closed both geographically and psychically. As Neil Armstrong takes man's first step into extraterrestrial dust, we are made to see, if we haven't already, that that familiar slogan, "whole earth," means by an implication startling in its necessary simplicity "whole cosmos" as well. With his good looks and blue eyes, Armstrong is the new Adam awakening to the new Eden, the Eden of space. "Dawn in Erewhon," then, is an aubade, a hymn; the nowhere of Erewhon is the plenum of infinity, through whose magical lens one may glimpse the back of one's head, if one has vision heroic enough.

This motif of travel as the means of achieving closure informs the other important elements of the plot. As befits the universality of paradox and contradiction, "The Dawn in Erewhon" is a sort of *ave atque vale,* an intricate satire à la Swift as well as a hymn to the new age. (pp. 954-55)

What do I find to criticize, then, in such an intelligent effort? The problem is one of achieving that proper blend of language and action, of securing for each an interest which will justify its density as well as carry the reader forward. . . . Not only does Davenport push too far in his searching out of fancy words for inessential purposes, but there is a corresponding thinness in the actual human doings which exacerbates the matter. Again, I am speaking only of "The Dawn in Erewhon." Comical prolixity ceases to be funny if overextended; and even idyllic hedonism has, for onlookers anyhow, decided limitations. The voluptuous Kaatje is a case in point: how little, really, we know of her beyond her bedding habits. There is ardor and trust and kindliness in all these characters, but not much warmth and curiosity. Or should I say, perhaps, attentiveness—attention to all the things which lie between the riot of copulation and the antipodal calm found in philosophic thought.

This "middle zone," as it were, is where the most important action in our literature occurs. Earlier I said that most of the characters in *Tatlin!* lead disjunctive lives, lives alleviated by periods of happy conjunction. "Erewhon" appears to be an exception to this rule, but in fact it is not. Probably our lives *are* for the most part lived disjunctively; and I admire Guy Davenport for expressing his impatience with the usual sorts of relationships on which our fiction gluts itself. But the fact still stands that his particular sort of realism, of conjunction-in-disjunction, inverts the essential condition of intimacy as most of us know it, and as the Western novel has known it for a couple of hundred years. The tension in most fiction, both good and bad, results from a revelation to someone—someone "close" to someone else—that the conjunctive state by which they have been habitually defining themselves has become, or is becoming, a fraud, a mask, a mere formality. It is then that the painful fragility of human relationships opens up into something which can only be rendered fully by means of a visible social act. It is only then, for instance, that tragedy—a word used often in the pages of *Tatlin!* to describe the intellectual quandaries that modern man has fallen into—can possibly occur. The point at which the lovers have arrived at the conclusion of "Erewhon" is pregnant with suggestions of just such complex human developments. But it is as if the story's form has conspired with authorial reticence to keep them from maturing.

It had occurred to me, along the way, to cite Hawkes's *The Blood Oranges* as a piece of fiction whose merits and problems are parallel to those of "Erewhon." But *Tatlin!*, even "Erewhon" alone, dwarfs John Hawkes's novel. It dwarfs many another novel to have appeared in recent years as well; it is, for all the complaints which I have marshalled here, a brave and magnificent undertaking—arrogant, individual to a nearly perverse degree, endlessly rewarding in its bestowal of special benefits. *Tatlin!* is not likely to attract a wide following—such works never do, at least not quickly—and it is not very likely to encourage imitation. This would suit Guy Davenport. *Tatlin!* is a *summa,* in design a cosmic comedy; it is tragical-comical-historical-pastoral; scene indivisible and poem unlimited. One could do worse. (pp. 955-57)

Richard Wertime, "Book Reviews: 'Tatlin!'," in The Georgia Review *(copyright, 1975, by the University of Georgia), Vol. XXIX, No. 4, Winter, 1975, pp. 948-57.*

HUGH WITEMEYER

Tatlin! is historical fiction of an unusual kind. It is concerned more with the sensibility than with the events of the period it covers. That period is our own; four of the six stories are set between 1900 and 1970, and the collection is unified by a vision of modernism in art, science, philosophy, and politics. Like Hugh Kenner, Davenport believes that the intellectual life of the twentieth century is qualitatively different from that of any preceding period. *Tatlin!* attempts to do in the form of fiction what *The Pound Era* attempts to do in the form of literary criticism: to characterize the distinctive mental habits, or the unique intellectual "signature," of the modern age. . . .

[Pound's] influence upon the six stories is indirect but pervasive. To begin with, he affects the structure and texture of the book, which are consciously modernist. The structure is ideogrammic, in that the six stories are discrete and independent, yet unified by a network of recurring themes and images. The texture of the prose is dense, allusive, polyglot, discontinuous—"difficult" in the way that Eliot, Joyce, and the men of 1914 are difficult. These features are not uniquely Poundian, but Pound has clearly helped to shape them. Similarly, Davenport's sense of the integrity of human history, and of the power of the past to inspire and define the present, owes a great deal to the author of the *Cantos*. But again, the influence is not exclusive and cannot be demonstrated in terms of specific sources or passages. Some of Pound's most important contributions to *Tatlin!*, in other words, are difficult to isolate because they are integral to Guy Davenport's imagination, and inseparable from the very conception of the book. . . .

[Four other influences are also evident:] Pound's biographical presence; his influence upon Davenport's presentation of the Mediterranean world; the vision of a cultural vortex in the title story; and the fusion of eros and intellect in the long concluding story. These features of *Tatlin!* are not just modernist; they could not exist as they do if Pound had not been in the movement. (p. 57)

Pound, then, contributes several identifiable threads to the rich tapestry of *Tatlin!* He is, to be sure, only one presence among many in a set of stories that draws from an astonishing variety of sources. But discussion of this book should begin with its constituent elements, for *Tatlin!* is constructed according to a principle stated by Herakleitos in the story that bears his name: "Men who wish to know about the world . . . must learn about it in its particulars. Our knowledge will never be complete, just as our understanding will never be complete." (p. 60)

Hugh Witemeyer, "Ezra Pound's Presence in Guy Davenport's 'Tatlin!'" in Vort *(copyright Barry Alpert, 1976), Vol. 3, No. 3, 1976, pp. 57-60.*

GEORGE STADE

Different styles, times, places, characters are juxtaposed [in "Da Vinci's Bicycle"] sans connective or commentary, except that they comment on one another. They reflect on one another in ways too complex and numerous for commentary to fix in words. Less is more. The gaps fill up with meaning. But there is more to it than that. For one thing, the stories reflect on one another with the kind of variable light that the parts within the stories also shed on one another. . . .

In Mr. Davenport's [stories], Mussolini, like Nixon, Mao, Nero and numerous others . . . , is one of a series of farcical and ferocious despots. Pound, like Leonardo, Gertrude Stein and many others, is one of a series of artists whose concern is to discover or create order. But then we remember that Mao, in the first story, is also a poet. Then we remember that Gertrude Stein, in the first story, plays Napoleon and that Alice B. Toklas calls her "Augustus Caesar." In the fifth story we will read that Stein "has cut her hair short to look like a Roman emperor and to be modern."

But by this time, halfway through the book, the motifs have become so numerous, so complex in their combinations, that the mind cannot hold them together. One can only enjoy them as they occur and recur and intertwine. . . . Behind the appearance of fragmentation and inconsequence, the various series distribute harmonies. And so it is with the world: Fourier, like his immediate predecessors, Cuvier, Linnaeus, Buffon and Swedenborg, "all searched out the harmonies, the affinities, the kinship of the orders of nature." Mr. Davenport, like the artists in these stories, searches out the attractions, proportions and destinies among the orders of history, literature and human nature. "All of nature is series and pivot," says Fourier, and so are all of Mr. Davenport's stories. (p. 9)

[Davenport's] methods and doctrines are pretty much those of high modernism, of Pound, Eliot and Joyce, as are its difficult beauties. With that observation in mind, the stories at first struck me as dated, as anachronistic, for all their formidable art and intelligence, as derivative, for all their unconventionality. The modernist moment is past; in theory, at least, different moments call for different methods. But on the second go-around my preconceptions crumbled before the human impact of the stories; they now struck me as simply very good, by any standard, except that of immediate accessibility. They struck me as good for the usual reasons, for the author's ear for dialogue, for his heart, his head, his sense of humor. (p. 28)

George Stade, "Fiction in the Modernist Mode," in The New York Times Book Review *(© 1979 by The New York Times Company; reprinted by permission), June 17, 1979, pp. 9, 28.*

JACK SULLIVAN

[Almost] everything about *Da Vinci's Bicycle* . . . is complicated. Writing in the tradition of Joyce, Pound, Beckett, and Eliot (all of whom appear in allusions or as actual characters), Davenport mixes chronologies, tones, voices, languages, and chunks of other learned books to create dizzying collages that are often impressive in their cleverness and intricacy, but sometimes wearying in their self-conscious erudition.

In several passages, both qualities appear at once. Of a balloon trip he writes, "It was like striding over a sea of gelatin, that bell-stroke swing of our nacelle through the rack of the upper air on elastic wicker, wind thrumming the frapping with the elation of Schumann strings *allegro molto vivace*." One admires the musical effect but resents the musical analogy. Schumann doesn't sound any more like balloons than Stravinsky ("The crickets sing around us, fine as Stravinsky") sounds like crickets.

The best stories, ironically, are the simplest. In "Ithaka" we meet an anguished Ezra Pound, back from the asylum for the criminally insane. . . . In "The Wooden Dove of Archytas," an ancient Greek narrative involving the ascension of a steam-operated dove is juxtaposed with a 19th-century tale of sorcery. . . . With its double crescendo and deftly orchestrated imagery, the story carries the reader to some nice heights too.

It is appropriate that these enticingly experimental stories are about explorers and pioneers. At his best, Davenport belongs in the same company as his "foragers" of language and experience.

Jack Sullivan, "Books in Brief: 'Da Vinci's Bicycle'," in Saturday Review *(© 1979 by Saturday Review Magazine Corp.; reprinted with permission), Vol. 6, No. 14, July 7, 1979, p. 46.*

HUGH KENNER

"Ten stories" is the publisher's description of *Da Vinci's Bicycle*. Davenport's own word for what he makes is *assemblages*. His paragraphs array and elaborate discrete themes: the Paris of Miss Stein and Picasso, the anatomy of the wasp, the myths of a Dogon cosmologist, the Wrights, Charles Fourier; also the young photographer Jacques-

Henri Lartigue, and Da Vinci drawing a bicycle (as he did). All are found actualities. All are foragers, enamored of the particulate. All make up worlds out of innumerable acts of perception. And all are themselves made on these pages out of words, more than half of them monosyllabic, the way Seurat made large intricate pictures out of little spots of paint.

Nothing attracts Guy Davenport like a world almost impossible to imagine, requiring reconstitution atom by atom. (p. 1240)

Imagine. But we cannot imagine more than we are, and even Davenport's personages are all oblique self-portraits, even the Richard Nixon who utters banalities in China, a thing we are all of us doing much of the time. The most remarkable is the voice of the last strict fantasy, Robert Walser of Biel, who has experienced the world as widely as Odysseus. . . . [He] assembles memories and bizarre observations, and writes above the final blank space, "But let us desist, lest quite by accident we be so unlucky as to put these things in order."

There is an order which is death, placid in brains wherein thousands of words have died, and people suppose that they know what they are saying when they say (Richard Nixon said it), "The world is watching us." Five little words. And who knows the meaning of "The"? (p. 1241)

Hugh Kenner, "Assemblages," in National Review *(© National Review, Inc., 1979; 150 East 35th St., New York, NY 10016), Vol. XXXI, No. 39, September 28, 1979, pp. 1238-41.*

* * *

DELANY, Samuel R. 1942-

An American science fiction novelist and short story writer, Delany is an experimental writer who calls his works "speculative" fictions. He has been awarded science fiction's Nebula Award four times. (See also *CLC*, Vol. 8, and *Contemporary Authors*, Vols. 81-84.)

MICHAEL GOODWIN

Samuel Delany has been the cutting edge of the SF revolution for more than ten years. He works within the traditional SF iconography (i.e., spaceships and cyborgs), but his characters come straight from Desolation Row.

Triton is set in a sort of sexual utopia, where every form of sexual behavior is accepted, and sex-change operations (not to mention "refixations," to alter sexual preference) are common. But Bron, Delany's anti-hero (who becomes, for the last quarter of the novel, an anti-heroine) doesn't know what he wants. All he knows is that he's miserable. When his lover tells him, "Your confusion hurts people," Bron replies, "Then people like me should be exterminated."

Bron's downhill drift is underscored by carefully fragmented syntax, the withholding of crucial bits of information, and a series of deliciously self-conscious set-pieces. In one, Bron enters a booth on which a sign reads: "Know Your Place In Society." The booth is supposed to display taped sequences from an individual's life, but when Bron puts in his money the tape breaks, and he doesn't even get his dough back. In another sequence, as he's reading a brutal get-lost letter from the woman he's in love with, a full-scale interplanetary war breaks out around his ears, gravity fails, and only negativity pulls him through.

Triton is an alienated, ambiguous novel. Delany's running concern with characters on the fringe of society (poets, musicians, actors and prostitutes), his stylistic departures (an incomprehensible 14-page lecture on "metalogic"), and his open bisexuality have put off many longtime SF readers. Yet Delany may very well turn out to be as important a writer as Thomas Pynchon. At the very least, he's taking up where [Theodore Sturgeon] left off; that's not very least at all. (pp. 62-3)

Michael Goodwin, "A Giant Step for Science Fiction," in Mother Jones *(copyright © 1976 by the Foundation for National Progress), Vol. I, No. VI, August, 1976, pp. 62-5.**

GEORGE EDGAR SLUSSER

The fiction of Samuel R. Delany seems a striking example of what Robert Scholes calls the "structuralist imagination." . . . Instead of reflecting some objective "reality," the fictional work is seen as primarily a word-construct, a self-contained system whose relation to our familiar world is homologous, but in no way necessary or determined by it. Both in theory and in practice, Delany's "speculative fiction" (SF) is structuralist. Delany is a rare combination of imaginative writer and articulate critic. Because both of these operations are informed by the same imagination, they are reflexive, mutually illuminating. . . . To Delany writing an SF novel is a verbal activity that is simultaneously visionary and analytical. In this sense, his claims (and his works) are far-reaching and revolutionary. Indeed, he turns the tables on the defenders of the "mainstream," for he sees his chosen (and much maligned) genre as the one, among all modern forms, most supremely suited to this structuralist task. (p. 3)

Delany makes a distinction between SF and what he calls, respectively, "naturalistic fiction" and "fantasy." This distinction is drawn in terms that are primarily linguistic (and structuralist), and repays close attention. What differentiates these two modes of fiction is not "truth to life"—which implies some absolute and determined relationship between external "reality" and words—but what Delany calls their "level of subjunctivity": "Subjunctivity is the tension on the thread of meaning that runs between word and object." The various forms are described as inflexions in tense and mood: in fantasy the events "could not have happened"; in naturalistic fiction they "could have happened"; SF is distinguished from these by the fact that events here simply "have not happened." (p. 4)

Delany's work may seem, at first, highly stylized or lushly ornate. This rigidity is merely a facade. All the various verbal screens, the disquisitions on symbolic logic, blend into a basic weave of imagery that is far more dynamic than static. Talk of paradox resolves into paradoxes, these in turn decomposing in ceaseless patterns of thrust and counterthrust. The dynamic nature of Delany's fiction comes from the fact that its central rhythm is not (as with Le Guin) binary alone, but rather continuous shifting between binary and ternary combinations, odds and evens. On all levels it is a fiction of unstable twos and broken threes: one boot, one bare foot, Prince Red's missing socket. Central to this process of change is the pivotal figure of the "intersection" —the point at which some duality, irreconcilable and unstable, intersects with a third term that suspends it. Here, as on a palimpsest (another favorite Delany image), double and triple rhythms are momentarily superimposed. Each of

Delany's major novels has its intersection: Babel-17, Goedel's Law, metalogic.

A striking example of intersection—and one which preoccupied Delany the critic long before he incorporated it into the heart of his latest novel, *Triton*—is that of utopia and "heterotopia": Michel Foucault's "other place," the "shattering" of syntax and fable, the dissolving of the cement that holds the fabric of the known world—words and things—together. (p. 7)

[Delany] sees SF as a mode of writing more akin to poetry than to the traditional realist novel. Each separate word for Delany, as for the symbolists he admires, is precious, the key to some magic world, and a value to be regenerated as it passes through new and more visionary word-systems. . . . Successively, Delany has turned to two major modes of prose fiction. First, in a series of adventures in time and space culminating in *Nova* (1968), he embraces the heroic epic. Then, after a period of experimentation which may in the long run prove to be transitional, he turns this basic pattern of the quest in the opposite direction, inward rather than out. If the conventional patterns upon which *Nova* is built are those of initiation and adventure, *Triton* (1976) works upon a different base—that of psychological fiction. Pivoting around these two novels, this study examines Delany's fiction at still a different intersection: the point where freedom to deconstruct and reconstruct worlds and the abiding conventional patterns—the narrative of deeds and the narrative of motives—meet and interact. (pp. 8-9)

Contrary to what it may seem, Delany's universe remains a human one. True, Delany has a fascination with cyborgs, catmen, and other para-human forms. Yet there is far more here than what some have seen—a cosmic freak-show. If we look closely, we see that, beneath this surface, the human form divine tenaciously resists—just as at the center of these cultural explosions that lead to the wildest, most far-flung galactic civilizations our own twentieth century earth remains the key. Once again, this relationship between human and nonhuman, man and system, functions as a dynamic series of displacements and balances. Thus the dehumanization of the human form has its counter-thrust. . . . (p. 10)

The Tides of Lust (1973) and *Dhalgren* (1975) [are] essentially transitional, elaborate fictional experiments that lead the author in a new fictional direction. . . . What is explored in these two novels is less the relation of questing man to myth than the relation of myth to the collective mind. This preoccupation is summarized in the statement (central to *Tides*) that man today has confused Faust and the Devil. From here it is only one step to exploration of a new relation—myth and the inner mind, the quest within of *Triton* (1976). . . .

In one sense, [*Triton*] reads like an elaborate refutation of the existential novel, where even personal 'bravery' becomes little more than a subjective possibility constantly placed at the intersection with some other, indifferent system of logic. *Triton* also recreates the patterns of traditional psychological fiction, and not just to parody its hero's self-searchings. This is not a case of one form distorting an older one to overthrow it, or render it obsolete. On the contrary, we have intersection, an attempt to build a new mode of fiction upon this tension between two systems of narrative logic—the traditional *fabula* and its suspension in chaos. Delany has said that the speculative writer should explore, not condemn or condone. In his treatment of the "hero" of *Triton,* however, he is brought to do both. Here as in *Nova* he is clearly aiming at creation on the level of system. And yet the very nature of the convention chosen makes this stance more difficult. Tension in this novel approaches the breaking point. (p. 11)

On one hand, Delany's concept of tragedy is expansive: man must avoid the old patterns rather than blindly repeating them; thus he learns they are not binding in any absolute way. On the other, however, his view is contractive, for his heroes still follow the old hard way, the way of tragedy. Man must repeat the patterns that both myth and literary convention have set forth for him. Again, this is not inconsistency but intersection. From it comes that curious tension that gives Delany's best work its fascination and strength. For what he creates, at this point of tautness, is a new world in which the hero is both free and bound. Out of its construction (and his awareness or lack of awareness of his state) new truths about man can perhaps be glimpsed. (p. 12)

[*The Fall of the Towers* is a trilogy of novels including] *Out of The Dead City* (originally called *Captives of the Flame*), *The Towers of Toron,* and *City of a Thousand Suns.* Despite certain excesses, *Towers* is a very accomplished piece of writing. . . . In terms of the science fiction conventions it exploits, *Towers* is a highly unusual work. It is billed as space opera. . . . [Yet it] is not a trilogy in the sense this "genre" calls for—the string of episodes, each written as a self-contained entity, and grouped in progressive fashion to mark off the steps in a hero's or society's development. On the contrary, *Towers* is clearly one novel—a long, densely-interwoven structure obviously conceived as a whole. Nor is it an "opera"—the usual panorama or "fresco" of colorful characters and events. In fact, all such spatializing terms, with their implication of surface superficiality, are inadequate here. There is, in *Towers,* a horizontal sweep, but this cross-movement is merely dynamic, not progressive. There is depth as well, not that of character or social analysis, but that of system—interlocking patterns, on many levels, engaged in ceaseless change. (pp. 12-13)

[Delaney] gives us a trilogy that, although it retains [the basic tripartite] pattern, suspends the anthropomorphic vision that traditionally lies behind it. In these three novels, neither heroes nor society evolve in any clear linear pattern. And yet, triads penetrate the texture of the work on all levels. This pattern is exploited for the dynamic ambiguity it contains; such groupings may be as easily stable as unstable. . . . In his use of the trilogy form, Delany gives us an ironic reflection of this deeper dynamic. The three titles promise a progression: Dead City, Human City, Radiant City. And in a sense, in the fall of the towers, this order is realized: the first two cities—rivals—sink so that the third can be born. Yet, in numerous counter-currents, as these three elements come together in different patterns, such order is lost. As various arrangements are played against each other, we see nothing less than the labyrinth of possibility. (p. 13)

If *Fall of the Towers* has a fault, it is a too abstract focus on the workings of this system to the exclusion of the flesh and blood people who "function" in it. Characters here are counters, little more than pieces in some great chess game.

Delany's later works, while they continue to explore the dynamics of this human structure, also build upon the individual lives that must give flesh to the system. Gradually, counters become agents, and agents become human beings who feel and suffer. What Delany discovers is that this feeling and suffering becomes a powerful variable in the system. His best fiction creatively exploits a new tension: with one eye, man may see his world as an indifferent construct, a set of patterns; with the other, however, because he remains individual and mortal, man is forced to grasp it in existential terms. (pp. 13-14)

[The] abstract interplay of parts over a vast surface is more an art of arabesque than of narration. It forces us to read *Towers* less as a story, than a system of relationships. Indeed, what Delany calls "orchestration" occurs primarily on this level. At any given point we find him ordering his patterns on two planes simultaneously—vertical and horizontal. . . . Roughly, there are two axes in *Towers*. Vertically, the intersection is situated at the point where reality meets dream—an epistemological intersection. Horizontally, the junction comes at the point where being and becoming, progression and stasis, overlap. We can call this the existential intersection.

The landscape of *Towers* has a surreal feeling, as if its texture were formed of the constant interpenetration of waking and dreaming states—the familiar world forever intersecting with something that transcends or suspends it. . . . We cannot determine whether life is a dream, or whether the dream is a mad or a sane one, until we understand how these two elements interact—the system that governs their relationships one to the other. The focus of Delany's "surreal" narrative is less on states (waking or dreaming) than on transitions—the workings of the epistemological processes by which men relate to their universe. (pp. 16-18)

[*Towers*] is a marvellously constructed work. . . . If anything, it is over-constructed. What we have essentially is a logician's design, in which both the surreal and human axes converge to expose a problem which is neither epistemological nor existential, but essentially logical in nature. (p. 27)

In *Towers* the reader sees more of the system than the characters who live it. For us the interplay of change and permanence, order and chaos, would seem to be explained by the triple rhythm: perfection, death, transition. . . . Delany's characters are only potentially interesting here—in the end, they remain counters in a vast game, puppets in the hands of the Romantic ironist. Still, *Towers* is a marvelously realized beginning, a work which thoroughly explores the dynamics of a human system. In a series of later novels, Delany will loosen the web, expand upon the minds and feelings of his heroes and heroines as they too "deal with" the random. He moves toward the much more subtle balance of man and system which will mark a work like *Nova*.

Three novels, *Babel-17* (1966), *The Einstein Intersection* (1967), and *Nova* (1968), form a whole in Delany's canon and represent what is probably his best work to date. All of these novels are relatively short. In complexity and intricacy of design, however, they equal *Towers,* and even surpass it in many respects. If the early trilogy remains abstract—an anatomy of the system that underlies human existence on both the individual and collective level—it nonetheless exposes the themes that Delany will explore in the sharper analytical focus of these later works. In *Towers,* within the coordinates of change and permanence, chaos and order, various relationships appear: language to reality, freedom to order, art to crime or violence. More firmly rooted in the destiny of an individual hero, these themes are given flesh and bones in *Babel* and its successors.

This deeper probing comes from a change of perspective, most radically visible in *Babel.* The structure contracts and polarizes around a single point—the individual and his quest. Already the world of *Towers* is strangely constricted. Its base is an isolated island world. In this small compass all the various functions of the system are potentially there; gradually, as more and more elements interconnect, the microcosm expands to fill a universe of relationships. The base upon which *Babel* rests is rather different. Here it is the individual man who reaches out to fill the space between himself and another. And the reaching out, this time, is horizontal. The form of this novel, ostensibly, is that of the linear quest.

The patterns of circle and web are of course implicit in the structure of *Towers.* In each of these new novels, however, they not only dominate, but are dominated by the hero's quest—they have become living, energized forms. . . . In the three newer novels, the questing hero has become the maker and breaker of webs. This new hero is artist as well as actor. (pp. 28-30)

In *Towers,* the function of art is merely discussed, in terms of how it orders the randomness of existence, how the pain of that ordering, the experience of order in chaos, in turn destroys the artist. *Babel* and its two successors act out the process of artistic creation itself. Each follows a similar pattern. On the surface there is action and adventure. Within these conventional forms, however, the accent shifts in a most unconventional manner—away from the external world of deeds toward a much more private battlefield, where the hero struggles to give communicable order to words. In the beginning, in Delany's universe, is the word. . . . In these novels, the hero discovers his place in the world only when he establishes solid links between word and object. . . . In these novels, the quest for meaning in a world of verbal multiplicity is simultaneously a search to control the language structure as well. Not only are the webs which are made or broken essentially verbal ones, but the shadow each character casts is primarily a language shadow. Of these, the hero's is merely the biggest and most inclusive. In the same way, his story is the biggest circle. The artist-hero solves his problem, or reaches his goal and closes the circle of action only to open another: he is ready to write the work we have just finished reading. (p. 30)

As with *Towers* (but to quite different ends), *Babel-17* takes a number of stock SF themes and situations and shapes them into a new construct. Old familiar elements are given new functions, and we are prevented from suspending disbelief, and forced to read the tale on a level both ironic and analytical. (pp. 30-1)

Fabulous hero, super-language, the final shedding of light—all these elements belong traditionally to the celebration of reason, the triumph of will. In *Babel,* however, [Delany] uses the energies of space adventure to probe a contrary notion: the divided state that resulted from just such scientific presumption—the first Babel and the fall that drove men and their languages apart. (p. 31)

Playing on [the] disparity between conventional expectations and fictional reality, Delany manipulates the reader. In *Babel,* we run the gamut of genres—from epic beginning to tragic middle to comic end. (pp. 31-2)

In accordance with its titular image, *Babel* conceives of the fall of man primarily in linguistic terms. But here too we have the *felix culpa,* for differences in language separates men, only to unite them all the more firmly in the end. (p. 32)

In *Babel* the extremes of *Towers*—perfection and death—are given a different spatial relationship: that of circle and center. The circle can be both harmony and confinement. . . . [The] image pattern—the circle with hunger at its core—is mirrored in a second configuration, the web and its weaver or breaker. Again the object stands, simultaneously, for unity and isolation, interconnectedness and entanglement. And at its center is one who joins and cuts—the artist-hero. These two central images structure the complex panorama of *Babel-17.* (pp. 34-5)

If *Babel* is not a novel of action, neither is it a novel of fatality, celebrating the web that binds men together despite their will. To control is to name. Thus the webs in *Babel* are constructs of language; as such, they can either entangle and isolate, or unite. To break this ambiguity of the web, the heroine plunges not into action but into the language system itself. She starts by exposing a web of sabotage, and ends by investigating how webs themselves are made or broken. (p. 39)

Delany's world is clearly fallen. [The] new language may seem the perfect instrument of communication. In its speakerless perfection, however, this seventeenth variation on Babel, far from reuniting men only divides them further. . . . As an abstraction, Babel-17 is dangerous precisely because it denies that diversity of language that resulted from the fall of the original tower. . . . Delany's is a fortunate fall, for the necessary condition for unity in this world seems to be the broadest possible diversity—Babelian variety itself. In this novel true union of human beings occurs only where speech centers are most disparate; communication is most creative when tension between the speakers is at a maximum. Each man, in fact, weaves his own language web. To the extent that he knows himself, each is potentially an artist. (p. 40)

The Einstein Intersection (1967) is short, but still a work of extreme complexity and resonance. Like *Babel,* it is tightly patterned; yet, in its greater suggestive power, its structures resist analysis, forcing the reader to "bite through the shells" of their meanings. *Einstein* also approaches the human condition on the level of system; but it goes somewhat deeper. . . . *Einstein* deals with the fall in terms of . . . myth. Not only is there a similar profusion and confusion of myths, but they too are seen essentially as language constructs: verbal scenarios for human action sanctioned by tradition or authority. Delany's sense of the language act, in this novel, has a broader social valence. (pp. 42-3)

[Delany seeks] to redefine what is human; instead of physical norms and mythified codes of conduct, there emerges a basic rhythm of existence. In his discussion of the Einstein intersection, Spider describes this rhythm. As he displaces these intersecting explanations of man's relationship to his physical universe into the moral sphere, he himself ironically becomes an example of this dynamic at work. . . . To establish limits is simultaneously to deny them. Each character finds himself at every minute at this Einstein intersection. In approaching humanity at this level of system, Delany turns the traditional novel of initiation and quest upside down, freeing his narrative from the tyranny of a "realism" that itself is but another myth. In this world of dynamic bipolarities, there is constant "slippage" between coordinates. . . . If the hero remains on the Einsteinian edge ("which did I choose?") his journey is a linear fact that has forced stable contours to emerge in this seemingly chaotic world. These patterns, we discover, are both familiar and eminently human. (pp. 44-5)

However provocative, *Einstein* remains (in the structuralist sense) a novel of potentiality: it separates more than it remakes. Moving parallel to the narrative present, but not touching it, are the traditional past and the future promise of form.

To a greater degree, that promise is fulfilled in *Nova* (1967). Here too is mythical adventure narrated on a "structural" level, a novel aware of itself as literary process and system. In this work, however, Delany broadens both the sweep of action and the structural coordinates themselves. *Nova* has a genuine diachronic axis, a historical dimension. Past and future provide not only a theoretical but a dynamic, evolutionary frame for the present moment. . . . *Nova* is different: the coordinates now are history and system themselves, the intersection falling on individual man in a new position. In earlier novels, to control the world one first had to name himself. Here, on this historical axis, names take on a life of their own: they are hollow masks dropped in the stream of time, the focus of change. A name is worn by a succession of individuals or peoples who discover their own identity in the process of living the one they have inherited. The central question of *Nova* is: what's in a name? (p. 53)

In its cultivation of paradoxes *Nova* is highly stylized, to the point almost of preciosity. Yet somehow the adventure story carries it—we experience love, violence, memorable actions. If these two lives balance, it is in a particular way. In developing his tale, Delany has inverted the traditional epic relationship, in which the human subject (the quest) dominates the "form." Here instead is a "subjunctive epic." Men do not struggle against an inhuman system so much as *inside* an unhuman one. At the extreme limits of patterns indifferent to human values this human "content" is re-introduced and heroic actions re-examined in a context that frees them from the anthropocentrism of views such as "glory" or "absurdity." Everywhere in *Nova* seekers after meaning or meaninglessness pass beyond to encounter the neutral dynamic of change-in-order. Instead of absurdity they find ambiguity; instead of doubt uncertainty. . . . Everything in this narrative occurs on the subjunctive level. If man is placed at the center of systems, he is haunted by the possibility that relation between the two (homological or causal) is lacking. . . . What gives *Nova* its strength is [its] reaffirmation at the indifferent heart of system of collective human action—not isolated . . . in the arena of the mind, but bursting into the cosmic one of life and death. (pp. 59-60)

[*The Tides of Lust, Dhalgren* and *Triton*] are not inferior to . . . the *Nova* cycle, but rather (as Delany might say) "different." Yet even that must be said with reserve, for the patterned dynamics of threes and twos, the intricacies of palimpsest and filagree exposed in the earlier novels are repeated here, complicated in fact to a degree many find intolerable. The question to ask, with a writer of this sophistication, is why these complications, to what end? . . . These novels investigate less man's relation to linguistic or natural systems than the role he plays as maker of chaos at the heart of a human or social system. Increasingly, Delany places shadowy, uninteresting, dubious beings at the center. (pp. 60-1)

In both *Einstein* and *Nova* the realm of action is one of crime and chaos. The compensating order is brought about by art. In these novels the intersection remains the questing hero—Lobey narrates, Lorq's example drives his companions to "speak out of the net." The protagonists of *Tides* and *Dhalgren,* however, as artists or examples, are powerless to restore order. In *Tides* traditional moral opposites, Faust and the Devil, become artist-doubles, alike in their inability to create an artistic whole: on one hand there is the primitive "log" of the Captain, on the other the decadent Proctor "doomed to restoring old work with the energy I want to put toward new." Yet the novel itself, structured from without, is elaborately circular. The ordering of triple themes (sex, time and art) is [artificial and precious]. . . . The artist remains unconcerned with morality—symmetry comes first. This novel places us not at an intersection but at a split. On a far vaster scale, *Dhalgren* does the same. Its hero is neither hero nor artist; he is unable to act or create. As protagonist in search of his name, his maze is verbal and mythical (Kidd, the Kid, Apollo and Daphne, Newboy the poet, new boy in town, Grendalgren . . .). Primarily, however, his labyrinth is moral: the landscape he wanders through is made of the scattered and shifting fragments of one life. Again, we have a highly patterned work, simultaneously circular (the final line joins the first) and linear. . . . But this form is imposed from without—within there is 900 pages of chaos, the novel as notebook, mirror of a world that is itself the projection of the hero's moral confusion. The burning city is also utopia (everything is free), racial and sexual union is structured but meaningless in terms of values, violence is inconsequential. . . . Kid enters and retreats; aesthetic balance does not bring us to pass moral judgment but to suspend it. This novel with its "brass orchids" (a poem and a weapon) is Delany's ultimate garland of flowers of evil.

Triton is more problematical—as such it clearly marks a new direction, perhaps (as with *Towers*) a retreat from preciosity toward the human and tragic implications of man-in-the-system. If so, it turns *Nova* inside out. There, as man confronts systems he didn't make, heroic vanity and collective action (by sympathy if nothing else) take on positive moral value. If *Triton* pits a man against his systems, however, it does so from inside—the struggler against nets becomes more than ever their weaver. (pp. 61-2)

The recent Delany himself seems a Triton. On one hand he pursues his arduous career as theoretician of SF—expanding the domain of his chosen genre by claiming it the modern mode of fiction *par excellence,* the one most suited to deal with the complexities of paradox and probability, chaos, irrationality, and the need for logic and order. On the other he has, in his latest novel, returned creation on the level of system to conventional SF space, and in doing so raised the problem of returning man as moral center of an overwrought universe. It is this split that runs through our "literature of exhaustion" in general. Let us hope that here, at this intersection of descriptive system and moral judgment, there will be fusion, some new form of dynamic creation. (p. 63)

George Edgar Slusser, in his The Delany Intersection: Samuel R. Delaney Considered As a Writer of Semi-Precious Words *(copyright © 1977 by George Edgar Slusser), The Borgo Press, 1977, 64 p.*

T. A. SHIPPEY

Drawing themes out of Samuel Delany's story collection *Driftglass* is made much more difficult by the author's preoccupation . . . with texture, immediacy, being-not-meaning. Just occasionally this leads to a sort of sentimentality—the self-selecting singers who make spontaneous poetry for the masses and never go commercial, the nice adventurers who relate mysteriously to the natives wherever they go and never get taken for tourists. But these icons of dropout piety are superficial reader pleasers. . . . The stories make their impact through an immense zest for complication and an unrivalled ability to crystallize this in scenes, people, and objects.

T. A. Shippey, "Natural Alternatives," in The Times Literary Supplement *(© Times Newspapers Ltd (London) 1978; reproduced from* The Times Literary Supplement *by permission), No. 3976, June 16, 1978, p. 662.**

JOHN CLUTE

The book in question is Delany's collection of critical essays and reviews called *The Jewel-Hinged Jaw; Notes of the Language of Science Fiction*. . . . [Grammatical,] stylistic and factual howlers [abound]. . . . But when one actually experiences the clotted precocity of his prose, . . . [with] its uneasy condescension and agglutinative gumminess, then the multitude of typos and other errors does seem more forgiveable, because translatorese is always hard to get a grip on; the Rube Goldberg *unworkableness* of much of the writing in this book, especially in the earlier and middle essays collected, does in fact make the task of winkling out paraphrasable content almost impossible. . . . Ultimately I failed. . . . I could not even patch together an adequate sense of what I had failed to understand; after all, as Delany does say in a clear moment, style and content are intersecting models of one another. I'm paraphrasing him. At the heart of this failure of mine—beyond the word-deaf gaucheries of the style, beyond the intrusive self-congratulatory garish foregrounding of the auctorial voice with all its morose cheeriness and duckpond aggro—lay a sense that when I *did* think I understood the terms and assumptions shaping a paragraph, by the dint of a lot of deconstruction work, what I was left with was a kind of shambles strewn with disqualified data and beheaded arguments, a spastic *Guernica*. (pp. 45-6)

Bits of the arguments about the nature of sf as opposed to "mundane" literature, though tendentious and embarrassing in their attempts to restrict the imaginative scope theoretically realizable within a "mundane" text, are at least arousing. And the late long essay on Ursula K. Le Guin's *The Dispossessed* (1974) is a brilliant demolition job. Delany is at his best when he's forced to stick close to a given text. . . . (pp. 48-9)

John Clute, "Books: 'The Jewel-Hinged Jaw; Notes of the Language of Science Fiction'," in The Magazine of Fantasy and Science Fiction *(©*

1978 by Mercury Press, Inc.; reprinted from The Magazine of Fantasy and Science Fiction*), Vol. 56, No. 1, January, 1979, pp. 45-9.*

GERALD JONAS

"Tales of Nevèrÿon" strikes me as superb science fiction, although it deals with an ancient civilization, vaguely Mediterranean in flavor and presumably antecedent to the Sumerians, Egyptians and so on. As in his earlier science-fiction novels . . . , Mr. Delany explores the ways in which politics and economics affect our sense of identity, as expressed in art, sex and other forms of play.

His principal characters . . . are memorable. But Mr. Delany never makes the mistake of treating them as autonomous. They exist, as all characters in science fiction and fantasy must, as reflections of the world they inhabit. And because that world itself is a creation of the author, we are never very far from the realization that this story, like all stories, is simply a string of words, whose relation to "reality" is always problematical. Mr. Delany confronts this issue directly in an appendix, which "explains" that the tales of [his fictive] Nevèrÿon are an expansion of a 900-word "narrative fragment" called the Culhar' Text, which may be the oldest written document ever discovered.

The reader will do well to question at least some of the "facts" cited in this appendix. In doing so, the reader may pause to wonder about the possibility of separating fact from fiction in any archeological recreation of the beginning of civilization. At this point, he may conclude that the "science" in science fiction is not always what it seems—a fruitful insight that may, all by itself, justify the arbitrary genre label. (pp. 16, 18)

Gerald Jonas, "Science Fiction: 'Tales of Nevèrÿon'," in The New York Times Book Review *(© 1979 by The New York Times Company; reprinted by permission), October 28, 1979, pp. 16, 18.*

* * *

de la ROCHE, Mazo 1885-1961

De la Roche was a Canadian novelist and playwright, best known for her series about the Whiteoak family of Jalna. Although accused by critics of exaggerated romanticism and popular escapism, de la Roche's novels continue to attract a wide readership. (See also *Contemporary Authors*, Vols. 85-88)

B. K. SANDWELL

It is just 25 years since that excellent American magazine, the *Atlantic Monthly,* having offered a very large cash prize for the best novel submitted to its editors during a year, decided to award that prize to a young author with the romantic-sounding name of Mazo de la Roche [for her new novel *Jolana*]. . . .

[It] always comes as something of a shock when an author who not merely got born in Canada but still lives there scores a first-class hit in one or other of the two larger English-language countries; and I shall not readily forget the sensation caused by the announcement of Miss de la Roche's prize. . . .

And then to our amazement she did not do it again, not of course in the shape of another gigantic prize, but at least in the shape of another highly successful novel about the same family as the first one, the first prize one; and this was followed by a whole series of novels, until the Whiteoaks family has become one of the great imaginary families of the world, something like the clerical families in Trollope or the rather less religious families in Balzac, and is known not only to the English-speaking world but also to vast numbers of others who can read about it in translations. . . .

When it became obvious that the Jalna series could not be written off as a lucky accident but would have to be accepted as one of the great literary creations of the second quarter of the century, some of my Canadian friends began to find another fault with it; it was not "Canadian." It is true that none of the Whiteoaks family bear much resemblance to Jack Canuck, or to Old Man Ontario as depicted in a Toronto *Star* cartoon. But that is a rather limited concept of Canadianism, and one the acceptance of which would seriously hamper the scope of any Canadian writer of fiction. . . .

[We] know that Miss de la Roche is by no means limited to the Whiteoaks family in her powers of creation. She has written about many other and quite different kinds of people, and her next volume, which will shortly be in our hands, and which is entitled "A Boy in the House," has nothing to do with Jalna at all. Yet its title is thoroughly and perfectly Mazonian. What fascinates her as material for fiction is not the casual relationships which we develop with those whom we meet in business, in social intercourse, in professional contacts and the like, but the tight and often tense relationships which develop between people who are willy-nilly spending a good deal of their lives in one another's pockets. The house is the symbol of the things that tie us together in these tight family bundles, the pressures that we not only cannot escape but do not want to escape. It is significant that the word "house" or the name of a house occurs so often in her titles. It need not be Jalna, but wherever it is the household is the unit she studies, the forces that play within it are the warp and woof of her tale.

B. K. Sandwell "The Work of Mazo de la Roche," in Saturday Night *(copyright © 1952 by* Saturday Night*), Vol. 68, No. 5, November 8, 1952, p. 7.*

GEORGE HENDRICK

Jalna contains virtually everything which was included in [Miss de la Roche's] later novels. . . . (p. 60)

[Her] audience was one that much admired ornate style. Her readers were obviously entertained by [*Jalna*'s] appeal to snobbery, its romanticism, its erotic scenes, and its titillating incidents. All of these help to explain the popularity of *Jalna* and the novels which followed it.

Jalna began with a genealogical chart listing the twenty-or-so members of the Whiteoak family who were to be prominent characters in the novel, plus a few often-referred-to deceased members. Given this large cast of characters, the story inevitably moves ponderously. . . .

Since the outside world does not really intrude on the Whiteoaks, the scandal of their lives is heightened. There is great stress on family tradition and a justification of Anglo-Saxon snobbery. The Whiteoaks are praised inordinately, both for their strengths and for their weaknesses. Though their sexual activities are as plentiful and fanciful as those of the lower classes on the fringes of their lives, the Whiteoak family scandal assumes respectability. The Whiteoaks are, after all, landed gentry. . . . (p. 61)

[*Jalna*] is in fact, a glorification of much the same life, lacking only slaves, that Margaret Mitchell pictured in the beginning of *Gone With the Wind.* As befits such a legend, Captain Whiteoak was handsome; his wife was imperious and headstrong.

In keeping with English domestic drama, Miss de la Roche has many of the scenes played out at dinner or at teatime. Conversations run on rather interminably, for each member at the table or fireside is talkative and is put through his paces, performing in a highly predictable fashion, once one has grasped (and one does so easily) the character's personality. (p. 62)

Artistically, Miss de la Roche had come to a most advantageous place to end her Jalna saga [including *Jalna, Whiteoaks of Jalna,* and *Finch's Fortune*]. But with the urging of publishers and readers, she chose not to do so.

Miss de la Roche began to realize that if she wanted to go on making her living off the Whiteoaks, she needed to deal with them not only in the near present but also in the past; that is, before the beginning of the first volume of the series [and so she wrote the six books which present the Whiteoaks' history before *Jalna*]. (p. 68)

While most of the volumes, after the first three in the series, are certainly less fresh, they contain scattered incidents which are of some interest: there are scenes of comic relief and occasional good dramatic episodes; there is an embarrassing imitation of *Jane Eyre;* there is shameless exploitation of the American Civil War and a glossing over of the 1930's; there is a total immersion in Playland; and there are touches of incest and sadism. There is no real indication, however, that Miss de la Roche's narrative style or artistic understanding were much different in 1960 than in 1927. If her literary abilities progressed at all, the direction was downward. (p. 69)

Miss de la Roche was clearly captive of her own fantasy world, her publishers, and her public. She had no delusions about the "importance" of her Jalna novels. . . . (p. 114)

But the question remains: was she aware of what makes the readers interested? Clearly she had several groups of readers. Lonely ranchers' wives in Wyoming and teen-aged girls in Canberra found the novels appealing in different ways. For the frustrated woman, hungering for a virile male, Miss de la Roche could offer Renny, who smelled of the stables but was found irresistible by the neighboring ladies. For high-school girls, she could offer escape into a fantasy world far different from dull parents and staid schools. For garden-club types, yearning after culture, she offered various artistic types: Finch, the musician; Eden, the poet; and Wakefield, actor and playwright—three artists idealized and exaggerated. The culturally hungry could feel they had partaken of some of the so-called glamor of the bohemian world. Philistines, on the other hand, could feel superior, but at the same time they could relish descriptions of Eden's troubled life, his affair with Pheasant, his losing his first wife to Renny, his illegitimate daughter. Philistines could cluck over Wakefield's incestuous attachment to Renny's natural daughter, and they could be properly aroused by Finch's sadistic son and by the horrible deaths of Finch's wives. (pp. 114-15)

In *Morning at Jalna,* her last and perhaps worst novel, she added the American Civil War to her saga, no small feat since even southern Ontario is a long way from the South. . . . [However], it was hard to burn Atlanta from Ontario. Her attempt to exploit the Civil War was a complete fiasco.

To those readers unable or unwilling to grapple with the subtleties of a Henry James, or a James Joyce, Miss de la Roche offered an easy-to-read story and strong characterizations. (p. 116)

Miss de la Roche was interested in telling a story, and her prose was a means to this end. She obviously did not labor over her style, did not experiment, did not strive for organic imagery. She concentrated on a lively narrative and concerned herself with characters and episodes which held the reader's attention. Her readers clearly approved of her approach to literature. Over twelve million copies of the Whiteoak volumes . . . have been sold; it is evident that Miss de la Roche found the key to popular success and that she fulfilled a public need. She entertained a huge audience. (p. 117)

Even after *Jalna,* Miss de la Roche's success with non-Whiteoak fiction and non-fiction was not what she hoped for. Her short stories and novels, children's stories and autobiographies were published; and some readers, no doubt out of loyalty, did buy and read them, reviewers did take notice of them, but the reception was generally cool. Miss de la Roche was fond of some of these failures, and thought they were quite well done, but none of them were artistic achievements; they were not the great works of art popular writers often say they *really* want to be producing, if only they were not forced to write what the public wanted. (p. 119)

In *Lark Ascending* the Whiteoaks were temporarily abandoned, but she continued the tradition of presenting passionate, strong-willed characters caught in various love poses. She obviously hoped that her romantic characters gamboling about romantic Sicily would also enthrall the legion of Whiteoak fans. (p. 120)

Miss de la Roche's primary concern [in *Lark Ascending*] was showing the clash of American and European cultures. She was trying to write an International Novel. To find that she failed is hardly surprising.

She was an expatriate for ten years; and, had she kept on working on serious themes instead of the hermetically sealed world of the Whiteoaks, she might have written an International Novel of value. The novel she did write, however, had several interesting themes, though they were never explored and were largely covered over with romantic claptrap. (p. 121)

As *The New York Times* reviewer noted on August 14, 1932, *Lark Ascending* is a "cheerful book" which lacks depth and craft. One must conclude that the characters are not motivated and that the many serious and frivolous themes are introduced and never really examined. Miss de la Roche could have moulded this material into an international comedy of manners, but the melodrama of the adolescent Play [her youthful fantasy game] made this impossible. In truth, Miss de la Roche had a sense of humor but rarely a sense of comedy. (p. 124)

[*Lark Ascending*] must be relegated to the merely ludicrous, and . . . much of the fiction that follows is of no higher quality. . . . (p. 125)

Unfortunately Miss de la Roche did not peer deeply into the world of early childhood [in her book about her adopted children, *Beside a Norman Tower*]. What she did write was an episodic account of certain scenes in which the children appear as rather pert actors. There is no controlling point of view; there is no entry into the minds of the children; there is, instead, a series of "cute" stories; as a result the book is an inane failure. (p. 130)

Ringing the Changes: An Autobiography (1957) was one of those peculiar Victorian-flavored documents which tell more and less than the author intended. The most intriguing sections of the memoirs dealt with the Play. (p. 133)

Except for the description of the Play and its meaning in her artistic life, the memoirs are extremely peculiar. Scenes are presented in such dramatic fashion that it is clear a novelist with a romantic imagination has improved upon them greatly. Most of the dramatized scenes are set in a timeless world, as if the author were perpetually fifteen; it is virtually impossible to date any happening described. In Victorian tradition, the description of the emotional bonds [between members of her family] are presented in a naïve, girlish fashion. Did Miss de la Roche deliberately reject modern psychology; and, in doing so, did she not reveal more than she intended?

The description of her creative life is most unsatisfactory. If Miss de la Roche had worked out esthetic concepts, she was not able to formulate them when writing her memoirs. Her greatest skill was in telling stories for romantically-inclined readers, and esthetic views would perhaps have ruined this ability of hers. (pp. 133-34)

[Her] fans wanted to read about the Whiteoaks and largely ignored her non-Jalna fiction. Her audience was perceptive: the Jalna stories (except for *Delight*) are certainly more entertaining than Miss de la Roche's other writings. She had no major themes, made no profound comments on the human condition. (p. 135)

She may not have written works as critically acclaimed as the Brontës, Dickens, and Galsworthy, but she clearly gave much pleasure to millions of readers. Such an achievement is, in itself, significant. (p. 136)

George Hendrick, in his Mazo de la Roche *(copyright © 1970 by Twayne Publishers, Inc.; reprinted with the permission of Twayne Publishers, A Division of G. K. Hall & Co., Boston), Twayne, 1970, 149 p.*

DOUGLAS M. DAYMOND

Although the success of the Jalna novels has tended to overshadow [de la Roche's] earlier works, they represent some of [her] most interesting writing and suggest the principal characteristics of all her work and the nature of her contribution to the development of the Canadian novel. At a time when Canadian fiction was dominated by historical novels and sentimental stories of village and rural life, de la Roche challenged the code of conduct associated with Victorian morality and dramatized the tension between instinct and convention. *Possession,* her first and in many respects one of her most successful novels, reveals her efforts to turn away from the typical local colour story and to temper the essentially pleasant world of escape with realism.

Possession is a mixture of elements of the romance and the novel. On the one hand, the lively and convincing presentation of highly individualistic characters, the immediacy with which domestic action is dramatized, the absence of a stable conclusion, and the realistic scenes depicting the way of life at Grimstone, contribute to the feeling of realism. On the other hand, the episodic nature of events, the sudden shifting from melodramatic confrontations to comic or pastoral scenes, the artificiality of some of the dialogue, and the emphasis on individual freedom and instinct, suggest the extent to which elements identified with the romance are incorporated in the novel. The result is romantic realism or . . . a "romance novel" in which the strict realism of the naturalist is blended with a conception of character and plot which is often sentimental and romantic. (p. 87)

Possession is divided into two parts which are equal in length though somewhat different in tone and development. The first twelve chapters, more tightly constructed and realistic, concern the experiences of Derek Vale. . . . In the following episodes, less credible twists of plot as well as romantic and sentimental vignettes tend to slow the novel's development until the sudden and somewhat unconvincing departure of Derek's Indian wife and the death of their child. (p. 89)

The theme of ownership and the ironies attached to it permeate *Possession.* Among the most interesting groups of characters in the novel are the original owners of the Grimstone estate, Indian families like the Sharroes and the Rains who have been forced to become itinerant fruit pickers. Their fate is implied in their way of life. . . . (p. 90)

The realization of the social landscape of the Grimstone region is supported by the presentation of the physical setting. *Possession* reveals de la Roche's sensitivity to this setting as well as her talent for sketching the landscape and her use of it as a means of reinforcing mood. In general, her descriptive passages are relatively short and often serve as introductions to episodes or as breaks in the narrative. The most convincing descriptions reveal a particular feeling for seasonal change. . . . (pp. 90-1)

Although the early chapters of *Possession* focus on Derek's experiences as a novice farmer, attention is increasingly directed toward his involvement with two women. Grace Jerrold and Fawnie Sharroe. . . . This traingle is carefully developed and creates the central tension in the novel—conflicting appeals of instinct and convention. (p. 91)

The contrast between Fawnie and Grace is the most fully developed of several contrasts in *Possession* which emphasize the primitive and instinctual as opposed to the civilized and conventional. (p. 93)

Possession is the first novel by a writer who was to become one of the most popular and prolific of Canadian novelists. Despite its limitations, *Possession* marks Mazo de la Roche as a prominent figure in the movement toward realism that characterized the Canadian novel in the early decades of the twentieth century. (p. 94)

Douglas M. Daymond, "'Possession': Realism in Mazo de la Roche's First Novel," in Journal of Canadian Fiction *(reprinted by permission from* Journal of Canadian Fiction, *2050 Mackay St., Montreal, Quebec H3G 2J1, Canada), Vol. IV, No. 3, 1975, pp. 87-94.*

JO-ANN FELLOWS

The Jalna novels are a fictional expression of [the Loyalist

Myth]. . . . The Jalna novels describe obliquely some very basic ideas of the Canadian national identity, at least of the English-speaking identity. Leaving aside a consideration of the novels as literature, they provide a most interesting source for the student of social and intellectual history.

From the time that Philip Whiteoak and his young bride emigrated to Southern Ontario . . . , the family accepted intrinsically the idea that they held a certain position in society. This position was one of a kind of squirearchy, or to quote de la Roche, the Courts and Whiteoaks were "gentlemen, soldiers, 'goddamming' country squires." The family dominates the immediate neighbourhood—which means that they claimed a kind of feudal authority over a small, miscellaneous collection of country bumpkins, maiden ladies of humble means, the local clergymen and a few farm hands. (p. 284)

The elemental, basic quality of the authority exercised by the Whiteoaks is repeated often in the books. It is organic and timeless, based on the family group, the tribe, the clan and eventually the kingdom, with a religious re-inforcement. . . . The maintenance and the function of the family on the basis of these forces is the most important value in the novels. This authority demands a limiting of the choices available to the individuals in the family, but it is also provides for mutual protection and responsibility. (p. 286)

It is interesting that for all the obvious praise of "Britishness" in the book, de la Roche draws a romantic, vibrant young American woman on one side and offers for the British opposition, Aunt Augusta, old, quarrelsome and rather stupid. Aunt Augusta puts on superior airs that the other members of Jalna do not like and she makes occasional cracks about "colonials". The main contradiction of the Loyalist inheritance is illustrated in this comparison. The Loyalist tradition admired British ways and institutions but not necessarily the British. (p. 287)

The Whiteoaks . . . are not as important as the place itself, Jalna, and it is significant that Mazo de la Roche so titled the first novel in the series. The house and the land represent the traditions that are maintained, albeit in rather a run-down state, in the face of urban development, of the profit motive and of increasingly democratic political institutions. . . .

The novels are a kind of cross between those of Faulkner and those of the Brontë sisters. The decay of a regional culture is aptly illustrated, and the flight into fantasy in the maintenance of the set of values that have lost their validity is obvious. Jalna and its neighbourhood are gorgeously unrealistic. The novels describe a world that has internal consistency, but that is decidedly detached from the real world. Jalna is an ideal, a kind of regional type, but it has no real connection to the hinterland and specifically, since mention is made occasionally of realistic details, to North America in the first half of the twentieth century. Jalna is a dream world with more similarities to Xanadu or Shangri-la than to Southern Ontario.

Jalna is the Loyalist Myth. It is the dream of the descendants and followers of the United Empire Loyalists. The family is of primary importance. Everything is subservient to the maintenance of strong family ties, and behind this feeling of kinship lurks the basic, fundamental feelings of a clan or kingdom or any sort of organization based on a hierarchical authority and a respect for inherited power and position. (p. 288)

Jo-Ann Fellows, "The 'British Connection' in the Jalna Novels of Mazo de la Roche: The Loyalist Myth Revisited," in The Dalhousie Review, *Vol. 56, No. 2, Summer, 1976, pp. 283-90.*

* * *

DIDION, Joan 1934-

Didion is an American novelist, short story writer, essayist, journalist, and editor. Her work depicts without false sentimentality and in prose noted for its intensity and elegance the fragmentation of societal institutions and values. (See also *CLC*, Vols. 1, 3, 8, and *Contemporary Authors*, Vols. 5-8, rev. ed.)

JOHN LEONARD

["The White Album" is] full of Miss Didion, the dreamer of bad dreams. Doris Lessing, she says, registers "every tremor along her emotional fault system." So does Miss Didion—the migraine headaches; the "vertigo and nausea;" the "condition" that has "the kind of name usually associated with telethons;" the contemplated divorce; the bottle of bourbon in the hotel room; the dread in the sunlight; an inexplicable desire to be in Honolulu; her conviction that "narrative" no longer suffices, the script has been mislaid, happy conclusions are impossible, certain images refuse to make sense, and life ends up like so many feet of film on the cutting-room floor of a movie never finished. Her nervous system is a San Andreas Fault. (pp. 269-70)

"The White Album" is full of Miss Didion as a reporter and a Californian. Perhaps because her last two novels, "Play It as It Lays" and "A Book of Common Prayer," were so sinister and deracinated, so daunting in their stare at the soul, I forgot what a splendid reporter she is. The self is always there but, unlike too much New Journalism, so are the facts—on orchid breeding, on the theory of the shopping mall, on how water moves around in aqueducts, on Bogotá and the Hoover Dam. . . .

The reporter, the Californian and the sleep walker with bad dreams conspire in "The White Album"—the very mood of dread in the sunlight—at a cyanide lollipop. It is as if the absurd and the irrational were harder to bear under a blue sky, with the temperature in the 70's. (See Camus.) Violence, instead of opinion, crackles but doesn't short out. No wonder she wants to eat lunch in a greenhouse. Language is her seismograph and style her sanity. Nobody writes better English prose than Joan Didion. Try to rearrange one of her sentences, and you've realized that the sentence was inevitable, a hologram. . . .

[Miss Didion] experiences precisely that "fracturing of a sensibility" she finds in Doris Lessing. Mrs. Lessing continues to burrow toward a solution; Miss Didion, alas, settles for fragments. But what brilliant fragments! It is as if some clever editor at Trend Magazine had assigned Samuel Beckett to write a series of articles on the dazzling blankness where we live. (p. 270)

John Leonard, "'The White Album'," in The New York Times, *Section III © 1979 by The New York Times Company; reprinted by permission), June 5, 1979 (and reprinted in* Books of the Times, *Vol. II, No. 6, 1979, pp. 269-70).*

ANNE TYLER

Admirers of *Slouching Towards Bethlehem,* Joan Didion's

first collection of essays, will recognize at once her skewed, wry world, which often resembles the setting for a story by Donald Barthelme. *The White Album,* her second collection, is a kind of battle report from the '60s—brief notes from someone who manages to be an outsider, observing dispassionately, even when she is wounded in the crossfire. (p. C1)

Unease, foreboding and even terror color Joan Didion's perceptions of the '60s, but something cool and still in her voice prevents *The White Album* from being too disturbing to read. It's as if she were gazing through the wrong end of a telescope. Describing a man's intrusion into her house, she says, "We looked at each other for what seemed a long time, and then he saw my husband on the stair landing. 'Chicken Delight,' he said finally, but we had ordered no Chicken Delight, nor was he carrying any. I took the license number of his panel truck. It seems to me now that during those years I was always writing down the license numbers of panel trucks. . . . I put [them] in a dressing-table drawer where they could be found by the police when the time came." Her grave style of speech lends the scene an eerie motionlessness. We share her apprehensions, . . . but this is something oddly finer and more tightly focused than our own experiences. In a strange way, it's even funny; ourselves, our times, our bogeymen written up as anthropological curiosities. (pp. C1, C6)

Some phrases in *The White Album* are so exact, so supremely accurate, that you almost hear a little *clink!* as they fall into place. . . .

A warning: this is not a book to read at one sitting. The very tone that is so appealing—the ironic voice, the distance—can distance even the reader, if it goes on too long at a stretch. On what remote cliff is this person standing, anyhow? we begin to wonder. What would she not view from outside? It's best to read these essays as they were written: one by one, slowly, reflectively—like very good olives. Properly savored, *The White Album* is a true satisfaction. (p. C6)

Anne Tyler, "California Nightmares," in Book World—The Washington Post *(© 1979,* The Washington Post*), June 17, 1979, pp. C1, C6.*

ANNE HULBERT

The "temperamentally unobtrusive" reporter of a decade ago is now a literary figure who is taking her own pulse in her pages, not just observing American styles and states of mind. And that pulse is racing with anxiety. In the title essay of [*The White Album*] Didion announces "I began to doubt the premises of all the stories I had ever told myself." . . . Obsessed by this radical disorder, Didion writes in an intense and agitated style—the style of the haunted characters of her novels. Instead of the often insightful, ironic, deft stories of her first collection, her new essays tend to lose their shape and sharpness in her angst.

The world outside this new and larger self in *The White Album* looks strikingly familiar. In most of the essays . . . Didion is still writing about the 1960s, and the golden land. But the revealing stories, the little ironies she once found in the 1960s aren't there anymore. Janis Joplin, Eldridge Cleaver, Huey Newton, Hollywood people, music people, students demonstrating, bizarre murders—the old cast, the old dramas—flash quickly in and out, signifying very little. If Didion serves up the bewildering 1960s warmed over and without neat narrative lines, her literary imagination resumes its exertions when she writes about California. (p. 35)

But this collection of essays is not mainly about society, the 1960s or the California style. It is the woman who grew up "convinced that the heart of darkness lay not in some error of social organization but in man's own blood" who is at the heart of this dark book. . . .

If it seems presumptuous that Didion feels no need to offer any justifications for sharing her nightmares, it turns out not to be very enlightening when she tries to. When she announces that she and her husband are in Hawaii "in lieu of filing for divorce," she immediately takes off on an explanation of this confidence (not nearly the most noteworthy of her many):

> I tell you this not as an aimless revelation but because I want you to know, as you read me, precisely who I am and where I am and what is on my mind. I want you to understand exactly what you are getting: you are getting a woman who for some time now has felt radically separated from most of the ideas that seem to interest other people. You are getting a woman who somewhere along the line misplaced whatever slight faith she ever had in the social contract, in the meliorative principle, in the whole grand pattern of human endeavor.

What, *precisely,* is this torrent supposed to tell us? . . . What is all this about? Is Didion chastising herself for her past "stylish shell-games," making people Michelins to their time and place, or is she trying to say something about her vision of the ultimately personal nature of experience, and if so, what? This radical confusion about why Joan Didion is baring her soul is not the best way to trick us into reading her dreams. In fact, we don't even want or need tricks; I think we just want to know *why* Didion wants to expose such raw, private experience, to feel that we are walking around with her bad dreams for some other reason than that she's self-indulgent and we're morbidly curious. . . . Apparently writing about herself is more of an ordeal than a release for Didion. And since she has said she doesn't expect anyone else to enjoy reading her dark dreams, it's puzzling and disconcerting that she has made them the grim feature story of this collection. (p. 36)

Anne Hulbert, "Books and the Arts: 'The White Album'," in The New Republic *(reprinted by permission of* The New Republic; *© 1979 The New Republic, Inc.), Vol. 180, No. 25, June 23, 1979, pp. 35-6.*

DAPHNE MERKIN

Try to imagine Franz Kafka speeding along a California freeway, or sitting around with some rock musicians, or lolling on a Honolulu beach. You can't quite, can you? Nevertheless, such images—in their very incongruity—pinpoint the *what-is-wrong-with-this-picture?* feeling I had while reading Joan Didion's new collection of essays, *The White Album*. . . . I was tempted to dismiss the sensation altogether: Maybe the problem resided with me, rather than Didion, who is, after all, a very good writer. But it lingered and I had to pay attention.

The author, I finally realized, is the purveyor of a very streamlined model of *angst*. Like tubular furniture, there are no cumbersome appendages or unnecessary details. Everything is pared down for maximal depressive effect. . . . [This way of arranging reality] is not, at any rate, in itself objectionable as a style. It worked, for instance, supremely to her advantage in her first collection of pieces, *Slouching Towards Bethlehem*, and it has worked intermittently well in her three novels. It has ceased to work, most of the time, in *The White Album*. The *angst* is no longer believable; it has become too savvy and too clean. The famed delicacy of nerves . . . is now completely strategic. Calculated from first to last, her frailty is mere intellectual teasing. . . .

Like all great teasers, Didion nonetheless gets what she wants; her insistent vulnerability exercises—and this is the cunning of it—a tyranny of its own: We are not to hold her to anything, for migraine-ridden as she is, it is a wonder she is able to jot down her thoughts at all. She can still make the most astringent of judgments when she pleases. . . . When she doesn't feel up to drawing conclusions, however, she starts to act dazed-and-breathless, in the manner of Marilyn Monroe. (p. 16)

That Didion invests the fictional world of "the invisible city" with greater drama and authority than the real world is hardly surprising. . . . Yet the fact is that Joan Didion is a successful writer, with her wits firmly about her. Thus I cannot help finding her empathy with the nonfictional Maria [of *Play It As It Lays*] ultimately sinister in its inventiveness, if only because it so blithely overlooks the actual misbegotten instance for the sake of a dubious poetics. "We tell ourselves stories in order to live," Didion proclaims in her opening line; fine and well, but it is imperative that we differentiate between our stories and real lives.

What it comes down to in the end, I think, is a question of declaring one's ground. Can you honestly claim to be peering over the abyss from first-class cabins and suites in the Royal Hawaiian? . . . [Bluntly] honed juxtapositions clue the reader only into Didion's ambivalence about the world of moneyed pleasure, how she condescends to it, how she desires it and how she manages to play every angle every which way by inserting different parts of herself at different lulls in the action. Sometimes things become too confusing, even for so provisional a sensibility as hers, but when that happens she simply turns around and shapes a manifesto out of the confusion. . . .

It may be an indication of our times that Didion is to be found observing the contemporary wreckage—the misfits, the failed public projects, the unmitigated boredom—from the toniest of surroundings. Her imagination is exceedingly modern in being disaster-prone, yet also modern in ruthlessly appropriating the journalistic-voyeuristic elements of disaster and then retreating into irony, safely removed from the social and political implications. . . .

I am simply not convinced that Didion's radar-like attunement to fringe people and marginal situations is evidence of a profound response to anxiety. Rather, it seems to be a kind of magical displacement, an inverted stroking of the rabbit's foot: In you're busy keeping track of misery, maybe it won't happen to you.

Having said all this, I would like to note that Didion as a writer has little to fear from the competition. She is an expert listener and her snatches of conversation or overheard dialogue are like no one else's. . . . And she has about her a genuine receptivity to the odd nuances in seemingly straightforward occurrences that makes for an undeniable originality of perspective.

When Didion is good . . . she is very good, primarily because she has an uncanny ability to translate essentially private fascinations into matters of compelling general interest. When Didion is bad, when she is whistling her tune of High Weariness and coining phrases of disengagement that sound as if they were lifted not from Kafka but from the Top 40—"I lost track of information. I was blitzed by opinion" ("On the Road")—she is horrid. (p. 17)

Daphne Merkin, "Didion Looking Down," in The New Leader *(© 1979 by the American Labor Conference on International Affairs, Inc.), Vol. LXII, No. 15, July 30, 1979, pp. 16-17.*

BARBARA GRIZZUTI HARRISON

When I am asked why I do not find Joan Didion appealing, I am tempted to answer—not entirely facetiously—that my charity does not naturally extend itself to someone whose lavender love seats match exactly the potted orchids on her mantle, someone who has porcelain elephant end tables, someone who has chosen to burden her adopted daughter with the name Quintana Roo; I am disinclined to find endearing a chronicler of the 1960s who is beset by migraines that can be triggered by her decorator's having pleated instead of gathered her new dining-room curtains. These, and other assorted facts. . . . put me more in mind of a neurasthenic Cher than of a writer who has been called America's finest woman prose stylist. . . .

[In "Some Dreamers of the Golden Dream" from *Slouching Towards Bethlehem*] Didion reports, or purports to report, on the murder case of one Lucille Maxwell Miller, who was convicted by the State of California of having killed her husband by dousing him with gasoline and allowing him to burn to death while he slept in a Volkswagen she had been driving.

Until I sat down to write this essay, I could not, in fact, remember whether Lucille Maxwell Miller had been convicted or acquitted. Now, unlike the heroines of Didion's fiction, I do not regard memory as an affliction; I remember. I remember in part because I have no choice, but also in part because (unlike Didion's heroines, whose fate depends less upon memory and volition than upon selective amnesia), I believe that without memory there is no civilization. To complain ("I am so tired of remembering things") of remembering is to express a wish to be dead, to return to some pre-Edenic state in which good and evil, right and wrong, do not exist. It is a wish to erase, not only one's personal painful past but our collective past—which, in turn, is an invitation to believe that we cannot, individually or collectively, affect the present or the future.

I remember; so why didn't I remember what was surely a salient fact to Lucille Maxwell Miller if not to Ms. Didion? The reason—and I ask you to understand that this is directly related to lavender pillows and matching lavender orchids—is that Didion was not in truth engaged in reporting about Lucille Maxwell Miller; Didion was reporting on Didion's sensibility, which in this essay, as in all her essays, assumes more importance than, say, the existence of the electric chair. . . . The crime for which Didion indicts

Lucille Maxwell Miller is of being tacky—of not, that is, being Didion. This, you see, is where the lavender pillows come in: The body of Lucille Maxwell Miller's husband—burned black—offends Didion less than the fact that Lucille Maxwell Miller wore hair curlers. It isn't Didion's sense of morality that has suffered a blow, it's her sense of style. . . . Which is why, although I have nothing in principle against pretty houses or lavender love seats, Ms. Didion's lyrical *Angst* strikes me as transparently ersatz. . . .

Didion's "style" is a bag of tricks. Some of the effects she produces are quite pretty, even momentarily beautiful. But make no mistake: These are tricks—techniques—that can be learned (I don't know why they have evoked so much wonder). If, for example, I put Al Capone and sweet williams in the same sentence, I can be fairly sure that a certain number of readers will be jolted by the juxtaposition—their eyes will cross, and they will assume that they are in the presence of genius. They will be wrong, of course, because unless I use this technique to draw them into meaning, I will have cheated them. . . . And, as Didion will gladly acknowledge, she is interested only in the *what* (the "empirical evidence"), not in the *why*.

Didion uses the Capone-sweet williams trick often, sometimes with dazzling effect. . . . (p. 277)

[The] juxtaposition of nihilism with all the ripeness and plenitude of the physical world—the emptiness/cornucopia syndrome—is what passes for style. . . .

(I am also not unaware of the danger of confusing Didion with the narrators of her novels. I am aware of the danger, but I discount it, because the sensibility of her female narrators is indistinguishable from that which informs her essays.) . . .

Here is another kind of trick, a trick used to round off a paragraph or an essay that threatens to be going nowhere. From *The White Album:* "James Jones had known a great simple truth: the Army was nothing more than life itself." Nonsense. Tell it to the Marines. Look hard at that capricious sentence, and it wilts—for the very good reason that there is no truth in it, only contrivance. . . . Actually, as I think about it, it's worse than that: There is just enough truth in that sentence for it to slip by unnoticed. Sentences that contain half-truths should not be allowed to slip by unnoticed. (p. 278)

Didion makes it a point of honor not to struggle for meaning. (I have yet to meet anyone who has offered a satisfactory explanation for the first and last sentences of *A Book of Common Prayer:* "I will be her witness." "I have not been the witness I wanted to be." Witness to what? one asks. Some ask. I no longer ask.) I do not require that a novelist eradicate all mystery, which is in any case impossible. . . . Compare the sensibility of the existentialists to that of Didion—which also stems from the 1950s—because while Didion chooses to call attention to that which is ludicrous (Huey Newton spouting rhetoric), the existentialists, and Camus in particular, chose to call attention to that which was and is tragically absurd. The difference between the ludicrous and the absurd is the difference between the mirror (Didion) and the void (Camus). Reports from the mirror are likely to be jaundiced, puling and debilitating; reports from the void can, not so strangely if you think about it long enough, inspire courage and the will to act. You will remember that transcendent moment when Camus's Sisyphus, bound to his absurd fate, poised on top of the mountain, sees his rock, his burden, plummet to the earth; at that moment, lucid and aware, Sisyphus knows that he will once again and forever push the rock, the burden, up the mountain; but in that moment, wrestling with meaning, he becomes truly human. The essence of human dignity resides in that struggle for meaning. (pp. 278-79)

Now listen to Didion:

"I prefer not to know."

"The meaning continues to elude me."

"Nothing applies."

"Trying to find some order, a pattern, I found none." . . .

Nothing matters, Didion writes. What one hears is, "Only what I have to tell you matters." And, for Didion, only surfaces matter. . . .

Part of Didion's appeal, I am convinced, lies in her refusal to forge connections (notably between the personal and the political or between the personal and the transcendental). In spite of the sense of dread that suffuses her work, it contains this implied message of (false) comfort: If Didion—who is so awfully smart—doesn't trouble to make connections, why should we? (p. 279)

While I am sure that Didion would deny that she romanticizes insanity . . . , her revulsion against the struggle for meaning is so overwhelming that, in the world of her fiction, only the cruel, the blindly sentimental, or the mad are functional and/or attempt to interpret data or analyze facts. . . . [What Didion] romanticizes is privilege and terminal lassitude. What contempt Didion has for those who "look for the sermon in the suicide, for the social or moral lesson," for those who "interpret what we see"! For Didion, the *only* appropriate response to suicide, revolution, to all the ills the flesh is heir to, is "vertigo," "nausea." (pp. 279-80)

Didion is interested in "personalities." And she reduces politics to personalities. She has been called a minimalist; better to think of her as a trivializer. . . . [For example,] when she reports—selectively and superficially—on the Black Panthers, on campus disorders, she zeroes in on the most foolish of spokespersons, making a mockery of the causes that inspired good men to good action by ridiculing the worst of the best. (p. 280)

To assert that there was much about the 1960s that was bizarre, ludicrous, hedonistic and muddle-headed is like coming out in favor of white wine in carafes and fresh daisies—most of us recognize the obvious when we see it. Many of Didion's observations about the self-serving "children" of the 1960s are dead accurate; but that doesn't give her the right to fiddle while Watts burns. (pp. 281-82)

"Of course," Didion says, pandering to our worst instincts, our careless and selfish desires for political quietude, "we would all like to 'believe' in something, like to assuage our private guilts in public causes, like to lose our tiresome selves." The essay in which that sentence appears was written in 1965: Vietnam. In 1965, Didion told us that "all the ad hoc committees, all the picket lines, all the brave signatures in *The New York Times* . . . do not confer upon anyone any ipso facto virtue." Well, whoever said they did? Believing as I do in original sin, I am not so crazed or so simple-minded as to believe that human nature can be redeemed by an act of Congress; but I also believe that the consequences of not acting are as drastic as the consequences of acting: One marched because it was right and fitting to do so, and one allowed Providence to handle the rest. . . .

I think it's fine and dandy to poke fun at radical chic—I rather like it when someone like John Simon does it, because, say what you will about Simon, he operates from a moral base, however eccentric, and he includes the words *right* and *wrong* in his vocabulary. But Didion is incapable of divorcing *radical* from *chic;* she hangs out with a sorry crowd. . . .

Read *A Book of Common Prayer* again, and you will see that what is implied is that having politics paralyzes the potential for performing good deeds: to swallow Didion it is necessary to swallow the notion that all acts of virtue are—*must be*—divorced from politics. . . . I wonder if Didion is acquainted with the Manichaean heresy.

Didion—reporting from what she calls "the quintessential intersection of nothing," "the hard white core of the world" (her vanity table)—is obsessed with the child trapped in the fridge, the "children burning in the locked car in the supermarket lot," the honeymooners killed in their thermal blanket by a coral snake. Yes; this is the stuff of nightmare. How mean-spirited would it be to point out that this is also the stuff that calls attention to Didion's Exquisite Sensibility? It's hard to fault people for their obsessions, but Didion's proclivity for "aimless revelation" does tell us something: To attach oneself only to the unanalyzable incident (especially when one's subject matter intersects with the political passions of our times) is to prefer to love one's pain; it is to caress and nourish one's pain, to find it of infinitely more value than the pain of "acquaintances [who] read *The New York Times* and try to tell me the news of the world." (p. 282)

(If I have seemed, up to now, to be unfair to Didion, if I have neglected to say that her conservatism can sometimes be a refreshing antidote to doctrinaire radicalism-by-rote, to the shiny new baubles of current public opinion . . . if I have not acknowledged that some of her sentences leap off the page and find their way to the heart, in which her sentiments have already, inarticulated, been lodged, it is because that is a path well worn: When a writer has been so much overpraised, it is difficult, if not pointless, to join the chorus.) . . .

[For] Didion to have any sympathy with anyone who aligns herself with any cause, any movement, is too much to hope for. She informs us balefully that she feels "radically separated from most of the ideas that seem to interest other people." Like Grace in *A Book of Common Prayer,* she is *de afuera*—the outsider: "I have been *de afuera* all my life." I think she wears that singularity like a badge. *I am different* translates into *I am superior.* (p. 284)

That coddled singularity/superiority is, I am afraid, one of the reasons readers love Didion. To delight in her sensibility is to say, "I'm different, too—better than other people. I see that she sees what I see."

Didion, who can manage, maddeningly, to sound smug and remorseful at the same time, tells us that she has no opinions. . . . To pretend to carry no mental baggage at all makes one a voyeur at the party, a detached onlooker at the execution. There is a precariously thin line between voyeurism and decadence; and I am bound also to conclude that Didion, the participant-observer—at Hollywood parties, at the Manson trial, etc., etc.—titillates her readers with faint whiffs of decadence which emanate not only from the observed but from the observer—a poseur who does indeed have consistent opinions, although they are disguised as instinctual, idiosyncratic reactions to ephemeral phenomena, and thereby rendered less threatening and more winsome.

The reason I don't love Didion, after all is said and done, is that I need to be told forthrightly what a writer loves or more precisely what she values. I don't like to be seduced by indirection. (pp. 284-85)

In an essay called "Self-Respect," she lets us know that she abhors "sins of commission and omission, the trusts betrayed, the promises subtly broken, the gifts irrevocably wasted through sloth or cowardice or carelessness." These are pretty sentiments, prettily expressed; but her sense of tragic regret rings hollow to me; it is as nonspecific as her proposed remedy: "the willingness to accept responsibility for one's own life is the source from which self-respect springs."

"Except on that most primitive level—our loyalties to those we love—what could be more arrogant than to claim the primacy of personal conscience?" Then to what *does* she give primacy: If not to personal conscience, to authority? To a "social code," she answers: "I want to be quite obstinate about insisting that we have no way of knowing—beyond that fundamental loyalty to the social code—what is 'right' and what is 'wrong,' what is 'Good' and what 'Evil.'" But to what social code? framed when, and by whom? *for* whom? How can I trust her when I do not know the answers to those questions? . . . I can't trust her because when she talks about "the long golden afternoons that [are] no more" in her native Sacramento, her language is suffused with that peculiar sentimentality one associates with an Englishman who once enjoyed the glories and the privilege of the Raj—an imperialist mentality is at work here, a gentlemanly, aristocratic sensibility that obdurately ignores the realities of class and economics and remembers only the long shadows on the green grass on a summer afternoon. Both are real—the golden afternoons and the sale-lease-backs (the money); Didion dismisses half the equation. (pp. 285-86)

In the 1960s, she says, "no one at all seemed to have any memory or mooring." But to what is she moored?

What she is moored to, of course, is her *Angst.* And her *Angst* is not the still point of the turning world.

Anyone whose love is reserved almost entirely for the past can have only disdain for the present. And can consequently not be trusted to tell us the truth. Be wary.

Make no mistake: I too am interested in visits to the interior. I know that what happens in the recesses of the human heart is at least as interesting as what happens at the Center for the Study of Democratic Institutions. Yes, everything begins in the human heart. But the human heart is not vacuum-packed. The pulsebeat from any breast, however armored, is felt, not just in private contracts—"doomed commitments"—between private persons but in Selma, in

Haight-Ashbury, in Vietnam, in South Africa, in East New York. Reports from those locations are also reports from the heart. And Didion's heart is cold. (p. 286)

Barbara Grizzuti Harrison, "Joan Didion: The Courage of Her Afflictions," in The Nation *(copyright 1979 by the Nation Associates, Inc.), Vol. 229, No. 9, September 29, 1979, pp. 277-86.*

* * *

DOOLITTLE, Hilda
See H. D.

E

ELKIN, Stanley 1930-

Elkin, an American novelist, short story writer, editor, and critic, writes parodies of contemporary absurdity and violence, aptly called (although he dislikes the term) black comedies. Although he is generally highly regarded by critics and his fellow writers, Elkin has not received the popular acclaim that many feel he deserves. Josh Greenfeld praises him as "a bright satirist, a bleak absurdist, and a deadly moralist. . . . I know of no serious funny writer in this country who can match him." (See also *CLC*, Vols. 4, 6, 9, and *Contemporary Authors*, Vols 9-12, rev. ed.)

CHRISTOPHER LEHMANN-HAUPT

["The Living End" is] the work of a man who is desperately trying to joke away death. . . .

[Any] little thing that may go wrong with "The Living End" is justified by the marvelously funny gags and sketches that lie in wait around the next corner. And even in the unlikely event that you get through the first 140 pages without cracking a smile, the novel is worth reading alone for its four-page vision of the Day of Judgment. . . .

But what [God] does because He never found His audience needs the effect of the whole book to be appreciated. So please read it. (p. 248)

Christopher Lehmann-Haupt, "'The Living End'," in the New York Times, *Section III (© 1979 by The New York Times Company; reprinted by permission), May 25, 1979 (and reprinted in* Books of the Times, *Vol. II, No. 5, 1979, pp. 247-48).*

ROBERT BROWN

[*The Living End*] stretches from the moment of Ellerbee's murder until the end of time and space—doomsday. We follow the fortunes of Ellerbee and one Ladlehaus, an accomplice to the crime, through what there is of eternity. We see the Lord in action, giving and taking away, damning and saving, making the occasional error, *explaining* the ways of Him to men. I leave the reader to discover the explanation, the "state of the art" for himself, suggesting only that it hinges on those attributes of divinity emphasized when we speak of Him as "Creator."

And readers there must be. Through the years Elkin has garnered all the critical superlatives and deserved them, never more so than with this astonishing book. But he has remained something of a cult figure, and there is no reason for this. It may be said that anyone who reads this book without admiration and delight does not really know how to read at all. (p. 71)

Robert Brown, "Music When Soft Voices Die," in New York *Magazine (copyright © 1979 by News Group Publications, Inc.; reprinted with the permission of* New York *Magazine), Vol. 12, No. 25, June 18, 1979, pp. 70-1.*

WILLIAM PLUMMER

Stanley Elkin is a "writer's writer," a designation at once happy and sad. Sad because his older titles are not to be found at the nearest paperback store but, with luck, in the used book stalls. His is the sort of name publishing houses like to trot out when accused of Harold Robbins or Robin Moore.

Elkin does close-order dialogue as snappy as Heller or Roth, and his eye for contemporary detail is as sharp as Barthelme's. So what's amiss? Let him tell you. Like many modern writers, he's forever talking about what he's up to through the guise of his narrator. . . . (p. 33)

["The Bailbondsman"] is one of the great works in the language—right up there, perhaps, with [Faulkner's] "The Bear" and [Melville's] "Bartleby." But you must grant Elkin his premises. He has no interest in "the arduous, numbing connections" in plot or even structure. He's not anti-story, . . . but rather has an insatiable "sweet tooth for instance," which he treats with gags, interpolated tales, catalogues and assorted set pieces. Like Tristram Shandy, he believes in progress by digression.

Two more discomforting things. Character leaves him cold: he is exclusively "distracted by personality," the outré—no middle-range intensities for him. Thus, he is always *on;* there are no readerly reliefs, no rest stops on his highway. (pp. 33-4)

Elkin's new collection of novellas, *The Living End,* will probably disappoint his faithful; it's slighter, less fiercely written than *Searches & Seizures*. The lead story, "The Conventional Wisdom," is of interest, however, as a sort of parable about Elkin's fictional method. . . .

The motive force of Elkin's writing is "the conventional wisdom" itself. His aggressive, high energy rhetoric comes into being under the pressure of cliché, which is not to suggest that his métier is either satire or camp. Rather, he seems to share with Emerson the vaguely platonic idea that the hackneyed is "fossile poetry"—the Truth in tatters, in its fallen condition. When he is good, Elkin inhabits the interstices of stereotype, wherein he cracks jokes, performs prodigies of description, wonders mightily, and as a by-product, comments acutely on the way we live.

"The Conventional Wisdom" is joined in *The Living End* by two other long stories inspired by pat phrases: "The Bottom Line" and "The State of the Art." The three works are contiguous: they feature the same cast and take place mostly in Heaven and Hell. If "The Bottom Line" is unconvincing, "The State of the Art" has brilliant moments. Especially outrageous and curiously moving are the passages in which Elkin elaborates the old gags about the Virgin Mary's sluttishness into an anguished interior monologue and in which he perceives a brittle-talking Christ (the Lord's "designated hitter") and God Himself through an antic grid of father/son stereotypes. . . .

[The novellas in *The Living End*] are streamlined, tailored to the ear, not the eye. It is in *Searches & Seizures,* where Elkin has room to dilate, that he is most incorrigibly himself. . . .

["The Bailbondsman" is] where Elkin shines. It is riddled with routine, caparisoned with catalogue. The novella follows Alexander Main through a more or less ordinary day. . . . Main is Elkin's most brilliant monitor of the conventional wisdom. In his mid-50s, he has re-invented himself as a cliché, as "a cross between a railroad conductor and a deputy sheriff." (p. 34)

In no other work does Elkin more clearly reveal the root of his obsession with the tired and overly true. "We die drop-outs," Main says to Mr. Crainpool, in between taking shots at him. . . .

The future leans on Alexander Main "like a mountain range." Were he plugged into its hokey quotidian, were he fluent in the conventional wisdom to come, he would be impervious to death. For Elkin, cliché gives life a sacral intensity and mastery of it confers, perhaps, a certain immortality. (p. 35)

William Plummer, "'The Living End' and 'Searches & Seizures'," in The New Republic *(reprinted by permission of* The New Republic; *© 1979 The New Republic, Inc.), Vol. 180, No. 25, June 23, 1979, pp. 33-5.*

DORIS GRUMBACH

I think you will find Stanley Elkin's *The Living End* either hilariously funny or not funny at all. I managed to hover between the two extremes, finding some of the ripostes very good (a man in hell says, "It's too hot to harbor a grudge") but the main story-line labored and the humor often over-extended. *The Living End* is divided into three parts to parallel the sections of *The Divine Comedy,* but there the resemblance ceases. Some of the dialogue is Beckett-like, some of the inventions upon the theme of death and life after death are reminiscent of Mark Twain's later fooling around with such ideas, but mostly the humor is black and bitter. The writing is wonderful, the language rich and varied, and the Jewish dialect accorded Joseph and Mary successful, at least at the start. (p. R13)

Doris Grumbach, "A Season Redolent of Worthy Fiction," in Books & Arts *(copyright © 1979 by The Chronicle of Higher Education, Inc.), Vol. XVIII, No. 16, June 25, 1979, pp. R12-R13.**

HENRY ROBBINS

The Living End is Stanley Elkin's comic fable of Heaven, Hell and the Last Days, a small book big in every way but length. And I should say at once that this "triptych" . . . is the work of a master, a story eloquent in its gestures and amazing for the ease with which it moves from a liquor store hold-up in Minneapolis to the "wall-to-wall Wall" of damnation, from Heaven as a "theme park" to Hell as "the ultimate inner city." Half farce, half morality play, *The Living End* puts God himself on trial, the Lord faced off against the damned who in their countless number equal Everyman. Quite possibly only Stanley Elkin possesses the exact blend of irreverence and care, of hard-core realism and fabulous invention, to have pulled this off.

Elkin knows that clichés are the substance of our lives, the coinage of human intercourse, the ways and means that hold our messy selves and sprawling nation intact. To exploit their vigor and set them forth with unexpected force has been the basis of his success as a novelist; no writer has maneuvered life's shoddy stock-in-trade into more brilliantly funny forms. . . .

[Desperation] relieved by raucous humor slips into *The Living End,* where Elkin takes on the ultimate cliché, death and the preposterous protocol of Hereafter. (p. F1)

There is a kind of vulgate glory to Stanley Elkin's prose, and much of the power of *The Living End* depends on how things are worded. Elkin is the *magister ludi* of American vernacular, and for sheer stylistic brilliance no other writer can top him. The American novelist he most resembles is Nathanael West, but whereas West allowed us to feel superior to life's lunacy through savage irony, Elkin refuses us this distance, this illusion. And unlike others of his generation, Thomas Pynchon and William Gaddis for example, Elkin does not identify with the laughter of the gods, he does not dissociate himself from the human spectacle by taking out a franchise on the cosmic joke. Hard and unyielding as his comic vision becomes, Elkin's laughter is remission and reprieve, a gesture of willingness to join the human mess, to side with the damned, to laugh in momentary grace at whatever makes life Hell. (p. F4)

Henry Robbins, "To Hell and Back with Stanley Elkin," in Book World—The Washington Post *(© 1979, The Washington Post), July 1, 1979, pp. F1, F4.*

GEOFFREY STOKES

As a novelist, Stanley Elkin has often been too smart for his own good. The outrageous vision . . . that animates his stories—among the most tightly brilliant published by a contemporary author—has tended to become flaccid over the long haul of a novel. *The Dick Gibson Show* (1971) offered some hope that Elkin had become able to harness his enormous gifts and deal with the demands of form. But in retrospect, that novel's success seems to have more to do with the accidental confluence of Dick Gibson's performing style and his creator's weakness for spectacular schtickery than with Elkin's learning to provide us with something beyond mere astonishment. That, at least, was the judgment forced on even sympathetic readers by his more recent long work, especially *The Franchiser* (1976), a lumpily indigestible porridge of small boffos and Big Thoughts. Thus the triumph that is Elkin's *The Living End* comes at once as a stunning surprise and as a temptation to say we knew he could do it all the time.

In *The Living End* Elkin has finally found a subject worthy of him. No more does he diddle with the surrogates, no more leave us wiping the laughter from our eyes and wondering if we really care quite all that much about One-Hour Martinizing. This time, Elkin goes directly for the big one: God, He Who, etc. . . .

This is, of course, vintage Elkin; *everyone* is a standup comic. But precisely because it's God talking, the question of why He does what He does is genuinely important—especially when it turns out that Elkin is ultimately addressing the obligations of all creators. And suddenly—when the eternally-disfigured Christ learns that his suffering occurred solely because God thought it would make a better story—the laughter stops, and the very funny, very serious Elkin goes deeper than he's ever gone before. *The Living End* makes it at once possible to forgive God, and unnecessary to forgive Stanley Elkin.

Geoffrey Stokes, "Short Circuits," in The Village Voice *(reprinted by permission of* The Village Voice; *copyright © News Group Publications, Inc., 1979), Vol. 24, No. 34, August 20, 1979, p. 82.*

* * *

EMECHETA, (Florence Onye) Buchi 1944-

Emecheta is a Nigerian-born novelist and screenwriter now residing in England. Her native Nigeria and the problems of contemporary black women are the focal concerns of her work. (See also *Contemporary Authors*, Vols. 81-84.)

ALICE WALKER

Though [*Second Class Citizen*] is not stylistically exciting and is no doubt heavily autobiographical, it is no less valid as a novel. And a good one. It raises fundamental questions about how creative and prosaic life is to be lived and to what purpose, which is more than some books, written while one's children are banished from one's life, do. *Second Class Citizen* (and the title is unfortunate) is one of the most informative books about contemporary African life that I have read. (p. 106)

Alice Walker, "A Writer Because of, Not in Spite of, Her Children," in Ms. *(© 1975 Ms. Magazine Corp.), Vol. IV, No. 7, January, 1976, pp. 40, 106.*

The clash of Christian and African cultures, of generations, of ancient and modern pieties, and of group custom and the individual will are all vividly portrayed in this pure, fluid novel about a young Nigerian girl ["The Bride Price"]. . . . The author has a plain, engaging style and manages to convey all the lushness, poverty, superstition, and casual cruelty of a still exotic (to Western readers) culture while keeping her tale as sharp as a folk ballad. (pp. 170-71)

"Books: 'The Bride Price'," in The New Yorker *(© 1976 by The New Yorker Magazine, Inc.), Vol. LII, No. 13, May 17, 1976, pp. 170-71.*

VALENTINE CUNNINGHAM

The cumulative achievement of [Buchi Emecheta's] *Second-Class Citizen* (1975), *The Bride Price* (1976) and *The Slave Girl* (1977) has commanded my mounting admiration. In narratives of attractively readable simplicity (the sort that requires terrific art to bring off) she has successively charted the efforts of a Nigerian woman and her burgeoning family to survive the bleaknesses of a hostile London, and the problems of love and marriage in present and recently-past Nigeria. With the compelling warmth of an extraordinary capacity for investing her fictional world and her characters—even the grisliest—with deep affection she rebukes whole arrays of hostile forces. London racists, husbands, tribal traditionalists, missionary functionaries: the inhuman is everywhere laid bare. Buchi Emecheta speaks particularly, of course, for educated Nigerian women struggling against their more ignorant menfolk. But she speaks, too, for all women, for all the oppressed. . . . (p. 747)

Valentine Cunningham, "The Jock Campbell New Statesman Award: The Feeling of Onslaught," in New Statesman *(© 1978 The Statesman & Nation Publishing Co. Ltd.), Vol. 95, No. 2463, June 2, 1978, pp. 746-47.**

ANITA KERN

The London-based Nigerian writer Buchi Emecheta continues to grow in talent and craftsmanship. The novel *The Slave Girl,* her fourth book, is her most accomplished work so far. It is coherent, compact and convincing. It also represents a considerable achievement for a writer who . . . has worked under very difficult conditions. . . .

[In] general the slave girls are not too badly off. Emecheta describes their life in the context of early twentieth-century Onitsha society, in which buying and selling people was accepted as a situation that "could not be helped." It provided labor on the one hand in exchange for a roof and food on the other.

[The novel's framework is simple], but Emecheta has unobtrusively woven into it a great deal of sociological detail. All the background information is skillfully integrated, and the young girl's story makes fascinating reading. Emecheta displays considerable insight and a broadly-based knowledge of people's character traits and foibles, and she manages to endow even those characters who make only brief appearances with believable personalities.

Emecheta shows and states throughout the novel that a woman is never free, that she always belongs to others, be it a father, a brother or a social group. . . .

The Slave Girl describes an aspect of Nigerian life which has so far been little explored. Buchi Emecheta's novel is sympathetic and honest, her style clear and straightforward and her characterization skillful. Ojebeta is a welcome addition to the still-too-small gallery of Nigerian heroines.

Anita Kern, "Africa & the West Indies: 'The Slave Girl'," in World Literature Today *(copyright 1979 by the University of Oklahoma Press), Vol. 53, No. 1, Winter, 1979, p. 172.*

ANDREW MOTION

Buchi Emecheta is . . . concerned with tyranny, but her attention is more precisely fixed on the trials of a specific gender than of a particular nation. Although the action of *The Joys of Motherhood* is confined to 20th-century Nigeria, it teaches lessons which could equally well be learnt elsewhere. The economic and familial pressures exerted on women in Western communities are less obvious, but no less pervasive, than those which surround others in and around Lagos. The novel's heroine, Nnu Ego, is first living and then dead proof of this. . . .

Emecheta describes [her heroine's death] with moving simplicity. By viewing her heroine's fate with a compound of anger and pity, she avoids sounding either didactic or sentimental, and intensifies the force of her bleak conclusions.

Andrew Motion, "Land of Lost Content," in New Statesman *(© 1979 The Statesman & Nation Publishing Co. Ltd.), Vol. 97, No. 2510, April 27, 1979, p. 600.**

ADRIANNE BLUE

[*In the Ditch* is] derived from a diary Emecheta had kept for years, it depicts life at Pussy Cat Mansions, a public housing project, where Adah and her cockney neighbors develop a transient sense of community. . . .

The "ditch" of the title is a metaphor for poverty. The book is sad, sonorous, occasionally hilarious: an extraordinary first novel. . . .

Emecheta tells [the story of *The Joys of Motherhood*] in a plain style, denuding it of exoticism, displaying an impressive, embracing compassion. Like any village storyteller whose tale is sad and meaningful, she laces it with humor. Her three generations of unlettered Africans can be as ornery and individualistic as any California voter.

Expatriate writers often dwell in a fertile country of the mind and body, but are denied the soil. . . . Exceptionally, Emecheta writes compellingly and utterly without condescension of agrarian African modes she personally rejected. Hers is an urbane sensibility, and her novels—very much of our time—even reverberate upon each other.

Adrianne Blue, "Buchi Emecheta: A Nigerian in London," in Book World—The Washington Post *(© 1979,* The Washington Post*), May 13, 1979, p. K8.*

PETER KEMP

The Joys of Motherhood, by Buchi Emecheta, is that rarity, a quiet piece of feminism. Its main character, Nnu Ego, is also out of the ordinary. (p. 93)

Both the old way of life which shaped Nnu Ego, and the new one she has to cope with, are described in absorbing detail. On the one hand is an Ibo village world of guardian gods, dream-readers, tattooed beauties and polygamous protocol; on the other, a shanty-town existence of back-breaking toil and petty trading—sales of smuggled cigarettes, fried locusts or laboriously-toted firewood. Sturdily unmawkish, the narrative movingly depicts the humiliations, ingenuities and small satisfactions of the poor. What emerges is a strong sense of exploited decency. As time passes, Nnu Ego discovers that the code of her culture—a code she has spent her life trying to conform to—is now obsolete.

Realistically, however, the novel does not write off her life as simply waste and exploitation. Its title is both ironic and unironic. Though she is a victim of conditioning and transition, Nnu Ego has found, in her restricted life, some cause for pleasure and pride, and celebration parties with palm wine. That these are faithfully recorded, too, in no way weakens Mrs Emecheta's indictment of repressive attitudes; it adds both strength and subtlety to an impressive book. (pp. 93-4)

Peter Kemp, "Older Wife's Tale," in The Listener *(© British Broadcasting Corp. 1979; reprinted by permission of Peter Kemp), Vol. 102, No. 2620, July 19, 1979, pp. 93-4.**

JOSEPH LELYVELD

[Buchi Emecheta's account in "The Joys of Motherhood"] of three generations of Ibo women and their changing values with regard to the children they raise and the men they wed is refreshingly straightforward. . . .

The values of her women change, of course, so history can be seen through the lives of these characters. But they don't see themselves as acting in history. (p. 15)

A reader who has no real feeling for village traditions in Nigeria may suspect that Miss Emecheta is romanticizing them to advance a cause. . . .

Nnu Ego is aware of "new rules" governing the relationship between man and wife in Lagos and spells them out, sometimes as if she, rather than Miss Emecheta, had the degree in sociology from London University. . . .

The basic argument is put in the novel [schematically] . . . , but as episode piles on episode, the texture of the changing society becomes palpable. And this is not just any changing society but proud, rambunctious Nigeria. Dangling between two standards, Nnu Ego starts to ask basic questions herself: Why, for instance, can't women value their daughters as much as their sons? "God, when will you create a woman who is fulfilled in herself, a full human being?" she asks. It's a good question, but it is less than convincing coming from Nnu Ego, whose discovery of abstract feminist principles is too abrupt. (p. 39)

Joseph Lelyveld, "Out of Africa," in The New York Times Book Review *(© 1979 by The New York Times Company; reprinted by permission), November 11, 1979, pp. 15, 39.**

* * *

ENDO, Shusaku 1923-

Endo is a distinguished Japanese playwright and novelist. As a Catholic, Endo is thematically concerned with both the confrontation and the harmony between Oriental and Christian customs. (See also *CLC*, Vol. 7, and *Contemporary Authors*, Vols. 29-32, rev. ed.)

JOHN MELLORS

By way of demonstrating [the] difficulties of Christianity in Japan, Endo has written a novel [*Silence*] based on the persecution by the Japanese in the 17th century of missionaries from Italy and Portugal, and of their native converts. The apostate Ferreira maintains that Christianity is wholly alien to the Japanese mind, and unable to grow there to maturity. 'The sapling I brought quickly decayed to its roots in this swamp,' he says. But there is an underlying theme that is even more important—the 'silence' of the title, 'the silence of God . . . the feeling that while men raise their voices in anguish, God remains with folded arms, silent'. . . .

Silence is an object-lesson to committed writers. Endo never sermonises. He has a strong, calm narrative style. . . .

John Mellors, "Japanese Cross," in The Listener *(© British Broadcasting Corp. 1976; reprinted by permission of John Mellors), Vol. 95, No. 2458, May 20, 1976, p. 654.**

LOUIS ALLEN

Endo is likely to be struggling with ["the Japanese Graham Greene"] label for many years yet.

And, of course, the relation between literature and religion *is* one of his main themes. . . .

But he is far more versatile than this suggests. He is one of Japan's major comic writers, for one thing, and, in *When I Whistle,* he explores yet another vein, a plain realism behind which lingers a discreet but clear symbolism. . . .

Two threads run through the book. Ozu, an unsuccessful 'salary man', bumps into someone on the train who recognises him from the prewar past at Nada Middle School. Ozu cannot place him, but the incident jogs his memory, and his childhood at Nada and friendship with the grotesque and singular Flatfish unfold. . . . Both boys fall in love with one of the girls, Aiko. . . .

Interwoven with this is the story of Ozu's son, Eiichi, whose life is Endo's unflattering version of postwar Japan. Eiichi is a house surgeon who despises his father—and his father's generation—as sentimentally humanist. He also loathes him for being a nonentity. . . . He uses people, a nurse, a doctor's daughter, a colleague, and does not hesitate to experiment with a new drug on the body of a terminal cancer patient.

By a more than Dickensian coincidence, the patient is Aiko. . . . (p. 530)

There is no *Citadel* ending, though. Aiko dies, but Eiichi flourishes. . . . Ozu, at the end of the book, makes a journey back to Nada, and the inevitable happens: the old train has been scrapped, Aiko's house has been bulldozed to make way for a block of flats, the river-bed the boys wandered along is filled in. But the nadir of disillusionment is the manipulation of the sea. . . .

It is the price that Japan, more than most countries, has paid for keeping herself up to date. Yet the contrast will not work that simply. Ozu's nostalgia does not blind him to the reality of prewar Japan. . . .

Even so, Endo implies, something carefree survived which is missing from the calculating, ambitious Japan of his son, Eiichi. There is, really, a poverty of choice here, and the gap into which the individual slots his own remembered happiness—or the possibility of his son's—is still narrow. No change depicted by Endo summons up the fierce rejection of a Mishima. Sadness is the keynote, and its symbol the changed Aiko: a delicate beauty, unhoused and brought to penury by war, and ultimately devoured by a disease which is merely a pretext for experiment by the new, predatory generation of young Japan. (p. 531)

Louis Allen, "Rastignac of Tokyo," in The Listener *(© British Broadcasting Corp. 1979; reprinted by permission of Louis Allen), Vol. 101, No. 2606, April 12, 1979, pp. 530-31.*

VALENTINE CUNNINGHAM

When I Whistle shows how telling a novelist Shusaku Endo can be when he stops straining to live up to his dubious label as 'the Japanese Graham Greene' and settles more for being Japanese. This latest of his works to be translated into American ('Gee, teacher') rises powerfully above the limitation of its awkwardly dubbed sound to examine modern Japan—worldly, wealthy and riddled with cancer patients—in relation to the Second World War. It does so by having its narrative shuttle nicely back and forth between mediocre businessman Ozu's memories of growing up during the War, and his son Eiichi's ruthless efforts to scrabble into prominence in the medical profession. The plotting is sometimes pretty bare and occasionally close to melodrama; what's more, Endo's manner is always so absorbent that his taking the cancer ward as the typical symbol for present Japan must seem more than a nod towards Solzhenitsyn. But the link between cancerous militarism and cancerous materialism is convincingly Endo's own. Rightly, he doesn't rely merely on indignation, though there is plenty to grouse about in the Japanese wartime enthusiasms—the *Banzai* zeal of women sending recruits off draped in the Rising Sun to be slapped and beaten daily into fighting shape—as there is in the custom of lying to patients about their illness and using them as unknowing guinea-pigs.

There's plenty of wryness too. . . . And Endo's plea for ruth and fondness, the human nexus, against the inhumanitarian medical view of people as objects, cannot be bad. But, we wonder, was everything really that much better before the War? Endo's sentimental regret for the 'beautiful things' of 'the treasured past' finds paltry support in the novel's own picture of pre-war puritanism, rigidly class-bound education and rampaging behaviour of the drill-sergeants.

Valentine Cunningham, "Death in the Afternoon," in New Statesman *(© 1979 The Statesman & Nation Publishing Co. Ltd.), Vol. 97, No. 2508, April 13, 1979, p. 527.**

FRANCIS KING

Of all Japanese novelists, Shusaku Endo is the most accessible to Western readers. This is not merely because he spent many years in France and has obviously been influenced by a variety of European writers, but because he is also a Roman Catholic. . . .

Whether we are Christians or not, a heritage of Christianity permeates all our thinking; but that heritage is wholly alien to all but a small section of the Japanese population.

Once again, in *When I Whistle,* Endo returns to the theme, already used by him in his masterly *The Sea and Poison,* of human vivisection. (p. 23)

The one flaw of the novel lies in the Iago-like character of Eiichi, whose evil is so calculated and complete that it is difficult to believe in him. Graham Greene, to whom critics like to compare Endo, would have shown some faint illumination of grace even in a heart so dark. Ozu on the other hand—unintellectual, ordinary, decent, hardly understanding his attachment to the memory of his dead school-friend—is a beautiful creation. . . .

In describing Aiko's illness and death, there are moments when Endo seems to escape sentimentality only by a hair's breadth; but each time he withdraws from the edge just in time. There is a terrible sadness in his account of the war years and their humiliating aftermath; and the story of the doomed woman, who has already lost both her child and her husband in the war, is profoundly depressing. . . .

One senses in Endo a profound hatred of change: the beautiful things that are disappearing are not only trees, rivers and old houses but also such intangibles as decency, humanity and idealism. Eiichi, with his destructive egotism, and his efficiently soulless hospital are symbols of a new Japan that frightens and awes the author.

Weaving back and forth in time, this book suffers from none of the feebleness of construction so common in even the best Japanese fiction. Saner than Mishima, closer to us than Kawabata and more universal than Tanizaki, Endo is one of the half-dozen leading novelists of the post-war period. (p. 24)

Francis King, "Experiments," in The Spectator *(© 1979 by* The Spectator; *reprinted by permission of* The Spectator*), Vol. 242, No. 7866, April 14, 1979, pp. 23-4.*

EDWARD BUTSCHER

Shusaku Endo has wisely set his gripping novel about one man's struggle for belief in early 18th-century Japan when medieval samurai still held sway and the brutal process of expelling Christianity (and other Western influences) was in full flower. . . .

At the heart of *Silence,* whose title refers to God's muteness in the face of evil's savage triumph, throbs the sensitive, if vain, awareness of Sebastian Rodrigues, a young Portuguese Jesuit who has slipped into Japan with a fellow missionary to tend whatever native Christians they can find and to discover why Christovao Ferreira, a former teacher and hero, has apparently renounced his faith rather than endure a glorious martyrdom. Sebastian's own capture by the authorities, which had seemed inevitable from the start, gives the novel much of its impressive narrative power, as does the dramatic series of climactic confrontations with both Ferreira and Inoue, the Japanese magistrate who embodies a very contemporary marriage between intellect and detached inhumanity.

Although flawed by a somewhat simplistic grasp of philosophical complexities and a taste for elemental characterizations, Endo's terse tale has a subtle way of penetrating sophisticated thresholds into the cellar of self where more primitive emotions rule. We root for Sebastian to find salvation even as we reject the terms of his inner dilemma.

Edward Butscher, "Books in Brief: 'Silence'," in Saturday Review *(© 1979 by Saturday Review Magazine Corp.; reprinted with permission), Vol. 6, No. 15, July 21, 1979, p. 50.*

IVAN GOLD

The final chapter of this profoundly moving, profoundly disturbing book [*Silence*] consists of excerpts from the diary of a Dutch clerk in Nagasaki in which the drama that we have been so intimately exposed to is seen from the remote perspective of a man concerned with commercial matters. The feeling is similar to viewing the action off in a corner of a Brueghel painting, or to watching a figure almost lost in the mists of a Japanese scroll. . . .

Shusaku Endo . . . is described on the dust jacket as "the leading writer in Japan." On the strength of this splendid novel, he may very well be. The quotation from Graham Greene on the front cover—"In my opinion one of the finest novels of our time"—does not seem like hyperbole. (p. 5)

Ivan Gold, "The Cross and the Sword: The Anguish of Faith in 17th-Century Japan," in Book World—The Washington Post *(© 1979,* The Washington Post*), September 2, 1979, pp. 4-5.*

PAUL WILKES

[Shusaku Endo's Jesus in *A Life of Christ*] is approached carefully, quietly, as if his story is to be told accompanied by a simple tune on a hand-carved flute. . . .

[The pace is] slow, the history interesting, the tone reverent, as would befit a man who is trying to tell his people, the Japanese, of a man they know as little about as we do of Buddha. I quickly flagged. Good intentions, my friend, but. . . .

I felt I was in the company of a good, old friend, a baker of substantial whole wheat loaves. Perhaps, as we sometimes reject those plodding, well-intentioned friends of ours, I'd not waited long enough for him. I'd wanted to be swept away and all my friend Endo wanted to do was take me along for a walk.

Paul Wilkes, "Jesus, East and West," in Commonweal *(copyright © 1979 Commonweal Publishing Co., Inc.; reprinted by permission of Commonweal Publishing Co., Inc.), Vol. CVI, No. 18, October 12, 1979, p. 574.**

* * *

EVERSON, William 1912-
(formerly Brother Antoninus)

An American poet formerly associated with the San Francisco Renaissance, Everson was a Dominican monk from 1951-69. He began his poetic career as a disciple of Robinson Jeffers; however, many critics feel that Everson's contribution has surpassed that of his master. Everson, whose deepest concerns are with the sexual union of man and woman and the analogous ecstatic communion of man and God, views his entire body of work as a spiritual autobiography. (See also *CLC*, Vols. 1, 5, and *Contemporary Authors*, Vols. 9-12, rev. ed.)

KENNETH REXROTH

It's long ago now, another epoch in the life of mankind, before the Second War, that I got a pamphlet of poems from a press in a small California town—*These Are the Ravens*—and then a handsome book from the Ward Ritchie Press in Los Angeles—*San Joaquin.* They weren't much like the poems being written in those days, either in *New Masses, Partisan Review* or *The Southern Review.* They were native poems, autochthonous in a way the fashionable poems of the day could not manage. Being an autochthon of course is something you don't manage, you are. It was not just the subjects, the daily experience of a young man raising grapes in the Great Valley of California, or the rhythms, which were of the same organic pulse you find in Isaiah, or

Blake's prophecies, or Whitman, or Lawrence, or Sandburg at his best, or Wallace Gould, or Robinson Jeffers. This, it seemed to me, was a young fellow out to make himself unknown and forgotten in literary circles. The age has turned round, and the momentary reputations of that day are gone, and William Everson, now Brother Antoninus, is very far from being unknown and forgotten.

I say this, not in a spirit of literary controversy, but to try to bring home to a time that accepts his idiom and his sensibility, how unusual these poems were thirty years ago. Everson has won through, and in a very real sense this whole book [*The Residual Years: Poems 1934-1948*]—a new edition of his early poems—is a record of that struggle. It is a journal of a singlehanded war for a different definition of poetic integrity. There is nothing abstract or impersonal about these poems. They are not clockwork asthetic objects, wound up to go off and upset the reader. T. S. Eliot and Paul Valéry told the young of the last generation that that's what poems were, and the young dutifully tried their best to make such infernal machines, never noticing that their masters never wrote that way at all. Everson paid no attention. He cultivated and irrigated and tied up the vines and went home in the sunset and ate dinner and made love and wrote about how he felt doing it and about the turning of the year, the intimate rites of passage, and the rites of the season of a man and a woman. He used the first person singular pronoun often, because that, as far as he could see, was the central figure in the cast of the only existential drama he knew. (pp. xv-xvi)

Everson has been accused of self-dramatization. Justly. All of his poetry, that under the name of Brother Antoninus, too, is concerned with the drama of his own self, rising and falling along the sine curve of life, from comedy to tragedy and back again, never quite going under, never quite escaping for good into transcendence. This is a man who sees his shadow projected on the sky, like Whymper after the melodramatic achievement and the tragedy on the Matterhorn. Everything is larger than life with a terrible beauty and pain. Life isn't like that to some people and to them these poems will seem too strong a wine. But of course life is like that. Night alone, storm over the cabin, the sleepless watcher whipsawed by past and future—life is like that, of course. . . . (p. xvi)

I don't think there is any question but that William Everson is one of the three or four most important poets of the now-notorious San Francisco school. Most of the people wished on the community by the press are in fact from New York and elsewhere. The thing that distinguishes Robert Duncan, Philip Lamantia, William Everson and their associates is that they are all religious poets. Their subjects are the varied guises of the trials of the soul and the achievement of illumination. Everson's poems are mystical poems, records of the struggle towards peace and illumination on the stairs of natual mysticism. Peace comes only in communion with nature or momentarily with a woman, and far off, the light is at the end of a tunnel. So this is an incomplete autobiography—as whose isn't?

How deeply personal these poems are, and how convincingly you touch the living man through them. . . . As I turn over the pages, some of them thirty years old, I feel again, as always, a comradeship strong as blood. Evil men may have degraded those words, but they are still true and apposite for the real thing. Blood brotherhood. (p. xvii)

Kenneth Rexroth, in his introduction to The Residual Years: Poems 1934-1948 *by William Everson (copyright © 1968 by William Everson; copyright © 1948, 1968 by New Directions Publishing Corporation; all rights reserved; reprinted by permission of New Directions Publishing Corporation), New Directions, 1968, pp. xv-xvii.*

FREDERIC I. CARPENTER

"The Poet Is Dead" is a moving elegy [to Robinson Jeffers] in which the living poet who is with us now, mourned the passing of the poet recently dead. But instead of writing a conventional elegy, Everson remembered Jeffers' own earlier poetry, especially "Post Mortem"; and, borrowing some of Jeffers' imagery and poetic phrases, spoke as it were with the tongue of the dead poet, in order to realize his presence in the world which he had just left. These two poems complement each other—the first looking forward to the time when the poet should have died; the second remembering the dead poet and naturalizing him in our living world. (p. 4)

The strophes of "The Poet Is Dead" alternate between images of nature (the natural environment in which Jeffers lived), and images of human nature (the nature of the dead poet). . . . The parallelism and repetition of the imagery subtly emphasize that the poet, both in body and in spirit, was integrally a part of physical nature—his "pen, splintered on the excesses of vision." Then, throughout one extended metaphor, the poet's body seems magically to become one with the wild rock coast which he loved. . . . The poem succeeds in *naturalizing* Jeffers, both body and spirit, in the larger world which he had just left.

Further, this process of naturalizing the visionary poet has the effect of assuaging some of his own fears, expressed in "Post Mortem." In this new poem, which might have been entitled "Post Post Mortem," the poet's ghost becomes no longer an "impotent voice on the sea-wind." By means of his naturalization in the world after his death, the poet's body is rescued from the embalming process which has been called "the American way of death," in which the reality of death is disguised with rouge and cosmetics. In Everson's poem the impotent ghost becomes refleshed. (pp. 6-7)

Finally, even the voice of the poet who is dead seems to speak again through the voice of his disciple. Not only the dead body, but the "voice on the sea-wind" returns, and both body and spirit become realized anew. For Everson's poem remembers phrases and recalls images from the earlier poetry of Jeffers: from "Post Mortem," from "The Bed by the Window," from "The Wolf Who Died Snapping," and from "To Death"—a poem in *Hungerfield,* the last volume published in Jeffers' lifetime. Addressing "Death," Jeffers had written: "I think of you as a great king," and continued: "You have a sister named Life, an opulent treacherous woman / Blonde and a harlot. . . ." Now Everson's poem echoes these words:

> Now the opulent
> Treacherous woman called Life
> Forsakes her claim. Blond and a harlot
> She once drank joy from his narrow loins.
> She broke his virtue in her knees.

But these particular words and phrases, first used by Jeffers and now repeated by Everson, seemed to me to emphasize the life-denying aspect of Jeffers, which had increased as he grew older. And as I read and reread the poem, this single strophe disturbed me. Everson seemed to accept Jeffers' characterization of Life as "blonde and a harlot," and even to universalize the metaphor. Flatly stated, he seemed to agree: "Life is a harlot." And so, about five years ago, I formulated my objections, and spoke to the author about them.

Everson readily agreed that the personification of Life as a harlot violated the norms of language and morality. But when I accused him of adopting the phrase, he emphasized that it was a quotation—as of course it was. But it seemed to me that he also had adopted it, and to the degree that he had identified himself with the dead poet, had made it his own. Moreover, his own final line had declared, "She broke his virtue in her knees," and this seemed to reaffirm the justice of Jeffers' metaphor. If "Life" destroys man's virtue by seducing him to sex, then "virtue" is not manhood in its fulness, but a repudiation of Life.

Well, that is the problem. There are several possible answers.

First, and most personally: when Brother Antoninus wrote "The Poet Is Dead," he was a monk in the Dominican order. These lines echoed the religious convictions of the "Brother." In his "Foreword" to the poem, he suggested this interpretation: "my incorporation of direct figures from Jeffers' work" represented "my need to bury, once and for all, those elements of my own past with him." But now, once again, Brother Antoninus has become the secular poet, William Everson.

Second, and more important: "The Poet Is Dead" changes and develops as it progresses toward its conclusion. After remembering Jeffers' early life, and after seeming to identify with his "excesses of vision," the poem not only naturalizes Jeffers, but also naturalizes his poetic vision in the modern world. . . . As the poem moves toward its conclusion, it moves toward a larger vision.

For "the dark thoughts" to which Jeffers' poetry gave expression have become increasingly the preoccupation of the modern world. The "sheer / Excesses of vision" upon which his "pen / Splintered," projected only too realistically the "bad dreams" of many modern poets and authors. Even the violent hatred of civilization which gave rise to Jeffers' grotesque metaphor of "Life" as "blonde and a harlot" has found realization. (pp. 7-9)

Finally, the two lines of "The Poet Is Dead" which first seemed flawed and distasteful, may actually focus most clearly the crucial problem, both of Jeffers' poetry and of modern civilization. Jeffers conceived of "Life" as "blonde and a harlot." Brother Antoninus developed the metaphor: "She broke his virtue in her knees." But the very language which Antoninus used to describe the life of Jeffers echoes not only the poetic language of Jeffers but the conventional language of orthodox Christianity as well. It suggests that much of the imagery and metaphor of the English language which we all use has been borrowed from the iconography of Christianity. There is the suggestion of sin in "She once drank joy from his narrow loins"—a suggestion which the final line makes explicit.

The apparent flaw in Jeffers' poetry derives from its failure to resolve the fundamental dilemma of our civilization. That most natural of human instincts, sex, inherits not only the guilt-feelings of traditional Christianity, but also the denunciations of futurists who fear "the women's abundance." The greatness of his poetry lies in the completeness of its expression of both conflicting values: the narratives describe sexual emotions so vividly that they sometimes seem pornographic, yet they also describe frustrations and guilt so vividly that they sometimes seem moralistic. If the poetry fails to produce the catharsis of classical tragedy, it is because it realizes this ambivalence so completely that it refuses to ascribe any "tragic flaw" to the protagonists. The flaw lies rather in that "monster," civilization; yet when his modern maenads roam the barren hills of Point Sur they find only madness. Jeffers' poetry speaks to us the more urgently because it prophesies our problems, although it does not solve them. (pp. 9-10)

Frederic I. Carpenter, "'Post Mortem': 'The Poet is Dead'," in Western American Literature *(copyright, 1977, by the Western Literature Association), Vol. XII, No. 1, May, 1977, pp. 3-10.**

[*River-root: a syzygy for the Bicentennial of these States*] deals with a "syzygy," a coupling, in this case viewed specifically in the act of intercourse. Taking the act as both psychical as well as physical, an act of creation and thus true communion with the divine, Everson exercises delicacy in depicting the physiological concomitants. His juxtaposition of images from nature, such as the river as a seminal force, however, does not altogether succeed. Reminiscent of Whitman, Robinson Jeffers, Allen Ginsberg, his San Francisco colleague, and occasionally Hart Crane, Everson fits into a somewhat old-fashioned tradition in American poetry. He is in full command of the techniques, producing a free-flowing and supple verse, with occasional over-alliteration and exaggerated imagery. A worthwhile example of an erotic poem that succeeds, as few do, as a depiction of sex and as good, sometimes inspired verse.

"Language and Literature: 'River-Root: A Syzygy for the Bicentennial of These States'," in Choice *(copyright © 1977 by American Library Association), Vol. 14, No. 7, September, 1977, p. 860.*

ALBERT GELPI

[If] T. S. Eliot is the most important religious poet in English in the first half of the twentieth century, Everson // Antoninus is the most important religious poet of the second half of the century.

The extreme contrasts between those two poets point to a symptomatic tension in the religious commitment. The differences are less doctrinal than temperamental: Eliot the conservative classicist submitting the weaknesses of the individual to the reasonable authority of tradition and institutional structures in order to absolve him from the exigencies of personality; and Everson, the romantic individualist, trusting reason less than the undertow of passion and instinct to write out a life-long poem, as Whitman did a century ago, of the struggles with himself to realize himself. (p. 355)

[The] explicitly Christian poets of the twentieth century have, by and large, tended to stress the constraining limits of a radically flawed creation through which the refractions of the Spirit penetrate at best tenuously and elusively, and they have generally insisted on working within the limitations of formal conventions as a way of testing and fixing "hints and guesses," as Eliot described our experience of the Incarnation. The means and the meaning, the norms and the measure have therefore been ruminative, guarded, Apollonian in the main. (p. 356)

It is the very history of religious—especially Christian—poetry in the twentieth century, with its fixation on human fallibility and its consequent insistence on necessarily prescribed forms, that makes Everson's poetry seem radical, original, transformative. Most of the Dionysians in recent poetry—Allen Ginsberg, Jack Kerouac, Lawrence Ferlinghetti, like Hart Crane in the twenties—have used alcohol or drugs for release into vision. . . . The distinctiveness of Everson's achievement springs, rather, from the Dionysian character of his Christianity. This has evolved in two complementary phases: from the beginning, his surrendering to primal experience until at last it yielded him the Christian mystery; and his surrendering, then, to the Christian mystery so unreservedly that it enflamed and illuminated, below and above structured rational consciousness, that dark area, at once the center and circumference of psyche, where passion and spirit reveal themselves as personhood incarnate. (pp. 356-57)

William Everson's life has been punctuated again and again by interruptions, abrupt changes and seeming reversals. . . . [In] 1934 he discovered the master whose work made him a poet: Robinson Jeffers. Jeffers represented an "intellectual awakening and the first religious conversion, all in one." "When Jeffers showed me God in the cosmos, it took and I became a pantheist," and "that pantheism was based on a kind of religious sexuality," a sense of the universal life-force compelling all things in the sexual rhythm. . . . "August" is characteristic of much of the early poetry in its identification with the female earth so deep that masculine intellect relinquishes sovereignty and the poet yields virginal to the God of Nature. . . . (p. 357)

Everson's pantheism made him a pacifist [during the Second World War]; death and destruction in nature were part of the ecological cycle, but in the human order were violational because egoistic and malevolent. The figure of the bloody warrior from his Nordic ancestry stalks the poetry of the late 30's as the Shadow-inversion of the feminine pacifist-pantheist. But when the holocaust broke, Everson retreated to nature and spent the years 1943-1946 as a forester in an Oregon camp for conscientious objectors. "The Raid" describes war as rape, and "The Hare" acknowledges the Shadow in himself with the awareness, "father of guilt," that we are all killers. Still, fascinated as he was and remained with assertive masculinity (Jeffers was similarly ambivalent), he chose the C.O. camp in the name of his feminine susceptibilities. . . .

In 1946 he came to San Francisco to join the pacifist-anarchist group around Kenneth Rexroth who as writers were opposing the established academic poets and critics in the cause of open form and spontaneity. There he met and married the poet-artist Mary Fabilli. The sequences *The Blowing of the Seed* and *The Springing of the Blade* hymn their union and move the nature mysticism of the earlier poetry more explicitly into the area of human sexuality. But she was a lapsed Catholic undergoing a rebirth of faith, and through her ordeal Everson found his own life unexpectedly altered and clarified. . . . (p. 358)

At Midnight Mass, Christmas 1948, Everson was overwhelmed, psychologically, almost physically, by the divine presence in the tabernacle, and that mystical encounter led directly to his conversion the next year. However, by a grotesque twist of irony, the previous marriages of both partners and the prevailing Church procedures at the time made it impossible for them to remain husband and wife. *The Falling of the Grain* deals with the wrenching ironies and the overriding commitment which underlay their decision to separate. Two years later he entered the Dominicans as a lay brother and served for almost nineteen years, during which time the poems written as Brother Antoninus made him a figure in the San Francisco Renaissance and the Beat Generation. . . . (p. 359)

Everson's conversion and Antoninus' monasticism did not so much "break" his pantheism and erotic mysticism, as break them into a new set of circumstances and a new psychological and spiritual dimension. Now his life was centered on the Incarnation. Not an isolated historical event, but a daily miracle: the ongoing infusion of Creator into creation, supremely expressed in Jesus, the God-Man. The individual hangs on that cross, where all the contradictions of the human condition take on new consequence. The natural and the supernatural, soul and body, sexuality and spirituality—the Incarnation means that those seeming polarities, often vehemently at cross purposes, are meshed at the point of tension.

From the human point of view the Incarnation cancelled out Original Sin, so that God could redeem man from the sinfulness which was part of his freedom. Everson had seen the killer in himself; like Eliot, he knew that the fallible will needed to be curbed by ethical restraints and external norms lest creative freedom become oppression or anarchy; and his penitential bent sought the stricter discipline of monasticism. But from God's perspective the Incarnation is the completion of the creative act. On the one hand, God could be seen as driven to descend into flesh to save soul from body: the vision of Lowell and Eliot. But on the other hand God could be seen as having saved man in his human condition: not Spirit charging into flesh but Spirit embodied; not sinful flesh but transfigured body. The implications of this mystery were tremendous and dangerous, and Everson was driven to search them out. For when God became man, did He not submerge himself in the sexual element? In fact, was not sexuality the manifestation of that submersion? Had He not chosen from eternity to move in and through the sexual polarity, so that our sexual natures disclose their divine impulsion? Then in the heart-beat, pulse-throb, sex-urge, the Incarnation unfolds the contingencies of time and space, and subsumes them. Now Antoninus found himself confronting these paradoxes in exactly the situation which would test them most severely: separated from the wife who was the saint of his conversion, bound by his own election to a vow of celibacy.

Consequently the poetry of Brother Antoninus is almost obsessively concerned with the Feminine—that is, not only women, but his own sexuality and the feminine component in his psyche which mediates his passional, instinctual and poetic life. Decades before he had read Jung's psychology his poetry was recording his own often conflicting encounter with the major archetypes: in the psyche of a man, the Shadow, who represents his dark, repressed, even violent aspects; the Anima, the woman within, who is his soul and leads him into engagement with his erotic and spiritual potentialities; and, most dimly, the Self, that achieved and transcendent personhood realized through the resolution of polarities, who reveals himself as the God within and of whom, Jung says, Jesus is the symbol and reality. Everson's poetry through the war had enacted an initial rejection of the Shadow; now the Anima became the primary archetypal focus in the struggle toward transcendence. (pp. 359-60)

Many of the poems in *The Crooked Lines of God,* written soon after converting and becoming a Dominican, excoriate the flesh, and the poems in the first half of *The Hazards of Holiness* churn in the frustration not just of lust but of his passionate nature. They recount, Everson has said, his own "dark night." (p. 360)

However, by 1954 the stresses of the monastic life had dried up the inspiration, and it could resume again in 1957 only after a profound, shattering "breakthrough into the unconscious" the previous year, made possible by Antoninus' association with the Dominican Jungian Victor White, and by saturating himself in archetypal psychology. The result was a long narrative poem called *River-Root,* which is the most sustained orgasmic celebration in English, perhaps in all literature. Amongst the Antoninus poems collected into *The Veritable Years, River-Root* can be seen as a watershed: the turning away from the often austere asceticism of the years just after conversion back down again to primal nature, now transfigured in the mystery of the Incarnation. The narrative objectivity of the poem permitted Antoninus, while still under the vow of chastity, to render the intercourse between the husband and wife with a candor that, far from detracting from its sacramentality, climaxes in a vision of the Trinity. God's entry into flesh locates the sexual mystery, its source and activity and end, in the very Godhead.

River-Root, then, represented at once a recovery and synthesis and turning point. It opened the way back to poetry —and to the world. In *The Hazards of Holiness* the ascetic Antoninus struggled with and against the drift that had already begun to carry him, unaware, back to Everson. The last section of that divided volume expresses the full range of his experience of the feminine archetype: from the sexual force leading men to their death in the title poem (whether demonically, like Salome and the Baptist, or heroically, like Judith and Holofernes) to the Virgin mother and spiritual Wisdom of "A Canticle to the Great Mother of God." (pp. 361-62)

The Rose of Solitude tells of an encounter which moved him to his most exalted realization of the Feminine. The highest recognition that I can give the book, the final validation of poetry which refuses to distinguish between art and life, is the fact that it will leave the reader, too, shaken and transformed. The plot is not remarkable: Antoninus falls in love with a Mexican-American woman, breaks his vow of chastity with her, is led by her to repentance and confession; in the end they part. The remarkable quality stems from the character of the Rose herself. The sequence gradually reveals her and extols her as the apotheosis of the Feminine. . . . The sequence is so densely and intricately woven that it is difficult to excerpt passages, but "The Canticle of the Rose," "The Rose of Solitude" and "The Raging of the Rose" are prodigious feats of rhetoric, the poet pitching language to the extremes of articulation (the prolonged compounding of multisyllabic philosophical concepts in the "Canticle"; the wild incantation and imagery of "Solitude"; the synthesizing of the two modes in "Raging") in order to express the inexpressible fact that, in her, sexual sin becomes *felix culpa* and the Incarnation is accomplished. (pp. 363-64)

But the relationship ends in separation: the monk returning to his cell, releasing her to her own life and to another relationship. The end of the book is muted—necessarily so, since the Rose has had to be experienced, for all her glory, as forbidden, alien finally to his chosen existence. (p. 364)

Thus, after all the years as Brother Antoninus, he still had not recovered, except in exalted moments, that unquestioned oneness which he had felt with nature in the mid-thirties. (pp. 364-65)

It could be no simple duality. Everson had experienced Christianity "as a Dionysian phenomenon" at the time of his conversion and in subsequent moments of mystical transcendence; and, as he later recalled it, "this same movement took me into the monastery—to exclude everything from the ecstatic Dionysian core" in the life of Brother Antoninus. Dionysus symbolizes the Anima-dominated man, whose creative energy comes from his feminine affinities. (p. 365)

He could be Dionysian Christian, but could he remain a Dionysian monk? In the late sixties he moved toward taking final vows, even while sounding more emphatically the erotic basis of spirituality. . . . *Tendril in the Mesh,* Antoninus' last poem as a monk, strives to assimilate and terminate another love-relationship with a woman by subsuming its graphic sexual details in an "Epilogue" which experiences Incarnation not as idealized humanity but as animistic totem. . . . After the first public reading of this poem in December, 1969, Brother Antoninus stripped off his religious habit and announced to his shocked audience that he was leaving the Dominican Order. Shortly thereafter he married. . . . (pp. 365-66)

The precipitate departure indicated how much like a thunderclap it came, even to himself; and the poems of *Man-Fate* (1974) are the words of a man caught in a psychic crossfire: Antoninus become Everson again. During the years as Brother Antoninus, nature had remained a strong religious presence for him. The elegy for Jeffers, *The Poet is Dead,* works almost completely through images of the California coast, and poems like "The South Coast," "A Canticle to the Waterbirds," and "In All These Acts" project pantheism into Christian mystery. Now Everson withdrew again to nature to validate his break with Antoninus, but with a consciousness heightened and complicated by all that Antoninus had come to realize and value, and by the monastery life that Everson found it excruciating to leave behind. In the opacities of the elemental matrix he would be healed or torn apart.

That venture into the primeval is enacted in a sequence of dreams and archetypal fantasies which comprise the climax of *Man-Fate.* (p. 366)

The nightmares [in *Man-Fate*] tell what Antoninus already knew: that one cannot give over to the Shadow; abandonment to the powers of darkness without a guide will end in dissolution, chaos, death. For the man, the Anima can be such a mediator. She is grounded in the Shadow-area so strongly that at times she seems merely his vassal and instrument: the Feminine as temptation or threat. But in coping with the Shadow the man also engages *her*. And if trusted and loved, she can free him from enslavement to the Shadow, mediating the unconscious and the passions, drawing them from blind automation into activity and actualization in masculine consciousness, and thus opening the way gradually to Selfhood: the apocalypse of the polarized personality into androgynous, undivided identity. The Self is the psychological equivalent of the Beatific Vision, glimpsed in our supreme moments, but mostly striven for through the polar rhythms of living. For in Selfhood the individual attains not just what is uniquely himself, but thereby attains participation in the Godhead in which we shall all find ourselves at last.

Under the onslaught of the Shadow in *Man-Fate* Everson's response is instinctive and right: he turns to touch his wife. She is the objective verification of the Anima: a somnolent but locating presence, waiting for his return from lonely contention with the Shadow. For after the powerful consolidation of the Anima in *The Rose* and the subsequent poems, now no longer alien and suspect but tallied in his marriage, she lies ready to wake again from drowsy abeyance to spring him into the next thrust towards Selfhood. . . . Expressed in the archetypal terms of the human psyche, the Incarnation is God entering into, permeating and operating through the Feminine, just as the Annunciation proclaims. The concluding image above, physical yet suggestive of the sacramental act, constitutes, more immediately and elementally than with the Rose, the personalizing of the regenerative, redemptive mystery in the witness of the wife to the power of the Anima. Mother and wife and priestess in one, she administers him nourishment needed now for the way ahead. (pp. 367-68)

Albert Gelpi, "Everson/Antoninus: Contending with the Shadow" (copyright © 1978 by Albert Gelpi), in his afterword to The Veritable Years 1949-1966 *by William Everson, Black Sparrow Press, 1978, pp. 353-68.*

JAMES FINN COTTER

A poet whose religion was of as much interest as his writing, William Everson (then Brother Antoninus) has republished the work of his eighteen years as a Dominican lay brother. [*The Veritable Years: 1949-1966*] is the second in a trilogy called *The Crooked Ways of God*. Reading these poems again several decades later, one wonders what the fuss was all about. . . . Everson falls back on imitations of Jeremiah and Jeffers. Did Everson's reputation depend on the verbally sensational, the mock-biblical, and the autobiographical shock rather than on content and style? It appears so. Tip over the first exclamation point and line after line of poetry collapses like dominoes. Here pseudo-Donne ("Make me! Slake me! Back me! Break me!"), pseudo-Song of Songs (the poet's affair with "Rose"), and pseudo-Aquinas (Being exists, etc.) exploit the Christian tradition, not explore it. Everson explains too much, whether about his sexuality or his spirituality. (p. 117)

James Finn Cotter, "Familiar Poetry," in The Hudson Review *(copyright © 1979 by The Hudson Review, Inc.; reprinted by permission), Vol. XXXII, No. 1, Spring, 1979, pp. 109-22.**

ROGER TAUS

What a beautiful thing that William Everson's *River Root* comes out in a period of such sexual derangement. For what this epic and magnificent poem does is restore the love making between a man and a woman to its voluptuous and shuddering essence. It is as if Walt Whitman saw from the grave, with somber yet newly startling visage, that all the democratic vistas have long since been shattered like so many burned out tenements in the South Bronx, but still believed. . . . [Everson] gets to a vision of bonding in this poem that is enrapturing. Quieter, for obvious reasons (a century's difference), than Whitman, his celebration is nonetheless ecstatic, ceremonial and deeply erotic.

In a most intelligent foreword, the poet speaks of this work as "a monolithic anacronism, a core of primitive exultation out of the past." Its *presence*, however, sings, and calls us together.

Roger Taus, "Books in Brief: A Syzygy for the Bicentennial of These States," in The Minnesota Review *(© 1978* The Minnesota Review*), n.s. No. 12, Spring, 1979, p. 113.*

F

FAULKNER, William 1897-1962

Faulkner, an American novelist, short story writer, and poet, is considered one of the greatest writers America has produced. Although a variety of attitudes and themes are evident in his work, Faulkner is best known as the chronicler of the decadent South. His genius transcends regionalism, however: in his evocation of the mythical Yoknapatawpha, Faulkner's brilliant narrative technique, complexity of characterization, and innovative use of time sequence mark him as a major figure in American letters. Twice the recipient of the National Book Award and the Pulitzer Prize, Faulkner also received the Nobel Prize in 1950. (See also *CLC*, Vols. 1, 3, 6, 8, 9, 11, and *Contemporary Authors*, Vols. 81-84.)

JOHN T. IRWIN

My sense of the relationship between Faulkner, Freud, and Nietzsche is that they were writers who addressed themselves to many of the same questions, and that at numerous points their works form imaginative analogues to one another. (pp. 2-3)

It is precisely because I understand Faulkner, Freud, and Nietzsche to be related specifically as *writers* that I treat the works of all three as literary texts whose implications are ultimately philosophical. (p. 3)

The figure of Quentin Compson—the narrator locked in an incestuous, suicidal struggle with his dark twin, the story—is the shadow that falls in one form or another across the works of most postwar American novelists; it is a presence, a pervasive influence that the novelist who aspires to major status must come to terms with. (p. 20)

Of the many levels of meaning in [*Absalom, Absalom!*], the deepest level is to be found in the symbolic identification of incest and miscegenation and in the relationship of this symbolic identification both to Quentin Compson's personal history in *The Sound and the Fury* and to the story that Quentin narrates in *Absalom, Absalom!* (pp. 25-6)

One reason that the voices of the different narrators sound so much alike is that we hear those voices filtered through the mind of a single listener: Quentin's consciousness is the fixed point of view from which the reader *overhears* the various narrators, Quentin included. Since Quentin is the principal narrative consciousness in *Absalom,* and since the story of the Sutpens contains numerous gaps that must be filled by conjecture on the part of the narrators, it is not surprising that the narrative bears a striking resemblance to Quentin's own personal history and that of his family. . . . This is not to imply that the factual similarities between the stories of the Sutpen and Compson families are a product of Quentin's imagination, but to point out that, given these similarities of fact, Quentin as creative narrator could easily presume similarity of motivation. It is a mutual process in which what Quentin knows of the motivations in his own family life illuminates the story of the Sutpens and, in turn, the events in the Sutpens' story help Quentin to understand his own experiences. (pp. 26-7)

Faulkner did not need to make Quentin Compson a narrator of *Absalom,* nor did he need to involve the Compson family in the story of the Sutpens. The fact that he did both indicates that what we know of Quentin Compson and his family from *The Sound and the Fury* is somehow material to the meaning of Sutpen's story. . . . [For] Quentin the objectification of subjective contents is an effort to give a personal obsession a more than personal significance.

To what extent, then, does the story that Quentin tells in *Absalom* resemble his own life story in *The Sound and the Fury*? We noted first of all that Quentin's failure to kill Candace's seducer and thus fulfill the role of protective brother has its reverse image in Henry's murder of Bon to safeguard the honor of their sister. Also, Quentin's incestuous love for Candace is mirrored by Bon's love for Judith. That Quentin identifies with both Henry, the brother as protector, and Bon, the brother as seducer, is not extraordinary, for in Quentin's narrative they are not so much two separate figures as two aspects of the same figure. Quentin projects onto the characters of Bon and Henry opposing elements in his own personality. . . . This separation of the unacceptable elements from the acceptable elements in the self, this splitting of Quentin's personality into a bad half and a good half, with the subsequent tormenting of the good half by the bad and the punishment of the bad half by the good, involves a kind of narrative bipolarity typical of both compulsion neurosis and schizophrenia. The split is the result of the self's inability to handle ambivalence, in this case, Quentin's failure to reconcile his simultaneous attraction to and repulsion by the incestuous desire for his sister. The solution is primitive and effective: one simply splits the good-bad self into two separate people. . . . If at points during the narrative Quentin divides his personality between the characters of Bon and Henry, at other points Henry and Bon merge into one figure by exchanging roles. (pp. 27-9)

Clearly, the relationship between Henry and Bon is a form of doubling: the hero-worshiping Henry imitates Bon's manners, speech, and dress, while Bon . . . looks at Henry and thinks "*not* there but for the intervening leaven of that blood which we do not have in common is my skull, my brow, sockets, shape and angle of jaw and chin and some of my thinking behind it, and which he could see in my face in his turn if he but knew to look as I know but there, just behind a little, obscured a little by that alien blood whose admixing was necessary in order that he exist is the face of the man who shaped us both out of that blind chancy darkness which we call the future; there—there—at any moment, second, I shall penetrate by something of will and intensity and dreadful need, and strip that alien leavening from it and look not on my brother's face whom I did not know I possessed and hence never missed, but my father's, out of the shadow of whose absence my spirit's posthumeity has never escaped." . . . (pp. 29-30)

In the doubling between Bon and Henry, Bon plays the role of the shadow—the dark self that is made to bear the consciously unacceptable desires repudiated by the bright half of the mind. Throughout the novel, Bon is identified with the image of the shadow. (p. 30)

As Otto Rank has pointed out in his classic study of doubling [*The Double*], the brother and the shadow are two of the most common forms that the figure of the double assumes. Rank locates the origin of doubling in narcissism, specifically in that guilt which the narcissistic ego feels at "the distance between the ego-ideal and the attained reality." . . . Rank points out that in myth and literature the appearance of the double is often a harbinger of death and that just as often the ego attempts to protect itself by killing the double, only to find that this is "really a suicidal act." . . . It is in the mechanism of narcissistic self-love that Rank finds the explanation for that "denouement of madness, almost regularly leading to suicide, which is so frequently linked with pursuit by the double . . . ". . . . (pp. 33-4)

Both the narcissistic origin of doubling and the scenario of madness leading to the suicidal murder of the double help to illuminate the internal narrative of Quentin Compson's last day given in *The Sound and the Fury* and in turn to illuminate the story he tells in *Absalom*. . . . [It] is only when we see in the murder of Bon by Henry what Quentin saw in it—that Quentin's own situation appears to be a repetition of the earlier story—that we begin to understand the reason for Quentin's suicide. And this whole repetitive structure is made even more problematic by the fact that the explanation which Quentin gives for Bon's murder (that Bon is black, i.e., the shadow self) may well be simply the return of the repressed—simply an unconscious projection of Quentin's own psychic history. (p. 35)

Like Narcissus, Quentin drowns himself, and the internal narrative of his last day, clearly the narrative of someone who has gone insane, is dominated by Quentin's obsessive attempts to escape from his shadow, to "trick his shadow," as he says. (pp. 35-6)

Quentin's narcissism is necessarily linked with his incestuous desire for his sister, for as Otto Rank points out, brother-sister incest is a substitute for child-parent incest—what the brother seeks in his sister is his mother. . . . Quentin's drowning of his shadow, then, is not only the punishment, upon his own person, of the brother seducer by the brother avenger, it is as well the union of the brother seducer with the sister, the union of Quentin's shadow with his mirror image in the water, the mirror image of himself that evokes his sister lying on her back in the stream. The punishment of the brother seducer by the brother avenger is death, but the union of the brother seducer and the sister is also death, for the attempt to merge the shadow and the mirror image results in the total immersion of both in the water on which they are reflected, the immersion of the masculine ego consciousness in the waters of its birth, in the womb of the feminine unconscious from which it was originally differentiated. By drowning his shadow, Quentin is able simultaneously to satisfy his incestuous desire and to punish it, and . . . it is precisely this simultaneous satisfaction and punishment of a repressed desire that is at the core of doubling. For Quentin, the incestuous union and the punishment of that union upon his own person can be accomplished by a single act because both the union and its punishment are a *liebestod,* a dying of the ego into the other. (pp. 43-4)

Quentin's incestuous desire for his sister and the disabling fear of castration that she embodies for him have made Quentin in effect Candace's eunuch—impotent with his sister and yet obsessed with preventing her from making love to other men. . . . Quentin's brother Benjy is in certain respects a double of Quentin—in his arrested, infantile state, in his obsessive attachment to Candace, in his efforts to keep Candace from becoming involved with anyone outside the family, Benjy is a copy of Quentin, and when their brother Jason has Benjy gelded for attempting to molest a little girl, Benjy's physical condition doubles Quentin's psychological impotence, acting out the fate of the brother seducer at the hands of the brother avenger. Jason is, of course, named after his and Quentin's father. (pp. 51-2)

As Quentin's suicide is associated in his mind with the image of the general resurrection, so the dating of the other sections in the novel associates Quentin's death with Christ's death and resurrection, establishing for Quentin's suicidal murder of the brother seducer by the father-surrogate a religious context in which the archetypal son sacrifices his life to appease the anger of the archetypal father. (pp. 52-3)

[The] sense of a cyclic repetition within whose grip individual free will is helpless presents itself in Faulkner's novels as the image of the fate or doom that lies upon a family. Certainly, it would be difficult to think of two words used more often in *The Sound and the Fury* and *Absalom* than "fate" and "doom." (p. 60)

[The] feeling that an ancestor's actions can determine the actions of his descendants for generations to come by compelling them periodically to repeat his deeds is the form that the fate or doom of a family takes in Faulkner. Often in his novels the actions of a grandparent preempt the life of a grandchild. One thinks immediately of *Light in August* . . . , where the three principal characters . . . have had their destinies determined by the lives of their grandfathers. (p. 61)

Rank notes that for primitive man the earliest image of the immortal self was his shadow—the shadow which departs with the death of the grandfather but returns with the birth of the grandson. It would seem, then, that in the reversal fantasy we have the archetypal form of the temporal aspect of doubling. (p. 66)

[The crux] of Quentin's problem is repetition, the temporal form of doubling, for it is those inevitable repetitions inherent in the cyclic nature of time that seem to rob the individual will of all potency. Yet it is not just repetition that is involved here, it is recollection as well—the awareness of repetition. . . . (p. 69)

Surely, there can be no question that Quentin reconstructs the story of Bon, Henry, and Judith in light of his own experiences with Candace and Dalton Ames. . . . Quentin's recollection or reconstruction of the events in the story of the Sutpens turns out to be a reincorporation or reliving of [earlier] events. (p. 74)

[The] most striking example of the way in which Quentin's narrative act becomes a reincorporation of the lives of the people in that narrative is to be found in Quentin and Shreve's identification with Henry and Bon. Indeed, that identification becomes so complete that Quentin and Shreve supply the missing information in the story with the authority of participants and not simply narrators. . . . [The] interchangeability of the persons with whom [Quentin and Shreve] identify springs from the interchangeability of the roles of brother seducer and brother avenger, for in Quentin's case they are, of course, simply two aspects of a single personality. Since the relationship between the brother avenger and the brother seducer is a substitute for the father-son relationship in the Oedipal triangle, it is not surprising that when Quentin and Shreve identify with Henry and Bon, the narration turns into a father-son dialogue. . . . This basic interchangeability of the roles of father and son is present in both the reversal fantasy and the incest complex, and it is internalized in the father-son relationship of the roles of the superego and the ego within the self. (pp. 76-7)

[The] latent homoerotic content in the story of Bon and Henry may well be simply a projection of Quentin's own state made in the act of narration. (p. 78)

What Quentin must face . . . is that in terms of the content of an event no actual repetition in time is possible. . . . It can only be the internal compulsion to repeat, that compulsion to repeat which is rooted in the unconscious and thus operates without or in spite of the conscious will, that compulsion to repeat which . . . is always frustrated, a frustration that is experienced by the conscious mind, paradoxically, as a failure of will. (p. 80)

[There] is a clear connection between the repetition compulsion and doubling, a connection which Freud discusses at length in his essay on the uncanny. He points out that doubling is one of those structures that commonly evoke the feeling of the uncanny. . . . (p. 82)

[According to Freud] it is not every repetition that evokes the feeling of the uncanny, it is only certain events whose repetition reminds us of that inner compulsion to repeat, and the specific character of those events, according to Freud, is that they all represent the recurrence of something that has been repressed. Freud points out that every emotional affect, whatever its quality, is transformed by repression into morbid anxiety, and that that class of morbid anxiety that is associated with the return of the repressed is what we refer to as the feeling of the uncanny, irrespective of whether the original event aroused dread or some other affect. . . . (p. 83)

One can, I believe, construct a model showing the structural links between the repetition compulsion, the regressive character of the instincts, and the morbid anxiety evoked by the return of the repressed through the involuntary repetition involved in doubling, and this model will serve as an imaginative analogue to Faulkner's texts, shedding light on the structure of Quentin's personal history and the story he narrates. (p. 88)

If the involuntary repetition experienced in doubling recalls the helplessness sometimes experienced in dreams, it is because the double as the return of the repressed evokes by both its form and its content that primal threat of the son's being rendered permanently helpless by the castrating father—an overruling of the will from outside that has as its analogue the internal overruling of the will by the unconscious through the return of the repressed, the same overruling by the unconscious that we meet in dreams.

This sense of helplessness, of impotence, is, of course, the very core of Quentin's dilemma, for when Quentin tries to play an active, masculine role, his will is always frustrated and overruled and he is shifted into a passive, feminine role. . . . [It] is not just *within* the scenarios of brother avenger and brother seducer that Quentin's will is frustrated and Quentin rendered helpless, it is also by the very unwilled recurrence of those scenarios within the story that he narrates and in the events with the Italian girl and Gerald Bland that he is again rendered passive in the grip of fate. (p. 97)

In his interviews at the University of Virginia, Faulkner repeatedly pointed out that *Absalom* is a revenge story—indeed, a double revenge story: Sutpen's revenge for the affront that he suffered as a boy and Bon's revenge for the affront that he and his mother suffered at Sutpen's hands during Sutpen's quest for revenge. . . . Sutpen wants revenge not against the injustice of that mastery which the powerful have over the powerless, but against those "artificial standards or circumstances" that determine who are the powerful and who the powerless, against the artificial standard of inherited wealth and the circumstances of one's birth. Faulkner says that Sutpen in his quest for revenge violated all the rules of decency and honor and pity and compassion. But there is one rule that Sutpen does not violate, and that is the rule of power. For the rule that Sutpen follows is that real power springs not from the external, artificial advantages of birth and inherited wealth but from something internal: for Sutpen the source of real power is the force of the individual will. . . . [The] central paradox of Sutpen's quest [is] that he seeks revenge on the artificial standards of birth and inherited wealth as the determinants of power by setting out to establish a dynasty—that is, by trying to confer those very same artificial advantages on his son. Faulkner gives us the key to this paradox when he says that Sutpen "wanted revenge as he saw it, but also he wanted to establish the fact that man is immortal, that man, if he is man, cannot be inferior to another man through artificial standards or circumstances." (pp. 99-100)

[What] is at work in Quentin's struggle to bring the story of the Sutpens under control is the question of whether narration itself constitutes a space in which one can be original, whether an "author" possesses "authority," whether that repetition which in life Quentin has experienced as a compulsive fate can be transformed in narration, through an act of the will, into a power, a mastery of time. . . . At the beginning of the novel, Quentin is a passive narrator. The story seems to choose him. . . . But in the second half, when he and Shreve begin their imaginative reconstruction of the story, Quentin seems to move from a passive role to an active role in the narrative repetition of the past. (pp. 113-14)

[In the novel the] primal affront that the son suffers at the hands of the father and for which the son seeks revenge throughout his life is the very fact of being a son—of being the generated in relation to the generator, the passive in relation to the active, the effect in relation to the cause. . . . [But] the son can never really effect that reversal by which he would become his father's father. The son's only alternative is to take revenge on a substitute—that is, to become a father himself and thus repeat the generative situation as a reversal in which he now inflicts [revenge] on his own son, who is a substitute for the grandfather. . . .

When Sutpen takes revenge on a substitute for the affront that he received as a boy, he takes revenge not just on Charles Bon but on Henry as well. (p. 117)

Keeping in mind this notion of revenge on a substitute, we can now understand how Quentin's act of narration in *Absalom* is an attempt to seize his father's authority by gaining temporal priority. In the struggle with his father, Quentin will prove that he is a better man by being a better narrator—he will assume the authority of an author because his father does not know the whole story, does not know the true reason for Bon's murder, while Quentin does. Instead of listening passively while his father talks, Quentin will assume the active role, and his father will listen while Quentin talks. (p. 119)

As Quentin had to listen to his father tell the story in the first half of the novel, so in the second half Shreve must listen while Quentin tells the story. But what begins as Shreve listening to Quentin talk soon turns into a struggle between them for control of the narration with Shreve frequently interrupting Quentin to say, "Let me tell it now." That struggle, which is a repetition in reverse of the struggle between Mr. Compson and Quentin, makes Quentin realize the truth of his father's argument in *The Sound and the Fury*—that priority is not necessarily originality, that to come before is not necessarily to come first. For Quentin realizes that . . . Shreve will [in turn] try to take revenge on him by seizing "authority," by taking control of the narrative. What Quentin realizes is that generation as revenge on a substitute is an endless cycle of reversibility in which revenge only means passing on the affront to another who, seeking revenge in turn, passes on the affront, so that the affront and the revenge are self-perpetuating. (p. 120)

[If] for Quentin the act of narration is an analogue of . . . revenge on a substitute, then narration does not achieve mastery over time; rather, it traps the narrator more surely within the coils of time. What Quentin realizes is that the solution he seeks must be one that frees him alike from time and generation, from fate and revenge: he must die childless, he must free himself from time without having passed on the self-perpetuating affront of sonship. What Quentin seeks is a once-and-for-all solution, a nontemporal, an eternal solution. (pp. 122-23)

As the central enigmatic event in *Absalom* is Henry's murder of Bon, so its equivalent in *The Sound and the Fury* is Quentin's suicide, and the structures of both books, with their multiple perspectives in narration, point up the fact that the significance of these events is irreducibly ambiguous. . . . Certainly, by putting Quentin's suicide in the context of Christ's death, Faulkner makes the significance of Quentin's act more ambiguous, but this strategy works in two directions, for it also points up the irreducible ambiguities in the significance of Christ's death itself. With characters like Quentin and Joe Christmas, Faulkner uses the context of Christ's death to raise questions about the actions of these characters, and he uses their actions to question the meaning of the Christ role. His most explicit questioning of the ambiguous significance of Christ's redemptive act occurs in *A Fable* (1954), where Christ's passion and death are reenacted during the First World War in that struggle between the old general and the corporal, between the father who has supreme authority and the illegitimate son who is under a sentence of death. (pp. 124-25)

[In the structure that is central to Faulkner's work], the struggle between the father and the son in the incest complex is played out again and again in a series of spatial and temporal repetitions, a series of substitutive doublings and reversals in which generation in time becomes a self-perpetuating cycle of revenge on a substitute, the passing on from father to son of a fated repetition as a positive or a negative inheritance. . . . [Religious] sacrifice as an institutionalized substitute for those impulses is also a conscious, communal preserver and transmitter of those impulses. . . . (p. 157)

[Since this] structure is created by means of an interplay between texts, it must be approached through a critical process that, like the solving of a simultaneous equation, oscillates between two or more texts at once. The key to the critical oscillation that I have attempted between *Absalom, Absalom!* and *The Sound and the Fury,* is, of course, the figure of Quentin Compson—Quentin, whose own oscillation constantly transforms action into narration and narration into action. (pp. 157-58)

John T. Irwin, in his Doubling and Incest / Repetition and Revenge: A Speculative Reading of Faulkner *(copyright © 1975 by The Johns Hopkins University Press), The Johns Hopkins University Press, 1975, 183 p.*

WARREN BECK

As a fictionist Faulkner was not of any school, nor would he have abetted or blessed the recruitment of one. . . . In each work, and throughout each, he is his own man; and at his truest and best he has not yet been proved imitable. In various ways at many points he brilliantly intensified and refined effective fictional practices, by apt extensions of known artistic techniques. . . . [His] accomplishments remain unparalleled; and with the conspicuous tangentiality and cultural dispersions in more recent American fiction, it becomes plain that no one since him draws any such strong bow so closely aimed. What is still to be fully appreciated . . . is that despite some extravagances and excursions into the baroque, Faulkner stands as the central and preeminent American novelist, and if that fabulous entity the great American novel has already loomed above the horizon, it must be one of his major displays of mastery, such as *Absa-*

lom, Absalom!, Light in August, Go Down, Moses, or the Snopes trilogy. (p. 144)

Realistic regionalist, regional realist—the factors are reciprocal in the substantive and artistic unity of a Faulknerian work. This will be felt if the thrust of his realism and the focus of his regionalism are closely discerned. Their interrelations are complex yet harmonized. Faulkner cannot be given two discrete faces, even though sharply drawn, as a kind of realist and conversely a kind of regionalist. . . . His realism and regionalism are most distinctly recognizable in their complementary aspects, the local matter broadly conceptualized in a sustained artistic unity. For Faulkner realism is something more than naturalism, and quite the opposite of its extreme forms. His narratives do not move at an automated pace along determinism's constricted path, nor are his protagonists wholly indentured to milieu, no matter how weighty its impingements. . . . Faulkner feels too nearly and concernedly for his major characters to consider any of them wholly explicable, and yet he ventures to represent them in their conscious active lives as discernibly motivated, and suggests in each some bent toward congruence, so that through successive actions there aggregates the suggestion of a personal trend in which character becomes the more defined to others as also more deeply committed to its intentional self. (pp. 145-46)

In Faulkner's stories a moving force operates through some major characters in their disinterested and magnanimous advocacy of [certain values] overtly in a socioethical context but also at deep subjective levels of their private realizations. Recognized in this aspect, Faulkner's realism can be termed humanistic. . . . While Faulkner's fictional proponents of humanistic values resolutely combat unprincipled men, they cannot always prevail, nor can they stave off further offenses by such as Flem Snopes and lesser villains; therefore a weighty element in many of the stories is at a subjective level, in the protagonists' frustration, somber doubt, and sometimes outrage under the stress of a resisted temptation to give up. Through their uncertainties, disenchantment, and exacerbations in the struggle against socioethical offenses and incorrigible disorderliness there comes to be heard as a recurrent undertone the artist's own melancholy apprehensions. By some this has been felt as morbidity, but these readers may not have fully assessed Faulkner's realism, with its humanistic imperatives. . . . His recognition in his fiction that the well-intentioned are often deflected and even defeated and the innocent may be basely betrayed, while moral victories are transient in the flux of ever-changing circumstances only proves the honest percipience of Faulkner's realism and makes more exemplary the persistence of his agents of justice and mercy. (pp. 148-50)

It is with primary reference to character that humanistic-realistic aspects merge in Faulkner's art, through works rising to an enhanced organicism and authenticity beyond the inconsistencies of average behavior and the transient improvisations of expedient men in societal contexts. . . . Faulkner is objectively-subjectively aware of his characters not only as individual but intrinsically solitary beyond any conforming or gregariousness or even the remedies of love; his narratives comprehend such isolation, yet treat of it not with that autographic mock-pathetic solipsism often exhibited in modern novels, but as under the genuine ordeal of onerous, frustrating, sometimes disastrous human involvement. For Faulkner as oriented artist the existential being always is of primary interest and importance. . . . (pp. 150-51)

A vitalizing factor in the flow of Faulkner's subjectively realistic narratives enters through recurrence in some characters of recollected awareness, whether out of earlier acts or observations or information, and now returned to in a not merely extended but experientially modified perception and evaluation of them. This strategic use of repetition is acutely illustrative of Faulkner's constant basic concern with existential motion and change. . . . [Some] of Faulkner's most penetrating effects are to be found in such repetitions, where substance previously communicated, especially as a character's subjective experience, is transposed by further instance into another mode and reorchestrated with a fuller significance. . . . When read with response to this mode of a ranging subjectivity, Faulkner becomes a most absorbing storyteller, paradoxically the more so by his repetitions, in which matter is modified within the character's further realizations under changed circumstances, and this is to be valued not only in itself for its honestly realistic relativism, but in the artist's tactical use of it in the total narrative structure. Such a basic progressional-consequential setting-forth is of course the plain main way of all fiction; Faulkner's unique, dynamically objective-subjective use of it show genius at its height. (pp. 154-55)

Faulkner the humanistic realist is never sensational. He does not embroider events for their separately arresting effects, and while aspects of his stories are startling and in some degree shocking, yet the more intense this is, the more pervading is the created sense, in a many-toned, subjectively-attuned composition, that the issue is one of basic values. Concurrently there is always Faulkner's strategic narrative momentum, which does not dwell unduly upon event in itself . . . , but draws action into the modulations of consequence as realized and ethically evaluated by at least some of its enactors. His practice seems a careful avoidance of preoccupation with mere incidents, lest they overshadow the realities of a continuum. . . . Not just plotted event . . . , but conception and embodiment of such a deepening fluidity of experience, conveyed primarily through a directly represented awareness in his characters, is at the heart of Faulkner's humanistic realism, and is what his dramaturgically apt composition is designed to undergird.

It is only as seen in the unified functioning of such complementary factors that Faulkner's realism can be adequately estimated. Within the conceptualized and imaginatively rendered unity of a Faulkner novel the abstracting of verities increasingly apprehended by the working consciousness of protagonists is in an intuitive and responsive relationship with reality. Here the subjective and the societal are interactive and indeed symbiotic. . . . [Relativism] becomes dynamic in narrative actions, since it sharpens delineation of any human life in the endured fluxions that are its cumulative lot, and in particular makes fully veritable a conveyance of the matter through the turbulent counterpoint of a protagonist's objective-subjective experience. Herein Faulkner's searching realism is unflinching in its admission that grave threats to humanistic values persist. . . . (pp. 159-61)

[For] Faulkner as humanistic realist, men individually are the undependable but essential and possibly effective agents of melioration and can most fully realize themselves within such orientations. This is of course not unique in Faulkner, but he stands supreme in modern American fiction through the primacy and potency he gives this fundamental view. (p. 161)

Faulkner as fictionist concerns himself with stresses, frustrations, and miscarriages even under the law and more often under the looser rule of custom, yet he postulates that while implemental conventions and institutions as well as personal attitudes ask for reassessment situationally, certain value-concepts though pragmaticaaly arrived at have proved abidingly applicable and hence imperative whatever the pains. Faulkner discovers this again and again as an active kind of folk knowledge among common people tempered in the brunt of their beset lives, and he finds it equally operative among men and women whose good fortune imposes a strict sense of obligation. (p. 162)

The declared "Sole Owner & Proprietor" of that variously peopled and fabled "Yoknapatawpha Co., Mississippi" is one of the greatest of regionalists and irresistibly solicits consideration as such, yet as a rigorous realist. Moreover, in the light of his relativistic humanism and his corresponding attention to his characters' subjectivity as the way of close approach to theme and a medium of the matter's full imaginative realization his regionalism may be termed romantic in the most central and persistent sense of the term. (p. 163)

It would be erroneous to characterize Faulkner as self-indulgent in any aspect of his art. . . . Even when his style is copious it is to a point and of a calculated weight; and his narrative structures however complex are not loosely rambling but of proportionate and effective design, entirely to serve his brooding reflectiveness even in proximity to a throng of characters in a flood of events.

Faulkner not only illustrated as transcendental reality that one can go venturing in one's own back yard, he showed that what a fictionist has seen most of he may be able to see into most deeply. . . . (pp. 164-65)

The broad dimensions of Faulkner's genius are to be estimated both from the magnitude and substantiality of his conceivings of regional subjects and from his commensurate imaginative penetration into a continuum of events given their coloration through characters involved by their awareness as well as in their actions. Thus his regionalism, humanistically realistic, goes deeper than the data of naturalism; thus his representations of subjectivity, going beyond that of an isolate introverted life, show involvement in matters of wide relevance and personal interrelation, and more than single import. Not that the narrative may not include characters' states of mind concealed from all but the reader, but those transpire in a context of circumstances; these are contributively particularized by the subjective responses to them, an interaction that epitomizes Faulkner's basic idiosyncratic fictional mode. In this fusion of scope and subjectivity his fictional art achieves an equilibrium and a steadily operative reciprocation, with a suggested symmetry, a uniquely potent aesthetic effect. It is indefinable, and its factors are scarcely to be analyzed, but it is there, the characteristic Faulknerian tone, an extraordinary achievement in the craft of fiction, that distinctive resonance which in some novels and in portions of others may seem comparable to the sostenuto of a perfected lyric poem or an unintermitted musical composition. (pp. 167-68)

Though racial interrelations constituted a major and in some ways central theme in Faulkner's regionally focused fiction, that was not his whole story. Tensions arising from racial antipathies and anxieties may have widest societal significance, and he seems to be probing most deeply when it comes to that, but there are other kinds of conflict on less extended grounds to which he gives as much intensity. . . . The socioeconomic and psychological stratifications in the South as typified in Yoknapatawpha County are not only a matter of race but of antecedents and ongoing tendencies and consequent distinctions in the whole society, within the perspectives of regional history. Yet quite possibly an adequate appreciation of Faulkner's works was retarded, perhaps even impeded for a while by the emphasis some critics put upon considering it a kind of epic in many episodes and books, even a saga of the South. . . . [Throughout] the *oeuvre* from novel to novel there are great differences in magnitude, narrative structure, and mode; and this may well be noted not only as evidence of a profuse imagination but also as a passion at that particular point for its own focus and concentration of effect. It seems especially the characteristic of his artistic temperament to be susceptible to absorbing commitments. With each work the artist appears to have given himself completely during the process of its creation, bent upon the most intense realization of its potentials. No doubt such absorption in the singular task and its opportunities was made easier by a continuing familiarity with regional materials, but the perfected autonomy in each novel as a work of art is closer to the essence of the Faulknerian achievement than the sense of locale or of recurring racial tensions, and a proof of the matter is that when an already known character enters into yet another narrative action he or she is absorbed into it, depending on no credentials from another country, and manifesting a fresh aspect in his new surroundings. This, however, is not by subordination of identity, but in fresh instancing of the subjective element as the pervading factor imaginatively uniting a humanistic reality and a romantic regionalism. (pp. 173-74)

Faulkner's works are each so particularly formed, colored, and consummated that he continues to defy the sort of imitation which can produce a school. . . . What was characteristic that could be an influence (in addition to a brilliant example of the regional transmuted into dynamically representative art) was his alertness to the forceful centrality of the subjective element, as he had found it in the strongest fiction of his times, and as he had gone along with this trend but to his own ends, with rapidly acquired skills, through adaptations less conspicuously technical than in *The Sound and the Fury* and *As I Lay Dying*. Therein he became more various, with a greater tonal range even if in less extensive subject matter and with less sophistication than James. . . . Faulkner was also more originative than Conrad, whom nevertheless he resembles greatly as a spirit, a temperament that must have some place in the work, though Faulkner's felt infiltrations, while more forceful, are less frankly personal. (pp. 218-19)

In Faulkner's narrative art a progressive modulation operates regulatively within the mingled flow of objective-subjective matter. Such gradations result in a more complex texture than that in pure stream-of-consciousness narration or in the typical uses of a central intelligence, whether first- or third-person. Both these modes, as well as overt omniscient narration, enter into Faulkner's practice; the difference is that often they are refracted from a formal, sustained employment of one or the other into transitory uses in a complexity that fluctuantly combines modifications, sometimes of them all, always with variances between objective-subjective extremes. Faulkner is not unique in this, but he was an independent pioneer in such synthesizing of representational modes within a unitary fictional narrative, and what is extraordinary is the intensity of his achieved effects, combining a fluidity of subjective penetration and an enhanced momentum. . . . Faulkner in his most characteristic bent left still further behind the easiness of a preempted and constantly presiding authorial omniscience, to achieve instead an almost Flaubertian aloofness. Even when narration is in first person it is the verified player speaking; and the widely proved advantage of such distancing in modern fictional art is that the characters, left on their own whatever the mode of expression given them, are made to stand forth and represent themselves in deeds, words, and states of inner being, as these are the immediate passing aspects of their roles. . . . By their involved, responsive, and projective imaginations Faulkner's protagonists become impressionistic poets of situation and involvement. . . . (pp. 220-21)

Faulkner has followed the main way of much of [modern English and American fiction at its most serious levels]. He is not an eccentric artist; he does not differ essentially from those in the fertile modern trend that derived its aesthetics of fiction, including control of point of view and narrative use of subjectivity, primarily from James and Conrad, and produced a remarkably various yet instrumentally conventionalized flowering in Faulkner's own time. Faulkner's distinction, which requires that he be named among the most distinguished of his contemporaries and immediate predecessors, is not in a difference from the most significant trends in fiction; rather it is in his superlative accomplishment, in its scope, grasp, vigor, and intuitive penetration, and the sheer virtuosity of his greatest compositions. (pp. 257-58)

That Faulkner's closely centralized regionalism was not an opportunistically chosen fixed stance is apparent not only in his fictional excursions from native ground but in the thematic range of his Yoknapatawphan novels themselves as unique artistic autonomies. (p. 270)

Regionalism provided the rich substance and fluent modes of Faulkner's work, but the profound idiom of his communications is a humanistic realism. . . . While naturalism in fiction is not without objective grasp in its constancy to profuse materials, in this aspect Faulkner's regionalism, though forcefully authentic, was more selective of detail, to further ends. For him emphasis by comparative limitation of substance and selective ordering of narration itself served to implement a dynamic realism stressing what in the local instance also suggests the more widely typical. Thereby as a regionalist whose developing concepts . . . had feeding roots which ran close and deep in an immediate acquaintance, his fictions transcended entirely the dimensions of typical naturalism. (pp. 271-72)

Under Faulkner's synthesis of regionalism and realism what his technical accomplishment most differed from was not a simple objective naturalistic fiction but its opposite, stream-of-consciousness narration, with its narrowed exclusive subjectivity along a more random and desultory way, with a greater self-preoccupation and less involvement, in a diminution of dramatic tensions. The very life of each of Faulkner's greatest fictional works is in its lives figured as interpersonally situated, through which there fluctuantly interpenetrates a variable fusion of forces, objective-subjective, communal and individual, overt events and private responses tinged with relevant individual concern. Regionalism sharpens issue through its situational immediacy in the pressures of milieu, and thus frames the singular qualities of individual responses; correspondingly through that medium a humanistic realism makes the local representative and further sanctions its specificity. In this totality the private awareness of Faulkner's characters is shown moving through attitude into action, and such purposeful consciousness implies subjective configurations, the gestalts of organismic thought and feeling. Presumably out of comparable imaginative awareness and response there may have loomed more largely the cloudy silhouettes of not impossible fictional entities for this greatly gifted artist to arrest and perfect into the totalities of inclusive concept and aesthetically containing form. This apparently he had proved as the one thing needful for himself, given the fruitful juncture of regionalism and humanistic realism in an achieved objective-subjective juncture and functioning. That unity, ultimately validated in the holistic work of art itself, could have increasingly stimulated him to the pure sorcery, through style and structure, which liberated his genius and enabled consummate masterpieces. (pp. 273-74)

Warren Beck, "Realist and Regionalist" (revised by the author for this publication), in his Faulkner: Essays *(copyright © 1976 The Regents of the University of Wisconsin System), The University of Wisconsin Press, 1976, pp. 144-274.*

MICHAEL GRIMWOOD

William Faulkner's "address upon Receiving the Nobel Prize for Literature" is a classic statement of humanist affirmation. (p. 366)

The text that appears in freshman anthologies is a noble statement, a model of rhetoric transcending platitude. But the text that Faulkner delivered to the Swedish Academy—albeit an identical one—is false and insincere. It lacks eloquence, because Faulkner did not fully believe what he was saying.

The first half—yes. He did believe what he said about other writers: that they had "forgotten the problems of the human heart in conflict with itself which alone can make good writing," and that those who fail to confront the "old verities and truths of the heart" doom themselves to write "not of the heart but of the glands." These sentiments reflect principles he had always held. But the final, longest paragraph of the Speech presents a teleological defense of his foregoing remarks which contradicts not only the pessimism implicit in his early works but opinions he was expressing in current books as well. That paragraph will be familiar to most students of modern literature:

> Until [the writer] relearns [the old universal truths], he will write as though he stood among and watched the end of man. I de-

> cline to accept the end of man. It is easy enough to say that man is immortal simply because he will endure: that when the last ding-dong of doom has clanged and faded from the last worthless rock hanging tideless in the last red and dying evening, that even then there will still be one more sound: that of his puny inexhaustible voice, still talking. I refuse to accept this. I believe that man will not merely endure: he will prevail. He is immortal, not because he alone among creatures has an inexhaustible voice, but because he has a soul, a spirit capable of compassion and sacrifice and endurance. The poet's, the writer's, duty is to write about these things. It is his privilege to help man endure by lifting his heart, by reminding him of the courage and honor and hope and pride and compassion and pity and sacrifice which have been the glory of his past. The poet's voice need not merely be the record of man, it can be one of the props, the pillars to help him endure and prevail.

This stirring assertion of immortality for the human spirit, and of the writer's contribution to that immortality, presents only one side of an internal debate that preoccupied Faulkner throughout the 1940s and into the fifties. It therefore provides a false resolution to a question Faulkner was then still struggling to answer, a question that touched him personally in a way the Speech conceals: not only "Will mankind prevail?" (that is, does human history have meaning?), but also "Is it meaningful for me, William Faulkner, to write?" (is *my* voice "inexhaustible"?).

This context of internal debate can best be demonstrated by tracing the history of the central image in the last paragraph of the Speech—that of the lone man standing upon the last rocky island in an apocalyptic seascape. From early in his career, Faulkner used this image as a metaphor for his own literary situation; and variations in his use of it reflect important shifts in his attitude toward his vocation. (pp. 366-67)

While, in the Speech, Faulkner admonished writers to contribute their words to the construction of a refuge for mankind, in *The Sound and the Fury* the words themselves are a force from which the speaker seeks refuge. The Speech denies the possibility that man's voice will exhaust itself, but the novel seems to accept such a possibility as desirable: the ultimate goal of language is to move "beyond the need for words." A major change *has* occurred between 1928 and 1950; but it has less to do with Faulkner's supposed conversion to humanist affirmation than with the advent of severe doubts about the efficacy of his vocation—doubts he had to appease in order to continue writing. In 1928, Faulkner felt the imperative voice within himself too strongly to resist an attempt to move beyond it; but in 1950 he was too fearful of his own exhaustion, and too disillusioned with the idea that language can transcend itself, to speak favorably of the condition of silence.

The debate within him between faith and doubt began in earnest in the late thirties, when he complained for the first time of an intermittent inability to write. Financial difficulties, family responsibilities, and his failure to reach a comprehending audience contributed to this dilemma, but it also derived from his growing pessimism about the future of mankind. . . .

[In *Go Down, Moses* the] river is an instrument of oblivion, embodying all of Faulkner's fears for his own vocation and for world history. The admonition in the novel's title to "go down" bespeaks his prevailing awareness of decline.

Yet *Go Down, Moses* also contains a hopeful vision, and it was within a confrontation between the two opposite attitudes that Faulkner first composed the germ of the last paragraph of the Nobel Prize Speech, using language that became formulaic for him even before he received the prize. As a young man, Ike McCaslin had become disillusioned with his social heritage. He chose to reject the past, to erase his historical memory, and to begin life hopefully anew. Consequently, he was willing to dispense with written records, for they only preserve past injustices without actively accommodating change. An exponent of oblivion, the younger Ike articulates Faulkner's own deep suspicion of the inertia and ineffectuality of words. Against this position stands Ike's cousin Cass Edmonds, who defends inherited evils and cultivates book-knowledge—consulting a volume of Keats's poetry, for example, in order to explain an experience Ike would rather leave to instinct. Thus, Faulkner entrusted his optimism about the human race to a man who belittles the value of writing and his defense of literacy to a man who accepts a bleak vision of history—a confusion he only artificially untangled in the Nobel Speech. (pp. 370-71)

Despite his covert pessimism, Faulkner adopted an affirmative pose before the world, and probably for his own benefit as well, during his laureateship. He frequently repeated the sentiments of the Nobel Address in interviews and in other speeches he delivered, as if he were consciously fulfilling the writer's duty to uplift the human heart which he had asserted in Stockholm; and he used the same language in many of his later books. (p. 373)

The immortality of mankind and, implicitly, the future of Faulkner's artistic legacy remain doubtful in *A Fable*. The debate between the general and the corporal—which they have no more resolved than Ike and Cass have theirs in *Go Down, Moses*—articulates the division between faith and despair that afflicted Faulkner throughout the forties and into the fifties. He tried to persuade himself that he, *and* mankind, had a future; and toward the very end of his life he may have succeeded in doing so. But in the Nobel Prize Speech he voiced only half of what was within him. While advising his listeners to write about "the human heart in conflict with itself," he was wishfully ignoring the conflict within himself, which his books revealed whether he wished them to or not. (pp. 374-75)

Michael Grimwood, "The Self-Parodic Context of Faulkner's Nobel Prize Speech," in The Southern Review *(copyright, 1979, by Michael Grimwood), Vol. XV, No. 2, April, 1979, pp. 366-75.*

ALICE SHOEMAKER

As I Lay Dying is a remarkable illustration of [the fusion of form and content], for in this tour de force the author blends the architectonic structure of a wheel within a wheel with subject matter based on the age-old quest resulting in geographically, psychologically, and philosophically cyclical movement. Two antithetical perspectives are represented in this novel, that of Bundrens and non-Bundrens toward the journey to Jefferson. These perspectives can be conceived of architectonically as the rims of two concentric wheels moving in opposite directions through time and space. The Bundren perspective is the inner wheel with the somewhat varying viewpoints of the individual family members represented as points on the wheel directed toward the hub of the wheel, Addie Bundren, the primary motivation for the journey. An outer rim, that of non-Bundrens, constitutes a different perspective toward the Jefferson trip. This rim of perspective views Addie and the Bundrens themselves in the process of their peregrination and regards the trip as absurd. (pp. 101-02)

Despite the fact that Addie has but one segment, written as though she were still alive and yet significantly placed *after* her death, her consciousness suffuses the entire book. (p. 108)

[All] of the Bundrens, in one way or another, sense and acknowledge Addie's continued presence, just as the entire family has internalized Addie's distrust of words—"the high dead words in time." . . . Thus the Bundren perspective focuses on Addie and her will to be buried in Jefferson. . . . (p. 109)

Those outside the Bundren family do not share this perspective. Addie's lover Whitfield does violence to Addie's central concern—the matching of word with deed. (p. 110)

The Bundrens seem oblivious to the spectacle their journey elicits and to the stench which Addie's unembalmed body produces. . . . Hence, the outsiders, the non-Bundrens, view the family and their journey as some kind of grotesque and ridiculous joke. To them the Bundren quest, although it cannot be ignored, is not to be taken seriously. Thus, the two perspectives—a wheel within a wheel—move through time and space to help reveal the complexity of modern consciousness in regard to life and to death.

Addie serves not only as the hub of the inner wheel but as the central metaphor of time and space. (pp. 111-12)

Another way in which Faulkner achieves this fusion of time and space is by stopping or elongating time. We have already noted how Addie's dying is elongated. Darl, who is Faulkner's chief spokesman regarding time, compares Addie's continuing consciousness to a road, one of Faulkner's favored time-related analogues. (p. 112)

However, there is one more aspect to be considered, that of the reader's perspective; for Faulkner, in his novels, relied on the reader's creative energies to form a heuristic concept. Thus, the reader's view toward the Bundrens' journey (a quest in many ways analogous to that of the reader's own journey through life to death) may not coincide with the Bundren perspective of heroic necessity or with the non-Bundren perspective of grotesque absurdity. The reader's perspective may encompass more than that of Bundrens and non-Bundrens so that the fusion of parts, by means of the heuristic process, results in a whole which is greater than the sum of its parts. Subtly, Faulkner acknowledged the creative role of the reader when, near the end of the novel, he has Cash say "It was like he [Darl] was outside of it too, same as you." . . . (p. 113)

Alice Shoemaker, "A Wheel within a Wheel: Fusion of Form and Content in Faulkner's 'As I Lay Dying'," in Arizona Quarterly *(copyright © 1979 by Arizona Board of Regents), Vol. 35, No. 2, Summer, 1979, pp. 102-13.*

PAUL ROSENZWEIG

In *Absalom, Absalom!* the richness of texture and detail is so great that the full effect of the many narrative frames is easily obfuscated. The comparison between the present (the narrative frames) and the past (Sutpen's story) accentuates many of the central themes of the primary story, imparting a sense of timelessness to the story and showing how myth is created to contrast with the reality from which it grows. Yet a far more subtle and revolutionary effect of the novel's overlapping and interwoven frames is the manner in which they—as they reflect and distort both the primary story and one another—comment on the problems of epistemology, the imagination, art, and the creative process.

While Faulkner is centrally concerned with the imagination in all his novels, . . . he never directly extended this concern to the province of art. . . . Perhaps this omission was caused by a more traditional attitude toward art than, for instance, such a novelist as Gide or Mann had—one which both did not so radically question the possible conflict between the traditionally moral function of the novel and a more purely esthetic perspective, and one that accepted art's traditional function of representing an ultimate reality. Such an attitude might seem inconsistent with Faulkner's depiction within his novels of the imagination as a distorting mechanism that limited rather than increased man's contact with reality; but Faulkner . . . never fully applied his perceptions of the mind's inherent distortions to the functioning of his own artistic imagination. It is for this reason that *Absalom, Absalom!*'s narrative frames are of particular interest, for they set up an implicit—even if partially unintentional—metaphor for the artistic process, thus extending a concern for the imagination to the province of art.

Although the novel's themes, like its structures, are complex and diverse, the central theme of the primary story of Sutpen deals with love, which the novel seems to define as the ability to see and care for another *in his own right*. All the characters in the primary story lack this ability and this ubiquitous lack is the ultimate cause of evil in the novel. (pp. 135-36)

However, while this theme of love denied is central to the primary story, in the secondary narrative framework the central theme is the search for truth—the truth about Sutpen's, Bon's, and Henry's complex motivations, and, more generally, the truth about all human motivation. . . . As the novel progresses, we along with Quentin seem to progress toward the truth. (p. 136)

There is an ironic element to this sense of progress toward the truth, for each successive narration of the story appears to be told by a narrator who is further removed from the original action both in time and in direct involvement. . . . Such an inverse relationship between distance and truth suggests that a type of detachment, an emotional and artistic distance on events, is needed to discover the truth. (pp. 136-37)

However, there are problems with such a neat thesis. For one thing, the progression is not so clearly defined as it at first might seem. . . . More importantly, while in some ways we seem closer to the truth as the novel progresses, in others we seem equidistant or further removed from it, although the fact of our removal is subtly, even deceptively, made. The successive versions of the story are increasingly products of the imagination. Therefore, while they are more fully and vividly told, this sense of their reality is in inverse proportion to the actual knowledge the narrators have. (p. 137)

[A radical twist occurs near the end of the novel.] Not content to embellish upon and flesh out the truth upon the skeleton of bare facts, Shreve changes one of these facts. He insists that it was Henry, not Bon, who was wounded in the war. . . . The radical nature of this statement goes far beyond the one fact it alters. Although we may reject Shreve's logic as applied to this one case, it serves to suggest how tenuous is our hold on even the "facts" of the story. (pp. 138-39)

All the narrators' accounts are distorted by their own interests and needs. . . . [In Quentin's case] his concern with manhood, impotence, and incest is reflected throughout *Absalom, Absalom!* and it is not hard to imagine how he receives and in turn creates the various versions of the primary story. From this perspective, *Absalom, Absalom!* becomes a novel about the narrators rather than about their narratives. (pp. 139-40)

To fully appreciate the problems inherent in this question of narrator interference is to open a Pandora's box on rampant skepticism as to the reliability of any fact and to consign oneself to the impossibility of knowing anything absolutely. To the initial problem of deducing from an incomplete set of mere external facts complex motivations is added the consideration of a myriad of reasons and ways in which each of these facts may have been distorted. To separate the actual occurrence from narrator distortion and addition is an impossible task, for we cannot merely compensate for idiosyncratic reflections of the narrator in his narrative since there always remains the possibility, and in many cases, probability, that some such "reflections" have originated in the story itself and colored the narrator's personality. Thus it is not merely one distorting lens that we are faced with but two opposing, distorting mirrors, each reflecting the distortions of the other. Moreover, because of the series of narrators involved in most of the products we receive, we have a whole series of distorting lenses and mirrors, each conditioned by the distorted version received from an earlier narrator. Even such distortions, however, are only the tip of the iceberg. There is the more egregious problem of outright fabrication. . . . (pp. 140-41)

From this perspective, while the central theme of the primary story is the inability of any character to truly love another, the central theme of the secondary frames as they reflect that story is the inability of anyone to know the truth. Nor are these two themes of love and truth so separate. . . . [Both] failures—to love and to know the truth—have the same source, the overbearing ego that imposes and projects upon everything outside itself, itself. (p. 141)

Yet, although such speculations lead to a radical appreciation of the illusive and illusory nature of all truths, the case that *Absalom, Absalom!* presents for the attainment of truth is not so unilaterally bleak. The contrasting nature of the other imaginative level of truth does not allow so simple a skepticism. In a sense Faulkner seems to be playing a game with the reader. In the search for truth we are continually teased with facsimiles of the truth which, to the degree they seem real, are in fact false, for the meagerness of knowledge about the primary events forces any scrupulously scientific reportage to exist as mere skeletons, ghosts of truth, while the more truly imagined and thus more detailed scenes take on more readily the semblance of reality. What seems real and what is seen to exist in an inverse relationship to one another. (pp. 141-42)

[The] form of the novel, the interaction between narrative frames and primary story, introduces a concern for the imagination and the artistic process. . . . In fact, in what might seem a largely pessimistic novel, the only source of transcendence comes, not in the primary story through an individual's power to love, but through the secondary frames of the narrators, primarily Quentin and Shreve. Through the power of their imagination they transcend time and self, uniting with each other and with Bon and Henry. . . . In fact, if there is any sense of love shown in the novel, it is displayed by these two narrators as they work together, their imaginations united.

This link between the moral and esthetic sphere and the identification between imagination and love as transcending factors, so that the esthetic factor, the imagination, becomes a criterion for judging the moral sphere of love, are themes found usually in a more purely esthetic writer such as James or Nabokov. The paradoxes that *Absalom, Absalom!* inevitably creates because of its form—the paradoxical nature of truth and the necessity of creating esthetic distance to bridge emotional, psychological, and spiritual distances—link it with the involuted, self-conscious fictions of such writers as Nabokov, Barth, Cortazar, Borges, Robbe-Grillet, and Beckett. All are writers who deal with the problems of the relationship between reality and the mind as bridged by the imagination and who use the metaphor of the novel itself to discuss and reflect these relationships. By placing a representation of himself as novelist in his novel, the self-conscious novelist automatically creates a series of mirrors that not only reverberate within the novel but between it and the "objective" external reality of author and audience. In so dispelling the conventions of the novel form that established qualitative distances between the characters, the novelist, and his audience, the self-conscious novel challenges that absolute nature of any reality and investigates the relationship between truth and illusion, not merely as they undercut, but as they contribute to one another.

Absalom, Absalom! is Faulkner's most self-conscious novel and by internalizing narrators equivalent to himself he implicitly sets up the metaphor of novel-writing and creates truncated versions of many of the same effects that can be found in the fictions of more fully involuted writers. Like such fictions as Nabokov's *Pale Fire* or Barth's *Lost in the Funhouse,* but to a far lesser degree, *Absalom, Absalom!* is a novel about its own creation. Once the narrators, primarily Quentin-Shreve, are seen as novelists of a sort in the process of writing and rewriting a novel, each time moving a bit closer to the finished product, embracing a truer picture through a purer use of the imagination, all that has been said here becomes a series of statements about the artist's relationship to his art. (pp. 143-44)

Faulkner seems to be suggesting that the ideal artistic relationship between the artist, his material, and his audience is a symbiotic relationship in which each partakes of and is changed by the others and all are simultaneously active and passive. (p. 145)

In the application of this thematic duality of simultaneous creator and audience to Faulkner's relationship to his readers and his novels, it is interesting to note that not only does he force on his readers in many of his novels a greater participatory role than in most traditional novels, but in talking of his relationship to his characters he often places himself in the more passive role. (p. 147)

The involuted novels of Nabokov or Barth invariably describe themselves and in *Absalom, Absalom!* there are numerous passages that on a second reading can be seen to describe the novel itself. (p. 149)

The double metaphor that Judith Sutpen employs to describe the restrictions each individual encounters both from others and apparently from on high can also be read in this manner:

> . . . you are born at the same time with a lot of other people, all mixed up with them, like trying to, having to, move your arms and legs with strings only the same strings are hitched to all the other arms and legs and the others all trying and they dont know why either except that the strings are all in one another's way like five or six people all trying to make a rug on the same loom only each one wants to weave his own pattern into the rug; and it cant matter, you know that, or the Ones that set up the loom would have arranged things a little better. . . .

Both metaphors have their source in art and describe not merely the interaction between characters in the primary story but both the interaction between narrators, each attempting to impose his own patterns on events, and our trouble as readers attempting to separate our own meaning or pattern from the apparent chaos of narrator-imposed patterns. The two levels of the double metaphor imply a double level of patternmaking, not merely by the individual weavers or puppets but by the Puppeteer or the "Ones who make the looms"—that is, the artist-narrators and Faulkner. Judith's problem of asserting her will is thus not merely limited by her contemporaries (the other characters in the primary story) but by those succeeding generations of narrators who impose their own obscuring patterns upon hers. Yet the apparent chaos of this triple imposition of patterns is resolved—although Judith cannot see it—in the larger pattern of the novel (or Loom or Puppet Show) which uses the interwoven patterns of apparent chaos (the interwoven narrative frames) to form a clear, if intricate, meaning. (pp. 150-51)

[An] artist's imaginative patterning replaces outside fate and becomes a comment on the imaginative psychology of the creator of the pattern rather than a statement about an external fate.

The stylized nature of all the primary characters, who never seem to truly emerge as full characters, should also be viewed from this perspective. We are not viewing them directly through Faulkner's eyes but through the intermediary multiple veils of narrator-artists who, quite contrary to Faulkner's own realistic aims, are involved in mythmaking. That the primary characters, although we know far more about them, seem less real than the narrators, is Faulkner's comment on the limits of his narrators' imaginations. Although they create, their inability to fully conceive another person is a comment not on Faulkner's artistry but on Quentin's, Shreve's, and Mr. Compson's shortcomings. (p. 152)

Paul Rosenzweig, "The Narrative Frames in 'Absalom, Absalom!': Faulkner's Involuted Commentary on Art," in Arizona Quarterly *(copyright © 1979 by Arizona Board of Regents), Vol. 35, No. 2, Summer, 1979, pp. 135-52.*

ELIZABETH M. KERR

Faulkner was *both* a realist and a romanticist and was positively Gothic: an artist can view life from various perspectives if his vision is sufficiently comprehensive and penetrating. Faulkner loved his land and his people too much to reject them in their everyday aspects, without romantic or Gothic makeup and lighting, and some of his characters share his love of the ordinary. He was enough of a romanticist to feel keenly the difference between the reality he observed and what his land and his people had been at their best, between the sometimes nightmarish present and the fine dreams they had cherished.

Faulkner achieved the fusion of dream and reality in his Yoknapatawpha novels. . . . By assuming many points of view and imaginatively sharing the experiences of many diverse characters, by showing the outer world as it appeared to the mentally deficient, the psychologically disturbed, or the romantic idealist, Faulkner revealed the inner worlds of dream and nightmare and the razor's edge which separated them. As the omniscient author or through a rational, humanistic central intelligence or narrator, he showed a world of everyday experience, cherished in its multiplicity and uniqueness. The scope provided by this fictional world, despite its short history and limited boundaries, accommodated a variety of approaches, within a single novel or within the Yoknapatawpha cycle. In this cycle, only *As I Lay Dying, The Town,* and *The Reivers* are more in the romance vein than some version of Gothic novel or romance. (Although *As I Lay Dying* has a macabre quality and a partially Gothic effect, I deal with it in my article as an ironic version of quest-romance.) For Faulkner, it is apparent, Yoknapatawpha was essentially a Gothic realm. (pp. 220-21)

Faulkner never abandoned the advantages of the omniscient author but tried various limitations of omniscience, always with the purpose of getting inside a character and involving the reader as fully as possible. With an inarticulate character or one of limited awareness and self-knowledge, such as Mink or Joe Christmas, the style must be the author's. The restriction or the relinquishment of authorial omniscience, however, had great advantages in securing reader cooperation and involvement in a Gothic tale. The most difficult and successful experiments with multiple points of view, with interior monologue or soliloquy, came early, in *The Sound and the Fury* and *As I Lay Dying.* Faulkner's predilection for the oral tradition, strong in *The Hamlet* and dominant in *The Town,* in much of *The Mansion,* and in all of *The Reivers,* is perhaps the most original feature of narrative method in his Gothic novels and the closely related romances. By never telling a Gothic tale in the first person from the point of view of the hero or heroine at the time of the action or in retrospect, Faulkner dissociated himself from the multitude of run-of-the-mill writers of Gothic romance.

In Yoknapatawpha the equivalents of the Gothic castles, symbols usually of past splendor and present decay, appear in most of the novels: the Sartoris plantation house in *Sartoris* and *Sanctuary;* the ruins of the Old Frenchman's place in *Sanctuary* and *The Hamlet;* the Compson house, in a state of dilapidation, in *Absalom, Absalom!* and *The Sound and the Fury;* Sutpen's Hundred in *Absalom, Absalom!* from creation to destruction; Miss Burden's house in *Light in August;* the McCaslin plantation, still a going concern, in *Go Down, Moses* and *Intruder in the Dust;* the Backus plantation in decline in *The Town* and as transformed by Mr. Harriss in "Knight's Gambit" and *The Mansion;* the old De Spain mansion as transformed by Flem in *The Town* and *The Mansion.* All these "castles" represent the plantation days of the past, and all of them had or have neighboring slave or servant quarters. Only one novel, *Intruder in the Dust,* lacks a "castle": the Mallison house is a comfortable middle-class residence in which the family live happily and usefully in the present. Although Will Varner's house, the only two-storey one in Frenchman's Bend, was scarcely a "castle," it housed a princess, Eula Varner, the Helen of Frenchman's Bend.

The scenes of enclosure, the "other rooms," in these "castles" or in other buildings, signify isolation, whether captivity or withdrawal or self-imprisonment. . . . External nature ranges from the waste land despoiled by man, in *The Hamlet* and *Sanctuary* and *Absalom, Absalom!* and *Light in August,* to the pastoral and elegiac views of nature in *The Hamlet* and *The Mansion,* respectively. Productive plantations in *Sartoris* and *Go Down, Moses,* small farms in *Sartoris* and *The Hamlet,* and worn-out sharecroppers' or tenants' acres in the Frenchman's Bend area epitomize the agricultural economy and in context may be either Gothic or realistic. The most extended views of the natural scene in Yoknapatawpha are Gavin's panoramic survey from Seminary Hill in *The Town,* in which nature is least often a setting, and Chick's observations of his land and his vision of its place in the continent in *Intruder in the Dust.* Both Gavin and Chick show the romantic sensitivity to nature which is typical of Gothic fiction, but neither lives close to the land. Conversely, Ike McCaslin, despite his mystique of the land and the wilderness, shows little feeling for the areas which provide a living for man. (pp. 226-28)

[We] not only find all the traditional Gothic character types, but we find them in every novel, played straight, ironically inverted, or parodied: the Romantic, Byronic, or Faustian heroes and, for good measure and medieval flavor, the courtly lovers; the tragic villain-heroes, the revenge villain-hero, the rational villains, the villain seducer, and the arch-villain of melodrama. The heroines, who may or may not be Persecuted Maidens, are less prominent than the heroes—in *The Sound and the Fury* Caddy appears only as a memory. What with adolescent heroes and heroes who can do without women, heroines would sometimes be as extraneous as in a horse opera. There is no traditional heroine in the action of *Intruder in the Dust* or *Go Down, Moses.* And *Snopes* makes do with two real heroines in three volumes, Eula Snopes and her daughter Linda, but they come closer to being romantic or romantic-Gothic heroines than do any other female characters. Evil Women or Temptresses are less numerous than villains and sometimes are disguised as heroines, like Narcissa, or beneath a bawdy exterior conceal a heart of gold, like Miss Reba. *Snopes* seems to lack a female villain until, at the end of *The Mansion,* Linda appears to qualify.

The parental figures who produced many of the heroes, heroines, and villains may be tyrannical or benevolent, but rarely were they successful as parents or grandparents. . . . In the record of ineffective or unloving parents, emotionally crippled children, and broken lives in Yoknapatawpha, Faulkner directly continued the Gothic tradition into the new American Gothic in which, Irving Malin said, "almost every work in the canon contains family terror."

The grotesques, which are the most easily recognizable of Gothic character types, appear in all the Yoknapatawpha novels, in part because Faulkner was both a Gothic and a comic novelist and combined the horror story with the comic tall tale. . . . The fact that Faulkner's grotesques, except those who are willfully or insanely evil, are presented with sympathy distinguishes them from those of some other Gothic writers and suggests the influence of Dickens in this as in other aspects of Gothicism.

Visible grotesqueness may or may not indicate psychological abnormality or sexual perversion, but characters who display such deviations from normality usually are indicative of themes typical of Gothic fiction, especially southern Gothic. . . . Narcissism, homosexuality, incest, and miscegenation are the specifically sexual themes in Yoknapatawpha which reflect the southern concept of upper class white women. (pp. 228-30)

The strongest theme in this group is that of incest, involved in some characters . . . with narcissism and homosexuality. (p. 231)

The recurrence of these Gothic themes in Yoknapatawpha points to a basic weakness in the society, an inability of its members to enter into harmonious, vital relationships in family and social groups, which is confirmed in other Gothic themes. One group of themes deals with individual problems and the attempts to solve them. Isolation, alienation, and lack of love appear [in many of the works]. (p. 232)

In contrast to the themes of individuals but not necessarily irrelevant to them are the extremely Gothic themes of family relationships and family heritage, often a heritage of doom. Only rarely does the positive and un-Gothic aspect, a heritage of love and fidelity, occur. . . . In the Yoknapatawpha novels the Gothic theme of family and social heritage signals the doom of those who look to the past and glorify the dead and implies Faulkner's abiding concern for the continuance of the family by those who have love, vitality, and courage to face the future.

Transcending individual concerns are themes based on the community, such as the theme of Negro-white relationships in *The Unvanquished, Go Down, Moses,* and *Intruder in the Dust.* The theme of truth recurs in various aspects: the themes of truth and justice *(Sanctuary),* of the truth of history *(Absalom, Absalom!)* of life-saving and spirit-saving truth *(Intruder in the Dust),* of essential human truth *(The Town* and *The Mansion).* When these themes involve a search, it is not primarily self-centered or self-seeking. (p. 237)

The extent to which Faulkner retained essential Gothic

elements is impressive. He also transformed the Gothic mode in significant respects: by reducing it, by inverting it, and by parodying it. In *Sartoris* he undercut the Gothic effect by counterpointing the story of young Bayard with that of old Bayard and by using Aunt Jenny to deflate the Sartoris vainglory; both these effects are stronger in *Sartoris* than in *Flags in the Dust,* where the romantic-Gothic and grotesque-Gothic characterizations of Horace and of Byron Snopes divert attention from the Sartoris story. In *The Sound and the Fury* Faulkner provided a cheerful present scene in Benjy's and Quentin's sections and substituted psychological horror and pathos for mystery and suspense; the deaths take place offstage.

Omission of horror scenes is a favorite device with Faulkner. . . . In *Sanctuary* after the omission of the rape and the understatement of the two murders, the lynching scene is a devastating shock. Similarly, the omission of the actual murder of Joanna Burden in *Light in August* leaves the reader unprepared for the retrospective account of Joe's death in horrible detail. . . . The murders in *Intruder in the Dust* are distanced and understated, but the state of mind of Chick provides tension to lend Gothic suspense and mystery to setting and characters which in themselves are not Gothic. In *Snopes* the combination of Gothic and non-Gothic narrative sequences serves to modify the Gothic effects. Mink's two murders, of Houston and of Flem, admirably illustrate the two extremes of Faulkner's method, completely Gothic treatment and ironic understatement of violence.

In addition to diminishing some of the Gothic horror by such devices, Faulkner frequently, extensively, and significantly used ironic inversion, wherein characters and action are the reverse of what the Romantic or Romantic-Gothic tradition leads one to expect. This is done most completely in *Sanctuary,* to satirize the values and actions of respectable society. . . . (pp. 237-38)

Closely allied to ironic inversion is parody, which is inherent in Gothic romance. Parody is more comic in effect than irony, which may be bitterly satiric. (p. 239)

In addition to the ways in which Faulkner transformed or modified the Gothic elements he used are the ways in which he added new elements. First of all, he based the setting and characters on actual places and contemporary times or the relatively recent past, in an interrelated series of novels. He added individual characters which are not derived from traditional Gothic types. . . . In his experiments with point of view Faulkner covered all levels of intelligence, from speechless idiots to highly intelligent, sensitive, and articulate characters. . . . These are additions to the basic ingredients, as it were. Other additions are related to new purposes to which Faulkner adapted the Gothic.

These new purposes were rarely achieved in a single novel; the limited area and society made realistically possible the recurrence of characters, the repetition of incidents, the allusions to local legend, and the continued development of accounts of families and related themes. . . . The Gothic novel which deals with the more or less remote past or with a very limited scene and society in the present and with characters who are oriented to the past cannot attempt such a broad view as Faulkner's of social change and its impact on successive generations. (p. 240)

Of all the failures and weaknesses with which he dealt, Faulkner seemed most concerned with the failure of the family and society to preserve and observe meaningful rituals by which to initiate the young into mature life. . . . One of the great strengths of Faulkner's characterizations in his Gothic novels is his intense sympathy with and understanding of young people; his indictment of families and society is that they have failed to give their children love and emotional security or to instill in them by precept and example sound moral and ethical principles, truths to live by.

By great good fortune Faulkner had at his disposal what the original Gothic novelists, and even those of the generation before his, had lacked: the insight into the unconscious provided by Freud. Thus, in dealing with the irrational and instinctual aspects of the psyche, Faulkner was able to combine the subjective techniques of modern fiction with knowledge of depth psychology. . . . To pour into a whole row of old bottles of Gothicism a new wine fermented by a powerful creative imagination, stimulated by technical knowledge, and irradiated by intuition, this was Faulkner's distinctive achievement in Gothic characterization.

The Gothic revival of interest in the irrational side of man's consciousness tended to undervalue the rational side which had been too exclusively the concern of the age of reason. This lack of balance Faulkner could avoid because the scope of the Yoknapatawpha cycle allowed him to include characters who combined imagination and sympathy with reason and whose lives were more satisfactory and useful than those of either the irrational or the too rational characters. . . . Such characters are naturally rare in Gothic novels but can be accommodated in the Yoknapatawpha cycle because, first, the ample scope permits non-Gothic elements, and, second, the point of view of normal characters under stress involves multiple levels of consciousness and irrational phenomena which serve to illuminate the dark and secret areas in man's psyche. (pp. 241-43)

As the omniscient author, Faulkner could express his moral and ethical convictions, or he could use normal characters as spokesmen or reflectors. . . . He could always convey his meaning through the narrative events and thematic ideas. Instead of the good-evil polarity that Gothic romance often took over from medieval romance . . . Faulkner represented evil as white. . . . The same principles, Faulkner showed, apply to all men, black or white, and human dignity must be respected, regardless of caste or class. *Intruder in the Dust* dramatizes both the American Dream and the American Nightmare by revealing the unconscious reasons for and the conscious reactions to race hatred which violates these principles. No more serious new purpose could be conceived for revitalizing the Gothic tradition. (p. 243)

Faulkner belonged naturally to the tradition that accepts change and will not be held in bondage to the past. By choosing the Gothic mode, he was recognizing that man's "moral conscience is the curse he had to accept from the gods in order to gain from them the right to dream." He recreated the motivating dreams of the past in a specific region and showed how its society was destroyed by what was wrong with its dreams or by its failure to attain and maintain what was right. (p. 244)

The influence of Faulkner is not necessarily the chief source of Gothicism in later writers; but his work, like that of Dickens, contributes significantly to the Gothic tradition and to its capacity to accommodate the dreams and nightmares of modern civilization. . . . (p. 248)

Elizabeth M. Kerr, "From Yoknapatawpha to the World: Faulkner's Gothic Bequest," in her William Faulkner's Gothic Domain *(copyright © 1979 by Kennikat Press Corp.; reprinted by permission of Kennikat Press Corp.), Kennikat, 1979, pp. 220-48.*

* * *

FRISCH, Max 1911-

Frisch is a Swiss novelist, playwright, and architect. Translated into many languages, his writings involve not only themes of personal identity but such social concerns as dictatorship, anti-Semitism, prejudice, and justice and injustice. (See also *CLC,* Vol. 3, 9, and *Contemporary Authors,* Vols. 85-88.)

GERTRUD B. PICKAR

Frisch has never employed time as an inexorably forward-moving totality, carrying characters to an inevitable fate and moving the action to its ultimate prescribed conclusion. . . . Instead he employs undeniably 'undramatic' techniques—the extension of time, the suspension of time, repeated portrayal of the same time period, the interaction of separate time spheres, movement back and forth in time, and the presentation of incidents of the past and future which are interjected into the dramatized present.

Not all these features are present in all the works nor do they appear in identical form or degree; some, however, are found in each work and are frequently even substantial in effect. An examination of Frisch's manipulation of time considerations in these works and of the time structure which results indicates that the time sense they manifest is essentially a narrative one. It demonstrates as well that the relationship of Frisch's . . . play, *Biografie,* to its predecessors is an evolutionary, rather than an innovative one.

Frisch's interest in exploring the possibilities of time and his utilization of a narrative time sense is evident from the outset. His first play *Santa Cruz* (1944) is constructed upon a duality of time paralleling that of place in which the clearly delineated and progressing time of the castle is contrasted with the non-time of Santa Cruz. The framework of the play, from the *Vorspiel* to the final tableau, spans seven days, yet within the work, a period of seventeen years is encompassed. (p. 1)

The oscillation between the time spheres of the present and past and the fusion of realities and unrealities, together with the confrontation of time-oriented progression with the time-denying fantasies of mind and memory, represent a time manipulation which is clearly narrative in nature. It reflects a consciousness which inserts itself between the material to be presented and the viewer or reader and restructures that material in a manner which is unmistakably conscious and which cannot be ignored.

In addition, *Santa Cruz* exhibits a further narrative time feature—simultaneity of time, a phenomenon which is alien to the dramatic concept of temporal sequence. (p. 2)

Like a postscript, the final brief and dream-like scene ends the work on a note of timelessness, as figures from the past and future, representations of lost opportunities and experience, Death, and the promise of the future held by the daughter Viola gather around Pelegrin as he lies dying. It is a fitting conclusion for a work whose time structure exhibits such variance and fusion of fictional, experienced, and fancied time and such contrast and interaction between time oriented and time suspended events. As a result of the interwoven complexion of times and places and the timelessness which is intentionally achieved, *Santa Cruz* is not located in time, but seems to float unmoored in the expanses of eternity. . . .Frisch's second dramatic work, *Nun singen sie wieder* (1945), manifests a duality of time similar to that found in *Santa Cruz,* though of less thematic and structural impact. The scenes among the 'living' are time-oriented. They take place in a sequential order with repeated references both to previous events and to those which are to follow. The scenes among the dead, however, are devoid of time consideration; their existence revolves around the continual baking of bread and the nourishing of the dead. The time awareness of earthly life with its daily concerns and pathetic hopes for the coming spring thus forms a contrast to the timelessness of eternity 'jenseits' and provides the work with a dual basis in time. This duality of time experience and portrayal which the time consciousness of the work encompasses, however, is not structurally maintained. The removal of the demarcation of death prevents a distinction in cast, setting or action between the living and the dead. (p. 3)

The time concepts which appear to be suspended in *Nun singen sie wieder* are directly and consciously violated by the structure of *Die Chinesische Mauer* (1946, revision 1955), as three time perspectives are brought together and interact: that of the present of 'heute abend' represented by the performance itself and the figures of der Heutige, Frack, and Cut; that of ancient China presented as a fictional present in the 'play within the play' pivoting around members of the Imperial court of Emperor Twing Sche Hwang Ti of the third century B.C., and that of a timeless consciousness of the past, represented by the series of historical and literary figures, the 'Maskenfiguren' which repeatedly cross the stage singly or in groups and contribute to the revue-like aspect of the work. (p. 4)

Die Chinesische Mauer is the first of Frisch's plays in which an attempt is made to utilize the 'present' of the stage performance and integrate it into the time considerations of the work itself. 'Zeit der Handlung: heute abend' announces der Heutige as the work opens and proceeds to move from that time sphere to the other fictional levels of the work. As a result, the 'present' of experienced time interacts with the fictional present produced on the stage. . . . The situation in *Die Chinesische Mauer* is further complicated by the addition of a third time perspective, for the 'experienced present' is brought into contact with both the fictional present of a historical time and the continuing, yet timeless present of the 'Maskenfiguren'. The latter represent figures from the historical past from fictional times and places and, if the intent of the author succeeds, they are to be accepted as manifestations of man's continuing consciousness of the past. . . . *Die Chinesische Mauer* represents a significant attempt to counteract the historicism of time with its sequential order by creating what may be termed a simultaneity of time or a recapitulative time-denying structure. Of special interest here is the fact that the time concept inherent in *Die Chinesische Mauer* is unquestionably alien to the dramatic concept of time and strongly suggestive of a consciously directed narrative will. Clearly, the time oriented bounds of the dramatic medium have been exchanged for the more fluid and complex time dimensions associated with the narrative mode of expression.

Relevant here, too, are the discussions of time by the protagonists in *Die Chinesische Mauer*. It is the first play in which time is consciously a concern of the dramatic figures, gaining thus theatrical consciousness. Not only do they integrate the concern with time into the thematic framework of the piece, but they also elucidate the philosophical bias with which both form and content are constructed, as well as bringing the phenomenon of time into relation with concepts of time in modern science. (pp. 4-5)

In contrast to these thoughts and the format of the first three works, *Als der Krieg zu Ende war* (1947/48) displays a far more 'traditional' use of time. Time is limited, though not severely so, for the action of the play stretches over a 'spring' (specifically indicated as that of 1945), and the thematic content of the work is very definitely bound to that period. Yet, *Als der Krieg zu Ende war,* too, displays a narrative element related to its temporal constitution. . . . Though not assuming the function of a chorus, the way [the character] Agnes speaks out of the framework of the work and suspends its time-flow as she relates incidents which have a bearing upon her attitudes or the events in the drama tends to relativize the time-experience of the work itself. The inclusion of anecdotes and incidents from the past and future disrupts the time consciousness of the work and reveals its narrative bias. (pp. 5-6)

Graf Öderland (1951) displays yet another format of time structure. The scenes, while maintaining an impression of chronology, are episodic in nature and references to incidents in preceding or pursuant scenes are minimal. As in *Nun singen sie wieder,* scenes in which the same protagonists, or in this case specifically the Staatsanwalt, do not participate are not dovetailed to fit in temporal sequence between those in which they are present, and acquire rather a feeling of simultaneity. A duality of time awareness, so frequent in Frisch's works, is achieved by the contrast between the opening and closing scenes [with their temporal references] . . . , and the intervening scenes, which are essentially unrooted in time, and seemingly take place in a simulated fairytale-time of 'once'. . . . The ambivalence of [the] dual time and the dual characterization of the Staatsanwalt is crystalized in the final scene, where the ambiguity of time-experience becomes thematic [and the time perception of the Staatsanwalt is challenged by the maid Hilde and her recounting of specific events]. (pp. 6-7)

[The] intrusion of the subjective experiences of the intermediary scenes into the 'objective reality' of the framework of the work, rather than dispelling their fantasy quality, tends to relativize the entire work. This feeling of a subjective time-consciousness which exists above and beyond the individual scenes and impinges upon their dramatic objectivity is a narrative one, to which the uses of extended and undefined time, also found in the play, are correlative.

In *Don Juan oder Die Liebe zur Geometrie* (written 1952 and revised in 1961), the first acts display a dramatic time sense, a chronological sequence of events is maintained, no variance in time experience or interplay of time realities occur, and the time portrayal is tight and limited. The final two acts do not affect the natural time sequence of the work nor insert new time elements, but they do extend the time span to narrative dimensions. The fourth act takes place a number of years after the third, and the final act is set after a further but indefinite period of time has elapsed. The intervening time is telescoped, and the earlier scenes recede into a prepast perspective. (p. 7)

Frisch's [next] four plays are characterized by a contrast between the scenes in which the validity of time is recognized and portions associated with narration or commentary in which time concerns are excluded. . . . The nature and effect of the contrast in time considerations thus created are significant and reveal more clearly than in the preceding works Frisch's intense concern with this aspect and the development of a time formulation which culminates with that found in [*Biographie*].

In *Biedermann und die Brandstifter* (1957/58), the story line proceeds lineally from the arrival of the first lodger until the fiery holocaust, though the time factor is usually only vaguely indicated. The timelessness of the chorus forms a temporal counterpoint to the portrayed events. Its admonitions and generalizations, chanted intermittantly throughout the work, provide a loose framework for the story development on stage. [In addition, the action is temporarily 'frozen' during brief interludes, during which Biedermann and Babette step out of the fictional present to comment upon proceedings or to justify themselves].

In *Die große Wut des Philipp Hotz* (1957/58), the time sense is fractured, as scenes between the dramatic figures, which progress in a linear fashion, are suspended in the alternating conferencier scenes, in which Hotz steps from the platform on the stage to comment on the proceedings or to provide additional information. At other times the action continues 'on stage,' as he proceeds with his commentary in the time vacuum of 'off-stage'. . . . Within the dramatization of the portrayed scenes, a different incongruity of time flow is in evidence. Dorli is presented . . . in an uninterrupted time continuum, [while] Philipp [is] functioning in an accelerated, telescoped time stratum. . . . (pp. 8-9)

In conjunction with this discrepancy in time experience, an interesting use of tense occurs. The narrative past, associated with the narrative mode, is used in those passages where Philipp is acting as the raconteur, and the present tense is employed in the scenes with Dorli. . . . His action acquires thus a narrative perspective, while the others continue in the fictional present of theatrical illusion. This interaction of time strata, supported by the accompanying variation in the use of tense, destroys any pretense of a dramatic unity of time and reveals the essential nature of the work's time structure as a narrative one.

In *Andorra* (1958-1961), the episodic scenes depicting the chain of events which mold the figure of Andri and lead to the final denouement of the work are chronological and extend over a considerable period of time, reaching narrative proportions. These scenes are transposed from the immediacy of their presentation to the nebulous realm of the past by the statements of the witnesses which frequently follow them and which reveal the events as long passed. The 'present' of these figures, manifested by their appearance at the witness stand and often accentuated by a change in clothing, contrasts with the 'present' of the dramatized action, lending to the latter a narrative distance. (p. 9)

In its treatment of time, *Biografie: Ein Spiel* (1967), draws upon the experimentation with the dimension of time found in earlier plays. Movement back and forth in time, which was structured into acts in *Santa Cruz,* is used extensively, and as in *Santa Cruz* an attempt is made to secure on the stage a continuum of time in which past, present and future freely intermingle. As in *Andorra* and *Die gro e Wut des Philipp Hotz* (and more tentatively in *Als der Krieg zu Ende war*) characters both function as performers within a dramatized present and withdraw from that dramatization to function outside of its fictional and temporal framework. The time concept of the work, as in *Santa Cruz* and *Graf Öderland,* fuses fictionally 'real' events and their time dependence with projected reality (whether of dream, fantasy, or suggestion) and its inherent temporal antipathy and permits the protagonists to experience them in one time continuum and to be affected by their interaction. As in *Andorra,* scenes from the fictional past are presented in a theatrical present; however, in *Biografie,* these scenes are not absolute and their integrity is not preserved. Rather the staging present is maintained throughout the work and often [intrudes] into the scenes. A theatrical simultaneity similar to that found in *Die Chinesischle Mauer* dissects variant time spheres and is essentially anti-lineal and anti-historical in effect. *Biografie,* however, strengthens the use of the stage found in the other works by granting it domination over the entire work and radically expands its significance by utilizing the rehearsal as the structural basis of the work. The effect upon the role of time within the work is striking and substantial. (p. 10)

[Drastic in effect] is the irrelevance with which the time factor is treated in the structuring of the work. The play opens and closes in a fictional 1960—yet the opening scene is soon revealed to be a reenactment of an evening experienced by the protagonist Kürmann at some prior time. The 1960 setting is thus eliminated as a contender for the fictional present of the play, which must now be assumed as having begun *in medias re.* The true fictional present remains undefined, as the play proceeds, revealing in cornucopian fashion its temporal complexity and variety. (p. 12)

The kaleidoscopic interplay of the scenes and general disruption of temporal precepts encountered in *Biografie* is fostered by the rehearsal situation into which the play is cast and the unique formulation of time inherent in that mode. The rehearsal situation . . . extends the limits of theatrical tolerance. It allows an extensive range in fictional time . . . without effecting the bounds of theatrical time; it can justify a simultaneity of presentation not otherwise tenable, and permits a time period to be repeated, its events to be recalled, reiterated or cancelled without prejudice. It is conducive to an intermingling or interaction between varying time spheres or time perceptions and promotes minimal use of a sequential time structure. In effect, it sustains an otherwise narrative time use in a theatrical medium.

Believing that the very use of the stage possesses the power to place events and things in a sphere beyond time, Frisch has repeatedly removed his plays from a strictly dramatic time context and chosen to treat time in a predominantly narrative fashion. In the course of his dramatic works, Frisch has experimented with the employment of multiple time periods, the interaction of 'objective' and 'subjective' time, and its suspension, acceleration and extension. Protagonists, situations and thematic interests have been affected by and in turn affect these temporal variations in varying degrees and manners, until in [*Biografie: Ein Spiel*] the temporal concern is fully integrated into an artistic one. In [this work], Frisch, by rejecting time-structuring and proffering in its stead the vehicle of the rehearsal, has created a stage situation which parallels the narrative condition. Narrative time aspects have been synthesized within a theatrical format formalized by the work itself, and the narrative time sense has become bonded with theatrical form, thus effectively concluding Frisch's experimentation with temporal formats. (pp. 12-13)

Gertrud B. Pickar, "The Narrative Time Sense in the Dramatic Works of Max Frisch" (revised by the author for this publication), in German Life & Letters, *n.s. Vol. XXVIII, No. 1, October, 1974, pp. 1-14.*

V. S. PRITCHETT

["Sketchbook 1946-1949"] is not a hotchpotch of things and persons seen or of random ponderings but a coherent narrative, an ingenious mosaic. The fragments hold together as the portrait of a sensitive moralist responding to the chaos in Europe in the years immediately following the Second World War; they also reveal the artist's eager greed for people and what is behind their faces. One is really reading two men at once. Frisch may be a travelling conscience, shocked by what he sees and reporting it all, but he is also at his business of imagining. So that, in a sense, the "Sketchbook" is an incipient and earnest *Bildungsroman,* quick-witted and vivid. Every anecdote may have its bearing on some play or story he thinks of writing. . . .

[The people Frisch describes] will reappear in the "Sketchbook" from time to time, transfigured. Indeed, the image of the forester will turn up powerfully at the end of the book, in the long account of a lawyer's nervous breakdown, which is closely related to the writer's own fears and guilts as he travelled through Germany, Austria, Poland, Czechoslovakia, France, and Italy; Kafkaesque fantasies of the impassive interrogation, the false trial, the confiscated passport, the concentration camp, and the firing squad haunt his innocence. . . . And this eventually leads Frisch the artist on to questions of political commitment. Can writers have any real influence in stopping future wars? When they gather by the hundred in international meetings, do they not stick to their national or ideological factions? And what about the "good man" living in a safe and tolerant society —may not his tolerance conceal a sleepy or disingenuous attachment to the status quo? How embarrassing it is to notice that success in writing a very good sentence may keep unpleasant reality at arm's length, if only for a moment.

Anyone of Max Frisch's generation will recognize how especially painful such difficulties were felt to be at the end of the Second World War. We all remember the worried neutrals who, released from their claustrophobia, encountered the other claustrophobia of war, which had trapped the rest of us. One remembers the questions and answers in ruined Germany when one broached the question of German guilt. (p. 87)

There are many wise remarks on writing scattered through the book. One is particularly important to Frisch, as readers of his brilliant "Montauk" will recall:

> Every experience basically defies description as long as we try to express it through the actual example that has impressed us. . . . Essentially only fiction—things altered, transformed, shaped—can convey impressions—and that is the reason why every artistic failure is always linked with a stifling feeling of loneliness.

Finally, we come to the long sketch of the breakdown of lawyer Schinz, a fiction that can be said to dramatize the facts, fantasies, symbols that have been at the back of the author's mind throughout the "Sketchbook." Story or play? Whatever it is, we see the artist pushing the moralist out the door and finding a possible self in the rich mosaic he has created. (pp. 88-9)

V. S. Pritchett, "A Peripatetic Conscience," in The New Yorker *(© 1977 by The New Yorker Magazine, Inc.), Vol. LIII, No. 21, July 11, 1977, pp. 87-9.*

FRANCINE du PLESSIX GRAY

Few contemporary writers have attacked the traditional borders between fiction and nonfiction more systematically than Max Frisch. . . . "Montauk," and two sets of diaries, "Sketchbook 1946-1949" and "Sketchbook 1966-1971,". . . rebel against the tyranny of genre more vigorously than any contemporary work I can think of. (p. 3)

Mr. Frisch's literary mosaics could have become a mere hodgepodge in the hands of a lesser artist, and yet, few works I know prove the increasing irrelevance of distinctions between literary genres. The power and consistency of the writer's sensibility—that of a very sophisticated, concerned, acerbic Western liberal probing the conscience of our time—binds his disparate styles into a powerfully unified structure. They are like metal filings kept in perfect order by an unseen magnet, held together by an order of energy not unlike that which unites Kierkegaard's and Nietzsche's disparate aphoristic jottings. . . .

Mr. Frisch's novels differ from the mainstream of post-war Existentialism in several important ways: They are essentially studies of marriages and relationships between equally independent male and female protagonists, and it is in great part his heroes' unwillingness to commit themselves to their strikingly liberated women that leads them to destruction. Also, Mr. Frisch is more interested in concrete problems of "honesty" in our technological age, in a concrete "telling of the truth" in contemporary life and art, than in expressing the prevalence of the absurd or the sweet indifference of the world. . . .

In "Montauk," his boldest work to date, Mr. Frisch recounts the impact of the American press on a famous European writer's consciousness—his very own. . . . With the same deftness with which he assembles the disparate genres and styles of his "Sketchbooks," the author moves among several personas: the novelistic "he," Frisch of the American media romance, and the autobiographical "I.". . . The contemporary writer's attempt at ultimate candor is both the theme and the process of this book. . . .

"Montauk" is Mr. Frisch's biggest gamble to date. It involves his most meticulous violation of novelistic taboos, his most aggressive attack against whatever boundaries remain between fact and fiction. Like the heroes of his novels, Mr. Frisch's books have always seemed to rebel against any process of pegging, naming, classifying; they defy the useful and worn labels of the literary trade. And Mr. Frisch's tour de force is that "Montauk," like the "Sketchbooks," remains rigorously devoid of any confessionalism. The author is in such control that these bluntly honest documents are infinitely less subjective and more elegantly impersonal than the thinly masked life histories that emerge in the fiction of Updike, Mailer and countless other contemporary novelists. The liberating effect of Mr. Frisch's rebellion against the tyranny of traditional genres, as well as the breadth of his human message, make him a more fitting candidate for the Nobel Prize than any other writer I can think of. (p. 34)

Francine du Plessix Gray, "Max Frisch Considered," in The New York Times Book Review *(© 1978 by The New York Times Company; reprinted by permission), March 19, 1978, pp. 3, 34.*

FRANZ P. HABERL

The dramatic action [of *Triptychon*], such as it is, consists of a funeral during the first tableau, a series of conversations in Hades during the second one, and a conversation on a park bench in Paris between a couple of lovers (one alive, one dead) during the last one. The innovative device which Frisch uses to propel his "action" and to advance his thesis is to have dead and living characters intermingle and even speak to each other. The dead retain the age which they had at the moment of death; the living continue to grow old. This device results in some comic relief in the second tableau, as when a seventy-year-old son encounters his forty-one-year-old father who scolds him for still not being able to fish properly.

Essentially, though, this is a very serious work. As the eighteen disparate yet related characters confront each other in Hades, as they recount important events in their lives, as they try to justify their acts and omissions to each other, Frisch's familiar themes reappear: his condemnation of social injustice and of prejudice, but most prominently his exhortation that we should love a person without trying to change him or her, without forcing him or her into a preconceived mold. The eighteen characters in the second tableau had been unable to live up to Frisch's standards while they were alive, and they persist in their imperfections even in Hades. This is why Hamlet's question (uttered by a clochard) is answered at the end of the second tableau with the lapidary phrase: "Eternity is banal."

The banality of the characters in the second tableau is contrasted to the seemingly extraordinary couple in the third one. (p. 283)

[But] Frisch's stage directions specify that the banality of life is to assert itself: the very last sounds of the third tableau are the roaring noises of contemporary city traffic. (pp. 283-84)

Franz P. Haberl, "World Literature in Review: 'Triptychon'," in World Literature Today *(copyright 1979 by the University of Oklahoma Press), Vol. 53, No. 2, Spring, 1979, pp. 283-84.*

STEVEN KELLMAN

[*Montauk*] takes its title and its authority from the town on Long Island where Frisch spends a weekend in the company of a woman who works for his American publisher and whom he refers to simply as Lynn. Montauk is no literary invention, and Lynn's identity is no secret to the New York publishing world. We enter the book *in medias res* and in the present tense, as Lynn and the author find themselves on foot, lost in the thickets of the Long Island coast. It is the palpable disorder of immediate sensation.

A thing of beauty is a joy forever, precisely because of our faith that art transcends the bagatelles of specific time and place. Frisch acknowledges that "Literature cancels the moment—that is what it is for," yet he eschews literature. His avowed purpose in *Montauk* is to meet the moment on its own terms. Describing himself, not without perverse satisfaction, as "a writer without very much imagination," his goal is very nearly that of *l'ecriture blanche,* writing that denies its own resources. Frisch would be a humble servant of present verity, and for such fealty impositions of past and future would be churlish. His modest proposal is:

> to describe this weekend: in an autobiographical way. Completely autobiographical —without inventing a single character; without inventing happenings of more significance than his own simple reality; without taking refuge in inventions of any kind; without seeking to justify his writing as a duty toward society. A story without a message. He has none to give, and yet he is alive. He wants simply to tell it (though not without some consideration for the people he mentions by name): his life.

Montauk is to be an aging writer's effort to capture life, though its Gnostic premise is that life defies the wiles of narrative. (pp. 433-34)

Published confessions often thrive on the *frisson* of wondrous indiscretions toward self; but *Montauk,* a record of their weekend together, is an exercise in self-effacement. Jean-Jacques Rousseau exalts himself even when broadcasting his problems over premature ejaculation. However, Max Frisch's disparaging remarks about himself, such as the disclosure of impotence during his final night with Lynn, are consistent with his entire project of abandoning the self. Individual identity, like plot, possesses shaped chronology, and it is to flee both that the Swiss novelist finds himself in Montauk. . . .

[Throughout] *Montauk,* Frisch escapes to the freedom of "he." Yet atavistic reappearances of "I," sometimes even within the same sentence as "he," are reminders of how very difficult it is to live outside the fictions that are our selves.

Aware that language and plot are desecrations, Frisch struggles valiantly to resist the temptations of art. Yet his diary is an artifact. He declares that: "It is just the present moment he wants, nothing more," but his account of the weekend with Lynn is crowded with flashbacks to other times and other places. . . . Diarist, historian, and fabulist are uncomfortably confounded. (pp. 434-35)

The publication of a diary, especially one with intimate details so embarrassing and lacerating, is an exercise in the mortification of personality. Yet, as in the case of Gide's journals, such an act can also enhance an author's reputation. Frisch's epic question "Why am I telling all this? Whom am I telling it to?" remains unanswered. But it is clear that his is a Romantic quest to lose oneself in the Other. Individual imagination becomes distortion, a flight from the here and now. In seeking "to describe this weekend, this thin present weekend, exactly as it is, without inventing anything," Frisch is desperately attempting to embrace Nature, which, *an sich,* is immediate—and feminine. When the self and its fictions are discarded, "All that remains is the mad desire for present identity through a woman." "Every first time with a woman is the first time all over again," and repetition breeds not only boredom, but history.

The diary, with its shifting point of view, is the appropriate form for an epistemological skeptic. It aspires to the unmediated experience of a fundamentally fragmented, shapeless world devoid of the consoling patterns of past, present, and future. (p. 435)

Steven Kellman, "The Diary As Fiction: The Days of Max Frisch," in Book Forum *(copyright © 1979 by The Hudson River Press), Vol. IV, No. 3, 1979, pp. 431-35.*

* * *

FRY, Christopher 1907-

Born Christopher Fry Harris, Fry is a British dramatist, screenwriter, translator, critic, and children's author. Using the form of the verse play, he mingles drama and poetic language, humor and tragedy, metaphysics and wit in an Elizabethan richness that invites comparison with Shakespeare and T. S. Eliot. Also Elizabethan is his incorporation of verbal ornament into the actual meaning of the play, creating an elegant view of reality. The unconscious effect of poetry and word sounds is drawn upon for dramatic impact. Fry celebrates life in his work, often using religious and historical themes. His optimism has been criticized by some as escapism. (See also *CLC*, Vol. 2, 10, and *Contemporary Authors*, Vols. 17-20, rev. ed.)

J. A. COLLINS

Unfortunately (and unjustly as well) the name of Christopher Fry has been linked with that nebulous monster, The Establishment. And since the mid-fifties responsible theatre in England, as elsewhere, has been out to get the Establishment. Fry, in my opinion, deserves more than a summary dismissal, a dismissal (for some) decided on by applying the criterion of guilt-by-association. . . .

Christopher Fry has defined comedy as 'an escape, not from truth but from despair: a narrow escape into faith', a definition which suggests an attitude towards—rather than a solution for—the central paradox: the mystery of existence itself. And in Fry's plays the attitude of faith is always love —romantic love, brotherly love, love of God and the universe; but even in love (the acceptance of faith) spirit and flesh refuse to harmonize and the old battle continues. Fry's dramas usually end on this absurd note of discord, however muted.

The absurdity however has its point: Fry advocates a theatre of 'purpose' over a theatre of 'behaviour', which is to say that he is more interested in what man is than in what he does—or when he does it. . . . (p. 63)

And the human being, Fry constantly reminds us, is paradoxical; and the heroes and heroines of his comedies (as well as many of the minor characters) have that touch of absurdity which makes men sane. They fly in the face of convention, as did the mad poets of life in the novels of G. K. Chesterton. Their actions are outrageous—and highly entertaining—but behind their actions lies the mystery of a conflict as ancient as the seasons: Dynamene (*A Phoenix Too Frequent*), preposterous in her husband's tomb, dies into life through her love for Tegeus Chromis; Thomas Mendip (*The Lady's Not for Burning*), tired of killing, yearns for death but falls into life through his love for Jennet Jourdemayne, yet tells her, 'Girl, you haven't changed the world'; the Duke of Alstair (*Venus Observed*), mouldering in autumn, praises 'A sudden illumination of lumbago' and the solitude of late love, but his enthusiasm for love and existence is tempered by the reminder of death in Reedbeck's snore. . . .

Fry's characters are usually the poles of paradox and their mutual attractions and repulsions the actions of dramas which do not 'conclude' but suggest, rather, a perilous means for continuance; but it is the quality of the thought which gives the plays texture and fibre and this quality finds expression in the verse idiom of the character.

Paradox is not only a mode of thought, it is also a way of verbalizing that thought. Its frequent manifestations are within Fry's case often a metaphysical wit, verbal irony, puns, exaggeration for the sake of rhetorical inflation (rhodomontade), humorous invective, and conceits. These, as would be expected, often overlap, and an exchange between characters will sometimes exhibit them all—and at the same time state the play's theme and advance action as well as incident. (p. 64)

[Combination] of incident and verse, the outer and the inner lives of the characters, is both the action of [a Fry] play and the unfolding of its theme.

Fry relies strongly on incident, not only in his comedies but in all of his plays, and in that respect he is a conventional realist. Incident, however, in Fry's dramas is not primarily 'to advance plot' or 'to reveal character'; it is present, more importantly, to illustrate paradox. It is the gesture which complements the words, and the result is the play's action. In the comedies incident is fantastic—as fantastic as an allegory—but so is the verse, in its obvious poetic effects, fantastic.

But Fry is aware of the need to keep his fantasies under control and he does this, as did Ben Johnson, by turning lyric effect into satiric. Thomas Mendip's 'faintly festive' hiccups do occur in spite of his eloquent denials of them; and their counterparts in language and/or incident and gesture are continually turning song to satire. Doto, for example, the promiscuous maid of *A Phoenix Too Frequent* (another of Fry's characters given to hiccuping), is constantly (and most often unconsciously) topping her mistress's elegies with passages of lusty and mock-bathetic humour. . . . (pp. 65-6)

The technique of turning lyric effect to satiric is central to Fry's comedies and is responsible for much of their humour. But contrasting as it does the ideal with the real, the spirit with the flesh, it is illustrative also of paradox; and the themes, however humorously they may be realized, are serious.

While no verse dramatist of this century has been as audacious, and as indulgent in the use of the poetic devices of imagery, metaphor and simile as Fry, few have been as nonchalant as he in their attitude towards prosody. Although he has disagreed with Eliot and defended the conventional iambic line as an adequate expression of contemporary speech accents, *The Firstborn* is the only one of his plays which has a conventional iambic pentameter base. But even there the norm is so elusive that departures from it fail to take on rhythmic significance. Examining the verse of Fry's plays for the dramatic implications of its prosody is something like looking for a needle in a haystack—only to discover that the needle was never placed there at all. (pp. 66-7)

Fry's concern is to bring poetry onto the larger convention of the theatre and not to bring the theatre into the convention of verse. Fry's dramatic language is, as is Eliot's, an elevation of colloquial speech, but his verse is more sensationally styled (through his 'poetic effects') than is Eliot's. His diction is, generally, less precise: his syntax closer to the stumbling spontaniety of contemporary spoken speech. There is little variation in Fry's rhythm—either from play to play or within the individual plays. Although he has tended toward a shorter, more trochaic line in his plays since *A Sleep of Prisoners*—one can imagine Eliot having scanned *The Dark Is Light Enough* with some satisfaction—orchestration, in all of Fry's plays, would seem to be missing. Rhythm doesn't change with mood, character or action; although diction, imagery and syntax do. (p. 67)

Fry has written of the 'tension' between the prosaic and the poetic that verse can convey, favouring sometimes the prosaic sometimes the poetic:

> The prosaic or colloquial can be rhythmically just sufficiently charged to resolve into the implication of verse at a moment's notice even half way through a sentence and back again without disturbing the unity of the speech, in the way that the spirit and flesh work in ourselves without noticeably sawing us in half.
>
> The writer's responsibility is to know when he can safely break free of this, and relax for contrast into the rhythms of prose.

This observation . . . can best be understood in the context of *The Dark Is Light Enough* and *Curtmantle*. In both of these plays Fry has alternated verse and prose, although in *The Dark is Light Enough* only servants and soldiers provide the contrast and relaxation Fry desires. *Curtmantle* is a much more subtle, and at once a more conscious and more artistic admixture of verse and prose than is *The Dark Is Light Enough*. In *Curtmantle* all the principal characters speak both in verse and prose; and the various 'low' characters—who both begin the play and end it—speak always in prose. Much of the play's narration is in prose, as well as the arguments involving the political—as opposed to the spiritual—side of the law. Henry is, usually, truculent, boastful, vulgar in prose; sincere, friendly conciliatory, at times even humble in verse. And, as would be expected, the prose passages are much more colloquial—often vulgar and/or racy—than are the passages in verse. Fry moves with ease from one medium to another. There are no jolting levels of reality, unless a jolt is intended, because the material quite naturally (but not without art) imposes the medium. . . . (p. 68)

One reason for [Fry's colloquialism] is that all of Fry's dramas have at their centre an eloquent man of action, like Henry, whose syntax is direct and virile, but whose sensitivity to others and to the world about him is extraordinary. Words, undoubtedly, are sometimes 'wasted' in Fry's verse—as they are in colloquial speech—but constructions are kept simple and in an order that is true to that of conventional speech. Eloquence in Fry is, usually, a spoken—as opposed to a literary—eloquence, and the 'poetry' . . . is often flashes of quick-silver on the surface of the verse. (p. 70)

Fry's strength as a poet lies in his appreciation of nature, but it is a difficult task indeed to harness this appreciation to truly dramatic ends. And what often happens in Fry's dramas is that the very eloquence of his central characters lures them into a plethora of images taken from nature; the images, it is true, do relate but too vaguely to turn the drama into the intensity of a vision. Fry has overcome this in *The Dark Is Light Enough* by making the Countess Rosmarin the quiet centre of a storm; and the strength of his one tragedy, *The Firstborn,* is that he has made its hero, Moses, more eloquent in action than he is in words—and created an admirable cast of minor characters whose own verbal eloquence is governed by the themes they are meant to represent. They express themselves in the images of nature—and it is, largely, this controlled expression of imagery which gives to the play its cohesion of action, character and theme. (p. 72)

On the strength of its imagery alone, *The Firstborn* comes close to being a masterpiece. But—as is the case with so many other fine plays of this gifted craftsman—it has received neither the critical attention nor the popular acclaim it deserves. Christopher Fry remarked in a recent interview that there were times when he doubted whether he was capable of writing anything at all that would not be met by 'contumely'. Let us hope that those times are over. (p. 73)

J. A. Collins, "Poet of Paradox: The Dramas of Christopher Fry," in Literary Half-Yearly, *Vol. XII, No. 2, July, 1971, pp. 62-75.*

JAMES WOODFIELD

[*Phoenix*] is a secular drama whose final statement is essentially religious. This statement results from a highly integrated structure that fuses the ancient tale with pagan myths and a Christian sub-structure—all subsumed within a vital, entertaining piece of dramatic craftsmanship. (p. 4)

Phoenix embraces all three levels [of myth classification: Legends, based on historical fact, Folk or Fairy Tales, and Religious Myths]. . . . At the level of Fairy Tale, the title indicates the traditional pattern Fry wishes to evoke of the fabulous bird, the symbol of love, which is consumed in flames only to emerge from its ashes with renewed youth to live out a further cycle. Also in the Fairy Tale tradition, Dynamene is a Sleeping Beauty awakened by her Prince. On the level of Religious Myth, *Phoenix* is a comic analogue for the Christian pattern of atonement and resurrection. (pp. 4-5)

The effect of [the numerous] mythic associations is to suggest that beneath the surface comic action lies a pattern of meaning which has a timeless significance. The Christian cycle is not isolated, but is a recurring phoenix-like pattern with modern relevance. (p. 7)

A great deal of the success of *Phoenix* lies in Fry's creation of [well-motivated, vital] characters, whose internal changes and external relationships capture the imagination of the audience. (pp. 7-8)

Whereas the first method by which *Phoenix* is made relevant to a modern audience is through its vital characters, the second method is through the use of a universal mythological pattern of death and resurrection which also incorporates Christian rituals. The relationship between the characters indicates a pattern of atonement. Dynamene and Tegeus attain a reconciliation through the sacrifice of Virilius in reparation for Tegeus' sin of losing the body and for Dynamene's sin of choosing to die. . . . The atonement brings resurrection after death, but not before a series of rituals has been enacted signifying the process. Four of the Seven Sacraments are performed during the play. . . . These rituals form part of our modern consciousness, and their effect is to suggest a deeper content in the play's action.

The interfusion of death, life and love forms the central concern of the play. . . . *Phoenix* and *The Firstborn* have a similar death-and-resurrection pattern, but an essential difference in *Phoenix,* in addition to the comic rather than the tragic direction, is the emphasis on love. The regenerative power of love is suggested in *The Firstborn* . . . but the idea is not expanded or fulfilled in the action. In *Phoenix* the whole pattern of action evolves from the burgeoning love between Dynamene and Tegeus. . . . Through the suggestion that love is a cosmic force, Fry links the *eros* of sexual love with the *agapé* of brotherly or divine love. Similarly, an appreciation of the world of the senses is not opposed to an appreciation of the spiritual world—rather it is an essential step towards it. . . . Fry's attitude is that of the Affirmative Way, that God is immanent as well as transcendent, and "mystery and goodness and beauty are primarily mediated through created things, if not wholly through them." . . . The literal reality of the phoenix may be questioned, but the reality of the love-phoenix rising from its ashes, of the interrelationship of life, death and love, is an unquestionable pattern of truth which the play reasserts.

Despite the ancient setting, Fry succeeds in giving the play a distinctly modern flavour. The language captures the contemporary speech idiom demanded by T. S. Eliot, broken only by reference to the gods . . . whose names are valuable mainly for their humorous and euphonic effects. Fry is extremely successful in combining the poetic and colloquial styles. . . . [Poetic] imagery and association shift smoothly into the mundane and back to the poetic. The movement in language between the two styles parallels the concertina-like structure of the action. There is no harsh juxtaposition for effects of contrast, rather a blending of style with style and subject with subject to show the essential unity in diversity: an exchange of levels of language in which the poetic acquires an everyday quality and the colloquial some of the stature of poetry. . . . Fry also gives the events of a past era modern connotations. For example, Doto explains how Dynamene circumvented the eternal official mind:

> . . . at first
> Madam had difficulty with the Town Council. They said
> They couldn't have a tomb used as a private residence.
> But madam told them she wouldn't be eating here,
> Only suffering, and they thought that would be all right. . . .

This comic encounter with authority foreshadows the more serious life-and-death matter of the missing body. . . . [Both] the ludicrousness and the inhumanity of institutions, Fry implies, are by no means confined to past eras. . . . The assertion of *Phoenix* is that in any era, love can transcend senseless killing, the oppression of institutions and deadening materialsim.

It has already been suggested that the flow of language parallels the structural movement between antithetical positions, and results in a blending of the oppositions. A further language-structure-theme parallel is the manner in which the imagery reinforces the comic pattern of action by affirming a positive view of the world. . . . Contrasts of death-life, dark-light, cold-hot, and down-up, pervade the language, revealing the tensions of which life is composed, yet always asserting the positive. (pp. 11-16)

In *Phoenix,* as in *The Firstborn,* Fry is manipulating antitheses to show that ultimately they form a unity which transcends their difference. The alternatives are not mutually exclusive, but mutually dependent. Death and resurrection form the overriding pattern, but the treatment is different from the anguished manner of *The Firstborn.* The deeper concern is distanced by the comic pattern, and less vital antitheses present figural patterns of the basic archetype. The internal tensions of the play lead to a series of delightfully comic ironies. . . . *Phoenix* exemplifies this process: night is distilled into dawn, the tragic is transcended, and the movement of the play traces "the figure of a dance" as Dynamene and Tegeus concertina in the throes of Langer's "life rhythm," which is part of the eternal mystery of death and resurrection embodied in the Christian and Phoenix myths, and in the plot and language of the play. This demonstration of unity is far from "too frequent." (pp. 17-18)

James Woodfield, "'The Figure of a Dance': Christopher Fry's 'A Phoenix Too Frequent'," in Ariel *(copyright © 1978 The Board of Governors The University of Calgary), Vol. 9, No. 3, July, 1978, pp. 3-18.*

PATRICIA BEER

Can you find me is precisely what its subtitle states, a family history. . . . In this case, although Christopher Fry has distinct recollections of the first eleven years of his life . . . , there is no question of our being given his own version of them. This is no child among you taking notes; there are no ruthless revelations. Neither is there any self-deception, which can be so much more alienating than any amount of ruthlessness. The "I" is almost purely formal.

Not entirely formal, of course; for the fact that the writer is Christopher Fry, the successful man who was once the child, accounts for the pleasantly authoritative tone, and indeed for the circumstance that the story was written at all, for nobody but a famous man would devote a book to very ordinary ancestors and only an experienced writer could make them interesting if he did. . . .

Mr Fry makes them memorable by portraying them precisely as they were, with no descent to the picturesque. . . .

Christopher Fry's organization of what mounts up to a considerable body of material is ingenious and inventive. The method is more cinematographic than historical, and sometimes the continuity goes astray but not often.

Patricia Beer, "Life Before Birth," in The Times Literary Supplement *(© Times Newspapers Ltd. (London) 1978; reproduced from* The Times Literary Supplement *by permission), No. 3994, October 20, 1978, p. 1197.*

HAROLD HOBSON

Christopher Fry was the first dramatist after the war to bring to the English theatre not merely a national, but also an international, fame. It is difficult to exaggerate the sense of freshness and excitement that swept through the theatrical world when *The Lady's Not for Burning,* with the extraordinary brilliance of the fancies, the conceits, and the imagination of its dialogue, the originality of its verse-form, and the joyous mediaeval paradox of its story seemed to shatter the by then somnolent reign of naturalism on the British stage. (p. 13)

[*Can You Find Me*] is a book of unique character. It is the autobiography of an outstanding international dramatist of our time, who has achieved some of the most notable successes, and been played by some of the most famous actors and actresses of the age. Yet no mention is made of these things in *Can You Find Me.* They could, it is true, hardly be discussed at length, for the book finishes when the author reaches the age of eleven. But there is not even the slightest premonition of them, no suggestion of the things to come. From the perfect form and completeness of the book I should guess that Mr. Fry does not intend to give it a sequel. It is one: indivisible and unadditionable. Not only is there no reference in it to, for example, *Venus Observed,* or *The Boy with a Cart,* but it scarcely ever mentions the theatre at all. . . .

It is a book that is full of echoes rather than of foreshadowings: a series of minor events that happened to small people out of which there slowly emerges a pattern of life magically surrounded with a sense of mystery and even of awe. Mr. Fry is a great hand at jigsaw puzzles. . . . As each piece in a jigsaw is of little or no importance in itself yet combines with its fellows to present a total work of art, so out of a multitude of tiny incidents, trivial hopes, and unmomentous disappointments, which are rescued by Mr. Fry with the help of a few old letters and diary entries of the baldest kind, out of what one would have thought an impenetrable past, there is created a feeling about life, about its strangeness, and its inexplicability that is poetic in its sensibility, and poignant in a gentle and all-pervading sadness. . . . [*Can You Find Me* is] subtle in its inspiration, and in the quietness of its establishment of a universal melancholy; and since our sweetest songs are those that tell of saddest thought it is the most beautiful, and in the end the most haunting.

Does anything of the past, as revealed in these unobtrusively masterly pages, live on in Christopher Fry? Is he what he is because his parents and his grandparents, his aunts and his cousins are what they were? He asks this question wistfully, but he does not answer it in set terms; it is left to the understanding and sympathetic reader to judge for himself. The question is present in our minds all the time we are reading his book, and it remains to tease us long after we have put it down. . . . Basically Mr. Fry's book is the evocation of a troubled and bewildered suburban and rural family flanked by wild adventures at opposite ends of the globe. (p. 14)

Can You Find Me demonstrates Fry's instinctive searching for another world than that in which we live: for a world that is perhaps not wholly comprehensible to ordinary human reason, but which is free from sordidness and restlessness and baseness and insecurity. He has discovered in this remarkable work that such a world is not to be found in the past, at least not in the past of his own family, in spite of its aspirations, its many gifts, and its fatal weaknesses; and it is this perhaps that has made him in the theatre an inhabitant of a glittering romance founded ultimately on a sense of deep religious faith and commitment. (p. 17)

Harold Hobson, "Christopher Fry's Other World," in Drama, *No. 132, Spring, 1979, pp. 13-17.*

ANDREW AROS

Christopher Fry, has fashioned a chronicle of his family—a mini "Roots" if you will. While some of the more colorful relatives draw one's interest, the greater part of [*Can You Find Me*] is just plain dull. (p. 54)

A biography of Christopher Fry might have been far more interesting, and much of the material in this book could have been boiled down to a very interesting introductory prologue, rather than an, at times, pointless family history. (p. 55)

Andrew Aros, "Non-Fiction: 'Can You Find Me: A Family History'," in Best Sellers *(copyright © 1979 Helen Dwight Reid Educational Foundation), Vol. 39, No. 2, May, 1979, pp. 54-5.*

*   *   *

FUGARD, Athol 1932-

Fugard is a South African dramatist. His plays feature a small cast of characters whose minds he probes. Although Fugard depicts lives of desolation and ennui, he is most concerned with apartheid and its consequences. He collaborated with John Kani and Winston Ntshona on three of his most recent works, *The Island, Sizwe Bansi Is Dead,* and *Statements after an Arrest under the Immorality Act.* (See also *CLC,* Vol. 5, 9, and *Contemporary Authors,* Vols. 85-88.)

MARY BENSON

"My job," Athol Fugard has said, "is to witness as truthfully as I can the nameless and destitute of one little corner of the world." Packed into those words is a loving, fierce, unremitting confrontation with the outrageousness of the existence of the nameless many who inhabit that corner: the Eastern Cape region of South Africa. . . . The characters in his plays reverberate with life. . . . Poverty, pain, dumb dreams are their lot yet—battered, bruised, with their violence and mockery directed against each other—they are alive. Forced to face the facts of their wretchedness, outraged they yet survive. And because Fugard writes as close as he can get to the bone—"meat is something that must rot or be cut away before the hard white truth is exposed"—essentially local characters from the littered slums around the industrial center of Port Elizabeth become universal; his language, often stemming from crude Afrikaner earthiness, is harsh, lyrical, comic. (p. 55)

He formulated the 'pure theatre experience' back in 1961: "The actor and the stage, the actor on the stage. Around him is space, to be filled and defined by movement; around him is also a silence to be filled with meaning, using words and sounds, and at moments when all else fails him, including my words, the silence itself." Now he adds that "this means an existentialist standpoint in theatre: space and silence equals nothingness; the actor's confrontation with our being and nothingness." (p. 57)

[*No Good Friday* and *Nongogo,* "The Family" trilogy, and *People Are Living There* are all plays] about survival—his favorite word. And in each play through a faceless catalyst the characters are precipitated into a confrontation with the facts of their lives, a sense of the here and now; *This* is my life. It is from the confrontation that outrage springs. Why this faceless character; Fugard says he doesn't fully understand, yet. (p. 58)

After *Boesman and Lena,* Fugard felt he was about to take a leap. This proved to be [*Orestes*]. . . . Some years ago he became impatient with the sequential logic of his play; music, poetry, painting had broken from such rigidity. . . . [He] continued to ask himself how he could escape. Meanwhile the writings of R. D. Laing led him to "a more direct access to inner space." . . . He fused a statement of the murder of Iphigenia by Clytemnestra and Orestes' revenge, with the act of protest of John Harris who, in 1964, placed a suitcase containing a bomb beside a bench in Johannesburg station concourse: a woman sitting on the bench was killed. Fugard, describing himself as "scribe"—"this was not being pretentious but accurate"—took the writer into the rehearsal room to be on a par with the actors. . . . He formed the mandate, fed challenges to them and, out of their responses, their own inner sources and identities, he shaped the play. *Orestes,* he emphasizes, did not come out of a vacuum; it tapped an energy in that society. (pp. 59-60)

Mary Benson, "Athol Fugard and 'One Little Corner of the World'," in yale/theatre *(copyright © by* Theater, *formerly* yale/theatre *1973), Vol. 4, No. 1, Winter, 1973, pp. 55-63.*

ATHOL FUGARD

[It was during a period in Europe in 1960 that] I began to keep a notebook. It became a daily ritual to record anything that happened to me which seemed of significance—sensual fragments, incidents, quotations, speculations. Writing now, I find in them the content of all that I can possibly say about my work. (p. viii)

I began working seriously on *Hello and Goodbye* towards the end of 1963. My notebooks have [an] extensive record of both the genesis of this play and my problems in writing it.

[5/19/63:]
From time to time I keep remembering, and still see occasionally on the streets, one face from my youth. That of a man who, for as long as I can remember, could be seen at night standing motionless against the wall on the corner of Jetty and Main Streets. Large unsmiling eyes, heavy lids. Bitter mouth. Must have seen him a hundred times, yet I have no recollection of any expression other than this one of morbid withdrawal. (p. xii)

[9/16/63:]
Last night before sleep found myself thinking about Johnnie—the local street-corner derelict I made a few notes about some months back. I remembered a thought I had about a sister and suddenly I saw very clearly the germinal situation of a play. (p. xiii)

[9/25/63:]
Almost certain now that the next play is going to be about Johnnie and Hester Smit. Central images becoming increasingly obsessional. How many themes does a writer really have? How *few* can he have? This play—the idea is in one sense a fusion of elements in *The Blood Knot* and *People Are Living There*. If I can realize my intentions though, it should be closer to the former in style and structure—tense and tight. Main problem remains whether to have only two characters, or whether the father should also be seen.

[9/29/63:]
Certain now that there will only be two characters—Johnnie and Hester. At one level this worries me a little because it means the inevitable comparison with *The Blood Knot*. Once I get past this fear though and concern myself only with what is real, it seems so pointless to even consider 'adding' another character. In Hester and Johnnie I find a *complete* expression of the complex of ideas and images that have generated this play. (p. xiv)

[12/19/63:]
Thinking and making notes almost continuously now about the Valley play. Difficulty in the mechanics of the climax, when Hester 'loses hope' and 'learns she must die'. Suspicious of what I feel is a stock pattern or formula in my resolution of the climactic moment, i.e. *growing desperation*, leading to *emotional crisis*, leading to *the leap*.

Thinking about it for a moment I realize that I am wrong to see this as a formula common to all my other plays. *The Blood Knot* doesn't have it. Far from leaping, Morrie and Zach wake up heavy and hopeless, almost prostrate on the earth.

Yes, that is it! What I am searching for in the new play is the moment when Hester 'wakes up'. Three experiences: Loss of hope, knowledge of death, and finally the only certainty, the flesh . . . 'truths the hand can touch'.

What could be more obvious than that I should be drawn to, overwhelmed by Camus. Wasn't I trying to do that to Morrie and Zach at the end of *The Blood Knot*—two men who were going to try to live without hope, without appeal. In effect Morrie is trying to say, in that final beat of the play: Now we Know. (pp. xiv-xv)

[9/4/64:]
Hester gives me a chance for the ruthless honesty I so admire in Faulkner. Also Camus' 'Courageous Pessimism'. Isn't Hester the closest I've yet come to the bone? Even in Milly (*People Are Living There*) there is still too much 'meat'—something that must rot or be cut away before the hard, white truth is exposed. (p. xv)

[1/11/65:]
Strong sense of Hester's moral anarchy. Have abandoned the idea of Hester forgetting about the money while she searches through the boxes for something *specific* and *special* from her childhood, and which when found will trigger off a cathartic reliving of a moment in her youth. Instead, she still forgets the compensation from time to time, but is searching for something she herself cannot identify.

What does Hester want? To begin with, the compensation. But only *to begin with,* because she walks into that room unconscious of her life; 'in it' as she says at the end. But one level of her experience with the boxes and all that comes out of them is a growing alienation, a removal from her characteristic intense 'being myself'. At this level she is searching for something that will counter the absurdity spilling out of the boxes. (pp. xv-xvi)

[1/14/65:]
Important step forward yesterday. Plotted the sequence that takes the play through to the last box and Hester's climax on discovering that the next room is empty, that her father is dead. Two major gains in my rough outline of the play. First, and specifically, I see the way to a full and complete expression of the absurdity that overwhelms Hester ('There is no God!'). Secondly, and more generally, I see a pattern, not just a plot, a chance to weave together all that Johnnie and Hester mean separately—the 'simultaneous' moment with all its complexity in design and depth that I achieved unconsciously in *The Blood Knot* and was not able to repeat in *People Are Living There*.

[2/18/65:]
A question I cannot fully answer. (Yet? Ever?) What is it that draws Johnnie to the crutches? Any number of 'little' answers. Tantalized by the thought that there is one 'final' answer that still eludes my thinking? Do I need to know it? Because I *feel* the absolute reality of his fascination with his father's crutches, I see him so clearly drawing closer and closer to the moment when he goes onto them permanently.

[2/28/65:]
To master the idiom—thought and speech—of a character. The problem is never 'what' Hester and Johnnie think, but 'how' they think it. A constant challenge in all the plays. (p. xvi)

[Concerning the play *Boesman and Lena,* the notebook includes the following entries.]

[10/25/67:]
An essay on the translation of poetry—form and content of one language as opposed to another (English and Afrikaans here in S.A.)—prompts the thought that an important element in my own writing is this question of 'translating' from Afrikaans to English. Particularly conscious of it this time with *Boesman and Lena*. To begin with so much of it was in Afrikaans—some phrases are still and seem to defy translation into an English equivalent that will have the same texture or feel, e.g. *nog 'n vrot ou huisie vir die vrot mens*. . . . (pp. xix-xx)

[7/4/68:]
First act down in the roughest of rough drafts, skeleton for the second. More difficulty than I expected in finding the substance to this man-woman relationship. Struggling for objectivity and distance. For example: Boesman's hatred and abuse of Lena. Easy enough to formulate this as an 'idea' but a struggle to reveal the full carnal reality of it in incident and dialogue.

Unrelieved squalor of their situation demands that I write this one very carefully. . . . Realised that the genesis of this play lies possibly in an image from over ten years ago—Coloured man and woman, burdened with all their belongings, whom I passed somewhere on the road near Laingsburg. It was sunset and they were miles from the nearest town. (p. xx)

[7/19/68:]
To be careful that I do not pitch Boesman at a level of monotonous hatred and abuse. Not just the technical problem of variety of tone and tempo—the more basic issue that

it is not as simple as Lena being the victim and Boesman the oppressor. Both are ultimately victims of a common, a shared predicament, and of each other. Which of course makes it some sort of love story. They are each other's fate.

So for Boesman as total a statement as for Lena. What is mutilated and why? The key I am sure is to reveal and dramatise his self-hatred as focused on Lena. What he really hates is himself. (p. xxii)

[8/21/68:]
Strong and clear sense of the dynamics to the first act. Most important consequence is that Lena now has a drive, is 'moving' and not just sitting there in the mud floundering in her predicament. Reading Laing's *Politics of Experience* and *Bird of Paradise* has added new dimensions to my thinking about Boesman and Lena. Ontological insecurity: Lena in her demand that her life be witnessed. Not just a sense of injustice and abuse. . . .

[8/23/67:]
An example of [what I call the 'accident' in my writing] five minutes ago. Sorting out my ideas and images for the ending of Act One—Lena at the fire with Outa, sharing her mug of tea and piece of bread, kept hearing her say 'This mug . . .' 'This bread' 'My life . . .'. Suddenly, and apparently irrelevantly, remembered Lisa the other day reading a little book on the Catholic Mass. Suddenly there it was. Lena's Mass—the moment and its ingredients became sacramental, the whole a celebration of her life. (p. xxiii)

Like everyone else in this country, black and white, my horizons have shrunk [with the threat of censorship], and will continue to do so. Today's future barely includes tomorrow. [At times I see the situation deteriorating still further, to the point where even] the thought of a tomorrow will be a luxury. I'm trying to live and work in preparation for that eventuality. (p. xxv)

Athol Fugard, "Introduction" (copyright © 1973, 1974 by Athol Fugard; reprinted by permission of Viking Penguin Inc.), in his Three Port Elizabeth Plays, *Viking Penguin, 1974, pp. vii-xxv.*

RICHARD EDER

Athol Fugard's plays about the knife-edge life of blacks and coloreds in South Africa furnish some of the strongest and most moving stage literature being written in the English language.

"The Island," "Boesman and Lena," and "Sizwe Banzi" bob their human cockleshells just upstream from a giant whirlpool. The jaunty resilience of their characters has a tragic significance in the face of the racial and social rigors that will crush them.

These works are masterpieces, but Mr. Fugard, like any playwright, had to learn his trade. . . . ["Nongogo"] has some interest, but the main part of that may lie in the demonstration that a large talent can stumble quite a lot before it finds its way.

"Nongogo" . . . has found its theme: fearsome surroundings breed hope, and then destroy it. But the play is awkward and thin. It is unable to communicate very much about its characters, or make them much more than the servants of a noticeably ticking plot.

"Nongogo" means prostitute, and that was Queenie's trade before she set up her shabeen, or unlicensed bar, in one of Johannesburg's black shanty towns. . . .

Queenie and Johnny are both vulnerable through their past. Johnny has spent a year in a mining camp where he was abused sexually. When Sam drops hints about Queenie's previous career, and she confirms them, Johnny is shattered. Their venture collapses. He is determined to pull himself out of the mud; but he cannot bear the idea that Queenie comes from the same mud. It is a vision that Mr. Fugard will continue to develop: society's degradation does not bring its victims together, it keeps them apart.

Queenie is the most real of the characters. Her sense of herself and where she wants to go makes her believable, and the crumbling of her dour defenses at a touch of hope makes her affecting. By contrast, Johnny is unreal. His warmth and hopefulness at the start crumble too suddenly and too completely; we have an explanation for it but explanations on a stage are like apologies in real life.

The three other characters—Sam, Blackie and a neighbor—are mere dabs of characterization, used only to drive the machinery. And once Johnny has learned about Queenie's past, the machinery pretty well stops. The last third of the play is little but speeches made in anger and pain.

Richard Eder, "'Nongogo', a Drama," in The New York Times *(© 1978 by The New York Times Company; reprinted by permission), December 4, 1978, p. C15.*

EDITH OLIVER

If ever there was a born dramatist, it is the South African Athol Fugard. . . . ["Nongogo"], one of his earliest, was written and performed in South Africa in the late fifties. . . . Mr. Fugard appears to have found his subject and, to a large extent, his talent immediately. Himself a white man, he has written play after play about the various races—singly and in combination—imprisoned in his racist country, but in doing so he has never stooped to propaganda or case history. . . .

The small touches in the play and the excitement they generate—the whipping of the bright cloths on and off the table, for example—more than make up for its occasional awkwardness. If the plot seems melodramatic and arbitrary, and its hopeless ending forced, it is because the playwright has not yet learned to conceal his hand, but he has learned—or is on his way to learning—everything else of importance. The characters, their feelings, and the lines they speak (when the lines are not too openly expository) are admirably done, and there is enough suspense and wonder to keep things on the boil.

Edith Oliver, "The Theatre: 'Nongogo'," in The New Yorker *(© 1978 by The New Yorker Magazine, Inc.), Vol. LIV, No. 43, December 11, 1978, p. 57.*

JOHN SIMON

Fugard has not only become South Africa's leading dramatist, he has also, as much as any man, made the world conscious of the horrors of apartheid. But good as some of Fugard's later work is, this piece of juvenilia [*Nongogo*] is creaky, predictable, unconvincingly simplistic, and afflicted with a particularly awkward dramatic failing: overacceleration. . . . As in ancient newsreels, where people seem to move in a funny little quickstep, the plot skips ahead from expected twist to unsurprising reversal. What, in more experienced hands, could have had the measured pace of the inevitable, displays only the tugging of a nervous puppeteer. (pp. 88, 90)

John Simon, "Futile Fandango," in New York *Magazine (copyright © 1978 by News Group Publications, Inc.; reprinted with the permission of* New York *Magazine), Vol. 11, No. 51, December 18, 1978, pp. 88, 90.**

TERRY CURTIS FOX

Athol Fugard is a political tragedian, a very rare kind of writer indeed. His characters—sometimes consciously, more often not—revolt against the social order, but they are neither beaten back by it nor do they defeat it. They destroy each other instead. The idea of personal growth, of change, of effective individual action is banished by the very nature of South Africa. Fugard does not cry for the beloved country—he describes with painful detail a nation in which daily activities are turned into recurrent horrors by constant oppression.

Fugard wrote *Nongogo* 20 years ago, but the play's themes remain current in his work. This is not a failure of the writer to evolve, but the continued presence of apartheid. It is one thing to tell a story of personal distruction. It is another to have to tell it over and over and over again, because the world of oppression never lightens. Then the outcome of all human intercourse becomes tragic. Nothing in any one of Fugard's plays is nearly so horrific as the fact that he has been writing about the same thing for over a generation. What is astonishing is that Fugard can continue to write at all. (p. 126)

Terry Curtis Fox, "20 Years Ago Is Now," in The Village Voice *(copyright © 1978; reprinted by permission), Vol. XXIII, No. 51, December 18, 1978, pp. 126, 128.**

G

GELBER, Jack 1932-

Gelber, an American playwright and novelist, is best known for his depiction of the drug culture in his play *The Connection*. Though original and intriguing in its conception, the quality of Gelber's work is generally considered to be uneven. (See also *CLC*, Vols. 1, 6, and *Contemporary Authors*, Vols. 1-4, rev. ed.)

EDITH OLIVER

Jack Gelber is, and has been from "The Connection" on, a dramatist who makes his own rules. His "Sleep," a play of sorts, . . . is based on the research that has been done over the past few years on sleep itself, and especially on Rapid Eye Movement Sleep and the kinds of dream that accompany it. The setting of the play is a sleep laboratory. A man called Gil is lying on a bed, upstage center, with his head in a metal contraption that looks something like a hair dryer. . . . Two doctors, Morphy (dim joke) and Merck (another), give Gil a few instructions, and he goes to sleep. The duration of the action is the duration of his first night in the lab, where, by tracking the dreams he acts out as he passes from one stage of sleep to the next and in and out of REM Sleep, we reconstruct his life . . . and his emotional spectrum—the heights he scales and the pockets he falls into. . . . [Many] of the scenes are quite good. We see Gil trying to make love to his wife; she refuses, to his dismay and anger, and the marriage cracks into pieces before our eyes. A threatening dream figure forces him to strip, and suddenly his horrified modesty changes to joy, and he goes scampering and dancing around the stage to make the funniest nude scene on earth. Nevertheless, the play is not a success—is not, I think, quite inventive or imaginative enough—nor does the character of Gil, as it is written, seem worth all that attention. But the idea is certainly original. There is a lot of work still to be done on "Sleep," and I hope that Mr. Gelber doesn't abandon it.

Edith Oliver, "A Hard Night's Sleep," in The New Yorker *(© 1972 by The New Yorker Magazine, Inc.), Vol. XLVIII, No. 2, March 4, 1972, pp. 82-3.*

CLIVE BARNES

What is a play? How does it happen? What makes it work? These were the basic issues behind Jack Gelber's new play, which is called, beguilingly enough, "Jack Gelber's New Play: Rehearsal." It is directed by the author. And it is not a rehearsal. But it tries to be the substance of a rehearsal—which might be something less or might be something more. . . .

It is a play about a play, or at least about a play that was being rehearsed. The fictional author is a white ex-convict. His play is about "a prison rebellion that doesn't work out." It could be Attica. But then, Mr. Gelber and even his fictional author play everything cool; it could be anywhere. But, just as a tip, the fictional director, directing the fictional play, has a paperback of "Attica" on his fictional desk. The paperback could have been fictional.

Mr. Gelber's purpose is very clear. He is fascinated by the machinery not only of playwriting but much more of the business of getting a play on. . . .

Mr. Gelber's playwright indeed even gets involved in the play itself, as an actor. Even more indeed, he finds himself playing in a male rape scene that he neither wrote, witnessed, nor envisaged. He is learning about the theater the hard way. But so is everyone else, including the play's fictional cast, its fictional director and its fictional producer. The only nonfiction part of this particular show is the audience. For much of the time it learns things the hard way as well.

Just as in his first and probably best-known play, "The Connection," Mr. Gelber is dealing with life. In that case it was the reality of drug addiction; so here he is dealing with the actual process of a play passing through its first read-through to production. . . .

All of Mr. Gelber's points seem perfectly pertinent. . . .

The play is neatly structured, and the idea is a good one. But unfortunately it is not particularly well-written. It neither has the raciness of vernacular speech nor perhaps the more measured tread permissible in dramatic literature. As a result the end product never convinces to the extent the original concept might promise. Because despite the good premise, Mr. Gelber often falls into cliché thought and predictable action.

Clive Barnes, "Gelber's 'Rehearsal', A Play Within a Play," in The New York Times, *Section C (© 1976 by The New York Times Company; reprinted by permission), October 8, 1976, p. 4.*

ALAN RICH

My first reaction to *Jack Gelber's New Play: Rehearsal,* now at the American Place, is the fervent hope that Mr. Gelber will spare us the sequel, *Jack Gelber's New Play: Play*. The most distressing part of the current show, whose title ought to be self-explanatory, is the play that his group of actors and other stage folk occasionally get down to rehearsing, in between long bouts of palaver about what the play means, what theater means, what being an actor means, and so forth.

Yet, I did not mind Mr. Gelber's little theatrical exercise as much as my colleagues apparently did. Yes, the dialogue is utter trash, but I suspect that that was the aim. Actors, especially the seedy, out-of-luck bunch that people Mr. Gelber's theater, do tend to mistake the language of their work—soap operas, commercials, and the like—for intelligent speech, and they do go around, if they're not careful, saying things like "we're all in this together."

Mr. Gelber obviously knows his theater folk, and some of his observations in this new work are deadly accurate. . . . His show may not be much as drama, but as a learning experience I can, from my own days as a theater groupie, vouch for its authenticity.

Alan Rich, "Balderdash in the Bayou," in New York *Magazine (copyright © 1976 by News Group Publications, Inc.; reprinted with the permission of* New York *Magazine), Vol. 9, No. 43, October 25, 1976, p. 77.**

ARTHUR SAINER

Gelber's *Jack Gelber's New Play: Rehearsal* is fascinating to the degree that it allows us to see . . . [a] communal breakdown, at work. Like *The Connection,* its people not only damage one another but collaborate in a situation which allows a force outside the group to set the conditions for survival. In *The Connection,* all are waiting for the fix. In *Rehearsal,* all are dependent on a financial fix. If the producer, like the pusher, fails to arrive with the fix, general and/or personal collapse ensues. The individual is at the mercy of the marketplace, at the mercy of the whims of the entrepreneur who can give or withhold. Neither the value of the individual nor that of the communal goal is given weight in these transactions. But it is the individual who allows the conditions. If the communal goal were worth enough to him, collaborative ways might be found to support it, obviating the need for the entrepreneur.

Near the end of *Rehearsal,* one actor suggests that the company simply go on with rehearsals, mount the play off-off Broadway, *without* financial support if need be; but no one else, not even the writer of the play, gives that serious consideration, failing to understand that a true communal effort invests not only the goal (which is the furtherance of the communal good) with meaning but everyone involved in the effort. . . .

A further complication implicit in the situation that Gelber sets up in *Rehearsal* is that though everyone wants the play to happen, few in the company are agreed as to what play it is they are trying to make happen. . . .

And within those contradictions, irony: Gelber gives *Rehearsal's* political ideology to the middle-class Rufus, while Danny, the author, and Fat, his prison buddy, both victims of society's brutal penal system, are innocent of ideology and reflect the political virginity of America's blue-collar men and the destitute. In America, those who have been most hurt economically by the system are often the ones to support the system unthinkingly; perhaps the system comes to take on the character of the retributive father who possesses all the riches and must be kept alive even as the sons attempt to rip him off.

Others in the play never consider the play's nature seriously—it is entirely a vehicle within which they can at worst keep alive for another few weeks, at best use as a stepping stone to classier productions. Since the play cannot be all things to all men, it declines into no thing for no one, it takes on the character of whoever has it by the throat at any given moment.

If Gelber, consciously or not, sees the rehearsal of the play as a metaphor for the kind of molding we do in order to get the society we want, his writing and direction reveal curious inconsistencies. Gelber seems to dwell on improvisation as an aesthetic good in theatre, but he also wants to control it, so we get examples of seeming improvisation that are really staged. They provide the audience with the vicarious thrill of thinking it is witnessing life in theatre without *allowing* that life in the theatre. As director, he has allowed the movements to be too-planned, he has minimized the risks (which is supposedly what responsible directors should and usually do), but in effect his controlling undermines the very value of improvisation the play implicitly condones.

And further, the play hardly gives us a sense of the forces that go to make up prison society. While Gelber beautifully sets up a capitalist order in miniature, seen through the rehearsal process, he barely sketches the world of prison hierarchy and prison values that have created the explosive situations in our various Atticas. . . .

But for all its inconsistencies, for all its lack of sufficient risk-taking, Gelber's script and his direction of it evoke a keen sense of humanity under the system's ax, of theatre people tearing at each other, often without knowing it, to keep themselves going in this economic jungle.

Arthur Sainer, "Gelber Revisits the Survival Junkies," in The Village Voice *(reprinted by permission of* The Village Voice; *copyright © The Village Voice, Inc., 1976), Vol. XXI, No. 43, October 25, 1976, p. 95.*

* * *

GELLHORN, Martha 1908-

Gellhorn is an American novelist, short story writer, journalist, playwright, and essayist. Stylistically as well as thematically, her fiction shows strong evidence of years spent as a war correspondent. Gellhorn's is a skillfully crafted, frequently reportorial prose, often compared for its hard-edged clarity to that of her late ex-husband, Ernest Hemingway. (See also *Contemporary Authors,* Vols. 77-80.)

DIANA TRILLING

["Liana"] is for me reminiscent of . . . "Tropic Moon" by the French writer Simenon, not only because both novels are triangular love stories of the French tropics and share a sophisticated concern for the way colored people are treated in the colonies, but because they both manage to achieve an emotional, almost a literary, effect quite beyond their literary merits. Possibly this is the result of their non-intellectuality—or rather, of their perfect blending of intellectual and emotional pitch. There is more atmosphere, for instance, in Miss Gellhorn's book than the author seems to work to produce, and more suggested meaning in the human relationships than characters such as hers usually yield. On the surface, or even several layers down, "Liana" is not much more than another stereotyped, not-so-lush-as-it-could-have-been narrative of tropical miscegenation. . . . Still, there are reverberations from Miss Gellhorn's simple story, as there were reverberations from Simenon's novel, which must be recorded on the credit side of the ledger; it is always a good thing when a novel gives off more effects than can be readily accounted for. (p. 104)

Diana Trilling, "Fiction in Review: 'Liana'," in The Nation *(copyright 1944 by the Nation Associates, Inc.), Vol. 158, No. 4, January 22, 1944, pp. 104-05.**

MARK SCHORER

[In "Liana"] Miss Gellhorn, who is a sober and skillful rather than a powerful novelist, challenged herself to bring to life the most worn materials of cheap fiction: a beautiful native girl in a lush tropical setting, a brutal white man to whom she is tied, a beautiful and sensitive white man who is hired to teach her and who is promptly gripped by the conflict of love and honor. In 1944, the beautiful and sensitive white man is, of course, sensitive to fascism; specifically, this one is a Frenchman who has fled Vichy and determines to return to fight Vichy, a sound and obvious conclusion which leaves Liana in the familiar dilemma of Madame Butterfly. . . . Miss Gellhorn is pitiless: she does not hesitate to include even the heroine's heartbroken letter which, by misrepresenting her true feelings, releases the hero from his scruples about her. Where she breaks sharply with her trite materials is in the handling of the relationship between the two men: they come to understand, almost to love, each other, and Liana is faced with utter exclusion. This is a delicate psychological situation which Conrad, for example, would have developed with circumspection; but most of Miss Gellhorn's novel is devoted to blackening her villain, and her last chapters hardly give him time to take off his mustache. (p. 286)

Mark Schorer, "Exotics," in The New Republic *(reprinted by permission of* The New Republic; *© 1944 The New Republic, Inc.), Vol. 110, No.9, February 28, 1944, pp. 286, 288.**

[*Two by Two*] consists of four long short stories, or four short novels, depending on how you look at it. "For Better for Worse," "For Richer for Poorer," "In Sickness and in Health," "Till Death do us Part"—these are the themes and titles. All four are extremely readable, for Miss Gellhorn has a brisk narrative style, her writing is founded on the sure belief that human relationships are the essentials of life, and she is able to judge women through men's eyes as realistically and dispassionately as she is able to examine the male ego with the torn feelings of the woman.

Miss Gellhorn has been a newspaper correspondent and these stories move about the important capitals of the world with an easy familiarity. London, New York, Paris, Rome, come to life not as tourist centres, holiday stop-offs, but as places of work, where roving men and roving women have to subordinate emotion to career. Miss Gellhorn's characters are high-level professionals, politicians, war photographers, journalists, and she manages to suggest the urgency of their lives, bound up with the times, and the consequent disruptions of their marriages. For these four stories are analyses of the marriage relationship, in each of which money, ambition, sickness, career play crucial parts.

The final story, a running report on the life and loves of a photographer who races towards his death from one warspot to another, is a remarkably sustained and moving affair. Miss Gellhorn creates in Tim Bara a faithful symbol of our time; it is a portrait that goes deep, is rich in revealing touches, and is formed with great technical mastery. *Two by Two* is not always successful, but the characterization, even when at its glossiest, shows a true understanding of what hazards disturb the rarely calm waters of marital love.

"For Better for Worse," in The Times Literary Supplement *(© Times Newspapers Ltd. (London) 1958; reproduced from* The Times Literary Supplement *by permission), No. 2923, March 7, 1958, p. 125.**

DAVID DEMPSEY

One accepts [the characters in "His Own Man"] as artificial, polished and pleasantly unreal; their problems are not real problems, but those of a novelist experienced enough to know that all's well that ends badly. . . . "His Own Man" is sensibly restricted to less than 200 pages, and is written with such verve, such an effervescence of wit, that it is like taking a bubble bath, with a well-iced absinthe on the side. One emerges refreshed—and a little groggy.

David Dempsey, "All's Well That Ends Badly," in The New York Times Book Review *(© 1961 by The New York Times Company; reprinted by permission), August 6, 1961, p. 4.*

CHARLES ROLO

[Martha Gellhorn's *His Own Man,*] an elegant entertainment which is also a morality tale, is felicitously conceived and executed with wit, gaiety, toughness of mind, and perfect control. The story is a topical variation on the theme of the American abroad. Its hero—or, rather, antihero [Ben]—belongs to a new class which is the contemporary counterpart of the intellectuals of an earlier era who lived abroad on small private incomes. (p. 101)

Ben is a thoroughly convincing, if unusual, amalgam of pride, irresponsibility, and the Puritan conscience, and Miss Gellhorn shows with finesse and humor how such a man gradually, reluctantly makes compromises with his precious principles and drifts into corruption. The other characters are impeccably drawn, and there is a rich fund of high comedy. The book is a delight. (p. 102)

Charles Rolo, "La Dolce Vita," in The Atlantic Monthly *(copyright © 1961 by The Atlantic Monthly Company, Boston, Mass.; reprinted with permission), Vol. 208, No. 3, September, 1961, pp. 101-02.*

MARY HOPE

Martha Gellhorn is curiously dated and sentimental [in *The Weather in Africa*]. The three stories are set in Kenya before and just after Independence. . . . In all three stories, Africa changes the lives of people; but somehow, the resolutions are achieved in spite of the characters' interactions which remain on the most basic level, and in their recounting seem to me to retain the crudest of racial assumptions. Love scenes are either stilted, if between whites . . . or torrid, if between black and white . . . which is a cue for disaster). However, the heart is in the right place.

Mary Hope, "Books: 'The Weather in Africa'," in The Spectator *(© 1978 by* The Spectator; *reprinted by permission of* The Spectator*), Vol. 241, No. 7828, July 15, 1978, p. 25.*

EMILY HAHN

Martha Gellhorn is a gentleperson. For 42 pages in ["Travels with Myself and Another"] she writes about an Unwilling Companion on her trip into China's interior in 1941, always referring to him as U. C. and never mentioning that he was in fact her husband, Ernest Hemingway. This—at a time when to have been Hemingway's wife . . . seems excuse enough to publish every possible remembrance of the great man—entitles Miss Gellhorn to a medal, at least. But her excellence does not stop there. She renders U. C. justice: she makes him a sympathetic as well as amusing figure, although perhaps a wee bit maddening. . . .

U. C. apart, Miss Gellhorn can be exceedingly funny on her own. Often, reading of her travels—in China of course, the Caribbean . . . , Russia and Israel, to name the headliners—I chuckled in a ladylike, repressed manner, but sometimes I had to stop to laugh really loud. Not that Martha Gellhorn is merely entertaining. She is a thoughtful woman with a lot of serious opinions, and whether or not one agrees with her, as I often didn't, it is worth reflecting on her reflections. (p. 15)

I have a lot in common with Miss Gellhorn, and it's not merely that we both come from St. Louis. Never mind the Chinese sense of humor that she doesn't dig. Never mind various other small, small points on which one could, if one wished, take issue. I agree with the important things she says, and I loved the book. (p. 30)

Emily Hahn, "Moving Lady," in The New York Times Book Review *(© 1979 by The New York Times Company; reprinted by permission), September 23, 1979, pp. 15, 30.*

Miss Gellhorn writes in the merry, self-depreciating manner of those who came of journalistic age in the grin-and-bear-it thirties, and it is a blessing that she does, for the journeys recounted [in *Travels with Myself and Another*] . . . would be unbearable in the hands of a complainer. All her trips are unwilling, either on assignment from *Collier's* or as the helpless result of an unrelenting addiction to travel, but all her senses are fully involved (including a painfully keen sense of smell), and her eye is notably sharp ("We saw ostriches, an untidy weird bird, with an upper thigh like a ballet dancer and feet like high-laced black shoes"). She also has the courage to voice unpopular observations. . . . (p. 198)

"Books: 'Travels with Myself and Another'," in The New Yorker *(© 1979 by The New Yorker Magazine, Inc.), Vol. LV, No. 36, October 22, 1979, pp. 198-99.*

AARON I. MICHELSON

[Martha Gellhorn's *Travels with Myself and Another*] is written with a piquant wit and a fervent compassion for human folly and suffering.

Yet, whether by accident or choice, *Travels with Myself and Another* is a depressing travelogue of disasters and exasperating hardships somewhat savagely narrated in an almost continuous account of frustrations, crises and even horrors. With the termination of each trip the reader will find it difficult to feel any glowing sensation of vicarious satisfaction; contrariwise, he will more likely sigh, "Thank God it's over!" Perhaps our traveller is deliberately following her own advice that the only aspect of travel guaranteed to hold an audience is disaster. . . .

Also, most readers would be greatly aided by a few maps to assist in better understanding the accounts. . . . Still, *Travels with Myself and Another* is an interesting, informative and worthwhile book if for no other reason than most of us need to be jolted to an awareness that we are fortunate enough to repeat after Ms. Gellhorn, "Oh what a beautiful place I live in . . . I will count my blessings every morn and night . . ."

Aaron I. Michelson, "Non-Fiction: 'Travels with Myself and Another'," in Best Sellers *(copyright © 1979 Helen Dwight Reid Educational Foundation), Vol. 39, No. 8, November, 1979, p. 295.*

* * *

GENET, Jean 1910-

Genet is a French novelist, dramatist and poet. An abandoned child, he spent his youth in prisons and reform schools. Instead of reforming him, he claims, these institutions led him to defy society and to dedicate his life to the pursuit of evil. In his quest for identity, Genet aligned himself with criminals and homosexuals, choosing them as his heroes and their world as his. He posits that evil is superior to good because it is nothingness expressed in its purest form. Susan Sontag wrote of him that "only a handful of twentieth-century writers, such as Kafka and Proust, have as important, as authoritative, as irrevocable a voice and style." (See also *CLC*, Vols. 1, 2, 5, 8, and *Contemporary Authors*, Vols. 13-16, rev. ed.)

DAVID I. GROSSVOGEL

Genet is an outcast amid outcasts, a criminal and a pederast —outlaw to society, female to the fraternity of outlaws. When he writes for the stage, he wants his writing not to be fiction, not to be entertainment, not to be a mirror held up to whatever the stage is supposed to mirror, but to be a genuine act of aggression; his play is the continuation of a gesture performed by an outlaw against society.

No social protest enters into this outrage; Genet needs the existing order of things. He is Lucifer turned Satan, an aristocrat of Evil—the inverted world in which he dwells—and cannot desire to right the social structure without jeopardizing that which confers upon him his titles of nobility. . . . For Genet, Evil is the resplendence of Lucifer, the criteria evidencing the beauty of an act, an object, or a human being. Society is a sealed package, familiar, drab, secure—scarcely the right climate for what should be alive, significant, beautiful. Beyond this closed and sterile world is another into which society cannot expand without disintegrating; that outer planet is its mystery, short of which there is no poetry—something which society is intent on destroying but which is also its secret fascination. The outlaw inhabits this exotic world, and this is his first virtue. His second virtue comes from being the only one possessed of "that will, that daring to pursue a destiny that is against all rules" ("The Criminal Child"). These words should not, however, imply volition: the criminal is the one *necessary* being, the one who has not been shaped with another end in view. His is a world of subversion and death and beauty. The "saintliness" of the criminal (the two terms are frequently linked by Genet) is his rigor in not returning to the blandness of society, in resisting its blandishments.

But it is not a systematic evil which Genet will pursue in his drama: this is not a moral theater, even in reverse. Genet has a string of prison sentences sufficiently long to evidence the sincerity of his criminal leaning. It is not the crime itself that he will propose as an artist, but the flavor of crime; not the subversion, but the beauty of an order subverted. The ritual of this stage, its properties and actors, will be the sacred objects that reveal the mystical horror, the dread, and the supreme beauty of that which is beyond the usual purlieus of man (sometimes simply because it is beyond those purlieus). To begin with, in the image suggested by Sartre, Genet will redeem for man those false objects which God cannot see (since they are false) and which only man can contemplate as beautiful. He is able in this way to assume a beauty that exists only for man, and he achieves in so doing the touch of the esthete that turns into something imaginary what would be otherwise real. Much that defines the world of Genet also defines poetry.

But such objects cannot have the stillborn dimension of static things. Their reality is in their symbiotic relation to man, meaningful only as long as a human being anticipates their promise and is frustrated by their refusal ever to keep that promise. Only man can provide such a victim for the never-familiar talisman that remains both human, because of its human respondent, and more than human, because of its own ultimate unresponsiveness. The sacred object on stage touches man only in that part of him that strains to transcend his human essence. Genet's is an esthetic drama in which the spectator remains conscious, in his identification, of his necessary detachment.

Analysis of a play by Genet is most difficult in its incipience: how does one enter Genet's maze of interreflecting mirrors? (pp. 137-40)

[The] physical level of [*The Maids,* Genet's first play to be performed, is] the part with which Genet is not truly concerned. It may indicate the lineaments of its action, but it fails to account for the protagonists, their circumstances, or the climate in which they move about. It does not even describe them. Who are these "maids"? At the level closest to reality, they are actresses playing a role which Genet has written for them. But that is precisely what Genet does not want. In the preface to the play, he complains that "the occidental actor does not try to become a symbol laden with symbols; he wants merely to identify himself with a character." A genuine maid on a stage would not be a stage-worthy person: the quality of her presence would not make of the stage a significant moment in the consciousness of an onlooker. If an actress—not a maid—plays a maid and if her "play" is to be more than the mere exhibition of what a maid might be off stage, the quality of this new maid (the actress-as-maid) must be derived in part from the spectator's inability to dismiss her presence with the statement, "She is a maid." Instead, she is a hybrid, part actress, part maid. As an actress, she is the half-goddess, the remote creature of beauty and of luxury, the emanation of the multiple desires of those who see her as such and inform her with their longing. On stage, she is more—she is the flesh-and-blood creature, a woman to whom a spectator (or a spectatress), also of flesh and blood, will respond through animal calling. Her impersonation of the maid is going to awaken a complex response in the spectator. A part of him goes out to the creature of his dreams, the star; another reaches to the woman, the scented and pulsating reality before him; a third is being drawn into the words and action upon which the character "maid" leaves her impress. The author, the director who believes that it is this last form of the "maid" who provides the most important of these stimuli, will subdue the star and the woman (to the extent that she is something besides a maid). Genet's intention is different. Maids exist outside the theater; so do women—and even actresses (though to a lesser extent, since their world carries forever with it at least a part of the stage). But only in the theater are these several realities blended within the irreality of the stage. It is the *stage* that Genet wants to preserve, a justified bias that defines an art form in terms of its ability to do what no other form can do as well, as totally, or in the same way.

It is the quality "actress" that Genet wishes to emphasize, not the quality "maid." These will thus be actresses acting —not actresses enacting maids, as this would start a descending line away from the theatrical illusion. They are playing at being, in an ascending line, maids who are in fact actresses and maids who think of themselves as actresses "laden with symbols," only the first of which is the inverted social order which they "represent."

The actress who plays at being a maid justifies one part of her being—she is a woman playing a woman. The tension provided by the equivocal actress-woman-maid breaks down at the point where "woman" and "maid" fuse. Genet has required for this play that the tension be carried forward along another upward spiral: the two maids are to be played by two young boys. Now the actor cannot identify himself immediately with any part of his creation. Or can he? For the ambiguity of the stage does not confine itself to the relation of the actor to his role; there is still another point of view represented by the spectator, a part of whom responds to the physical truth of an animal like himself, whatever its role and attributes. And the maids, young boys disguised as women, are acting out a strange, inverted relationship [as they also pretend to be mistress and maid] that involves the spectator directly in this stifling hothouse of flowers, phantasms, and the pomp of a weird ceremony.

The relationship of the maids is homosexual; is not a homosexual someone consciously enacting a role? The dress which each maid wears is part of an inverted sex-play which is not confined to the unreal stage, for beyond that stage the participant actors and spectators have been directly contaminated. But then, are these two figures? They are "sisters," they look alike to the extent that they can exchange roles—the homosexual polarity requiring two similar partners. Up to a point they are indeed distinct. Claire, the luminous one, incarnates the esthetic half of the homosexual act; she is the female principle within the male. Solange, the angel now in heaven, now fallen, is generally the male or destructive principle, the antiesthetic; she will destroy the symbol Claire. For a while, both performers are willing to conform to these parts. Solange is "in adoration" of Claire, and Claire acts the distant, detached, and desirable figure who is both the hierarchical and sexual mistress of Solange. She is haughty ("avoid touching me"), ironic, and cruel (Solange: "Madame is forgetting herself, Madame . . ."; Claire: "And what about your hands? Don't *you* forget your hands"), and these imperatives rouse the desire of Solange while confirming Claire in her role as an object of desire that is conscious of its empire.

But even as she is playing the role of the maid, Solange is drawn into the intensity of its significance and becomes the destroyer—the avenger of all servants, the immolating male. In those moments, the love relationship becomes one of hatred on the part of Solange who turns from active lover to executioner, while Claire, at that very same time, asserts the depth of her own meaning. She is beauty against which the slap of Solange and her hatred are unavailing; they can provide only a supplementary glow to her beauty: "Danger is my halo . . . ; and you, you dwell in darkness . . .". Thus, by merely extending in depth the significance of the principle which each symbolizes, the sexual and spiritual love that informs these principles turns into reciprocal and bitter hatred. (pp. 142-45)

The homosexual singleness of the two maids has already been alluded to—they are in reality one. . . . The entire ritual, their dialogue with its crises and its depressions, is a monologue, or, in Sartre's definition, the lonely and isolated sexual experience of the invert. . . . The patterns of this drama are like the sterile turgescence and deflation of the homosexual act, conceived in loneliness and fraud and ending in deception. This is also the way in which each of Genet's plays is constructed. (pp. 148-49)

[The] ultimate significance of the maids is in their recurrent frustration, failure, and, withal, their comprehension of that which they cannot achieve. They exist only to perform a ritual that will never become more than just that. They have a sacred concept of their performance. (p. 149)

The purpose of the ritual killing that stands at the center of this drama is twofold. Death is first a form of splendor. Solange genuinely loves Claire, as her alter ego, as an embodiment of beauty, and in her role as the male immolator. Therefore, her words to Claire that confess her desire to murder her are significant: "I wanted to free you. I couldn't bear it any longer. It made me suffocate to see you suffocating. . . ." Solange does not want to free Claire romantically from the clutches of her mistress, but to give her, with death, a splendor that will elevate her above her mistress, that will allow her a conclusive triumph. . . . But why, then, is there only a play-murder in this play? Here again, the answer lies in the esthetic concern of the maids, and to them is added still another dimension: they are the ordainers and the officiants of the dramatic act, the esthetic commentary. . . . The symbol of sacredness is not required to create, but merely to convince. The maids, no more than the theater, need produce the corpse of their victim. Their responsibity is only to make the spectator feel that he has witnessed a murder in that he felt the splendor of the act and thrilled to its mystery. For this to happen, the ritual must remain sterile. The reality of a corpse turns the play away from ritual as the spectator moves from awe to identification, as the mystery of an act becomes the reality of that corpse. Horror unalloyed must not be allowed to replace the more subtle feeling that blends with horror the image of beauty and the stirring of a singular experience. That is why the maids fail, why Solange is carried away from her homicidal act into the dream of homicidal magnificence. That is why it is also safe to assume that the climactic moment when the curtain comes down on Claire drinking the poisoned tea is a murder performed only in the spectator's intimation of it, but no more real for its priestesses than were any of their previous gestures. (pp. 150-151)

[*Deathwatch* recalls] Sartre's *No Exit* and that play's comment, "Hell is the others." But whereas in the play by Sartre each person exists as a witness to the incompletion of the others and exercises his destruction as part of a cooperative set of constants, each executioner [in *Deathwatch:* Green Eyes, Maurice, and Lefranc] is an independent and fluctuating quantity in the play by Genet. (p. 151)

[Green-Eyes, on trial for murder,] is he-who-is. He has killed, or rather, a part of him has killed while another part of him stirs restlessly under the onus: "I ran right and left. I squirmed. I tried every shape so as not to be a murderer. Tried to be a dog, a cat, a horse, a tiger, a table, a stone!" (p. 152)

Lefranc experiences the temptation of the saint to live by his vision alone, to settle symbiotically upon Green-Eyes in a relationship that Genet calls "the eternal couple of the criminal and the saint" (in *The Maids*). Lefranc has the vision, not the reality; in reality, he is a fraud. In a world where tattoos are worn as a mark of distinction, Lefranc has a chest decoration, but it is not even skin-deep. . . . If Lefranc is to move into the aura of Green-Eyes, he must strangle Maurice; he must perform . . . the sacrifical gesture upon the appointed victim. This he . . . does, and the play becomes a commentary on what happens when esthetic distance is not preserved. Green-Eyes is not a killer. He is an incarnation of his own fatality—greatness is as much a part of him as his beauty, his green eyes. He is simply a force, blind and selfish, with no allegiance but to that force. (p. 155)

[Green-Eyes is] indignant at Lefranc's useless murder, at the crude manner by which he has attempted to force his way into the company of the fated. And Lefranc, still lucid, is compelled to acknowledge the legitimacy of Green-Eyes' indignation. As the final curtain drops, he comments, "I really am alone." (p. 156)

Green-Eyes rejected the crime that signified his sanctity; Lefranc assumes the crime that marks his ineradicably as an outcast. Is the curse on both not similar? . . . In the baroque drama of Genet, *Deathwatch* is strangely stylized and relies on an espousal by the spectator of the characters. Therefore, in this theater of blood and death occurs one of its rare murders: it cannot construct the horrific puppet necessary for Genet's black art. Because they must be accepted as people rather than as significances, these beautiful and fatal murderers and their bloody and exotic deeds lack substance, and the dramatic experience evaporates in a redolent puff of sentimental expressions and incredible deeds. (pp. 156-57)

The balcony [in Genet's dramas] is a stage upon Genet's stage, a place of sumptuousness, triumph, and make-believe.

The Balcony is a conscious stage from the first. . . . But this stage is also . . . "the most artful, yet the most decent house of illusions." A house of illusions is the traditional French name for a brothel, a place for the creation and enjoyment of intimate fancies. . . . No problem, says Genet, should be resolved in the imaginary realm, especially since the dramatic solution is an indistinct part of the closed social structure. It is rather the play that should bring its reality to the spectator. And so Genet has placed a mirror on the right-hand wall of his set which reflects an unmade bed that would be, if this stage room had a normal extension, in the midst of the orchestra's spectators. The playgoer does not enter into *The Balcony* with impunity—once the curtain is up, he *is in* a bawdyhouse.

But he is also in the theater. The set *appears* to represent "a sacristy," formed by three folding screens of blood-red cloth: The sacristy is where the priest puts on the holy vestments, the alchemist's kitchen (in *The Maids,* the scullery was referred to as the sacristy). Note that the setting merely appears to represent; this is a stage, not the real thing. The spectator must not attempt to fool himself; if he makes of this a real sacristy, it loses its virtues of staginess and mystery, and the wellspring of ritual turns into a dressing room. It is made of folded screens [a later play is called *Folding Screens*], those tenuous walls that are suggestion, not substance. And finally, the set is blood red, the color of the sacrificial and the sexual acts—the sacred ritual of death and rebirth as life, or as beauty, according to its moment. (pp. 158-59)

[There are in *The Balcony*] moments of illusion . . . for the private enjoyment of certain people on stage who are not so very different from the spectator—that participant watching the proceedings from behind a peephole that has the full dimensions of the proscenium. The half-naked girls in the sadistic sex play are exhibited to the spectator as well as to the actor in his role as brothel customer—bishop, judge, general, and so on. The world which these create in the stage privacy of their own mind is just as much the spectator's; the objective stimuli are the same.

To this dimension which incriminates him, the spectator is asked to add another for which the evidence is less explicit: it is that of the revolution [taking place outside the brothel], echoed in the gunfire and the concerns of the principals on stage. The contaminated spectator participates immediately in only one level of the actor's reality, for the actor on stage plays a role concerned with events other than merely those of the brothel. (pp. 161-62)

[Genet] contrasts with the sealed world of the Balcony the world of the revolutionaries. These are by definition the ones who don't play; they are . . . the reality of their action. The brothel is their symbolic enemy since its life principle —esthetic distance that separates the performer from his act—would be their death; for them, "hand-to-hand fighting eliminates distance." These priests of factuality are solemn. The danger to their revolution does not come from want of strength; it comes from lack of purity. The moment their solemnity is in doubt, the moment their action takes on the appearance of a game, they will find themselves defeated even in victory, having merely replaced the old order by another image of itself. Theirs is the struggle of the purposeful against the purposeless; when they have won, they will *organize* their freedom and their relaxation, their festivities and their ritual. Their greatest victory has been won not in the streets but through conversion: one of the revolutionary leaders, Roger, has brought over to their side a prostitute from the Balcony—the singer Chantal. And it is out of that victory that defeat will spread to the revolutionary camp. Chantal becomes the illusion which even the revolutionaries now require in the fire of action, the myth—a symbol singing on the barricades. The revolutionary image must die, confused with the image of that against which it was directed, in order for the revolution to succeed. (pp. 162-63)

The Balcony is largely an expository play, a commentary upon the nature of reality and illusion and upon the function of the stage. *The Blacks* . . . is the play based on that theory. . . . In *The Blacks,* Genet demands a public of whites. He is insistent upon this to the extent of asking for at least one ceremonial white spectator if the play were performed for an audience of blacks, in which case the entire performance would be addressed to that single figure. Lacking even that single sacrifice, the blacks would have to wear white masks. "And if the blacks refuse the masks, then a dummy will have to be used." Thus the magic object has now moved beyond the footlights into the hitherto privileged realm of the spectator. This play forces implementation of Genet's admonition: "Let no problem be resolved in the imaginary world."

The stage of Genet is more important than the spectator since it requires a specific spectator and, barring that, a spectator disguised. (If the stage should have to settle for a dummy white, Genet will have succeeded in inverting completely the order of things: the performers will then be playing for only themselves.) The play is first of all a game, a diversion whose full meaning will be made clear later on; on stage, it is a performance put on by blacks for the benefit of other blacks dressed and masked as whites. It will be, as conceived by blacks, a definition of blacks by whites for the benefit of an exclusively white audience. Its paraphernalia will be the customary flowers and a coffin, the sacred objects in a ritual concerned with beauty and death.

Genet begins this act of play by eliminating the stage. The curtain does not come up mechanically, but is drawn—the human hand, portent of human mystery, replaces the machine. Thereafter, Genet adds the aspect of reality that ultimately defiles the mystery of the figureheads in *The Balcony* by making the reality of their first vision dependent upon the vision of someone else: these blacks are played by Negroes. At this level of reality, the spectator cannot detach himself from the stage. (pp. 165-67)

Having stated the primacy of the stage-as-reality, Genet proceeds to subvert that reality in order to make of the stage the place of magic and mystery which it must also be if it is to sustain a genuine ritual; something is going on somewhere beyond this stage—an emissary occasionally breaks into the play with news from a world alien to the one of the play. The pseudo-whites on the dais are obviously actors, and not very good ones. Those who are below, performing for them, although they are ostensibly actors and spectators in a yet unspecified ritual are likewise learning their parts as actors and spectators. On each of these levels, the actual reality is being transformed into an artifact—something which will acquire a dimension other than that of its immediacy as existence.

The "whites" upstairs have come to witness the ritual murder of one of their number. The "organizer," who is a central performer in every one of Genet's plays, is a black by the name of Archibald, and he begins the ritual. This is built around a catafalque on center stage which supposedly contains the remains of a white savagely murdered by the blacks. The play is defined by Archibald as ritual: tonight again, the play goes on, the scene is to be enacted once again. The theater is asserting its own reality; these blacks are *ideas* of blacks—white pictures interpreted by the blacks themselves. Although they are Negroes, they now exist at their own level of the stage. In addition to being the generic reprobates, the outcasts that people each of Genet's stages, they are the shoeshine blacks, bad-smelling, lustful, murderous, childish—and, withal, exotic symbols because of these nonwhite attributes and because of their physical power and beauty. The whites are similarly mental images, though less complex. They are the black's notion of white authority. . . .

These "whites" try to see themselves as a necessary radiance; they are the born masters whose being legislates and justifies. The blacks, in addition to their own definition of themselves, are able to legitimate their personal feelings by this view of the "whites": their "black" hatred, their desire to possess and kill, rape, and obliterate those who need not justify their own rule over them, returns the stage gradually to the reality of that which encompasses even the stage. Genet is transferring to these blacks the prerogatives of the criminals, the perverts, and the inverts of his plays and novels. They are automatic forces attempting to become more consciously and more hugely *themselves,* in order to "deserve [the whites'] reprobation . . .". . . . (pp. 167-68)

The ritualistic killing . . . (for what is in the coffin is of little importance, "an old horse will do, or a dog or a doll"), that symbolic gesture, must thus not only destroy an individual, aiming at the destruction of a historical moment, but also the mask which that individual wears—the black hatred worn by the white. (p. 169)

This grisly tribal dance of passion and murder is suddenly broken short by Genet; the esthetic and voodoo object is cast aside. News comes from the outside which all the blacks gather about to hear, including those on the dais who remove their false white faces. . . . [An emissary announces that a] congress has elected the one who is on his way to organize the fight: "Our aim is not only to corrode and dissolve the idea they'd like us to have of them, we must also fight them in their actual persons, in their flesh and blood." The Negroes on stage were real as "blacks," not as actors in their various roles. Now Genet actualizes even the roles which they were playing. Not only were the blacks representing to the symbolic whites on the dais the metaphor of an off-stage reality, but it turns out that the real plot is being performed beyond the theater. Blacks are rising the world over . . . , while these blacks on stage were providing a screen with their ritualistic actions . . . , with whites drowsing in the illusion of a play as blacks rise to action before their sinking figures. (p. 170)

This drama is fraudulent. The white spectator (any spectator) who has seen *The Blacks,* or any play by Genet, has been deceived. He has seen a conjurer, or what Sartre calls an elegant ballet which is the orchestration of those interreflecting mirrors. At the moment of his most intense perception, that which he derives from the human revelation of the magical object, he has been concerned with only a small part of man, the part giving the illusion status as an essential human perplexity. But the human perplexity is far more complex. Man does not live by any single anguish—nor, incidentally, by the raptures of an esthetic experience. . . . [A] single fiber, however vibrant, does not define man. (p. 171)

[*Folding Screens*] is the leisurely chronicle in seventeen scenes of the customary outcasts of Genet on their way to oblivion. This time, the outcasts are a normal couple, man and wife, the Arabs Leïla and Saïd, outcasts in the homosexual's view. Their isolation assumes many forms. They are ugly, as only Genet can portray ugliness, with its physical horror, its stench, its vulgarity (the euphemism of Leïla's hideousness is the one-eyed hood she wears). Like the Negroes in *The Blacks,* the Arabs are outcasts within a world dominated by another race, and as in *The Blacks* again, they are at war with their foreign overlords. For their isolation to be absolute, these outcasts turn traitors to their own kind (following a pattern already noted in *Deathwatch*) so as to remain isolated even within the world of the outcast. And in a hallucinatory ending, the very dead are seen waiting for this damned couple in vain: their death is an extinction beyond even the power of death to conceive.

Genet has woven this chronicle into the reality of present events, in a setting which is presumably Algeria. He has provided a lush fauna of whores with their traditional ritualistic dignity and the heavy burden of sacred isolation (symbolized by their heavy brocade skirts that are weighted down with lead); caricatural *colons* (the white landlords, similar to the caricatures performing on the dais of *The Blacks*); and soldiers, whose ritual of sex and savagery makes of them yet other exemplars of a total exclusion associated with what Genet praises most—beauty, evil, splendid remoteness, the qualities of purity and election that denote his saints.

The themes are old. What is fresh is Genet's scenic imagination. Significantly, the play is not named for the people or its action, but for its props. . . . The screens are the manifest irreality of the stage. Its people and its tangible props are its symbolic reality, for they are to be transformed by the irreality of the stage, just as the screens are to bring to life the imaginative reality of the play.

In this play whose actors play many roles . . . , the reality of the human being can be little more than symbolic. . . . In a similar way the physically real people give up their corporeality in order to create the wind and the rain, their bodies and their manner responding to the reality of nonexistent elements. Thus Saïd's mother creates the tree to which she is talking, through gestures that convey the Platonic Idea of an otherwise invisible tree.

This is the area of Genet's mastery: the ritual which is the stage performance, the reality derived from its objects, the sacredness conferred by that stage upon its objects and its people, so that their former being outside the magic circle of the stage is transcended. The image is of course hollow. But in addition to the hollow image which Genet demands, since the ritual starts with a fetish, there is a great hollowness at the center of his drama. In "The Criminal Child," Genet speaks of his love of Nazi horror camps. His "envy" of their suffering is disproportionate, however, because he has shown himself incapable of assuming either the imaginary "crimes" of those tortured or their innocence. He is naïvely juxtaposing the pin in the voodoo doll and the beast-inflicted torture, confusing the automatic criminal (whose automatism is no better than that of the bourgeois) with the slaughtered innocent; there is little in common between the mechanical acts of the first and the imposed suffering of the second. Genet's very saintliness—the rigor involved in remaining a criminal—constitutes a dereliction of freedom that bears too great a resemblance to the dereliction of others whose objectives are less admirable: both are equally illegitimate in the long run. There are other ways to beauty.

The magic of his stage holds the spectator under its spell for the duration of the performance. But on reflection, the absolute assertion of a force greater than man is sterile because there is nothing with which to compare the absolute assertion. Such reflections are outside the realm of the theater, however. Within it, no one has yet so magnificently duped an audience, and there is no playwright writing today who is more legitimately possessed of the theater. (pp. 172-74)

Existence is not a collective phenomenon for Genet. As Saint and Sinner, man and homosexual, aristocrat and thief, asserter and outcast, Genet has lived a double life, remaining consciously mask and marrow, ritualist and renegade. His single constancy was that of his double vision, the inherent self-consciousness that kept him at all times an actor. The effortlessness of his plays reflects his intimacy with every form of the dramatic ritual, antedating his very knowledge of the stage. And every one of his plays grows out of his personal need to define within the texture of being the warp and the woof that are reality and illusion. (pp. 177-78)

David I. Grossvogel, "Jean Genet: The Difficulty of Defining" and "Postscript," in his Four Playwrights and a Postscript *(copyright © 1962 by Cornell University; used by permission of the publisher, Cornell University Press), Cornell University Press, 1962, pp. 135-74, 175-99.**

LEONARD CABELL PRONKO

There has always existed a certain kinship between the spirit of Eastern theater and that of Jean Genet. In the plays written after 1955, however, this affinity becomes much more evident. There is a sharp difference between the visual simplicity, for example, of *Deathwatch* and *The Maids* and the richness of later plays like *The Balcony, The Blacks,* and *The Screens.*

The appearance of monsters, masks, exaggerated costumes, music, the stress on ritual and ceremony, all indicate a fundamental change in technique. *The Balcony, The Blacks,* and *The Screens* show the triumphant use of Oriental theatrical devices which, consciously or unconsciously, Genet has appropriated and made peculiarly his own, transforming them in a way that is meaningful and effective within the framework of Western drama.

While the decors of the early plays are meant to suggest solid masonry, stone, or Louis XV frills and lace, *The Balcony*'s set, with its false mirror reflecting what is obviously not in front of it, and its stable chandelier which remains when the scene shifts, establishes the stage as a purely theatrical milieu. Decor as decor is still present, however. In *The Blacks* we are confronted with the bare stage of Chinese opera, with the addition, however, of gallery, runway, and platforms. The catafalque in the center of the stage, we later discover, is, like Chinese stage walls, created by chairs and a sheet. In *The Screens* the decor is created from screens rolled on and off stage as needed, the set changing before the eyes of the audience. Often the screen is bare and the decor itself is drawn upon the surface by the actors: as an orchard catches fire, the Arabs draw flames in yellow and red; when night falls, an actor quickly sketches in a moon.

Costumes and makeup again recall the theatricalism of Chinese opera by their sumptuousness, violence, and brightness. Particularly striking is a resemblance between the so-called figures of *The Balcony*—the bigger-than-life General, Bishop, and Judge perched on their cothurni, their shoulders built out to great breadth—and the generals of Chinese opera, their figures enlarged by the banners rising from their shoulders, a high headdress topped with two 6-foot-long feathers. Warda, the great hieratic whore in *The Screens,* is equally impressive. Genet describes her thus: "Dress of very heavy gold lamé, high-heeled red shoes, her hair coiled up in a huge blood-red chignon. Her face is very pale [it is in fact painted white]. . . . Warda has a very long and very thin false nose." As the scene progresses Warda's feet and hands are painted with lead white, and blue veins are drawn upon them. The other characters wear equally unrealistic makeup. . . . (pp. 65-6)

Genet often adds notes to his text regarding the production. It is interesting to compare the advice regarding actor's movement in his first play with that given in the last. In *Deathwatch* we are told that "the actions of the actors should be either heavy or else extremely and incomprehensibly rapid, like flashes of lightning." In other words, the author wanted to draw attention to the movement as an integral part of the performance by treating it in a stylized way, but his ideas regarding the stylization were quite vague. By 1960, although there are few specific indications, the directions to the producer indicate that the dramatist has given up the "incomprehensibly rapid," in order to stress the significance of each movement: "The Acting: To be extremely precise. Very taut. No useless gestures. Every gesture must be *visible.*" It is plausible to think that the choreographic, highly controlled, economical, and suggestive movement of the Chinese actor revealed to Genet a way of moving and gesturing toward which he had been tending, but which until then he had perhaps not succeeded in clearly visualizing for himself. (pp. 66-7)

As in [a] Chinese play, night scenes [in *The Screens*] are presented in bright stage light and darkness is suggested by the actors' movements. . . . Following the Chinese, Genet is here giving back to the actor the central role in the drama, a role often usurped from him by the decorator and lighting technician. He is also putting more faith in our imagination, forcing us to find a childlike creativity we seem to have lost. (p. 67)

Leonard Cabell Pronko, "Servitude and Grandeur of the Chinese Opera: Jean Genet," in his Theater East and West: Perspectives toward a Total Theater *(copyright © 1967 by the Regents of the University of California; reprinted by permission of the University of California Press), University of California Press, 1967 (and reprinted by the University of California Press, 1974), pp. 63-7.*

HARRY E. STEWART

In order to defend Lefranc as "hero" of *Haute Surveillance,* an examination of the structure of the criminal-religious hierarchy as Genet views it becomes imperative. Certainly the most accessible theme in Genet's early works is the theme of the criminal hierarchy, and this theme is stressed in . . . *Haute Surveillance*. Particularly revealing is the original title of the play, *Préséances,* which may be translated as "the right to assume a position above some-one or to precede him." . . . Furthermore, the text of the play explicitly establishes this criminal hierarchy. (p. 365)

Coexisting with the criminal hierarchy is a religious hierarchy. Although Sartre [in *Saint Genet*] clearly distinguishes between the two opposing aspects of the eternal couple of the criminal and the saint, it is not at all certain that this distinction exists in Genet's mind. Indeed, it seems that Genet often blurs this distinction, that the saint and the criminal may sometimes have separate identities, but more often the murderer and the saint are merged into one figure with a dual, paradoxical nature. The explanation of Genet's attitude may be found in the *Journal du Voleur* where he says that his goal is saintliness, that saintliness is the moral procedure that leads to it (i.e., theft, betrayal, murder, solitude, etc.). . . .

The religious hierarchy has levels of achievement analogous to those of the criminal hierarchy. Boule de Neige is at the top of the criminal hierarchy because he is a convicted murderer who has been sentenced (Yeux-Verts has not yet been sentenced). He is at the top of the religious hierarchy. . . . (p. 366)

Immediately below Boule de Neige is Yeux-Verts. His criminal status is that of a convicted, but as yet unsentenced murderer. His lower religious station derives from the fact that his crime had less prestige than Boule de Neige's, but it was still of more consequence than mere petty thievery. Yeux-Verts claims that he, like Boule de Neige, "killed in order to live." . . . [The play] stresses the hierarchical difference between the two murderers by pointing out that Yeux-Verts murdered a defenseless girl, and essentially by accident.

In the religious hierarchy, Yeux-Verts may be considered a saint. Since one of the rarest yet most impressive signs of sanctity has been the resurrection of the dead, it is only natural that Yeux-Verts should believe that he possesses this power. . . .

Lefranc is the petty thief who seeks to advance to the rank of murderer and consequently to the religious status of saint. . . . Lefranc's position in the religious hierarchy is that of a supplicant, or petitioner. He collects photos of famous murderers (like Genet), and then he prays to them and says mass to them. . . . (p. 367)

Maurice's criminal status is that of a young delinquent who feels that he was "born to crime." . . . [His] religious status is not as clearly defined as is the status of the other characters. Although he is referred to by Lefranc as "un démon" . . .—perhaps because he represents the female principle—Maurice seems to best symbolize the sacrificial lamb which Lefranc will offer to the higher deities in his effort to ascend in the criminal-religious hierarchy. . . .

As befits his role as god, Boule de Neige never appears on stage, yet his presence and his actions influence the others. We know that he rules the fortress from on high, that he sends [gifts, encouragement, and orders to his subordinates. We also know that he can inspire jealousy, admiration, and dissension.] . . . Furthermore, like most gods, he is a source of comfort and inspiration during times of stress. . . . (p. 368)

Lefranc's imitation of the "saint's" crime is as complete as the situation will permit. Maurice, an obvious homosexual, replaces the girl in Yeux-Verts' murder, both victims are strangled, and the esoteric symbol of the murders—the lilacs—are involved in both crimes. . . . (p. 369)

In the same way that Lefranc must commit the murder of a saint to advance in the hierarchy, Yeux-Verts, in order to confirm his status as a saint, must betray those who trust or love him [in accordance with Genet's definition of betrayal]. . . . Yeux-Verts incites Lefranc to murder Maurice, and then denounces this murder—a double betrayal of both Maurice and Lefranc. . . . Yeux-Verts' judgment of Lefranc's crime is an aspect of his betrayal and not necessarily a valid assessment of it. Yeux-Verts' reasons for rejecting Lefranc's murder of Maurice are particularly difficult to support by examples from either the life or works of Genet. Yeux-Verts rejects the murder as a failure because, unlike his own crime, it was not accidental . . . , or imposed from without, or [predestined]. . . . Yeux-Verts insists that he did not want his crime, and that he did everything possible to undo it. . . . On the other hand, Lefranc wanted his crime, and he is condemned precisely because he consciously chose it. The evidence found in Genet's life and works clearly indicates that he would prefer that criminal who opts for prison, who chooses his acts and his crimes in the same way that Genet chose to be a thief and a traitor. . . . Like Genet, whose "chief concern has always been to be responsible for my acts," Lefranc has chosen his universe, he does not regret his crime, and he accepts the responsibility for his act. In short, Yeux-Verts' judgment of Lefranc's crime is invalid, he is merely fulfilling his saintly nature by betraying Lefranc whom he had incited to murder.

In conclusion, when one accumulates the criteria favorable to Lefranc as preferred "hero," the list is imposing: he strives toward saintliness by imitating the crime of a criminal-saint, he opts for prison life . . . , he murders Maurice out of love of misfortune . . . , he cheats in order to advance in the criminal-religious hierarchy . . . , he chooses and accepts his crime and its consequences, which makes him stronger than Yeux-Verts . . . , and finally, he successfully attains the "moral solitude" which is so important to Genet. It is this final condition of solitude that clinches Lefranc's claim to preferred "hero" of *Haute Surveillance*. Genet, speaking of the connection between saints and criminals, says: "They both live in solitude. Don't you have the impression, if you examine the matter closely, that the greatest saints resemble criminals? There is no visible link between society and the saint." . . . Although there are degrees of solitude, and, although Yeux-Verts does achieve a certain measure of solitude by his betrayals, it seems quite clear that Yeux-Verts, whose murder was exterior and accidental, does not attain the same high degree of solitude as Lefranc. (pp. 369-71)

Lefranc's final statement, "Je suis vraiment tout seul!" . . . , is not a cry of despair, nor of astonishment, but of "orgueil" [pride]. Lefranc has triumphed. . . . (p. 371)

Harry E. Stewart, "Lefranc As a 'Hero' of 'Haute Surveillance'," in The French Review *(copyright 1971 by the American Association of Teachers of French), Vol. XLV, No. 2, December, 1971, pp. 365-72.*

DORIS Y. KADISH and L. BRIAN PRICE

[Both "Le Balcon," a poem by Baudelaire, and Genet's play, *Le Balcon,*] contain forceful yet subtle images of sensuality and sexuality, presented in climactic terms and serving to express a transcendence of reality. This dramatic process is furthermore presented in both works on a backdrop of nocturnal obscurity. The complex mysteries and depths of space, present throughout the two works, create a tension between the worlds beyond and within the physical barrier of the balcony. . . . [Both] worlds are evoked in highly sensual and strangely similar terms and . . . both works present similar expressions of temporal and spatial movement. . . . (p. 331)

First impressions of the two works are obviously very different: generally sensual recollection of an individual woman as opposed to a blatantly sexual description of "perverted," impersonal acts; a warm and open evening atmosphere as opposed to an artificial and hermetic setting; a tone of tenderness and nostalgia as opposed to one of cruelty, eroticism and coldness. Although a balcony may be posed in the setting of both works, in Baudelaire's poem it would seem to open onto the "real" world seemingly denied by Genet's characters. Women may play a role in both works, but does any relationship exist between the seemingly cherished individual the poet recalls from his past and the paid strangers with whom Genet's clients play out their sexual fantasies in the present? (p. 332)

[In the poem, what] may appear at first glance to be a purely tender and natural experience of a relationship with woman perhaps contains preconditions and distinctions as artificial in nature as those demanded by the clients in [Le Balcon's] house of illusions. (p. 333)

Each of the first three tableaux of the play seems to contain the total experience expressed in the first four stanzas of the poem: a didactic process of both sexual and transcendental nature. (p. 335)

Genet's imagery is not confined to the coldly erotic and utilitarian object. Sensual properties of the real or imagined setting are stressed in each tableau: among others, effects of light and color in the first, of warmth in the second, and sound and moistness in the third. The one quality of the setting, however, which is consistently stressed, as in the poem, is the redness of the evening atmosphere. This combination of warmth and color, intermingled with references to the increasing darkness of night is clearly a significant aspect of the analogy. More important yet is the subtle interplay of this reddish quality outside and within the rooms of poet and playwright. Just as the fire in Baudelaire's room extends outward and permeates the evening setting, the glow of blood and fire in Genet's city colors the otherwise cold, brightly lit room of the brothel. Initially only intermittent reminders of what is occurring in the city are to be found. Yet gradually (in the third tableau in particular) the two realities appear to fuse, as the General's imaginary vision of war assumes the very coloration and spirit of the "real" revolution.

The third element of Baudelaire's response to woman, physical response defined as *baisers infinis,* appears at first glance as substantially different in the play. For the poet does evoke what is generally called "normal," or at least direct, physical contact with woman as opposed to the "perverted" acts in the play. And yet in the final analysis for both writers the sexual partner's body is merely a "vehicle" (literally so in the third tableau), one object out of many which when artificially combined induce the moment of exaltation and fulfillment. (p. 336)

Although the dramatic rhythm of the sexual experience is picked up at different points in the three scenes [of the play], each presents an increase in intensity, a progression from mundane subjects such as price, hour, props, etc. to exalted lyrical passages strangely reminiscent of Baudelaire. . . . (p. 337)

Granted that what is presented as concrete reality is social and "outside" Genet's balcony whereas it was individual and "inside" Baudelaire's room, that *au-delà* and *pure apparence* are vastly different, that the poetic experience differs from the dramatic, the fact remains that a moment of transcendence is reached in two works of the same title, and that it occurs in the strangely similar, equivocal region between the inside and outside of a room, a balcony. (p. 339)

Le Balcon by Genet is a play and "Le Balcon" by Baudelaire is a poem, and this choice of genre is not accidental. . . . If Genet's balcony opens onto a chaos of social upheaval, whereas Baudelaire's opens onto a vague, symbolist beyond; if the perverted acts which occur in Genet's room have specific socio-political implications, whereas Baudelaire's room is the scene of an exclusively personal albeit universal experience, is it not appropriate and even necessary that this be reflected in the literary form each chose? Balanced between the ephemeral beyond of external reality and the sensual experience of woman is glimpsed a poet. Poised between the problematic realm of society and *le public* on one hand and the interior aspirations of a ceremonial world of illusions on the other hand appears a dramatist. Curiously enough, the image of a balcony serves the literary exigencies of both. (p. 342)

Doris Y. Kadish and L. Brian Price," A View from the Balconies of Baudelaire and Genet," in The French Review *(copyright © 1974 by the American Association of Teachers of French), Vol. XLVIII, No. 2, December, 1974, pp. 331-42.**

NEAL OXENHANDLER

Jean Genet's play *The Blacks* is preceded by the words: "One evening an actor asked me to write a play for an all-black cast. But what exactly is a black? First of all, what's his color?" What color is a black? And, by extension of this paradoxical question, an extension already implicit in its more ambiguous French phrasing, What color is black itself? Or rather, if blackness is not a matter of complexion but a question of how one exists, what one is, then who among us is entitled to say that he is black? For Genet's play, played by black actors and designed to raise in excruciatingly direct ways the question of racial conflict, uses blackness as a metaphor for a condition more vast, more profound than a question of skin tones and genes; blackness, in Genet's play, has two meanings.

In the first meaning, blackness is the hallmark of all those who suffer exclusion, deprivation, degradation; all those who are oppressed, minorities of all kinds, men of all castes and classes; homosexuals and thieves as well as blacks and Jews; women; and all those whose role in society is to realize themselves as outsiders, alienated persons, those whose being in the world is one of abasement, exclusion and loss.

All these are "black" and figure, behind the metaphor of blackness, as the protagonists of Genet's play. (p. 417)

[Blackness], again as expanding metaphor, embodies the nihilistic values that Genet, the creative metaphysician, propounds in opposition to the positive values of Western bourgeois Graeco-Christian society, values such as work, family, country, love, respect for life and property, the high values of art and culture; to these Genet opposes a mystique of murder and sexuality, a diametrical reversal of the society's values in which hate is proclaimed as superior to love and murder becomes sainthood. . . .

Genet approaches [a unity with himself, a unity of total solitude] through the mediation of others (his lovers), through the mirrors that reflect his own image and through the fictional heroes who are also so many mirror-images. This possession of Self is a religious attitude, the infernal equivalent of union with God. . . . Saint Genet mounts toward this beatific vision through crime. (p. 418)

[There is crime], the heroic crime of murder, committed by Genet's young criminal heroes—Querelle, Green Eyes, Harcamone. Through the love that he vows to these heroes, Genet participates in their power and shares the process by which they attain solitude through the destruction of the other and of the good. . . .

There is another path to unity for those, such as Genet himself, who cannot choose (or be chosen by) the crime of murder. This second path is the way of abjection—degradation, humiliation, nausea. . . .

All reality is dialectical. Evil leads to good; good leads to evil. By stressing negativity, by sinking as deep as possible into abjection, one arrives at the positive. (p. 419)

This is a ferocious and deliberately preverse Hegelian dialectic, a form of idealism that aims not at the realization of Absolute Idea but at total annihilation and the void. I have called it an infernal system and it is clear that the feelings generated by Genet's plays—suffocation, anxiety, alienation—are precisely those feelings that are associated with the solitude of damnation. (pp. 419-20)

It is necessary to grasp this ontology if one is going to understand the mirrorings and doublings and projections of *The Blacks;* for in this play Genet has adroitly seized the objective situation of the black man and used it as a foil for his own highly special (and pathological in the sense of inimitable and dangerous) way of being himself, or of playing at being himself. . . .

Genet, like Dostoevsky or Proust, is seeking first and foremost his own fulfillment through a parody of religious ecstasy. . . . [His "religious"] experience is conveyed to us through theatrical conventions that have considerably evolved since the original production of *Deathwatch*.

Genet's first two plays, *Deathwatch* (1949) and *The Maids* (1954), show the obvious influence of Sartre's *No Exit* and have the classical economy and inner strictness of that model. They use a limited cast of characters, have unity of time, place and action, and unfold with algebraic inevitability to their tragic conclusions where transcendence and death coincide.

Beginning, however, with *The Balcony* (1957) and continuing with *The Blacks* (1959) and *The Screens* (1961) Genet shows new theatrical influences. There is first of all Antonin Artaud, with his emphasis on a greatly expanded palette, above all mytho-poetic resources and ritual; and, as in Artaud, there is emphasis on the theatrical experience as one of violence and cruelty. Brecht is an even more immediate model than Artaud, and the sweep and openness of these later plays of Genet reflect the epic theater. (p. 420)

Genet did not have to discover Artaud to see the theater as offering a ritual experience, one that is essentially liturgical in nature. For Genet, that inverted "saint," had early on proclaimed the Mass as the most perfect and most overwhelming of all theatrical events. . . . (p. 421)

The Blacks begin [the play] by dancing a minuet to a Mozart melody around a catafalque which occupies center stage. Even though the element of parody is apparent in their movements, the minuet signifies the enslavement of the Blacks to white culture. That enslavement is both the starting point and the ending of the play; and, in a certain sense, it is the dramatic fact closest to contemporary reality.

We have spoken of the mirror and of man's relation with his image. Black and white are mirror images of each other. The relationship is therefore an intense and passionate one. (pp. 422-23)

Each sees in the other what he may become. Each sees the negative to his positive, the positive to his negative. There is no hard and fast separation between them; because, as Genet has told us, what color is a Black? No more black than a white man is white, only some shade in between. (p. 423)

From a simple narrative [Village's story of the murder and rape of the white women] becomes a mime-show. Here, as elsewhere in Genet's theater, the actors imitate or give a "simulacrum" of another action which the audience has not seen. So in *The Maids* Claire and Solange mime their interaction with their employer, Madam. In *The Blacks* we have the rape and murder of a white shopkeeper, mimed and recited although not recreated in a full realistic reenactment. This episode is clearly the pivot of the play and our understanding of the play as a whole depends on what we make of the mime-show.

The mime-show is a play within a play and a ritual within a ritual. It has several functions. First, as ritual, that is hieratically stabilized gesture system, it brings into being that "beauty" which is, for Genet, one of the attributes of the divine. He says: "No doubt one of the functions of art is to substitute the force of beauty for religious faith. At least that beauty must have the power of a poem, that is to say, of a crime." Beauty is crime, that is to say, the act by which the transcendent is realized in life, the attainment of that experience through which mystical union (within the self and between spectator and author) may be achieved. The subject of the mime-show is self-defilement and the radical act by which one being separates himself from society; here the powerful schizoid strain in Genet comes to the surface. And yet, through the ritual, the schizoid act of separation is transcended, and union occurs. The mime-show portrays a crime; but the incitement of poetic language perpetrates a second crime, this time against the audience, revealing it to itself and forcing it to intuit itself in the ugliness and abasement of its passions.

The second function of the mime-show is to carry to a new

extreme the dialectic of illusion and reality that the play spells out. The mime-show is presented as ultimate truth yet it is also ultimate illusion, since the events recorded in it never happened. Yet there *is* a deep truth in the mime-show, a hieratic truth, one that is ritualistically and sacramentally revealed. (pp. 424-25)

The black mass unfolds in three moments—elevation. consecration, communion, with the addition of a fourth step, the incarnation of the god. (p. 425)

One level [of the play] always invokes its mirror image: black invokes white, freedom invokes slavery, presence invokes absence, life invokes death. All reality describes a circle from which there is no escape. In Genet's suffocating work, the way up is the way down, and there is no way out. So appearance and reality cohere as in the astonishing anecdotes, told repeatedly by Genet, of beggars who put false sores over real sores or criminals who disguise themselves as criminals. The addition of the mimetic or histrionic element and the consequent rejection of reality raise beggar and criminal to the level of sainthood in Genet's pantheon. But sainthood too is only a moment on the spinning wheel of illusion and reality. (p. 428)

[For Genet] death is a passage to the other side of the mirror. Genet, however, . . . is in love with death and, in his ontology, equates loving with murder and dying. The basis for this view of death is the schizoid inability to tolerate intimacy: hence loving closeness brings with it the wish for the death of the beloved. Genet's vast negativism also contributes here its celebration of absence, void, annihilation. Finally, Genet's paradoxical dialectic defines things always by their opposites. And death is the ultimate opposite, hence evoked in all situations where there is a strong positive affect. (p. 429)

Genet's effect on his audience is complex, yet two strands can be detected. There is first the creation of a communion-in-passion between actors, playwright, and audience. That passion may be alternately, as it is for Genet himself, shame, hate, ecstasy: yet the fact of passion is undeniable, passion which both separates and unites. The fact that Genet, through his ritual, places us in an emotional space means that he is concerned with authentic human behavior; and the very complexity of the emotions testifies to their authenticity. . . . Genet's theater opens up the emotional wounds that we disguise with false wounds just as he has seen beggars do; and in the coinciding of our illusion with our reality, he forces us to confront our multiple duplicity. (pp. 430-31)

Although the plays are constructed around a dialectic of illusion and reality that seems to offer no way out, they do nevertheless provide us with a living symbol of our human complexity that helps us to understand and grasp that complexity. These plays, in their striving toward ritual and myth, lift us toward the poetization and even the consecration of our experience. (p. 431)

Neal Oxenhandler, "Can Genet Be Saved? Remarks on 'The Blacks'," in Contemporary Literature *(© 1975 by the Board of Regents of the University of Wisconsin System), Vol. 16, No. 4, Autumn, 1975, pp. 417-32.*

L.A.C. DOBREZ

The gap between *Les Bonnes* (1947) and the journal (1948) on the one hand and *Le Balcon* on the other represents a turning point in [Genet's] life. The crisis was obviously of some magnitude and to a large extent it must have been prompted by [Sartre's] *Saint Genet,* whose revelations doubtless proved too much for a Genet unused to being the object of such sustained and merciless analysis—so much of it relating to Genet's private life as homosexual and criminal and all of it embarrassingly accurate. . . . Certainly, no one who has made a thorough study of Genet's work could doubt that Sartre's chart is at least very close to the truth. But *Saint Genet* follows Genet's progress only up to 1951 and, in Genet's later work, from 1956 onwards, it is clear that old preoccupations are still being aired, that the search for what I have termed "solitude" is far from over.

Genet is obviously dissatisfied with the impasse of *Les Bonnes*. Now he panics to the extent of questioning the possiblilty of a way out of his predicament. In *Le Balcon* he reasons in the following way. Granted that the basic issue is one of retaining the initiative over the Other, is it not true that, even as I struggle with my opponent, I am in fact reliant on his being there? Solitude, if it is attainable, means complete autonomy. But there can be no autonomy in the relation of the Look since, even if I escape being object and objectify the Other instead, I cannot be a dominant subject without the existence of a corresponding object. The very struggle against the Other suggests that he is *necessary,* that I need him even as he needs me. This in turn suggests something more disquieting, that each side exists *only* in the other, that I *am* only in so far as I relate to the Other and that he *is* only as related to me, in short, that to *be* is to *act out a part*. Now the struggle of subject and object takes on the appearance of a ghostly duel, a battle of roles, each entirely dependent for its existence on a complementary opposite, a mirror. Thus I play the role of object made possible by the Other who plays the role of subject made possible by me—and so on, ad infinitum. The struggle for solitude has degenerated to a play of shadows, a *giuoco delle parti*. No *real* victory or defeat is possible because the rules of the game require two players. (pp. 57-8)

[In *Le Balcon*] Genet is . . . depicting an interdependence of opposites: subject and object, that is to say, bishop and sinner, judge and thief *need* each other. But there is more to it than this, for mutual need suggests to Genet a mirror game in which each term of the relation is no more than a reflection, exists *only* by virture of the mirror. . . . There are no people left, only mirrors. Of course bishop, judge and general are in any case fakes. They are visitors at madame Irma's establishment who wear elaborate costumes for the purpose of sexual titillation, in short, actors. Even as they play their parts machine gun fire outside proclaims the reality they are trying to exclude. Later, a further complication is introduced. As the revolution proceeds and the chief religious, judicial and military figures are killed, it becomes necessary for the fake dignitaries of the brothel to assume the roles of *real* bishop, judge and general. In these new roles they are able to quell the revolt. Why not? If role is everything then a fake bishop acting the part of a real bishop *is* a real bishop, since a real bishop is simply one who acts the part of a bishop. Genet has made his point twice. First he presents us with a fake dignitary playing the part of a true one. Already the implication is that real dignitaries too are actors. To underline the conclusion, Genet goes further and actually demonstrates the interchangeability of true and false. (pp. 58-9)

Similar conclusions emerge from another major relationship of the play, that of the Chief of Police and madame Irma. It is, in one sense, the old subject-object relation. . . . With respect to the Chief, however, there is a special point to be noted. In contrast to those of bishop, judge and general his role has little tradition behind it, it is historically recent. The Chief's power is very real, of course—it is he who leads the conservative forces against the rebels—whereas bishop, judge and general are merely figureheads. And yet it is thanks to the figurehead, to the dignitaries and to Irma in the role of queen, not to the Chief, that the revolution is crushed. Illusory power, power based on myth, is more effective than actual power. And the Chief knows it. He is aware that real power is worthless unless it is operative in the realm of appearances, that is, of fantasy, that what one must have is not actual power but a powerful *image,* a power-filled *role*. (pp. 59-60)

There is a third relationship to be considered in this play. In addition to that of bishop and sinner, judge and thief and so on and that of police and brothel, *Le Balcon* presents us with the conflict between revolutionaries and the establishment. Now the primary aim of the revolutionaries is to do away with the old game of roles, to substitute reality for illusion and for this reason they are enemies of the brothel as well as of the police. Moreover, whereas the usual Genet rebel, from Divine to the maids, *accepts* the law he breaks, the revolutionary, in seeking to go beyond all mere forms, all appearance, necessarily rejects the rules, customs and morality of the establishment. This means that the revolutionary, although an enemy of society in the tradition of the murderer and the saint, represents a new type in Genet's work. His way represents a *sadist* solution, not the fake sadism—submission in the guise of aggressiveness—of the killer, but a genuine attitude of Sartrean hate, a real attempt to overcome the Look of authority not by any form of submission but by a direct assault. The revolutionary tries to do what the killer fails to do, to transcend the Look, objectify the Other, and regain the initiative of the subject. In other words he tries to achieve Sartrean freedom by a direct confrontation. From the standpoint of the mechanism of willing one's Fate the change in tactics is simple: instead of adopting the masochist solution, the revolutionary seeks to *alter* his Destiny, not to submit to it, to alter what the Other has decreed, in short, to *will freedom*. This represents yet another Genet attempt to realize the ideal of solitude in a particular character type. . . . (p. 60)

Genet now toys with the idea of a new solution to the problem of the Look. Since appearance has the victory, since all is illusion, perhaps one may go to solitude by way of appearance and illusion. If every action represents the acting out of a part it may be that there is an ultimate role to be assumed, that solitude itself is a role. Conceivably, one might retreat into *pure appearance,* one might become a symbol or an image and, discarding all else, exist in a pure heaven of eternal Ideas. What if by this means one might reach a state of independence from the Other? An image is not a vulnerable human being, it is dead, a mere shell containing nothing. Perhaps it exists in an impregnable Platonic paradise, utterly alone, utterly perfect. Clearly the great symbol of the victorious establishment and of victorious illusion in *Le Balcon* is the Chief of Police. Thus the Chief comes to represent a third Genet type, following the murderer and the saint, and his way a third alternative for the attainment of solitude. . . .

And yet, in *Le Balcon,* Genet is throwing us into confusion. Despairing of ever realizing his ideal of solitude he opts once more for a very dubious solution. The resemblance between the Chief as image and the murderer type should put us on our guard, since in each case we are concerned with a power that is essentially "hollow." Moreover the triumph of the Chief is the triumph of illusion, which, as already argued, would seem to be incompatible with the realization of solitude. It is the triumph of the game of mirrors, the I-depend-on-you-and-you-depend-on-me relationship, a veritable *negation* of the possibility of solitude—and this could hardly be otherwise. Role implies the status of the object. A role, an image, an appearance, all these presuppose the Other. (p. 61)

[The] Chief-Irma relationship must be referred back to the Mignon-Divine, Harcamone-Genet and Solange-Claire couples. In each of these earlier cases the real search for solitude is associated not with the hollow dominant figure—who is inevitably revealed as a passive object in disguise—but with the saint, whose passivity conceals aggressive initiative. In *Le Balcon* it should be Irma. In fact it is that other complement to the Chief, the revolutionary Roger. . . . Unfortunately, Roger is no improvement on Claire of *Les Bonnes*. At the end of the play, having lost all hope after the defeat of the revolution, he capitulates to the forces of illusion and arrives at the brothel to impersonate the Chief of Police, that is, to imaginatively *become* the Chief. Then, at the crucial moment of the impersonation, he castrates himself. Like earlier Genet saints he *wills* his Fate, confirming by a free act what has already come about, namely defeat. But the action raises the same problems as does the suicide of Claire: who is castrated, the Chief or Roger? On the one hand it looks like a final submission, a masochistic acknowledgement of failure, as if the revolution admitted the impossibility of breaking out into reality and bowed to the sexual power of the Chief. On the other it may be interpreted as an act of self-assertion, that is, it may be said that Roger has emasculated himself *as* Chief, in short, emasculated the Chief in *himself* and so rid himself of the power of illusion—and the illusion of power. Of course the significance of the act is meant to remain ambiguous. Like the ending of *Les Bonnes* which it so closely resembles, Roger's castration is a victory-in-defeat, something of a victory and something of a defeat. (pp. 62-3)

In spite of overwhelming frustration and failure, however, something of a positive nature does occur in *Le Balcon.* Genet's timid attempt to create a fourth character type—the revolutionary, a real sadist in the Sartrean sense of one who overcomes the Look—fails because the author undermines it by means of the theme of illusion and the image. This ensures a reversion to the doubtful masochist solution at the end of the play. . . . [Relations] in *Le Balcon* presuppose an *equality* of terms. A judge needs a thief *as much as* a thief needs a judge. If this is so, then the masochist approach has lost its force. . . . [The] underdog in *Le Balcon* is as necessary as his master and consequently he has his own kind of dignity in the relationship. Genet is beginning to transcend the masochist stance precisely because his insistence on the theme of illusion leads in the direction of relativism.

This is the positive achievement of *Le Balcon:* that for the first time Genet is suggesting that the subject, master of the Look, is simply the object *in reverse*. The Genet of the novels and early plays accepts society: the murderer acknowledges the law he breaks and the saint is ambivalent about it. Now it becomes possible for Genet to visualize a character who does *not* acknowledge the power of the Other, in short, a true sadist, the revolutionary. That the sadist revolt is betrayed and crushed in *Le Balcon* simply reflects the author's indecision, the fact that *Le Balcon* is a transition play. From now on Genet's work concentrates on the figure of the rebel, as willing-one's-Fate is replaced by the mechanism of willing-freedom, of forcibly *altering* one's situation. But even as Genet works his way out of the masochist impasse he necessarily raises up a new obstacle to the search for solitude. If all existence is role-playing and all role-playing requires a partnership, then solitude is abolished. Out of the masochist's chamber of horrors, Genet finds himself in the maze of mirrors. (pp. 63-4)

This is exactly the position in *Les Nègres* (*The Blacks,* 1958), a play dominated by the—ultimately successful—revolt of black against white. (p. 64)

Genet calls upon his entire repertoire of ambiguities. There is, first of all, no escaping the fact that the ritual recalls the masochism of the murderer. Even if we overlook this, there remains a disturbing echo of the masochism of the saint. . . . The killing which is acted out . . . is not that of a white, only of a black who stands for the whites, that is, it represents the destruction of whiteness *in the negro,* just as Roger's castration represents the Chief's death in Roger and Claire's suicide the death of Madame in Claire. Nevertheless, a new element has been introduced into the Genet ceremony. In this case the purge is successful and without the need for an actual black sacrifice. Indeed, the tone of *Les Nègres* is not at all defeatist. . . . [The] play dramatizes a rejection of guilt rather than an actual struggle with the Other, that is, . . . it is concerned with the expulsion of the Other *from oneself.* The blacks are rejecting their status as objects, in short, the masochist's desire to regain the initiative and to transform submission into aggression is in the process of being realized as the ritual of the saint gives way to that of the revolutionary.

There is a final complication. It appears that, while the ritual is going on, a *real* drama is being enacted elsewhere and one which is an exact counterpart of what is taking place on stage: a black traitor is being tried and executed. This once more underlines the message that black revolt consists essentially of the obliteration not of the enemy, but of the enemy-within-oneself. In this bewildering series of about-turns, however, we are forced once more to the questions raised in parallel contexts by earlier plays: who has paid, the victim or the oppressor? All that can be said here is that, in spite of Genet's game of boxes-within-boxes, *Les Nègres* represents an advance beyond the old masochist solution, since whiteness *is* in the end defeated, since the blacks are able to free themselves of attachment to the enemy. But we are still left with the problem of illusion, for if the *real* revolt of the blacks offstage exactly mirrors the stage *ritual* of revolt, may it not be that *both* are fakes, that no clear distinction can be made between appearance and reality? . . . It is simply a question of role-playing. This returns us to the question raised in *Le Balcon.* If both sides are acting out a part, then perhaps each side is merely relative to the other, that is, a mirror. Both whites and blacks in *Les Nègres* believe this to be so. Consequently we must see that what the black revolutionary envisages is not the destruction of whiteness, which is not possible, but an *exchange* of roles. . . . Masochism did not lead to solitude, although it asserted the dignity of the individual in a roundabout way. Sadism asserts his dignity directly, but in so doing brings him no closer to solitude. Thus at the end of *Les Nègres* Genet is uneasy. . . . [For] all its usefulness a Sartrean framework cannot adequately explain the pattern of Genet's imagination. The ascesis of the fourth Genet type, the revolutionary, leads to Sartrean freedom but no more suffices to encompass the dimension of solitude than that of murder, saint and, it would seem, image. Genet's only alternative is to grope towards another type, as it happens, a development of a previous experiment. Significantly, we are drawn to the unknown black traitor of *Les Nègres,* the one man who is said actually to die. In Genet's next play, *Les Paravents* (*The Screens,* 1961) this character is revived.

Before considering this character we may note that *Les Paravents* clarifies other conclusions arrived at in earlier plays. It appears that the revolt of the blacks is a success and that, even as a success, it leads nowhere: *Les Paravents* confirms these two assumptions. Now the conflict is between French and Algerians, two sides which function as complements in the old master-slave relation, each allowing the other to stand out. . . . Eventually the revolt, which is completely free of even the masochist echoes of the previous play, is shown to be unambiguous success. Of course it was a war of images, of revolutionary symbols against the old symbols of France, so that victory means a substitution of roles. Thus in the end the rebels are depicted as Sartrean subjects, conscious of their freedom and dignity which, however, makes them nothing more than a mirror reflection of the defeated colonials—as they themselves realize. . . . The move, foreseen in *Le Balcon* and *Les Nègres,* is now out in the open. Having conquered their masters, the Algerians become masters in turn, requiring new creatures of abjection to provide a new complementary opposite. . . . In the end . . . little has been achieved by the success of the sadist revolt. Everything is a facade, a "screen," as suggested by the title of the play, and Genet's fourth character type finds solitude as unattainable as ever.

There is only one thing for Genet to do and that is to return to the abject hero once more with the insistence of a Beckett returning to his tramps. (pp. 64-7)

[With his protagonist] Saïd Genet has developed his concept of the image considerably beyond the examples offered in *Le Balcon.* Saïd in fact represents what the author has wished to depict from the beginning. He has remained an underdog to the end, yet without the masochism of the saint. If he does not hate, he does not love either and in this resembles the revolutionary. But unlike the revolutionary he has committed his crimes for no social or political cause, indeed, for no human motive, only in order to distance himself from other men, to be *alone.* He does not will his Fate, as does the saint, nor does he seek to alter it, as does the rebel. Simply, *he does not care,* he is indifferent—and this is the essential element of his achievement. It is also what clearly distinguishes him from Genet's earlier experiments with the image. We must see why this is so. So far all attempts to escape the subject-object relation have failed and they have all been based on an attitude of masochism or sadism, Sartrean love or Sartrean hate. Clearly as long as one takes a stand which relies on a social complement, one is playing the game of roles and neither the sadist attempt to destroy the Other nor the masochist attempt to surrender to him will succeed in realizing the ideal of solitude. But to be indifferent is to *refuse to play the game*. . . . (pp. 68-9)

[The] only real dying to self and consequent living-in-the-image is one which goes by the way of indifference. Judge, bishop, Chief of Police, as depicted in *Le Balcon,* merely represent a starting point in the development of the type of the image. . . . In the end, then, Saïd is the only character in Genet's plays to illustrate a way out of the dilemma of *Le Balcon*. However repugnant when viewed outside the context of the author's desperate search for inward peace and integrity, he is the apotheosis not only of the image but of all the Genet types, an example of solitude achieved. (pp. 69-70)

Throughout his writing career Genet returns obsessively to his double, the figure of the outcast, hoping, through a total rejection of relationships which compromise individual autonomy, to enter a magical realm where revolt itself turns into an absolute, an area deep within the human being where revolt ceases to be a struggle *against* and becomes something in its own right, an affirmation of particularity, essential difference, singularity. Not unexpectedly, at this point he is driven, like Beckett, to a language of negatives. . . . There is a sense . . . in which solitude, like Beckett's Unnamable, is an impossibility, a blend of being and nothingness, as if Genet were to sever one after another all the bonds which link him to the Other: eventually he would reach a threshold, on one side, minimal relations, on the other, absolute particularity, a uniqueness of being indistinguishable from *nothing*. Solitude, as Genet conceives it, must be seen as residing in that no-man's-land which is the domain of irreducibles. It is here that spiritual presence expresses itself as a form of absence, an absence which is not mere nothing but a nothing which *is:* "l'Impossible Nullité," the Impossible Nullity. Of such nothingness works of art, human and non-human, are made. (p. 71)

L.A.C. Dobrez, "The Image and the Revolutionary Sartrean Relationships in the Work of Jean Genet," in Southern Review *(copyright 1978 by L.A.C. Dobrez), Vol. XI, No. 1, March, 1978, pp. 57-71.*

* * *

GOLD, Herbert 1924-

An American novelist, short story writer, essayist, and editor, Gold presents various aspects of contemporary life. His successful novel *Fathers* is an account of Jewish immigrants in America. (See also *CLC*, Vol. 7, and *Contemporary Authors,* Vols. 9-12, rev. ed.)

ANATOLE BROYARD

While still in his 40's, Gold had published perhaps a hundred short stories and as many articles, most of them knowledgeable, polished and promising. He was considered by many "a writer to watch," one of the possible heirs apparent of the Bellow-Malamud generation. . . .

By the time "The Great American Jackpot" and "Swifty the Magician" appeared, the pendulum had swung and reviewers were ready to pan books that were not so very different from those that had been praised.

It is easier to point out what is wrong with Gold's novels than to discover why critics and the public were so slow to react to these flaws—or why they reacted to them at all. Though Gold often substitutes shtik for character development in his novels, so do quite a few other authors . . . without suffering any loss of popularity. . . .

Perhaps Mr. Gold's trouble is not that his books are pretentious, but that they are not pretentious enough. . . .

W. B. Yeats defined rhetoric as the attempt of the will to do the work of the imagination. Gold's rhetoric might be defined as the attempt of the head to do the work of the heart. He seems to prefer theoretical people to real ones, characters who might say: "I talk, therefore I am." "Waiting for Cordelia" is a relentless talkathon, everybody reaching for effect instead of for us or each other. (p. 14)

Anatole Broyard, "Gold, Simenon, Latham," in The New York Times Book Review *(© 1977 by The New York Times Company; reprinted by permission), May 22, 1977, pp. 14, 28.**

FRANCIS KING

What Mr Gold has succeeded in doing with considerable success [in *Waiting for Cordelia*] is to give a picture of modern San Francisco. . . .

Mr Gold has an amusingly 'scummy' wit. . . . He also has a gift for creating pathetic and grotesque characters. . . . [One such character, a Russian agent,] eager always to be in the vanguard, sexually, socially or philologically, asks the narrator what word has now succeeded 'groovy'. Flash, fly, cool? the Russian suggests. The narrator tells him: neato. Mr Gold's novel is neato, as well as being flash, fly, cool and groovy. But it is like an organism without a backbone. The disparate elements show a hectic vigour; but there is nothing to hold them together, much less to coordinate their movements. (p. 21)

Francis King, "Neato," in The Spectator *(© 1978 by* The Spectator; *reprinted by permission of* The Spectator*), Vol. 241, No. 7832, August 12, 1978, pp. 20-1.*

JOHN MELLORS

Waiting for Cordelia is soggy with stale crumbs from the bottom of the Great American Crackerbarrel—'perfection means you are what you are'—and the earth-mother heroine is too sweet'n'sad to be true. When she is not big-heartedly giving her clients 'specials' at a cut price, Cordelia is 'squeezing away at the fret in her heart'. Al is a sad sack, too. He wants 'to link my stiff wet lonely soul with the welcoming wet soul of someone'. There is altogether too much 'wet soul' in this ramblingly episodic book. Gold is at his best when he abandons his folksy philosophising and just tells funny stories. (p. 319)

John Mellors, "Roman Road," in The Listener *(© British Broadcasting Corp. 1978; reprinted by permission of John Mellors), Vol. 100, No. 2576, September 7, 1978, pp. 318-19.**

H. T. ANDERSON

Not long into *Slave Trade* I found myself wondering what I was doing reading a novel about pederasty and male prostitution. . . . The whole thing is in the private eye genre. Sid Kasdan is wry, glib, and underwhelming. He is also rather boring even though what happens to him can hardly be construed as tedious. . . .

He is hired by an international ring that supplies very vulnerable young men to very invulnerable old ones. . . . His job is to escort the escorts all over the world to their appointed destinations and when possible to do a bit of recruiting. The fact that he even considers doing it produces the novel's minor tension. He does have some reservations about it which produces a little bit more.

Slave Trade has been heralded as a detective story that spins its own fable. Perhaps—but fabulous it isn't.

H. T. Anderson, "Fiction: 'Slave Trade'," in Best Sellers *(copyright © 1979 Helen Dwight Reid Educational Foundation), Vol. 39, No. 3, June, 1979, p. 85.*

ROSS THOMAS

[*Slave Trade*] features Sid Kasdan, one of the most morose private eyes in recent memory. Kasdan's wife has left him, his investigator's license has been revoked, he's broke, he's getting old, and sometimes, when nothing else is convenient, he broods about his big toe, or at least the part of it that got shot off in Korea. . . .

Gold writes well enough when he really wants to. Unfortunately, the style that he has adopted for this book, a kind of San Francisco flip, is relentless and ultimately wearying. And his hero's continuous maundering over his lost wife, lost youth, lost chances and lost toe really doesn't help matters much. (p. E4)

Ross Thomas, "The Thrill of the Chase," in Book World—The Washington Post *(© 1979,* The Washington Post*), June 3, 1979, pp. E1, E4.**

* * *

GOYEN, (Charles) William 1915-

Goyen is an American novelist, short story writer, playwright, and translator. His style and subject matter place him in the tradition of the southern Gothic novel, but he has been largely overshadowed by the more prominent authors associated with that tradition, such as Flannery O'Connor and Carson McCullers. His first novel, *House of Breath,* is considered by many critics to be his best. (See also *CLC,* Vol. 5, 8, and *Contemporary Authors,* Vols. 5-8, rev. ed.)

E. R. CURTIUS

Alive in William Goyen is a primal affinity with the first things of creation. . . . He has the keen senses of the woodsman, whom no creak or rustle can elude. He registers the sensual qualities of natural things, and it is as though he himself had experienced, from within, the cycle of germination, budding, flowering, and withering of all created matter. We seem to be hearing the voice of an aboriginal American that is being constantly pushed back by industrial civilization and forced to languish in its big cities. (p. 458)

[*House of Breath* is a] fledgling work—but a mature one. We are accustomed to a first novel being an eruption on which ore, slag, and ashes are whirled up together; or a so-called confession; or the reaction to the shock of growing pains on the nerves. Goyen's art is of a different sort. He has pledged himself to silence and waiting; to wait until he should find the word, "strong, small, but hard as a stone," which would utter his loneliness to the world. . . . The breath of lived life has merged with the breath of the artist. William Goyen had the power to attend this moment. He was able to wait because this breath was energy, an energy that wanted to be caught and directed so as to become the driving force of a power station. (pp. 459-60)

Like all modern art Goyen's book is the testimony and result of a sincerity that refuses to draw the line at cruelty. . . . [Goyen] lays bare the cancer of the flesh and of the soul; he . . . proclaims the passion of man. But with him suffering and torment include compassion. The tragic agony is carried through to the catharsis. The harmony with the elemental power of earth operates in this book as a stream that washes away all stains, that purifies and heals. (p. 461)

It is no accident that this book recalls poetry. The element of poetry entirely pervades Goyen's novel. It is not as if it had isolated "lyrical passages." No, its very substance is poetic in nature. Everything that the author experiences presents itself to him in the aggregate state of poetry; a primary poetry in which the epic and the lyric have not yet been sundered. The mode of discourse is not descriptive but imaginative. This is already shown by the title. . . . Goyen's mode of lyrical epic is related to myth and legend. The muse of the book is the blind girl sitting on a blue, rolling, cosmic sphere, bent over her lyre, and reciting her memories in a lyric lament. . . . *The House of Breath* tells us of Charity and East Texas; when it ranges farther, it only crosses the border of the neighboring state of Louisiana. And yet this book is something other than a local novel. What we are given here is not regionalism. The language and the landscape of East Texas are only the ground here of a fabric in which living and neighboring people talk and move. . . . To the boy whose story is related to us the outlines of the countries and continents seemed like the organs of a human body. The articulation and conformation of the earth has impressed itself with the utmost vividness upon his child's consciousness. In the sleepy town of Charity he has had an intuitive apprehension of the wide world and known that he himself was part of it. That is why this novel of a childhood has become a book containing a universal experience. (pp. 462-63)

From the American novel we expect brutality and cynicism; intellectual overrefinement but also primeval eruptions; morbidity and neurosis. In William Goyen's book we shall find very different elements: substantive poetry . . . ; harmony with the deepest simplicities of existence; reunion of sexuality with love; but also an artistic discipline that is more reminiscent of Flaubert, Proust, Joyce than of Melville, Wolfe, Faulkner. (pp. 463-64)

E. R. Curtius, "William Goyen" (1952), in his Essays on European Literature: Kritische Essays zur europäischen Literatur, *translated by Michael Kowal (copyright © 1973 by Princeton University Press; reprinted by permission of Princeton University Press), Princeton University Press, 1973, pp. 456-64.*

LOUISE Y. GOSSETT

[Goyen] differs markedly from his contemporaries in his lyrical, poetic translation of material into his imagined world. Mood finally supplants place. When the specifications of place and people fade, the violence becomes grotesqueness. The shadowy, elusive figures drop the forthrightness of violence and take on the half-lights, the mysteries, and the freakishness of the grotesque. Although their existence often seems other-worldly, these ghosts are related to the fear of crass industrialism and standardization which haunts or has haunted many Southerners. (p. 131)

Each [of Goyen's five books] is a collection of short pieces related in theme and mood. [*The Fair Sister* (1963)] is the briefest and the most unified, having been developed from a single story. (pp. 131-32)

Foremost in Goyen's work is a sense that human life now has no integrity. People are isolated from one another and from the past. They have lost their purpose, their ideals, and their capacity to communicate with one another. These psychological and moral disorders parallel the intrusion of industry, which has obliterated natural beauty and set profit above love and community. The grotesqueness of spiritual injuries and of physical malformations which manifests these conditions as well as overt violence interests Goyen. He creates an atmosphere of horror and ugliness in which characters are suspended like figures in a half-forgotten nightmare. (p. 132)

The subtlety with which Goyen perceives introspective characters and expresses their reveries approaches a kind of literary neuroticism. The dominant mood both of the characters and narrators is self-pity; hence there is little analysis of motives and causation. Action, conflict, and change as elements of drama in fiction are less important than the meditations of the narrator upon them. In this temper Goyen conveys something of the emotional stagnation and isolation of modern man as seen by Albert Camus in *L'Etranger* and Jean-Paul Sartre in *La Nausée*. Goyen's characters, however, do not engage in philosophical quests to define existence, for they are solaced simply by reciting their laments. (pp. 132-33)

In Goyen's fiction the feeling of being isolated is not so much expressed in dramatic situations as it makes up the circumambient mood in which life looks broken like a stick refracted in water. A view of this brokenness is made possible by the emotional distance between the narrator and the people he writes about. Because the narrator's role is to convince the reader to accept the vision of distortion, the method of narration is especially important.

To make vivid the malady of isolation and the consequent violent disintegration of human relationships, Goyen relies upon a point of view which might be called multiple refraction. This method is best exemplified in *The House of Breath* in which the narrator is a young man who speaks for himself both in the present and in the past, a period he captures by reconstructing the biographies of members of his family. The one quality he is able to respond to in each person is isolation. The fact that these people are warped further disjoints the narrative line. Before the grotesque personalities reach the reader, their characterization has been filtered through their own consciousnesses and through two time levels in the narrator's mind. Wrapped thus in several layers of subjective responses, the people tend never to come alive. Under this treatment violence is chiefly a matter of tensions which are repressed and action which occurs only in report. In the novel *In a Farther Country* the relation between the reader and the event is less distant because part of the narrative is conveyed dramatically, but the dream device which forms a large portion of the book forces the reader's attention to follow a refraction again from . . . actual life into . . . fantasies and on to the narrator's commentary. . . . No other writer [of recent Southern fiction] makes use of such refraction to enhance the distance from the norm which grotesque characters already represent. The effect is to heighten the sense of isolation in Goyen's work and simultaneously to reduce its dramatic impact. Because the themes which the violent and grotesque underscore are presented obliquely and at several removes from everyday actuality, Goyen seems to construct his fictional world from an entirely private view. . . . (pp. 133-34)

Criticism of modern life as being impersonal, mechanical, and ruthless is implicit throughout Goyen's work. Hostility to industrialism is expressed by the unhappy lives of characters passed in dreary surroundings. The maladjustments caused by the change from a farm economy to an industrial economy alarm him less than the destruction of natural beauty and social graciousness. (p. 136)

Goyen views the lack of community in the modern world fundamentally as a failure of communication. Although in *The Faces of Blood Kindred, The House of Breath,* and *In a Farther Country* he considers factories and cities obstacles to communication between human beings, he indicates that the state of mind which denies the past isolates people even more dangerously and thrusts them into eccentricity or violence. Because it is never clear what form a positive relationship with the past would take, most of the characters remain caught in confusion and disorder as if these conditions were nets which tightened in direct proportion to the pressure of the struggle against them. The past which the narrators in Goyen's fiction wish to restate in terms of a unified present has little relation to the historical past of the South. Instead they work from private memories of grotesqueness, violence, and ugliness which they have noted in the lives around them. Their sense that it is evil to cut off the past is, however, a peculiarly Southern heritage. (p. 139)

Goyen's experiments with themes and narrators culminate in the voice of Ruby Drew in *The Fair Sister*. The words and rhythms of this voice encompass only so much violence and grotesquerie as are needed to complete the myth in which the claims of flesh and soul, mind and heart, words and acts cross one another like threads in a tapestry. (p. 142)

The battle in this tale is no longer between the self and an outside world ruined by machines and warehouses but between the body and the soul, neither sufficient by itself to make a complete human being. The frenzy which in Goyen's earlier books broke into violence is now channeled toward tolerance. The narrating voice speaks with assurance in its own rhythm and imagery; it retains the incantatory tone of preceding narrators but with increased authority and extended range. (p. 143)

Because Goyen's fiction is introspective and descriptive of moods rather than objectively dramatic, it depends more upon grotesqueness than upon violence to portray the author's vision of a world askew. Although Goyen reacts to many of the same flaws of man and society which arouse his fellow writers in the South, his method creates a nebulous haunting effect at the opposite pole from the naturalism of Erskine Caldwell. . . . [Goyen's] prose is finely wrought. Vowels are arranged for their melody. Rhythms—whether of folk speech or of standard written prose—are subtly adjusted to the tone and mood. The metaphors and symbols suggest the death, coldness, and isolation which permeate much of Goyen's world. Such technical adroitness sometimes calls excessive attention to itself, and the language becomes a trick obfuscation of simple materials. When this happens, Goyen's mourning for beauty and truth seems a private elegy too fragile for translation. When he succeeds in controlling and uniting both subject and style, as he does notably in *The Fair Sister,* he leads the reader along the uncertain line between the normal and the abnormal, the sane and the insane, the actual and the myth. (pp. 143-44)

Louise Y. Gossett, "The Voices of Distance: William Goyen," in her Violence in Recent Southern Fiction *(reprinted by permission of the Publisher; copyright 1965 by Duke University Press, Durham, North Carolina), Duke University Press, 1965, pp. 131-44.*

DAVID DILLON

The adjectives *lyrical* and *poetic* have often been applied to William Goyen's first novel, *The House of Breath.* They are not so misleading as most critical cachets because Goyen *is* a singer whose prose keeps time to the mysterious inner music of his characters.

Whether so much lyricism is a virtue, however, is another matter. I don't believe finally that it is. Being skeptical of epiphanies in general, I get annoyed with someone like young Ganchion, the narrator, who has one on every page. "Spit it out, boy," I keep thinking, "Say it straight." Instead, he trills it out in long plaintive songs about family tragedies and homesickness and some terrible yet ineffable loss of innocence that has transformed him into an Ishmael. Even when we acknowledge that the past is a foreign country and the flutterings of memory difficult to capture, Goyen's prose is frequently so convoluted, so self-consciously sensitive, that we are reminded more of the pre-Raphaelites than the Piney Woods. The simple homely events that obviously mean so much to him, and on which much of his best writing is based, dissolve into inscrutable private symbols that seem devoid of specific meaning.

The most intriguing voices in the novel—and *House of Breath* is a novel of voices, of interpolated monologues really—belong to Granny Ganchion and the scarred outcasts like Follie and Hattie. Talkers rather than singers, their speech is seasoned by place and folklore and a flinty, self-deprecating kind of humor that young Ganchion lacks. . . . Goyen [is] at the top of his form [when] his eye [is] fixed squarely on East Texas and his ear tuned to the cadences of local speech rather than the distant strains of violins and cellos. While it would be wrong to think of him only as a regional writer, especially given the acclaim his work has always received in Europe, it is fair to say that the farther he strays, geographically and psychologically, from familiar territory the more unsteady his writing becomes. Though cosmopolitan by nature, he is not a good traveler.

This is even clearer in his short stories [in *The Collected Stories of William Goyen*], which can be divided roughly into those that are set in East Texas and those that are not. Except for the uproarious "Savata, My Fair Sister," the second group is a disappointing mixture of inert mood pieces and ambitious but ultimately rather murky fables. Again, it's as though Goyen is trying so hard to escape the label *provincial* that he forgets about character and situation.

The first group, on the other hand, contains a number of memorable stories like "Rhody's Path," "Pore Perrie," "The Thief Coyote," and "Tapioca Surprise." These are solid achievements that have what Goyen says interests him most in a short story, a dramatic teller-listener situation, and in which the rich oral tradition of East Texas, that unique combination of the King James Bible, Negro spirituals, and Barnum and Bailey, works most impressively. . . . [These] stories stay with us long after we've closed the book. Not a false note anywhere. Which is not to say simply that Goyen writes better folk songs than arias but that when he listens intently to the rhythms of his own particular place, and allows characters and events to speak for themselves, he expresses truths that touch us all. (pp. 433-34)

David Dillon, "Uneven Rhythms in Prose," in Southwest Review *(© 1976 by Southern Methodist University Press), Vol. 61, No. 4, Autumn, 1976, pp. 433-34.*

JAY S. PAUL

As befits an age of universal solitude, in which art often is *about* art, William Goyen's stories are a testament to the essentiality of telling. He regards such communication as a form of love, a process including seeing and saying: to tell one must know; once one knows he *must* tell. The teller devotes his life to shaping an "anxious shapelessness" into truth. (p. 77)

The willingness to discipline himself in the use of language underlies his entire achievement as a writer. His stories ring with precision because they are language told to someone, not simply private, inchoate voices. . . . *The Collected Stories of William Goyen* . . . presents his ideas with remarkable continuity and seems to have been his means of experimenting in form and of finding "a language I thought I could use." Whether he writes of homelessness, fragmentation of individuals, elusiveness of the past, or the miracle of human love, Goyen is playing his main theme—the essentiality of telling—and orchestrating speech to render the "marvelous reciprocity" of a genuine relationship. (pp. 77-8)

Goyen has always written of human relationships—solitary people who fail to connect, solitary people who succeed in loving. The latter have been Goyen's hope: they are alert to surroundings; they have patience and imagination to comprehend others. One must keep in mind that story-telling . . . is both a means and a metaphor of loving, and that although knowing moves one to tell, comprehension is often simultaneous with telling for Goyen's characters. Restoration of self during the process of telling is one aspect of "marvelous reciprocity," but Goyen sees love as social. . . .

The most lucid metaphor of the story-teller's activity occurs in a pair of stories, "The Enchanted Nurse" and "The Rescue," depicting the relationship of the nurse, Curran, and his patient. In the first, Curran is an old man remembering how Chris, brought to St. Albans hospital with a severely injured leg, became comatose after surgery, occasioning Curran's complete dedication to his recovery. "The Rescue" is set during the time Chris is in the coma and is tangential in plot to "The Enchanted Nurse": while a flood threatens the hospital, which becomes a sanctuary for all living beings, Curran more fully understands the miraculous reciprocity of healing. (p. 78)

[Like] many of Goyen's characters, Curran has been diminished—"my body is vanished, almost," but reduction has clarified what is essential, "this tale that lives within my senses." Chris, too, has been diminished, by the crippling of the leg. . . . (pp. 78-9)

The story-teller . . . immerses in the mysterious, fathoming what cannot be immediately perceived . . . without compromising the individuality of the unknown patient. Comatose, Chris grows in Curran's mind just as a fictional character emerges in the writer's. . . . (p. 79)

Goyen's favorite voice is the boy grown up, a man haunted by his past, longing to know enough to tell it. He is compassionate and gentle, attracted to minute detail and to the capacity to sense and understand. Grown, he is solitary and displaced. Loving, his preoccupation, may not be impossible, but it has proven difficult. Goyen often presents the teller as a writer who, like himself, resides in a large city, away from his family home. These pieces are shaped by the act of remembering and are meditations upon the past . . . and upon human memory. (p. 85)

Most of Goyen's stories are not the musical tours de force which have been used to illustrate the potential of lyric speech. More often the narratives are subdued, sometimes ironic, but the stories are "lyric" in the sense that they are ringing with the vitality of said language. The story that exemplifies his control of tone is "Bridge of Music, River of Sand," a captivating, but difficult piece. The teller is "making a sentimental trip through home regions" . . . when he sees a naked man plunge from a railroad trestle and disappear into the sand that once was the bed of the Trinity River. The self-conscious "sentimental" reflects the guarded flippancy he tries to maintain, but his excitement over the puzzling, apparently supernatural phenomenon keeps breaking through. . . . [The] teller never can explain the image.

Goyen's handling of tone, though, is one key to its meaning. On the one hand the teller relates his *will to* return, on the other the *feel of* return. Perhaps he has never resolved his ambiguous memories of the bridge, that curious mixture of beauty and impracticality—his mother's fear and his father's scoffing at her fear. Or the teller may be disoriented by return; for whatever reason, he experiences a confusing combination of immediate perception and detached skepticism. . . . He *sees,* but cannot *believe*. (pp. 89-90)

Goyen's tellers are obsessed with finding calm, moments when, flesh and spirit unanxious, one sees clearly, loves. Like the writer in "Nests in a Stone Image," the teller hears in his mind "a language that created the speakers as it spoke, that seemed yet to be his own voice and his own speech, so that it all seemed one." . . . Telling occurs under the threat of anxiety. . . . (p. 90)

The whole of Goyen's work must be thought of as a meditation upon story-telling, which ideally is a means of rescuing one's past, one's self, one's listeners. His concern has been art's power to transform human life, that in shaping and telling a story one "restores the unity and wholeness of the world." . . . Goyen's fiction published from 1947 through 1963 offers the possibility of self-realization and community through telling. Then, in 1974, after a long silence, Goyen published *Come, the Restorer*. Whereas the earlier stories are cells of hope in a roiling world, the recent novel offers no such possibility. A symphonic work relating careers of several "restorers," the book is told by an anonymous figure who, like the would-be saviors, is fascinated by sensuality. No one is able to synthesize the sensual and the spiritual. Whether *Come, the Restorer* tells of Goyen's disillusionment or parodies the modern age that he is out of patience with, it is certainly a chilling rendering of the chattering compulsiveness that he jokes with in *The Fair Sister*. The new book underlines the truly sobering point made in all his work: telling—or loving or healing—often seems no more than a fantastic possibility. . . . (pp. 90-1)

Jay S. Paul, "'Marvelous Reciprocity': The Fiction of William Goyen," in Critique: Studies in Modern Fiction *(copyright © by James Dean Young 1977), Vol. XIX, No. 2, 1977, pp. 77-91.*

JAY S. PAUL

What makes "Nests in a Stone Image" [in *Ghost and Flesh*] much more than an indulging of an all-too-writerly propensity to write about one's own writing is Goyen's use of imagery of the life of Jesus. The writer's vigil is patterned on Jesus' night of prayer and doubt in Gethsemane and overlaid with allusions to other aspects of his life. But "Nests in a Stone Image" is not updating of Jesus' story: the writer may agonize, but he is acutely aware of his mortality. Goyen utilizes Christian imagery to show both the writer's capacity to love and his anxieties that preclude loving. Goyen believes that belief is an individual possibility, and that each person *can* be as vital and dynamic as Jesus himself. Given this hope, Goyen has the writer in "Nests in a Stone Image" seek, as Jesus does in Gethsemane, knowledge of his destiny so that he might pass it on; surreal Christian imagery establishes the debilitating effects of his all too human anxiety.

The significance of "Nests in a Stone Image" is that it identifies the full spiritual implications Goyen perceives in the act of telling. His characters often resemble Jesus in their use of speech to further a sense of community; stories about healing and love treat themes identical to Jesus'. . . . "Nests in a Stone Image" depends not only upon conventional biblical material, but also upon Goyen's personal understanding of Jesus. Study of "Nests in a Stone Image" in this light reveals Goyen's abiding concern with the restorative effects—upon oneself and upon one's companions and hearers—of the act of telling.

Goyen patterns the writer's vigil upon Jesus' in Gethsemane. . . . The writer's vigil braids together memories of the woman he has not loved well, other incidents from his past, and goings-on in the hotel. Jesus returns three times to his companions; the writer remembers the woman three times. This pattern of meditation and looking backward informs both stories, and both principals are forced to realize the profundity of their solitude and the inappropriateness of their self-doubt, their looking back. (pp. 415-16)

The emphasis upon Jesus' love of human beings and upon his mistaking their mortality suggests that Goyen sees the writer in "Nests in a Stone Image" as more Christlike than he might seem at first glance. For the writer, too, feels himself fill with compassion for the woman and admits his betrayal of her, his misunderstanding her nature, his *fear* of her humanness. . . . (p. 417)

But the writer is not Christ: Goyen's biblical imagery makes that clear. The writer's agony is overlaid with allusions to Jesus' birth, ministry, and passion, causing the reader to understand that the writer is confused and falls back on aspects of Jesus' experience to try to comprehend his own. In fact, he does so consciously—self-consciously, aware of his pretense, but determined to experience a revival of his spirit through understanding what haunts him. Thus, Goyen's surrealism makes Jesus a foil for the writer; furthermore, Goyen's emphasis in *A Book of Jesus* upon the availability of the "Kingdom of God," in this world, for every person, justifies doctrinally the writer's hoping to be like Jesus. He spends the night to this end: to love and thus restore himself. Keenly aware of his humanness, he eventually does participate in the spirituality he has longed for.

The most obvious biblical imagery is of Easter, rebirth. The story opens "on the Eve of Easter" . . . and ends when "The morning sun was abroad" and the writer senses that he is part of reviving life. . . . Not surprisingly, the hotel in which he spends the night reminds him of a "celled, stone skull," . . . which evokes the tomb of Jesus as well as Golgotha, the hill upon which he was crucified, "The place of a skull." . . .

Yet the hotel also is an allusion to the inn at which Jesus was born. The symbol's ambivalence is central to the story and made explicit in the final sentence: "Now he knew that something was all over, that through all the little hotel, in every room, something was finished, and that another long beginning had begun." . . . Goyen fuses imagery of birth and death from the outset: the writer lies across his bed "like a five-point star in the sky of this city hotel world," this "in all that winter weather." . . . (pp. 417-18)

Additional allusions to Jesus' life reinforce the writer's attraction to Jesus' potency as message, Logos. The writer wants to bring what *he* has to tell out of the "darkness" and have it "be like a good word." . . . Though he constantly compares himself with Jesus, he falls short of the ideal. . . . Imagery of fishing and the desert are frequent and ironic, parodying the writer's presumption in comparing himself with Jesus. For instance, one woman whose loud talk disturbs him is Mrs. Fisher, and the subject of her conversation is one Finney Robinson. Alluding to two Christian symbols—Jesus as fisherman, Jesus as fish—, these names heighten the taunting effect the overheard talk has upon the writer. Though he tries to see the women as "fiends" and "hellshades," . . . he notices that Mrs. Fisher's terrifying laughter resembles "the cry of a woman in childbirth." . . . Goyen also alludes to the Gethsemane story to deflate the writer's presumption. The writer likens the sounds of a bed during love-making in the room above him to "the breathing of a chased thief hiding in a dark place." . . . (p. 418)

As the night lengthens—it is, the writer is painfully aware, Easter—, what frustrates him is his failure to love as Jesus said every man could. Upstairs the lovers have "made each other still," and their footsteps cause the writer to observe, "The bridegroom has come forth from his chamber." . . . Again, he refers to someone else in terms of a metaphor Jesus used for himself . . . , implying the writer's unresurrectedness. He remains suspended between the hell of the lobby and the earth above where the love-making has culminated.

Before he succeeds in reviving his spirit, events in the hotel more intensely parody the resurrection he desires. . . .

He is able to affirm his love of the world. "He thought how all things glow, glimmer out and fade and fall away and how we must let ourselves be claimed by all passing things, vanishing bit by bit in them, but flourishing in them too. . . ." . . . The word "glimmer" evokes Fitzgerald's Father Schwartz, who goes mad at the end of "Absolution" because he has tried to suppress his attraction to sensuous things. The writer's relation with his surroundings has the immediacy of the love Goyen sees Jesus preaching: "Jesus loved the physical world and the suffering creature in man. He was so much a part of the substance of nature that it was the very material of his teaching. . . ." . . .

All along the writer has sought wholeness. He has been dissociated from his home region and felt "the most painful sense of dismemberment" . . . when he has returned there; he needs to rediscover his "beginnings," which are his "heritage" and his "truth." . . . "What matter what else he had gained, if he did not possess, as it existed, the shape of his own life . . . ?" . . . he asks, echoing Jesus' question, "For what is a man advantaged, if he gain the world, and lose himself, or be cast away?" (p. 419)

Self-integration is critical in Goyen's stories: it precedes any form of reaching out. It is also quintessential to Jesus' message as Goyen perceives it: "Curing and healing the afflicted . . . meant for Jesus making them whole again. He wanted people clean and whole. . . . He wanted a unity of the physical being as well as of the spiritual being, and he set great stock in mending fragments, putting together what was broken, and so bringing back physical dignity and fullness to the individual." . . . Once this is achieved, the ultimate goal may be pursued: "Jesus wanted to heal up this society around him by *reforming* it, and he wanted to restore to all human beings the sense of membership, fellowship, brotherhood, kingdom." . . .

Like many other characters of Goyen's, the writer in "Nests in a Stone Image" can find relief from confusion. Goyen arrays biblical imagery to depict the writer's agony, but the man, though not Christ, can approach in his resolution of his problems the exuberance that Goyen considers the essence of Jesus. . . . Goyen writes about many people who are anything but devout, but one must not confuse his work and his beliefs. He speaks repeatedly of the chaotic condition of the world (and devotes *Come, the Restorer* [1974] to depicting the absurdity of seeking a Messiah when oneself is unrestored), but he hopes because one *can* love. He believes, despite the fact that those beliefs are not always manifest in human activity. He recognizes that everyone is subject to anxiety—even Jesus—but hopes for the emanation of some word from the whole person. (p. 420)

Jay S. Paul, "'Nests in a Stone Image': Goyen's Surreal Gethsemane," in Studies in Short Fiction *(copyright 1978 by Newberry College), Vol. 15, No. 4, Fall, 1978, pp. 415-20.*

ROBERT PHILLIPS

[*The Collected Stories of William Goyen*] is the book William Goyen has been writing all his career. A born storyteller, even his four novels (*The House of Breath, In a Farther Country, The Fair Sister, Come the Restorer*) are composed of stories joined together by a common thread of locale or circumstance, so many beads on a string. . . . Covering a creative span of nearly thirty years, the book reveals what too few have acknowledged: William Goyen is one of our most distinguished and uncompromising fiction writers.

In the past, some critics have dismissed Goyen's work as too "poetic" or too "regional." (He was born in and writes most frequently of the Southwest.) Yet the surprise of his *Collected Stories* is the extraordinary range of his work. These stories not only transcend the regionalism from which they sprang, they also are more than poetic or symbolic. They are, in fact, prefigurative—or, to use a term more in currency, they are "mythic." The world of Goyen's imagination reveals the mythic manner in which all of us reexperience life, the way we live on a variety of levels: thought and action, dream and reality, past and present, appearance and reality, personal and collective. Goyen sees, or more probably intuits, how these levels can work together in harmony in works of art.

This is not to say William Goyen consciously employs the "mythical method" of James Joyce or Thomas Mann. Nowhere does he appear deliberately to appropriate a myth or set of myths and weave a fictional tapestry about them, hoping to add depth or counterpoint to the current secular reality through mythic underpinnings. Goyen is, rather, one of those rare mythopoeic artists, like Franz Kafka, whose best work unconsciously reflects archetypes from the collective unconscious—a fiction writer whose work exemplifies not mythology-consciousness but rather a true mythic imagination. (pp. 234-35)

"Children of Old Somebody" is obstensibly the tale of a child disowned by his elderly parents and left to grow up in a log. Later the child is removed, but too late: already it is unfit to live in society, having grown up among wild things. The sin committed against this child is our own heritage and ancestry. The innocent but disowned son roams the world, knocking on every door, reminding us of our own sins—a Christ figure, recalling Holman Hunt's famous Pre-Raphaelite painting of Jesus at the door. But the babe in the log is also a Childe Percival figure; indeed, Goyen's story relates perfectly to Jung's special phenomenology of the child: Abandonment, exposure, and danger are all elaborations of the child's insignificant beginnings (in Christ's case, in a manger) and of its mysterious and miraculous birth (in Goyen's child-character's case, not an immaculate conception, but a rather miraculous one between elderly parents). The child is a symbolic content, then, manifestly separated from its background (the mother), but sometimes including the mother in its perilous situation (as when she comes to nurse it). In Jungian terms, the log-baby is that third thing of an irrational nature which the unconscious psyche creates during a collision of opposites, on the way to "wholeness."

The log-baby recurs frequently in world mythology, and consciously or unconsciously Goyen . . . has struck upon a timeless archetypal situation. The fact that his child is delivered helpless unto the dangers of nature, but is endowed with superior powers to pull through, represents the strongest and most ineluctable urge in every being—namely the urge to realize itself, to achieve wholeness. (pp. 235-36)

These brief comments can only hint at the richness to be found in Goyen's stories. The collected volume is a book to be read, to be studied, to be explicated, with no fear of "spoiling" the stories through dissection. Goyen dives down deeper and stays down longer in the human psyche than most American writers practicing fiction today. In these twenty-seven stories he depicts the timeless conflicts between the past and the present, the visible and the invisible. Characters who on first encounter seem bizarre—bearded sisters, a solitary flagpole sitter, a man who lives in a child's playhouse—come to be perceived as archetypes for man's great struggle for wholeness, what Jung calls the process of individuation. The waking and dream lives of Goyen's characters create a meandering pattern in which meaningful individual strands become visible, then vanish, then return again—shifting patterns of water and dust, ghost and flesh, lost and found, dismemberment and wholeness. William Goyen's central vision is finally seen as man in the process of psychic growth. (pp. 236-37)

Robert Phillips, "The Mythopoeic Imagination of William Goyen," in The Southern Review *(copyright, 1979, by Robert Phillips), Vol. 15, No. 1, January, 1979, pp. 234-37.*

* * *

GRAY, Simon 1936-

A British novelist, editor, short story writer, and playwright, Gray is a master of the double entendre and comic situation. Gray's dramas are often seemingly domestic, but they transcend domesticity to deal with the conflict between individual expression and such repressive social institutions as the church, government, and marriage. (See also *CLC*, Vol. 9, and *Contemporary Authors*, Vols. 21-24, rev. ed.)

EDITH OLIVER

["Molly"]— not a comedy but often funny—is about a woman who allows herself to become overwhelmed by feeling. . . . Molly is an Englishwoman, presumably still in her thirties, who has just moved back to England from Canada with her elderly, deaf Canadian husband. . . . There is quite a lot of action. They hire a local boy—a pimply adolescent —as gardener and chauffeur, and before long Molly seduces him. The plot is concerned with that seduction and its consequences, yet the drama is primarily one of character and mood. When we first see Molly, she is distracted and half out of her mind with boredom and sexual frustration, trying to conceal her irritation with her bumbling, impotent husband. . . . Her sharp, witty lines need no muffling, since they fall on literally deaf ears. . . . The play is also about casual double-dealing with deaf people and *its* consequences. In the climactic scene, the husband talks of the bored, contemptuous expression he always sees on the faces of those around him, and how it is belied by their foolish, cheerful words, and then, revealing his awareness of what has been going on, furiously spits at the boy. . . .

"Molly" ends with a burst of melodrama that I wouldn't dream of revealing (the play is based on an actual event in England in 1936), and while it is not a flawless work, it adds up to a generally accomplished evening.

Edith Oliver, "The Theatre: 'Molly'," in The New Yorker *(© 1978 by The New Yorker Magazine, Inc.), Vol. LIII, No. 51, February 6, 1978, p. 68.*

JOHN SIMON

If you look to *The Rear Column* for philosophical illumination, you will not find it exceptionally enlightening or original. But it is a highly intelligent piece of craftsmanship, with shrewd command of dramatic strategy, blessed with sharp but not unduly clever dialogue (Gray has displayed *that* skill elsewhere; here he is after other things)—and firm control over character development and interaction. (p. 148)

John Simon, "Oh, Dad, Poor Dad," in New York *Magazine (copyright © 1978 by News Group Publications, Inc.; reprinted with the permission of* New York *Magazine), Vol. 11, No. 49, December 4, 1978, pp. 146, 148.**

EDITH OLIVER

["The Rear Column"] is based on a historical episode. In the late eighteen-eighties, Henry M. Stanley, the explorer of the Congo, led an expedition to relieve one Emin Pasha . . . in the Sudan. Stanley's officers were British volunteers, and he left a column commanded by two of them—a Major Barttelot and a civilian named Jameson—behind at a camp in the Congo jungle, to wait for a promised contingent of porters. Three other officers, on their way to join Stanley . . . stopped off at the camp for supplies, as they had been instructed to do, but Barttelot was so furious at Stanley for abandoning him that he refused to give them any without specific written permission; unable to go forward, they were forced to remain at the camp. I set forth all this history and name all these characters, who actually lived, to demonstrate that, although it rarely occurs, a play—a powerful play, at that—can be written about real people who happen not to be Henry IV, Part II. . . . [The] play tells the story (as imagined by Mr. Gray) of that terrible year and of a misunderstanding so profound that it becomes lethal.

"The Rear Column" is essentially a play of character, ironic and tragic—of English gentlemen bearing up, or appearing to bear up, under unbearable circumstances, and of the demoralization of all of them as their reserves of physical and mental and nervous strength are eroded. . . .

Each of these characters is written with admirable subtlety and clarity. . . . (p. 84)

Edith Oliver, "The Theatre: 'The Rear Column'," in The New Yorker *(© 1978 by The New Yorker Magazine, Inc.), Vol. LIV, No. 42, December 4, 1978, pp. 84-5.*

TERRY CURTIS FOX

Simon Gray's *The Rear Column,* an anti-adventure of Stanley's years after the discovery of Livingstone, is pure revisionism. Gray goes into Africa with modern eyes; Stanley has marched off to a year-long diversion and his rear guard —five on-stage British officers and several thousand off-stage natives—is left behind to degenerate at will. The play is the progress of falling apart.

It is a curious work, written in the language of the adventure movie with all the romantic myth removed. . . . The exceptional has been banished in favor of the ordinary; Gray, anxious to dwell upon that modern cliche, the banality of evil, robs his characters of the values of their own time.

The story of *The Rear Column* is one of men who fail not only in the judgment of history but also by the standards they set for themselves, and, as such, it should have provided material for a fascinating work. Jameson [the British gentleman-dilettante who is second in command] in particular shows how great the moral dilemma in the play should have been. He, alone of the quintet, is fascinated by the African continent. . . . There is no largeness of purpose possible in this play, and that, ultimately, is what belittles the script.

For as the characters' integrity diminishes, peripheral issues outdistance fundamental ones. The relationship between the younger men and Major Barttelot, the lunatic commander who constantly threatens to turn himself into Captain Queeg, becomes more compelling than their relationship to imperialism. . . . Their attachments to Barttelot are literally unnatural. . . . (pp. 121-22)

Something is badly wrong here. In a world in which private London societies would conspire with the entrepreneurial King Leopold to enslave a continent, the worst evil does not come from being gay. (p. 122)

Terry Curtis Fox, "Heart of Grayness," in The Village Voice *(copyright © 1978; reprinted by permission), Vol. 23, No. 49, December 4, 1978, pp. 121-22.**

PETER JENKINS

In the course of one Sunday afternoon we encounter drunkenness, homosexuality, dishonesty, adultery, abortion, and more besides, until the stage [for *Close of Play*] is knee-deep in skeletons. . . . The point, I think, is that [the members of the family] have all destroyed each other. In an embarrassing moment they chant, Eliot-like, 'The door is open, we'll send them towards it', i.e. the door of death yawns from the moment of birth.

Simon Gray tries to solve the problem of the family play by the device of sitting [the father] down in an armchair and having him speak not a word till the end. It is not quite clear whether he dies at the end, is dead throughout, or whether the whole play is intended to take place at his moment of dying. Whichever it is his silent presence serves as an excuse for the family to expose themselves, relentlessly and at times indecently, to us outsiders.

Peter Jenkins, "Two for Tea," in The Spectator *(© 1979 by* The Spectator*; reprinted by permission of* The Spectator*), Vol. 242, No. 7874, June 9, 1979, p. 30.**

HAROLD HOBSON

Before the ending there are two parts of *Close of Play* which are entirely successful. The first is a brief conversation between the mercurial Marianne and the controlled Margaret, on the subject of the reviews of Margaret's latest novel. The *faux pas* of the not altogether unmalicious Marianne will be familiar to everyone who has friends and has written a book. This brief episode is both amusing and authentic. The second incident is not at all funny, but it is very brilliant. . . . [Henry] in his story showing how a doctor may without realising it until it is too late become a seducer of one of his patients, and unable to rescue himself from the sequel of his mistake, passes with enviable ease from confident insouciance to desperate bitterness in his accusations against his silent and unresponsive father for having brought him into the world. Mr. Gray takes a sour view of the world; and this sourness is . . . reflected in Henry's sexual stumble. . . . (p. 41)

[The] resemblance in plan of *Close of Play* to *Otherwise Engaged* is deceptive. The effect that . . . Mr. Gray is building up to in *Close of Play* is the shock of surprise contained in the piece's last revelation, which is the confession made to the whole family by Daisy. This revelation has been signalled all through the play. We await it, and we expect that it will be the culmination, the climax, the crowning point of all the horrors whose existence have been revealed to us during the evening. But when it comes it is nothing of the kind. It is not the demonstration of climactic misery, but the assertion of a radiant happiness . . . [which] gives to the play a truly magnificent ending. (pp. 41-2)

Harold Hobson, "Hobson's Choice: 'Close of Play'," in Drama, *No. 133, Summer, 1979, pp. 41-2.*

* * *

GREENE, Graham 1904-

A British novelist, short story writer, editor, children's author, essayist, and playwright, Greene is highly respected and widely read. His literary world is one of paradox and seediness where the sinner is often the saint, the idealist a destructive agent, and evil is everywhere while innocence is suspect. Greene's Catholicism figures prominently in his fiction, providing him with a system of concepts, situations, and symbols that he uses to dramatize human nature. (See also *CLC*, 1, 3, 6, 9, and *Contemporary Authors*, Vols. 13-16, rev. ed.)

EVELYN WAUGH

Of Mr. Graham Greene alone among contemporary writers one can say without affectation that his breaking silence with a new serious novel is a literary "event." It is eight years since the publication of "The Power and the Glory." During that time he has remained inconspicuous and his reputation has grown huge. . . .

Mr. Greene has long shown an absorbing curiosity in the [existence of Hell]. In "Brighton Rock" he ingeniously gave life to a theological abstraction. We are often told: "The Church does not teach that any man is damned. We only know that Hell exists for those who deserve it. Perhaps it is now empty and will remain so for all eternity." . . . Mr. Greene challenged the soft modern mood by creating a completely damnable youth. Pinkie of "Brighton Rock" is the ideal examinee for entry to Hell. He gets a pure alpha on every paper. His story is a brilliant and appalling imaginative achievement but falls short of the real hell-fire sermon by its very completeness. We leave our seats edified but smug. However vile we are, we are better than Pinkie. The warning of the preacher was that one unrepented slip obliterated the accumulated merits of a lifetime's struggle to be good. "Brighton Rock" might be taken to mean that one has to be as wicked as Pinkie before one runs into serious danger.

Mr. Greene's latest book, "The Heart of the Matter," should be read as the complement of "Brighton Rock." It poses a vastly more subtle problem. Its hero speaks of the Church as "knowing all the answers," but his life and death comprise a problem to which the answer is in the mind of God alone, the reconciliation of perfect justice with perfect mercy. It is a book which only a Catholic could write and only a Catholic can understand. I mean that only a Catholic can understand the nature of the problem. (p. 322)

Mr. Greene divides his fiction into "Novels" and "Entertainments." Superficially there is no great difference between the two categories. There is no Ruth Draper switch from comic to pathetic. "Novels" and "Entertainments" are both written in the same grim style, both deal mainly with charmless characters, both have a structure of sound, exciting plot. You cannot tell from the skeleton whether the man was baptized or not. And that is the difference; the "Novels" have been baptized, held deep under in the waters of life. (pp. 322-23)

[Mr. Greene's style of writing is] not a specifically literary style at all. The words are functional, devoid of sensuous attraction, of ancestry and of independent life. Literary stylists regard language as intrinsically precious and its proper use as a worthy and pleasant task. A polyglot could read Mr. Greene, lay him aside, retain a sharp memory of all he said and yet, I think, entirely forget what tongue he was using. The words are simply mathematical signs for his thought. Moreover, no relation is established between writer and reader. The reader has not had a conversation with a third party such as he enjoys with Sterne or Thackeray. Nor is there within the structure of the story an observer through whom the events are recorded and the emotions transmitted. It is as though, out of an infinite length of film, sequences had been cut which, assembled, comprise an experience which is the reader's alone, without any correspondence to the experience of the protagonists. The writer has become director and producer. Indeed, the affinity to the film is everywhere apparent. It is the camera's eye which moves from the hotel balcony to the street below, picks out the policeman, follows him to his office, moves about the room from the handcuffs on the wall to the broken rosary in the drawer, recording significant detail. It is the modern way of telling a story. . . .

Mr. Greene is a story-teller of genius. Born in another age, he would still be spinning yarns. His particular habits are accidental. The plot of "The Heart of the Matter" might well have been used by M. Simenon or Mr. Somerset Maugham. (p. 323)

[Mr. Greene] makes of his material a precise and plausible drama. His technical mastery has never been better manifested than in his statement of the scene—the sweat and infection, the ill-built town which is beautiful for a few minutes at sundown, the brothel where all men are equal, the vultures, the priest who, when he laughed "swung his great empty-sounding bell to and fro, Ho ho, ho, like a leper proclaiming his misery," the snobbery of the second-class public schools, the law which all can evade, the ever-present haunting underworld of gossip, spying, bribery, violence and betrayal. There are incidents of the highest imaginative power—Scobie at the bedside of a dying child, improvising his tale of the Bantus. It is so well done that one forgets the doer. The characters are real people whose moral and spiritual predicament is our own because they are part of our personal experience.

As I have suggested above, Scobie is the complement of Pinkie. Both believe in damnation and believe themselves damned. Both die in mortal sin as defined by moral theologians. The conclusion of the book is the reflection that no one knows the secrets of the human heart or the nature of God's mercy. It is improper to speculate on another's damnation. Nevertheless the reader is haunted by the question: Is Scobie damned? One does not really worry very much about whether Becky Sharp or Fagin is damned. It is the central question of "The Heart of the Matter." I believe that Mr. Greene thinks him a saint. Perhaps I am wrong in this, but in any case Mr. Greene's opinion on that matter is of no more value than the reader's. Scobie is not Mr. Greene's creature, devised to illustrate a thesis. He is a man of independent soul. Can one separate his moral from his spiritual state? Both are complex and ambiguous. (p. 324)

Mr. Greene has put a quotation from Péguy at the beginning of the book *"Le pécheur est au coeur même de chrétienté . . . Nul n'est aussi compétent que le pécheur en matière de chrétienté. Nul, si ce n'est le saint,"* and it seems to me probable that it was in his mind to illustrate the *"Nouveau Théologien"* from which it is taken, just as in "Brighton Rock" he illustrates the Penny Catechism. The theme of that remarkable essay is that Christianity is a city to which a bad citizen belongs and the good stranger does not. . . . If Péguy is saying anything at all, he is saying something very startling and something which people seem to find increasingly important. Mr. Greene has removed the argument from Péguy's mumbled version and re-stated it in brilliantly plain human terms; and it is there, at the heart of the matter, that the literary critic must resign his judgment to the theologian. (p. 325)

Evelyn Waugh, "Felix Culpa?" in Commonweal *(copyright © 1948 Commonweal Publishing Co., Inc.; reprinted by permission of Commonweal Publishing Co., Inc.), Vol. XLVIII, No. 14, July 16, 1948, pp. 322-25.*

KATHLEEN NOTT

The framework of absolute Catholic theory employed by Greene . . . in his serious novels, really implies that sexuality is sinful and is not more than condoned by marriage. When Greene is writing about a real psychological situation he writes powerfully and movingly. Such a situation may well be one in which the particular actions of a character result from the reaction between a certain type of education and his concrete circumstances. This applies to the priest in *The Power and the Glory*. Compared with this the psychological situations of the policeman in *The Heart of the Matter,* and the novelist in *The End of the Affair,* seem factitious, even *ad hoc*.

To be artistically satisfying the situation must be objectively described. The author must not imply that, for esoteric reasons, he knows more about the answers to the problem than the characters do. You can write a human book about a Catholic if you do not at the same time write a book about Catholic theories of human nature.

The Power and the Glory is about the effect of Catholic belief and dogma on someone for whom that belief affords his whole *raison d'être*. We are allowed to concentrate our attention of the priest as a suffering human being. In *The Heart of the Matter* and *The End of the Affair,* which are about sexual and marital relations, the problems, while they are not less specialised and also peculiar to those who have had a Catholic education, are not resolved in their own terms, that is, also, in human and therefore artistic terms. The priest, a minor character in each of these two later books, is yet of major importance to Greene. He is a *deus ex machina*. He supplies the answers, dogmatic ones, not artistic.

The End of the Affair, for instance, is a book about sexual sin and about a superstitious bargain to evade punishment. The main 'answer' seems to be 'Catholicism is right, for look what happened' (some of it very odd). One of the concrete forms of the answer is that superstition is a good idea because anything is better than trying to resolve one's problems in rational terms. This is the answer given to the main character, who seems to be impressed by it, although not himself a Catholic.

Greene never shows the effects of Catholicism on the temperamentally cheerful and balanced, yet some of these people must surely exist without being too insensitive to merit either attention or salvation. In his books, moreover, the refined agonies of conscience which Catholicism may induce in the more sensitive do not bear impressive fruit of charity or even greater understanding of fellow-sufferers and fellow-sinners. For pathological types like Pinky in *Brighton Rock,* it only provides a certain security of vaingloriousness and self-satisfaction which is deeply offensive to a merely humane and ethical conscience.

When Evelyn Waugh writes as a Catholic, e.g. in *Brideshead Revisited* and *Helena,* he also writes about Catholic theory. His satirical novels are artistically successful because they are written outside the scope of Catholic dogmatism. It seems to be much easier for Catholic writers who are born Catholic, for instance Mauriac, to stick to psychological truth than it is for converts. (pp. 309-10)

Kathleen Nott, "Augustinian Novelists," in her The Emperor's Clothes *(reprinted by permission of Indiana University Press; in Canada by Hope Leresche & Sayle), William Heinemann Ltd., 1953 (and reprinted by Indiana University Press, 1958), pp. 299-311.**

FRANK McCONNELL

After the revolution of sorts in fiction's faith in its own adequacy to describe the world wrought by Nabokov, Robbe-Grillet, Murdoch, and Pynchon, we can appreciate [*The End of the Affair,* Greene's] own most deliberate gamble with the limits of art as good taste. But when it appeared in 1951, it seemed in very bad, indeed scandalous, taste. Greene had already, with *The Power and the Glory* (1940) and *The Heart of the Matter* (1948), established his reputation, for better *and* worse, as the most complex and challenging religious novelist of his day. But even for many of his most sympathetic readers, he took things a bit too far in this story of a contemporary Magdalene, an adulteress named Sarah Miles who utters a prayer for her lover as he is trapped by a V-2 explosion outside their bedroom, finds herself drawn more and more to Catholic mysticism, finally dies, having caught a bad cold. . . . (pp. 35-6)

Scandalous, literally: one of the crucial New Testament meanings of *skandalon* is an event, divine or demonic, that upsets our notions of the way the world is supposed to work. . . . But the word can also mean fanatical, outrageous, silly. And not the least of Greene's accomplishments here is to have put these two meanings, scandalously, together. To tell a story that seriously insists a woman can love God enough to transform, *physically,* the world around her is to risk turning the novel into what Orwell called the "smelly little orthodoxies" of sectarian pamphlets. . . .

[Greene] takes even bigger risks with our credence than many of the absurdists and fantasists who have lately populated fiction. A Nabokov may say that "reality" is the only word that must always be used in quotes. But he well knows the dangers of trying to remove the quotes, and whenever he does so, as in *Pale Fire* or *Ada,* he is careful to nudge us at the moment of removal, reminding us that he shares our basic sense of how things "really" are. But Greene withholds that comforting nudge. It is no accident that *The End of the Affair,* his eleventh novel, is the first to feature as its central character a professional novelist, and the first to be narrated from the first-person.

"I can be trusted," Bendrix insists, whenever he says anything favorable about Sarah or her God: "I am writing against the bias because it is my professional pride to prefer the near-truth, even to the expression of my near-hate." It is a device of remarkable subtlety: the novel's insistence on its own quality *as* a novel demands that we take seriously the conventions of "reality" to which the story at last does such systematic violence. The effect is intensified when, in the middle of the action, Bendrix acquires Sarah's journal, which seems to be written to her new lover. Only after some pages of apparently erotic musings do we—and he—discover that the "You" Sarah keeps addressing is God. In other words, Greene constructs with his usual mastery an absolutely convincing tale of human passions and betrayals, which entraps the reader who has swallowed it all into accepting, *at the same level of narrative reality,* the facts of sainthood and miracles. . . .

[The] central fascination and central problem of *The End of the Affair* [is:] why does Greene write such an unpromising, offensive, perhaps fanatic book, and, beyond that, why does it, against all odds, *work*? For work it does, as one of the richest novels he has written. . . .

[*The End of the Affair* is] an extended demonstration of the priest's last-minute discovery, articulated so as to upset the very religious complacency that might give it too easy an acceptance. Some of Greene's most withering scorn has always been reserved for what he calls the "habit of piety," the smugness of ritualized "goodness" that denies a world of pain. And Sarah's conversion, if that is the word, does not so much obliterate as it complicates and humanizes her relationships with the people around her, including her lover Bendrix. It is in fact her initiation into that truly political community of concern and charity that Greene calls elsewhere the ministry of fear. . . . (p. 36)

But when Matthew Arnold suggested that art would become the modern age's substitute for a dead religion, he could not have imagined that the religion of art would itself grow into a ceremony of self-consciousness as arrogant and rigid as the liturgies it supplanted, a religion of technique and taste as paralytic as the habit of piety and perhaps a good deal more current. Call it the habit of Culture. Its superstitions have by now wrecked or spoiled quite a few writers. . . . Bendrix is such a writer, but his creator is not. And Bendrix's terminal failure to comprehend what has happened to him is one of Greene's most effective reminders that the function of storytelling, even at the expense of esthetic form, is to make available to us clearer modes of feeling, of loving and hating, and of living humanly in this world: to help us . . . to live our lives. . . .

The affair whose end Greene's 25-year-old book records is not just Bendrix's, but the century-long affair of an art divorced from moral energy, and a religion unconscious of its human responsibilities. He has not since experimented so daringly with the limits of the novel and the limits of belief. But the book's fierce intelligence, tempered and deflected, is present throughout his later, brilliant political novels, defining as they do a world whose salvation lies, if at all, not with its theologians or strategists but with the messiness, passion, and brave bad taste of its saints—that is, its martyrs and comedians. (p. 37)

Frank McConnell, "Books Considered: 'The End of the Affair'," in The New Republic *(reprinted by permission of* The New Republic; *© 1978 The New Republic, Inc.), Vol. 178, No. 10, March 11, 1978, pp. 35-7.*

RICHARD JONES

After more than 50 years before the reading public, Graham Greene has become an institution, the living proof that a contemporary novelist can tackle important subjects and still enjoy immense popularity. As a result, a new work by him is a major event in the international publishing season. (p. 338)

It is difficult to pin down unerringly the source of Greene's popularity. His appeal cuts across several classes of reader, and the link is probably his readability. For Greene, the novel still tells a story, and all his considerable craftsmanship is directed towards this end. He is uninterested in technical innovation, although he has been open to the influence of many different fashions from English historical romance and spy thriller to the French Catholic moralists—with glances at Conrad, Hemingway, and even Faulkner and the existentialists. Accents and passages can reflect these influences, but nothing deflects Greene from the main business of holding the reader's attention. To do this, he resorts to the tricks of the cinema—swift juxtaposition of scene, character, and tone—and is often, because of this, slick and ambiguous in his effects. . . . [What] makes Greene stand out is that from 1938, the year of *Brighton Rock,* he has used popular forms to explore his own very special obsessions, such as the operation of divine grace, man's moral responsibility to himself and other people, and the nature of love and disloyalty. The serious reader likes to recognize in these obsessions the proof of Greene's seriousness and claim to greatness. They respect his obsessions, even though the vocabulary of Greene's Catholicism and of his mysterious brand of radicalism is not shared.

Anyone writing about Greene has to face up at once to the Catholicism, not in order to argue with it, as many Orthodox Catholics have done. . . . Nor to dismiss it, as some free-thinkers tend to . . . , but rather to recognize that a Catholic novelist like Greene brings restraints to the novel that the Anglo-Saxon tradition is not used to. George Orwell's statement that "the novel is a Protestant art form, requiring the free play of mind" never seems truer than at the end of those novels in which Greene has drawn most heavily on his beliefs, such as *The Power and the Glory* and *The Heart of the Matter.* The reader is left as uneasy by the locked gears of the novel's progress as by the rigid optimism of Soviet socialist realist fiction. . . . Greene may be right to claim "not to be a writer of Catholic novels, but a writer who in four or five books took characters with Catholic ideas for his novels," but the influence is there: it is the religious sense that Greene himself believes was lost to the English novel with the death of Henry James. . . . [His] sounding the religious note has been of the utmost value in reminding an increasingly agnostic century that man has existed on another level of being. This leads to the most interesting aspect of Greene's work: that despite the special nature of his obsessions few readers feel that they are being preached at. Each novel is really a private exploration of the possibilities of certain lines of conduct which Greene later shares with his public. . . . [There] is much that is ideologically dubious in Greene's work, but for the general public this matters less than the simple fact that Greene is a superb entertainer. . . .

[In] considering the mass of his work, a line of demarcation wavers through it. On the one side are the novels that operate in what might be called a free market, and they include *Our Man in Havana, Travels with my Aunt,* and most of the early work. The other side of the line are the works that are the products of a closed market, where Greene's obsessions distort the values. By this rough and ready classification, *The Human Factor,* because it lacks either Catholic or left-wing dialectic, ought to belong to the free market, but in fact it belongs to the second. What we see operating, in place of Greene's acquired ideologies, is his native passion, not far removed from Thomas Hardy's, for plotting the destruction of small men and the half-baked hopes that inspire them. The fact that Greene is on the small man's side for most of the novel does not soften the inexorable way he so shapes events that his hero ends up cornered by actions of his own devising. In some respects, the novel is a throwback to the ones Greene wrote in the thirties, a spy thriller set against important political events. . . . Fascism was the accepted evil of many of the 1930's novels; apartheid is the one that dominates *The Human Factor.* In publishing his novel at this time, Greene once again shows his flair for producing a topical document. (pp. 338-41)

The South African situation dominates the novel, but the reader is never taken there except in flashback and conversation. The "beautiful, doomed country" plays the same role in *The Human Factor* as Paraguay does in *The Honorary Consul.* It is the place of injustice, where the main characters cannot, may not, live, and it is also their private climate. Greene's version of South Africa offers no surprises; it is accepted as a police state and, as such, fair game for subversion and harassment.

In establishing Castle as the non-political, non-religious, non-ideological man of good will, Greene had to give him qualities of heart, even of passion. He tries hard, but the result, perhaps from lack of practice, is little more than banal. Greene lavishes much detail on establishing the Castles' mousy life with Sarah's child by a black professor—accepted as Castle's—and a dog; but after years of writing about the horrors of marriage, Greene can only fumble for the essence of a happy match. . . . (p. 343)

At the end of this unconvincing story, Greene seems to be saying: this is where foolish affections and gratitude get you. Men of good will beware. Castle is a traitor, but he is a traitor that the reader has sympathized with for the simple reason that there is no one else in the novel capable of rousing any feeling. In this respect, Greene has produced a variation on an old theme. Otherwise, Castle as a hero is a washout, a soft-centered bumbler. His activities have been, on the whole, trifling, and he lacks the ability of the true ideologic spy, to claim that he is in some way "on the side of history." Why should Greene have given us such an old softie as hero? Was he trying to produce the anti-spy novel hero or to show us that the man without a real ideology is nothing and that it hardly matters what becomes of him since his actions are devoid of any real significance? (p. 345)

It is easy to accept that Greene is moved by poverty, exploitation, and corrupt dictatorships—the classic ills of the Third World—but does he classify as a political animal? It is hard to say "yes" on the strength of *The Human Factor*! It is not that anyone expects Greene to fill a novel with half-baked propaganda, but we are entitled to expect from him a greater resonance. Everything Castle does lacks common sense and gravity, and this failure in the central character exposes the defects in the framework of the novel.

What comes as a surprise is the realization that despite the sleaziness of many of Greene's settings and his capacity for converting any given place into a landscape in Greeneland, Greene is not a realistic writer. What is important for him is the poetic idea. In *Brighton Rock* he had the idea of the good-natured, rather beery woman become avenging angel; in *A Burnt-Out Case,* Greene was moved by the notion of a great man at the end of his moral rope, as it were, burying himself alive among lepers in steamy central Africa; in *The End of the Affair* he worked out the battle between the loves of this world and the love of God. The reader recognizes the poet's insights, but he expects the novelist's working out. This demands that the writer pay frequent tribute to the great god Probability, the one who presides over the fiction writer's desk. Nearly all of Greene's books are flawed by the schism between the poet's dream and the novelist's realization. (pp. 346-47)

[*The Human Factor*] sets up the great poetic idea of a love that wipes out traditional loyalties and then unsuccessfully tries to support it with a novel that is neither genuine thriller nor comedy of errors. Suspense is missing except at the end, and the exploration of character is minimal. Nowhere is this more evident than in the character of Sarah. She and Castle are an archetypal Greene pair, the elderly man and the young woman available for bed and domestic service. Greene's women are the least contemporary aspect of the novels. In book after book the reader is faced with the same subjugated type, incapable of sharing the battle of ideas. Nothing is less convincing than the scene in *The Human Factor* after Castle has confessed to his wife that he has been a double-agent. Given the hard, even pitiless, rhetoric of some female political activists at this time, Sarah is an Aunty Tomasina.

There are so many things off key in *The Human Factor* that it is difficult to know where to begin. The Castle household is wrong; the setting in Berkhamsted is not right; the handling of the details of the child's education is clumsy; the impact of such a strangely assorted couple in a conservative community is misjudged. Then, London is inaccurately placed. In some cases the mistakes are nugatory: errors that could have been put right by careful editing. In the end, so perfunctory is Greene's English setting that one wonders why he bothered, after so many years living abroad, to return home for a fictional enterprise.

Greene's absence from England had appeared to be an

important factor in his youthfulness as a writer. . . . Greene has made the world his province and has found exotic settings and themes which excited him in places as diverse as Africa, Southeast Asia, Haiti, and Spanish America. Greene has made himself a true man of the world, in the best sense, and has been an eyewitness for a generation of readers for whom he has made concrete the great bugbear of our time, the reality of political power that ignores the will of the people and refuses to be restrained by any moral consideration.

In *The Human Factor* there is no electricity between Greene's eye and the landscape. Southeast England is too well-known to be exciting, and to see Greene trying at one or two points in the book to create an uneasy nighttime London—a city that goes to bed about eleven o'clock—is to see that there are certain tricks he has grown used to employing that do not work on the home scene. Greene is really quite limited in his atmospheric effects, and the reader of his novels must often be struck by how much a cliché the sudden storm has become . . . although realizing that it makes highly effective cinema. This is fine in Mexico, West Africa, or Vietnam, but the English, grown stoic in their oceanic climate, do not recognize rain as the stuff of melodrama. (pp. 347-49)

Richard Jones, "The Improbable Spy," in Virginia Quarterly Review *(copyright, 1979, by the* Virginia Quarterly Review, *The University of Virginia), Vol. 55, No. 2 (Spring, 1979), pp. 338-49.*

* * *

GUARE, John 1938-

An American playwright and recipient of several important awards, including New York Drama Critics awards for 1971 and 1972, Guare is generally thought to be the most promising playwright to appear in America since Edward Albee. His plays are distinguished by their variety, wit, and strong sense of theater. (See also *CLC*, Vol. 8, and *Contemporary Authors*, Vols. 73-76.)

EDITH OLIVER

[John Guare] is a naturally comic writer whose indications of high spirits and an original turn of mind are all but muffled by Brechtian tricks and by the plastic pranks, the empty conventions, and the all-round hooey of "America Hurrah." (p. 91)

There are funny ideas and funny scenes scattered through ["Muzeeka"]. . . . But Mr. Guare keeps insisting on the significance of things that he does nothing to *make* significant . . . and his generalizations about America have a weak, second-hand ring to them. (pp. 91-2)

Edith Oliver, "Mr. Lowell and Mr. Haigh," in The New Yorker *(© 1968 by the New Yorker Magazine, Inc,), Vol. XLIV, No. 12, May 11, 1968, pp. 85-6, 91-2.**

HAROLD CLURMAN

John Guare's most striking talent is for savage farce. There are scenes in Act II of his first full-length play, *The House of Blue Leaves* . . . , in which his fancy boils over into a tempest of hilarity. They are the best things in the play; they provoke wild laughter and merit enthusiastic applause. Still, the play remains unfulfilled; the reasons are worth careful attention.

Guare is not simply a prankster. What motivates him is scorn for the fraudulence of our way of life. In *The House of Blue Leaves* he has been aroused by the obsession with big shots, "personalities," stars, the "in" tribe. That is a way of saying that we no longer see people as human beings; we worship "names." The imbecile, the villainous, the irredeemably mediocre possess glamour (even when we profess to despise them) if they have been sufficiently publicized. No wonder advertisement is the country's prime industry.

The central figure of *The House of Blue Leaves,* Artie Shaughnessy, a man who tends the animals in a zoo, has wanted all his life to be a pop songwriter. His tunes are atrocious. He is not only ungifted—which is no great matter—he is a fool. He is abject in the fetishism of his fellow citizens. The only people who count for him are those who have "made good." . . .

Artie really knows nothing about himself or anyone else. . . . His stupidity is apparently the cause of his wife's insanity, though she too is infected with the craving for the smile of the blessed public heroes. . . . Artie stands for the half-wits who constitute the bulk of the audience for Hollywood's typical product.

There is a certain grimness in all this but Guare turns it into a roar of clownish mockery. *The House of Blue Leaves* is crazy fun. But something disturbs it. That "something" may be (this is only conjecture) a personal pain—an autobiographical memory?—which causes Guare to inject elements of cruel sorrow into the proceedings. There is nothing at all mirthful about the madness of Artie's wife nor in the play's final moment when he strangles her.

The play suffers, thus, from a discrepancy of style, but that need not have been fatal. What damages the total effect is that nobody—not the director, the producers, nor apparently the author himself—appears to have been aware of what was required to make the play a workable whole for the stage. . . . I have just now suggested that Artie's obtuseness may have caused his wife's insanity, but that connection is not made in the writing. As the play stands, she is an unexplained hospital case: a raw wound that cripples the play's comic nature. (p. 285)

While *The House of Blue Leaves* possesses real and valid content, it cannot, given Guare's gifts, be articulated as realism. (p. 286)

Harold Clurman, "Theatre: 'The House of Blue Leaves'," in The Nation *(copyright 1971 by the Nation Associates, Inc.), Vol. CCXII, No. 9, March 1, 1971, pp. 285-86.*

STANLEY KAUFFMANN

In the current crop of overpraised young American playwrights John Guare is one of the few with readily discernible talent. It was discernible even in his disappointing *House of Blue Leaves*. . . . His early short plays like *Muzeeka* had imaginative release and exuberant humor, but nothing of his that I have seen, including his screenplay for the Milos Forman film *Taking Off,* came close to satisfying.

So it continues with his [*Rich and Famous*]. . . . It consists of the fantasies of a young playwright on the night of the first preview of his first produced play, after writing 843 previous scripts. (pp. 28-9)

A great deal of Guare's dialogue is sharp and resourceful. He wrote several songs, music and lyrics, that are pleasant and clever. Some of the set-pieces . . . are show-stoppers, patently manufactured but nonetheless effective. But I'm left again with the feeling that what Guare needs is a sympathetic collaborator. After he has shot all his fireworks, and he has some, almost every one of his scenes is residually trite and static. The scene with the former sweetheart is full of familiar, grubbily overtugged heartstrings. The scene with the uncomprehending parents is *that* scene again, this time Irish instead of Jewish. Even the scene with the *doppelgänger* film star at the end concludes with a flashy gag, with only a strained relevance to the play. The script has no dramatic conclusion or thematic issue. Guare is the writing equivalent of a talented actor who needs a good director and flounders without one. (p. 29)

Stanley Kauffmann, "Off-Broadway Offerings" (copyright © 1976 by Stanley Kauffman; reprinted by permission of Brandt & Brandt Literary Agents, Inc.), in The New Republic, *Vol. 174, No. 11, March 13, 1976, pp. 28-9.**

EDITH OLIVER

What an odd mixture of inspired comedy, sudden horror, and plain guff is John Guare's "Landscape of the Body"! Whenever his imagination takes over, whenever his astonishing dramatic talent for creating characters and lines and scenes is let loose, he is invaluable; it is only his abstract thoughts, as spoken by the characters in a number of set pieces, that tend to become trying. The play . . . begins aboard a ferry from Cape Cod to Nantucket. Betty, the heroine, burdened with overflowing shopping bags, walks to the rail, where she is joined by a man in a Groucho Marx false face. When he removes the mask after a few unsuccessful attempts at pickup conversation, she recognizes him as the Greenwich Village detective who has been questioning her for months about the murder of her fourteen-year-old son, Bert, and attempting to trap her into a confession. Her story is then played out in bits and pieces—episodes and songs (delightful ones, also by Mr. Guare) and fantasies and a sprinkling of those tiresome monologues. The brimming action moves back and forth in time—from the ferry to Betty's apartment on Christopher Street, to the police station, and finally back to the ferry. . . .

The application of [the] title line to the proceedings onstage is tenuous at best; a song, "I Used to Believe," . . . provides a better clue, for the theme of unpredictability—of the chanciness of everything, especially death—runs through the script. Whether or not that is what the play is about I cannot tell you, but no matter: the imagination—and this is surely true of Mr. Guare's—was not put on earth to illustrate the intellect. The form of the play may be catch as catch can, but it is filled with surprises and theatrical resourcefulness. (p. 144)

Edith Oliver, "Betty and Bert in New York," in The New Yorker *(© 1977 by The New Yorker Magazine, Inc.), Vol. LIII, No. 36, October 24, 1977, pp. 144-46.**

BRENDAN GILL

Much as we may enjoy [Guare's] plays from one line to the next, we almost always end by wondering what on earth they are intended to be about. Specifically, what is his latest work, "Bosoms and Neglect," about? . . . [Both] the ravaged bosom and the two species of neglect remain more like stated topics than developed themes. . . . Although the author is very good indeed at writing funny one-liners, and from time to time gives us one-liners that are, by calculation, not at all funny, the lines have a tendency to remain attached to him, and not to his characters. They are the exclamations of a mischievously self-delighting artist, and behind them we seem to hear, to our unease, a whispered "What a bright boy am I!" . . .

In the last few minutes of the play, something true and touching emerges: Why had Henny provided Scooper with such a miserable, unloving childhood? And just then the curtain falls. Horseman, pass by! (p. 83)

Brendan Gill, "Family Troubles," in The New Yorker *(© 1979 by The New Yorker Magazine, Inc.), Vol. LV, No. 13, May 14, 1979, pp. 83-4.**

TERRY CURTIS FOX

In the first scene of *Bosoms and Neglect,* Henny, the blind, 82-year-old mother of a 40-year-old man who calls himself Scooper, hides behind a curtain and shows her son her cancerous breast which she has been treating with Kotex and St. Jude for the past two years. John Guare would do well to take that scene and burn it, interpolating what little exposition it contains into one of the speeches that follow. For this prologue hovers like the Vulture of Significance over the rest of the play, a false, pretentious, utterly unsatisfying scene that masks a beautiful, painful, and frequently hilarious show. Guare can be like that—brilliant fits after false starts and casual comedy collapsing into too-believable melodrama.

Bosoms and Neglect is an ill-made play. Its first act is a screwball comedy about two analysands, Deirdre and Scooper. . . . The second act takes place in Henny's hospital room and is about what Guare's plays are always about—the paralytic hate that grows out of family love. (pp. 95-6)

Guare is a fine writer of farces; he has the moralist's outrage at the imperfection of the world and the good satirist's delight in the foibles of his own kind. The comedy in *Bosoms* is full of pain. Scooper is a quintessential Guare hero: a man who is successful in business but an utter emotional failure. . . . Scooper and Deirdre revel in neglect; for them, calling a book or author "neglected" implies idolization. But if they love neglected works, they also love to neglect everyone around them, including each other.

As a result, all they can do with each other is attack. . . . When the two run off together, you expect them to enter "The Loveliest Afternoon of the Year," Guare's playlet about a perfect couple on a perfect day who get perfectly machine-gunned. Only Guare no longer sees the world as his hostile enemy. The enemy consists of the people who love you. . . .

Henny is at once the most appalling and sympathetic character in the play. For she has truly been driven mad by love: in the last scene she lies alone in her hospital room and solves Scooper's great psychological mystery. In a chillingly beautiful curtain speech, Henny explains how she lost her lover to his Quaker mother and how she took a revenge that destroyed her and her son.

In all his plays, Guare has dealt despairingly with the uses to which parents put their children, even when, as here, the "children" are 40 years old. It's clear in this play that

Guare believes the only way for Scooper to survive is to break his bond with the past, but at the same time Guare trusts the psychoanalytic explanation: Henny really did influence Scooper for life; nothing he can do at 40 will free him. Both parental and romantic love are perceived as forms of bondage, as the attachments people make with each other become inevitable sources of pain. The need for bosoms breeds neglect. . . .

In the few days since this review was written, *Bosoms and Neglect* has folded, so this intelligent and deeply-felt play can no longer be seen. Some years from now, it will doubtless be revived—probably in the midwest—and everyone will wonder how New York could be so dumb as to miss its points. (p. 96)

Terry Curtis Fox, "Premature Burial," in The Village Voice *(copyright © 1979; reprinted by permission), Vol. XXIV, No. 19, May 14, 1979, pp. 95-7.**

JOHN SIMON

[*Bosoms and Neglect*] consists of three levels that stubbornly refuse to blend, and are not worth much individually either. . . .

[We] have the mother, psychiatry, and book levels that prove grotesque and outlandish but only very sparsely funny, and also unrelated and immiscible. Someone else might have put them believably together; in Guare's unsure grasp they fall apart like a card castle being built by a sufferer from Parkinson's disease. The play, moreover, fluctuates between the absurdist and the naturalistic, the scandalous and the would-be endearing, the obvious and the arcane. (p. 77)

John Simon, "Folie à deux," in New York *Magazine (copyright © 1979 by News Group Publications, Inc.; reprinted with the permission of* New York *Magazine), Vol. 12, No. 21, May 21, 1979, pp. 76-8.**

MARTIN GOTTFRIED

[*Bosoms and Neglect*] was an important work for an author who is at a difficult time in his career. Though predictably a commercial failure (too abstract and disorganized), *Bosoms and Neglect* should not have been treated as a play without a right to exist. It was a serious attempt by a serious writer. Guare's previous plays—*Landscape of the Body* and *Rich and Famous*— were not satisfactory, but he had demonstrated a literary flair and comic originality in such early works as *Muzeeka* and *The House of Blue Leaves*. This new play showed that exhilarating talent still strong.

Martin Gottfried, "An Unmerry Month of May," in Saturday Review *(© 1979 by Saturday Review Magazine Corp.; reprinted with permission), Vol. 6, No. 14, July 7, 1979, p. 40.**

H

H(ilda) D(oolittle) 1886-1961

An American poet connected with the Imagist school, H. D. wrote poetry infused with the rhythm of emotionally charged speech. She was greatly affected by the terror of the Second World War, a fact evidenced in the tone of desolation in her poetry, notably the group of poems known as her "War Trilogy." (See also *CLC,* Vols. 3, 8.)

DENISE LEVERTOV

Like so many others, I was for years familiar only with a handful of H. D.'s early poems, "Peartree," "Orchard," "Heat," "Oread." Beautiful though they were, they did not lead me to look further, at the time. Perhaps it was that being such absolutes of their kind they seemed final, the end of some road not mine; and I was looking for doors, ways in, tunnels through.

When I came, late, to her later work, not searching but by inevitable chance, what I found was precisely doors, ways in, tunnels through. One of these later poems, "The Moon in Your Hands," says:

> If you take the moon in your hands
> and turn it round
> (heavy slightly tarnished platter)
> you're there;

This was to find not a finality but a beginning. The poem ends with that sense of beginning. . . . In "Sagesse" the photograph of an owl—a White Faced Scops Owl from Sierra Leone, which is reproduced along with the poem—starts a train of thought and feeling which leads poet and reader far back into childhood, by way of word origins and word-sound associations, and back again to a present more resonant, more full of possibilities and subtle awareness, because of that journey. The interpenetration of past and present, of mundane reality and intangible reality, is typical of H. D. For me this poem (written in 1957) was an introduction to the world of the Trilogy—*The Walls Do Not Fall* (1944), *Tribute to the Angels* (1945), *The Flowering of the Rod* (1946). (pp. 244-45)

What was it I discovered, face to face at last with the great poetry of H. D.'s maturity? What was—is—the core of the experience? I think this is it: that the icily passionate precision of the earlier work, the "Greek" vision, had not been an *end,* a closed achievement, but a preparation: so that all the strength built up, poem by poem, as if in the bones, in the remorseless clear light of that world . . . was *there,* there to carry darkness and mystery and the questions behind questions when she came to that darkness and those questions. She showed a way to penetrate mystery; which means, not to flood darkness with light so that darkness is destroyed, but to *enter into* darkness, mystery, so that it is experienced. And by *darkness* I don't mean *evil;* not evil but the Other Side, the Hiddenness before which man must shed his arrogance; Sea out of which the first creeping thing and Aphrodite emerge. . . . (pp. 245-46)

The "style"—or since style too often means *manner,* I would rather say the *mode,* the means—is invisible: or no, not invisible but transparent, something one both sees and sees through, like hand-blown glass of the palest smoke-color or the palest water-green. And in this transparent mode H. D. spoke of essentials. It is a simplicity not of reduction but of having gone further, further out of the circle of known light, further in toward an unknown center. Whoever wishes a particular example, let him read part VI of *The Walls Do Not Fall.* . . . (pp. 246-47)

After I had begun to know the later poems I returned to the *Collected Poems* of 1925 and saw them anew. . . . The poems I had thought of as shadowless were full of shadows, planes, movement: correspondences with what was to come. But I, and perhaps others of my generation, could come to realize this only through a knowledge of the afterwork. (p. 247)

There is no poet from whom one can learn more about precision; about the music, the play of sound, that arises miraculously out of fidelity to the truth of experience; about the possibility of the disappearance, in the crucible, of *manner.* . . .

Her last book, *Helen in Egypt* . . . is (like *Bid Me to Live* in its different form) a world which one may enter if one will; a life-experience that gives rise to changes in the reader, small at first, but who knows how far-reaching. The alternations, in *Helen,* of prose and poetry are not alternations of flatness and intensity but of contrasted tone, as in a Bach cantata the vocal parts are varied by the sinfonias, and each illumines and complements the other. *Bid Me to Live* and *Helen in Egypt* are neither of them works to be idly dipped into: one must go inside and live in them, live them through.

Indeed this is true of all her work: the more one reads it, the more it yields. It is poetry both "pure" and "engaged"; attaining its purity—that is, its unassailable identity as word-music, the music of word-sounds and the rhythmic structure built of them—through its very engagement, its concern with matters of the greatest importance to everyone: the life of the soul, the interplay of psychic and material life. (p. 248)

Denise Levertov, "H. D.: An Appreciation" (originally published in Poetry, *Vol. C, No. 3, June, 1962), in her* The Poet in the World *(copyright © 1962 by Denise Levertov Goodman; reprinted by permission of New Directions Publishing Corporation), New Directions, 1973, pp. 244-48.*

VINCENT QUINN

["Hermetic Definition"] is an important revelation of [H. D.'s] understanding of the life of a poet. At the start of her career in 1913, by the act of adopting the pen name "H. D.," she had separated her identity as Hilda Doolittle from her role as poet. In this poem, written almost fifty years later, she offered a "hermetic definition" of what that separation had meant. . . .

The poem consists of three parts—"Red Rose and a Beggar," "Grove of Academe," and "Star of Day"—and each part has a pair of dates appended to its title. . . . [By] including these dates H. D. calls attention to the importance of time in the poem. Her real subject, in fact, is the relationship between the timeless state in which completed poems exist and particular moments in the life of the poet, especially those involved in the writing of poetry. (p. 52)

Throughout "Hermetic Definition" [a young man H. D. had met only twice] is present as both human being and symbol; in the first part his symbolic role predominates, and [in "Grove of Academe"] his reality is stressed. In addition to their ages, H. D. gives several other personal details: his remark "'You look well'" when they last met "in a strange place / with others there," . . . his promise to write to her, their exchange of letters, her fear that her "*Notre Dame* revelation" . . . may have seemed bizarre to him, his failure to write again, and her conclusion that "apparently, it was over." . . .

In this sad, resigned state of mind, she has been reading Perse, whose perception of vast cycles of time and nature appeals to her as an alternative to the anxieties of a personal relationship. His detachment is welcomed as:

> the exact emotional opposite,
>
> your cool laurel, the olive silver-green,
> to compensate or off-set the reddest rose,
> this enigmatic encounter. . . .

Yet she cannot accept this impersonal alternative. Perse has transcended human emotion so far that even her plea to him for pardon for her "deflection" would go unheard. She sees his detachment as part of his greatness, but she cannot share in it. Her place is with ordinary humanity, fearful and pious, hoping against hope that wishes may be fulfilled. . . . (p. 58)

[Part Three, "Star of Day"] brings the poem to its climax with the announcement that the young man has died "in the winter, / . . . in the depth of night, just as my Christmas candles had burnt out." . . . Her reaction provides the key to the deepest meaning of the poem.

The significant fact is that she expresses no grief at all. The physical reality of the young man, which has hung in unsteady balance with his symbolic role, now almost completely vanishes. Instead of lamenting the death of a man, H. D. at once absorbs herself in the supportive implications of the myth of the Egyptian goddess Saïs, whom she associates with Isis and *Notre Dame,* the childbearing archetypes she has invoked throughout the poem. H. D. introduces her at this point because "They say, Saïs brought forth the Star of Day, / at midnight when the shadows are most dense, / the nights longest and most desperate." . . . Patterning her situation upon this myth, H. D. transforms the death of the young man at the winter solstice and Christmastide into a birth by which he has been "integrated with the Star of Day." . . . (pp. 58-9)

Looking back upon her relationship with him, she sees in it a sequence that is now complete. Their first meeting took place in April, they met once more in May, and he has died in December. From their first meeting to his death, nine months elapsed. This detail supports her intuition that she has given birth to a spiritual child in what appears to be the death of a man. Like Saïs, Isis, and *Notre Dame,* she has played the role of mother. . . .

As a consequence of their nine-month relationship, H. D. has written a poem resurrecting the young man in art; he now has a "life" in poetry. The stages of this "childbearing" are charted in some detail. H. D. says that when in August she became aware of her "'condition,' / you were five months 'on the way'." . . . It is now clear that the statement "the reddest rose unfolds," which is repeated throughout Part One, refers to the swelling caused by the growth of the poem within her. (p. 59)

She now understands Part Two, "Grove of Academe," in the context of her "pregnancy." Meeting Perse had strengthened her commitment to art. Momentarily, as we have seen, she was attracted to his poetic world of "*transhumance,*" his "*iles de promesse,*" but she had recognized the error of following a way "not mine but another's." . . . (pp. 59-60)

Having created a poem which transforms a death into a birth, H. D. feels that her role as artist-mother has been completed. Her potentiality has been realized, and she is ready for her own death. She has met the responsibility of her "condition"; through art she has shared in the life-giving power of Isis and *Notre Dame.* The "hermetic definition" of her nature has been found and realized in the poem, which ends with a reference both to herself and to the young man whose fate became entwined poetically with her own. . . .

The process of transforming life into art is, then, the "hermetic definition" of the artist. The metamorphosis of Hilda Doolittle into the poet H. D. is paralleled by the metamorphosis of the events in H. D.'s life into the material of art. (p. 60)

Essentially, the poem is not about the young man. Regardless of his physical reality, his main function here is to be a figure of speech for the process of writing a poem. H. D. has succeeded in using the apparent subject of her poem to represent the stages she went through in writing it. The young man's first appearance germinates the creative impulse: the mysterious conception of a poem within the poet. The completion of the poem is the Poet's delivery of her child, noted explicitly by H. D. as occurring nine months after they met. Ironically, this poem is born in the old age of its poet mother at the same time as the death of the "father" who inspired it. This concurrence shows both the kinship of art to the process of natural creation and its separateness from nature's ordinary time-cycle. (pp. 60-1)

H. D. wrote this poem at the close of her career; she died the year the poem was completed. Nearing the end of her life, she was perhaps better able to understand and accept the paradox of art. She knew that the artist is a creator (the word "mother" is her recurrent image), but she also knew that art is totally independent of the life that bears it. The self-sacrifice demanded of the poet might be too painful to choose, if a choice were given, but her deepest perception is that there is no choice. To those born to be poets, writing is the only condition on which they can live at all. . . . (p. 61)

Vincent Quinn,"H. D.'s 'Hermetic Definition': The Poet As Archetypal Mother," in Contemporary Literature *(© 1977 by the Board of Regents of the University of Wisconsin System), Vol. 18, No. 1, Winter, 1977, pp. 51-61.*

MARGARET NEWLIN

How to satisfy the needs of both woman and poet without betraying either is the major theme of [H. D.'s] work and must surely have been the cause of her breakdown as well. Over and over she expresses the struggle between her longing for love and her equally great desire for freedom and solitude. (p. 223)

Margaret Newlin, "'Unhelpful Hymen!': Marianne Moore and Hilda Doolittle," in Essays in Criticism, *Vol. XXVII, No. 3, July, 1977, pp. 216-30.**

SUSAN GUBAR

One of H. D.'s most coherent and ambitious poetic narratives, her war *Trilogy,* explores the reasons for her lifelong fascination with the palimpsest. . . . H. D. presents herself as an outsider who must express her views from a consciously female perspective, telling the truth, as [Emily] Dickinson would say, "slant." Inheriting uncomfortable male-defined images of women and of history, H. D. responds with palimpsestic or encoded revisions of male myths. Thus . . . , she discovers behind the recalcitrant and threatening signs of her times a hidden meaning that sustains her quest by furnishing stories of female strength and survival. In the *Trilogy,* through recurrent references to secret languages, codes, dialects, hieroglyphs, foreign idioms, fossilized traces, mysterious signs, and indecipherable signets, H. D. illustrates how patriarchal culture can be subverted by the woman who dares to "re-invoke, re-create" what has been "scattered in the shards / men tread upon."

While there is never any question for H. D. that she can avoid reinvoking or re-creating, such a posture implies that she never expects to find or make a language of her own. It is significant, I think, that H. D. sees in her famous vision at Corfu a tripod, symbol of "prophetic utterance or occult or hidden knowledge; the Priestess or Pythoness of Delphi sat on the tripod while she pronounced her verse couplets, the famous Delphic utterances which it was said *could be read two ways*" [italics mine]. Throughout her career, H. D. wrote couplets which have been read only one way. Placed in exclusively male contexts, the poetry of Freud's analysand, Pound's girlfriend, and D. H. Lawrence's Isis has been viewed from the monolithic perspective of the twentieth-century trinity of psychoanalysis, imagism, and modernism. While none of these contexts can be discounted, each is profoundly affected by H. D.'s sense of herself as a woman writing about female confinement, specifically the woman writer's struggle against entrapment within male literary conventions. Furthermore, the fact that H. D. wrote her verse so it could be read two ways demonstrates her ambivalence over self-expression: she hides her private meaning behind public words in a juggling act that tells us a great deal about the anxieties of many women poets. Reticence and resistance characterize H. D.'s revisions in the *Trilogy,* where we can trace her contradictory attitudes toward communication: in *The Walls Do Not Fall,* H. D. demonstrates the need for imagistic and lexical redefinition, an activity closely associated with the recovery of female myths, specifically the story of Isis; in *Tribute to the Angels,* she actually begins transforming certain words, even as she revises apocalyptic myth; finally, H. D. translates the story of the New Testament in *The Flowering of the Rod,* feminizing a male mythology as she celebrates the female or "feminine" Word made flesh. (pp. 197-99)

The title of the first volume, *The Walls Do Not Fall,* reveals the primacy of spatial imagery in H. D.'s analysis of a splintered world where "there are no doors" and "the fallen roof / leaves the sealed room / open to the air." . . . All of civilized history has failed to create forms that can protect or nurture the inhabitants of this wasteland, and the "Apocryphal fire" threatens even the skeleton which has incomprehensibly survived. The poet is especially vulnerable in a world that worships coercion, for the sword takes precedence over the word. (p. 199)

It is only in the context of her psychological and physical dispossession that H. D.'s famous poem about the spell of the seashell can be fully understood. In her first attempt to "recover the Sceptre, / the rod of power" associated with the healing powers of Caduceus . . . , H. D. portrays herself in the image of the "master-mason" or "craftsman" mollusk within the seashell. . . . Hidden and therefore safe, the mollusk is protected in precisely the way the poet craves asylum: neither fully alive nor fully dead, half in and half out, the mollusk in its shell becomes for H. D. a tantalizing image of the self or soul safely ensconced within the person or body, always and anywhere at home.

But the fascination goes much further because the "flabby, amorphous" mollusk not only protects itself with such impenetrable material as "bone, stone, marble" but also transforms living substance into formal object, and thereby mysteriously creates the beautiful circular patterns of its house and also the perfectly spherical pearl. Shells are associated traditionally with art because the shell is a musical instrument expressing the rhythm of the waves. . . . (p. 200)

The self-enclosed, nonreferential completeness of pearl and shell recalls H. D.'s own earlier imagistic poems, but the limits of imagism are what emerge most emphatically since the mollusk can only combat the hostile powers of the sea by snapping shut "shell-jaws.". . . . H. D. has spoken of the power of her verse to"snap-shut neatly," and the analogy implies that these tidy, enclosed poems may be unable to communicate or unwilling even to admit a content. Imprisoned within what amounts to a beautiful but inescapable tomb of form, the mollusk will not be cracked open or digested, but instead remains "small, static, limited," just as H. D.'s early poems refuse any interaction with the external world when they reproduce images that seem shaped by a poet rigidly and self-consciously in control of herself and her material. Far from representing the ultimate statement of her poetics, the seashell poem is a very limited statement, altered and superseded by transformations of this image as the *Trilogy* progresses.

While H. D. discusses her craft in terms of the crafts*man* mollusk, clearly she was drawn to the shell and pearl because of their feminine evocations. Associated iconographically with Venus and the Virgin, the shell is also said to represent the female genitals. It may represent pregnancy, since the pearl is a kind of seed in the womb of the shellfish, or a hope of rebirth, as in the traditionally termed "resurrection shells." . . . H. D. was careful to elaborate on these aspects of her initial self-portrait in succeeding images of female artistry. But as the poet progresses in her identification with overtly feminine forms of creation, shells become associated with "beautiful . . . yet static, empty // old thought, old convention" . . . as she draws her old self around after her like a "dead shell." . . . She wants not a shell into which she can withdraw but, on the contrary, an escape from entrapment. . . . The locked-in image of female sexuality and creativity provided by male culture, complete with its emphasis on purity and impenetrability, is finally a "jar too circumscribed," . . . and the poet renounces "fixed indigestible matter / such as shell, pearl, imagery // done to death" . . . in her attempt to forge more liberating and nourishing images of survival.

In her next attempt to recover the scepter of power that is Caduceus, H. D. wittily decides not to become the rod itself, which is transformed into an innocent blade of grass, but the snake/worm which travels up the rod in a circuitous spiral toward heaven. (pp. 201-02)

It is significant that Denise Levertov centers her discussion of H. D.'s poetry on [the sequence of worm poems in *The Walls Do Not Fall,* see excerpt above], voicing her appreciation for poetry which provides "doors, ways in, tunnels through." (p. 203)

Of course, women from the Fates to Madame Defarge have traditionally been associated with the spinning of fate, the weaving of webs, the ensnaring of men with serpentine allies or embodiments. But H. D. and Levertov reinvent the Lamia-Eve, testimony to modern defilement of Isis, in the innocuous form of the lowly worm who recalls the speaker of Psalm 22: after crying out, "I am a worm and no man; a reproach of men, and despised of the people," the petitioner in the Psalm asks that the God "who took me out of the womb" provide a loving substitute for that loss. Both H. D. and Levertov emphasize the ways in which the worm, like the woman, has been despised by a culture that cannot stop to appreciate an artistry based not on elucidation or appropriation but on homage and wonder at the hidden darkness, the mystery. Both emphasize the worm's ability to provide another womb for its own death and resurrection. With visionary realism, both insist that the only paradise worth seeing exists not behind or beyond but within the dust. While "the keepers of the secret, / the carriers, the spinners" of such "Earth Psalms" are surely men as well as women, they are all associated with traditionally female arts of weaving, with uniquely female powers of reproducing life, and with a pre-Christian tradition that embraces gods (like Ra, Osiris, Amen) who are "not at all like Jehovah." . . . (pp. 203-04)

The "other side, the Hiddenness" which H. D. and Levertov seek to penetrate consists precisely of those experiences unique to women which have been denied a place in our publicly acknowledged culture, specifically the experiences of female sexuality and motherhood. (p. 204)

[The need for self-transformation leads to] H. D.'s confusion when she feels ready "to begin a new spiral" . . . but finds herself thrown back on outworn vocabularies and the terrible feeling that she has failed to achieve metamorphosis. . . .

Perhaps she has failed because she has tried to evoke Ra, Osiris, Amen, Christ, God, All-father and the Holy Ghost, all the while knowing that she is an "initiate of the secret wisdom, / bride of the kingdom." . . . Specifically, she recalls now that the spinners who keep the secret that links humanity to the ancient wisdom are aspects of the female goddess, Isis. She must remain true to her own perspective. . . . (p. 205)

Seeking the "one-truth," to become as wise as "scorpions, *as serpents,*" . . . H. D. can now read her own personal psychic map to find the external realities. . . . [The stars toward which the worm moves in its slow spiral toward the sky] contain a promise of revelation not very different from shells and cocoons, which can also disclose secret treasures. Modern words, too, may reveal hidden meanings, thereby relinquishing their alien impenetrability, if the poet can somehow perceive their coded, palimpsestic status. . . . H. D. learns how to decipher what that other H. D.—Humpty Dumpty—called "portmanteaus," words which open up like a bag or a book into compartments. By means of lexical reconstruction, she begins to see the possibility of purging language of its destructive associations and arbitrariness. Viewing each word as a puzzle ready to be solved and thereby freed not only of modernity but also of contingency, H. D. begins to hope that she can discover secret, coded messages. Surely these must be subversive to warrant their being so cunningly concealed by her culture. (pp. 205-06)

Although the walls still do not fall, continuing to testify to the divisions and barriers between people, between historical periods, within consciousness itself, they also preserve remnants of written messages—anagrams and cryptograms—which, by providing the link from the present back to the past, allow H. D. to evade the destructive definitions of reality provided by those who utilize the word for modern mastery.

The poet's response in the subsequent volumes of the *Trilogy* to the shattered fragmentation of her world is stated in the first poem of *Tribute to the Angels:* dedicating herself to Hermes Trismegistus, patron of alchemists, H. D. undertakes not merely the archeological reconstruction of a lost past, but also a magical transfiguration not unlike Christ's creation of the sustaining loaves and fishes or the transubstantiation of bread and water into body and blood. Since alchemical art has traditionally been associated with fiery purification that resurrects what is decomposing in the grave into a divine and golden form, even the destructive lightning and bombs can now be associated with melting that fuses a new unity, heat that transforms the contents of the dross in the alchemist's bowl into the philosopher's stone. The seashell of *The Walls Do Not Fall* becomes a testimony to such displacement, reappearing as a bowl which is cauldron, grave, and oven, yet another womb in which a new jewel can be created. Now the poet sees the function of the poem/bowl as the transformative redefinition of language itself. . . . Seeking a noncoercive vocabulary, a new language that will consecrate what has been desecrated by her culture, H. D. tries to re-establish the primacy of what masculine culture has relegated to a secondary place as "feminine." (pp. 207-08)

The miraculous transformation in the alchemical bowl and the equally mysterious flowering of the rod find their culmination in [a] revelation of the muse who is not only the veiled goddess, Persephone, the *Sanctus Spiritus, Santa Sophia,* Venice, Isis, and Mary, but most importantly the female spirit liberated from precisely these mystifications. . . . (p. 209)

As she evokes and thereby reinterprets the inherited signs of her culture which are said to contain the secret wisdom necessary for the attainment of paradise, H. D. implies that "the letter killeth but the spirit giveth life" (2 Corinthians 3:6). It is life that she sees finally created in the crucible "when the jewel / melts" and what we find is "a cluster of garden-pinks / or a face like a Christmas-rose." . . . In the final book of the *Trilogy,* the escaping fragrance of such flowering within the pristine glass of a jar represents the poet's success in finding a form that can contain without confining. No longer surrounded by splintered shards, H. D. makes of her jars symbols of aesthetic shape not unlike those of Wallace Stevens or Hart Crane, beautiful and complete objects but also transparencies through which a healing content is made manifest. Purified of their opacity, shell, bowl, and box are now ready to reveal their previously secret and therefore inaccessible hoard. This promise of release is realized fully in *The Flowering of the Rod:* dedicated to the Lady who has escaped conventionally defined categories, the poet readies herself for flight as she asks us to "leave the smouldering cities below," . . . the place of deathly skulls, to follow the quest of Christ, who was "the first to wing / from that sad Tree" . . . and whose journey is similar to that of the snow-geese circling the Arctic or the mythical migratory flocks seeking paradise.

Not only does H. D. move further back in time in this third volume of the *Trilogy,* but her initial focus on seemingly insignificant animals and her subsequent naming of angelic powers seem to have made it possible for her to finally create human characters as she retells the story of the birth and death of Christ from the unexpected perspective of two participants in the gospel—Kaspar the Magian and Mary Magdala. Furthermore, after two sequences of poems progressing by allusive associations, complex networks of imagery, and repetitive, almost liturgical invocations, the final book of the *Trilogy* embodies the emergence of the poet's sustained voice in a story—if not of her own making—of her own perspective. She takes an unusual stance toward the ancient story to distinguish her vision: claiming to see "what men say is-not," to remember what men have forgot . . . , she sets out to testify to an event known by everyone but as yet unrecorded. . . . (pp. 210-11)

Like Christ, who was himself "an outcast and a vagabond," . . . and like the poet who is identified with the thief crucified by His side, both Kaspar and Mary are aliens in their society. (p. 211)

Only after we have recognized the seemingly antithetical wise man and the whore as common representatives of reverence for the ancient principles of female fertility and creativity does H. D. . . . fully describe the vision granted to Kaspar through the intervention of Mary. Here, at the climax of the *Trilogy,* Kaspar recalls the poet's experience with the Lady, for he is graced with a remembrance of "when he saw the light on her hair / like moonlight on a lost river." . . . In a fleck or a flaw of a jewel on the head of one of three crowned ladies, Kaspar discovers "the whole secret of the mystery." . . . He sees the circles of islands and the lost center island, Atlantis; he sees earth before Adam, Paradise before Eve. Finally, he hears a spell in an unknown language which seems to come down from prehistorical times as it translates itself to him:

> Lilith born before Eve
> and one born before Lilith,
> and Eve; we three are forgiven,
> we are three of the seven
> daemons cast out of her. . . .

This is an extremely enigmatic message, but it does seem to imply that a matriarchal genealogy had been erased from recorded history when this ancient female trinity was exorcized as evil, cast out of human consciousness by those who would begin in the Garden with Eve. Since Lilith is a woman who dared pronounce the Ineffable Name and who was unabashed at articulating her sexual preferences, her presence among the crowned or crucified queens seems to promise a prelapsarian vision quite different from that of Genesis: Lilith, Eve, and the unnamed daemon are three of the seven who establish a link back to Kaspar's pagan daemons; together they promise a submerged but now recoverable time of female strength, female speech, and female sexuality, all of which have mysteriously managed to survive, although in radically subdued ways, incarnate in the body of Mary Magdala. As a healer, a shaman of sorts, Kaspar has in a sense recaptured Mary's stolen soul, her lost ancestors; he has established the matriarchal genealogy that confers divinity upon her.

Reading Mary like a palimpsest, Kaspar has fully penetrated the secret of the mystery. H. D. then reverses the chronology of his life, moving backward from his confrontation with this Mary over the jars of myrrh to his delivery of the gift of myrrh to the Virgin Mary. (pp. 211-13)

Dramatically ending at the beginning, moving from Apocalypse to Genesis, from death to birth, from history to mystery, H. D. illustrates the cyclical renewal she personally seeks of dying into life. Calling our attention to her own narrative principles, H. D. proclaims: "I have gone forward. / I have gone backward." . . . [Her] point is precisely the need of going backward in time to recover what has been lost in the past, for this justifies her own progress backward in chronological time throughout the *Trilogy:* proceeding from the modern times of London in *The Walls Do Not Fall* to the medieval cities of *Tribute to the Angels* and back to the ancient deserts of Israel in *The Flowering of the Rod,* she dedicates herself to finding the half-erased traces of a time "When in the company of the gods / I loved and was loved." . . . Such a discovery, as we have seen, involves not a learning but a remembering. However, instead of moving backward in a linear, sequential manner, she chooses three time bands that seem to be relatively self-contained, like ever-narrowing circles enclosing some still point of origin. Furthermore, she calls our attention to the disconnectedness of her three time spheres by isolating each within a book of the *Trilogy*. These three distinct periods in time, when taken in themselves, are senseless and directionless, each repeating the other. . . . (p. 213)

The poet who understands the palimpsestic symbols of the past in today's imagery can interpret the "mysterious enigma" that merges "the distant future / with most distant antiquity." . . . Similarly, seeing down the "deep, deep-well // of the so-far unknown / depth of pre-history," Kaspar realizes "a *point* in time— // he called it a fleck or a flaw in a gem" on a circlet of gems on a lady's head. . . . Since historical time is envisioned as a series of circles enclosing a prehistoric center, H. D. can describe how Kaspar heard "an echo of an echo in a shell,". . . a language he had never heard spoken and which seems translated "as it transmuted its message // through spiral upon spiral of the shell / or memory that yet connects us // with the drowned cities of pre-history." . . . (p. 214)

In *Tribute to Freud,* H. D. returns to the image of the echoing shell when she describes how her unspoken expressions of gratitude go on singing

> like an echo of an echo in a shell—very far away yet very near—the very shell substance of my outer ear and the curled involuted or convoluted shell skull, and inside the skull, the curled, intricate, hermit-like mollusk, the brain-matter itself.

Clearly the spiraling echoes of the shell are a way of recognizing the intimate yet convoluted relationship between a central origin and its distant reaches. (pp. 214-15)

Echo, we should remember, was punished for her only "failing," her fondness for talk, by being deprived of the power of speaking first. In this respect, she serves as a paradigm of the secondary status of women who have traditionally been reduced to supporting, assuaging, serving, and thereby echoing the work, wishes, and words of men. Specifically, she serves as a model for H. D.'s sense of her own belatedness as she repeats the warped words she experiences as prior authorities on her own spiritual and psychic experiences. Echo does manage, however, to express her desires, even as she mocks the speech of those she mimics. Like Echo, H. D. felt cursed because she was denied control over her own speech, destined to repeat the language of another's making, and therefore hidden, if not obliterated, from her own creations. However, just as Echo manages to express her desires, even making sexual advances by dropping certain words and altering her inflection, H. D. manages to get her secrets sung, making of her echoes a personal response to the literary and linguistic conventions she inherits. Moreover, as a symbol of retreat from the danger of meaning into protective obscurity, the echoing shell is an understandably attractive image for H. D., who can define her art as "merely" derivative. Using the language of another's creation is, after all, a foolproof defense against being defined by one's verse and thereby confined within the prisonhouse of language. H. D.'s story is always "different yet the same as before," . . . and therefore "only" a repetition. Herein lies both the strength and the weakness of her art, as well as the reason why the echo is yet another infinitely decipherable (and therefore indecipherable) palimpsest.

Whether derivative or transmuted sound, however, the spiraling echo of the shell makes all of the enclosures of the first two poems comprehensible as metamorphoses of the circle. The shell with its spherical pearl, the bowl containing the gold, the boxes hatching butterflies, even the jars are circles surrounding a magical potent center. . . . The poet seeks this center because it can serve as an escape from the repetitions of history and because it is an entrance to creative stasis. Such a center is neither temporally nor spatially bound: its potential for unfolding gains it extension in space as detemporalizes the present into an emblem of both the past and the future. (pp. 215-16)

Participating in a mystical literary tradition that extends from Dante to Roethke, H. D. evokes the unbroken, unfolding circle to satisfy her longing to "equilibrate" . . . the antagonisms between desert and arctic, spring and winter, silence and sound, to heal the struggle between father and mother, thereby establishing a harmony dramatized by the recognition of commonality between Kaspar and Mary Magdala and by the image of the androgynous center of the flower. Seeking to be drawn into the center, H. D. finds in resurrection "a sense of direction" taking her "straight to the horde and plunder, / the treasure, the store-room, // the honeycomb" to "food, shelter, fragrance." . . . While H. D. never denies the place of men in such an origin, she does end the *Trilogy* with an emphasis on the feminine that extends Kaspar's consciousness of prelapsarian time as a time of woman worship: she celebrates the baby or myrrh cradled in the arms of a woman whose sex is represented as a circle on a stem ♀—the sacred *ankh* which is the symbol of life in Egypt. The medieval definition of God as the sphere whose center is everywhere and whose circumference is nowhere has been radically feminized by a writer who sees the outstretched wings of the butterfly or the beauty of the "lunar rainbow" . . . as alternative examples of the "arc of perfection." . . . Here again H. D. serves as a paradigm for other women writers. . . . (p. 217)

H. D. would not and does not deprive the center of its inaccessible mystery or the circumference of its distance from origin. On the contrary, as one of Jung's precursors, she testifies to the continued need for approaching the center, for retelling and rewriting and adding to a palimpsest even as she realizes that such an approach is a regression, and that—as the word "re-cover" implies—she hides what she seeks to reveal. Denise Levertov celebrates just this reverence for the unknowable in H. D.'s poetry when she explains that H. D. went "further, further out of the circle of known light, further in toward an unknown center." This center is the secret; for example, the final transaction between Kaspar and Mary Magdala which is never represented in the *Trilogy* or even adequately explained. If in some ways Kaspar the Magian was right that "no secret was safe with a woman," . . . he nevertheless failed to realize that the woman who models her speech on that of Echo or Sibyl, or (less hopefully) Cassandra or Philomel, would be telling a secret that retains the power of its hidden mystery. Singing a spell which conforms to none of the words she had ever heard spoken, H. D. reveals the ways in which one woman mythologizes herself and her gender, asserting herself as the center of the universe in a radical reversal and revision of the inherited images she so brilliantly echoes. (pp. 217-18)

Susan Gubar, "The Echoing Spell of H. D.'s 'Trilogy'," in Contemporary Literature *(© 1978 by the Board of Regents of the University of Wisconsin System), Vol. 19, No. 2, Spring, 1978, pp. 196-218.*

RACHEL BLAU DuPLESSIS

In her life's work, H. D. returned constantly to a pattern of personal relations that she found perplexing and felt to be damaging to herself and other women: thralldom to males in romantic and spiritual love. In her later writing, she invented a number of strategies to transform this culturally mandated and seductive pattern of male-female relations. Romantic thralldom is a feature of many literary plots because of conventions surrounding love and marriage, quest and vocation, hero and heroine. These conventions could be termed "Scripts" for both literary plots and personal relations. In order to transform these psychocultural scripts, H. D. had to invent in her works patterns for male-female relationships less damaging than, but . . . as satisfying as those she and other women had experienced.

Romantic thralldom is an all-encompassing, totally defining love between unequals. . . . Viewed from a critical, feminist perspective, the sense of completion or transformation that often accompanies thralldom in love has the high price of obliteration and paralysis, for the entranced self is entirely defined by another. (pp. 178-79)

Female thralldom occurs with startling, even dismal frequency throughout H. D.'s published and unpublished works. In particular, H. D. was vulnerable to the power of what she termed the "héros fatal," a man whom she saw as her spiritual similar, an artist, a healer, a psychic. Again and again this figure that she conspired to create betrayed her; again and again she was reduced to fragments from which her identity had once more to be painfully reconstructed. She states, for instance, that one famous "Héros" —D. H. Lawrence—"conditioned me to deception, loss, destruction," and that another, "Lord Howell," "was the perfected Image" of this former lover. Though H. D. lived for many years as the companion of Winifred Bryher, her work returned obsessively to the "héros" figure and to the damage she suffered in her relations with him. Whatever personal and sexual arrangements she made could not obliterate the culturally reinforced plot of thralldom. She had to remake this psychocultural pattern in her writing in order fully to break with it.

The impact of sexual subordination on H. D. as woman and artist can be seen in two autobiographical novel-memoirs written about her early adulthood: the unpublished *Her* (c. 1927), an ungainly but interesting work which justifies H. D.'s decision not to marry Pound, and the more serious and desperate *Bid Me to Live* (1960), a *roman à clef* about the London Bohemian set during the First World War. In tandem, these works describe the situation of a woman of artistic leanings and achievements within a male-dominated society in the early part of this century. In every role in which she is cast, the woman is unsatisfied and tormented: as courtesan, as deceived wife, as muse, as consort. She is prevented from claiming the end to that torment: equality. (pp. 179-80)

[*Her*] concerns a classic dilemma for woman: the necessity to choose between being a muse for another and being an artist oneself. . . . The heroine's authentic identity, indicated in the image of a tree which recurs throughout the novel, and . . . in the contrast between austere Greek and sensual Roman pantheons, is mirrored and intensified by Her's relationship with Fayne. Fayne represents self-love, self-identification, and a twinship between spiritual sisters. Through Fayne, Her makes contact with herself and her vision. Instead of being George's muse, she takes Fayne as her inspiration.

The name "Her" has a particular meaning bound up with the image of Fayne. Whenever H. D. writes "Her realizes" or "Her says," she is using the wrong form of the pronoun in subject place; and every time this ungrammatical usage occurs, one is jarred into a recognition of the situation of generic woman. Though "Her" is the object form, the very ungainly quality of the name used as the subject of a verb ("Her does," "Her realizes") suggests that we are in the presence of some resistant, stubborn matter which will not be captured. The contradictory features of this striking nickname are brought into focus and then resolved as Her strokes Fayne's forehead with "healing hands" and says, "I will not have her hurt. I will not have Her hurt. She is Her. I am Her. Her is Fayne. Fayne is Her. I will not let them hurt HER." By identifying with another wounded woman, the heroine perceives her own hurt and her own capacity for self-protection. The heroine must love herself through another woman as a sign of selfhood. However, the novel does not deal directly with the alternative loves which are so clearly delineated within it. In any case, thralldom to males has been only temporarily rejected. *Her* is a first skirmish in the almost endless battle of H. D.'s psychic life.

At the end of her life, H. D. returned to this formative World War I period in her novel *Bid Me to Live*. The title epigram, from Herrick, wittily presents the life of the emotions as a playful religion of love:

Bid me to live, and I will live
  Thy Protestant to be:
Or bid me love, and I will give
  A loving heart to thee. . . .

The poem refers to the time in a relationship when adoration is mutual and commands are not burdensome. The novel explores the attempt by Julia and Rafe Ashton to sustain such a "blithe arrangement." But equal comradeship and romantic love appear to be contradictory states. The circumstances faced by the couple—the war, the birth of a dead child—make it difficult, even impossible, to sustain equality and interdependence. She becomes vulnerable, neurasthenic, needy; he is bluff, willful, callous. They fall into stereotypic behavior, their needs at cross-purposes. Therefore the woman in *Bid Me to Live* feels completely inadequate—a sexual failure and a professional anomaly within the group of male artists that surrounds her. (pp. 180-82)

In Julia's encounters with Rico and Rafe, we confront the unedifying spectacle of male poets compelling a female poet to curtail her ambition, to dissolve the complete world she strove for, to concentrate on the item, not on the *oeuvre*. . . . *Bid Me to Live* shows male poets limiting the shape and force of a woman's material by using sexual and personal acceptance as a weapon. Julia's response reveals the internalization and acceptance of these demands, which diminished her ambition and limited or negated her power. The issue is larger than the relationship of these three writers. The encounter raises the question whether male writers, in complicity with prescribed roles for women, have helped create poetesses where there could have been poets. This is the issue underlying the censorship with which H. D. grappled. The stakes were poetic achievement itself. Thralldom to male power had to be attacked; yet it was the most difficult thing to attack. For the pain of thralldom seemed to fire H. D.'s creativity even as it undercut the conditions necessary for her fullest, uncensored flowering.

While resistance is one solution to thralldom, H. D. also tries to articulate a creative and psychic power transcending the claims of romantic love. (pp. 185-86)

H. D. was trying to construct some perspective that avoided the constant subordination of the woman to the man in normal sexual and cultural life. In her view, men and women are equals in the spiritual realm, not seeking the distinctions of fixed sex roles, but rather a mutual suffusion of insight and wisdom. (p. 187)

H. D.'s profound psychic damage from sexual and spiritual thralldom continued to torment her. The kinds of rejections she suffered were coupled in her mind with the First World War as linked aspects of that destructive force which shattered the possibility of a cultural life. Yet the themes of the first war recurred to be resolved during World War II, which H. D. spent, by choice, in the London of the Blitz. In her inner patterning of these events, the first war was death, and the second was rebirth. The long-awaited consummation of her poetic force did occur; the evidence can be seen in the brilliance of *Trilogy*, for its symbols of resurrection, its vision of a new city, and its invention of the role of Mary Magdalene constitute the materials of a psychic and cultural reconstruction. At the same time, however, H. D. returned to the forms of sexual polarization and entrapment represented by the thralldom of women to men. (p. 188)

The strategy of outright resistance and confrontation of male by female forces is not paramount in H. D.'s poetry. The transposition of conflicts to a spiritual area beyond conflict . . . sometimes makes H. D. lose contact with her materials. I surmise that these exits from the script of thralldom do not wholly succeed for H. D., although the transposition of conflicts into a spiritual area of unification remains an important end in her writing. The first option represents conflict and defiance, the second represents sheer resolution, unity by the suppression of conflict. Only in the final solution to romantic thralldom—what I term the sufficient family—do both conflict and resolution exist in a complex and nuanced balance, with a full account both of the engendering conflict and of the transpositions that create resolution. This solution, paramount in *Helen in Egypt,* builds a new structure of relationships to substitute for thralldom. (pp. 189-90)

H. D. wrote this poem in the aftermath of strong spiritual and psychic attraction to men on whom she had depended for some kind of self-justification. She suffered rejection; her response is the poem. But although the poem was provoked by rejection, within it the pattern of thralldom is broken: the same needs are met by different relationships, and nurturance and vision are achieved without sexual or spiritual damage from men.

Helen in Egypt is engaged with one particular literary "order of reality," a prominent myth of Western culture. H. D. has not precisely displaced the *Iliad* or the story of the war following an abduction; that tale is taken for granted as the plot that precedes this new alignment of characters and actions. But criticism of the epic realm is present, if indirect. Before the poem begins, H. D. has replaced the sexually centered woman and her bellicose lover with two liminal figures, wavering between worlds of fragmentation and wholeness: Achilles, the vulnerable "New Mortal," and an incubating psyche, still in chrysalis but nonetheless fully winged (Helen-Thetis). H. D. chooses her characters not because of their capacity for sensual love or savage war but because of their visionary ability to crystallize the dissolved or latent meanings hidden in the former story. The characters act as catalyzing precipitants of nonepic material already "dissolved" in culture. By postulating that another shape to traditional stories occurs necessarily, H. D. mutes the critique she is making. In her view, stories are not created but recovered; they are not new-made but really old. *Helen in Egypt* is the archeological site where those recovered stories are found. . . . H. D., like other women writers, had difficulty establishing an authority sufficient to remake a culturally sanctioned story. So the story is "the same"—the old legend—when she felt her own authority most weakly, and "different"—the "flame of thoughts"—when she could plumb the depths of her desire for critique and transformation. (pp. 191-93)

The form of *Helen in Egypt* also dramatizes the question of the poet's authority to remake this story, and that question becomes part of the strain of remaking it. There are prose passages preceding every poem which summarize the contents of that section. This is helpful, because the material is difficult and obscure. But the prose also has the effect of making the events seem more elusive, challenging both their place in time and their reality. Sometimes the prose passages make a statement implying that something has happened, while the poetry which comes later poses the same fact as a question. After having read the two statements, the reader is unsure whether or not something has occurred. While generally the prose and poetry are simple retellings of the same events, at other points a degree of difference is emphasized: the event is first present, then absent or obscured.

The poem concerns the parallel quests of Helen and Achilles which are not journeys to each other, but quests for access to the unifying mother. Helen's quest is emphasized, but both have found Thetis at the end; this is what finally unites them. (p. 193)

[All] the males in *Helen in Egypt*—Achilles, Paris, and Theseus (the figure of Freud)—have begun to form a postheroic personality, and all give Helen permission to make her quest, which must include understanding herself as a post-romantic woman. The granting of permission by all three males is a female fantasy, based on extraordinary need for male approval and fear of male judgment. All the male characters know of and approve of her desire for reintegration within Thetis, the mother: all instruct her in one way or another to "call on Thetis." . . . Yet they want different Helens. She must avoid the polarized roles which the two lovers give her while at the same time retaining their approval. . . . [Her] multiple identities indicate her own lack of inner integration. This dilemma is solved when she transcends these opposites through the healing mediation of Theseus in Part II, who "reparents" her, acting as both mother and father and healing the divisions found in the traditional nuclear family. She becomes Helen-Thetis in Part III, uniting Troy and Greece and uniting her own torn consciousness in love and death.

Making Achilles and Helen into fellow questers is the first move in H. D.'s strategy for breaking the script of romantic thralldom. The lover and woman are imagined as brother-sister questers, so that totally spiritual, not sexual, forces define the relationship. The quests of Helen and Achilles are finally not journeys toward love for each other, but a single quest to identify the source: the mother. Further, Helen avoids a replay of the drama of sexual thralldom by asking Paris, too, to join her on a brother-sister quest. Paris then emerges as Helen's child by Achilles; for the lover, displaced from dominance in the plot of thralldom, can return in the role of a child. (pp. 195-96)

The "child-mother, yourself" is a way of moving beyond both war and romantic love, beyond the strains of the heroic and romantic scripts. Helen is both the Great Mother, avatar of Thetis, and the baby in her mother's arms. "Helen in Hellas forever" is the climactic, reverberating phrase which suggests an ongoing exchange of force in the closed circuit of mother-child-mother. . . . This closure solves for H. D. the needs and themes of her major work—the needs for undamaging nurturance and undamaging powers. Helen is the complete family represented by the petals of the nenuphar, but most particularly she is "the child in the father, / the child in the mother," the child-mother herself. . . .

By this set of solutions, H. D. was attempting to end her submission to male power, constructing from available male and female roles, especially from parent and child roles, some set of relationships that would be less emotionally damaging to her as a woman than those she had actually experienced with men. To do this she creates a female quest whose final answer is the central revelation of mother and child, flanked by father and brother; "the thousand-petalled lily" contains and presents all the relations of the sufficient family. . . . (p. 201)

Through the superficially bizarre connections among her characters, H. D. constructed an answer to thralldom to male power, inventing relationships that would make specific kinds of transformations of that damaging script. In the hieroglyph of the sufficient family, a strict division of sexual roles is often retained, but female insight is approved of and assisted as if it were a valued cultural and personal resource. Under the system of romantic thralldom, love, care, and nurturing come with a very high price: sexual bitterness and despair. But in the system of the sufficient family, the father or mother figure, and more rarely the brother, give care and nurturing to the female character without exacting the debilitating price which the male lover always seemed to extort.

Further, in the system of thralldom which H. D. experienced, male power always stood first, and female power was unequal to it. This meant that a man expected a woman to be subsumed under him and to experience a loss of identity, as in *Her*, while the woman at once desired to be equal and experienced guilt about that desire. Certainly it is an old story. Within the sufficient family, rather than being subsumed in an unequal power relation, the woman has two special sources of force—in biological creation (as the mother through the child) and in self-creation, as the child through herself as mother—on the psyche quest.

While the sufficient family composed of brother-sister questers, reparenting fathers and mothers, and the psyche madonna is not the product of any social or political analysis, this family could nonetheless be taken as an accurate postulation of all the relationships that would have to be transformed in order for a new kind of male-female sexual and spiritual relation to exist; that is, in order to end romantic thralldom. Some sense of the enormity of the task of cultural reconstruction is revealed by the immense changes that H. D. makes in her poetic family. Since psychocultural patterns are learned within the family, it must surely be recast in order to change our images of women, culture, and society. (pp. 202-03)

Rachel Blau DuPlessis, "Romantic Thralldom in H. D.," in Contemporary Literature *(© 1979 by the Board of Regents of the University of Wisconsin System), Vol. 20, No. 2, Spring, 1979, pp. 178-203.*

* * *

HALPERN, Daniel 1945-

Halpern, an American poet, is noted for his cool, almost emotionless poetry in which he explores man's interior landscapes. *Life among Others* is his most recent collection. (See also *Contemporary Authors,* Vols. 33-36, rev. ed.)

PETER COOLEY

Traveling on Credit has an ease, depth, assurance and picaresque range of subject matter rare for a first volume. Halpern takes us out of the house, out of America, but remains himself in any adventure, mastering experience while in it. "I've been after the exotic for years," the book begins, but this poet shows us (in the title poem and elsewhere) that the journey is made with imagination and language as much as lifted thumb. . . .

Though his catalogues, his peripatetic quality and his flipness relate him to the "New York poets," Halpern focuses on an image just long enough to take it, make it, without the obsessive repetitiousness one has come to associate with that movement recently. He's hip *and* sophisticated, somebody to watch. (pp. 83-4)

Peter Cooley, "Turning, Turning: 7 Poets Moving In and Moving Out," in Michigan Quarterly Review *(copyright © The University of Michigan, 1974), Vol. XIII, No. 1, Winter, 1974, pp. 79-84.**

Calm and melancholy in tone, the poems in [*Life among Others*] are diminished, weaker than his earlier work, at best simple sketches or dream scenes. A few, like the last piece, "I am a Dancer," have a strong, clear voice, but most are less elegant, less animated, and rich in metaphor, a backing away from illuminating intelligence towards blankness, suspension, "white images that lift away." Nature is good, man evil in the scheme proclaimed by the title; and an orderly life excludes relationships, so that one lives among, not with, others.

"Poetry: 'Life among Others'," in Virginia Quarterly Review *(copyright, 1978, by the* Virginia Quarterly Review, *The University of Virginia), Vol. 54, No. 3 (Summer, 1978), p. 100.*

JAY PARINI

[*Life Among Others* is Daniel Halpern's] best work to date, not different in kind but in degree from *Traveling on Credit* and *Street Fire*. The new poems intensify and extend Halpern's earlier visions of isolation and loss, and they push outward into the real world of lovers, houses, friends, food. The dreamlike quality of his previous collections persists, as does the claustrophobic aspect of heightened self-consciousness, but with a difference. A newfound transparency, an almost embarrassing directness and simplicity, presents itself here; the poet casts a net over (into) his experience of himself in the world. This is psychic fishing, so to speak, an attempt to retrieve from strange personal depths something of the subliminal energies which charge the dream-world with meaning.

Halpern obliterates normal boundaries of day and night. In doing so, he also blurs the usual limits between self and others or between subject and object. . . . Halpern traverses an interior world in pursuit of what Yeats called "radical innocence," a condition in which the world outside of the mind and the world within find a natural balance, a dwelling in the evening air. Halpern longs for this sense of equilibrium and acceptance wherein "You are no longer the stranger / who made too little sense."

This ideal state of being remains, as it must, at the edge of Halpern's experience, a luminous stillness like a clearing deep in some dark wood. (pp. 117-18)

With eery precision, Halpern discovers the intersections of consciousness at various levels; he generates a sense of being wound backward into memories, collective and personal. The epigraph to "Long Distance" (taken from Kierkegaard) isolates this sense of concentric worlds: "Back in the world in which we live, far in the background, lies another world." This criss-crossing of layers thickens as the poet moves rapidly between past and present events, between memories and dreams. . . . (p. 118)

Life Among Others has its weaknesses: some lame rhythms, some pancake flat lines ("I sit on the edge of the bed / and think about this"), some mannerisms ("My 800-pound arm / is sex, all man between us"). One has, indeed, to get used to Halpern's laconic style, his refusal to make similes or "pretty" lines. The poems derive from conversation, which makes the title of this book all the more appropriate. Although a good number of the poems are interior monologues, strictly speaking, most are concerned with the tensions between the individual sensibility and the world-at-large. In general, Halpern examines these tensions with admirable detachment, much less self-consciously than before. His search for the "central mind" is begun here and points a way into his future work. (p. 119)

Jay Parini, "Short Reviews: 'Life among Others'," in Chicago Review *(reprinted by permission of* Chicago Review; *copyright © 1979 by* Chicago Review*), Vol. 30, No. 4, Spring, 1979, pp. 117-19.*

WILLIAM PRATT

Solitude. Silence. Stillness. Whiteness. Otherness.

These words and others like them resonate through [*Life Among Others,*] a sequence of short poems that seem to be about almost nothing. But the nothing penetrates, as Paul Valéry once said. Here, deliberate reticence sometimes becomes potent with meaning. . . . *Life Among Others* is a quiet book, like a conversation in whispers, conducted by strangers who meet for the first time but somehow seem intimate. Their world is the city—no particular city, but a peopled space where meetings are casual and inconclusive, anonymous encounters with others, faceless souls in limbo seeking some human contact. The voice that speaks them is less a talker than a silent listener, one who says, "My work is to stand still and see everything."

This . . . collection of Daniel Halpern's poetry is mostly impressive for what it is *not* about, for he seems to have passed through the rather slick cosmopolitan world of his earlier books, *Traveling on Credit* (1972) and *Street Fire* (1975), where exotic, forbidden places beckon with a leer, into a purer world where everything is white, clear, transparent: "It is winter. The trees / march away from the window / like the ghostly skeltons of fish." Lines such as these are reminiscent of the later poems of Wallace Stevens, and it is probably significant that this volume begins with a few verses from "The Final Soliloquy of the Interior Paramour." But Halpern's poems move at their own pace through this bare inner landscape, with an air of attentive and at times compelling anticipation, as if the poet were on tiptoe, a somnambulist walking through a dream. The dream never wholly materializes, but the mood of expectancy lingers, like breath in cold air, giving hope that someday, perhaps in his next book, Halpern may stumble on a revelation of what all this stillness means. It is a faint hope, but amid the myriad slim, forgettable volumes of poems, it is something. (pp. 293-94)

William Pratt, "World Literature in Review: 'Life among Others'," in World Literature Today *(copyright 1979 by the University of Oklahoma Press), Vol. 53, No. 2, Spring, 1979, pp. 293-94.*

DAVE SMITH

For me the severely spare and squeezed distillate of human experience in most of Daniel Halpern's third book, *Life Among Others,* is interesting but not, finally, enough. The poems haven't a sufficient dirt on their feet, however earnest their hearts, however they fully disclose an aesthetic intelligence. Twenty of Halpern's thirty-six poems commence with the same monosyllabic conjunction of a personal pronoun and a verb of the most modest action, if any, ("I take the hand of others.") which makes a flat statement whose value depends on our interest in Halpern's emotional life, his travel, or his ennui. I would guess he has come to a dead end mannerism not unlike "It is night. The snow is falling." . . . [Yet] beautiful poems have a habit of rising out of the most arid zones. . . . Three of Halpern's poems seem to do as much as we might ask and more; they are "The Hero at Midnight," "Letter To The Midwest," and "The Dance." If we are lucky, and if we look for what is and not what isn't there, we may see more poems with Halpern's own stamp of joy, such as ["The Dance"]. . . . Mr. Halpern is dancing pretty nicely in his poem and I am dancing for the pleasure it gives me. . . . (p. 33)

Dave Smith, "Dancing through Life among Others: Some Recent Poetry from Younger American Poets," in The American Poetry Review *(copyright © 1979 by World Poetry, Inc.; reprinted by permission of Dave Smith), Vol. 8, No. 3, May-June, 1979, pp. 29-33.**

PETER STITT

Daniel Halpern's *Life Among Others* has been criticized for the stance expressed by its title—the speaker of these poems is seen as an observer of rather than a participant in life, as one who doesn't live *with* others. It is assumed that this situation weakens the book, that the reader's sympathies cannot be given to a protagonist so withdrawn from humanity, seemingly so cold to it. This view, I think, ignores certain important features of the book. In many of its poems, the speaker does in fact reach out to, and express real sympathy for, other human beings. Then there is the tone of most of the poems, which seems to me more stunned and psychically defensive than downright cold. The book has an inner plot of sorts, and we must attend to this if we are to understand the speaker's seeming coldness.

It is not until the second of the book's two sections that we learn the reason for the speaker's strange withdrawal from humankind—a broken love affair. This theme is carried by several poems—"For You" and "I Hear Nothing" among them—but appears centrally in the beautifully written "Sad Endings," which concludes:

> And how simple it all is. Someone finally just walks
> away. It might be sunset, but it mustn't be.
> The one who leaves is moved
> less than the left,
> but both are touched, and touched in different ways.
> One leaves, one remains:
> For you who go, for me who stays, two autumns.

The pacing and precision, the rhythmical balance of the phrases, are impressive, and I like the self-conscious literary joke in the second line. Meanwhile, the words tell of pain and loss, said to have a greater effect on the abandoned speaker than on his departing lover.

It is as though this experience has led the speaker to choose solitude for a while, to seek companionship in his memory and his imagination rather than in reality. . . . It is chiefly through memory, imagination, and dream that the speaker maintains contact with society.

This stance is almost entirely solipsistic, and seems to place Halpern squarely in the middle of the New York School, amid the Sons of Marcel Proust. Work of this sort generally has a strong imaginative charm, as in the closest thing to a love poem in the first section of Halpern's book—"Person Smoking." . . . In the purest solipsistic way, imagination controls and determines the course of reality in this poem. So it is throughout most of the book.

What finally draws me most strongly to these poems is the quality of Halpern's writing. The level of craftsmanship here is very high, and shows itself in passages as in entire poems. The language is generally very clear, simple, precise, but allows for startling effects sometimes: "the air of memory, // the distal air of avatars." The imagery too is precise, striking: "the palms flap, rooted / birds with green tropical wings." Occasionally Halpern's images sound like John Ashbery's: "Outside another cheery day is going on. / The gay life in the sun that breeds / the darkness that lasts into night. / . . . The days last / as long as they can."

Halpern's technical excellence shows best in complete poems, where he is clearly in control at all times. . . . [For example, "Photograph"] is a poem of deep feeling—directed, it is worth noticing, towards an "other," a human being separate from the speaker. The poem is unified by not just the concept of feeling but also by plays on the verb, *to feel*. This is a good book, rich in nuance and in technique, beautifully written and intelligently conceived. Halpern's success as an editor and teacher, as a force in the New York literary scene, may be tending to overshadow his success as a poet, but it shouldn't. This book, his third and best, deserves to be read and admired. (pp. 463-66)

Peter Stitt, "Book Reviews: 'Life among Others'," in The Georgia Review *(copyright, 1979, by the University of Georgia), Vol. XXXIII, No. 2, Summer, 1979, pp. 463-66.*

* * *

HAMBURGER, Michael 1924-

Hamburger is a German-born English poet, translator, and critic. Hamburger has achieved a solid reputation as a poet; in addition, he is the outstanding translator and interpreter of German poetry for English readers. His collected translations of Hölderlin and Hugo von Hofmannsthal are considered definitive. (See also *CLC*, Vol. 5, and *Contemporary Authors*, Vols. 5-8, rev. ed.)

[It] is the combination of poet and critic which makes the special interest of Mr. Hamburger's book [*Reason and Energy*]. Whether he is analysing Hölderlin's "Patmos" or the fifth Hymn of Novalis, Kleist's *Die Marquise von O* . . . or Büchner's *Woyzeck*, or the hysteria of the German Expressionists, it is a poet's preoccupation with their characteristic use of language which provides the insight and the illumination.

At first sight the poets assembled between these covers seem strange bedfellows, and one may well ask what they have in common. The answer is implied in the title—Reason and Energy—taken from an aphorism by Blake which states that "without Contraries there is no progression." All these German poets were the victims of—and were often obsessed with—contraries and contradictions, dichotomies and dualisms. . . .

It is clear that none of these poets ever gets any farther by his "progression" through contraries. And from the Novalis motto which also stands sponsor to his book, it is doubtful whether Mr. Hamburger would have wished them to. He evidently has little liking for the real "progress" through contraries made by the one great German poet who, like Blake, knew this to be a law of existence and acted on the knowledge throughout his life and work—Goethe. From the essay on Hölderlin it might even seem that Mr. Hamburger envisages contraries being resolved, not by accepting them, but rather by denying or abandoning them. But in all fairness it should be noted that the unity of his book is "a theme discovered in retrospect, rather than a thesis driven towards a foregone conclusion," and this, as we know from similar collections of essays brought under a single head, does not always make for clarity of argument at every point. . . .

An important contribution to Hölderlin scholarship is Mr. Hamburger's interpretation of "Friedensfeier," for the discovery and identification of which he was mainly responsible. . . .

[Mr. Hamburger] is not only poet and critic but scholar as well, and these three often warring persons seem in him to live in harmony. The outward and visible signs of their fruitful collaboration are the accurate and poetic translations with which he is able to set the seal on his critical interpretations.

"Studies in German Poetry," in The Times Literary Supplement *(© Times Newspapers Ltd. (London) 1957; reproduced from* The Times Literary Supplement *by permission), No. 2883, May 31, 1957, p. 337.*

M. L. ROSENTHAL

Michael Hamburger is an English poet of recent German ancestry, a fact that makes it easy to understand the unhappy historical consciousness that marks his work. The title of his book, "Weather and Season," seems rather commonplace—until one realizes the importance in it of the two poems, "Homage to the Weather" and "In a Cold Season." The former of these is a beautiful evocation of remembered moments in many places, summoned up by the sudden appearance of bees—"a tide, high tide of golden air"—in a garden. The other is a poem about Eichmann, and about the poet's grandmother who perished in Nazi Germany. The range of Mr. Hamburger's work lies between these extremes.

He is an exquisitely perceptive lyric poet, at his best close in the nature of his talent to Charles Tomlinson, reveling as best he can in each moment's "weather." And he is a poet of modern political Europe, living in our tragic "season." A humanistic intelligence informs his work, and a melancholy constantly eluded through the sudden sensuous awareness of an angle of light, an unexpected color, a blaze of red geranium against the city grime. His long poem "Anachronisms" perhaps best brings together the varied facets of this somewhat complex poetic personality. (p. 10)

M. L. Rosenthal, "Surrender to Despair," in The New York Times Book Review *(© 1963 by The New York Times Company; reprinted by permission), December 22, 1963, pp. 4-5, 10.**

JOHN FULLER

Hamburger writes honestly, without fudging his feelings, but he has admitted into [*Travelling*] too many poems that are simply dull. His ironies tend either to lack sharpness (as in a poem on the erroneous bombing of friendly villages in Vietnam) or to be unconvincingly high-pitched (as in the pessimism about the consumer society in 'Report on a Supermarket'). The fact that his perception and criticism in these poems is so unfailingly right does not guarantee their impact on the reader. Yet Hamburger is a poet who blossoms marvellously when he has found the convincing images.

All is saved by those poems which show that he has found them, poems like 'Observer', 'The Cello' or 'For a Family Album'. They are moving poems because there is no spare snarling or flabbiness in them: the feelings are powerfully conveyed by the images, and Hamburger's preponderant sense of the hero as victim, even when he is merely the suffering observer, finds moving expression. They remind one that even when Hamburger is less than exciting he still deserves respect. (p. 414)

John Fuller, "Abandoners," in The Listener *(© British Broadcasting Corp. 1970; reprinted by permission of John Fuller), Vol. 83, No. 2139, February 26, 1970, pp. 413-14.**

M. B. BENN

The second edition [of *Reason and Energy: Studies in German Literature*] contains only one essay that is quite new: a comparative study of Milton and Hölderlin entitled 'The Sublime Art'. . . .

'The Sublime Art' has the merit of dealing with two poets whose likenesses and differences are sufficiently interesting to make a comparative study worth while. And it has the further merit of focussing attention on *Samson Agonistes* and *Empedocles,* works which are genuinely comparable. But it is unfortunate that Hamburger should have chosen to base his interpretation on the *second* version of *Empedocles.* Few firm conclusions can be drawn from the extant brief fragments of this version. . . .

Hamburger is in general too prone to inaccuracy. A candid critic will pardon some slips in a first edition, but not so easily in a second. And it is indeed difficult to understand how Hamburger could have permitted so many obvious errors to reappear in this new issue of his book. . . . In two pages of the essay on Büchner I find no less than six false or misleading statements which have now been published for the second time. (p. 702)

A writer who can be so unreliable in such elementary matters cannot expect to inspire much confidence when dealing with the more difficult questions of critical interpretation and evaluation. (p. 703)

M. B. Benn, "Reviews: 'Reason and Energy: Studies in German Literature'," in The Modern Language Review *(© Modern Humanities Research Association 1972), Vol. 67, No. 3, July, 1972, pp. 702-03.*

RUSSELL DAVIES

It is shameful to be curt with Michael Hamburger, but I feel his *Real Estate* suffers . . . from its travels. It is the fairly depressive constancy of Hamburger's personality that is emphasised by the movement, not the variousness of moods and worlds. The phrase 'Ah well' came somewhere in the book, but it could have come everywhere. A possible exception might have been the long philosophical poem 'Travelling', which Hamburger has been working up to this definitive length for some years; but by now, the title-term seems to me to have become over-loaded with meanings—and the one that suffers the worst damage is that condition of swishing weightlessness of spirit which I suspect the poet most highly prizes. (p. 448)

Russell Davies, "Ah Well," in New Statesman *(© 1977 The Statesman & Nation Publishing Co. Ltd.), Vol. 94, No. 2428, September 30, 1977, pp. 448-49.**

GLAUCO CAMBON

[The miscellaneous pieces about British and German authors contained in *Art as Second Nature: Occasional Pieces 1950-74*] are more than just crumbs of an intellectual banquet, and one remarkable trait is the extent to which they penetrate their respective topics in depth, within the generally very narrow compass allowed by literary journalism. Quick sharp probings they are, and it is no wonder that Hamburger should turn out to be so frequently quotable in a book that introduces itself to us in the demure guise of a miscellany. He is of course a poet, as the short unpretentious self-analysis called "A Writer on his Work" reminds us and as any reader of his translations from Hölderlin knows. . . . (p. 663)

With Hamburger the critic is the right arm of the poet. Only a poet could start an essay-review of Kierkegaard in this fashion: "To review this book is indecent, like giving a running commentary on the eruption of a volcano, from a safe distance." Only a poet could tell the story of Dostoevsky's daughters as Hamburger has done in the verse recently contributed to the first issue of *Canto*. But I am not implying that Hamburger's criticism is colored by his poetical disposition to the point of bias. He is, on the contrary, unbiased, scrupulously text-oriented, refreshingly objective. Technique is something he knows firsthand, as the chapter on "Metrical Verse, Free Verse, and Prose" proves, but listen to its conclusion: "Scansion, at best, confirms what the ear knew all along." And the reader's ear, if consistently applied, has no trouble catching the tone of Hamburger's voice through its several performances in the book that is a book only because of this voice. (pp. 663-64)

Indeed the author of *Reason and Energy* . . . knows the value of "energy" because he never lets go of "reason." He persuades, unrhetorically; he does not overwhelm; and in this he reminds me of that other Apollonian critic, Francis Fergusson. . . . (p. 664)

Glauco Cambon, "The Poet's Self—and the Poem's," in The Sewanee Review *(reprinted by permission of the editor; © 1977 by The University of the South), Vol. LXXXV, No. 4, Fall, 1977, pp. 660-67.**

ANNE STEVENSON

[Reality] is Michael Hamburger's theme, and he seriously confronts it in his title poem [in *Real Estate*] about almost but not quite buying an old house where the 'pure idea of dwelling' seems 'too real for us to meddle with'. All through this book Hamburger explores the endemic dilemmas of the bourgeois poet: what to have, what to dream about, what to kill, what to keep in the garden? This is a thoughtful book by a poet who is more personal than philosophical. (p. 487)

Anne Stevenson, "Snaffling and Curbing," in The Listener *(© British Broadcasting Corp. 1977; reprinted by permission of Anne Stevenson), Vol. 98, No. 2530, October 13, 1977, pp. 486-87.**

* * *

HARRISON, Jim 1937-

Harrison is an American poet and novelist. He is generally considered a poet of the natural world. Sensory images play an important role in his richly descriptive poetry, which is usually set in his native northern Michigan. (See also *CLC*, Vol. 6, and *Contemporary Authors*, Vols. 13-16, rev. ed.)

PARKMAN HOWE

A midlife crisis, as in Oedipus's case, may be distressing; on the other hand, one may discover that an adolescent trauma has simply been delayed several decades.

Take, for example, Joseph, the schoolteaching hero of Jim Harrison's novel of rural Michigan, "Farmer." Joseph has been teaching 20 years in one of those small farming towns where one's private life and the talk of the town tend to be the same. Joseph has also been courting fellow teacher Rosealee since she was widowed by the Korean War. He has always had plans to marry, but the advent of gorgeous, citified Catherine in Joseph's senior class one September postpones that decision for another academic year.

Melodrama? Undoubtedly Harrison draws hollow distinctions between downtown Catherine and hometown Rosealee. But what annoys a reader most about the farmer's discoveries (marriage is a trap, women always scheme against men's tranquility) is that Harrison manages little ironic distance: Joseph's tribulations are treated with teenage seriousness.

The book does have descriptive passages, nonetheless, which flare up appealingly behind the ghost figures, such as the almost indiscernable, relentless coming on of seasons in upstate Michigan. These are the book's true touches.

Parkman Howe, "Two Novels Accent Self-Discovery," in The Christian Science Monitor *(reprinted by permission from* The Christian Science Monitor; *© 1977 The Christian Science Publishing Society; all rights reserved), January 27, 1977, p. 23.**

HAYDEN CARRUTH

[A couple of years ago] *Letters to Yesinin*, a minor masterpiece, was hardly noticed; it was minor because its mood was so thoroughly bleak that probably it could appeal to only a minor segment of sensibility. But it was magnificently written, and I hope somehow it will still find its proper audience. Harrison's new book, *Returning to Earth*, seems not quite so successful—perhaps because it is more low-keyed—but still notable. It is a loose sequence of poems and *aperçus* in which the poet gradually moves away from despair toward a tentative, tenuous acceptance of the natural world, his own world of farm and woodland in northern Michigan. Still, the old pain is dominant—alcoholism, a blind eye, sexual disillusionment, the wrack of the land. "At nineteen I began to degenerate," he writes, meaning, among other things, that then he discovered the degeneration of the world. . . . It is hard-boiled poetry, some of the best of its kind, and one is not surprised to know that Harrison has written very tough novels and many magazine pieces about sports and outdoor life. His poetic vision is at the heart of it all. To stay alive now is primitivism. And that is the hard best that we can know. (p. 87)

Hayden Carruth, "The Passionate Few," in Harper's *(copyright © 1978 by* Harper's Magazine; *all rights reserved; reprinted from the June, 1978 issue by special permission), Vol. 256, No. 1537, June, 1978, pp. 86-9.**

VANCE BOURJAILY

In "Legends of the Fall," the title piece and best of Jim Harrison's collection of three novellas—and it seems fair to rank them good, better and best—the usual way of combining intensity and breadth is discarded with engaging recklessness. In place of a single point of view and a restriction of time, place, number of scenes and characters, Mr. Harrison delivers, in 87 pages, a complete two-generation family saga. . . .

The opening line establishes both the voice and the manner of the epic storyteller, who deals in great vistas and vast distances. . . .

There are tragedies, accidental and inflicted, a vendetta against Tristan [the protagonist] by Irish mobsters, insanity—enough melodrama for a thousand-page novel. Yet in a novel, these events might seem too many and too much. In "Legends of the Fall," the steady, singing, epic voice assures and reassures us that we are hearing—as the title claims—legend, not reality. In compression, unexpectedly, lies credibility.

In "Revenge," where Mr. Harrison tries to expand dramatically upon events, he is less successful—although, like "Legends of the Fall," this story begins auspiciously: "You could not tell, if you were a bird descending (and there was a bird descending, a vulture), if the naked man was dead or alive." Here is one author who knows how to word an invitation. (p. 14)

The time span of the story, a tale of violence unleashed by [Cochran's] adulterous liaison with the wife of a Mexican gang lord, is only a couple of months, long enough for Cochran's recovery and revenge. But the complicated sequence of events that unfolds in this brief span . . . is difficult to make convincing. "Revenge" is readable and at times exciting, but about halfway through, the author is betrayed by his own recognition that his characters must be reduced to believable proportions. It was the right intuition, but what was needed for it to work was the resourceful art to be found in "The Man Who Gave Up His Name."

"Nordstrom had taken to dancing alone." Thus begins the story of a character more interesting, more individual, more *imagined* than Cochran, the protagonist of "Revenge." (pp. 14, 27)

Nordstrom, like Mr. Harrison's other two characters, is compelled to acts of violent revenge on his way to self-realization. But this time the offense is both plausible and preposterous, the sequence of revenge scenes surprising and colorful—almost, in fact, lighthearted. It is in "The Man Who Gave Up His Name" that Mr. Harrison comes closest to combining the traditional economy of the novella with the more comprehensive narrative that works so well for him in the title story. The result is a character more affecting, perhaps, than the others. Though this story may not have the flawless, controlled quality of the title piece, Nordstrom is by far the most sympathetic figure in these three absorbing novellas. (p. 27)

Vance Bourjaily, "Three Novellas: Violent Means," in The New York Times Book Review *(© 1979 by The New York Times Company; reprinted by permission), June 17, 1979, pp. 14, 27.*

KEITH OPDAHL

It's as though William Butler Yeats had written a scenario for Sam Peckinpah. Or as though James Dickey had done a Western—though Dickey wraps the violence in *Deliverance* in a context that attempts to explain and redeem it, while Jim Harrison gives the pure, raw, *macho* daydream. Harrison's three long stories [in *Legends of the Fall*] are full of silent men and lovely women who desire to be ravaged. The bad guys are nightmare figures with names like "Slats" who just won't listen to reason. You have to zap them hard. . . .

The violence [in *Legends of the Fall*] is a norm, a daydream, a fantasy of male power that we could call adolescent if it weren't so clearly middle-aged. . . .

And yet Harrison's style can be pretty decent, as you would expect from a man who has published four volumes of poetry. (p. 23)

Harrison sees the weather and the countryside clearly. He too often doesn't see the characters, and particularly the women. In the first story, "Revenge," the wife who seduced Cochran is vague, which is unforgivable since it is love for her that drives the protagonist. Or is it? You would think, in any case, that Harrison's preference for event over character would make him careful in his plots, but not so. . . .

The best of the stories, "The Man Who Gave Up His Name," suggests that Harrison has better fiction within him. The protagonist is a second-generation Norwegian named Nordstrom who is emotionally reticent. He is also an American who has found our dream empty, and a somewhat clumsy man who is too sincere, too diligent not to act once he has seen through the sham. . . . Nordstrom is a moving figure. At 40, divorced, he dances alone in his apartment, trying to get in touch with himself. A cliché? Perhaps, though Harrison has caught something both recognizable and fresh. Nordstrom is too innocent, too efficient, not to seek health.

At the very least, he points to a peculiar result of our melting pot, for when the stiff-lipped children of Northern European immigrants see a Latin mama hugging and crying and loving in the movies, they don't shrug it off, regretting their ancestors didn't use more garlic. They feel cold, deprived, emotionally stunted, or so Harrison suggests. And in this story they *do* something about it, for Harrison finds his point of departure in the emotional sterility that so many other writers take as their shaping revelation. . . .

This too is fantasy, of course, but it is honest and revealing. Harrison's style is right, too, for it consists mostly of summary, as though we looked from a distance, with a tone that catches the large perspective and mute struggle of the character himself.

But this style cannot redeem the title story, . . . for it is the crudest fantasy of the three, and makes one wonder about the state of the American male. . . .

[It] is really the death of his brother in World War I and then of his true love by a stray bullet that Tristan cannot forgive. He throws away his life in angry, brooding, romantic adventure on the sea and as a bootlegger. Never mind that he hurts other people far more than life hurts him. He is our protagonist, and we are to see him as sensitive rather than as a sorehead. When he lays another brother's pathetically insane wife, whom he had abandoned earlier—the point of his name—we are to understand that he is driven to it by his unhappiness.

Has Harrison seen too many gangster movies, too many Westerns, too much TV? He seems to *believe* all this, though I would guess that he is either doing movie scenarios, attempting to tap into the great American Dream Machine, . . . or has trained himself as a poet to be too honest, too direct to soften these American fantasies. They are not after all so very different from Grimm's fairy tales. The bad guys must be destroyed. The good guy provides a catharsis of self-pity and resentment.

Every once in a while someone like Calvin Trillin confesses his hunger for Twinkies, as though his body had a real need for all those chemicals. If our culture has a similar need for junk lit—the so-called "romantic" fiction of lonely people engaged in preposterous and violent pranks, usually in picturesque places—why not have our poets write it? Give them a monopoly, if we cannot stamp it out. Enrich our endowment of the arts. In the hands of Jim Harrison, these fantasies are so open we can indeed see what we are or what we dream. At the very least, such clumsy plots and vacant characters, such ill-concealed self-pity and anger, such male posturing and fearful fantasies would find expression in precise language. (p. 24)

Keith Opdahl, "Junk Food," in The Nation *(copyright 1979 by the Nation Associates, Inc.), Vol. 229, No. 1, July 7, 1979, pp. 23-4.*

[Mr. Harrison] stands high among the writers of his generation, and he is also one of the few not to have been drawn into navel-gazing introspection, but his ideas have never quite matched his technical and artistic skills until now. [*Legends of the Fall*] three long stories, or short novels is a triumph. The subject here is obsession. . . . The last, the title story, is perhaps the best, but all are strong stories, rich almost to the point of melodrama yet alive and shatteringly visceral.

"Books: 'Legends of the Fall'," in The New Yorker *(© 1979 by The New Yorker Magazine, Inc.), Vol. LV, No. 24, July 30, 1979, p. 89.*

Jim Harrison is a stylist. For him, this means great use of simple declarative sentences, cast out like fishing lines in pursuit of an elusive catch. As Hemingway discovered long ago, this kind of writing can carry immense emotional power, and it is the chief virtue of *Legends of the Fall,* a collection of three long stories about men in crisis.

The comparison to Hemingway is inevitable, for Harrison's plots as well as his prose are tough, masculine, and deliberately understated. The heroes of these tales, well-educated, well-off men in their early forties, move through barren landscapes of their own choosing where passion and action are inseparable. . . . In the title piece, an impressive, impassive novella set in Montana in the early 1900s, the characters circle one another in a silent pool of relationships marked by loss and desire. These are men to whom life reveals itself in primitive ways, through primitive acts of will.

"Some of our strangest actions are also our most deeply characteristic," writes Harrison, and *Legends of the Fall* goes a long way toward proving that contention. But there is something facile here; the taut lines of prose eventually reel in only small, bland truths. These stories skim dangerously near the category of thrillers, and while they are exciting to read, they leave a disappointing aftertaste.

"Life & Letters: 'Legends of the Fall'," in The Atlantic Monthly *(copyright © 1979 by The Atlantic Monthly Company, Boston, Mass.; reprinted with permission), Vol. 244, No. 3, September, 1979, p. 92.*

ANNE V. KISH

[*Legends of the Fall*] is a trilogy of tough, masculine stories reminiscent of Hemingway in terseness of style, sardonic philosophy, and even in heroes who are not too far removed from the much over-used and abused "grace-under pressure" code. . . .

These are three good stories each with a neat epilogue that adds a sense of completeness to the story, each involving fascinatingly rare characters whose singlemindedness, if not their particular brand of grace under pressure, is to be admired.

From the viewpoint of fictional technique, "Revenge" seems the most nearly perfect, not only because the action is limited in time to the few months between the assault and the vengeance, but because the subject matter is confined to the single major thread of revenge. "The Man Who Gave Up His Name" spreads itself a little thinly over twenty years. "Legends of the Fall," which promises the most by virtue of its hero's "supernatural constitution," actually suffers the most simply because it should have been a novel. There is too much time covered, there are too many actions, too many involvements to be squeezed into 81 pages. It should be a trilogy in itself.

Anne V. Kish, "Fiction: 'Legends of the Fall'," in Best Sellers *(copyright © 1979 Helen Dwight Reid Educational Foundation), Vol. 39, No. 6, September, 1979, p. 197.*

* * *

HAWKES, John 1925-

Hawkes is an American novelist, playwright, and short story writer. Jonathan Baumbach calls Hawkes "something of a naturalist in reverse"; in his experimental fiction he outlines and defines life as a surrealistic, often terrifying, dream world. Hawkes has said that his novels attempt to renew the form of that genre. According to critic Albert Guerard, in whose writing class Hawkes wrote his first novel, *The Cannibal,* he is "perhaps the most original American novelist since Faulkner." (See also *CLC,* Vols. 1, 2, 3, 4, 7, 9, and *Contemporary Authors,* Vols. 1-4, rev. ed.)

MARC RATNER

Since the appearance of his first novel, *The Cannibal,* in 1949, the work of John Hawkes has proven him to be a writer whose technical control, poetic imagery and content demand critical recognition. His novels challenge the reader's imagination and force him to read them with the care necessary in reading most modern poetry. The variety of experimental techniques in dealing with time and space in his fiction, the use of fantasy and dream and the pervasive, naturalistic theme of the determinacy of history and myth over men's lives suggest the influence in his work of naturalism and symbolism. In this he belongs to a tradition which combines the Gothic fiction of Charles Brockden Brown and Poe with the compressed symbolism and ironic view of Crane, Bierce and, on occasion, Hemingway. In Hawkes's particular view of the novel and the function of the novelist, the imagination dominates the fact. . . . Because of his "detached" approach, Hawkes achieves sympathy without sentimentality. His credo might be shared by Djuna Barnes, Nathanael West, Bernard Malamud, James Purdy, and Flannery O'Connor among contemporary writers. . . . Where Hawkes excels over the tried-and-true "realistic" writers is in the uses of imagination and the power to excite that faculty in the reader. (pp. 345-46)

[His technique of reworking myths to convey his perspective of modern man] is most evident in *The Beetle Leg* (1951), a novel set in the American desert near the site of a dam. The dry season and the figure of the fisherman at the dam are not unfamiliar images from T. S. Eliot's *Waste Land*. Beyond these, Hawkes's concept of the buried Christ-Osiris in the slowly sliding wall of the dam ("the sarcophagus of mud") is a prime example of his mythopoesis. The imperceptible movement of the retaining wall becomes the inevitable force and movement of the universe and the small absurd heroes, whether their activity is directed towards the wall or the fields, below, cannot check the cosmic flux. (pp. 346-47)

Images of sacrifice, particularly horses and chickens, occur as a motif and the elaborations on the theme of the buried fertility god are skillfully worked into the novel. These recognizable myths are combined with Hawkes's own creations. . . . (p. 347)

Hawkes returned to a European locale in his next works, *The Owl* and *The Goose on the Grave* (1954). These complementary novellas set in Italy, have received more adverse criticism than his other fiction, mostly because they rely more on religious imagery and historical fact than on characterization. The ritual sacrifice of the prisoner proscribed by the hangman-dictator of the principality of Sasso Fetore reenacts the death of Christ. But the sacrifice is of a human being, not a god. . . . While the religious symbolism of the sacrificed geese on the prisoner's grave and the image of the destroyed Madonna link the two novellas, the second novella is more concerned with the end of innocence. . . . Following a more direct narrative line and using [a] dream as a basis for connecting incidents, Hawkes indicates here the changes in method apparent in . . . *The Lime Twig* (1961). This novel fulfills the prediction of Albert Guerard in the introduction to *The Cannibal* that "Hawkes will move still further toward realism." Along with a closer adherence to a chronological development, Hawkes has shifted gears in his use of time. Instead of scanning the cultural history in the context of the everpresent past, Hawkes in a method slightly similar to Robbe-Grillet and Nathalie Sarraute arrests time to present a situation through the emotional, irrational acts or gestures of his characters. What Hawkes does in *The Lime Twig* is to present us with his superreal characters, victims of the ironic mesh of human affairs. . . . *The Lime Twig* finds Hawkes's technique directed more towards characterization, although his view of man as victim has not changed.

Hawkes's technique is that of the modern poet. His language and images are modes of dramatic delimitation, condensed flashes of action which convey intellectualized emotions. Characters and incidents operate on several strata, much in the way that they do in Dante's *Divine Comedy* where the situation can be viewed realistically and allegorically at the same time. Not that Hawkes's work is solely allegorical in nature—it is not fixed to a sharply defined view in that sense—but he is able to free the reader's imagination to range over the cultural past of a nation, and always with a comprehension of the pastness of the present. The influence of Yeats and Eliot is evidenced by his use of personal symbols, his sense of history, his objective view of contemporary society, and his compressive technique. However, it would be unfair to consider him solely as a derivative writer. He is an experimental writer and his challenge to the reader's imagination, his use of symbol, psychology and language mark him as a writer who does not accept the limitations placed on fiction by traditionalists.

Because of his experimentation, Hawkes has been mistakenly cast as a surrealist by most critics. The nightmare events in his novels do appear as expansions rather than evasions of reality but his objective technique, his deterministic themes, and his control of imagery are not part of the surrealist manifesto. Like Nathanael West, Hawkes's imagery resembles the products of automatic writing but his conscious themes and use of symbols invalidate the view that his work is autistic. Instead of the freedom from the past and present that the surrealists aspire to, he projects his symbols and the myths of the past on the modern world to give an original view of reality. (pp. 347-49)

In *The Cannibal* the three part narration moves from Germany, 1954, to 1914 and back; the main action is roughly based on the assassination of the faceless, one-man army of occupation, Leevey, by the neo-Nazi and sometime narrator, Zizendorf. In the interval between the description of the town at the end of World War II and the death of Leevey, Hawkes presents a diorama of German life between the two wars. (p. 350)

Hawkes, like Faulkner, only gradually reveals the significance of [his] characters by giving fragmentary views which integrate as the novel develops. Thus, Zizendorf's plot, which will restore the Reich, Stella's "ancestral fears" and "undersea life", or the Duke's pursuit of the child, continue a suspenseful line through the book, representing the corruptibility of the future in Germany, to give us a current action. Interspersed with the main action of Parts I and III set in 1945 are the related incidents from the inescapable "sack of the past" presented in Part II, 1914.

The imaginative incidents of the 1914 section of *The Cannibal* range through the pre- and postwar periods and are divided into four sections: "love", "Stella", "Ernst", and "lust". The private lives of Stella and Ernst, her husband, including her relationship with the Englishman, Cromwell, are connected to the political and social changes in Germany. . . . Hawkes here is viewing the personal lives of man, their involvements and passions, within a simultaneous setting of historical determinism which far more affects their lives. (p. 351)

The dramatic quality of Hawkes's work lies only partially in his images; much of his strength comes from his characterization. Again this aspect of his work cannot be thought of as circumstantial realism but more in terms of the figural realism used by Dante. Although Hawkes's universe is the obverse of Dante's ordered cosmos, in their weaving of myth and history and in their characterization the two authors use parallel methods. Hawkes's futile world most resembles the *Inferno* and his characters appear as part of a sensuous, irrational reality which finds acceptance perhaps only in the imagination. This is evident in the two women who are central to [*The Cannibal*], Madame Snow, the aristocratic Brunhilde of the Teutonic past, and her sister, Jutta, a more natural creature who always remains that part of a nation which never surrenders to the state; or the two male characters, Ernst, the saber-scarred victim of the Prussian ideal who turns toward the ascetic life, and Zizendorf, duped by the bankrupt promise of Nazism. All four reflect not only their own personal betrayals and the lack of love, but also the betrayal of Germany itself to false ideals. (p. 355)

Instead of being embodiments of sin as Dante's creations are, Hawkes's figures, set in their landscape of dreams and death, are symbolic of the social and political forces at work in twentieth century Europe. Throughout his novels the dominance of history over men's lives and their inability to escape their past is reiterated. Trapped by their past, the Europeans in these novels and the Americans in *The Beetle Leg* are caught in inevitable forces too strong for them to overcome. A certain dignity belongs to those comic-ironic heroes who try, like Ernst, to break with the past and in turn are broken. Perhaps the idea of the lime twig can stand as a symbol for Hawkes's view of man's condition, for he sees humanity as trapped birds, victims of internal and external forces. One can see this in Zizendorf's recognition of the futility of his efforts reflected in his annoyed tone at the novel's end. (p. 356)

Hawkes's work continues to reward the reader not only with revelations of individual characters but also with the wider meanings of their lives.

John Hawkes's economy of surreal effects, achieved by the juxtaposition of objects and incidents, his compressed poetic prose, not unlike the prose poems of the French symbolists, and his vaguely symbolic characterization similar to the figural realism of Dante all combine to achieve the intensity of the concentrated emotional moment of good modern poetry with the chronicling power of the novel. Hawkes opens to us the ironic vision of twentieth century man through the imagination of the poet and the objectivity of the novelist. (p. 357)

Marc Ratner, "The Constructed Vision: The Fiction of John Hawkes," in Studi Americani, *Vol. 11, 1965, pp. 345-57.*

JAMES L. GREEN

Like the typical fairy tale "Charivari" is a nightmare with a happy ending. However, the happy ending of fairy tale denies nightmare, preserves childhood innocence; the happy ending of "Charivari" is ironic, undercutting the false security of dream, affirming the reality of nightmare. (p. 83)

Charivari denotes "a serenade of 'rough music,' with kettles, pans, tea-trays, and the like, used . . . in mockery and derision of incongrous or unpopular marriages" (OED). "Charivari" is a satiric epithalamion to the marriage of Henry and Emily Van, two forty-year old children. Provided with money and a country estate by their parents, Henry and Emily have played house for fourteen years, though both subconsciously desire to break out of their fairy-tale world of parties and games. Henry has a nightmare in which he views Emily with a child. The next day during one of their parties, Emily announces her pregnancy. The news is terrifying because the birth of a child will force the couple to acknowledge their age, to accept time and the inevitability of death. Henry flees, a runaway child, but is found and brought back by his father. In a parallel action Emily is taken by her mother to a doctor, who finds that the pregnancy is hysterical. Returned home, Emily again appears youthful, and the children resume their games. This marriage is Hawkes' microcosm for twentieth-century Western society, affluent, hedonistic, committed to the preservation of youth and to the establishment of paradise on earth. Henry's nightmare and Emily's hallucination correspond to nightmare realities in Western civilization—to world war, which is the result of, and a threat to, utopian social and political dreams. Henry and Emily's parents, representatives of the Victorian age, are immediately responsible for their children's marriage, for the world in which Henry and Emily live. Hawkes implies that these parents were victimized by their own parents, and so on back through history. Ultimately, both dream and nightmare are grounded in man's existential condition. Life evokes in man the desire for eternal life, but man is also condemned by nature to death. Attempting to deny or escape his human condition, man has created systems of order, which in denying death, deny life as well. (pp. 83-4)

Hawkes' concern with the recurrence of nightmare and the recurrence of equally destructive dreams is reflected in his fictional technique. . . . "Charivari" is divided into four sections: "Courtship," "The Bachelors," "The Wedding," and "Rhythm." The story telescopes two periods of time, the original courtship and marriage of Henry and Emily and a two-day period fourteen years later, during which the couple experience fears and desires which parallel their ambivalent emotions during courtship. Hawkes also renders parallels between the experiences of Henry and Emily and those of their respective parents. Allusions to figures in literature and myth evoke other, ironic, parallels. Thus Hawkes expresses the recurring pattern of nightmare and dream, from which his characters cannot escape. "Charivari" is a closed system, ending where it begins. (pp. 84-5)

The fairy tale of "Charivari" has its happy ending. But Henry has escaped the death-in-life of isolating alienation only to become locked with Emily in the death-in-life of adult childhood. The story ends where it begins. Childhood is a time of fairy tale and nightmare. For Henry and Emily the nightmare will increase and ultimately shatter their bright, cold world of fairy tale.

"Charivari" is not a perfectly achieved work. The novelette is marred by occasional snickering intrusions of the omniscient narrator. For example: "These poor people. We should pet them; we should take care of them . . . Send them a painted teapot, perhaps . . . They are so flimsy, apt at any moment to be blown away forever." . . . Such commentary is the result of Hawkes' desire, as he says of Djuna Barnes, to focus "the most baffling of unsympathetic attitudes . . . upon the grudges, guilts, and renunciations harbored in the tangled seepage of our earliest recollections and originations." Hawkes writes that this "extreme fictive detachment" produces "extreme fictive sympathy," results in the "delicate malicious knowledge of us all as poor, forked, corruptible." In "Charivari" the "malicious" commentary works against this ultimate sympathy, expresses and provokes an attitude of superiority. The commentary is all the more regrettable, because by itself the rendered experience of "Charivari" evokes the "knowledge of us all as poor, forked, corruptible." To some readers, the numerous allusions to other works of literature in "Charivari" may seem self-conscious and obstrusive. The technique is probably borrowed from T. S. Eliot. A result of Hawkes' desire to combine poetic and novelistic method in fiction, it serves to add depth and range of implication to the narrative, to establish the determining influence of the past on the present, and, by inviting comparison with more vigorous ages, to reveal the enervation of the modern world. Though the allusions may seem self-conscious in "Charivari," the technique becomes increasingly subtle in Hawkes' later works, where mythic and literary parallels are implicit, or, as in the brilliant *Second Skin,* where literary allusions are naturally located in the mind of the self-conscious, first-person narrator, whose mode of expression is ironic self-parody. Finally, the parallels in "Charivari" between the microcosm of Henry and Emily's fairy-tale marriage and the macrocosm of a materialistic, luxury-seeking, neurotic twentieth-century society are more asserted than established. At least, in comparison with the perfect coherence of microcosm and macrocosm in *The Cannibal,* Hawkes' second work, the relationship between the personal experience and the social and historical situation in "Charivari" seems tenuous.

In spite of these faults, "Charivari" is an impressive first work. In his analysis of the equally destructive worlds of dream and nightmare, Hawkes focuses attention on fundamental problems of human existence. Faced with a nightmare reality, terrified by devouring time, by the perception that life is a process of death, the characters in "Charivari" repress their natural desires, which, if allowed full expression, would commit them to the natural, creative-destructive process. In so doing, they enter the world of dream, of fairy-tale denial of reality, commit themselves to death-in-life. But repressed human impulses reassert themselves in tormenting nightmare and neurosis. And ultimately the cannibalistic processes of nature will break through the walls of protective fantasy. (pp. 93-5)

James L. Green, "Nightmare and Fairy Tale in Hawkes' 'Charivari'," in Critique: Studies in Modern Fiction *(copyright © by* Critique, *1971), Vol. XIII, No. 1, 1971, pp. 83-95.*

* * *

HAYDEN, Robert 1913-1980

Hayden, an award-winning American poet, deals with the black experience in America. His poems revolve around concepts of suffering, and his use of alliteration and complex sound structure has often elicited comparisons between his work and that of Wallace Stevens and Hart Crane. (See also *CLC*, Vol. 5, 9, and *Contemporary Authors*, Vols. 69-72.)

WILLIAM LOGAN

Offered the chance that all selections offer, to expunge, silently, the errors and excesses of early work, Robert Hayden has retained [in *Angle of Ascent*] all but two of the poems which formed his 1966 *Selected Poems.* This is a poet secure about the past, and the past work. That work, continued here by eight new poems and the bulk of two interim volumes, has shifted its emphasis, gradually, from narrative to symbolism. The earlier poems, heavily dependent on story, have broken down now entirely into words, some of rich personal association: "Plowdens, Finns, / / Shefeys, Haydens, / Westerfields. // Pennsylvania gothic, / Kentucky homespun, / Virginia baroque." The new poems have a spareness that resists first reading, but which eventually rewards with the radiance of hard-earned, hard-edged memory. (p. 226)

Hayden exploits the classics and the contemporary, historical anecdote and personal encounter, to demonstrate that what grants history poignancy—that it cannot be altered—also gives pathos to the personal. His explorations of Black history appear in choice of subject matter and a slight widening of technique to include occasional swatches of song and dialect, rather than as impenetrable anger or voguish posture. He produces homages to both Mark Van Doren and Malcolm X; his poems conjure up a variety of lives caught in the desperation of poverty, or that of decadence. His most extreme emotions, and successes, reserved for the era that began with the arrival of slaves in America and ended with the Civil War and Reconstruction, produce a number of serious, haunted poems, including *The Dream, The Ballad of Sue Ellen Westerfield,* and the stunning *Middle Passage.*

Middle Passage is a deceptive piece, a perfectly modulated pastiche of voices contained in diary, deposition, and reminiscence, that has for its subject the slave trade between Africa and America. The poem exhibits a toughness of language and a variety of method, including prose, parody, and prayer, that create effects of horror and anger in service of a passage through history, the "voyage through death / to life upon these shores." . . . *Middle Passage* is the best contemporary poem I have read on slavery. It is a singular performance, one which Hayden's later poems have not matched, in part because it is a poem whose special construction does not invite imitation.

Hayden has not discovered other methods rich enough to encompass public or private history so well. The defects which mar his poetry include compositional tics (repetition, for example: "the name he never can he never can repeat") and, especially in the newer poems, occasional opaqueness. Some recent poems are contrived from feelings so momentary that only a fleeting satisfaction is achieved. At worst, in the new work the phrases break up, the words fly apart, and the associative structure holds no meaning. The poems may shatter into component images, individually attractive but fragmentary. There are few first-rate metaphors; the poems that remain in the mind persuade by narrative, not image. As one moves through the book, it is disconcerting to find the older poems last. Such as ordering places the newer poems, whose methods are smaller, and which should be seen as the product of development, at a disadvantage; as the older poems drape themselves in description and narration, the newer work seems insubstantial. (p. 228)

William Logan, "Language against Fear," in Poetry *(© 1977 by The Modern Poetry Association; reprinted by permission of the Editor of* Poetry*), Vol. CXXX, No. 4, July, 1977, pp. 221-29.**

ROBERT G. O'MEALLY

Hayden is a poet of many voices, using varieties of ironic black folk speech, and a spare, ebullient poetic diction, to grip and chill his readers. He draws characters of stark vividness as he transmutes cardinal points and commonplaces of history into dramatic action and symbol.

The slender, potent *American Journal* is well named. For here we peruse, at close range, portions of America's visible (public, documented) and—to use Octavio Paz's term—"invisible history." We ascend "The Point" at Stonington, Connecticut, and in the brilliant air, alive with wild swans and terns, we salute the revolutionaries who repelled the British there: "we are for an instant held in shining / like memories in the mind of God."

The Afro-American past is of special concern here. In "A Letter From Phillis Wheatley," Hayden uses understatement to reveal what historians have recently discovered: that Phillis, the 18th-century slave poet, viewed slavery and prejudice with horror, wonder, and well-guarded humor. . . .

The title poem is a tour de force framed as the jottings of an otherworldly visitor reporting on the American people during the bicentennial. The visitor, in earthling disguise, finds Americans noisy, vain, wasteful, and cruel worshippers of machines; yet the "charming savages enlightened primitives brash / new comers lately sprung up in our galaxy" are attractively vigorous and ingenious. (p. G6)

The most compelling section of this book is the sequence of poems ironically called "Elegies For Paradise Valley," (named for a tough Detroit neighborhood of yesteryear), a place vividly recalled from the poet's boyhood, and captured in terse, sometimes gritty language. . . . (pp. G6-G7)

American Journal, by Hayden the "poet of perfect pitch," is a book of unforgettable images of America and her people, a prayerful report from one of our most hauntingly accurate, and yet hopeful, recorders. (p. G7)

Robert G. O'Meally, "Poems and the Nation," in Book World—The Washington Post *(© 1978,* The Washington Post*), June 25, 1978, pp. G6-G7.*

REGINALD GIBBONS

[*American Journal*] is characteristically spare and lyrical. Hayden chooses his words with more care than most poets use, and there is also a kind of formal ghost hovering behind his lines, so that his free-verse stanzas seem almost to have resolved themselves into something more traditional. Their holding back is what gives them their charm, however. (p. 87)

What is most pleasing about his work is the delicacy and care with which he takes the common tongue, including nicknames and slang, and manages to place every word so cleanly in his lines that a kind of bright, varied mosaic emerges. On a larger scale, this is tied esthetically to his method in "Middle Passage" (*A Ballad of Remembrance,* 1962), which cuts and splices documents as well as the spoken word. But here, as in the central sequence, "Elegies for Paradise Valley," the individual tiles are plucked from the language we speak, and that common language is balanced against the strictness of the form of each brief section. As in section V, where the form is the counter-weight to the sadness and risky catalogue of names:

> And Belle, the classy dresser, where is she,
> who changed her frock three times a day?
>   Where's Nora, with her laugh, her comic flair,
>   stagestruck Nora waiting for her chance?
> Where's fast Iola, who so loved to dance
> she left her sickbed one last time to whirl
> in silver at The Palace till she fell?
>   Where's mad Miss Alice, who ate from garbage
>   cans?
>   Where's snuffdipping Lucy, who played us
>   'chunes'
> on her guitar? Where's Hattie? Where's
> Melissabelle?
>   Let vanished rooms, let dead streets tell. . . .

The sequence is unsentimental and compassionate. It has a great sense of timing, and utilizes this fully as a poetic resource—Hayden is far too good a poet to rely solely on images to do the poem's work. His rhythmic sense is stronger, and more appealing, in any case, and his use of syntax superb. (pp. 87-8)

Reginald Gibbons, "Hayden, Peck, and Atwood," in The Ontario Review *(copyright © 1979 by* The Ontario Review*), No. 10, Spring-Summer, 1979, pp. 87-94.**

MICHAEL S. HARPER

Mr. Hayden's precision and economy is ubiquitous in ["American Journal"]; his use of slang, nicknames and the common parlance of the street is full of charm and never overdone. . . .

The appeal of "American Journal" is enhanced by its organization, the lyrical economy with which sequences of poems develop the historical perspective; for Mr. Hayden the desire for beauty is a very human wish to resist the inevitable pain of life. . . . (p. 18)

Mr. Hayden's thematic attention to history reflects an attention to the vernacular and to the uses of the literary mask; the title poem is a devastating commentary on the contrast between the celebration of ancestral rituals and the damage to our spiritual lives wrought by a materialistic world. . . . [His] poems promise a blossoming evident in the continuous journal of an America he has both named and penetrated. (p. 20)

Michael S. Harper, "Three Poets," in The New York Times Book Review *(© 1979 by The New York Times Company; reprinted by permission), October 21, 1979, pp. 18, 20, 22.**

* * *

HEANEY, Seamus 1939-

Heaney is an award-winning Northern Irish poet. Although most of his poetry is set in Northern Ireland, it is only recently that Heaney has considered its political turmoil in his writing. Many critics consider him the best poet now writing in Ireland. (See also *CLC,* Vols. 5, 7, and *Contemporary Authors,* Vols. 85-88.)

PATRICIA BEER

Geographically [Heaney's] landscape [in *Wintering Out*] is still the Irish countryside, past or present. . . .

Sometimes the countryside is seen, dramatically, through the eyes of others, not very human others and one of them an outright mermaid, who returns to the sea wrapped in the smoke-reeks, straw-musts and films of mildew from the thatch of her lover's house. . . . As to metaphorical landscapes, there is little in this book, apart from the prefatory poem, which deals specifically with the present troubles, but of course 'specifically' is the operative word, and even if it were not, what Heaney chooses to tell us is his own business.

The tenacity with which Heaney, superficially the most urbane and least urban of modern poets, clings to his chosen rural setting is certainly not at this stage due to any limitation of actual experience. It comes perhaps from the spirit which makes compilers of anthologies for children still include such a vast majority of poems about the countryside. . . . The scenery of *Wintering Out* is predictable—misty and waterlogged and exhausting, with very black darkness—and its motifs are recognisable and recurrent: half-doors, cobblestones, swinging lanterns. It is an orderly realm of cause and effect. Desirably or undesirably, one thing leads to another. . . . There is none of the relief of surrealism, as when Ted Hughes's cat is found sitting outside the front door when his murderer gets back from the river.

Out of this sort of order come well-ordered poems, of the well-made kind which, significantly, the younger Irish poets have been giving us. Seamus Heaney's technique is as brilliant and idiosyncratic as ever. His poems do remind us of someone but it always turns out to be Seamus Heaney, except for such odd echoes as, for example, 'huge pleasures in the water', which necessarily recalls Dylan Thomas's 'huge weddings in the waves'. 'Smaller and clearer as the years go by'—Larkin's words about the young lady in the photograph album—could apply to Heaney's work. The poems in *Wintering Out* seem to be smaller in the best sense of the word: condensed even in their look on the page, concentrated, a long story made short. They are clear in every sense of the word: intelligible, confident, vivid. Every so often a metaphor starts showing off.

> The moon's host elevated
> in a monstrance of holly trees

would have pleased Polonius. But most are more subtly memorable:

> A nimble snout of flood
> licks over stepping stones
> and goes uprooting.

Heaney is not only concerned with sound but obsessed with pronunciation: in poem after poem, vowels, consonants, the organs of speech themselves provide metaphor: in 'Toome', 'Broagh', 'Traditions', 'The Wool Trade', 'A New Song'. Like its two predecessors, *Wintering Out* is an impressive collection.

Patricia Beer, "Seamus Heaney's Third Book of Poems," in The Listener *(© British Broadcasting Corp. 1972; reprinted by permission of Patricia Beer), Vol. 88, No. 2280, December 7, 1972, p. 795.*

WILLIAM H. PRITCHARD

I've admired Seamus Heaney's work, but have preserved my distance from it: almost no human beings, but grainily humble perceptions in terse lines. There are some further capable poems in this mode in . . . [*North*]; yet I confess to being more interested in the group of poems from the book's Part II. There, because he has been pressed to, Heaney writes about being a poet in Ulster in time of The Troubles. "What ever you Say Say Nothing," one of these poems has it; Heaney's way is the way of an Irish poet writing sixty years after Yeats's "Easter, 1916" or "Meditations in Time of Civil War." He carries it off with both dignity and gallows humor; in fact I hadn't fully realized until these poems showed me, how sly and expert is the presence of their poet. . . . I found the relative talkiness of these concluding poems, their reach towards some kind of social sophistication and manner—even put to the purposes of more elaborately saying "nothing"—an attractive new direction I hope Heaney will keep on taking. (pp. 457-58)

William H. Pritchard, "More Poetry Matters," in The Hudson Review *(copyright © 1976 by The Hudson Review, Inc.; reprinted by permission), Vol. XXIX, No. 3, Autumn, 1976, pp. 453-63.**

KENNETH McROBBIE

North is the latest collection of verse by Ireland's most significant living poet. The theme is Ireland, but in a new regional and particularly temporal sense. *North* works less as bleak geographical than as bleaker historical force: from the Vikings of Dublin to the retributive Ulstermen wreaking atrocities in the present. . . . Ritual brings on and legitimizes the round of punishings. Individual and tribal deaths surface in this secret and retentive landscape, where the poet steps "through origins" "kinned by hieroglyphic peat" and reverses Yeat's line: "This centre holds."

More than coherence of place, there's coherence of action. Action is the key to Heaney's poetics. "'Description is revelation,'" yes. But this means here the imaginative retrieval of place, objects and people, and then the naming of these and their movement toward expression. This must be the direction for the modern lyric, away from the reflexive indulgence of "poets who sing like Onan." There is the personal. . . . And there's the glorious spectacle of the poet's faculties employing a vocabulary of richly restorative sensual and especially temporal particulars in archeology, topography, physiognomy. . . .

Kenneth McRobbie, "World Literature in Review: 'North'," in World Literature Today *(copyright 1977 by the University of Oklahoma Press), Vol. 51, No. 3, Summer, 1977, p. 446.*

DONALD HALL

North is Seamus Heaney's fourth book of poems. *Death of a Naturalist* was his first, a fully achieved book, followed by a second volume—so often observed in young poets—which was hasty and inferior, *Door into Dark;* followed in Heaney's case by an excellent third volume, *Wintering Out,* and now by *North* which is the best of all. One has the sense in Heaney that politics is forced upon him by the combination of nationality and circumstance. . . . Circumstance invades this volume. . . . The second and final section of this book [is politically inspired]. It is good poetry—and there is not a single poem among them that ranks with Heaney's best. It's a poetry written out of social necessity. No man or woman in Northern Ireland at this time could avoid social statement without loss of humanity.

But when mad Ireland teases Heaney into the truest poetry, in *North* it is confrontation with the long dead which provides us the favor. Heaney writes of the bog people [in "The Grauballe Man"], corpses preserved in the humus of Ireland. . . . Here in the short lines, sentences elegantly broken across them, contemporary man touches down at an ancient source. In the title poem he makes the same motion downward through to the "longship's swimming tongue," which weds him present and past to poet's journey and task. (pp. 156-58)

Donald Hall, "The Nation of Poets," in Parnassus: Poetry in Review *(copyright © Poetry in Review Foundation), Vol. 6, No. 1, Fall-Winter, 1977, pp. 145-60.**

ARTHUR E. McGUINNESS

"Kinship" and "Funeral Rites," two poems in Seamus Heaney's latest volume *North* (1975), suggest a theme that recurs in many of his poems, namely, the importance of connection in human experience, the personal and social value of a cultural matrix within which behavior can have intelligibility. (p. 71)

Heaney's first two volumes, *Death of a Naturalist* (1966)

and *Door into the Dark* (1969), are almost totally concerned with farming and domestic life in the rural area of Northern Ireland where he grew up. Profoundly aware of the traditions that once gave meaning to rural Irish life—the land, the rhythms of farming and fishing, family customs, the mysteries of nature and love—he is equally aware that rural Ireland has nearly lost its customary life. Many of the poems in *Death of a Naturalist* and *Door into the Dark* look back longingly to the old ways. Heaney's more recent volumes, *Wintering Out* (1972) and *North* (1975) both broaden and deepen his subjects. Aware of the need to develop his own imagination on the one hand and conscious of being part of a violent and ungovernable society on the other, he looks for answers in the bogland, in the goddess-mother whose "wet centre is bottomless" ("Bogland"). His imagination is stimulated by traces of the ancient Irish language he finds embedded in bogland placenames that have survived the imposition of English. These words may enable one to make contact with an ancient Irish spirit. For a present-day Northern Ireland, which has lost its cultural roots, he finds "antecedents" in the traditions of prehistoric societies recently discovered buried in Danish and Irish bogland. The archaeological evidence reveals people apparently obsessed with violence and murder, sometimes ritualized, more often merely self-indulgent. (pp. 71-2)

The poems in [*Death of a Naturalist* and *Door into the Dark*] are generally more direct, less figurative, less allusive, and less "literary" than those in *Wintering Out* and *North*. In his first two volumes he proposes to dig into the darkness of the earth and his own imagination with his spade-pen to discover his roots. Knowing that Heaney was born a Roman Catholic and attended Catholic schools until he went to the university, one might expect the traditions and rituals of that faith to have a central place in his poetry. But actually there is little reference to Catholicism. (p. 73)

While Heaney makes few direct references to Roman Catholicism, his consciousness is certainly structured by the myth of the Fall. His poems typically move from "then" to "now," first looking back nostalgically to a time when life had value, and then describing the present as a time without value. (p. 74)

The myth of happy times once long ago is most obvious in *Death of a Naturalist* in "St. Francis and the Birds," a poem very like Yeats's "Byzantium," where time is fixed and evil has no place. Here are not the rotting blackberries, the drowned kittens, dead child, and aging parents one finds elsewhere in the book. In this poem the artist can connect with his environment, creating the possibility of love. Our present world is quite a different sort of place, where things have fallen apart and the center cannot hold. The poem which follows "St. Francis and the Birds," a poem called "In Small Townlands," also deals with an artist, this time the painter Colin Middleton, whose imagination "creates" a new world. Its qualities starkly contrast with the ordered and beautiful world of St. Francis and suggest the waste land of Northern Ireland. "His eyes, thick, greedy lenses, fire / This bare bald earth with white and red, / Incinerate it till it's black / And brilliant as a funeral pyre: / A new world cools out of his head."

The strongest figures in *Death of a Naturalist* and *Door into the Dark* are those, like Heaney's father, who were devoted to the land and whose lives were ritualized in harmony with their environment. (p. 75)

"Lough Neagh Sequence" represents Heaney's most sustained effort in *Door into the Dark* . . . to recapture the traditions and rituals of rural Irish life. The subject of the seven poems is eel fishing and the sequence moves from the traditional lore of the fisherman in "Up the Shore" and the beginning of the instinctive return of the eels to spawn ("Beyond Sargasso"), to the rituals of "Bait," "Setting," and "Lifting," and finally of the death of the eel at the end of its life cycle ("Return") and a boy's fear and fascination at being witness to these natural rhythms ("Visions"). Heaney is intrigued by creatures so instinctively connected to their environments that their actions are ordered and beautiful ("The Trout," "Cow in Calf") and by rural people who participate nearly as instinctively in traditional ways.

Seamus Heaney does not have the naïve romantic notion that nature never betrays the heart which loves her. His poems present nature as a random power that sometimes rewards but more often frustrates human [efforts]. "At a Potato Digging" describes the ritual worship of a fickle mother-earth. . . . The laborers who operate the mechanical harvester in "At a Potato Digging" contrast sharply with Heaney's noble individuals. . . . Heaney sees neither harmony nor rhythm in them at work or at rest. When set against the easy natural movement of the gulls, their awkwardness is even more apparent.

This life-denying and graceless ritual of mechanized labor contrasts with another ritual clearly life-affirming, the ritual of sexual relations and marriage. Of the several marriage poems in *Death of a Naturalist* . . . , *"Poem For Marie"* is most obviously [concerned with tradition and ritual]. (pp. 76-7)

The last poem in *Door into the Dark* . . . , "Bogland," connects Seamus Heaney's first two volumes to *Wintering Out* . . . and *North*. . . . Moving beyond the traditions of rural Irish society . . . , "Bogland" suggests another kind of history and culture that has more recently interested Heaney. His realization that the traditions of rural Ireland have had a relatively brief and contingent existence leads him to seek other "connections," other older and more stable reference points. He continues to trust in his homeland, but now he wants to learn more about himself and his society in relation to the archaeology of that land. . . . [The final line of the poem], "The wet centre is bottomless," suggests the religious and sexual aspects of the earth. Heaney develops this notion of the earth as goddess-mother more fully in *Wintering Out* and *North*. (pp. 77-8)

Heaney's own uprootedness has intensified his search for broader cultural and historical roots in *Wintering Out*. Several of the poems such as "Bog Oak," "Anahorish," "Toome," "Broaghe," and "A New Song," find traces of the Irish language surviving in Northern Irish placenames that could open a door into that dark. As an Irishman, Heaney resents England's centuries-long effort to take away his culture and especially his language. But some of the old words have survived the imposition of English, and they are resonant with the old ways. Poems like "Gifts of Rain," "A Northern Hoard," and "The Tollund Man" continue Heaney's "soundings" for "antediluvian lore" to help him comprehend Northern Ireland's present nightmare. (p. 78)

"Gifts of Rain" and "Toome" bring together . . . two kinds of "digging," digging for the roots of language and digging for the archaeological roots of history. (p. 79)

Heaney does not presume that the pressure of English ways alone is responsible for loss and powerlessness in Ireland. Had he done so, his poetry would be provincial. . . . [He] understands that ours is an age without sacred time or space. In *Wintering Out* he develops this theme most fully in the five poems that make up "A Northern Hoard." (p. 82)

Each of the poems in "A Northern Hoard" sets the present chaotic state of Northern Ireland against a time of ritualized behavior and the contrast dramatically highlights the psychological, religious, and cultural impoverishment of that unfortunate country. "Roots" begins with the impossibility of sexual love in a barren and uprooted place reminding Heaney of the Old Testament Gomorrah, and then moves to the only space where sexuality can still express itself in deeply rooted mythic forms, the space of dreams. "No Man's Land," "Stump," and "No Sanctuary" set the terrors of our present rootless time against terrors in a time of faith. The Judeo-Christian experiences of Passover, plague, and All Souls' Day were times of tribulation and testing, but likewise times when men believed in divine purpose. "Tinder," the final poem of "A Northern Hoard," introduces a quite different cultural reference, the Danish Iron Age, which provides Heaney with a rich source of inspiration for other poems in *Wintering Out* and especially in *North*. In "Tinder" Heaney stresses the similarity between the Judeo-Christian experience and the "antediluvian lore" revealed in the excavation of bogs in Denmark and Ireland. In other poems, particularly in *North,* he will be less confident about the faith of this Iron-Age culture, and will emphasize instead its distressing similarities to our own age. (pp. 82-3)

The idea of an Iron-Age society structured around ritual . . . changes radically in *North*. . . . Many poems in this volume, including the title poem, consider the "antediluvian lore" and "new history" to be found buried in the bog. . . . Heaney moves from the Iron-Age people of Denmark to the Danish presence in Ireland in "Belderg," "Funeral Rites," "North," "Viking Dublin: Trial Pieces," "Bone Dreams," and "Bog Queen." These tribal societies now seem to Heaney much more like our own. He no longer contrasts an older, ritually structured society with current loss of faith. On the contrary, in *North* the social behavior of the ancient peoples reveals depressing similarities to our own. (p. 87)

Life-enhancing experiences in *North* occur only in the private world of the poet's memory, imagination, and dreams. Or, put in the ritual terms of "Kinship," the benevolent goddess of one's private world becomes in society-at-large an indifferent goddess who "swallows / our love and terror." One of Heaney's most ambitious poems, "Kinship" again celebrates intimacy with land, language, and family. But intimacy with society is not possible. (p. 89)

However, in the narrowed world of family and self, life-enhancing relations are still possible. "Kinship" begins characteristically with Heaney walking in the bog searching for "antediluvian lore." The redemptive powers of the earth do not flow into society-at-large, but only to the sensitive and trusting spirit. He speaks in section I of "hieroglyphic peat" and the "coopered secrets / of process and ritual." For the enlightened one, the bog remains a source of sacred rings: "the unstopped mouth / of an urn, a moondrinker." Digging into the bog becomes a sexual experience in sections III and IV, as the poet himself becomes part of a fertility ritual. . . . Heaney's kinship with his father is presented in section V as a sacred ritual as well. Interestingly, the small boy has a patriarchal rather than matriarchal concept of primordial power. Only later does he learn of female power. (pp. 89-90)

"Funeral Rites" provides an excellent final example of Seamus Heaney's concern for tradition and ritual. The poem attempts to replace a ritual-of-memory, the family observances of a Catholic wake, with a ritual-of-imagination, a burial service that could incorporate the ancient symbols of Iron-Age peoples. While the senseless murders of the young continue in Northern Ireland, the victims' families dare not risk the exposure of a traditional burial service. Heaney himself has lost faith in the symbols of the traditional Catholic wake and burial. So, for different reasons, poet and community are without ritual: "We pine for ceremony, / customary rhythms." In "Funeral Rites" a burial rite is imagined that might give these violent deaths the dignity of association with the elemental, life-sustaining female powers revealed elsewhere in his poems. Heaney does not presume that such imagined ritual can actually happen in the afflicted communities of Northern Ireland. But the ritual is obviously important for him, and he may feel that this imagined link with what he regards as fundamental truth is the only sort of "connection" he can make with the society of Northern Ireland. (p. 90)

"Funeral Rites" concludes . . . with Seamus Heaney's most dramatic use of the "sacred ring" motif. Just as on the domestic level—in a significant reversal of the Pauline adage—husbands must be submissive to their wives in order to experience the richest possibilities of marriage ("Poem for Marie"), so in an ideal society the energies of the hero must be channeled through female power to have order and value: "he turned with a joyful face / to look at the moon." Heaney nowhere else presents the case for ritual more unequivocally. Provided that it has not degenerated into platitude and habit, ritual can still give order to life. Digging into the "bog" of his imagination as well as into the archaeological lore of the real bog has convinced Heaney that, even in these desperate times, one might hope to connect with life-enhancing elemental powers and, through the discipline of language, to give these connections shape. (p. 92)

Arthur E. McGuinness, "'Hoarder of Common Ground': Tradition and Ritual in Seamus Heaney's Poetry," in Éire-Ireland *(copyright Irish American Cultural Institute), Vol. XIII, No. 2, Summer, 1978, pp. 71-92.*

PETER PORTER

Heaney has plenty of magic in his poetry: that moving on from the first unusual word, the right placing of which is probably in the gift of every poet, to a second one which clinches the insight, and thence to the confirming vision which makes the poem memorable.

You can see this in the first poem in [*Field Work*], entitled 'Oysters.' Clearly, such a mundane subject is going to be made to yield dividends in seriousness, even solemnity. He says his tongue was 'a filling estuary' and that he tasted 'the salty Pleiades.' In the next stanza the sigh of ocean is given the adjective 'philandering'; the poem moves to celebrate friendship in oyster-eating and a further stanza recalls the privileged Romans who carried oysters over the Alps 'packed deep in hay and snow.' The final stanza picks up that touch of philandering, and turns away from poetry and freedom to an unplaced disquiet which is countered only by his resolution to eat the day and be quickened 'into verb, pure verb.'

The poem has a sense of an ending, but what does the vision perpend? Heaney pleases critics because he is at once accurately plain and resoundingly obscure. He is lyrical and pastoral, yet the lights of great city quarrels flicker over his horizon. Ambivalence and a sort of archaism run through the book. Nevertheless, it strikes me as a finer performance than 'North,' which was such a chilly standing-about in the niches of the Pantheon.

The magic I referred to has been too often used by Heaney in the past to tie tighter the knots in his poetry, so that nobody might strip him of his Yeatsian robes. He just wasn't going to concede place to any rival. . . . But he relaxes more often in *Field Work,* and is just as magical and far more human when he does. 'The Skunk' is a beautiful poem which re-mystifies the love of man for wife in terms of that unloved but graceful animal. . . . I would like to see Heaney move to themes which demand that he takes greater risks. He has the grand style at his command, but there is no insurance available to those who use it.

Peter Porter, "Landscape with Poems," in The Observer *(reprinted by permission of The Observer Limited), No. 9819, November 4, 1979, p. 40.**

DONALD HALL

Seamus Heaney's new volume is *Field Work,* containing poems written since *North* in 1976. *North* was a superb volume; I suppose *Field Work* is even better, though it is possible that I merely hear more of his voice as I come to know him better. . . . Heaney's land is Ireland . . . ; but what Ireland? He is a northerner who lives in the south; he writes the English inherited from centuries of oppression, sweetened by the excellence of earlier Anglo-Irish poetry. These conflicts make for energy, I suspect. If Heaney is the best Irish poet since Yeats, a sentiment often expressed, it is less known that there are half a dozen other living Irishmen who could run for the title without fear of disgrace.

Heaney's subjects in *Field Work* range from troubles in Ireland to skunks in California, but his geographical spread never suggests the tourist. The voice speaks of love with an astonishing and wholly captivating tenderness. It speaks as well of violence, desire and memory, and it speaks with deliberate intelligence—willful, diligent and playful. For all the qualities I list, the most important is *song,* the tune Heaney sings which is poetry's tune, resolutions of cherished language. (p. 473)

Donald Hall, "The Music of What Happens," in The Nation *(copyright 1979 by the Nation Associates, Inc.), Vol. 229, No. 15, November 10, 1979, pp. 472-73.**

DENIS DONOGHUE

Seamus Heaney . . . has learned his trade so well that it is now a second nature wonderfully responsive to his first. And the proof is in "Field Work," a superb book, the most eloquent and far-reaching book he has written, a perennial poetry offered at a time when many of us have despaired of seeing such a thing.

Heaney published his first book of poems, "Death of a Naturalist," in 1966. It was a book of promise, and of promises made mostly to his father, family, race and country. A local book, in the sense that our household gods are local. . . . In his second book, "Door Into the Dark" (1969), the dark is a blacksmith's forge, to begin with, and then the other forms of darkness that shadow the security of earth, time and the seasons. One poem speaks of "the smells of ordinariness." The art of poetry is likened to other arts, including thatching and smithery. In a few poems the young poet's veins bulge more than the occasion warrants, but mostly the rhetoric is true, well-earned. The poet in these two books is walking the land, training his eyes, getting the measure of things right. Landscapes are tactfully moralized, pressed to disclose values and meanings so gracefully reasonable that they hardly need pressure at all, only a few of Heaney's "time-turned words."

"Bogland," the last poem in "Door Into the Dark," made a new promise, that Heaney would go further, dig more deeply into Ireland's past. . . . In his next book, "Wintering Out" (1973), Heaney included some political and civic poems, mainly about the competence in pain you acquire by living in it—he was still writing in the North of Ireland and pondering its "little destiny"—but the most far-reaching poems reached down into the bog and magma of the country. (pp. 1, 45)

It is my understanding that in "North" Heaney draws upon the long perspective of an ancient buried race to release himself from the appalling syntax of a modern Irish history. There are a few poems, such as "Whatever You Say Say Nothing," in which there is no perspective and therefore no respite. The scene is Belfast, Heaney's town, where the only vantage points are held by soldiers. But the more typical, and indeed the richer poems, take the long view of the dead, going down through the dictions, fossils, quernstones, Norse, Viking—evidence you read like braille. . . .

"Field Work" is the record of . . . four sabbatical years in [rural County Wicklow]. The book is continuous with "North" in its values, but far stronger in its craft, what Yeats called its trade. Heaney is still "the etymologist of roots and graftings," Irish poetry's contact-man: seeing is still believing, but the strongest belief is touching and hearing. "North" was animated by those convictions, but the new poems listen even more movingly to "the music of what happens" and find a second music to respond to the first. (p. 45)

Heaney is now writing more powerfully than ever, more fully in possession of his feeling, more at home in his style. He has given up, at least for the moment, the short line of his earlier poems, which often went along with a brittle, self-protective relation to his experience. The new long line is more thoughtful, it brings a meditative music to bear upon fundamental themes of person and place, the mutuality of ourselves and the world.

Heaney's confidence, entirely free of vanity, is so finely adjudged that he can allude to other poets in the spirit in which, as Eliot said, "there is no competition." The strongest allusion is to Robert Lowell, as in the poem "Sibyl," where the abruptions of tone are lessons well learned from the Lowell of "Life Studies" and "Near the Ocean." (pp. 45-6)

The only poem that falls short in "Field Work" is a version

of the Ugolino episode in Cantos 32 and 33 of Dante's "Inferno." For once, Heaney's confidence faltered, as well it might. There are fine things in the version, but much of it is flat. . . .

[The] superlative poems in "Field Work" are the personal lyrics. I wish I could go through the book, quoting, reciting from the "Glanmore Sonnets," and for an encore, "The Otter," "The Badgers," "An Afterwards," "The Skunk," "The Harvest Bow" and "A Dream of Jealousy." What is exhilarating in these poems is the relation between their two musics: the music of what happens comes first, and Heaney listens to it, receives it as a gift, like the first line of a poem; the second music is what he makes of the first, taking it into himself and finding a voice for it there.

These poems make you feel that the best part of poetry is given not as inspiration but as something you have had the luck to see, hear, smell or taste, and that the poem adds only a grace note here and there to a music virtually complete. It is doubtless untrue. But Heaney's new poems sound, yes, so natural that you believe them to be forces of nature, like rain and sunset, and forces of culture only by the way. (p. 46)

Denis Donoghue, "Poets Who Have Learned Their Trades: 'Field Work'," in The New York Times Book Review *(© 1979 by The New York Times Company; reprinted by permission), December 2, 1979, pp. 1, 45-6.*

* * *

HEINLEIN, Robert 1907-

An American science fiction novelist and short story writer, Heinlein established his reputation writing stories for *Astounding* in the forties. Today he is, along with Isaac Asimov, the dean of American science fiction writers. His *Stranger in a Strange Land* became a cult novel among the college youth of the mid-sixties, drawing attention to science fiction as a literary genre warranting more serious consideration than had previously been granted it. Heinlein has also written under the pseudonyms of Anson MacDonald, Lyle Monroe, John Riverside, and Caleb Saunders. (See also *CLC*, Vols. 1, 3, 8, and *Contemporary Authors*, Vols. 1-4, rev. ed.)

DENNIS E. SHOWALTER

In 1959, Robert Heinlein's *Starship Troopers* won the Hugo award as the year's best science fiction novel. Critics and reviewers have been apologizing for that fact ever since. Even admirers of Heinlein as a logician and story-teller condemn *Starship Troopers* as a "militaristic polemic" glorifying a violent, proto-fascist ethic, creating a polarized society in which heroic war veterans rule over "draft-dodgers, effeminate snobs, pacifists, and other animals of low standing." (p. 113)

Evaluating [the charges of fascism and militarism] is complicated by the fact that Heinlein's society is not presented in detail. It is a framework supporting an adventure story, and any scholarly analysis runs the risk of pedantry, of burdening the novel with such a weight of footnotes that it sinks without a ripple. Nevertheless, consideration of the social structure outlined in *Starship Troopers* in the context of recent scholarship on fascism and militarism suggests that, in fact, neither ideology is embodied in this work, and that critics of Heinlein's views and visions must find new pejorative terms with which to condemn the novel.

The charge of fascism can be most easily dismissed, since the world of *Starship Troopers* has literally none of the characteristics commonly associated with fascist societies. Such concepts as a revolt against bolshevism, a reaction to liberalism and positivism, and a desire to restore an organic community, can be neither supported nor extrapolated from the novel's context. . . . More significantly, Heinlein offers no other common bench marks of fascism. There is no indication of a ruling party, a secret police, a charismatic leader, or an official ideology. (p. 114)

At least as significant in demonstrating that Heinlein's society is not fascistic is the absence of racism and xenophobia. . . . [*Starship Troopers*] can be called fascist only if fascism is used in the contemporary sense, as a generalized term of opprobrium, impossible to refute on an intellectual level. (p. 115)

If the charge of fascism cannot be substantiated, the accusation of militarism requires more careful consideration. Militarism can be narrowly defined as the tendency of armies to serve themselves instead of war, to seek glory, diversion, or narcissistic gratification at the expense of efficiency. The military system of *Starship Troopers* is as far from this concept as can be imagined. (p. 116)

But there is another definition of militarism as well, one which speaks both of the exaltation of military ways, military attitudes, and military authorities over their civilian counterparts, and of the permeation of society by military behavior patterns. At first impression, the world of *Starship Troopers* seems perfectly tailored to these specifications. Flogging is a punishment for minor crimes. Assaulting a serviceman is a serious offense. Police forces are composed of retired career men. Military law takes precedence over civil. . . . These are points to chill the heart of the civil libertarian. . . . And for those who might still question the militaristic nature of Heinlein's society, there remains the main theme . . . —the making of a soldier, described in loving detail and with evident approval.

To evalute the elements of militarism in the world of *Starship Troopers,* however, it is first necessary to understand that Mobile Infantryman Juan Rico [the protagonist] cannot be regarded as a spokesman for and reflection of his society. He is the universal soldier, and the quintessential career man. He is competent enough at what he does. But he is not that common Heinlein protagonist, the Individual, the Man Who Knows How. (pp. 116-17)

[The society depicted in the novel] is neither militarist nor fascist in the scholarly sense of these concepts. . . . [Critics] might do well to familiarize themselves carefully with the past from which they believe a given work draws its social and political inspiration. Such knowledge can make possible conclusions and extrapolations in areas where an author intent on telling a story may present no more than the hint of an explanation. It might also indicate that science-fiction writers are not entirely prone to rely on custom and analogy in developing their future societies. (p. 120)

Dennis E. Showalter, "Heinlein's 'Starship Troopers': An Exercise in Rehabilitation," in Extrapolation *(copyright 1975 by Thomas D. and Alice S. Clareson), Vol. 16, No. 2, May, 1975, pp. 113-24.*

GEORGE EDGAR SLUSSER

[What] is a "classic" Heinlein work? Most criticism of

Heinlein begins and ends here. Invariably, each individual critic has chosen the works he likes best, dubbed them classics, and consigned the rest to oblivion. . . . The years to be covered in this study include, basically, the 1940s and 1950s —the period of the stories and novellas, and the novels of juvenile adventure. Unfortunately, there is no touchstone which allows a reader infallibly to pick "classics" out of this span. What is possible, however, is a definition of process that will permit us to study Heinlein's evolution as a writer over two long and full decades. (p. 3)

[If] chronological periods are marked off at all [in Heinlein's work], they must be ordered in terms of genre. The use of a given form, in Heinlein's case, was dictated in large part during [his] early and middle years by the vagaries of science fiction publishing. His first (and only) market was pulp magazines, so he wrote short stories and novella-length serials. The switch to novels after the war . . . demanded that he adopt the strict formulas and conventions imposed by his market—in this case, juvenile adventure. The middle period, then, begins with Heinlein's first full-length novel conceived as such, the space epic *Rocket Ship Galileo* (1947), and ends when what I call the subverted adventure finally rears its ugly head in *Starship Troopers* (1959). . . . Not all the novels of this period were juvenile, however. Two old serials were quickly published as novels: *Beyond the Horizon* (1948) and *Sixth Column* (1949). In 1951, Doubleday published Heinlein's first original "adult" novel, *The Puppet Masters*. The novels of this decade are basically of two sorts: the adolescent space adventure dominates—these are novels of initiation to manhood, in which a boy comes of age in outer space. The adult works are novels of political intrigue. But they also, in a sense, are stories of initiation. The heroes are young men instead of boys, and their field of action the "grown-up" world of nations and espionage. Still, they have as much to learn, and the situation is meant to test (and teach) them. In fact, these two modes tend to conflate in the later novels of the period. *Citizen of the Galaxy* (1957) has a boy hero who grows to be a young man; it has space adventure, political intrigue, and much more. (p. 4)

[Conventional] patterns of heroic adventure and formation dominate the works of the 1950s. And yet, as patterns they seem in many ways contrary to Heinlein's deep-seated vision of things. In contrast to the juvenile novels, few of his early narratives have tight construction, or even "plots" at all. Indeed the episodic, almost impressionistic nature of these works has always puzzled critics. They expect "character studies" in the traditional sense, where an individual shapes himself and is shaped in the matrix of free choice and chance event. They do not get them. On the contrary, Heinlein seems most willing to exploit the other, anecdotal tradition of the short story. In like manner, the tendency of serialized narratives to decompose into a row of autonomous units appears to favor rather than hinder his sense of construction. Behind the looseness of these forms, in fact, lies a much different basic pattern—call it predestination. In Heinlein's stories, man's acts do not carry through, nor do they link future sections in causal fashion, so much as illustrate, in any number of particular, exemplary moments, the workings of an immutable higher order.

In light of this, it is tempting to set aside the juvenile novels, and seek the germ of Heinlein's later problem fiction solely in these early stories and novellas. . . . The middle novels, however, cannot be ignored as anomalies. On the contrary, they are the crucial step in Heinlein's development as a writer. There is no sudden conversion from formless episodic works to tightly wrought stories of adventure. . . . Nor are these adventure patterns simply abandoned, either. Heinlein retains them in his late novels, but has modified their form and function. (pp. 5-6)

A pattern of election and predestination is dominant throughout Heinlein's work. It exists most visibly and openly in the early tales and novellas, and here it should first be grasped. Significantly, among these stories tight plots occur only in those that celebrate the workings of inexorable destiny—time-travel paradoxes, and various tales of sacrifice. In the latter, a man (he may be any size or shape, with results ranging from "tragic" to comic) is chosen, and simply accepts to do the job. He neither rebels against the machine, nor sets himself above it—he takes his place unhesitatingly in its workings.

The looser structures seem, contrarily, to center on the exploits of one powerful personality. If we look more closely, however, we see that he too, paradoxically, is more chosen than chooser. He achieves rank and power, but less through personal actions than by a special "vision," a predisposition. (p. 6)

Heinlein's elite are not known by physical signs, nor do they bear the traditional hero's stamp. Their deeds do not really designate them (they may give sample displays of power, no more). Instead, their true work is a common mental disposition: they believe in individual freedom, and are willing to band together to fight entangling bureaucracy and mass strictures. The goal of these libertarians is simply to keep the channels of election open. . . . Significantly, once their own society within society is formed, they proceed to develop even tighter regulations than the structures they replace. What was custom on the outside takes on the force of code and ritual inside. (pp. 6-7)

[Heinlein's *laissez faire* "philosophy" is rooted] in patterns that are both cultural and mythical. The advent of religion in *Stranger* and the other later novels is no accident, nor is the harshly Calvinistic nature of this creed. Calvinistic figurations are present in Heinlein's earliest stories—they run throughout his work in one form or another. These variations, however, are important: there are three discernable phases. The first, essentially but not exclusively that of the early stories and novellas, could be called the Puritan phase —Heinlein's emphasis in these stories is on worldly hierarchies of the elect. At the point, in the juvenile novels, where predestination and conventional heroic patterns meet, we have a second, more "democratic" phase: the rule of the visionary company gives way momentarily to the possibility of Everyman as hero. The third phase, that of *Stranger* and its kindred novels, is more purely Calvinist. The mechanisms of election are reaffirmed; but, as with the Everyman hero, the group also pales before the all-absorbing problem of superman before grace. (p. 7)

In Heinlein's latest novels, however, such groups wane beside the rising star of one supreme existence, and we find something comparable to Calvinist "supernatural grace." Election . . . overleaps regular channels, elides everything into one epiphanic moment. This contrasts with the early stories, where, if election takes place, it is analagous to what was once called "common grace," the form most amenable to the worldly Puritans because it sanctioned their theocratic order. Its path was visible both in the ritual and social structures of their group—it was God's will incarnate. Indeed, Heinlein's characters in these stories do little more than act out such concrete designs of providence. The thrust of election is both worldly and functional; its result is a firm and efficient social hierarchy.

The roots of Heinlein's basic pattern go deep into the American past. They can be found at that point where the social forces of the Puritan Church and the new mercantile elite of the enlightenment cross and blend, where church member and property owner meet. Indeed, behind the seemingly "democratic" facade of "inner light" grace stands the Puritan theocracy, interpreting their own worldly success as a sign of election. In the same way, behind the Enlightened doctrine of "liberty and justice for all" lies the basic inequality of entrepreneurial society; add this to the sanction of Puritan doctrine, and it becomes incontestable; add a "Darwinian" sanction, and it becomes hereditary as well. Heinlein holds up the same masks of freedom and individual liberty. And yet he despises the incompetent and weak, the democratic processes that enfranchise what he calls "homo sap."

In taking up the juvenile adventure, Heinlein must adopt quite a contrary pattern. However unlikely the channel, through it he taps a tradition that, if not egalitarian, is eminently humanistic. Heroic action at least implies that man makes his way in the world through moral qualities that many humans (not just the happy few) recognize and to some extent possess. The novels in which Heinlein develops this pattern are full of a strange tension. Can the individual help shape his destiny through willed action? Or are deeds futile in a fallen world? Is not election rather irrational and unearnable, a gift beyond all sense of personal merit? Born of this tension, perhaps, is the new emphasis, in Heinlein's novels of the 1960s and 1970s on the ambiguities of election. Out of it rises the new Heinlein hero: supreme man alone before his hidden god. (p. 8)

No matter what their intended audience, all [Heinlein's] stories share one structural characteristic—they are loosely episodic. This openness fits Heinlein's purpose admirably. Only in the most external sense does a Heinlein story focus on a crucial moment in the life of a character. His protagonists do not, through some process of self-discovery, come to a climatic recognition of identity or place in the world order. Nor are there "surprise endings" in the classic sense, where an ironic twist of fate reveals a man's character to himself. On the contrary, the heroes of Heinlein's tales seem to know from the start what they must do: they face their destiny, accepting it with a singular lack of resistance or self-searching. But there is more here than "doing one's duty": the hero seems chosen, compelled by some inner predilection that goes against all reason or common sense. What the narrative invariably examines, as step by step it becomes visible, is the mechanism of election itself. This can take myriad forms—the more involuted the better—but there is always the same underlying pattern. If the story ends with a surprise, it is the wonder of destiny, always fortunate in some higher sense, if not for its immediate agent. Indeed, the final emphasis is not on the disparity between individual aspirations and the whole, but on their harmony. In amazing ways, the two strands unite, the expendable acts of one being spill over into the larger ongoing process of racial destiny, apparently advancing according to a predetermined plan toward some glorious end. Only in the later Heinlein will that end itself become problematical. (pp. 9-10)

[Heinlein's first story, "Life-Line,"] is a work directly antipodal to the adventure story and its well-hewn plot. Indeed, the center of this sequence of episodes is less a character than a problem. Pinero is more than a model of how we should act. The man and his machine embody a much more general pattern, not of conduct, but of universal law. Instead of enacting destiny, they literally incarnate it. This tale, then, is clearly allegorical. As such it stands, at the onset of his career, as a microcosm of Heinlein's world. (p. 10)

If "Life-Line" is an allegory, what does it signify? The theory behind Pinero's machine [that measures each human life] is simple: a human life span, like that of the race as a whole, is a material entity. . . . In this purely physical sense, each individual life is pre-determined. The machine gives man foreknowledge. For the majority, however, this knowledge is intolerable: life is livable only in uncertainty. And yet, Pinero proves that struggle and a clear vision of one's fate are not incompatible. In contrast to the others, he sees the moment of his death and its cause—the defense of his own machine—and still pushes on, meeting his end with calm dignity. What else can he do? Man can know his destiny, but not alter it. . . . (p. 11)

Pinero is the prototype for Heinlein's elite man: all are marked by what might be called a creative capacity to accept the inevitable. But where does this superiority come from? It is nothing the hero develops—this would imply that any man could do it—but rather something he already has. Indeed, its existence is clearly placed on a level outside commonality. It is not a biological trait in the ordinary sense, for Pinero possesses neither physical beauty nor strength. Nor, apparently, does he have the craft or cunning necessary for blind survival at all costs—if anyone has these, it is his opponents. Pinero puts his great intelligence to a much different end—martyrdom. But it would be wrong to give this a tragic sense either, to see it as protest against a world without transcendence. (p. 12)

In "Life-Line," there are two states: nature, and a secular form of grace. In the first, "wisdom" is ignorance and darkness; the way of nature is irremediably perverted. Only Pinero is lifted above this: he receives his illumination, and goes to meet his end with the serenity of the elect. His martyrdom is part, not of nature, but of some higher evolution. The fallen state is merely sifted, the chaff abandoned. The destiny of man is that of the chosen few.

The interplanetary job corps in "Misfit" (1939) serves the same function as Pinero's machine—it places all men on an equal footing, so that the new elite may emerge. . . . Again, from outward appearances alone, [the protagonist, Andy Libby,] would be the least likely choice: he is an awkward, gangling lad from the Ozarks. In Heinlein's parables, our standards constantly fail to discern the elite. Yet, despite appearances, Libby is an intuitive mathematical genius. . . . There is no rational explanation for his talents: they were given him, and providence allows them to unfold. Libby's destiny fits neatly into the larger one of man's expansion into space. In this tale, he performs the minor task of moving an asteroid—man is rearranging the heavens. He will go on (as we learn in *Methuselah's Children*) to invent the space drive that will open up the boundless universe. If things are predestined, they also seem open-ended: already we see a phobia of the end that will haunt Heinlein increasingly in later years. (pp. 12-13)

In Heinlein, names like Andrew Jackson Libby (or Johann Sebastian Bach Smith) are microcosms of election—the everyman's last name is a mask covering the true lineage of genius. Libby comes into his world trailing clouds of glory, and merely acts out his predestined role. The story has become a ritual more than anything else. (p. 13)

"We Also Walk Dogs" provides a transition between the early tales and those written during the years immediately following Heinlein's wartime silence—especially 1947 and 1948. Like the early stories, it is partly an allegory of election, a demonstration of the processes of destiny. And it is partly an exemplary tale as well, one of an openly didactic nature. As it seeks to define the complex relationship between the individual and his universe, it also sets forth exemplary types. We are not only told who the elect are—we are told or taught to admire them. (p. 18)

[Heinlein's novellas] should not be considered as something intermediary or transitional, a step on the way to the novel. Theirs is rather an alternate mode of narration. Compared with Heinlein's more orthodox novels of adventure and intrigue, the novellas have a quite different structural logic. The adventure novel is fundamentally synthetic in form; successive episodes are subsumed in the gradually evolving mystery, resumed in the culminating denouement. In the same way, on the private level, the hero's consciousness unfolds in time and space until, at the moment of self-discovery, all previous experiences are encompassed in a flash. Heinlein's novellas often contain numerous episodes. These are organized, however, not in a linear series, but in concentric layers around a single center. In each novella, "action" is restricted to one pivotal problem or adventure. This is rapidly set forth and circumscribed; ensuing events tend to gloss it, building upon this center in analytical fashion. Heinlein's novellas often appear excessively digressive. Indeed, it is this centrifugal structure that generates most of those disquisitive passages that so annoy readers of Heinlein. . . . [We] do not find linear movement toward a point, but pulsatory movement away from it. The "action" will expand into various satellite realms, and then suddenly (irrationally, if we persist in thinking in terms of linear construction) contract upon the point in order that the story may end.

These early novellas seem to hold the key to the excessively digressive, actionless form of Heinlein's latest work. . . . More importantly, however, their structure sheds light on the unusual nature of some of Heinlein's juvenile novels. In certain of these "classics," it seems almost as if this vertical, analytical pattern has been superimposed over the initial horizontal impetus of the action novel. In this way, the "fast starts" we find in many Heinlein novels of the 1950s—where hero and reader are thrown at top speed into the middle of a train of events rushing forward toward denouement—are literally sabotaged. The forward thrust is made to coagulate around a problem center. This may indicate a preference for the novella form; but it does not necessarily mean Heinlein has lost structural control. . . . [He] can write adventure novels of a more conventional sort when he so wishes. We can only assume, from the persistence of these hybrids, that Heinlein intends this fusion of forms, and is actively seeking some structural advantage from it. Not only are Heinlein's early novellas strongly didactic; they illustrate, in their expansive and contractive structures, a vision of man in which the individual's relation to the whole is predestined and unchangeable. Fusion of this form with the patterns of heroic adventure in the middle novels allows Heinlein to redirect a view of man that must have been basically alien to him. Freedom of individual action, rational control of destiny—values implied in the narrative of heroic quest, no matter how debased—are gradually cancelled out as this axial form spreads from the center of these novels. (pp. 24-5)

[The] high points of action and intrigue in Heinlein's work are *Rocket Ship Galileo* and *The Puppet Masters*. Heinlein is often praised for the quality of his intrigue. . . . [These two works] best measure the extent to which intrigue leads an independent existence in his fiction. We will find it, even here, oddly qualified, mitigated by the need to shape parables. Billed as "the classic Moon flight novel that inspired modern astronautics," *Galileo* remains a narrative very much in the tradition of the pulp serial. Brassy chapter headings like "Let the Rockets Roar," and melodramatic cliff hangers like "Danger in the Desert" betray its origins. As is typical of certain pulp adventures, flamboyant scenes of action alternate with fictionalized lectures to young scientists. . . . [Digressions] are always controlled in this novel by the exigencies of intrigue. Once the action starts on the Moon, there is no time for school. Things are just the opposite in an earlier narrative like "Beyond this Horizon" (1942). Here, the characters hardly find time to act. The few episodes of intrigue seem added merely to enliven the series of dialogues that expose the central problem of genetic engineering. These, rather than the feeble actions of the Order of the Wolf, dominate and impel this story. In *Galileo,* there is hardly enough time to explore the city of the original lunar dwellers. The heroes are too busy with the Nazis; and though the Nazis used these ancient tunnels as a base, they neither noticed nor cared where they were. In the compass of this novel, the mystery is hardly touched: the heroes bring back some pictures, and the Moon dwellers remain in limbo. In later novels, however, similar mysteries suddenly expand to overwhelm the initial conflict. As early as *Red Planet,* the enigmatic Martians awake, and Heinlein's subplot suddenly suspends and invalidates the intrigue. (p. 44)

[In addition to intrigue, the] other major shaping pattern in Heinlein's novels of adventure (a pattern present in most of his fiction to some degree) is that of initiation. Several kinds of initiatory experience must be distinguised here: First, there is the novel of *Bildung*—the individual is mysteriously chosen for admission in some select group, and actively guided by its members through a series of trials to the goal. These works are the most backward-looking; often, they seem little more than elaborate extensions of a novella like "Gulf." Then there is the novel of false heroic formation—individual deeds and accomplishments turn out, in the end, to be superfluous: all along the hero has been following the guiding hand, intimate and invisible, of grace. In this overleaping election, the heroic conventions are subverted. Finally, there is *Have Space Suit, Will Travel.* This seems an unusual novel for Heinlein, for not only is the hero a free agent to an appreciable degree, but his individual acts have a real bearing on the outcome of events. Has the author simply relaxed his stance, and fallen back upon the stock juvenile formula? On the contrary, *Space Suit* is very much Heinlein, very much concerned with election and the destiny of the human race. A marvelous dynamic balance has been struck here between two states—heroic insecurity and sureness of the elect—which elsewhere function as contraries. In spite of its infelicitous title, this novel is a masterpiece.

Heinlein's period of juvenile adventure is roughly bracketed by two works that bear much resemblance to each other—*Space Cadet* (1948) and *Starship Troopers* (1959). Both represent a crude variation on the novel of *Bildung* as Goethe practiced it. In Goethe's work, coming of age is seen as a process which prepares the individual to assume his social responsibilities. To this worthy (and classic) goal, some modern factors are added. The hero (as the name Wilhelm Meister implies) is both everyman and a special man. Or rather, the "master" is somehow immanent in the bumbling commoner, and only waits to be drawn out. Mysteriously, he is chosen to become part of a powerful secret society, and guided until he discovers his true vocation. The hero is separated from the ordinary world; the society to which he accedes is an elite within the general society of man—benevolent, aristocratic, above the law. *Space Cadet* is exactly this kind of tale. Here, the dream of the inner circle is incarnate in an even more romantic vision of the military organization. The bulk of this story focuses on the apparatus that trains the hero. Individual action is relegated to a brief coda, in which Matt Dodson (now aware of his role in this elite group) performs a mission. The heroic act is illustrative rather than formative.

In a later novel, *Starman Jones* (1953), we have a significantly different process of initiation. Not only is the shaping group gone, but the hero finds himself apparently thrown against a select clique which stands for repression rather than election. . . . Growing up, it seems, is a much different process here: this boy appears to shape his own future through acts of perseverance and courage. But does he really do so? Traditionally, heroes are superior men. But if they differ from us, it is more in degree than in kind: they possess a greater force of will, or a higher capacity for suffering, or more willingness to risk their existence in perilous actions. If we look twice, we suddenly see that Jones is not such a hero at all. Far from smashing the caste system, his acts only serve to confirm its validity by revealing that he (by inalienable right) belongs among their number. . . . As ever in Heinlein's universe, the attempts of the non-elect to rule are only self-damning. In *Starman Jones,* Heinlein offers the promise of heroic adventure and of growth in action, and then cancels them out in a flash.

In both cases, Heinlein forces us to read the adventure of initiation allegorically. On one hand, the process of *Bildung,* is made to incarnate an older, more familiar form of "common grace." On the other, the classic adventure story is overturned by the revelation that its "free" hero has been following a preordained path all along. Here things turn in a different direction. In the surprising career of Max Jones, there is perhaps the analogue of that other direct and overleaping mode of grace. In a later novel like *Stranger in a Strange Land,* Heinlein strikes a new balance between the elect group and the individual recipient of "supernatural" grace. Here is a new centrifugal form in which grace, as an expanding center, comes to dominate the structural rhythms of the whole. Heinlein has also given us another alternative to this dichotomy. The one tale of initiation that escapes this easy conversion into allegory is *Have Space Suit, Will Travel* (1958). . . . [This novel] looks across the gulf of a year at Heinlein's next effort in the vein—*Starship Troopers*. It is hard to imagine two more disparate treatments of the same theme—the coming of age. *Space Suit* remains a tale of election and destiny. Its patterns are relaxed, while those of *Troopers* are harsh and rigid. This time, within the broader frame, there is latitude for individual action. True, the story has a typical Heinleinian confrontation: a young boy stands at the bar of universal justice, and is called upon to defend the human race against the charges of these superior aliens, to thwart the menace of punishment—man's extermination. Again, the center makes direct contact with the circumference. Rather than elision, this time there is unbroken linear development from one extreme to the other: the adventure pattern holds. Symbol and concrete object relate to each other in a manner resembling causality. If Kip's actions are exemplary, it is not at the expense of his personal drama of formation, but because of it. . . . [He] would never have evolved as a chosen representative of the human race had he not also grown as an individual. Election is only the starting point, and destiny the end. If the path here seems too full of twists and fortunate surprises, these are interlinked each step of the way with real, believable human agents. The plan works in *Space Suit,* but it is not so absolute or restrictive. The elect are less obvious, less certain. Mankind is not so rigidly divided, nor are human will, heroic deeds, always blatantly superfluous. In its more tentative nature *Have Space Suit—Will Travel* is interesting Heinlein. Somehow in this novel, the contrary patterns of heroic adventure and predestination reach a moment of miraculous balance.

In *Space Suit,* Heinlein achieves the conflation of personal adventure and exemplum through skillful use of the first person narrator. . . . This exemplary situation, where a young American dreamer and his battered space suit come to stand for humanity as a whole, is not the product of ellipsis. It results instead from a clearly triadic rhythm—thesis, antithesis, synthesis—in which the logical action of the hero's mind becomes inseparable from the progression of events. (pp. 49-52)

The truly "classic" Heinlein is [an] allegorical writer. . . . There is a basic pattern, shaped in the earliest tales, and carefully elaborated in his subsequent work. But there is also a distinct development of allegorical forms on a diachronic axis as well. The early stories and novellas are more obviously parables, and whatever action and adventure there is has an overtly symbolic or illustrative function. The middle novels are different: here, an allegorical purpose gradually informs and transforms conventional adventure. Rightfully, then, Heinlein's later "problem" novels are hybrids. In their didactic and "philosophical" emphasis, they mark a return to the more static patterns of the early stories. At the same time, however, their form has benefited from the development of Heinlein's art during the decade of juvenile writing. The curious subversion of the linear patterns of intrigue and initiation in these works has contributed as much to the form of *Stranger* as the vertical configurations of a story like "Waldo."

In spite of this merger, these adventure forms have a certain life of their own in Heinlein. Running parallel to the revival of openly philosophical works on a grand scale in the 1960s is a current of shorter works in which the impetus of a decade of action and intrigue is sustained. . . . True, these novels eventually blend with the philosophical stream, if only through the fact that their heroes get progressively older. We go in the span of a decade from youth to middle age, and finally to senescence. In Heinlein's latest work, *Time Enough for Love,* adventure of all sorts (intrigue as well as the drama of coming of age) is absorbed into a new narrative center—the exemplary life of ancient and deathless Lazarus Long.

One novel of the 1960s does stand out—*Glory Road* (1963). The last of Heinlein's juvenile adventures is an interesting work, both from its position in this decade, and in itself. It has many of the faults of the Heinlein novel in general, and a dogmatic edge that places it unquestionably in his late period. Yet somehow it remains a satisfying piece of work. Again, in a novel apparently about the formation of a hero, there is no individual growth. . . . In terms of traditional patterns initiation, the action centers here in another huge elision—the hero doesn't face his world, he circumvents it. But might it not have been (as the rival convention demands) only a dream after all? Heinlein strikes, it seems, a new note of ambiguity. In openly stressing the dream-motif, which has propelled the hero of many a romance into fabulous adventure, and brought him safely back again, Heinlein seemingly seeks to parody his own process of suppressing the middle. (pp. 57-8).

[*Glory Road*] shares with *Space Suit* the same creative interplay (if to a lesser degree) between Heinlein's persistent patterns of election and predestination, and those of the action genre he adopts. . . . [As] with *Space Suit,* the meaning of this novel is to be found not in a separation of these two strands, but in their interaction. The message, however, is a different one—and a poignant sign of the alteration in Heinlein's world view that occurred during the '60s. Scar goes down the "glory road" to the heart of a universal order that would seem a Heinleinian paradise. Instead of big government, there is no government. . . . Democracy and freedom for all? Far from it. In this universe, the ablest rule, and order is strictly maintained. Yet even in an Eldorado such as this, Scar becomes restless—without his heroic task, the hero feels "useless." An alien on the planet Center, Scar goes back to Earth, only to discover that he is alien there too. Glory is the goal of Heinlein's man. Here, between center and circumference, it can be found only on the endless road that moves back and forth. Here begins that pattern of perpetual motion from one meaningless extreme to the other which receives its ultimate incarnation in Heinlein's latest novel. Lazarus Long moves forever between what for him are the mutually cancelling terms of time and love.

Glory Road, then, is both a "classic" and an anomaly in Heinlein's canon. Less overtly allegorical than most of his works, it remains nonetheless a superb parable, in which the higher workings that control man's destiny are deftly exposed to view. On the other hand, as the last of those novels of juvenile adventure in which the patterns of action not only co-exist but actually interact with those of election, it represents in Heinlein's fiction the current that lost. (pp. 59-60)

George Edgar Slusser, in his The Classic Years of Robert A. Heinlein *(copyright © 1977 by George Edgar Slusser), The Borgo Press, 1977, 63 p.*

IVOR A. ROGERS

The "best" science fiction writer for most [readers] is a composite entity: Heinleinasimovclarke—usually in that order. . . . Omitting the enthusiastic burblers who can neither see, hear, nor speak evil of Heinlein, most critics have managed a certain consensus—they like his writing, but the sins of commission and omission in his writing are staggering: poor use of language, weak and inadequate plotting, poor storytelling techniques, and incapacity to handle mature sexual themes being the worst offenders. Yet people, even his severest critics, like his writing, and he sells well. Most importantly, he is capable of attracting readers with a wide age differential and with widely disparate educational backgrounds.

The most common criticism of Heinlein is based on his (supposed) political ideology, and much of the political philosophy expressed by some of his characters does set the teeth on edge; but Liberal knee-jerk reflex has no more place in a mature consideration of his work than Conservative knee-jerk adulation does. Ideological considerations aside, Heinlein appeals to and is criticized by a wide variety of "-ists," "-ats," "-ites"; and there is little consensus on what is his best work. (p. 222)

The problem facing the archetypal or mythic scholar who applies his talents to popular culture is a simple one: the myths or *topoi* remain constant, but the thematic treatment suffers from changing styles in form and language. What is a deeply moving experience to one generation, because it has been phrased in forms and words most vital to their unconscious needs, withers to unreadability as attitudes, language, and form change. . . . The true classic has a universality or greatness that can transcend writing styles and formalistic devices so that it has greatness for the present generation and for generations to come, and I believe that at least one-fourth of Heinlein's work *may* have this universality, especially portions of his last work to date, *Time Enough for Love* (1973). (p. 223)

Heinlein's critical theory is simplistic: he has read many books but knows little theory. For him there are only two kinds of fiction: realistic (or possible) and fantasy (or impossible) fiction. He breaks these two categories down into three subclasses each. Fiction may be set in the past, the present, or the future. He makes a strong point that most of the best science fiction (or speculative fiction as he prefers) is realistic fiction set in the future, but this is not an inflexible dogma. A novel may be set in both the past and the present, or any other combination of the temporal classifications, including a combination of past, present, and future.

For our purposes his most meaningful use of his classifications is when he declares that it is perfectly possible for a story to combine fantasy and realistic writing, have historical, contemporary, and future settings, and it may include comedy, tragedy, burlesque, and straight hortatory propaganda. . . . Heinlein knew that it was possible to write such a story, even though it posed serious technical problems, because he had read and liked a book which did all of these things: *Caleb Catlum's America* by Vincent McHugh. In writing *Time Enough for Love* I believe that Heinlein, either consciously or unconsciously, patterned his book on the earlier work. . . . (pp. 224-25)

If there is this relationship between the two books, and if Heinlein's book follows the pattern set out above, then *Time Enough for Love* is not science fiction *as its own author defines it* in his article "Science Fiction": ". . . such exotic creatures as to defy almost any method of literary taxonomy." . . . There are extensive elements of fantasy in the book: most of the love sequences, references to Gilgamesh and the Wandering Jew as real people, and the claim that Shakespeare—a brother to Queen Elizabeth—was a red-haired immortal who dyed his hair to conceal his identity. Heinlein also claims in his essay that any story involving a talking mule is fantasy. . . . Note that he does not say donkey or ass, the traditional talking animal of Fable and *Märchen*. Heinlein states that a talking mule equals fantasy, and in the Dora/Lazarus section of *Time Enough for Love* there are talking mules—who can reproduce their own kind. To a former farm boy, I don't know which would seem more fantastic: the ability to reproduce or the ability to talk. Heinlein has an out for this sort of implausibility in his essay under the rubric of "imaginary but possible," and there is a quick gloss in the novel about "special mutations." Possible, perhaps, but so little explained that it is closer to the old magic wand than the genetics laboratory. . . . Heinlein may be pulling our leg, or even trying to tell us something about his fantasy. So much of *Time Enough for Love* is imaginary but (not very) possible, that it is difficult to classify it as anything short of fantasy.

What is this exotic creature if it isn't science fiction? Unlike the horse put together by a committee it isn't a camel, nor is it even a talking mule. It has elements of a picaresque, but surface elements only, and is actually a romance masquerading as a novel. . . . I believe that McHugh and Heinlein are . . . [true] writers in the [romance] genre. This is particularly seen in *Time Enough for Love* where the fear which one might feel at the death of a hero or demigod (Lazarus Long) is transformed into the adventurousness, the marvelous, and pensive melancholy (the latter is especially noted at the beginning of *Time Enough for Love* and the end of *Caleb Catlum's America*). It turns pity into chivalrous rescue and tender charm, and pity without an object into creative fantasy.

Because there is a good deal of amatory adventure in both *Time Enough for Love* and *Caleb Catlum's America,* it should be made clear that the term romance as used in this chapter has nothing to do with sentimental novels (although Heinlein exudes sentimentality at every paragraph) [or] love stories (although there are several love stories in *Time Enough for Love*. . . . (pp. 225-26)

The true romance is a medieval (primarily) genre which succeeded the epic and *chanson de geste*. Although the romance . . . has been called a predecessor of the novel, it is one by several removes at least. A romance is typically a collection of adventures tied together with a central theme or around a central character, often developing minor characters into adventures of their own. (p. 226)

The major stumbling block to consider *Time Enough for Love* as a romance is that it is written in a moderately realistic manner with little attention paid to metaphorical, rhetorical, and literary techniques. It is baldly written where it does not descend to sentimentality and awkward prose (especially the embarrassingly written sexual episodes). (p. 227)

In Heinlein's later novels the characters sweat, vomit, and have normal excretory functions—usually signs of realistic writing. Because of the prudish censorship of the science fiction magazines these elements are lacking in his earlier novels and short stories, but he prizes tough, realistic writing styles. . . .

Despite realistic elements in Heinlein's later novels, the final determination of his genre or mode of writing revolves around his use of the hero. Lazarus Long, the hero of *Time Enough for Love,* and the hero of *I Will Fear No Evil,* are both men who are superior in degree to other men rather than superior in kind, which would make them divine beings. (Even Valentine Michael Smith of *Stranger in a Strange Land,* for all of his "Thou art God," is still different only in degree.) Lazarus Long is different in degree; but even in relationship to the other members of the Howard Families—who are of a similar kind of human—he is so different that he is considered something special among his kin, and his exploits approach the realm of myth. (p. 228)

Heinlein's later novels have been obscured for us critically because of his incurable penchant for diatribe, hortatory propaganda, and his blending of heroic/romantic modes and irony. I believe that there is a parallel situation between Heinlein and the very first speculative fiction writer, Aristophanes. (p. 229)

Aristophanes' *The Birds* is the story of two disaffected Athenian citizens who "split the scene" and decided to found their own perfect polis. It is called Cloudcuckooland, and is built in the air—about as close to No-where as one can get. . . . [Consider] what Heinlein's later work, especially *Time Enough for Love,* is like, while reading [Northrop Frye's description] of Aristophanes: "Old Comedy, like the tragedy contemporary with it, is a blend of the heroic and the ironic. In some plays this fact is partly obscured by Aristophanes' strong desire to get his own opinion of what the hero is doing into the record, but his greatest comedy, *The Birds,* preserves an exquisite balance between comic heroism and comic irony." . . . Conservative, polemical, and libertarian, Heinlein and Aristophanes have much in common, including the fact that both were writing speculative fiction about society, thus clouding their status as writers of high mimetic comedy.

If *Time Enough for Love* is high mimetic comedy and a romance, there are still many areas of the book that do not fit these descriptions easily. Part of the problem lies in the inadequacy of the critical tools we have to handle popular culture, but more important is Heinlein's writing what purports to be a novel in an age of low mimetic fiction—and we expect a fictive piece in prose to be a novel. *Time Enough for Love* is just about everything that a novel is not, and most of his "novels" since 1960 (excepting the juveniles) are neither novels nor low mimetic fiction. This major change in his writing has irritated most of his critics who find his plots diffuse and his structure rambling. This irritation may well be due to differences in political views . . . , but some of the irritation may also come from the fact that there is a conflict between the ostensible form and the actual content of his works.

The final argument on form rests on the similarities between *Time Enough for Love* and McHugh's *Caleb Catlum's America*. . . . McHugh wrote the definitive folktale adventure-romance of the United States of America, and

Heinlein attempted to write the definitive equivalent of outer space adventure-romance. As Caleb is the quintessential American hero, Lazarus is the folk hero of the Howard Families and, hence, of the human race. . . . (pp. 229-30)

The major content element which convinces me of the similarities of the McHugh and Heinlein books is the question of immortality and red hair. Caleb is an immortal—that is a given by the author, and Lazarus is a presumed immortal (he was three hundred years old before his first rejuvenation). For Heinlein there is a mystique about red hair. Many of the heroes and heroines of his earlier fictions are redheaded. . . . Heinlein provides no explanation for the immortality of Lazarus, but [Caleb and Lazarus] are both redheads, and it is these linkages between the books which make me believe that *Caleb Catlum's America* was the source for Heinlein's Lazarus.

There is a curious similarity between the politics expressed in both novels. . . . Both [writers] might be classed as Jeffersonian, populist, libertarians. . . . McHugh's book is an affirmation of what he considers the American spirit: unbounded, free, open, and founded upon the natural, innate goodness of the common man. (pp. 231-32)

[The] element that apparently appeals to [Heinlein] is the libertarian quality in McHugh; a man ought to be able to do whatever he damn well pleases—unless it conflicts with the wishes of a Heinlein hero. . . . [The] overlap of Heinlein and McHugh comes in their belief that the Nietzschean superman must experience his intense emotions without let or hindrance from men of lesser breed or governmental systems that prohibit and restrain beyond the minimum necessary for survival of society. . . . Both recognize that the free man is a fiercely independent man, capable, competent, and master of his desires, but both recognize the legitimacy of all man's desires that do not conflict with rationality. (Lazarus is perfectly willing to impregnate his clone sisters or have intercourse with his mother if he is convinced that the offspring of the first situation will not carry lethal or defective genes, and in the second case when he is sure that there will be no issue.)

Both writers apparently find the sexual act as the ultimate expression of personal freedom. . . . Both heroes are restricted in their freedom by social and political considerations, but neither are restricted sexually, and both are breakers of sexual taboos. (pp. 232-33)

This brings us to a consideration of Heinlein's sexuality, as expressed in his novels. I have earlier made reference to *Time Enough for Love* as Heinlein's last and greatest novel. I believe that he considered it to be the capstone to his career as a writer, and there are unconscious elements which lead one to the conclusion that his entire writing career was a working out of his oedipal conflicts. Most authors go through cycles in their development, and I believe that *Time Enough for Love* is the culminating work of his final cycle. (p. 233)

Heinlein's ["All You Zombies" (1959)] was a shocker compared to what had come before. [The story] involves time travel that allows a single transsexual individual to impregnate himself and be both his own father and his own mother. The narrator of the story declares that he knows where *he* comes from, "—but *where did all you zombies come from*?" and in the final line, speaking as his female self, Jane, says, "I miss you dreadfully!"

Psychologically this is the tremendous first step in working out the oedipal conflict in the writer. Earlier stories have commented on the fact that adults do have sexual intercourse, but he is still denying that *his* father and *his* mother would ever do such a thing. So he does it to himself. This is a perfect denial of oedipal desires; since it does not resolve the conflict of desiring intercourse with the mother and supplanting the father, it merely avoids the problem. . . .

[The] implication of this story and the stories that are to come in this period of Heinlein's writing shows strong, unresolved sexual conflicts, *until we get to Time Enough for Love*. Resolving a conflict does not mean *solving* a conflict, however, and even in this last work we see unsolved problems obscuring the quality of the writing. This may simply be that Heinlein lacks the technical skill to write explicit sexual scenes without resorting to embarrassing clichés and coyness. (pp. 236-37)

In *Time Enough for Love* there is a recapitulation of sexual development through several stages, each development clearing the ground for the next stage. (p. 237)

From the moment that Lazarus lands in Missouri we start on a sequence that viewed psychologically might lead one to suspect that the author is "putting us on." Does Lazarus land at the place of the author's birth? No, he lands *below* the site of his birth, and after a bit of plot fooling around, gets into this long thing (a train where the little sperm cell of Lazarus waits, ready), passes through his birthplace, still in the train, and is finally ejected into the womb/home/egg of Kansas City. The author's stand-in has finally returned to the womb in a symbolic sense, and is eventually destined to return to his mother's womb via his actual penis. It is either brilliantly humorous or mordantly grotesque—I can't make up my mind.

In any event, this return to the womb, solving both the aggressive and retrogressive desires of the author surrogate, clears the air of a great deal of sexual tension. (pp. 237-38)

[In the sequence describing the Dora/Lazarus relationship we find] Heinlein at his very best. He is dealing from his special area of expertise, how to do something—in this case how to explore and homestead in a totally uninhabited wilderness. The writing is compact, believable, well plotted, and it is a believable treatment of a mature sexual love. Only a little of his fatal coyness remains in the love sequences, and the ending is at least highly charged with pathos if not full-fledged tragedy seen through a rose-colored framework. Reemphasizing that last point is crucial. The ending is not pathetic, although there is an element of pathos; the ending is not sentimental, although he sentimentalizes to a certain degree; and in the end, an old man learns wisdom (to paraphrase the ending of *Antigone*): the arrogant pride of an immortal being brings the final catastrophe home to Lazarus. His *hubris* over his greatness is what eventually brings him to the point where he see no further point in living. I do not know if Heinlein intended this interpretation. He has obviously read Greek tragedy and Shakespeare, but, even if unplanned and unintentional, it is the only reason why Lazarus wishes to die: he has done everything, *including the experience of a complete love.* And Heinlein, like Lazarus, has written everything, including a mature love story. (pp. 238-39)

Ivor A. Rogers, "Robert Heinlein: Folklorist of Outer Space," in Robert A. Heinlein, *edited by*

Joseph D. Olander and Martin Harry Greenberg (copyright © 1978 by Joseph D. Olander and Martin Harry Greenberg; published by Taplinger Publishing Co., Inc., New York; reprinted by permission), Taplinger, 1978, pp. 222-39.

ELIZABETH ANNE HULL

In an attempt to account for the extraordinary popularity and influence of the novels of Robert Heinlein, it would be all too easy to assert that the masses are asses and let it go at that. Those of us academics who read Heinlein are likely to admit it with an apology, acknowledging that we realize his literary merit is probably small and our weakness in enjoying his work a minor character defect. We feel we should not relish his opinionated expressions. . . . We note that frankly didactic literature has always had a relatively small but devoted readership, especially among those whose prejudices and biases coincide with the author's.

But Heinlein's appeal somehow seems to be broader than these general apologies account for. The fact is, though many of us disagree with Heinlein, or what we assume are Heinlein's "true" opinions, we're usually caught by the questions he raises. . . . [Contrary] to the most widely accepted critical theories, the Heinlein addict reads his work, *not in spite of* the sermons Heinlein crafts, but actually *for* the pleasure of the challenge of considering the moral and political questions Heinlein raises. I also believe the secret of his successful sermons lies in his provocative use of irony and in his *not* providing clear answers to these vital questions; rather, at his best he raises issues for the serious adult mind to consider and trusts the reader to draw his or her own conclusions.

SF in general and Heinlein's work in particular have often been considered as different—a thing apart—from the "mainstream" of literature. But I believe Heinlein's craft can be analyzed best by first placing it in context. (pp. 38-9)

[When] Heinlein began writing novels in the 1940s, we find an ironic tension in our public morality and attitudes toward the traditional questions of religious and social duties. Heinlein exploits this cultural schizophrenia by combining our interest in external and pragmatic problems with our need to justify the ways of Man to God. The practical question of how to live, how to cope with our mechanization, technology, overpopulation, scarce resources, pollution, human orneriness; this is entirely inseparable from the ethical and moral issues of personal freedom and responsibility. Yet the separation of state and religion remains our national ideal. A citizen must be free to choose.

The most fascinating questions Heinlein raises are in the field of political power—our outward responsibilities to one another—and in the realm of personal freedom, particularly sexual freedom. In the former area, Heinlein's mastery of irony creates some of the most intriguing, albeit secular, sermons of modern literature. In the latter, he often lacks the perspective and balance required to intrigue someone not already in agreement. One feels he or she is being told rather than shown, and the viewpoint seems manipulated to fulfill the author's wish-dreams.

Heinlein's most successful device in writing is the exploitation of irony and existential absurdity. His protagonists must act without any assurance that they will ever know objective reality. In *Farnam's Freehold,* the eponymous hero-protagonist calls himself an Existentialist and explains his pragmatic agnosticism in performing religious ceremonies even though he refuses to assert a creed: "If there is no good and no God, this ritual is harmless. If God is, it is appropriate—and still harmless."

A master of paradox, he shows that machinery is "human" both in the sense of being created by people and in the notion of capacity to produce good or bad results in terms of our continued existence. What is good in the short term may prove ultimately bad, and vice versa.

Being human, Heinlein shows, is a process of becoming; only changes are permanent. His protagonists are usually becoming better or more aware, but whatever state of awareness in which he leaves his protagonist at the end of a novel, the reader is assured he has not stopped developing. "Truth" exists only in pragmatic moments when decisions must be reached on whatever evidence is at hand. (pp. 41-2)

Heinlein's most successful way of creating this intriguing ironic vision is through the use of a first person narrator. Contrary to prevalent critical assumptions, Heinlein is freed rather than artistically limited by this narrative technique. Using the persona of a likable enough but not heroic or objective or omniscient narrator allows Heinlein to let readers draw their own conclusions about the significance of the events, apart from the meaning the narrator draws from his experience. . . . Heinlein's most successful novels using this technique are probably *Double Star, Starship Troopers, The Puppet Masters,* and best of all, *The Moon is a Harsh Mistress.* Aside from the overall length, these stories contrast sharply in craftsmanship only because of their first person narrative. *Stranger in a Strange Land* and *I Will Fear No Evil* are both told in the third person. The excessive length and repetitiousness of these latter novels may be Heinlein's effort to regain the immediacy and control of the involved first-person narrator. But what he loses more importantly than involvement is the excuse to reflect on the significance of the events, which the participator-narrator can plausibly do to explain to himself why he does what he does next. And the third-person narrator cannot be used ironically to suggest the possibility that the author knows more or has more insight than his protagonist.

But in order to air his sermons, Heinlein typically uses an older man figure: the mature Lazarus Long or Jubal Harshaw in his many forms. Whereas the protagonist-narrator has wasted potential and narrowly specialized skills, the older man has accomplishments to boggle the mind and a broadly impressive range of admirable qualities. Whereas the protagonist just happens to be in the crucial place at the opportune time, or at least not by his own design, the wise mentor's history reveals that he was at the very least responsible for his own destiny and often for bringing the present crisis to a head. The only limits to his control are of cosmic proportions, e.g., the collective ignorance, laziness, or avarice of the masses, or of some powerful special interest group, or the invasion of the earth by an interplanetary menace. The separation of the heroic figure from the main plot concerning the naive narrator-protagonist permits the older man to function as a *raisonneur* for the author, extending the feeling to the reader that he or she is free (as the protagonist is) to accept or reject the conclusions of the author-hero. (pp. 42-3)

The secular theme of the small man rising to meet the great challenge is one of Heinlein's favorites. In *Double Star,* for instance, Lorenzo is as apolitical as Juan Rico when the book opens—and he also resists being called to duty. . . . But by the end of the story Lorenzo is as resigned as Camus's Sisyphus to serving external demands which he cannot avoid. . . .

Not only do we have humanity justifying its ways to God [in this novel], but elevating the listener-reader to the position of judge. Again, however, because the plea is a personal one in first-person narrative, the reader is free to question Lorenzo's conclusions. The very fact that Lorenzo is aware of his own fallibility is powerfully moving, but the reader is free—even invited—to decide whether Lorenzo has outdone himself or whether human existence in the universe is simply totally absurd. (p. 45)

[Let] us look at *Stranger in a Strange Land.* Told by a third-person narrator from the point of view of Valentine Michael Smith, the first part of the novel succeeds fairly well as an exercise in anthropological perspective. Mike is a human raised by Martian ghosts without contact with his own species. Through Mike's unspoiled, unbiased eyes we see how strange our world really is. The question of what it means to be human biologically but alien environmentally is enough to help the reader willingly suspend disbelief through parts one and two. But part three might be the education of any rube and part four reeks of the corruption of Elmer Gantry or worse. By part five the story bogs down hopelessly in the silly and repetitious sexual exploitation of Jill, Patty, Dorcas, Maryam, Anne, Ruth, Dawn—until one gets lost in the proliferation of characters. With growing competence at manipulating the world, Mike loses his appeal as a human being. Jubal Harshaw is the epitome of Heinlein's *raisonneur.* He is good at absolutely everything. . . . But his seduction by Dawn seems unimportant because it comes *after* his pronouncements about the evils of our sexual mores. The seduction is typical of Heinlein's rather vague and summarized description of sexual relations, "Jubal cursed and reached for Dawn . . . and cooperated with the inevitable."

Lacking clear political perspectives, the novel ends on a note of extreme cynicism. . . . The mystery of life is reduced to its ultimate absurdity. If one could believe in the nature of the universe Heinlein postulates, hedonism would be the only sane way to live. But if not, nothing fills the gap but elusive sexual gratifications (from a rather limited and conventional viewpoint). Through sheer repetition and summation, sex loses all meaning as human experience. Everyone loves everyone and all are happy. The secret? Heinlein's fiat. Using Gillian or Ben Caxton as narrator might have focused the story and certainly would have eliminated the silly Foster-in-heaven episodes.

In *I Will Fear No Evil* Heinlein has even less control of his subject—again sex as an end in itself. . . . Not only does the story lack a modicum of integrity and plausibility, it has no particular moral or political question to give it the zest of his better works. Whether Smith survives his brain transplant or has another affair matters to no one else in the world. Freud notwithstanding, as Heinlein treats it here, the question of how to live one's sex life lacks vitality, compared to how to get along in the world politically and economically, which Heinlein masterfully makes graphic in other novels. In *I Will Fear No Evil,* these elements are not entirely missing; they are simply subordinated so they seem incidental to the plot. A first-person narrator might not save this book, but it might allow some ironic reflection on Smith's "wisdom" gleaned from his/her experience. As it is, the reader is either compelled to accept the essentially preposterous or reject the entire story for lack of credibility of narrative voice.

In *Time Enough for Love,* Heinlein returns to first person narration but does not make the narrator the protagonist. Aside from the fact that this book is probably not self-coherent without the rest of the future history series, it lacks strong unifying elements beyond the character of Lazarus Long, who is both protagonist and *raisonneur.* The narrator-historian is effaced completely by the ending so that for practical purposes the reader is listening to the author lecturing on the vulnerability of men to sexual love and the value of family commitments. Again, one feels that this could have made an interesting story if it were tightened and unified.

The question now is: will Heinlein return to his most successful technique of naive *persona*? Or, having brought this to perfection in *The Moon is a Harsh Mistress,* will he go on to evolve an even more effective way of persuading his fans to consider the eternal question: how to live? Heinlein has been accused too often of being merely brightly imitative both of himself and of others; so was Shakespeare. We can clearly see that he has not stopped experimenting with technique. We fans are waiting to consider his questions if Heinlein will trust us to make up our own minds. My bet is on Heinlein, even as the odds grow longer. . . . (pp. 46-8)

Elizabeth Anne Hull, "Justifying the Ways of Man to God: The Novels of Robert A. Heinlein," in Extrapolation *(copyright 1979 by Thomas D. and Alice S. Clareson), Vol. 20, No. 1, Spring, 1979, pp. 38-49.*

* * *

HELLMAN, Lillian 1906-

An American playwright, screenwriter, and director, Hellman has also published three highly successful memoirs. Both her plays and memoirs are characterized by scrupulous diction and economy of language. Hellman's most recent memoir, *Scoundrel Time,* has proved to be the most controversial of all her writings. (See also *CLC,* Vols. 2, 4, 8, and *Contemporary Authors,* Vols. 13-16, rev. ed.)

MARVIN FELHEIM

Probably no play of the American theater (and I am including that feeble adaptation *The Wisteria Trees*) is more completely Chekhovian than Lillian Hellman's . . . most charming original drama, *The Autumn Garden.* Although the piece was only mildly successful when presented during the 1950-1951 season on Broadway, to the discerning (and here I quote Alan Downer) it is "Miss Hellman's most original play."

The Autumn Garden is remarkable for its skill. Miss Hellman herself (in her Introduction to *Four Plays*) lists the two faults most enumerated by her critics: that her plays are "too well-made" and that they are "melodramas." These two limitations are strikingly absent from *The Autumn Garden.* As a matter of fact, the play successfully contradicts Miss Hellman's own statements about the nature of drama. In her Introduction, she states: "The theatre has limitations: it is a tight, unbending, unfluid, meager form in which to write." But *The Autumn Garden* is just the opposite kind of drama; it is loose in structure, bends easily but without breaking, is fluid and, far from being meager, overflows with characters and situations; indeed, so diffuse is the play that a first reading presents the same difficulties as does *The Cherry Orchard:* one must keep a finger poised to search out identities in the cast of characters.

In all of Miss Hellman's first six plays, the initial situation is presented in terms of some kind of problem, and in three of these pieces (*Days to Come, The Little Foxes* and *Watch on the Rhine*) the first actors the audience sees and hears are servants behaving in the traditional opening scene fashion. The Negro servants, Addie and Cal, who are on stage in the first scene of *The Little Foxes,* are there to give us a feeling of elegance and richness and a sense of power, all of which help establish the character of Regina Giddens before her delayed entrance allows her really to dominate the stage. In *The Autumn Garden,* the opening is quite different. "On stage at rise of curtain" are six of the main persons of the play. They do not direct their conversation or their actions toward any one situation, but indeed are behaving in a manner which we have come to call Chekhovian. Each is concerned with himself, his own problems. We, the audience, seem to have interrupted a series of activities which have been going on for some time. . . . The house serves a symbolic function, just as do the houses of Madame Ranevsky in *The Cherry Orchard,* of Sorin in *The Seagull* and of the Prosorovs in *The Three Sisters*. It is the old home to which cling many memories but which has grown somewhat shabby with the passage of time; it is the autumn garden where flashes of brightness only emphasize the proximity of wintery sterility.

In both *The Children's Hour* and *The Little Foxes,* widely regarded as Miss Hellman's best plays, once the initial situation has been established, the whole movement of the plays is direct and without embellishment toward the climax. Both are "well-made" plays in the narrow sense that in neither are there any characters or any actions which do not contribute directly to the unfolding of the central incident. Here we might consult Miss Hellman's definition; "by the well-made play," she writes, "I think is meant the play whose effects are contrived, whose threads are knit tighter than the threads in life and so do not convince." But all art is contrived and better organized than life. The trouble in *The Children's Hour* and *The Little Foxes* is that the contrivances are too obvious; they are *theatrically* convincing, but they do not have the high artistry which makes them consistent with themselves, true not to life but to dramatic art; the contrivances in these pieces render them merely realistic, good enough for exciting (even meaningful) theater, but not great art. Again, Miss Hellman's words suffice. The dramatist, she asserts, "must represent." These plays do, merely.

The Autumn Garden does all this and more. Without seeming to, in this play Miss Hellman organizes her materials in terms of artistic principles, dramatic principles (what Coleridge called "organic" principles). The realism is to the essence of human existence, not to the representation of life. There are many threads of action and of thought playing through *The Autumn Garden*. By the end of Act One, we have established the moral and artistic principle upon which the play is based: people must do the best they can; to do less is immoral. And Miss Hellman, as she hastens to admit, is "a moral writer." But the difference in *The Autumn Garden* is that the moral is within the situation and within the characters, not superimposed upon them by a skillful playwright. . . . Lillian Hellman lets her characters alone to act out their destinies, regarding them only with love and understanding; in her earlier play, she took sides; one can list the characters she admires and those whose behavior and beliefs she dislikes; in *Days to Come,* for example, she admits she even tried to balance characteristics: good against bad, well against sick, complex against simple. In *The Autumn Garden,* she does not make this kind of breakdown. The result is true complexity, both in dialectics and mechanics.

Mechanically, *The Autumn Garden* has Chekhovian grace. The characters all belong on the set: each has a legitimate reason for being at the Tuckerman house at this particular moment in history; each is searching for the meaning of life, and for love. (pp. 191-93)

These people arrive and depart constantly. The superficial stage action consists of noise and bustle; the director is provided with inexhaustible opportunities for stage effects of the most varied sort. This movement supplies the external tension, a tension partly produced by confusion and stir, but a tension which accurately mirrors the inner states of mind and emotions of the characters.

This is a Chekhovian cast, appropriately set in the American South; they are upper middle-class people, with their roots in money and traditions, but caught in the essential tragedy, the tragedy of life. This is not Shakespearean; it is Chekhovian. It is social drama, not classical tragedy. As such, it has two necessary dialectical principles. First of all, as Miss Hellman reminds us, it is "sharp comedy. . . . The world these people [she is discussing *The Cherry Orchard*] made for themselves would have to end in a whimper." But, and here is the second significant point, even though the dramatist does foresee the end of this world, he has what Miss Hellman calls "the artist-scientist hope" for a better one. The pity and terror are present, but they are not for the single, noble (however representative) individual, the Hamlet or the Lear; the pity and the terror are spread out, they are for all. Pity and terror have been democratized and made the proper subject for prose.

The Autumn Garden is written in prose. By the very nature of the medium, the tragic intensity and, to a lesser degree, the tragic nobility of the characters and their situations are rendered less magnificent than if the play were phrased in poetry. In one sense, this is a purely mechanical problem. But prose can take on certain of the qualities of poetry, or, I should say, certain poetic devices are available to the prose writer, particularly to the dramatist. Perhaps the most significant of these is symbolism. . . . In *The Autumn Garden,* aside from a few incidental references to roots and trees, there is no mention of a garden, but the title adds a necessary symbolic note to the whole play. Miss Hellman has used a number of such titles, particularly those which emphasize the organic, natural aspects of human existence: in both *The Searching Wind* and *Another Part of the Forest,* she has used the significant relationship between man and nature to extend the meaning of her dramas. So in *The Autumn Garden,* the symbolism inherent in the title adds a poetic dimension to the scope of the play.

In fact, this is my central point: that the kind of drama we have in *The Autumn Garden* is the only kind which makes for modern tragedy. It is not merely psychological (as in Tennessee Williams) nor sociological (as in Arthur Miller) but it is artistic (poetic) and moral—and all in the Chekhovian sense. And so Miss Hellman's movement in this direction is a movement toward seriousness. (pp. 194-95)

[Miss Hellman's movement in the direction of Chekhov] was natural in light of the life-long study which Miss Hellman has made of Chekhov, a devotion which culminated in her edition of *The Selected Letters of Chekhov*, published in 1955. In her various editorial notes, Miss Hellman pays tribute to Chekhov's "common sense," to his workmanship, and to his "deep social ideals"; of all his plays she thinks *The Three Sisters* is the greatest. These opinions throw some light on *The Autumn Garden*, for they support our idea of its careful design and, in particular, they give a point of reference. For the central themes of the two plays are similar: nostalgia for a no-longer existent past and the individual's frustrating search for love and the meaning of life. The central "message" of both *The Autumn Garden* and *The Three Sisters* is also the same: the inevitability of disaster in the kind of world presented. Miss Hellman has quoted this pertinent remark from one of the letters: "A reasoned life without a definite outlook is not a life, but a burden and a horror." (p. 195)

Marvin Felheim, "'The Autumn Garden': Mechanics and Dialectics," in Modern Drama *(copyright © 1960, University of Toronto, Graduate Centre for Study of Drama; with the permission of* Modern Drama*), Vol. 3, No. 2, September, 1960, pp. 191-95.**

ELIZABETH HARDWICK

It is nearly always said that Lillian Hellman's plays are triumphs of craftsmanship. Actually the question of motivation, the construction of a plot, are quite awkwardly managed in most of them. . . . The plays are full of thefts and letters discovered. The basic plot device is so often unfortunate that the efforts to work it out, skillful enough in a technical sense, become more and more visible and disturbing. This craftsmanship of climaxes and curtain lines and discoveries is a sort of know-how, useful enough in the commercial theater, but paralyzing to the natural development of characters in action. We are too often asked more on behalf of the plot than we can sensibly give assent to.

Behind Lillian Hellman's plays there is a torn spirit: the bright stuffs of expensive productions and the hair-shirt of didacticism. Between these two, her genuine talent for characterization is diminished. . . . [That Hellman's characters] should be squeezed to death by the iron of an American version of Socialist Realism and the gold of a reigning commercialism is a problem of cultural history. (p. 5)

Elizabeth Hardwick, "'The Little Foxes' Revived," in The New York Review of Books *(reprinted with permission from* The New York Review of Books; *copyright © 1967 Nyrev, Inc.), Vol. IX, No. 11, December 21, 1967, pp. 4-5.*

DAVID HUNT

[*Scoundrel Time*] is the story of the 67 minutes that [Lillian Hellman] spent before the House Committee on Un-American Activities in Washington in May 1952, of what preceded the hearing, and what its consequences were. (p. 656)

It is a moving story that she tells, but it must be said that, with all her skill in writing, it is not very easy reading. She assumes too much knowledge in the reader, and there is too much vagueness about dates and places. She is equally vague on her connection with communism: 'Whether I signed a party card or didn't was of little importance to me.' . . .

[The] abiding impression that remains is of the warmth and endurance of Lillian Hellman in her ordeal, and the splendour of her declaration of faith: 'I cannot and will not cut my conscience to fit this year's fashions.' (p. 657)

David Hunt, "Clean Conscience," in The Listener *(© British Broadcasting Corp. 1976; reprinted by permission of David Hunt), Vol. 96, No. 2484, November 18, 1976, pp. 656-57.*

WILLIAM F. BUCKLEY, JR.

[When *Scoundrel Time*] was first published, in the spring of 1976, only the cooing of reviewers was heard. . . . Then . . . then, in *The New York Review of Books*, Murray Kempton interrupted his own paean to Miss Hellman to make a comment or two which, however gentle, quite ruptured the trance. It was as if, in Paris during the occupation, an anonymous arranger had, by fugitive notation, insinuated the motif of the "*Marseillaise*" into a great Speer-like orchestration of "*Über Alles*." Others, after that, came rushing in. It would never be quite the same again for Miss Lillian.

Even so, one has to hand it to her. Though the book is slender, the design is grandly staged, in self-esteem as in presumption. To begin with, here is someone described in the introduction to her own book as the greatest woman playwright in American history. (p. 101)

And here is a writer [Garry Wills] introducing an autobiographical book by a woman who is publicizing now her complaint against an America that, as she might put it, victimized her because of her alleged championship of the regime of Josef Stalin. And what, then, does Wills go and do in his introduction? Quote from the author's pre-McCarthy works, to demonstrate the impartiality of her opposition to tyranny? Not at all. He goes on (and on and on—Mr. Wills consumes 34 pages with his introduction, one-fifth of the book), blithely—offhandedly—describing the era of Miss Hellman's travail as the era in U.S.-Soviet relations during which horrible old us, led by Harry Truman, promulgated a cold war against reasonable old them, the startled, innocent Communists, led by Josef Stalin. . . . *That* introduction, which might have been written in the Lenin Institute, introducing *that* book, under the circumstances of Miss Hellman's apologia, was a venture either in dumb innocence (inconsistent with Hellman's persona), or in matchless cheek. . . . (pp. 101-02)

But the difficulties had only just begun for her. Is Ms. Hellman a nice guy? In a way, it shouldn't matter. A sentence from her book, much quoted, asks, "*Since when do you have to agree with people to defend them from injustice?*" By the same token, we shouldn't require that someone be endearing as a prerequisite to indignation at unfair treatment of her. But Ms. Hellman, author of *The Little Foxes*, is quickly spotted as being no less guileful than one of her characters. It's another case of Germaine Greer, filibustering against male chauvinism, while stripteasing her sexual biography across the magazine rack. Ms. Hellman, affecting only a disinterested concern for justice, twanging the heartstrings—with, however, more sleight of hand than craft. . . . If, unlike the earlier reviewers, you finish the book believing that you have read anything less than an episode in the life of Thomas More, you are either callous—or else her art has failed her. . . .

All in all, her performance is about as ingratiating as a post-Watergate speech by Richard Nixon, and so we quite understand it when Murray Kempton is driven to saying, in concluding his review, that, really, he would not want Lillian Hellman "overmuch as a comrade." Thus, the scaffolding of the book is pretty shaky. It is, after all, implicitly entitled, "*The Heroism of Lillian Hellman during the Darkest Days of the Republic,* by Lillian Hellman." It would have been a little seemlier if her book had gone out as: "*Scoundrel Time,* by Lillian Hellman, as told to Garry Wills." Or—why not just "*Scoundrel Time: How Lillian Hellman Held Her Finger in the Dike and Saved American Freedom and Self-Respect,* by Garry Wills"? He would not have needed to increase the size of his contribution by all that much. In any event—an artistic point, and with apologies to Burke—this martyr, to be loved, should be lovelier. (p. 102)

What does one go on to say about a book so disorderly, so tasteless, guileful, self-enraptured? The disposition to adore her, feel sorry for her, glow in the vicarious thrill of her courage and decency (her favorite word, "decency": she is apolitical now, she says, desiring only "decency") runs into hurdle after hurdle in the obstacle course of this little book. (p. 105)

The author, though she attempts to project a moral for our time out of her own travail, does this less avidly than most of her critics, who seized greedily on this mincing tale of self-pity as the matrix of a passion play. It doesn't work. The heart of her failure beats in a single sentence. "*. . . whatever our mistakes, I do not believe we did our country any harm.*"

"Dear Lillian Hellman," the socialist Irving Howe writes, "you could not be more mistaken! Those who supported Stalinism and its political enterprises, either here or abroad, helped befoul the cultural atmosphere, helped bring totalitarian methods into trade unions, helped perpetuate one of the great lies of the century, helped destroy whatever possibilities there might have been for a resurgence of serious radicalism in America. Isn't that harm enough?" . . .

But it was Providence that provided the epilogue, the ironic masterstroke. Lillian Hellman, best-selling author of the diatribe against the Hollywood moguls who discriminated against her after she was identified as a Communist apologist. When Miss Hellman finally brought herself to criticize the Soviet Union, she singled out for special scorn Soviet censorship. "*The semi-literate bureaucrats, who suppress and alter manuscripts, who dictate who can and cannot be published, perform a disgusting business.*" And lo! the publishers of Miss Hellman's book, Little, Brown, instruct Diana Trilling to alter an essay on Miss Hellman in her manuscript. Mrs. Trilling declines, and Little, Brown breaks the contract—does its best, in effect, to suppress her book. "Miss Hellman is one of our leading successful authors," said Arthur Thornhill, president of Little, Brown. "She's not one of the big so-called money makers, but she's up there where we enjoy the revenue." The principled Miss Hellman, who condemns Hollywood for its base concern for profit, has not severed her relations with Little, Brown, never mind that they sought to suppress and alter a manuscript—in deference to *her*! But, don't you see, the vertebral column of her thought finally emerges. She can do no wrong. "*There is nothing in my life of which I am ashamed,*" she wrote to the chairman of the House Committee on Un-American Activities, setting herself, by that sentence, in a class apart from her fellow mortals. Well, it took a long time for her to learn about Communism. She is elderly, but there is time yet, time to recognize that she should be ashamed of this awful book. (p. 106)

William F. Buckley, Jr., "'Scoundrel Time': & Who Is the Ugliest of Them All?" in National Review *(© National Review, Inc., 1977; 150 East 35th St., New York, N.Y. 10016), Vol. XXIX, No. 2, January 21, 1977, pp. 101-06.*

DORIS V. FALK

[Lillian Hellman's eight] original plays fall into two principal groups, based on Hellman's view of human action and motivation—a highly moral view, interpreting both action and the failure to act in terms of good and evil.

The first two plays became signposts, marking the directions to be taken by the later plays. *The Children's Hour* concerned active evil. . . . The drama pointed the way toward the three plays whose chief characters are despoilers—those who exploit or destroy others for their own purposes. Hellman's second play, *Days to Come,* was not so much about the despoilers—the evildoers themselves—as about those characters who, well-meaning or not, stand by and allow the despoilers to accomplish their destructive aims. Often these bystanders may be the victims of their own naiveté or lack of self-knowledge.

The despoiler plays are *The Little Foxes, Another Part of the Forest,* and *Watch on the Rhine.* Each is a tightly constructed drama, leading to a violent climax that is the result of evildoing. Most of the characters are clearly defined as evil or good, harmful or harmless. But the so-called bystander plays—*The Searching Wind, The Autumn Garden,* and *Toys in the Attic*—are as different from the despoilers in structure as they are in theme. The action is slower, the plot more discursive and low-keyed, moving more within the characters and the events that befall them, than through their actions. For most of these people are unable to act positively or with conviction. They let things happen and they become the passive victims of the despoilers and themselves. Despoilers and bystanders appear in some form in all the plays, but Hellman clearly differentiates between evil as a positive, rapacious force in the first group, and evil as the negative failure of good in the second. (pp. 29-30)

Characterization in all Hellman's plays is trenchant, and her characters are looked at, objectively, from the outside; the playwright sees them but does not identify with them. Unlike many playwrights—O'Neill is the most obvious example—she does not use the stage to express her innermost, personal conflicts or sufferings; she is singularly intolerant of self-pity wherever she sees it. With a few exceptions, her compassion and empathy were to be saved for the memoirs, and there, too, it is highly selective. Even the persona of herself—the "I" who remembers and the "Lillian" who acts—is sometimes mocked in the memoirs and the plays. (p. 42)

The Children's Hour and, possibly, *Watch on the Rhine* are the only plays that approach the definition of tragedy, in the Aristotelian sense. Miss Hellman's customary detachment from her characters is related to the genre in which she writes—not tragedy, but "serious drama" or melodrama. For tragedy requires a protagonist whose fall—partly through his own fault, partly through circumstances beyond his control—can excite pity or terror in the spectator. Detachment, objectivity, or simple dislike or hatred rule out such emotional involvement. (pp. 43-4)

Melodrama, as Hellman used the term, was a logical outcome of realism in drama. . . . [Realism] assumes that life is seldom mysterious, seldom predetermined. When, in most of Hellman's plays, human beings fail or are destroyed, the powers of destruction are in human hands; they are not functions of a higher necessity or fate, or of naturalistic forces. (pp. 44-5)

The Children's Hour has many of the qualities of Hellman's later plays. Its mode and setting are realistic; its characters, strongly etched; its theme, serious; and its tone, indignant. The object of that indignation was both social and individual—a society made up of a group of individuals so bound by their own mores and conventions as to feel compelled, for the preservation of that society, to punish those who deviated from it. (p. 45)

In her later work, Hellman was to be drawn to causes only indirectly related to labor or the proletariat: the ruthless decadence of the southern capitalist in *The Little Foxes* and *Another Part of the Forest,* and the atrocities of fascism in *Watch on the Rhine* and *The Searching Wind. . . . Days to Come,* however, took Hellman's characteristic form—realistic melodrama. The play was a failure, partly because as Hellman said, she tried to say too much about the people in it. The labor cause was not enough to unify the action; Hellman had to explore the individual characters who were themselves often confused about their own motives. There were plot confusions, too—"accidental judgments, casual slaughters . . . purposes mistook" that did not necessarily, as in *Hamlet,* fall on "the inventors' heads," but on everybody's. (pp. 46-7)

As Hellman grew older, the more her misanthropy became like that of the preacher in Ecclesiastes, cynical and sad, rather than angry and rebellious. The anger that she had turned against the Tilfords of this world—Mary and her grandmother in *The Children's Hour*—rages through *The Little Foxes* and *Watch on the Rhine,* and flares up again, but almost as parody, in *Another Part of the Forest.* But in *The Searching Wind, The Autumn Garden,* and *Toys in the Attic,* Hellman is looking at . . . the ineffectual ones who let evil and decay attack and destroy the lives of others, as it consumes their own vitality. (p. 49)

In looking back at Hellman's work as a playwright, it is tempting to try to reduce all her plots and characters to repeated formulas and types. Such an exercise can be performed, of course, on any writer's body of work, but the demands of the stage and of her favorite genre, the realistic well-made melodrama, make Hellman's plays particularly vulnerable to this kind of analysis. . . . More interesting [than the similarities in structure and characterization in the plays] is the moral point of view that unifies both the plays and the memoirs. This is her concept of both active and passive evil, the sins produced by both commission and omission. (p. 92)

An Unfinished Woman is subtitled "a memoir" and *Pentimento* "a book of portraits." But the differences in mechanical structure are more apparent than real. The first book is built as a narrative, not strictly chronological, but still chiefly linear in movement from past to present and back again, relating events and persons to time and to each other. The second, *Pentimento,* is constructed as a series of portraits, each a unit, including group portraits and landscapes. But *An Unfinished Woman* also contains portraits. . . . And the portraits in *Pentimento* are strung together in a loose chronological sequence, over the same time span as *An Unfinished Woman.* (p. 98)

More interesting than the way Hellman organizes her materials is the way she sees them. The books are memoirs, rather than autobiographies, because their concentration seems, at least, to be upon the ambience of the writer rather than upon the writer herself. True, they reveal the author, but in carefully selected times, places, and company. Even in the anecdotes and diaries she is both narrator and protagonist, in a series of short, self-contained dramas.

As speaker and actress, Hellman is the principal unifier of the memoirs, but recurrent settings and characters also help to unify the books as they did her life. (pp. 98-9)

[Lillian Hellman] is a playwright: a maker of tightly constructed theater pieces, and the best of her memoirs are tales told by a playwright—with plot, character, and carefully paced suspense. Her biography provides a narrative line on which to hang the separate, loosely related episodes; and if some of these owe their mechanical structure to the well-made play and the film script, they owe their thematic, or symbolic structure (when it is there) to a combination of sources—including nineteenth-century American fiction, psychoanalysis, and Christianity. (p. 100)

[Hellman] seems to believe as Melville did, that ambiguity often presents a truer version of our perceptions than could clarity or sharp distinction. . . . [She] is influenced by her knowledge of the methods of literary symbolism and by her own predilection toward the religious mythic interpretations of experience, and not least, by her own experience of psychoanalysis, with strong religious associations.

The language of the memoirs is what Hellman would call "pretend cool." It is casual, slangy, objective, humorous, self-deprecatory. But these qualities are often deceptive. Sometimes they are masked, restrained expressions of intense and often irrational angers, fears, conflicts. (p. 101)

The most important difference between the two long books is in their thematic emphasis. *An Unfinished Woman* questions and explores the occasions and rites of initiation, the expiation of guilts, the meaning of suffering and survival—all of these in the context of a deepening insight into self. *Pentimento* seems to be thematically unified around the shapes of love; exploration takes the form of what Richard Poirier [in a review of *Pentimento*] has called "emotional range-finding." In the portrait chapters of *Pentimento,* Hellman ponders the nature of her deepest relationships to others. Of course, the two books combine or interchange themes at times: the last two chapters of *Pentimento* raise questions about suffering, guilt, and survival posed earlier in *An Unfinished Woman.* But this is an appropriate ending for the second book and brings the wheel full circle. (p. 104)

[In] *An Unfinished Woman* and *Pentimento,* Hellman faces

the fact that moral indignation may at times be only a mask for personal pique, for irritability at an insult or an invasion of privacy. . . .

The saving grace from either diatribe or sentimentality is the wry, often rueful humor with which Hellman looks at herself. (p. 111)

Compared to the other memoirs, *Scoundrel Time* (1976), is a minor literary performance that elicited a major political controversy. The book is a slight one. . . . The narrative itself is brief, with remembered sidelights and flashbacks. (p. 147)

The elliptical and often ambiguous style of the other memoirs was, in those books, a legitimate medium for describing the author's personal reactions to life. Most of the characters in those books were dead; names and identities could be changed and shifted to protect the living. Moreover, those memoirs were intended as artifact, not history; accuracy was not the point. But many of the people accused in *Scoundrel Time* of being bystanders to villainy are still alive, and Hellman attacked them by name. They fought—and are still fighting—back. Their charges are based on alleged inaccuracies and omissions in Hellman's facts, and on her stance as the lonely truth-speaker.

As a literary performance, the book has a certain understated charm. It is discursive and anecdotal, less tightly constructed than the memoir chapters I have called dramatic tales. The tone is less that of anger than of disappointment and weariness that Hellman's "old, respected friends" could have been parties to injustice. But she still constructs a series of dramatic confrontations—somewhat episodic now, and sliding forward and backward in time—to build toward the climax, her appearance before the House Un-American Activities Committee in May of 1952. And in spite of her sad or wry disillusionment, the old cantankerous, hot-tempered Lillian is still the protagonist—the Southern kid now grown up. . . . (p. 148)

Hellman has always been a bit dogmatic in her value judgements—especially if she has been personally offended—and sometimes is carried away by the opportunity to air an old grudge. So she let fly in *Scoundrel Time*—sometimes masking her anger under the tone, as I have said, of sorrowful disillusionment with old friends who belonged to the intellectual anticommunist left. (p. 152)

Hellman herself has not answered [the many critical attacks against her position in *Scoundrel Time*] . . . in any cogent, credible way. She claims that she was writing her personal story, not history. Some of her hostile critics have called the book "self-serving;" the character of "Lillian" too heroic, too put-upon and almost martyred, considering the comparative extent of her financial losses and persecution. But the readers who made the book a best-seller thought it was a modest understatement of heroism; that the portrait she presents is of a woman who, in evil times, stuck to her own values against odds and under pressure, and won. (p. 155)

Such a value system as Hellman's, whether in the plays or the memoirs, with its clearcut criteria of good and evil, has a reassuring emotional appeal; it makes us nostalgic for a child's world (where the worst crime is to tattle on your friends) and for the make-believe world of fiction and drama, of despoilers and bystanders, where such a system flourishes. But the adult realm of politics and history demands complexities of knowledge and fact, in which value judgments are painfully arrived at. (p. 156)

Lillian Hellman's insight is sharpest when it is most personal and specific. If some of her plays seem dated now it is probably because of their "well-made," realistic mode and their two-dimensional, good-or-evil characterizations. But three plays (and perhaps others) have had current repertory revivals—*The Autumn Garden, Toys in the Attic,* and *The Children's Hour.* These are the less structured ones, more concerned with psychology than plot, and with moral ambiguity rather than moral definition.

As a memoirist, Hellman was able to present her materials dramatically, without the limitations imposed by the stage. The memoir form allowed, too, for subtlety in the exploration of character; for unanswered questions, and for a certain mysterious quality that evoked a response from readers who knew that mystery for their own.

The personal, the ambiguous, were not appropriate, however, to the politics of *Scoundrel Time,* and Hellman has taken some punishment for that mistake. But she formulated her philosophy of survival when she was fourteen: "If you are willing to take the punishment, you are halfway through the battle."

Lillian Hellman is still producing, still battling, still surviving, still performing. Whatever we may think of her politics or temperament, we must rejoice in the energy, ingenuity, and skill of the performance. (pp. 156-57)

Doris V. Falk, in her Lillian Hellman *(copyright © 1978 by Frederick Ungar Publishing Co.), Ungar, 1978, 180 p.*

* * *

HIGHSMITH, (Mary) Patricia 1921-

Highsmith is an American-born novelist and short story writer now living in France. Her highly imaginative fiction is characterized by chillingly realistic explorations of crime and the criminal mind. (See also *CLC*, Vols. 2,4, and *Contemporary Authors*, Vols. 1-4, rev. ed.)

MARGHANITA LASKI

I used to be the only person I knew who loathed Patricia Highsmith's work for its inhumanity to man, but our numbers are growing and will be increased by [*The Animal Lover's Book of Beastly Murder*], short stories about animals killing or mutilating people, with a strong flavour of being motivated less by pity for animals than by distaste for men. (p. 685)

Marghanita Laski, "Long Crimes, Short Crimes," in The Listener *(© British Broadcasting Corp. 1975; reprinted by permission of Marghanita Laski), Vol. 94, No. 2433, November 20, 1975, pp. 684-85.**

NEIL HEPBURN

Highsmith's purposes are evidently sterner than the mere setting down of [a] sad chronicle of family life [in *Edith's Diary*]: her characters and their circumstances are transparently emblematic of the state of the Union, as well as of the union, in the horrible Vietnam years—the do-gooding that refuses responsibility and results too easily in death for the done-good-by, the lying and evasions of men unwilling to accept the consequences of their actions, the inheritance by the rootless and thoughtless of America the once-beautiful, the irrevocable passing of that patrician strain that, for all its shortcomings, carried within it the ideals of 1776. It is a very pessimistic view of America and, in Miss Highsmith's wonderfully insinuating prose, a very convincing one. Can it really be like that? (p. 699)

Neil Hepburn, "Nuclear Reactions," in The Listener *(© British Broadcasting Corp. 1977; reprinted by permission of Neil Hepburn), Vol. 97, No. 2510, May 26, 1977, pp. 698-99.**

Miss Highsmith has always been a strong and richly imaginative entertainer, and "Edith's Diary" is her strongest, her most imaginative, and by far her most substantial. . . . [Edith] is a firmly committed liberal with a clear view of the realities of world affairs, but her diary tells a different story: it gives her satisfaction there to soften, and even beautify, the rough edges of family and domestic truth. . . . The diary entries take on a brighter and brighter glow. "Edith's Dairy" is a work of extraordinary force and feeling. (pp. 86-7)

"Books: 'Edith's Diary'," in The New Yorker *(© 1977 by The New Yorker Magazine, Inc.), Vol. LIII, No. 28, August 29, 1977, pp. 86-7.*

TOM PAULIN

Alas, there's nothing revolutionary about *Little Tales of Misogyny,* a thin collection of failed fables in which various hairy, possessive or over-fecund women are murdered by their mates. It would be wrong to read these stories as indirectly feminist satires on dependency, because the real centre of their inspiration is the delight which Patricia Highsmith everwhere shows for the brutal ways in which these unlikely women are first murdered and then 'thrown away as one might throw away a cricket lighter when it is used up'. The style of these sterile anecdotes, moreover, is baldly second-rate: 'Christine was absolutely no loss to Philippe except for burial fees', and so on. (p. 745)

Tom Paulin, "Mortem Virumque Cano," in New Statesman *(© 1977 The Statesman & Nation Publishing Co. Ltd.), Vol. 94, No. 2436, November 25, 1977, pp. 744-45.**

BLAKE MORRISON

Critics have been unsure of where to place Patricia Highsmith's work, and it's easy to see why. To call her a 'crime writer' sounds limiting, even patronising, since, like Chabrol, Highsmith is less interested in the mechanics of crimes than in the psychology behind them. On the other hand you can hardly overlook the fact that most of her fictions end up with blood on their hands: she may command a high-art following, but there are those who read her to see how ingeniously and brutally she'll dispose of her characters. Very few of the 12 stories in *Slowly, Slowly in the Wind* slot neatly into a crime-suspense category, but there's no slackening of invention when it comes to the crunch. Vines sprouting out of a pond drag their victims underwater; a farmer's corpse is hung up as a scarecrow; Madame Thibault's Waxworks Museum acquires three additional exhibits . . .

The most chilling stories here are those in which the threat of violence or death, and the taking of measures to stave off that threat, have become a part of daily routine. . . . There's a good deal of class and racial tension in these stories (middle-class whites protecting themselves against down-and-outs and blacks), but the ultimate horror-show is one that a family inflicts on itself: a child dies after swallowing broken glass and sleeping tablets left on the floor by a neglectful mother and drunk father. This story, 'Those Awful Dawns', reads at times like an exaggerated case-study for trainee social workers, but Highsmith's grasp of current social problems is generally greater than she's given credit for and she's at her most macabre when most mundane. (p. 455)

Blake Morrison, "Hot Stuff," in New Statesman *(© 1979 The Statesman & Nation Publishing Co. Ltd.), Vol. 97, No. 2506, March 30, 1979, pp. 454-55.**

LORNA SAGE

[*Slowly, Slowly in the Wind* is] well up to Miss Highsmith's usual standard of nastiness, though perhaps more motley, not so insidiously interlinked as her last collection, the splendid 'Little Tales of Misogyny.' Though her talent for finding fresh horrors, still unspoilt corners of the mind, is exhilarating. Here, one theme that's striking is the furious violence of the meek (senior citizens, suffering wives, violated householders): they were always supposed to inherit the earth, but she's found characteristically ingenious and chilling ways of suggesting how that may come about. Such topical motifs rub shoulders with the classics (the wax museum, the encroaching vegetable) which are equally cleverly twisted, and even a couple of metaphysical/futuristic pieces, which are not. The best story, in some ways, is the oddest, 'The Man who Wrote Books in his Head.' In it she produces a dizzying and very funny illusion within illusion, a casual reminder of the skills behind the blacker magic.

Lorna Sage, "Black Mischief," in The Observer *(reprinted by permission of The Observer Limited), No. 9788, April 1, 1979, p. 37.*

* * *

HOLLANDER, John 1929-

An American poet, critic, and editor, Hollander is a formalist poet of considerable merit, a neo-Scholastic who looks to the seventeenth century for his poetic models. Along with Frank Kermode, he edited the *Oxford Anthology of English Literature*. (See also *CLC*, Vols. 2, 5, 8, and *Contemporary Authors*, Vols. 1-4, rev. ed.)

LOUIS L. MARTZ

Hollander has written his *Reflections on Espionage* in the form of a single long poem composed in strict eleven-syllable lines, except for twenty-one lines at the very end which contain a clever cipher carefully explicated in the author's notes. Hendecasyllabic verse, then, is the "eleven-phase transposition grid" used by the secret agent Cupcake for transmitting in cipher his messages to other agents and ultimately to his director, named Lyrebird. All this of course is derived from the recent flurry of revelations about espionage and counterespionage in the Second World War, as represented in Sir John Masterman's *The Double-Cross System* (1972), which reveals such code-names for agents as Biscuit, Dragonfly, Cobweb, Zigzag, Tricycle, Garbo, Lipstick, The Snark, and so on. Hollander takes off from here with a galaxy of names that would delight any counterspy: Thumbtack, Image, The Foot, Aspirin, Steampump, Artifact, Gland, Felucca. . . . It will already be evident from some of these names that the "transmissions" are concerned with poetry as a mode of enciphered communication, where enigmatic messages come from agents beyond the individual mind, while the mind attempts to "encode" them and transmit them to other agents—Reader, no doubt, being the ultimate receiver. Allusions to poetry, poetic inspiration, and poets become increasingly overt as the work proceeds. . . . It does not take much of a "grid" to decipher Kilo as Pound, or Puritan as Eliot. . . . I suppose the section on Moroz alludes to Robert Frost; and there is certainly a candid appraisal of Anne Sexton ("So widely thought—and who believed herself—to / Be an agent"). Other names will no doubt be decoded; but the important thing about them is that, as in Alexander Pope, these figures, while sometimes recognizable, are larger than life, types, images of the varied manifestation of poetical effort, failure, and achievement.

It is in the transmissions to Image that the discussions of poetry become most intimate and profound, for Image is the agent's other self, his deeper self, the real self that lives within the "cover." . . . [His] mingling of the cadences of both Eliot and Stevens is a measure of the way in which Hollander has absorbed the codes of other poets and made them his own. Yet of all the echoing we hear, the most persistent is that of Stevens's *Esthétique du Mal,* and Hollander's achievement here is worthy of that grand comparison.

Perhaps all this sounds a little coy in brief review, but it is not so in the reading. This is not just another "poem about poetry." No good poem ever is, in any limited sense of the word poetry. Like Stevens, when Hollander speaks of, or implies, poetry, he includes within that word the whole human power of imaginative creation, imaginative living, imaginative seeking. That is why he spends a section pondering with Image the meaning of the root of the word "spy," placing in each of the twenty-one lines here "some trace of the Indo-European root," as he points out in a note. (pp. 118-20)

The basic power of Hollander's conception here lies in the way in which he has maintained the literal details of his fable: the "Terminations" of failed agents, the tortures, the deceptions, the sordid traps, the fears, the suspicions, the frustrations of a world in which "Scattered outbreaks of terror do not abate," while he transmutes the details into a parable of the efforts of a creative seeker, a tragicomic saga of the human effort to explore the workings of ultimate truth, to probe the depths of one's own consciousness, and to discover the springs of human motive in others. The effort, we learn, can only hope to succeed through stout mental discipline (symbolized by the eleven-syllable grid). . . . And with discipline comes the hoped-for liberation: one must admire the flexibility and ease with which Hollander moves within his chosen grid; there is no sense of straining; the language, though frequently colloquial, moves with dignity and grace toward a measured eloquence. . . . With such a book, if we had not known his stature before, John Hollander surely stands forth as one of the two or three best in his generation of American poets now in their forties or early fifties. Indeed, I would say one of two.

In Hollander's poem one feels an acceptance of and reconciliation with a world of pain and struggle and terror—an attitude far removed from the outrage and fierce dissidence that invaded some of the poetry of the 1960's. By acceptance I do not mean resignation or indifference, but rather an attitude irradiated by the indestructible presence of hope: "the pleasures of hope," Hollander calls them, a kind of toughened hope that knows and sees and does not bow to Them. (pp. 121-22)

Louis L. Martz, "Recent Poetry: Mending Broken Connections," in The Yale Review *(© 1976 by Yale University; reprinted by permission of the editors), Vol. LXVI, No. 1, Autumn, 1976, pp. 114-29.**

ALICIA OSTRIKER

Hollander's tastes are eclectic, which enables him to write cogently [in *Vision and Resonance*] on poets as disparate as Donne, Jonson and Campion, Marvell, Milton and Pope, Wordsworth and Blake, Whitman, Pound, and William Carlos Williams. Since his cultural range includes European music and graphic art, classical literature and literary theory, and contemporary linguistics, the rifts of this volume are quite filled with ore. And his ear and eye are fine, so that his readings are usually reliable, which is more than one can say for many critics who attempt to write on prosody. He has excellent chapters dealing with contrastive stress, with enjambment, with rhyme. Each, if applied historically, would yield discoveries about ideas of order in English poetry over the last four centuries. The question of line-break has particular significance for modern poetry, where it serves as the single most important formal signal for a great number of poets (go back to Pound and Cummings, move up to Creeley), opening doors in hitherto plain blank walls. Here Hollander makes some brilliant observations about how the relations between line-break and syntactic juncture in the twentieth century consistently direct attention, create drama, produce meaning. There are also good chapters on the role of meter as frame, and on formal experimentation, both theory and practice, in Romantic and modern American poetry.

Hollander's consideration of "the poem in the eye," the poem as shape-on-page rather than sound-in-ear, undertakes an essential critical task, since the decline of traditional meter leaves the mantle of poetic form very much on the figure a poem makes visually. (p. 634)

Any critic of Hollander's stature must provoke arguments. Some of mine are fairly trivial. I disagree with a scansion of Donne's "Elegy on his Mistresse" which stresses pronouns and gets metrical regularity at the cost of rhetorical sense. I believe a comparison Hollander makes between Ben Jonson and James Joyce should have been made with Pound. Especially after Hollander's own sensitive description of Jonson (e.g. "his 'translations' proper never aim at preserving a particular poem . . . but at carrying over a method, a style, a way of writing, thought, and life"), what else can spring to mind but Pound's *Seafarer, Homage to Propertius, Cantos*? I am distressed by a treatment of William Carlos Williams's "Spring and All" which calls this poem "a soundless picture of a soundless world." (p. 635)

A more serious flaw concerns the ghost of sphery music haunting Hollander. He seems to occupy himself excessively with efforts to lay this ghost—belaboring poets and prosodists who have made misleading poetry-music analogies, extensively demonstrating, as if it needed demonstration, the inadequacy of musical settings to Donne's unsong-like "songs," recounting at length the differences between Greek meters, which were music-based, and English, which are not. We may all suffer from a nostalgia for primal harmony which we recognize as a fiction, but Hollander's repeated digressions from poetic to musical matters practically entitle this book to be called *The Elephant and the Music Problem.*

Finally, and unfortunately, both Hollander's organization and his prose leave much to be desired. This is a meandering, repetitive book, in which most of the essays read like occasional pieces or even worked-up footnotes, and the writing style is as stuffy as an overheated, over-furnished, close-windowed lamplit room. The possession of vast learning should not exempt an author from the lucidity and grace required of other mortals. In this case, non-specialists should brace themselves. Nevertheless, the ideas in *Vision and Resonance* deserve a wide audience for their solid discoveries and for their provocative suggestions, and for reminding us again, as at the outset of his first volume, that "particularly in the case of poetry, the functional relationship of form to content continues to pose the most demanding critical questions." (p. 636)

Alicia Ostriker, "Shapes of Poetry," in Partisan Review *(copyright © 1977 by Partisan Review, Inc.), Vol. XLIV, No. 4, 1977, pp. 632-36.*

JAMES K. ROBINSON

John Hollander began his poetical career with *A Crackling of Thorns* (1958) which, on Auden's recommendation, was the choice of the Yale Younger Poets series. Superficially, his early poetry resembles Auden's in its wit, its learned allusiveness, its prosodic mastery. There is a poem, "Under Aquarius / for W. H. Auden on his 65th Birthday," in *Tales Told of the Fathers* which reminds us that Hollander knows his Auden. . . . Indeed, Hollander owes a great debt to Auden. The final sentence of the Preface to his brilliant critical work *Vision and Resonance: Two Senses of Poetic Form* (1975) reads: "To the late W. H. Auden, whose ear for prosody was like a moral sense, my obligation is not easy to express in a sentence."

Yet, though the resonance of Hollander's poetry often reminds one of Auden, his vision is his own. He has paid his debt to the sassenach and is clearly an American poet. . . . [*The Head of the Bed*] is a remarkable long poetic sequence consisting of a prose prelude and fifteen cantos of five tercets each. . . . [The] poem, rich in implication, is . . . remarkably accessible to the fairly knowledgeable reader. (p. 356)

James K. Robinson, "Sassenachs, Palefaces, and a Redskin: Graves, Auden, MacLeish, Hollander, Wagoner, and Others," in The Southern Review *(copyright, 1978, by James K. Robinson), Vol. 14, No. 2, April, 1978, pp. 348-58.**

MICHAEL WOOD

[Cleverness] is not a vice, indeed I regard it as something of a virtue, and in John Hollander's poems it is the clearest sign of his extraordinary gift. *Spectral Emanations,* a book of "new and selected poems" which, read consecutively, takes us backward through Hollander's whole career, offers an abundance of examples. In a well-known early work, "Aristotle to Phyllis," Hollander translates the *sounds* (and some sense) of a Mallarmé poem into English, thus: "*La chair est triste, hélas, et j'ai lu tous les livres*" / "This chair I trusted, lass, and I looted the leaves"; "*le vide papier que la blancheur défend*" / "A wide papyrus . . . blanched and deafened"; "*Steamer balançant ta mâture*" / "Stammering, balanced, the master"; and "*Lève l'ancre pour une exotique nature*" / "dipped pale ink of an exotic nature"—this last item actually managing to pick up a pun (*ancre/encre*) which is lurking in the French. . . .

Hollander imitates Marvell and Pope with uncanny precision, and actually makes his imitations *work:* those old masters are momentarily revived and contemplate the present with the ironic glances of their respective ages. . . .

For an instance of [another] mode of wit, the leaning on a familiar phrase, we can't do better than look at Hollander's early poem about a divorced couple. "Quickly now," he asks, "which of you will keep the *Lares,* / Which the *Penates*?": "You have unmade your bed, now lie about it." This is a line which goes beyond cleverness, of course, as the imitations do, and suggests a considerable amount of sorrow and distress. (p. 27)

But of course even if cleverness is a virtue it does, quite often, keep bad company—or to change the metaphor, it belongs to a rather dubious family of qualities with names like diffusion, elusiveness, flippancy, and (my hand shakes as I tap out the word) insincerity. I don't mean that all good poetry has to be concentrated and confessional. I do mean that good poetry appears only when the poet is in touch with a set of genuine feelings, his own or someone else's or his culture's. A loose enough formula, but it is obviously possible for a poet *not* to be in touch in this way, and I think this is what happens quite frequently to Hollander: feelings are not available to him, or they flood the page, touch turns to rout. . . . [Certain passages from "Green" and "Departed Indigo"] seem to me merely stately: nothing is going on behind the perfect glare. It is not a question of artifice or manner . . . but of whether the language catches anything, or is simply idling. Compare the Popean "yowling chaos reassumes the streets," in "New York," which picks up energy and wit from its context, with Hollander's earlier "So frowning violence reassumes the crowded land," which is just vacant and grandiose.

Nothing there, then; when the flooding occurs, everything is there. In a witty poem about Sundays in New York, full of carefully emphasized locutions ("month of Sundays," "full of itself," "come to a bad end"), Hollander lets loose an unmanageable unhappiness, and tells us that on such Sundays "one" can go home, "one can have . . . climbed up a concrete hill to one's own walls / And quietly opened a vein." The wit and distance are swamped. It is a delicate notion, but it seems that the sincerity of the poem has been spoiled by the abrupt, excessive sincerity of the poet.

Hollander has diagnosed a good deal of this himself. His gift seems larger than his achievement; but his achievement, though sporadic, is substantial; and he has recently found a mode of writing in which the shady relatives of cleverness are paid off and put to work. The mode, in my view, is not the heavy myth which informs the most ambitious of the new poems in the new book, a legend about the lamp of the Second Temple, a seven-branched candelabrum, which Hollander associates with the seven colors of the spectrum, which in turn he plays through the hours from daylight to darkness. It is the mode of fragmentary, hinting narrative which Hollander used in his most recent book, *Reflections on Espionage*, a remarkably funny and quite haunting work. Here it appears in the central story about the Lamp, in the form of "Leaves from a Roman Journal" which tell a spectral, summary tale of love and adventure and loss and recovery. (pp. 27-8)

[Hollander] has found in the subdued, secretive world of such fictions a place for cleverness, indirection, insincerity, and himself. That he knows this is clearly indicated by a poem included in this new book and called "Collected Novels." Full of fine lines and gags ("terror firmer," *"My Brother's Reaper"*—the title of a novel), it shows a novelist who confesses that all the books he published under various names are in fact his. They are now "collected"; the title of one of them is a literal quotation from Hollander's earlier poem "The Ninth of July." It is a portrait of the poet in a mirror: Hollander is a number of quite different people, but he signs with a single name. (p. 28)

Michael Wood, "Calculated Risks," in The New York Review of Books *(reprinted with permission from* The New York Review of Books; *copyright © 1978 Nyrev, Inc.), Vol. XXV, No. 9, June 1, 1978, pp. 27-30.**

HAROLD BLOOM

It is exactly 20 years since the appearance of John Hollander's first book of poems. I read the book then, soon after I first met the poet, and was rather more impressed by the man than by the book. It has taken 20 years for the emotional complexity, spiritual anguish, and intellectual and moral power of the man to become the book. The enormous mastery of verse was there from the start, and is there still, so augmented that only James Merrill in his own generation seems to me Hollander's peer as an *artist*, as a stylist equal to Auden and to Wilbur. But there seemed almost always to be more knowledge and insight within Hollander than the verse could accommodate. (p. 42)

As a poet, Hollander was not truly Hollander until the volume, *The Night Mirror*, published in 1971, when he was past meridian. [*Spectral Emanations: New and Selected Poems*] is strongest in his work of the 1970s, in the sequence or long poem "The Head of the Bed," in the title sequence of "Tales Told of the Fathers," and in "Spectral Emanations," the superb and difficult long poem that should make a new beginning for him.

Hollander began as an Audenesque poet of the 1950s, merging the American Auden back into the Jonsonian line of measured wisdom. But from *The Night Mirror* on, Hollander surprisingly blends Jonson and Shelley in a single body, with Stevens inevitably displacing Auden as central precursor. Quite explicitly, Hollander has developed into an American-Jewish High Romantic, esoteric and elegiac, and daring to write long poems in the Sublime mode. . . . "The Head of the Bed" concealed something of its complexities and its profound design beneath a graceful mythological pattern, baroque in its interwindings. "Spectral Emanations" brings its difficult vision directly to the reader, demanding extraordinary energy of response, and a genuine labor of reading. With this poem, Hollander adds another to the formidable group of major achievements by poets of his generation. "Spectral Emanations," in scope and splendor, is comparable to Merrill's "The Book of Ephraim," Ashbery's "Fragment," and Ammons's "Hibernaculum" and "Sphere." But it is the most recondite and elaborate of these poems, and indeed is as difficult as the Stevens of "The Auroras of Autumn." It demands rereadings, and greatly rewards them.

At once an American and a Jewish fable, the poem moves out from a suggestion in Hawthorne's *The Marble Faun*, for a seven-branched allegory celebrating the recovery of the golden lamp that Titus robbed from the Second Temple in Jerusalem. Hollander restitutes for the lost sacred illumination by seven color-visions, each supported by a prose-poem as commentary. The 40 pages of verse and prose constitute a brief epic marked by bitter wit, by an impressive awareness of the painful burdens of literary representation this late in tradition, and by an authentic and very surprising communal passion, which hesitates upon the verge of allowing itself expression in the accents of the Jewish religion. At least two of the sections, "Yellow" and "Violet," seem to me individually great poems, but it is the total coherence of the entire sequence, its difficult rightness, that is most admirable and that promises to make this work canonical. (pp. 42-3)

Hollander is a restless and very varied poet, and many readers prefer him as a satirist, or as a comic writer, or in poems of ironic self-reflection. This selected volume gives much of its space to those modes, as well as to shaped poems and to philosophical meditations. . . . The poems that I urge upon new readers, besides "Spectral Emanations" and "The Head of the Bed," would include "On the Calendar," "Tales Told of the Fathers," "Mount Blank," "The Night Mirror," "Under Cancer," the versions of the Yiddish poet Halpern, "Ad Musam," and "From the Ramble." But there are many more nearly as good, and my sensibility is narrower than Hollander's. What this volume brings us is another poet as vital and accomplished as Ammons, Merrill, Merwin, Ashbery, James Wright, an immense augmentation to what is clearly a group of major poets. . . . (p. 43)

Harold Bloom, "Books Considered: 'Spectral Emanations: New and Selected Poems'," in The New Republic *(reprinted by permission of* The New Republic; *© 1978 The New Republic, Inc.), Vol. 179, No. 11, September 9, 1978, pp. 42-3.*

RICHARD POIRIER

"Spectral Emanations," the extraordinarily brilliant and ambitious work in poetry and prose which leads off [the collection by the same title], is prompted in part by a passage, quoted in the volume's epigraph, in which Hilda of Hawthorne's *The Marble Faun* talks about the menorah, the golden lamp of seven branches. . . . Hilda proposes a parable in which the lamp will be recovered and its seven branches kindled, each with a different color, until the world is illumined by "the white light of truth."

"It will," she says, "be a seven-branched allegory, full of poetry, art, philosophy, and religion," and she goes on, in a passage not quoted by Hollander, to say that she will propose such a project—a project by which the imagination will create a poem in lieu of a lamp—to seven poets.

In effect, Hollander is these seven poets in one, and in "Spectral Emanations" he has written a poem in seven parts, one for each color, each of which is, to a different degree, political because it provokes the doubt that any one mode of consciousness or state of being or "color band" can be exclusive of any other.

This is a matter central to all of Hollander's work, and is responsible for his now being, to my mind, the most intellectually daring, poignant, and thrilling poet writing in the Emersonian tradition of our poetry. He is passionately absorbed in the transitional, what Emerson called the "vehicular" nature of substantial things. . . .

With its sense of the transitional, of crossed boundaries, Hollander's poetry never indulges in the contemporary taste for fragmentation. As his critical writings alone would suggest, he is a master of classical and English forms; he can do a poem like "Fireworks" in strict Pindaric triads or a book length sequence like *Reflections on Espionage,* the unflaggingly brilliant and haunting book that preceded this one, in the hendecasyllabics favored by Catullus. He is forever playful about forms. There are included here six pieces from *Types of Shape*—one in the form of a car key, another of a light bulb—which are a delight to eye and ear. He is a formalist but a decidedly witty one. The changes that can be worked within form are made incumbent upon the discovery that any form is implicitly a substitute for or an interpretation of some other. Any form exists in the shadow of some other, and is on the verge sometimes of eliding into it; and the more you are aware—as Hollander asks you to be—of the form even of particular words, the more they are on the brink of those puns into which he sometimes lets them drop.

It is also crucial to any appreciation of Hollander's demonstrably major achievement that his sense of losses, deprivations, and transformations is never satiric in a distancing or disdainful way. His satiric manner is meditative, affectionate, and, above all, self-questioning. His is, in fact, a more radical self-questioning than any found in the confessional poetry, so called, of these times. Hollander escapes the limits of confessional poetry because he will not imagine the self—his or any other—in isolation, as a "substantive," to recall [William] James, deprived of the relational and blurring effects of "and" and "if," of "but" and "by."

He suffers as true poets often do, not because he centralizes himself, as a confessional poet would, but because he does not and will not. Instead he finds himself, culpably, in everything, including responsibilities for loss. Thereby we are given the extraordinarily moving conclusion to the new "Collected Novels," in which the speaker has been going over, with the woman he loves, some imaginary novels that might have been written while they were together. . . .

Form in Hollander is inextricable from visionary experience, from seeing things within a mode that can be shared because it is in part inherited and in part the result of some common pursuit, some corporate enterprise. The price is a necessary pain of complicity in the labors of composition, whether in the making of love or the making of poetry. Things are "safe for the heart because unenvisioned," he writes in "From the Ramble," and it is his human and poetic accomplishment, one of the very highest order, not to be satisfied with that kind of safety.

Richard Poirier, "Crossing Poetic Boundaries," in Book World—The Washington Post *(© 1978,* The Washington Post*), December 17, 1978, p. E5.*

ANDREW MOTION

[*Blue Wine*] describes a wide range of experience in confidently rhetorical terms, and seldom seems more than swaggering or pompous. To [Hollander's] credit, he is conscious of this tendency, but he is never sufficiently self-ironising to get away with it. Poem after poem slips into posturing, and object by object is buried in a plethora of detail. Even a turd becomes 'The half-dried, grey serpent-stump an unleashed dog left / To affront the carelessness of our steps'. Such wordiness is as reductive as the other poets' discretion—mainly because it does not allow him to build a firm enough foundation for his more abstract thoughts. This is particularly evident in the title poem, 'Blue Wine'. As each section comes to an end it closes in on itself, hiding its meanings and their relationship to the world. It is a form of literary narcissism; not surprisingly the wine 'broods on its own sleep' just as—elsewhere—a sunset is 'absorbed in itself' and clouds 'read their own shadows'. (p. 311)

Andrew Motion, "In Retreat," in New Statesman *(© 1979 The Statesman & Nation Publishing Co. Ltd.), Vol. 98, No. 2527, August 31, 1979, pp. 311-12.**

RICHMOND LATTIMORE

John Hollander does not become easier as he goes, nor does the somewhat frustrated pleasure of reading him grow less. He is always on the point of being fully comprehensible and never quite arrives at that point. The poems [in *Blue Wine*] are poems with beginnings middles and ends; not parts of a continuum you could hack into pieces, without its mattering where you hacked, here would do as well as there, and call the pieces poems. Hollander's poems have not only structure but subject and substance. . . . Put it briefly, Hollander is a master poet with an eye for image, a sense of line (and a sense of humor), and a rightness of composition; all of which qualities makes him a delight to read, whether or not we come out more fully informed than when we went in. (pp. 443-44)

Richmond Lattimore, "Reviews: 'Blue Wine'," in The Hudson Review *(copyright © 1979 by The Hudson Review, Inc.; reprinted by permission), Vol. XXXII, No. 3, Autumn, 1979, pp. 443-44.*

PAUL RAMSEY

[The prose poems of Hollander's *In Place*] are not so much lyric, though light and shadow pass and interplay, as about what constitutes or fails to constitute lyric; that is, what constitutes (or fails) poetry; that is, what constitutes (or fails) knowledge; that is, what constitutes uncertainty. A major theme is the unknowability of reality, hence the impossibility of validating poetics, ethics, or ontology. Explorings, nostalgias, beseechings and unbeseechings inconclusively conclude, sometimes with tentative hope, sometimes not. While one can hardly claim that the poems are affirmative, they are less consistently self-parodying and skeptical than Hollander's book *Reflections on Espionage.* In tone, subtlety of intelligence, control of imagery and prose rhythm, they are very fine, a grand pleasure to read. "In Place of Place" is a philosophical and poetic meditation well worth serious philosophical as well as poetic attention (whether or not its author will keep its distinctions and beliefs for five minutes or two separate poems). As it ends, it sounds theistic, earned, and composed. (p. 690)

Paul Ramsey, "Lyric—Ways We Walk Now: American Poetry in 1978," in The Sewanee Review *(reprinted by permission of the editor; © 1979 by The University of the South), Vol. LXXXVII, No. 4, Fall, 1979, pp. 686-92.**

PHOEBE PETTINGELL

One of the most urbane poets writing, [Hollander's] mercurial mind sparkles with the iridescence of an opal. In the notes to [*Blue Wine*], he engagingly explains the genesis of his title poem thus: "I visited Saul Steinberg one afternoon and found that he had pasted some mock (or rather visionary) wine labels on bottles, which were then filled with a substance I could not identify. This poem is an attempt to make sense of what was apparently in them." The 11 meditations on the subject attack the puzzle from a bewildering variety of angles. . . . In the end, Hollander decides that his "Blue wine in bold bottles" is for the poet to "take home with him / in the clear cup of his own eye, to see what he will see."

The poems that follow are seldom so full of fey humor. Melancholy plays a *continuo* throughout them. The themes are absence and loss. All roads lead inexorably into darkness, and this is often expressed through Hollander's obsession with dreams and journeys. "The Train," for example, is an extended stream of musings on the conventional associations between journeys and life. . . .

I would guess from the evidence of *Blue Wine* that John Hollander is now at the crossroads of his own midlife journey, picking out a new direction to follow. (p. 22)

Phoebe Pettingell, "Midlife Journeys," in The New Leader *(© 1979 by the American Labor Conference on International Affairs, Inc.), Vol. LXII, No. 21, November 5, 1979, pp. 21-2.**

* * *

HORWITZ, Julius 1920-

Horwitz is an American novelist whose work reflects his sociological interests. (See also *Contemporary Authors*, Vols. 9-12.)

JAMES R. FRAKES

[David, the protagonist of "The Married Lovers," a "journal of high-fashion *angst*," wants] everybody to learn not to be frightened of each other. The sense of fear actually structures this disturbing novel. The sense of fear seems to be the cause of everything—the ecology movement, communes, drugs, marital distancing, Kent State, Bangladesh, and the screwed-up Paris peace talks. No mention of Watergate.

Not only do all the characters think and speak in epigrams, but they all make speeches at each other—in letters, phone conversations, doctor-patient colloquies, confessional narratives of stark horror. From these speeches emerges a list of things about which we know nothing: sex, marriage, suicide, "life," conception, children, women, existence, and why people do what they do. . . .

The final near affirmation (off to Maine to fix the roof and walk along the beach and air the blankets!) is hard-earned and honestly tentative but sadly unpersuasive.

James R. Frakes, "Fiction: 'The Married Lovers'," in The New York Times Book Review *(© 1973 by The New York Times Company; reprinted by permission), September 16, 1973, p. 4.*

PETER STRAUB

Most novels which conceal a tract can be immediately sensed as dishonest, for they have little of the energising flow of discovery which marks the most authentic fiction—novels of ideas usually flatten out characterisation and schematise plot for the sake of the propagandising. Julius Horwitz's *The Married Lovers* is a rare and honourable exception: certainly as much essay as novel, it also reduces its characters to examples (and has almost no plot at all . . .), but the book solves the problem by meeting it head-on. Horwitz makes the brave choice of turning most of the novel over to monologue. The subject is the nature and survival of marriage; and his point is that marriage represents escape from fear. . . . *The Married Lovers* has a felt depth and solidity: though not really a successful novel, it is a successful and moving human statement.

Peter Straub, "Hot & Cold," in New Statesman *(© 1974 The Statesman & Nation Publishing Co. Ltd.), Vol. 88, No. 2276, November 1, 1974, p. 627.**

D. A. N. JONES

The title of this quiet, sad American novel [*The Married Lovers*] is bound to recall Coventry Patmore's poem, "The Married Lover". A comparison is not frivolous, since both writers are, in their generation, far superior to the average in their command of the English language. Like Patmore, Mr Horwitz seems eager to repudiate the notion that marriage is too dull and familiar a subject for imaginative writing; but Patmore's narrator, Felix, is made to exult in the everyday excitement of his situation, whereas Mr Horwitz's narrator—a middle-aged surgeon, called David—is appalled and driven to desperation by both the concept and the reality of marriage. . . .

David is anxious to reason things out—the novel is stiff with argument and generalization—and his wife, Anne, is equally articulate and explicit. There is a third prominent character, a Miss Wharton, who offers David advice about marriage in much the same tone of voice. All three speak in the best sort of American English, a spare, graceful, aphoristic style, which is pleasing to read but makes the novel implausible—as if Socrates, Xanthippe and Diotima were all on one wavelength. . . .

It is not until the last four brief chapters that the immediate cause of David's breakdown is revealed. . . . It seems a disappointingly simple explanation, after all the sociology and metaphysics. But it comes at the right place in the book, as if David had only just managed to spit it out, get it off his chest: he is refreshed, ready for more advice from Miss Wharton—whom he then neatly characterizes to Anne as a woman who "talks about herself like a film editor who takes bits and pieces of film and puts them together to make a movie". That is just how all three of them talk about themselves.

The argumentation, we begin to recognize, reluctantly, is leading nowhere, but within the fiction it has a healing property: it is a kind of exercise or massage. In the final chapter, David is ready to leave the hospital. There is another dialogue with Miss Wharton, the rhetoric still heady but much simpler, with the word "good" musically reiterated. All the dialogue, however sensible and stimulating, has been sort of impressionistic music. . . . The music of Mr Horwitz's language is quite different from Patmore's: the Victorian Catholic's mysticism is sustained by a faith in reason and rational discourse, whereas Mr Horwitz uses exceptional verbal fluency merely to illustrate confusion, irrationality and failure in communication. His elegant book is well worth reading, particularly by the married and the marriageable.

D. A. N. Jones, "Married Dialogues," in The Times Literary Supplement *(© Times Newspapers Ltd. (London) 1974; reproduced from* The Times Literary Supplement *by permission), No. 3797, December 13, 1974, p. 1405.*

RAYMOND SOKOLOV

["Natural Enemies"] is Julius Horwitz's seventh novel, and he has learned a few tricks along the way, but, as in an earlier book, "The W.A.S.P.," his shrill kvelling over the decline of urban civilization tends to discredit his story. Horwitz is always exaggerating some social catastrophe that is not really so bad as he claims. For instance, I would like to see the proof of [one character's] statement about the up-swing in mass murders of a family by the father. I cannot believe such events are accelerating to the point at which they constitute a trend. But Horwitz seems to need to validate his story of one man by sociologizing it into an exemplum of modern life.

In a way, Horwitz mitigates this problem by writing in the first person, which puts the sociological overkill in the mouth of his unhinged protagonist. The overall effect, nevertheless, of Horwitz's highly realistic diary technique is that of a case-study presented for our edification. The author must, we are eventually convinced, think that most men, or even larger numbers of them, live on the edge of parricide.

Unfortunately, this obsession deflects Horwitz's energies from fictional tasks he does well. He has a gift for portraying middle-aged resignation in long monologues. . . . I like [his] slightly wacko irony. If only there were more of it, instead of so much unconvincing psychosocial pathology.

Raymond Sokolov, "Three Novels: 'Pride of the Bimbos', 'Slammer', and 'Natural Enemies'," in The New York Times Book Review *(© 1975 by The New York Times Company; reprinted by permission), September 14, 1975, p. 41.**

JANE MILLER

Considering that [*Natural Enemies*] is about the awfulness of a marriage, of middle age and of pretty much everything that is going on these days, it manages to be disconcertingly original. Its preoccupations are Western, but its artistry and compression go well with its implicit acceptance of the Buddhist belief that all evil resides in the individual's will to stay alive. Paul Steward, the successful owner and editor of a magazine called *The Scientific Man,* wakes up one morning and loads his gun. He plans to shoot his wife, his three children and himself at the end of the day. The novel is a lucid record, stylish and abbreviated, of the events of that day, his last one and representative of all his days. Packed between long train journeys to and from New York are conversations he has with strangers, with his messianic contributors, with five haranguing whores, with a deliciously compliant lady, with his best friends: a famous psychologist and a famous expert on catastrophe. . . .

The novel works so well because the vision of the world provided by the hero's disintegration is always understandable as the product of his state of mind and the circumstances of his life. . . .

It is easy to make the novel sound too big for its boots, but that is exactly what it is not. Crammed explosively into the tricky plot and teasing, innocent dialogue is a turbulent inner life. There is a temptation to look for strain in a novel so contrived and violent, but, strangely, it evades that criticism.

Jane Miller, "The American Disease," in The Times Literary Supplement *(© Times Newspapers Ltd. (London) 1975; reproduced from* The Times Literary Supplement *by permission), No. 3841, October 24, 1975, p. 1255.*

* * *

HOWARD, Maureen 1930-

Howard, an American novelist and autobiographer, uses polished and precise language to write of ordinary domestic life. Her autobiography, *Facts of Life,* explores many of the same themes that her earlier *Bridgeport Bus* had explored fictively. (See also *CLC,* Vol. 5, and *Contemporary Authors,* Vols. 53-56.)

DAVID R. SLAVITT

The improbable heroine of [*Bridgeport Bus*] is a flat-chested, hawk-nosed, five-foot-eleven-inch, 35-year-old virgin from Bridgeport, Conn. Not surprisingly, she departs both from Bridgeport and virginity, but she is less interesting rather than more for having done so. . . .

Pregnancy and death are not so terrible as dullness—in novels, anyway—and Mary Ag gets dull. The careful, tight writing gets loose, diffuse, and self-indulgent. Mary Ag keeps a journal, writes a play, records the irrelevant story of a wayward, show-girl cousin, as if she were filibustering and reading cookbooks into The Congressional Record. It is almost enough to make one forget the initial pleasure of meeting a finely drawn, amiable character with which the book began.

David R. Slavitt, "Running Out of Gas," in Book Week—New York Herald Tribune *(© I.H.T. Corporation; reprinted by permission), October 3, 1965, p. 16.*

ROGER SALE

Maureen Howard's *Before My Time* is not as good as it should be, and not as good as admirers of *Bridgeport Bus* had reason to hope, but it is in many places a very impressive work nonetheless. (p. 618)

When Howard is dealing with the Cogans of Bruckner Boulevard—mother Millie in a flashback as a stenographer, daughter, and lover, "failed" father Jack in a marvelous friendship with a retired Jewish millionaire, Siobhan and Cormac trying to settle in to an unoccupied highrise apartment—she is at her best, and that best is very good. But the major focus of the book is really on Millie's Boston cousin, Laura Quinn, discovering she is still before her time. Howard locates Laura's resentful but loving unfulfillment very well early on, but then sputters because the feeling itself does, and when Howard's pressure leads not to action but to repetition, the writing becomes less free, more insistent. One is tempted to say, simply, that Howard knows New York better than Boston, Catholics better than Protestants—and while that may be too simple, with her style she needs all the knowledge she can get to keep the action evolving out of the details. With Laura Quinn she either has the wrong kind of character for herself, or she doesn't know enough about her, and so, despite many brilliant passages, *Before My Time* disappoints as much as it satisfies. I hope she can go on to write *My Time;* it is the book no American woman has yet written, so far as I know, and no one is better equipped to write it than Maureen Howard. (p. 619)

Roger Sale, "The Realms of Gold," in The Hudson Review *(copyright © 1975 by The Hudson Review, Inc.; reprinted by permission), Vol. XXVIII, No. 4, Winter, 1975-76, pp. 616-28.**

ALFRED KAZIN

My first impression of *Facts of Life* was of sheer novelistic skill, of so many stories, moods and time-shifts turning up in every chapter that it looked as if the author was stuck with a lot of effects that she couldn't unload in a novel. But it turned out to be a ruthlessly personal story told, like all good self-histories, to deliver the author from evil, to liberate her from some pressing burdens.

The fact that Maureen Howard doesn't seem much happier at the end of her brilliantly told story than she does at the beginning doesn't diminish her achievement. She is a dogged snipper of the human heart who, despite life with other breeds, retains a narrowly focused Catholic suspicion of enthusiasm, especially her own. . . . Since it is easier to write a book than to liberate oneself from all pain, sin and error, it doesn't surprise me—though Maureen Howard's bitterness sometimes does jar me—that she communicates her stirring hatred of pretense and false gentility better than she does any great personal liberation. The style is very, very bright; the other characters are wonderfully alive; the suffering and resentment out of which the book was written stick to it like a burr.

The story is of an extremely perceptive but family-tied Irish Catholic girl in Bridgeport who realizes bit by bit . . . that the life to which she is submissive is full of lies, absurd ambitions, nonsense culture. (pp. 37-8)

Beyond Bridgeport and the academy, and just like them, only worse, was the great self-promotional world of American publishing. There is a description of a book-and-author luncheon . . . that makes one see in the clearest and most painful tones the utter contrast between the honest soul of Maureen Howard and the world we all have to live in. "There was something pure in the utter filth of the experience." If she has a "devastating" tongue and an obstinate "grudge," her book ends on a vision of herself at 23, about to get married and with perfect faith in her coming happiness, that turns the reader over. A painfully strong, good book. (p. 38)

Alfred Kazin, "Books Considered: 'Facts of Life'," in The New Republic *(reprinted by permission of* The New Republic; *© 1978 The New Republic, Inc.). Vol. 179, No. 11, September 9, 1978, pp. 37-8.*

KATHA POLLITT

I can understand why a friend of mine groaned when I told him that Maureen Howard's reminiscences [in *Facts of Life*] centered on her childhood in Bridgeport, Connecticut: Life in that grim and prosaic city is a pretty daunting subject. But as readers of her novels know, Howard cannot be grim or prosaic for two seconds. (p. 43)

The facts of life, as Howard sees them, are three—culture, money, and sex—and how her parents shaped her adult attitudes in these matters is the central concern of these witty and vivid memoirs. But others also had their say, and *Facts of Life* is packed with sharply drawn sketches. . . .

If *Facts of Life* has a flaw it is that it is not a novel. Howard's people have the vitality of fictional characters, and her efforts to use them to explain her own life sometimes diminishes them. A moving description of her mother's senility—surrounded in the end by the wealth she had rejected, Loretta washed dollar bills in the sink because they seemed so dirty—is followed by Howard's own confession that "I declare myself to be absolutely sane in the matter of paying bills." The central revelation of her memoir is not self-knowledge but a climax straight out of a novel: Her mismatched parents did indeed love each other, and the poverty in which they reared their children was a fantasy they had invented, two grownups playing house in the shadow of the mansion Loretta always knew would someday be hers. (p. 44)

Katha Pollitt, "Midlife Writing," in Saturday Review *(© 1978 by Saturday Review Magazine Corp.; reprinted by permission), Vol. 5, No. 27, October 28, 1978, pp. 43-4.**

FRANCES TALIAFERRO

Maureen Howard's "autobiography" is the work of a fine novelist. . . . She disclaims the title "memoir," and certainly this book has nothing in common with those memoirs that are part name-dropping and part narcissism. *Facts of Life* is a writer's notebook, a rich source of portraits any one of which might turn into a novel. Maureen Howard observes that "hindsight is common and bland as boiled potatoes," and perhaps it is only the true novelists who can cut through the barrier of "memoir" as she does. (p. 92)

Frances Taliaferro, "Books in Brief: 'Facts of Life'," in Harper's *(copyright © 1978 by* Harper's Magazine; *all rights reserved; reprinted from the November, 1978 issue by special permission), Vol. 257, No. 1542, November, 1978, pp. 91-2.*

[*Facts of Life*] weaves disparate parts into a surprising unity. Its style is excellent; its content, rather sad. It is often reminiscent of *The Women's Room* by Marilyn French —only this is for real. Its voids are the voids of French's novel: faith and lasting love. . . .

Throughout the book the author shows a special gift for vividly depicting people. So expertly done is this, that much of the time they sound like people you might rather not know.

Howard has written a bitter book (with Hobbes-like tones— life is nasty, brutish), but not a complaining book. She has a curious kind of stoic courage, and wryness. Of her father she writes, "I learned more from his cruelty than from my mother's care."

The fact that Ms. Howard seemingly needed to purge herself of her pain does not mean that the reader will enjoy her exorcism.

"Books in Brief: 'Facts of Life'," in The Critic *(©* The Critic *1979; reprinted with the permission of the Thomas More Association, Chicago, Illinois), Vol. 37, No. 14, February 1, 1979, p. 8.*

HUGHES, Ted 1930-

Hughes is an English poet, playwright, editor, and author of books for children. He is a nature poet in the sense that his poems express, in their descriptions of wildlife and landscape, the brutal savagery of nature. (See also *CLC*, Vols. 2, 4, 9, *Children's Literature Review*, Vol. 3, and *Contemporary Authors*, Vols. 1-4, rev. ed.)

A. E. DYSON

[*The Hawk In The Rain*] is, to my mind, the most distinguished volume of verse by a poet of Mr. Hughes's generation to have appeared, and it notably escapes the various poetic labels that the last ten years have thrown up. . . .

The major theme in the poems is power; and power thought of not morally, or in time, but absolutely—in a present which is often violent and self-destructive, but isolated from motive or consequence, and so unmodified by the irony which time confers. For Ted Hughes power and violence go together: his own dark gods are makers of the tiger, not the lamb. He is fascinated by violence of all kinds, in love and in hatred, in the jungle and the arena, in battle, murder and sudden death. Violence, for him, is the occasion not for reflection, but for *being;* it is a guarantee of energy, of life, and most so, paradoxically, when it knows itself in moments of captivity, pain or death. (p. 220)

[In] Ted Hughes's poems, there is a constant striving towards moments of significance; moments of greatness which will last, as symbols if not as facts; ideal events more enduring than their agents, whose death, indeed, is their own occasion to be. Love, like death is valued for its power of providing such moments. First, there is the violence of encounter, restless, compulsive, pitiless

> There is no better way to know us
> Than as two wolves, come separately to a wood.
> Now neither's able to sleep . . .

but after, the lovers break through to a moment of glory; they duck and peep,

> And there rides by
> The great lord from hunting . . .

Ted Hughes values such moments for their intensity; but he has to isolate them from past and future, cause and effect, reflection and evaluation before he can savour them to the full. Hence the absence of compassion, anger, humility, nostalgia, disgust and the other attitudes belonging to the perspectives of time. His intelligence is often wholly absorbed in the battle to embody moments of power in words: it is the purity of intoxication, not the complexities of hangover, that engage him. (p. 221)

Instead of the opposites coming together, and generating the complexities which modify them in sober reflection, they are resolutely segregated, and so kept pure and strong. In this way, the poems recreate the intensity, the absolute quality of each state—union and disunion, romanticism and cynicism—treating experience not as parable or text but as sacrament. Articulation itself becomes a mode of participation, at least for the moment when feeling is being grasped.

All of this, of course, is exactly similar to Donne. And as in Donne, one finds explosiveness of utterance; imagery which is developed intellectually, but assimilated at every point to the central emotional experience; vividness and even grotesqueness of phrase and metaphor; metre which twists and turns in its wrestling with meaning

> Love you I do not say I do or might either.
> I come to you enforcedly . . .

and a general sense of being at the white-hot moment of experience: directly involved, so that the experience of the words is inseparable from the insight with which they grapple, and is, indeed, the high point of awareness itself. (p. 222)

[Hughes celebrates] the frozen moments of greatness—the photograph, the cenotaph, the martyr burning, the hawk riding the storm, the jaguar free in his cage, the lover at the moment of consummation. To remember these things can give meaning to birth and life, and incite to vigour and endurance. To some degree it can put magic back in life, and also meaning; but no human can stay on such heights for long.

What, then, can be a provisional judgment on these poems? . . . There is a temptation (for a radical, at any rate), to make easily adverse judgment upon them—as, for example, that the pre-occupation with violent death is adolescent, or sadistic; or that there is something sinister about a creative intelligence which can devote itself to the recreation and celebration of violence rather than to critical reflections upon it. Such objections may have some point, but they are less relevant in considering poetry than they would be (say) in drama or the novel. For one thing, Ted Hughes's control of words and metre in his best poems is profoundly mature already: the style is clearly the expression of a serious and adult intelligence, and a guarantee of validity in itself. Then again, poetry need not always evaluate experience. Sometimes its main function is to extend awareness, creating new areas which the reader can assimilate into his own total morality later, as he will. Ted Hughes, more than any recent poet I can think of, has the skill to do this. (pp. 225-26)

His own obvious values are not unimportant—the quest for resilience and endurance, the response to birth as miracle, the sense that being able to ask 'Why?' may still be more important than hearing answers. But beyond these, he offers us the *feel* of power, as something inescapably to do with life, however we may feel its deadly qualities too. The God of the tiger must be known today, whether we choose to worship or not. Also, refusal to worship might, we are reminded, be itself another kind of death. . . .

Summing-up will have to be personal. Though for my own part I dislike violence, and even more the acceptance of it as a norm, I find in these poems something powerful and compelling. The tone is strong and honest, individual and unmistakeable. Ted Hughes's voice is the most distinctive we have heard in poetry since Dylan Thomas and this, in itself, marks him out—especially since he is swimming against the prevailing currents of detachment, irony, urbanity and Neo-Augustan influences generally. Our present literary scene is full of very *good* poets, who offer varied and deep pleasures: Poetry is flourishing these days as seldom before. But Ted Hughes is more than very good. I don't doubt that, hydrogen bombs and his own ethos of violence permitting, he will be one of the select few to be read a hundred years from now. (p. 226)

A. E. Dyson, "Ted Hughes," in Critical Quarterly, *Vol. 1, No. 3, Autumn, 1959, pp. 219-26.*

DERWENT MAY

[When *The Hawk in the Rain* was published] it was evident that there was a gifted new poet on the scene who was prepared to make strong, confident assertions about the importance of strong—even confused or blind—feeling. And not only assertions; for the poems were often simply like assaults, designed to provoke the reader into vigorous—and in this poet's view, it seemed, perfectly healthy—responses of scarcely rational dismay or anger. *Lupercal* was the title of Hughes's second book, but what it suggests about the character of that volume could equally well be applied to *The Hawk in the Rain:* Lupercalia was a Roman festival at which the priests struck women to make them fertile. (p. 134)

Many of the assaults and arguments in *The Hawk in the Rain* are marked by [an] aggressive exaggeration that it is difficult after the first impact to take seriously, though one respects often in the same poems the justice—as it were, the sound theatrical imagination—with which the effects are managed: the impression the book made on its first appearance is wholly understandable. (p. 136)

Some poems in *The Hawk in the Rain* engage . . . specifically in assertion and argument concerning the desirability of a certain kind of emotional and moral life. Two that seem to be presented as a pair, one following the other, are 'Egg-Head' and 'The Man Seeking Experience Enquires His Way of a Drop of Water'. They are about two contrasting kinds of self-assertion, that may remind us respectively of the way of life of the dove-breeder before and after the hawk struck. 'Egg-Head' represents, with explicit scorn, a man who establishes his individual existence in the world (his 'I am') by resisting all those experiences that might upset his settled and complacent ways. . . . The second poem is about a man who is supposed to be learning a lesson from a water-droplet—a lesson that the man in the previous poem would obviously not listen to. To this man the water-drop seems to show how it is possible to go through extremes of experience and take full cognition of that experience—at the same time, casting benefits about one—and survive with unimpaired capacity to go on doing the same thing. (pp. 138-39)

It is neither possible nor relevant to treat the 'arguments' in these poems as forms of sustained rational disquisition. There is neither evidence nor ratiocination offered here; nor, what is more, is there really any appeal *by demonstration* to our feelings. The first of the two poems is just a brilliant—and, taken in this way, also rather funny—display of abuse and verbal bullying from a wholly unargued viewpoint; the second might be described as a sort of awed comedy about fascinating but tantalisingly obscure ideas that the poet does not get down to scrutinising at all seriously in the end. At most we are left with hints at possibilities that we may be inspired to follow up.

More of Ted Hughes's work is marked by an extravagant but sardonic humour than has, I think, been stressed before (though, as we have seen, it sometimes shows lurches into portentousness that suggests he has not always been quite sure where the humour begins and ends). (p. 140)

Any poem in some degree establishes simultaneously for the reader the presence of a speaker, and the independent presence of a situation external to the speaker to which he is responding. What characterizes Hughes's most remarkable poetry to date is the large part played in that 'external situation' by objects from nature—mountains, plants, birds—and the intricacy and force of the speaker's response to them. It is in these poems, rather than those more concerned with shock and assertion, that he most successfully conveys his sense of the importance of strong feelings and desires: important in some cases as being rewarding, in others simply as being present in human existence and necessary to recognize and cope with, and perhaps most often, in a tangled way, for both these reasons together.

The art of establishing those simultaneous presences is, all the same, only very intermittently present in Hughes's first two volumes. A good example is the title-poem of [*The Hawk in the Rain*]. What such a poem calls for is a voice that in speaking of the objects it is concerned with conveys the speaker's reaction to them implicitly. The meaning-associations of the words, and their delivery under the thrust of the conventional rhythm and the supporting or contrary pull of the stresses normal to speech tax: these must offer as a composed whole a sense of the scene and its responsive occupant.

The poem 'The Hawk in the Rain' is the work of a poet prodigal with effects that are in this particular case over-employed: an undercommitted armoury, as it were. (pp. 140-41)

It would obviously be quite wrong to suggest that the hawk in ['The Hawk in the Rain'], and the stones, animals, other birds and so on in other poems by Hughes, are simply there as vehicles for reflecting human situations in which they ultimately have no place. This poem would not have been possible without the existence of hawks . . . : the human sensations and emotions that the poem is about could only have been evoked by observation of the bird itself, and indeed to some extent by sympathetic feeling for it. Yet the poem, opening up as it does a shareable experience of a man living intensely through a certain situation, manages to establish a set of human possibilities for the feelings and the will, and of dangers and failures, that it might be possible to apply more largely, by making our own analogies, in our lives. Other poems in *The Hawk in the Rain* that recreate a response to natural phenomena—envy, in some cases, at unmatchable simplicity or ease, or in other cases fascination and fear at the fierce spectacle—are 'The Jaguar', 'The Horses', 'September', 'A Modest Proposal' and, perhaps best of all, 'Wind', where the constant flicker of humour at his own exaggeration lends, this time, a greater air of authority to the speaker's description of the wind's violence. (p. 144)

To my mind, [*Lupercal*] does not show any great advance in the poet's powers of development or in his themes. There are forcefully-phrased pieces of thin argument or specious exhortation, dazzling curses and outbursts of hero-worship, but only a few poems in what I think is his most satisfying vein. The more aggressive poems assert points of view already familiar from *The Hawk in the Rain.* 'Strawberry Hill' is a zestful scarer: a symbolic 'stoat with the sun in its belly' who 'danced on the lawns' of Horace Walpole's Gothic castle but also 'bit through grammar and corset' was nailed to a door—

> But its red unmanageable life
> Has licked the stylist out of their skulls,
> Has sucked that age like an egg and gone off . . .

Any number of vague threats are shaken at us in those two lines—all the forces of life and death at once, it seems. However, this poem, with its challenge to the playful macabre of Walpole's, does not lack its own lightness of touch—no stoat has licked the stylist out of Hughes's skull here. . . . (pp. 144-45)

[The best poems in *Wodwo* are] the poems of direct—though complex and imaginative—response to nature. And some of these in *Wodwo* are magnificent. Poems like 'Skylarks', 'Thistles', 'Still Life', 'Fern', or 'Sugar Loaf' wholly fulfil the promise of the earlier books. These poems, together with a number of marked successes in other modes, easily make *Wodwo* Hughes's best book yet. (p. 152)

Wodwo also contains some excellent poems [such as 'Public Bart'], in Hughes's fierce, critical style, offering as little argument as usual but powerful in the intensity of their scorn. (p. 158)

[His sequence of poems called, provisionally, 'Crow Lore' represents Hughes's] most successful attempts so far at finding a 'mythical' situation and characters to dramatize both his sense—apparently growing—of the cruelty and arbitrariness of life, and some form of acceptable human riposte to it. What is especially interesting is that it is a bird, once again, that has provided him with the necessary inspiration. . . . Crow seems to represent, at the same time, various forces in the universe and various human attitudes; but he is always a bird, and in fact always easy to visualize immediately as none other than a crow. He is destructive and has a small, callous sense of humour; but he is heroically stubborn and indeed apparently indestructible. God, who in these poems is well-intentioned but not very bright, is usually worsted by him. (p. 160)

Many of Hughes's themes and arts come together in these poems. It is as though in his earlier work birds, animals and plants gave him a sense of certain possibilities of instinctual life or of simple moral life with a certain similarity to the life of natural phenomena; while human life mainly offered a spectacle of failure that he could only hold up to contempt. In the Crow poems he has found a way of drawing these intuitions into a unity. We follow the acts of Crow with the same closeness, and the same sense of ambivalent human possibilities being delineated, as we do with the earlier non-mythological birds (though the possibilities are rather different now). But these acts take place now in a different sort of setting, still always vividly physical but reflecting—through its scenery and characters—a wider range of human emotions and decisions, and impersonal forces, that enter powerfully into our lives. The fable-form both gives scope for a multiplicity of mirrorings of human experience, and fixes them in a single dramatic narrative of a kind that does not allow us to say—as we so often feel obliged to say of Hughes's more direct poems about human life—that he is over-simplifying. And all his powers of mimicry are splendidly and relevantly on display.

Looking back at his work as a whole, so far, it is as a *mime* that it is perhaps most useful to consider Ted Hughes. Though he is a traditional poet of the written word, and the normal action of the meanings of words is essential to his effects on us, he has an exceptional gift for making words act out the processes they are describing. . . . At any rate, the kind of instinctual, physically responsive life that Hughes has a particularly strong feeling for is displayed in action in the best of his work rather than simply argued for. He argues for it, too: but as I have tried to show, though he does this with wit and aplomb, he never really makes a case until he goes back to the poems in which he 'imitates' and embodies it. (pp. 162-63)

Derwent May, "Ted Hughes," in The Survival of Poetry: A Contemporary Survey, *edited by Martin Dodsworth (© 1970 by Derwent May; reprinted by permission of Faber and Faber Ltd.), Faber and Faber, 1970, pp. 133-63.*

MARY KINZIE

No patently sexual or scatological motifs are present in Ted Hughes's book, *Moon-Whales,* but the poems here suffer . . . from trying to be cutely hard-headed. . . . Hughes is often trying to write metrical, rhymed verse. The eeriness of the poems is that they are not even decent doggerel. . . . The scheme is sometimes to translate earthly lessons to another sphere and thereby make them more interesting and palatable as lessons. In *Moon-Freaks,* we find that when moon-people want to read, they look into a friend's face, "And thereupon / Each holds the other open and reads on." *Moony-Art* succinctly advises, "If you can't draw perfect / Better not draw. What you draw you get." But by and large Hughes is content to indulge in fantasy without much thought for the point of the analogy. The dracula vine is a moon-pet that transforms trash into fruit:

> So this is a useful pet
> And loyal if well-treat.
> But if you treat it badly
> It will wander off sadly
>
> Till somebody with more garbage than you
> Gives its flowers something to do.

One would prefer the more innocent, mild, and accomplished poetry of Milne, the marvelous ghostliness of Lear, and certainly the ballad wit of a Plomer or a Betjeman to the messy versification and sluggish monsters here. (pp. 34-5)

Mary Kinzie, "How Could Fools Get Tired!" in Poetry *(© 1978 by The Modern Poetry Association; reprinted by permission of the Editor of* Poetry*), Vol. 132, No. 1, April, 1978, pp. 31-52.**

JOHN MOLE

Moon-Bells and Other Poems [published in the United States as *Moon-Whales and Other Poems*] is, in a very real sense, a young person's guide to Ted Hughes. It does not aspire to the density and subtle orchestration of his recent *Season Songs,* but neither is it . . . a parcel of left-overs. At the festive level, closest to the nursery, there are several examples of Hughes's verbal juggling and wizardry of scansion . . . and the comic-strip invention, which is there as an element in much of his most complex work, has a field-day in some of the moon-fantasies which give the book its title and are deployed at intervals throughout it, providing a delightfully airy and bizarre linkage between the more substantial pieces. . . .

Only Ted Hughes could have given us that Beano WHOP placed just there, or the delightful/groan-making rhyme of *electronic* and *chronic*. It is a productive complicity between the poet and his young readers. They meet on a common ground, at odds with all the grammars, and set out from there together. With Hughes's fantasies there is a sense of shared, illicit invention. . . .

However, the real strength of this collection lies in the handful of poems which arise from direct, natural observation. Their force gathers, detail by detail, with a kind of note-taking intensity. Like the Roe Deer, in the poem of that title, things (for Hughes) appear to have "happened into my dimension / The moment I was arriving just there." . . .

John Mole, "The Real Thing," in The Times Literary Supplement *(© Times Newspapers Ltd. (London) 1978; reproduced from* The Times Literary Supplement *by permission), No. 3966, April 7, 1978, p. 384.**

CHRISTOPHER REID

After [his] youthful, somewhat amateur-carpenter exercises in stanza-form, [Hughes] has abandoned this in his later work for a narrative mode that is largely his own invention — characterised by a disdain for rhyme, lines of *ad hoc* length, a jerky movement from incident to incident, etc.

At times Hughes seems to be going for a primeval effect, as though his verses were really translations of fragments lucky to survive from some remote and rather butch culture. So, in *Cave Birds,* his latest sequence, we get:

> Big terror descends.
>
> A drumming glare, a flickering face of flames
>
> Something separates into a signal,
> Plaintive, a filament of incandescence,
>
> As it were a hair . . .

This is more mannered than anything we find in *Crow.* I once attended a reading of Hughes's where he gave us a number of songs from that work and accompanied each with a narrative preamble—the story that lay behind the poems in their published form—so inventive and so strong that one wanted it to continue long after the verse had taken over. I do not believe that *Cave Birds* hides any equivalent story, and the absence of even such a dubious hero as Crow is significant. The Cave Birds themselves are . . . a variable lot—some, entirely ornithological; others, very nearly human. But, mercurial as they may be, their persistent presence does suggest that, if not a drama, then at least a ritual is being enacted in these abrupt, declamatory verses, and it is our business to find out what this ritual is about.

The answer, as it becomes clear, is death. . . . Death is always there, the poet hints, as the ultimate answer, to be arrived at, or evaded only for a time, by means of sophistry, metaphor, myth—all the apparatus of a mind unwilling to let a bare fact go unclothed. Every physical and metaphysical aspect is looked into and Hughes's performance has a suitably strenuous, virtuoso quality. . . . Through [his] relentless enquiry, in poem after poem, Hughes builds up a mythology of death and survival, in which birds and humans and bird-humans, whether alive or dead, are seen in heroic contrast to their own annihilation. But the question remains: is such myth-making worthwhile? Well, there is a partial answer in the book's subtitle, 'An Alchemical Cave Drama'—by which I understand Hughes to mean that the endeavour to extract a golden mythology from the dross of death is comparable, in one way at least, to the age-old ambition of the alchemists: the deed may be impossible, but there is courage in attempting it.

However, granted all this, the book still has serious faults. To begin with, I do not see how one can write with telling irony about death, when there is so little of observed life in one's writing. . . . Hughes's poems tend to turn themselves into rigmaroles and chants—tremendous periphrastic lists. One lights with such pleasure on any appearance of the real, human element (e.g. in 'Something was happening') that the birdiness of the rest of the book begins to look more and more of an evasion. A pity. (pp. 106-07)

Christopher Reid, "Flapping and Other Motions," in The New Review *(© TNR Publications, Ltd., London), Vol. 5, No. 2, Autumn, 1978, pp. 106-08.*

CRAIG RAINE

Ted Hughes is the least academic of poets, totally unfazed by the unpoetical nature of the age. In *Gaudete,* whatever its structural obscurities, his confident, unselfconscious talent simply assimilated awkward items like the W. I. and Jaguar cars—rather as if Hughes was some X-ray visionary who could see the myth throbbing under the bonnet. The common criticism of Hughes is that he is a kind of linguistic Quilp, forcing huge beakers of boiling language down the throats of his readers and wolfing down words with their shells on. . . .

Occasionally in *Cave Birds* the rhetoric seems excessive but it is nevertheless a very successful book. . . . Much simpler than *Gaudete,* it is an 'alchemical drama' devoted to the single subject of death: death as an irrelevance that suddenly and sickeningly becomes relevant; death as something to be dreaded in a variety of ways; death as cosmic salvation.

As a subject, it is equal to Ted Hughes's strenuous verbal gifts. One could spend a good deal of time simply quoting: 'Mountains lazed in their smoky camp'; 'Calves' heads all dew-bristled with blood on counters'; 'a seed in its armour'. The achievement, though, isn't in the fine touches; it is in the way Hughes has taken something impossibly abstract (as death and dying must be) and made it convincingly concrete: 'And you flare, fluttering, black-out like a firework.' . . . *Cave Birds* has faults, idiosyncratic shorthand like 'a filament of incandescence', but it is a stupendous work, far better than *Crow,* from which it grew. (p. 20)

Craig Raine, "Promises, Premises," in New Statesman *(© 1979 The Statesman & Nation Publishing Co. Ltd.), Vol. 97, No. 2494, January 5, 1979, pp. 19-20.**

MARTIN BOOTH

The importance and validity of place to the English poet has long been of prime importance. . . .

For Ted Hughes, not surprisingly, it is the West Riding of Yorkshire, more especially the area around the Calder valley at Hebden Bridge, and to the north of it. In Celtic times, this area was the domain of Elmet, the last of the native tribal lands to fall to the Angles. It subsequently became uninhabited moors and was, 200 years ago, invaded again, this time by industrial progress. . . .

Ted Hughes was born and raised in the area and it has been a binding source for all of his poetic talent and power. The violence in his work, so harsh yet so acceptable and understood, stems from his landscape—whether he be writing the

Crow poems, *Gaudete,* or verse directly related to the moorland parishes. The harshness of his work is abundant in the physical aspect of Elmet as it is now.

Remains of Elmet is about the place but that is only the surface matter. The poems reach far below that to produce a book of stunning value, an intensely private yet paradoxically public statement of a man for his roots, not merely historical and romantically, poetically imagined, but real. . . .

The poems are of a power and strength that even Hughes has not yet really reached in his career until now. They seek to delve and explore in a way he has not attempted with such love and knowledge before: they rely upon truths and observed realities for their immediate impacts, but are enigmatic and hold much deeper truths in what they are saying. . . .

The poems are a coming face to face. Their diction, which is easily understood yet vast in implication, tells of the real things Hughes knew, which move in his soul and are all accessible to any reader.

Hughes is not seeking to expand the photographs. That is too easy; besides, that is the eye's job. What he is doing is drawing personal, intellectual parallels to each picture, thus widening the range of the reader's awareness by introducing additional emotions.

It is in the handling of facts, though, that the book succeeds. It is a highly charged emotional journey into a poet's (and a nation's for the relevance to the "lost kingdom" ideal is not limited merely to a small tribal homeland) background, totally without sentimentality and with complete conviction and objective acceptance. . . .

The book as a whole is a modern attempt at a similar task as Wordsworth sought to present in *The Prelude,* the understanding of where the individual has come from and what that background has made of him. It is an attempt that works magnificently. It is safe to say that this book stands as one of the most outstanding volumes of verse this century. And it is a crowning achievement to this incredible man's poetic skills. What will come next? We wait in terrible fascination and not a little longing.

Martin Booth, "A Poet's Journey to His Roots," in Tribune *(reprinted by permission of* Tribune, *London), Vol. 43, No. 25, June 22, 1979, p. 11.*

PETER PORTER

All Ted Hughes's books since 'Lupercal' in 1960 have been mixtures of poems and some other element—drawings, photographs, prose, dramatic exchanges, folklore. . . .

It is important to stress that [in *Remains of Elmet*] the pictures came first and that Hughes wrote the poems to them, since the connection of verse and scene is by no means close in many cases. . . .

Hughes's poems are annotations of the scene and, though they have some sense of the deep past, with references to the Brontës and the mills of the Industrial Revolution, they do not attempt to refashion the reality of distant Elmet through a modern sensibility. . . .

In general the poems suffer from two faults—a muscle-bound galvanism expressing itself in packed and tensile phrases listed down the page, often with no verb at all, and an excessive use of the pathetic fallacy, which goes beyond observing what men have made of Elmet, and turns the land into a malicious godhead. Very little is allowed to stand in its own right: it must brood, symbolise and portend. . . .

The reader is so consistently battered by language that he has to turn to the heavily inert photographs to look for some clue to Hughes's intentions. It seems to me that Hughes takes the land by the scruff and shakes it—he wants it to be more significant, more death-dazzled than it is. In the process, the real pain of the industrialised centuries and the true beauty of their detritus is concealed by a grimacing expressionism.

In the middle of all this, there are some finely presented poems, chiefly honouring the daily life of the working towns, mills and farms. . . . [And] occasionally there is a poem which has that illuminating sense of mystery which has always been Hughes's greatest gift, but which is too often replaced today by an arrogant arbitrariness. 'Churn Milk Joan' and 'The Sheep Went On Being Dead' are two such, and in 'Rhododendrons' he proves my list of complaints momentarily irrelevant by writing a poem which offends as much as any in the book and yet stands vindicated by the authority of its imagination.

Cenotaphs and the moor-silence!
Rhododendrons and rain!
It is all one. It is over.
Evergloom of official titivation—
Uniform at the reservoir, and the chapel,
And the graveyard park,
Ugly as a brass-band in India.

Peter Porter, "Landscape with Poems," in The London Observer *(reprinted by permission of The Observer Limited), No. 9803, July 15, 1979, p. 37.*

I

IGNATOW, David 1914-

Ignatow, an American poet, employs deceptively simple poetic language to reveal what James Dickey terms "a strange, myth-dreaming vision of modern city life." Many of his poems are set in his native New York City. (See also *CLC*, Vols. 4, 7, and *Contemporary Authors*, Vols. 9-12, rev. ed.)

WILLIAM CARLOS WILLIAMS

[The poems in "Poems"], the best of them, ought to be printed on pulp and offered at Woolworth's, a dime a copy. They'd sell, too. For these are poems for the millions, in the cities and out of them, those who would read, and read poems too, poems such as these, if only they could get to them: manna in the wilderness. . . .

[The] work can be respected by those who know what good writing means and yet it touches and illuminates the humblest lives about us—without that offensive patronage which uses humanity for the effects of art. When I first picked up the book I paged through it lightly in the usual way, but soon came to a poem that attracted me, "To a Friend Who Has Moved to the East Side." It starts:

What did you expect you were getting?

That's enough, in a short review, to give the effect of my meaning. There's the language and there's the straight look that goes with it. From that point on I read with interest. But the Fifth Section convinced me that I was dealing with a first-rate poet. Here you will find five poems, the accumulated work of Mr. Ignatow's thirty-four years at the craft, whose tragic force, economy of language and plastic sense governing the words begin to shape up into something impressive. I was deeply moved. . . .

[It is] from such a man as Mr. Ignatow, to whom language is like his skin, [that we must] look for those innovations which will set us upon our feet in our writing. . . .

Mr. Ignatow writes of what he knows. Therefore most of the poems come from the New York City "underworld." There's no slang. Slang is mere escapism. But this is almost an odor, foul with love. Such poems as those in the Fifth Section would be understood by a North Dakota farmer's wife in January and cheer her against the snow. . . .

Mr. Ignatow, in the best of the work, gives a new sense of a low, melodious humming.

William Carlos Williams, "Poetry with an Impressive, Human Speech," in The New York Times Book Review *(© 1948 by The New York Times Company; reprinted by permission), November 21, 1948, p. 50.*

ROBERT BLY

David Ignatow's poems have an unusual openness to the consciousness of the collective. We are more used to poets open to the personal unconscious. If the "dark side" is thought of as a part of the personal unconscious, we notice that David Ignatow sees his dark side clearly only after he has seen it reflected in the angers and frustrations of the collective, when he sees it embodied in a stabber moving through a subway car. He is a poet of the community, of people who work for a living, as Whitman was too, but he is also a great poet of the collective. Reading him we experience in a deep way our union with the collective. (p. 127)

"Rescue the Dead" is a mysterious and marvellous poem, in which the meanings of "to live" and "to be dead" keep shifting, as well as the meanings of "to love" and "to be alive." There is some sort of ecstasy in the poem as well, perhaps from having faced these intricate ideas so imaginatively.

Like Rilke, Ignatow notices that human emotions are not becoming less insistent, but more insistent, and they have greater influence upon events. The sorrow cannot be dissipated. The stairs he goes down in a dream, if not "built by human hands," then perhaps were built by God, or by hard, chill instincts. The poem with those stairs in it is another hint that Western man is moving again into the nonhuman, into a state that interested the Greeks.

It is thought that rituals are a form that instinct behavior takes in human beings, modified by civilization. It is interesting that Ignatow has written three "Rituals."

His work says that we are caught in the collective consciousness, and therefore we are unable to rescue the dead, who now live helpless in that vast consciousness, longing to be rescued. "You who are free, rescue the dead." I think one of David Ignatow's loveliest qualities is that unlike Shelley, who claims he is free and we are all imprisoned, Ignatow does not claim to be free. He asks those who are free to rescue the dead. (p. 128)

Robert Bly, "An Afterword" to David Ignatow:

Selected Poems *(copyright © 1975 by Wesleyan University; reprinted by permission of Wesleyan University Press), Wesleyan University Press, 1975, pp. 127-28.*

PETER COOLEY

David Ignatow can no longer be considered "anti-poetic." American poetry in the last few years has finally caught up with what Ignatow has been working on for years, and the flatness of his idiom, the decided effort to write out of the here-and-now, the search for a commonality between poet and ordinary citizen can be found in hundreds of his imitators. For Ignatow's influence to be so late in coming (his first book was published in 1948), he had to be ignored for years. He was. Perhaps only the "discovery" of William Carlos Williams, to whom he willingly acknowledges a debt, allowed Ignatow, too, to be recognized in the 1960's.

[*Facing the Tree*] is no radical departure from the Ignatow tradition but a development of it. The poet can assume now that we understand his basic aesthetic; that understood, he can sometimes step beyond it. This poem ["Content"] from *Say Pardon* is his famous observation on "what is":

I should be content
to look at a mountain
for what it is
and not as a comment
on my life.

Ignatow still likes to make a poem out of almost nothing, daring us to take it as poetry, to question its slightness. (pp. 473-74)

Like the Black Mountain poets—with whom he otherwise has little in common—he envisions a poem as one continuous speech, not image, unit. Ignatow, unlike Olson or Creeley, however, sees the poet as a definitive moral force; he is the witnesser of the thing, the thing as total experience, not image nor construct. (p. 474)

[His] plain speaking is deceptive enough to cause one critic mistakenly to insist, "nothing should be taken for more than it says on the surface," when describing this poet. Ignatow is shot full of tonal ambiguities and ironies in almost every poem, though, and paradoxes, too, if I can dare to pull on another term out of favor at the present. The prose poems in this volume contain his usual virtues, but their form stretches out the flatness we find in the verse and that parable-quality found in so many of his poems is slacker and more indulgent in his prose. (pp. 474-75)

Peter Cooley, "Visions and Revisions: Four Poets," in Michigan Quarterly Review *(copyright © The University of Michigan, 1976), Vol. XV, No. 4, Fall, 1976, pp. 473-80.**

JAMES K. ROBINSON

"Dry mustard with a tinge of dun" might well be used to describe the color of a good deal of the poetry in David Ignatow's *Facing the Tree*. . . . Ignatow is a poet with modest ambitions. . . . Ignatow, born the same year as Berryman and Jarrell, is clearly a poet of a different order. Berryman could not conceivably have written for Ignatow as Ignatow writes in "For John Berryman." The final stanza is compact of fuzzy sentiment, feelings of omnipotence and of self-righteous self-pity. . . . Yet it is not fair to say of Ignatow that flatness is all. There are poems which clearly establish a slender claim to survival. In "For Marianne Moore" he praises Miss Moore's affirming joy over flowers in her garden not yet named.

for though she saw
them it was not for her
to name them
and to lose their life
in words.

In such poems as "The Future," "Birds in Winter," and "Autumn," Ignatow's feeling for the mystery of existence does not lose its life in words. (pp. 351-52)

James K. Robinson, "Sassenachs, Palefaces, and a Redskin: Graves, Auden, MacLeish, Hollander, Wagoner, and Others," in The Southern Review *(copyright, 1978, by James K. Robinson), Vol. 14, No. 2, April, 1978, pp. 348-58.**

HAYDEN CARRUTH

The first poem in David Ignatow's ["Tread the Dark"] is "Brightness as a Poignant Light." We know its importance to him because he has placed it first and has taken his book's title from it. But beyond that it is important to the book itself, a statement of the major theme, and will become important, I think, to all who read it. . . .

Notice that Mr. Ignatow has made his poem from the most conventional ideas in our culture: intellectual light, the darkness of reality, silence, the passing of generations. Notice as well the spareness of language, the absence of trickiness. In an age of artifice, such as we appear to be inhabiting, many may fail to respond to this conventionality and simplicity, which will be their loss, for another definition of poetry is a new perceiving of the roots of convention, a reseeing. This is Mr. Ignatow's gift, to bring the inevitable conventionality of human response to new expression. (p. 14)

Each word of the poem is right, i.e., practical, practiced. . . .

His poems are lyrical meditations, many in the shape of parables, which go directly to the sources of our fear, hope, hatred, etc. With never an expressly religious or philosophical word, he nevertheless speaks to us from the spirit of humankind that created religion and philosophy to begin with. And the spirit is genuine. It is new; not because of invention, since anyone can create a new metaphor or think up a new twist on an old story; Mr. Ignatow despises invention. He writes because he sees, and what he sees is perennial human experience, the hardship of joy as well as the hardship of pain, here and now in our changed, urbanized and, in many respects, secularized civilization.

To write like this entails risk. In every poem Mr. Ignatow brushes against triteness, sentimentalism, the banality of our imagination, which has been overworked for millennia. Yet he avoids these. Or perhaps, more accurately, his vision penetrates them, leading us with it. We come out on the other side, where experience is genuine again. His poems move us deeply, carry and sustain us, I think exactly because meaning is their whole existence. . . .

One cannot say ["Tread the Dark"] is his best book because earlier ones contain many very fine poems, but it adds greatly to his best. He is the kind of poet whose primal feeling does not play out, but instead moves steadily forward to greater purity, coherence, inclusiveness—the sign of a profound sensibility. His new book gives us the power of meaning—human spirit exemplified, this poignant light. (p. 15)

Hayden Carruth, "Poems That Mean," in The New York Times Book Review *(© 1978 by The New York Times Company; reprinted by permission), July 30, 1978, pp. 14-15.*

JOYCE CAROL OATES

[*Tread the Dark*] contains some of the best work of [David Ignatow's] that I have seen. Ignatow . . . is contemptuous of "perfect form": in Poem 88 he mocks, in one of his few explicitly angry statements, the American poetry establishment which at one time made a virtue of well-groomed, fastidiously-wrought incapacity. It is hardly a revelation to say that Ignatow writes in the tradition of Whitman and Williams, and that he has developed a conversational, understated tone that would make a poem of his immediately recognizable anywhere. Yet in *Tread the Dark,* in the parable-like prose poems especially, there is a quizzical, highly intellectual consciousness at work, an intelligence that hides itself, paradoxically, behind what might be called the "simple speech" of everyday life. Ignatow's art isn't simple, however, any more than Williams's was. One encounters in their poetry the casual ease of common speech employed to record distinctly uncommon states of mind and the effect, when most successful, is far more striking than a well-wrought infinitely self-conscious poem of Wallace Stevens's. . . . Ignatow's poems in *Tread the Dark* seem to be almost exclusively about poetry, even when they deal, metaphorically with images far removed from the poetic consciousness. . . .

Ignatow always reads like a confessional poet, which is one of the disguises he takes; he sounds defiantly personal, yet the reader comes away with almost no knowledge of his personal life. His vision is austere, as well as ironic and frequently self-deprecatory: you may think he is speaking of Ignatow, but how *can* he speak of Ignatow since his very identity is a mystery to him? There are many "I's" in *Tread the Dark* and they are all convincing. . . .

[The] book is constructed like a journal: one has the impression of reading the poet's thoughts as they move, and change, from day to day. Images of death, pain, and despair appear to be transformed gradually into images of acceptance, even pleasure, but the transformation is certainly not a mechanical one, and it is not without that quirky reasonableness in the face of the unbearable that is a characteristic of Ignatow's poetry. (p. 28)

Joyce Carol Oates, "Joyce Carol Oates on Poetry," in The New Republic *(reprinted by permission of* The New Republic; *© 1978 The New Republic, Inc.), Vol. 179, No. 24, December 9, 1978, pp. 25-30.**

MICHAEL BENEDIKT

David Ignatow has one of the strongest, strangest voices, and one of the most unique histories as a writer, of any contemporary American poet. Privileged with an extraordinary gift—that gift evident even in his earliest poems, published during the 1930's, but not represented in book form until two small collections published mid-century (*Poems* . . . and *The Gentle Weight Lifter* . . .), Ignatow was not really recognized as a major writer until the 1960's with [the] publication during that decade of three collections, *Say Pardon, Figures of the Human,* and *Rescue the Dead.* Today Ignatow continues to be both one of the most curiously rewarding and perhaps most unrewarded poets of his period. Like Miró's well-known dog, barking into more or less unresponsive darkness in a well-known painting, Ignatow has been a kind of watchdog of the American conscience and consciousness (not to mention his own conscience and consciousness) for some 40 years now. It seems increasingly a kind of modest tragedy in the history of American poetry that critically the poet received little attention until the 1960's. . . .

Still, if the quietly intimate, self-searching (and therefore universal-psyche-searching) voice of David Ignatow was not really heard until relatively recently, the problem is partly Ignatow's own fault. This is a poet who needs an editor. It is an aspect of Ignatow's talent that he is a truly *copious* poet, who pours out his gems quite generously—assuming that gems ought to be found in cornucopias. Still, the work at its best is irreducible and right, even if unlike a prolific poet Ignatow seems to have adopted as his spiritual father, Walt Whitman, alluded to increasingly in the work, Ignatow's visions have their limits, turning inward as determinedly as Whitman's turned outward. . . .

Like its predecessor, *Facing the Tree,* . . . [*Tread the Dark*] shows a poet at the height of his powers, secure in his mastery—and, therefore, relentlessly exploring. . . . In form, the book reflects, with similar sanguineness, Ignatow's disinterest in quasi-academic "testings"—one being that great canard in contemporary American literary cocktail-party chit-chat, the so-called "argument" between prose poem vs. verse poem. Ignatow stomps on that distracting snake with a sure, which is to say, implicit foot. He denies it! While *Tree* contained a number of prose poems, in a manner tentatively contemptuous of merely categorical distinctions, in *Tread the Dark,* verse poems and prose poems often alternate. To the extent to which Ignatow's book develops a philosophical or psychological argument . . . , the prose poems serve the same purpose as the verse. Stylistically, taken poem-by-poem, all one can say is that this poet's work has—in several senses—a lot of nerve. . . . Ignatow's poems in this book have, tonally speaking, unshakeable poise, sitting comfortably as if in literal armchairs (though deskchairs would be more like it), in the midst of the Human Dilemma. Echoing Whitman . . . the writer (in poem #32) phrases it:

> I am an affectionate man.
> I love the differences
> That compose me.

Fair enough. If there is one thing we know from the thrust and posture of contemporary poetry, it is that one must learn to love internal differences. But Ignatow goes a step further [in poem #16], taking into account the realistic fact that some of those factors in the poet's interior may be horrifying. . . . Thus, this odd step in the long, continuing, contemporaneous dialectic of self-awareness as Good. It is Ignatow's essential contribution: his lendscape: If the self is to be accepted, what then if one doesn't like that self? . . .

[I believe a certain quality of the Double Bind to be] characteristic of *Tread the Dark,* not to mention a certain direction in Ignatow's work in general. . . . [The] "Double

Bind" is descriptive of a circumstance in which one has two choices, both alternatives seemingly leading to disaster or even annihilation. . . . These implicitly self-imposed double-binds are a most rambunctious, problematical part of Ignatow's philosophy if not esthetic (for it is an aspect of Ignatow's art that the poems work, even when they do not "work out" these double-binds). They lead, at their most extreme, almost inevitably, to such visions of total self-attrition as one finds in "The Suicide." . . .

Ignatow is a poet who, while psychological and (to use Bly's by-now rightfully celebrated term) "Inward" in interest, is far from regarding his job as being The Lyricizing of The Psyche. . . .

One of the dangers of this almost relentlessly melancholy, perhaps doomful, view of existence is, quite naturally, the writing of a poetry of pure Complaint. Curiously enough, Ignatow's work in *Tread the Dark* skirts that danger by various strategies of style and tone. After all, double-binds (or "Conflicts" as they are sometimes called) are potentially, if properly framed in thinking or writing, manageable. Ignatow is a master composer in the interest of that composure in the presence of difficulty; the bleak burden of this book is lightened by access to grace notes of interior poise and humor. Indeed, Ignatow is not afraid to invite the invigoratingly bizarre into his writing. . . . (p. 4)

Ignatow, in the midst of a certain sadness, is not above making a recognizable and sensible joy, even to the point of making fun of himself. Such a poem is surely the one in which the poet equates the act of continuing to go on living, with the watering of his plants, "knowing that the world would end with the demise of all plants" (#77). Perhaps the ultimate gesture in this direction, for the reader of Ignatow's poetry generally, occurs in "I'm a Depressed Poem" (#86), in which the poet says with finality: "You probably understand [this], from experience; gone through something like it yourself which may be why you hold me this long. I've made you thoughtful and sad and now there are two of us. I think it's fun. . . ." (p. 5)

Michael Benedikt, "'Tread the Dark'," in The American Book Review *(© 1978 by* The American Book Review*), Vol. 1, No. 5, December-January, 1978-79, pp. 4-5.*

PETER STITT

[There] is an almost total absence of human sympathy [in *Tread the Dark*], of concern for others' suffering. The poems are utterly solipsistic, outgrowths of a single, self-conscious, meditating sensibility. . . . (p. 469)

Over the years, Ignatow has worked to become a kind of poet of the people, in the tradition of Whitman and Williams. In order to carve out his own territory, Williams had to attack the elitism and intellectualism of Eliot—and a refreshing attack it was. Ignatow has a poem here directed against the elitist and Platonic concept of "perfect form" in poetry. He makes some telling points—unless you are an upright citizen, stolidly middle-class, white, prosperous, you do not belong in the poetry of perfect forms. . . . The great American writers have almost always been rebels and outcasts, shaggy, writing poems and novels in a clearly imperfect form.

I sympathize. But this is an elitist book that violates its author's own concerns; it forms an exclusive little world of one. The only citizen is David Ignatow, who carefully excludes even his readers. Poem after poem is preoccupied only with the imagined death of the author—he meditates on his potential suicide, on his decay, on his inevitable alienation and isolation. Humanity finds all doors into this book locked. The sufferings of others, their deaths in a loneliness and a pain we can easily imagine because we see them every day—these are as nothing to David Ignatow. It is impossible to empathize with the cold, self-absorbed solipsist who speaks these poems, despite the obvious skill with which they were written. (pp. 469-70)

Peter Stitt, "Book Reviews: 'Tread the Dark'," in The Georgia Review *(copyright, 1979, by the University of Georgia), Vol. XXXIII, No. 2, Summer, 1979, pp. 469-70.*

MANLY JOHNSON

A reader will be struck at once by the call for attention of [the poems in *Tread the Dark*]—the way, in Heidegger's apt expression, that they "presence" themselves. The poems are convincing as authentic personae. Though they have one voice, Ignatow's, they are the different guises he speaks through: an abandoned animal in a cage, himself as his own child, an old man who regresses to an ovum, a suicide, a zebra, a wax figure in a museum, a vase, an explorer, a leaf. They reveal Ignatow's compulsion to accumulate all the things of the world in himself. But they will not stay there, separating themselves to sit regarding him from a distance, or inside his head.

The collection is in fact not ninety-one separate poems, but a series of probes into the nature of individual being by one whose poetry has long been established as messages from a particularly alert, original imagination. Most are linear and in free verse, but nearly a third are block poems, displayed in paragraphs. The block poems are effective word by word from beginning to end because the amplitude of the form accommodates itself to the matter-of-fact metamorphoses of fairy tales, which Ignatow utilizes for startling effects. The linear poems more often provide a different effect—of struggle, of contest, of unresolved inner debate.

There is a reason for these differences in structure which underlies what the poems are saying about essential form. In one poem Ignatow satirizes the idea of a national award to a poet for the "perfect form" of his poems. He itemizes the categories of dreadfulness in this age . . . to ask ironically of each whether it can become a poem of "perfect" form. Ignatow does not trust form, as he does not trust life, though loving both.

For Ignatow, the perfect form is in essence, not appearance. In the "Epilogue" the essence is seen to consist in the attitude itself of creating poetry, an attitude receptive to the "presencing" of created things: "The trees are tall gods / commanding a view / of my study. I bow / my head over my typewriter / and start the ceremony / of a prayer." To arrive persuasively, as Ignatow does, at this metaphysical conclusion through poems of the utmost physical particularity is an achievement which marks this collection as one of the most significant and satisfying recent volumes of poetry. (pp. 509-10)

Manly Johnson, "Verse: 'Tread the Dark'," in World Literature Today *(copyright 1979 by the University of Oklahoma Press), Vol. 53, No. 3, Summer, 1979, pp. 509-10.*

INNES, Michael
See STEWART, J(ohn) I(nnes) M(ackintosh)

* * *

ISHERWOOD, Christopher 1904-

Isherwood is an English-born novelist, playwright, poet, essayist, filmwriter, translator, and editor. Like other members of the "Auden group," he was influenced in the 1920s by the philosophies of Marx and Freud. He is generally considered at his best when writing detached social satires, depicting a tragic view of life that is outlined with humor. Describing himself as "a born film fan," he has experimented with cinematic and episodic techniques in his fiction. Much of his work is autobiographically oriented. Isherwood collaborated with Auden on three plays, works of fantasy which combine verse with prose. He has also explored an interest in Hindu mysticism, translating and editing several books of Indian philosophy. (See also *CLC*, Vols. 1, 9, 11, and *Contemporary Authors*, Vols. 13-16, rev. ed.)

EVELYN WAUGH

There is only one portrait in Mr. Isherwood's collection [*Journey to a War*] that does not recall a familiar type; that is the host of the Journey's End Hotel, Mr. Charleton, and for the few pages of his appearance the narrative suddenly comes to life, and one is reminded that Mr. Isherwood is not only the companion of Mr. Auden, but the creator of Mr. Norris and Miss Bowles. Not that his work ever falls below a high literary standard. It is admirable. The style is austerely respectable; not only does he seldom use a *cliché,* he never seems consciously to avoid one; a distinction due to a correct habit of thought. Anyone of decent education can revise his work finding alternatives for his *clichés;* a good writer is free from this drudgery; he thinks in other terms. Mr. Isherwood writes a smooth and accurate kind of demotic language which is adequate for his needs; he never goes butterfly-hunting for a fine phrase. It is no fault of his technique that *Journey to a War* is rather flat; he is relating a flat experience, for he is far too individual an artist to be a satisfactory reporter. The essence of a journalist is enthusiasm; news must be something which excites him, not merely something he believes will excite someone else. Mr. Isherwood—all honour to him for it—has no news sense. In particular, he is interested in people for other reasons than their notoriety. The quality which makes Americans and colonials excel in news-reporting is the ease with which they are impressed by fame. Mr. Isherwood met nearly all the public characters in his district; he felt it his duty as a war correspondent to be interested in them. But they were bores—or rather the kind of contact a foreign journalist establishes with a public character is boring—and he is too honest a writer to disguise the fact. (p. 498)

Evelyn Waugh, "Mr. Isherwood and Friend," in The Spectator *(© 1939 by* The Spectator; *reprinted by permission of* The Spectator), *Vol. 162, No. 5778, March 24, 1939, pp. 496, 498.*

KINGSLEY AMIS

There must be plenty of people who, like myself, read their Isherwood during the war period and recognised in him a novelist not only admirable but congenial. Although quite capable of powerfully haunting effects (witness the closing scene of 'The Nowaks'), he offered clarity, common sense, easy-going humour and detachment as distinct from the more insistently literary or prophetic qualities of some of his elders. They constructed; he evidently re-created. There may have been something suspect about that detachment of his, something that ceased at times to look like an authorial strategy and became a mere personal reticence; but the rest was genuine, the gift for atmosphere and for location in place and time, the ability to fix a bar or a tenement or a beach or a Berlin street by the swift unfussy selection of concrete objects. The study of this was worth giving one's days and nights to.

The year 1945 brought *Prater Violet,* which incorporated an unwelcome novelty. Herr Issyvoo was discovered to have a sex-life after all, and about time too, but the whole thing was treated in a chary, allusive manner, with the other people given initials instead of names. Much better to have gone on being 'detached' than to roll up the bedroom blind a quarter of the way, so to speak. This kind of self-editing brings a danger of self-indulgence: the novelist can say whatever he likes about what he hasn't actually described. So here sex got fitted into generalisations, talked *about,* made the subject of anguished self-communing. And this from a writer who had acquired his tone of voice, indeed his whole world, by dint of never stirring an inch from the straight path of event and on-the-spot emotional reaction. Still, the first five-sixths of the book, in which a relationship was treated in the old Isherwood way and just shown happening, was all right.

It was not long, of course, before it became as apparent as such things can be that that first five-sixths had crossed the Atlantic in Mr. Isherwood's trunk, constituting a marble torso that was to be eked out with a plaster leg or so when he reached Hollywood. Until somebody writes *Christopher Isherwood in America* I suppose we shall all go on saying, whenever and wherever we bring up the question why his talent took a nosedive as soon as he left England, that this is neither the time nor the place to attempt an answer. . . .

Passing over *The World in the Evening* in tactful silence and coming at last to *Down There on a Visit,* I note my first twinge of disquiet—or recognise occasion for one on second reading—at the first sentence: 'Now, at last, I'm ready to write about Mr. Lancaster.' More follows in the same strain. No barker at the entrance was needed in the case of Mr. Norris, a character of almost incredible all-round superiority to the poor buffoon here commended to our attention. To be sure, I find things picking up for a time after the opening paragraph, or looking as if they're going to. The persona of the eager, talkative, flatteringly confidential and self-deprecating, 'engaging' narrator seems a bit overdone, but he is obviously some sort of kin to Herr Issyvoo, and after all, I reason, this is the 1962 Isherwood consciously looking back at the 1928 version. And there are references to Hugh Weston, Allen Chalmers and the Enemy. . . .

The paradoxically claustrophobic atmosphere of [the setting in the second sketch presented in the book] with its endless farcical-nasty quarrels and momentary revelations of paralytic depression, comes over here and there with jolting effectiveness; but the reader is left in some doubt whether either narrator-Isherwood or author-Isherwood fully appreciates what a fearful Sartrean hell is being portrayed. Again, there are times when we see how that tolerance which is the condition of a homosexual mode of life—a tolerance arising not out of benignity but out of a fear of making demands which may be humiliatingly rejected—slides into the condonation of any and every kind of nauseous behaviour and thus into total moral and emotional chaos; but it is hard to tell whether we are being shown this or just deducing it for ourselves from material offered with nothing particular in mind. There are, or ought to be, limits to detachment.

After a meticulously bitchy, but otherwise unremarkable, account of a Hollywood lunch-party, the final sketch comes slowly and as it were reluctantly to life, in spite of periodic descents into coy amorous semi-revelation on the part of the narrator, the initial-dropping mode of the worst episodes in *Prater Violet*. Paul, a bisexual remittance man with a long history of bed-oriented globe-trotting, seeks out Christopher to be saved from suicide and, with the aid of a contemporary-style mystic called Augustus Parr, is so saved. Parr is the one assured success of this volume. Highly educated, charitable, remorselessly articulate and just faintly silly, he is depicted with a blend of reverence and irreverence that I think is unique, and funny and sympathetic too. Paul, similarly, is witty and tough as well as whatever else he is in a way that recalls the author's pre-war work. It's a pity that Paul's later career is so foggy and remote, his eventual death so meaningless—this as a result, presumably, of the real Isherwood's loss of contact with the real Paul. (In heaven's name, can't the fellow *invent* occasionally?)

I don't mean to be smart, let alone patronising, in calling this book promising. There's just about enough in it to foster the hope that that old glassiness may turn out not to be chronic after all. The novelist is a less differentiated and specialised, altogether simpler life-form than the poet, and can survive shocks and amputations which would mean total death to the higher organism. Anybody who cares for the novel in English must hope that Mr. Isherwood is going to be a case in point.

Kingsley Amis, "A Bit Glassy," in The Spectator *(© 1962 by* The Spectator; *reprinted by permission of* The Spectator*), Vol. 208, No. 6976, March 9, 1962, p. 309.*

CAROLYN G. HEILBURN

[Christopher Isherwood] is the best British novelist of his generation. . . . [His] fictions have achieved the integrity of art while illuminating the human tensions of our time. Muted in tone, self-effacing in manner, his works continue to make a quiet but persistent claim on our attention. . . .

To read . . . his "autobiographical" *Lions and Shadows,* is to find oneself not only committed to the reading of all his other books but surprised into an appreciation of the rarest literary conjunction of our times: readability and high intelligence. . . . Readability is usually allied with superficiality, best-sellerdom, or, at best, competent nonfiction, and there can be little doubt that Isherwood's readability has preserved him from academic sanctification. It is difficult to be properly serious about a writer in whose literary presence one feels so relaxed. (p. 3)

Certainly the effect of ease in Isherwood's writing is deluding: it persuades the reader to overlook the enormous skill of his prose. . . .

No one, in these works, is romanticized, condemned, or even judged; if the narrator, named Christopher Isherwood, responds at all, he does so only from personal pique or inconvenience. The brilliantly unobtrusive prose allows us to watch violence, brutality, and compromise with pain, and to realize only when the book is finished that in doing so we, like the narrator, have failed in humanity. Isherwood's Berlin Stories are the best rendering of early Hitler Germany we have: an artistic re-creation of a society's self-betrayal. (p. 4)

In a consideration of Isherwood's major work, a division clearly suggests itself: Documentaries and Novels. I call "documentaries" those works in which "Christopher Isherwood," the ventriloquist's dummy, appears; "novels," those works in which he does not. . . . The division is less arbitrary, or superficial, than may at first appear. If, for example, we call the books with the "Christopher Isherwood" narrator "political," we begin to see that it is precisely in the use of this particular device of point of view that Isherwood's success as a political novelist lies. Even his so-called factual books, *Lions and Shadows, Journey to a War, The Condor and the Cows,* are documentaries in their presentation of events, in their selection of incident, and in the character of the dummy who tells the story. In all of these, emotion has been transposed or dissolved, and the distance which political novels require has been achieved. (p. 15)

Be that as it may, a comparison of Isherwood's portrayals of characters in his documentaries, and his "factual" portraits of actual people, reveals immediately the particular and peculiar art of the documentary. His factual portraits of Ernst Toller, Virginia Woolf, and Klaus Mann . . . , and his sketch of Aldous Huxley . . . , are lifeless and unevocative. Without the dummy, without the touch of the artist, Isherwood is strangely feeble. The reporter without the artist is only a competent journalist. (p. 17)

The rare gift of touching a portrait with life is discovered by Isherwood only in the documentaries; the lifelessness of his actual portraits attests to this. (p. 18)

The whole question of point of view and the reliability of the narrator has been seen as central in modern studies of the novel. It is the more extraordinary . . . that critics have failed to recognize that Isherwood alone developed the form of the documentary and the particular narrator who makes it possible. Not even Wayne Booth, whose *Rhetoric of Fiction* is devoted to the relationship between the chosen point of narration and the sense of truth and morality conveyed by the story, has seen how Isherwood's first-person dummy makes possible a kind of veracity that is freed from an intrusive sense of morality or ideological bias. Yet a study of Isherwood's fictional technique makes clear the apparent anomaly that political novels are best narrated by a first-person viewer of bland personality, while interior novels of sensibility are, as Henry James of course discovered, impossible successfully to render in the first person. Furthermore, the bland first-person narrator saves the political novel from too strident a presentation of ideology so that, in the end, the moral point of view for which Wayne Booth hankers, is, in fact, created. (p. 19)

"Christopher Isherwood," who refuses to judge the characters, who, indeed, allows himself to be charmed by them, provides the perfect unity: the focused, the unjudging camera, which visualizes but does not preach. Isherwood is fond of referring to some of his works as dynamic portraits; it is in the dynamic portraits, with the dummy as the focal point, that Isherwood . . . gains for himself the obviously essential aesthetic distance. Distance, of time as well as of narrator, is essential to Isherwood. . . . (p. 21)

"Christopher Isherwood," throughout *Lions and Shadows,* is seen as immature, passive, always admiring some stronger, more forceful or attractive figure. In fact, . . . Isherwood was a markedly active and dominating figure among his friends. . . . The dummy has been formed to serve its particular purpose in this masterful book in the documentary form. (p. 23)

Prater Violet is a brilliant novella which re-creates the whole lunatic process involved in the making of a successful film. Isherwood, in fact, had been working on the writing of films for many years prior to 1945, but "Christopher Isherwood" of the story assumes no expertise as he trails after the director in England during the early thirties. Indeed, the dummy is depicted here rather more harshly than before, complete with mother and brother who are amiable and long-suffering in the presence of arrogant, German-speaking Chris. (p. 26)

Down There on a Visit, particularly in its two best sections, "Waldemar" and "Paul," is a brilliant example of how suffering (or, as we say, life) can be transmuted into art. . . . It is the extent and subtlety of the transformation that intrigues us. Isherwood has managed, astonishingly, to keep separate "the man who suffers and the mind which creates." (pp. 31-2)

Yet one cannot go on to discuss the "novels," as opposed to the documentaries, without pointing to the extraordinary accomplishment of this last of the documentaries. The four sections of *Down There on a Visit,* although uneven, do precisely and uniquely reveal the four versions of hell which modern man has most consistently chosen to explore. . . . The dummy "Christopher Isherwood" has visited every hell except that of complacency. Immensely readable, as always, one of the most fascinating and accurate record of several eras, *Down There on a Visit* is perhaps the best of Isherwood's documentaries, because it took the most courage to write. It is clearly the best work of fiction we have on the spiritual odyssey of his generation. (pp. 32-3)

What is remarkable about [*All the Conspirators*] is its accomplished technique, style, and tone: Isherwood might not have discovered his true voice, but he was clearly a born writer, and his novel is still in print. Cyril Connolly . . . called it mature, readable, concentrated, and perceptive; it was all of these despite its author's early age, and, despite Isherwood's youthful fascination with private worlds, it is an available book, not only to another generation of "angry young men," but also to readers the same age as the novel itself, or older. (pp. 33-4)

[*The Memorial*] is divided into four sections, each superficially independent as though it were a family photograph. . . . The technique [used in this novel] has been compared, astonishingly, with Faulkner's *The Sound and the Fury,* a work Isherwood admits to never having read through. The comparison, however, is suggestive: if the two writers could not be more different in style, setting, tone, and theme, they are alike in evoking societies which have largely destroyed themselves. . . . Here, as in all of Isherwood's novels, the relation between the private life and the public event is closer, more vital than it was in the novels of the previous generation. Yet differing from the documentaries, the novels allow the private individuals greater development, a more richly perceived interior life, a deeper intelligence. (pp. 35-6)

It is Angus Wilson who points out that Isherwood, in *The World in the Evening,* explores for the first time "the complex patterns of emotional love" [see *CLC,* Vol. 11]. His readiness for this exploration perhaps persuaded him to return to the "novel" form; certainly his special achievement is to have created, in 1954, a novel in which the women characters are not, as in the novels of almost every other writer in the fifties . . . , objects of the hero's scorn, leers, lusts, and aggressions, twice as simple as the hero, and five times as evil. (p. 38)

The letters . . . [used in the novel] constitute the book's chief failure, which is one of over-all technique. Isherwood apparently wrote the letters from Elizabeth Rydal with fatal ease. Many of them are beautifully done. . . . But all the other letters, and particularly that written by Stephen at the end of the book to his wife-of-the-doll-house, are little more than admissions of defeat. The difficulty, of course, is to get inside a character (the dummy had only to look, listen, and, later, respond) without the use of diaries, letters, or first-person narration: to show inner struggles without requiring that the characters expound them personally. This use of letters more seriously weakens Isherwood's . . . *A Meeting by the River;* he has yet to master the rare technical skill of the novelist, to which James devoted his life, of being able to manifest in act, dialogue, and image the inner spiritual quality and growth of the characters. (pp. 38-9)

A Single Man (1964), that masterpiece of a comic novel, is the story of one day in the life of an expatriate English professor in Los Angeles. It contains the best American college classroom scene ever portrayed, and a series of stunning portraits, not least of all George, the central character who, like Leopold Bloom, is allowed no single moment of privacy, but who, unlike Bloom, is not surrounded by a wealth of literary symbols or endowed with a shred more dignity than he can muster up for himself. . . .

Not that *A Single Man* ever mentions spiritual experience; that is its greatness. Here is only the portrait of an inhabited body and the attempts it makes at living. (p. 42)

A Meeting by the River (1967), is a failure, an attempt to use insufficiently digested material gathered on a visit to a monastery in India. Unable to find the proper narrative technique . . . , Isherwood falls back on letters which are unsuccessful on even the most superficial level: in an age of telephone calls and jet flights, it is simply improbable that the two brothers in the book would write, for the few days they are together, as compulsively as Clarissa Harlowe. (p. 44)

If his religion of Vedanta simply has not worked when incorporated wholesale into his novels (as in *A Meeting by the River*) it appears to have worked well enough in his life and therefore indirectly in his art. Certainly it is essential for anyone who would understand him to realize that his religious conversion has made him closer to, not more distant from, the problems of his time. (p. 46)

Carolyn G. Heilburn, in her Christopher Isherwood *(Columbia Essays on Modern Writers Pamphlet No. 53; copyright © 1970 Columbia University Press; reprinted by permission of the publisher), Columbia University Press, 1970, 48p.*

W. H. AUDEN

In reading Mr. Isherwood's latest book [*Kathleen and Frank*]—since in it he always refers to himself as Christopher, I shall henceforth call him by his first name—it may be helpful to recall the three crises through which, according to Erik Erikson, anybody who merits an autobiography must pass: the crisis of Identity, the crisis of Generativity, and the crisis of Integrity. Roughly speaking, these occur in youth, middle age, and old age respectively, but they usually overlap, and the intensity and duration of each varies from individual to individual.

In the Identity crisis, the young man is trying to find the answer to the question, "Who am I *really*, as distinct from what others believe or desire me to be?" This is a crisis of consciousness. The Generativity crisis is a crisis of conscience. The question now to be answered is: "I have done this and that; my acts have affected others in this way or that. Have I done well or ill? Can I justify the influence that, intentionally or unintentionally, I have had on others?" Both the Identity and the Generativity crises are preoccupied with freedom and choice. The Integrity crisis of old age is concerned with fate and necessity. As Mr. Erikson puts it, it demands:

> . . . the acceptance of one's one and only life-cycle as something that had to be and that, by necessity, permitted of no substitutions, the knowledge that an individual life is the accidental coincidence of but one life-cycle with but one segment of history.

As I read it, *Kathleen and Frank* is Christopher's attempt, wholly successful in my opinion, to solve his Integrity crisis. . . .

The trouble for the reader of a diary who does not know its author personally is that he can only judge it, firstly, by its entertainment value—it must amuse him—and, secondly, by its historical value, the light it sheds upon the social mores and political events of the time in which it was written. I must frankly confess that, taken by itself, that is to say, without Christopher's comments and explanations, I do not think Kathleen's diary very interesting. (p. 19)

[Christopher's] descriptions of the family and their life in Cheshire are . . . fascinating both personally and historically. . . .

I have [a bone to pick with the author]. . . . The narrative would be easier to follow if [he] had provided genealogical tables. . . .

A fine book though, I cannot imagine any reader, whatever his social background and interests, not being enthralled by it. (p. 20)

W. H. Auden, "The Diary of a Diary," in The New York Review of Books *(reprinted with permission from* The New York Review of Books; *copyright © 1972 Nyrev, Inc.), Vol. XVII, No. 2 and Vol. XVIII, No. 1, January 27, 1972, pp. 19-20.*

PAUL PIAZZA

With matriarchal arrogance, the mother rules Isherwood's first two novels, *All the Conspirators* and *The Memorial,* written just before his Berlin books. . . . In the later novels, after [Isherwood's] conversion to Vedanta, mother figures become kind, even saintly, as [he] no longer postures as the young man "angry with the family and its official representatives." . . . (pp. 19-20)

Although Isherwood chafed against all authority, particularly its initial manifestation in his mother, his first novel cannot be classed either as a manifesto of independence or as a polemic in the same way that D. H. Lawrence's *Sons and Lovers* and James Joyce's *A Portrait of the Artist as a Young Man* can. *All the Conspirators* is a portrait of the artist as a hapless mother's boy unable to sever his ties to mother and to home. Isherwood exposes not only the Edwardian manners of the older generation but also the postwar sensibility of the younger generation as bogus and smug. His targets are pretentiousness and Prufrockian escapism, neither trait exclusively possessed by either generation. Rather than "a call to sound the cry to the barricades," *All the Conspirators* is an autopsy of a malignant family with Isherwood a coroner dissecting "the great malady, horror of one's home" and "Acedia, 'the malady of monks,' that deadly weakness of the will . . . the root of all evil" that sickens unto death. (p. 20)

Isherwood assembles his book as if he were editing a film, juxtaposing snips of action and dialogue with sparse descriptive passages. . . . [The critic's] charge of sketchiness stems from the novel's jerky, cinematic technique and Hemingwayesque dialogue, which needlessly obfuscate. (p. 21)

All the Conspirators ultimately fails because Mrs. Lindsay looms too large for the young Isherwood: at the end, Isherwood either retires her in the wings or renders her bland and inept. In his second published work, *The Memorial,* Isherwood is competent and versatile enough to create a world with the ambience and time not only for a character like Mrs. Lindsay to flourish, but also for her opposite. In Lily Vernon, Isherwood presents a masterful portrait of the "Evil Mother, fierce, obstinate, tearful and conventional." Lily's antithesis, Mary Scrivens, is a dilettantish, exuberant mother who lives only in the present; nevertheless, like Lily, she too destroys her children. Both women bequeath unrest and death to their families.

Isherwood's method is a sophisticated refinement of the jerky, stop-go cuts in *All the Conspirators.* Isherwood still composes like a film editor, but in *The Memorial* he lengthens his vignettes, clarifies his dialogues, varies and develops his characters. . . . To avoid an "I remember" digression, he does not construct a continuous narrative but arranges his story "in self-contained scenes, like a play: an epic in an album of snapshots." . . . We see the characters at four critical periods through the subjective eyes of other characters and through the writer's own descriptions. What emerges is a chilling, prescient portrait of a family dominated and damned by its women. (pp. 30-1)

[Although] sentimental, at times flabby, [*The World in the Evening*] nonetheless augurs a fresh start for Isherwood. . . . [In *The World in the Evening*] Isherwood strives mightily to chart the spiritual awakening and growth of Stephen Monk, who, under the tutelage of Aunt Sarah and Elizabeth, his mothers in the spirit, learns how to live. What they teach him is succinctly recapitulated by an entry in Katherine Mansfield's diary [which defines individuality as the consciousness that one has a will and can act]. (pp. 49-51)

Stephen Monk's journey from anger to appeasement mirrors Isherwood's own change of attitude toward himself and his life. (p. 51)

Two father types appear in Isherwood's fiction: in the early novels, the forbidding ghost whose legend, kept alive by Kathleen, emasculates his son; and in the later books, after Isherwood's settling in America and adoption of Vedanta, the sympathetic, broadly human, anti-heroic father.

The father of the Others is fully fleshed in *The Memorial.* There, seen through the admiring eyes of Edward Blake or the love-beclouded eyes of Lily, Richard Vernon (Eric's father) is a cynosure of classical manhood, "a hero and a great man . . . sure of himself . . . brave." . . . (pp. 55-6)

For his own sanity, Isherwood had to cut himself free from the father of the Others. Hence he plays so often and so well the role of Heathcliff, the fatherless child, the mysterious outsider without home and country. Only in *Prater Violet* does Isherwood, still without father and country, transcend these losses and convert them into spiritual gains. *Prater Violet* is significant because it bears witness to Isherwood's reinterpretation of reality in terms of Vedantist philosophy and because, for perhaps the first time, his hero establishes intimate contact with another human being whom he fittingly calls "father." But this is not the father of the Others.

Vedanta presented a religious version of Isherwood's anti-heroic hero. And for this reason—as much as for any other—Isherwood converted to Vedanta. In an article explaining this conversion in the collection *What Vedanta Means to Me,* Isherwood clearly shows that the search for a father and the search for a religion had become inextricably interwoven in his consciousness. (p. 57)

Vedanta answered Isherwood's every need. It is nondualistic: God is not above and beyond man, but the Atman is within man. Unlike Christianity, Vedanta is not narrowly moralistic. . . . To be more precise, unlike Christianity, Vedanta does not condemn homosexuality but views it as "merely another form of attachment, neither worse nor better" than heterosexuality. (p. 59)

For a book that begins with persistent self-confirmation (the book opens: "Mr. Isherwood?" "Speaking." "Mr. Christopher Isherwood?" "That's me."), *Prater Violet* is Isherwood's longest journey, from inveterate ego reinforcement to a loss of name and identity. (p. 67)

[The] final pages carry the lyrical mysticism of a miniature *Bhagavad-Gita,* the struggle for affirmation of Wordsworth's "Resolution and Independence," even the transcendence of Tennyson's *In Memoriam.*

At the spiritual center of *Prater Violet* is Bergmann, father to Christopher or, in Vedantist terms, guru. (p. 71)

Perhaps because Isherwood's creative subconscious is responsible for the spiritual dimension in Bergmann, Bergmann is Isherwood's most successful portrait of a father-guru figure. Isherwood's deliberate attempt in "Paul," the fourth part of *Down There on a Visit,* is far less successful. Modeled on Huxley and Heard, the guru Augustus Parr is too self-consciously religious. . . . Though Parr's appearance in "Paul" is brief, his function is as essential as Bergmann's in *Prater Violet.* Parr is Christopher's guru, someone whose presence and faith compel Christopher into belief. Nevertheless, in the book he comes off as little more than a cardboard saint. (p. 72)

Only in *A Meeting by the River* does Isherwood create a convincing guru gifted with both the irresistible genius of Bergmann and the other-worldliness of Parr. (p. 73)

[As Evelyn Waugh writes in *Journey to a War*], Isherwood's definitions are exquisitely hewn—but, more than ever, Isherwood is the outsider looking in, the *Berlin-Stories* narrator observing a holocaust in which he is not involved. Perhaps because he was unable to penetrate the enigma of the Orient, much less the enigma of man's violence to his fellows, his style is rhetorical, even rehearsed (Waugh's term was "respectable" [see excerpt above]). It is as if . . . Isherwood is masquerading "as a war correspondent." . . . [While] lacking clichés, Isherwood's diary entries also lack the authenticity and anguish of his war novels. Perhaps his braced, deliberately wrought style derives from this fact—that to Isherwood, the *idea* of war is far more nightmarish than the actual *fact* of war. (p. 80)

Isherwood cannot curb his own pathological war obsession from rearing its ugly head in his books. E. M. Forster's clear-eyed appraisal of English prose between the wars is pertinent here. Forster reads the books of that period as the "product of men who have war on their minds." Their works "need not be gloomy or hysterical—often they are gay and sane and brave—but if they have any sensitivity they must realize what a mess the world is in." (p. 81)

[War] taints the atmosphere of a major portion of Isherwood's works. . . . The little lives of Isherwood's characters are rounded by nightmare: not yet recovered from the bitter sorrow of one war, they discover themselves madly careering toward another. There is nothing in Isherwood of the idea often found in Michael Roberts or Rupert Brooke or Rex Warner, that war would purge the country of pettiness and selfishness and eventually invigorate. Rather, in Isherwood's world the idea of war conjures up a legion of Eumenides, or in Lawrence's terminology, a pack of jackals, hounding Isherwood's characters to the death. (pp. 81-2)

Because Isherwood brilliantly recorded what he saw, *The Berlin Stories* is a valuable social document which provides an insight into Isherwood's handling of political themes. (p. 88)

Isherwood's stories achieve political significance not because of their ideological content, but because of their heightened sensitivity to the obscure dread, the vague, unnatural menace inherent in the last days of the Weimar Republic. . . . Even in summations of this sort, [with] extreme selectivity of detail . . . , Isherwood's method is to catch the unrest and shabby chaos of the larger life around him in the microcosm of the individual. Isherwood is not an archivist like Orwell, prying into totalitarian atrocities, but rather a seismographer capable of reading the subtlest tremors that ripple across his personal landscape. . . . The "essential human element" in Isherwood's Berlin pieces composes all, gives the various genres a sustained, unified impact, and reveals the main lines of the epic he originally intended. As the political situation deteriorates, Isherwood's portraits darken. There is an increasing sense of suffocation, a sinking of human consciousness, as people discover themselves locked in hopeless situations, trapped by the approaching horror of Nazism. Indeed the subjects of Isherwood's portraits support [John] Lehmann's assertions that anyone reading *Goodbye to Berlin* with *The Last of Mr. Norris* will catch "glimpses of the bigger work which never materialized," which Isherwood planned to name *The Lost,* or its German equivalent *Die Verlorenen.*

If we take *The Berlin Stories,* then, as the epic Isherwood intended, the first piece we encounter is a novel, *The Last of Mr. Norris,* narrated by Isherwood's namesake, William Bradshaw. Norris is an essentially comic character, a colorful *flaneur* delighting in mysteries, dabbling in communism and fascism, reveling in the decadence of wigs and scents and vintage wines. (pp. 88-91)

While Norris flits about with the epicene pomp of a *fin-de-siècle* aesthete, tragedy is all around him. . . . Berlin is in a state of civil war. But the reader's attention is focused on Arthur Norris' comic inferno and Bradshaw's amused toleration rather than on the tragedy. Even the ending is ironic. . . . (p. 91)

The sequel to *The Last of Mr. Norris* is *Goodbye to Berlin,* which begins and ends with Isherwood's two Berlin diaries. Here the tonal change is immediately clear from the very first line, a sentence fragment: "From my window, the deep solemn massive street." . . . [There is a] gradual shift from edgy watchfulness to icy despair. (p. 92)

["Waldemar," the third section of *Down There on a Visit,* reveals] an anguish and passionate despair that recall Quentin Compson's breakdown in William Faulkner's *The Sound and the Fury.* "Waldemar" is one prolonged, desperate scream from beginning to end. . . .

Isherwood is so engrossed with himself that he does not see his despair macroscopically reflected in Europe's; instead, he sees England's and Europe's problems mirrored in his own manic behavior. (p. 103)

The political crisis stokes Isherwood's personal crisis. Though studded with citations from newspaper pundits, his diary is really another mirror in which Isherwood can glare at his sweating self. Stylistically, the selections shudder with self-interrogations, curses, and ranting *non sequiturs.* (p. 105)

Because his mother, invoking his dead father, wanted him to attend and because an award given by the Others enabled him to attend with the highest scholarship of his year, Isherwood had no choice but to detest Cambridge. In *Lions and Shadows,* he calls it a "city of perpetual darkness . . . the country of the dead." . . . He vigorously rejected Cambridge and in its place substituted, with [Edward] Upward, his own imaginary country of the dead, located somewhere near the Atlantic and peopled with a menagerie of ghouls. This macabre fantasy of Mortmere schooled Isherwood for the real nightmare he was to encounter in pre-Hitler Berlin.

Mortmere became the mad nursery in which Isherwood and Upward grew up as writers. (pp. 110-11)

With its aberrant characters, pornography, and gothic plots, Mortmere is as flamboyantly bizarre as a Dali painting, its stories clever pastiches of Sir Thomas Browne, the Brothers Grimm, Edgar Allan Poe, Lewis Carroll, Conan Doyle, Beatrix Potter, Anatole France, and many others. (p. 111)

Isherwood and Upward eventually repudiated Mortmere precisely because they were unable to connect its lunacy with the prose of everyday life. They gave it up, however, reluctantly, and only after repeatedly trying to impose sense on its essential nonsense. (p. 112)

Berlin with its Mortmere monstrosities uncannily pandered to Isherwood's predilection for the grotesque. . . . [Unlike the Mortmere stories, fantasy] does not alter reality; rather, reality in Berlin assumes the Caligari-like perspective of dream and surpasses even fantasy's tendency toward extremism: life heightens art. And life drastically alters the writer. The callous observer of *The Berlin Stories,* whom Isherwood repudiates in the late fifties and sixties, not only describes the Mortmere monstrosities about him, but, by the time of *Down There on a Visit,* actually becomes a monster. (pp. 116-17)

Isherwood's technique, as he himself expounds it, is that of a camera; however, too many readers stress the objectivity of the camera, forgetting that the Isherwood camera is subjective, highly expressive, and, in fact, Germanic. The influence of German film on Isherwood's writings is no surprise—Isherwood cites German film as captivating his generation. . . . The peculiar German contribution to film was the creative use of the camera—what the gestures of the actors could not communicate was to be conveyed by the symbolic language of the moving camera which "had the power of giving meaning even to lifeless things." (p. 117)

[It is not] that the camera as a metaphor for Isherwood's technique is identical with the actual camera of film-making. The two art forms are vitally different and, of course, Isherwood achieves certain effects which can be produced only by the choice and arrangement of individual words. . . . However, the characteristically visual properties of this style are achieved by Isherwood's placing his so-called camera in the proper position at the proper time. . . .

The very simplicity of *The Berlin Stories*—in plot, lack of clutter, and use of cogent incident only—may well be a result of Isherwood's schooling in the German cinema. On its simplest level, *The Last of Mr. Norris* is a serial biography of Arthur Norris who, surrounded by lesser characters, commands the reader's eye. (p. 118)

The novel's action is episodic, bracketed into single chapters or a series of chapters, like sharp cuts in a film, often with little connection to preceding incident. . . . The progression of the book resembles a film serial in which each installment presents, almost independently, another phase in the life of its picaresque hero.

In *Goodbye to Berlin,* Isherwood abandons the novel form to compose what he feels he can write best, a sequence even simpler and more compact—individual portraits. Against the bleak but garish background of a falling city, Sally Bowles, Peter and Otto, the Nowaks, the Landauers, and other Berlin denizens shuffle through their shabby cabaret choreography. Even more compressed than *The Last of Mr. Norris,* these portraits are succinct and direct. It is as if Isherwood, rather than making a full-length feature as he did in *Norris,* contents himself with shooting vivid, loosely joined shorts, startling in their severity and power. (p. 119)

[It] is important to note that the camera technique itself embodies the theme of *The Berlin Stories,* for, as Hitler's grasp on the city tightens, the narrator becomes more remote. In the beginning of *The Last of Mr. Norris,* Bradshaw feels excluded from a communist meeting, standing "outside it. One day, perhaps, I should be with it, but never of it." . . . By the time of "Sally Bowles," however, the narrator is isolated from the mass of men. . . . In "Ambrose," this personal detachment dilates to cosmic proportions.

But what separates Isherwood's camera from the documentary camera which churned out reel after reel of undistinguished footage is the way Isherwood's camera is highly sensitive to nuance, capable, because of its selectivity, its angles, its juxtaposition of light and dark, of catching what Stephen Spender calls "the terrifying mystery of cities."

Isherwood's camera captures the terror of Berlin very early in *The Last of Mr. Norris*. Bradshaw's walk to a New Year's party in chapter three is actually an archetypal journey to the land of the dead. So closely allied is Isherwood's technique with that of the early German film-makers that, merely by the insertion of camera directions and a slight rearrangement of the text, Isherwood's account of a New Year's festivity could have been excerpted from an early fantasy feature similar to *Dr. Caligari*. (pp. 119-20)

[Even] after Berlin's nightmare, Isherwood's narrator is still as uninvolved as he had been after the New Year's party in *Norris*. When he catches his reflection in a store front, he is quite shocked to see himself smiling. In *Down There on a Visit,* however, the same narrator is not so detached. Then looking into the mirror, he is startled by his terrible transformation. Although Isherwood's narrator flees Berlin's Mortmere atrocities, he cannot escape them—for the truth, as Isherwood discovers, is that Mortmere is not a place, but a state of soul, more pernicious than his wildest imaginings at Cambridge. (p. 126)

Throughout his career, Isherwood has constantly been reassessing and reinterpreting his life and work. For a writer who sought escape from the past, this continual remembrance of things past is, as we have seen, an unexpected irony. The rebellion against Kathleen and Frank, the camera technique of *The Berlin Stories,* which won him instant acclaim, the bizarre Mortmere fantasy of those stories, the concealment of his homosexuality—of these Isherwood, as an older man, takes a second, very different view. With his conversion to Vedanta he even revises his conceptions of character and conflict, conceptions basic to the work of any novelist.

Very early in his career, as he relates in *Lions and Shadows,* Isherwood formed four concepts which fired his creative imagination and which were to figure in his major fiction: the Enemy, the Test, the Truly Weak Man, and the Truly Strong Man. (p. 136)

Impossible to pass, the Test doomed Isherwood to continual aberrations in behavior. . . . Even the flight to Berlin is a search for the ultimate experience, the absolute Test, as the squeamish public school boy willfully samples the perversion of a foreign capital.

In Isherwood's early fiction, the Test exists only for the Truly Weak Man, Isherwood's version of the modern neurotic hero, feckless and impetuous, plunging where angels fear to tread. Yet, "no matter whether he passes it [the Test] or whether he fails, he cannot alter his essential nature" . . . , for he is damned by his ponderous sense of failure and inadequacy. (pp. 139-40)

All of Isherwood's early characters—those conceived during his English period, before he left for America in 1939—easily slip into the categories of the Truly Weak Man and the Truly Strong. (p. 141)

Isherwood's characters and conflicts are no more than the desperate attempts of a Truly Young Man straining to exorcise his demons, for the fictional possibilities of this early scheme lead nowhere. The Truly Weak Man is on an endless journey without a destination. . . . In all cases, the options, in terms of the novel, are cramped, even solipsistic.

The options of the Truly Strong Man seem equally feeble for a novelist. In Isherwood's early career this figure suffers from such superficiality that he is a mere heroic cutout. . . . (p. 142)

[In] the books of his American period, or more properly his Vedanta period, beginning with the publication of *Prater Violet,* his characters become markedly more interior as Isherwood discovers more potential in them. Bergmann in *Prater Violet* is the first indication of Isherwood's deeper understanding of the Truly Strong Man. Alternatively, Stephen Monk in *The World in the Evening* is as spoiled as Philip Lindsay (*All the Conspirators*), as lost as Eric Vernon (*The Memorial*), and as miserable as Edward Blake (*The Memorial*). But Stephen does learn the futility of imposing harebrained tests on himself, because the Test for the deeper Isherwood hero is inward and the Enemy is his own deficiency, not his mother or his father or his two wives. (p. 143)

[At] least from the time of *Prater Violet,* Isherwood is writing from an altered perception of what a novel should be. . . . [The] basic ideas of the Enemy, the Test, the Truly Weak and Truly Strong Men, though still with him, become modified. Now Isherwood's Truly Strong Man is a saint, the most interesting subject to write about because a saint responds to life more creatively than anyone else. (p. 147)

[The] Test is no longer the somber spectacle of insurmountable odds, the Truly Weak Man's inevitable failure. By now Isherwood has grown to view the Test as the risk-taking inherent in maturing into one's better self. The . . . Test is more akin to a conversion than to an ordeal. . . .

Once the hero is converted, Isherwood sees the writer's task as demonstrating that the saint is not insane when he turns his back on "the whole scheme of pleasures, rewards, and satisfactions . . . accepted by the Joneses, the Smiths, and the Browns, and goes in search of superconscious, extraphenomenal experience." (p. 148)

What about the portrait of the perfected saint? Here Isherwood despairs, for nothing short of genius can succeed in such a task. . . . Isherwood concludes: "Perhaps the truly comprehensive religious novel could only be written by a saint—and saints, unfortunately, are not in the habit of writing novels."

This new depth and awareness of saintly possibilities are salient characteristics in Isherwood's last two novels, *A Single Man* and *A Meeting by the River*. (pp. 149-50)

Though radically different in technique, *A Single Man* and *A Meeting by the River* both point to an extra dimension, a "superconscious, extraphenomenal" aspect in reality. In *A Single Man,* Isherwood presents a day in the life of a Truly Lonely Man, George, a middle-aged homosexual and professor of English literature. George is very much like Jones or Smith or Brown, for his life is not particularly rich or luminous: if he is different, it is only in degree. His homosexuality, his education, his pathetic mourning for Jim, his dead lover, actually intensify George's very human condition of loneliness. The spiritual, even mystical aspects of George's life are suggested by Isherwood who, throughout the novel, sustains a delicate dialogue with the reader. Isherwood's description of George's late-night encounter with Kenny, one of his students, as a symbolic Platonic dialogue, defines the book's narrative method: a symbolic dialogue between the author as a kind of guru and the reader as a disciple meditating on the ephemera of George's day.

George has no idea that his confusion and monotony contain mystical ramifications; he is the early Isherwood hero as he might have been without Isherwood's conversion. The dialogue remains between author and auditor only—George is unaware of his dimensions. (p. 150)

In *A Meeting by the River,* however, Isherwood abandons any stylistic individuality in favor of an epistolary novel—it's as if in his last novel he is trying to bring the book as near as possible to the experiences of the Joneses, the Smiths, the Browns, by casting the book in the form of letters and diary jottings. The style here is simple, energetic, but in comparison with the subtle, delicate prose of *The Memorial, The Berlin Stories, Prater Violet, A Single Man,* it is deliberately undistinguished. (p. 161)

What begins as a dispute ends in a fraternal dialogue as Isherwood deftly manipulates the double viewpoints [in *A Meeting by the River*] to fulfill his chief requirements for a religious novel. He makes his saints-to-be very much like Messrs. Jones, Smith, and Brown. More important, Isherwood surpasses his own expectations, for the novel's thrust is that both Oliver and Patrick are incipient saints, brothers in the deeper sense that both are seeking sanctity. It is not the richly evocative language of *A Single Man,* but Isherwood's placing of the letters and feuilletons of the brothers which contrasts their individual strivings and thus makes two points intrinsic to Isherwood's conception of the religious novel: that Oliver's behavior is not at all insane but, in essence, is similar to that of Patrick; that Patrick's flamboyance is not merely mindless bustle but actually an expression of his longing for the same realities Oliver seeks. Their two paths, therefore, represent complementary roads to holiness, the religious and the worldly. (pp. 162-63)

Does Isherwood give us the portrait of the perfected saint? No. But he does present the Isherwood hero as no longer lost, but as having found himself; if he is still an outsider, he is so not because of neurotic hostility but because of spiritual growth. (p. 168)

In the early novels, Isherwood's treatment of the homosexual is, at best, conventional; only later, as Isherwood's own vision deepens, does he alter his vision of the homosexual's place in the world.

Not surprising, Isherwood's first references to homosexuality in *All the Conspirators* are, like other aspects of the novel, strained and self-conscious. (p. 172)

By the time of *The Memorial* and *The Berlin Stories,* . . . homosexuality has become a staple of the anti-myth, a characteristic of both the Truly Weak Man and of the Lost, who are alike shunned by society. Edward Blake in *The Memorial* is severed from society by the nightmare of the Great War and by his sexual preferences. Blake's homosexuality, though, is a perversion characteristic of his peculiar malaise. (p. 173)

In *The Berlin Stories,* homosexuality takes on a new dimension and becomes a resonant metaphor for Berlin's Mortmeresque depravity. Isherwood's portrait of the Baron Kuno von Pregnitz, for example, like all the Mortmere parodies, is a caricature of perversion: loathed by Bradshaw, the Baron is drawn as a sinister storybook monster. His advances to Bradshaw are always made to appear farcical. (p. 174)

Isherwood's recent reflections on Berlin confirm the notion that his use of homosexuality as a symbol of depravity is only a literary technique and not a realistic representation. . . .

Isherwood's artistic reason for turning Bradshaw-Isherwood into what many consider a chaste prig are well-intentioned and understandable. To have made the narrator heterosexual would have been to capitulate to the heterosexual dictatorship and to distort his own experience; to have made him homosexual would have been to affront his readers and to detract from the story. (p. 179)

As the narrator began to develop into a human being in the later novels, and as Isherwood's own understanding of how he might use homosexuality as a theme in his novels matured, the fictional treatment of the narrator drastically altered. Rather than a Mortmere curiosity, the narrator becomes a human being. . . .

In *The World in the Evening,* for the first time, Isherwood begins to probe the perilous dilemma of the homosexual in an intolerant society. He gamely attempts to draw Bob Wood, Dr. Charles Kennedy, and Michael Drummond as complex human beings who are also homosexuals. Their loneliness and alienation are unmerited: they suffer because they are different. But like almost every other character in the book, they are cardboard figures, another series of exhibitions. Nonetheless, Isherwood's failure here shows an advance in his handling of homosexuality: he has indeed tried to imbue them with flesh-and-blood characteristics. (p. 180)

Isherwood's later frankness about his personal life also accounts for a change in his style. In the last four novels, Isherwood's writing is, as always, a perfect instrument for his perceptions; but, lacking the distant I-Christopher narrator, the books contain less posturing, fewer rhetorical gestures. In *A Single Man,* the style is plain, at times even bare. The only metaphoric passages are religious—George's midnight swim and the rock-pool description. In both passages, because Isherwood is trying to communicate the mystical, he is forced to speak in imagery and parable, for, as he has written, the mystical experience can only be hinted at. (p. 190)

Isherwood has always asserted and maintained his identity in a world that operated from diverse, chiefly antagonistic values. His nine novels are nine autobiographical glimpses —blurred, darkened, partial—into a mirror. Taken together, these nine glimpses coalesce to form a reflected image of what might be called the "essential Isherwood," always investing his life with epic proportions, always creating his ironic anti-myth, the subject of which is, always, the anti-son of Kathleen and Frank. Each new frontier crossed, each new shock survived, each new revelation declared, entails a further probing and fresh articulation of the counter-myth. . . . [One might] say that Isherwood wrote one novel which he constantly amended, incorporating new, original insights so that the final copy is a palimpsest recording the results of his modified interpretation of the anti-myth; or that he actually wrote a Proustian remembrance of things past with nine books, as well as three autobiographies, which organically expand and change as Isherwood matures, recalling and reliving his past. (pp. 196-97)

As the man and the myth change, so does the style. As always, Isherwood is a master, his writing exact and unclichéd, a superb medium for his observations. In the books since his conversion, the style is still masterly, but different, simpler, at times more lyrical, and, in the seventies, certainly more honest and straightforward. Isherwood's last three books—*A Meeting by the River, Kathleen and Frank,* and *Christopher and His Kind*—are based on letters and diaries. Intent on telling the truth, Isherwood seems to regard the manner of his early work as a hindrance to revelation. The writing is energetic, subtle, but compared to that of his early works, austere and unembellished. The style here is nonstyle. In these books one . . . sees realized the hope expressed in 1949 by a critic in the *Times Literary Supplement:* "What could he do if he really tried." (p. 197)

Paul Piazza, in his Christopher Isherwood: Myth and Anti-Myth *(copyright © 1978 Columbia University Press; reprinted by permission of the publisher), Columbia University Press, 1978, 245 p.*

D. S. SAVAGE

Isherwood set out initially to be a novelist, not an autobiographer; but his apprentice efforts as well as later attempts to dramatize characters and situations and to write confidently about adult emotions, are all relative failures. Most of his best work, written in Europe in the thirties—*Sally Bowles, Goodbye to Berlin, Mr. Norris Changes Trains* and *Lions and Shadows,* together with the later rechauffe of much the same material in *Down There on a Visit* (1962)—is artfully artless reportage by a naif 'I' who bears one of Isherwood's own christian names, or it is direct if slightly fictionalized autobiography.

With Isherwood's self-absorption is associated both his recessive orientation towards the past and his preoccupation with the immature. . . . Isherwood's style at its early best has a bare particularity which accords well with the triviality of his subject-matter. (pp. 71-2)

[An] admission by one of Isherwood's later mouthpieces that he is one to whom things happen in a disconnected, meaningless way seems to express facetiously his author's own unreadiness, for all his self-concern, to grasp, evaluate and comprehend experience so as to grow inwardly to maturity through its creative assimilation. (p. 72)

[It] becomes apparent that Isherwood's characters have one especial feature in common. They are simultaneously both *naughty* and *innocent*. . . . It is this odd combination of innocence and guilt which fascinates Christopher/William . . . , as if he too were in some respect guilty and innocent. He accepts Sally Bowles so uncritically because the more *naughty* she is the more she reveals her irrefragible *innocence,* so reflecting his, Christopher's, own moral perplexity or equivocalness. (p. 73)

The central issue for Isherwood is an irresolvable ambiguousness concerning innocence and guilt which, for him, has always a sexual focus. While for the Isherwood man, sexuality is everything, it is at the same time the realm of the wicked, the forbidden, above all, the dangerous. Its forbiddenness makes it irresistibly enticing; its dangers make it a Test. And the approach to sexuality is surrounded with an inadmissible guiltiness which must be denied by re-phrasing it in terms of innocence. (p. 81)

What that curious memoir, *Kathleen and Frank,* sets down in factual terms is precisely that which is implied, though never more than implied, in the novels: its author-editor's lifelong reluctance to grow out of a cosily reassuring homoerotic phase. To become adult Isherwood had an inner task to perform which proved against his will or beyond his strength, a movement towards self-possession which should free him from the compulsiveness of an unresolved Oedipal attachment, both positive and negative, to his Daddy and Mummy, and the consequent determination, as on a fixed track, of his life-pattern throughout by this never ending travelling 'in the parental train'. . . . Here the desperate need for self-justification, deadly to a writer, constrains Isherwood to parade his continued determination by the homosexual mother-fixation as though it were a form of self-liberation. But a man does not escape from or transform his own inwardly infantile emotions by putting himself at a physical distance from his mother or by defiantly adopting modes of living of which she disapproves, but by an inward and spiritual de-conditioning and emancipation which removes him altogether from the child-parent context into the dimension of personal autonomy and moral responsibility. As elsewhere in this writer, the overt pronouncement is in conflict with the covert meaning of the words. It is only necessary to compare this piece of bland self-approbation with the cool self-analysis of *Lions and Shadows* to see how far, and in what direction, the later Isherwood has diverged from the earlier; and yet the two are related, and the same. Both are summed up in the guileless observation concerning the unfulfilled quest for Christopher's identity. —'Impossible to say exactly where Kathleen and Frank end . . . they merge into each other . . . Christopher has found that he is far more closely interwoven with Kathleen and Frank than he has supposed, or liked to believe.' On a railway journey one may change trains, but the train never leaves the tracks. (pp. 87-8)

D. S. Savage, "Christopher Isherwood: The Novelist as Homosexual," in Literature and Psychology *(© Morton Kaplan 1979), Vol. XXIX, Nos. 1 & 2, 1979, pp. 71-88.*

* * *

IVASK, Ivar 1927-

Ivask is an Estonian-born poet and scholar now residing in America. His love and homesickness for the natural beauty of his native land inform his poetry. His verse is further marked by a palpably physical lyricism and acute sensitivity to nature. Ivask has been the editor of *World Literature Today* since 1967. (See also *Contemporary Authors,* Vols. 37-40, rev. ed.)

ALEXANDER ASPEL

[Dr. Ivar Ivask], whose scholarly and incisive criticism has won him unanimous recognition also as the best literary critic of the younger generation in free Estonian literature, reveals himself in [*Tähtede tähendus*], which is his first [volume of verse], as a poet of remarkable talent and unusual depth. The title "Meaning of the Stars" . . . refers to a sentence written long ago by the grandmother of the poet, but it refers through the poems of the collection also to the Milky Way, to companionship and, last but not least, to the correspondence between macrocosm and microcosm in a unified world.

Pointing to the poet's origins, the title summarizes aptly the poetic substance of the volume which lies in the discovery of the poet's inner identity and of his relation to the world through the experience of an immediate contact with fundamental realities. This contact occurs in situations of everyday life, which release suddenly the sensation of a breakthrough and of participation with the fullness of life. (pp. 373-74)

Condensed to few striking images and elliptic statements, the pattern of reduction and rebirth runs through most of Ivask's dramatic poems. It runs also through the whole cycle of travel poems, where Vienna, Paris, and the Mediterranean world are met as revelations of their particular essences.

The dramatic poems of rebirth are balanced in this collection by a series of simple, often epigrammatic yet singularly transparent poems, in free verse, where the poet senses the faint echoes of his ancestral past. . . .

Ivask's poetry meets the age-long current of elemental and animistic realism in Estonian poetry, yet it shows close affinities also with the new poetry of Being apparent in many countries of Europe and Latin America. (p. 374)

Alexander Aspel, "Books in Various Languages: 'Tähtede tähendus'," in Books Abroad *(copyright 1965 by the University of Oklahoma Press), Vol. 39, No. 3, Summer, 1965, pp. 373-74.*

MALL JÜRMA

Ivask's fifth collection of poetry has a remarkably meaningful title, *Verikivi* (Bloodstone), which sounds somewhat like an anagram of his name. Actually the title refers to a family ring that Ivask inherited from his father. The ring symbolizes not only the latest cycle in the poet's life, but other cycles as well. . . .

It is the author's most personal book of verse, reflecting his innermost feelings. Alongside meditative nature poetry, motifs of life and death, separation, loss and rediscovery of love dominate. Death of family members and the loss of a close friend have influenced the author's verse.

The loss of his fatherland is . . . deeply felt after a visit to Estonia. The poems reflect the rediscovery of one's home as an intimate and secure place and a new appreciation of the world. They speak about the search for "life's vein of gold in the dust and ashes of dreams." Such lines were inspired by the exhausted gold mines of Colorado. Themes of loneliness, rootlessness, alienation, homelessness and assimilation occur. The forests of Colorado remind the poet of the pines and fir trees of his northern homeland. He compares his co-exiles with aerial rooted mangroves, detached from their native soil, yet continuing to grow in a foreign environment. (p. 470)

Despite all disillusionment, the poet's creative spirit forges forward with unsubdued vitality. . . . Ivask's latest poetry is not only a reflection of sad and painful memories, it is a creative act that gives significance and substance to his life and work. . . . His free verse is supple, and its often deliberately simple wording seems to engage the reader in a direct dialogue. (pp. 470-71)

Mall Jürma, "World Literature in Review: 'Verikivi. Luuletusi 1973-1976'," in World Literature Today *(copyright 1977 by the University of Oklahoma Press), Vol. 51, No. 3, Summer, 1977, pp. 470-71.*

VALEV UIBOPUU

"Life Collection" is [a volume] of selected Estonian poems . . . illustrated with [Ivask's] own pen-and-ink drawings which reflect well the spirit of the book. He has elected not to arrange the material chronologically, but rather thematically and associatively. This proves to be an excellent idea, as it has permitted the poet to impart to this selection nuances which transform it in many ways into something completely new. It presents the author's profile in sharper relief and through recurring motifs points out what he considers most essential.

This way of looking at a poet's production reminds us of studying growth rings in a tree—we see the individual's personality at the same time as we see his development. The fact that the recurrence of images through the years and even decades does not become a burden to the reader is proof of the vitality and freshness of Ivask's poetic gift. The very titles of the seven sections in the volume dramatically embody his thematic reach. . . . "Time Is the Artery of Space," in which the philosophical implications of the author's world view are particularly evident, is perhaps the most aptly named section.

Ivask has, without doubt, added considerably to the already varied landscape of Estonian poetry. Even the dimensions of its themes have been widened in a manner which might be called geographic expansiveness. Ivask's subject matter shows a Viking-like agility. Since the day of Gustav Suits (1884-1956), no Estonian poet has worked within so open a system of international coordinates, remaining at the same time deeply Estonian. In this respect he has fulfilled the promise of his first collection, "The Meaning of Stars." . . . Homeland as a space has grown in Ivask's work to almost global proportions, both through the discovery of similarities with his native land or, then, their absence. The relationship between native country and the world has become for Ivask an interaction between micro- and macrocosmos, the first being contained in the second. Where this is not so, it is the poet's task to look for it. . . .

It is not surprising that one of the main aspects of Ivask's verse is nature poetry. In this he might seem to be following in the footsteps of Bernard Kangro, but his poetry has an individual, nearly mystical cast. Merging with nature is part of this, as is experiencing it on equal terms and looking in it for similes of life and death: "I fall with every drop of rain / And I am freed in every flaming leaf / I fly with the wind from tree to tree / To be reborn in your womb of earth" (1965). Poems like "Close to Earth, Close to Soil, Close to Grass" (1971) or "Forests of Pine, Fir, Alder, Birch" (1969) are poetic expressions of pantheistic faith. Trees and shrubs, mushrooms and moss, flowers, berries and rocks, cats and fish all represent it symbolically and become means of incantation for the poet-shaman. Yet nature is for Ivask universal, including Mediterranean olive trees as well as the pines and firs of the North. . . .

A fundamentally nature-worshiping, pantheistic world view is but a step away from the cosmic experience of reality, and Ivask's poetry proves this. The cycle "Time Is the Artery of Space" contains the largest number and the best poems giving expression to this feeling. The entire universe is to Ivask as much a poetic object as any detail in nature. . . . (p. 324)

The present selection shows that Ivask has followed in his verse technique the general evolution of our period: the full rhyme of his early years has disappeared completely in later collections. He has retained and perfected the already mentioned gift for poetic imagery. By a fusion of concrete and abstract elements, he often achieves surprising results, as in the poem "The Moon's Skull in the Lake" (1965). Summing up, we may say that in twenty years of poetic activity Ivar Ivask has created for himself in Estonian poetry a distinct place which without him would not have existed. At the same time, the generous universality of his life perception raises him above the limits of narrowly restrictive nationalism. (pp. 324-25)

Valev Uibopuu, "World Literature in Review: 'Elukogu: Valitud luuletused,'' in World Literature Today *(copyright 1979 by the University of Oklahoma Press), Vol. 53, No. 2, Spring, 1979, pp. 324-25.*

J

JACOBSON, Dan 1929-

An English novelist, short story writer, and essayist, Jacobson was born in Johannesburg. His skillful fiction explores problems of identity and environment in South Africa. (See also *CLC*, Vol. 4, and *Contemporary Authors*, Vols. 1-4, rev. ed.)

The Trap is a skilfull short story padded out to look a great deal longer than it is. In fact, Mr. Jacobson . . . has worked up an anecdote of life on a small veld farm suggestively enough to make the reader interested in what he may write next. *The Trap* probably should have formed part of a book of short stories rather than a volume on its own, for it offers not much more than a tale, in the Conrad manner, of a white man being influenced against a trustworthy black servant by an untrustworthy one. The setting is vividly and economically created, and Mr. Jacobson handles his stolid *baas* and his unfortunate employees very professionally. Patently, he is a writer of considerable promise, whose ability to write ironic dialogue is matched by a telling restraint in the use of descriptive prose. He has style; when he has more to do with it than embellish a familiar and basic plot with a slick twist it will be possible to see how deep his talent runs.

"Mingled Shades," in The Times Literary Supplement *(© Times Newspapers Ltd. (London) 1955; reproduced from* The Times Literary Supplement *by permission), No. 2793, September 9, 1955, p. 521.**

SIMON RAVEN

Mr. Jacobson [in *The Price of Diamonds*] presents his people with subtlety and intelligence, carefully sets them down in an unappetising South African township, and then, with the reader's interest fully and skilfully aroused, sets them ticking at a nicely calculated pace. But alas, the nicely calculated pace can apparently neither be varied nor halted, and one can only pray for the breakdown which Mr. Jacobson is much too efficient to allow. . . . After a promising and almost striking start, and with the evident talent at Mr. Jacobson's disposal, it is a pity the total performance should be so utterly futile.

Simon Raven, "Upstairs, Downstairs . . . ," in The Spectator *(© 1957 by* The Spectator; *reprinted by permission of* The Spectator*), Vol. 199, No. 6756, December 20, 1957, p. 879.**

A. ALVAREZ

Violence makes a strange ending for a love story, even if the setting is South Africa. But because Dan Jacobson has the ability to create sensitive, intelligent people and make them act sensitively and intelligently despite the background of guilt and shock, *The Evidence of Love* is neither propaganda nor sensationalism. It is, instead, a considerable artistic achievement, all the more impressive because it was written calmly out of the same tensions as created the South African explosion.

It is the story of a love-affair between a Cape Coloured boy and a white girl. . . .

The Evidence of Love might have been just another case-history. But since Jacobson is a novelist, not a politician, he knows none of the answers in advance. Despite the ending, I'm not even sure he knows them in retrospect. He has only an artist's answer—people. It is a matter not of dogma, but of the moral intelligence. And even that is an uneasy, unwilling affair, with conscience instead of theories, feelings instead of principles, and insights which are unpredictable, fluctuating, not to be controlled. Jacobson, in fact, is political against the grain. His book is less a tirade against the South African set-up—though all that is implied—than a drama of the profound difficulty of being South African. . . . There is an answer to all this, but it is an implicit, an artist's answer. It lies in what gives Jacobson's work its distinction: the witty, compassionate writing which creates a dimension of detachment, honesty and judgment in which his characters take on their full significance. . . .

His lovers are neither isolated at heart and battering against their isolation, nor are they romantically afloat in a warm continuum of passion. Instead, they are rooted in a world made solid and alive by the precision of Jacobson's observation. There is a certain sharpness about his writing which draws everyone and everything—major figures and minor scene and mood—into a tight circle of mutual commitment and mutual illumination. . . . Jacobson has a great reputation as a stylist. He does write beautifully, but never in the show-off manner of the professional littérateur. His style is a function of his meaning, a sign of his intelligence and control. It gives a hardness and density to the world he creates. It imposes values without preaching. . . .

His subject is not class and snobbery, it is race. And race is not so much a theme as a dimension of the world he creates. In this he has the edge on William Faulkner who, for all his genius, is forever slipping out of the racial issue: he either treats it as though it *were* class, or uses it as a cipher for good and evil. . . . [Where] Faulkner excuses the moral issues or shuffles them out of the way, Jacobson faces them squarely. (p. 827)

[Jacobson] is not only South African, he is also Jewish. It is this, I think, that gives him his extraordinary awareness of racial tensions; they are deeply part of his sensibility, as rich in creative possibilities as ever class was to Trilling's European tradition. . . . For race, from the inside, is not a separate problem with a separate answer. It is not a cause or a 'larger issue' in which to submerge one's identity. It *is* one's identity, and the answers, Jacobson shows, are in the complexities of life itself.

This is both the strength and the weakness of the book. He has transposed on to a Coloured boy the difficulties of being Jewish, and then geared them up until they seem appropriately more extreme. It doesn't altogether work. Jacobson commands great eloquence and he uses it to raise the necessary intensity. But eloquence is a tricksy gift; handled wrongly it topples into rhetoric. . . . Granted the subject hardly encourages detachment, but the whole of Jacobson's power depends on his tone. The more he strains, the less effective he seems. In a way, Kenneth [the protagonist] is less convincing than the figures who surround him and matter less.

But strain or no strain, I can think of no other novelist with the range and compassion and insight to tackle the theme at all. *The Evidence of Love* may not be such an assured artistic success as Jacobson's earlier novels, but it is considerably more ambitious, more important, and promises heaven knows what to come. (pp. 827-28)

A. Alvarez, "The Difficulty of Being South African," in New Statesman *(© 1960 The Statesman & Nation Publishing Co. Ltd.), Vol. LIX, No. 1525, June 4, 1960, pp. 827-28.*

GRANVILLE HICKS

I have had a feeling all along that some day Jacobson would write a "big" novel, big in scope. Some fiction writers do better with small canvases, and that's fine, but others need room to move around in. The diversity of Jacobson's experiences has seemed to demand the development of a large and complicated pattern. This is what he has worked out in *The Beginners,* which portrays several generations in several countries. . . .

[The] prologue, beautifully told, gives us the character of Avrom, the strange blending of true generosity with sentimental self-indulgence. None of the other characters in the book is made like Avrom, but we come to see the mixed motives out of which they act. (p. 37)

The cast is large, and not every character can be fully developed, but each one is alive, even if he is on stage for only a few minutes. One also has a strong sense of the vitality of groups of people, whether they are gathered for a family conference or are watching a political demonstration. These people live, and they live in our times, the troubled years since World War II. They are truly beginners, whether they are immigrants to South Africa or descendants of those pioneers, searching for a new life in Israel or England or America. Jacobson lets his novel sprawl a little, but it is hard to do anything else when one works on so ambitious a scale. (p. 38)

Granville Hicks, "No End to Beginnings," in Saturday Review *(© 1966 by Saturday Review, Inc.; reprinted with permission), Vol. XLIX, No. 8, February 19, 1966, pp. 37-8.*

DOUGLAS DUNN

Childhood is frequently thought of as the staple source of the short story writer's inspiration. Standard themes of short stories are the conversion of childhood into adolescence, adolescence into adulthood, and the contrast of an innocent world with one not so innocent. Dan Jacobson's stories [in *Inklings: Selected Stories*] fit, like an illustration, into this pattern. His setting is, of course, South Africa. . . .

The peculiar and vicious social arrangements in South Africa are, to a writer, as much interesting as something to flee from or be hurt by. Stories like Mr Jacobson's thrive on subdued tensions and recognitions. His Jewish background makes these more than a simple black-white antithesis. And in order to convey the complex realities of racial and national oddities, Jacobson has devised a plain, natural prose, from which the engaging humanity of his concerns is imparted to the reader with beautiful, almost poetic, balance. . . .

An immense human sadness is common to . . . Jacobson's stories. Within a bewildering range of imperfections and dissatisfactions, [his] characters find self-knowledge and the future dispiriting. . . . Adding up these stories, one gets the impression that Mr Jacobson's achievement is at least on the same level as *Winesburg Ohio,* with an apt burden of 'characters', events, detections, and a convincing portrait of 'how it is.'

Douglas Dunn, "Disturbing Stories," in The Spectator *(© 1973 by* The Spectator; *reprinted by permission of* The Spectator*), Vol. 230, No. 7560, May 19, 1973, p. 623.**

TOM PAULIN

[The] Republic of Sarmeda is located somewhere outside the geography of history. It is the setting of Dan Jacobson's *The Confessions of Josef Baisz,* an account of a systematic traitor and police-spy whose confession of "my days as a petty functionary" is, at least partly, an allegory of the artist as political Judas. Like Judas, Josef Baisz "can love only through betrayal", and his justification of his sins contains occasional insights into the psychology of disloyalty. Baisz is disloyal to the bureaucrats who employ him, and his autobiography is offered as a translation. . . . It's a witty parody of the standard academic preface, and as Dan Jacobson lectures at an English university there are sound reasons for thinking that *The Confessions of Josef Baisz* is on one level an account both of the situation of a writer employed by an academic institution and of the spirit that now pervades many such institutions—a spirit of complacent irrelevance, bland scholarly courtesies, and outmoded, autocratic habits of thought.

What is remarkable about this story is the clammy, stifling atmosphere of the one-party state that is the Republic of Sarmeda. . . . It might be somewhere in the Balkans or an oblique vision of South Africa. The whole country seems "to lie in that trance-like state which so often precedes a great change." Everywhere "the pathos of inexpectancy, the fragile stillness that precedes a violent disruption" can be sensed. And on the afternoon of a coup by "the Armed Forces Purification Grouping" there is a sudden feeling of "attentive stillness . . . glittering silence and vacancy" which is the atmosphere of a state or institution which is about to be forcibly reconnected to the historical process. . . . (pp. 70-1)

Jacobson designs a mysterious political landscape of clandestine meetings in misty parks where alleyways open out "into circular, apse-like spaces where statues and metal benches faced one another." . . . [Baisz's dream of unconditioned freedom] is impossible, and he can only confess his wish to escape being a servile functionary. . . . [He] is the rebellious victim of a process of cultural conditioning, though Jacobson (since he has invented a whole culture) has a much surer sense of the workings of such a process, and so is able to explore Baisz's wish to understand and transcend it. However, it's also possible to view Baisz's longing for the unconditioned as one side of Jacobson's private dialogue with himself—another part of his mind seems to be screaming to be released from the pure freedom, the unconditioned territory, of this fiction. Baisz's demand for complete irresponsibility is in fact Jacobson's way of reminding himself that the extremities of dreams can be the beginnings of responsibilities. (pp. 71-2)

Tom Paulin, "Books & Writers: 'The Confessions of Josef Baisz'," in Encounter *(© 1978 by Encounter Ltd.), Vol. L, No. 1, January, 1978, pp. 70-2.*

KATHA POLLITT

For all the grimness of its subject, Dan Jacobson's facility of invention makes [*The Confessions of Josef Baisz*] a surprisingly lighthearted book. He obviously had a lot of fun inventing Sarmeda. . . . As a political fantasy it is at once playful and provocative, and as a study of the psychology of betrayal—that complex tangle of love, pity, self-hatred, and power-seeking—it is compelling. While a certain offhandedness makes me wonder if Jacobson was bringing all his considerable energies to bear on his subject, he has brought enough of them to make this a supremely amusing fable for our time.

Katha Pollitt, "Books in Brief: 'The Confessions of Josef Baisz'," in Saturday Review *(© 1978 by Saturday Review Magazine Corp.; reprinted with permission), Vol. 6, No. 3, February 3, 1979, p. 44.*

Josef Baisz, citizen of an imaginary totalitarian state, recounts every detail of his adventures as an informer and duplicitous bodyguard [in "The Confessions of Josef Baisz"]. . . . Josef's meticulous descriptions of the world around him—the people, the machines, and the land itself seem ugly and hostile—suggest that the habit of cynicism has narrowed the range of his emotions; it is his notion that the thrill he feels at the moment of betrayal must be love. When he declares, in the final pages, that he plans to take his own life and thereby outwit his superiors, his boneheaded self-satisfaction is at once pitiable and repellent. A chilling portrait but an enthralling one, because Dan Jacobson lets this lucid and deluded creature betray his folly with his own—for once, candid—words. (pp. 144-45)

"Books: 'The Confessions of Josef Baisz'," in The New Yorker *(© 1979 by The New Yorker Magazine, Inc.), Vol. LV, No. 4, March 12, 1979, pp. 144-45.*

DEAN FLOWER

Jacobson's austere narrative [*The Confessions of Josef Baisz*] follows out with the clarity of a syllogism its chilling logic. As a newly-conscripted soldier, Josef Baisz finds himself through a series of absurd chances and petty enmities in a position to betray a friend. When he does so, the effect stuns him:

> Everyone had got Judas wrong! That was my great discovery. When he pressed his lips to the master's, he did it passionately, with a breaking heart and expectant eye, full of excitement and curiosity, trembling with pity. . . . He was one of those who loved only what he betrayed; who could love only through betrayal.

And Baisz is another. We follow his appalling career with fascination because its psychology and politics ring so true.

There is never any question about Jacobson endorsing his hero or using him as a stand-in. Baisz reveals himself with terrifyingly flat honesty. . . . The book suffers from predictability of character types, outside of the narrator, and situations; the cost, it would seem, of Baisz's violent and reductive temperament appears in his contemptuously narrowed vision. Yet his fate too turns out to lie in the despised past. (pp. 303-04)

Dean Flower, "Picking Up the Pieces," in The Hudson Review *(copyright © 1979 by The Hudson Review, Inc.; reprinted by permission), Vol. XXXII, No. 2, Summer, 1979, pp. 293-307.**

* * *

JENNINGS, Elizabeth 1926-

Jennings is an English Catholic poet and critic who established her literary reputation as a member of "the Movement," a group of writers that included Kingsley Amis, Thom Gunn, and Philip Larkin. The dignity and composure that characterized the early work of the "Movement" writers are evident in all of Jennings's poetry. (See also *CLC*, Vol. 5, and *Contemporary Authors*, Vols. 61-64.)

P. N. FURBANK

The good things about Elizabeth Jennings are as good as ever in [*Recoveries*], and the limitations just the same. When a poem of hers comes off, she manages to cancel the impression made by those fluent, limp, iambic lines by some line (often a last one) which, equally fluent and rhythmically unexciting, concentrates the whole meaning of the poem, hits the bull's-eye in fact. The measured stillness sometimes comes out just as dullness, but much more often it is rescued in this way. Her best and natural state is contemplation, and the poems tend to be about the debits and credits of the contemplative attitude. . . . By a fine and conscious stroke of art Elizabeth Jennings places in the middle of her own grey and cloistral verses a translation from Camus, ecstatically hymning an Algerian morning, which has, in that context, the effect of blazing sun through cloister arcades.

P. N. Furbank, "Books: 'Recoveries'," in The Listener *(© British Broadcasting Corp. 1964; re-*

printed by permission of P. N. Furbank), Vol. LXXII, No. 1843, July 23, 1964, p. 137.

JULIAN SYMONS

The characteristics of [Elizabeth Jennings's] poetry, from her first remarkable Fantasy Press volume 14 years ago, have been ingenuity, wit, and a persistent interest in the relationship between visible and imagined worlds. The tone is often lyrical, but the poems [in her *Collected Poems*] are metaphysical conceits. Some are about love, all are basically involved with the nature of reality. Can we really trust what we see? . . .

These are Miss Jennings's poetic concerns [in *Collected Poems*], and she carried them through from the first with intelligence and a powerful sense of form. It is a pleasure to see poems that are organised, like those of Graves or Housman, that start from an evident point, move to a designed coherent end, and are written in a language that is always clean and clear. As a stylist she sprang ready-armed with her first book and has developed little, but her subjects have changed. In a British Council pamphlet she defined the function of poetry as the discovery of

> order amid chaos, meaning in the middle of confusion, and affirmation at the heart of despair.

Many of her own later poems make this kind of affirmation. They are about admission to a mental home, diagnosis and treatment, psychiatrists, attempted suicide, a nurse going sick, a friend's relapse and return to a mental clinic, and almost all are composed with the cool firmness of the early poems. Nobody can have written less hysterically about hysteria, yet the sense of personal involvement is always there.

The most exact tribute one can pay to Elizabeth Jennings's poems is that among chaos and personal unhappiness order is always there, not merely pushing through but triumphantly asserted. The dreams are dark enough, but they are both wild and serene.

Julian Symons, "Clean and Clear," in New Statesman *(© 1967 The Statesman & Nation Publishing Co. Ltd.), Vol. 74, No. 1909, October 13, 1967, p. 476.*

MICHAEL MOTT

Elizabeth Jennings has been accused at times of quietness, if not tameness, but it would be grossly unfair to accuse the poet of *The Animals' Arrival* of any such thing. Like Abse's recent poems, if these are not shrill, they are bravely concerned with harrowing experience and a still more harrowing vision of it. . . . (p. 110)

Seeing disorder within and without, Elizabeth Jennings seeks courageously for order. In such poems as *A Pattern,* she achieves it at least in the high standard of her own art. But where order is not to be had outside her poetry she admits it. (p. 111)

Michael Mott, "Recent Developments in British Poetry," in Poetry *(© 1971 by The Modern Poetry Association; reprinted by permission of the Editor of* Poetry*), Vol. CXVIII, No. 2, May, 1971, pp. 102-14.**

ALASDAIR MACLEAN

Elizabeth Jennings has been a poet of solid if modest achievement, but her decline [in *Relationships*] is catastrophic. This new collection includes a poem addressed to Emily Dickinson, and one guesses that the American served as the model for much of it. For Emily Dickinson's apparent simplicity, however, Miss Jennings too often supplies bathos, and for phrases like'zero at the bone' substitutes a language colourless to the point of invisibility. The trouble seems to be a lack of any real pressure in the creation of these poems. (p. 389)

Alasdair Maclean, "Marble Fun," in The Listener *(© British Broadcasting Corp. 1973; reprinted by permission of Alasdair Maclean), Vol. 89, No. 2295, March 22, 1973, pp. 389-90.**

ALAN BROWNJOHN

It's good to see a poet breaking back out of a lean period. Elizabeth Jennings, one remembers, was brought in as the 'sensitive' dimension to the no-nonsense Movement of the Fifties. Her early poems were precise, beautifully rounded and very personal broodings on topics which her immediate contemporaries refused to have truck with: love, childhood, religion, travels in southern places. Her work was never less than accomplished, and could be memorable in its quiet, unstrained way. But subsequent books tended to be only as interesting as the new things she had to say, and these were few. And new *ways* of saying them were fewer still. Now, just when she seemed set to take a minor, if very respectable, place as a gentle mid-century romantic and modest allegorist, *Growing Points* shows us a poet who has suddenly and impressively increased the scope and richness, and the technical variety and command, of her writing.

The change is not always a matter of the form of the poems —though it is heartening to see how the longer poems here, especially some with a new long line allowing a freer, less circumscribed diction, achieve a much more successful release than some of her previous experiments (those occasional, uncomfortable prose poems in books like *Recoveries* and *Lucidities*). The real improvement is in the ordering of ideas within the familiar Jennings framework, and a new freshness and surprise in the ideas themselves: all at once the neat stanzas have a new bite. . . . As before, her poems of formal tribute or address ('Hopkins in Wales', 'Mozart's Horn Concertos') are a bit stiff and reverential, and she can still turn out too easily the kind of small-scale, sensitively introspective poem which loses its point in vagueness. But there are more poems here which turn the recognisable Jennings themes and properties to good, and moving, effect than in any volume we have had from her for a decade. *Growing Points* is a book which amply merits its title. (p. 732)

Alan Brownjohn, "Hymenoptera," in New Statesman *(© 1975 The Statesman & Nation Publishing Co. Ltd.), Vol. 89, No. 2306, May 30, 1975, pp. 732-33.**

ANNE STEVENSON

Women's poetry has become an industry since Elizabeth Jennings began to publish in the 1950s. It is to Miss Jennings's credit that she has not allowed herself to be swept along with the tide. In her new collection, *Growing Points,* the poise and tenderness of her early work is reaffirmed. She is still too nice to stand up and spit at life—a gesture not incompatible with the reverence she obviously feels for it—but in some of these poems she shows us that she probably could if she would.

> I feel I could be turned to ice
> If this goes on, if this goes on.
> I feel I could be buried twice
> And still the death not yet be
> done.

If only there were a few more poems like this in the book; but too often, 'literature' takes over. . . . Miss Jennings is a better religious poet. The sequence with which the book begins is masterly in technique, and enhanced by perception and deep feeling, but it has little force. A few lines, though, do possess the necessary cutting edge that makes poetry stick in the mind after the book has been closed. (pp. 572-73)

Anne Stevenson, "A Need for Reverence," in The Listener *(© British Broadcasting Corp. 1975; reprinted by permission of Anne Stevenson), Vol. 94, No. 2430, October 30, 1975, pp. 571-73.**

TERRY EAGLETON

Elizabeth Jennings's [*Growing-Points*] reveals most of her strengths and fewer than usual of her weaknesses. All the Jennings hallmarks are here: scrupulous deployment of the iambic, purity of diction, psychological shrewdness, that parabolic movement from particular to general which crystallises in eye-catching, aphoristic last lines. Some of the limitations are also sporadically in evidence: a slightly too kidgloved, reverential, excessively wistful treatment of emotional states, a faint tremulousness which seems inseparable from the attractive delicacies of feeling, a lack of irony, suggestive ambiguity and dramatic dynamism. Nevertheless, the collection shows more variety, vigour and open-endedness than has been evident in Miss Jennings's recent work, and even though her best effects still work in terms of meanings rather than physical images, the purity of structure and verbal clarity she always strives to sustain can now accommodate richer, more complex realisations without being overloaded. If Miss Jennings's poems give the impression of being shapely, crystalline distillations from pain, . . . [her writing] aims for a compensatory coolness and poise. (pp. 79-80)

Terry Eagleton, "New Poetry: 'Growing Points'," in Stand *(copyright © by* Stand*), Vol. 17, No. 1 (1975-76), pp. 79-80.*

JOHN MATTHIAS

Throughout [*Growing-Points*], poems in Ms. Jennings's familiar meters and stanzas alternate with largely unsuccessful attempts to find a substitute for the largely unsuccessful experiments with prose poetry and free verse of earlier volumes in experiments with long lines, irritatingly printed in ugly run-ons.

My guess is that Ms. Jennings writes too much and probably publishes all of it. There are some very good poems and passages here, all right, but you need to do a lot of weeding. What is particularly upsetting is to find, say, a truly exceptional quatrain—and there are several of these—in a poem that is otherwise uninteresting, or a distinguished and original line sandwiched between banalities. It's too bad. My objections, in general, are to clichés of diction and imagery which appear with some regularity, from the autumn leaves of the first poem to the sunrise and sunset of the last; to the habitual and unoriginal use of literary stereotypes; to breathless questions at the conclusions of poems . . . or, alternatively, barren unresonant statement . . . ; to awkward hyphenating . . . ; to gushiness of all kinds . . . ; to the abstractions, sentimentality, and laboriousness I mentioned earlier; to the frequent lack of energy. . . . There are a lot of bad moments in poems about artists and thinkers. . . . And there are things that "ring true", gardens which inevitably become "a metaphor for Eden", "pangs" upon seeing, "breath-taking" beginnings and "breath-regaining" pauses, "worn-out thoughts", "scars of doubt", and even poems which should never have been seriously considered, like the monologue spoken by Christ on the cross.

The extraordinary thing is that Ms. Jennings can turn two-thirds of these faults into virtues. It is, in a way, a matter of taking risks. Had she not been willing to risk writing the unresonant statement "I / Am amazed still at the authority of your perception, your gentleness", she might well not have written elsewhere the equally abstract but very resonant "Self-portraits understand, / And old age can divest, // With truthful changes, us of fear of death." . . . [In] many of the best poems in *Growing-Points* Ms. Jennings is very particular, very specific indeed. . . . One often finds the precision, the sensuousness, and the exactness of observation she admires in Christina Rossetti's work. She is on record these days as aiming chiefly at clarity and simplicity. . . . Ms. Jennings is not the kind of poet who is likely to find it acceptable to "say something a bit more interesting" than she means. And that will indeed limit her range, her development, and her appeal. But perhaps it will also yield poems and passages—in *Growing-Points* there are only passages—that achieve something like Yvor Winters was asking for when he wrote of "the ability to imbue a simple expository statement of a complex theme with a rich association of feeling, yet with an utterly pure and unmannered style." She achieves this, I think, in certain lines of several poems in *Growing-Points*, notably, for example, in the conclusion of *Rembrandt's Late Self-Portraits*. . . . (pp. 348-50)

John Matthias, "Pointless and Poignant," in Poetry *(© 1977 by The Modern Poetry Association; reprinted by permission of the Editor of* Poetry*), Vol. CXXIX, No. 6, March, 1977, pp. 340-55.**

ANNE STEVENSON

[Elizabeth Jennings's] title, *Consequently I Rejoice*, is a brave and appropriate one for her new collection, in which she shows herself better able to face up to the realities of anguish than many more self-indulgent poets. Her themes are the naturally dramatic themes of the religious poet: pain, longing, hope, faith, love and, finally, if not victory, at least triumph. (p. 487)

Anne Stevenson, "Snaffling and Curbing," in the Listener *(copyright © British Broadcasting Corp. 1977; reprinted by permission of Anne Stevenson), Vol. 98, No. 2530, October 13, 1977, pp. 486-87.**

PETER SCUPHAM

In *Consequently I Rejoice*, a substantial collection of eighty-eight poems, experiences are ordered with that meticulous precision we have grown to expect, and the whole book is marshalled impeccably so as to lead us from the preliminary night-thoughts, stirrings of creative activity, through a cycle of the year, dominated by bird-flight and bird-song, to a world of men and women: the old, who have attained wisdom or declined from it. Conscious of the timeless equation of bird and soul, we pass to a sequence of meditations on the Christian faith, some cast in the form of dramatic monologues by Christ and Mary, and so to a group of poems whose theme is the relationship between the artist and his achievement.

Elizabeth Jennings's world is lucid, topiaried. When she moves deeply inside herself, the poems have that edgy feeling of the convalescent for whom the small event bears a press of tears or anger. . . . It may not be the function of a poet to count the streaks on a tulip, but substance in these poems is refined again and again to essence. The sudden metaphors . . . enter her landscapes with particular felicity. Her poems for people are warm and moving: the understanding shown in "Old People's Nursing Home" makes Larkin's "The Old Fools" seem a piece of theatre, and her tribute for Edward Thomas illuminates both poets, a description and self-description. . . .

Peter Scupham, "Sacred Encounters," in The Times Literary Supplement *(© Times Newspapers Ltd. (London) 1977; reproduced from* The Times Literary Supplement *by permission), No. 3953, December 30, 1977, p. 1530.**

* * *

JOHNSON, Eyvind 1900-1976

Johnson was a Swedish novelist and short story writer who wrote political and historical novels. He reached prominence in Sweden after publication of his autobiographical tetralogy, *Romanen om Olof,* in which he employed interior monologue similar to that used by Joyce. He is best known to English-speaking audiences for his *Return to Ithaca,* a modern recapitulation of *The Odyssey.* Johnson received the Nobel Prize for Literature in 1974 along with his fellow countryman Harry Martinson. (See also *Contemporary Authors,* Vols. 73-76; obituary, Vols. 69-72.)

GAVIN ORTON

["Stad i ljus" ("Town in Light") (1928)] is the apologia of a young Swedish writer, hungry and wretched in an illuminated and festive Paris. Eyvind Johnson described it as a chapter out of his own life—"two hundred pages of diatribes, reflections, prose-poems, and cries of woe". His hero declares that his generation has seen its revolutionary faith disintegrate into despair in the shadow of a generation of war-profiteers. He looks hopelessly for the meaning in the miserable life he has lived:

> I want to arrive at my century. I mean, I want to know what it is like. Do we know what it is like? No. And I want to arrive at myself . . . *I want to know who I am!*

Not surprisingly "Stad i ljus" has often been compared to Hamsun's "Sult" ["Hunger"], whose hero finds himself in a similar predicament. But while Hamsun was compelled by his experiences of starvation and failure to create a new form for his novel, Eyvind Johnson could appeal to the theories of Bergson and Freud and use methods developed by others—among them Hamsun. Like Hamsun, the young Eyvind Johnson considered it is his duty to tell his backward countrymen that the contemporary novel must be devoted to psychological analysis. Following in the Strindberg-Hamsun tradition he dismissed the concept of "character", for man is an infinitely complicated structure of impulses and states of mind. And the whole is undergoing a continuous change, for every moment of experience alters the complex and creates a new person. (pp. 111-12)

"Stad i ljus", Eyvind Johnson's first tentative approach to the modern novel, was his third novel, preceded by "Timans och rättfärdigheten" ("Timans and Justice") (1925) with its somewhat abrupt changes of scene and motivation, and by a collection of predominantly satirical vignettes from a wintry Arctic town, "Stad i Mörker" ("Town in Darkness") (1927). Both novels reflect the author's political beliefs and his personal despair and disillusion, though in the second novel the anarchist schoolmaster comes to see human companionship as a defence against a cruel and pitiless universe. However absurd the town and its council may seem, however ridiculous its inhabitants, he feels a kind of love for them. But "Stad i ljus" showed that bitterness and nihilism were by no means conquered in Eyvind Johnson's works, and when he returned to a northern town in "Minnas" ("Remembering") (1928), existence proved to be more horrifying than ever. He could draw on Proust and Freud to portray people tortured by sexual desires and memories they try vainly to suppress. They seek escape in drink, in religious fervour, or in intellectual detachment, but when their guard is down some detail reawakes their memories, or they are ambushed in their dreams. The author himself withholds his sympathy, following them only with a desperate mockery. (p. 112)

"Kommentar till ett stjärnfall" ("Commentary on a Falling Star") (1929) repeats some of the themes from "Minnas" and composes them into a convincing demonstration of what Eyvind Johnson considered the modern novel should be. Like Gide he follows the untidy destinies of a group of characters whose paths meet and part in a random fashion. Like Joyce he presents their thoughts directly in all their apparent meaninglessness. At the same time "Kommentar" is a work of imagination, not a psychological document, for the author does not disguise his presence but comments on the course of events, plays with his characters, indulges in strange flights of fancy—in fact he sets the whole tale in motion by playing on the word "stjärnfall" (a shooting-star or an award of decorations). Technically speaking Eyvind Johnson has now mastered his material, but the characters themselves are still unable to come to terms with the universe. Magnus Lyck provides a fitting example of this unhappy period in Eyvind Johnson's novels. He declares defiantly that he is no Hamlet; he is a clear-sighted revolutionary who knows love is merely a matter of biology. All the same, he goes to pieces because of a romantic attachment to a dissolute actress, and at the end of the novel, while the May Day processions pass through Stockholm, he stands aside, stripped of everything but the will to keep living—somehow.

Eyvind Johnson spoke of his next novel as a continuation of "Kommentar" but also a liberation from it, an effort towards a more positive social commitment. The title of "Avsked till Hamlet" ("Farewell to Hamlet") (1930) promises a greater determination than the contents justify. The character struggling with a Hamlet disposition is Mårten Torpare, who reappears in several novels of the decade. He is a man "who stands beside the author and sees what he sees and tries to look with his eyes". However doubtful his literary farewell to Hamlet, when he appears in "Bobinack'' (1932) his personal difficulties seem to be overcome, and although he is sufficiently sceptical of society he is no longer nihilistic. The target for his criticisms in ''Bobinack'' is capitalist middle-class society, which, he thinks, is about to give way to a less inhibited form of life. (pp. 112-13)

In [his] novels of social criticism abstract discussion often gets the upper hand. That the abundant imagination Eyvind Johnson had shown earlier in his works was not lost is clear from two collections of short-stories: ''Natten är här'' (''The Night is Here'') (1932), which includes some thoroughly unclassical and unheroic tales from Ancient Greece; and ''Än en gång, kapten'' (''Once More, Captain'') (1934), with stories from his childhood province of Norrbotten. . . . Norrbotten immediately provided the material for the four-volume ''Romanen om Olof'' (''The Novel About Olof'') (1934-37), which has established itself as one of the classics of Swedish literature.

The novel is the story of Olof Persson from the time he leaves his foster-parents at the age of 13 to the moment five years later when he leaves Norrbotten altogether. It is based on Eyvind Johnson's own experiences during adolescence. ''Romanen om Olof'' is usually considered to be the most straightforward of Eyvind Johnson's novels, but although the action is centred on one character and is unfolded in short scenes in chronological order, the author's main interest is in his subject's psychological development, and he follows Olof's thoughts in all their confusion of memories and impressions, backwards and forwards in time, hither and thither as his associations freely lead them. When Eyvind Johnson comes to describe Olof's environment he chooses what he called ''a roundabout way''—''sagor'' (fairy-tales), for the reality that surrounds Olof is so bleak and depressing that it can scarcely be approached directly. It needs a little romanticizing, since it is a world where tuberculosis rages, where dreams of love end in wretched seductions, and where emigrants' hopes of an earthly paradise, far from Norrbotten, end in Brazil in disease and snake-bite. (p. 114)

Eyvind Johnson's war novels are both exhortations to armed resistance and reservations about the use of force, while with his usual interest in psychological analysis he tries to discover the psychology of a free society and how it differs from that of his enemies. (p. 116)

The enormous ''Krilon'' trilogy . . . represents, its author declares, his military service. . . . Personal misfortunes have turned Krilon not into a neurotic with a grudge against the world but a balanced human being who has overcome the bitterness in his memories. . . . With Johannes Krilon, Eyvind Johnson said he had attempted to describe a human being as thoroughly as possible, and he used all his technical ingenuity to this end. In one section he describes Krilon's past in terms of his collection of keys. In another section he uses six pages for a description of Krilon's face—''I wanted it to be exhaustive''. But Krilon is more than a Stockholm estate-agent, just as the novel is about the triumph over forces that threaten not merely the integrity of Krilon and his friends but that of all Europeans, and ultimately of all mankind. Krilon becomes the representative and saviour of humanity—for example, he is ''crucified'' on Good Friday. And he stands too for a particular person in a particular situation, since the novel is also an allegory in which the war is reflected in terms of the Stockholm property-market. . . . As an additional complication the novel contains a number of miscellaneous items, such as news bulletins on the real war, merciless satires on the Swedish government's inelegant antics in the cause of non-involvement, an attack on one of Eyvind Johnson's personal antagonists, and even short stories which are told merely for their own sake. More directly here than in ''Romanen om Olof'' the author discusses the principles that have determined the style of the novel—its ''half-realism'' and its strange subtitle: ''A Novel About the Probable''. For reality is many-faceted, and the author can only see parts of it. His duty is to convey to his readers what he sees, which does not, strangely enough, mean that he should describe exactly what he sees. The reality behind Krilon, like the reality behind Olof, must be approached indirectly. The way to World War II leads through the fantastic allegory and morality-play that is ''Krilon''. (pp. 116-17)

Eyvind Johnson's next novel is a retelling of the ''Odyssey'', but bears the subtitle ''A Novel About the Present''. ''Strändernas svall'' (''The Swell on the Beaches'') (1946, English translation ''Return to Ithaca'', 1949) is a grateful pupil's tribute to both Homer and Joyce. Eyvind Johnson has followed Homer's story closely, but his style is as devious as his hero's thoughts, and the actions and conflicts are essentially psychological, fought in a less resolute Ulysses and a less faithful Penelope, middle-aged mortals with time no longer on their side. . . . In telling the ''Odyssey'' in realistic terms, Eyvind Johnson revealed once more the ingenuity and imagination that accomplished the ''Krilon'' allegory. Yet here again reality and ''saga'' are scarcely distinguishable, for with all its down-to-earth pictures of the Greek heroes, ''Strändernas svall'' is, at the same time, a ''saga'' about the Second World War.

Eyvind Johnson's post-war novels develop naturally from ''Krilon'' and ''Strändernas svall''. He consistently defends principles of democracy and humanity, both in his literary and journalistic writings; but his narrative position constantly changes, as he attempts to capture and exhibit an elusive, transient reality. He comes to the conclusion that reality is no more than the result of a way of looking at the world, and consequently his novels generally include a number of narrators who view the same events from different angles, while his style reflects uncertainty, hesitation and qualification. The tangles of past and present in his earlier novels become even more confused as the historical past begins to play a crucial role in his characters' lives.

Eyvind Johnson's production since the war has included a number of autobiographical documents. . . . His greatest successes, however, have been with a series of historical novels.

The first of these, ''Drömmar om rosor och eld'' (''Dreams of Roses and Fire'') (1949), is based on the trial for witchcraft of a priest in seventeenth-century France. The author follows the historical documents closely but makes explicitly the reservation that he is a man from the 1940's attempting to interpret distant events. Man himself changes little over the centuries, but his way of seeing himself inevitably differs. Eyvind Johnson lets his characters explain in their own words how they interpret events in terms of witchcraft, and he explains how he sees it in a post-Freudian age; in addition he interleaves his own account with the entries of a contemporary diarist. . . . ''Drömmar om rosor och eld'' has, as the title suggests, an intensity unusual in

Eyvind Johnson's works. Its characters are consumed by the fires of love and hate, destroyed slowly or violently by the aphrodisiac perfume of roses. (pp. 117-19)

"Lägg undan solen" ("Put Away the Sun") (1951) is not at first sight a historical novel, for it is the account of a group of twentieth-century Europeans as they are tossed about in an age of war and revolution. But some of the characters are uneasily aware that they are merely repeating a sequence of events acted out in a slave revolt in Ancient Rome. Here Eyvind Johnson develops the important concept of *simultaneity*. For many years he had worked with the knowledge that an individual's past was, through memories, as real in his consciousness as his present. Now he extends the idea to include the historical past, for the twentieth-century intellectual is so well aware of his historical background that it forms an integral part of his present.

It is almost impossible, Eyvind Johnson writes in "Lägg undan solen", for an author to convey the simultaneous presence of different periods of time in a man's mind, for however he shuffles his pictures from the past and the present he can never really convey them simultaneously to his reader's consciousness. He attempts one solution in "Molnen över Metapontion" ("The Clouds over Metapontion") (1957), which is formed of two stories, one centred on a retelling of the retreat of Xenophon's "Anabasis", the other on an Italian journey in the 1950's. (pp. 119-20)

The organization of "Molnen över Metapontion" is tighter than some critics have supposed, for the characters and events of the two distinct stories are everywhere related, the characters in their fates and emotions, the events in their order and outcome. (p. 120)

Eyvind Johnson's next novel, "Hans nådes tid" ("His Grace's Days") (1960), proved to be his biggest critical success since "Strändernas svall". It is a complicated story of Charlemagne's Europe, compiled from the accounts of a number of real or imagined chroniclers, whose words have to be interpreted with due allowance for their political and personal discretion. Consequently, the novel demands careful reading, but it can also be enjoyed as a straight-forward love-story. (p. 121)

"Livsdagen lång" ("Life's Long Day") (1964) is the lyrical complement to the Carolingian epic—again the themes are love and tyranny. The novel is an expansion of the technique of "Molnen över Metapontion". Here one basic story is repeated in seven different periods of time. It begins when a young man and a girl meet but are parted; the man falls into a hunters' pit, which he shares with a bear; later he returns to the earth's surface to pursue the girl and relate his search, as a different lover in another country and another century. The elements of this story reappear in ingenious guises. The pit, which is in a sense the grave, may reappear as a dungeon or a hostelry, while the bear, a symbol of man's less noble instincts, may be a prison-warder or a servant. One story flows so easily into the next that the separate periods of time merge into one, the characters become contemporaries, and even their relative individualities are blurred—the prisoner and his warder exchange roles, are ultimately *man*. The literary form is intimately connected with the ideas that the young man expounds from his pit. Man's great enemy, he declares, is time, and man's great dream to be liberated from time. . . . To be freed from time is, he says, to be like the Rhine, where the past flows into the present and the present bears the past into the future—"a river where many ages flow abreast". An additional exemplification of the theme is provided by the narrative frame-work, for the narrator who tells his story to a group of friends in a succession of Roman restaurants is himself part of his hero's destiny. (pp. 122-23)

[As a character from "Life's Long Day"] studies himself in his mirror, he echoes Eyvind Johnson's thoughts from "Stad i ljus":

> I do not know who I am. No man will ever come to know who he is . . . No man can rest in his past, no old man in his childhood, there is no one who can be fully sure of himself. But we can grasp the present and say: "This is what I am like now, at this moment."

Eyvind Johnson's works reveal his untiring attempts to meet the challenge in these words, to present an intelligible picture of a bewildering world to his fellow-men, and to build up a common defence against its insecurity and impermanence. (p. 123)

Gavin Orton, "Eyvind Johnson—An Introduction," in Scandinavica *(copyright © 1966 by Academic Press Inc. (London) Limited; reprinted with permission), Vol. 5, No. 2, November, 1966, pp. 111-23.*

As an evocation of that special time when a boy is neither a child nor a man, eager yet troubled, hopeful yet afraid, *1914* is remarkable. Nor is it easy to cite among Scandinavian novels familiar to this country a more telling picture of the darkness of life on the edge of the Arctic Circle where people picture the south of Sweden as a warm place where apples grow. . . . It is clear, even from this first volume of the tetralogy [*Romanen om Olof*], that Johnson is a major contemporary European writer.

"Northern Lights," in The Times Literary Supplement *(© Times Newspapers Ltd (London) 1971; reproduced from* The Times Literary Supplement *by permission), No. 3602, March 12, 1971, p. 285.**

LEIF SJÖBERG

Några steg mot tystnaden is subtitled "A Novel about Imprisoned Ones," and, true to this intent, it gives a panoramic view of human cruelty, suffering, oppression, injustice, vanity, passion, infidelity, estrangement, revenge and anguish—all seen in the mirror of the past but directly reflected, by implication, in present-day human behavior. Surprisingly, however, the result is not a totally pessimistic work. The narrative's emphasis on the interdependence of people and actions, along with its sheer energy, creates a positive and exciting atmosphere; and despite the gloom and frequently harsh turns of fate depicted, the novel is imbued with a thirst for freedom, a hatred of tyranny, an appreciation of artistic imagination . . . and a love of justice. . . . (p. 137)

In his historical novels, Eyvind Johnson deals with time and its transformations. Not the least of his concerns is that of contemporary events and problems, however. That is why *Några steg mot tystnaden* should be read and reread. (p. 138)

Leif Sjöberg, "World Literature in Review: 'Några steg mot tystnaden'," in Books Abroad *(copyright 1975 by the University of Oklahoma Press), Vol. 3, No. 2, Winter, 1975, pp. 137-38.*

LEIF SJÖBERG

[Eyvind Johnson's] way of writing is quite complex and cannot easily be classified under any specific rubric. He varies his techniques and devices with each novel, mixing the styles of classical writers with those of such moderns as Thomas Mann and William Faulkner, yet maintaining his integrity and his own personal style. In *Krilon* Johnson sometimes turns to the reader. Even in *Molnen över Metapontion* the narrator is more noticeable than is usual in modern novels. Sverker Göransson rightly observes that Eyvind Johnson's attitude is that of the scientist. "He is by no means 'omniscient'; he only organizes a certain material. The reader thus can form his 'own' opinions about the protagonists, without immediate directives or guidance from the author. Johnson views the action from different angles and in that way attempts to give as much intensity and truth as possible. Scandinavian, French and German critics have proclaimed him a master; he nonetheless continues to experiment with form in his novels, as if never really satisfied."

Johnson has long been interested in problems of time, that mysterious stream which continues to occupy so many minds with its riddles. He has been specially concerned about parallelisms and simultaneity. To him the past is often a parallel of the present. (p. 417)

Leif Sjöberg, "The 1974 Nobel Prize in Literature: Eyvind Johnson and Harry Martinson," in Books Abroad *(copyright 1975 by the University of Oklahoma Press), Vol. 49, No. 3, Summer, 1975, pp. 407-10, 415-21.**

LARS G. WARME

In Eyvind Johnson's total production of half a century we can follow a line of protagonists, narrators, and observers who mirror the author's own development, his aging, and change of social and intellectual status, from the young and struggling writer Torsten in *Stad i ljus* (1928) to old Favel-Hyth, the "professional spectator and narrator," in *Favel ensam* (1968). . . . It is interesting to note that no Johnson novel since the *Krilon* books has been exclusively set in Sweden. The "international" protagonists could be seen to personify the author's ideal of European cultural unity through a breaking down of national boundaries, paralleling similar attempts, in the historical novels, to obliterate time barriers between epochs. (p. 452)

Några steg mot tystnaden presents a number of familiar themes and technical preoccupations from earlier Johnson novels, such as the exploration of personal and historical pasts and the tenuous line between fact and fiction, and recapitulates the author's views on Western culture and humanism in the face of overwhelming odds. (p. 453)

In *Några steg mot tystnaden* the time perspective transcends that of the living memory of any of the novel's characters and extends far back into historical pasts. (p. 454)

[At times Johnson uses] characters often extraneous to the main action charged with the task of demonstrating how the fictional world is set in motion and of commenting on the difficulties and uncertainties connected with the apprehension of an elusive reality. The process, particularly evident in Johnson's explorations of the past, is characterized by a balance between two principles—one scientifically objective and one imaginatively creative. In *Drömmar om rosor och eld* (1949), for example, the two principles are subjected to a critical test, the first in the form of epistemological research of the documented "facts," and the second in the form of a demonstration of the ontology of the fiction. The intrusion of this selfconscious, "meta-fictional" element, constituting a third principle or dynamic impulse in Johnson's novels, is sometimes made in the author's own name, by a first-person "I"; more frequently, Johnson delegates the task to one or more *scenbetjänter* within the fiction, a writer or historian (or both, as in the 1964 novel *Livsdagen lång*), a chronicler of events, or a person in charge of ordering letters, journals, or other documents. The discussion which is carried on through and around the fiction in *Några steg mot tystnaden* is the vehicle for Johnson's apologia. With a polemic edge perhaps directed at contemporary "documentary" literature, it makes a fervent plea for *fantasi,* for imaginative creation, as an inevitable complement to scientific objectivity. (pp. 454-55)

Eyvind Johnson's technical preoccupations in novel after novel, his perspectivism which searches for new vantage points, could be seen as attempts to find a way out of subjectivity, an Archimedian point outside his own insulating selfhood through a playful or desperate manipulation of distances and experimentations with optical lenses. . . . The captive's escape from the self through delvings into the past does . . . , ironically, lead back to the self. The same reflection, or rather *projection,* of the self in the past is experienced by Roquentin in Sartre's *La nausée*. (pp. 455-56)

In *Några steg mot tystnaden,* as in a number of earlier novels, Johnson uses the device of juxtaposing historical events and contemporary reality. The method has raised some critical comments. The relationship between the different time levels may strike the reader as tenuous, even gratuitous. . . . In accordance with Johnson's vision of a basic sameness of human existence through the ages, of an eternal recurrence of phenomena, the device may be justified. At the same time the very universality of this vision with its unlimited number of potential applications threatens to weaken the impact and lose itself in a demonstration of the obvious. The perspective chosen by the author may at times seem too "Olympian," yet lacking in that depth dimension, a reaching down to the mythical or the archetypal, which is so evident in Thomas Mann's *Joseph* novels, for example. (p. 457)

It is not difficult to recognize . . . Johnson's own commitment to an ideal of "human culture" and to see his efforts as a writer as attempts to preserve those values that ensure a continued civilization and lend dignity to human existence. The greatest threats to these tenuous values are tyranny, oppression, willful contributions to human suffering. The delvings into the past are aimed at bringing to light those forces which, according to Johnson, have always been part of human reality with an unbroken extension down to our own day and age. In this context, Johnson's own experience of *evil* in the form of Nazism and political oppression and his active resistance to these forces must be seen as something of an *Urerlebnis,* a very fundamental trauma, which was to affect the direction of all his writings from the late thirties to the present. In the contemporary part of *Några steg mot tystnaden* the honeymoon couple have a jolting realization of unmitigated evil through a collection of photographs of victims of Hitler's concentration camps. (pp. 458-59)

Johnson's concept of evil is that of a rationalist. As *écrivain engagé* he carries on a tradition from Voltaire, who raised his voice in the Calas trial, to Zola and Anatole France, who publicly defended Dreyfus, to Thomas Mann, Sartre, and Camus, who actively opposed Nazism, to Solzhenitsyn, who wrote the *Gulag Archipelago* as a major monument to man's unending inhumanity.

What kind of resistance does Johnson suggest to oppose evil? He believes in the power of the rational individual. . . . In the *Krilon* books he advocates freedom of speech as a means of keeping communication channels open for dialogue, discussion, criticism, and enlightened conversation; man's actions should be motivated by *hygglighet*, common decency, and an honest desire to seek the truth. (p. 460)

In Johnson's novels the spirit of freedom and resistance to tyranny, the sense of traditional values and virtues, are often invested in isolated individuals of low social origin, in servants or members of the common people, who generate the impulse of protest and turn to their social and intellectual superiors for articulation and action. (p. 461)

In Johnson's description, the art of story-telling becomes something miraculous, mysterious, an autonomous force. . . . Throughout Johnson's writings [a] storyteller asserts himself again and again: in the "fairytales" of the *Olof* novels, in the fantastic story about the octopus in the *Krilon* series, in the haunting tale about the moon flight in *Hans nådes tid*.

Några steg mot tystnaden presents Eyvind Johnson's views on life and art as an apologia for his vision and his methods of conveying it. It is *en roman om fångna,* about captives in the literal sense, but also about prisoners of the human condition, facing the inescapable fate of death. . . . As in the case of Scheherazade, the story-telling becomes a means of staying the power of death, of dispelling the ultimate *Silence*. . . . (p. 463)

Lars G. Warme, "Eyvind Johnson's 'Några steg mot tystnaden': An Apologia," in Scandinavian Studies, *Vol. 49, No. 4, Autumn, 1977, pp. 452-63.*

* * *

JONES, (Everett) LeRoi
See BARAKA, Imamu Amiri

K

KEMAL, Yashar 1922-

Kemal is a Turkish novelist and journalist. He is Turkey's most famous novelist, both at home and abroad, as well as an outspoken political activist. The material for his novels is drawn from his native rural area, and is presented in a forceful yet lyrical prose style. He has often been mentioned as a possible candidate for the Nobel Prize in Literature.

TALÂT SAIT HALMAN

In the 1950s Turkish fiction moved out of the centers of urban culture into rural Anatolia, giving rise to an impressive output which is often referred to as the "Village Novel." The practitioners of this brave new genre are, unlike earlier pioneers in the field, writers who were born and reared in poverty-stricken villages. Their work has the poignancy of personal agony experienced during their formative years.

The leading figure of the "Village Novel" is Yashar Kemal. (p. 181)

The Wind from the Plain . . . is actually the Turkish village novel par excellence: It typifies the strongest features as well as some of the basic defects of this genre. The narration is fluent and forceful, dialogue crisp and colorful, and the plot engrossing. Its principal failing is also typical: The characters, while serving admirably as stock-types, are devoid of individual traits and lack psychological motivation except for the pressures of poverty.

The Turkish title *Ortadirek* means "mainstay" and symbolizes Yasar Kemal's faith in the peasant as the central force of Turkey's future. *The Wind from the Plain* lionizes the dauntless spirit of the peasant to survive. (p. 182)

Talât Sait Halman, "World Literature in Review: 'The Wind from the Plain'," in Books Abroad *(copyright 1970 by the University of Oklahoma Press), Vol. 44, No. 1, Winter, 1970, pp. 181-82.*

Kemal is above all a chronicler of his people. In *Memed, My Hawk,* which brought him worldwide recognition, he created the folk-hero of post-Ataturk Turkey—the noble outlaw, the latter-day Robin Hood of his villagers still dependent on the patronage of the *aghas.* In *Iron Earth, Copper Sky* there are only hints that, a million miles away in Ankara, bureaucrats sit at office desks, jets land, the telephone exists. Here in the hills above the cotton-growing plains of Chukurova life has not changed for centuries; the animals are bred as much to provide body-warmth in a frozen mud-hut as for food; mad old women pad barefoot over the snow to brew potions for a fever; a third wife, barely pubescent, is bought by the village headman for the price of a cow—to be returned once it has calved. . . .

Kemal has a gift, clear even in translation and overriding the boundaries of sophisticated literary heritage, for compelling concern for the simple people he creates. Simple? Even the village madman, Spellbound Ahmet, is wise enough to revile the village for hypocrisy when two young lovers, unable to tolerate family pressures, elope to death in the snow; even the child Hasan, whose box of matches is worth guarding with his life, senses that the flowering of a plant beneath a stone when spring comes is as much a miracle as any "saint's" cure. There is no condescension in Kemal's analysis of the problems of his countrymen. Even if we find it hard to share his involvement, the reader who embarks with idle curiosity is likely to find himself stirred and sobered.

"Tamberlaine Country," in The Times Literary Supplement *(© Times Newspapers Ltd. (London) 1974; reproduced from* The Times Literary Supplement *by permission), No. 3765, May 3, 1974, p. 465.*

PETER PRINCE

A sure sense of setting is certainly one of the strengths of the Turkish writer Yashar Kemal. At all times in his funny and tragic story of a peasant who is raised up against his will to be a saint [*Iron Earth, Copper Sky*], he makes the reader vitally aware of the background—the mountains, the steppe, the huddled village, the forest. Indeed, these are not really 'background' at all: they are in there in the thick of it, conditioning events, limiting human action, rewarding some, killing others. Together with the elements, they constitute practically the novel's main character. . . . [*Iron Earth, Copper Sky* is a] title that gets its priorities just about right.

Peter Prince, "Intramural," in New Statesman *(© 1974 The Statesman & Nation Publishing Co. Ltd.), Vol. 87, No. 2257, June 21, 1974, p. 894.**

PAUL THEROUX

[There is a native witness of Turkey] who, in the half-dozen books of his that have been translated, has depicted his country with a close attention to detail and yet with a majestic, almost epic sweep.

Yashar Kemal has been compared to Thomas Hardy and Tolstoy, and has several times been short-listed for the Nobel Prize. This is interesting news, no doubt, but hardly illuminating. The author with whom Kemal feels a special kinship . . . is William Faulkner. This strange pairing-off becomes less strange once you know how closely the cotton-growing plains of Chukurova in South Anatolia resemble those in Yoknapatawpha County, and how similar are the blood-feuds, rural past-times, barn burnings, old time religion and incidents of local heroism. . . .

[Kemal's] first novel, "Memed, My Hawk" achieved enormous celebrity when it was published in English in 1955. He has written many since, and though they appear regularly in translation, he has not received the critical acclaim or wide readership he deserves in America. He is revered in Turkey and read avidly in Sweden, France and in the Soviet Union, where his novels are—mistakenly, I think—assumed to be the result of some great access of Marxist indignation.

His newest novel to be translated here is, happily, a sequel to "Memed, My Hawk" and indeed it was published in Turkish as its second part. The title [is] "They Burn the Thistles." . . . (p. 11)

The landscape, the seasons, the wildlife, the flowers: Kemal works on a huge canvas but there is interest in every inch of it. This novel is a worthy successor to "Memed, My Hawk" and ought to send readers swiftly to "The Legend of the Thousand Bulls" "Anatolian Tales" or "The Wind From the Plain." . . . I doubt that anyone who reads "They Burn the Thistles" will hesitate in seeking these out and concluding that Kemal is an important literary figure. (p. 40)

Paul Theroux, "Turkish Delight," in The New York Times Book Review *(© 1977 by The New York Times Company; reprinted by permission), July 10, 1977, pp. 11, 40.*

TALAT SAIT HALMAN

The Undying Grass is Kemal's eighth book of fiction to become available in English translation. . . . It is the third and last volume of his trilogy, which started with *Ortadirek* (*The Wind from the Plain;* 1960). . . . The second part of the trilogy, *Yer Demir Gök Bakir* (1963), is also available in English: *Iron Earth, Copper Sky*. The concluding volume, *Ölmez Otu* (1969), now makes its appearance in English under the title of *The Undying Grass,* which connotes both the reference to the generic "everlasting plant" and the book's central theme—the indomitable spirit of the Anatolian to survive and to endure. (p. 676)

[The plot of *The Undying Grass*] is one of Kemal's most elaborate and complex story lines ever. The author has described it as the tale "of a people in the throes of adversity who make up a dream world for themselves and try to escape into it from the hard realities of their existence." (pp. 676-77)

The Undying Grass, with its epic power and dazzling insights into human drama, ranks as one of Yashar Kemal's masterworks and underscores the immense strength of his fictional art. (p. 677)

Talat Sait Halman, "World Literature in Review: 'The Undying Grass'," in World Literature Today *(copyright 1977 by the University of Oklahoma Press), Vol. 51, No. 4, Autumn, 1977, pp. 676-77.*

LARRY ROHTER

No one knows the world of the Turkish peasant better than Yashar Kemal. In a half dozen novels and collections of short stories, he has been remarkably successful in making their way of life comprehensible to the Western reader, writing with respect, affection and understanding about their customs and beliefs and the hardships they face.

Something is definitely awry, though, in *The Undying Grass,* the final volume of Kemal's trilogy of life in an Anatolian village called Yalak. The gruff, earthy characters, with names like Spellbound Ahmet, Home-Leave Memet and Gooey Apti, who peopled earlier Kemal novels, are still there, and their surroundings are described with the same loving detail, but this time they sound different. Their speech, colorful and coarse, has suddenly become awkward and artificial.

It is hard to tell who is responsible for this disappointing turnabout, Kemal or his translator. In all likelihood, the latter is probably the culprit: *The Undying Grass* has not exactly been rendered into the most idiomatic English. . . .

So irritating is the stilted dialogue that it is nearly impossible to appreciate the intriguing tale Kemal proposes to tell. His preferred themes of social and political protest and exploitation, in which the line between good and evil is always clearly drawn, have been muted here, enabling him to write with unaccustomed subtlety about another timeless problem: man's need for heroes, created out of thin air if necessary.

Larry Rohter, "'The Undying Grass'," in Book World—The Washington Post *(© 1978,* The Washington Post*), April 30, 1978, p. E4.*

KATHA POLLITT

Yashar Kemal's novels, set in the backward villages of his native Taurus Mountains, have an abundance of . . . exotic verisimilitude. Perhaps there are other reasons for his wide popularity in Turkey . . . , but for American readers the fascination of his novels lies largely in his depiction of a way of life as utterly alien to us as life on Mars. (p. 14)

Yashar Kemal has been compared with Tolstoy, a burden no one deserves to bear, and has been praised for the epic quality of his novels. I don't know about "epic"—among reviewers it seems to mean something like "a tale of simplified passions set among primitives," which leaves any genuine epic out in the cold—but Mr. Kemal, who grew up in a village much like Yalak, gives a much more astringent picture of peasant life than the aristocratic Tolstoy. His villagers possess neither earthy wisdom nor natural piety—nor, one might add, class consciousness. They are gullible, cruel and calculating; their feuds and quarrels are so hotheaded as to seem positively whimsical. If they are as tightly knit as a family, they are also as mutually destructive as only close relatives can be. Ignorance and oppression, Mr. Kemal seems to be saying, drive them to turn on one another. And yet they are a spirited bunch, capable of great exertions, imbued with poetry and myth, and much given to falling in love. Life in Yalak may be grim, but it's never boring.

Yashar Kemal is a devoted admirer of Faulkner, and it shows—in ponderous prose and a penchant for long descriptive passages, as well as in a web of violence and intrigue that would keep Yoknapatawpha County busy for years. As a novel "The Undying Grass" is a bit slow-moving, but as a portrait of a people and a way of life it couldn't be better. It should do much to humanize our patchy and stereotyped picture of the Moslem world. (pp. 14, 37)

Katha Pollitt, "Turkish Trouble," in The New York Times Book Review *(© 1978 by The New York Times Company; reprinted by permission), June 18, 1978, pp. 14, 37.*

TALAT SAIT HALMAN

Kuşlar da Gitti (The Birds Too Are Gone) stands in contrast to the epic sweep of the huge novels for which . . . [Kemal] has gained his international reputation. It is short and spare, but it contains, in compact form, almost as a synecdoche, the strengths which have become Yashar Kemal's hallmarks.

The plot and the characters hold a firm grip on the reader's attention for their universal values, although they do not lack the authenticity of the Turkish context. The style is enchantingly lyrical in the narrative passages and fully attuned to the rhythms and colors of the Turkish language in the dialogues. The way Kemal establishes links between scenery and psychological states is nothing short of magical. Like Faulkner, to whom Kemal has always felt akin, he creates a mythic framework, and like much of the best fiction produced by the major Latin American writers in the past twenty years, he provides several levels of literary experience and a concentric metaphorical structure.

Kuşlar da Gitti is a masterly evocation of the hopes and frustrations of proletarian life in Turkey's most bustling city, Istanbul. Yashar Kemal's aviary—birds of all colors, birds of prey, captive birds—functions as a metaphor of society. Each episode, as it unravels, offers symptoms of social ills as well as symbols of freedom, happiness and a dignified life. Yashar Kemal's newest is also one of his best quintessential statements about how the common people will ultimately overcome and prevail.

Talat Sait Halman, "World Literature in Review: 'Kuşlar da Gitti'," in World Literature Today *(copyright 1978 by the University of Oklahoma Press), Vol. 52, No. 4, Autumn, 1978, p. 689.*

ANTHONY THWAITE

[The setting of Kemal's "Iron Earth, Copper Sky"] is the southern central part of his country, Antalya, in the foothills of the Taurus Mountains. As Mr. Kemal presents it, it is a timeless, primitive world; though there is brief mention of radios and tractors, the Government in Ankara is unbelievably remote—certainly much more remote than specters, saints, devils, witches and jinns, all of whom are real rather than metaphorical. In fact, the timelessness is such that legends ("in those days there were two holy persons in the world . . .") float easily into modern village happenings. . . .

Even more than his earlier books, ["Iron Earth, Copper Sky"] comes from and lives on the borderland between fiction and legend, its events drawing on the atmosphere of rumor, superstition, fear and the wild fancies of ignorance that possess his Antalyan villagers. . . .

Mr. Kemal is both closely involved with his characters and capable of remaining ironically detached. "Saints in this atom age? Mehdis in this space age? I'll break every bone in his body. I'll show him how to be a mehdi in the twentieth century," a skeptical army man says; and yet, such is the intensity of Mr. Kemal's other characters that one almost wants to accept Tashbash as a miracle worker. In a society in which a box of matches is a luxury, and in which a man can say without affectation, "I'd rather die than have my honor stained in this village," we are closer to the Middle Ages than the space age. Even the names of Mr. Kemal's characters, in translation, have a fairytale flavor. . . .

The pacing of all this, as distinct from the plotting, is sometimes too leisurely and discursive, perhaps, for Western urban readers—an audience Mr. Kemal has presumably never had in mind. Folklore and oral epic, comic interludes, moments of sexual passion, lyrically "poetic" bits, satirical realism, participants who inexplicably come and go are all intermittently present without being woven together. Clearly, Mr. Kemal is not a naïve writer, but his concentration on a naïve world can betray him into being an odd mixture of simple, solemn and portentous. But at his best one can see why some people have seen him as the Hardy, if not the Tolstoy, of his country. (p. 13)

Anthony Thwaite, "Turkish Delights," in The New York Times Book Review *(© 1979 by The New York Times Company; reprinted by permission), August 19, 1979, pp. 13, 21.**

* * *

KENEALLY, Thomas 1935-

An Australian novelist, Keneally is an ex-seminarian of Irish-Catholic descent. Best known for his *Blood Red, Sister Rose*, a retelling of the Joan of Arc legend, Keneally has been praised both for his realistic characterizations and his use of history. (See also *CLC*, Vols. 5, 8, 10, and *Contemporary Authors*, Vols. 85-88.)

BLAKE MORRISON

Thomas Keneally's fictions are widely travelled: medieval Normandy, an 18th-century penal colony in the South Pacific, France in 1918, the Antarctic (twice)—you name it, they've been there. *Passenger* happens in the most exotic place of all: 'I sat in the black duchy of the amnion. Through the blood vessels of the placenta I took bounties from my mother's body—oxygens, minerals, carbohydrates.' This is no ordinary pregnancy: . . . [the foetus-narrator] has a precociously clear vision of the outside world. It's the Romantic idea of insightful childhood pushed one step further—the wise womb—and it makes for an old-fashioned omniscient narrative: the wide-awake foetus can see for miles and miles. His overview, though, is not exactly one of fingernail-paring detachment, for our unborn hero is threatened with the knives of abortion. . . .

It may not be Keneally's best novel (*The Chant of Jimmy Blacksmith* takes some beating) but it's his wittiest and most inventive. So strong and original is the narrative voice that he manages to work in a great deal—the foetus's Oedipus complex, the Gnome's shady business dealing, extracts from Sal's novel—without letting the main events lose their grip. And though it's not anti-abortionist in intention—the foetus is careful to stress that it's only his own life he wants to save—Keneally's lyrical responsiveness to the womb, with its 'rich lakes of wild and plentiful cilia, of browsing bacteria, of hearty corpuscles and of those flabbergasting denizens, the chromosomes', makes *Passenger* a quietly effective little protection campaign for the unborn child.

Blake Morrison, "The Wise Womb," in New Statesman *(© 1979 The Statesman & Nation Publishing Co. Ltd.), Vol. 97, No. 2496, January 19, 1979, p. 88.**

HERMIONE LEE

Keneally's newest narrator [in *Passenger*] is a foetus, a pugnacious little fellow who's been jolted into omniscience by a hologram taken to establish his sex. As the laser beams 'pepper up his cortex,' lovely Sal Fitzgerald's passenger becomes 'arrantly awake' to his family history, his father's infidelities, and the threats to his own existence. . . .

Passenger is a witty variant on the picaresque tradition, jauntily sustained, and versatile, in that the narrative contrivance, itself fantastical, allows the fantastical developments. But we have to be insistently reminded of how much the foetus-hero knows, and it's hard for Keneally not to be cute about the little man ('I ground my fist against my sealed left eye') nor to indulge in this kind of amniotic rhapsody: 'I rode the warm estuaries of Sal's blood and heard it singing.'

Fortunately the novel is solidified by a recurrent parallel between the foetus and one of his ancestors, Maurice Fitzgerald, servant to a revolutionary naturalist, who travelled in 1799 from Cork to Australia in the hold of a convict ship. Sal is writing a book about him, and Keneally might easily have done so had he wanted to prove again his talent for historical reconstruction. Instead he uses that story to enforce his treatment of bondage: knowledge helpless without power. Both 'heroes' have been 'assigned a narrow billet by a higher authority'; both know 'there was no princedom on earth where anguish could not make its run.' The analogy turns a whimsical experiment into something more considerable and earnest than it first seems.

Hermione Lee, "A Womb with a View," in The Observer *(reprinted by permission of The Observer Limited), No. 9778, January 21, 1979, p. 35.**

D. J. ENRIGHT

At first sight, the *donnée* of Thomas Keneally's new novel [*Passenger*] lies in its narrator, a foetus. . . . 'The rose or weed of knowledge opened in my hand, and I, as it were, fingered all its petals.' . . .

This sounds like science fiction, but in the event the book is much farther from that genre than was Thomas Keneally's earlier novel, *A Dutiful Daughter,* which was also much more horrific. There, children had to cope with parents who turned into physical monsters; and the son declared that moral blindness towards 'freaks' derives from 'our poisonous concept of what's *natural*'. Here, a foetus has to cope with a mildly barbarian father and his concept of what is convenient to him: the *natural* is now at risk. But the privileged foetus simply serves as the novelist's eye, a necessary convention, and—more importantly—as an essentially conventional character in its own right: indeed, as the hero, or potential victim, in that (like many another foetus) its arrival at birth is by no means certain.

If the author enjoys the benefit of the foetus, the foetus (in the way that Hamlet was a poet) enjoys the benefit of the author, who endows him with a pungent prose style and an exciting pre-life, even a rather cultivated one. . . .

It is a tribute to the engaging qualities of *Passenger* that the reader (one, at any rate) leafs tremulously towards the last pages, hoping against experience to find a happy ending. What a novelty such a novel would be!

D. J. Enright, "Fortunate Foetus," in The Listener *(© British Broadcasting Corp. 1979; reprinted by permission of D. J. Enright), Vol. 101, No. 2594, January 25, 1979, p. 174.*

LUCY HUGHES-HALLET

The narrator of Thomas Keneally's *Passenger* hasn't been born yet and at certain points in the course of the story it begins to look doubtful whether he ever will be. . . .

The tone, suitable to an unborn narrator, is one of innocent cynicism. The foetus, absorbing human knowledge with one pulsation of the umbilicus, finds it all acceptable but for the squalid fact of birth and views the antics of those unlucky enough to have left the womb with a high-flown pity tempered by the horrid knowledge that he must soon join them. There is a taste of syrup in the prose, as in the premise, which might deter some readers and the plot meanders with no apparent purpose other than that of giving the foetus lots to talk about. But Keneally carries it off beautifully. Archaic words and elaborately convoluted clauses abound but they don't snag up the sentences, only twist them in smoothly attractive eddies. His writing has a lovely lilt to it that carried me through his disjointed story as unprotesting as the narrator placidly swimming in the amniotic fluid.

Lucy Hughes-Hallet, "Thomas Keneally's 'Passenger'" (© copyright Lucy Hughes-Hallet 1979; reprinted with permission), in Books and Bookmen, *Vol. 24, No. 6, March, 1979, p. 56.*

DAPHNE MERKIN

"Passenger" is a wonderfully poised novel. It rattles along at great speed without ever missing out on the telling, piquantly humorous detail. Mr. Keneally has taken on a bold range of subjects—parenthood, sexuality, psychiatry—and serves them up with a rare, Nabokovian verve that yet manages to sound the depths. His novel should be read for the sheer *jeu d'esprit* of it, although "Passenger" is more than fun.

Daphne Merkin, "Parents and Their Problems," in The New York Times Book Review *(© 1979 by The New York Times Company; reprinted by permission), July 8, 1979, p. 13.**

STEPHEN VAUGHAN

War, like the sea is slow to give up its dead; any verdict on a novel of war so immediately overwhelming as Thomas Keneally's ['Confederates'] should similarly be the slow fruit of rumination.

Since there is no such breathing space for the reviewer, one is tempted to risk the opinion that this author has excelled the achievement of his 'Gossip from the Forest' and 'Season in Purgatory' and that 'Confederates' deserves some comparison with the two great war novels of the last hundred years in the language, 'The Red Badge of Courage' and 'Her Privates We,' one of which stemmed from the bloody springs of experience and one from an imagination of genius.

It is stock-in-trade nowadays that the poetry of war is in the pity, but compassion at the finger tips is another matter from Keneally's compassion of the heart. The setting is the American Civil War, specifically the Stonewall Brigade of the Virginia Volunteers bound for the hinge of fate and Antietam. Thus the title on the face of it applies to the scarecrow army of the South with a clinching elusive victory in the sights of its (inferior) rifles. But the scenes of battle and forage are contrapuntal to the theme that envelops them all, haters, fraternisers, whores, deserters, farm boys, slaves and brass hats alike, all victims and confederates in the pity and madness of war.

Huge and sprawling as the canvas is, the individuality of these fighting and yearning men is retained in spare, telling prose, with few of the purple sorties that this author sometimes ventures. And how many war books bring home the feel of the earth itself, the ever-present earth that takes the blood and the shit and the dreams of tired infantrymen?

As an Australian writing about events so thronged with ghosts, altars and portents for our time but also so fervently and proprietorially American, Kenneally is treading on holy ground. Dangerous ground, too, with such forerunners as Crane, Faulkner, Bierce, Sandburg, but he avoids the pitfalls of pastiche in this noble book.

Stephen Vaughan, "Boys in Blue," in The Observer *(reprinted by permission of The Observer Limited), No. 9817, October 21, 1979, p. 39.**

MICHAEL RATCLIFFE

I confess to finding the randy villain of that uterine jest [*Passenger*] a more sharply conceived and executed figure than any of those who toil through the mud and blood of the North Virginian Army [in *Confederates*] as it desperately seeks through 1862 to bring the British Government, politically, into the war.

Confederates, in short, is Keneally's American Civil War Novel. He has done his reading thoroughly, listed the main sources at the end, made a craftsmanlike fiction out of them, and moved on to the next job. Hard not to feel that the precariously sustained subplots of adultery and amorous espionage are there for the attention of casting-directors and that a brief appearance by President Lincoln should not be there at all. Hard, too, not to feel that the proximity of the sources is responsible for the faintly inspirational, sentimental and portentous tone which dogs *Confederates* as so much other writing about this war. . . .

Homework is the key to all historical novels, and should ideally be felt and not seen. . . . [Keneally] is very good on detail, and on the nature of battles which he rightly describes as the accumulation of such, but his chief sympathy is with the suffering, boredom, panic and, above all, the pathos of a volunteers' war, and when he keeps those in focus he is very good indeed. (p. 683)

Michael Ratcliffe, "Booker Dark Horse," in New Statesman *(© 1979 The Statesman & Nation Publishing Co. Ltd.), Vol. 98, No. 2537, November 2, 1979, pp. 682-83.**

* * *

KEROUAC, Jack 1922-1969

Kerouac was an American novelist and poet. Along with Ginsberg, Burroughs, and others, he was an original member of the group which, in the middle 1940s, became the Beat movement. Kerouac's own work was an effort to "invent a new prose," specifically American, which was to reflect in its spontaneity and formlessness the vastness and beauty of this country. (See also *CLC,* Vols. 1, 2, 3, 5, and *Contemporary Authors,* Vols. 5-8, rev. ed.; obituary, Vols. 25-28.)

SEYMOUR KRIM

With each passing book Jack Kerouac begins to come down to earth a little more, to reveal what he's made of and allow for some practical judgments. There has been such a gossip campaign about our so-called wild man, the King of the Beats, that ordinarily serious literary people have come to assume a fighting stance (either for or against) that has little to do with Kerouac's actual performance. . . .

[Ray Smith in *The Dharma Bums*] adds mountain-climbing and meditation to the typical Kerouacian staple of batting madly around the country. In a sense, this book is gentler and less pretentious than both *On the Road* and *The Subterraneans;* Kerouac-Smith is in a more thoughtful and introspective mood than previously, and spends much time by himself digging the beauties and possibilities of nature. A genuine pastoral charm can be found in the *Bums,* and it is quite refreshing until it becomes overdone. But although this new facet of Kerouac's sensitivity has been seized upon by some conventional critics who couldn't see what all the fuss was about before, Kerouac's sensuous response to nature should not be hoisted high as proof that he is a good boy after all, wholesome and bracketable. (p. 359)

The most widely quoted reviews of *On The Road* compared Kerouac to Thomas Wolfe as a rolling, roaring, all-American type of prose bard. As his writing . . . tumbles out into book form . . . , we can see that this original comparison was misleading. Kerouac does not have the classic verbal equipment or majesty of Wolfe at his best, and anyone who goes to his books looking for the same thrilling bombast won't find it. As a handler of words, Kerouac is often careless and slangy, the language often dripping colorlessly into an undifferentiated puddle. And in this latest book we see that the writing is thin as well, with none of the rotundity or resonance that the Wolfe-Whitman comparisons implied.

I think it is illuminating to poke into his actual prose itself because so much hazy misinformation has found its way into the press concerning it. The most interesting writing of Kerouac's three recent books can be found in *The Subterraneans,* where the sentences are thick, clotted, almost unreadable in their fidelity to what the "I" experiences, down to the most hair-fine detail. I have been told that this is the only one of Kerouac's books that has not been edited; and it shows in the final tediousness of the writing and, more importantly, in the attempt on Kerouac's part to tell *all* about his painful affair with a young colored girl. It is a strong and vivid piece of writing, one that stays in the mind like a burr, but it also points up the recklessness of his method of composition and, probably, his entire philosophy. This is important, I think, because Kerouac's virtues and excesses are yoked very tightly, almost inseparably, together. (pp. 359-60)

Thus I believe that Kerouac, by throwing over the literary restraints, has succeeded in letting some of the real experience of our decade escape into his pages in crude, free-swinging, even shapeless form. Unlike most of his contemporaries, who haven't been spared a similar life, Kerouac doesn't apologize for his pursuit of pleasure; he refuses to look down on his experience or to measure it against any ideal. He is determined simply to find joy in his life, even at extravagant cost and risk.

What sets Kerouac apart from the "writer writers," and makes his voice carry despite its comparative frailty and childishness, is that he has the courage to put down the unaccustomed rhythm and details of the frantic modern scene exactly the way he's lived it. This may not be a literary achievement which will survive beyond the present. But can we be sure what will? (p. 360)

Seymour Krim, "King of the Beats," in Commonweal *(copyright © 1959 Commonweal Publishing Co., Inc.; reprinted by permission of Commonweal Publishing Co., Inc.), Vol. LXIX, No. 14, January 2, 1959, pp. 359-60.*

WARREN TALLMAN

Kerouac's sound starts up in his first novel, *The Town and the City,* and anyone who grew up with or remembers the sentimental music of the 1930s will recognize what he is doing. The New England nights and days of his childhood and youth are orchestrated with slow violins, to which sound the children whose lives he chronicles are stirred into awareness as the stars dip down and slow breezes sweep along diminishing strings towards soft music on a farther shore. It is the considerable achievement of the novel that Kerouac is able to sustain the note of profound sentimentality his style conveys even as he is tracing, with remorseless intelligence, the downfall of the New England family. . . . (p. 65)

The jazz is in the continuity in which each episode [in *On the Road*] tells a separate story—variations on the holiness theme. And it is in the remarkably flexible style as Kerouac improvises within each episode seeking to adjust his sound to the resonance of the given moment. Some moments come through tinged with the earlier *Town and City* sentimentality. Others rock and sock . . . , the sentences jerking about like muscles on an overwrought face. Still others are curiously quiescent, calm. And the melody which unifies the whole and lifts the cockeyed star up into the jazz sky is the holiness of life because this for Kerouac is the meaning of words, the inside of his sound. . . . To read *On the Road* with attention to the variations Kerouac achieves is to realize something of the very impressive talent for meshing his sound with the strongly-felt rhythms of many and various moments. It is not possible to compare him very closely with other stylists of note because his fiction is the first in which jazz is a dominant influence. (p. 69)

[*The Subterraneans*] is written with the driving but hungup rhythms of a hurrying man who is also, always, alas, looking back over his shoulder. . . . A failure of love by reason of deep fissuring guilts emerges from the depths on the rush but not exactly on the wings of Kerouac's spontaneous Bop style. As Percepied says, 'I'm the Bop writer.' As one might expect, the spontaneity falters in a good many pages. Yet I do not doubt that the method does permit Kerouac to tap his imagination in spontaneous ways. Nor do I doubt but that *The Subterraneans* is his most important novel and a very important one indeed. (pp. 70-1)

The easiest way to approach *The Dharma Bums*—the truth bums—is to imagine an exceptionally talented musician trying out a new instrument in an interested but nonetheless very tentative way. The instrument is Zen Buddhism, American fashion. The novel is full of hummed songs, muttered chants, self-conversations carried on in railroad yards, on beaches, in groves of trees, in the mountains. The half-embarrassed, half-serious mutterer is Ray Smith, Zen amateur, and the style which Kerouac floats through the novel is part of an obvious attempt to adjust the practices, the flavour, the attitudes of Zen to an American sensibility. (p. 71)

It is . . . significant that in the opening paragraph [of the novel] Smith travels past the place where the 'king and founder of the Bop generation', the jazzman Charlie Parker, 'went crazy and got well again'. Kerouac might be hinting at the strain of writing eleven books in six years and about the need for a temporary so-long to jazz, hello to Zen. But the hello is most tentative. To put the very best construction on the novel, always advisable when dealing with a versatile writing talent, is to read it as a kind of primer of Zen experience. . . . [If] the Zen attitude is consistent with Kerouac's own, it is nonetheless apparent that the meditative world in which this attitude is best cultivated hasn't much affinity with his essentially nervous and agile sensibility. Unsustained by the driving intensities which make *On the Road* and *The Subterraneans* swing, *The Dharma Bums* frequently goes flat. There are dull scenes, mechanical passages. If there is one superb mountain-climbing episode, that is less because Zen catches hold for Kerouac, more because the mountain does. Certainly, representation of the final trip to the Northwest, where the protagonist attempts to live in the Zen way on Desolation Peak, is so sketchy as to amount to a default. And it is here that one touches upon Kerouac's limitations.

In *The Dharma Bums* distinctly and in his other novels in less evident ways, one becomes aware of Kerouac's receptive, his essentially feminine sensibility. Sensibility, I repeat. This receptivity is certainly his main strength as artist, accounting as it does for his capacity to assimilate the rhythms, the sounds, the life-feel of experience into his representation. When Kerouac is at his best he is able to register and project the American resonance with ease and accuracy. But on the related, weaker side of the coin, he has only a limited ability to project this sound up to heights, down to depths. Moments of climax, of revelation, of crisis, the very moments which deserve the fullest representation, frequently receive only sparse representation. The climactic Mexican journey in *On the Road* suffers from this limitation. Beginning with the madcap afternoon in the Mexican whore house, followed by the night-time sojourn in the jungle, the creation-day morning in the mountains, and subsequent arrival in Mexico City, the hipster Zion, where marihuana cascades like manna into the streets, the entire sequence is as brilliantly conceived as any in recent fiction. But representation in these scenes which show Moriarity's life sweeping up to climax, is sparse, fleeting, even sketchy. No reader will be convinced that Moriarity, the true traveler, has made it to a mountain-peak of our present moment from which creation-day is glimpsed. Nor will any reader be convinced that Ray Smith has gained access to the Zen Way in his mountain fastness.

Yet I do not think that this defect traces so much to want of creative force, though that is what it appears to be, as to Kerouac's almost animal suspicion of the meaning values toward which words tend. When his fictions converge toward meanings something vital in him flinches back. His sound is primarily a life sound, sensitive to the indwelling qualities of things, the life they bear. To be Beat is to be wary of moving such a sound into the meaning clutter. It might become lost, the life. So Kerouac draws back. Which is his limitation.

But also his strength. For in the jazz world of the Bop generation where Charlie Parker is king and founder, Jack Kerouac in a different medium is heir apparent. . . . [His] emphasis upon a from-under sound made spontaneous by adherence to the jazz principle of improvision is right for our time, I think. The jazz vernacular is just that, a vernacular, and Kerouac has demonstrated that it can be transposed into fiction without serious loss of the spontaneous imaginative freedom which has made it among the most vital of the modern arts.

Although Kerouac's art is limited, I am convinced that his sound is more nearly in the American grain than that of any writer since Fitzgerald. The efforts of his outcast protagonists to get life into their lives seem more closely related to our actual moment than those of any since Jay Gatsby, similar across worlds of difference, tried to shoot the North American moon. Gatsby failed and finished like a sad swan, floating dead on the surface of a pool. And Kerouac's protagonists fail too. . . . Fitzgerald's efforts got lost in the personal, national, and international chaos from which he summoned Gatsby into presence. But it was only after his energies lost coherence that Fitzgerald woke up in the ruins of that dark midnight of the soul where it is always three o'clock in the morning. Kerouac starts in with the dark midnight and it is his effort to bring his protagonists through the jazz of that night, naked, into something like a new day. He fails too. The moment, NOW, which is the only promised land, shrugs off [his protagonists] Moriarity, Percepied, and Smith, shrugs off Kerouac too. Outcasts they began and end as outcasts. But very distinctly Kerouac's protagonists press more sharply close to the truth about our present moment than have fictional protagonists for many years. And that's a help. And very distinctly he has created new ground of possibility for fiction to stand upon with renewed life. And that's a help. (pp. 71-4)

Warren Tallman, "Kerouac's Sound," in The Tamarack Review, *No. 11, Spring, 1959, pp. 58-74.*

KINGSLEY WIDMER

[Central] to Beat writers, though little noticed, is the desperate flight from lower middle class life and its culture of anxiety. The unredeemable horrors of petit bourgeois meanness and restriction combine, as also in Céline's *Death on the Installment Plan,* with dissociated child fantasy, savage forbodings, and strange moments of tenderness. This characterizes most of the Beat confessions. Kerouac's lyrical-ruminative documentaries of his anxious *wanderjahrs—On the Road* (1958), *The Dharma Bums* (1959), the travel sketches not masquerading as fiction such as *The Lonesome Traveller* (1960) and his later imitations of his earlier work (such as *Big Sur*)—depend essentially on the softness of the child in flight from a petty order. This is not only the guilty-ecstatic adolescent romanticism and its poignant muddle (and its artistic correlative of the inability to realize character and scene other than in ragged detail and forced private mood—in the Thomas Wolfe manner) but the yearning for the return to innocence, both of the self and the American order. Identifying his wanderings with the quest for freedom, from that of Zen monks and American hobos through the prophetic outcasts ("Jesus was a strange hobo who walked on water"), hardly modifies the personal pathos.

Kerouac touches at moments on the existential intensity and profundity of the traditional wanderer: the defiant separateness, the sharp moral comment of a life denuded of surplus, the suspension of time by those wedded to motion, and the outcast's brilliant perceptions of most of what passes for humane order and meaning. But childishness usually takes over. On looking at the lights in the night, Kerouac comments: "I wish I was a little child in a crib in a little ranch style sweet house." In similar forlorn need, and incisive prose, he describes "kid dreams," juvenile ideas and adolescent tastes. As he notes of his "gang" of rather over-aged "boys," "We sorta wander around like children." The ideal is to return to "the happy life of childhood again." The style corresponds, with inflated and run-on sentences (perhaps an attempt to give a literally breathless heightening) and cute expletives ("comfy," "heavenly," "raving great," "glady," and the catatonic "Wow!"). The insights show similar quality, it being a great revelation of Kerouac that everybody walks around with a "dirty behind," or that most people are "crazy," or that buddies are "great," or that America is a "nutty" place. Of course there is a rather burbling charm about intensifying the commonplace, such as eating a hot dog or hungering for home. LIFE is unalterably "sad" or "fun," we are regularly told. Recurrent paranoid episodes, the guilty sexual fears, the eager and then disillusioned identifications with more manly or purposive buddies, and a constant anxious inadequacy block any more incisive ordering of experience. Yet intermittently Kerouac's kid-world, as heightened by a series of trips across America in the late 40s and middle 50s, opens into some suggestive responsiveness of a rebel on the road, junior division.

Kerouac's aesthetic, if such we can call a widespread quasi-art ideology of salvational self-expression, claims rebellion against intellectualized literature and thought. This generally comes out as free-associational confession but also, as with Ginsberg, includes efforts to "spiritualize" the flight from American lower middle class sensibility. While the material of *On the Road* mostly consists of some of the history of the coterie which became publicly identified as the Beat Generation, the novel attempts something more. Focusing on a touchingly flamboyant psychopath, Dean Moriarity (the late Neal Cassidy), it presents him as profound wanderer and "HOLY GOOF," the wild pilgrim. To achieve romantic apotheosis in an otherwise blandly repressive society, Kerouac exalts a delinquent intensity, an amoral posture and personality without much specific content. Awe, more adolescent than sacred, covers "the ones who are mad to live, mad to talk, mad to be saved, desirous of everything at the same time, the ones who never yawn or say a commonplace thing, but burn, burn, burn, like fabulous roman candles exploding like spiders across the stars and in the middle you see the blue centerlight pop and everybody goes 'Awww!'"

The fireworks hardly light up the intellectual and social vagueness, any more than do the temporary Buddhist trappings put on in *Dharma Bums*. There the hero-narrator is the outdoors American boy turned contemplative, with Japhy (Gary Snyder) providing Kerouac's pattern for a religious-therapeutic summer in the mountains and woods. The mystagoguery, and an excess of reportage on fatuous Bohemianism in the Bay Area, muddle an interesting larger theme—a call for a style of "rucksack wanderers," "Dharma bums," American Don Quixotes of tenderness who refuse to be imprisoned in a system of pointless work, forced consumption, and control by the "Master Switch" in a wired-up civilization. That moving ideal is still with us, still a leading edge of the "youth culture" in its perceptive disaffiliation and poignant vagary.

The interest of Kerouac's writings is mostly documentary. Sometimes they give apt details, hardly ever developed, about the American scene, when not obscured by "real straight talk about souls." (pp. 160-62)

On the Road ends with a frenzied journey in Mexico with glimpses of what is taken to be a more real and primordial life; *Dharma Bums* ends with the trip down Desolation Mountain with glimpses of what is taken to be a primal therapy and spiritual transformation. Somewhere on those journeys, the author hopes, he has rediscovered life as it has eternally been, and will be again after the "Apocalypse" willful and arbitrary and mad American civilization is inevitably creating.

In spite of the childishness of much of the writing and thinking, Kerouac's yearning flights show us something about the American scene of the time with its harshly alienating places and lavishly fraudulent order and forlornly dissociated young. The "road is life," we are told with typical sententiousness and repetition of an old American metaphor, but it leads to both a vaguely visionary sense of a different life, "the ragged and ecstatic joy of pure being," and a "senseless nightmare road," in which even an inadequate sensibility recognizes our existential failures and foresees the collapse of the old culture. (pp. 162-63)

The soft rebellion in sensibility of a Kerouac, the All-American boy as Beat cynosure of the spiritual vagrant, melts away. Jack Kerouac went on in the 60s to mere idiosyncratic legendizing of himself (books about his own ancestry and dreams) and further pathetic withdrawal. The literature, like the figure, seems mostly symptomatic. (p. 163)

Kingsley Widmer, "The Beat in the Rise of the Populist Culture," in The Fifties: Fiction, Poetry, Drama, *edited by Warren French (copyright © 1970 by Warren French), Everett/Edwards, Inc., 1970, pp. 155-73.*

ALLEN GINSBERG

Kerouac was the first writer I ever met who heard his own writing, who listened to his own sentences as if they were musical, rhythmical constructions, and who could follow the sequence of sentences that make up the paragraph as if he were listening to a little jazz riff. . . .

[He] would model sentences on the choruses, on the particular squiggly little "dadadadadadaduhdada"—"As I was goin' walkin' down to Larimar" of "Lester Leaps In" is "dadada dadadada dadada, dadadadadadada dadada, dadadadada dada dadada, dadaadadaydyadadda." So it was a definite rhythmical squiggle that he was hearing when he was writing his prose sentences, a funny body rhythm, a breathing rhythm and a speech rhythm that he was conscious of writing when he was writing prose. So he added a dimension to prose which most prosateurs have not yet actually discovered exists or is necessary for epic or historical prose.

Kerouac got to be a great poet on that basis, 'cause he could hear American speech, and he could hear it in musical sequence. (p. 152)

Allen Ginsberg, "Kerouac" (originally a lecture delivered at Kent State University on April 6, 1971), in his Allen Verbatim: Lectures on Poetry, Politics, Consciousness, *edited by Gordon Ball, (copyright © 1974 by Allen Ginsberg; with permission of McGraw Hill Book Co.), McGraw-Hill, 1974, pp. 151-60.*

J. MEREDITH NEIL

[Kerouac's novels], taken together, exemplify a change of consciousness so subversive to prevailing American values and institutions and so attractive, at least within a decade, to millions of Americans that all defenders of the Establishment felt compelled to shout them out of existence. Kerouac's novels are more readily summarized than Ginsberg's poetry or the Beats' innovations in life styles, but all three manifest a rebellion against the Establishment—the goals and habits of middle-class America. . . . (p. 435)

On the Road, written in 1951 concerning events of the preceding four years, superficially appears to be much as the book's cover brazenly proclaims, a "wild Odyssey of two dropouts who swing across America wrecking and rioting—making it with sex, jazz, and drink as they Make the Scene." . . . It all seemed to be an unrestrained Whitmanesque celebration of the open road, that peculiarly American joy in moving for its own sake: "I didn't know where all this was leading," Sal once confessed: "I didn't care." . . .

The ambiguity of the enterprise, however, crept out almost immediately and persistently reappeared throughout the book. Sal's friends "rushed down the street together, digging everything in the early way they had, which later become so much sadder and perceptive and blank." . . . The innocent early pleasure repeatedly confronted the meaninglessness of such a life. Compulsively rushing across the continent, Sal could not avoid an impasse: "Here I was at the end of America—no more land—and now there was nowhere to go but back." . . . The trip always turned into a bummer. The somber warning of Carlo Marx (i.e., Allen Ginsberg) kept returning to haunt them: "Now I'm not trying to take your hincty sweets from you, but it seems to me that the time has come to decide what you are and what you're going to do. . . . The days of wrath are yet to come. The balloon won't sustain you much longer. And not only that but it's an abstract balloon." . . . (pp. 435-36)

Their dilemma [was] how to find the good life without falling into a whirlwind of movement. . . . (pp. 436-37)

On the Road, it seems to me, is not all what it first appeared to be. Rather, it is a metaphor exposing the pointlessness of American enchantment with a kind of progress that involves constant, compulsive movement, occasionally spiced with wistful notions of relaxing and enjoying life. . . . Having failed to understand what *On the Road* was saying, most Americans could scarcely be expected to follow Kerouac in his next novels. After *On the Road* Kerouac's audience quickly dwindled to those who were actually or potentially beat. (p. 437)

The Subterraneans picked up where *On the Road* left off. . . . The author-narrator, no longer celebrating the open road, has become desperately self-conscious and writes for therapy. The result is little more fulfilling than had been tripping *On the Road.* Compulsive movement had only been internalized. The sole gain appeared to be that, finally, Sal-Leo [the protagonist] recognized that compulsion, rather than movement, was the barrier to existential meaning. (pp. 437-38)

Kerouac's protagonist was now ready for beatness. In Timothy Leary's terms, Sal had dropped out, Leo had tuned in, and Ray Smith in *The Dharma Bums* proceeded to turn on. The unpretentious pseudonym suggested the loss of self-consciousness and his potential as Everyman. . . . [The characters] and their friends, mainly non-students in Berkeley, had a mission: ebulliently witnessing a new consciousness. (pp. 438-39)

J. Meredith Neil, "1955: The Beginnings of Our Times," in South Atlantic Quarterly *(reprinted by permission of the Publisher; copyright 1974 by Duke University Press, Durham, North Carolina), Vol. 73, No. 4, Autumn, 1974, pp. 428-44.**

ERIC KORN

[*Doctor Sax*] was Kerouac's favourite book: it's easy to see why. It was much abused by the critics: it's easy to see why. Now, twenty years after its appearance in the United States, and a generation after it was written, a canonical book, this hash-brown study of the demons and angels of adolescence achieves hardback publication in Britain. For Kerouac *Doctor Sax* was a myth of puberty, the second chapter after *Dreams of Gerard* in the vast envisaged "Legend of Duluoz", the mythification of the author's life. . . .

A literary nomad needs an origin and a promised land. Kerouac was multiply exiled: pelagic in the city the smalltown boy from Lowell, Massachusetts, where he was one of the Francophone expatriate community from Quebec, land of exiles (as it seemed then) looking back to a lost Brittany, land of miracles. It is a good pedigree for nostalgia.

Ti-Jean Kerouac's childhood was seemingly uneventful: the family moved from Pawtucketville to Centralville; meals, illnesses, devotions, baseball and ice-hockey, companions, a death, a flood. But "I was a scared kid"; there is a furious fantasy life; fumy horrors distilled from Street and Smith pulps stalk the dingy alleys. Reorganized by hindsight, they are rock gothic, Firbankian werewolves: Emilia St Claire, Boaz the Butler, Amadeus Baroque. Among them moves silently Dr Sax—who has somehow acquired the physical attributes of William Burroughs—much more than a lonely child's invisible playmate: the pilgrim of a cabalistic quest, possessor of a great secret—"He knew something that no other man knew; a something reptilian; pray, was he a man?" . . .

But Lowell takes its place with Winesburg, Ohio and Hannibal, Missouri in that child's America of fixed habitations, as opposed to Greyhound America, Route 66 or the Mississippi. How much the reader shares Kerouac's enjoyment depends on how he feels about the prose. . . .

In the book's first paragraph Kerouac exhorts himself to "describe the wrinkly tar of this sidewalk . . . don't stop to think of words when you do stop, just stop to think of this picture better—and let your mind off yourself in the work". It is a naive prescription, and not one he had the least intention of fulfilling; but as long as he keeps the tar in focus, he carries the reader along.

Eric Korn, "Off the Road," in The Times Literary Supplement *(© Times Newspapers Ltd. (London) 1977; reproduced from* The Times Literary Supplement *by permission), No. 3919, April 22, 1977, p. 477.*

* * *

KNEBEL, Fletcher 1911-

Knebel is an American novelist. His experience as a journalist in Washington has enabled him to write suspense stories with credible political settings and complex characters. These novels reveal his liberal ideals and his interest in the struggle for power. He has coauthored novels with Charles W. Bailey II. (See also *Contemporary Authors*, Vols. 1-4, rev. ed.)

SANDER VANOCUR

It would be a mistake to dismiss [*Seven Days in May*], as some already have, because it reads like a thriller. The authors [Fletcher Knebel and Charles W. Bailey II] obviously believe that it is not necessary to be dull if a subject is serious. It will be a runaway best-seller because it is well written, because it is virtually impossible to put it down once you have picked it up. The same thing was true of *Advise and Consent.* The main difference between the two books, apart from the weight, is that the characters in *Seven Days in May* are plausible. (p. 23)

This is an important book. Somehow in this country, we have not produced any first-rate modern novels about the uses which men make of power. We have had limited exercises in certain localized areas like California in Eugene Burdick's *The Ninth Wave* and in Louisiana in Robert Penn Warren's *All the King's Men.* But we have not had, until this book, any serious, or successful, literary effort which explores what men do with the power thrust upon some of them, or seized by others, at the national level. This book is no masterpiece. It will, however, both defy and endure the efforts of those who attempt to dismiss it as superficial. (pp. 24-5)

Sander Vanocur, "Drunks, Babies and the USA," in The New Republic *(reprinted by permission of* The New Republic; *© 1962 The New Republic, Inc.), Vol. 147, No. 14, October 1, 1962, pp. 23-5.*

ROBERT HATCH

[The prophetic entertainer] is a writer who makes no pretense to literary art; in matters of character, narrative devices, style and psychology, he models his work on formulas developed by the large fiction magazines, by television family drama, by the commercial movies. He is out for the very largest market (and he is reaching it), but the fuel that drives his vehicle is not love or success or adventure—it is doomsday. (p. 291)

The true application of the method is to be seen in *Seven Days in May* . . . , [which is] at present leading the domestic fiction market and . . . which, it seems inevitable, will soon be on film for world distribution. [This novel is] built firmly on the foundations of suspense, sustained and sweeping action, the verisimilitude of technical detail, and simplistic but strongly projected character. These ingredients of success could be predicted; more important is the fact that [the book does not allow] a gap of time or place between the reader and the fiction. *Seven Days in May* . . . [is] as immediate, in the inevitable phrase, as tomorrow's newspaper.

Knebel and Bailey . . . write as men intimately acquainted with the public streets and private channels of the capital. Their tale is of a narrowly averted plot by the military leadership to unseat the President and seize the country. . . .

The authors shape their narrative, not only to carry the reader on an unbroken chase after excitement, but to neutralize his skepticism. . . .

I would give *Seven Days in May* a very high mark for probability. Its authors resort to no *outre* gadgetry, they envision no circumstance so bizarre as to lend distance and comfort. Beneath the blood-stirring excitement of their melodrama lies the clammy suspicion that just such a plot might be hatched, almost any day now, across the Potomac from the Washington Monument. . . .

[The book] may point a way to communication in a noise-engulfed world. [It weaves] probabilities with human interest into a design that the reader can feel as intimately as the rug under his feet. (p. 292)

The literature to which *Seven Days in May* [belongs] achieves its popularity at the cost of falsifying—or, to be kinder, simplifying—human experience. And in the area of world crisis this may be a high price to pay for information, let alone entertainment. True to type, [the book deals], not in flesh and blood, but in super cardboard. And, true to type, they glorify man (including the reader). You come from them feeling refreshed, keen-minded, about ten feet high. It is the well-known Walter Mitty effect and it lies at the base of all mass entertainment.

The crises, described may well come to be part of history, but the solutions offered belong to the worlds of Eric Ambler and Clark Kent. Coincidence and accident are used impartially to set up and dissipate disaster, and the men who walk the edge of catastrophe have feet that falter, for the sake of the excitement, but never slip. . . . [In] the Knebel-Bailey thriller the last-second arrival of a tiny but conclusive bit of evidence will cause the least impressionable reader to cheer—and leave him safely in the grandstand.

The effect of reading these books is certainly to make the perils more credible. At the same time, if we are not wary, it is to make us believe that Someone Up There is watching over us and that our leader, no matter how late the hour, can be depended on to extricate us and themselves from the maelstrom. . . .

[This book is] good medicine, but very careful note should be taken of the ingredients. (p. 293)

Robert Hatch, "Making Tomorrow Convincing," in The Nation *(copyright 1962 by the Nation Associates, Inc.), Vol. 195, No. 4, November 3, 1962, pp. 291-93.**

WILLIAM BARRETT

[*Seven Days in May*] had a freshness and suspense of melodrama to recommend it and was a great popular success; . . . [*Convention*], however, is corny and mechanical, and at times it seems an echo of Mr. Vidal's play [*The Best Man*]. . . .

To [various] stock villains the authors have added another that is bound to become a staple of the new political thriller: a computing machine used to store data of the most personal kind on the delegates so that they can be shamelessly pressured into voting the way the big bosses, big business, and big labor, miraculously banded together, want them to. In their serenade to political virtue, Messrs. Knebel and Bailey have pulled out all the stops, but the notes are sour.

William Barrett, "Problems of Power," in The Atlantic Monthly *(copyright © 1964 by The Atlantic Monthly Company, Boston, Mass.; reprinted with permission), Vol. 213, No. 4, April, 1964, pp. 146-47.*

CHAD WALSH

Night of Camp David begins with a standard plot: a junior senator summoned to a mysterious conference with the President, and informed that he is being considered for the vice-presidential nomination. Predictably, the senator—a handsome, lazy lout—has a lush lady friend hidden away, though his own wife—as demonstrated later when she doffs her pajamas and goes swimming by moonlight—is adequately endowed. Predictably, our hero finds himself torn between newly born ambitions and old lusts, and quickly votes for the former.

So far, almost the archetypal political novel, complete with worldly-wise lawyers and cynical political advisers. But what gives Mr. Knebel's tale a fresh twist is the personality of the President, who slowly reveals himself as a top-drawer paranoid with delusions of persecution and grandeur. . . .

The story is swift-moving, and the characters, though not studies in depth, seem plausible enough. There is even a certain poignancy in the unexpected nobility of the President when he donates the surprise ending. For a political thriller—which does indeed dramatize the awesome problems surrounding the office of President—this is distinctly above average.

Chad Walsh, "Split Ticket," in Book Week—New York Herald Tribune *(© I.H.T. Corporation; reprinted by permission), May 30, 1965, p. 14.*

MARION ARMSTRONG

George Orwell's 1984 is still a relaxing 14 years away [note date of this essay]; if in the interval we refuse to be shunted into its inhuman and insane approaches, we may yet avoid our indicated psychic and political annihilation. But 1973, the year of Fletcher Knebel's new novel [*Trespass*], will be with us in another 36 months, and the book is so perfectly credible that one can imagine reading it as faintly fictionalized history in—say—1978. Rapidly paced, absorbing in the adventure-story mode and rather gaudily written, *Trespass* hypothesizes a sample and small-scale but tightly plotted thrust against white money and white power by a dedicated group of black militants known as the B.O.F.—Blacks of February 21st (the date of Malcolm X's assassination). . . .

All the characters are well developed, all momentarily fascinating. . . .

As the word *trespass* cuts two ways it it clear that in the given context neither white landowner nor black assailant has a lien on righteousness; nor is either quite guiltless of bad faith. *Trespass*'s strength lies in its unwelcome plausibility, its assumption that our racial troubles are just beginning. I should like to find it melodramatic, but I don't. . . .

Marion Armstrong, "Perfectly Credible," in The Christian Century *(copyright 1969 Christian Century Foundation; reprinted by permission from the December 24, 1969 issue of* The Christian Century*), Vol. LXXXVI, No. 52, December 24, 1969, p. 1646.*

MARTIN LEVIN

"Dark Horse" recalls those old Jimmy Stewart and Gary Cooper movies, where Mr. Smith or Mr. Deeds outsmart the corrupt hotshots of the System. The lifestyle here is different (the author has projected his plot four years ahead, into the climax of election year 1976), but the platitudes are familiar.

In Mr. Knebel's heavy-footed political comedy, the Jimmy Stewart role is taken by Eddie Quinn, an ex-trucker who is processed into instant Presidential timber when his party's candidate drops dead three weeks before the voting. If the bosses think they can manipulate Eddie, currently a New Jersey Turnpike Commissioner, they have another think coming—from the moment he throws away the predigested text of his acceptance speech, and comes out foresquare against "the elitists, the men from prestige universities, Wall Street lawyers, rich men's clubs." Commissioner Quinn is a "plain man" as his mother puts it, but he has picked up plenty of savvy out on those highways, along with the fumes. Some of his ideas are O.K., and some are as wild-eyed as campaign promises in real life.

Martin Levin, "Fiction: 'Dark Horse'," in The New York Times Book Review *(© 1972 by The New York Times Company; reprinted by permission), July 23, 1972, p. 21.*

GENE VENABLE

Phony plus phony equals funny. That is the formula for [*Dave Sulkin Cares!*]. It works, within limits.

Fletcher Knebel . . . here scores a mild success, pitting two con-persons against each other. The plot suggests a new answer to the old paradox: what happens when an irresistible force meets an immovable object? Knebel's answer is that if the forces are a con man and con woman, they fall in love, give up their bogus ways for normal lives, and abandon their glamorous lives for the same dull round of ordinary existence.

As you can see, I was saddened when this lively couple decided to quit their evil ways at the end of the book. For me, the height of the book comes at the beginning, with the hilarious description of the career of Gail Sunderling, who cuts a swatch of chicanery across the U.S., all the while half convincing herself that she had done nothing really wrong. She meets a guru on Hawaii who is her match.

Gail and the guru set out to stop land developers from defiling land in Hawaii. The guru enlists the aid of other hyper-strange cult leaders, and the reader meets the most endearing character to grace the pages of a novel for some time. He's "J. J. Jenkins of Jeff City", who thinks the letter "j" is holy, and therefore includes it as often as he can in conversation. (pp. 29-30)

Any novel with preposterous, delightful speech like [J.J.'s] calls for jocose but justified joyful jubilation. (p. 30)

Gene Venable, "Books in Review: 'Dave Sulkin Cares!'" in West Coast Review of Books *(copyright 1978 by Rapport Publishing Co., Inc.), Vol. 4, No. 6, November, 1978, pp. 29-30.*

* * *

KOTZWINKLE, William 1938-

Kotzwinkle is an American novelist and writer of books for children. His work ranges from the urban fiction of *The Fan Man*, with its authentic dialect of New York's hippies, to the high-class pornography of *Night Book*. (See also *CLC*, Vol. 5, and *Contemporary Authors*, Vols. 45-48.)

RICHARD P. BRICKNER

While technically sportive and sometimes successfully lyrical, William Kotzwinkle's novel about man's inhumanity to rats, dogs, snakes, lions, elephants, bears, whales, turtles, etc. is so recklessly sentimental in its argument as to be food fit for Lynette (Squeaky) Fromme and other such fauna children. "Doctor Rat" did not quite make me want to go out and shoot dachshunds; but it did not persuade me, as it seems to have meant to, that laboratory research, using animals, into the causes of cancer is the equivalent of Dr. Mengele's experiments at Auschwitz. . . .

The novel drips with gruesome experiments committed by humans on animals. . . . Kotzwinkle acknowledges that snakes are dangerous to rats, and badgers to elephants, but there is not a mention in his book of snakes biting people, or dogs biting people, or lions eating people. There is, for "balance," a bunch of musicians on board a ship playing lovingly to whales and then musically warning them of a harpooning expedition. But the heaved burden of the novel, so irritatingly easy to dodge, is that animals are beautiful (not dumb; they all talk or think here, talk or think like people) and humans hideous with lip-smacking sadism. . . .

Kotzwinkle has us fail to realize we are all one, as if a sense of all-oneness among all animals were the answer to human or zoological problems, as if the problem (and necessity) weren't differentness and the answer the intelligent handling of differentness.

In "Elephant Bangs Train," his short-story collection of a few years back, Kotzwinkle performed subtly and with conspicuous skill and charm. Here he appears to be the Marx of zoology, hoping to inspire the proletariat to revolution (and mass death?). Is "Doctor Rat" to be sold to animals in research labs, slaughterhouses, zoos? Or are we, shamed by reading it, to turn universally vegetarian, close down our labs, slaughterhouses, zoos? In that case, *we'll* get creamed. This novel, which appears to be so feeling, is in fact disturbingly frivolous. It is zoö-radical-chic.

Richard P. Brickner, "Fiction and Poetry: 'Doctor Rat'," in The New York Times Book Review *(© 1976 by The New York Times Company; reprinted by permission), May 30, 1976, p. 8.*

ROBERT STONE

Doctor Rat is a very contemporary novel by a writer who

knows what the contemporary novel is for, and it tries to deliver what the times demand—an examination of modern society and a little conscience-forging for the race. It's an unashamed moral statement which upends verismo to get at basic truths. Although it's often funny, it's a very serious work which demands to be taken seriously. In spite of the respect for the author's talent that reading it inspires in me, taking it seriously involves me in a fundamental quarrel with the validity of its posture.

It's a novel about the Revolt of the Animals. Its principal character is a laboratory rat who has been castrated and driven mad by rat-running vivisectionists. (p. 97)

In the lab, where oppression is most acute and the rat population highly socialized, something like a classical Marxist uprising takes place—and Kotzwinkle has a good time making some amusing comic analogies as the rats transform themselves into rodent *fidelistas* to smash the unspeakable status quo.

All this throws the insane and embittered Doctor Rat into paroxysms of antisocial reactionary rage, and he single-handedly sets out to crush the life-affirming struggle of his fellow victims, with considerable energy and resourcefulness. . . . Kotzwinkle is what would ordinarily be called a humanist and he does not want a full-scale horror story on his hands, so The Man never shows his hated face. (pp. 97-8)

In part, *Doctor Rat* is about the phenomenon of revolution. . . .

What I find particularly irritating about *Doctor Rat* is the way it seeks to gather to itself every loose piece of more or less revolutionary sympathy left lying about the ruins of Consciousness III. (p. 98)

In *Styles of Radical Will,* written back in 1969, Susan Sontag called the white race "a cancer on human history." *Doctor Rat* follows through with the ultimate reductio, the final payoff on the same number—every prospect pleases and only man is vile.

Because humans are oppressors by their very nature, right? The cruelty inflicted by vivisectionists is only one aspect of the arrogance with which the humanoid colossus squats astride the fair face of biology, enslaving and destroying life forms older and finer than itself. Our very languages are oozing with injustice. Terms like "lower animals," the "evolutionary scale," "bestial," "varmint," "pest" all betray the cunning with which we have deadened our sensibilities to our own tyranny.

If this is not the moral that I'm meant to take, I find myself led toward it by the relentlessness with which the author introduces every artifact of man's inhumanity to man—from cyclon-B gas to tactical air strikes—for service as reference points. And even though I know I'm not supposed to, I object to the way all the animals are equipped with human emotions, human speech, and human mystic speculations to demonstrate their superiority to people.

In the sections set outside the lab, there are fanciful descriptions of animals which are often genuinely poetic and sometimes moving, but their cumulative effect is sentimental in the extreme. For one thing, they are anthropomorphized to a degree beyond anything Thornton W. Burgess or Ernest Thompson Seton ever attempted. (pp. 98, 102)

As a result, sympathy fails progressively and when the mother bear and her chirpy cub are about to be search-and-destroyed we find ourselves confronted with the imminence of Bambi-time, the whole parable trembling on the brink of ecological Disneyana.

Kotzwinkle is a good writer, and he is not afraid to take the kind of risks that are necessary for the production of a serious novel. But, taken on its own terms, *Doctor Rat* does not deliver, and the reasons it does not will be plain to any sympathetic reader. It's too contrived, too ingratiating, too soft at the center to carry the weight of its own intentions. (p. 102)

Robert Stone, "Soft in Tooth and Claw," in Harper's *(copyright © 1976 by* Harper's Magazine; *all rights reserved; reprinted from the June, 1976, issue by special permission), Vol 253, No. 1514, June, 1976, pp. 97-8, 102.*

ANNE LARSEN

[I imagine that *Doctor Rat*] is going to *sound* funny as hell (it isn't). I imagine that we will be told by some otherwise intelligent people that it's the kind of funny book that's going to make a lot of angry people a whole lot angrier (it won't). And worse, it's simply a bad book, a puffed-up book, claiming humility.

An animal fable with a presumed moral purpose behind it, the book, at a glance, might seem promising enough. A satire on the atrocities of human experimentation on animals, it does have behind it the traditions at least of Aesop and the allegorical satire of Orwell. But for this, for what Kotzwinkle has really given us, I was not prepared. I am not speaking of the grotesqueries of the science lab, though there are those, many of those, but of the out-and-out shallowness, the sophomoric arrogance of the book itself. It's worse than banal; it is finally, I would say, a misleading, manipulative book that is likely to pass for a highly "moral" statement, when, in fact, it has nothing very moral in it, and little that's even good. I include especially those intended-to-be moving and "eloquent evocations of animal consciousness" that are used throughout the book as interchapters punctuating the main story.

The better half of the book is its main story. . . .

[The story] is heavy-handed satire, though occasionally worth a laugh or two. It becomes after a time repetitive and dull, but there is a point in it that anyone can sympathize with. After all, nothing is really asked of the reader: *nobody* is in favor of maiming and pain.

Yet the exaggerated horrors of the experimentation in this fictional lab are another matter, as though Kotzwinkle himself, in spite of what he implies, is more than willing to *use* pain for all it's worth. . . .

[It] is interesting that Kotzwinkle's book is an animal fable that, in the end, remains about *animals,* not people. In this it departs radically, one might say foolishly, from Aesop and Orwell. Compared to what's happening to *people,* animal experimentation seems, frankly, less serious and less important—particularly when we read about experimentation that has been done on human subjects, who, like their animal friends, didn't realize they were subjects at all.

[The] rebel rats in the lab have been a very mixed bag: there were strung-out Pleasure Rats (drug-addiction), a

Christian minister rat who wore a "pink identity tag" and said things like "I can give you a profound relationship" (homosexual, of course), and several other very familiar stereotypes. They're being satirized, of course, and yet at the same time they're part of the "good" enemy force that is, justly, fighting for its freedom. One doesn't know whether Kotzwinkle is for or against them—probably both, since sentimentality is not much bothered by mutual exclusivity.

And yet the contradictions here are as nothing to the subtle and insidious contradictions implied by the interchapter sections of the book—those relentlessly gushy, misty-eyed, and nostalgic vignettes of animals in their "natural" state. I don't question, certainly, the use of animal fable or allegory, especially not when it's less excessively and more honestly done. I do question the ethics, however, of anthropomorphizing a pig or a cow to death, while at the same time crying murder.

What Kotzwinkle has done is make the dreadful and thoughtless slide from Aesop and Orwell to a flower-child's lamentable and embarrassing vision of Walt Disney. For even Walt Disney made sense: his characters were, in truth, simply people who rather charmingly looked like mice or long-eared dogs. Kotzwinkle, however, does not use one to explain the other, he just distorts both: His humans are purely, wholly, and simplistically villainous; his "good" animals are the essence of the passive, mind-blown counterculture, housed in the skins of hippopotami and chipmunks.

But let Kotzwinkle explain—I, for one, cannot.

Anne Larsen, "Did Doctor Rat Sell Out?" in The Village Voice *(reprinted by permission of* The Village Voice; *copyright © The Village Voice, Inc., 1976), Vol. XXI, No. 26, June 28, 1976, p. 45.*

HOLLIS ALPERT

There is nothing that says a suspense novel need not be well written. . . .

As familiar, even overly familiar, as the form is, it nevertheless allows for wit, cleverness, displays of arcane knowledge, daring invention, and, every now and then, good writing. A case in point is *Fata Morgana,* by William Kotzwinkle, a fine young writer previously known for such "serious" novels as *The Fan Man* and *Doctor Rat.* The title of this new work is taken from the Italian and means a mirage, especially one that is the work of a sorceress or, as employed here by Kotzwinkle, a sorcerer. (p. 23)

[Kotzwinkle takes] us on an almost dreamlike journey. The details seem real enough, but real in the way a movie is real. Though the atmosphere of nineteenth-century Paris is there—the smells of food and perfumes, the mode of dress, the dingy cafés and the great salons—it's as if the author had used a film, *Children of Paradise,* say, for research. . . .

[It] is obligatory for a suspense novel to provide answers, along with a flashy finale. But Kotzwinkle quite obviously wants to employ the form for the opportunities it provides for indulgences; for escape from the dreary realism, the psychological delving the minutiae of experience, the philosophical anguish of the important novelists. The form allows him to tell an adult fairy tale. And so the possibilities widen.

This sets him well above the more ordinary practitioners, the specialists in modern terror, the revivalists of the private eye. . . .

Kotzwinkle deals in mysteries rather than mystery; they have to do with the practice of magic, and magic is always real in imagination, if not in life. The ending of his tale might seem to be a cheat, yet it fits his theme—and the title. (p. 24)

Hollis Alpert, "Mysterious Mirage," in Saturday Review *(© 1977 by Saturday Review Magazine Corp.; reprinted with permission), Vol. 4, No. 15, April 30, 1977, pp. 23-4.*

JEROME CHARYN

"Fata Morgana" is a curious mingling of genres: detective story *and* fairy tale. It manages to pull the reader in, because William Kotzwinkle, who has written for both children and adults, is able to move from the mundane to the grotesque, from magic to hard-nosed fact, without bruising his story. . . .

Toys form a constant motif in the novel. They are "much finer than men, and much worse." The men and women in the book have all the appearances of animated dolls, with a system of "springs and balances." . . .

The novel itself reads like a small, relentless engine, fueled by whimsy and a powerful froth. The intentions are narrow; the realities are nearer to cardboard than to flesh, but the book does entertain all the way through.

Jerome Charyn, "Conjuring Tricks," in The New York Times Book Review *(© 1977 by The New York Times Company; reprinted by permission), May 1, 1977, p. 11.*

ROBERTA TOVEY

Kotzwinkle knows that mysteries are the most satisfying of books not because everyone gets his just deserts but because in the best of them there are no gratuitous elements, no existential occurences. [In *Fata Morgana*] Inspector Picard follows the trail of the gypsy Lazare, and the elements which emerge from the fraudulent glitter of Paris—the abandoned lavishness of the *masques,* the tarot cards, the jeweled gowns trailing in the filth of the Paris streets—fall magically together. The world created has a sensuous order; the ending is a necessary irritation, and Kotzwinkle rather gracelessly disregards it. But the chase itself is perfect.

Roberta Tovey, "Books Considered: 'Fata Morgana'," in The New Republic *(reprinted by permission of* The New Republic; *© 1977 The New Republic, Inc.), Vol. 176, No. 22, May 28, 1977, p. 40.*

PHOEBE-LOU ADAMS

Mr. Kotzwinkle has done the unforgivable [in *Fata Morgana*]; he has bailed out of a fantasy by turning it all into a dream. Naughty, naughty—and besides, the climactic scene is pilfered from an old movie.

Phoebe-Lou Adams, "PLA: 'Fata Morgana'," in The Atlantic Monthly *(copyright © 1977 by The Atlantic Monthly Company, Boston, Mass.; reprinted with permission), Vol. 240, No. 1, July, 1977, p. 87.*

KUNITZ, Stanley J(asspon) 1905-

An American poet, editor, essayist, translator, and journalist, Kunitz has been a critically neglected but important voice in contemporary poetry. His work is skillfully crafted, incorporating the rhythms of natural speech, and evidencing a fine ear for the musical cadence of phrases. Often considered metaphysical, his is an intensely personal poetry, exploring the mystery of self and the intricacies of time. Kunitz won a Pulitzer Prize in 1959 for *Selected Poems, 1928-1958*. (See also *CLC*, Vols. 6, 11, and *Contemporary Authors*, Vols. 41-44, rev. ed.)

A.J.M. SMITH

[*Passport to the War*] is a sincere and sound achievement. It is the work of a talented craftsman, with a sharp and elegant mind, and it concerns itself with the most significant problem of the modern world—the murderous and efficient mechanization of our environment that has invaded and corrupted the mind itself. This problem is implicit everywhere in Mr. Kunitz's poems, where under the pressure of our failure, energies that might have been concentrated upon the service of humanity or the love of God are dissipated in frustration and hysteria. This is the inescapable theme of serious modern poetry, and the war gives it the immediacy of an explosion. "How shall we uncreate that lawless energy?" is the question forced on us as we stand with Mr. Kunitz

> in the center of that man's madness,
> Deep in his trauma, as in the crater of a wound.

And the lawless energy, we realize, is not that of the enemy alone, but that of the undirected forces of mechanization and "progress" that the western world, and especially the Anglo-American world has lived by for nearly two centuries.

"In the destructive element immerse" has been the practical wisdom forced upon this poet, but the method, which has the virtues of necessity and honesty, has also its nullifying weaknesses. Mr. Kunitz is intensely sensitive, intelligent to the point of scepticism, and so agonizingly aware of the pity and horror at the base of the modern dilemma that he has been thrown off balance and has come to the point of making his most effective case against the evils of the time by illustrating them himself. Many of the war poems succumb in language and imagery to the violence, distortion, and hysteria that are the symptoms of their (and our) illness. They are the poems of a sick man in a sick world. (pp. 165-66)

"The staunchless word, my language of the wound" is the way Mr. Kunitz speaks of his poetry. The clinical themes and neurotic imagery may well be inescapable and perhaps are justified by their intensity; but they have a special danger, which is not lessened when the Grand Guignol manner is repeated in poem after poem. Specifically, the danger is that the horror and pity, which ought to be felt as universal, may seem only individual and eccentric. . . . [The] validity of the poet's tortured sense of the evil of the modern world is jeopardized (though certainly not destroyed) by the frankness with which the source of so much of it is shown to be in personal ill-adjustment. Sometimes the poet is betrayed into self-pity. "The burden of the personal" is a heavy one, and it contains much that isn't worth carrying, but Mr. Kunitz knows only too well that it cannot be laid down. (p. 166)

To risk a generalization, one would say that under the stress of the war and the long preliminary period of disintegration Mr. Kunitz has not been able to avoid developing the personal elements of distortion found in the more mannered of the early pieces. Many of the poems, early and late, are built on a scheme of simultaneously poeticizing language and distorting imagery to convey an intense experience. But we are seduced or distracted by the conceits so that we do not realize, or do not care, that the experience is not being defined and therefore not faced. . . . It is good to see that in one or two lyrics at the end of the group of war poems Mr. Kunitz has recaptured the clarity, strength, and suppleness that characterized such fine poems as the early *Change*, *Promise Me* and *The Words of the Preacher*. . . . The final poem in Part I of *Passport to the War* ranks with [*The Words of the Preacher*] as one of the great lyrics of our time. (pp. 167-68)

A.J.M. Smith, "Language of the Wound," in Poetry *(© 1944 by The Modern Poetry Association; reprinted by permission of the Editor of* Poetry*), Vol. LXIV, No. III, June, 1944, pp. 165-68.*

JOHN CIARDI

I have carried some of [Stanley Kunitz's poems] in my head for twenty years, and they still ring there in delight. Listen to the opening lines of "Deciduous Branch":

> Winter, that coils in the thickets now,
> Will glide from the fields; the swinging rain
> Be knotted with flowers; on every bough
> A bird will meditate again.

How sweetly the usual word slips fresh into the line—coils, glide, swinging, knotted, meditate—and how sweetly the rhythm sways the thought alive! Such lines are not only in the purest lyric tradition of English poetry, but do honor to that tradition. To be sure, Kunitz is not always that immediately clear. He is a poet of intellectual passions. At times one must labor to follow the subtleties of his perception. The point is that the labor will not be in vain. Kunitz is certainly the most neglected good poet of the last quarter-century.

John Ciardi, "Poetry: 'SR's' Quarterly Roundup," in Saturday Review *(entire issue copyright 1958 by Saturday Review Associates, Inc.; reprinted with permission), Vol. XLI, No. 39, September 27, 1958, p. 18.*

FRANK KERMODE

Mr. Kunitz is, after thirty years' writing, brought to us [in *Selected Poems: 1928-1958*] with rich plaudits from his fellow-American poets. He is indeed a big poet, given to traditional poses and metres, but holding them both with muscular professional skill. He is a rift-loader, a maker of weighted lines, elaborating complex figures with goldenmouth magniloquence. He will frankly use the big word, the large statement qualified only by the cleanness of its expression. 'I suffer the twentieth century,' he says, sardonically converting his suffering into pleasure before the *hypocrite lecteur*. There is variety here, and a rather Gravesian humour—note a splendid maledictory poem on a Roman pickpocket. But the central position is stilt-jack Yeatsian:

Imagination makes
Out of what stuff it can
An action fit
For a more heroic stage
Than body ever walked on.

It is good to feel such power nakedly used.

Frank Kermode, "Matters of Life and Death," in The Spectator *(© 1959 by* The Spectator; *reprinted by permission of* The Spectator), *Vol. 203, No. 6838, July 17, 1959, p. 81.**

ROBERT B. SHAW

Even if change were not so prominent among his themes, the reader of Kunitz's life work [in "The Poems of Stanley Kunitz: 1928-1978"] would have to be aware of changes time has wrought upon his style. From his first book, "Intellectual Things" (1930) through the "Selected Poems" (1958) . . . Kunitz pursued a style that even for those times was formidably ornate. His rhythms and diction harked back to the Elizabethan sonneteers and the Jacobean dramatists. In the 1960's he altered his style decisively, eschewing grand effects and writing in a language both contemporary and determinedly direct, as if in penitence for having earlier dallied with rhetorical convolutions. (p. 1)

I suspect that [Robert Lowell's "Life Studies" served as a potent example] to Kunitz, for his poems in "The Testing-Tree" (1971) and after, besides being metrically relaxed, are frequently given to autobiography and anecdote with something of Lowell's calculated casualness.

It is hard to imagine a reader liking early and later Kunitz equally well; and one can conceive of a reader who would not much care for either. To some tastes the earlier work must seem hopelessly over-upholstered. To others, the newer, pared-down poems must reflect a drab, Danish-modern esthetic that is just now beginning to seem as dated as iambic pentameter seemed to the 60's. I think it could be said, not so much in complaint as in description, that Kunitz has rarely mastered a middle style. . . .

[This] poetry is very evidently aware of its precedents in theme and tone. Aside from the Renaissance precursors I have mentioned, one can discern Yeats and Blake in the background of several of the earlier poems. One thinks also of Theodore Roethke, who became Kunitz's friend and enthusiastic reader in the 1930's. . . .

The two men have a remarkable amount in common. . . . Both write of women in a tone of Petrarchan exaltation. . . . Both are acutely sensitive to the mysteries of organic life around them. . . . Both attempt in writing to reconcile themselves to a father too soon dead for them as sons to have truly known. Both see man as an oxymoron, immortal and perishing at once, spirit at odds with flesh; and both make forays into Christian mysticism as they endeavor to transcend this condition. . . .

If the "principal of being" that unifies this collection remains somewhat obscure, there are numerous triumphs to be found in each of the poet's intelligently assumed manners. There are enough poems that succeed on their own terms to outweigh the deviations into fustian or flatness.

Among the more memorable early pieces are several in quatrains that well display Kunitz's rhythmic finesse: "Particular Lullaby," "Deciduous Branch" and "He." . . . "Benediction," in trimeter couplets, is distinguished among the love poems for delicacy of form and feeling. "Careless Love" and "Geometry of Moods" are brainy and dense conceits sustained with authority from their first to their final lines. So is "The Science of the Night" in its more ample way. Kunitz often writes memorably of the world of sleep and dreams, as in this poem. (It must be admitted that his dream imagery can run away with him: "Father and Son" has to fight hard to survive the notorious line "The night nailed like an orange to my brow.") "The Dragonfly" is beautifully and minutely observed . . . and the fine detailing intensifies the impact of the macabre conclusion.

Some of the newer poems stand out for the candid and compelling use they make of memory: "The Testing-Tree," "The Magic Curtain," "Quinnapoxet" and "River Road." "Words for the Unknown Makers" celebrates American primitive art with a geniality and charm that are scarce in today's verse. "King of the River" is a startling, incantatory poem in which the Pacific salmon's awesome trip upriver to spawn . . . symbolizes the aging ego's approach to death, which is at once a dissolution and a consummation. . . .

This poem is emblematic in more ways than one: Kunitz's willingness to risk bombast, platitude or bathos in his contemplation of what he calls "mystery" is evident in it. Mystery—of the self, of time, of change and fate—is not facilely dispelled but approached with imaginative awe in his work; in our rationalistic century this is swimming against the stream. This is a form of artistic heroism; and when Kunitz's scorning of safety meshes firmly with his technical skills, the outcome is poetry of unusual power and depth. (p. 20)

Robert B. Shaw, "A Book of Changes," in The New York Times Book Review *(© 1979 by The New York Times Company; reprinted by permission), July 22, 1979, pp. 1, 20.*

HARRY MARTEN

[Stanley Kunitz is] forthright in facing and communicating the hopes and hazards of man's right knowledge [in *The Poems of Stanley Kunitz, 1928-1978*]. "A poet," he tells us, "needs to keep his wilderness alive inside him," seeking his "darkest Africa." The pursuit of dangerous places takes Kunitz through several poetic incarnations. His verses go from dense and highly figured to almost transparently clear. The Platonic abstractions of a young man experiencing mostly *Intellectual Things*—as Kunitz aptly titled his first volume—mature into poems firmly fastened to the realities of our day. Kunitz relies increasingly on a mix of memory and immediate observation to trigger his poetic discoveries. He perceives universals in minute particulars, and his loving attention to detail is telling. . . .

The verses can seem relentlessly grim. . . . Yet Kunitz offers "Signs and Portents" of both pain *and* possibility. Throughout the volume we explore with him the depths of his own being, and find there, even in "darkest night" when the poet "roamed the wreckage," the promise of life energies renewed. . . .

While Kunitz's art has changed with the years, his preoccupations and themes have not. The epigraph for his first book marked the path clearly: "For the tear is an intellectual thing." Mind and emotion cannot be separated whatever the difficulties of their interweaving.

Harry Marten, "Warren and Kunitz: Poets in the American Grain," in Book World—The Washington Post *(© 1979,* The Washington Post*), September 30, 1979, p. 10.**

L

LEVINE, Philip 1928-

Levine is an American poet, critic, and editor. His poetry is peopled with unhappy, unlucky characters depicted at the dramatic moment of personal defeat. He is the recipient of the 1980 National Book Critics Circle award in poetry for *Seven Years from Somewhere* and *Ashes: Poems New and Old.* (See also *CLC,* Vols. 2, 4, 5, 9, and *Contemporary Authors,* Vols. 9-12, rev. ed.)

IRA SADOFF

At a time when much American poetry has become *self*-conscious, exploring the psyche almost to the point of narcissism, Philip Levine, one of our finest poets, continues to write poetry that explores the relation between self and other, between the personal and social worlds. His poetic ancestors are the most vulnerable and feeling Spanish surrealists, Vallejo and Hernandez, and he uses many of their poetic devices in his work: the catalogue, repetition, and the interrogative. Levine is also a born story-teller, and he uses his narrative gifts in his latest book, *The Names of the Lost,* to name, to call back, the metaphoric and literal dead, to tell their stories, stories which they could not tell themselves. (p. 241)

A number of poems serve as dedications to political revolutionaries, those who have lost their lives in causes not yet won; Levine cries out for explanations, a sense of moral justice, really, to compensate for their tragedies. These poems are often melancholy, powerful, though occasionally a little sentimental. But it is the memory of the poet's own Detroit childhood, where political realities take on a haunting particularity, that calls forth his greatest powers, his descriptions of the nobility and harsh realities of urban life. . . . (pp. 241-42)

Memory, then, becomes an important center for the book. To remember, to recall, is to honor the "lost," the dead, to learn from, if not recover, the past. As he says in "To the Poets of Chile": "Someone / must remember it over / and over, must bring / it home. . . ." Memory is also central because the book begins, in a Job-like fashion, to question the irrevocable process of time, the process which leads us only to death. The personal obsession of the book (and of Levine's previous and brilliant book, titled *1933*) becomes the justification of loss: the loss of those we love and those who touch our lives, and our own inevitable death. (p. 242)

The Names of the Lost creates a process of discovery, beginning by questioning the inevitability of loss: "Shall I ask / how many men, dying, passed me / the blood of their voices, the spittle / oiling their groins?" And is it possible that the poet himself, with strong memories of his youth and a history with the woman he loves, "will come at last / to dirt and stone and love them?" Gradually the book attempts to move toward acceptance. . . . Still, there is a dialectic between community and decay, imagistically between blossoming and burning, a link between him and the past, personally and politically. As for the future, "which grows like a scar," Levine fears these connections will be lost; this fear is usually confronted when dealing with his own son, to whom he carries, via the fables of story-telling, the lessons of the past. . . .

Finally, by the end of the book, in "And the Trains Go On," he returns to the necessity and limitations of his need to bring the past forward. . . . (p. 243)

Ira Sadoff, "A Chronicle of Recent Poetry," in The Antioch Review *(copyright © 1977 by the Antioch Review Inc., reprinted by permission of the Editors), Vol. 35, Nos. 2-3, Spring-Summer, 1977, pp. 237, 241-44.**

STEPHEN YENSER

Auden once observed that every poem testifies to a rivalry between Ariel and Prospero. Ariel urges the poet to make "a verbal paradise, a timeless world of pure play" that affords some relief from the historical world with all its dilemmas and suffering. Prospero, concerned more with truth than with beauty, exhorts him to reveal life as it really is, to bring us face to face with "the problematic, the painful, the disorderly, the ugly" and thus to "free us from self-enchantment and deception." While any poem will owe something to each of these advocates, it is usually possible to decide whether a poem and occasionally whether a poet is "Ariel-dominated" or "Prospero-dominated." Few have listened as attentively to Prospero as Philip Levine. Ariel sometimes draws him aside, but Levine is too much a product of the fallen world to be comfortable for long in the realm of "pure play." (p. 101)

[The world of Levine's poems] is all bleared and smeared with toil and pain. Selections from Doré's *Inferno* illustrations might have accompanied the poems in Levine's most recent and grimly impressive volume [*The Names of the*

Lost]. . . . For Levine, the plight of the man in "Waiting," convicted on the testimony of a lying witness and sweating out the ninth year of his sentence, merely exaggerates an all too common condition.

Since that condition is political, so is much of Levine's poetry, as he had to insist in a recent *Partisan Review* [interview]. . . . When [Levine] speaks of "the agony of living" he is thinking chiefly of the life of the working class in a system in which "the people in power have no compassion." While his own compassionate skepticism saves him from being narrowly partisan, Levine is our notable heir to the radicalism of the 1930s, a descendant of Henry Roth who has read Neruda and Vallejo closely. (pp. 101-02)

Buenaventura Durruti, the leader of the left wing of the anarchist movement during the Spanish Civil War, to whom Levine dedicates *The Names of the Lost,* stands at the center of this volume. . . . Levine follows his dedication . . . with an epigraph—*"and the world he said is growing here in my heart this moment"*—that echoes Durruti's comments in an interview. . . . (p. 102)

Prospero counsels realism; Levine's epigraph is no declaration of faith. Seen in the light of many of these poems, it might even be read as a bitterly mocking epitaph, not only for Durruti and the *anarquistas* but also for the vision behind the movement. Levine recalls Durruti's vow in a derisive passage in "Gift for a Believer." In a friend's vision Durruti whispered that he would never forget his comrades "who died believing they carried / a new world there in their hearts"—but when Durruti died, "he forgot." Levine knows how lesser exigencies paralyze conviction: later in this poem he tells how he once swore never to forget an early, radicalizing experience at the Chevy plant, and yet eventually "the memory slept, and I bowed / my head so that I might live." If Durruti's faith survives today, he implies, it survives as tenuously as the wretched garden at the end of "Autumn Again," where "Down the oiled path of cans / and inner tubes in the field / by the river" a young mechanic struggles to keep his beans and herbs alive.

The garden recurs so often in *The Names of the Lost* that it becomes a unifying element closely related to the *"world growing here in my heart this moment."* The poet's wife almost always appears tending her plants ("New Season," "Autumn Again," "The Falling Sky," "Another Life," "My Son and I"), as though she embodied Durruti's spirit, or as though the growth he envisioned depended upon such steady, intense devotion. Levine's own detachment from the family garden reminds us that he has little faith in a new world, and the advent of the "New Season" seems to bear him out. While "the future grows / like a scar," the garden, so painstakingly cultivated each day, suffers at night the slow fury of the snails: "the rhododendrons shrivel / like paper under water, all / the small secret mouths are feeding / on the green heart of the plum." Surely Levine is playing those lines against the memory, continually imperiled, of Durruti's words. But of course—and from this qualification spring both the tension and the occasional self-righteousness in this book—Levine does finally remember. Nullifidian though he might be, he has his own plot, as the poems prove. His grafting of irony on to idealism is an attempt to develop a sustaining belief. (pp. 103-04)

The need to bring it all home, in both senses, shapes a number of these poems, including "For the Fallen," a moving elegy for Durruti. . . .

> The comrades must have known
> it was over, and Joaquín
> Ascaso, staring at the earth
> that had opened so quickly
> for his brothers must
> have whispered *soon.*
> Soon the boy rose
> from his desk and went
> into the darkness
> congealing in cold parlours
> or in the weariness
> of old pistons, in the gasps
> of men and women asleep
> and dreaming as the bus
> stalls and starts on the way
> home from work.

Technically austere, as befits both the scene and Prospero's temperament, this passage is nonetheless subtly put together. The images in its narrow gauge lines flow as smoothly as in a film. Like much of his work, it calls up Eisenstein, some grainy black and white silent picture (for Levine's work is unusually chiaroscurist, his people rarely speak), the point of its montage unmistakably political. The covert analogy between the uneasy sleepers and the poorly running engine implies and implicates a society in which people with dreams but no power become worn parts in the machinery. As the boy rises from the desk, years pass; and with the unobtrusive shift in tense the past dissolves into the present, elegy into indictment. Levine sometimes considers Durruti's acts alms for oblivion, but he cannot forget their pertinence.

This volume's title, just near enough paradox to snag the attention, joins these barely reconcilable feelings. It derives from "And the Trains Go On," a highly concentrated meditative lyric which grows from memories of riding the rails with an unidentified companion some twenty-five years ago. Levine starts in the past tense, then shifts to present and future tenses in combination with images drawn from the Korean War to conjure the future, and finally modulates into a present tense that recovers the past. . . . [The] poem's real achievement is its conclusion, where Levine and his friend come "back the long / tangled road that leads us home":

> Through Flat Rock going east
> picking up speed, the damp fields
> asleep in moonlight. You stand
> beside me, breathing the cold
> in silence. When you grip
> my arm hard and lean way out
> and shout out the holy names
> of the lost neither of us is scared
> and our tears mean nothing.

These lines bring the past incident rushing into the present, thus accomplishing in small one of the book's aims, and they image the movement into the future. (pp. 104-06)

The lost began to haunt Levine in *On the Edge* (1963), although he did not yet know they were to be his abiding subject. . . . [The] first volume's more interesting poems, not all political, try to shock us into [a sort of awareness]. "Gangrene" does so as literally as possible. Beginning with a description of electrical and other tortures of political prisoners, packaged in fussy syllabic stanzas, it then rounds on the reader, *ipso facto* "secretly thrilled by / the circus of excrement." . . . For the American who might really believe himself innocent, Levine juxtaposes "Gangrene" with a searingly objective poem about a horse flayed alive by the bomb dropped on Hiroshima. In various ways, "L'Homme et la Bête," "Small Game," and "The Turning" serve the same end: Levine means to strip the reader of his own integument of moral pretension.

"Political facts" motivated many of the poems in *Not This Pig* (1968), but frequently Levine's animus took the form of satire on bourgeois conformity, viewed once more as the spiritually bankrupting price of admission to the system. (pp. 106-07)

"Heaven" is an eerie, softly-hued poem, but these others, although smooth enough—no, partly because so smooth seem thin and dated as old coins. The poem with the wonderfully skewed title, "Animals Are Passing from Our Lives," will always seem newly minted. A parable of the blinkered "progress" of the consumer society, it fascinates both because of its framing concept (how many poets would dream of adopting the point of view of the first little pig in the children's game?) and its execution of detail. (p. 107)

But such a poem is a tiny territory discovered and fully exploited at once, just as "Heaven" is an enchanting island to which one does not return. "The Midget" might stand for Levine's entrance into a country large and potentially productive as the Spain in which it is set. The poet is accosted, in a workers' bar in Barcelona once frequented by Durruti, by a midget who will not be bought off or discouraged by pleas to be left alone. . . . Few poems deal as ruthlessly with our attempts to dissociate ourselves from the world's grief or dramatize as convincingly our utter moral defenselessness in the face of the claims of the poor and powerless. . . .

Levine has never shaken that obstinate midget. His paradoxical image of potency was prophetic: from such narrow circumstances, whether in Spain or the United States, most of his finest poems have come. (p. 108)

Levine's home turf is the urban setting, so it makes whimsical sense for *Not This Pig* to be dedicated in part to "the cities that are here, Detroit, Fresno, Barcelona." But often in *Red Dust* and throughout *Pili's Wall,* both published by small presses in 1971, Levine explored the rural areas of the country of the spirit that he had settled in. . . . None of *Pili's Wall,* a sequence of ten lyrics, has ever been reprinted, perhaps because the accompanying photos would pose a problem in a larger edition. Its limited printing is a pity, but one has to approve the decision not to publish the poems alone; for although they never refer to the wall's graffiti, reproduced in the photos, the two media come to seem inseparable. Levine never quite says so, but it seems that Pili, a "Spanish girlchild," chipped these figures into the wall. They are her poem at the same time that they inspire Levine's, which is also primitive, elliptical, out of perspective—and written in a tight free verse rather than the syllabics that predominate in the earlier volumes.

Through most of the sequence Levine assumes Pili's point of view, while she in turn merges with the elements of her small but inexhaustible world: a lost and frightened dog, a weary shepherd, even the wall itself, as in section VII, the germ of "They Feed They Lion":

> Out of saying No
> No to the barn swallow, No
>
> to the hurled stone
> No to the air
>
> out of *you can't*
> to the crying grain, *you won't*
>
> to the lost river
> of blackening ivy
>
> out of blind
> out of deaf, closed, still
>
> I stand and stand and stand into
> this wall.

While the syntax of this section owes an obvious debt to Whitman, the definition of self in terms of gritty negation is pure Levine. Again, the identifications at the heart of the sequence recall "There Was a Child Went Forth," but only Levine could so vitalize a wall that it could give a detailed, inventive account of its birth. . . . The concluding negative, Levine's cachet, is more positive and specific than that in "Not This Pig." In this context of "The low houses of the poor" and a hardscrabble life the wall embodies the refusal of those who built it not to exist.

The force that drives the wall up also powers the rough beast in the ferocious, exhilarating title poem in *They Feed They Lion* (1972), but here the focus is once more on the city:

> Out of burlap bags, out of bearing butter,
> Out of black bean and wet slate bread,
> Out of the acids of rage, the candor of tar,
> Out of creosote, gasoline, drive shafts, wooden dollies,
> They Lion grow.

The tremendous compression corresponds to the constraint of the energy Levine at once eulogizes and stands in awe of, like Michaelangelo's slaves, their bodies straining to free themselves from the marble. And like the sculptures, the poem catches moments at which raw material converts itself into raw power, and it too elicits a kinaesthetic response. . . . Or perhaps we should take our cue from the black dialect it draws much of its strength from and think of it as a sort of apocalyptic jazz. In any case, Levine's Lion is plainly a later, fiercer version of his wall and an earlier, more joyful version of the world growing in the workers' hearts.

Someone is always asking whether the good political poem is possible in the United States today. An affirmative answer can only be concrete, and to confront the question with "They Feed They Lion." . . . "They Feed They Lion" celebrates latent power at least as much as it condemns oppression, and its union of labor and nature (as in "caves," "reeds," and "grained") augurs something closer to the proverbial inheritance than to revolution, but it is not the less political on those accounts—though it might be the more visionary. (pp. 108-11)

In spite of the harshness of the lives depicted, [many of the poems in *They Feed They Lion* are] laced with a certain delicacy, which in strange combination with repugnant subjects generates some of Levine's most original work. At one end of the spectrum is "¡Hola Miguelin!", a lovely lyric about a young Spanish neighbor just risen from love-making, which is all delicacy except for its last line's hint of a *frisson*. At the other end is "The Children's Crusade," an inscrutable tale in which a little girl who is an accomplice in the gruesome murder of her father wears, very precisely, "silver ignition keys hooked in her / pierced ears." . . . [If] "They Feed They Lion" is Levine's "Second Coming," "Angel Butcher" is his "Dialogue of Self and Soul," its "dark valley" being analogous to Yeats's ditch and its burning cities Levine's special object of love and hate.

But Yeats's Self praises life as he has known it, and to the extent that Levine does likewise his anger at its political facts must be affected. His discontent can afford only so much nostalgia. In *1933* (1974) Levine's emphasis shifted. As he said in the interview, this volume is "less aggressive" than its predecessor. It includes a number of his best realistic vignettes, but as its title hints, its wistfulness at least balances its rancor. (pp. 111-12)

Yet Levine's nostalgia encourages the soft and the sentimental. Sometimes one cannot believe—or does not know how to believe—his claims, as when he says in "1933" (the year of his father's death) that "Once in childhood the stars held still all night / the moon swelled like a plum but white and silken." The standing still of the stars is patently symbolic and the image of the moon hardly calculated to substantiate the "Once." In "Once in May" he recalls that he stood "all afternoon under heaven / with water in my pockets, / salt in my socks, naming / the grains of the sea." But it is no more clear what that too familiar "naming" might really mean than it is where else he might have stood on the beach. At such moments Prospero yields the floor to Ariel, but Ariel, flustered and out of practice, blurts out the first thing that comes into his head.

Nostalgia perhaps breeds another kind of self-indulgence in "Letters for the Dead," an ambitious elegiac poem 350 lines long which is crisply written, particular at every step, yet confusing as a whole. The problem is simply that it needs the fleshing out one often gets at readings. The relationships among its people remain stubbornly obscure, and the reader is so bedeviled by ambiguous second person pronouns that he can hardly tell how many people are involved. What is the purpose? I am not certain, but the vivid obscurity gives one an especially strong sense of being privy to an intensely personal transaction. For some readers the poem will prove the exceeding tolerance of Mill's definition of successful poetry as "feeling confessing itself to itself in moments of solitude." Yet one values just this quality of seeming "*over*heard" in Levine's recent political poems. They spurn what Mill called "eloquence"—"feeling pouring itself forth to other minds, courting their sympathy, or endeavoring to influence their belief, or move them to passion or to action." "And the Trains Go On" and "For the Fallen," far from having designs on us, allow us to eavesdrop on meditations. If occasional obscurity were the expense of the mode, it would be worth the price.

The Names of the Lost often reworks the political themes of *They Feed They Lion* in the elegiac manner of *1933*. . . . [A lost black] man rambles on about his prison terms and other things [in "Another Life"]:

> about the poem he can write will follow
> me all the way home, try my chair,
> eat from my plate, take my voice
> until I'm the one walks all night
> in the rain, gets stopped by the cops
> at dawn, and with the sky reddening
> spread my arms and legs against the car
> and feel the gloved hand
> slide over my balls and pause
> and go on, leaving nothing.

The transition is flawless. If it is impossible to say whether the frisking is Levine's experience too or just the convict's, that seems to be the point.

At exactly this point one has to voice a reservation. The question—which threatens to raise itself even in the case of "I was the man, I suffered, I was there"—is whether the identification does not trivialize the experience it means to bring home, whether the technique has not subverted the subject. The final image means something for the convict that it cannot mean for Levine. He confronts the difficulty in "For the Fallen": "Look at your hands. They / are not scarred by / the cigarettes of the police." But then "For the Poets of Chile" opens with these lines:

> Today I called for you
> my death, like a cup
> of creamy milk I
> could drink in the cold dawn,
> I called you to come
> down soon.

Could any poem accommodate this passage? It might illustrate one problem with Mill's concept of poetry, which does not allow for the awareness of audience that can cut the grease of mawkishness that often films over conversations with the self. When Levine concludes with an image of the daughter of a slain political prisoner setting the breakfast table with "the tall glasses / for the milk" that she and her mother must drink each morning, the easy symmetry and the presumptuous equation betray whatever emotion has survived the opening lines.

Levine's rhetorical questions can also lead him to the brink of the bathetic. . . . [Take] the passage in "Ask the Roses" where Levine demands: "Has anyone told the sea it must count / its tears and explain each one / has anyone told the blood / how long it must crust the sheets." Isn't this really a way of making witty images, a means of setting in motion a machine that can process, in the name of suffering, any material that comes to hand?

Still, such moments are rare in this volume. Besides "And the Trains Go On," "For the Fallen," and "Gift for a Believer," *The Names of the Lost* contains several other poems nearly as compelling, including "New Season," "My Son and I," "On the Murder of Lieutenant José Castillo by the Falangist Bravo Martinez, July 12, 1936," and "No One Remembers." A few others, such as "A Late Answer" and "Wednesday," are admirably done though more modest attempts. (pp. 113-15)

References to rising and falling run throughout this volume ("You," "Let It Begin," "Another Life," "Gift for a Believer," and "For the Fallen," for example), and the tension between the impulses they embody—parallel to that between remembering and forgetting—is at its very heart. A section of "For the Fallen," where Levine transports us to the cemetery in which Durruti is buried, will serve as synecdoche:

You
can go down on your knees
and pray that the spirit
of men and women come back
and inhabit this failing flesh
but if you listen well
your heart will ask
you to stand, under
the fading sun or
the rising moon, it
doesn't matter, either
alone or breathing as you
do now the words
of the fallen and the slow
clouds of diesel exhaust.

Within the intricate local counterpointing, we might take as summarizing lines the two on "the fading sun" and "the rising moon," where the attribution of "rising" to the weaker "moon" nearly redresses the slight imbalance caused by the stronger position of that second adjective. In the sentence as a whole, the foreknowledge of the futility of rising up nearly frustrates the urge to do so. The standing must be accomplished, after all, within sight of "the fallen." And the "heart" (again one remembers Durruti's words) is saddled with the "failing flesh."

Not that bowing down is to be despised. On the contrary, the endurance it represents has often approximated heroism in Levine's work. . . . Lacking the dynamism of "They Feed They Lion," "For the Fallen" might not be as immediately appealing, but it just might be more accurate, a poem Prospero could approve more quickly—as well as a harder one to write, or at least to be felt through, to have brought home.

If few others in this volume can stand with the prodigious poems in *They Feed They Lion,* we must remember that we do not have the right to expect such poems and can only be grateful when they appear. Perhaps not even Levine has the right to expect them. Randall Jarrell told us that a good poet is "someone who manages, in a lifetime of standing out in thunderstorms, to be struck by lightning five or six times." Levine has already been struck at least that many times, and Lord knows no one is more likely to continue standing out in thunderstorms. (pp. 116-17)

Stephen Yenser, "Bringing It Home," in Parnassus: Poetry in Review *(copyright © Poetry in Review Foundation), Vol. 6, No. 1, Fall-Winter, 1977, pp. 101-17.*

SYDNEY LEA

Philip Levine's characters are specifically not the masters of their need. The opening passage of *The Names of the Lost* signals that it too will be filled with wakenings, but not into home:

When the streetcar stalled on Joy Road,
the conductor finished his coffee, puffed
into his overcoat, and went to phone in.
The Hungarian punch-press operator wakened
alone, 7000 miles from home, pulled down
his orange cap and set out. If he saw
the winter birds scuffling in the cinders,
if he felt it was the dawn of a new day,
he didn't let on . . .
("On the Birth of Good and Evil During the Long Winter of '28")

The punch-press operator is literally—as so many of Levine's lost are metaphorically—a Displaced Person, his life and mind mysterious. Does he expect or even want the revelation, the dawn of a new day, the revolution which Pack has dismissed? We don't know; hence the poet's own frustration, for he at least yearns to transform this gritty tableau. . . .

But Levine moots his general desire to make large changes, to forge grand significances, by honestly presenting all that stands in the way. Neither breast-beater nor self-styled vatic, he reveals the perilous longings of the Inquiring Spirit, Coleridge's Mariner, say, or Milton's Satan, and he confronts the full implications of the latter's famous contention that "the mind is its own place." It is as if some god had indeed fated the heirs of such subjectivism always to lack a home. (p. 118)

[A] poet's titles are telling, and Levine includes "No One Remembers," "For the Fallen," "For the Poets of Chile," "And the Trains Go On." He is a master of the tragedy of transience and alienation, of the wide meeting of souls. For him, even the family . . . is unfamiliar: he frequently tells us that his children "have grown away." . . . The very closest associate is almost uncanny, so that all fellows are strangers, all moments of tenderness exquisitely tenuous. . . . (pp. 118-19)

For Levine's lost, the mind *is* its own place, a fact which persistently vetoes the poet's wish for a revealed wholeness and community. . . .

Belief in and doubt of a possible sharing; satisfaction and dissatisfaction with surfaces: simple differences in temperament affect all detail, including the way in which [Levine] stands in the natural world. (p. 119)

[In "New Season"] Levine summons recurrent loss and strife, not peaceable continuity, from his reading of the landscape: he runs together his senile mother, the Detroit riots of '43, the feebleness of his aged cat, and ends by undercutting [durability and gentle gradualism.] . . . [The burning willow in the poem] subtly reminds us of Levine's urge for revelation—his search for some means to integrate and ennoble this frankly sordid and fragmented instant—but the poem acknowledges its unattainability. The search for a cohering Truth is vitiated by things-as-they-are: the foliage shrivels like paper under water, and we cannot miss the bitter implications for Levine's own writings. It is the bitterness that closes his volume in "To My God in His Sickness," for this sickness is that He does not exist, that there *is* no transcending Principle to gather up and redeem the names (or the poems) of the lost. Levine anticipates a great blank page. (p. 120)

Sydney Lea, "Wakings in Limbo," in Chicago Review *(reprinted by permission of* Chicago Review; *copyright © 1978 by* Chicago Review), *Vol. 30, No. 1, Summer, 1978, pp. 116-24.**

PHOEBE PETTINGELL

The title of Philip Levine's new collection, *7 Years from Somewhere,* . . . refers to an encounter with Berber herdsmen in North Africa, where the disoriented poet was seeking directions. Though they shared no common language, a fleeting communion was achieved that seems, in retrospect, highly significant to the writer. "I have been lost since," he mourns, "and I could sleep a moment and waken / in the world we made / and will never call ours." . . .

Although Levine has a better idea of where he's going than most of his contemporaries, a sense of displacement in his work sounds a continual threnody for the disunity of mankind. He is particularly concerned with the class struggle and the resistance to injustice. "A lot of the rage one encounters in contemporary poetry has to do with the political facts of our lives," he has said. But cynics who associate "political poetry" with strident declamation or simple-minded dogmatism will have to revise their thinking in the face of his humanism. "When I say I'm a romantic poet," he insists, "it seems to me that I feel the human is boundless." This conviction that each man is everyman, and worth more than any impersonal system or cause, underlies both the rage and the tenderness evident in his work.

Over the years, Levine's style has become increasingly straightforward, spare, unadorned. His poems are charged with emotion, yet are never sentimental: He does not substitute literary reactions for actual feelings. Material is often drawn from his own epiphanies and revelations. . . .

The heroism of defiance is often expressed in Levine's poetry through his obsession with the anarchist martyrs of the Spanish Civil War. . . . (p. 16)

In *7 Years,* "Francisco, I'll Bring You Red Carnations" makes the witness of the anarchist Ascaso a brilliant symbol for man's unquenchable spirit. Evoking the dream of freedom "that goes on in spite of slums, / in spite of death clouds," the poet promises Ascaso, "when we give it up with our last / breaths someone will gasp / it home to their lives." The red carnations of the title remind us that the flower's name derives from the same root as "carnal," and will "celebrate the unbroken promise" of lives that once were "frail and flesh," but have become symbols of hope. "The hammered little blade" of Francisco Ascaso's spirit proves to be a more obdurate object than all the "industrial filth and / the burning mists of gasoline" that defile modern Barcelona, or than the pollution of Franco's police state. None of the many bouquets Levine has offered his spiritual comrades is more beautiful than this one.

In another sense, however, the martyrs are merely aspects of Levine's death-haunted imagination. A character speaks for the poet when he complains during World War II that "except for the dying / this would be heaven and I, / 37 years old would be a man I could talk to." Paradoxically, this refusal to dissociate oneself from the suffering of others is an affirmation of as much wholeness as we can hope to achieve. . . . [The] movement of *7 Years from Somewhere* is toward reconciliations, and the belief that one must "love his life because it is like no other." . . .

Believing that poetry is a "public good," he makes his the antithesis of art for art's sake (even if, characteristically, he appreciates different styles in others). And the high seriousness of his verse shows up the frivolity of expression, the insipidness of imagination of many contemporary poets. Philip Levine's integrity is salt to our jaded palates. (p. 17)

Phoebe Pettingell, "The Politics of Philip Levine," in The New Leader *(© 1979 by the American Labor Conference on International Affairs, Inc.), Vol. LXII, No. 16, August 13, 1979, pp. 16-17.*

HERBERT LEIBOWITZ

[From] the beginning of his poetic career, Philip Levine has focused on two themes with ritual consistency: the tribulations of the powerless and the Spanish Civil War. A child of the working class who grew up in Detroit during the Depression, Mr. Levine has returned again and again in his poems to the lives of factory workers trapped by poverty and the drudgery of the assembly line, which breaks the body and scars the spirit. The lurid fires of the foundries serve as a backdrop to the prevailing greyness. In the best poems of his three major volumes—"They Feed They Lion" (1972), "1933" (1974) and "The Names of the Lost" (1976)—Mr. Levine became the elegist of lost souls beaten down by forces they could not understand or control. By providing brief verse chronicles of their struggles to survive . . . and by conferring names on their anonymous selves, Mr. Levine could partially reinstate these victims in our consciousness, even if he could not rescue them from the malevolence of history. . . . The empathy of these poems made them seem like urgent political acts.

Mr. Levine's other obsession has been that "kingdom of agony," the Spanish Civil War. Though he was too young to fight in that war, it embodies for him the historical exemplum: a people's uprising that succeeded, quixotically, for a few rare days in hinting at what a genuine egalitarian society might be, only to be crushed by Franco's brute force. Like Orwell in "Homage to Catalonia," though far more sentimentally, Mr. Levine is driven to celebrate the common people ground down by exploitation and pain. The poet's "Spanish self," as he calls it, is kin to his Detroit self. Both bear witness to a visionary ideal destroyed.

These themes and emotions continue in Philip Levine's two new books ["Ashes" and "7 Years from Somewhere"]. . . . An uneven collection of lyrics, "Ashes" is quietly introspective, thoughtful, impersonal. The style of "In the New Sun" and "The End of Your Life," for example, achieves a heightened simplicity. Objects take on a luminous presence and delicate tints so that we see them freshly. . . .

Despite occasional lapses into frayed surrealism and mechanical "On the Road" poems, "Ashes" seems balanced and modest, a relief from Mr. Levine's preoccupation with exorcising his demons.

"7 Years From Somewhere," by contrast, is a real disappointment. Reading these poems is like watching a veteran prospector digging for gold in a nearly exhausted vein. There are a surprisingly large number of poetic reveries about childhood and adolescence, embarrassing for the reader to eavesdrop on. . . .

Slack language and imagery also mar Mr. Levine's Spanish Civil War poem, "Francisco, I'll Bring You Red Carnations." (p. 15)

"7 Years From Somewhere" is filled with . . . threadbare language. Mr. Levine once remarked in an interview that he was not interested in language itself; he wished his words to be so transparent that the reader could see through them. But when language calls attention to itself by its lackluster appearance on the page, as in most of the poems in "7 Years From Somewhere," all the reader sees through is the poet. . . .

Mr. Levine has always shunned rhetoric as if it were the gilded speech of reactionary politics, somehow synonymous with beautiful, sordid lies. . . . There are perilous limits to a plain style when it is used carelessly under the pressures of strong feeling: bathos and flatness, the absence of texture. Mr. Levine's inner critic needs more leeway to demand rigor and invention. (p. 31)

Herbert Leibowitz, "Lost Souls, Lost Cause," in The New York Times Book Review *(© 1979 by The New York Times Company; reprinted by permission), October 7, 1979, pp. 15, 30-1.*

W. S. Di PIERO

The simultaneous publication of [*Ashes* and *7 Years From Somewhere*] . . . persuades us again that if poetry comes as naturally as leaves to a tree—as Keats said it must—it will be singular and exciting and new, however wintry its theme. Levine's high theme is the tragic detachment of self from the world, sometimes an embittered withdrawal, sometimes a brutal cutting off by outside forces, a course redeemed in rare moments by desperate joinings and communings. His subject, as in all his books since *They Feed They Lion* in 1972, is his own history . . . as it overlays and collides with modern Spanish history. From these materials he has drawn an occasionally stern and moving elegiac poetry.

Levine's best poems are those in which he finely calibrates the brooding presence of past configurations—friends and family, places, historical events—as they compel his imagination here and now. History is no plodding continuity of events but an instantaneous presence, and Levine's language seeks to accomodate this intense pressure. He has always been a poet of rage, but now, in his middle age, much of it is directed toward the weariness of words, "as though the earth / were tired of our talk / and wanted peace, an end / to promises, perhaps / an end to us." He still points his anger at anything that mocks or diminishes life, as in the cruel poetry of the factory in "The Life Ahead." His anger feeds on yearning, his wish to discover and speak from "the place within me / where I am every / man and woman, the trees / floating in the cold haze / of January." This kind of wish may strike some readers as overextended, gross, Romantic, but I think its intensity is redeemed by the purity of its origins in the felt life, in situation, character and event.

But Levine is not always as demanding of himself as he ought to be. There are poems in both books ("Here and Now" and "Milkweed" in *7 Years,* for example, and "Everything" and "Montjuich" in *Ashes*) which lack the clear intellectual focus of his better poems; when his *rigor* of feeling weakens, the poems sink into an almost pietistic complacency. And when his passion goes undisciplined, the poems' sentiments seem little more than an obligation to contemporary conventions or to his own sense of charming endings. . . . Because his poetry is for the most part placed in dramatic situations, and because these dramatize the decisions of selfhood (how, for example, we must learn to live with what suffices, and how this may be an unexpected richness), Levine risks a kind of melodrama which has the absolute look of sincerity I mentioned earlier. It must be said, however, that in Levine's case this is a flaw of a high order, commensurate with his high ambition.

There is a sentimentality peculiar to American poets entering mid-life, and it touches Levine as it does Hugo, Stern, Ignatow and others. They tend to exaggerate the drama of endurance and to make cult of experience, of their griefs and hardships, though their tone is generally stoical and composed. The result is a facsimile of self-knowledge, soft answers instead of stern Yeatsian truths. (This may have something to do with the long time these poets had to wait before their voices were widely heard.) Levine is strongest when he disciplines himself away from this temptation. When his poems display little or no sense of self-importance, they become the most important poems of all. . . . (pp. 567-68)

W. S. Di Piero, "A Poet of Rage," in Commonweal *(copyright © 1979 Commonweal Publishing Co., Inc.; reprinted by permission of Commonweal Publishing Co., Inc.), Vol. CVI, No. 18, October 12, 1979, pp. 567-68.*

* * *

LEWIS, C(live) S(taples) 1898-1963

Born in Ireland, Lewis was an English novelist, essayist, critic, author of children's books, poet, and autobiographer. Although a distinguished medieval scholar, Lewis is known predominantly as a writer of fantasy literature. His conversion to Catholicism was perhaps the most important influence on his work, for Christian humanism informs both his literary and critical output. The conflicts presented in his fiction are easily discernible as allegories of good and evil, and in his literary criticism he is concerned with the religious and moral content of a work of literature. Lewis was a traditionalist in his approach to both literature and life. He opposed the modern schools of literary interpretation in favor of explication free of biographical or psychological connotations. He also published under the pseudonyms of Clive Hamilton and Nat Whilk. (See also *CLC*, Vols. 1, 3, 6, and *Contemporary Authors*, Vols. 81-84.)

RUTH Z. TEMPLE

Mr. C. S. Lewis [in *The Allegory of Love*] was moved to attack the personal heresy in modern criticism. The first essay in the elegant small book is his spirited, and to some extent salutary, denunciation of contemporary critics and readers who regard poetry as a means of contact with the poet's personality. So shocking does this seem to Mr. Lewis, that he has boldly taken up the extreme negative position: ". . . when we read poetry as poetry should be read, we have before us no representation which claims to be the poet, and frequently no representation of a *man,* a *character,* or a *personality* at all." (p. 596)

No doubt a corrective was needed for the psychological-biographical school which, not content with using the biography to illuminate the work, rather lays the work under contribution to complete the portrait of the man, and makes the poet rather than his very title to consideration—his poetry—the proper end of enjoyment. But reduction of the poet to mere linguistic interpreter of the natural world to man could not, of course, go unchallenged. Mr. Lewis was fortunate enough to provoke a distinguished adversary, Dr. E.M.W. Tillyard . . . whose study of Milton he had cited as exemplifying the personal heresy. From this point the discussion becomes a controversy in due form [resulting in a collection of essays published jointly by Lewis and Tillyard entitled *The Personal Heresy*]. (pp. 596-97)

One follows [Mr. Lewis] with more confidence when he is attacking vulgar errors in the understanding of the function of poetry than when he is faced with the uncongenial necessity of substituting for these errors a true and plausible system of his own. Here he appears to suffer from what might be called "the Oxford orthodoxy". Though not incapable, as he has plainly demonstrated, of rigorous speculative thought, he here falls back to the gentlemanly level where all men of "polite imagination", in Addison's phrase, may follow him. Poetry, he says, takes for its subject matter anything that may be the subject of conversation, excepting only the attempt to prove (which is the province of science and philosophy) and the attempt to accomplish an immediate practical purpose [propaganda?]. Most poetry, indeed, tells stories. Poetry, like any other utterance, should be interesting; poetry, like any other utterance, should make us happier, wiser, or better. Surely this is no dangerous departure from the respectable Victorian tradition and surely it is not illuminating. (pp. 597-98)

It will seem, I imagine, to most contemporary critics that for the personal heresy Mr. Lewis has substituted one as ancient and at least as damned: the heresy of the separation of form from matter. . . .

Mr. Lewis makes the appreciation of poetry too easy. In so far as the poet gives intelligible expression to the concrete reality of experience, he is bound, Mr. Lewis seems to say, to communicate that experience. We are all mute inglorious Miltons, inferior to the poet only in linguistic aptitude. Therefore when the poet tells us what it is like to meet an elm, whether the poet be Tennyson or Donne, we know what it is like to meet an elm. Naturally, on this view, there is no necessity for biographical or historical elucidation of poems. If poetry is by definition accessible, the critic as mediator between the poet and the common reader is superfluous. We are all equal before poetry. But the very disagreements which arise between Mr. Lewis and Dr. Tillyard as to the interpretation of poems called in as concrete illustrations belie this comfortable conclusion. . . . And Mr. Lewis is not without misgivings. He has been able to differentiate two kinds in the experience which poetry communicates to him: such experience as all men have had, and "a new and nameless sensation, or even a new sense, to enrich me with experience which nothing in my previous life had prepared me for". This surely raises important questions. (p. 598)

Ruth Z. Temple, "Pool of Bethsaida," in The Sewanee Review *(reprinted by permission of the editor; © 1939 by The University of the South), Vol. XLVII, No. 4, Autumn, 1939, pp. 596-99.*

CHARLES A. BRADY

Not many writers nowadays are on such terms of cordial insult with His Infernal Majesty as the ruddy Ulster-born . . . Mr. Clive Staples Lewis has shown himself to be in what is by now the most phenomenally popular household book of applied religion of the twentieth century, *The Screwtape Letters*. Not since another Oxford don chose to divest himself of his academic robes and slip down a rabbit-hole with Alice and the White Rabbit has the reading world been given such a divertissement by a race of spectacled savants. . . .

For himself, [Mr. Lewis] has preferred to treat of [the devil] in these latter stages of degeneracy, when, like a certain Scottish thane, the forsworn recreant to a greater lord than Duncan has indeed grown old in evil and underneath the sinister mask the ravaged face begins to look faintly comic; but the button slips off both foils at times, as when, in *Perelandra,* Our Father Below decides to take a hand in the game; then Screwtape draws back, and the wrestling with Principalities and Powers begins. (p. 213)

[When] John left Puritania in Mr. Lewis' spiritual autobiography, *The Pilgrim's Regress,* he left John Calvin behind forever—more irrevocably, in fact, than many Catholic Irishmen manage to do; and the book then carries us to a *Paradiso* as well as to an *Inferno*. Mr. Lewis' fantasy or, if you prefer, vision of Paradise, here and in *The Problem of Pain,* is, in one fashion, like the Irish myth of Tir-n-an-Og, the Land of Youth and, in another, like some Platonic archetype of English hearth and nursery, a blend, almost, of Sunday's house in *The Man Who Was Thursday* and Barrie's nursery under the nightlights, where dog Nana keeps guard over the sleeping children. (pp. 213-14)

Mr. Lewis' teleology does not invoke the dour Calvinistic dogma of "you can't take it with you," but rather the exactly opposite doctrine of that sweet Scottish mystic, George Macdonald, his and Chesterton's "owne maister deere," who used to preach in sermon, poem and fantastic novel that you really can take it with you in the last analysis —all that counts, anyway, wife and child and candlelight and old cat purring on the hearth; toy theater and tavern; for man will remain man. . . .

Mr. Lewis makes two other major demands upon our attention, the first of which, I am sure, needs no belaboring. He is the only truly popular champion of Orthodoxy. . . .

But it would be a shame if his critical work and scholarly essays were confined to the lamp-lit circle of those dull persons who subscribe to *English Studies* and *Modern Language Notes*. Mr. Lewis' veins run blood, not ink; there is no mildew in his bones; nor mere jargon on his lips.

He has to his credit in *The Allegory of Love,* . . . the best critical treatment in English of Chaucer's psychological romance, *Troilus and Criseyde;* the finest book of general commentary I know of on *Paradise Lost* in *A Preface to Paradise Lost;* and, I will go bond, the most superb single essay consideration of the sweet Prince of Elsinore in *Hamlet: The Prince or the Poem*. . . .

Even the non-professional reader, who has but slight concern with matters of prosody and literary history, will find much to delight him in these pages; and no enthusiast of Lewis, English scholar or not, can afford to overlook the humane scholarship, as excellent in its respective fields as Ker's or Chambers' in theirs, of this very humanistic, and therefore Catholic, don.

It is true, however, that there are two lobes to the Lewis brain, both working at once to produce a more than three-dimensional stereoscopic reality, but one coloring the field of vision more at one time, the other at another. This was also true of Chesterton, his great congener, in whom one could distinguish a rationalistic and a mystic lobe. In Lewis' instance both lobes turn at once on a pivot of wit; but there is a lobe of Swiftian fancy and a lobe of Dunsanyesque—the term is used to indicate kind, not degree—imagination, both crossing and criss-crossing in bewildering simultaneity, with Swift predominating in *Screwtape* and the Tir-n-an-Ogish Dunsany in *Perelandra* and *Out of the Silent Planet,* where instead of Eighteenth Century efts and ouphs of fancy à la Voltaire or Alexander Pope we sight our crossbows for the great Albatross, the splendid Oyarsa of the imagination, who haunts the ringing crags of myth rather than the pleasant upland slopes of allegory.

This latter charming qualification applies to *The Pilgrim's Regress,* in which Lewis, who, as a scholar, had found himself in reaction against today's contemptuous depreciation of that old-fashioned form, seems to have set out to prove he could write as good allegory as Bunyan. The resultant, half medieval, half seventeenth-century Puritan, reveals the Bedford Tinker's iron somewhat mitigated by the sweetly silver musical alloy of nursery rhyme, of *Boys and girls come out to play, The moon is shining bright as day.* Wisdom's wanton children gambol in the moonlight; the moon shines soft and clear on Mother Kirk's pool of Baptism; but it is still the familiar moon of earthly nurseries after the Fall. Malacandra and Perelandra gleam fair with the further radiance of Mars and Venus cleansed of the perilous stuff that Original Sin brought into our silent world, the pure planets of Chesterton's dream, freed of the incestuous associations of mortal legend. . . .

I consider [the] Miltonic grandeur of conception [in *Out of the Silent Planet* and *Perelandra*] the greatest exercise of pure imagination in immediately contemporary literature. . . . (p. 214)

Charles A. Brady, "Introduction to Lewis," in America *(© America Press, 1944; all rights reserved), Vol. LXXI, No. 8, May 27, 1944, pp. 213-14.*

CHARLES MOORMAN

The popular reputation of C. S. Lewis depends to a large extent upon his prominence as a modern day "apostle to the skeptics." His theological writings are designed for and directed toward skeptical laymen who have been, in Lewis's opinion, unduly influenced by nineteenth-century liberalism and scientism and so have left the Church for the greener pastures of "humane science." Lewis's theological writings are thus designed to woo mankind away from the laboratories and the secular reform movements back into the arms of the Church. In books such as *Mere Christianity, The Problem of Pain,* and *Miracles,* Lewis is a propagandist; his cause is orthodoxy in religion and in morality; his methods are those of his enemies. At all times, he views the world from the vantage-point of the church steps.

Yet in order to provide a suitable literary vehicle for orthodox ideas, Lewis creates his own cosmic myth. Science fiction provides him with a method and a plot, the theology of the Church with a theme. . . . In Lewis's three novels—*Out of the Silent Planet, Perelandra,* and *That Hideous Strength*—the earth becomes "Thulcandra," the "silent planet," cut off from the rest of the cosmos by the rebellion of Satan, the "Bent Eldil" (angel), and the subsequent fall of man. In the first novel, Elwin Ransom, the philologist-hero of Lewis's cycle, is kidnaped by Edward Weston, a physicist, and so is accidentally involved in a trip to Mars. There he learns that the universe, apart from Earth, exists in harmony and peace, having a common language and a common interplanetary religion and government. In describing this theocratic arrangement Lewis seeks to translate the usual Christian terms into some sort of pseudo-scientific and mythical terms, without at the same time losing or distorting the basic Christian concepts with which he is working. Thus the two sets of terms involved can only approximate each other; the Martians, inhabiting as they do an unfallen world, cannot view Christianity from the same point of view as do fallen earth men. (p. 401)

Lewis's main aim in the creation of his silent planet myth is thus to create and maintain a metaphor which will serve to carry in fictional form the basic tenets of Christianity and present them from a non-Christian point of view without reference to the usual Christian symbols. This general method is graphically illustrated in *Perelandra,* the second novel of the trilogy. Ransom, summoned by Maleldil through the Oyarsa (tutelary eldil) of Mars, journeys to Perelandra (Venus). There he finds a young world, a Paradise. He meets the queen of that world, who tells him that Maleldil has forbidden that she and her husband sleep on a certain fixed island (most of Venus's islands are floating). Weston, the physicist, again appears, but it is immediately apparent that Satan has taken possession of Weston's body in an attempt to induce the queen to sleep on the forbidden island in order to bring about another Fall. The novel from this point on settles down into argumentation—Ransom, the emissary of Maleldil, seeks to preserve the queen's innocence; Weston, the devil incarnate, attempts to confound her with arguments glorifying the knowledge of evil.

It is apparent that Lewis is here expounding, from the point of view of his own cosmic myth, the doctrine of the fall of man. The theological problem, as Lewis sees it, centers upon the validity of that interpretation which sees the Fall as fortunate. . . . Lewis's conclusion would thus seem to be that the Fall on Earth was fortunate in that God, almost by definition, brings good out of evil. Yet had the Fall not occurred, some equally great good, forever lost to man, would have been revealed.

The main point to be made concerning the first two books of the trilogy is this: Lewis, using the literary methodology of the science-fiction writer, is attempting, as in his tracts dealing with Christian apologetics, to justify the ways of God to skeptical man by presenting the core of the Faith. He must, however, describe and define the theological tenets with which he is dealing from a point of view which, of necessity, cannot make use of the normal vocabulary of the Church. This is, of course, both a strength and a weakness. The old terms have the advantage of producing stock responses, which is one of the great advantages of literary allusion to known and accepted myth. Yet this calling forth of stock responses may have serious disadvantages in that it may repel the very people whom Lewis is trying hardest to attract. Thus it is that Lewis's seemingly non-Christian point of view in the novels is one of his chief sources of strength; it functions in the same way as does his sophisticated prose style in the popular theological books. In both cases, Lewis would seem to be working on the principle that the usual approach to Christianity is no longer effective, so that new and totally different terms must be found to express the old and, for Lewis, still valid doctrines.

In *That Hideous Strength,* the last of the novels, Lewis retains his general method in that he presents orthodox Christianity by means of non-Christian terms, but in this novel he shifts his emphasis away from the silent planet myth developed in the first two novels. The primary structure of that myth is still retained: Ransom, appearing as Mr. Fisher-King, is Lewis's hero; we have allusions to Weston, the physicist; the moon is Earth's battle perimeter. But the field of action shifts from Heaven to Earth. Evil takes the form of a sociological and scientific society whose professed aim is the amelioration of social and economic conditions by means of the creation of a cooperative state. Yet this society, ironically called the N.I.C.E. (National Institute of Co-ordinated Experiments), is in reality only a facade for the operations of Satan who is attempting to conquer the world by appealing to ideals of secular humanism, science, and material progress. (pp. 402-03)

Lewis in *That Hideous Strength* deliberately plays down the cosmic myth of the first two novels. The reason for such a decision seems obvious: Lewis's cosmic machinery cannot properly function in an "earth" story. He thus introduces another myth to take the place of the cosmic adventure story—the Arthurian. (p. 403)

What Lewis seems to see in the Arthurian myth is a metaphor which will at once fit within the overall scheme of the silent planet myth and at the same time reinforce his general plan by expressing it in another and more overtly literary set of terms. Thus, the Arthurian material in a sense can be said to exist within the silent planet myth and parallel to it.

It is evident that Lewis in emphasizing the eternal war between Logres, the Arthurian ideal, and Britain, the secular reality, is attempting to develop a symbol which will parallel roughly the war between good and evil forces, fallen and unfallen angels, on Earth, the silent planet. Just as in the other novels he had so carefully delineated the position of Earth as "enemy-held territory," so here is he expressing the same concept in Arthurian terms.

In the personage of Mr. Fisher-King, Lewis has portrayed a new and almost divine Ransom; he has become the Fisher King of the Grail story, the guardian of the Grail, and thus the head of the new Logres. Perhaps the most significant detail which Lewis uses in his description of Mr. Fisher-King is the bleeding foot, the result of Ransom's struggle with Weston-Satan in *Perelandra.* The wounded heel becomes a symbol of Mr. Fisher-King's heritage both as a keeper of the Grail and as a man among men. It is thus, by extension, a symbol of the waste land of modern society, land laid waste by the victory of the Bent Eldil and doomed until Logres captures Britain and the battle line of the moon's orbit is broken. The purposes of Logres and the dream of the eldila of Deep Heaven are thus identified through the symbol of the wounded Mr. Fisher-King, who is also the space traveler, Elwin Ransom.

The identification of Ransom / Fisher-King with the Pendragon can also be said to extend the implications of Lewis's theme. Lewis thinks of Arthurian Britain as the ideal secular civilization awaiting a reconciliation with its religious counterpart. Lewis is thus able to join the Grail (Mr. Fisher-King) with the ideal kingdom (the Pendragon) with Deep Heaven (Ransom the voyager). The menage of Mr. Fisher-King thus comes to represent a microcosm of the Arthurian court, the true remnant of Logres. Lewis dwells on the idyllic and co-operative aspects of this civilization in order to provide a contrast with the secular civilization (if it can be called that) represented by the Belbury headquarters of N.I.C.E. (pp. 403-04)

Lewis's introduction of Merlin is the last of his interpolations of Arthurian materials. Merlin is, in a sense, the key figure in the novel. Both sides desire the "mantle of Merlin," the supernatural power which the great magician represents. What Lewis finds in Merlin is a figure, half-mythical and half-real (in terms of Lewis's imposed theory of history which claims that the story of Arthur is historical fact), whom he can use as an active force of good and whom he can ally naturally with the Arthurian myth and artificially with the cosmic myth. (p. 404)

Lewis's general use of myth, along with his statements concerning the nature of myth, would seem to point to a unified concept of the place of myth in literature: Myth itself represents an ultimate and absolute reality; myth in literature represents a reflection of that central reality, capable of conveying the meaning and, to some extent, the power implicit in the myth itself. Lewis thus implies that myth functions in literature as a suggestive archetype to which ordinary fictional situations may be referred by allusion. In this way, myth lends its own total meaning and inherent power to the fictional situation. . . .

In *That Hideous Strength* Lewis's theme is not a theological dogma, but a moral dilemma. Lewis is here opposing the sanctity and morality of Mr. Fisher-King, who symbolizes the whole weight of an ordered and Christian society, and the chaotic and turbulent secularism of the N.I.C.E. The war between these forces, and thus, in terms of the silent planet myth, between the angels and devils who direct them, is reflected in the inward struggles of a young couple, Mark and Jane Studdock, to choose sides in the great battle, and it is their personal struggles which become the real subject of the last novel. But these personal struggles have no meaning except as they are interpreted against the background of the mythical structure which gives reality and force to their deliberations. *That Hideous Strength* represents Lewis's most complex and impressive use of myth in fiction. Here he uses myth to give force and meaning to a modern story of conversion, by placing that conversion against a backdrop of myth which presents the problems of the two young people as manifestations of a universal and cosmic struggle. (p. 405)

Charles Moorman, "Space Ship and Grail: The Myths of C. S. Lewis," in College English *(copyright © 1957 by the National Council of Teachers of English), Vol. 18, No. 8, May, 1957, pp. 401-05.*

JOHN H. TIMMERMAN

The driving motif of *Till We Have Faces* is the development of the soul, a motif explored allegorically in one of Lewis' earliest works, *The Pilgrim's Regress.* Here Lewis has recast the familiar myth of Cupid and Psyche, possibly attracted initially to the enchanting symbolism of the butterfly frequently associated with Psyche. Transformed from a creature of the earth to a creature of the air, from a creature that gropes in the darkness to a creature that flutters in the light, the butterfly seems to encapsulate the glory of the resurrection in which fallen man is transformed from a creature of dust to a spirit received in God's radiant glory. (p. 498)

The novel is a tale of transition in character, but more than this it is a tale of pursuit of a vision. . . . (p. 500)

The philosophic cast to the novel is stronger than in any other of Lewis' work. In fact, it would not be far afield to point out the remarkable parallels between the three sisters of the court and the Platonic view of the tripartite soul. Orual, the eldest sister, is a convincing portrait of the philosopher-king, . . . one whose life was governed by reason and whose center of soul physiologically rested in the head. Psyche fits the Platonic description of the spirited person of courage and impulsive daring whose center of soul rested in the chest or heart. Plato foresaw this kind of person constituting the guardian, or warrior, class, the person who will uphold and guard the state at whatever cost, which clearly does not apply to Psyche. Yet, one should recall the dire schooling Plato prescribed (train them like dogs, he said) to form the guardian thus. The natural virtue of this class, the natural trait of soul which Psyche does share, is spontaneous belief and unfaltering courage in pursuit of that belief. Redival represents the appetitive soul, whimsical, sensual, uncontrollable, whose center of soul rests in the lower regions of the body.

As Plato's philosophy turned on the crucial distinction between reason and belief, so too does Lewis' theology, albeit with markedly different answers. These answers lie at the heart of the novel. Plato, of course, had little use for *doxa,* or knowledge based upon what one "believed" to be true—that is, not revealed by reason but apprehended existentially. These "opinions" Plato considered to be deceptive and bound in what only seems to be true. Instead, he argued that true knowledge arises only from reason, that only mental processes grant certain truth as they gain access by recollection and mathematical study to the eternal world of the forms.

In a sense, the Western world has never recovered from Platonism, for many still wish to argue that faith is absurd and that only reason (or "scientific method" to adopt the post-Enlightenment term) gives certain knowledge. Lewis' wish is not simply to reverse this popular notion, but to define the function and limit of reason and belief in Christian epistemology. For Lewis reason is a guide, but not the goal; never an end in itself, it can nonetheless lead to an end that is achieved finally by belief. (p. 501)

The error that Lewis believes modern man has committed was to assume that reason is the exclusive organ of truth. Notice that Psyche begins at one point to call Orual—the philosopher-king—*Maia,* which means the way of illusion. Reason as self-sufficient means of obtaining knowledge is ultimately illusory, for it limits man to the boundaries of his own mind. Reason, to rephrase Kant, must be seen within the limits of belief.

The Fox, cast as rationalist philosopher, thus plays a crucial role. For much of the novel he is always at hand to adroitly "explain away" mysteries that lie beyond process. Dreams, illusions, heightened emotions—the glimpses into spiritual reality are anything for him but the truth. Yet, the Fox's system fails to hold, even for the Fox. It precludes the tears that too often fall down his cheeks. It counts his often searing emotions as puerile poppycock. It leaves no room for the songs and festivities that fill the Fox with uneasy joy. In short, it is a system that denies life; it is the skeleton abhorring the flesh and viscera that grant being. . . .

The Fox [however, is no] facile arbiter of value and truth. He is seeking, by his own innate means of reason, to discern certain verities in life. It is significant that the Fox is selected as a guide for Orual through the Deadlands, for by reason he sees many things clearly. One mistakes Lewis' epistemology if he sees it as exorcising reason altogether as some malevolent demon preying upon faith. Reason does grant us conveyance down the path of belief; it just doesn't take us far enough.

Perhaps Lewis' most precise statement concerning reason and imagination . . . [is that] "reason is the natural organ of truth; but imagination is the organ of meaning." Imagination reaches beyond the grasp of reason to seize the meaning of "what is," or fact. Its method is mythic, or the use of allegory or symbolism to reach "after some transcendental reality which the forms of discursive thought cannot contain." Belief consists of assent to the meaning disclosed through imagination. (p. 502)

Psyche does act impulsively, wildly, on her belief. By a leap of faith she seizes the spiritual reality. Perhaps for that reason, Psyche often seems more Christlike, more spiritual than human, in the novel. Although her anguish in mortal life is real and agonizing, her quest for the spiritual god is almost heroic. (pp. 504-05)

Orual is inescapably a part of [the] world of clouded belief and distorted reason, and no act of her own can lift the clouds nor clear the mind. . . .

Orual's spiritual sight operates on two levels, the pragmatic reality and increasing experience of the transcendent meaning of reality. Her own pragmatic vision begins to show to her the reality that she attempts not to see. (p. 506)

[In] her vision Orual comes to the understanding that all the angry words of her writings, the bitter acrimony, the blazing ire, break down in abject terror at the realization that the gods are real and the mysteries of their will can never be fathomed by man. All of man's reason and will are in the presence of divine wisdom but a babbling wind. Man has no voice, no face to present before the gods. (p. 507)

Through [a] gesture of ultimate love, [Psyche's] descent into hell whereby man is redeemed, man is truly transformed. By this act he receives the face by which he can behold the gods face to face, the face [which] can only be bestowed by the One who has borne all the anguish. It is this act of Christ to which the myth points, for this act transforms the Orual in us to the Psyche . . . , the fallen man to redeemed man. (p. 508)

John H. Timmerman, "The Epistemology of C. S. Lewis: Reason and Belief in 'Till We Have Faces'," in Religion in Life *(copyright © 1977 by Abingdon Press), Vol. XLVI, No. 4, Winter, 1977, pp. 497-508.*

A. K. NARDO

In the orderly cosmos of his Space Trilogy (*Out of the Silent Planet* [1938], *Perelandra* [1943], *That Hideous Strength* [1945]), Lewis repeatedly presents his characters (both terrestrial and celestial) speaking and acting in accordance with a system of propriety which literary theorists label decorum. . . . [Lewis uses various] examples of generic variety and propriety to demonstrate both the plenitude of being that fills Maleldil's (Christ's) fertile universe and the cosmic harmony by which this proliferation is ordered. Several times in the trilogy he presents pageants in which countless exotic animals, different races of *hnau* (rational beings), and *eldila* (angels) arrange themselves into patterns which seem intrinsic to their natures. (pp. 118-19)

The Renaissance, the period of specialization for Lewis the critic, generated much interest in decorum among literary theorists who tried to systematize the rules of propriety. . . . Despite disagreements on details, most theorists agreed that epic and tragedy should portray the nobility of kings and heroes, that pastoral should sing of shepherds and nymphs in a Golden World, and that satire and farce should expose the vice and folly of low-life characters such as servants, sailors, and hostlers. In his Space Trilogy Lewis follows a similar system of decorum in order to characterize the three planets (Mars, Venus, and Earth) which form the settings of the novels. . . .

Malacandra [the setting for *Out of the Silent Planet*] is Mars, an undeniably martial and epic world. Hardship and struggle were imposed upon its *hnau* early when the surface of the planet was ruined by a blow from the Bent Eldil (Satan) in his rebellion against Maleldil. Now its people labor for food, shelter, and knowledge in caverns beneath the barren surface of a planet they know is old and will soon die. Yet they accept the death of their planet and death in general with heroic fortitude, seeing it as the final glorious moment which completes life. (p. 119)

Perelandra [the setting for *Perelandra*] is Venus, an undeniably pastoral and lyric world. Whereas Malacandra is old and dying, Perelandra is young and, when Ransom arrives, its King and Queen await "the morning" of their birth into the unfallen life of glory which was lost by Adam and Eve. . . . Protected from the sun's harsh rays, safely insulated from the conflicts of inter-planetary politics, and flowing in the rhythm of the divine will, the planet is a Golden World of prelapsarian bliss created for the joy of its two inhabitants. (p. 120)

As the reader travels with Ransom into Deep Heaven, he too is introduced to worlds where myth comes true and where what are merely artificial constructs to delineate kinds of poetry on earth become living realities in the heroic world of Mars and the pastoral world of Venus. Through identification with Ransom, the reader tastes what, Lewis seems to believe, is almost impossible in the modern world: pure epic and pure lyric experiences. (p. 122)

On earth, however, the reader is not encouraged to immerse himself in the experience of the planet because Thulcandra is a sinful world under the rule of the Bent Eldil, Satan. To characterize earth, therefore, Lewis uses a genre that necessitates an emotional distance foreign to epic, pastoral, and lyric—satire. . . . It is precisely this distance that allows the reader to experience the response to wickedness that is proper in a universe governed by an omnipotent and beneficent God—laughter. From the perspective of divine providence (or from the glimpse of that perspective man can attain), it is easy to see that "the Devil is an ass."

On fallen earth, however, surrounded by the effects of Satan's attempts to subvert God's providence, it is difficult to maintain the distance necessary to laugh at evil. When a good man feels the power of Satan at work, his usual response is terror. . . . In the universe of the trilogy, only earth is terrifying, not outer space which is filled with the radiant light and life of Maleldil. The gothic novel is thus an earthly genre, and the reader shares its terror when Lewis immerses him in the works of the Devil, which from a cosmic perspective always appear ludicrous.

With this understanding of proper (laughter) and partial (terror) responses to evil on the silent planet, we turn to the third novel of the trilogy, *That Hideous Strength,* which is set on Earth. Ransom, now the leader of a godly remnant at St. Anne's on the Hill, wages a covert war against the hellish N.I.C.E. (National Institute of Co-ordinated Experiments), in which the resurrected Merlin is a secret weapon. . . . [Lewis] gives the reader a normative stance outside worldly wickedness, the godly community at St. Anne's on the Hill [and] the reader is assured of the emotional distance necessary to laugh at the meaningless bureaucratic jargon of the N.I.C.E., the petty squabbles for power in the "inner circle," and the obsequiousness of Wither and Frost, the N.I.C.E. deputy directors, who roll out the red carpet for a tippling hobo they believe to be the resurrected Merlin. When the real Merlin calls down the curse of Babel upon the N.I.C.E., satire again becomes farce as those who have sold their souls to the Devil are forced to babble jibberish only slightly more outlandish than the "bureaucratese" they have been spouting all along. . . . As their tongues are confounded, all Hell (literally) breaks loose: experimental animals seek bloody revenge, "the Head" demands new sacrificial victims, and the Satanic Wither and Frost complete the self-destruction their names imply.

These last events are, however, not farcical. In the final scene at Belbury, the N.I.C.E. headquarters, the reader is granted a disturbing double perspective. Because the reader watches humans like himself chanting the nonsense of Devil worship and being slaughtered by wild beasts, he feels the terror all sinful mortals must feel in the presence of Satanic anarchy and divine justice. But, because the reader has been encouraged to grant his allegiance to St. Anne's Christian community, he can laugh as Ransom's pet bear, Mr. Bultitude, smacks his lips over a chance to get at "the Head" and as Merlin forces Lord Feverstone (Devine) to drive over the old Roman road to Edgestow. In other words, this scene elicits the reader's sense of kinship with all fallen men, thereby producing the horror appropriate to a gothic novel; but because the reader has emotionally joined the redeemed community at St. Anne's, the scene also elicits the reader's sense of distance from these fools who have damned themselves, thereby producing the laughter appropriate to satire and farce.

St. Anne's, while providing the reader with a stance from which to view the vice and folly of damned Belbury, has a characteristic genre of its own—medieval romance. (pp. 122-25)

[The] genre itself is appropriate to characterize the group at St. Anne's because medieval romance so often portrays a quest for the ideal in an all-too-real world. As Arthur hoped to create Logres in the chaos of Britain, as Perceval and Lancelot sought the Holy Grail despite their repeated sins and failures, as Gawain tried and failed to resist the tempting offers of his host's wife, so the remnant at St. Anne's strives to keep Christianity alive in a fallen world of hellish bureaucracies. Medieval romance is indeed the appropriate genre to mediate between immersion in the sinful world, which produces terror, and distance from it, which produces laughter. (p. 125)

Now that we have surveyed Lewis's system of decorum and seen what genres are appropriate to Mars (epic), Venus (pastoral and lyric), fallen man (gothic novel, satire, and farce) and redeemed man (medieval romance), we are ready to see how, in the radiant light of the genre appropriate to the cosmic harmony, all these genres are both partial and central. (pp. 125-26)

If all these responses are partial, what genre leads the reader to the fullest response to the cosmic harmony? We glimpse it in the pageant scenes that conclude each of the three novels of the trilogy. The chant of the *hrossa* at Hyoi's funeral, the song of rejoicing which all Perelandra sings, and the dancing of the elephants on the lawn at St. Anne's introduce the reader to a universe whose characteristic genre is Divine Comedy. (p. 126)

In the festive conclusions to all three novels, the reader sees that Lewis's cosmos is ordered and loved by the same smiling God whom Dante tries to describe in his beatific vision. . . . Like Dante, who experiences, then rises beyond the horror and farce of the infernal depths, the struggle required to climb the purgatorial mount, and even the joy of the earthly paradise at the summit in order to gaze on the fullness of God, so the reader of the Space Trilogy makes a similar pilgrimage to catch a glimpse of (if not to gaze upon) the cosmic (and comic) harmony.

The genres that form Lewis's system of interplanetary decorum are not, however, arranged in a rigid hierarchy like the *genera dicendi* proposed by Renaissance theorists. Each genre performs its function in each planet, and all merge in the harmony and rejoicing of a dance, the characteristic ending of comedy. . . . Paradoxically, each planet's genre is both central and subordinate to the Divine Comedy. Although on earth we may seem doomed to experience only the horror and farce of the modern world, even that, says Lewis, is a significant movement in the decorous Dance before God's throne. (pp. 127-28)

A. K. Nardo, "Decorum in the Fields of Arbol: Interplanetary Genres in C. S. Lewis's Space Trilogy," in Extrapolation *(copyright 1971 by Thomas D. Clareson), Vol. 20, No. 2, Summer, 1979, pp. 118-28.*

M

MACDONALD, Ross (pseudonym of Kenneth Millar) 1915-

An American detective story writer in the tradition of Raymond Chandler, Macdonald is the creator of Lew Archer and the author of such best-selling novels as *The Goodbye Look, The Underground Man,* and *The Moving Target.* He has also written under the pseudonym of John Ross Macdonald. (See also *CLC,* Vols. 1, 2, 3, and *Contemporary Authors,* Vols. 9-12, rev. ed.)

MICHAEL WOOD

In Ross Macdonald's novels, the past is always falling in on top of the present. Lew Archer, a wise, tired, divorced and lonely private eye, is hired to investigate a theft or a kidnapping or the disappearance of a child, and immediately, as if released by Archer's appearance on the scene, murky old cats begin to leap out of poorly sealed bags. Archer uncovers guilt wherever he goes, and his job, once the cats are all out and howling, is to put them together into a theory, to tie the past to the present, and to catch the whole case in what Macdonald calls, in an early novel, "the final amber." In Macdonald's new book, "The Blue Hammer," Archer tracks the past more obsessively than ever, and the result is the best work Macdonald has done in a number of years. . . .

All detective fiction is fairly theological, given to displays of ultimate coherence, but what interests Archer is the first hint that there may be a coherence. . . .

"I was in trouble, and Lew Archer got me out of it," Macdonald wrote of his early career. Archer, a figure he could hide behind, rescued him from an autobiographical novel and "sloppy feelings and groping prose." The resulting work was "The Moving Target," published in 1949, and Archer has helped Macdonald to nineteen novels since then. A few years ago he seemed to have got Macdonald back into trouble, and "Sleeping Beauty" (1973) was full of sloppy feelings and groping prose, and Archer was offering shabby and easy consolations to himself and others. . . .

I'm happy to report that Archer and Macdonald, in "The Blue Hammer," have pulled themselves together and are out of trouble. . . .

The risk of writing novel after novel within the same convention is that you will come to understand your methods too well, and your preoccupations and your style will then turn simply into a program or a recipe. . . . [There is, perhaps] an excess of self-consciousness, but in "The Blue Hammer," it is not at all a crippling excess, and this intricate tale of multiple murder and transposed identities moves fast and is full of surprises. There is one flaw in it, and I think I am not giving too much of the story away if I say what it is, since it arises from what is a sort of occupational hazard for writers of detective fiction. . . . [In] "The Blue Hammer," even the least suspicious of readers is going to be ahead of Archer, who is still waiting for the earth to move, waiting to make his first connection.

Michael Wood, "Fiction and Poetry: 'The Blue Hammer'," in The New York Times Book Review *(© 1976 by The New York Times Company; reprinted by permission), June 13, 1976, p. 4.*

WILLIAM McPHERSON

Until now I had never read a Ross Macdonald novel. My loss. For on the basis of *The Blue Hammer* alone—and there are 19 earlier Macdonald novels in the Lew Archer canon—this writer of cracking detective stories is as good as the more relentlessly "serious" American novelists of the declining years of our 20th century, and better than most. A snap judgment, perhaps, but that's what we're paid for.

And a shameful admission. For Ross Macdonald is as easy to read as he is hard to overlook. . . .

It is [his] perfect blend of style and action that hooks the reader at once. . . . (p. G1)

[A] tantalizing possibility, hinting of further mysteries neither acted out nor directly revealed, gives Archer his dimension of flawed innocence. Macdonald once described him as "a deliberately narrowed version of the writing self, so narrow that when he turns sideways he almost disappears. Yet his semi-transparent presence places the story at one remove from the author and lets it, as we say (through sweat and tears), write itself."

And so it appears to do, with clarity and brilliance, a stunning use of dialogue and metaphor and, of course, an ingenious, constantly moving plot. The sweat and tears are left back on the office floor in Santa Barbara.

Archer's—and Macdonald's—venue is Southern California, the space between the Sierras and the sea where the past comes reluctantly to rest and the future, blank and inscrutable, plays atop the subterranean fault, waiting for something to slip, as it inevitably will. This is Joan Didion's territory—the world of the Santa Monica Freeway, of moral fatigue, controlled hysteria and raw nerve ends—but with a difference: the nerves are frayed but still intact (Archer has great dignity and never loses it) and redemption is a possibility, however slight. More closely than Didion, Macdonald resembles another artist obsessed with guilt and retribution: Nathaniel Hawthorne, moved ahead a century and waking up in California, there to unravel the tangled past in the hope of exorcising it.

It is an obsession perhaps most novelists have, but a vision only fine novelists can bring off. . . .

In a world where traditional forms of absolution have lost much of their power but the necessity remains, Archer serves as a surrogate priest, without the power to absolve but with the power to bring to light. (The truth may make you free.) . . .

Archer takes plenty of grief. There are no happy people in this novel, but the possibility of at least a transitory happiness, "a temporary kindness," exists. "The combination of the speeding car and the sleeping woman made me feel almost young, as if my life might have a new beginning after all," which is, at bottom, what mystery novels are all about: old crimes and new beginnings.

Lew Archer tries to believe, like the wiser, tougher altar boy he still is, in "the controlling forces of the world, if any," a vision ultimately theological though not exactly hopeful:

"'It doesn't seem to make sense,'" he says at one point. "'But nearly everything does when you understand it.'

"'You really believe that, that everything makes sense?'" he is asked. And replies, "'I work on that principle, anyway.'" It is the principle of coherence that every writer must work on: that seemingly inexplicable events, small man-made mysteries, can be solved. Figure those out and the rest may take care of itself. (p. G2)

William McPherson, "Archer with a Deadly Aim," in Book World—The Washington Post *(© 1976,* The Washington Post*), June 27, 1976, pp. G1-G2.*

PETER WOLFE

[Ross Macdonald's] novels are well-built, suspenseful, and easy both to read and enjoy. His best work gives equal weight to invention and execution. His intellectual power, social conscience, and bright, crisp style promote both impact and resonance. He has something to say, knows how to say it, and deserves to be heard. (p. 1)

A good example of his ability to write books that everybody can read inheres in his treatment of sex. He never denies the force of sex; sex always plays a large part in the troubled lives he depicts. But because erotic descriptions would cut the range of his readership, they never appear in his work. Nor does he let his preference for searching out criminal causes, rather than merely recording crime's sensations, outrank his sense of mission as a storyteller. . . . [He] translates motive into both physical *and* psychological act. In depicting the inner man, he does not forget the outer man—how he looks and what he does. He tells how characters have become the way they are; he reviews his main issues; he will remind you of the main currents of his sometimes highly complex plot. Though most thrillers start quickly, his set their own pace, adding characters and information when both reader and plot are ready for them.

Thus the novels give a great deal—action and credibility, sound plotting and something to think about: the meaning and the mechanism of crime. The crime points to serious issues. Almost all his work shows how far society at large, the family, and the individual have veered from what they should be. The idea is neither original nor profound. Ross Macdonald's strength lies not in idea but in his moral seriousness and power to convert idea into sharply observed and well-integrated details. He convinces us, through his artistry, of both the complexity and mystery of life. While persuading us that life is full of meaning, he does not define that meaning; rather, he invests detective fiction with a psychological dimension that fits well with its traditionally complex plot. More interested in private than in public crime, he uses psychology rather than applied science to probe motives and causes. This turning-away both from the gadgetry of the novel of international intrigue and the secular rationalism of the 'tec-yarn helps him reveal his characters through speech and action. (pp. 1-2)

Ross Macdonald does not analyze or explore motives. He shows, instead, the effects of deeply seated, sometimes obsessional, motives. Characters reveal themselves, if not at their worst, then at their most deeply surprised and tested. What will these nerve-raked souls do next? Who will be their next victims? Ross Macdonald conveys a sense of untold menace lurking behind the reported action. The bipolar pull of conscious and unconscious forces both energizes and controls the blend—the dark subject-matter of the novels resonating against a bright, limber style and Kenneth Millar's use of both a penname and a persona, in his narrator-detective Lew Archer. The tensional field of Ross Macdonald's art hums with imaginative possibilities. (p. 2)

Though Ross Macdonald links detection to psychology, he ignores criminal pathology. Crime in Ross Macdonald is usually murder; its motive, always personal and specific. Each book has only one killer, but he will kill three or four times. His motives? Gain and self-protection. Though the first victim dies because he stands between his murderer and something his murderer wants, the other ones die because they have incriminating information. . . . [The] killer cannot stop killing.

Ross Macdonald works harder to justify the motives of murder than to supply a conventional ending, where the murderer is caught after a setting-forth of the evidence. He cares about telling a good story because he cares about people—even killers and thieves. . . . Treating characters with respect, the Archer novels portray wrongdoers but, in recent years especially, no villains. Nobody chooses evil. Violence isn't simple; nor does it lend itself to moral absolutes. . . . (p. 3)

Ross Macdonald can be rightly accused of stretching probability past the breaking point and also of relying upon contrivances to resolve major issues. Examples to support the charge of implausibility come easily: Archer's habit of eavesdropping on conversations that just happen to deal directly with an important aspect of the case he's investigating; an identity-switch involving two women who look alike; the killing of the Most Likely Suspect soon after he rouses suspicion; the obligatory scene near the end where charges are made, evidence is brought forth, and the killer confesses. . . .

These stratagems, or staples, while not fresh, are usually freshly perceived. What is more, they fit well with both Ross Macdonald's use of narrative form and his overall imaginative intent. Though he documents his settings realistically, Ross Macdonald is not a realist. (p. 4)

The novels magnify rather than imitate or copy. Highly compressed, they are metaphors for stress. The characters stand larger than life, and the crises that claw them would wreck most of us. According to Ross Macdonald, his novels do not break away from reality so much as give a poetic documentary. . . . Though living in the twilight of faith, Ross Macdonald's characters believe certain truths worth living and fighting—even, sometimes, worth killing—for. These truths are given in everyday experience. Nor are they described in night language, dream symbolism, or hallucination. Though the novels use the same filial-sexual materials as Joyce in the Circe ("Nighttown") section of *Ulysses,* Ross Macdonald writes objective narratives in straightforward prose. His style obeys the natural controls of conventional syntax and word choice. The inner world of his characters is intelligible. His plots, though full of strange meanings, are continuous. Without trivializing the complex process of causation, the plots transcribe bizarre events accurately.

But, crackling with ingenious twists and turns, they do not develop simply. . . . A relentless interior logic and a carefully regulated tempo controls the novels. At the same time, the energy building from their robust style, Archer's moral sympathy, and the mood of desperation cast by murder make them human dramas rather than technical diversions. Their strength stems chiefly from their dramatic force—an intensification of existence. Their gyrating plots mesh well with the larger-than-life impressions created by the characters and their crises. The abundance in each book imparts a sense of peopled space, even, in view of the pent-up energies driving the characters on, of overflowing life. The conjuction of Ross Macdonald's plots with the human drives impelling them also dramatizes today's leading concept, in psychology as well as in literature, of the city as maze. (p. 5)

Aesthetically, historically, and socially, Ross Macdonald belongs in the private-eye tradition of pulp crime fiction; early Archer is as much the hard-boiled dick as Dashiell Hammett's Sam Spade (*The Maltese Falcon*) and Raymond Chandler's Philip Marlowe. (p. 6)

Ross Macdonald's other work adapts the novel of English village life to American social dynamics. Murder in Ross Macdonald is never ideological or crudely mercenary. The killer will come from the same social set, maybe the same family or street, as his victim and the other suspects.

Archer must find the connection between killer and victim(s). Both the openness and the mobility of America today make his job different from that of the English gentleman-sleuth of Dorothy L. Sayers and Margery Allingham. . . . Although Archer's search for the connecting principle can take him twenty-five years into the past, once he finds it his case virtually solves itself. . . . (p. 7)

Like other good detective writers, [Ross Macdonald] distributes suspicion evenly among the suspects; he displays his clues clearly, so that the reader has the same chance as Archer to solve the mystery; he reasons from the clues. But most of these clues do not come from close study of the physical evidence. . . . Usually, he reasons *a priori* from psychological patterns. His clues are based on behavioral rather than material evidence. Any crime occurring during his investigations comes from an earlier one and may cause others later on. . . . Logical analysis helps Archer less than a generous heart and an imaginative grasp of the moral complexities of daily life. . . .

Finding criminal impulses in all [people, Ross Macdonald] shortens the moral distance between murderer and victim, even between investigator and suspect; a popular murder-motive in his book is blackmail. Because we are all capable of crime, he extends both charity and moral sympathy to wrongdoers. This tenderness gives him more heart-knowledge than any of his counterparts today—not only in the area of the British detective story but also in that of the hard-boiled private eye, reaching all the way from Hammett to Mickey Spillane. (p. 8)

Evil does not win out in Ross Macdonald. The many last-chapter confessions, besides making for artistic symmetry, relax psychic strain. The killers feel relieved, first, to unload their guilt and shame and, next, to stop killing. Despite the greed and violence they describe, the Archer novels often taper to quiet, even peaceful, conclusions. Yet the fast-changing society the novels accept tallies well with the hard-boiled tradition, which is where most readers correctly place them. (pp. 8-9)

Ross Macdonald is one of America's few male novelists, let alone male crime writers, who use women as major characters. What interests him more than the hardiness of the Leatherstocking hero is the egalitarianism stretching from the eighteenth century to our day. The carrier of this tradition is spoken language. "Democracy is as much a language as it is a place," said Ross Macdonald in 1966. Archer's terse, middle-register speaking style confirms his freedom and equality. He communicates easily with witnesses, understanding them and being understood in turn. His street language subsumes both tower and gutter; down-and-outers and college deans come within his linguistic purview. A man who starts out knowing nothing and who knows only what people tell him, he has mastered, in his clear, straightforward speech, the basic working principle of his trade.

And so has his creator. Both the form and the build of a detective novel depend on the give-and-take of dialogue, the checking and rechecking of witnesses' stories, and the exchange of information among investigators. Thus Ross Macdonald writes in an oral, rather than in a literary, register. Fiction, he claims, should be written "more or less" in the rhythms and vocabulary of spoken language. . . . (p. 10)

Archer's *ex parte* role makes him more of a *deus ex machina* than a principal. Though his moral sympathy helps the later Archer cope with banality and grime, his accommodation is not tragic. He doesn't suffer enough and, by withholding both moral and emotional response, doesn't share any heightened perception with us. . . . Moreover, any literary form leaning as heavily as detective fiction does on dialogue comes under the aegis of social comedy. . . . Ross Macdonald excels in the skills that count most in social comedy—quicksilver dialogue, trim, inclusive plotting, and the creation of characters who need no reintroducing. The people and their problems range along the arc of comedy. Though Ross Macdonald looks deeply into character, he does not give many-sided pictures; the crimes energizing the plots call for a sharpening rather than a development of character. Character pre-exists Archer; instead of developing or changing, it struggles to survive. Variety comes from the range of character-types; each figure in a novel differs from all the others in age, job, and social-level. (pp. 13-14)

Ross Macdonald's sociological nightmares describe the pitfalls of new world energy. His characters don't understand freedom because they don't respect the freedom of others. Their freebooting individualism, a romantic perversion of the Protestant spirit, overrides secular, scriptural, and moral law. I feel, therefore, I am, is their guiding principle. What they feel most keenly, in Ross Macdonald's best work, is the loss of security; insecurity charges the novels with crisis. Characters deny the reality of both facts and persons; they twist, suppress, even kill. Violence becomes the natural outlet for insecurity; when force is the only social control, chaos, isolation, and despair follow soon after. (p. 16)

Psychology in Ross Macdonald, criminal or otherwise, does not reach us as applied doctrine. . . . Ross Macdonald uses Freud as an idea-bank. Much of the theory he bypasses as artistically unusable, unsuitable, or irrelevant. What he keeps he varies, even reverses, depending on his needs. Freud's influence, though strong, is implicit and absorbed. The novels do not read like psychoanalytic case studies, and Ross Macdonald does not explore character with the cold eye of the analyst. The hard purity of the doctrine is warmed and reshaped by the artist's imagination, moral charity, and sensitivity to the technical demands of his art. (pp. 21-2)

[Ross Macdonald's] belief in the inescapability of the past has led him to seat his characters in the family. The family, even if it encompasses only two generations, gives him access to one of the few surviving pasts in the instant society of California. This continuity generates force. The family is the greatest single influence on character in his fiction. (p. 23)

The moral equilibrium created by the past and the toil of solid literary craftsmanship weld the rich variety of the Archer novels. Little more can be asked of any novelist than that he control his deeply perceived and clearly realized materials. This strenuously achieved razor-balance of penetration and control, effortless look and all, has made Ross Macdonald an important novelist. (p. 36)

He has the Dickensian gusto—the stamina, curiosity, and genius for organization—both to create a megalopolis and to pull it together. For all its variety and sweep, California rides easily on the narrative rigging of the Archer books. The job of communicating with the reader claims equal rank with subject and idea—that which is being communicated. The bestowing of equal priority upon different narrative elements is, in fact, one of his leading aesthetic tenets. . . . Ross Macdonald's well-built books glow with bright interscenic commentary. We are never put into a room without knowing how we got there and what the room looks like. The room takes shape through well-observed details carefully chosen both for atmosphere and idea. The rundown frame shacks, the stucco ranch houses, and the elegant mansions Archer visits have the same authenticity. Often Ross Macdonald will insert a retrospective passage which reviews and summaries the plot for the reader's benefit. (pp. 36-7)

At the top of their form, [the Archer novels] vibrate with suspense, undertones, and classical inevitability. The success of most crime fiction depends on plot, and nobody builds a plot more ingeniously than Ross Macdonald. . . . Everything before [the conclusion] is so unforced that the resolution surprises us. The form of an Archer stays hidden until the novel is over. . . .

The beauty of the narrative construction lies more in its process than in its conclusion. The inclusiveness of the dialectic—the many-sided plot and Archer's method of finding out and then using information—depicts the vitality of life. The cases move forward with the precision, gait, and confidence of *Bleak House* or a Simenon. They make us feel we are in the hands of a master; we may be tricked but not mocked. (p. 37)

[Ross Macdonald's] style has flaws and blemishes, some of which come from his use of stage, rather than narrative, techniques of plot-structure. These, built into the brickwork of the novels, could not be smoothed without a major dismantling. The novel is not a stage play; it uses different rhetorical conventions to generate a quite different illusion of life. The need for the detective to collect evidence from many different people crams most detective fiction with more dialogue than it can bear. Ross Macdonald, too, has a topheavy proportion of dialogue to narration. This imbalance squeezes the characters into the shrill, small spotlight of present time, a handicap offset in part by the presence of old letters, old photographs, and old people. . . . A flaw just as serious is that the characters sometimes talk like novelists. The too-sharp eye for detail, the encompassing summation, the measured speech—these all violate the realism of spoken language. (p. 44)

An aesthetic contribution . . . that reaches past the purview of detective fiction, is . . . [the use] of Archer as an "open narrator." The open narrator is a corollary of the continuing detective. He is easily recognizable and needs no reintroducing; since we know basically what to expect from him, we can watch his personality unfold in its own good time without growing anxious. . . . By adding to him in each book, Ross Macdonald keeps options alive; Archer reveals himself over many novels and remains fluid, besides. As with Anthony Powell's Nicholas Jenkins (*A Dance to the Music of Time*) and C. P. Snow's Lewis Eliot (*Strangers and Brothers*), a real self emerges from the Archer novels without dominating any single action. (p. 47)

A licensed private detective, [Archer] stands for authority, or the father. His reordering of time to the logic of detective-work enables him, first, to stop time and, supremely, to connect far-flung events; he becomes both the connecting principle and justicer in the lives of people he has only known for two or three days.

Some of Ross Macdonald's projections of him as God or man-God are . . . pointed. At different times, he is called altruist, do-gooder, Crusader, a zealot in his trade, even Mr. God. (pp. 47-8)

Archer's fate is that of all man-Gods. Though physically

damaged, he stays spiritually whole; his professional honor and compassion, if dented, will serve him again. Though he pays compliments graciously, he doesn't like to receive them. Though he stops crime, he often gives the police the credit. His clients do not know how hard he has worked or what risks he has taken for them. Yet his modesty and professional stoicism do not wane into quietism. The West's twentieth-century man-God cannot reign or preside. Of our time, he must certify his divinity in movement and action. (p. 48)

Ross Macdonald's early tendency to judge can convert dramatic events into moral issues. . . . Archer loses us when he does . . . moral calisthenics or when he turns a case into a crusade. He is a much better Leatherstocking than an evangelist.

Always ready to sermonize, the early Archer doesn't shrink from reminding people of their moral duties or from telling them, especially policemen, how to do their jobs. But one wonders whether some of his cocksureness comes less from within than from his author's artistic unreadiness. If Ross Macdonald has become an important novelist, his growth has been slow. His first seven or eight titles, though rich in lively characters and scenes, creak with implausibility. Archer's double role as narrator and plot-mechanism makes him, unfortunately, the focus of the novels' structural flaws. (p. 57)

[Not] all Archer's personal failings come from problems in narrative form. He is often priggish in his own right; he stretches and even breaks the rules. Known to bully and to threaten witnesses, he is capable of brutal sadism. . . . At least once a novel he will blunder badly—misjudging a witness, mixing sentiment with detection, even exploiting people. (p. 58)

Archer acts from conviction, and his work, like that of God, mirrors him. Lew Archer has a firm sense of himself —moral integrity as well as moral passion. He has tried to heal himself by fitting his needs to those of others. His charity is rooted in pain. Born too of pain, Lazarus-like, is the overarching virtue irradiating the novels. (p. 67)

[The four novels] published between 1944-48 under the byline of Kenneth Millar introduce the family as a major influence; both family conflict and the repetition of obsessive behavior by members of the same family in *The Dark Tunnel* and *The Three Roads* prefigure similar struggles in *The Underground Man* and *Sleeping Beauty*. Introduced, too, in these four fledgling works is the idea that crisis engulfs whole families, not just individuals. Any unit comprising sub-units will be controlled by the least stable one. Accordingly, anybody drawn into a crime will draw in others. As his family rallies round to protect him, normal work routines break, trips are made, and long-dormant relationships revive. The nightmare reunion of Dr. Herman Schneider and his son, a Nazi intelligence officer in *The Dark Tunnel,* causes the same havoc as that of the elderly Macready sisters in *The Chill,* a work published twenty years later.

The first quartet of novels also establishes the importance of the Midwest in Ross Macdonald's thought. . . . Besides storing many indelible memories, the Midwest, because of its conservative tradition, also symbolizes the buried past where the California detective sometimes digs for answers to old mysteries. (p. 68)

Tunnel is both a spy thriller and an academic novel. The two fictional strains don't fit well because [the voice of Branch, the narrator] wavers between the bookish and the hard-boiled. . . . Branch has a literary quotation for every occasion. Many come at dangerous moments, when his instincts should turn to survival, not to Shakespeare. He also has the habit of working a literary reference into a sarcasm or a private joke with the reader; at times, he'll display the academic temper and then belittle it.

The reason for all this? Ross Macdonald conceived of Branch as an all-purpose man—an impromptu patriot-sleuth with the fast fists and street sense of the private eye and also the thoughtfulness of the college professor. . . . Ross Macdonald's own attempts to confer superiority upon Branch fight the plot. (p. 77)

Ross Macdonald's handling of Sam Drake [the narrator-hero of *Trouble Follows Me*], reflects a maturity in technique, if not in attitude and outlook. In principle, anyway, the intellectual and the athlete in Drake do not obtrude as in Branch. Drake is touched but not tainted by commonness; he doesn't parade his humanism or patriotism as Branch did. He is a journalist by trade, not a Ph.D. in English; in fact, a career officer in the U.S. Navy, he may never have gone to college. His crime-hunting takes less agility, endurance, and physical strength than Branch's did. Yet, in spite of this restraint, Drake, too, comes across as an all-purpose man, gratifying the reader's moral superiority. He says, "I'm an intellectual among roughnecks and a roughneck among intellectuals." His choosing duty over love affirms his manliness as do his Hemingwayish references to Midwestern towns, as if the Midwest had a corner on tough-minded, grainy honesty. (p. 78)

Hector Land, ex-prizefighter, ship's steward, and Black Israelite [in *Trouble Follows Me*] remains Ross Macdonald's only portrayal of a black American. Much of his brawn and biddability stems from the pseudo-scientific notion of post-Darwinian man. Like O'Neill's Emperor Jones and Hairy Ape, Land shows more intellectual development than a gorilla, but less than a human.Even more important than Ross Macdonald's conception of him as an evolutionary throwback or "missing link" is his place in the plot. Land is a good bad man, whom Ross Macdonald neither patronizes nor uses as a peg on which to hang his views on racial injustice. But without intending it, he makes Land his main character. Drake's ubiquity makes the book's title a misnomer. Drake is not singled out for trouble or bad luck. . . . Because he is no fugitive, *Trouble* lacks the tension and drive of *Tunnel*. The suspense it does rouse comes largely from Land. Although neither hero nor villain, he's the novel's title character, embodying both the heroic and the base. (p. 81)

The morality of *Trouble* is not cheap or trite. Ross Macdonald never presents Negroes or Jews as the oppressed noblemen of nature. . . . Though Ross Macdonald doesn't sympathize with the methods they used to get into the political mainstream, neither does he favor the white Christian society that made communism and black nationalism last refuges for the powerless. This complex political attitude he conveys as a novelist should—through character, incident, and setting rather than manifestos. (p. 82)

But [his] indirect plea to look for meaning and value in neglected places leaves out women. . . . [Their] moral lapses determine the characters' worth for Ross Macdonald. The moral identity he foists on his women is as shabby as the political identity he accuses the white establishment of foisting on blacks.

But no lowering comes from Ross Macdonald's style. The bright, crisp language of *Trouble* reflects both a sharp eye and tender heart; the narrative materials are well selected, imaginatively perceived, and carefully arranged. (pp. 82-3)

Blue City mars its *verismo;* the slice of life it serves up is locker-room fare. Though it has a rough strength, it lacks any offsetting humor, irony, or comparison. The wit is malicious, not affectionate, absurd, or funny. (p. 91)

[The cynicism of the narrator, John Weather, and his] breakneck life style rob the book of a humanizing perspective. *Blue City* is too closely tied to the cult of the hard-boiled. Its evil characters are neither understandable nor sympathetic. Though it has some good scenes, its characters lack life. . . . And though Weather's stepmother and dead father give Weather more family background than Branch or Drake had, the background exerts no psychological force. Weather's individualism has no ancestry.

The move from hyper-masculine police drama to psychological realism brings both a slowing of pace and more introspection. *The Three Roads* (1948) includes only two killings, one of which is done by the police. . . . Like John Weather, Bret Taylor is an actionist, a doer rather than a thinker or talker. . . . Like his brutal counterpart, Weather, Taylor finds out more in a day than the police do in months. Yet, though police corruption is no issue in *Roads,* other similarities between the two books come to mind. The characters, if not sexually determined, are sexually explainable; most of their problems springing from a troubled libido. This sexuality isn't treated commercially, as in *Tunnel.* Though there's a mystery whose solution depends on sex, the book is no whodunit, either. The solution forms but part of the hero's search for wholeness. Again following *Blue City,* the family crisis and unsolved murder carry the action into the past. The most overtly Oedipal of Ross Macdonald's novels leans most heavily on events that took place before the dramatized action begins. (pp. 92-3)

The Three Roads is his first California novel and also his first novel which stresses the vitality of the past. . . . Endorsing eternal recurrence, the novel has a classical flow, in which acts of passion and retribution occur. (p. 96)

Rich in character, setting, and style, [*The Barbarous Coast*] is a strong book. But its strength lacks coordination. Ross Macdonald's marvelous material suffers from vagueness and lack of dramatic follow-through. Notably weak is dramatic selection. We don't move close enough to the characters to imagine ourselves capable of their crimes. Instead of finding pieces of ourselves in the book, we examine the motives of strangers. . . . *Coast* is a driving good novel. Had Ross Macdonald sharpened its motivation, he could have supplied the conviction to make it a memorable one. (pp. 166-67)

The writer was right to view *The Galton Case* (1959) as both "a turning point" and a personal favorite among his books. Though he had already written about exile and semi-recovery, two of the crucial problems of his own American-Canadian life, he hadn't given them the power that pulsates through *Galton.* The novel, the only one Ross Macdonald has singled out, in "Writing *The Galton Case,*" for critical discussion, sustains a higher level of inspiration than any previous work from his pen. Though well planned, it doesn't look preconceived, alternating smoothly between California and the northern Midwest, rich and poor characters, simplicity and complexity. . . . This elaborate dialectic, no technical self-indulgence, imparts truths too sheer for straightforward presentation. If not an attack on reason, *Galton* has little faith in intellectual systems. Characters with formalized plans for the future meet bad ends; recurring blunders by Archer and the police break with the assumptions of the Sherlockian tradition; also humanizing the cosmopolitan scope of the book is the primitivism underlying it: people want families they can call their own. (pp. 178-79)

Ross Macdonald's calling *Galton* "a breakthrough novel" refers not only to aesthetic distance and control; the book also probes the deep meanings of the author's life. . . . This highly personal novel cried to be written. Coping with the deprivations of not-having and not-belonging, it confronts "the poverty and brokenness" of Ross Macdonald's "worst days." He never dug deeper for material than in *Galton.* The threat of dispossession and displacement lurking behind the action shows in early ideas for titles like "A Matter of Identity," "The Castle and the Poorhouse," and "The Impostor." Ross Macdonald's "Preface to *The Galton Case*" yokes this alienation to the Oedipus myth. The essay repeats the workpoint from his notebook that was to give shape to the novel: "Oedipus angry vs. parents for sending him away into a foreign country." . . .

Subjects like dual citizenship and the lost father (Kenneth Millar's father left the family when Ken was three) makes *Galton* a landmark for Ross Macdonald both as a writer and a person. The novel did for him what *Sons and Lovers* did for Lawrence, allowing him to face and understand his past. (p. 187)

Galton is less of a parade of Ross Macdonald's obsessions than an artistic expression of them. Craftsmanship tempers feeling throughout. Resisting any temptation to identify the auctorial self with young John, Ross Macdonald scatters bits of himself into other characters. Archer mirrors him as accurately as ever; in fact, the detection done by Dr. Howell, relieving Archer of some mechanical sleuth-work, lets him live more fully and generously; Tony Galton, whom we never meet, was born in 1915, the same year as the author; and, though he studied engineering, his real work was the writing of imaginative literature. Finally, Ross Macdonald has explained how Tom Lemberg both foreshadows and serves as an opposite number to John, his own boyhood double: Archer's meeting with Tom in Chapter 5, when Tom steals the detective's car, "prefigures Archer's confrontation with the boy impostor John." The parallels continue. . . . The ability to express deeply felt subject matter would go to waste unless Ross Macdonald worked John smoothly into the plot. Again, artistry modulates obsession. Ross Macdonald only puts John before us long enough to certify his reality; the youth has no marked personal style, quirk, or skill other than his acting. He is kept colorless for a reason. His character is developed from the outside, through the complex reactions of others to him. Maria Galton, Ada Reichler, and Dr. Howell, all having a vested interest in him, read their needs into John; he expresses their hopes and fears. Had he been portrayed with psychic depth, he would have blocked this variety. The plot thrives on his indefiniteness. Ross Macdonald hides his identity as long as possible. Even Archer can't make up his mind about John—doubting, challenging, being both puzzled and impressed. . . . Ross Macdonald keeps changing Archer's mind and bringing in new evidence in order to mystify us. The more we learn about John, the less we know. Our curiosity rises accordingly. His shifting role amid several developing dramas keeps us wondering and, what is more important for any writer, reading. (pp. 188-89)

Galton is richer than either *Target* or *Grin;* the love triangle . . . has a far more complex effect, both dramatically and structurally, than anything like it in the past; its three participants struggle blindly to bring on the calamity that destroys them.

Archer also helps make *Galton* the writer's most moving and intense work to date. He doesn't let what he might be, the ideal, blot out what he is—a fallible person working at a hard job. . . . Ross Macdonald challenged himself deeply in *Galton* and, thanks to the introspective effort the challenge posed, grew as an artist. (p. 190)

An apposite successor to *Galton, The Ferguson Affair* (1960) contains many moments worthy of Ross Macdonald's later work and none of the easy cynicism riding his early fiction. The book, a non-Archer, is deeply imagined: its probes the anxieties of Ross Macdonald's life as doggedly as *Galton;* it delivers action, suspense, and atmosphere; it balances hidden fears and ingenious warmth. (p. 191)

[*The Ferguson Affair*] shows how completely, if unconsciously, a writer can reveal himself in his work. The likenesses between [the title character] and Ross Macdonald's forerunner, Raymond Chandler, are too glaring to overlook. . . . Chandler and Ross Macdonald both set their novels in greater Los Angeles, use Oedipal materials, and couch their rhetoric within the hard-boiled literary tradition. But Ross Macdonald had all but given up hard-boiled fiction in *Doomsters*. Why should Chandler exert such a strong spell on him two novels later? The laying-to-rest of the literary father looks pointless. Ross Macdonald had to make the gesture, even though he did it without malice. Chandler influenced him more than any other writer. . . . For most of the 1950s, Ross Macdonald was a better writer than the more celebrated Chandler. Knowing this, he lets Ferguson, whom he likes, gain his hopes, but only after putting him through the direst ordeals inflicted on anybody in the canon. (pp. 200-01)

Ferguson stands closer to traditional detective fiction than do most of the Archers. Many of the riggings of the sleuth novel are here—the legwork, the red herring (Pike Granada), the laborious but necessary work of checking old out-of-town telephone books, the all-purpose secretary. . . . The book also includes scientific detection. . . .

Ferguson is a rich, robustly told novel that exerts force at several levels. Gunnarson allows Ross Macdonald to include things that wouldn't fit into an Archer. Yet because the book has too much material, some of these things lack definition. The domestic subplot doesn't fuse with the main action. Some events occur out of view. . . . The ending is clogged and contrived. . . . The unveiling of criminal motives counts as much in detective fiction as the catching of the criminal; the one wouldn't make sense without the other. Structurally, Speare plays a role as bogus as that of the *deus ex machina* of classical drama.

Most of the way, the structure is trim and smart. Though the novel ends badly, it has a strong start. (p. 203)

In its way, the book breaks as much new artistic ground as the more admired *Galton Case*. Strewing its red herrings discreetly and using solid police work to unravel the mysteries, *Ferguson* relies heavily upon the conventions of standard literary detection. These it rubs to a deep, mellow gloss. The detective novel has more sinew and suppleness thanks to *The Ferguson Affair*. (p. 205)

The books from *The Wycherly Woman* (the earliest and least successful of the group) to *Black Money* deal with tragic sexual passion. Some of the tragedy is caused by money; money cuts across the passion in all the books. . . . In no case is a relationship or commitment inviolable. Price tags appear on human hearts everywhere; the sacred and the precious becomes items for barter. (p. 206)

The plots raise both moral and sociological questions, with characters of all backgrounds joining in the investigations. This inclusiveness promotes a realism usually reserved for the mainstream novel of manners and morals. Yet Ross Macdonald holds his ground. Literary conjurer as well as psychologist of repressed feelings, he builds plots expressive of the tensions undergirding them. The works published between 1961-66 grow more elaborate and complex. Red herrings abound; options spring open and slam shut; characters surprise us while acting in line with their ruling passions. Some of these, it needs saying, are women. As he gains artistic seasoning, Ross Macdonald imparts new depths and shadings to his female characters; women bear more and more of the narrative burden. What is more, the killer in three of the five novels in the group is female.

The years have brought other changes. Titles like *The Chill* and *Black Money* show Ross Macdonald's vision darkening with the years. Reality has become tougher; experience offers more pain than it does joy, and we feel the pain more keenly. Desperation becomes more common. Middle-aged and elderly women now kill as well as adolescents (*Pool*) and wives in their early twenties (*Way* and *Doomsters*). Whereas the soldiers and sailors in the four pre-Archers were men of derring-do, their older counterparts in *The Wycherly Woman, The Zebra-Striped Hearse,* and *The Far Side of the Dollar* all invite pity. The harshness of routine living also accounts for Archer's frequent mistakes, hesitations, and acts of compassion; the recent works are both tougher and more tender-hearted than their predecessors. One reason why people need compassion and charity is the growing danger of living a dream. In the earlier works, a fantasy might become a fact without causing widescale damage. . . . The fantasies spun by the heroes of the novels published between 1961-66 end in isolation or death. No longer livable, the dream bursts, its fragments, often storing a twenty-years' charge, shattering violently. Dreamers use up their options quickly in these dark novels. The past tears away their disguises and smokes them out of their hiding places; in *The Wycherly Woman* and *The Far Side of the Dollar,* the killers end up as suicides.

But gloom and waste don't engulf all. To recognize darkness is not to sink into it. The later works of Ross Macdonald express more than despair. Resisting cynicism and moral quietism, he maintains moral balance, stylistic flair, and control of his characters. To write about evil constitutes an honest attempt to cope with it. Unlike most American novelists, he improves with the years. Evil bores, inhibits, and confines. On the other hand, the Archers published between 1961-66, broadening their human base, display new strengths, with *The Chill* and *Black Money* pushing to the top of the canon. (pp. 206-07)

The thriller is an action story, a narrative with a drive and moral simplicity lacking in most mainstream fiction; suspense, movement, and the intellectual exercise of naming the killer replace character analysis and subtle moral discriminations. Ross Macdonald's contribution to the genre consists of bringing depth and resonance to plots depending on swiftness of execution. In thrillers, action usually supercedes character. The Archers maintain a brisk tempo without allowing the crisis to dominate. They keep action and character in healthy balance by seating many of their key events in the past; channeling a dramatic event through a twenty-year shaft of time creates intensities that safeguard rather than blur individuality. The presence of psychiatrists, social workers, and policemen helps create a forum where the meaning of these intensities is debated. Because detection isn't an exact science, it thrives on discussion and debate; the detective writer's need to conceal both the killer's motive and identity till the end invites speculation, much of it historical or psychological, in the Archers.

Murder brings the tensions undergirding the Archers into the material world. Ross Macdonald said in a 1972 radio broadcast in London that his books try "to take the psychic event which has occurred in all of us, the guilty loss of togetherness and innocence, and put it back in the external world where it has had its repercussions." One of these repercussions is a craving for security, which usually translates in the late Archers to an urge to find and then reunite with a lost parent. The shuttle between chaos and order forms one of Ross Macdonald's basic narrative rhythms. . . . Murder energizes the rhythm. Unlike killing, which is often accidental, murder has roots in relationships that go back in time. Because it usually happens close to home, its solution will lie in the home life of the murderer. But this life depends on secret ties. The detective's discovery of these ties includes both intellectual challenge and bodily risk. Murder taking place in a close-knit social structure becomes harder to detect because, based on motives deeper than money or political differences, it is more desperate.

Archer's job in Ross Macdonald's four latest books [*The Instant Enemy, The Goodbye Look, The Underground Man,* and *Sleeping Beauty*] is his usual one—that of finding the connection between the people, places, and motives informing the crisis. . . . Rather than describing reality realistically, the Archers are metaphors for crisis. Ross Macdonald doesn't inform so much as he creates and communicates the shatter-effects of crisis.

The four latest Archers maintain the sharpness of their predecessors while broadening and strengthening their thematic base. The forest fire in *The Underground Man* and the oil spill in *Sleeping Beauty,* by fusing moral guilt and ecological disaster, bring Ross Macdonald's inventiveness new scale and dignity. The lesson of these last two works hinges on the dangers of urbanization: cutting yourself off from nature causes almost all your troubles. (pp. 274-75)

Enemy extends the scope of [Archer's] mind. He surprises us by recognizing a Klee, a Kokoschka, and a Picasso in Jasper Blevins's private art gallery; later, we wonder where he acquired the learning to identify Erik Erikson, Erich Fromm, Paul Goodman, and Edgar Z. Friedenberg as "the freer spirits" in social science today. This learning doesn't enter the investigation, though, as it would in an English detective story featuring a highly informed gentleman-sleuth. . . . His best insight, which owes little either to formal learning or the mechanics of detection, comes when he explains Sandy's leaving her diary where her mother could find it as an indirect plea for help.

But even insights like this can't humanize Ross Macdonald's most ingeniously plotted novel to date. The writer plants his clues fairly, sets forth his subjects clearly, and reminds us tactfully of the shifts and changes taking place in the fast-moving action. But the mixture of events is too rich. Though brilliantly observed and organized, the novel isn't lifelike; it has more material than it can assimilate. . . . The book is too thickly worked. Missing is the openness and good-natured indeterminacy that left unexplained the deaths of Ronald Jaimet in *Hearse* and Roy Fablon in *Chill.* The logic of the plot is the only logic the characters obey. Without being rushed or coldly analytical, *Enemy* is all execution. Besides Laurel, who dies early, none of the other murder victims matter to us. . . . Weak characters mean weak resolutions. Archer's last-chapter demonstration of the evidence gives only mild intellectual pleasure. The evidence comes from a tape recording. Furthermore, . . . the hunt for the killer isn't a race to stop him from killing others.

The narrative curve of the action expresses negation. *Enemy* opens at daybreak, everything looking "fresh and new and awesome as creation." It ends in darkness; Archer is eating cold, stale chicken as he looks out of his office window. . . . The final image of *Enemy* settles nothing. Nor is it meant to. The people who pass under Archer's office window portray urban futility. Archer's floating the torn yellow flakes of Ruth Marburg's $100,000 check onto their heads neither redeems nor blesses them. Solving the Hackett case has drained Archer. Lonely, bitter, and tired, he is one with the passers-by he describes in the urban barrens.

The elaborate narrative mode sought in *Enemy* emerges brilliantly in *The Goodbye Look* (1969). The plot runs in tangents and oblique lines; it splits into parallel strands which cross and recross; spanning four generations, it attempts new turns and variations with time (one character accuses Archer of having a tortuous imagination). This flashing silver neither blinds nor tarnishes, thanks to the book's well-regulated style and sensitive, thoughtful narrator-hero. In short, *Look* has found a controlling voice for the intricate narrative technique of Ross Macdonald's maturity. The superiority of *Look* over *Enemy,* in fact, makes the later work the cornerstone of a technical achievement new in the history of crime fiction. (pp. 288-90)

The last chapter [of *The Goodbye Look*] is a sad comedown. Ross Macdonald hadn't left a loose thread up to the finale. . . . [The] first thirty-five chapters of *Look* are nearly flawless. The novel resembles *Chill, Dollar,* and *Money* more than it does *Enemy,* which stands closer to it in time but not in quality of performance. *Look* has the elaborate design of *Enemy,* and its plot begins with a childhood trauma. But Ross Macdonald infuses it with more understanding than he did *Enemy;* Archer's greater thoughtfulness in *Look* giving the other characters added warmth and insight. *Look* also has more detection. (p. 301)

The Underground Man (1971) is Ross Macdonald's most ambitious book to date. . . . Serious and thoughtful, *Man* both absorbs and reflects experience with a high degree of sensitivity. Ross Macdonald doesn't merely conjure up emotions but, rather, helps us understand them. (p. 306)

[The finale of *Sleeping Beauty*] lacks force because it isn't prepared for. Ross Macdonald hides Marian Lennox most of the way; her murderousness doesn't flow from any observed set of traits or human values. . . . The problem she raises is more structural than motivational. The novel's design is out of tilt. We don't know Marian well enough to care about her guilt. (p. 331)

Ross Macdonald's unswerving eye for detail and fine timing gives the well-turned plot [of *Sleeping Beauty*] a temporal and spatial structure that adjusts easily to the many changes in the action. This interplay of logic, structure, and incident represents a high-order achievement. . . . Ross Macdonald is challenging himself with new ideas and putting detective fiction to new uses. His imagination grows wilder, stronger, and more mystical with the years. Steady in focus, everburgeoning in range, the Archers form a cumulative masterpiece. No student of American detective fiction can imagine the development of the genre without them. (p. 337)

Peter Wolfe, in his Dreamers Who Live Their Dreams: The World of Ross Macdonald's Novels *(copyright © 1976 by The Popular Press), Popular Press, 1976, 346 p.*

NEWGATE CALLENDAR

[Macdonald's "Lew Archer, Private Investigator"] covers a 30-year span. It also has an introduction by the author, in which he makes the point that the American private eye "speaks for our common humanity" and demonstrates the shift from aristocracy (as represented by such investigators as Sherlock Holmes and Lord Peter Wimsey) to democracy. Macdonald enthusiasts will be rushing to get their hands on this book, and so should everyone else.

Newgate Callendar, "Crime: 'Lew Archer, Private Investigator'," in The New York Times Book Review *(© 1977 by The New York Times Company; reprinted by permission), December 18, 1977, p. 25.*

* * *

MacLEISH, Archibald 1892-

An American poet, playwright, and editor, MacLeish is a man of eclectic achievements and has been involved in literature, art, government, and other facets of American cultural life. Often focusing on political topics in his work, MacLeish is, as James Southworth says, "not political in the party sense of the word, but in its larger connotation of the problem of man's relation to society." MacLeish's thematic concerns also encompass nature, love, and reminiscences. He has won three Pulitzer Prizes. (See also *CLC,* Vols. 3, 8, and *Contemporary Authors,* Vols. 9-12, rev. ed.)

R. P. BLACKMUR

The past is a living creature with a talent for seeming stable at particular moments. The use of an old myth today may provide a scaffold for contemporary feelings and ideas. It may offer a form, capable of any degree of solidity, for the most abstract subject. Mr. MacLeish in his play, *Nobodaddy,* deals with "the dramatic situation which the condition of self-consciousness in an indifferent universe" seems to present. For his scaffold he has arbitrarily employed certain incidents in the myth of Eden. He has made an intense and very "modern" poem out of his theme, even though he has chosen blank verse as his method. There is of course no argument, no discussion, in the play; these are attitudes presented with the force of poetry, not ideas demonstrated by logic.

Nobodaddy was the name Blake used for the god of jealousy and reason, for the god of this world, the devil. Presumably, Nobodaddy is here also the human selfconsciousness. (p. 339)

From the entry of Abel to the end of the play amid rain and thunder, the drama is real in the finest sense. The action results from the conditions given, and the words rise out of the action and have themselves the force and density of physical movement. (pp. 340-41)

But Eve was ill-served in this play. She was the source of both Cain and Abel; surely the pattern of the play demanded that Eve at the last should connect, or understand, the terrifying disparateness of her two sons. Their fate would have been the sharper, and her own; the plot would have seemed complete, and the interpretation, within its limits, final. Surely she might have understood her creations, and in her own voice have combined them, giving the play a kind of poetic, even philosophic finality which it now lacks. (p. 341)

The reason for the comparative failure of *Nobodaddy* is that its subject-matter was not completely exhausted. An attitude, more than an act, has its consequences; and in art they must all be dealt with. If irrelevant to the artist's interests, they may be swept out of sight, their figures excised from the emotional pattern. If relevant they must enter the structure and complete the symbol, and not otherwise than as their particular character demands. More than the popes, poets are the servants of the servants of God. (p. 342)

R. P. Blackmur, "A Modern Poet in Eden," in Poetry *(© 1926 by The Modern Poetry Association; reprinted by permission of the Editor of* Poetry*), Vol. XXVIII, No. VI, September, 1926, pp. 339-42.*

JOHN WAIN

Mr. MacLeish has a weakness for the large subject; he finds convenient fairways in the major myths; previous works of his have rehandled the material of *Hamlet* and of the Book of Job. In [*Herakles*] he is at one with many or most 20th-century poets. . . . Mr. MacLeish has certainly made it a central part of his business to "manipulate a continuous parallel" between the immemorial and the modern. . . . But I must admit that the grounds of his considerable success are, for the most part, opaque to me. I cannot understand why *The Hamlet of A. MacLeish* was ever taken with much seriousness. . . . His epic, *Conquistador,* is hardly any more readable than the general run of long narrative poems in our time, which means virtually that it is not readable at all. His most successful verse play, *J.B.,* had a good run in the theatre, and I can only assume that it had some sort of theatrical vitality that made it worth watching; but on the page it is so disastrously inferior to the original as to be positively agonizing. I think if I were to spend an evening in the theatre following the story of Job, I would rather have someone come on to the stage, open the Bible and just read the story aloud; it is one of the greatest works of literature, quite arguably *the* greatest, and in MacLeish's treatment of it, as in his treatment of *Hamlet*, one has the uncomfortable sensation of watching the original "stiffen in a rented house."

In spite of all this, a new work by MacLeish is always worth looking into; there is always the chance that he might have rung the bell; the evidence of his shorter poems is there to remind us that he is, or has been, a poet of true sensibility and originality. One of these, "Ars Poetica" (1926), must be one of the most often quoted of all modern poems, partly no doubt because it has provided a slogan for the modern criticism of poetry, but also because it is genuinely impressive. . . . *Herakles,* I am glad to report, is rather more successful in "being" than *J.B.* was. It is deftly constructed as one large-scale metaphor: of man's achievement resulting in a sharpened confrontation with what is tragic in his destiny. The play has two acts, and it presents two great achievers. . . . (p. 25)

MacLeish has got hold of a real subject, and he is too experienced to miss the opportunities inherent in it. Also, since there is no one clearly defined masterpiece, like the Book of Job, towering in the background, but only a tangle of stories which can well bear being told again, there isn't that crippling sense of secondhandness. The writing, line by line, is not very interesting, but probably speakable by actors. Rhythmically—and for the writer of verse drama rhythm is by far the most important single technical problem—MacLeish has kept well clear of the ten-syllable iambic that makes any play sound like sub-Shakespeare; the verse he uses most is a brisk four-beat line that derives, I suppose, from Eliot's *Sweeney Agonistes*. Eliot, one is bound to add, used it much better. . . . MacLeish has very few passages which come off quite successfully; the best writing, on the whole, is in set-pieces like Herakles' description of going down into Hades to fight Cerberus. . . . [Given the] general poise and expertness of the verse, *Herakles* should be attractive to directors, players and audiences; perhaps, to readers on the page also. Certainly, on the coolest analysis, it has something to say and it succeeds in saying it. (pp. 26, 30)

John Wain, "Mr. MacLeish's New Play," in The New Republic *(reprinted by permission of* The New Republic; *© 1967 The New Republic, Inc.), Vol. 157, Nos. 4 & 5, July 22-29, 1967, pp. 25-6, 30.*

HAYDEN CARRUTH

[My] rereading of MacLeish's poems in [*New and Collected Poems, 1917-1976*] has reaffirmed my admiration and has shown me excellences I had overlooked before. Above all I see a devotion to excellence in general, artistic excellence, which means not simply the excellence of craft but that of mind and heart, perhaps especially that of mind and heart. MacLeish began, like most other poets in the period of World War I, with more or less conventional, Georgian verses, but quickly fell under the influence of Eliot. Is that right? Was there a direct influence? (I am not a student of biographies.) Did Herrick write like Jonson because Jonson told him to or because that was the only way he could write —he and many others—with the example of Jonson before him? Certainly we know, with the example of "The Waste Land" (1923) before them, what American and British poets did, scores and hundreds of them who had no more acquaintance of His Grace than the look of his verses on the page (and who would have actively disliked him if they'd met). We know what MacLeish did. . . . The echoes [of Eliot] are unmistakable, cadences, modulations of sound, syntactical patterns. . . . One is distracted by these echoes at first, even irritated by them, but as one reads further, with closer attention to what MacLeish himself was doing, one comes to see—at least I have—that although the whole impact is slighter—yes, still, 50 years later; one is bound to acknowledge it—nevertheless MacLeish's poems contain passages better than anything Eliot ever wrote, more lucid, better integrated, with a more sensitive judgment of the qualities of diction: in short, *in* the manner, unquestionably, but not as *mannered*. It is the achievement of a very intelligent craftsman, and not many were able to do it.

With *Einstein* (1929) and *New Found Land* (1930), MacLeish began to hear his own voice more surely, a discovery coinciding more or less with his return to the U.S. after the years of expatriation. It came to full flower with *Conquistador* (1933). We know its characteristics, the faint rhymes, the falling line-breaks and sudden enjambments, the heavy reliance on connectives, the mixture of rough pentameters and hexameters and sometimes shorter lines. (pp. 147-49)

What to say of *Conquistador,* that splendid poem? One can hardly imagine a more compelling theme for our time, the conquest of Mexico, the confrontation between Cortés and Montezuma, those great men, incorporating everything we have come to feel about the European take-over of America, our pride and its voidance, our helplessness and self-reproach in the face of historical process. And the writing fits the theme; they are welded, they cling together. Still the poem is flawed. One can see how (again speaking as a poet) MacLeish was tempted by the chronicle of Bernal Díaz, the only account of the Spanish expedition possessing contemporary authenticity: there it was, all laid out, the plan and plot of the poem. But in the end MacLeish was hampered by Bernal, who became in the poem only a testy old warrior recalling the exploits of his youth, a tedious narrator. There is too much description in the poem, not enough drama. . . . I wish MacLeish . . . had been more willing to fictionalize, to *mythologize;* for isn't that what epic is all about—myth? And do not doubt me, MacLeish was writing the American epic. That is what he had in mind. Epic needs fiction, however, needs myth, and usually a good dose of it, not just history. Does anyone, for example, believe the argument between Achilles and Agamemnon was really that important in the siege of Troy? (And incidentally, what would Hart Crane have done with the long poem he was projecting on Montezuma, during those same years when MacLeish was writing *Conquistador,* if he had been able to carry it through?) Still and all, *Conquistador* is what we have, it is our best epic (and I do not except *The Bridge*), it is coherent, complete, and strongly conceived, and it contains many, many magnificent passages. It merits a good deal more attention than it has been given lately. (pp. 149-50)

After *Conquistador,* as we know, MacLeish moved further into poetry of political and social feeling, and we may as well say bluntly that these poems don't stand up. Plenty of strong feeling, no doubt, and sound reasoning too; ringing declarations, prophetic ironies, angers and maledictions; but in effect they were versified editorials, not poems. MacLeish committed the same error made by many young radical poets of the 1960's and early 1970's, namely, the failure to transmute feeling and ideology into dramatic or lyrical structures through the intercession of the artistic imagination. Asseveration does not make art; the Declaration of Independence is a political, not a poetic, document. . . . I think the main point to be made about MacLeish's politically inspired poems, once we aknowledge their artistic defect, is that they were definitely of the sustaining, not the destroying order. . . . MacLeish wrote not as a personal crusader, never as a political crank or lonely visionary, but instead as the spokesman of the people, and like all such spokesmen, if they are true to their roles, he wrote with humility, while his "ideology," if you can call it that, was humanitarian common sense and liberalism, as these could then still be understood without the taint of bourgeois insincerity they have acquired more recently. His poems were outgoing, in other words, products of basic poetic and human loving kindness, and whether or not they succeeded as poems they were works of humane purity and valor.

Without abandoning his political predilections, during the 1950's and 1960's MacLeish moved back again toward the personal lyric, where he has always been at his best: poems of love and death, friendship and other attachments, landscapes and seasons, cosmological and moral disconcertions. To my mind his most often quoted lyrics are not his best, such poems as "The End of the World," "Ars Poetica," and "You, Andrew Marvell," though because of their pointedness and self-containedness they make good anthology pieces. Others are better. (pp. 151-52)

Hayden Carruth, "Homage to A. MacLeish," in Virginia Quarterly Review *(copyright, 1977, by the* Virginia Quarterly Review, *The University of Virginia), Vol. 53, No. 1 (Winter, 1977), pp. 146-54.*

JAMES K. ROBINSON

MacLeish's *The Great American Fourth of July Parade* is subtitled *A Verse Play for Radio.* It is a public speech to be broadcast—MacLeish's contribution to the bicentennial. It marks a return to a mode and to an obsessive theme. The mode was poetic drama for radio. . . . The obsessive theme, of course, is America. . . . [In his thirties poems such] as *Frescoes for Mr. Rockefeller's City, Land of the Free* and *America Was Promises,* and in *Colloquy for the States* (1943) MacLeish agonizes over the dark fields of the republic. The agony has become excited reverie in *The Great American Fourth of July Parade*—promises forty or 200 years after. To Jefferson's characteristically sanguine "A sovereign people never can despair," Adams, foreknowing Watergate, can respond

Even a sovereign people that's no longer sovereign?
Even a sovereign people that has learned
its servants have become its masters?
That those who govern, govern for themselves?
A knave in office and a palace guard of fools? . . .

MacLeish has already lived longer than Jefferson; may their common dream live long beyond them. (pp. 348-50)

James K. Robinson, "Sassenachs, Palefaces, and a Redskin: Graves, Auden, MacLeish, Hollander, Wagoner, and Others," in The Southern Review *(copyright, 1978, by James K. Robinson), Vol. 14, No. 2, April, 1978, pp. 348-58.**

PETER BRUNETTE

The danger in reading a poet's prose is that one can too easily be swayed by sounds and syntax, forgetting that words must make sense, too. Fortunately, Archibald MacLeish's passion extends to meaning as well and, for the most part, what he has to say in [*Riders on the Earth: Essays and Recollections*] is worth listening to. In the first part of the book, he discusses from an intensely humanistic point-of-view subjects as various as Thomas Jefferson, the place of science in our lives, and contemporary fiction's flirtation with the absurd. The rest of the book is composed primarily of short autobiographical pieces, where the poet is at his most revealing and, consequently, his most entertaining, and brief mediations on other poets like Pound, Frost, and Sandburg.

Yet, no matter what the particular theme of a given piece, the general theme is always the continuing possibility of making men whole again. . . .

Throughout, one senses a man who suspects he may really be one or two generations behind. He needn't worry. The book is not free of a few tiny blemishes, like the occasional, unconscious sexism. But by the end, one is left thinking how fine it would be simply to know this person who seems to care so extraordinarily much for his fellow human beings.

Peter Brunette, "Brief Notices: 'Riders on the Earth: Essays and Recollections'," in Book World—The Washington Post *(© 1978,* The Washington Post*), April 30, 1978, p. E4.*

TOM JOHNSON

Ten years ago Archibald MacLeish published a prose collection called *A Continuing Journey;* it was a public book, addresses and essays on topics ranging from literary theory to the fate of the nation. Now he has published a new prose collection, *Riders on the Earth;* this one is a private book, filled with MacLeish's reminiscences, meditations, and convictions. They reveal behind the fine mind a generous spirit.

There are two kinds of essays here. In the more formal ones MacLeish examines the course of humanism in the last decade and makes a case for its future. In the others he discusses, fondly but with unsoftened clarity, his own past and the lives and careers of some of his friends and colleagues. He is the last of the race of literary giants that created modernism, and he has had to write these eulogies for some time now. (pp. cxxvi, cxxviii)

MacLeish has, and has long had, a bad name in literary circles that call themselves sophisticated because he is an optimist. Indeed, examining the events of the late sixties, MacLeish finds grounds for hope where many have seen despair. (p. cxxviii)

MacLeish's optimism is not born of naiveté; we should be naive to presume it of a man whose close friends have included not only Ezra Pound and Ernest Hemingway but also Niels Bohr and Franklin Roosevelt. The very range of his experience is astonishing. Perhaps the best reason we might have to take heart about our own futures is the optimism of a man such as this. (p. cxxx)

Tom Johnson, "Sturdy Sense and Vital Humanism," in The Sewanee Review *(copyright © 1978 by The University of the South), Vol. LXXXVI, No. 4, Fall, 1978, pp. cxxvi, cxxviii, cxxx.*

* * *

MacLENNAN, (John) Hugh 1907-

A Canadian novelist, essayist, and editor, MacLennan has emerged as a major voice in Canadian literature. Dealing almost exclusively with nationalistic themes in his work, he has created many vivid portraits of the Canadian character and experience. If not strikingly innovative, his work is skillfully crafted, and has played a positive role in the development of a Canadian identity. (See also *CLC*, Vol. 2, and *Contemporary Authors*, Vols. 5-8, rev. ed.)

GEORGE WOODCOCK

The reason for MacLennan's reputation, and for his undoubted importance as a novelist, are to be found in the original way in which he has interpreted the Canadian scene to his fellow countrymen rather than in any originality of approach to the art of the novel itself. Indeed, if we are concerned with fictional technique, one of the most striking characteristics of *Barometer Rising* and MacLennan's four later novels is their relative conservatism. They are unashamedly didactic; they rely heavily on environmental atmosphere and local colour; their characterisation is oversimplified and moralistic in tone; their language is descriptive rather than evocative; and their action tends to be shaped externally by a Hardyesque use of circumstance and coincidence. What does distinguish them is MacLennan's combination of theme and symbol—his development of the problems of individuals in an emerging nation by means of action built on a simple but powerful foundation of universal myth.

The myth is that of Odysseus translated into terms of modern living; the *Odyssey* itself was the product of a people in the process of becoming aware of itself, and, appropriately, the theme which MacLennan uses it to illuminate is the growth of a Canadian national consciousness. Indeed, the most striking—and in some ways the most jarring—feature of MacLennan's books is the degree to which the national theme in its various aspects forms an imposed pattern within which the lives of the characters tend to be worked out rather than working themselves out. . . . This predominance of the national theme is a factor that must be taken into account in any attempt to understand MacLennan's work, since it bears a close relationship to his most evident weaknesses as a novelist, and also since its progressive assimilation into a fictionally viable form runs parallel to his growth towards maturity as a writer. (pp. 7-8)

MacLennan not merely establishes in *Barometer Rising* a Homeric plot of the wanderer returning to a mysteriously changed homeland. He also uses for the first time a group of symbolic characters which will recur in various permutations in his later novels; the returning wanderer, the waiting woman, the fatherless child, the wise doctor—sometimes transformed into the wise old man, and the primitive, violent, but essentially good giant. If we wish to seek a Homeric parallel, the quintet of Odysseus, Penelope, Telemachus, Mentor and Eumaeus seems obvious, though MacLennan is too good a writer to follow the pattern slavishly, and we shall see the relationships of these five basic characters changing from novel to novel until, in *The Watch that Ends the Night,* the wanderer, the wise doctor and the primitive giant are finally united in that super-Odysseus, Jerome Martell.

There are some satisfying things in *Barometer Rising*. The atmosphere—the very physical feeling—of Halifax four decades ago is admirably recreated, and the action moves with the right momentum towards the grand climax of the explosion. And this event is celebrated in a passage of fine reconstructive reporting which establishes at the outset the power of describing action in which MacLennan has always excelled. The later chapters narrating the rescue work are maintained at a level of sustained vigour, and the diminuendo from catastrophe to the saddened realisation of human happiness when Neil and Penelope are finally and fully reunited gives the appropriate last touch to the novel's balance.

But these virtues, which make *Barometer Rising* a constantly interesting book, are balanced by defects which are due partly to deficiencies in technique and partly to MacLennan's view of life and the world. For example, the relationship between the lovers is the least convincing of all the relationships in the novel because of a curiously embarrassed clumsiness which makes MacLennan incapable of dealing with any aspect of sex except in high-mindedly sentimental terms. (pp. 9-10)

More serious, because it seems to spring from a philosophic fatalism perennial in MacLennan's attitude, is the mechanical impetus that at times—and particularly during the explosion—takes the action wholly out of the hands of the characters. (p. 10)

The final flaw of *Barometer Rising* comes from the too articulate concern of the major characters with the destiny of Canada. There are times when this theme assumes a crude and abstract form which tears like a jagged spur into the unity of both feeling and style. . . .

MacLennan's second and third novels, *Two Solitudes* and *The Precipice,* are even more dominated than *Barometer Rising* by the effort to create the arch of Canadian unity, and, because everything else in them is eventually subordinated to the elaboration of the national theme, they are the least successful of MacLennan's novels, in human understanding and formal cohesion alike. (p. 11)

[The] first part of *Two Solitudes* has a close unity; it is bound together by the common anxieties of war and by the virtual identity of the larger problem of racial conflict with the actual lives and relationships of the characters. The problem seems to grow with the story rather than the story being fabricated to suit the problem, and the characters, Father Beaubien, Captain Yardley, the financier Huntly McQueen, Athanase himself, are up to this point well-knit and self-consistent. If *Two Solitudes* had ended with Tallard's death, it would have been a moving and cohesive book. But up to this point it merely presents the problem of racial relations; it does not have the logical completeness of presenting a solution, and this MacLennan seeks, at the expense of his novel, in its later chapters.

After Tallard's death the central character becomes his second son, Paul, a Telemachus fated to complete his father's unfinished Odyssey. . . . [He] can speak English without a French accent and French without an English accent, and so personifies racial reconciliation. (p. 12)

MacLennan is so anxious to make his point that he is not content merely to show Paul as the obvious human symbol of two traditions united; at the end of the novel he actually steps out of the novelist's garment and assumes that of the social historian to deliver a final chapter of authorial reflection, not on the fate of his characters, but on the destiny of the Canada they represent.

The conclusion of *Two Solitudes* is in fact contrived to fit a nationalist message, and this divides it so sharply from the earlier chapters that, while the story of Athanase seems written by a novelist acutely sensitive to concrete human predicaments, the story of Paul reads as if it were written by a man in whom this very kind of sensitiveness had been wholly submerged under the abstractions of a destiny-ridden view of history.

The same rather startling dichotomy is evident in *The Precipice,* MacLennan's worst novel. In *The Precipice* the life of a sleepy and narrow-minded Ontario town, intended to represent Canada between the wars, is shown in opposition to the "precipice" of New York, which attracts so many innocent Canadians to moral destruction. This is the only novel in which MacLennan's principal character is a woman, and his inability to penetrate the feminine with any profundity . . . is undoubtedly one of the principal reasons for its failure. (pp. 12-13)

Like *Two Solitudes, The Precipice* begins well; the early chapters on the small town life of the three sisters are alive, self-consistent and perceptive. But in New York, among the brassy glitter of familiar clichés on city life, the sense of an original world disappears, and the novel slumps into a stock romance. . . . As a tract it is doubtless admirable; as fiction it is extremely dull.

Again, the fault lies in the attempt to force a lesson, and one notices in *The Precipice,* as in *Two Solitudes,* how far the effort to work out a social problem in logical terms tends to weaken the mythical structure that MacLennan brings forward from *Barometer Rising*. In each of these intermediate novels we encounter again the Odyssean pattern of journey and return, and also, at least in part, the Homeric group of characters. But both plot and characters lose strength when the author seeks to state explicitly what should be suggested figuratively. (pp. 13-14)

In contrast to the novels that preceded it, *Each Man's Son* is a tensely constructed and well-unified book, in which the balance of theme and mythical structure is re-established. Central to the novel is the tragedy of the failing boxer, Archie MacNeil, and in the portrayal of Archie's world of prize fights and shabby gymnasia MacLennan writes with an extraordinary descriptive power. But Archie's fate, the fate of a basically good primitive in an environment of cynical exploitation, does not suggest the only theme of the novel; there is also the even stronger theme of Calvinist guilt, which afflicts Archie and all the other people. . . .

The structure within which MacLennan develops these two themes differs considerably from that used in *Two Solitudes* and *The Precipice*. There he allowed the statement of a problem to be followed in chronological sequence by its solution, and the result was a linear pattern whose lack of inner tension undoubtedly contributed to the anti-climax into which both books eventually fell. In *Each Man's Son* MacLennan returns emphatically to the counterpointed pattern of the Odyssey. (p. 14)

[In *Each Man's Son* as] in his earlier works, MacLennan cannot avoid seeing life running in the lines of Greek tragedy, and the mechanics of a classical destiny grind their pattern all too heavily and harshly on the human weakness of his characters. Yet this incorporation of destiny, with its corresponding weakening of the sense of human freedom, is not entirely inappropriate in a novel so permeated with the ambient darkness of Calvinist guilt. For the people MacLennan creates, destiny is an inner reality, and so for once the novelist's own fatalism accords with his subject. MacLennan suggests with powerful effectiveness the fear that always seems to overtop hope in the hearts of his Cape Bretoners, and he portrays equally effectively the relationships of classes and persons in a little society bound together by a common faith in its own damnation. MacLennan himself comes from Cape Breton, and it is likely that the immediacy one feels in this novel, the tension that unites structure and theme and myth, and makes the characters convincingly human even when they are most the slaves of circumstance, stems from its closeness to his own experience. (p. 15)

The Watch that Ends the Night [is] a novel constructed in receding vistas of time, and in handling the leaps of memory MacLennan's craftsmanship is unobstrusively sure. (p. 16)

Jerome, though not technically the hero of *The Watch that Ends the Night,* is a figure in the heroic mould, the wanderer and the giant and the medicine man all in one, an energumen in the thirties, a man of sorrows and saintly wisdom in the fifties, who seems for most of the novel too far above common clay to be either true or tolerable unless we accept him as myth incarnate. Yet there is one point at which even Jerome becomes authentically human; that is when another tunnel of time opens up and takes us back into the New Brunswick woods, to the childhood of a boy born of an illiterate Central European immigrant and brought up in the primitive turn-of-the-century logging camps where his mother works as cook. The mother is murdered by one of her lovers; the boy escapes downriver and is adopted by a simple-minded pastor who finds him starving on a railway station. This part of the book is written as admirably as MacLennan has ever written of primitive action; the woods of New Brunswick take shape in one's mind as a distinct physical presence, different from any other woods one has ever read of or walked in, and the night scene in the sleeping camp when the boy escapes from the murderer is powerfully thrilling. (pp. 16-17)

[By the end of the novel] Jerome has enabled [Catherine] and George to find themselves, to face their pasts, and to wait tranquilly in a world of gathering shadows for death. In fact, in a sense he has passed them through death, and so the three main characters become united at that key point of the Odysseus myth, the descent into the underworld that precedes rebirth into the sunlight.

There is a flavour of pietistic smugness about this ending which is hard to accept; there is also, throughout *The Watch that Ends the Night,* a suave mawkishness in talking about sex which amounts almost to diplomatic evasion.

MacLennan still suffers from his Calvinist background. But, granting such shortcomings, granting also the difficulty one experiences in really believing in Jerome, *The Watch that Ends the Night* is still a novel that impresses one for a number of reasons—its craftsmanly construction, its descriptive power, its ambitious grasp of the variety of Canadian social situations. . . . (p. 17)

MacLennan is still clearly developing as a novelist. His didacticism, which will probably never leave him, is at least presented now with a discreet indirection; his fatalism has largely acquired meaning in terms of the content of his novels—it is a fatalism proceeding rather from within his characters than from the world outside. He has, in other words, largely neutralised some of his most evident defects as a writer of fiction. It is true that his handling of any kind of sexual relationship remains almost as clumsily romanticist as ever it was; indeed, in this respect *The Watch that Ends the Night* is a regression from *Each Man's Son*. On the other hand, in his three successful novels, *Barometer Rising, Each Man's Son* and *The Watch that Ends the Night,* he has steadily widened and varied his portrayal of the character of Canadian life. Ultimately, perhaps, he is best as a social novelist, using his central myth to demonstrate the underlying universality of the personal and national experience he re-creates. And doubtless it is this function that really explains the consideration we accord him. Few Canadian critics, even among those who praise him, would seriously claim him as a great writer adept at exploring the intricacies of the human heart and mind; most accept him as the best example of a kind of novelist that may be necessary in Canada today, the kind of novelist who interprets a rapidly maturing society to its own people in the same way as Dickens and Balzac interpreted the society of the industrial revolution to the English and the French a hundred years ago. MacLennan may not have the variety or the abounding vigour or the sheer greatness of texture shared by these imperfect giants, yet in his way he is of their kind and no writer has yet come nearer than he to writing a Canadian *Comédie Humaine*. (pp. 17-18)

George Woodcock, "A Nation's Odyssey: The Novels of Hugh MacLennan," in Canadian Literature, *No. 10, Autumn, 1961, pp. 7-18.*

DOROTHY FARMILOE

Over the years, through a steadily deepening analysis of the national scene, Hugh MacLennan has been exploring the meaning of Canadianism; each of his novels, in some manner, has been a variation on this theme. His long study of all aspects of the Canadian character has peculiarly fitted him for the writing of *The Watch that Ends the Night* in which he traces Canada's coming-of-age. More important, in this novel he has gone back to examine what he feels are the character-shaping protoforms of the Canadian identity as exemplified by the fur trader. In one magnificent chapter of *The Watch that Ends the Night* in which the boy Jerome escapes down the wilderness river in his canoe, Hugh MacLennan is giving us his version not only of the Canadian character, but of the Canadian myth.

The most rewarding, and probably the shortest, route into MacLennan's latest novels is through his essay "The People Behind this Peculiar Nation." In this brief study MacLennan wrote that the fur trade has been as basic to the Canadian character as the sea has been to England's; that nations as well as children tend to forget the events of early years; that these events sink into and become part of the national subconscious. The true makers of Canada, he maintains, were not the Victorians whose ghastly statues surround the Parliament Buildings in Ottawa, but the voyageurs. . . . If we accept true myth as originating in either the historical or the religious background of a people and belonging to their collective subconscious, then it becomes clear that Hugh MacLennan is leading us, in this essay, toward his definition of the Canadian myth. In the significant section dealing with Jerome's childhood in *The Watch that Ends the Night* . . . , MacLennan has consciously embodied in narrative form all the mythic elements of our early history that he had outlined in his essay.

This chapter is a flashback episode, one of many, in the life of Jerome Martell told partly in his words and partly in the words of the protagonist George Stewart. The boy's experience is a mythologized version of the early years of this country. Jerome, having inadvertently witnessed his mother's murder, flees the community of the lumber camp to face the utter loneliness of the virgin wilderness. The social myth pursues him in the form of the Engineer; here is Jerome's description of him:

> "There was a man that winter," he said, "that used to frighten me the way a snake frightens me now. There was nothing snake-like about his appearance, but there was a look in his eye, the way he had of looking at everybody. He never talked at all, and when he drank he drank sullenly. We all called him the Engineer because . . . he was the only man in camp who could keep the motorboat in repair. He was dark and lean and he had this queer, drawn look in his face, and he used to carry a spanner wherever he went. . . ." . . .
>
> (pp. 1-2)

The entire chapter is related with deliberate simplicity and understated emotion in passages that, like the one above suggesting the sullen ugliness of a mechanical civilization, are cumulatively and powerfully effective. In contrast to the Engineer, Jerome symbolizes the Voyageur. His lonely struggle to escape, his attitude to his predicament, his native fortitude and resourcefulness, all add up to a display of the same survival tactics that enabled the early coureurs de bois to exist in the wilderness. (pp. 2-3)

Although his foster father is English, the name Martell, as Jerome finds out later, is of Huguenot origin, implying, in a Canadian adaptation, ambiguities of French Catholicism and English Protestantism. Both his first and last names have this significance. "Jerome," his foster father speculates, "generally only Roman Catholics are called Jerome." Thus MacLennan has cleverly and economically incorporated the four important ingredients of our native make-up into the personification of Jerome Martell—French, English, Protestant, Roman Catholic—for a genuinely Canadian symbolic figure. When Jerome says at one point that he does not know who he is, he exemplifies not only the search for the Canadian identity but the split personality caused by the two cultures in our national consciousness. This goes a long way towards explaining the paradox of his character as George sees it in the novel: "He was so boyish and yet he was so competent, he was so rugged and yet so vulnerable, so intelligent in some things and yet so naive in others." . . . (p. 3)

All the characteristics Jerome displays as *The Watch* unfolds are the inherent traits of bravery, stubbornness, pride —and "loneliness past modern comprehension" . . . —that were exhibited in the lives of the voyageurs.

There is also a suggestion of restrained strength in the significant river section where the writing flows with the fluid ease and hidden power of a great northern river. In the wonderful paragraph after Jerome knows he is safe from the Engineer, the river and the forest come to life for him; but more important than the stylistic felicity is that the boy and the canoe are an organic part of the environment. . . . (pp. 3-4)

Beginning with the violence of the mother's murder (violence is a favourite device of MacLennan's to initiate change) the adventure on the river becomes the traumatic experience—something of which always remains in the subconscious—that shapes the nation as well as the child. (p. 4)

Jerome's trip in the canoe is a Canadian counterpoint to Huck Finn's flight down the Mississippi on the raft and ought to occupy the same place in Canadian literature that Huck's holds in American. The tradition that has grown up around Mark Twain's tale involves the American myth of the hero who escapes from the dehumanizing restrictions of society to the freedom of the frontier. Both Huck and Jerome are fleeing from a civilization they consider vicious. . . . Huck's way of life is that of the outcast; so too is Jerome's. In the struggle for survival both boys transcend the world they leave to achieve mythic significance. (pp. 4-5)

As in *Huckleberry Finn* it is the river that gives the important Part Five of *The Watch* its form and its mythic quality. It is as much a river-god as the Mississippi with a will and a mind of its own. (p. 5)

It is significant that George holds a degree in history; as the story opens he is lecturing part-time at the university. He is well-qualified, therefore, to comment on the past as well as the present, particularly the important thirties and forties that form the backdrop for much of the novel's setting. . . .

It is easier to accept what MacLennan is doing with myth when we view Jerome's story through the eyes of a historian. George is a logical and acceptable spokesman for the author; he quietly relates events in the life of Jerome Martell that parallel the growth of Canada itself. (p. 7)

Each of [MacLennan's] novels expresses the Canadian character in one of its social aspects: *Barometer Rising* proclaims the leap from colonial mentality to a new Canadian identity; *Two Solitudes* probes the French-English conflict with considerable insight and sympathy, while *The Precipice* does the same for Canadian-American relations; *Each Man's Son* explores the vestiges of Calvinist influence. On the surface level *The Watch* examines the depression years when people "caught politics just as a person catches religion." . . . The latest work, *Return of the Sphinx,* picks up many of the earlier arguments and weaves them into a father-son relationship, a sequel to *Each Man's Son*. In this novel, as in most of the others, the social ideas tend to over-balance the imaginative handling of the material with the unfortunate result that the lesser characters become stereotypes. Bulstrode and Latendresse in *The Sphinx* are cardboard caricatures. Only *The Watch that Ends the Night,* in every way MacLennan's best work, avoids this failing. Even the minor characters in *The Watch* —Norah and Harry, for example—are well-rounded.

Some of MacLennan's best writing is in his unforgettable descriptions of the Canadian climate and countryside. If there is a common denominator in his work, it is that of the land itself. (pp. 7-8)

MacLennan sees this vast land with its lakes and rivers as one of the basic elements in our unique myth, and the love for the land remains, conscious or unconscious, in us as part of our collective personality; the continuing popularity of the nature poets attests to our peculiar bond with the land. (p. 8)

Dorothy Farmiloe, "Hugh MacLennan and the Canadian Myth," in MOSAIC: A Journal for the Comparative Study of Literature and Ideas *(copyright © 1969 by the University of Manitoba Press; acknowledgment of previous publication is herewith made), Vol. 2, No. 3 (Spring, 1969), pp. 1-9.*

RONALD SUTHERLAND

[*Return of the Sphinx*] contains a great many insights which are pertinent and valuable. . . . [It] is probably the most important Canadian novel to appear for many years. I emphasize the word Canadian, and I am going to make a general observation about the works of Hugh MacLennan which may disturb some critics in this country. As I have become more and more deeply involved and conversant with Canadian literature in both languages, it has become increasingly evident to me that Hugh MacLennan is one of the few writers in the emerging mainstream. By mainstream I mean that sphere of experience, consciousness and identification which is essentially and peculiarly Canadian. (p. 15)

[The] main distinguishing feature [of that sphere of consciousness] would have to be dependent upon the main distinguishing feature of the Canadian Nation—the co-existence of two major ethnic groups. To be in the emerging mainstream of Canadian literature, therefore, a writer must have some awareness of fundamental aspects and attitudes of both language groups in Canada. It is just such awareness on the part of a few which is slowly moulding a single, common Canadian mystique out of the previous parallel threads of evolution. The parallel threads, of course, are still there, and the majority of Canadian writers seem content, in some cases consciously determined to continue the process. But Hugh MacLennan is one exception. And not only is MacLennan one of the few in the mainstream; his body of works is the current which has given that mainstream definition and momentum. It is not surprising that the perceptive American critic Edmund Wilson, in describing his reaction to Hugh MacLennan, should say, "I came to recognize that there did now exist a Canadian way of looking at things." . . . So many other Canadian writers . . . are in the tributaries rather than the mainstream. And what is more, they are in the tributaries of American literature, not Canadian. Which does not mean, of course, that the work of these authors has any less literary merit. Indeed, in terms of universality of theme and appeal it could mean, and in some cases has meant, the very opposite. The mainstream is a matter of sphere of consciousness, not artistic skill; although sometimes the latter can be conditioned by the former. (p. 16)

Ronald Sutherland, "The Fourth Separatism," in

Canadian Literature, *No. 45, Summer, 1970, pp. 7-23.**

WARREN STEVENSON

It has become almost a commonplace of criticism of Hugh MacLennan's *Two Solitudes* to say that the novel succeeds brilliantly up to the end of the twenty-ninth chapter, portraying the death of Athanase Tallard, but is less convincing in the last twenty-three chapters portraying the symbolic resolution of the theme in the education and maturation of the members of the second generation, Paul Tallard and Heather Methuen, and their eventual marriage. . . . I think the time has come for a reassessment of this position. (p. 53)

It has also become a commonplace of criticism of *Two Solitudes* that "the idea of Canadian unity becomes the main symbolic theme," which MacLennan attempts to embody in the lives of his characters. Without pretending to deny the primacy of the theme of Canadian self-awareness and unity, I would like to suggest that the novel contains an important subsidiary theme which most critics have overlooked and which helps to unify the novel. I refer to the theme of individual self-awareness, worked out in terms of a contrast between two types of persons, those who learn to come to terms with what MacLennan calls "the ultimate solitude" and those who don't. The title thus has another dimension than the French-English dichotomy to which it is usually applied. The quotation from Rilke which constitutes the novel's epigraph is an important clue to its meaning: "Love consists in this, that two solitudes protect, and touch, and greet each other." Rilke was almost certainly referring to individuals, not societies, though it would be pedantry to attempt to limit the range of applicability of the quotation; and the novel's dedication which precedes the epigraph, "To Dorothy Duncan with admiration and love," suggests that MacLennan was also thinking of individuals and their personal relationships. (pp. 53-4)

[Those] characters in the novel who learn to come to terms with "the ultimate solitude" are most notably Captain Yardley, Paul Tallard, and Heather Methuen, who becomes Paul's wife. The characters who most dramatically fail to come to terms with the ultimate solitude are Athanase Tallard, his second wife Kathleen, his son by his first marriage Marius, such satiric figures as Huntly McQueen, General Methuen, et al, and Janet Methuen. (p. 54)

The loneliness within Paul the acceptance of which leads to self-knowledge finds its objective correlative in the sense of desolation in the northern forests as he recalls a trip to Lake Superior on a lake boat. . . . The result is what Robertson Davies has somewhere called a kind of northern mysticism. In coming to terms with the inner loneliness, Paul is also coming to terms with the outer loneliness, and the growth of MacLennan's protagonist towards self-knowledge parallels a similar development in the young nation. (p. 57)

MacLennan describes Paul's recurring feeling of loneliness [in Athens]: "the city surrounded him like a giant presence of loneliness. It was no new feeling; most of his life he had known it, and now it was recurring again like a periodic disease. . . . He wondered if Heather had ever felt as he did now. Two solitudes in the infinite waste of loneliness under the sun." This is the only occurrence in the novel other than the title and the epigraph of the phrase "two solitudes"; and it is significant that, in its context, it refers not primarily to the fact that Paul is of French and Heather of English extraction, but to the existential and individual aloneness which both characters are learning independently to face as part of maturation. The passage from which I have just quoted ends with Paul rejecting the opportunity to have a casual affair with a woman sitting at a nearby table, and the statement: "He wasn't equal to that kind of loneliness today." Again, there is the solitude of those who learn to come to terms with their existential loneliness, and the solitude of those who don't. MacLennan suggests that the latter kind of solitude is potentially dangerous, causing wars and other social upheavals. . . . (p. 58)

When Paul returns to Canada and marries Heather, MacLennan emphasizes the solitude of the lovers in a way that reminds one of a line from Kahlil Gibran: "Let there be spaces between your togetherness." (p. 59)

The concluding chapter departs from the private lives of the novel's human characters to emphasize the coming together of the nation's energies to meet the wartime crisis. The portrayal of the autumnal face of the Canadian landscape reminds us that the country both human and natural is the real hero of this novel. The theme of solitude—what MacLennan previously described as "race memories lonely in great spaces"—is also evident, along with its counterpart, the theme of self-awareness:

> Then, even as the two race-legends woke again remembering ancient enmities, there woke within them also the felt knowledge that together they had fought and survived one great war they had never made and that now they had entered another . . . And almost grudgingly, out of the instinct to do what was necessary, the country took the first irrevocable steps towards becoming herself, knowing against her will that she was not unique but like all the others, alone with history, with science, with the future.

Canada in relation to the European countries is like Paul and Heather in relation to the older generation: neither has made this war, but both recognize the importance of seeing it through. And like Paul and Heather, Canada is approaching self-knowledge and the self-sufficiency that comes from an acceptance of the ultimate solitude. (p. 60)

Warren Stevenson, "A Neglected Theme in 'Two Solitudes'," in Canadian Literature, *No. 75, Winter, 1977, pp. 53-60.*

DAVE GODFREY

[The] charge of turgidness or parochialism which comes from misunderstanding MacLennan's novels cannot in all fairness be levelled at [the essays in *The Other Side of Hugh MacLennan*]. Indeed, what he seems best at is the light, the witty, and the exotic. The evocations of English eccentrics are delightful and precise, the recreations of the Halifax past acknowledge that it has all fled and gone, while even the high-table pieces on "Literature and Technology" or "Scotland's Fate: Canada's Lesson" admit that one should be concerned not so much with outdoing George Grant as with keeping the audience awake before the brandy arrives. (p. 57)

MacLennan's way of looking at the world, like that of

James Reaney and D. H. Lawrence, has been shaped by apocalyptic Christianity. But whereas Lawrence fought the shaping and Reaney carefully sought external situations through which that shaping power might express itself, MacLennan has lived in uneasy truce with it all of his life. The terms of surrender have never been signed.

The very concern with audience that lends his lighter work so much charm works against the full expression of this deeper current, while his concern with history leads him to give voice to the more powerful strains of Christianity which existed in his society and which were non-apocalyptic. . . . But the apocalyptic vision is not rooted in social change or expressed through social change; it is far more absolute, random, and mysterious, and its dichotomies do not find resolution. In his fiction, MacLennan lets this vision have its way at the deepest levels, which is why the critics are always fundamentally disquieted by his novels: their social framework is so near, so historical, but their mythology is disconnected from our central (and unexamined) mythology. It is at once too dark and too hopeful: too dark for the liberals and too hopeful for the cynics and the disco-conservatives.

MacLennan himself has remained true to his convictions all these years. In terms of his audience he has been willing to make many concessions of style, content, and attitude because he has never really made any concessions in terms of his vision. (pp. 57-8)

Dave Godfrey, "The Apocalyptic Christianity of Hugh MacLennan," in Saturday Night *(copyright © 1978 by* Saturday Night*), Vol. 93, No. 9, November, 1978, pp. 56-8.*

CATHERINE SHELDRICK ROSS

The six novels that form the MacLennan canon explore for us, in specifically Canadian terms, a familiar pattern of the humanist's quest for an ideal society, consequent disillusionment and despair, and finally spiritual transcendence. There are striking parallels between the narrator's sense, by the end of *Barometer Rising,* that he is witnessing "a great country move into its destiny" and the Renaissance humanist's feeling of historic participation in rebirth from Gothic darkness. In their desire to provide an ideal literary model for Canada's development, MacLennan's early novels resemble the numerous mirrors for Christian Princes and the literary models for ideal societies written during the Renaissance. The increasingly sombre tone of the later novels is an acknowledgement that the gap between the ideal model and the actual Canada is as unbridgeable as the gap between Erasmus' "Philosophy of Christ" and the statecraft of Henry VIII. (p. 5)

MacLennan's six novels, from *Barometer Rising* to *Return of the Sphinx,* develop according to this pattern. The national odyssey of the early novels to find an ideal Canada becomes a quest for the otherworldly Celestial City. The change occurs midway in *The Watch That Ends the Night* and accounts for that novel's noticeable shift in tone from the detailed, realistic account of the Thirties experience at the beginning to the spiritualized conclusion in which the everyday world of Canadian life is "becoming a shadow" and politics "seemed the most unreal of all." Erasmus' comment on the need to move "through the labyrinth of this world into the pure light of the spiritual life" . . . forms an apt summary of the thematic movement of *The Watch That Ends the Night* and explains the abstractness, the detachment from action in this world, and the apocalyptic intimations that characterize *Return of the Sphinx.* (p. 6)

Not surprisingly, in view of MacLennan's own Calvinist inheritance and his consequent familiarity with the doctrine of the two worlds, guilt and transcendence are the twin dynamic forces of a MacLennan novel. Awareness of guilt . . . becomes intolerable and drives its possessor forth on a quest for transcendence. (p. 7)

[The novelist] must cope somehow with the dark domain that belongs to the beasts of experience. MacLennan tends to cope in two ways with the necessity of finding his materials in the fallen world. He writes satire and, secondly, he idealizes, turning the physical world into a symbol of the spiritual world. The satiric strain, consistently an important element in the novels, expresses MacLennan's sense of the betrayal of humanist values in the world as he finds it. . . . Usually, whenever MacLennan is at his most realistic and convincing in his handling of specific detail, his tone is satiric.

Not contrary but complementary to the satire is MacLennan's idealism. This is expressed in his favouring of heroines of spectacular virtue and purity, in his development of symbolic characters and allegorical central episodes, and in his consistent use of the quest pattern. Since, within the Calvinist scheme of things, the disintegrating physical world is fitter as an object of satire than as a source of values, the characters in MacLennan's novels are constantly in search of something that proves to lie outside the world of experience. The novels are all shaped in the form of a quest, and the characters yearn, like Jerome Martell and George Stewart in *The Watch,* "to belong to something larger than themselves." In the first three novels, the quest is for an ideal national identity for Canada. . . . Consistently in the novels the characters become symbols and the quest ends with some ideal that transcends the literal.

Characteristics of MacLennan's fiction that have troubled readers—the "unnovelistic" endings that jettison characters and transcend the human situation, the didacticism—these are likely products of a two-world theory. The novel's subject is the world of change: "A novel's chief value lies in its capacity to entertain and in its characters," says MacLennan. But MacLennan also desires to instruct, and truth belongs to the spiritual world. (pp. 8-9)

It is in *The Watch That Ends the Night* that the various tensions between the visible world and the ideal world, the characters and the spiritual meaning, the actual country of Canada and the ideal model finally become irreconcilable and the two worlds split apart. The early novels support the belief that the barometer is rising. They depict journeys that end in lovers meeting and show a model new society forming itself around the united young couple. The last two novels emphasize the isolation of their now middle-aged protagonists, who end up sojourners and exiles in a disintegrating world. As MacLennan becomes increasingly disillusioned with the effectiveness of action, he turns from romance and comedy to irony and tragedy. (p. 9)

Hugh MacLennan's novels, taken together, form the record of a process which, one suspects, has been completed, with the gap between the two worlds now too wide for a novel to span. . . . [We] can say that MacLennan's Calvinist brand of humanism has shaped this dualistic pattern and goes far to account for many characteristic features of the novels: their tendency to be didactic and rhetorical rather than representational and mimetic; the use of symbolic characters and incidents; the vividness of the satirical sketches of minor characters in contrast with the often unconvincing and abstract major characters; the use of apocalyptic imagery; the turning away in the later novels from romance and comedy to irony and tragedy; the persistence of the quest motif; and the shifting of the geography of the quest from this fallen world of shadows to the spiritual world. To us MacLennan is important because his national odyssey puts the recurrent humanist dilemma into a Canadian context. In his six published novels, we see the completed process of the political quest for an ideal model of Canada, despair and the repudiation of the "labyrinth of this world," and finally the movement into "the pure light of the spiritual life." (pp. 11-12)

Catherine Sheldrick Ross, "Hugh MacLennan's Two Worlds," in Canadian Literature, *No. 80, Spring, 1979, pp. 5-12.*

* * *

MACPHERSON, Jay 1931-

Macpherson, an English-born Canadian poet, nonfiction writer, and critic, writes sophisticated, intricate verse, focusing on intellectual and spiritual awareness. She is best known for *The Boatman,* a collection of poems for which she won the Governor General's Award. (See also *Contemporary Authors,* Vols. 5-8, rev. ed.)

ARNOLD EDINBOROUGH

That [ballad poetry] still is the main stem from which poets can put forth their own shoots is shown in *The Boatman.* All the symbols of balladry—the fish of fertility, the golden apples of love, the suggestive shape of Cupid's bow as it shoots an arrow, the red rose of sex, the unicorn—are here, with just the same technique of double and triple meaning. Indeed, so much in the tradition of ballad punning and suggestiveness is Miss Macpherson that she has a collection of riddles as part of her book.

This is not to say that she is derivative except as all new poets are derivative of the poets who have written before them and from whom they have learned their technique. *The Boatman,* in fact, presents a new and intensely personal voice in Canadian poetry which has an assurance, a breadth and depth which is as arresting as Miss Macpherson's splendid control of her lyric medium.

Steeped in the symbols of our culture, both pagan and classical, she chisels one exquisite lyric after another in completion of her central task which is to make the reader see with new eyes, assess with newly-rediscovered values and to turn his world upside down to see if it looks any better. (pp. 20-1)

She makes us meditate on the central facts of life, of love and of death, wittily but mercilessly, not scrupling to make us think hard to get her point. (p. 21)

Arnold Edinborough, "High Cockalorum in Verse," in Saturday Night *(copyright © 1957 by* Saturday Night*), Vol. 72, No. 15, July 20, 1957, pp. 20-2.**

JAMES REANEY

[*The Boatman*] has made a great difference in the world of Canadian poetry. Let us proceed to explain the greatness of this difference.

First, what one must remark about Miss Macpherson's whale or "Leviathan" is that it is so very skillfully carved, and so are all the other beasts inside it, for her Leviathan turns out to be a Noah's Ark as well. It can also be said that she is the first Canadian poet to carve angels at all well. No one before had ever told Canadian poets that the Angel was or could be a very suitable and good topic for poetry.

Miss Macpherson's angels, of course, have a lot to do with the fact that she does some very natural but very hard things connected with the Bible. The Bible is still a vexatiously ill-known work in Canada. . . . I mean that it is ill-known as a key to art and as a source for new art. Miss Macpherson knows her Bible, knows that the natural world about us is not natural, knows how her Bible shows you how to deal with this unnaturalness; so nothing seemed more amiable probably than to have lots of angels, for they are the structure of the Bible and they prove to be a subject that immediately creates a tension in which any object or animal or being—Egg, Abominable Snowman and Mary of Egypt—begins to have an outline that glows. In *The Boatman* there is the "faceless angel" of the Storm, the angel who knows what "sways when Noah nods", the "inward angel"—of a poem called that—who has a "diamond self". There are the angels who look on as Leviathan frolics and there are the seraph forms within the "caverned woman" which are later named "flowers, fountains, milk, blood". In this equation we see that what the poet means by an angel is anything or anybody or any being seen in its Eternal aspect, that is, at its most glorious and most real, its most expanded. Actually, in leafing backwards through *The Boatman* and tracking down the angels, I've forgotten to mention the very important angel in the last poem:

> The world was first a private park
> Until the angel, after dark,
> Scattered afar to wests and easts
> The lovers and the friendly beasts.

This angel represents the giant and supernatural force all Creation lost at the Fall. This force, like a cork in a bottle, stands between us and Paradise in the sense that we must attain to it again before we can return to Paradise. This significant angel and his companions are a great part of the reason why *The Boatman* is such an exciting book. . . . To have landed and handled [the concept of the angel] is a real achievement.

Not only is this poet able to arrive at a skill with a very important symbol; she knows also how to deal with a great variety of topics in a carefully modulated variety of ways. The variety of methods or ways or tones is so cleverly arranged that by the time the reader has finished the volume he has boxed the compass of the reality which poetry imitates. This should be an ability an enthusiast for poetry would naturally expect from the author of any volume of lyrics. (pp. 23-5)

One of the proudest conclusions the author of *The Boatman* might draw about her own volume is that very few of the experiences described are "real" or "natural" experiences. The situations, the beings, the speakers are all gloriously artificial like the themes of Bach, which no "real" bird, no "real" train whistle could imitate or has ever imitated. If the tyranny of the "natural" or unorganised results in the ragbag approach to a volume of lyrics, then the monarchy of the better than "natural", the monarchy of the organised, has resulted in the beautifully articulated structure of this book, and it is a monarchy that shows the way to future ones. (pp. 25-6)

In a poem entitled "The Anagogic Man" we are presented with a figure as interesting as the angel, the figure of a sleeping Noah whose head contains all creation. "Consider that your senses keep / A death far deeper than his sleep". . . . [It represents] the slumbering imagination of all life, a slumbering imagination that slowly through art and science rearranges the sun, moon, stars and figures of the gods until they are once more under human control. This Noah is the artist, a man who has brought and still brings all of society safely through the flood and tempest of a fallen world's whirlwind of atoms and death-wishes. But Art must be allowed to decide for itself when the time for universal apocalypse has arrived. If we waken him or it beforehand it is akin to building the Tower of Babel, to attempting a leap into Paradise when we are by no means ready for it. The whole collection of poems requires the reader to transfer himself from the sleep our senses keep to Noah's sleep, and from Noah's sleep eventually to the first morning in Paradise. Miss Macpherson's book is a dream that starts off in the world of the senses and slowly lifts us higher and higher until in the final half dozen pages we are as high as we can be. (p. 26)

One clue to the mystery of Miss Macpherson's hold on one's imagination is the feeling she constantly gives of things inside other things. This idea of things within things can be expanded into the most satisfying explanation of existence I think I know of. We live in a Leviathan which God occasionally plays with and is always attempting to catch. Once we played with it and tried to catch it but it caught us instead. This myth is the essential design of Miss Macpherson's book. (pp. 29-30)

[The] point of the Ark poems is that when Man found himself sinking in the fallen world he had enough sense to build an imitation of that world which met it and himself halfway. One day he'll regain his island or Eden, but a floating island will do for now. . . . The Ark is a Leviathan within Leviathan and it prophesies to Noah that one day he will swallow his own Ark, that is, make mental and controllable what was physical before and not so easily controlled. (p. 33)

If the reader has really tried to turn himself inside out, that is, discipline and organize his life around a focus of Eternity, then the riddles of the last suite of *The Boatman* are easy. Each riddle is the top of a spiral staircase leading down through the book. In all the riddles the effect is very much like that of the dancing sequence of those naked ladies on the Acidalian Mount in Spenser's *Legend of Courtesy*. There is an air of release in Spenser—the Mountain of Contemplation is also at last the mountain of love and joy, nakedness and beauty. So here, after learning how from the other poems in *The Boatman,* the reader can look at anything in the world and find joy in it, from a lungfish to an abominable Snowman. . . . The last section in effect says to the reader that Creation, Fall and Redemption are part of a dance whose final figure is the scene in which the Fisherman, in the very last poem, having corrected the Fall is himself corrected for all time. But perhaps in Eternity we would never dream of playing with lungfish and mermaids completely scrubbed of their fallen characteristics, which would be their firm graspable outline. Even when one finally achieves the freedom of being outside one keeps very wisely a delight in the perils of insideness.

Perhaps the best way to conclude what should be said in praise of *The Boatman* is that it shows you how to get from "here to there". If "here" is this world and "there" the world of Eternity, then this book of poems shows the reader all the necessary steps of the way. These are steps that I am sure an increasingly great number of readers and writers in Canada are going to find very exciting to take. (pp. 33-4)

James Reaney, "The Third Eye: Jay Macpherson's 'The Boatman'," in Canadian Literature, *No. 23, Winter, 1960, pp. 23-34.*

DAVID BROMWICH

Welcoming Disaster collects roughly a decade of Jay Macpherson's light verse and mad jottings and brilliant mythmaking poems. The volume . . . is full of bright designs and dark conceits, amphisbaenic or yin-and-yang emblems; invocation, asides, and acknowledgments have all been severely dealt with. . . . [There] is really no describing a production like this—no substitute for having it. The book has a plot of sorts: at the end of a special and intimate friendship, presumably a love affair, the poet tries to get her capsized vessel afloat through a return to the terrors of childhood and the necessary unmourned losses of adult life. Her injunctions of self-command are directed to, or rather deflected off, a splendid toy bear called Tadwit or Ted, as the sequence moves from consolation to guilt to terror and finally to a deepened consolation. Miss Macpherson looks at her own life as well as Ted when she beckons to a "needed, familiar pain. / Come, little thorn." Surely, Blake would have smiled in baffled delight at the woman who could ask, "Having so much, how is it that we ache for / Those darker others?"; or speak of the search for a blessed monster "through the caverns wild / Where the giant led the child"; or hint, so calmly, at the difficult weight of love. . . . Yet I am reducing Miss Macpherson's grandness and verve by giving them a name. She will put readers in mind of Graves and Wordsworth, of Auden and Dickinson and Stevie Smith, of every poet who ever wrote truly about innocence and its unlucky master, love.

Dickinson most of all has formed her style. Vast and yet terse-seeming nouns, often new compounds, from physics or fairy tales or the ordinary world; shocks of defiance, longing, propitiation; pet cadences and turns and even a surprising verse form out of the Protestant hymn book; hyphens and dashes, with the queerest kinds of enjambment; above all the conviction that self-scrutiny, an act of unswerving authority and intensity, is the way to self-possession in art: these impressive habits and ideas, odds and ends of a craft, Miss Macpherson has absorbed so that they become her own. (pp. 236-37)

Throughout her sequence Miss Macpherson's "they" refers to nothing in particular: it is the abstract plural of absolute portent, proper to certain types of allegory, which one understands at once in Auden, Kafka, or Edward Lear. . . . [Her] respect for things-in-general which goes with a belief in their ultimate triumph over herself, makes her not a finer poet than Dickinson but, to my mind, a more neighborly person in her poetry. (pp. 237-38)

A poet who worries about her ability to summon creatures of the imagination, who she knows can never be creatures of the will, is worried about memory and its sovereignty over her: that is Miss Macpherson's theme and her single story. . . . When she writes of her monsters, Miss Macpherson is tender, high-spirited, mayhem-loving, and filled with awe, as at an Eastern Tale, and then she comes back to Ted. . . . [The] toy bear looms up cheerfully and strangely, a little god of departed things. (p. 238)

On the cover of her book, Miss Macpherson has a nameless devourer of the deep about to snap its jaws on a boat that drifts helplessly in the sun. The space is two-thirds black with only a sunny triangle left at the top. It gives a curious impression, however, for one of those reasons only the imagination knows not of engulfing darkness but of penetrating light: and it is the perfect emblem for Miss Macpherson's art. (p. 239)

David Bromwich, "Engulfing Darkness, Penetrating Light," in Poetry *(© 1976 by The Modern Poetry Association; reprinted by permission of the Editor of* Poetry*), Vol. CXXVII, No. 4, January, 1976, pp. 234, 236-39.**

SUNITI NAMJOSHI

Superficially, there seem to be some obvious differences between *The Boatman* and *Welcoming Disaster*. The second in some ways seems much "simpler." It is my purpose here to explore some of the similarities and differences. . . .

As Reaney makes clear, the central myth of *The Boatman* is that of the ark [see excerpt above]. The ark appears to contain us, as though we were trapped in the belly of some monstrous creature, and its contents appear to be hopelessly miscellaneous; but properly perceived, Man, in fact, contains the ark, and its contents are ordered. . . . (p. 54)

Noah's salvaging operations at the time of the flood correspond to the activity of the poet, the man who perceives or "dreams" and thus makes "a Cosmos of miscellany." In other words, Noah, Endymion (the sleeping shepherd) and the poet merge into one another. The type of the poet is, of course, Orpheus; and Narcissus, Orpheus and Psyche are interconnected figures. Narcissus is not seen in a negative light by Jay Macpherson. He also is the type of the poet, and the elegiac Orpheus engages in the same activity. But the poet as an Orpheus or as a Psyche are conceptions that are of greater importance to the second book (*Welcoming Disaster*) than to the first, because both stories contain an element that is missing in the stories of the other figures. Both Orpheus and Psyche have to make a journey underground. Redemption is no longer a matter of starting with the world of the fall and gradually proceeding upwards. In the second book it becomes necessary to hit bottom and then to make the journey up with a fully regained or "half-regained Eurydice." Now the problem is not simply to get the animals outside, but to find the way to that perception again, the source of dreaming. . . . (pp. 54-5)

[As] Reaney makes clear about *The Boatman*, the separation of the sexes corresponds to the separation between Man and Nature. . . . In *The Boatman* it is enough to say that in a fallen world all attempts at union are bound to be somewhat unsatisfactory. . . . In *Welcoming Disaster* the corpses that result from this disjunction have to be recognized and acknowledged. They have to be given their due. It is only then that they can in any way be recovered. "Naked spectres, come for shrouding, / Those I failed and snubbed and crossed, / In the deadly waters crowding: / Angel, let not one be lost." In *The Boatman* the Ark appears simply as a much misunderstood creature that has been needlessly at odds with Man: "Why did your spirit / Strive so long with me?" In *Welcoming Disaster* it is the self itself that is lost, and that is the corpse that must be recovered.

The obvious place to go looking for corpses is, of course, the world of the dead, the Kingdom of Hades, the world undersea, the world of memory, the world of the past. This is the world that *Welcoming Disaster* is primarily concerned with. Noah the boatman can be turned quite easily into a fisherman, and this is, in fact, done in *The Boatman*, but the action is kindly rather than expiatory. To restate the matter, Noah is not a diver. Again, sleep imagery can be used to point the contrast between a drugged sleep and the sleep of the dreamer who sees with the third eye of real perception. This also is done in *The Boatman*, but in *Welcoming Disaster* the world of nightmare must first be explored. It becomes necessary to come to terms with or at least to face the past before the process of dreaming can begin again. . . . The descent into the kingdom of Hades is not a search for the waters of forgetfulness, but for the source of dreams, for, in a sense, "pools where I fished with jamjars for minnows," for "strangeness of water." Rivers are lifegiving, the sea is destructive. (In "Revelations" there is no more sea.) The boatman appears as a type of Charon. The corpses to be brought back are their own, the kid and the teddy bear (doll-god). This is, in fact, done, and expiation is achieved by a kind of acceptance of wrongs done and wrongs endured. The prayer to "infallibly restore my share in perdition" is granted. (pp. 55-6)

In *Welcoming Disaster* there are two kinds of movements. The first of these is concerned with the two lower levels, and the five sections of the book indicate the pattern. It is after a descent into the underworld that it is possible to return to the ordinary world of everyday life, the world in which "Some are plain lucky—we ourselves among them: / Houses with books, with gardens, all we wanted, / Work we enjoy, with colleagues we feel close to— / Love we have, even." . . .

While, in one sense, there is a movement from the fallen world to the world of nightmare and back again to the daylight world, there is another kind of movement as well. To put it simply: If you dig deep enough, the way down becomes the way up, and you eventually see the stars. (p. 56)

It is evident, of course, that the ark for Jay Macpherson represents not a withdrawal into isolation, but a merger into a community, a sealing of the "rift in Being," the externalization of the dream. (p. 57)

[Placed] side by side, *The Boatman* and *Welcoming Disaster* reveal that the distance between the mythopoeic and the familiar is less great than might be supposed. (p. 58)

Suniti Namjoshi, "In the Whale's Belly: Jay Macpherson's Poetry," in Canadian Literature, *No. 79, Winter, 1978, pp. 54-9.*

* * *

MAILER, Norman 1923-

Mailer, a novelist, essayist, social critic, and filmmaker, is

one of the most prominent contemporary American writers. *The Naked and the Dead* is considered one of the major novels of the Second World War, but his fiction since has been of uneven quality. He has shown a much more consistently capable hand in his nonfiction, most of which is written in the style of New Journalism. Foremost among these works are *Armies of the Night* and *Of a Fire on the Moon*. A writer of powerful prose, he is at his best when attacking the materialism and spiritual malaise of contemporary American society. (See also *CLC*, Vols. 1, 2, 3, 4, 5, 8, 11, and *Contemporary Authors*, Vols. 9-12, rev. ed.)

GEORGE ALFRED SCHRADER

Soren Kierkegaard has . . . provided us with an exquisitely precise description of the kind of program which Mailer has adopted for himself. Mailer calls it the "philosophy of Hip" and "good orgasm"; Kiekegaard terms it "the despair of defiance." They come to much the same thing. (p. 82)

Mailer is no existentialist—unless we are to consider his brand of self-styled "American existentialism" as an existentialist heresy. Whereas Mailer claims to be a confirmed *romantic* who hopes to find his destiny through Hip and "good orgasm," the European existentialists have been consistently opposed to all varieties of romanticism. Kierkegaard expressed the antiromantic orientation of existentialism pungently and succinctly in his assertion that "there is no immediate health of the spirit." Yet, it is just such an "immediate health of the spirit" which Mailer professes as the fundamental doctrine of his "existentialism." Although he is referring specifically to the psychopath rather than the hipster, what Mailer says about orgasm expresses the basic tenet of "the philosophy of Hip": "At bottom, the drama of the psychopath is that he seeks love. Not love as the search for a mate, but love as the search for an orgasm more apocalyptic than the one which preceded it. Orgasm is his therapy—he knows at the seed of his being that good orgasm opens his possibilities and bad orgasm imprisons him." The very notion of "orgasm," which might be construed as a self-chosen caricature of romantic imagery, is typical of the language and point of view of romanticism. Through the deliberate and repeated use of what is ordinarily considered to be obscene language, Mailer seeks to give his version of romanticism a more virile expression. He fails to recognize, however, that in obliterating the distinction between the sacred and the profane, he deprives obscene language of its shock value. When the language of the soldier becomes the language of the schoolboy—and even of female novelists—obscenity is transmuted into a pale vulgarity. Mailer is, if he only knew it, the worst enemy of Hip. As in so many instances, Mailer must depend upon the "squares" to preserve the purity of the distinction for him.

Whereas the existentialists have been sharply critical of romanticism, charging it with naiveté, "bad faith," or both at once, Mailer wants to recover the primeval vitality of romantic passion and reestablish it in a new power and glory. His quarrel is never with romanticism as such, but with those forms of romanticism which have become effete through social domestication. The chief difference between Mailer and earlier romantic reformers is that he is more violent in his attack upon social decadence and more desperate in his advocacy of the return to primitivism. Moreover, primitive freedom, as Mailer conceives of it, is far from the serene and idyllic affair envisioned by Rousseau. Mailer's faith, he tells us, is in the essential goodness of the uncorrupted (which means socially untrammeled) vitality of man's libidinal energies. Like Nietzsche, he represents himself as an antinihilistic nihilist who is summoning us to rebellion against a society which threatens to emasculate us. (pp. 85-6)

In his search for the *interesting*, for unexplored possibilities of human choice, Mailer has become fascinated with antisocial and psychopathic behavior. "For I wish to attempt an entrance into the mysteries of murder, suicide, incest, orgy, orgasm, and Time. These themes now fill my head and make me think I have a fair chance to become the first philosopher of Hip." But it is not as a *spectator* that Mailer sought to understand Hip; he was experiencing something of a psychic rebellion (liberation?) in himself. He reports that after his unhappy experience with the publication of *Deer Park* something broke in him and he was "finally open to my anger." . . . This anger, for which Mailer had become "open," was no ordinary anger, but the defiant rage of what Kierkegaard termed "demonic despair." "Now my will was a dictator; like all tyrants it felt the urgency of the present as unendurable." (pp. 86-7)

Unlike French existentialism (the only variety with which Mailer appears to be acquainted), "Hip is based on a mysticism of the flesh, and its origins can be traced back into all the undercurrents and underworlds of American life, back into the instinctive apprehension and appreciation of existence which one finds in the Negro and the soldier, in the criminal psychopath and the dope addict and the jazz musician, in the prostitute, in the actor, in the—if one can visualize such a possibility—in the marriage of the call girl and the psychoanalyst." Mailer is surely correct in calling attention to this difference—*so great a difference, in fact, as to differentiate it completely from all other forms of "existentialism."* Hip, as Mailer portrays it, is, indeed, a "mysticism of the flesh," a romantic glorification of the primordially instinctual. The trouble is that, like most nostalgia for the primitive, Mailer's advocacy of Hip is *phony*. Rape, murder, suicide, orgy, and even orgasm are anything but primitive "instincts." They are in their very nature culturally determined modes of behavior and highly sophisticated forms at that. And, what is more important, they depend for their meaning in Hip on their *negative* quality as rebellious acts against a predominantly square society. There are and could be no hipsters in a primitive African society, nor could hipsterism ever become a prevalent mode of conduct. If enough people became hipsters they would of necessity all turn out to be squares. Were the revolt which Mailer advocates to succeed, all would be lost. The Hip ideal is all too typical of romantic programs which have an essential term outside themselves and are, thus, negatively determined. Even as the romantic novel is over and, perhaps, ruined when the obstacles are finally removed, so it must be, also, with Hip as a program. It can succeed only in failure and be advocated only in "bad faith." (pp. 87-8)

The capacity to float gracefully on the surface of desire seems to be the very essence of the Hip view of life. . . . Mailer recognizes that the more highly the life founded upon desire is developed, the more it tends to lose its vitality. . . . He seeks to live only in the *instant* which is unchanged in being repeated. Unfortunately, this view ignores the fact that natural energy is intrinsically and incorrigibly temporal. To affirm the natural and reject *development* is practically absurd. Incurably a romantic, Mailer cannot tolerate the fruits of the romanticism which he embraces. His rage is not so much against the world or anything within the world as against the impossibility of finding ultimate satisfaction within the sensuous while refusing to give up the attempt. He wants to sweep aside the refinements of civilization in order to begin once more at the beginning with an upsurge of primitive vitality. But can the result be any different? Isn't Kierkegaard perfectly correct in maintaining that as the erotic is developed the *rapist* becomes a *seducer*? It is strange indeed for an artist to set himself in violent opposition to the life of art.

The fact is that Mailer, in his new self-consciousness, has come to the point of what Kierkegaard termed "despair over the worldly." . . . Mailer has discovered what countless men before him have known, namely that the world offers us no self-sustained meaning, no ultimate satisfaction. And he is enraged, blaming everything on the "squares" who have spoiled evervthing for him. He sees himself now as in the position of having to "make his own kicks."

But even though it is in some respects the rage of a man who has come to consciousness of himself, Mailer's rage is, also, like that of the small boy who has discovered that there is no Santa Claus. Disappointed as we all are at this discovery, Mailer is enraged and refuses to accept the fact. (pp. 89-90)

If Mailer is an existentialist he is an odd one, for he clearly cannot tolerate existence. He is enraged at his own freedom because it is finite. He will settle for nothing short of an omnipotence which would enable him to actualize every possibility. Failing that, he yearns to become fate itself in the hope that it might extinguish his miserable finitude. . . . It is not so much his action as the *infinity* of the murderer's passion which intrigues Mailer. As he half-knows, he is obsessed not simply with violence, but with *death*. (p. 90)

Mailer's hero, the hipster, corresponds nicely to Kierkegaard's esthetic hero, the "sensuous-erotic genius." Although Mailer chooses a primitive rather than a poetic expression of the erotic, the categories are essentially the same. The esthetic man, Kierkegaard argues, bases his life upon sensuous desire, lives only in the *instant*, and has no reality either for himself or others. The paradox of the esthetic life is that as the individual develops his own sensuousness he develops, also, his capacities as spirit and, hence, transcends immediacy. It is the inescapable fact of transcendence within immediacy which leads the sensuous-erotic genius more and more deeply into despair. For he is ultimately confronted with the choice: either to surrender the attempt to live within natural immediacy and go on to the ethical mode, or to hold himself defiantly within immediacy. To have discovered that an immediate fulfillment of the human spirit is *impossible* and, yet, to refuse to abandon the attempt to achieve it, is to be in *conscious* despair. This is, I would argue, essentially Mailer's predicament as set forth in *The White Negro*. (p. 91)

Hip is the incarnation of the flesh from which spirit has been excluded and in which rape and murder are as significant as love and self-sacrifice. This is precisely what Kierkegaard means by "esthetic indifference." There are no genuine contradictions, no irreconcilable oppositions, within esthetic immediacy. . . . (p. 92)

Mailer's advocacy of Hip represents a curious blending of nihilism (demonic defiance) and a pagan faith in the essential goodness of elemental power. He identifies with the hipster both because the White Negro is in full-scale rebellion against civilization (defiant) and unleashes the life-giving force of primitive emotion. The very notion of the White Negro symbolizes the opposition between civilization (White) and instinctual passion (Negro). It is not only a *dialectical* but a *contradictory* idea in that rage and rebellion derive their force and meaning from civilized passion and can by no act of violence gain reentry into the innocence of immediacy. Mailer refuses to accept original sin as a fact of human life and would undo the Fall of mankind. He will, if need be, carry the human race back to the Garden of Eden on his own shoulders—even if he must tread upon all the edifices of civilization to do it. The courage he wants is heroic, epic, Promethean, but, also, futile. (p. 93)

Mailer has fixed himself in the esthetic mode of defiant despair. It is the *demonic* which he affirms as the heroic courage of Hip. The hope for redemption, as he sees it, lies in our capacity to surrender ourselves to a "dark and mysterious unconscious power" in which we must trust *blindly*. If we are fortunate, it will carry us along to a freeing and purging release in "good orgasm." But such a project cannot arrest despair, for it is based upon an illusory view of the natural. It evades the recognition that it is *spirit* which posits the flesh as flesh and that, once developed, spirit cannot be reabsorbed into the flesh. It only postpones the problem of ethical and religious choice. It is the dread of being responsible for himself that Mailer is as yet unwilling to confront. Either he must go on to an ethical-religious courage in which he affirms existence with all its finite blemishes—or remain in pathos. And, whether personally or as a novelist, for him the pathetic has only a limited scope. If he can free himself of his self-established bondage to the esthetic, he may yet be the outstanding novelist he so desperately wants but does not yet will to be. (p. 95)

George Alfred Schrader, "Norman Mailer and the Despair of Defiance," in The Yale Review *(© 1960 by Yale University; reprinted by permission of the editors), Winter, 1961 (and reprinted in* Norman Mailer: A Collection of Critical Essays, *edited by Leo Braudy, Prentice-Hall, Inc., 1972, pp. 82-95).*

RICHARD POIRIER

[To] write history in Mailer's style requires even more strenuous efforts with language than does the writing of a novel or a play. Having more claims to preexistent forms of reality than novels do, history will give up the shape it has assumed to some other shape only under enormous stylistic (or scholarly) pressure. In the absence of such pressure, we're left to contemplate only the failure of the efforts to exert it, to study the drama of confrontation between a doughty self and resistant historical forces. (p. 168)

His books are about Mailer, to be sure, about the man as he writes history as well as about the man who tried to participate in its making. But they are meant to reveal the true nature of the historical events and issues with which he has involved himself. Similarly, while his metaphors do reveal the workings of his mind, in its probing, contradictory, fluid movement, they also, he would insist, expose the reality of America. He'll settle for nothing less. It's a heroic ambition, but except in the special circumstances of *Armies*, where the nature of his participation in events is beautifully synchronized with his writing about them, the ambition is seldom achieved. Mailer is more often than not the over-reacher of his times.

His metaphoric and melodramatic versions of society and history are of course full of revelations; they tell us more than would a Mailer gone sane and sedate. . . . There is nothing more seductively entrapping than a repetitive commitment to one's own inventions. It is not the weak, but rather the exceptionally strong writer, a Mailer or a Faulkner or a Hemingway, who finds himself eventually constrained by the persuasiveness of his own fictions, his own metaphors, his own stylistic manners. These come to dominate his mind, to tether the imagination far more than the "reality" they were meant to displace.

Of a Fire on the Moon suffers precisely because he has come to believe so staunchly in the orthodoxy of what he has already written, to believe so literally in his own metaphors, and in the efficacy of his peculiar management of them. They are almost invariably laid down in pairs, for example, in a dualism, like "mystery" and "technology." Each side is imagined tied to the other in a continual struggle. As a consequence, these tensed pairings express for him the schizophrenia he finds in the country and, as a responsible part of it, in himself. But they do much more than that: their interaction is a stay against the complete disruption of the American community and of communication among its parts. In this respect, as in others, Mailer's style is a conservative rather than a radical instrument. The induced give-and-take between the factions is a necessary alternative to a more dreadful possibility: a drawing apart of the factions, the end of any dialectical relationship between them. The consequences would be either the one-dimensionality which is the condition predicted for us in *Of a Fire on the Moon,* or revolution, the dread eventuality in *Armies*. Revolution for Mailer would mean that he could no longer live *within* his dualisms, no longer partake of the characteristics of both sides; he would have to opt for a fragment of the country and of himself, and in the choice would be final madness. This commitment to necessary oppositions, both as a form of writing and as a form of society, has so far been given its most eloquent expression in *Armies* where the language shuttles back and forth over the various conflicting elements, political and stylistic, with almost unflagging assurance—but in the moon book the shuttling becomes mechanical. (pp. 168-69)

Perhaps more important than odors to Mailer as a writer is the possible demise of the verbal equivalent of odors, blasphemies and dirty words. Since World War II, obscenity has lost those enlivening powers that Mailer wistfully remembers in *Armies* as part of the language of his buddies. . . . (p. 170)

Making it one of the most anxiously, sadly patriotic books in our literature, Mailer's perplexities in *Armies* are as culturally and stylistically rewarding to his writing as are any of the comparable perplexities of Yeats.

Yet roughly the same position operates to his disadvantage in *Of a Fire on the Moon,* which is, I think, a quite messy performance. Everything he wrote before made it likely that he would have to write about the moon shot; but what was not required of him was that he meet the challenge with techniques used in earlier and lesser confrontations. The landing on the moon raised for him an old question: what will finally be left to the literary imagination by the exploitations of science? In combination with every political, financial, and industrial institution in America, science has empowered technology to the point where it can invade the very symbol of romance and dream. Such big words, such a tried issue—it's really a factitious and phoney issue, I suspect. The real issue is how well it, like any myth or fiction, can be explored, especially by a writer who has already locked himself into those metaphors, those dualisms, those large turns of mind which dictated that this was the question he would want to ask.

It's to the point that the best parts of the book are the ones most freed of Mailer's larger ambitions. Some part of him seemingly wants less to reinstate magic and romance than, deeply, to get away from the lure of them, like Rojack at the end of *An American Dream* who "wanted to be free of magic, the tongue of the Devil, the dread of the Lord . . . to be some sort of rational man again, nailed tight to details." His most impressive performances are descriptive ones, which isn't to join the tiresome chorus of those who step away from the difficulties of his achievement by saying that he is a great journalist and a lesser novelist. The distinction, not much good to begin with, is trivializing in the case of a writer who reveals here a genius for even the quickest characterizations . . . , for Proustian social observation. . . . And he is sometimes close to Lawrence in his capacity for imaginative drifts and extensions, all the while being moved forward by what seem to be the accidental associations of language. Not in his intellectual superstructurings, but in these more open evidences of his powers as a writer is assurance enough that the Machine has not yet collapsed the language or stilled the imagination. His magnificent description, the product of intense research, of the cratered face of the moon excels anything made available in words or pictures by the machined men of the Apollo flights.

The book is messed up by ambitions in excess of what is done brilliantly. Too much of it is put on loan to one dualism or another: technology and intuition, the Sanitary-Lobe and the Wild-Lobe nesting together in every American, technological reality and the reality of death, Von Braun as a man of opposites, NASA as having in it the sound of Nazi even though technology and Nazism may be inimical to one another, the space program as insane or noble, "a search for the good, or the agent of diabolisms yet unglimpsed." On and on it goes. . . . Old ways of facing new problems produce old questions and answers, but he goes ahead anyway; divide and conquer. Divide the material, argue the differences, reach a kind of stalemate and call it a "mystery."

It is by such means that the book gets hooked on the subject of dreams. After all, the only life other than the irredeemably evident one that Mailer can propose for men of such rectitude has to be in the unconscious. (pp. 171-73)

Having decided to create a division in the astronauts by populating their unconscious, he must then up the ante still more: their unconscious can't be individuated; it must instead contain the historical, metaphysical, and social components Mailer needs for the on-going rhetoric of his book. Obviously he wouldn't allow their dreams to be the result of anything so merely personal as sublimation. While he can't supply it, he must therefore call for a theory of dreams beyond Freud, thus showing, if only for a moment, his alignment with a kind of intellectual who thinks that questions not answered by Freud or Marx have not yet even been asked. But there's more to come. Once he's escalated his terms to this point, Mailer is scarcely going to settle for the idea that the voyage itself represents merely a larger, corporate effort at the sublimation "of aggressive and intolerably inhuman desires." Even as he allows that possibility, he prefers to divide the matter more ostentatiously: the astronauts and their flight may be the instrument of "celestial and satanic endeavors."

I don't think I am being unfair in schematizing what might be called the incremental technique of Mailer's writing. But why, it still has to be asked, must he engage in these banal acts of cosmic division? Their function is best understood, and made altogether less debilitating, I suspect, if the reader takes them less as part of the substance of the book than its necessary fuel, its lubricant even. They get him moving, get him involved and boosted to a level of intensity where he will then be able to produce the masterful straight stuff in the book, like his description of the Vehicle Assembly Building at Cape Canaveral. (p. 173)

[He] still can, in his own phrase, "climb to capture the language again." He and not the space program, not Technology, is responsible for making the climb harder than it need be by carrying intellectual luggage that is always heavy, usually excess, and now manifestly a hindrance. (p. 174)

Richard Poirier, "The Ups and Downs of Mailer," in The New Republic *(reprinted by permission of* The New Republic; *© 1971 The New Republic, Inc.), Vol. 164, No. 4, January 23, 1971 (and reprinted in* Norman Mailer: A Collection of Critical Essays, *edited by Leo Braudy, Prentice-Hall, Inc., 1972, pp. 167-74).*

JAMES WOLCOTT

Writing in brief, widely spaced-apart paragraphs, Mailer laces together a string of disquieting anecdotes [about condemned killer Gary Gilmore in *The Executioner's Song*], creating an atmosphere of friction and frayed nerves: fear at the heart of an empty calm.

The early chapters are suspenseful—doubly suspenseful: The reader not only waits for Gilmore's nerves to snap, but also for Mailer to make an all-trumpets-raised-in-tribute entrance as Aquarius or The Reporter or The Existential Detective. Instead, Mailer slyly—wisely—cloaks himself in invisibility and keeps a watchful distance. . . . He shadows Gilmore, shooting him from a dozen angles, darting in and out of the minds of his victims, lovers, enemies, and kinfolks. Free of psychometaphysical bombast (remember the anagrammatic analysis in *Marilyn,* the apocalyptic epiphanies of *The Faith of Graffiti*?), *The Executioner's Song* is a study of shallows and surfaces, of moods that curl like smoke or harden into hateful fists.

Nearly 800 pages into the book, Mailer reports *New West* writer Barry Farrell's reaction to Gilmore's tapes of his *In Cold Blood* escapades "His account fell into the same narrative style every hustler and psychopath would give you of the most boring, or of the most extraordinary evening—we did this and then, man, like we did that. Episodic and unstressed." Gilmore's narrative style becomes Mailer's: Episodic, unstressed, *The Executioner's Song* is an epic-scaled psychopathic reverie. Can such a book become a boomer on the best-seller list? Doubtful. Just as a lot of readers declined to ride with Aquarius to the moon, they may refuse to take an 1100-page trek in the company of a scrawny, hollow-cheeked Mormon-killer. Too bad; it's their loss. For the book is often crisp, absorbing, scary, and startlingly funny—the first near-to-greatness book that Mailer has published since *Miami and the Siege of Chicago.*

Nearly everybody in Book One (titled "Western Voices") lives in other people's spaces, in hollows carved out by drugs and indifference. Mailer writes about Utah as if it were a foreign country, as if he were Peter Handke just off the Greyhound, dazed and fascinated by America's eerie splendors. Stretching out into the distance is a twilight-toned suicide landscape. Yes, if murder is a symphonic explosion (muses Rojack in *An American Dream*), suicide is pale light, soft dreams, seductive whispers. Moving through a world of bland, dreamy ominousness, Gilmore emerges not as an outlaw or demon but as a bright cruel force contending with other forces; and contending with himself, as he pops Fiorinal to soothe his migraines. His homicidal longings make dead air crackle into sinister life.

Karma, reincarnation, occult reckonings, suicide, murder, machismo, cancer, sex, WASP authoritarianism, psychopathic rage—all of Mailer's obsessions are in Book One of *The Executioner's Song,* and he's dramatized them in a slangy, unadorned style that carries a light lethal chill. It's a heartening recovery for Mailer after the sluggishness of *The Fight* and *The Faith of Graffiti,* and one suspects (and hopes!) that he's on his way to composing a Dreiserian classic.

Unfortunately, the second half wobbles and wavers and does corkscrewy spins. In Book Two (titled "Eastern Voices"), Gilmore finds himself strapped into the cockpit of a death-propelled fame machine. (p. 46)

The cast soon becomes crowded with celebrities. . . . The pace picks up . . . and yet none of this noisy intrigue is as compelling as the catastrophes that quietly uncoil in Book One. Mailer's I-am-a-camera technique isn't nearly so evocative when the lens is trained on lawyers and TV producers instead of losers, nymphos, nickel-and-dime drug peddlers, and stricken Mormon widows. Moreover, he's written so ringingly about the monkey-see, monkey-do conformity of the media in past pieces that their antics here make for stale comedy. At times nothing seems to propel the author (and the reader) forward except inertia, duty, and Spartan will. And when Mailer starts giving you the life story of every lawyer before the bar, you long for a swashbuckling editor to gallop in like Zorro and start slashing away.

Worse: Mailer makes the grievous blunder of trying to rehabilitate the reputation of his all-star researcher Lawrence Schiller. (pp. 46, 48)

In a "true life novel" in which a psychopath's innocent victims are sketched in quick sharp strokes, it's an insult to trot out the celestial violins for a slap-happy beaver like Schiller.

So many things go wrong in this thick doorstop—chapter after chapter cries out for cutting, sentences slacken and shrivel, a prison ditty lifted from *Maidstone* mars the final page. . . . And yet you feel that Mailer has pulled off something phenomenal—that he's captured loneliness, discontinuity, and druggy squalor better than anyone, even Joan "Bad Nerves" Didion. If only Mailer had remained faithful to the Western Voices and let the Eastern Voices be damned. (p. 48)

James Wolcott, "Norman Mailer and the Dream of Death," in The Village Voice *(copyright © 1979; reprinted by permission), Vol. XXIV, No. 40, October 1, 1979, pp. 46, 48.*

JOAN DIDION

It is one of those testimonies to the tenacity of self-regard in the literary life that large numbers of people remain persuaded that Norman Mailer is no better than their reading of him. They condescend to him, they dismiss his most original work in favor of the more literal and predictable rhythms of "The Armies of the Night"; they regard "The Naked and the Dead" as a promise later broken and every book since as a quick turn for his creditors, a stalling action, a spangled substitute, tarted up to deceive, for the "big book" he cannot write. In fact he has written this "big book" at least three times now. He wrote it the first time in 1955 with "The Deer Park" and he wrote it a second time in 1965 with "An American Dream" and he wrote it a third time in 1967 with "Why Are We in Vietnam?" and now, with "The Executioner's Song," he has probably written it a fourth. (p. 1)

[In] a meticulously limited vocabulary and a voice as flat as the horizon, [Mailer has written] a novel which takes for its incident and characters real events in the lives of real people. "The Executioner's Song" is ambitious to the point of vertigo, and the exact extent of its ambitiousness becomes clear at the end of the first chapter, when a curious sentence occurs, a sentence designed as a kind of Gothic premonition. Brenda Nicol . . . has gotten a call from the penitentiary at Marion saying that her cousin Gary Gilmore was coming home—by way of St. Louis, Denver, Salt Lake—to Provo. "With all the excitement," Chapter One of "The Executioner's Song" closes, "Brenda was hardly taking into account that it was practically the same route their Mormon great-grandfather took when he jumped off from Missouri with a handcart near to a hundred years ago, and pushed west with all he owned over the prairies, and the passes of the Rockies, to come to rest at Provo in the Mormon Kingdom of Deseret just fifty miles below Salt Lake."

Against the deliberately featureless simple sentences of "The Executioner's Song," sentences that slide over the mind like conversations at the K-Mart . . . , the relative complexity and length of this sentence at the end of Chapter One is a chill, a signal that the author is telling us a story of some historical dimension. Notice the intake of breath on the clause "and the passes of the Rockies," notice the long unbroken exhalation that ends in a fall on "just 50 miles below Salt Lake."

It is a largely unremarked fact about Mailer that he is a great and obsessed stylist, a writer to whom the shape of the sentence is the story. His sentences do not get long or short by accident, or because he is in a hurry. Where he does or does not put the comma is a question of considerable concern to him: his revisions on "The Deer Park" are instructive in the extreme. Brenda Nicol may not have been taking into account that handcart, those prairies, those passes of the Rockies, but Mailer was, and, in that one sentence, the terms of the novel had laid themselves out: a connection would be attempted here, a search for a field of negative energy linking these events and these people and the empty melancholy of the place itself.

"The Executioner's Song," then, was to be a novel of the West, and the strongest voices in it, as in the place itself, would be those of women. Men tend to shoot, get shot, push off, move on. Women pass down stories. (pp. 1, 26)

I think no one but Mailer could have dared this book. The authentic Western voice, the voice heard in "The Executioner's Song," is one heard often in life but only rarely in literature, the reason being that to truly know the West is to lack all will to write it down. The very subject of "The Executioner's Song" is that vast emptiness at the center of the Western experience, a nihilism antithetical not only to literature but to most other forms of human endeavor, a dread so close to zero that human voices fade out, trail off, like skywriting. Beneath what Mailer calls "the immense blue of the strong sky of the American West," under that immense blue which dominates "The Executioner's Song," not too much makes a difference.

In a world in which every road runs into the desert or the Interstate or the Rocky Mountains, people develop a pretty precarious sense of their place in the larger scheme.

"The Executioner's Song" is structured in two long symphonic movements: "Western Voices," or Book One, voices which are most strongly voices of women, and "Eastern Voices," Book Two, voices which are not literally those of Easterners but are largely those of men—the voices of the lawyers, the prosecutors, the reporters, the people who move in the larger world and believe that they can influence events. The "Western" book is a fatalistic drift, a tension, an overwhelming and passive rush toward the inevitable events that will end in Gary Gilmore's death. The "Eastern" book is the release of that tension, the resolution, the playing out of the execution. . . . (p. 26)

The women in the "Western" book are surprised by very little. They do not on the whole believe that events can be influenced. A kind of desolate wind seems to blow through the lives of these women in "The Executioner's Song," all these women who have dealings with Gary Gilmore. . . . The wind seems to blow away memory, balance. The sensation of falling is constant. (pp. 26-7)

Control is fugitive. Insanity is casual. The love-death seems as good a way of hanging on as any other.

These women move in and out of paying attention to events, of noticing their own fate. They seem distracted by bad dreams, by some dim apprehension of this well of dread, this "unhappiness at the bottom of things." Inside Bessie Gilmore's trailer south of the Portland city line, down a four-lane avenue of bars and eateries and discount stores and a gas station with a World War II surplus Boeing bomber fixed above the pumps, there is a sense that Bessie can describe only as "a suction-type feeling." She fears disintegration. She wonders where the houses in which she once lived have gone, she wonders about her husband being gone, her children gone, the 78 cousins she knew in Provo scattered and gone and maybe in the ground. She wonders if, when Gary goes, they would "all descend another step into that pit where they gave up searching for one another." She has no sense of "how much was her fault, and how much was the fault of the ongoing world that ground along like iron-banded wagon wheels in the prairie grass." When I read this, I remembered that the tracks made by the wagon wheels are still visible from the air over Utah, like the footprints made on the moon. This is an absolutely astonishing book. (p. 27)

Joan Didion, "'I Want to Go Ahead and Do It'," in The New York Times Book Review *(© 1979 by the New York Times Company; reprinted by permission), October 7, 1979, pp. 1, 26-7.*

FRANK McCONNELL

[One] of the many edges on which Mailer has always precariously balanced his career and reputation is the edge between fiction and what we like to call (forgetting how fictive it really is) "real life." The subtitle of his best political book, *The Armies of the Night*, is *History as a Novel: The Novel as History*. And, seriously as that subtitle may have been meant in *Armies*, it takes on even more serious meaning in *The Executioner's Song* (subtitled *A True Life Novel*). For if "fiction" means anything at all, it means an intelligent shaping and ordering of the inchoate stuff of life itself.

He was lucky in his subject. Gary Gilmore was a loser, a violent thug who, after spending half his life in jails, chose to accept his sentence of death rather than spend the rest of his life there. But he was—*is*, in this book—also a walking compendium of everything that had, long since, become characteristic of the archetypal Mailer hero. (pp. 28-9)

Moreover, by the time he became front-page news, Gilmore had begun to realize another and less savory aspect of Mailer's own career: that of the existential hero trapped among clowns and hucksters capitalizing on his private decision, and even seducing him into complicity in the packaging of what ought to be, in its purity, unpackageable. (p. 29)

Gilmore (like Jim in *Lord Jim*) is both the center of this book and its least visible, least knowable character. Mailer never once allows himself to narrate events from Gilmore's own point of view: even when telling the story of the first, solitary killing, he does not indulge in any speculations about what the killer may have thought or felt at that crucial moment. It is a narrative technique of real genius, particularly since the narrator at one point or another enters and paraphrases the consciousness of every other character of the book. For all the explanations with which he is surrounded, Gilmore remains a mystery—and in remaining a mystery remains (like Jim) one of us.

Granted that Mailer has forged a tale that catches the full ambiguity of life on the edge: can we really call it a creative work, or even more seriously, a work of creative fiction? What has he done, after all, but transcribe, transpose into indirect discourse, and edit the reminiscences of some sad people who happened to cross paths with a penny-ante punk and killer?

Well, in a way he has done nothing more than that. But that is enough, and more than enough. The style of *The Executioner's Song* is remarkably flat, even at times ungrammatical and improvisational: partly, to be sure, as a result of writing the narrative from the tapes of semiliterate people. But the very clumsiness of these characters' narratives achieves an authentic and very moving rhetoric. Especially in the first half of the book, the half describing Gilmore's life and friends, it is like finding yourself surrounded by corrupted Huckleberry Finns, innocents whose inarticulateness is no longer a shield against the ravages of history, but is still the only shield they have. The prose is like black-and-white stock in documentary filmmaking: we know it is consciously chosen, and yet we also know that it somehow, magically, underscores the reality of what we watch.

Indeed, the association with documentary film makes more sense than that. For what Mailer, like a talented director, has done in *The Executioner's Song* is to select, cut, and shape preexisting material into a creation that reflects equally the reality of his own time and the reality of his own imagination: so much so that we do not know whether to be more dazzled by the reflection outward or the one inward. If the novel is a mythology constructed to catch the moral ambiguity of its age, then *The Executioner's Song* is a brilliant, maybe a great, novel. And if *The Executioner's Song* is not that, we had all better revise our definitions. (p. 30)

Frank McConnell, "Books and the Arts: 'The Executioner's Song'," in The New Republic *(reprinted by permission of* The New Republic; *© 1979 The New Republic, Inc.), Vol. 181, No. 17, October 27, 1979, pp. 28-30.*

ALDEN WHITMAN

The good news is that Norman Mailer's *The Executioner's Song* . . . is a superb piece of writing. It has the scope and wallop of Theodore Dreiser's *An American Tragedy;* its realism contains echoes of Zola and Frank Norris and James T. Farrell; and it reaffirms the vitality and the validity of the social novel, which, having fled underground with the advent of the Cold War, has now re-emerged with incredible pulsing power. *The Executioner's Song* is (or should be) the occasion for rousing cheers.

In spare, detached, almost journalistic prose Mailer demonstrates that he is a master of suspenseful narration and of character building through adroit use of quotations, dialogue, and stark personal interactions. The result is a camera-eye focus on the underside of American society; on the loathsomeness of some of its inhabitants who exist in mirror image to cultivated society; on the failure of our penal system to regenerate its inmate-victims; and on the devilish role of the press in publicizing Gilmore's final days.

Mailer eschews tractarian moralism: It is enough to grip the reader and to fix his gaze steadily on the human lemons that American society produces. . . . With its relentless authenticity, Mailer's volume forces us to confront the fact that life in the Lower Depths is just as American as sour apple pie.

The first part of the book centers on Gilmore, Nicole, their circle, and the killing. It is written (deliberately, I am certain) in very short paragraphs and in the voices of those who supplied the information. Mailer's aim is to create an atmosphere of authenticity from which the authorial presence is absent. He does not judge; more difficult, he asks understanding.

In the second section, as in the first, Mailer writes in many voices, none of them his own. The effect is eerie. In twang and drawl his people strive for the pretentiousness of schooled speech, yet slip easily into television colloquialisms, into phrases right out of beauty-shop magazines. The legal voices of the second section, dry and drained, bespeak the inhumanity of justice and dessicated law and lawyers.

Mailer has written a fascinating and wholly disturbing book that captures the rawness, the crudity, the violence and the inhumanities in American life. He raises basic questions that cry out for answers. Why a Gilmore? Why a Nicole Baker? Why wasted lives? Why a cheap killing? Why the firing squad? Has the American Dream turned, for too many, into a Nightmare?

You won't find the answers in *The Executioner's Song*. What you will find is the daring work of a man who is willing to raise the basic social issues of our age.

Alden Whitman, "The Dissonance of the American Dream," in Books & Arts *(copyright © 1979 by The Chronicle of Higher Education, Inc.), n.s. Vol. 1, No. 5, November 9, 1979, p. 9.*

TED MORGAN

The Executioner's Song is a "plain, unvarnished tale," stitched together from hundreds of hours of interviews, about half of them conducted by Mailer, with supporting characters and bit players in the Gary Gilmore saga. The story is told from several dozen points of view. . . .

Mixing the different voices proved to be Mailer's highest hurdle. "I was brought up not to jump from one person's mind into another," he says. "I thought that was what poor writers did when they didn't have enough imagination to find a form. But then, I thought, the shifting point of view was a 19th-century form, it went back to a time when people believed in God and the novelist could play at being the All Knowing Supreme Deity."

In this case, the deity orchestrates the voices, but does not join in the song. The qualities (or flaws, depending on one's point of view) we look for in Mailer's work—the ripe style, the existential musings, the outrageous ideas, the over-characterizing—are nowhere in sight.

What then, one might ask, is there of Mailer in the book, and why could it not have been written by any competent journalist who knows how to edit taped interviews? Mailer insists that "only someone who has been writing for 30 years would be willing to relinquish his ego. I couldn't have done it 15 years ago. It's hard for a writer who takes himself seriously to be nothing but a transmission belt."

But there is more to it than not getting in the way of his material. Mailer saw in Gilmore a character that he might have invented in a novel, for Gilmore personified the main theme of his entire *oeuvre*—namely, that the soul could conceivably have a separate existence from the body. Gilmore believed so fervently in an afterlife that he worried about bumping into his murder victims. Mailer wanted to show that Gilmore's wish to die was not a put-on or a publicity stunt; he wasn't just a proud con trapped in a role. He was doing it because he felt he deserved to die, could no longer tolerate life in prison, where he had spent half of his 35 years, and wanted to reach the Other Side. That was the kind of existential gamble Mailer could appreciate. (p. 57)

[*The Executioner's Song*] is Mailer's best book since *The Deer Park,* which may be a backhanded compliment in light of the author's unprecedented restraint. My first thought was, "How in the world can Gary Gilmore be worth a thousand pages?" But I found myself swept up and carried along by the narrative, and I began to see now artful the design is—how, by letting the characters speak in their own voices, and by having the events unfold as they appeared to witnesses, Mailer achieves an effect that is not unlike the homespun credibility of Thornton Wilder's *Our Town.* But this is the underside of *Our Town,* dealing as it does with misfits and murders. The overall tone made me think of Conrad's remark in *Lord Jim* concerning "that mysterious, almost miraculous, power of producing striking effects by means impossible of detection, which is the last word of the highest art."

This book is much more than the story of a man who wanted to die. It is a panorama of American life in the Seventies, of people at every level of society responding to an extreme situation. . . .

Mailer devotes one-third of his book to the transformation of a criminal case in Utah into a national media event, the shift from the saving of Gary Gilmore to the merchandising of Gary Gilmore. The man and his bizarre crusade were overshadowed by the deal—the movie and TV rights, the articles and interviews, and the foreign sales, which Larry Schiller kept hustling.

One end-product of this merchandising is Mailer's book, which redeems itself from the accusation of cheap (no, make that expensive) checkbook journalism by showing how the press distorts, makes over, and becomes a part of the event. Gilmore began to like the part and to play up to it, striking poses, chuckling over his mail, and enjoying the attention. Eventually, he got his way, and was shot by a firing squad early in 1977. The book is strewn with clues to explain his behavior, but it ends without a pat, predigested, conclusive answer. . . .

The point Mailer makes is that even when we know everything about another human being we can never understand his ultimate moral nature. "I put in all I knew," he says, "and I have the answers we have in life, not hard concrete answers, but that Gilmore was a deck of cards, as many of us are. Perhaps he killed because he knew that what was best in him could never be expressed." (p. 58)

Ted Morgan, "Fine Lines: Last Rights," in Saturday Review *(© 1979 by Saturday Review Magazine Corp.; reprinted with permission), Vol. 6, No. 22, November 10, 1979, pp. 57-8.*

DIANE JOHNSON

However powerful one finds [*The Executioner's Song*] there are reservations one may feel about the genre and about its social implications—if only what to make of the literary ambulance-chasing that the true-life novel encourages.

Perhaps the contradictions embodied in the idea of true-life fiction reflect Mailer's ambivalence about whether to take a journalistic or novelistic direction with this fascinating material, involving as it does both dramatic elements of love and death and matters of worldly significance. Gilmore's assertion of his right to have the death sentence carried out and the legal bases of efforts to save him, the evident failure of the penal system to do anything for or with him in his nineteen years of prison, or to protect his victims from him either, the role in the story of Mormonism and Utah history —these and many other matters would repay the attention of a journalist of Mailer's penetration and energy. On the other hand, Gilmore's story partakes something (too little, it turns out) of popular literary traditions about tragic lovers and defiant condemned men . . . , cowboys, *On the Road* types, *Tobacco Road* types which would attract any novelist, especially one with Mailer's romantic turn of mind. . . .

Gilmore's history, Nicole's history are horrifying, sad, moving, and skillfully told in Book One ("Western Voices") in short, forceful paragraphs with extra spaces between, allowing quick shifts among a welter of interesting characters. . . . Mostly these are trustful, hapless, well-meaning people whom Mailer wisely neither judges nor sympathizes with. He thereby nearly avoids patronizing them on the one hand and on the other associating them too obviously with his own known preoccupations with violence, execution, female masochism, and other tough stuff. Technically he keeps out of the book altogether; there is no evident point of view and no comment, only a matter-of-fact tone perfect for the baroque tale it will unfold, and even enough to conceal that here is, of course, a work of selection and interpretation. . . .

The book is written in an apparently simple style—pure tape recorder, it seems at first—and given the fact that no one can make up things better than the things people actually say, this mode of quiet attention seems right. But maybe it's all made up and Mailer infinitely artful; the text is mined with Mailerisms when you look closely. . . .

The language mainly fits, convinces, but the voice of Mailer himself, once heard, lingers with strange insistence over the voices of the others, except perhaps that of Gilmore himself.

Then you begin to hear the great parodist in Mailer straining to get out, especially when he's representing the thoughts of Lawrence Schiller, his colleague and the central consciousness for much of the book. Schiller is given a number of callous, greedy, self-important, and dishonest thoughts and reactions, presented in a mock Hemingwayese perfectly catching his moral pretentiousness and inherently despicable pursuit. . . .

On the whole the writing is fastidious and, given the lurid material, tasteful. It's just that you keep wondering which are the true parts. . . .

It is finally the fact that all this really happened that moves us most. Thinking about Debbie and Ben is like looking at the photograph of the starving child in the CARE poster. Because that is so serious it demands explanation and reflection that are not forthcoming. Not even a writer of Mailer's skill can make us suspend our realization of history, can stop us from remembering the world and not this shadow of it. Since this is so, to make fictions of them exploits and trivializes these people at the same time that it may seek to ennoble or project them; in the service of a private (but popular!) mythology it takes over their words and thoughts while they are still around to speak for themselves, leaves them, as it were, without words, and diminishes their humanity. (p. 3)

Mailer's misunderstanding or underestimation of Mormonism is a little disappointing; for instance, he makes a lot of Gilmore's ideas about life after death, without realizing the extent to which these are orthodox Mormon beliefs. (pp. 3-4)

The author of a true-life novel tries to have it both ways—to improve the dull, invent the spicy parts, leave out the inconvenient things, and not be held accountable for veracity or completeness. Yet he hopes for significance too. Playing neither by the rules of fiction nor by the rules of fact, he is in danger of sinking into facile sensationalism. The handling of Gilmore's letters is an example here of the inconsistency. Sagaciously edited by a fine writer, they are pretty impressive. Mailer has abridged them "because it seemed fair to show him at his best, not his average." "One wanted to demonstrate the impact of his mind on Nicole, and that was best done by allowing his brain to have its impact on us." Yet Nicole presumably read the letters entire. Mailer finds the real Gary Gilmore a good enough writer only at times, but he gets the advantage of Gilmore's real life death.

No one has mythologized Son of Sam, so fat and creepy. You wonder whether if Gary Gilmore had looked less like a cowboy, this book would have been written. It does have sweep and charity and power; but in the long run it is a kind of socialist-realist ballet, where the redneck killers are recognizable by their bandannas, the nymphos by the "couple of bruises on those juicy thighs," a cast Mailer has assembled before. He seems to have grafted an Eastern urban dream of the Wild West, complete with sixpacks, CBs, and pickup trucks, onto a conventional paradigm about poverty and child abuse eventuating in anomie and murder. This doesn't seem to be quite the truth of Utah or Nicole or Gilmore—and Mailer has given us so much of a powerful and absorbing story, one can only wish to know how it really was. (p. 4)

Diane Johnson, "Death for Sale," in The New York Review of Books *(reprinted with permission from* The New York Review of Books; *copyright © 1979 Nyrev, Inc.), Vol. XXVI, No. 19, December 6, 1979, pp. 3-4, 6.*

* * *

MARTINSON, Harry 1904-1978

Martinson was a Swedish novelist, poet, essayist, and dramatist. Travel motifs run throughout Martinson's work, stemming from his early years as a seaman. His verse contains many symbolic references, and critics have compared him stylistically to Strindberg. Martinson received the 1974 Nobel Prize for Literature along with his colleague Eyvind Johnson. (See also *Contemporary Authors,* Vols. 77-80.)

LEIF SJÖBERG

Hardly ever has a Swedish author led a life more fantastic than that of Harry Martinson; in Swedish literature no exoticism is more captivating than that in his autobiographical books and travelogues; and the tender devotion to Swedish nature expressed in his *naturprosa* is unsurpassed—which is apparent in such works as *Svärmare och harkrank* (1937), *Midsommardalen* (1938), and *Det enkla och det svåra* (1939). . . . In later writings such as *Utsikt från en grästuva* (View from a Tussock, 1963), the author has still managed to retain the larger, even cosmic, perspectives. (p. 364)

After his autobiographical books Martinson broadened his view of people on earth and became a humanist (in the traditional old European sense) and a scholar. There were ups and downs (especially *Verklighet till döds,* about the war in Finland, "a subject that was too close") and *Den förlorade jaguaren* which satirized the hyper-efficiency of contemporary times, his first real novel ("written in too great haste"). But if there is a common denominator in his many-faceted work, it is his belief that everything is interrelated, which is "why one can feel secure in it." . . . (p. 365)

Martinson the humanist did not neglect the study of the natural sciences. In the essay "Tekniken och själen" ("Technology and the Soul," published in *Daedalus,* 1955), he admits that he enjoys keeping in touch with scientific developments through books on popular science. (pp. 365-66)

Martinson is aware of the fact that there is a great deal of "kindness" in technology and its servants, and much that is praiseworthy "if you stick to the bright side." Our duty now is to dare see even the darkness, and even to make ourselves familiar with the dark imagination's images of the clouds of destruction. . . .

Martinson's vision of destruction developed over a period of years. The epic poem *Aniara,* which appeared in 1956, tells the story of a space ship hurtling toward its annihilation in time, a mirror of our space ship earth. Here, from lack of foresight, or as a result of plain greed, man has left behind him simple, traditional research, embarking instead on the utilization of a device that is fatally complex: nuclear power. . . . It is a modern apocalypse, a poetic revelation of the future: a Völuspá of the twentieth century. (p. 367)

Almost since the atom bomb was exploded over Hiroshima and Nagasaki in 1945, Martinson has warned us of man's capacity for destruction, in a way that is sometimes reminiscent of Lewis Mumford, whom he has read and still admires. (p. 368)

Martinson considers himself by temperament a romantic, a man of feeling, but with strong attraction for science. . . . (p. 369)

Leif Sjöberg, "Harry Martinson: Writer in Quest of Harmony," in The American Scandinavian Review *(copyright 1972 by The American-Scandinavian Foundation), Vol. LX, No. 4, December, 1972, pp. 360-71.*

LEIF SJÖBERG

It remains to be seen if even a very considerable author like Harry Martinson will be able to make an impression on the English-speaking literary world—and, if not, it is not at all his fault . . . , yet it is beyond any discussion that he has been of great importance to the Swedish (and Scandinavian) literary world. Indeed, he has helped form a specific consciousness for an entire generation of his compatriots at large and not just the literary gourmets. (p. 478)

The storyline of *The Road* is occasionally extremely thin, and miraculously, as in folk tales, sometimes it disappears and becomes entirely invisible. What made *The Road* such a great success in Scandinavia and such an average affair in the English-speaking world? Part of the answer, no doubt, is Martinson's poetic language. He is a stylistic innovator comparable to Strindberg and an imaginative coiner of words. . . . Martinson's assertion that translation is impossible (?) is not entirely an exaggeration. Dealing with facts and subtleties, proceeding with his stories and meditations, in a most leisurely way, Martinson's book cannot possibly be read in a hurry, like an ordinary novel. *The Road* is a book one must read slowly, with pauses, and to which one must return as to a book of maxims. . . .

Why did Martinson select a tramp as the main character [of *The Road*]? Possibly because in his rather extensive rovings about the world he had acquired competence as a latterday itinerant and because in vagabond literature he would be allowed liberties with the real world and imagination similar to those enjoyed by so many of his predecessors, from Eichendorff to the later Kerouac.

An additional benefit of employing a "wandering lookout tower," such as Bolle the tramp as protagonist, is that the countryside, the full terrain of the Swedish realm, as it were, can be described through a unique point of view, yielding more intimate geographic information than any geography book. (p. 483)

In Martinson's epic poetic cycle *Aniara* (1956), . . . poet-technological man has rejected Earth after having made it uninhabitable. "The possibilities of imagination" had been neglected and rejected: *Aniara* deals with a journey into outer space, and it is thought to occur in a very distant future. However, as Martinson has pointed out,

> this is essentially a pretext. What it offers is above all a vision of our own time, of the life journey through our own emptiness. Its perspectives are those of the expanded afterthought, with the narrator's instrument moved into a symbolic world where the poem's symbols connect with those of natural science. . . .

Through lack of foresight and restraints, or as a result of plain greed, man has left behind him relatively simple, traditional values and delves instead into utilization of a device that turns out to be fatally complex—nuclear power. . . . (p. 484)

Leif Sjöberg, "Harry Martinson: From Vagabond to Space Explorer," in Books Abroad *(copyright 1974 by the University of Oklahoma Press), Vol. 48, No. 3, Summer, 1974, pp. 476-85.*

MICHAEL MEYER

Martinson, now well over seventy, is (or was) a genuine proletarian poet who served for years as a merchant seaman and made his mark in the 1920s and 1930s with splendidly simple yet perceptive poems and prose memoirs, a sort of Swedish W. H. Davies. Sadly, there exists a deep-seated belief among Swedish critics that to achieve top rank a writer must prove himself *djupsinnig* (literally "deep-minded"), which in practice means writing [a kind of woolly pseudo-philosophy] . . . , and after the war Martinson turned to this depressing genre, producing novels such as *The Road to Klockrike* and poems like "Aniara", both of a pretentious emptiness. (But they paid off; had he stayed simple, I am sure he would never have won the Nobel Prize last year.) Fortunately, Mr. Bly [editor and translator of *Harry Martinson, Gunnar Ekelöf and Tomas Tranströmer: Friends, You Drank Some Darkness*] has avoided this side of Martinson's work and stuck to the simple poems, like "Out at Sea":

> At sea you know spring or summer just as a faint wind.
> Sometimes in summer the drifting Florida-weed puts
> out blossoms,
> Or one spring evening a spoon-billed stork flies in
> towards Holland.

Michael Meyer, "The Call of the Deep," in The Times Literary Supplement *(© Times Newspapers Ltd. (London) 1975; reproduced from* The Times Literary Supplement *by permission), No. 3842, October 31, 1975, p. 1287.**

CHRISTOPHER HOWELL

The first thing one notices about Harry Martinson's poems is their precision and over-all exactitude. . . . Always the precision takes on its own life, moves from impression to expression but without disturbing its own clear-pond-like surface. . . . [His] attention to actual "things" is nothing less than reverence, the everyday magic that keeps banality out of the everyday and out of Martinson's poems. Thus he can write a difficult (borderline sentimental) Wright-like elegy like "No Name for It" [in *Friends, You Drank Some Darkness*] with almost frustrating ease. . . .

The second thing one notices about these poems is stillness. It is the blood of every word Martinson writes, and it winds without a seam around a major theme in Scandinavian literature from Strindberg to the present: the holy solitude of travelers. The small lyric "March Evening" . . . is a made-to-order example. . . . (p. 76)

Using precision, stillness, and the solitude of travelers, Martinson strings a tense, thin field between the mechanized, human-dominated world and the dance of nature. Like all lyric poets, Martinson draws heavily on his place in the natural flow. Nature, therefore, is in his poems true power. All else is counterfeit. In the poem "Hades and Euclid," it is the human world, the mathematical and mechanical one, which is flat and burning. Life, in Martinson's work, is depth, depth is power, and power is at its most luminous in the natural world. Though this conviction can be seen in nearly every poem collected here, nowhere is Martinson's moral ecology more explicitly outlined than in the poem "Winds of Passage." . . . [The] source of the tragic in Harry Martinson's work [is that new worlds do not exist—but in the world being left behind and in dreams]. It is not personal tragedy . . . but the unutterably huge sorrow of our species and, ultimately of our gleaming planet as well. (pp. 76-7)

Salvation? If Martinson believes in it, he locates it in the solitary mind, the unconscious surfacing from deep down without letting go the soil-clogged roots of existence. All things (even planets, species) die, but the deep-given perceptions of a reverent life stop time and are deathless. . . . (p. 77)

Christopher Howell, "Swedish Mystics," in Moons and Lion Tailes *(copyright © 1976 by The Permanent Press), Vol. II, No. 1, 1976, pp. 75-82.**

* * *

McCARTHY, Mary 1912-

McCarthy is an American novelist, essayist, short story writer, critic, and travel writer. Her work is highly moral in tone and temperament, revealing the writer's concern for an aesthetic encompassing political, social, and philosophical beliefs. (See also *CLC*, Vols. 1, 3, 5, and *Contemporary Authors*, Vols. 5-8, rev. ed.)

JEAN GARRIGUE

Contrast is all: Mary McCarthy starts off [*The Stones of Florence*] with a racy, highhanded fault-finding. As if from the petulant mouth of the tourist, she speaks; hustling a cranky mirror down streets, she echoes that never-hypothetical creature's complaints: that the city is drab, provincial, harassed by Vespas, overrun by occupying armies of tourists, stuffy like Boston, not naughty, with too much rusticated stone and too many "academic" masterpieces.

After the reader has been caught and nettled, she changes her stride and her "true" eye takes over. But the tone emerges, ever so often, that launches the book—a kind of talking down to, with tongue in cheek, or a kind of bringing things down to the level we can *all* understand. Therefore the ambition of the Renaissance artist to excel everyone, even the Ancients, is compared to some millionaire's boast of ordering a building bigger and better than the Parthenon —which is like comparing John D. Rockefeller to Lorenzo the Magnificent. (p. 14)

The Renaissance and Florence, its chiefest lily, have been written about voluminously, and usually with painstaking scholarship and in a spirit of submission to their enchanter powers. Like a cool member of this age, McCarthy stands off from it to just a degree, and delivers a work of another hue. But it is a brilliant assemblage of anecdotes, observations interlaced with history, some accounts of painters' lives, *à la* Vasari, all in a swift, energetic and highly charged style. Its excellence lies in part in the way things are made to hang together; the city, that work of art, and its works of art, is seen in firm relation to the checkerwork of its history. Its excellence also lies in the visual pleasure it has to give us. The look of things, the grand joy of Italy after all, is wonderfully caught, from the "enchanted economy" of Italian gardens and the plotted colors of the countryside to Florence at its stoniest. (pp. 14-15)

Shying off somewhat from that almost unbelievable unicorn that the Renaissance has a way of seeming to us, with its profundities of many-mindedness, magnificence and daring, giving, in fact, almost more emphasis to the iron-tempered time preceding it, of Guelph and Ghibelline frays and feuds, she brings a fresh insight—and an interpretation unexpected (at least to me)—on Florence, with its "wise ruling of space —the only kind of government the Florentines ever mastered," when she says that it has about it the look of the ideal city of reason and justice as dreamed of by the Greeks and Dante, and that its great statues in the Bargello and in the Piazza della Signoria are like "admonitory lessons or 'examples' in civics, a part of the very fabric of the city—the *res publica*." (p. 15)

Jean Garrigue, "Books: 'The Stones of Florence'," in Arts Magazine *(© 1960 by The Arts Digest, Inc.), Vol. 34, No. 6, March, 1960, pp. 14-15.*

BENJAMIN DeMOTT

The interest of Mary McCarthy's *The Group* . . . stems in part from the ingenuity of its argument that rules aplenty exist in every age, and that old ways of judging people aren't really outmoded. The news will not astonish this writer's followers; a Puritan in Upper Bohemia, Miss McCarthy has for years approached her characters as a stern objective moralist. Sly Professor Mulcahy in *The Groves of Academe* is a knave; it is wrong to take advantage of innocence, no matter whether the innocent is a college president or a college girl. Clever Martha Sinnott in *A Charmed Life* receives the wages of sin; it is wrong to commit an act of adultery whether in the name of reason or of passion. The elegant European anti-Americans chided in *On The Contrary* are irresponsible; it is wrong to deny the connection between American ugliness and European apathy about the education of its poor. These books, like the author's earliest works, regularly invoke standards of decency and propriety that current fashion finds boring and irrelevant. And this consistency has helped Miss McCarthy win regard as a novelist of manners with a better than even chance of achieving moral clarity and significance.

Such clarity never comes cheap, as is well known: novelists of manners buy it by narrowing their social range and emotional sympathies. Sitting in judgment upon poor people, for instance, looks inhumane; the focus must be upon privileged, well-brought-up types who "ought to know what's right," and need not be understood from within. Nor can these types survive much exposure to the times they live in; they have to be kept at a remove from historical events of the kind that drain meaning from personal foibles.

Miss McCarthy's method of meeting these demands in *The Group* is to center her attention upon a clique of Vassar girls making its postgraduate way in New York in the mid-1930s. None of the members of the clique can be described as dumb, and each is solvent enough to experience the Depression as an "exciting period," rather than as a disaster. This in itself would provide an old-style Marxist moralist with a text for a sermon on the sin of obliviousness. And Miss McCarthy's reluctance to mention that sin may well disconcert more than a few readers of non-Marxist persuasion. . . . No doubt a direct comment on the triviality of [her characters'] agonies compared with the sufferings of non-groupers of the period would be excessively flat—but shouldn't the writer hint that the absurdities of the rich sometimes do spring from feelings of powerlessness and guilt?

Perhaps—but hints of that sort would open this dramatized *Alumnae News* to foreclosures, bankruptcies, unemployment statistics, and a mass of other facts whose moral meaning, if any, remains obscure. And Miss McCarthy is too fond of the moralist's position to run that risk. Keeping a cool distance between herself and her characters, using history largely for color rather than as a force shaping human behavior, she tells the interlinked stories of her girls as though each were free to choose between good and evil, and wholly unjustified in blaming failures of humanity and intelligence upon the age. (p. 98)

[The] pleasure afforded by *The Group* resembles that afforded by an eighteenth-century novel. The reader always knows where he is in moral terms. Each of the contemporary objects that crowd the pages—prescription Scotch, Forward House at Macy's, Russel Wright cocktail shakers, Jones Beach, Radio City, the Communist party, Venetian blinds—seems to point a moral. (The moral is that liberation, progress, and folk art from the factory are but dreams of naïveté.) Each of the pathetically Modern seductions, assignations, and sexual experiments thrusts forward an "improving" lesson. (The lesson is that stupidity alone seeks to transform sex or any other ancient area of human experience into a technical problem.) . . .

Yet for all its ingenuity, *The Group* fails to put every reservation to rest; its moral clarity often seems too mechanical to trust. . . . Miss McCarthy is a knowing woman, a shrewd reporter and entertainer, and among the most original—and most readable—Puritans this country has produced for years. She is, however, at once a shade too clear, too unforgiving, and too conscious of fashion for her art's own good. (p. 102)

Benjamin DeMott, "Poets, Presidents, and Preceptors," in Harper's *(copyright © 1963 by* Harper's Magazine; *all rights reserved; excerpted from the October, 1963 issue by special permission), Vol. 227, No. 1361, October, 1963, pp. 98-110.*

GORDON O. TAYLOR

'There is always one theme in Mary McCarthy's fictions', writes Alfred Kazin in *Bright Book of Life:* 'none of these awful people is going to catch *me*. The heroine is always distinctly right, and gives herself all possible marks for taste, integrity and indomitability. Other people are somehow material to be written up.' Whether or not one accepts this as fair, one *is* inclined to agree that a pattern of identification exists between the novelist and her fictional heroines. A reader of McCarthy's *non*-fiction is also often struck, particularly of late, by the extent to which self-portrayal can become central to her treatment of a subject. The inward play of her imaginative response is frequently as much the substance as the servant of her outwardly avowed literary purpose, or the onward momentum of her narrative line. The intellectual, aesthetic or moral assurance of her self-characterization exerts defining pressure on her materials, be they those of the critic or the polemicist, the autobiographer or the reporter. This pressure of personality indeed relates more than it distinguishes, sometimes even fuses, these various literary roles, along with a number of their respective techniques.

This seems particularly true of *Vietnam* (1967), *Hanoi* (1968) and *Medina* (1972), McCarthy's short books about the American presence in South Vietnam, the impact of the war on the North and the psychic as well as legal aftermath in America of the killing at My Lai. . . . [These] volumes convey a coherent narrative of experience absorbed as much as observed by McCarthy, and of her shaping personality correspondingly shaped. The circumference of her attention progressively contracts (as her titles suggest) from the abstract illusions underlying American involvement in Vietnam, to a more geographically and humanly specific consideration of the view from Hanoi, finally finding in Captain Medina a 'juncture-point' of the war's contradictions, more accessible to the novelist's than to the professional reporter's eye. So, too, one's sense of McCarthy's personal investment in her accounts progressively intensifies.

'Facts', those she accepts as given at the outset and reaffirms at the end, together with those she discovers or revises along the way, gradually become internalized, their secure possession by the reader increasingly a matter of McCarthy's *self*-possession. The 'integrity' of the novelist-heroine impugned by Kazin is in these works to be understood as a process through which the author-protagonist integrates the factuality of her material with her sense of herself, strives to complete herself in relation to it. This process, moreover, depends for rhetorical and moral persuasiveness on McCarthy's willingness to risk through self-questioning that safe certainty which Kazin suggests is an *un*questioned premise of her fictional self-projections. She *is* in these books, whatever the case in her novels, 'caught' in situations in which her *own* 'awfulness' or innocence eventually becomes a central issue, one determinant among many of the 'truthfulness' of her reportage. In order to 'write up' others she must, in the literary situation evolving around her here, write up herself. (pp. 103-04)

McCarthy's own 'interest' as a writer at the outset is to document further an existing case against the war, the prosecution of which case indeed concerns her throughout all three books.

From the start, however, there are signs of more subtle

problems and possibilities involving self-representation. Personal pronouns gradually become charged, stress-points in a structure through which McCarthy begins to negotiate the issue of her own Americanness in relation to American acts or attitudes she is attacking. This web of self-reference is further complicated as it expands by the developing relationship between author and reader, a relationship with its own points of presumed contact or tension. 'I' and 'you', 'we' and 'they'—the problematical quality as well as the grammatical necessity of such designations emerges early as a condition of McCarthy's probing of relations between her subjective resources and her objective aims. Early suggestions also arise of a mind deflected inward by, as well as reacting outward to, its encounters; of involuntary as well as deliberate forays into the personal past for perspective on the national present. (pp. 104-05)

At times [McCarthy] wishes to explode by the force of her disgust the Americanized surface, verbal strategy appropriate to a cultural impact as violent as any bomb-crater. At times it is a matter of 'excavating' an imaginative truth by careful siftings of immediate observation through memory or association, the strategy now an 'archaeological' procedure of patient verbal brushwork. (p. 105)

[In *Hanoi,*] the questionings of a more prominent self are from the first more central to the shape, tone and pace of the discussion, borne inward by the pressure of personal implications: 'Quite a few of the questions one does not, as an American liberal, want to put in Hanoi are addressed to oneself.' (p. 106)

Just as there is no real solution to McCarthy's immediate problem of social behaviour, there is no clear solution to her vaguer sense of a problem of symbolic meaning. Wedded . . . to a personal predicament of association with and aversion to the war—in some ways a microcosm of the national dilemma—she can settle the 'score', solve the 'mystery', only, if at all, by an inquiry into the nature of her responsibilities as a writer in relation to the material of these volumes. (p. 108)

[The] claim to objectivity, the certainty of being able to write out of that aspect of oneself, has over the course of the volume been 'shrinking', not so much disappearing as being compressed by experience into a different substance, a 'cherry stone' of self in which acknowledgment of complex personal interests is the prime literary source: 'a subject, an "I", asserting itself.' (p. 110)

A trip initially undertaken for 'my own peace of mind'—as if using one's literary influence might help end the war and restore one's life to normal—becomes an inward search for 'my own salvation', the fossil remains of a Catholic girlhood yielding up the phrase. Salvation, such as it is for this American writer as she confronts the interior consequences of an American 'crime', consists in possessing the aluminium ring, never forgetting even if not wearing it. (The aluminium POW bracelets so popular for a time tended rather to be conspicuously worn, then easily discarded.) McCarthy knows—along with the heroes and heroines of Henry James—that 'Nothing will be the same again, if only because of the awful self-recognitions', not least her own, 'the war has enforced'. . . .

Later, having contracted to report on the Medina trial, McCarthy brings to this ostensibly straightforward assignment, through the continuing assertion of a cumulatively shaped 'I', her experience as author-protagonist of the earlier books. Even without the epilogue to *Hanoi,* having travelled a psychological as well as geographical distance to and from Vietnam, she would inevitably be drawn to this dimension of American self-encounter on home ground. (p. 111)

[*Medina* is] a single statement of the protagonist self as well as an observer's report on the trial. If the personal presence seems more static than in *Hanoi,* it is because McCarthy now seems the possessor rather than the pursuer of her literary soul *vis-à-vis* the war as a literary subject. She knows who 'I' is, having learned through the process of the preceding texts, at some psychic risk and cost. . . . If McCarthy's voice in *Medina* is more dispassionate than in *Hanoi*—even cold, as it becomes apparent that the test of acknowledgement will fail—it is not necessarily therefore less personal. If she subsides from the subjective intensities of *Hanoi,* she does not revert to the formal argumentation of *Vietnam.*

The courtroom atmosphere is familiar to McCarthy's persona: one of boredom as pervasive and enervating as August heat in Georgia, where the trial is situated, or in Saigon. Seeming to fix the participants in tableaux of ennui, threatening to numb an observing intelligence, this atmosphere nonetheless begins to communicate its message. She is rasped into noticing fragments of the truth which the proceedings seem designed to ignore more than to deny. (pp. 111-12)

Medina is available to McCarthy as a 'transition figure' through whom the military abstraction was not so much distorted as inevitably translated into the human horror. 'A figure of speech, overworked, takes its revenge by coming to life', she had written in *Hanoi* of the dehumanized reiterations of propaganda on both sides. A moral vocabulary without reference to consequences, its weaponry in words as well as ordnance, will eventually have the consequences it denies. (p. 113)

Mary McCarthy's particular personality, an opposite attitude the key to the growth of its literary design in these volumes, has been felt throughout as the precipitating energy of her narrative. Now at the end—her final 'Amen' bearing personal witness to a record of experience uneasily sustained—that force seems to have united the books, ringlike, interlocking the orbits of their prose. (p. 114)

Gordon O. Taylor, "Cast a Cold 'I': Mary McCarthy on Vietnam," in Journal of American Studies *(© Cambridge University Press 1975), Vol. 9, No. 1, April, 1975, pp. 103-14.*

MARY GORDON

McCarthy's voice has always been perfectly reliable; the stirring and disturbing tone of the born truth-teller is hers, whether she is writing essays or fiction. Her perspective is always feminine: Antigone grown up, her absoluteness not diminished as she takes on sex. She has never been easy on herself or her characters, or tried to make anyone look better. (p. 1)

This represents the essence of McCarthy's sensibility: the fineness, the formality, the stance that cannot imagine any but a moral perspective. . . . [McCarthy's] ease and balance, largely moral, suggest a lost world.

Where are we, then, to place "Cannibals and Missionaries," which its publishers present as "a thriller," in the context of Mary McCarthy's work? She is not the sort of writer who would toss off a book as a lark or a diverting experiment, so why has she done it?

It is clear to me that this, the most political, the least autobiographical of her novels, would have been impossible without her experience of traveling to Vietnam as a reporter. Many of the details of that experience, particularly those about physical fear and communal bonding, find their way into this novel in the accounts of the passengers' ordeal. "Cannibals and Missionaries" is the story, among other things, of a committee of liberals who are hijacked while traveling to Iran to examine the atrocities of the Shah's regime. It speaks, with McCarthy's habitually unsentimental voice, to the problem of witness and political responsibility among nonprofessional men of good will. For McCarthy, terrorism is disturbing in the same way that sexual promiscuity would have been for Emily Brontë: it is political activity without manners, without form; therefore it is incapable of yielding much meaning and is inevitably without hope. (p. 33)

The most important achievement of "Cannibals and Missionaries" is McCarthy's understanding of the psychology of terrorism, the perception . . . that terrorism is the product of despair, "the ultimate sin against the Holy Ghost." Once again, McCarthy is asking the difficult question, confronting the difficult problem. For surely, terrorism threatens us all, not only physically and politically, but morally and intellectually as well. It postulates a system of oblique correspondences, a violent disproportion between ends and means, against which we have no recourse. She comes to terms as well with our peculiar but irrefutable tendency to see human beings as replaceable, works of art unique. For the lover of formal beauty who is also a moralist, it is the most vexed of questions. I'm not sure McCarthy has anything new to say on the subject, but she does not imply that she does.

Often, artists have responded to the prospect of atrocity by creating a well-crafted work of art. . . . In response to the truly frightful prospect of anarchic terrorism, Mary McCarthy has written one of the most shapely novels to have come out in recent years: a well-made book. It is delightful to observe her balancing, winnowing, fitting in the pieces of her plot.

The tone of "Cannibals and Missionaries" is a lively pessimism. Its difficult conclusion is that to be a human being at this time is a sad fate: even the revolutionaries have no hope for the future, and virtue is in the hands of the unremarkable, who alone remain unscathed. (pp. 34-5)

Mary Gordon, "A Novel of Terrorism," in The New York Times Book Review *(© 1979 by The New York Times Company; reprinted by permission), September 30, 1979, pp. 1, 33-5.*

PEARL K. BELL

More than thirty years ago, Elizabeth Hardwick and Mary McCarthy began their literary careers with precocious works of fiction (*The Ghostly Lover* and *The Company She Keeps*). Both of them went on to become literary and cultural critics of considerable authority. But in the novels and stories they continued to write (Miss McCarthy has of course been the more prolific novelist), their fierce analytic intelligence often seemed less an asset than a meddlesome intrusion. Their highly developed skills at critical generalization diminished their imaginative freedom; they preferred commentary to the disorder of human experience, and their characters were personifications of the writers' fervent—in Miss McCarthy's case, belligerent—opinions about politics, society, culture, and woman's estate. Their fiction displayed such perfect command of an intellectual "position" that the well-heeled bohemians of Miss McCarthy's *A Charmed Life* and the academic voyeurs of Miss Hardwick's *The Simple Truth* seemed encased in preconception.

Now each of them has again produced a novel, testing her strengths against more complex structures—more complex because the novel form has been declared exhausted, and the political world has lost its simpler faiths—and one has the opportunity to judge whether their large critical gifts have worked for or against their imaginative vitality. . . .

At first reading, [Miss Hardwick's] *Sleepless Nights* appears to be a haphazard assemblage of fragmentary portraits, anecdotes, aphorisms, meditative generalizations, wayward bits and pieces of "transformed and even distorted memory," and it is extremely puzzling. Its elegantly wrought randomness and calculated air of improvisation yield almost no clues to the author's intentions. (p. 65)

In sharp contrast to Elizabeth Hardwick's fascination with subjective experience, Mary McCarthy's *Cannibals and Missionaries,* her first novel in eight years, is a sort of thriller about terrorism and hijacking—albeit a thriller with high intellectual gloss. What the story lacks (at least until the genuinely spectacular denouement) in manipulative tricks of suspense, it makes up for in a wealth of information—some of that wealth no figure of speech.

In her famous essay, "The Fact in Fiction," Miss McCarthy argued that "the distinctive mark of the novel is its concern with the actual world, the world of fact, of the verifiable, of figures, even, and statistics." By this touchstone, *Cannibals and Missionaries* is a novel with a vengeance. (Whether it is also the political novel she seems at times to have had in mind is another matter.) The book is as densely packed with fastidiously researched data—about everything from varieties of helicopter landing-gear to the brush strokes of Vermeer—as a computer print-out. Unlike the tedious accounting of clothes, furniture, luggage, cooking, and contraceptives in *The Group,* which sometimes seemed less a work of fiction than a household inventory, much of the factual plenty in her new novel is pertinent and amusing. But it is dispensed with too zealous a hand, and there is just too much of it. (p. 66)

Miss McCarthy operates the complicated machinery of her plot skillfully, but one wonders what has become of her once bright clear voice and unsleeping indignation, the scourge of hypocrites here, intellectual poseurs there, and fools everywhere. *That* Mary McCarthy is not entirely absent from this talky "thriller," but her witty and aggressive self-confidence is not what it used to be. Her satiric lance has a dull edge, and her thrusts are neither well-aimed nor damaging. Indeed, she seems surprisingly out of touch with the prototypes of her character, who appear out of sync with the present-day realities they are meant to represent. For example, one liberal is allegedly the president of a "good New England women's college," but this chattering goose, with her busy earrings and artful makeup, sounds like a provincial teacher of high school French; she is inconceivable as the president of Wellesley or Smith. . . . The art-loving plutocrats are in the main anachronisms who belong not to the America of 1975 but to *New Yorker* cartoons of the 40's. As for the "New Left" journalist traveling with the liberals, she is beautiful, intelligent, sensitive, and erudite, and during her captivity she fills a journal with arresting comments on art, life, and love (so she will have something to read the next day). This intriguing woman, one would guess, far from resembling any New Left journalist of the moment, is a hindsight and somewhat gilded version of the young Mary McCarthy.

What is especially strange about the novel is the superficial attention Miss McCarthy pays to the political and moral aspects of terrorism—an opportunity she would not have missed in the old days—and the excessive space and energy she devotes to the paintings and the fine points of collecting. She has chosen a political topic but failed to write a political novel, perhaps because she is not completely sure where her sympathies lie. . . . In *Cannibals and Missionaries*—the title comes from an old puzzle: how to ferry three cannibals and three missionaries across a river, in a boat for two, without having cannibals outnumber missionaries at any stage—political ideas are subordinated to pedagogical gamesmanship. The serious intent of the book —and I don't doubt that she started out with one—remains cloudy.

Elizabeth Hardwick's critical sensibility is the source of a venturesome effort to work out a new aesthetic idea, and as a result her novel is hobbled by the abstract severity of that idea. Contrarily, *Cannibals and Missionaries* suffers from its author's failure to decide what she wants the story to mean. Can it be that Mary McCarthy, surely for the first time in her life, has been unable to make up her mind? (p. 67)

Pearl K. Bell, "Elizabeth Hardwick and Mary McCarthy," in Commentary *(reprinted by permission; all rights reserved), Vol. 68, No. 4, October, 1979, pp. 65-7.**

MARY McCARTHY

Most of my books have been in some way political, but I suppose ["Cannibals and Missionaries"] is the first one which deals directly with what you might call headline material: terrorism, hijacking and so forth. . . .

[Once] I started the book it came to me that I had to show at least one of the terrorists from the inside. I realised that it would be refusing the jumps not to describe such an event from a terrorist's point of view as well. It was as if they were speaking out of the dark: 'Hey, teacher, we're here too.'

I don't think this means I've romanticised them—terrorism is terrifying. But we've seen, after all, that in many of these cases the terrorists find it impossible to commit murder or use extreme violence on someone they've gotten to know. . . .

It's true, I suppose that I have a certain sympathy for the main terrorist character in my novel: it would be hard not to respond to his kind of total dedication and self-sacrifice, though not of course to extorting sacrifice from others. But I also show how terrorists paint themselves into a corner because their aims are impossible—that's the whole point.

Actually it wasn't really hijackings which got me started on the book. People aren't the only hostages in the story: there are works of art. . . . [The] whole question of the value people put on works of art is very interesting, especially for someone who cares about art and beauty in every way, as I do.

I think really my criterion is aesthetic or I think the aesthetic and the ethical are the same—to me, a beautiful action is a good action and a good action cannot be ugly. Nevertheless, one can't help questioning one's own way of life and one's principles, the fact that one cares so much about art and about the appearance of things. . . .

[The] main thing that came home to me while I was in daily contact, amid the air-alerts, with the North Vietnamese was religious—their current religion was Marxism-Leninism though with a wayback Buddhist background; and this made me realise how much I was a Christian. It was not even a matter of confronting it, but, let's say, of noticing it. I don't believe in God—that's just a fact, it's not an act of will; I can't even conceive of God, so there it is. But ethics came to me in the frame of Christian teaching, and even though I don't believe in an afterlife I'm still concerned with the salvation of my soul. I'm quite incapable of switching to an atheist's ethics, if there is such a thing. . . .

Aside from Christian doctrine, the thing that has most formed my cast of mind has probably been Shakespeare. Whether the two are connected in some way I'm not sure, but it seems to me that throughout Shakespeare there is a deep rejection of the will. The will naturally allies itself with abstractions, and abstractions in Shakespeare are always wrong. In comedy they simply lead to comic conclusions, beginning with 'Love's Labour's Lost' where the young men make their absurd vow and try to stick to it. And anyone who thinks that he embodies what Ibsen called 'the claim of the ideal' is shown to be wrong in Shakespeare, like Angelo in 'Measure for Measure' or Lear or Coriolanus or Shylock with his insistent idea of a pound of flesh—a bloodless abstraction, evidently.

Shakespeare's view of the will and its capacity for abstractions, as opposed to the things of nature, to the instinctive and the concrete, spoke to me very young and still speaks to me. I believe in humility, in a certain modesty towards what is outside, towards what is not I. Or not me. The assertion of any absolute idea is really a claim on the part of the mind to control the world, to control reality. It's a proclamation of sovereignty, and I don't want that, I don't believe in it; I think one must respect the created world which has its own laws, including unjust laws, and its own harmony. We must listen to messages from that world, and this comes over very strongly in Shakespeare where the rustics are always right, they have the last word. The rustics and the clowns and even the fools. That corresponds to my sense of the way things ought to be. . . .

Every time I write a book I face the problem that people—and that includes book-reviewers—can't read any more. In my last novel, for example, the hero is attacked by a black swan. One reviewer described it as a white swan, another as a goose. And in the very first review I read of my new novel, I found one of the characters described as 'a narrow, venal woman.' This is the poor dumpy collector who tries to lay down her life for her painting. This is terribly discouraging. . . .

I do think that people have lost touch with language, which

is, after all, a kind of silting in of human knowledge and of the human capacity for definition and identification. . . .

I've said to myself that 'Cannibals and Missionaries' is my last novel. Something I've observed is that one loses one's social perceptions, they get blunted and dimmer as one gets older—it's partly a matter of eyesight. You can continue writing poetry and essays and so on, but to be a novelist you have to have this alert social thing.

I've started working on a new book, but it's not a novel. It's what my publisher calls an intellectual autobiography. But again, you're working from memory, which doesn't improve with the years. I've always had a very good memory—though I wish I hadn't lost the letters from a crucial period of my life, in the 1930s: I didn't pay my storage bill, they were in a trunk. But anyway, that's what I'm doing. You know, one only has this much time on earth.

Mary McCarthy, "A World Out of Joint," in an interview with Miriam Gross, in The Observer *(reprinted by permission of The Observer Limited), No. 9816, October 14, 1979, p. 35.*

ROBERT M. ADAMS

['Cannibals and Missionaries'] is an old-fashioned thriller with modern decor and modern overtones. It is a high comedy of mixed motives, inept calculations, and personal weakness; and, by no means incidentally, it is also an informal colloquium on a variety of general topics. No character in the book runs true to form—his own form, or anybody else's estimate of his form; none of the discussions is pushed to a distinct conclusion. Reviewing a macédoine containing so many ingredients and flavorings involves some necessary injustices; if one is to explain the issues, one has to destroy most of the suspense. Because it leaves unresolved so many of its equations, human and intellectual, this novel will get a great many different readings, of which the author clearly intended to render none definitive. . . .

As always, Miss McCarthy writes crisp, unsentimental prose, with a cruel eye for weakness and inauthenticity. Her title comes from a parlor game, which already suggests a measure of ironic detachment. If anything, the acerbity of her manner would seem likely to incline her toward sympathy with cannibals rather than missionaries; in fact, she seems to prefer the milder of the hijackers and the tougher-minded of their victims. But the catalyst of the situation, which by its mere presence changes the chemistry of the whole social mix, is an important work of art. (p. 38)

From the book's early pages, [we dangle] over an abyss of threatened violence, and to have it finally done with in [the cataclysm of the denouement] is a genuine relief: the carnage is larger than that in the fifth act of *Hamlet*. For most of the novel, the terrorists despite their menacing demeanor have been agreeably restrained. On the other hand, the liberals have been so self-important, the rich so spineless, and the terrorists so incompetent, it's hard for the reader to feel that anybody deserves to survive. As it is, the rich suffer no casualties at all, the liberals fairly heavy ones, and the terrorists are wiped out to a man. Does this distribution result from accident, moral judgment, or fictional convention? Once again, the author suggests no answer that I can see.

Most to be regretted is the lost Vermeer. Whether Miss McCarthy meant it this way or not, that is how the reader feels. Most of the people are commonplace, easily replaceable types. . . . Most of them remain paper characters on a paper page: we could see them going to wholesale slaughter, if the plot demanded it, without a twinge of compunction. But a genuine Vermeer! If it were not a museum-quality forgery (even that is left open to question), it would be one of no more than forty Vermeers; it would be a quiet, perfectly fulfilled instant of time, air, and light. By what she says of the painting and of people's reactions to it, Miss McCarthy persuades us that it is precious beyond any of the comedians standing around and gaping at it. (pp. 39-40)

Mary McCarthy has produced a carnival of such petty egotisms and, unlikely as some of it may seem, her clear swift prose and slightly mordant humor carry the reader around it, hoping that the intimations of significance will amount to something more. The reader can take pleasure in her precision of language about people who lack precision in their ideas. What is hardest to believe in the end is that there is much to be learned from this particular set of cannibals and missionaries. (p. 40)

Robert M. Adams, "Unhappy Landings," in The New York Review of Books *(reprinted with permission from* The New York Review of Books; *copyright © 1979 Nyrev, Inc.), Vol. XXVI, No. 16, October 25, 1979, pp. 38-40.*

Somewhere over Europe, a plane is hijacked, apparently because its passengers include the well-known members of a liberal committee traveling to investigate allegations of torture in Iran—ideal hostages, from the terrorists' point of view. . . . [The] thirty-two participants in this all-too-common drama [*Cannibals and Missionaries*] have little option, but to learn to live with one another, a situation that provokes a crucial question: Who are the cannibals, and who the missionaries?

This novelistic scheme presents a number of possibilities, and McCarthy takes advantage of it to raise some interesting points about social beliefs and behavior. She is skillful at exposing the subtle hypocrisies of class, and her arguments regarding the dangerous and unnatural position of art in our technological world are well taken. But as a work of fiction, *Cannibals and Missionaries* suffers from a lack of focus. Despite the exciting plot, the pace is leisurely, full of lengthy pauses during which various ideas are promulgated. Worse, the characters are maddeningly banal; chosen to represent a variety of types, they come to life only when given some concrete action to perform, and just one of them—the leader of the terrorists (a rather frightening choice)—is genuinely sympathetic. (pp. 93-4)

"Life & Letters: 'Cannibals and Missionaries'," in The Atlantic Monthly *(copyright © 1979 by The Atlantic Monthly Company, Boston, Mass.; reprinted with permission), Vol. 244, No. 5, November, 1979, pp. 93-4.*

RICHARD LINGEMAN

Reading Mary McCarthy's new novel, *Cannibals and Missionaries,* makes one worry about an apparent shortage of literary settings for novelists who trade in ideas, wit and observation of manners. Why else has McCarthy concocted a novel about an airliner hijacking? . . .

I can only assume that McCarthy adopted the hijacking device because she was pressed for a suitable fictional venue in which her shrewdly cast group of liberals, wealthy dilettantes and dedicated revolutionaries could perform. With these sharply drawn character types, articulate and representative in the case of the liberals, and devastatingly obtuse in the case of the rich, we might reasonably expect—given McCarthy's intelligence and political sophistication—a compelling symposium on a number of issues of our times, plus clashes of class and politics, respectively, between the liberals and the rich, and the liberals and the revolutionaries. In other words, ideas, talk, love, hate—people in the pressure cooker of captivity, in which essential psychological and social juices are sweated out.

Some of that we do get, especially in the first part of the book before the hijacking, as the ad hoc committee of liberals bound for Iran to investigate torture in the Shah's dungeons are assembled. But then, one-quarter into the book, McCarthy must deal with the logistics of the hijack and tinker with the mechanics of the plot; soon our potentially exhilarating mix has dissolved into a rather tepid soup.

When she is writing about people in social situations, McCarthy is fine, but a hijacked 747 is the wrong matrix. These people are the ingredients of a McCarthy-patented realistic intellectual comedy. It is as though they are in search of a 1979 version of Heartbreak House, or maybe a Wildean drawing room, or a grove of academe—a place where talk can flow, the new order confront the old, social types play off against one another. Nothing so lofty as a Magic Mountain, but maybe the Catoctins. And if the author's game is showing a motley group of people thrown together *in extremis,* then there should be revealing clashes. (p. 470)

[While] McCarthy has evoked the conditions of captivity vividly, one is never terribly worried about the hostages' lives. Only hard-core thriller fiends will mind that, and they shouldn't have picked up a book by Mary McCarthy anyhow. I mention it, though, because it is a small symptom of a larger offhandedness—a glancingness—about this novel. The novel is like an Aspen conference attracting a lot of star academic names that falls flat—or rather drones on inconclusively. . . .

[The] ideas [presented in the novel] are not really engaged; instead they are broken up and scattered about indiscriminately among various characters. (p. 471)

Cannibals and Missionaries describes its own circle and returns to a platitude—or rather the flatness that results when all views sink back into their common element. At the center of a circle is emptiness, and at the center of this novel there is an emptiness—a missing presence, the presence of the passionate heart and mind of the author herself. (p. 472)

Richard Lingeman, "She Gets No Kick in a Plane," in The Nation *(copyright 1979 by the Nation Associates, Inc.), Vol. 229, No. 15, November 10, 1979, pp. 470-72.*

THOMAS R. EDWARDS

In *Memories of a Catholic Girlhood,* perhaps her finest book, Mary McCarthy describes her youthful hopes for a career in an interesting way. Her ambition was literary, she says, but she does not put it as a yearning to become any one of the things she so notably *has* become: a novelist, a travel writer, a critical journalist of drama, literature, and public events; she wanted to be "a professional writer." Most people would call her a novelist, I suppose, but fewer than half of her 17 published books are works of fiction, and her latest, *Cannibals and Missionaries,* encourages the suspicion that she is best considered not as a novelist but as a professional writer who writes a novel from time to time—since the early 1950s, in fact, at steady intervals of eight years.

The earlier fiction had an obviously close relation to her own experience in the 1930s and early 1940s, as a bright young woman come out of Vassar to make her way in the literary-intellectual life of New York, with its fringes in bohemia, academia, and high society. And her provincial, Catholic background gave her useful ironic leverage upon an intellectual life governed by Freud, Marx, and literary modernism. *The Company She Keeps, The Oasis, The Groves of Academe, A Charmed Life,* and (later) *The Group* are skeptical responses to "advanced" attitudes and modes of living that are nonetheless recognized as attractive and necessary alternatives to what otherwise might have been. . . . The earlier fiction, with its cool, malicious portrayal of recognizable individuals and types, suggests a writer determined not to be fooled and utterly possessed by a life that nevertheless represents a welcome escape from narrow, spiritless possibilities.

This fascinating sense of self-division is much less evident in *Birds of America* and, now, *Cannibals and Missionaries.* Her interest has been shifting from personal history to public history, as her writings on Vietnam and Watergate suggest too. But such a change doesn't guarantee stronger novelistic performance, and while *Cannibals and Missionaries* is a considerable book, full of intelligent speculation about serious contemporary issues, it is not a terribly successful work of fiction. . . .

[The story of the novel] is of course the stuff of thrillers, and McCarthy does provide suspense and a climax of slambang violence. And she has worked hard to achieve the accuracy of surface behind which the larger improbabilities of this fictional genre may decently conceal themselves. . . . (p. 30)

McCarthy doesn't make her terrorists and their motives seem very convincing. . . . McCarthy suggests that they're showing off, turning terrorism into a work of art for the admiration of friendly competitors like "Carlos" or the PFLP, but such a notion removes the novel pretty far from real cases. (pp. 30-1)

Nor does McCarthy's picture of how hostages and terrorists get along together seem very credible. . . . And there's something both unreal and strangely condescending about McCarthy's way of depicting the non-European hijackers—Palestinian and Latin American—as, in effect, amiable, childlike, protective *servants* of both their comrades and the captives, as if it all were something like a rather edgy house-party down on the old plantation.

Depending on one's own political and moral outlook, it is possible to think of terrorists as common criminals, as crazed fanatics, or as tragic victims or heroic agents of significant political purposes. In each view they figure as extremely dangerous persons. But McCarthy's terrorists are cream puffs. . . . To the extent that it seeks to represent a frightening reality, *Cannibals and Missionaries* is fairly preposterous.

The book does better in describing personalities, or personality-types, under the pressures of bewilderment, anxiety, and fear. Here some significant categorizing is detectable. (pp. 31-2)

[The] two characters McCarthy likes best are both failed (or failing) Catholics, as well as being lawyers, successful politicians, poets, and men of the world. One, Senator James Carey, comes uncomfortably close to being a portrait of the author's namesake, Eugene, and it's enough to say here that for all Carey's charm, sophistication, and wisdom, his vanity and cynicism permit him to be killed off at the end. His counterpart, the Dutch statesman Henk Van Vliet de Jonge, has all of Carey's virtues and none of his flaws; he's also a better poet, and he gets out of the story with only a serious concussion. Carey and Van Vliet are the right spectators for the drama McCarthy means to present. Unlike the other hostages, they know how the world works, they can keep cool under pressure, they are humanly interested in their nominal enemies, they know as artists that larger issues are at stake in immediate actions. . . . Though Van Vliet's faith is lost and Carey's is in some doubt, both have been prepared to see the secular world in the concerned yet detached way the author sees it too.

This may be rather too convenient for McCarthy's purposes, and rather too hard on all the people in the book who haven't had the advantage of a Catholic upbringing. . . . But though I'm not convinced that the cultivated political man is the finest type our age affords, I must admit that Carey and Van Vliet (and the terrorist Jeroen, their peer on the other side) largely escape the outlines of caricature that enclose most of the novel's characters and achieve a considerable semblance of complex life.

I can't imagine not being interested in anything written by Mary McCarthy, and *Cannibals and Missionaries* has pleasure and instruction to give to anyone who values wit, intelligence, and seriousness of purpose. But as a realistic novel it isn't very convincing, and I wish that she had given us her thoughts on art, violence, and the inadequacy of most secular roles in some more direct, or more oblique and fantastic, form. (p. 32)

Thomas R. Edwards, "Books and the Arts: 'Cannibals and Missionaries'," in The New Republic *(reprinted by permission of* The New Republic; © *1979 The New Republic, Inc.), Vol. 181, No. 20, November 17, 1979, pp. 30-2.*

* * *

McGINLEY, Phyllis 1905-1978

An American poet, author of children's books, essayist, lyricist, screenplay writer, and editor, McGinley is best known for her light verse. Her technical skill combined with wise insights into everyday living save her poetry from sentimentalism. She gained an appreciative readership with *Six Pence in Her Shoe,* autobiographical essays on the satisfactions of being a wife and mother in suburban America. In 1961 she was awarded the Pulitzer Prize for *Times Three: Selected Verse from Three Decades.* (See also *Contemporary Authors,* Vols. 9-12, rev. ed.; obituary, Vols. 75-80.)

BETTE RICHART

Before McGinley, love and art were the proper (and almost only) subjects of à la mode light verse. Mrs. McGinley is famous for adding suburbia to the list, and I can't quite make up my mind how I feel about it. This is the mood I like least:

> For, though aware that life is what
> One ought to view with wrath and gravity,
> I live delighted with my lot
> Sunk in content as in depravity.

Who said one ought to view life with wrath and gravity? No one I know, no book I read. And after all, content *can* be depravity; in our society it often is. Mrs. McGinley occasionally sounds more complacent than content, diametrically opposed states, if one stops to think about it. Fine wit attacks pomposity and cruelty, but not the true, the good, the beautiful. Self-pity is a valid target for wit, but never discontent; discontent is its well-spring. Therefore I protest the coyness of this poem and its conclusion:

> Alas, alack, how well I know
> My kind's a draw-back to the nation!
> But here I am and here I go
> Contented with the status quo
> And quite beyond salvation.

That kind *is* beyond salvation, and the irony doesn't come off.

It was while reading Mrs. McGinley . . . that I began to realize that light verse has a moral obligation not to make a point at the expense of truth. To glorify the commonplace is one thing (poets have done it since time began) but to glorify the merely common is another. When she visits an art exhibit she has . . . reactions more surprising than amusing in a civilized being.

> Ladies whose necks are long and swanny
> Are always signed Modigliani.
> But flowers explosive in a crock?
> Braque.

The rejoinder is obvious enough:

> Flowers explosive in a crock
> I fear are more van Gogh than Braque.

In light verse more than other kinds, one must be chary of saying just anything for the sake of a clever rhyme. Occasionally Mrs. McGinley does this, and almost always in an appeal to the popular viewpoint. Fun at the expense of modern art ought to be as passé as the hula hoop. . . . (p. 278)

Her variety, her usual (but alas, not invariable) explicitness of observation, her humanity, are a tradition in themselves. Certainly it is true that she is, within her tradition, an important poet, and she writes as wisely and sadly of youth and old age as anyone since Cicero, perhaps. In the poem "The Doll House," a mother is planning to repair this outgrown toy, "a good house, artfully built," her relic of busier days with the children. The diction is as pure as possible, and the conclusion reverberates:

> And caught into this web of quietness
> Where there is neither After nor Before,
> She reached her hand to stroke the unwithering grasses
> Beside the small and incorruptible door.

In "Blues for a Melodeon," an aging woman visits the house of her childhood, finding the subtle corrosions of time a shock:

This is the house I knew by heart.
Everything here seemed sound, immortal.
When did this delicate ruin start?
How did the moth come?

Naked by daylight, the paint is airing
Its rags and tatters. There's dust on the mantel.
And who is that gray-haired stranger staring
Out of my mirror?

The shock of the rhyme and rhythm change in the fourth line of each stanza, the line that carries the weight of meaning, heightens to the breaking point the shock of recognition; the title is inept, but nothing else is. These two poems are beyond controversy, and certainly beyond the scope of light verse, even at its brilliant best. It doesn't seem possible that the philosopher who wrote them could ever be merely flippant, and this brings us to the major pitfall of this type of verse.

How long ago [Dorothy Parker] wrote:

And though to good I never come
Inseparable my nose and thumb!

[Mrs. McGinley is often] caught in this quintessential attitude of immaturity. . . . The inseparable nose and thumb are neither courageous nor funny; they are a child's protest, and a bore's. When light verse palls, for me at least this is the usual reason. (pp. 278-79)

The important, the most endearing function of this type of verse is to teach us to wear our rue with a difference. In her series on the saints, Phyllis McGinley does this most felicitously, making an object lesson of faults which would have been unforgivable, had they not been obliterated by love: St. Simeon stubbornly clinging to his pillar, St. Teresa shaking her fist at heaven, St. Bridget giving everything to the poor—other people's belongings, unfortunately, as well as her own. . . .

Amusing though it is, light verse is effectively didactic, and its lessons are tolerance, self-sacrifice, and joy in "littles," as Herrick called our every-day simplicities. (p. 279)

Bette Richart, "The Light Touch," in Commonweal *(copyright © 1960 Commonweal Publishing Co., Inc.; reprinted by permission of Commonweal Publishing Co., Inc.), Vol. LXXXIII, No. 11, December 9, 1960, pp. 277-79.*

The title [*Saint-Watching*] hardly promises a book of such exceptional erudition, wit and common sense. Not since Father Martindale produced his *What are Saints?* some thirty years ago has there appeared so lively and sympathetic an account of the diversity of holiness. . . . [Being] holy means being wholly human, and Miss McGinley provides a richly assorted variety of the young and the old, the learned and the ignorant, the men of action and the hidden hermits; whose only common factor is that they relate all that they are and ever might be to the enduring reality that is God.

Miss McGinley's purpose is to rescue the saints "from their pious niches; to celebrate their eccentricities and persistent mortality". Her gallery is a vast one. . . . There are intellectual saints and peasant saints; beggars and courtiers; mothers of families and cloistered nuns; peculiar, not to say neurotic, saints who may be hard to like but have to be loved for their single fidelity to God. . . .

Saint-Watching is a humane book, and that is what a book about saints ought to be. They are saints precisely because they are human. . . . Their lives, in all their variety of social circumstance and human achievement, are parts of a single spectrum, and Miss McGinley's book is an extended conjugation of the verb "to live" in the scriptural sense. . . .

"Holy Humans," in The Times Literary Supplement *(© Times Newspapers Ltd. (London) 1971; reproduced from* The Times Literary Supplement *by permission), No. 3602, March 12, 1971, p. 305.*

LINDA WELSHIMER WAGNER

[Miss McGinley] is something rather rare in twentieth-century literature, or so the social observers would have us believe. She is a woman who speaks her mind—and not a bad mind at that. She believes firmly in religion, in personal morality, in the beauty of fine, old things and of the finest of old principles. She responds to sympathy, enjoys nature, worrries about her children, grows impatient with trivia—and trivial people. McGinley enjoys good living, but not at the expense of other values or of other personalities. No paragon, no exemplar, no saint, she is a person—full, idiosyncratic, just, understanding, witty, recognizable.

Readers identify with her . . . ; readers laugh with her; they condone and admire her. They say, "Oh, Phyllis McGinley—yes, yes, I *know* her." And in a very real sense they do, for she comes through vividly in much of her writing. . . . The most essential quality of Phyllis McGinley, poet, is not, however, her approachability—not her humor. It is, simply, her poetic skill.

Miss McGinley has published widely and has been honored frequently because she is a good poet. She writes with a technical proficiency equal to that of the best-known poets through history. She knows how to use the full range of poetic devices; and she writes with the freedom, the innovation, possible only after a person has thoroughly mastered the ground rules of an art. . . . I suppose it is this reciprocity of abilities that makes Phyllis McGinley the outstanding literary figure she is: her humanity infuses her technically adept poem; and her respect for workmanship keeps even her most emotional poems from being mawkish. (pp. vii-viii)

McGinley's first books—*On the Contrary* (1934) and *One More Manhattan* (1937)—appeared while the United States was still in the throes of the Great Depression. The effects of that economic catastrophe are evident in some of her poems, but more often McGinley comments obliquely on social inequalities. Her moving "Trinity Place" . . . vividly contrasts starving men and fat pigeons; her sonnet "Love in the Depression" describes the difficulties of love for "the luckless brood, this generation's litter"

. . . who see their love's good metal
Moment by moment darken to their gaze
In the dank air of these corroding days. . . .

Poems more representative of McGinley's attitudes during these years, however, are "The Kingdom and the Glory," "Apostrophe to a Nephew," "The Further Off from England," and "Message from Mars." These poems ridicule the commonplace preoccupations of a nation—and a world—in which thousands were going hungry and as many thousands were being crushed by fascism. People went about their mundane concerns, thinking them "questions so profound." (p. 44)

In her 1960 selected poems, *Times Three,* McGinley has grouped these poems of social commentary under the title "The Threadbare Years." At first glance, we relate the title to the Depression; but, again, this title seems to be ambiguity at its best. Most of the poems in the section deal not with the economics of the world so much as with its morals. . . . Most of the poems in this group include epigraphs or quotations from daily newspapers. Their inclusion substantiates McGinley's irony: the world is like this; these things do occur.

What Miss McGinley does with these fragments of life is also interesting. She does not rant or rave. She very neatly deflates the hypocritical—as in "Wrong Formula." Irony appears to expert advantage in "Millennium." And she works with all her poetic art to emphasize the moral tragedy of war in "Carol with Variations, 1936." (pp. 44-5)

In collecting poems from the 1930's in *Times Three,* McGinley groups many of them under the heading of "Personal Remarks." Here are the poet's idiosyncrasies: her dislike of the "steadfast ration of ham" in Southern restaurants; her love of winter and its necessary laziness, of a hot bath, of a good bed; her criticism of "progressive" education, of mechanical "inconveniences"; her admiration for women. Here, too, is found McGinley's characteristic insistence on balance in living. (p. 48)

A commonplace of literature is that the social critic, the satirist, is a person who cares deeply about the state of affairs which he attacks, perhaps more deeply than his complacent brothers. . . . I think McGinley's love of her world is evident throughout her writing in many of her poems. One of the poems which most freshly expresses her joy in life is her parody "Intimations of Mortality," written "on being told by the dentist that 'this will be over soon'." . . . (pp. 49-50)

Many of the poems in the section titled "On the Town" are jovial by nature of their rhythm and structure, eight-line stanzas of iambic measure. "Midsummer Mediations" reflects on the mushrooming of outdoor cafes ("Give me a dim interior / And Let me munch alone. / For I am sick of sidewalks / Whereon to break my bread"). . . . (p. 52)

The poet's fourth category for her poems of the 1930's is entitled "The House of Oliver Ames." It includes poems written about her husband (she was married to Charles Hayden in 1936) and, more generally, about married life. In this vein of subject matter, McGinley is writing lighter verse than comparable poems from the decades to come. (p. 54)

Technically, the impression of McGinley's poems from the 1930's is that she relies on conventional forms (with occasional parodies of lines within an appropriate form . . .) or that she makes great use of one- or two-stanza forms which work well for her—the eight-line iambic stanza, or the alternately rhyming quatrain. In addition, McGinley begins experimenting with her own innovations within standard forms—with the long-short alternating line, which she uses on occasion throughout her writing career. Another is the three-line interval in a rhyme pattern, used to break the regular *a a* or *abab* rhyme scheme. A third is her willingness to vary a refrain and to substitute the rhythms of prose for those of poetry in a refrain.

Variation within refrain lines gives power to one of McGinley's strongest early poems. "Trinity Place" is composed of three quatrains, each one of which ends with a comparison of the busy, fat pigeons and the hungry, idle men of Depression years. . . . (p. 55)

There are many good early McGinley poems. Others from the 1930's are good light verse, without achieving what has come to be her usual excellence. Too frequently, McGinley's earlier poems are written in iambic tetrameter, as is "Dissertation on Furniture," with a heavy dependence on catalogues to provide content. Sometimes, of course, the latter can be extremely apt and/or funny, but any device becomes boring when used too often.

Some of McGinley's early poems contain the kind of "slant" rhyme considered legitimate for use in light verse, *Edison* and *medison, raw gust* and *August, luncheon* and *munch on, sandwiches* and *bandwiches.* Usually these rhymes only detract from the total poem, even though they spring from a long, light-verse tradition. . . . There are also in other of her poems the puns on familiar phrases or lines from well-known poems, "When the dew is on the milkman and the bacon's on the grill" or "I wandered happy as a cloud / Afloat with fellow-cumuli" or "What's so rare as a day in June / Without a gift to shop for?" (pp. 56-7)

Of all the technical practices of the 1930's, only McGinley's titles seem less than effective: "Lament of the Normal Child," "Ode to the Bath," "Song for an Engraved Invitation," "Dirge over a Pot of Pâté de Foie Grass," "Reflections Outside a Gymnasium." "Ballad of the Lord and Columbus." (p. 57)

[All in all,] McGinley's early writing illustrates her consistent verbal skill and her interest in the world about her—its admirable qualities as well as its foibles. For the most part, these are good poems; a great many of them show that McGinley is already beginning to move toward the "incredible brightness" of her later work. (pp. 57-8)

[In] the midst of an incredible amount of bad war poetry—gross, maudlin, overly sentimental, prejudicial—McGinley managed, on the whole, to write good poems. She wrote in a variety of attitudes; she wrote about a wide span of war-related subjects; she wrote "serious" poems and funny poems—and satiric poems. . . .

McGinley's versatile handling of the pervasive theme of war is proof that she can do whatever she wants, technically, in her poetry. . . . In "V-Day," McGinley captures the quiet hope of a country still powerful after a debilitating war, the hope of the people—"the women kneeling in churches, the people's laughter." Promises are not yet broken; ideals are still "coin-bright." To express the relative tranquility of this time, she uses a longer line than in many of her poems—a varied iambic pentameter. Characteristic of the pentameter line, many segments fall into two phrases as if they contained a formal caesura. The mood is stately. (pp. 59-60)

Another of McGinley's war poems, "Landscape without Figures," is frequently quoted. This poem presents the normal villages ("The shape of the summer has not changed at all") saddened, emptied of the vital young men who "boasted, and swam, and lounged at the drugstore's portal," never thinking "but that they were immortal." The images are reasonably successful, but the poem suffers from a too-long catalogue of the boys' activities. The same complaint might be made about the well-known "Soldier Asleep." (p. 61)

Variety in pace gives life to McGinley's group of war poems. She is not afraid to depict real fear; she attempts to re-create the homefront loneliness; but she is not above finding what fun must exist in nearly all human situations. (pp. 61-2)

Quatrains, couplets, sextains, sonnets—the stanzaic forms are varied as McGinley approaches the subject of war from a number of viewpoints. Despite—or perhaps because of—this assortment of techniques, the body of McGinley's war poetry reflects a dispassioned participant, *participant* because the poet is involved enough to see many facets of the conflict, both military and human. But she is *dispassioned* because she somehow avoids the emotional imbroglio evident in so much poetry from the 1940's.

Only about one quarter of McGinley's poems written during this decade deal with war, for more of her writing treats what she described in "V-Day" as "an island in time, secure and candid." McGinley's "island" . . . was the much maligned suburbia; and her "island in time" was her several years as a homemaker with a husband and two small daughters. McGinley's poems from the 1940's are about parades, Halloween, a village in spring, household budgets, Christmas, income tax, her children leaving for school. There is no shadow of war; she describes her village as if it were isolated; she compares it with Arcadia and Camelot. Most of her poems reflect the serenity of the complacent homemaker, but that attitude is coupled with the perspicacity of a sage social observer. (p. 64)

McGinley writes many poems of social criticism during the 1940's—a "brief history of modern man" condensed into the symbol of "Tiptoe, the weathercock"; a tirade against the City of Brotherly Love for refusing to erect a statue of Tom Paine; a critique of modern journalism; critical glances at elections, taxes, and unions. Though probably serious in intent, most of these poems are written in the lilting iambic tetrameter that the poet handles so well; and their rhythm and form makes their denotative impact less harsh.

Compared with McGinley's earliest poems, her work from this period does show innovation. Thematically, she has branched into areas like literary criticism and the Christmas season with its related warmth and foolishness. She has a few very short—almost aphoristic—poems about concepts instead of situations. These mark a departure in that most of them are written in the short-line quatrain form common to light verse—a form McGinley has seldom used—yet they make no pretense at being "light." (pp. 65-6)

Innovation is not, of course, the whole story in any poet's maturity. McGinley's body of poems from the 1940's show, too, that her familiar stanza forms still work very successfully. "To a Lady in a Phone Booth," one of her best funny poems, is written in the now-polished iambic tetrameter sextain. (p. 67)

In her work during the 1940's, McGinley shows her greatest insight—and the first signs of a real tenderness—in her writing about and for children. Her poem "Here Come the Clowns—Didn't They?" is as funny as "The Velvet Hand" is rueful. McGinley is to write stronger poems about her children as they reach adolescence, but this earlier parent-child relationship comes through vividly in poems like "One Crowded Hour of Glorious Strife." (p. 68)

One of McGinley's strengths—as poet and as person—is [an] ability to recognize her feelings, and to accept them as natural. . . .

[The] important thing about McGinley's view of children is that in it they are people; they do have "consciousness" and "passions." (p. 69)

Miss McGinley's poems from the 1950's show several kinds of technical development. There is a steady improvement in the poet's handling of the traditional forms, and, more noticeably, perhaps, there is increasing use of "free" forms. The greatest single change in prosody is, however, McGinley's move from accentual to syllabic verse. (p. 75)

Perhaps "In Praise of Diversity," one of McGinley's best-known poems, can be considered as both serious and light poetry. . . . [Written] during the McCarthy era of Senate investigations, the poem stressed the need for differences, for diversity, without making any reference to politics per se. (p. 78)

"Ballade of Lost Objects" shows McGinley's tireless poetic skills. . . . [The] ballade relates thematically to many of McGinley's best poems of the 1950's. "If I have done anything original," McGinley writes in 1965, "it is in my portrayals of childhood and adolescence, not subjects generally attempted—or bothered with." The progression of thought pleases McGinley in this poem since most ballades are only catalogues. And, as she restated the theme of "Ballade" . . . , "The human pathos of having one's children grown up and past their homes is as full of truth as, say, a tragic love affair—and much more frequent." McGinley's best poems of this decade show again and again those moments of truth in the life of any woman and/or person. Her best poetry has moved from timely concerns to timeless ones.

One of the most interesting of poems about an adolescent is the lightly phrased "Homework for Annabelle." (pp. 80-1)

In this poem as in much of her writing about "childhood and adolescence," McGinley is skirting dangerous ground. Because she is a woman and a mother, she is open immediately to the charge of "sentimentality." She herself has answered this objection by quoting G. K. Chesterton, "the meanest fear is the fear of sentimentality"; for writing must contain "genuine emotion" if it is to be effectual. At least partly, McGinley's technical prowess here (such a touch as the alternating rhyme pattern in the quatrains of each stanza) keeps this poem—and many others—from any such criticism of sentimentality.

McGinley's choices of subject matter in these poems—and the attitudes she expresses toward them—are well summarized in her short poem, "Apologia." . . . "All that I own / I celebrate"—family, home, village. McGinley "owns" the things she loves by assuming a responsibility for them, by caring for them. And the quick tenderness which her writing of the 1950's evinces has become as much a part of the present McGinley attitude as her perceptive view and her wry humor. (pp. 81-2)

With the publication in 1959 of her selected essays, *The Province of the Heart,* Miss McGinley discovered anew what it was to be a "public voice." . . . As she shamefacedly wrote in the introduction to the book, McGinley had "committed" a book of prose; readers of these essays were not surprised, however. McGinley's prose style had much in common with her poetry—exact yet apparently colloquial; personal, in that the poet was often the speaker of the essay; honest, in that her opinions echoed and reinforced those already expressed in her poems.

The Province of the Heart restates McGinley's premises in her defense of suburbia. But the collection does much more than defend the cosy neighborhood where women might thrive on their homey pastimes; it emphasizes again and again the right of women to do just that—thrive. (p. 87)

The 1960 *Times Three* was McGinley's last book of poetry until 1967 when *A Wreath of Christmas Legends* was published. Although some critics viewed the book of fifteen poems as a seasonal contribution, McGinley readers were enthusiastic about the legends as poetry. In direct line of descent from her series of poems on saints ("Reformers, Saints, and Preachers") and her many poems about Christmas, this collection gave McGinley another chance to write about her often recurring theme: love. Using Jesus's birth as the ostensible center, McGinley focuses on the emotion of love—or the lack of it—in most of these poems.

A Wreath of Christmas Legends made clear, too, that an expert craftsman had succeeded in writing single poems in which rhythm, form, and language expressed perfectly each story being told. The subject matter might sound limiting; but as McGinley handles each legend, we are conscious only of her great ease and her great technical freedom that are displayed in a wide variety of forms. (p. 96)

The poems of *A Wreath of Christmas Legends* are very much in the mainstream of McGinley poetry. These legends seem to be a continuation of the poet's search for meaningful concerns in literature, a search for ways to do more than belittle—rather, to build—for her readers. The typical understatement in each poem and in the series as a whole serves McGinley well: this art is based not on dogma or doctrine but on the always very human reaction to a more-than-human experience. The concern of each of these poems, shaped and figured with such evident care and warmth, is love. (p. 106)

Sixpence in Her Shoe, published in 1964, was McGinley's "reward" to the modern housewife. According to an English legend, a good housewife would sometimes find a sixpence in her shoe—her tribute for doing her work well. (pp. 106-07)

McGinley's theme in *Sixpence,* as in her earlier collection, is the "traditional concern" of woman—"Wifehood, the house, a family . . . each in its way represents one of the other great three—faith, hope, charity—which St. Paul sets down as the virtues of earth. (For how can one rear a family without faith? Or build a roof without hope? Or remain a proper wife without charity?) They are life's vital elements and no ordered world can endure without them." (p. 107)

In 1969, McGinley published a very interesting book, *Saint-Watching.* A "saint watcher, amateur standing," she writes in her customary casual but informative style of the real happenings, the real involvements of the revered Christian figures. In the earlier short poems, "Reformers, Saints, and Preachers," McGinley had focused on the humor, the telling single detail, which made each character memorable. In this book, humor has become compassion, the fullness of the lives treated bringing the weighty meaning of *saint* to the reader. It is as if McGinley has grown from thinking of these people as good subjects for poems to a view of them as real and admirable friends in themselves. . . . (pp. 107-08)

There is much about McGinley's poetry that is more "serious" than many poems being written today. There is a respect for the traditions of the poetic art form not unlike the reverence many a sane man holds for his religion. There is an altruistic impulse too often belittled by the younger artisans of modern poetry. And there are many moments when McGinley writes excellent poetry, especially in the 1950's. (p. 112)

Linda Welshimer Wagner, in her Phyllis McGinley *(copyright © 1971 by Twayne Publishers, Inc.; reprinted with the permission of Twayne Publishers, A Division of G. K. Hall & Co., Boston), Twayne, 1971, 128 p.*

JOHN B. BRESLIN

Whether her subject is religious or secular, Miss McGinley wields her wry wit and her deft prosody in the cause of mirth and sanity. W. H. Auden says it all in his Foreword [to *Times Three*]: "Phyllis McGinley needs no puff. Her poems are known and loved by tens of thousands."

John B. Breslin, "Book Reviews: 'Times Three'," in America *(© America Press, 1975; all rights reserved), Vol. 133, No. 11, October 18, 1975, p. 240.*

* * *

MILES, Josephine 1911-

Miles is an American poet, critic, dramatist, and editor. A respected scholar as well as an accomplished poet, she produces poetry noted for its quiet understatement and simplicity of style. The reserved quality of her verse has often prompted Miles's detractors to criticise what they perceive to be a narrowness of poetic vision. (See also *CLC,* Vols. 1, 2, and *Contemporary Authors,* Vols. 1-4, rev. ed.)

STEPHEN MOONEY

One of Josephine Miles's earlier poems is called "On Inhabiting an Orange." This poem, as much as any other in Miss Miles's early work, establishes a way of looking at the world that has made the total work possible up to the present. The world. Reality is too big to see all at once. But successive views of Reality are possible through the perusal and contemplation of segments or aspects or steps, and the poem can find a form within philosophic Reality without letting go of the tangible world at all. (p. 21)

[Miles's poems are] crisp and kind, modest but sometimes gnomic, and always content to know reality on a human scale. There is nothing superhuman in the poems. They are the words of a survivor. The superhuman goes down; the human seems to continue.

Josephine Miles's particular segment of the globe is America and, more particularly, parts of California, chiefly the cities. Proper names are abundant. . . .

Josephine Miles travels in and out of stores, harbors, streets, skies. The people in her poems (perhaps it is one person) buy shoes, look at beauty parlor signs, turn their attention to the sky, consider the smoke abatement problem, and discover housing projects. What kind of consciousness comes of turning the external globe around and watching it with so much human attention? Nothing didactic, nor programmatically social. Rather, we find the sense of a world grown inward, accepted for itself with at least "the idea of joy" and perhaps real joy, a sense of praising the American world in spite of its cheap or distressing or alarming moments. (p. 22)

There are kinds of affection, Miss Miles keeps telling us, not only for people but for places, for the world the way it is, since that is *what we have*. . . . Is it so bad to be human, and to pursue illusions? . . . We must love one another or die. So she does not carry on about the Waste Land. America is the space we can see about us. Affection is hope. The Platonic heaven is not forbidden, but we stay on earth. (p. 23)

Segments, stances, views, aspects, and kinds are parts and not the whole, hints and guesses and not the reality; but by such perception and intuition as are human, Josephine Miles evokes a reality that is of this place, of this time. (p. 24)

Stephen Mooney, "Josephine Miles: Successive Views," in VOYAGES *(copyright, 1968, by VOYAGES, Inc.), Vol. II, No. 3, Fall, 1968, pp. 21-4.*

ARTHUR K. OBERG

Kinds of Affection comes to us as a confirmation and an extension of Josephine Miles's best work. In this . . . book we again confront a poetry that is confident and skilled enough to consider no field of knowledge hostile to poetry and no poetic type sacredly or safely defined. The poems are at ease in a world that increasingly has had to acknowledge the sciences and social sciences as bedfellows of the humanities. As the poems hover between parable and conceit, and lyric and dialogue, they indicate how easy they can be with the shifting faces which the world may put on.

The poems in this . . . volume reveal the same scrutinizing delineation of Miss Miles's earlier verse. Such delineation, frequently taking the form of linguistic or metaphysical play(fulness), moves toward a poetry of vision in which seeing is made to accommodate things strange and even unpleasant. And the measure of that accommodation is the peculiar way in which the poet comes to her world. . . .

Josephine Miles has always proceeded, or given the impression of proceeding, obliquely in her world. But when the poems in *Kinds of Affection* utilize an attraction of mind to abstract exercise and conundrum, they do so in connection with the release of a fund of feeling conspicuously absent or too implicit in some of her earlier poems. To a manner of proceeding has been joined a sense of increasing substance and cost. The poems in *Kinds of Affection* are less willing to allow language and thought to deflect terror and joy. Previous poems of hers like "The Halt," "Reason," "Kind," and "Brooklyn, Iowa, and West" looked ahead to this book.

The poems in *Kinds of Affection* are so many more attempts at writing "this eventual song." However close the poems may move toward conversational speech, the best pieces move also toward song. In poems like "Down from another planet they have settled to mend," "Truth is never," and "Have I outgrown you?", there is a syntax of feeling that is unafraid to encounter vision and its potentially disintegrating power. . . .

[There] is the impression that nothing has changed neither the poet nor we have outgrown poems that deal responsibly and significantly with what cannot be taught and with what only love can do. But there is also the impression that something is different, that we are witnessing something like the writing of a new kind of poem. . . . (p. 27)

There is a new edge of restlessness and rest here. This at times had been intimated in her earlier work. But Miss Miles has also moved on to what would have once been unavailable to her. (p. 28)

Arthur K. Oberg, "A Review of Josephine Miles's Latest Book," in VOYAGES *(copyright, 1968, by VOYAGES, Inc.), Vol. II, No. 3, Fall, 1968, pp. 27-8.*

VERNON YOUNG

[Josephine Miles's] "To All Appearances" (keep your eye on the title as you read her) is a noteworthy publication, especially for critics who may have taken Miss Miles too readily at her own word in the past: the empiricist prepared to eliminate from her verse all the felicities save those of the denotative voice. She had her tongue in her cheek. Among the new poems in this collection are some scarlet with indignation, if you read them properly. Miss Miles is excruciatingly personal, never solipsistic; she is engagé but not yours for the keeping; her accent is mid-west; she sees ghost goal-keepers. (p. 592)

Vernon Young, "The Body of Man," in The Hudson Review *(copyright © 1975 by The Hudson Review, Inc.; reprinted by permission), Vol. XXVIII, No. 4, Winter, 1975-76, pp. 585-98.**

HELEN VENDLER

Josephine Miles's new and selected poems ["To All Appearances"] show a quirky commenting mind still finding things of interest in the American scene, reliving in verse the Berkeley riots. . . . There is a need for more poems of this sort, poems, so to speak, of the day's news, now largely a preserve of interested propagandists. But Miles can also be metaphysical, as in her fine poem on teaching, "Paths," about "going out into the fields of learning":

Ant labors, hopper leaps away;
too early for the bee,
The spider's silk hypotheses
unfold
Tenacious, tenable.

"The spider's silk hypotheses" is worthy of Emily Dickinson, whose voice, in its dryer tone, has entered Miles's voice as well; but Miles is more humane than Dickinson in her parables, of which my favorite is about the drowning man (in a poem called "Family") who hollers "help," caught in the undertow, while his unconscious family reply blandly:

Hello, they will say,
Come back here for some
potato salad.

For all its comedy and factuality (two qualities present in all Miles's verse) the poem has the ring of moral truth. . . . Miles has strict expectations of the world, a comic sense of her own unrealistic hopes, a stern judgment of her own failings, and an observant birdlike interest in classes of people unlike herself. She lacks the sweeter side of verse (or when it comes, it has an uncertainty about it) but her enterprise and sense of art are sure. . . . [Miles's poems] are almost too well-wrought, without yet having the inevitability of the best-wrought, but they never lack intelligence or feeling. (pp. 32-3)

Helen Vendler, "A Quarter of Poetry," in The New York Times Book Review *(© 1975 by The New York Times Company; reprinted by permission), April 6, 1975, pp. 4-5, 29-38.**

DAVID SHAPIRO

Parables, according to [theologian C. H.] Dodd, are "illustrations . . . designed to provoke thought rather than to close the question." Many of Josephine Miles's *New and Selected Poems* would fit Dodd's description very well. The didactic freshness of her poems makes them a complex pleasure, because, for her, pleasure itself is complex. . . . Her work may begin with an appearance as diminished or domestic as the doily, upholstery or curtains, but it ends as much more than a remark or perception, but rather as a little sermon without a pulpit. Her demotic phrases may be daunting, but her poetry is concerned with the value of fact and the fact of value. It is a rich collection and capable of a Dantesque fierceness. (pp. 230-31)

Josephine Miles's poetry is generous and full. Abundant and not merely copious, it reminds us that the domestic scene is as rich as any wilderness. . . . Laurence Lieberman has remarked on the poet's desire for and belief in a "community of the heart" and in Josephine Miles's best work the slowly revealed parable is a model for such cohesiveness, and slowly unveiled intimacies. Her poetry speaks of the ambiguities of unity, in which it is possible to question, sadly and fully: "Am I going away to your nearest distance?"

In Josephine Miles, the satisfactory and the unsatisfactory, as topics, the traditional resource and our agonies of resourcelessness, mingle and make a moderate poetry. Our favorite notion is that of a poetry open and flexible and never merely free, a poetry of wholeness conjuring up that recalcitrant old concept of *sophrosyne*. This maximalism in an age of competing minimalisms might be our curiously unprogrammatic programme. The only thing eclecticism cannot contain adequately is the advantage of dogmatics, but we will accept this deficiency. (pp. 231-32)

David Shapiro, "Into the Gloom," in Poetry *(© 1976 by The Modern Poetry Association; reprinted by permission of the Editor of* Poetry*), Vol. CXXVIII, No. 4, July, 1976, pp. 226, 230-32.**

JAMES K. ROBINSON

[Josephine Miles] is focused on American promises, but hers is the carved ivory rather than the bow-wow strain. In "Ride," for example, she describes her relation to the land realized from the dreams of Adams and Jefferson:

> It's not my world, I grant, but I made it.
> It's not my ranch, lean oak, buzzard crow,
> Not my fryers, mixmaster, well-garden.
> And now it's down the road and I made it.
>
> It's not your rackety car but you drive it.
> It's not your four-door, top-speed, white-wall tires,
> Not our state, not even, I guess, our nation,
> But now it's down the road, and we're in it.

As Randall Jarrell acutely remarked thirty years ago, Miles is a specialist in the sly, dry, minimal observation [see *CLC*, Vol. 1]. Yet sometimes, especially in the "Poems New" which open *To All Appearances*, the observations make an impact which is *not* minimal. In "The American Flag," a star-spangled morning takes its stripes, not red and white but "dry mustard to the tinge of dun," from a "Cad steering westward" and a "diesel, gray caul bobbing / VW after VW." (pp. 350-51)

James K. Robinson, "Sassenachs, Palefaces, and a Redskin: Graves, Auden, MacLeish, Hollander, Wagoner, and Others," in The Southern Review *(copyright, 1978, by James K. Robinson), Vol. 14, No. 2, April, 1978, pp. 348-58.**

* * *

MILLAR, Kenneth
See MACDONALD, Ross

* * *

MILLER, Henry 1891-

Miller is a self-educated American novelist, essayist, and critic who has long been involved with searching for truth and freedom. Many of his best-known and most controversial works, such as *Tropic of Cancer* and *The Rosy Crucifixion* trilogy, are autobiographical; in them he describes his quest, which culminates in a rejection of modern civilization, but with an eventual realization about personal truth. Karl Shapiro says of him, "As a spiritual example he stands among the great men of our age." However, due perhaps to the frank sexuality and scatological language in his writings, and to his somewhat dissatisfied attitude about America, his reputation has only lately been changing from notorious to influential and well respected. (See also *CLC*, Vols. 1, 2, 4, 9, and *Contemporary Authors*, Vols. 9-12, rev. ed.)

PAUL R. JACKSON

In Henry Miller's *Tropic of Cancer* an Emersonian epigraph announces the romanticized autobiography that would become the staple of Miller's art. "These novels," Emerson asserts, "will give way, by and by, to diaries or autobiographies—captivating books, if only a man knew how to choose among what he calls his experiences that which is really his experiences, and how to record truth truly." Along with Whitman—"In Whitman the whole American scene comes to life, her past and her future, her birth and her death"—Emerson stands as a clear, if surprising, link to those traditions of American writing that produced the prophetic autobiographer that Miller became. . . .

While Whitman has remained a perennial constant in Miller's literary enthusiasms, Emerson recurs only as a supportive figure in the Americanism that marks the volumes of a writing career that spans at least three decades and that binds the literary expatriate to the artistic roots of his own country. Yet Miller returns to Emerson often enough to suggest an attachment more significant than one would at first suppose. (p. 231)

Miller's indebtedness to general Romantic and Transcendental modes of thought emerges in his prophetic announcements, often with the cadences of a speaking voice reminiscent of that of Emerson himself. . . . Emerson's emphasis on intuitive understanding with its resultant reliance on childhood experience, dream, and vision is constantly echoed. . . . [The] ecstatic emerging of the emancipated individual with divine process is dependent, with the insistence of a contemporary Emerson, on self-reliance: "The world would only begin to get something of value from me the moment I stopped being a serious member of society and became—*myself!* The State, the nation, the united nations of the world, were nothing but one great aggregation of individuals who repeated the mistakes of their forefathers." . . . (pp. 232-33)

Throughout his career, Miller has been drawn to autobiographical writers of all sorts, and letters, diaries and confessions rank high in those books to which he has enthusiastically responded. . . . [But it was in] Emerson's *Journals* and essays [that] Miller found that the divided self of the visionary seer in his long journey of emancipation into life was his subject.

The completeness with which Miller has been willing to confront Emerson's simultaneous levels of selfhood is nowhere better underscored than in one direct borrowing from Emerson's *Journals* in *Sexus*. This long autobiographical romance records the trying years of the 1920's; it begins with the turmoil of Miller's first marriage to the Maude of the romances and his initial meeting with Mona, the fictionalized second wife, chronicles his escape from employment with the telegraph company, his early attempts to begin writing, and ends on the night of his second marriage. At the close a life stretches before him that is to be marked by the ambiguities of the trilogy's title. Through the process of personal crucifixion paradoxically will come the new life.

Sexus ends with two parallel fantasies, the first taking place in a burlesque theater on the night of Miller's marriage to Mona. Watching the show unfold and allowing his mind to play with elements of his own predicament, Miller begins to fantasize about the death of a young soapbox orator he names Osmanli. (pp. 234-35)

It seems likely that Osmanli is Miller's version of Emerson's Osman, the alter ego who appears throughout the *Journals* and in the essay on "Manners." The change in his name presumably suggests a "manly" version of the ideal man Emerson secretly defined over so many years, a more masculine projection than that of the author Miller found at once "daring" and the writer of "pabulum." A comparison of Osman and Osmanli makes clear the hopes Miller entertained for himself as a young man and substantiates the technique that is basic to his art—the simultaneous projection of himself as heroic paradigm and the honest admission of the personal failures that marked much of his early adulthood. (p. 237)

Certain elements of this portrait would surely appeal to Miller. In a book detailing its author's late arrival on the literary scene—Miller was in his early thirties during the period dramatized here—Osman's neglected youth and the obscurity of his early adulthood closely parallel Miller's account of his own early years. . . . Like Osman, he has been interested in the "rude self" and in "highway experience." In short, there is much in Emerson's portrait of Osman that corresponds to Miller's estimate of himself, at least with the "better side" he confessed to Anaïs Nin Emerson invoked. If he was a dog, he was also, in aspiration at least, many of the things Emerson hoped for himself.

There are, however, at least two essential differences between Osman and Osmanli, and Miller's fantasy creature is not the simple alter ego that his Emersonian counterpart had been. While Emerson's Osman is a "poor and simple man," without any touch of the violent, Osmanli is a desperado of action—in fantasy he cuts off the dog's head, rapes the maid, and spends a life promoting anarchy. Moreover, he is disguised as a dandy, "a boulevardier, a flaneur, a Beau Brummel." Both changes suggest the real pressures to which Miller felt himself subject in the twenties and the intensity with which he had to respond. The autobiographical hero of Miller's romances is generally conceived as a comic but nonetheless serious man of forceful, especially sexual, action. While other men vacillate in their responses toward women, Miller can depict himself as assertive and bold. (pp. 238-39)

Yet such heroics are undercut by the dramatization of himself as henpecked husband and canine lover. Hesitant and reluctant, Miller emancipated himself slowly and with the utmost difficulty. . . . Osmanli, the forceful emancipator, is in fact a perfect projection of the ideal actor Miller, at the time, felt himself incapable of being. Himself a dog bound to an ambiguous mate in Mona, he could neither decapitate a dog nor rape a maid. (p. 239)

But Osmanli is not a simple character of wish fulfillment, any more than he is a one-dimensional alter ego. He dramatizes a strength that, no matter how attractive, Miller felt was fictitious in himself, and he is presented as a hollow man, a straw hero who has to come to terms with his own hidden self. Beneath his ostentatiousness, Osmanli is essentially the kind of empty, trapped human being Miller evidently felt himself to be in the twenties. Bound and visionless, Osmanli is merely the mockery of heroic strength. Like the watch and money that he discards as he runs down the street, his outer self is mere sham, and behind the glibness of the words he finds it so easy to manipulate is a personal vacuum that turns words into empty gesture. Until emancipation is complete, freedom remains a fiction, strength an illusion. For Miller the hollowness of his life as he looked forward to it is symbolized by a dying man learning at the last moment that dogs were still there to bark in spite of his own futile acts.

By borrowing Emerson's own creation, Miller followed the direction the earlier American had indicated. If novels were to give way to autobiography, the personal statement would have to express the complexity of what it is to be human at any given time. For Miller in the twenties, his humanity involved the combination of competing hopes of forceful action and acknowledged fears that actions without selfhood would result at best in comic emptiness. Emerson's Osman eventually flowers into a wise and famous man; Miller's Osmanli dies the product of a freak accident, a parallel to the domestic dog who can only win blue ribbons for a demanding mistress. For Miller, the autobiographical novel has been indeed the vehicle with which he has presented "the truth of emotions, reflection and understanding, truth digested and assimilated." Emerson's secret Osman suggested the possibilities for dramatizing the simultaneous levels of being Miller felt in his own divided self. (pp. 240-41)

Paul R. Jackson, "Henry Miller, Emerson, and the Divided Self," in American Literature *(reprinted by permission of the Publisher; copyright 1971 by Duke University Press, Durham, North Carolina), Vol. 43, No. 2, May, 1971, pp. 231-41.**

GEORGE STADE

"Wear any uniform so long as it's not yours," advises

Henry Miller, and the various uniforms of bum, stud, psychopomp, jeremiah, and saint he wears in his books never quite fit the forms and motions we see behind the garb and the gab. The protagonist of his books, name of Henry Miller, describes himself as being such-and-such, and this so-and-so varies from book to book, from passage to passage. But we do not see him as he sees himself. The figure we make out from passage to passage exposes only new lineaments of its eternal consistency. The "I" of his books does not know itself, and what it doesn't know remains pretty much the same. The shiftings of Proteus configure a Prometheus bound to his obsession but sure he is free.

So far, then, we have two Henry Millers, one a wardrobe of costumes, the other their inhabitant. A third Henry Miller is the designer of the costumes, the author holding onto the shirt-tails of his protagonist. . . . Sometimes the author and the protagonist seem pretty close. "I have moved the typewriter into the next room where I can see myself in the mirror as I write," says the protagonist of *Tropic of Cancer*. From all the squirms and craning, we gather that the image lacks definition, Dracula eluding his own gaze into the pier-glass. Similarly, the author never sees through his reflections and so has to keep rewriting his single book under numerous titles, always one step behind a protagonist who keeps running in place, but in the very best form. (p. 616)

To this day Henry Miller the author is naive in relation to his protagonist. We can get a more-or-less direct look at the author through his letters, his literary criticism, his social commentary, his philosophizing. He has less grace, poise, aplomb than his protagonist, but he is more solicitous of our admiration; he is not as wise, but more opinionated; not as pure, but also less complicated; less original, but more cranky; not as desperate, but more self-pitying; less terrible, more of a trial; not an unliberated liberator, but a chide.

It is the protagonist we are interested in, rather than the author—the "I," the character written into the books, not the writer, not the costumes the other two write about. Let us call him Henry. Here, in a passage from *Tropic of Capricorn* . . . , is Henry's moment of conception:

> . . . in my dream life I frequently changed places with my sister, accepting the tortures inflicted upon her and nourishing them with my supersensitive brain. It was in these dreams, always accompanied by the sound of glass breaking, of shrieks, curses, groans and sobs, that I gathered an unformulated knowledge of the ancient mysteries, of the rites of initiation, of the transmigration of souls and so on. . . . I seemed to have absolute liberty and the authority of a god, and yet by some capricious turn of events the end would be that I'd be lying on the sacrificial block and one of my charming uterine relatives would be bending over me with a gleaming knife to cut out my heart. . . . I go completely off my nut and there is no more pain, no more terror, even though they are piercing me everywhere with knives. Suddenly I am absolutely calm and the body which is lying on the block, which they are still gouging with glee and ecstasy, feels nothing because I, the owner of it, have escaped. I have become a tower of stone which leans over the scene and watches with scientific interest. I have only to succumb to the law of gravity and I will fall on them and obliterate them. But I will not succumb to the law of gravity because I am too fascinated by the horror of it all. I am so fascinated, in fact, that I grow more and more windows. And as the light penetrates the stone interior of my being I can feel that my roots, which are in the earth, are alive and that I shall one day be able to remove myself at will from this trance in which I am fixed.

That day is still to come. He never removes himself from his fix. He continually rehearses its stations, which never occurred, except in a dream, as mankind rehearses Freud's myth of the Primal Horde, which also never occurred. In a dream of a scene from real life he soaks up punishment he deserves only by virtue of his uterine connections with other people. . . . (pp. 617-18)

The god tries to love the victim, for Henry is a narcissist (not a man who loves himself, rather one who works at it)—"My whole aim in life is to get nearer to God, that is, to get nearer to myself"—but neither the love of God nor of the Cosmological I is a substitute for the love of a mother. (pp. 618-19)

Henry's God . . . is the Imperial Self (the phrase is Quentin Anderson's) of Emerson and Whitman brought up to date. The relation is one of identity, which is the negation of relation. Between two things that are identical there are no dialectics. Therefore although Henry's prose is serial, it does not progress. It encounters nothing that might bounce it off the path of its return. . . . Henry's style never trips on itself; his balance is perfect because beyond the reach of gravity; he is as light on his feet as an acrobat in outer space. (p. 621)

A man with an Imperial Self is one who wants to generalize his void. His project is to destroy. His notion is that peace lies in an equalization of the pressures within and without him. His favorite sound is silence. (pp. 621-22)

"I put down everything which came into my mind, whether it made sense or not," says Henry, but his aim is a *Walpurgisnacht*. His way is not the way to rout habitual usage with new meaning, saturate words with consciousness, permeate them with mind, construct a world of words that is a reproach to the other one. Each word has to be emptied and refilled separately. The work goes slowly. (p. 624)

George Stade, "Mailer and Miller," in Partisan Review *(copyright © 1977 by Partisan Review, Inc.), Vol. XLIV, No. 4, 1977, pp. 616-24.**

LAWRENCE J. SHIFREEN

Miller begins his study [in his series of short fictions *Mezzotints*] by creating a clichéd image of society as a limiting environment which forces individuals into a patterned existence based on work and sleep. This concept affords no new insights into human nature but is a typical device used in the 1920's by writers who wished to study the "types" of people who inhabit New York. The routine Miller depicts of rising early to go to work and returning home to sleep, shows that he views man as a machine with no power or control over life and the world. (pp. 11-12)

The "Mezzotint," "Dawn Travellers," depicts the Williamsberg, Brooklyn world that Miller knows best. . . . These "Dawn Travellers" appear to be little more than drones, as Miller borrows Dostoevsky's metaphor of the "ant hill." . . . (p. 12)

[The] sick reality that characterizes a society of one dimensional people whose lives are monotones and who live in a dead world beneath the earth's surface forms the basis for Miller's term "cancer," an incurable disease that eats away at and destroys our society. The metaphor for this death is the subway, a machine that carries one from the land of the living and deposits one in the grave. This idea obviously haunted Miller's imagination; for, during this same era, his short story "Glittering Pie" uses this same image of death, as a train literally carries men and women to their end. Demise is the harsh reality that one faces again and again at dawn when one becomes a "Dawn Traveller" and perceives one's lot. . . .

The living death the workers experience horrifies Miller, who feels obligated to raise man above his meager lot in life. He accomplishes this transformation by calling him "the Great Beast," "Him," and "He." In each case, man's name is raised in capital letters and praised by the bard who sees man elevated above the role of beast of burden. Miller feels compelled to help men because they are his fellow beings, men who have suffered, like Miller, to attain an "American dream" of success. By "success," Miller does not mean the conventionally accepted better paying job; social prosperity appalls him. What he deems "success" is man's belief in and his attempt to reach his dream. (p. 13)

Besides hope, a second device that Miller uses to escape death's horror is humor. For when he entitles his following "Mezzotint," "If You're Dying, Choose a Mausoleum," he uses this undertaker's advertisement to mock the money making behind American success, a system which he believes finds its basis in undermining one man so that another can monetarily prosper. (pp. 13-14)

The need to find a better way of life comes with the realization that most men and women are takers. These entrepreneurs exploit others for their own personal gain. Such self-oriented beings are metaphorically depicted by Miller in his image of "Circe," the title of another "Mezzotint." . . . [The] everyday world of the subway [depicted in "Circle"] lacks the development of the images of the sewers and urinals found in *Tropic of Cancer,* and shows that the Miller who created the *Mezzotints* could not depict his environment as well as he would nine years later in *Tropic*. . . . Neither *Tropic* nor *Mezzotints* is a book of dreams. Each recounts the experiences that make up Henry Miller's "reality." For when he talks about the life in the streets of New York and Paris, he cannot couch the spit and urine in artistic images of love and beauty that are totally inapplicable to his life. It is for this reason that Circe cannot be described as having a Greek, Roman, or celestial nose. She must possess a real one and below it a mouth that is "gaping" and "red," for she is clearly a carnivorous animal, a meat-eater who is "carnal" and "lust[ing]" because her lips are "parched" and "seared" as they drain men of their blood and passions, leaving them empty shells.

The metaphor of the "vamp" who forces one to experience a living death is transformed into that of the whore when Miller's "Dance Hall" "Mezzotint" depicts the world as a place where one pays his nickel to have one's fun and lose one's virtue. . . . The puppets and machines that he creates by describing their mechanical and sexual movements are beings who "fuse" together, not as lovers, but as lusting animals who pay their nickels, dance, have sex, and then worry about an absurd sense of virtue totally unrelated to real life. These same beings, who are resurrected in the *Tropics,* make their first appearance in *Mezzotints* when Miller mocks their false morality by questioning our social standards. . . . (pp. 14-15)

This self-centered philosophy of survival leads to the creation of limited people. To Miller, life means much more than just endurance. He sees a more complete person as one who can integrate dreams and realities. This multi-faceted existence becomes the focus of the "Mezzotint," "The Awakening," a fiction about a man who hungers for a dream lover yet feels compelled to give her up for his wife and a life based on the struggling and fighting that Miller feels compose marital happiness—a many dimensional existence that carries him beyond the simplistic realm of dreams. . . . [A] basic realization that one's ideals are not equal to one's dreams provides Miller's protagonist with the first step in his movement towards self-awareness. The next step entails the growth of the individual to the point where he finds himself able to cope with the split between his dreams and actuality. . . . The cyclonic nature of this fiction seems most apparent when one realizes that the protagonist begins at home and ends up in the same place despite his journey. Yet he has left the confined world of the closely knit family for an adventure that Miller's married protagonist later experiences in *Capricorn* and *The Rosy Crucifixion*. Through the actual event of leaving home, he perceives a new path in his life, a road that affords him both peace and misery. By using the word "contrast" in this "Mezzotint," Miller suggests that a dual reality exists, a world that one must experience through getting beyond the escapes of home and sleep, and beyond the protective world of one's wife and child.

The reality that one finds by leaving the family's womb does not have to be the base, nightmarish world of "Dawn Travellers" or that of "Dance Hall" people. Instead, one can and should use one's experience to get beyond the depressing and grotesque aspects of life by rising out of the gutters and finding a world between heaven and earth, a state where base reality has been interwoven with the dream of an ideal existence, as in the final "Mezzotint," a "Bowery Phoenix." The combined image of man's baseness intertwined with his hopes leads Miller to present a dual being who appears as a gargoyle when seen in the earth's muck and mire, yet who becomes beautiful when he rises above his station. . . . By describing beings tied to the earth as "squat," "little," "monsters," "ugly," "misshapen," "bowlegged," and "devils," Miller shows that the men of our world who go nowhere and aspire toward nothing are grotesque beings whose minds are distorted because they fail to perceive change through growth. These monsters watch the world go by them instead of thinking and expanding their consciousness. To move forward, one must turn within and must realize one's physical and psychological short comings. Once aware of himself, man must aspire to rise above the world of limitation and must experience a new, "bronze" self. By hammering out a new being with a more positive and more realistic conception of himself, like Miller's protagonist in a "Bowery Phoenix," and like his later depictions of Thoreau and Whitman, Miller demonstrates his belief that man can and must move to a state of consciousness that displaces his basic acceptance of fear and limitation.

In this world combining such extremes as the bowery and the phoenix, Miller reaches a Whitmanesque realization that men are both saints and sinners. It is this knowledge that man has all possibilities which allows Miller's protagonist finally to accept his lot and flow with what he calls "life's river" in *Tropic of Cancer,* to enter and become one with both ancient and modern Greece in *The Colossus of Maroussi,* and to live the life of a pioneer united with the land, mountains, and sea in *Big Sur And The Oranges of Hieronymus Bosch.* Thus we see that although *Mezzotints* is an immature work, the images and metaphors it contains form the basis for Miller's literary ideas. His realization that life involves a process of growth that begins with self-awareness and leads to respecting others and finally moves to one's use of one's knowledge of people and one's world to change one's environment through expanding one's own consciousness, first takes shape in the sketches that compose *Mezzotints,* a collection of seven broadsides that form the basis for all of Henry Miller's major writings. (pp. 16-17)

Lawrence J. Shifreen, "Henry Miller's 'Mezzotints': The Undiscovered Roots of 'Tropic of Cancer'," in Studies in Short Fiction *(copyright 1979 by Newberry College), Vol. 16, No. 1, Winter, 1979, pp. 11-17.*

PAUL R. JACKSON

In the opening pages of *Tropic of Cancer,* Henry Miller announces the extravagant anti-art that will be his theme. Beyond the lice and the cancer of time, beyond hope and convention, Beauty and Art, the auto-hero offers his book as libel and insult, the studied rejection of accepted literary values: "I am going to sing for you," he promises, "a little off key perhaps, but I will sing. I will sing while you croak, I will dance over your dirty corpse." With fractured echoes of Whitman's celebration of the self, the passage insists on its own bellowing song. . . . If singing here is a last modern echo of Homeric invocation, music more generally becomes an insistant metaphor both for Miller's own discordant lyricism and for the collapsing world that *Tropic of Cancer* exposes.

Miller has his own inverted muse, the character named Tania, expatriate herself and wife of an American playwright. Fecund but conventional, Tania becomes at once both inspiration and the focal point of the chaos that Miller, singing only tunes of dying splendor, invokes as the hallucinated topic of the book. . . . Registering the death of time and the dissolution of the world itself, Miller announces the ultimate metamorphosis Tania inspires: "I am thinking that when the great silence descends upon all and everywhere music will at last triumph. When into the womb of time everything is again withdrawn chaos will be restored and chaos is the score upon which reality is written. You, Tania, are my chaos. It is why I sing." . . . Miller's song, then, will be a carefully adopted cacophony, the literary equivalent, off-key and triumphant, of the very chaos a conventional world generates.

Convention has its own music, though, and Miller's strident lyricism works constantly against the harmonies that predictability creates. Thematically, music is used throughout *Tropic of Cancer* as a sign of the flagging vitality Miller everywhere rejects. He will sing off key precisely because the rest of the world sings on key with the tunes that security composes and safety plays. As a sign of spiritual exhaustion, music pervades the book; people sing what is unreal, orchestras play what only soothes, down-and-outers turn to guitar and accordion, while stuffed-shirts of all varieties pompously and erroneously identify in the music of convention a false sense of life's possibilities. For Miller the music of habitual order is a pale tune indeed. (pp. 40-1)

[The accordion is represented as the] popular instrument of a commonplace world. Along with the guitar, it signals the humdrum and usual. Although Miller had linked the two at the beginning of the book as instruments irrelevant to his song, one is not surprised to find them assuming suggestive importance later. (p. 42)

Paris, alternating despair with ecstasy, either sings "a demented song" . . . , or—on pleasant days at least—is "like a piece of music for the pianoforte." . . . The flux of Parisian life is as aural as it is visual, its discordant music sounding the themes of the modern metropolis.

More personally, Sylvester and Tania, given to fads, pomposity, and dullness, rent a new piano, a concert grand. Positioning himself on a balcony to better announce his distance from their values, Miller sees the piano as proclaiming the end of his affair with Tania. The latter is playing "the adagio," and the music "says very distinctly: no more words of love." . . . With the violent rhetorical aggressiveness that marks his response to women throughout *Tropic of Cancer,* Miller looks down from the balcony: "The keys are black and white, then black, then white, then white and black. And you want to know if you can play something for me. Yes, play something with those big thumbs of yours. Play the adagio since that's the only goddamned thing you know. Play it, and then cut off your big thumbs." . . . (pp. 43-4)

[The] most extended thematic treatment of music as sign of this collapsed world is reserved for the concert hall. Appropriately, Miller has found a ticket for the concert in a *lavabo,* and the scene dramatizes the collision between the representative of the world of the sewers and the dead automatons, over-dressed, self-satisfied, cataleptic, the emblems of a rich world, bored but secure. While Miller immediately feels out of place, his insecurities are converted to rhetorical strength as he realizes that the concert is only a self-inflected form of torture for those who attend. Both Miller and the audience withdraw from the reality of the music. While the robots of the audience try to avoid thinking at all costs—for that way madness lies—they nevertheless recollect shop windows where an attractive scarf or hat stirs vital juices more profoundly than the music. Miller, on the other hand, becomes more intensely alive as he loses all sense of time and place, the pores of his body becoming windows through which glimpses of a felt world pass. (p. 44)

The harmony of a conventional world . . . consistently strikes Miller as a sterile expression of waning life and calls into being his own most grotesque and outraged gestures. Confronted by the music of ideas or music as sentimental evocation of female ties that bind, Miller violently, enthusiastically, rejects the harmonies he hears. . . . What exists as reality beneath the broken structures of form and meaning is finally the flux of life itself, the absurd flow of human passion, the sewer, the river, the discreet shards of buried emotional life. To these bits of life Miller directs his own song and dance. (p. 48)

Searching for the fragments of resuscitated life, Miller invites the reader to one final dance: "It may be that we are doomed, that there is no hope for us, *any of us,* but if that is so then let us set up a last agonizing, bloodcurdling howl, a screech of defiance, a war whoop! Away with lamentation! Away with elegies and dirges! . . . Let us living ones dance about the rim of the crater, a last expiring dance. But a dance!" . . . (p. 49)

Tropic of Cancer is precisely that last, expiring dance. Often criticized for his lack of dramatic skill, Miller is at his strongest in the sheer lyricism of the book. His ability to evoke both paralysis and life exists beyond his solipsism and the book's unevenness. . . . That lyricism informs not only . . . passages of acceptance—and the end of the book is an elegiac acceptance of the flow of time, of Paris and its past—but also the violently charged moments of rejection. Imagistic and concrete, the language at its best is the off-key cacophony, the score of chaos announced in his early invocation of Tania.

In *Black Spring* Miller continues to make much of the music theme. In "Third or Fourth Day of Spring" he identifies with Beethoven as he affirms creation and destruction. . . . [As] he says later, "Either you start with pure melody or you start with listerine." In *Tropic of Cancer,* Miller affirms a life, finally, without people. Acceptance at the end depends on a joy found outside the boundaries of Paris itself with the author insulated against those whose lifeless order had crippled earlier. Miller alone finds peace; the human world around him remains unchanged. That, too, had been anticipated: "I had moments of ecstasy, and I sang with burning sparks. I sang of the Equator, her red-feathered legs and the islands dropping out of sight. But nobody heard." . . . Alone or not, Miller has sung his song, his own aroused lyrical voice clashing with the harmonies of convention. (pp. 49-50)

Paul R. Jackson, "Caterwauling and Harmony: Music in 'Tropic of Cancer'," in Critique: Studies in Modern Fiction *(copyright © by James Dean Young 1979), Vol. XX, No. 3, 1979, pp. 40-50.*

* * *

MOSS, Howard 1922-

Moss, an award-winning American poet, an influential critic, and a playwright, has been the poetry editor of *The New Yorker* for almost three decades. (See also *CLC*, Vol. 7, and *Contemporary Authors*, Vols. 1-4, rev. ed.)

JOSEPHINE JACOBSEN

Howard Moss is pre-eminently—though certainly not exclusively—an urban poet. I know of no other contemporary poet who can so marvelously evoke a city—say, New York, but that is no matter. His relationship with the city is as complex as the city itself. It is a fine blend of distaste, faintly derisive love, and—one needs to say "nostalgia," though conscious of another injured word. The city is fragmented, and one of the prime strengths of Moss's poetry is its sense of fragmentations: of time, of love, of physical surroundings, of social relationships. The shards represent fragments of things which once were whole. . . .

Key words in Moss's poetry are "dark" and "light"; above all, he is fascinated by the mystifying and crucial moments in which they meet, the crepuscular encounter. In "Nearing The Lights" [in *Buried City*], for example, a whole series of speculations and relationships branch off from the narrow central shaft, as light penetrates and defines. There is always motion; at his most descriptive, Moss does not write a static poem. . . .

Wit, drama, the sharp collision of identities, are perpetually active. *Think of houses, dinners, all mendacious calm. . . .* All his calm is mendacious, a ferment of below-the-surface entanglements. There is in the work such a kinship with Proust that it comes as no surprise to read,

> . . . you will always bear
> two sacred marks of the interior:
> memory and art.

For years, Moss has been a brilliant technician. There was a period, in some of his early poetry, when that brilliance of technique seemed not always assimilated by the poem. By the time his *Selected Poems* appeared it was apparent that he had won that battle. There, and notably in *Buried City,* the technique is so fused with the poem's individuality that it cannot be separated, even for admiration. The long final poem which gives the book its name is one of the finest Moss has ever written, and that is saying a great deal.

Incidentally, one line alone would make the book worthwhile. It might be the nation's or the century's epitaph:

> Not to be loved is to crave power.

(p. 348)

Josephine Jacobsen, "The Spirit and the City," in The Nation *(copyright 1976 by the Nation Associates, Inc.), Vol. 223, No. 11, October 9, 1976, pp. 346-48.**

HAROLD BLOOM

[*A Swim off the Rocks* is] a superb book of light verse, which culminates in a marvelous poem, not so very light, called *Horror Movie,* with its sublime closing couplet: "Make the blood flow, make the motive muddy: / There's a little death in everybody." (p. 23)

Harold Bloom, "The Year's Books: (Part I)," in The New Republic *(reprinted by permission of* The New Republic; *© 1976 The New Republic, Inc.), Vol. 175, No. 21, November 20, 1976, pp. 20, 22-3, 26.**

W. G. REGIER

The buried life is encompassed by community in Howard Moss's *Buried City*. . . . Beginning in the Lascaux caves, the title poem wends through an art gallery, movie house, and "Hegelian doubletalk" to the centrifugal emblem of drollity, "Baked in lava, the figures at Pompeii." Moss twits wordplay while implying he takes little fun from it. Usually the jokes are toxic. . . . Moss's rhythms, at least, are infectious. But his techniques are not limited to the superficial; to the contrary, they are subversive. Internal patterns are more than trickery, breath is caught and released in precise art. Sometimes, as in "Sawdust," the effect is amusement. Elsewhere the same rigor, tied more tightly, exploits suspense, as in the crash landing at the bottom of "The Stairs." . . . Unlike the winding stairs of Yeats or Dante, Moss's go down only. It is rumored that there is no emigration from the buried city; these are the rumors. (pp. 386-87)

W. G. Regier, "Review: 'Buried City'," in Prairie Schooner *(© 1976 by University of Nebraska Press; reprinted by permission from* Prairie Schooner*), Vol. 50, No. 4, Winter, 1976-77, pp. 386-87.*

G. E. MURRAY

Perhaps no contemporary American poet writes so convincingly of the urban scene as Howard Moss. Indeed, it seems to me that, like roads and Rome, all city poems—especially those singing the virtues, vices and niceties of New York—lead to Mr. Moss. There is little question that in his National Book Award collection *Selected Poems* (1972) and, later, *Buried City* (1975), Moss staked a substantial claim on the strange, terrifying and wonderful territory we understand as the city. But Moss lays claim to other domains as well, specifically, the rarefied art of the light verse he assembles in *A Swim off the Rocks*.

In a time of cultural fallout, social shabbiness, and intellectual cribbing, when force-fed fad often supplants a good dose of whimsey, many have come to believe that writing that isn't "serious" isn't important. Not so, contends Mr. Moss. *A Swim off the Rocks* is at once clever, frivolous, well-crafted, outrageous, and, ultimately, genuine. Sometimes it's simply a matter of verbal fun, as in being a tourist "embarrassed in Paris in Harris tweed," or again when "Finding, in Frankfurt, that one indigestible / Comestible makes them too ill for the Festival," or pure pun. . . . (pp. 964-65)

Truth cast in the stone of understatement is a weapon with which Moss strikes home regularly. "Tennis: A Portrait" tells the real score of the game:

> Your triumph is to watch the set
>
> From the sidelines while you cheer the serves
> Smashed over by the stupid young.
> They do not know how the wind swerves
> The best-aimed shot from its target. Stung
> By age, high-strung among the doubles, only
> You are single. They miss the mark,
> Your verbal strokes—each lob, each volley
> As bright, and seedy, as New York, New York.
>
> You know the score—your nets of wit
> Hide your fine hand and, hand in glove,
> Time's racket lays no bets on it,
> Though it was once, at thirty, love.

This is heavyweight light verse, no vehicle for an amateur. It takes a daring and inventive poet to succeed in being so painfully funny without resorting to wearing a lampshade at a party. (pp. 965-66)

G. E. Murray, "Book Reviews: 'A Swim off the Rocks'," in The Georgia Review *(copyright, 1977, by the University of Georgia), Vol. XXXI, No. 4, Winter, 1977, pp. 964-66.*

J. D. McCLATCHY

A Swim Off The Rocks collects Howard Moss's light verse, written over a thirty-year span. It is a wry gathering. Sadly, light verse seems to be a dying or quiescent art, so that Moss not only delights us with his own work, but reminds us of past masters. . . . The elegant economy and anarchic absurdities of such poetry succeed in many forms and have simultaneous purposes—nowhere better described than by Moss himself, in an essay on Edward Lear, as "an entertainment, a release, and a form of criticism." These occur, first, in the poet's witty manipulation of language itself—outrageous rhymes, wicked puns, startling enjambments—and so at once reveal and revel in the tenuousness of meaning. And this preposterous dialect is joined with a distanced perspective that permits depths to be touched with biting satire or mock-heroic banter. . . . The best poems here are "Modified Sonnets" (clever Shakespearean parodies), "Fern Dying" (by any standard, a deeply moving poem), "Short Stories," "The Refrigerator," "Circle," and "Horror Movie." And to single out those poems says something about Moss's strengths and weaknesses. His merely playful poems sound too much like exercises or party lyrics. . . . But the poems I've mentioned, for all their digs and delights, are shot through with the same plangent melancholy that informs the sensibility of Moss's darker or "serious" poems. And that, in turn, reminds one of how often he has used a "light touch" to sound *their* depths. . . . Juxtaposed, the comic and querulous tones animate each other and comprise the poem's triumph. The most successful poems in *A Swim Off The Rocks* approach that same tension. You are smiling unconsciously, until second thoughts make you wonder why. (pp. 295-96)

J. D. McClatchy, "Grace and Rude Will," in Poetry *(© 1978 by The Modern Poetry Association; reprinted by permission of the Editor of* Poetry*), Vol. CXXXII, No. 5, August, 1978, pp. 288-98.**

N

NEWLOVE, John 1938-

Newlove is a Canadian lyric poet. His early work, characterized by a simple narrative and descriptive form, has evolved into a more complex poetry, featuring juxtaposition of fragments in his most recent verse. His poetry reveals an unremitting sense of alienation and despair. (See also *Contemporary Authors,* Vols. 21-24, rev. ed.)

GEORGE BOWERING

[*Black Night Window*] establishes for the wider literate audience what was previously known to sincere readers of Canadian poetry—that Newlove is one of our dozen really good poets. Period. (p. 187)

Newlove is a scholar . . . of the western American Indians, & finds their life style, history, thought, suffering, a major theme to return to, usually to start from. "The Pride" begins to make it because it is uncommonly rich in sound, image, historical resonances. In it the poet treats the Indians as men ("the indians / are not composed of / the romantic stories / about them")—yes, Newlove is aware of that word "composed." "The Pride" constitutes the great poem of the land. The Indians (not "The Indian") can be the origin of our own pride instead of our shameful human defeat. The Indians are carried inside us westerners—so poetry is not flakes of dandruff from the poet's long hair, but revelation of the whole body of poetry shared & put to use by men. (pp. 187-88)

Newlove is dedicated to his source, the West, & to that of which he is the source, the poetry. He provides a sense of real care & purpose to do the shaman's thing, get the spirit of the land's West into poetry as one thing, to make it permanent or at least available to like minds, & in other ways & degrees to Eastern strangers. . . .

Only with [his] unpretentious grip may [Newlove] begin to "Ride Off Any Horizon." In that well-known & well-made poem he makes clear his poetic intent & way, his sources & methods. With clear images & sure lines he provides in order, prairie particulars of landscape, prairie evidences of history, prairie phenomena in childhood, smalltown prairie people. . . .

A lot of poets & teachers in Upper & Lower Canada have askt me what makes the best Western poetry different from the best where they are. I'd suggest *Black Night Window* for an important part of the instructional reading list. (p. 188)

George Bowering, "Books Reviewed: 'Black Night Window'," in The Canadian Forum, *Vol. 48, No. 574, November, 1968, pp. 187-88.*

PETER DALE SCOTT

[John Newlove] is a formalist, alert to the tact as well as the audacity of the creative process. *North America* celebrates a poetic inebriation, moving the mind from "a medley / of sounds / from other men's / tongues" to "a disinterested / remembrance— / like a flower, / dried". A heroic fragment stops in his mind like a racial memory; and he asks "through how / many hands / have those words / / come?— to me, / so / that the noise / made / / of the continent / might be / recovered to / my mind".

This movement into *afflatus,* and return from it, illustrates the impersonal dimension behind the sparse and controlled movements of his *personae.* A historical irony, not always explicit, allows him to record these movements in minute and exact perspective. . . . Occasionally Newlove uses mannerisms from an older and inferior generation of Canadian ironists. At his best, he goes straight to "the root / of common penury for / all of us the same". (pp. 360-61)

Peter Dale Scott, "Comment: 'What They Say' and 'Black Night Window'," in Poetry *(© 1970 by The Modern Poetry Association; reprinted by permission of the Editor of* Poetry*), Vol. CXV, No. 5, February, 1970, pp. 360-61.*

STEPHEN SCOBIE

[In] the words of the epigraph to John Newlove's [*Lies*], a poet is someone who "often deceived himself and told the truth when he thought he was lying."

If the lie is one indirect form of getting at the truth, another is the dream; and Newlove's book is full of dreams. . . . The atmosphere of dreams pervades much of the book, especially dreams about water, the sea. Strange, surrealistic images float through the poet's mind, and arrange themselves in shapes which tease meaning towards the reader without ever declaring themselves fully.

And suddenly, in the middle of all these apprehensions, clear and stark come outright pictures of human misery: the desexed "it" who "loves company and company is disgusted by it"; the pitiful Harry who "just can't anymore, that's all"; the terrible complaint that "Nothing I'd read / prepared me for a body this unfair."

The latter quotation comes from a poem called "No Pleasure", which seems almost an understatement for the deep pervading pessimism of this book. "No world without demons, no island / not surrounded by sharks": these are the "Gross masks in the dreams." *Lies* deals with masks, illusions, self-deceptions; but in the end the most grotesque masks are true, and the dreams all turn into nightmares.

What makes this pessimism all the more pervasive, and yet at the same time a little less absolute, is Newlove's attitude of acceptance rather than outrage. . . .

[Newlove's poems] always seem to be moving out. He . . . has obscured connections, puzzling images; but always the emotional charge at least is clear.

Stephen Scobie, "Books Reviewed: 'Lies'," in The Canadian Forum, *Vol. LIII, No. 638, March, 1974, p. 46.*

ROBIN SKELTON

The poetry of John Newlove, as presented [in *The Fat Man, Selected Poems: 1962-1972*] begins in a dark and brooding whimsicality, and moves steadily into utter despair. From the very beginning the protagonist chooses to portray himself as a solitary dominated by fantasy and desire, making "poems babies & love-affairs / out of women I've only seen once," a wanderer on the side of the road "cold / & afraid." . . .

The safety he finds is in situations which do not involve him in affection or desire; he envies the hitch hikers and their aimless travelling, their "feeling safe with strangers / in a moving car." He reports in drab low-key language on those who are "emptied of desire," on the beer parlour and street life of the small town, where all is directionless and customary. . . .

He finds success a failure, for, recalling what he had wished to become and realizing he has succeeded, he finds that "complete, / I am more empty than ever." He observes the bird that declines "the privilege / of music" preferring to finger "the absolute / wood / beneath," just as he himself prefers plain and unvarnished speech. Sometimes this plain speech of pain results in self-pity as when in "The Dog" he recalls "never thinking anyone / would love me," but the self pity is countered by his sardonic envy of the dog, "damn fool / running and barking / away toward the town." (p. 101)

It is perhaps in contemplating the past, in sharing other lives, that we may discover something to admire, to revere, as in considering the strength of "The Doukhubor," and in "Remembering Christopher Smart" which concludes with the lines

> I see that we all make the world what we want.
> Our disappointment lies in the world as it is.

"Disappointment" is hardly an adequate word to describe the portrayal of humanity in the succeeding poems. The title poem is as brilliantly designed and as vigorous as a Daumier, and it has all Daumier's relish in the grotesque. "The Fat Man," waiting at the crossing light, is nameless, characterless, gross, and en route to an undignified and messy death. . . .

The man portrayed in "Harry" is also a creature of futility and despair. The universe, in the last poems of the book, has become a purgatory, even a hell. Earth is no place to live. (p. 102)

John Newlove's vision is indeed dark. His universe is one of solitude, failure, ugliness and nausea. The only driving forces of life are desire, which is always thwarted, and dreams which are never fulfilled. This world is a place of waste, despair, and desolation. . . . Newlove's vision is not qualified. . . . The comedy is never in the slightest life-enhancing, there is no discernible God, and the language is, in the majority of poems, bare of all but the most anguished flourishes. Newlove has, indeed, created a place where no other poet has yet had the courage to go without at least a Swiftian irony, a Websterian rhetoric, or a religious conviction as luggage. The Newlove man (and one is tempted to an ironic play upon the author's own name) is very much a creature of our times, however, as he is also a universal figure—the figure of need, solitude, despair. The poetry itself is enormously well crafted, subtly controlled in tone, and richly various in style, even while remaining consistent to what emerges as an over-all purpose to portray the human tragedy with an economy and elegance that succeed in making the whole book a tribute to courage and a statement of the awesome spiritual strength of man. This *Selected Poems,* omitting as it does many of the poems of pure reportage and of whimsy which lessened the impact of some of the separate collections is one of the most impressive to have been published in the English speaking world in the last twenty years. John Newlove is now at the height of his powers. One waits impatiently for further developments. (pp. 102-03)

Robin Skelton, "Newlove's Power," in Canadian Literature, *No. 79, Winter, 1978, pp. 101-03.*

* * *

NEWMAN, Edwin 1919-

Newman, an American critic, novelist, and reporter, is an advocate of grammatical precision and clarity. Once a well-known Broadway critic, Newman now writes about the humorous and misleading usage of English. He also writes and appears in television documentaries concerning the commonly accepted fallacies of language communication. Newman has recently written his first novel, *Sunday Punch.* (See also *Contemporary Authors,* Vols. 69-72.)

Most of [*Sunday Punch*] is mildly amusing, as are Newman's lightly satiric assaults in between the fights—on hog-washing Congressmen, chatty newscasters, the Washington in-crowd, bad sportswriters, gurus, and TV sit-coms. . . . But first-novelist Newman never really summons up a distinctive voice; it's all mixed echoes of Runyon, Lardner, Perelman, Wodehouse, and lesser sorts. A pleasant enough mix, but novel-length mildness (Perelman would have packed all the ideas here into a dazzling short story) may turn to tedium for all but the most sedate readers. (pp. 471-72)

"Fiction: 'Sunday Punch'," in Kirkus Reviews *(copyright © 1979 The Kirkus Service, Inc.), Vol. XLVII, No. 8, April 15, 1979, pp. 471-72.*

SPENCER PUNNETT

Never mind that you've seen the basic plot on a dozen old

"B" movies, or that many of the characters are familiar stereotypes. The star of "Sunday Punch" is really the English language itself.

Edwin Newman uses the scenes of this comic novel to poke fun at the linguistic behavior of sportswriters and Washington socialites, academicians and "happy talk" TV newscasters. He gleefully parodies regionalisms, makes plays on words, and points an accusing finger at assorted verbal fads and clichés.

Such attention to language is only to be expected from a veteran television correspondent who in past years wrote the nonfiction best sellers "Strictly Speaking" and "A Civil Tongue." Both these books humorously lambasted a variety of follies, foibles, and needless obfuscations in current American writing and speech.

"Sunday Punch" chronicles the meteoric career of an unlikely athlete named Aubrey Philpott-Grimes, who rises from the obscurity of British amateur boxing to become a contender for the middleweight championship of the world. . . .

[The book gives] a lot of chuckles, although few belly laughs. There is no element of depth to give it a more enduring appeal. But even for people like me, who reach to switch off the TV at the mere mention of boxing, "Sunday Punch" makes entertaining reading.

Spencer Punnett, "Pulling Punches," in The Christian Science Monitor *(reprinted by permission from* The Christian Science Monitor; *© 1979 The Christian Science Publishing Society; all rights reserved), June 6, 1979, p. 19.*

[In *Sunday Punch* Newman] cranks up a very ancient vehicle—the B-movie prizefight story. Every fixture is in place. There is the incongruous fighter [, the comic manager, the sinister gangster, the fighter's sweetheart, and the newspaper man who tells the story]. . . . It would be too much to call the result a comic novel. It is too lightweight, too frolicsome for that. It is merely extremely funny.

"Books: 'Sunday Punch'," in The New Yorker *(© 1979 by The New Yorker Magazine, Inc.), Vol. LV, No. 18, June 18, 1979, p. 110.*

Sunday Punch [is] a Wodehousian excursion that is lighter than air and twice as much fun as laughing gas. Its author, having honed his skills in nonfiction sorties against linguistic pretention and misuse, here reveals a merciless ability to mimic all that is silliest in the American way of talking. He also shows a fair eye for general inanity. . . . Newman pulls no punches; nobody is spared, not even television commentators. But his blows tickle more than they hurt, despite their accuracy. (p. 80)

"Life & Letters: 'Sunday Punch'," in The Atlantic Monthly *(copyright © 1979 by The Atlantic Monthly Company, Boston, Mass.; reprinted with permission), Vol. 244, No. 1, July, 1979, pp. 79-80.*

JOE FLAHERTY

Edwin Newman's first novel, "Sunday Punch," is a sad example of a man mesmerized by his inner music. The novel is ostensibly the story of an English middleweight named Aubrey Philpott-Grimes and his travails in America as he pursues the championship. The premise has promise. Nathanael West mined it well when he sent Lemuel Pitkin out to conquer America in "A Cool Million." The difference is that West used inspired madness, while Mr. Newman settles for smug pedantry.

Early on, Mr. Newman lets us know that the target for his Sunday Punch is not the novel's plot line, but sundry targets: editorial writers, airline menus, luxury apartments, sportswriters, Washington political and social life, and any other gnat that has landed on the estimable Newman brow across the years. . . .

But in his pursuit of cuffing around the booberies of our tongue (very little of it clever), Mr. Newman ignores Edmund Wilson's esthetic canon for the novel—a farrago is fine, if it lives.

Mr. Newman's novel doesn't live, because all his characters are cartoon characters. . . .

[If it hadn't been for Newman's celebrity status] he probably would not have gotten a chance to unload his "Sunday Punch."

Joe Flaherty, "Many Funny Names," in The New York Times Book Review *(© 1979 by The New York Times Company; reprinted by permission), July 15, 1979, p. 13.*

* * *

NIN, Anaïs 1903-1977

Nin, an American novelist, short story writer, and critic, is best known for her diaries. Living in Paris in the 1930s, she became part of several artistic and intellectual circles, where she became acquainted with Antonin Artaud, Henry Miller, and Otto Rank. Her study with Rank, a prominent psychoanalyst, is reflected in both her fiction and her diary, where she explores the power of the subconscious in imagery drawn from dream and myth. (See also *CLC*, Vols. 1, 4, 8, 11, and *Contemporary Authors*, Vols. 13-16, rev. ed.; obituary, Vols. 69-72.)

HENRY MILLER

As I write these lines Anaïs Nin has begun the fiftieth volume of her diary, the record of a twenty-year struggle towards self-realization. Still a young woman, she has produced on the side, in the midst of an intensely active life, a monumental confession which when given to the world will take its place beside the revelations of St. Augustine, Petronius, Abelard, Rousseau, Proust, and others. . . .

The diary is full of voyages; in fact, like life itself it might be regarded as nothing but voyage. The epic quality of it, however, is eclipsed by the metaphysical. The diary is not a journey towards the heart of darkness, in the stern Conradian sense of destiny, not a *voyage au bout de la nuit,* as with Céline, nor even a voyage to the moon in the psychological sense of escape. It is much more like a mythological voyage towards the source and fountain head of life—I might say an *astrologic* voyage of metamorphosis. (p. 33)

This diary is written absolutely without malice. The psychologist may remark of this that the pain inflicted upon her by the loss of her father was so great as to render her incapable of causing pain to others. In a sense this is true, but it is a limited view of the matter. My own feeling is rather that we have in this diary the direct, naked thrust which is of the essence of the great tragic dramas of the Greeks. Racine,

Corneille, Molière may indulge in malice—not the Greek dramatists. The difference lies in the attitude towards Fate. The warfare is not with men, but with the gods. Similarly, in the case of Anaïs Nin's journal: the war is with herself, with God as the sole witness. The diary was written not for the eyes of others, but for the eye of God. She has no malice any more than she has the desire to cheat or to lie. To lie in a diary is the height of absurdity. . . . Though the way is tortuous the direction is always the same, always inward, further inward, towards the heart of the self. Every encounter is a preparation for the final encounter, the confrontation with the real Self. To indulge in malice would be to swerve from the ordained path, to waste a precious moment in the pursuit of her ideal. She moves onward inexorably, as the gods move in the Greek dramas, on towards the realization of her destiny.

There is a very significant fact attached to the origin of this diary, and that is that it was begun in artistic fashion. By that I do not mean that it was done with the skill of an artist, with the conscious use of a technique; no, but it was begun as something to be read by some one else, as something to influence some one else. In that sense as an artist. . . . [The] diary is a silent communion with the father who has deserted her, . . . a gift of love which she hopes will re-unite them. . . . [The] father and child are kept apart for many years. In the legends which treat of this theme it happens, as in this case, that the meeting takes place when the daughter has come of age.

And so, in the very beginning of her diary, the child behaves precisely like the artist who, through the medium of his expression, sets about to conquer the world which has denied him. Thinking originally to woo and enchant the father by the testimony of her grief, thwarted in all her attempts to recover him, she begins little by little to regard the separation as a punishment for her own inadequacy. The difference which had marked her out as a child, and which had already brought down upon her the father's ire, becomes more accentuated. The diary becomes the confession of her inability to make herself worthy of this lost father who has become for her the very paragon of perfection.

In the very earliest pages of the diary this conflict between the old, inadequate self which was attached to the father and the budding, unknown self which she was creating manifests itself. It is a struggle between the real and the ideal. . . . (pp. 37-9)

Throughout the diary the amazing thing is [her] intuitive awareness of the symbolic nature of her role. It is this which illuminates the most trivial remarks, the most trivial incidents she records. In reality there is nothing trivial throughout the whole record; everything is saturated with a purpose and significance which gradually becomes clear as the confession progresses. Similarly there is nothing chaotic about the work, although at first glance it may give that impression. . . . It is a great pageant of the times patiently and humbly delineated by one who considered herself as nothing, by one who had almost completely effaced herself in the effort to arrive at a true understanding of life. It is in this sense again that the human document rivals the work of art, or in times such as ours, *replaces* the work of art. . . . We move amid boundless horizons in a perpetual state of awe and humility. We enter, with the author, into unknown worlds, and we share with the latter all the pain, beauty, terror and illumination which exploration entails. (pp. 40-2)

In the diary of Anaïs Nin there is a kind of desperation, almost like that of a shipwrecked sailor thrown up on a desert island. From the flotsam and jetsam of her wrecked life the author struggles to create anew. It is a heart-breaking effort to recover a lost world. It is not, as some might imagine, a deliberate retreat from the world; it is an involuntary separation from the world! (p. 42)

Nobody sees with his eyes alone; we see with our souls. And this problem of putting the soul into the eye is the whole problem of a diarist such as Anaïs Nin. The whole vast diary, regarded from this angle, assumes the nature of the record of a second birth. It is the story of death and transfiguration. (p. 44)

Whereas in the earlier volumes the accent was one of sadness, of disillusionment, of being *de trop,* now the accent becomes one of joy and fulfilment. Fire, audacity, dynamite, laughter—the very choice of words is sufficient to indicate the changed condition. The world spreads out before her like a banquet table: something to *enjoy.* But the appetite, seemingly insatiable, is controlled. The old obsessional desire to devour everything in sight in order that it be preserved in her own private tomb is gone. She eats now only what nourishes her. The once ubiquitous digestive tract, the great whale into which she had made herself, is replaced by other organs with other functions. The exaggerated sympathy for others which had dogged her every step diminishes. The birth of a sense of humour denotes the achievement of an objectivity which alone the one who has realized himself attains. It is not indifference, but toleration. The totality of vision brings about a new kind of sympathy, a free, noncompulsive sort. The very pace of the diary changes. There are now long lapses, intervals of complete silence in which the great digestive apparatus, once all, slows up to permit the development of complementary organs. The eye, too, seems to close, content to let the body *feel* the presence of the world about, rather than pierce it with a devastating vision. It is no longer a world of black and white, of good and evil, or harmony and dissonance; no, now the world has at last become an orchestra in which there are innumerable instruments capable of rendering every tone and colour, an orchestra in which even the most shattering dissonances are resolved into meaningful expression. It is the ultimate poetic world of *As Is.* (pp. 46-7)

There are some volumes, in which attention is focused almost entirely on one or two individuals, which are like the raw pith of some post-Dostoievskian novel; they bring to the surface a lunar plasm which is the logical fruit of that drive towards the dead slag of the ego which Dostoievski heralded and which D. H. Lawrence was the first to have pointed out in precise language. There are three successive volumes, of this sort, which are made of nothing but this raw material of a drama which takes place entirely within the confines of the female world. It is the first female writing I have ever seen: it rearranges the world in terms of female honesty. The result is a language which is ultramodern and yet bears no resemblance to any of the masculine experimental processes with which we are familiar. It is precise, abstract, cloudy and unseizable. There are larval thoughts not yet divorced from their dream content, thoughts which seem to crystallize slowly before your eyes, always precise but never tangible, never once arrested so as to be grasped by the mind. It is the opium world of woman's physiological being, a sort of cinematic show put on inside the genito-urinary tract. There is not an ounce of man-made culture in it; everything related to the head is cut off. Time passes, but it is not clock time; nor is it poetic time such as men create in their passion. It is more like that aeonic time required for the creation of gems and precious metals; an embowelled sidereal time in which the female knows that she is superior to the male and will eventually swallow him up again. The effect is that of starlight carried over into day-time.

The contrast between this language and that of man's is forcible; the whole of man's art begins to appear like a frozen edelweiss under a glass bell reposing on a mantelpiece in the deserted home of a lunatic. In this extraordinary unicellular language of the female we have a blinding, gemlike consciousness which disperses the ego like stardust. (pp. 50-1)

Henry Miller, "Un Etre Etoilique," in The Criterion, *Vol. XVII, No. LXVI, October, 1937, pp. 33-52.*

SHARON SPENCER

There is a particular sense in which Anaïs Nin's art is related to the Surrealist ideal of magical creation through combinations of entities drawn from different categories. But her work is not itself Surreal, and it is easier to understand the application of the collage idea in terms of a broad definition. Collage includes all works in which components belonging to separate intellectual or perceptual categories are combined, regardless of the nature of the materials or the techniques used to combine them. . . . (p. 5)

The degree of displacement in Anaïs Nin's writing is relatively slight, even though there is considerable variety among her works. Her most experimental book, the one in which displacements are the greatest, is *Collages* itself. The early books, *House of Incest* and the pieces collected in *Under a Glass Bell,* display juxtaposition less in a structural sense than in stylistic combinations. Nin's diction is based on collage; she chooses words from a wide variety of sources and is usually successful in achieving a striking yet authentic image, phrase, or descriptive passage. A lover of words *as* words, Nin uses them if they appeal to her, regardless of standards of usage; she also draws upon far-flung vocabularies. . . . Guided by the unpredictable lure of free association, Nin combines into a novel the incidents that seem most strikingly to project her characters' inner lives. (pp. 5-6)

Like Anaïs Nin's fiction, her Diary is also a collage composition. The assembled elements are the bits and pieces of her life. . . . Selected from the mass of materials of the unpublished diary, the passages that comprise each published volume are themselves a collage composition presenting a phase in the life of their creator. (p. 6)

[*Collages*] is a superb example of how an inventive writer can adapt a technique from the visual arts to literature, in this case fusing a variety of apparently unrelated materials into a striking composition. A more ambitious, a deeper book than its easy surface and gentle humor suggest, *Collages* is composed of nineteen short blocks of prose, beginning and ending with the same passage. This circular structure contains some twenty-two characters in an abundance of quickly sketched settings. . . . *Collages* gives the impression of having been put together from Nin's writer's scrap bag, conceived from the energy of her determination to create something interesting out of her leftover characters, situations, and settings. Again, she wants to use everything. (p. 9)

Collage art, like all art, works magic transformations. In this book Anaïs Nin repeatedly shows fantasy and dream enriching life, providing the loves that a narrow "reality" denies, dissolving the boundaries between the natural and the perverse, the impossible and the marvelous, comforting and reassuring the lonely and the isolated. . . . In *Collages* imagination is sovereign. (p. 10)

The concept of the self is very important in any exploration of Nin's writings, and it is difficult to isolate a single definition of "self," notwithstanding the many references to it. Nin does not seem to be concerned with the self as essence. Instead, she writes about the self in motion, in relationships with others, learning, searching, suffering, recovering, gathering still more experience. In short, Nin writes about the self as a process, almost as an urge toward the discovery and completion of itself. Gradually, though, it seems that Nin has come close to adopting a basically Jungian idea of the self. . . . It is particularly important to distinguish between the self and the *persona,* the mask or socialized dimension of a human being. (p. 12)

In dramatizing the journey of an "I" toward recognition of its self, again and again Nin chooses to explore the complexity of relationships or the impact of two selves on each other. She uses the terms "fusion" and "merging" to describe intense personal relationships. (p. 13)

The discovery of self becomes possible [for Nin] in the process of living relationships, of constant interaction between the individual and phenomena, the individual and other people. (p. 14)

House of Incest portrays the psychic torment of a woman who can experience love but not her physical nature. She cannot express sensuality or sexuality. The language of Nin's book evokes an oppressive atmosphere of erotic tantalization and paralysis; impossible pleasures beckon from every direction. The unnamed "I" is the center of the design. (p. 15)

Like the "I" of *House of Incest,* the young woman at the center of "Winter of Artifice" seeks to expand her identity through an act of psychic fusion. The novella is a collage of relatively homogeneous elements that are held into design by the consciousness of the dominant—again unnamed—central personage. Again, too, a psychic adventure with fusion has a strong individual tone which gives the book its appropriate metaphors and rhythms. Projecting the love of daughter and father, Nin in "Winter of Artifice" evokes and interprets the ambivalence of fusion that she described in her book on Lawrence, defending this ambivalence as an essential factor in all relationships of deep involvement.

Again the reader is shown that fusion, though necessary to the ego of the developing self, poses serious risks to identity. (pp. 15-16)

The quest that is traced again and again in Nin's writings actually involves a very radical concept: the abandonment of the idea of the self as a given fixed entity or essence. We create ourselves as we live, Nin explains poetically in her books and in the example of her own life that is revealed in the Diary. The idea of the self as a collage of experiences is central to Nin's psychological vision. (p. 17)

Nin has been searching for "another kind of language, the inspirational, which is the one that *penetrates our unconscious directly* [italics mine] and doesn't need to be analyzed or interpreted in a cerebral way. It penetrates us in the way that music does, through the senses." In denoting or pointing to objects and even to concepts, the word is more precise than the musical note or phrase, but verbal expression is more abstract, less direct in sensuous power than are the sounds, colors, forms, and rhythms of the nonverbal arts. That is why Nin, like so many other twentieth-century writers, has borrowed as widely as possible from the other arts. (p. 22)

Dispensing with plot and with the framework of conventional chronology, Nin portrays her characters again and again in a series of "shots" that depend for their power on the imagery of highly selective detail. Her language is metaphorical but never purely decorative. It is the language of lyrical poetry through which a personal attitude is compressed in a few words or phrases that express an individual sensibility. Nin does not describe. She interprets, and in the act of interpretation she re-creates her subjects over and over again, as she must do if she is to be faithful to their complexity and their growth. . . . Nin's writing is filled with patterns that are natural and spontaneous, having emerged from associations. The form is organic; it consists of repetitions; inversions; superimpositions; and, more and more often in Nin's later prose, of improvisatory flights in which images are often treated as are themes in jazz. Fluency, fluidity, a sense of motion, and of continuity are what Nin seeks in her writing, an orchestration of a great many elements into a composition that moves through time horizontally and vertically at the same instant, expressing emotion with a power that is impossible to attain in conventional realistic fiction. (p. 23)

[Two] of the main themes of Nin's later work [are found in *Under a Glass Bell*]: woman's conflicts (particularly with the role of mother) and the struggle of the artist to achieve joyous, unrestrained power of expression. The metaphors that Nin introduces in this collection appear again and again in her later work. She uses them not only to bind together her impressions in a single sketch but also to weave a unifying strand through the book. (p. 25)

The images of these early pieces appear again and again in Nin's fiction and in her Diaries: water, boats, musical instruments, mirrors, labyrinths, veils, shadows and fogs, blood, birds, voyages, dreams, births. But each image has an individual history of variations in presentation, diversity, and complexity, as Nin explores each one in a variety of moods and at various periods in her own development. (pp. 25-6)

["Winter of Artifice"] is a mature work, very sophisticated technically, in which Anaïs Nin first fully displays her talent for adapting the structure of the nonverbal arts to fiction. It is a ballet of words in which music and movement are so skillfully balanced and so subtly interwoven that, though the perceptive reader may be always aware of a musical quality as he reads, he isn't likely to be distracted by the search to identify the predominating musical medium. . . .

Dance unites several of Nin's most important themes: the power of art, which is itself its own goal; the possibility of turning to beauty for therapy and for healing; the association of movement and pattern with the life process. It is essential not simply to move but to move to a meaningful rhythm. . . .

Nin often imitates dance structure in alternating solos or duets with large group scenes. Parties and café ensembles occur throughout the novels of *Cities of the Interior* like rituals, bringing disparate elements into moments of splendid unity, moments of celebration. (p. 31)

The practice of alternating group scenes with more solitary or intimate ones gives a structure of alternating rhythms and moods. Thematically, this alternation stresses the subjective and objective worlds that Anaïs Nin constantly strives to bring together into moments of fusion. . . . Anaïs Nin ends each novel by reminding her characters—and readers—of new worlds. Instead of closing down with a neat, rounded-off (classical) resolution, she makes her novels open up at the end, exploding into a variety of surprising directions. . . . (p. 32)

When the five novels are regarded as a single composition, *Cities of the Interior* may be compared tn an abstract expressionist composition whose organization is dominated by huge areas of strong primary colors: yellow for Lillian who is exuberant and strong, garrulous, chaotic, passionate but inhibited; red for Sabina, a wild, dissatisfied woman who is always burning with unfulfilled desire; blue for the wise, reserved, self-controlled Djuna. These stand out against a more subtly colored background. Imagined in this way, the canvas seems to have been created by a series of improvisations. It is unfinished; it will lend itself to further elaboration, to the elimination of some elements and the addition of others, to redistribution of emphases, or even more drastic changes in the overall design. (p. 36)

In Anaïs Nin's writing perhaps no word appears so frequently in so many contexts or with so many nuances as the word "dream." Nin's vision of the dream gives continuity and profundity to her meaning as woman and artist alike. Dream provides the controlling image of unity and transformation in her fiction. . . . Her belief in the positive nature of the unconscious has given Nin many valuable insights. Even more importantly, it has given her processes for healing that range from the discoveries and consolations of psychoanalysis to a philosophy of creation that connects a theory of the development of the self with that of the artist. Although Nin's concept of the dream has altered slightly as she has experienced her life, it remains basically a vision of human love. (p. 44)

In particular the dream has given her a personalized approach to the creation of fictional characters, along with certain convictions about the structure and language that have by now become accepted tenets of twentieth-century thought. Her experience with psychoanalysis gave Nin personal proof of Bergson's theoretical and Proust's esthetic views of space, time and personality. Like the theory of relativity, which was made public at about the same time as Freud's *Interpretation of Dreams*, dreams show how time and space have meaning only when fused; they are not themselves reality but ways of orienting oneself toward it. (pp. 48-9)

The great importance placed by psychologists on the unconscious is the single most influential factor in Nin's approach to characterization. . . . The goal of Nin's fiction is the portrayal of her characters' hidden selves. She achieves this not with continuous linear description, but by portraying them quickly but repeatedly at certain highly selective moments. (pp. 49-50)

Nin's emphasis on states of feeling and awareness has meant that her readers miss such familiar guides in traditional characterization as family names, ages, occupations, places of residence, and similar details of surface. (p. 50)

One of the most common complaints against Nin's fiction is that her characters are "all herself." To voice this as a negative feeling is to reveal a misunderstanding of how characters in fiction are created; all are projections of some part of the author's self. It would be more to the point to criticize a novelist for drawing shallow characterizations based more nearly on observation than on empathy and emotional understanding. The women of *Cities of the Interior* are individuals; yet each symbolizes an aspect of woman: "Djuna, perception [it is she who bears the closest resemblance to Nin's public self]; Stella, blind suffering; Sabina, the free woman; Lillian, the one who seeks freedom in aggression." Nin's characters are perfectly individualized. . . . (pp. 52-3)

The position of the dream at the center of Nin's art may be wonderfully illustrated by looking at one of her most brilliant pieces, "The Voice." Here the dream is truly a vehicle of mobility. "The Voice" is a virtuoso piece that spins off from contrasting motions: soaring, plummeting, floating, sinking, spiraling, rushing, or flowing, along a horizontal or lying quietly on a bed to daydream. This thoughtful work is neither a story nor a sketch, but an animated essay or exposition of ideas through seemingly random selections of characters and incidents. (p. 58)

The spiral figure used by Nin to represent the dream [in "The Voice"] is a subtle choice, for its sweeping movement has four dimensions: from right to left; left to right; upwards; and downwards. At the center from which arises the spiraling dream, is the self. Passing beyond this center in one direction there is confrontation with self—life. (p. 67)

One of the remarkable aspects of the adventure of Nin's life has been her determination to explore the nature of woman as fully as time and energy would permit. An even more dangerous ambition has been her desire to make of this exploration an assertion of her own multi-dimensionality. . . . She has insisted that one role is not enough for a woman, particularly when this is a biologically determined role that covers but a third of her life span and makes no allowance for any but biological capabilities. Again and again Nin has proclaimed and has shown by her life that woman, like man, is complex and possesses the energy and the flexibility to play a variety of roles simultaneously. (pp. 68-9)

The Christian ideal of woman, worshipped and adored for centuries, is that of the Virgin Mary. Mary is a mother yet she is chaste. The supreme image of woman in the Western world combines two obviously irreconcilable conditions: virginity and motherhood. No woman can possibly live up to this ideal. (p. 69)

So powerful an influence has the Christian ideal of woman had on Western culture that woman feels ennobled by her own sacrifices and enriched by her own suffering. . . . Nin's books trace her own and her characters' struggles against the mother in themselves, for whether it is her sexuality or her impulse toward work that is blocked, the woman must —in each case—bring out of her self a will toward individuation that is strong enough to counter the force of the internalized mother image. (p. 71)

In Nin's writings the sexual woman is represented by Sabina, an important presence since *House of Incest*. . . .

In *House of Incest* Nin depicted—and with unmistakable agony—the split in modern woman which has divided her into parts, the body cut off from the emotions. The "I" of *House* struggles to attain a sense of union with her body, her sensuality and sexuality. Self-aware, responsible, the "I" is capable of love but cannot express her sexuality. (p. 80)

Nin goes beyond questions about woman's sexuality to probe the vast and very troublesome area of how individual sexual fulfillment can be reconciled with the human need for devotion, loyalty, and stability in a union of two. (p. 84)

The recovery of woman's complexity, which Jungian thought makes possible, has been immensely valuable to Anaïs Nin. The ancient relationship of woman to the moon serves to restore or bring back into the open two aspects of feminine nature which Judaism and Christianity have condemned and attempted to repress: her destructive power and her sexuality. Anthropologists and other scholars now know that the idea of a "virgin" goddess did not originally indicate a sexual condition but a social and psychological one. A "virgin" was—simply—unmarried. . . .

Anaïs Nin's discovery of this older ideal of woman had rich consequences, as well it might, for it enabled her to conceptualize a fuller, more complex idea of woman than that she inherited from Spanish Catholicism. As mother, woman is endowed with tremendous powers of destruction, something Nin had longed for ever since she met Henry Miller and grew to be in awe of his straightforward devotion to writing. (p. 89)

Rarely does Anaïs Nin receive credit for her daring social views or for writing about areas of experience that have previously been forbidden to women by force of public opinion. Her predecessor, the absolute mistress of the realm of eroticism and love, is Colette. . . . In their writing both women have explored homoeroticism and homosexuality (male and female); the friendships between homosexual men and heterosexual women; love between the older woman and the younger man; adultery; the psychic complications of the love triangle; and the grief and anger of the woman who, aroused, fails to achieve orgasm. Besides the topics that she shares with Colette, Nin has written of fantasized incest (see especially "Winter of Artifice"); or onanism ("The Voice"); of the white woman's sexual exploitation of the black man (*Spy*); of fellatio (*Collages*); and, most notoriously, of the female Don Juan. The last topic has never, as far as I know, been explored in the serious literature of England or the U.S. It is not surprising that *A Spy in the House of Love* was turned down by 127 publishers or that this book, once printed at Nin's own expense, met with misunderstanding and condemnation (even from women). (p. 91)

Nin's literary values have for too long been neglected, especially in the United States. The fact that she has expressed these values in so many ways places her at the center of a new movement, perhaps a countermovement, in American literature. Traditionally, writing that is intuitive, introspective, delicate, tentative, explorative, meditative, has been ridiculed as "precious" or "feminine"; this fact says more about our cultural values than about literature itself. Nin's statement of her beliefs, her articulate opposition to Miller and Durrell, gave her courage, once she saw her own thoughts in words. And now this courage has spread to other writers, male and female alike, who feel a greater confidence in their "sensitive" orientation toward writing. *The Novel of the Future* is "dedicated to sensitive Americans. May they create a sensitive America." (p. 112)

As the years passed and Nin developed as a writer, she began to make her Diary a work of art. It was never a typical writer's notebook or the "sketchbook" into which Otto Rank at one time hoped to transform it. Nin's Diary gradually became a work in its own right, one with all the polish and distinction of art. As a woman, with responsibilities and obligations to others that often seemed more important than her personal concerns, Nin has used her Diary to fill out her life; it is a complement; it is the expression of the dimensions of her self that her life has not always had room for. Nin's Diary is a more authentic, certainly a more complete, deeper, and fuller expression of her self than the actual life she has lived. Although her reasons for keeping the Diary have changed somewhat through the years, her faithfulness to it would seem remarkable were it not for the fact that this Diary has come to represent a self, a more developed, a vaster and more powerful self than that of the woman who wrote in it. (pp. 118-19)

Anaïs Nin's Diary is neither a diary in the usual sense—a candid, uncensored record of the events of a life—nor is it a work of fiction like the frankly autobiographical "novels" of writers like Leiris, Celine, or Henry Miller. From the 1930s on Nin clearly regarded her Diary not as a notebook but as a self-justifying and self-sustaining work. . . . [The] great paradox of the Diary is that, though it tells us much more than we have known about any living person, it tells us far less than we would like to know. (pp. 121-22)

Each volume of the Diary represents a phase in the unfolding life of the artist who is its author. Everything she records is filtered through a sensibility as fragile as a spiderweb that vibrates to every nuance of feeling yet is as tensile as a construction of fine steel. The individual Diaries are self-sustaining, each with a movement and a structure of its own; yet each moves from one to another in a fluent prose that is filled with the details of cultural history as the personal story evolves in a depth that probes the unconscious along with the external world. Comparable in this respect to the individual novels of *Cities of the Interior,* the individual Diaries are autonomous works that nevertheless assume an enhanced value and a richer texture when each is seen in context of the overall composition.

Viewed as a design, the Diary may be said to represent a spiral circling in a clockwise direction that signifies creative motion. The spiral rises from the central point of Nin's self, the voice that controls the Diaries; this spiral signifies the relationship between unity and multiplicity; it is related to the mandala. The spiral is also associated with dances of incantation that are used for healing purposes, and thus remind us of the circling dancer who is evoked at the close of *House of Incest*. It reminds us as well of the elaboration of the spiral as a metaphor for the dream that is part of the final rhapsody of "The Voice." A symbol of the evolution of the universe and of personal growth, the spiral of Nin's Diaries sweeps into motion from the point of the self, the "I" whose power of perception makes possible the apprehension and the interpretation of all that we experience. (pp. 123-24)

In being the first, Diary I has the advantage of announcing the unique qualities of the entire project. The impact of this book purely as confession can scarcely be underestimated. Hypnotically, it draws even a reluctant reader into the author's terrifying yet fascinating confusion, into the tangle of fears and desires, the sense of a psyche in labor (to use a perhaps impossible metaphor). The absorption with self seems unprecedented. For the introspective reader, it is a surprise that lures him deeper and deeper into the depths of Nin's personal reality, a maze of perceptions among which she gropes in an attempt to emerge with a lucid understanding of herself. (p. 124)

Beneath its apparently unorganized flowing surface there lies concealed a traditional structure based upon the ancient theme of the search for a father. In this case the search is conducted not by a young man, as in the epics of the past, but by a woman whose quest is for the artist father she has lost, along with a way of life she yearns to recover. (p. 125)

The second Diary describes a period of sadness, disappointment, and threatened loss. A different sort of struggle permeates its pages. The structure arises from conflict, various types of conflict in an interwoven presentation: the individual and the collective; Nin's personal determination to live and to create art contrasted to the struggle of Spain to free herself from political and economic tyranny; the undercurrent of the alliances and misalliances that were to lead to World War II. . . . Although the diarist often expresses depression and even a sense of defeat, the reader is always aware of her tenacious commitment to survival and growth. (p. 126)

The bright and glowing area of Diary II is an important journey to a source of artistic inspiration and personal renewal. This is the trip to Morocco. . . . Her language becomes brilliantly painted and pungent with odors, everything animated by her joy of discovery and fascination with the strange. The city of Fez especially attracted the author. . . . Nin burst forth with an articulate formulation of the goals that she was to adopt with growing assurance during the later decades of her career. "Woman must not fabricate. She must descend into the real womb and expose its secrets and its labyrinths. She must describe it as the city of Fez, with its Arabian Nights gentleness, tranquility and mystery." (pp. 127-28)

Diaries III and IV, 1939 to 1947, describe Nin's second enforced removal from France to the United States against the background of her continued war with herself and her absorption in the lives of a host of personages who were part of the cultural life of New York City. . . .

The theme of Diary III is loss. Again and again Nin laments the loss of Europe, its friendliness toward artists, the sense of camaraderie found in the busy yet relaxed cafes, the acceptance of the life of the senses, compared to the fear and disapproval of the Americans. . . . (p. 128)

Diary IV is the story of the writer's emergence into public life. . . . The great growth that animates Diary IV is found in Nin's speculations about the arts, their interconnections, and their influence on her own style and approach to literary structure. In the 1940s Nin's Diary began to become, in part, a meditation on literature. Meanwhile, the style of the diary adapted subtly to the new emphasis on ideas; there are fewer passages of self-analysis and many more brief essays on writing, literature, and the other arts.

Diary IV is populated with creative people, not celebrities but the young writers, dancers, and musicians with whom Nin identified in her sense of exclusion from the New York literary establishment. (pp. 129-30)

Near its conclusion Diary IV suddenly opens into the vista of a journey. Its author has grown. She has begun to think deeply about writing. She has resisted the neurotic lure of involvement with the sort of man she knows is bad for her. She is beginning to see through the "transparent" children and to understand how they exclude her. (p. 131)

The brilliant gold face on the jacket of the fifth Diary announces a rebirth. This is the presence, now vivid and magnificently self-confident, of the writer as a woman, for the emphasis of the fifth book reverses that of the third and fourth to bring us into the evolving consciousness, the newly asserted physical life of the woman. It seems that Anaïs Nin, having achieved her confidence as a writer, returns during the phase from 1948 to 1955 to balance her developing powers as artist with a renewal of sensuous feminity. (pp. 132-33)

Intermingled with the joyous mood of Diary V is a quiet sadness in the form of a new recognition; it is death that Nin admits to her writing at this time: the death of Dr. Hernandez in *Seduction of the Minotaur;* in her *Diary* the deaths, first, of her father, then of her mother. While the father dominated the earlier Diaries, Nin's mother is the central figure here. . . .

The air of gentle acceptance that pervades *Diary V* softens the moments of grief as they are not softened in earlier volumes. (p. 134)

Diary V, finally, is a success story. Privileged to share the life of a woman who is determined to seek her own evolution, the reader also shares her success. . . . This book is a tribute to tenacity. The success it depicts is entirely free from materialism or the desire to interpret one's success as a proof of superiority over others. A spiritual quality manifests itself in the pages of Diary V. There is an acceptance of a destiny that is very far indeed from a narrow concern with self. . . .

The sixth volume of the Diary brings Nin the realization of a cherished dream: the publication of Diary I. . . . Diary VI is strikingly different from its predecessors. Nin herself is now firmly established in the realm of the external. She is a mature artist with a total view of reality and of people that is a contrast to the delicate, tentative, evanescent feelings of the earlier volumes. Diary V glows with an aura of the sensuous. Diary VI is sometimes almost crisp. (p. 135)

In Diary VI the emphasis shifts from Anaïs, the woman who struggles to maintain her image as an artist, to the culture in which her battle for recognition is taking place. Volume VI is more nearly historical than any of the earlier volumes. . . .

Another of Nin's many faces is revealed in Diary VI. She becomes active as a critic of the arts. (p. 136)

Although the emphasis of Diary VI is on the outer life, the personal theme is always present, and the great concern in both spheres is transformation. As always psychoanalysis is Nin's personal faith and her means of achieving the transformations she desires in her personal life. And during the period chronicled in Diary VI the enemy that Nin had constantly to combat was the bitterness she felt at being overlooked by the literary establishment of the U.S. (p. 137)

To read Diary VI, which spans a decade ending in 1966, is a strange experience in which there is a measure of dramatic irony. Today we know what Nin did not know when she concluded her Diary entries for 1966: that she achieved recognition and fame; that she established an exchange of feelings and ideas with the world; that she was intensely involved in the process of transforming the cultural values of the U.S.; and that she was moving closer and closer to achieving her proper evaluation and respect as an artist. Although Volume VII of the Diary is not yet in print, the recent collections *A Woman Speaks* and *In Favor of the Sensitive Man* give a full portrait of the Anaïs Nin who emerged into public life after the Diaries began to appear in 1966. The woman who spoke in the 1970s was a gayer, happier, more powerful, and more fulfilled woman than the one we met in the Diaries of the earlier years. The woman herself was a tribute to her own steady belief in growth and in maturity.

It is an irony worth noting that Nin achieved fame in the culture in which she had felt uneasy for decades, and which she had frequently criticized for its insensitivity and its neglect of the artist. The explanation of this irony is not simple. It is partly that there actually *is* a subtle and gradual transformation of values occurring (to some extent as a result of Nin's influence); but it is also partly because Nin herself fit into the tradition of the popular American myth of the person who, without many advantages, "makes good" by virtue of persistence and hard work. Nin has often said that her "genius" is really a quality of tenacity. She was persistent in developing her talent, in combating her own self-defeating feelings and actions; in fighting illness; in maintaining artistic integrity against the pressure of more or less steady critical disdain; in sustaining a faith in the future of serious writing in this country (a faith that is more and more difficult for writers to sustain); and in her devotion to her friends and fellow writers. Nin's commonsense and her generosity are always evident. (p. 140)

The literary work that Nin's Diary most closely resembles is Proust's *roman-fleuve,* the great masterpiece of autobiographical fiction, *A la recherche du temps perdu.* This is both because of a profound affinity between the two authors and because of direct influence. (p. 142)

Proust's use of his own life to create the *Remembrance* gave Nin a magnificent example of what can be created in art by a sensitive and thorough exploitation of one's self. . . . Nin has defended Proust's power of realism for she sees that his vision, like her own, is comprehensive: an art of surfaces and of depths projected simultaneously within a flowing structure. (p. 143)

Nin's eye for . . . absurdity is sharp, but her empathy prevents her from mocking. Nin's evocations of places are as detailed and as appealing as are her portraits of the hundreds of people who appear in the pages of the Diary. When printed alone, Nin's descriptions of foreign cities and countries are self-sustaining and impressive, but they take on added vitality when read in the context of the Diary among the monochromatic scenes of Paris or New York. . . . The way that travel breaks the rhythm of Nin's life, giving it variety and providing periods of renewal, is an essential part of Nin's experience, and the alternating pace is a part of the Diary's underlying structure.

As in the *Remembrance,* in the Diary the structure wrought by the meditation of consciousness upon its own experience knows no boundaries; the flowing movement is a "tale without beginning or end." It is vast, capacious, and easily accommodates all that Nin responds to vividly before recounting these experiences in vivid language. Nin's Diary, like Proust's novel, is an act of devotion to art. He called his novel "a cathedral." Nin's Diary is the only sustained meditation on art that exists in the literature of the U.S. . . . In Nin's and Proust's writing alike, the love of art is so fervent that it cannot be satisfied by the *act* of making a work of art, but must also—and simultaneously—comprise a meditation upon itself. (pp. 149-50)

Nin has repeatedly given Proust credit for teaching her how to break down conventional chronology. . . . (p. 151)

Continuity and discontinuity. Both describe the nature of the self. The self is continuous because there is a center unique to each individual that remains stable, but not fixed, as it evolves through a lifetime. (p. 152)

Not everybody will wish to lay claim to Nin's Diary, and this is partly because Nin speaks with the voice of a woman, speaking not only for women and, beyond this, for the "sensitive Americans" to whom she dedicated *The Novel of the Future*. It is extraordinary but true that the first autobiography of the artist in the United States has been written by a woman. (p. 157)

Sharon Spencer, in her Collage of Dreams: The Writings of Anaïs Nin *(© 1977 by Sharon Spencer; reprinted by permission of Ohio University Press, Athens), Swallow, 1977, 188 p.*

BLAKE MORRISON

For readers who find it hard to stay with Anais Nin's novels for more than several pages (no, let's be fair: for more than one page), the publication of her collected fiction isn't going to be the major event which Sharon Spencer's introduction would have us suppose. Nin herself described *Cities of the Interior* as 'an endless novel', and for anyone wading faithfully through 589 pages of such sub-Lawrentian wisdom as 'A breast touched for the first time is a breast never touched before' the description is going to sound all too appropriate. Still, somewhere within all the gushing are a few pleasantly erotic moments. (p. 631)

Blake Morrison, "Looking Backwards," in New Statesman *(© 1978 The Statesman & Nation Publishing Co. Ltd.), Vol. 96, No. 2486, November 10, 1978, pp. 630-31.**

EMMA FISHER

In fiction [Anais Nin] tried to do something new, and she saw it as intricately linked with the fact that she was a woman; she was anti-intellectual, relying on feeling, and she was one of those people who believe that 'It is man's separateness, his so-called objectivity, which has made him lose contact. . . . Woman was born to *be* the connecting link between man and his human self.' . . . She wanted also to be a great artist; what is there in her books for people who do not find psychological guidance in the Diaries, and are not converted to her beliefs about men and women?

She was fond of using music, also painting and dance, as metaphors for writing. She wanted to communicate directly, to make words serve her intuitions that went beyond words. Rather than show you, she tells you, in fantastic, bright, rich images, woven together like a dazzling carpet. She often writes in the imperfect, less often in the past—describing the inner evolution of feelings over a span of time, rather than surface events moment by moment. Repetition is an essential part of the musical effect she wants. Her concern is always to see, to understand clearly the meaning of events for each character. . . . Because her female characters are all faces of Woman, it sometimes does not seem to matter which woman one is reading about; the characters melt and dissolve into each other, and indeed want to become each other.

By now it must be clear that I don't like her novels very much. She succeeds in making one feel immensely guilty about saying anything against her, because of her courage, goodness and persistence. She has an answer to most criticisms; if you say she was too self-absorbed, she will answer that it is only by concentrating on the personal, by sorting out one's own experience, that one can approach truth. But this is not what I have against the novels. 'I am not interested in fiction. I want faithfulness,' she said in an early volume of the Diary. She attacks Proust for his 'generalisation', adding: 'If only Proust had spoken for himself.' . . . [In her novels she herself] both generalises and says 'I, Anais', and the two do not fuse. The novels do not transcend their didactic origins: 'I would like to convert the diary into a long novel . . . I do want to dramatise the conflicts of woman. Conflict between maternal love and creation. Between romanticism and realism. Between expansion and sacrifice.' And yet, as well as being most of the characters in the novels, Nin is the air they breathe, the world they inhabit, and the way they think is the way she thinks. In fact she, the sensitive and brilliant writer, is too obviously doing their feeling and thinking for them.

Of course her method is not entirely unsuccessful. In *The Four-Chambered Heart,* the middle book of the five making up *Cities of the Interior,* the repetition, the revolving of the same situation as it gets worse and worse, is particularly suitable for the subject—the three-cornered relationship between Djuna, the fictional personality closest to herself, her lover Rango and his wife Zora. . . . This is a straight lift from Nin's own life and she tells it movingly. But I am moved in spite of her rolling, relentless style, with its many appositions and restatements. She speaks like a seer. The art of understatement is foreign to her. The states of mind she describes are real and powerful, but they produce in me the desire to escape, to flatten their reality and get out of the book, instead of a desire to believe and (to put it bluntly) to read on.

Her book of essays, *In Favour of the Sensitive Man,* is characteristic. As usual, she bravely plunges in with unsupported generalities about men and women, art and music, and the volume ends with travel pieces. . . . Her susceptibility to beauty makes her travel writing almost unreally beautiful; can Bali really be the Paradise she describes? Her optimism . . . is part of this desire for the best; admirable but not entirely convincing. (pp. 21-2)

Emma Fisher, "Female Faces," in The Spectator

(© 1979 by The Spectator; *reprinted by permission of* The Spectator*), Vol. 242, No. 7854, January 20, 1979, pp. 21-2.*

ROSALYN DREXLER

Anaïs Nin, better known for her diaries but better sold for her pornography ("Delta of Venus"), has left us another peep show in "Little Birds," a volume of 13 short stories that threaten to stir the erotic imagination.

In the preface to "Delta of Venus" she says that it was hunger that drove her and a number of starving writer and poet friends to collaborate on these droll tales. . . .

Her mysterious client had specifications; his orders were to "leave out the poetry and descriptions of anything but sex. Concentrate on sex." Nin felt that it was this exclusion of poetry from his life that forced him to resort to literary aphrodisiacs. . . .

The lubricous and sexually curious might, in time of need, find this volume of nostalgic sexware just the right thing to prod a lazy fantasy life; things are named, yet never become explicit enough to be judged obscene. . . . One imagines the wealthy gentleman who commissioned this charming curio to be a circumspect and discriminating connoisseur with a penchant for all sorts of erotica, one who would be shocked by today's insistence on the clinical close-up or the use of four-letter words in place of punctuation.

As I read "Little Birds" a common refrain seemed to unite the stories, that of impotence at the very moment it was inopportune to be so. Also rampant was the sadistic withholding of sexual favors, and the preference by males for females who were either virgins, statues or corpses (or acted as if they were). . . .

Are these perhaps attempts by Nin to help the male reader identify with her amorous heroes? The lapses of tumescence are only momentary, though, and every story in "Little Birds" becomes a sexual success story. Why not? The value of the stories lies in putting to rest feelings of fear and guilt, burying them at a great distance from the source. Once sex (in "Little Birds") is consummated, the object of desire and fantasy is allowed to disappear, never to bear witness against the main orgasmic character (or reader). This is ideal, is it not? Pleasure without repercussions? And this is what the reader will get from "Little Birds."

Rosalyn Drexler, "Peep Show Encore," in The New York Times Book Review *(© 1979 by The New York Times Company; reprinted by permission), April 8, 1979, p. 28.*

LINDA TAMKIN

Underneath the coarse brown cover [of *Little Birds: Erotica*] lies a treasure. Nin awakens the mind and senses with thirteen well-crafted tales. The settings range from a Parisian artist's studio to a moonlit beach. The combinations of lovers and settings mix the exotic with the erotic. Like a haiku poem, Nin captures with one image what other writers explore through endless words. The oriental quality is not surprising, since many of the stories draw upon material from the *Kama-Sutra*.

Nin was supposedly paid a dollar a page to write erotica. Yet her patron warned her to "leave out the poetry." Her glorious failure to heed his warning is evident. It is as if she wraps hardcore pornographic material in delicate gauze. The sexual gems on each page are rounded out with a luxuriance of detail. Unlike most writers of erotica, Nin's writing defies boredom. . . .

This collection continues the tradition established by the best-seller, *Delta of Venus*. (p. 43)

Linda Tamkin, "Books in Review: 'Little Birds: Erotica'," in West Coast Review of Books *(copyright 1979 by Rapport Publishing Co., Inc.), Vol. 5, No. 4, July, 1979, pp. 43-4.*

* * *

NORRIS, Leslie 1921-

Norris is a Welsh poet, editor, playwright, short story writer, and translator of medieval Welsh verse. His purpose as a poet is, in his own words, "to recreate, not to describe." (See also *Contemporary Authors*, Vols. 11-12; *Contemporary Authors Permanent Series*, Vol. 1.)

JOHN FULLER

Some of [the poems in *Finding Gold*] are bulked out with dull rhythms and language. He doesn't take short cuts enough, and is guilty of epithets ('brazen Africa', 'aching silences', etc.) that really needed a rethink. This said, he emerges as a very likeable new voice, fresh, elegiac, organized. . . . If he is sentimental sometimes, a little too eloquent perhaps, such defects are invariably smartened-up by neat observation and by touches of honesty that radiate thankfully in the rhetorical flow. . . . Norris can write, and though sometimes in danger of turning out the usual nature-notes, he communicates a real sense of life endured, of the flux tamed.

John Fuller, "Poetry: 'Finding Gold'," in London Magazine *(© London Magazine 1967), Vol. 7, No. 3, July, 1967, p. 88.*

CHARLES MOLESWORTH

[Leslie Norris's] views are ordered, rhymed, and syntactically finished. Poems such as *Old Voices* and *Early Frost* almost overflow with the melodious streams of Dylan Thomas . . . , but even then control and reason dominate. The typical mode is that of a weakly affirmative reverie tried out before a landscape, though the best poem in the book, *A True Death*, is a strongly reassuring elegy for Vernon Watkins. There are twenty-three poems on thirty pages, with very little stanzaic or prosodic inventiveness. . . . The phrases here place the objects in a temporal and spatial setting which is a trifle too set-up. Personal space loses itself in the traditional poetic environment. (p. 111)

Charles Molesworth, "Some Locals," in Poetry *(© 1972 by The Modern Poetry Association; reprinted by permission of the Editor of* Poetry*), Vol. CXX, No. 2, May, 1972, pp. 107-13.**

DOUGLAS DUNN

It is against a background such as the entrenchment of poetry in a previous tradition of thought about Nature that Leslie Norris's poem "Mountains Polecats Pheasants" has to be seen. It is elegiac, regretting the mortality of creatures and places before the encroachment of machines such as the motor car, which, in the poem, replace polecats as killers of pheasant. Norris's poem is reminiscent of William

Stafford's American version of the subject in "Travelling Through the Dark." But the attitude is familiar in any case, from society as well as literature. Nature poets, and others concerned with countryside and animals, become the guardians of wildness. They seek to preserve what is accidental and given. It is unremarkable that ideas of age and origin and accident should be involved in a description of natural beauty; or that Norris should write that

> The wind
> Over my shoulder
> Blows from the cold of time,

attempting not only to dramatise the rudimentary presence of the elements as ongoing, but, in a poem about cromlechs or dolmens, mystifying the permanence of the past. For it is the fault of contemporary nature poetry that it springs backward in thought too easily, uttering a global nostalgia. And this is an intellectual and human fault. It represents a state of mind which finds it too difficult to work within existing society, and by doing so contribute to its change.

Douglas Dunn, "Books & Writers: 'Mountains, Polecats, Pheasants'," in Encounter *(© 1974 by Encounter Ltd.), Vol. XLII, No. 4, April, 1974, p. 84.*

ALAN BROWNJOHN

Leslie Norris's personal seam of nature poetry is not a large one, but he works it with increasing sureness and pertinacity. In [*Mountains, Polecats, Pheasants and other Elegies*], he again emerges mainly as the ex-countryman for whom memories and sudden rediscoveries of country experience break in on the world of the indoors, or of mechanised civilisation, to bring regret at the increasing distance from us of the real world they represent. His best poems here—and they are very good indeed—come where he is poised between the harsh nature he reveres and the comforts he guiltily cherishes. 'Beachmaster' and 'Shadows' show him writing with splendid energy about marine and river life, too thoroughly immersed in what he is describing to be watching himself in case he is alienated from it by his indoor living. (p. 808)

Alan Brownjohn, "Scorch Marks," in New Statesman *(© 1974 The Statesman & Nation Publishing Co. Ltd.), Vol. 87, No. 2255, June 7, 1974, pp. 808-09.**

ROGER GARFITT

What one misses, for most of Leslie Norris's . . . collection, *Mountains Pheasants Polecats and other elegies*, is the sense of tension creating a movement of style. Elegy can be a paradoxical form, possessing an adroitness in direct ratio to its emotive charge. As Auden proved, the more risks you take with it, the more passionate the balance you can finally achieve. So, here, the human elegies have more daring, and more weight: whereas those for vanishing life forms seem a little inhibited, rather consciously even-handed.

Something in the form of long poems seems to over-extend them. . . . There is a cloying element in the diction, too: 'Black as nightfur', 'mortal stain', 'a fury of instinct'. The translations from the Welsh, however, have an energy that can carry the traditional phrasing: and in the shorter poems, particularly 'At Usk' and 'Stone and Fern', essentially the same formal approach, of repeated elements shaped into a cadence, works beautifully. . . . (pp. 117-18)

Roger Garfitt, "In Retreat to the Edges," in London Magazine *(© London Magazine 1974), Vol. 14, No. 4, November, 1974, pp. 111-20.**

MARTIN LEVIN

[The luminous short stories in *Sliding*] have the coherence of a novel. They are linked not by plot but by place and point of view. Most of them begin with a seemingly transient happening that signifies something much larger in the narrator's past. The title story, about a group of boys sliding on a frozen pond, captures the freshness of a first time experience and its bittersweet memory. . . .

All of the stories spring from the soil of the Welsh countryside, where even trivia is given a special radiance. . . . The quintessential story of the book—"Cocksfoot, Crested Dog's Tail, Sweet Vernal Grass"—refers to the grasses that border the village cemetery. The names of these grasses summon up the narrator's memory of "old intangible summers" before his father died; Mr. Norris compresses the turning points of a lifetime into his story beautifully. This and the other 13 interludes are a joy that one wants to read slowly, to make them last longer.

Martin Levin, "Fiction and Poetry: 'Sliding'," in The New York Times Book Review *(© 1976 by The New York Times Company; reprinted by permission), October 24, 1976, p. 47.*

ARDIS KIMZEY

The poems [in *Merlin & the Snake's Egg*] show a great regard for the young mind. The work is elegant, accessible, interesting and fresh in narration and content.

The range of the book is in itself an accomplishment. Singing trees weave lyric dreams, while the Winter Witch casts spells that "fill the dying year with the forest's moan." A strong mysticism and a mythic quality permeate the title poem. . . .

[The] poems are never abstract and never maudlin, but always alert to the "human beingness" of the situation. . . . (p. 25)

Ardis Kimzey, "Living Poets Are Coming Back," in The New York Times Book Review *(© 1978 by The New York Times Company; reprinted by permission), April 30, 1978, pp. 25, 38.**

O

O'CONNOR, Edwin 1918-1968

An American novelist, O'Connor drew many of his fictional settings and characterizations from his Irish-American Catholic background, creating novels that both entertain and contain important sociopolitical themes. Although his characters are at times reduced to caricature, his novels have been praised for their realistic dialogue and sensitive description. O'Connor won the 1962 Pulitzer Prize in Fiction for *The Edge of Sadness*. An earlier novel, *The Last Hurrah*, was subsequently made into a motion picture. (See also *Contemporary Authors*, Vols. 25-28, rev. ed.)

ANTHONY WEST

Edwin O'Connor's "The Last Hurrah" . . . arrives festooned with pre-publication laurels. . . . In view of all this, one is tempted to raise one's hat silently to the cortege and to let it pass on its way to oblivion with the best possible grace. The temptation is all the greater because it is difficult to discuss the book without infringing on a number of taboos that can be indicated by saying that its main subjects are the nature of city government in the New England states of the Union, the role of the Irish in municipal politics, and the relations between city machines and the Catholic Church. The approach chosen is to bring two clean-cut young persons, Adam and Maeve (get it? *Innocents*), into this thorny area by having them taken under the wing of the boy's uncle, old Frank Skeffington, as he launches his campaign for reelection to the mayoralty of a big Eastern-seaboard city. He loses the election, because he is an old-fashioned kind of political boss and times have changed, but in the course of his campaign Adam and Maeve discover what a charming, lovable, and heart-warming boss he is, what kindly, simple chaps—great-hearted, too, in their small way—his ward bosses and heelers are, and what a little thing peculation from the public funds really is, after all. (p. 121)

[From] the starting thesis—that a kindly thief is better than a plain greedy one—the line of thought advances to the conclusion that because some businessmen have been dishonest there is in general no difference between businessmen and crooked politicians, that there is no great gulf between charging a brokerage fee for handling a bond issue and slicing a little fat off the city budget here and there where it won't hurt. . . .

It is not immediately clear why Mr. O'Connor is laboring this puerile line of thought, and it can hardly be said that it becomes clear as the story develops; what does become clear is that the line of thought he advances is at once extremely simple and extremely confused. (p. 122)

One can imagine a powerful and convincing novel written tough-mindedly around the idea that the old-time city boss was a rococo ornament to the political scene and the source of a barrel of rough fun, but Mr. O'Connor's sentimental presentation of that barbaric figure as a fairy godmother of widows and orphans is more than hard to take. It persuasively pretends that mean vices are virtues, and it is that rare thing, a genuinely subversive book. (p. 124)

Anthony West, "When in Rome . . .," in The New Yorker *(© 1956 by The New Yorker Magazine, Inc.), Vol. XXXI, No. 52, February 11, 1956, pp. 121-24.*

JOHN KENNETH GALBRAITH

Currently, the leading prophet of the acculturation of the Irish, to give the phenomenon its technical name, is Edwin O'Connor. In my view, he is an excellent novelist and a master at showing how much can be made of moth-eaten material. His "The Last Hurrah," published in 1956, was a classic in one sense of the word: Frank Skeffington, the hero, was politically and sociologically a completely standardized phenomenon. . . .

There is evidence that when he began ["The Edge of Sadness"] . . . , O'Connor intended to leave the acculturation of the Irish for good and all, and deal with the simple but delicate problem of a priest who in his middle years turns to alcohol. The advance billing of the book made much of this theme. In fact, it forms only a small and not wholly plausible part of the story. The causes of the descent into drunkenness are not fully developed or entirely convincing. The lost weekdays are deliberately and mercifully left unchronicled. The cure, as recovery from alcoholism goes, seems to have been rather easy. . . . There being no story here, the author turns back to the struggles and torments of the Irish. But he has to find a new twist. (pp. 88, 90)

Because the author is not able to talk of the struggle between the Irish and their precursors, his solution is a struggle between the Irish and the Irish. He finds, or invents, a formidable tension between those who are fully acculturated

ated and those who are not. It is a remarkably ingenious solution, for it keeps a maximum of these fragile souls in torment for some little time longer. And it makes a very good story. (p. 90)

O'Connor is unquestionably one of the most skillful writers of the day. He has a gift for quick description and a singular purity of style. Moreover, in his own venue he has John O'Hara's ear for speech, and a gift for just the amount of exaggeration that provides contrast without loss of plausibility. . . . I do not think O'Connor's theme is excessively important. But out of his slender material I do think he has written a very good novel. (p. 94)

John Kenneth Galbraith, "Sadness in Boston," in The New Yorker *(© 1961 by The New Yorker Magazine, Inc.), Vol. XXXVII, No. 19, June 24, 1961, pp. 87-94.*

HUGH RANK

The extent of Edwin O'Connor's achievement in *The Edge of Sadness* has been concealed, ironically, by his own subtlety in craftsmanship. Although the novel was recognized by some as a major achievement in the realistic portrayal of a priest, there were just as many readers who found it merely an entertaining "re-hash" of the Irish-Catholic world of *The Last Hurrah:* Frank Skeffington had metamorphosed into Charlie Carmody and that was that. (p. 3)

[For] the reader (who has learned not to believe everything that the first-person narrator tells about himself) focusing on Father Hugh Kennedy as the protagonist, a subtle and highly dramatic conflict emerges as the priest reaches a crisis in his life.

It is extremely important to establish who the protagonist is in this novel. For if one [selects] Charlie as the main character, as some critics have, the book can be seen as [escapist literature]. . . . (p. 4)

But the book is Father Hugh Kennedy's story, whether he, as narrator, denies it or not. It is the story of the regeneration of a priest, a story of sanctity in the modern world, of a man coming to terms with himself and with God.

Part of O'Connor's widespread appeal is his ability to recreate the atmosphere of the New England Irish-Catholic environment through a mass of details, anecdotes, and informed commentary, which some critics have labeled sheer nostalgia. . . . It is true that O'Connor is a perceptive observer of the changing status of the Irish immigrant children, but he is more than a local colorist; the apparently rambling side-comments not only contribute to the versimilitude of the story, but also serve in *The Edge of Sadness* as necessary functional devices. If a writer is to describe accurately the world of Charlie Carmody and his octogenarian friends, he must concern himself with Johnny Corrigan's stroke, Rose Gormley's death, Albert's gallstones, and Sebastiano's blood poisoning because, in fact, the obituary page is the most popular reading for the aged, and medical case histories are the choice topics of conversation.

The Last Hurrah, for instance, is filled with memories of quaint and picturesque "characters" of the immigrant generation; however, *The Edge of Sadness* has very few nonfunctional anecdotes. The unity and coherence in the novel are frequently unrecognized by critics who may be distracted by the seemingly rambling episodes. The "death" scene of Mrs. Sanchez, for instance, early in the novel, allows O'Connor to establish some necessary material foreshadowing Charlie Carmody's "deathbed confession" later; random conversations in the early pages frequently become meaningful as the story progresses, thus indicating the structural design and control of the author.

O'Connor's basic technique is the use of a dialogue between the narrator and one other character. Even in crowded scenes, such as the dinner party or the wake, there are seldom any conversations in which more than two people are talking. O'Connor focuses sharply on one character for several pages, then, using the narrator's analysis as a transition, shifts to another character. In spite of the crowded stage, the reader never gets lost because of this device.

Structurally the novel is centered upon a few scenes rendered in depth. The dinner party, the rectory, the flashback to the Cenacle rest home, and the wake constitute the bulk of the novel. The forward motion is sustained by two suspense devices introduced early in the novel as O'Connor plants subtle foreshadowings concerning Father Hugh Kennedy's "problem" and Charlie Carmody's motive for friendship. By the end of the first section . . . , the priest's alcoholism has been revealed, establishing another suspense here as to whether or not he will be a backslider. The question of Charlie's motives for seeking Hugh's friendship is resolved in the "deathbed" scene. . . . [With] this suspense removed, the center of attention shifts to Father Kennedy's priestly life and the novel reaches its climax in the bitter invectives of Father John Carmody's denunciation of Father Kennedy's lethargy and egocentricity.

Realism takes time and space, sharp attention to detail and a relatively slow pace in order to be convincing. Characterization is a subtle thing and the failure of most "realistic" novels is a preoccupation of the author with action or idea. If we demand that a novelist present a realistic treatment of a character, then we must recognize the achievement of O'Connor in capturing the essence of Father Kennedy's situation and in exhibiting it in its seemingly rambling appearance which disguises the structure underneath.

O'Connor deals also with ideas. Among other things in this novel, he is concerned with the present status of the Catholic Church in America. . . . Satire, expressed through the narrator's analysis or through the dialogue of other characters, appear frequently; but although O'Connor and [J. F. Powers] often share the same targets for their barbs, O'Connor lacks the sustained irony for which Powers is noted. . . . Powers is the better satirist, but O'Connor is less interested in satire *per se;* the satire in *The Edge of Sadness* seems to accompany rather than to dominate the story and serves a valid function, however blunt it may be in certain passages, in helping to establish the characterization of the protagonist, Father Kennedy.

Father Kennedy is almost the antithesis of the traditional stereotype of the priest, a stereotype long established in Catholic popular literature, in the movies, and on television. The traditional stereotype pictures the priest as an authoritarian leader, a busy executive, a competent administrator, a wise counselor and shepherd to his flock, a gregarious, athletic extrovert, and an heroic celibate. With the exception of this last quality, which may have been deliberately retained to avoid sensationalism, Father Kennedy, as seen in the novel, fits into none of the traditional patterns.

To be more precise, at the beginning of the narrative he has either broken away from or failed in most of these categories; five years earlier, he too had once been a "typical" successful American priest. (pp. 5-8)

Father Kennedy is a reformed "whiskey priest," yet, in spite of the potential sensationalism here, this aspect is treated in a low key. Although the element of suspense, as to whether he will succumb to temptation again, is used as a device to move the story on, the primary attention is given to his own feelings of embarrassment as he is patronized by others on his return to society. The cause of his drinking problem is traced by him to his spiritual barrenness resulting from his priestly busy work; thus his alcoholism serves a functional part of the main theme of the story. In the emotional crisis after his father's death, the priest, lacking an inner strength which had been dissipated through his busy involvement in parish activities, turns to drinking; it could have been another outlet, "skirt chasing" for instance, but O'Connor remains true to a more common reality. (pp. 9-10)

[The] analysis by O'Connor of the priestly life is an extremely crucial and sensitive one for it points up . . . the dominant image of the American parish priest, as perceived by his people, is precisely that of the busy, overburdened, executive-administrator; the priest's preferable self-image, of course, is that of the shepherd-counselor. In this novel, O'Connor examines this confusion of roles and, through the self-analysis of Father Kennedy, points out and criticizes the attitude which allows the priest to envision himself as a shepherd doing "God's work" when in reality he may simply be a "cheerleader in a Roman collar." Father Kennedy's self-criticism here is really a scathing indictment of the dominant attitudes of the American Catholic clergy. . . . (pp. 12-13)

This novel could perhaps have been titled *Fathers and Sons* because of its great concern with the relation between generations of a patriarchal society. Three generations of the Carmody family are presented within this book, but a special attention here should concentrate on the filial attitudes of the three priests within this story—Father John Carmody, Father Casmir Danowski, and Father Hugh Kennedy. In this regard Father Carmody and Father Danowski act as contrasting foil characters, not only to each other, but also to Father Kennedy. (pp. 16-17)

The antagonistic obsession of Father Carmody was based not only on what [his father] Charlie had done to him, but also on how Charlie had wrecked the lives of all within the Carmody family. (p. 17)

Through the book, Father Danowski's simple loyalty and love for his father help to emphasize the malice and spite of Father Carmody's reaction to his father.

The importance of the father-son relationship between Dave Kennedy and his son, Father Hugh Kennedy, is indicated by the fact that Hugh's alcoholism begins in the period of emotional crisis after his father's death. . . .

The father-son relationship is central to most of O'Connor's work. Few writers have so consistently developed the variations and nuances of a patriarchal family; this is especially true in America where . . . there is a growing tendency toward a matriarchal society. (p. 18)

The varieties of love and hate, of guilt and shame, of responsibility and rejection, and of the ambivalences and the anguish of the conflict between generations is well done by O'Connor and deserves further critical exploration. (p. 20)

The crux of *The Edge of Sadness* is that Father Kennedy and Father Carmody, celibates who have renounced one outlet for an expression of love in order to seek another fruition of love, have lost love altogether. . . .

[When] a priest, who is "professionally" in the service of love, has no love, it is a most serious thing; much more serious, in fact, than the "skirt chasing" priest. For, as any reader of Dante or Aquinas knows, the sins of passion are far less grievous than the icy sins of a hardness of heart, a lack of love. . . . *The Edge of Sadness* with its exposition of lovelessness and egocentricity, and its criticism of administrative busywork, which is a most common temptation of the clergy, stands as a powerful critique of the American priesthood and a significant change in the image of the priest as seen in fiction. (p. 22)

There are other important violations of the traditional stereotype in this novel especially concerning the popular image of the priest as that of a gregarious person, open and friendly to all. Father Kennedy is established early, in the first chapter, as being aloof from the parishioners. . . . (p. 23)

Father Carmody, too, violates the stereotyped image of the gregarious priest, but his situation is different from Father Kennedy's. Whereas Kennedy is apathetic or indifferent to his parishioners, Carmody is aggressively hostile and misanthropic [as is Father Feeley, in *I Was Dancing*]. (p. 24)

[The] illusion-reality theme is important in the novel. It appears most obviously in Charlie Carmody's avoidance of reality and in Father Kennedy's recognition of it, but every other character can be seen in terms of his own fantasies. (p. 27)

[The] final scene could have been trite or could have been reduced to the level of a sentimental cliché about the priest-martyr giving up the world for God. . . . [The] problem of the novelist is to make such a story convincing, convincing perhaps to the skeptics who have seen so many two-dimensional characters, pious frauds, which have been offered to readers as "saints." Father Hugh Kennedy's choice, however, has been prepared for by over four hundred pages of honest writing and subtle characterization. After a dark night of the soul, not of alcoholism but of apathy, his choice becomes not a negative masochism, but a positive commitment to duty, to love, and to God.

Such idealism is rare in the contemporary novel and the book is apt to be dismissed by many who object not so much to O'Connor's craft as to this positive value judgment at the end. O'Connor has written a realistic Christian novel of hope, in a non-Christian age where the literature is more apt to reflect a pessimism or a nihilism. If idealism is rare in contemporary literature, realism is even rarer in the religious novel which has had a long-standing reputation for a bland optimism. The expression of faith, in a faithless age, is a difficult task because too many Pollyannas have debased the meaning of hope. Edwin O'Connor, in this novel, joins the company of Graham Greene, Georges Bernanos, and François Mauriac as a competent creative artist writing from a Christian ideological position. In American literature, O'Connor joins J. F. Powers as a leader in breaking away from a priestly stereotype which had dominated for nearly a century. (pp. 28-9)

Hugh Rank, "O'Connor's Image of the Priest," in The New England Quarterly *(copyright 1968 by* The New England Quarterly*), Vol. XLI, No. 1, March, 1968, pp. 3-29.*

DENIS DONOGHUE

There is a passage in *All in the Family* where the narrator, Jack Kinsella, something of a novelist, is thinking of his books:

> I think they were all good books of their kind: they were honest, decently plotted, with believable characters, and were reasonably well written. I was proud of writing them, in fact; I knew that not everyone could have written them, and indeed that many writers who were better than I could not have written them, either.

Kinsella is not O'Connor, but this seems to me a fair account of O'Connor's novels. Except for *The Oracle,* which is merely a caricature, the novels are serious studies of the relation between people and institutions. O'Connor's imagination was always concerned with the stress between an individual's nature and the public terms in which it is defined. *The Last Hurrah:* or what happens when the institution itself changes, runs to a new style. *The Edge of Sadness:* a priest-physician who cannot heal himself. The *Cardinal* fragment: the good man bewildered in a bewildered Church. There is no fault in the themes, except that they are never brought to the pitch of their possibilities.

O'Connor was variously gifted, but his gift of language was not remarkable. Notice, for instance, how often he resorts to italics, desperate to be heard, as if he feared that the words, left to themselves, would die on the page. *The Oracle* parodies the rhetoric of the radio commentator, but it reads as if O'Connor were trying to clear his own head, getting rid of all the turgid language he had ever heard or used. When we lose faith in his major novels we find ourselves trying to imagine another language, since nothing less will answer, capable of dealing with the things which O'Connor has merely provoked. We feel that his language has let him down at the first show of trouble, and that only a miracle of language could now save him.

In his characters, too, O'Connor seemed content with stereotypes. Father Kennedy in *The Edge of Sadness* conducts his confession, reciting matters which, given half a chance, would be poignant to hear; but he is given the language of *Going My Way,* and his life converges upon that of Father Bing Crosby Fitzgibbon. He is a whiskey-priest, but *The Edge of Sadness* is not *The Power and the Glory.* Graham Greene has imagined his priest so profoundly that he has only to release him, letting him live by his own force in word and deed. The only force O'Connor gives Father Kennedy is the force of the typical: the priest, like everybody else, has problems.

O'Connor came upon his characters soon or late—I have no information on that count—but he wrote as if characters needed to be verified rather than imagined. He liked to go back over his old characters, setting them now in a strange world, as *All in the Family* goes back over *The Last Hurrah,* but he never allowed the risk to go beyond another version of the typical. There is evidence that O'Connor tried to do most of the novel's work with character, but his imagination cared only for species and type. Reading the novels, we recognize many characters and situations, but the recognition is never a shock, the circle of the typical is never broken.

It is obvious that O'Connor was fond of broad effects. He was mainly interested in Irish-Americans, one of the broadest effects in American life. He liked to feel nostalgic for the bad old days, knowing they were bad and still, with half his heart, regretting that they could not survive. But he did not discover in South Boston anything more surprising than the predictable images already disclosed by rumor and gossip: his imagination merely confirmed the popular report. . . .

O'Connor writes well about vaudeville and the old-time professionals; lively, knockabout stuff, well-timed, well-paced. . . . If his books seem foursquare, the reason is that he left nothing to chance or risk, he never allowed a character to seize the book and run away, he would not even let his characters keep anything of themselves to themselves. Whatever is, is visible. There is no point in looking at those characters obliquely, hoping to find darkness and mysteries; they are only what they appear to be. The least that can be said for O'Connor's characters is that they are lucid: and this is also the most that can be said of them. (p. 21)

There is no doubt that O'Connor was writing well at the end [as we see in *The Best and the Last of Edwin O'Connor*], and "The Boy" is not at all broad. The improvement is clear, especially by comparison with the set piece chosen from *All in the Family,* the famous drowning scene. The unfinished fragment seems to me much more controlled, the language much sharper, more flexible. *The Cardinal* might have been good, too, but I doubt it; its feeling is too heavily compromised by *The Edge of Sadness,* those sad captains of the Roman Church. Again, it is a question of style. . . . I hope *The Best and the Last* will gain new readers for O'Connor, and that they will respond to his honesty. His world seems already to have died by its own hand, passing into history at once, abstract and allegorical. (p. 22)

Denis Donoghue, "Language Barriers," in The New York Review of Books *(reprinted with permission from* The New York Review of Books; *copyright © 1970 Nyrev, Inc.), Vol. XIV, No. 12, June 18, 1970, pp. 21-2.**

EDWARD R. F. SHEEHAN

The "Boy" fragment, at the very end of [*The Best and the Last of Edwin O'Connor*], is 40 pages of the novel that O'Connor was writing when he [died]. . . . It is a charming account of a boy growing up in a small, ugly mill city of New England; his friends . . . felt that in finished form it might have become his best book. The much shorter, and less polished, 16-page fragment of his "Cardinal" novel, however, seemed to me more ambitious of its intent and therefore more interesting for its unconsummated purpose.

The "Cardinal" of O'Connor's fragment is an eighty-year-old prelate, presumably of a New England see, staring death in the face. O'Connor's opening shafts are exceedingly veracious and well-aimed, not at the Cardinal himself, but at the insipid city newspapers which have thrived by nominating him every morning for sainthood. . . .

[The Cardinal] ruminates during the visit of an uproarious, slightly batty priest called Charlie Crimmins—the kind of character we are so accustomed to in O'Connor and which, had he lived to be eighty himself, he would never have ceased to conjure up—about the "silent, isolating, depthless and overwhelming" sadness of his own declining days. . . . He meditates as well on the confused laity—who are no more confused than the Cardinal himself—on the unsettled older priests and the rebellious younger ones, of the changing contemporary Church. Soon afterwards, the Cardinal is examined by his doctor, a cancerous node is discovered on his neck, and he is told he is going to die.

On the threshold of death the Cardinal, wondering like everyone else whether most of the lifelong devotional practices he had been raised on could now be considered worthless, and doubting even the value of his administrative legacy, contemplates the question of his successor. (p. 107)

What a pity that O'Connor committed so little of his prototypical Cardinal to paper, and that he did not live to persevere. One senses that it would have been not only an important book, but a necessary one. For this prototypical Cardinal exists, somewhere on earth or in space and time or all of these together, and whether he is assembled partly from the fragments of real life or partly or mostly from the caprices of an artist's imagination, does not matter in the end. The Cardinal exists, and we are still in need of an honest, full-length, full-blooded portrait of him. (p. 109)

Edward R. F. Sheehan, "'The Best and the Last of Edwin O'Connor'," in Commonweal *(copyright © 1970 Commonweal Publishing Co., Inc.; reprinted by permission of Commonweal Publishing Co., Inc.), Vol. XCIII, No. 4, October 23, 1970, pp. 107, 109.*

DAVID DILLON

Except for *Benjy* (1957) and his first novel, *The Oracle* (1951), a jejune satire on radio commentators, [Edwin O'Connor] wrote exclusively about Eastern, urban (Boston), Irish-American Catholics, and primarily about the effects of acculturation on their politics, religious beliefs, and family life. He concentrates on a late period of Irish-American history, approximately 1948-1968, with few immigrants or ghettos, when the battles against poverty, discrimination, and the Yankee establishment had already been won, and when, as a result, "nobody felt very Irish any more, or had much reason to." The dominant theme in his novels is the death of Irishness. Many of his characters have made it in America at the cost of their ethnic identity, while others, in apparent defiance of time and the world at large, cling stubbornly to traditional attitudes and customs. The result is a severe conflict between the generations, particularly between fathers and sons, and the widening gap between the values of the old world (Ireland, the ghetto) and those of the new. O'Connor is concerned not simply with the fact of change, however, but with individual responses to it. He is a novelist of manners preoccupied with the interaction between character and history.

Frank Skeffington, the hero of his first major novel, *The Last Hurrah* (1956), and Charles Kinsella, a central character in his last, *All in the Family* (1966), represent the extremes of Irish-American political styles and, by extension, of Irish-American thinking about the past.

Skeffington is the old politics incarnate. He has risen from precinct captain to ward boss to mayor to governor. For the past forty years he has ruled the city of his birth like a feudal lord. . . . In his fief personal relationships are everything. He spends his days dispensing patronage to widows and cronies, planning strategy with the local bosses, all of whom pledge him absolute allegiance, and appearing at wakes and testimonial banquets for disreputable but politically useful party hacks. His interest is politics, not government, specifically the acquisition and consolidation of power and the use of that power for personal, partisan ends. No machine exists apart from Skeffington himself; he has no municipal "program" except the satisfaction of the immediate human needs—food, jobs, housing—of his constituents. Abstract social theories and grand designs are considered profoundly impractical and dangerously Republican.

The Last Hurrah, covering Skeffington's final campaign, is a boisterous, funny, intensely verbal novel that is both the finest account of the Irish political process in American literature and a handbook of Irish-American speech.

For Skeffington, "politics is the greatest spectator sport in the country." . . . A campaign is not a test of issues, it is a carnival, a popularity contest, and, above all, a public ritual that enables the Irish community to reaffirm its ethnic and cultural identity. The successful Irish politician had to be an entertainer and an orator as well as a skillful anatomizer of ideas; Skeffington is a model of the type. He has a vaudevillian's sense of timing and theatrical effects (vaudeville, a recurrent topic in O'Connor's novels, represents not merely the past but individuality and eccentricity as opposed to colorless conformity—a metaphor for the older Irish character); his complete mastery of the art of Irish political oratory is a unique blend of anecdote, hyperbole, erudition, and invective that can be as subtle as a sonnet or as blunt as a hammer blow. *The Last Hurrah* is built around Skeffington's conversations with his relatives and cronies and his lively public jousts with his opponents. . . . [He] thoroughly enjoys the excitement of a campaign and the intricacies of the various factional power struggles. He has no Yankee sense of civic duty. . . . Politics appeals first to his emotions or, more accurately, his passions. . . . Even in defeat he talks about the "good times" he has had.

Charles Kinsella, on the other hand, is young, educated, polished, in short, the epitome of the acculturation process. He regards politics, at least in the beginning, as part avocation, part obligation, and part moral crusade. . . . Compared to Skeffington, he is an extremely aloof candidate. He works through an army of bright young aides, depends heavily on television and slick advertising, and avoids personal appearances whenever possible. He is very conscious of his image, which has been created by a group of New York public relations experts. More importantly, he is able to flout the conventional Irish taboos against social ostentation and elitism and get away with it. Glamour, urbanity, and conspicuous wealth are the ingredients of his style. . . . *The Last Hurrah* describes the end of tribal, paternalistic Irish politics; *All in the Family* presents the sophisticated, patrician politics that has replaced it. (pp. 108-10)

Whereas political discussions in *The Last Hurrah* are personal, anecdotal, and fiercely pragmatic, in *All in the Family* they are often theoretical and moralistic—that is, distinctly un-Irish. For Skeffington, an election is an occasion to strengthen the status quo and to reinforce the community's ties to its past. For Charles Kinsella, however, it is an opportunity to break with that past and to initiate a new era of reform and rectitude. (p. 111)

O'Connor accepts the passing of bossism as an inevitable and, on the whole, beneficial event. Skeffington is a charmer, but he is also a demagogue whose parochial, partisan ways finally work against the larger interests of his constituents. He dwells too much on memories of ancient injustices done to his family and race and seems to take childish pleasure in harassing old enemies. . . . He knows he is an anachronism and yet he attributes his final defeat to "some incomprehensible conspiracy of freakish circumstances" (defections in the ranks, faulty organization), not to history and its dramatic transformation of the Irish-American character. *The Last Hurrah* is not, therefore, a sentimental apology for graft, nepotism, and gerrymandering, as some critics have alleged. Skeffington's limitations are visible as well as his gifts, and although O'Connor sincerely admires the latter, he also agrees with Nathaniel Gardiner, the Yankee philanthropist who emerges as the conscience of the novel, that "a bigger man and a better man would have acted differently." . . . (pp. 111-12)

What O'Connor regrets and what accounts for the wistful tone of much of his writing is the demise of the humor, energy, and passionate sense of purpose that were characteristic of Skeffington's generation. Politics was once the only way up for the Irish, their sole entry into a society that otherwise excluded them. It was a collective cause. Because those who went first became tutors for those who followed, it was also a link between generations. . . . In O'Connor's novels, politics has become a disruptive force in family life. In fact, we find no stable families, only family conflicts. (p. 112)

[The "new breed"] are members of the establishment that their ancestors feared and hated and have no appreciation of the ancient struggles except as material for anecdotes and Hibernian pageants. They tend to regard the old people as quaint, semimythical creatures and to think of Irish history as a collection of legends without significance for the present. Revisionists without a purpose, they are essentially rootless, traveling everywhere but nowhere at home. They lack their ancestors' secure sense of place. Their only passions seem to be money and success; consequently, they are inclined to support candidates who remind them of their lace-curtain aspirations (McClusky, Charles Kinsella) rather than their shanty origins. They look back only to be sure that the past is not about to embarrass them.

Ironically, for all their noble pretensions, the "new breed" are, as O'Connor dramatizes repeatedly, rarely better than their predecessors and often a lot worse. . . . Charles Kinsella's committing his brother to a mental institution, with the help of the tractable Judge Kilrane, and his detente with Cogan's corrupt state machine are more cynical, self-serving acts than any in *The Last Hurrah,* a fact which does not beatify Skeffington but points out that Irish-American politics has changed in style but not in substance. The vices of the old boys have been refined while their virtues have been lost. (pp. 113-14)

Politics is only one aspect of Irish-American life with which O'Connor is concerned. Catholicism is another, particularly the Church's relationship to secular institutions and its declining moral and spiritual influence among the Irish. In the past the Church exercised the type of control over an Irish-American's spiritual life as the Democratic Party did over his political life. Both were hierarchical, authoritarian organizations that strengthened his commitment to the community and his sense of his own identity, his distinctiveness among other immigrants. In most parishes the pastor functioned as a tribal leader, as another boss-politician. He helped to keep cultural traditions alive and defended them against disruptive innovations. He also found jobs, settled disputes, gave advice on important social and political questions, rewarded friends and punished dissidents. His word was law because he spoke for both God and city hall. In return for his services he customarily received the devotion and unquestioning support of his flock.

O'Connor's novels have no clerical dictators, unless we count the aged Cardinal in *The Last Hurrah* and Father McGovern in *I Was Dancing,* but the ideal of the old-time parish and the old-time pastor, synonymous with traditional Irish Catholicism, is a powerful influence for good and bad on many of his characters. *The Edge of Sadness* . . . dramatizes two different reactions to this ideal, one dangerously nostalgic but ultimately constructive, and the other cynical and self-destructive. Both amplify the theme of the death of Irishness in America.

Hugh Kennedy, the reformed alcoholic who is the narrator, is pastor of Old Saint Paul's, a derelict slum parish. . . . The Irish have long since moved up to more fashionable, middle-class neighborhoods. (pp. 114-15)

For Hugh, being a "real priest" still means having a special rapport with the people. It means speaking their language, having one's advice solicited and followed, touching souls in intimate and decisive ways. . . . Earlier, he went through an emotional and spiritual crisis because he had given everything to his parishioners and kept nothing for himself. Now the situation is reversed: he does everything for himself and virtually nothing for his parishioners. His Irishness has become his spiritual albatross.

Charlie Carmody's eighty-first birthday party is a critical event in his rebirth. Once again he meets the gregarious, sharp-tongued old men who were such an integral part of his father's world and his own youth. He listens to their hilarious and interminable conversations about funerals, hospitals, and the sorry state of public transit, and in the process rediscovers his roots. . . . [He discovers a] basic truth about his vocation: a priest's marriage is to God, not to a particular ethnic group. His choice is either to become a model and teacher for his curate and a true shepherd to his alien congregation, or else to fail a second time as both priest and man. . . . At the end of the novel he refuses the pastorate of Saint Raymond's, the Gaelic jewel of the diocese, thereby expressing both his acceptance of his priestly responsibilities and his choice of the living present over the dying past. (pp. 115-16)

Unlike Hugh, [John Carmody] despises the Irish, finding them crude, sentimental, and provincial. His great ambition is to escape to some remote monastery where he will never have to listen to another brogue or another melancholy tale about a drunkard husband or a wayward son. He has lived a type of solitary, rigorously intellectual life that is generally disapproved by the Irish-American clergy. (p. 116)

If O'Connor's young people are ungrateful heirs of their cultural traditions, his patriarchs have been poor custodians of them. Charlie Carmody, Jimmy Kinsella, and Waltzing Dan Considine (*I Was Dancing*) are not charming Pickwickian rogues but belligerent, despotic, self-serving parents for whom "Honor Thy Father" is the first and only commandment. They are intolerant of other ethnic groups and blacks, blindly anticlerical, and hostile to any form of social change that is outside their limited experience. Charlie and Jimmy (also known as "The Irish Baruch") live by an Irish version of the Puritan ethic which says that wealth is merely just compensation for the past sufferings of the race. Charity and magnanimity are the enemies of business (both men are as ruthless as the Yankee financiers of the Irish horror stories) and should be shown to one's family only on special occasions, such as Christmas and birthdays. Moreover, their actions are often a travesty of genuine Irishness. (p. 117)

The "Cardinal" fragment suggests that O'Connor planned to expand a study of the contemporary Church to include the turmoil that followed Vatican II. The Cardinal is another aging patriarch who is caught between the fact of change and his own conservative training and sympathies. His disposition and attitude remind one of Skeffington, and throughout we find the outlines of the familiar O'Connor themes: conflict between generations, the revolt against tradition and authority. . . . Among contemporary authors, only J. F. Powers has written as knowledgeably and sensitively about the priesthood.

In focusing on priests and politicians O'Connor is not, of course, dealing with the total Irish-American experience, only with its most representative elements. Changes in these roles, which continue to be among the most appealing to Irish-Americans, inevitably reflect other cultural and psychological changes. O'Connor also captures the humor of his characters as rarely captured before. As he explained in an interview, "A great deal of Irish-American fiction has been written. I read it, and began to say to myself, 'Where the hell is the humor?' It was sullen stuff, depressed. Now the Irish writers—O'Casey, Joyce—they have humor, but the Irish-Americans never seemed to capture it. Irish-Americans can be very funny people, but no one seemed to set it down. I thought I'd try." His work lacks the bleakness and harshness of Farrell's or the cynicism of O'Hara's. The brutalities of the ghetto life are left behind along with the sentimental cliches. He is neither a satirist nor an apologist but a compassionate observer of a process. His legacy is a small but remarkably coherent body of work to which anyone interested in Irish-American life in the mid-twentieth century must turn. (pp. 119-20)

David Dillon, "Priests and Politicians: The Fiction of Edwin O'Connor," in Critique: Studies in Modern Fiction *(copyright © by* Critique, *1974), Vol. XVI, No. 2, 1974, pp. 108-20.*

* * *

O'CONNOR, Frank (pseudonym of Michael O'Donovan) 1903-1966

An Irish short story writer, novelist, critic, editor, and translator of ancient Gaelic works, O'Connor sets his stories in Ireland. However, his warm sense of humor, his realism, and his strong development of character give his writing universality. O'Connor lived in the United States during the latter part of his life. (See also *Contemporary Authors,* obituary, Vols. 25-28.)

JAMES T. FARRELL

There is a sensitive tenderness in Mr. O'Connor's ["The Saint and Mary Kate"] that overrides its patches of irony. Likewise, because of his skillful use of indirection, he is able to portray that melodrama and extravagance so apparent in many Irish lives without being himself melodramatic. The background of his novel is a tenement in the town of Cork that bulges with the sorrows and pitifulness of the poor. The two principal characters are Mary Kate and Phil, whose hopeful youth stands out in contrast to the frustrations of the older people they know. . . .

Mr. O'Connor's book is serious and genuine. Its strongest pages are those which retail the pitiful and almost heartbreaking lives of the poor. He is, unquestionably, an Irish novelist who should be read.

James T. Farrell, "'Inheritance', 'Sons' and Other Recent Novels: 'The Saint and Mary Kate'," in The New Republic *(reprinted by permission of* The New Republic; *© 1932 The New Republic, Inc.), Vol. LXXII, No. 934, October 26, 1932, p. 301.*

DIANA TRILLING

There is an Irish lilt to the dialogue and an Irish color to the scenery of Frank O'Connor's stories, even at their most melancholy, which, because it gives them a dimension of the strange, also acts to give them literary dimension. But emptied of local color, the stories in "Crab Apple Jelly" don't at all carry, for me, the weight that others have felt in them. I find them sweetly sad, sadly suggestive, or even a touch frightening at moments, but never more than in the way of the skilfully rendered pastiche. (p. 697)

Diana Trilling, "Fiction in Review: 'Crab Apple Jelly'," in The Nation *(copyright 1944 by the Nation Associates, Inc.), Vol. 159, No. 23, December 2, 1944, pp. 696-97.*

V. S. PRITCHETT

[Mr. O'Connor] has little or none of the professional Irishman in him or of the brothiness, feyness, sentimentality, that mar so much of Irish writing. At his best he is more truthful, lucid and substantial than any other Irish realist now writing and in . . . [*An Only Child,* his autobiography,] his talent is sure.

His story is by turns painful, hard, tragic, comical and sardonic. It is remarkable throughout for the portrait of his mother. . . .

[The] book ceases to be merely one more account of a life and hard times by a clever novelist and discloses the growth of a mind and a governing idea. To liberate himself from the humiliations of slum life and its picaresque slavery the boy made a religion of education. (p. 1049)

V. S. Pritchett, "A Fighting Childhood," in New Statesman *(© 1961 The Statesman & Nation Publishing Co. Ltd.), Vol. LXI, No. 1581, June 30, 1961, pp. 1049-50.*

DEBORAH AVERILL

A reader of Frank O'Connor's stories notices at once their atmosphere of warm intimacy. His concern with human contact originates in his sense of human isolation and it pervades his work; characters continuously touch each other, lie in bed discussing their problems or fall in love, and the narrative itself reflects a lively compassion which gives these stories their distinctive relevance. (p. 28)

His perceptions of emptiness lead him to seek an intensification of life. He delights in sheer animal vitality and encourages a full, waking life of the senses. . . . He dislikes abstractions, 'the Greek reasoning about life which are our daily bread', and thinks they have crippled modern literature as well as modern society by creating artificial barriers to communication. He tries to create an attitude of mind informed from within, from nature and the 'inner light', to overcome the literal application of sterile social mores, theories or religious doctrines. Consequently he avoids abstract speculation or burdening character or incident with a larger intellectual framework than is provided by the situation itself in relation to general human experience. (pp. 28-9)

He tries to locate within the complex, reflecting man the warm, vital animal which needs and seeks contact with others. His imagination dwells on the blood-ties which bind the human community together, on heredity, sex, reproduction, the family as an organic unit—the natural processes and conditions which create and sustain life. These natural relationships underlie and enhance human contact, so that it becomes not merely an interchange of ideas, but a communion, a sharing of experience expressed in the concrete acts of speaking and touching. (p. 29)

O'Connor's stories in particular convey a strong sense of family and community ties. They are remote from society, but not divorced from it; we can always feel a need for companionship, a pull towards contact and reintegration, and a desire to work out ways or reconciliation within the span of the individual life. He celebrates marriage as the institution in which natural bonds can best be maintained; at its best it combines romantic love with social acceptability. His attitude towards the more anti-social aspects of sexual contact is ambivalent. (p. 30)

O'Connor frequently casts his mind back to a childhood world for inspiration, because that period of his life exercised the most compulsive hold on him and because children have not yet lost their naturalness and innocence. (p. 31)

O'Connor's adult characters, like his children, are lonely innocents who determine their identity through contact. They reach from the changing complexities of their lives towards some kind of rooted primary condition in which they find rest and unity at least temporarily. Contact with others draws them out of themselves; the imperfect struggling animal in them impels them to overcome barriers to communication. To make his characters approachable, O'Connor often deflates them by using mock-heroic techniques; he tends towards caricature, towards a gentle puncturing of dignified poses and a revelation of the absurd.

He often contrasts characters who communicate easily with those who don't. The former are frank, self-revealing and naturally intimate, the latter are cautious and reticent. (p. 32)

His attempt to recreate the effect of a speaking voice, which he considers the physical body of a story, reflects a desire for direct contact and communication with the reader. . . .

The narrators through whom he tells his stories are loosely defined personae who are always either implicitly or explicitly present. They are not bound to a consistent point of view, so that they can speak either as a near-by witness of the situation, like a fellow-villager, or as an omnipresent creator, a kind of angelic observer. They move freely in and out of the characters' minds without identifying completely with anyone; even in stories told from only one person's point of view, we can see him from the outside as well as the inside. (p. 35)

The tone of the stories is conversational, animated and evocative, embodying O'Connor's own energetic vitality. It is intended to elicit an immediate emotional response from the reader. The language and idiom come directly from the situation. There is little obscure symbolism, stylization or abstract speculation. His easy, confident fluency creates a deceptive impression of casual off-handedness; he often narrates tragic events as if they were everyday occurrences which didn't really matter, but the underlying involvement builds up force until it is released at the moment of crisis in a passage which is overtly emotional, intimate and intense. Sometimes when these passages are too subjective and unrestrained they fail to be as convincing as he intended; he is too prone to making sweeping statements like 'I was a stranger to her, and nothing I could ever do would make us the same to one another again.'

He makes his greatest impact when he counterpoints the warm familiarity of the speaking voice with strict objective controls. Sometimes he uses a dramatic scene instead of the narrative to express insight. He thinks a 'sharp contrast should ideally exist between narrative and drama—the former should be subjective and persuasive, the latter objective and compulsive—in the one the storyteller suggests to the reader what he believes happened, in the other he proves to him that this is in fact how it did happen'. (p. 36)

O'Connor achieves chilling effects of distance by treating time and place in a way which suggests 'the eternal silence of those infinite spaces'. Sometimes he endues ordinary, familiar settings with a quality of remoteness which makes the living individual seem to shrink and flounder; efforts at contact become highly charged. (pp. 36-7)

Sometimes he distances events temporarily; the narrator speaks in an empty present of things that happened long before and which outweigh anything that has happened to the characters since. The future becomes subservient to the past, and the immediacy of the speaking voice is tempered by the backward pull of events. . . .

Although O'Connor sometimes fails to make human contact more than a momentary reprieve from inner conflict and intellectual complexities, at his best he fashions his stories into effective, lasting vehicles for communicating experience and uniting author and reader in a recognition of their shared humanity. He refines the idea of contact as the most significant response the living can make to the empty uncertainty of separation and death. (p. 37)

Deborah Averill, "Human Contact in the Short Stories" (copyright © 1969 by Deborah Averill; reprinted by permission of the author), in Michael/Frank: Studies on Frank O'Connor, *edited by Maurice Sheehy, Knopf, 1969, pp. 28-37.*

JAMES H. MATTHEWS

"I saw life through a veil of literature." This statement in his autobiography defines something important about Frank O'Connor. After writing, reading was his most consuming activity. He read without method or grace, because he was both a writer and a self-taught person. Since he knew what he liked and disliked, he seldom hedged his bets. Thus, when he wrote about literature he often seemed too opinionated, too flamboyant. But as Richard Ellmann has noted, O'Connor "thought he was stating conclusions that nobody in his right mind could miss. The strength of *The Mirror in the Roadway* and *The Lonely Voice* comes from this assumptive power. It begins in close observation, of course, but then, in an almost visionary way, renders writers, objects and themes malleable." O'Connor didn't just read books, he collaborated with them.

Like everything else he wrote, O'Connor's "literary criticism" reveals as much about him as what he happens to be writing about. . . . O'Connor's literary biases are seldom hidden; he has no use for Art that imposes itself upon Reality, that constructs its forms *a priori,* or that assumes to enlighten belated races. The distinction between living and museum art appears over and over again in his writing. Academic or aesthetic literature plays to pure intellect in the rarefied atmosphere of the private soul. Instinctive or folk literature plays to impure emotions in the clamorous, unpredictable, and ultimately ephemeral world of the communal marketplace. In *The Road to Stratford,* for instance, he says, "Jonson was Joyce to Shakespeare's Yeats, the literary theorist as opposed to the natural instinctive writer." (pp. 23-4)

Undeniably, literature in all its various forms was O'Connor's playground. On the other hand, he was incapable of absolute escape; he was an Irish writer and Ireland was his battleground. Consequently, his most powerful critical opinions were about Irish writing. Few other writers or critics have written as well or as widely about Irish and Anglo-Irish literature as Frank O'Connor. Shortly after finishing *The Lonely Voice,* O'Connor turned his hand to the book suggested thirty years before by Yeats—a history of Irish literature. *The Backward Look,* as it was eventually called, is actually a criticism of a larger life, a synthesis of a culture, and a personal statement. O'Connor's "backward look," then, is every bit as personally telling as his autobiographies or his stories. (pp. 27-8)

If any single assumption or attitude dominates O'Connor's critical writing it is his wariness of the intellect. In *The Backward Look* he argues that a literature heavy with political themes and oral techniques is necessarily a literature for "common readers" and not for the sophisticated. O'Connor was convinced that scholarship dries up the radical sources of poetry, that abstraction dulls the concrete impulses of the imagination. (p. 29)

Though it is the people that fascinate O'Connor, [*Irish Miles*] hardly lacks in scenic description. In fact, it contains some of his most impressive descriptive writing. In a characteristic passage he describes how "The country mounted on either side of us in bleak grey hills; gradually it came closer to the road, all choppy like a sea, threatening it here and there in bumpty, grassy hillocks, till all at once, as we reached the top of the hill and began our free-wheel down into Inchigeela, it rose and hurled itself on us, snapping at us with red sandstone teeth between purple lips of heather." O'Connor can picture in equally vivid and unself-conscious language a sunset over the Clare hills or the grey pallor of Connemara or a bitter wind at Tralee. It's just that Nature, though well enough in its own way, "produces a ravenous appetite for civilization." The irony is that civilization, at least that encountered by these cyclists, proves to be not altogether satisfying either.

Through it all, the persistent personality of the writer himself controls *Irish Miles*. One gets the impression not just of a voice speaking but of eyes seeing, ears listening, and a nose smelling. For that matter, everything he experiences and everyone he contacts, including his cycling companions, come to life. (pp. 42-3)

By his vigorous campaigns to salvage Ireland's past, O'Connor established himself as Ireland's slightly abrasive conscience. The same exasperated attachment to Ireland is evident in O'Connor's fiction, particularly his two novels. Both *The Saint and Mary Kate* and *Dutch Interior* were groping attempts not only of a writer for a suitable form but also of an Irishman for a cohesive consciousness. In them he was seriously confronting himself and his past; for O'Connor to do battle with the provincial narrowness of Cork was to attack his own provincialism. He once said that Ireland always looked out on the world through windows and doors. That notion, to a great extent, defines what O'Connor was trying to do in his novels. The two young people in *The Saint and Mary Kate* look outward from a Cork slum tenement toward the freedom and light of the outside world. The young people of *Dutch Interior* continually escape from respectable homes and jobs into darkened Cork streets and peer back through windows and doors, hoping to find warmth and life. Significantly, the doors are closed and the windows are heavily curtained. (p. 44)

As compelling and sensitive as it is, *The Saint and Mary Kate* is not a successful novel. On the one hand, O'Connor takes an abstraction too seriously and lets it dictate his characters. That is generally a weakness for a novelist. For a storyteller like O'Connor it is disastrous. The particular abstraction is the opposition between two conflicting ways of life, represented by Mary Kate, "Eternal Woman," and Phil, "Eternal Boy." The idea obviously plagued O'Connor, because it appeared so often and in so many forms in his later work. On the other hand, to O'Connor's credit perhaps, he is too easily diverted from his deterministic "tragedy of innocence." He appears so intrigued by the hero and heroine that he barely elaborates on the world in which they live, the world that supposedly crushes their dreams. By his own critical standards, though, a novel requires a society, not just a vague backdrop. O'Connor's inclinations as a storyteller get in the way. Even when he sketches a tenement feud, a striking face, or an overheard comment, it is almost an aside, a passing glance toward a momentary scene, rather than part of a carefully sustained totality. All in all, then, the part dominates the whole in *The Saint and Mary Kate*.

In *Dutch Interior,* O'Connor ostensibly turned that corner, perhaps with a vengeance. Being too close to the issue . . . , he sought detachment by way of technique. The impressionistic form, which really appears formless, is calculated to present a tapestry meaningful only in a large scale. The narrative, such as it is, develops from the static, suffocating atmosphere of a city, rather than from the motion of people's lives. The emptiness of the characters of *Dutch Interior* is the emptiness of the world of things that surround them—streets, clocks, churches, shops, and walls. The characters are not much more than symptoms of a diseased society. They are acted on almost solely from without. One is, in fact, meant to be less interested in the characters than in what has trapped them. The silhouettes of passengers seen by Peter Devane, for instance, through the portholes and doorways of a newly arrived steamer almost exactly equal what O'Connor allows us to see of his characters—vague silhouettes.

However, that's precisely the point. In the routines of the city, life has become vague and ghostly. Even the young people have been so deadened by things and customs that they are only shadows. (pp. 45-6)

Dutch Interior is richly impressionistic, but probably too full, too undisciplined to strike clear. It contains some of O'Connor's most lyrical prose. A reviewer called one of his plays a "novelist's play." *Dutch Interior* could be called a "poet's novel." But without a discernible voice to unify the images or to focus the drama, the novel lacks a sure emotional perspective. O'Connor's alienation from the piety, respectability, and half truth of his provincial past is too close to the surface, too unrefined. Furthermore, O'Connor appears unable to sustain a narrative about the blighted lives of two brothers without indulging quick glances toward the other lives they cross. The finest portions of the book, especially those concerning Eileen Madden, are almost diversionary, the subject perhaps of another novel. As a result, the larger tapestry is weakened, though it is in the whole that O'Connor has invested his cumulative effect.

Dutch Interior, as well as *The Saint and Mary Kate,* illustrates O'Connor's strengths as clearly as his weaknesses. He was a lyric poet who felt ill at ease behind the mannered mask of Poetry. He was a storyteller interested more in the flash points of human existence than in the sweeping artifice. . . . The sense of containment, of closed energy, that characterizes O'Connor's stories is precisely what hinders the progressive and differentiating strategy of the novel.

As flawed as they are, the novels deal with the issues that pepper all of O'Connor's writing—the incrustation of Irish life, the capacity of people to dream and to delude themselves, the failure of domestic relations as well as all institutions to provide love and genuineness, and above all, the pervasive burden of human loneliness. Then too, the characters of the novels are about the same as those one finds in the stories—little people, anonymous flecks of humanity, innocents, and outcasts. The novels also manifest the main traits of O'Connor's simple style. The prose is unpretentious, with no trace of literary allusion or intellectual ornamentation. The narrative is compact, carried not by exposition but by intense and brisk dialogue. But above all, the novels go a long way toward explaining why O'Connor inevitably stayed with the short story. (pp. 47-9)

The stories of *Bones of Contention* are typical of O'Connor's writing in the 1930s. By his own admission he was "fumbling for a style." Having found the exuberant romanticism of *Guests of the Nation* unproductive, he drew back his sights from the nation at large to smaller and less colorful social groups. The characters of these stories are not soldiers or lovers; they are peasants, drunken musicians, and tired old men. The narrative voice is casual and direct, calling attention to the persons in the story rather than to itself. Such phrases as "for as the old man said to me of him," or "as they all said," create in the story "Peasants," for example, the impression of a story overheard, almost like gossip, from the peasants themselves about the "unpleasant memories" left behind by a former priest. "Orpheus and His Lute," the hilarious account of the drinking habits of the Irishtown Brass and Reed Band, is told entirely as a *shanachie* tale. . . . For a writer so young these stories are surprisingly trim in form. What moral "comment" there is emerges from a natural and mature balancing of sympathy and judgment.

Though by no means its best story, the title story is indicative of the prevailing manner of the entire volume. The very phrase "bones of contention," suggests low-grade dissension, not revolution; the struggles within all of the stories are, for the most part, isolated, petty, and spontaneous. Set in Cork and narrated by the grandson of the central figure, "Bones of Contention" concerns the monumental and eminently funny feud that erupts when a stubborn, hard-drinking, opinionated old woman insists upon supervising the funeral of an old friend. The cliché title serves as ironic comment on the whole affair, for it is over a corpse that the "battle" is waged. The triviality of it all does not diminish the intensity of the conflict, so that all the fiery words and contentious bitching serve only to upset a normally serene community. (pp. 51-2)

O'Connor's struggle in *Bones of Contention* is primarily with himself, a struggle for a suitable style and for genuine concerns.

The finest single story in *Bones of Contention,* "Michael's Wife," contains no provincial edginess or verbal squabbling. Irony is noticeably quiet and, above all, the sense of occasion is carried by highly evocative description. In his best stories O'Connor provides just enough physical background to give a particular incident locality. Dan Bride, the old man of "Majesty of the Law," fits securely into his rough-hewn, almost archaic environment. Helena, the felon of "In the Train," is placed in momentary relief by the description of Farranchreesht. The sense of total occasion crystallizes both stories, completing for a hesitant instant the incomplete puzzle of life. "Michael's Wife" is like the dramatic lyrics of ancient Irish poetry because of the way O'Connor merges the presentation of Irish place with the drama of an Irish person. It is not lyrical, as some critics have argued, just because of the descriptive language. It is lyrical because the sound of the voice is heard within a supremely resonant environment. And it is dramatic because its occasion is so immediate that the voice is at once discreet and expansive.

"Michael's Wife" is probably the most perfect illustration of O'Connor's theory of collaboration. In it he does indeed grab the reader by the lapels, dragging him into the center of the story. (pp. 56-7)

As satisfying as it is, *Bones of Contention* is more or less of a piece. By the time he produced his third volume of stories O'Connor had not only explored the limits of his medium but had begun to expand them. The stories of the late thirties and early forties, many of which were originally published in *The Bell,* are consistently fine. Consequently, *Crab Apple Jelly,* published in 1944, is at once the most varied and the most disciplined single volume he was to produce. As its title implies, the volume is both sweet and tart, entertaining and serious. It contains some of the savage criticism of Irish life apparent in *Dutch Interior;* O'Connor was adamant that Ireland begin to look beyond its own shoreline. However, he does not cast blame or seek causes. His humanism accepts people for what they are. If there is a unity in the volume it is not a preconceived campaign, just a natural unity of manner and tone.

The first story, "Bridal Night," is powerfully impressionistic, and though it has more emotional impact than most of his stories, it is hardly sentimental. What strikes the reader is not just emotion, but the aptness of emotion. (p. 59)

O'Connor's so-called "lyrical" stories leave little doubt about the power of his prose to evoke highly poetic visual images. One of the most intriguing of these is "Uprooted," a story about two brothers, a teacher and a priest, both frustrated by the present and cut off from the past. Ned Keating, the teacher, is bored in Dublin by routine and judicious patterns. Tom, the more spontaneous and vigorous of the two, is a curate in Wicklow. Together they visit their home in the west. O'Connor's descriptions and conversational exchanges are forthright and swift. The momentum of the story is fierce, disallowing deep speculation. Neither of the brothers has time to think, time to be nostalgic, or time to regret. They are bustled about, sharing hospitable drinks and meeting forgotten relations. On the island home of their mother's people they enjoy the company of young people. Ned enjoys a moment of physical attraction:

> Everything had darkened and grown lonely, and with his head in the blinding folds of the shawl which reeked of turfsmoke and his arm about Cait, Ned felt as if he had dropped out of Time's pocket.
>
> (pp. 60-1)

The end of the story is sullen; the next morning the brothers share in drowsy recollection their distraught night. Ned is troubled by Cait, of course, and the shadowy possibility of marriage. Tom's turmoil is more profound, suggesting a false vivacity the day before. . . . O'Connor locates both men in the "subjunctive"—Tom for his vicarious experience of human relationship and Ned for his reticence toward love. The committed priest thinks of what might have been and the uncommitted teacher of what might be, but rather than go back on choices once made they simply fall back into "Time's pocket." As the two brothers leave home, the reader gets the distinct feeling that he is watching the final uprooting of the two men in a moment of suspended time. In the "magical light" of dawn over Carigan-assa, Ned's loss is the loss of childhood, of an intolerably vivid world. His future is as "remote and intangible" as Tom's is futile and lonely. The lyrical moment is the uprooting itself, the suspending of human personality between the irremediable past and the intractable future, between promise and regret. (pp. 61-2)

O'Connor once said that "An Irish writer without contention is a freak of nature. All the literature that matters to me was written by people who had to dodge the censor." The sexual repression of middle-class Irish life provided more than one Irish writer ready material for fiction. Even as the "in" Irish writer was expected to attack the clergy, so he was expected to "shock" Irish readers with a little sex, or to expose ruthlessly the sexual blight of a parochial society. O'Connor avoided both subjects until *Crab Apple Jelly,* refusing to wage a token war, to stoop to rhetoric. Later he was censored and to some he is only remembered for that. "The Mad Lomasneys" is one of his earliest and one of his most successful stories about the strange way of love among the Irish. The relationship of Ned Lowry and Rita Lomasney engages O'Connor's singular attention in the story from their first, awkward encounter as adolescents to their strained and unfortunate parting. Rita is an independent, rather rash girl, with a manner best described as audacious and a voice that seems to laugh casually at life. Ned is rather unperturbably automatic, though also "clever . . . precise and tranquil." But O'Connor is not just juxtaposing the predictable and the unpredictable. He is carefully accenting the subtle games played by the middle class. Consequently, much of the story takes the same dramatic form as "The Luceys," so that despite a lapse of time the effect is intensely immediate. (p. 65)

The stories of *Crab Apple Jelly* represent the refinement of O'Connor's technique of exploiting the "tone of a man's voice, speaking." He didn't see life steadily or whole; he heard it in bits and snatches. . . . Nowhere is his attention to voices more evident than in "The Long Road to Ummera," a simple tale about an old woman's eccentric wish to be buried in the mountain home of her people. By his own admission the main voices were those of his own father and grandmother. The story begins: "Always in the evenings you saw her shuffle up the road. . . ." The narrator is personal and informal, speaking about his own neighbors, not about strangers. Thomas Flanagan takes this fidelity to the community to be contradictory to O'Connor's theory of the "lonely voice." . . . The voice is lonely though it speaks within the community; O'Connor's voice is lonely not in spite of his fidelity to the community but because of it. (pp. 68-9)

Before the appearance of "The Drunkard," "Christmas Morning," and "My Oedipus Complex" he used first-person narration sparingly, and then generally as an interlocutor retelling a story told to him. The involvement of the narrator in "The Long Road to Ummera" or "Peasants" is genuine but not personal. However, one of the best stories in *The Common Chord,* "Judus," is the hilarious account by a settled bachelor of his first courtship; whether it was also his last we can only guess. He chuckles at his naive fantasies and foolish antics. But he fails to comprehend what the reader can't miss—his tragic dependence on his mother. O'Connor had listened to Irish life with brutal honesty. What he found was that people make themselves miserable, that they delude themselves, that they act in silly, indiscreet, or even vicious ways in spite of everything they know to the contrary. When he turned to situations closer to himself, his honesty still prevailed. He resisted the temptations of misanthropy and self-indulgence by adhering strictly to the limitations of his aesthetic: he was an observer, not a judge or an exhibitionist. (pp. 69-70)

A Set of Variations, twenty-seven stories written mostly in the 1960s, is not his best collection but it does suggest that in the last few years of his life Frank O'Connor had returned to whatever it was that produced the stories of the 1930s. Throughout the volume he is turning old sod, sifting through old themes, returning to old loyalties. However, the book is hardly the work of a tired old man resurrecting past glories. Rather, it is the work of one whose hand is steady, whose eye is keen, and whose voice is clear. As a whole, *A Set of Variations* has a range of interest and style comparable to *Crab Apple Jelly*. The domestic relations are mainly adult relations. In fact, there are more stories about old people and about death than in any previous volume. But O'Connor could never be grim or morbid; his humor is as wry as ever. (p. 75)

Scanning the entire course of Frank O'Connor's literary career, one is above all impressed by a remarkable unity of purpose working through a maze of conflicting impulses. He was a person of fierce sympathies. His idealism was often too buoyant, his bitterness often too heavy. But when it came to his writing he was a model of discipline and control. What this indicates, I think, is that . . . he never really ceased to be a romantic, by which he meant a way of seeing things, a style of life at once impulsive and searching. He rejected the romantic aesthetic, which he saw as the sentimental indulgence of the trite emotion, the reliance on the nostalgic or rhetorical generality. Likewise, he rejected the realistic way of seeing things—the "sensible" compromise, the cynical indifference to human needs, or the sterile, academic appraisal of life. But he completely affirmed the realistic aesthetic—the careful manner and sensitive frankness that are the trademarks of his writing from first to last.

Unquestionably, O'Connor's early writing represents some of his very finest work. His early stories and essays are especially impressive for the exuberance of their concerns and the unpretentious clarity of their style. His first volume, *Guests of the Nation,* was mainly about the insurrection. The energy of the entire volume emanates equally from O'Connor's unrestrained youthfulness and his idealistic fervor. That he later repudiated this early mode of writing does not repudiate its idealism. The violence of "Guests of the Nation" is a fresh, even creative sort of thing; but for him to have indulged it would have been to stagnate. Though he moved away from violence, he nevertheless continued for some time to operate within a context of youthful vigor. For example, his two novels, written while he was still trying to decide whether or not to write at all, were boldly uncertain efforts. In the first, *The Saint and Mary Kate* (1932), O'Connor's sympathetic idealism was too buoyant to control. In the second, *Dutch Interior* (1940), the unnaturally obtuse form was too flimsy to support the weight of O'Connor's embittered social criticism. Like the poems he was writing at about the same time, the novels were improvisational and imbalanced. But where the poems exhibited a mannered facetiousness, the novels were extremely serious and personal.

One of O'Connor's pet critical assumptions was that a person's art is an allegory of his life; one writes what he is. To that extent, then, his own writing is autobiographical. His two novels, especially, revealed his vacillation between such "counter-truths" as realism and romanticism, objectivity and subjectivity, judgment and instinct. (pp. 87-8)

All in all, the story of Frank O'Connor is the story. Invariably, his imagination forced itself through the picturesque, the historical and the abstract to some story, some point of vivid impact. For him human dignity and rationality inevitably yield to the sudden impulse, to the unpredictable and passing moment. O'Connor believed that it is "not for nothing that some of the great storytellers . . . have been tramps." . . . To O'Connor a story, whether it was about the Nun of Beare, Michael Collins, the Rock of Cashel, or those "displaced persons" of Cork, was nothing less than a "lyric cry in the face of destiny."

Frank O'Connor's stories were a sort of personal revolution. He took the form seriously and stayed with it despite modest financial benefits and pressures for a "major work." Only a secure vision of man and of himself as an artist explains this dedication to the Irish "common reader" and his constant focus on the "little guy." Everything he wrote displays his improvising and contending spirit, but his stories speak most eloquently of his lonely struggle for integrity and freedom. If any single attitude consistently looms large in O'Connor's work, it is a distrust of human reason, a suspicion of the abstract or the unnatural. Yet ironically, the principal strategy of his stories is containment, a deliberate scaling down of issues, situations and techniques. Simplicity requires conscious discipline and superb control—it's hard to be easy. . . . When all is said, his stories will stand as his most enduring contribution to modern literature and to Irish life. (pp. 89-90)

James H. Matthews, in his Frank O'Connor *(© 1976 by Associated University Presses, Inc.), Bucknell University Press, 1976, 94 p.*

PATRICK KAVANAGH

In 1922 [O'Connor], with O'Faolain, took the Republican side in the Civil War, and his early stories, like O'Faolain's, are based on those experiences. Unlike O'Faolain's, however, O'Connor's lack the somewhat cynical objectivity which the theme demanded. Next we find him interned. The Internment Camp was for him the equivalent of a university. There among his fellow internees were to be found a number of men with questioning minds. . . . O'Connor made contact with the humanist side of letters and with Yeats. He contributed poems, stories and reviews of Gaelic plays to [*The Irish Statesman*], and these are all full of the warm imagination of young genius. But they also suffer from a serious defect which can, I think, be attributed to the influence of Yeats. Yeats created a pose of swift indifference to the common earth, and the same isolation in the thin air of "literature" is to be found in O'Connor. . . . It would not be entirely true to say that O'Connor had entirely detached himself from his background, but he dimmed it into a literary mist.

The Yeatsian pose of aristocracy suited Yeats, for the pose fitted him perfectly. It was the essence of Yeats' verse. O'Connor also attempted in his own verse the ruthless hammer-blow arrogance of the older poet. (p. 41)

"He has his roots in the soil" is a well-known phrase and people who say it generally mean that the man was born and reared in a country place. But the real soil in which a man's roots are is the soil of common experience. You can follow the tracks of the writer whose feet are in that soil—Blake, Wordsworth, Milton, Shelley or Yeats—their clay trail is the trail we can follow. . . . However high they raised their mystical heads they all had their feet on the clay earth. That is why they felt the electric shock. Can one say the same of O'Connor?

As I pursue him I am continually losing the trail. Has he a direction? His feet are too seldom on the earth for me to follow. Is he merely a high-flying entertainer? Does his work hold the mirror up to life? Does he mean anything? (pp. 41-2)

[The] very fact that he began as a translator is somewhat of a key to his work—that his technical and imaginative machinery is greater than his material. For, like a great actor who is useless without a theme, O'Connor is inclined to be futile when left with only his own experience. Surely nobody has ever done such exciting translations as he has. . . . His own original verse which . . . was published in a volume called *Three Old Brothers* is obvious, honest verse. He uses a Yeatsian technique—the adjectiveless bang, bang of nouns. But what in the hands of Yeats becomes magic in O'Connor's use of it becomes a dumb wooden mallet. . . . As a poet he can only be seriously considered as a translator from the Gaelic. His actor's ability to give body and life to somebody else's ideas is shown by these translations.

O'Connor has written two novels but his reputation is rightly founded on his short stories. The first collection of his short stories to be published was *Guests of the Nation* based on his experiences in the Civil War. These stories touch the earth at more points than any of his other work, and yet for all that they lack a very vivid detail. . . . [Is] there enough poetic excitement and vitality in these stories to compensate for the dimness of the representation? He seems to me to fall between two stools. He is neither on the safe earth nor among the stars. What makes his work deceptive is the fact that he is very nearly on the earth. He is —as it were—about an inch from the top of the grass. . . . *Guests Of The Nation* has in lieu of real blood a good deal of the treacle of sentimentality. (pp. 42-4)

In some of these stories there is a charming poetic atmosphere, but even it is always half and half. You cannot damn it without being wrong and you cannot praise without being equally wrong.

His first novel *The Saint And Mary Kate* is a charming idyll of young people in Cork City. It is lyrical in a thin way. The heroine is a sentimental character. She is closely observed and heavily documented, but the lot doesn't add up to a fully alive human being. Once again you have that inch which is as bad as a mile, between its dangling feet and the earth. You can discern the characters moving vaguely beneath the literary skin. In so far as our straining eyes can pick out the landmarks this is something of a revelation of life in Cork—or anywhere. What I enjoy about *The Saint* are the too occasional episodes into which the author has put without stinting prudence the essence of his experience. . . . Unfortunately there is a lot of descriptive stuff in the novel, a desperate straining to give us all the facts. . . . (p. 45)

He has hardly ever written a story that is not entertaining. He has hardly ever written a story that does not bear some resemblance to reality. But as in his novels and other work there is a "kitchening" of the material, a tentativeness. He is a showman, getting the laughs where he can, but from the more serious point of view purposeless. His second collection of short stories called *Bones of Contention* has a number of very enjoyable pieces. "The Majesty of The Law" is a [brilliant burlesque]. . . . This is the best of comedy, and like the majority of comic writing it is detached—from Life. The main character is a lie, the sort of good-natured myth which makes good-natured fools, open-mouthed, uncritical, say: "Aren't these Irish charming?" The author is in that particular mood which most of us have experienced to our spiritual cost in which we are being corrupted by our audience. (pp. 46-7)

I have heard O'Connor compared to Chekhov. No two writers could be more unlike. Chekov's genius is the cutting edge of sincerity ruthlessly piercing through the crust of the ordinary. His courageous poetic mind is never the slave of his audience. One can see it in all Chekov's work—the continual surprise which vexes so many people who want a writer to run true to form. (p. 47)

Throughout all O'Connor's stories I am being continually mesmerised by the easy hum-hum of the narrative. Sometimes he says things which may shock but they are artificial shocks as when he takes pleasure in the weakness of human beings. The creative shock of truth revealed is a different thing. His next collection of stories is *Crab Apple Jelly*, and it is a very jelly-like book. (p. 48)

A great poet never sneers. He may show people sneering but he does not take part in it as [O'Connor sometimes] seems to take part. You cannot satirise fraudulent piety unless you stand on some dogmatic centre of truth. This is necessary even as a hypothesis. In so far as O'Connor has a centre it is in his unholy laughter which is fairly constant.

It would be hard to overpraise the skill with which the stories in . . . *The Common Chord*, are composed. Yet, these sexy stories are utterly unreal. How often as I read did I wish that the author could have thrown in a few spadefuls of the earth's healthy reality—roots, stones, worms, dung. In this patch intelligence could grow. It will be observed that the greatest writers never take themselves seriously—only their work. O'Connor takes himself seriously but his characters lightly. A Calvinistic leer grins from every page. O'Connor's Nora Lalor's, Tim O'Regan's, etc., are not people but silly "attitudes" which are to be found less in Ireland than in a war-hysterical England, and their intellectual level is that of the gossip columns. . . .

Passing an interim judgment on O'Connor I find that he is a purveyor of emotional entertainment, and that he has surrendered to this minor rôle. There is tension in his mind but most of this tension is expended on the construction of the container so that there is little left for the contents. He is like a powerful engine drawing a light load. The same is true of many writers who have achieved great contemporary fame—Joyce is a good example. Every generation produces fine technicians, designers, entertainers. But time destroys the tension of the wrapping paper, which their contemporaries mistook for inner excitement, leaving the dusty contents to be blown by the wind. (p. 49)

Patrick Kavanagh, "Coloured Balloons: A Study of Frank O'Connor" (reprinted by permission of Mrs. Katherine B. Kavanagh and Martin Brian & O'Keeffe Ltd.), in The Bell, *December, 1947 (and reprinted in* The Journal of Irish Literature, *Vol. VI, No. 1, January, 1977, pp. 40-9).*

* * *

O'DONOVAN, Michael
See O'CONNOR, Frank

* * *

O'FAOLÁIN, Sean 1900-

O'Faoláin, an Irish short story writer, novelist, critic, biographer, and playwright, is one of the foremost short story writers of the twentieth century. O'Faoláin spent his youth involved with politics and participated in the Irish Revolution of 1916-23. His stories deal with modern Ireland and its people; his lyrical prose evokes such Irish stereotypical charac-

ters as aging bachelors and priests without yielding to sentimentality. (See also *CLC,* Vols. 1, 7, and *Contemporary Authors,* Vols. 61-64.)

DONAT O'DONNELL

The "realists" of today, although apt to revolt or grumble against the rule of the past, have also a powerful and often creative sense of tradition. In the case of Sean O'Faolain this sense is especially, perhaps morbidly acute. It has animated some of his best writing with the mass-emotion of living history; it has also often fallen like an antique blanket smothering the life out of the beings he has created. (p. 3)

His first two novels, *A Nest of Simple Folk* and *Bird Alone,* are situated almost entirely in the shadow of preceding generations; a penumbra of folklore and historical conjecture in which however the living figure of a hero is clearly visible.

As a story of family life, a "saga" in the Galsworthian sense, *A Nest of Simple Folk* suffers from a great hiatus by reason of the author's failure to interest himself in the personality of any member of the middle generation. As the story of the fate of an individual it fails for a similar reason; towards the end the central character, Leo Donnel, although physically active, declines from the status of protagonist into that of phenomenon, a vague enigma of a potential symbol. In fact his creator is tired of him and wants to get on to Denis, his grandson. This gap in interest, enough to kill the attention of most readers, spoils the novel from any point of view. And yet *A Nest of Simple Folk* is a memorable work; memorable as an instance of the power and passion of memory.

Bird Alone is, in a sense, less deeply sunk in the past than *A Nest of Simple Folk.* Its narrator, Corney, an old man telling the story of his childhood and youth, was born in the 1870's, a quarter of a century or so after Leo Donnel and before O'Faolain. But behind Corney, and dominating the early part of his story, is again the figure of his Fenian grandfather, old Philip Crane. Old Philip, perhaps because he is described as seen by his grandson, and not merely reconstructed, is far more vivid and convincing than Leo Donnel. (p. 4)

The most obvious feature that *A Nest of Simple Folk* and *Bird Alone* have in common is atavism. In both novels the significant figures are an old man and a boy; in each the old man is a being of power, an accumulation of rage and lust, and ex-Fenian and an ex-fornicator; and in each the boy, under the old man's influence, becomes an outlaw in the world of his parents. The old man is the vital center, and seems to drag the temporal center of the story back into the past along with him; the youth receives from him the radiations of history and begins to turn into something like him. So in *Bird Alone,* Corney, the narrator, in his own lonely old age, an outcast from his tribe, enters easily now into the tormented mind of the "ageing wifeless man" who dominated his youth. Just as the middle generations are virtually "skipped" in both novels, the middle years of life are also "skipped" in *Bird Alone;* Corney is a youth listening to an old man, and then, quite suddenly, he is an old man himself. What happens in between is not a gradual process but a fracture: the youth has broken with the environment and beliefs of his youth and with the middle-aged people who represent them. Nothing remains real except the old man and the forces that through him went to cause the break. (pp. 6-7)

[Corney] finds, however, a natural ally in his grandfather and a flag in the traditions which his grandfather represents. The Irish rebels of the nineteenth century, so regularly condemned by the Hierarchy, were inevitable heroes for the spirited son of a pious and "loyal" family. Prometheus and Faust were remote and tenuous symbols but the Fenian dead, for whom, in that treasured episcopal phrase, "Hell was not hot enough nor eternity long enough," lived in the people's mind. In their names, revolt, that otherwise was doomed to futile isolation, found a way into the open, a fissure in the wall of acceptance. And even mightier than theirs was the name of Parnell, whose struggle not only against Church and State, but directly against the power of sexual prohibition made him the essential hero of rebellious youth. The sort of conversation that Joyce remembered in *A Portrait of the Artist* and of which O'Faolain captures the echoes in *Bird Alone,* the grown-up skirmishings about Parnell and purity and the priests must have been wildly exciting to hundreds of young minds. In young Corney's case, as no doubt in many others, such scenes helped, along with his grandfather's example, to establish a firm connection between the separate ideas of national, spiritual and sexual emancipation. As one name will be needed for this triple association we shall call it "parnellism" (as distinct from political "Parnellism"). (pp. 7-8)

A Nest of Simple Folk is planned to show the apotheosis of parnellism in a moment of historical decision. The 1916 rebellion frees Denis from his family and at the same time justifies the life of old Leo Donnel. The young rebel and the old, and their private rebellions, are merged in the national insurrection (in which, of course, their creator took part, at a later stage). They thus break out of their loneliness and recover through patriotism the unity with the people which they are unable to keep in religion. For them, and for almost all O'Faolain's central characters, this unity, perhaps because it is so difficult to achieve, is profoundly important, a condition of spiritual life, almost a religion in itself.

The dynamic element is also strong in O'Faolain's early short stories. The first collection, *Midsummer Night Madness,* published about the same time as *A Nest of Simple Folk,* is in one sense a sequel to it since most of the stories concern the Black-and-Tan war and the Civil War. Because these stories stress the brutality rather than the chivalry of the "Troubles" and because some of them are fairly outspoken about sex, they have been generally regarded as disillusioned and cynical or, by sympathizers, as coldly objective. Such views do not penetrate the surface, the impassivity of manner which thinly covers an excitement that is almost exultation.

The sad separateness of *Bird Alone* is also the predominant feeling in *A Purse of Coppers,* . . . but it shrinks into something more petty than Corney's stoicism. The protagonists of such stories as "The Old Master," "My Son Austin" and "A Born Genius" are all in their different ways artist-rebels and all are utterly defeated by the provincial life of Ireland.

The despair of *A Purse of Coppers* is unrelieved by any grandeur and the nearest approach to hope is contained in an unanswered question asked by the priest-narrator in the first story, "A Broken World": "What image of life that would fire and fuse us all, what music bursting like the spring, what trumpet, what engendering love . . ."

That O'Faolain has not answered this question is not surprising since history has not helped him. What is perhaps surprising is that he has continued to search history for an answer, digging deeper into the "racial mind" to find again the rebellious unity that Leo Donnel sought. His important biographies, *King of the Beggars* (1938) and *The Great O'Neill* (1942) develop and illuminate his half-mystical ideas of the nation. . . .

[*Come Back to Erin*] is so lacking in momentum and in any centralizing element that it is difficult to give a coherent account of it. It differs from the other novels in being situated entirely in "the present" and being free from grandfathers. But the pressure that Denis and Corney felt, the pressure of the Church through the family, is there again, impalpable and inescapable like the pressure of the atmosphere. It does not suffice to unify action, but hinders the divergent wills of a number of unequally interesting human beings. . . . (p. 9)

Through the gaseous flickering irresolution of *Come Back to Erin* there emerges the same rock of contradiction that contorts the structure of the biographies. However much he wants to, poor St. John cannot "be Irish" without "being Catholic," and as he cannot be Catholic he kills himself, thus making himself as sure of Hell as anyone can be. For Frankie on the other hand, and perhaps for some of the other characters, a sort of Limbo is reserved. He is, of course, Irish in the parnellistic mode, aggressive, anticlerical and "collectivist." He does not practice his religion but apparently continues, in some special way, to be Catholic. . . . The parnellistic way out is no longer valid for either of the brothers. It is a side-road that, after a brief historical detour, eventually leads back to the main enclosure where "being Irish" and "being Catholic" are the same. (pp. 10-11)

[*Teresa* (1947), a book of stories,] reflects very much the same world as *A Purse of Coppers* did ten years before. The clergy are still dominant, artists are still frustrated. The "fusing image" longed for in "A Broken Wheel" has clearly not been found. It still is being sought, however, perhaps less hopefully, but in the same places. The longest story in the book, "The Silence of the Valley" concerns the death of an old cobbler in the Gaeltacht, and the revelation to a group of visitors that this story-telling cobbler and his wife represented not merely the old Gaelic world but a primitive source of virtue, the natural state of innocence before the fall of man. This cobbler—the earthiness of whose stories we know to have brought on him the castigations of the clergy—is a necessary hero in the mythology of "Delphic nationalism." He is in fact the incarnation of the "true" Ireland: an Ireland before the Fall and therefore before Christianity, an Ireland which is its own religion and does not contradict.

This idea of the "true" Ireland has ceased to be an inspiring myth and has become a source of confusion and irritation. When O'Faolain was still writing out of the experience of his youth romantic Ireland was not dead. It was natural for him, whose own youth had coincided and mingled with his country's successful revolt, to fuse subjective and objective, identifying his own inner experience with the Irish revolution. This identification, extending back into the penumbra which had helped to produce it, established itself as a general association; nationalism was the communion of youth, freedom was a word of one indivisible meaning, the Irish-speaking districts of West Cork were a pagan Arcadia. Within a limited historical field, a period, ending in the early 1930's—during which a powerful revolutionary tradition ran not only against the Crown, but against the Church also—this association was coherent and a source of power. But revolution is little more permanent than youth. The Ireland in which O'Faolain now lives and writes is [at the time of this essay], the least romantic and the least revolutionary of countries. It is one in which Church and State exist in absolute harmony, as inexpugnable bastions of the family. Here the parents of Corney or Denis could live secure, for there is no fissure at all in the wall of acceptance. Parnell's place has been taken by a line of pious and blameless patriots and rebellion has become a praiseworthy but concluded activity. Ireland is now a middle-aged country. Youth can take it or leave it—and often leaves it.

O'Faolain will neither take it nor leave it. He sees of course, and bitterly resents, Ireland's staid paternalism, symbolized for him principally by the literary Censorship Board, which has banned three of his books (*Midsummer Night Madness, Bird Alone* and *A Purse of Coppers*). In scores of articles and letters he has denounced this institution and the spirit behind it. . . . His stories, with their great and increasing emphasis on the frustrations and stagnations of Irish life, show his oppression by that spirit and his knowledge of its power. But in combating it, which he has done more fearlessly than any other writer living continuously in Ireland, he has relied emotionally on something that has lost its meaning in the new environment—the old anticlerical nationalism. The clear-cut attitude of Frank O'Connor, who can laugh both at the people and at what they believe, is not for him, since he believes in the people. Corney's feat of believing in the people without sharing their beliefs is one that cannot be maintained for long, and *Come Back to Erin* is evidence of a sense that an Irish nationalist must, if only indirectly, be a religious man. Thus, starting as irreligion, or at least as anticlericalism, the patriotic emotion leads back to religion again. This flight involves a difficult mental revolution. It is hardly surprising that *Come Back to Erin* is a confused novel. . . . (pp. 11-12)

O'Faolain is not regarded in Ireland as a Catholic writer. . . . Abroad, however, he is a Catholic; his books figure in the American *Guide to Catholic Literature* (though not always with favourable comment), and one of them, *King of the Beggars,* was actually a choice of the Catholic Book Club of America. The difference of opinion is not surprising. O'Faolain is a complex writer, and in any case it has long been a matter of doubt whether any novelist (or poet or dramatist) can be properly described as being in his creative function "Catholic." If we apply the strict test of edification, and insist, like Maritain, that the Catholic novelist should abstract himself from the sinfulness of his characters, and contemplate it, without collusion, from the "altitude" then O'Faolain fails. (p. 12)

O'Faolain . . . is parochial. He neither affirms nor denies anything of universal importance. . . . [But he does not present] the "nationalism" of Dostoevski or Yeats or even Stefan George, which was in each case the vehicle for a general idea, apocalyptic or messianic. O'Faolain does not believe in "Holy Ireland," or in an aristocracy or in "the descent into the ancient Blood." The archaic nationalism which shows itself in his novels and stories is free from all taint of generality. His stories are illuminating about Ireland; an anthropological entertainment to the curious foreigner, an annoyance and a stimulus to the native. To Ireland the stimulus is of great value; in a time of sleepy simulation O'Faolain's irascible and dissenting temperament has struggled, not without success, to preserve some honest intellectual life among his people. What he may have lost himself in that struggle we cannot know.

We know that once, in *Bird Alone,* he managed to move from particulars to the universal and to write a novel of real importance. Corney is ripped away from everything he had been bound to; from his home, from the sentimental religion of his boyhood and the patriotism of his youth, from Elsie, from his native city. In the end he is a naked man, helpless, confronted with the God of his father. If at that point he had made an Act of Faith, *Bird Alone* would have been hailed everywhere, even in Ireland (outside Cork), as a great Catholic novel, for the whole book would have seemed to move to this end. The fact that he said "No" seems to me to put the book on a much higher plane than that of edification: the level of truth. The old man would not assent because he did not believe; and his creator was not willing to make him believe in order to please the readers of the novel. The reality of the character emerges in the stubborn rejection. *Bird Alone* is about human fate, which is harder than fiction. (pp. 13-14)

It is almost superhumanly difficult to be a Catholic writer in a Catholic country; the pressure of a community varies inversely with its size; ingrowing nationalism destroys a writer's scope. O'Faolain has been a living example of the truth and interrelation of these three propositions. (p. 14)

Donat O'Donnell, "The Parnellism of Sean O'Faolain," in Renascence *(© copyright, 1950, Marquette University Press), Vol. III, No. 1, Autumn, 1950, pp. 3-14.*

JULIAN MOYNAHAN

O'Faoláin is a virtuoso short story writer and teller of tales, an impressive historical biographer (of O'Connell, Newman, and Hugh O'Neill the second Earl of Tyrone among others), an urbane, learned and cosmopolitan travel writer, and a distinguished literary editor, critic and literary journalist who has written such works as *The Vanishing Hero* (1957) . . . which show a richness of original insight into the development of the nineteenth- and twentieth-century novel. Yet in his own creative practice he seems not to have got on with the task of novel writing all that well. (p. 19)

In his introduction to *The Heat of the Sun, Stories and Tales* (1966), O'Faoláin compares the novel to a giant aircraft carrier whose sole function is to launch a certain number of brilliant flights from the blank expanse of its flat deck. This seems a modern version of Poe's claim that there are no long poems, only short ones imbedded at intervals throughout such otherwise prosaic works as *Paradise Lost* and *The Divine Comedy*. However, one must not be misled by this comparison into thinking that O'Faoláin is only capable of short verbal flights. . . . Witness the magnificently sustained narrative performance of *The Great O'Neill,* the great narrative arches and edifice of *A Nest of Simple Folk*. (p. 20)

Henry James coped with the thinness of American social and cultural life by going abroad and by internationalising his literary concerns. O'Faoláin could have done the same thing. No one who knows his mind and talents will fail to recognise that he could have made a brilliant literary career in any of several countries, especially the United States and Britain. But he was drawn back to Ireland. . . . What was his reward? The Censorship Act of 1929. Would exile have been preferable? Perhaps it is time to get rid of this rather thrillingly Byronic term in the discussion of Irish literary dilemmas. It was appropriate when Stephen Dedalus considered his options at the end of the last century. But it had already outlived its usefulness by the early nineteen twenties when Joyce was established in Paris with a sufficiency of funds, a huge reputation, a circle of admirers and ready access to Ireland via correspondence, the habit of library research and an adequate public transportation system. In the modern world, writers are at home where they are. . . . Exile doesn't come into it. Let us emphasise then that O'Faoláin chose to tie his work as a novelist to the new, developing society of post-Treaty Ireland and that he encountered certain difficulties when this society developed, as he saw it, towards a condition of uniformity and conformism, towards a boring quality of life. (pp. 21-2)

[One] wonders why O'Faoláin as novelist pinned his hopes to Trollopian and Balzacian norms which were developed to render the more differentiated, dense, and complex societies of nineteenth-century Britain and France. Why has he not attempted something more exploratory and experimental in his novels, along lines established by Joyce and extended by such disciples as Flann O'Brien and the early Samuel Beckett? The parodies, internal monologues, and other formally 'decreative' devices and techniques of *Ulysses* effectively render Irish (or at least Dublin) amorphousness, while the works of the disciples, *At Swim-Two-Birds* and *Watt* in particular, carry the project further and update it as well. I suspect the answer is that O'Faoláin found the procedures of Joyce and his school too assaultive upon certain pieties and decencies of Irish life, and the impulse from which they proceeded too alienated. His choice was to be more constructive, by attempting in his novels a method of critical realism to some extent drawn from the example of the great Russian realists, who had managed to use the Balzacian novel—albeit transforming it in the process—to interpret a society and a national character very different from the French. This created some problems for O'Faoláin: Irish society was too unshaped for the method he wished to use; perhaps too the problem that his essential literary temperament, which is a lyrical and romantic one, illsorts with a method of critical realism. (pp. 22-3)

[Something] must be said about O'Faoláin's ascription of artlessness and simplicity to Irish society and character. This becomes a puzzle when we notice that he simultaneously and repeatedly makes reference in his writings to "the obliqueness and involution of Irishmen". Although a character, like a short story, may be oblique and simple at the same time, the combination is not usual and might well become the subject of a novelist's investigation over a lifetime. It may be surmised that O'Faoláin understands that Irish people can be complicated and artful but may prefer, for reasons of a historical nature, to keep their complexity out of sight, or else only expressed in privileged communications with representatives of [the Catholic Church which he calls the new Ireland's] "one firmly outlined social institution". . . . Joyce remarks somewhere that the first law of Irish moral life is *omerta,* the communal oath of silence sworn by Sicilians. Since O'Faoláin is himself part and product of that simple yet involuted, artless yet oblique, Catholic Irish community of the "cautiously silent" which came into its own after 1916, it was inevitable that his work with the novel—it is a genre, D. H. Lawrence reminds us, that thrives on indiscretion, letting a true state of affairs emerge even against the firmest censorship of the novelist himself—would not proceed smoothly or issue in copious productions. (p. 23)

There is a dialectic of liberation and constriction in the novels that has no happy issue. One way of focussing it would be to consider the figure of the policeman, in the novels themselves but first in O'Faoláin's life. As is well known, his father was a member of the Royal Irish Constabulary at Cork, staunchly loyal to the British power and therefore inevitably in bitter conflict with his gifted Republican son from Easter Week onward. The oedipal struggle is normal and universal, but not often in literary history has the authority of the disapproving father been arrayed in such visible emblems of power and prestige. . . . O'Faoláin *pere,* or rather Constable Whelan, survives and flourishes in the new Ireland. It's just that the uniforms, along with the official source whence flows repressive legislation, censorship and moral censure, have changed. (pp. 23-4)

A Nest of Simple Folk, one of the few great novels of modern Irish literature and a deeply satisfying one as well, begins in the remote countryside of East Limerick in 1854 and ends in the city of Cork in 1916. It is full of pain . . . but it is also rich with fulfillment: the fulfillment of certain limited dreams and aspirations as three generations of a family perform the slow, impeded change from country to town to city that epitomises an important phase of Irish social history during nearly a century; and the larger fulfillment which is the successful outcome of a bitter and painful struggle against the British colonial rule from the era of James Stephens and the Fenians to the year and very day of the glorious Easter Rising.

The novels that follow *A Nest of Simple Folk* are much less satisfying, much less fulfilled and fulfilling, and these begin and end with, and centre upon the city of Cork. On a simple view of O'Faoláin's longer fiction, one might surmise that it is a good thing to go to Cork but not to remain there. It is, therefore, more than a little surprising that all of O'Faoláin's novels should be so tied to his native city, especially since his short fiction, and of course his literary and travel pieces, range far and wide across the rest of Ireland and the entire civilised world. But it is equally surprising, since there is that tie in the novels, that Cork should be presented as such a clog and restraint on the adolescent aspirations and romantic hopes and dreams of a Denis Hussey or Corny Crone. With the somewhat older Frankie Hannafey the situation is scarcely improved, if we consider that the city contains on the one hand the police spies and detectives whose business it is to betray him and hunt him down, and on the other the gloomy family house on Morrison's Island in whose attic room he lies hidden for weeks at a time, as if already in prison, and where his mentally afflicted mother suffers her cyclic bouts of mania and melancholia.

Nevertheless, one must add that, on the evidence of the novels, O'Faoláin's quarrel with Cork, like his quarrel with post-Treaty Ireland as a whole, is a lover's quarrel. . . . [Note that young Denis, in *A Nest of Simple Folk*] comes to see that the city which he had heretofore beheld as "builded of light and loveliness", is in fact "dark and tawdry, old and deformed." His reaction to this shattering discovery is not to scorn, or to plan an escape to greener pastures, but instead to search the city until he finds some vista or image that will redeem it from its sad decay. . . . (pp. 26-7)

To save his city from its own isolate shabbiness and provincialism, [Denis] associates in his imagination a bit of Cork with the splendid and glamorous "Tuscan tower" of Italian medievalism and humanism—the tunnel in the passage working like a tunnel in time—and the link is not entirely specious, for there is the historic and inevitable connection between the Catholic culture of Ireland, including Cork, and the Latin culture of continental Europe. (Denis is doing imagistically and naively what O'Faoláin himself was to do in argument when he maintained in *The Great O'Neill* that Ireland would have joined the system of Counter-reformation Catholic Europe, instead of remaining isolated and cut off, if only the Earl had succeeded in his rebellion, becoming the first real king of a unified Catholic Ireland.) (pp. 27-8)

Regardless of what happened at Kinsale in 1601, the city and its associated deep water port of Cobh do lie open to the ships of the world. Why is the city yet so stagnant and isolated? Why, if the novelist in O'Faoláin remains so attached to Cork, can he do so little to liberate it from itself?

I suppose a large part of the answer must lie in the sad realities of the city's, and of Ireland's, history. . . . [In *Come Back to Erin,* Frankie] sees the entire port as a sort of open wound through which Ireland bled the victims of the Famine by the hundreds of thousands.

This sense of Cork's and the entire country's past, mingling with Frankie's distaste for present Irish developments—*Come Back to Erin* is set in 1936—makes for a dismaying vision altogether. To the extent that it was O'Faoláin's vision as well, one understands why he never again attempted a novel that took its setting from his native place. It remains something of a mystery why that decision has entailed his giving up novel writing altogether. (pp. 28-9)

Julian Moynahan, "God Smiles, the Priest Beams, and the Novelist Groans," in Irish University Review: A Journal of Irish Studies *(©* Irish University Review: A Journal of Irish Studies*), Vol. 6, No. 1, Spring, 1976, pp. 19-29.*

FRANK TUOHY

[*Selected Stories*] is great fun [and,] although O'Faolain himself has written of peasants and *petits fonctionnaires,* he approaches genius in his portrayal of Irish women. In half a dozen of these stories, where he allows himself enough space to escape from the professional knowingness of a story like "Two of a Kind", he brings the truth of a sexual relationship to life. "Lovers of the Lake", "Dividends" and "In the Bosom of the Country" are the calm triumphs of a writer who, having started as one whom Yeats would have called a "Cork realist", has transcended [provincialism] . . . without abandoning Ireland as his theme. After his years in the IRA, O'Faolain discovered that "the combination of an acquisitive middle class and a vigorous and uncultivated church meant that the fight—for a republic as I understood it—had ended in total defeat". The effects of this defeat are everywhere in the present collection, which covers the period since the Second World War.

In fact, one of the great qualities of O'Faolain's writing—remarkable in itself in a writer born in 1900—is its close connection with contemporary life. It is not part of his method to avoid contingent fact and place his reliance on the eternal verities—though it has been characteristic of Irish writing from Yeats to Beckett and beyond to do so. . . .

The earlier stories are fizzy with images, reminding one a little of the poems of MacNeice or W. R. Rodgers. Later the style grows calmer: its transparencies bring out the connection with Turgenev—O'Faolain's first novel was called *A House of Simple Folk*. But it would be wrong to think of O'Faolain as merely continuing a traditional technique. His narrative can contain complexities worthy of Nabokov. In "An Inside Outside Complex" he copes beautifully with such recent obsessions as mirror-images, role-playing and identity crises, without at all compromising the humanity of his two lovers, a middle-aged faker of antiques and the lady dressmaker he marries.

A story like "Lovers of the Lake" shows how different the major concerns of these stories are from any equivalent in America or England. The chief characters exist for themselves alone, outside class hierarchy or social group. . . . [As] always with this writer, the conflict between religion and the personal life is treated with admirable even-handedness: a poor young woman, who has had six children in six years, comes out of confession saying: "God bless the poor innocent priest, I wish I knew as little about marriage as he does", and returns to her husband with renewed ardour.

I look forward to returning to this and other stories in this collection. In the meantime, we must celebrate a writer to whom old age has brought no diminution of wit, style or force of attack.

Frank Tuohy, "Evidence of Defeat," in The Times Literary Supplement *(© Times Newspapers Ltd. (London) 1978; reproduced from* The Times Literary Supplement *by permission), No. 3961, February 24, 1978, p. 236.*

TOM PAULIN

Sean O'Faolain called the art of which he is such a brilliant exponent "an immense confidence-trick, an immense illusion, as immense a technical achievement as the performance of an adept magician." O'Faolain wasn't actually attacking the short story, but he was insisting that its characterisation is always simple and undeveloped, and that we mustn't look for the depths and mysteries of personality in a literary form which can only make people "appear to appear." (p. 64)

Whether the way in which literary opinion turned unconsciously against the short story was due to this sense of its being essentially a cheat, it's difficult to say, but what is certainly true is that this most difficult art has recently begun to emerge from a long winter of neglect. . . . That sweet, subtle, teasing art has returned from its exile in triumph—and it has returned to remind us that silence, exile and loneliness were often (though not always) what it was about, and that we should no longer view those qualities as being necessarily reductive and limiting. (pp. 64-5)

The socially marginal is the setting of "Admiring the Scenery" where three teachers stand on a little railway platform in the middle of a vast stretch of bogland. (p. 65)

Concealed behind the story's ostensible subject—three men sharing an anecdote about an eccentric character—there is another level of experience, and it is in the recognition of this hidden subject that we receive that formal pleasure which is one of the essential qualities of every good short story. It's as though the story casts a shadow which is the untold story of Hanagan's miserable love-affair. And it would be quite unfair to say that O'Faolain is a conjurer making flatness seem three-dimensional, because what we admire here is both his technical skill and the feeling of depth which he creates. His ending is not an empty trick.

In this element of formal pleasure, which is one of the results of its disciplined tightness, the short story resembles the sonnet, and like the sonnet many short stories playfully invite the reader to notice and share their technical self-consciousness. . . . One of the many joys of O'Faolain's work lies in noticing the play of hidden allusion and commentary in it. In "I Remember! I Remember!" he aims a clever joke at naturalism as well as giving an example of a typically Irish mnemonic tyranny. In "Of Sanctity and Whiskey" he pays oblique tributes to Browning and James in this tale of a proud and cunning cleric sitting for an alcoholic portrait-painter, and in "The Faithless Wife" and the variously clever "How to Write a Short Story" he knocks his detested Maupassant, while in "Something, Everything, Anything, Nothing" he returns to James and Browning. It is like glimpsing a series of sophisticated conversations in a literary heaven of witty spirits.

O'Faolain is a great story-teller, who can be wry, dreamily otherworldly, sensuous, ascetic, sad and funny. (p. 66)

Tom Paulin, "Evidence of Neglect," in Encounter *(© 1978 by Encounter Ltd.), Vol. L, No. 6, June, 1978, pp. 64-71.**

GARY DAVENPORT

Sean O'Faolain is one of the last and unquestionably the greatest of that generation of Irish writers that emerged in the Irish Revolution of 1916 and following. During his writing career of nearly fifty years he has firmly established himself as one of the great story writers in English, and [*Selected Stories of Sean O'Faolain*] is sufficient to demonstrate his stature to the most critical reader. (p. 143)

His stories are typically dense, lush, complex, and rich—his is not an art of understatement. He has two major themes: what it means to be Irish, and what it means to be an Irish Catholic. O'Faolain is a loyal but critical Irishman; he is capable of denouncing Irish provincialism of both the nationalist and religious genres, but unlike Shaw he denounces it from within: he lives in Ireland and he remains a Catholic. His chief allegiance is that of many other Irish writers, including Joyce, whose Leopold Bloom gave it a convenient name: "life for men and women." And these stories are full to bursting of life. Landscape provides much of this richness—especially the fecund landscape of his native Cork: low thick clouds, endless rain, sodden earth. And the characters who live in this environment partake of its sense of being outside time. In "The Silence of the Valley" the death of a cobbler is simply no match for the life force generated by his friends and relatives—the Brueghelian atmosphere of eel-roasting, singing, and whisky-drinking that surrounds the funeral is the real power here.

And there is another power, one which is woven inextricably through Irish life—the Church. . . . From the first

O'Faolain detested the sort of arrogant provincialism that is sometimes associated with Irish Catholicism, but he embraces the faith joyously at its human level. Catholic theology—invariably from the layman's viewpoint—is a major preoccupation with him, and his affection for the subject is visible in the good-natured comedy that often results. He is of course not a comic writer in the way that Frank O'Connor was, but when he does turn to comedy his mastery of the mode is impressive. I am thinking particularly of "Angels and Ministers of Grace," which ranks with the best of O'Connor's comedies of Irish Catholicism. (pp. 143-44)

Gary Davenport, "Reviews: 'Selected Stories of Sean O'Faolain'," in The Hudson Review *(copyright © 1979 by The Hudson Review, Inc.; reprinted by permission), Vol. XXXII, No. 1, Spring, 1979, pp. 143-44.*

JOHN MELLORS

Sean O'Faolain's *Selected Stories* are taken from collections published between 1947 and 1976. Every one of the 17 is a splendid example of the master's art of storytelling. It is quite remarkable how quickly the characters come to life and engage our sympathies; after one page of a story you feel you know them as well as if you had read 50 pages of a novel. O'Faolain has the gift of capturing in one phrase or sentence a look, a mood, a relationship: a faithless wife in bed with her lover tells him that her husband 'reminds me of an unemptied ashtray'. No other Irish writer has analysed so shrewdly and yet so charitably, and presented so entertainingly, the 'incongruities and contradictions' in his compatriots.

John Mellors, "Exuberant Lies," in The Listener *(© British Broadcasting Corp. 1979; reprinted by permission of John Mellors), Vol. 99, No. 2556, April 20, 1979, p. 510.**

ANDREW MOTION

The hero of Sean O'Faolain's [*And Again?* is] . . . anxious to find a social role which suits his authentic self. . . . Robert Younger doesn't die—or at least he reaches the age of 65 and is then invited by 'Our Celestial Divinities' to live backwards until he enters 'the womb of Time' again. . . . The point, O'Faolain and the Divinities insist, is to discover 'whether what you humans call Experience teaches you a damned thing'.

Given the silliness of its plot, *And Again?* manages to be remarkably serious and sympathetic. When O'Faolain deals with the process of 'younging' he involves himself in rather feeble absurdities, but he wisely prefers to concentrate on his hero's effort to reconstruct his past. A few clues quickly lead him to the arms of Ana ffrench—with whom he discovers he's been having an affair for 20 years—and so to the heart of the book. Its main concern is with the domination of love by time. Hence the supernatural elements, which add a special poignancy. . . . (p. 471)

Andrew Motion, "Time Trouble," in New Statesman *(© 1979 The Statesman & Nation Publishing Co. Ltd.), Vol. 98, No. 2532, September 28, 1979, pp. 470-71.**

* * *

OGAWA, Pelorhanke Ai
See AI

ONDAATJE, (Philip) Michael 1943-

Ondaatje is a Canadian poet, playwright, critic, editor, and film director who was born in Ceylon. The musical, rhythmic intensity of his poetry reveals Ondaatje's love of language and sensitivity to the meaning of words. (See also *Contemporary Authors,* Vols. 77-80.)

DOUGLAS BARBOUR

[*The Dainty Monsters*] is the finest first book of poems to appear since Margaret Avison's *Winter Sun.* Michael Ondaatje represents a healthy reaction in modern Canadian poetry. Although a completely contemporary writer, he eschews the "simple", almost barren, style of so many of the poets influenced by the Black Mountain group. He owes much of his originality to his background, I think. The exotic imagery which crowds the pages of this book appears to stem from his childhood memories of Ceylon. His poems are jungle-lush, but, unlike a jungle, they are cultivated and controlled. Their profuseness suggest a full and fertile mind always at work.

Imagery, in itself, is not enough, of course. Michael Ondaatje is also sensitive to poetic form, and he exercises a firm rhythmic control over his language. There is also, in his longer poems, his sense of plot, or story. In the poems of the second part of the book, he demonstrates a fine and subtle understanding of poetic narrative. This does not mean he longwindedly "tells the story." Rather, the story exists behind the poem, always present to focus the specific incident in a precisely imagined context. This suggestion of story context often occurs in the shorter poems, too. In "The Moving to Griffin", for example, there is a gain in density from the implied context of the poet's life story.

Ondaatje's imagery is obsessively natural: the book is a kind of modern bestiary, with birds, predatory and domestic animals, and the beast, man, always present, always active. Images of birds, especially, occur again and again. Yet in the poem, "Song to Alfred Hitchcock and Wilkinson", he does the unexpected, and the poem fairly leaps from the page as a result:

> Flif flif flif flif very fast
> is the noise the birds make
> running over us.
> A poet would say 'fluttering',
> or
> 'see-sawing with sun on their wings'.
> But all it is
> is flif flif flif flif very fast.

Although his poems are filled with images of violence and terror, his love poems are able to stand against this vision. Life is seldom gentle in these poems, but the love lyrics salvage and savour those moments of deep gentleness which cannot last but must be accepted joyfully in their passing. "The Diverse Causes", "She Carries a 'Fat Gold Watch'", "Christmas Poem, 1965", "Four Eyes", as well as the poems of love in the Troy Town section, all present the particular moments of communion with an intensity sufficient to command belief. We accept the validity of such moments because the poems poignantly create that validity. (pp. 86-7)

Yet Ondaatje's poetry never dissolves into sentimentality. His sure control, and the precision of his vision won't allow that. The ironies of his animal poems, his use of tone, the mythic vision of the Troy Town poems, the sense of the power in others, of our inability to control or protect others . . . all preclude sentimentality. He is too tough-minded, too aware of the complexities of life, and his poetry offers no answers or escapes, as sentimentality always does.

"Troy Town", the second part of *The Dainty Monsters,* is concerned with myth and the creation of myth. This is a difficult term; but it should be sufficient to suggest that, in these poems, Ondaatje tells "stories" which engender responses of awe and admiration. The life of these poems is violent, for they deal with the permutations of human violence. He has used the well-known myths of Troy and Lilith for some of these poems, but he has also created new myths out of history, or, in "Peter", probably the finest poem in the collection, out of his own imagination. The poem on Egypt, and the Elizabeth poems . . . are fascinating for their sense of the person. These are monologues, and, especially in "Elizabeth", he has achieved a high degree of dramatic realism. I have said that he has a clear imaginative understanding of violence, yet this violence never overwhelms the poet. The poetry is not voluptuous in its violence; it is chiseled and carefully wrought. The old idea of decorum applies perfectly to these poems. This is especially true of "Peter", where the poet deals with varieties of physical and mental violence in an almost virginally pure style and manner. The result is a tremendous gain in imaginative force over most modern treatments of the theme.

This is a beautiful book. It is this in both senses of the word, as a work of poet's craft and as a work of printer's craft. (pp. 87-8)

Douglas Barbour, "Controlling the Jungle," in Canadian Literature, *No. 36, Spring, 1968, pp. 86-8.*

ANDREAS SCHROEDER

The many lamely constructed similes of *Dainty Monsters* and the often lurid lyric excesses of *The Man With Seven Toes* are a far cry from the more carefully crafted, casually understated material of [*The Collected Works of Billy the Kid*]. Negotiating this book, I sensed a sure-footedness, a control which I have never felt in Ondaatje's earlier books. Indeed, if he hadn't used the historic framework of the adventures of Mrs. Fraser (*The Man With Seven Toes*) in a manner somewhat prophetic of his similar technique in *The Collected Works of Billy the Kid,* I would have found little area for comparison whatsoever.

The rather unusual choice of an old Wild-West saga—the story of Billy the Kid—as a literary vehicle struck me at first as dubious, but strikes me now as quite an intelligent choice to have made. For one thing, though much has been written about the incidents surrounding the Kid's life . . . , very little record remains (or has existed) of the Kid's own version of his story, of anything which might have given the reader more of an insight into his character than the descriptions of those who claimed to know him. . . . [The] Kid still remains essentially a silent, mysterious puzzle, an assemblage of pieces of hearsay and history representing a man whose deeds were clear, but whose reasons for perpetrating them were not. For this reason there was plenty of room for Ondaatje to develop and amplify, with few restrictions, an entire personage to whatever specifications he pleased, and, on top of this, to plunge quickly into deep water without having to waste unnecessary space with lengthy explanations and introductions, since the exterior, physical realities of his subject were already general cultural property.

In *The Collected Works,* then, Ondaatje projects himself into the minds of the Kid and Sheriff Garrett to retell the saga from the inside, writing down the reminiscences, jokes, casual thoughts, answers to simulated questions and even hallucinations which may have passed through the two men's minds. Using poems, prose sketches, "eyewitness" reports, diary-like notations and an ostensible newspaper interview with the Kid, Ondaatje restores to the saga the third dimension it had lost by having become an old tale always told from a single storyteller's point of view. Ondaatje's "new version", in fact, becomes one of the most intimate kinds of documentary imaginable, the camera having completely free access to both public and private sides of the subject(s); i.e. the incidents themselves as well as the minds of the men who provoked them are open to inspection.

Of course, the value of *The Collected Works* as a colourfully reconstituted account of the history of Billy the Kid has only little to do with the value of the book. . . . The success of the poetry and prose . . . goes well beyond its subject—a telltale hallmark of good literature in any style. And if the person of Billy the Kid consequently evolves into a character almost too sensitive to be a believable gunman, well—history must remain the slave of Art. (pp. 80-2)

Indeed, one is always conscious of Ondaatje speaking through the mask of Billy, Garrett, or any of the other characters in the book, but this never detracts from either the story or the verse; the characters, in fact, flourish by this method in a truly dramatic way. Whether any of the historic persons really appeared the way Ondaatje recreates them simply becomes irrelevant; they make a very credible amount of sense within the context of Ondaatje's version of the tale. His story takes on its own rhythms, entirely outside the realities of history. . . .

The clean simplicity, the uncluttered, toned-down, almost easy precision . . . generally characteristic of the book is probably the happy result of Ondaatje's being forced to assume, at least to some degree, the simplicity of speech his characters themselves would have used. This little exercise has done Ondaatje a world of good, and *The Collected Works* reflects it. Only occasionally, in precisely five poems, does he let his lyric overdrive run away with him to the detriment of the poem, which becomes not only nonbelievable in context, but simply bad or mediocre poetry outright. . . . I don't mean to imply that the rest of the work is therefore necessarily all undiluted genius, but it's certainly strong enough to keep one reading voluntarily and continuously. . . . (p. 82)

Andreas Schroeder, "The Poet as Gunman," in Canadian Literature, *No. 51, Winter, 1972, pp. 80-2.*

STEPHEN SCOBIE

[*The Collected Works of Billy the Kid*] *fixes* a certain view of the Kid into an intense, fully realized image. . . . (p. 42)

Ondaatje's mythmaking is a careful process, built up by various means, and he indicates in several ways the degree to which he is presenting a legendary or poetic image of the Kid. There is, for instance, the concern with photographs. The book opens with an account of photography at the time of Billy's life, indicating the difficulty (which is also Ondaatje's) of taking a sharp image of a moving object. . . . [And] what the photograph shows is always accurate. . . . Indeed, it was the reversed image of one famous photograph of Billy which led to the mistaken idea that he was left-handed. All contemporary authorities . . . remember Billy as right-handed; but his left-handedness fits in better with the legendary image of the outsider. . . . Ondaatje's subtitle, "Left Handed Poems" derives from [Arthur Penn's film on Billy the Kid,] *The Left Handed Gun*. (pp. 42-3)

The film image is a further way in which Ondaatje transforms the historical Billy into a legendary image. The subtitle casts the image of Penn's film across the whole book, and also recalls Penn's later masterpiece, *Bonnie and Clyde*, in which the outlaw figures are subjected to a mythologising process within the film itself. . . . Ondaatje uses comedy in much the same way as Penn: grotesque images of violence become almost simultaneously comic and horrible. . . . Finally, closely akin to the movie image is the comic-book legend which forms Billy's apotheosis. . . . This is the final transformation of Billy in pop culture into the upright clean-living hero. . . . (pp. 43-4)

But although Ondaatje's image of Billy the Kid may be influenced by the images of comic-books and the movies, these references are merely the context in which Ondaatje sets his own central image of Billy: and . . . it is the book's title which points to the nature of that image. . . .

Ondaatje gives a list of "the killed". To Billy he ascribes 20 victims (curiously, for the usual legendary number is 21), most of whom . . . are totally unsubstantiated historically. Then he gives Garrett's victims, ending

> . . . and Pat Garret
> sliced off my head.
> Blood a necklace on me all my life.

The strange, violent beauty of the image, together with the use of the first person, point towards the concept behind the title *The Collected Works of Billy the Kid*. Ondaatje's legendary context for Billy is poetry; the transformation will be carried out mainly through the poetic image; the book will present Billy himself as an artist. Of course, "works" is ambiguous: it can also refer to Billy's actions, the killings. But Ondaatje is clearly working within the Romantic tradition of the artist as outsider. . . . Billy's status as outlaw is intimately connected with the nature of his perception. He is placed outside society not only by what he does, but by the very way in which he sees the world. . . . (p. 44)

Of course, Billy's poetic personality is not entirely distinct from Michael Ondaatje's. The concern with animals—apparent throughout the book—is familiar to any reader of Ondaatje's poetry. What results from the title "*The Collected Works of Billy the Kid* by Michael Ondaatje" is in fact a composite figure: Billy the Kid, outlaw as artist, and Michael Ondaatje, artist as outlaw, meeting in one persona, which is part history, part legend, part aesthetic image, part creator of images. It is in terms of this complex persona that the book approaches its material. (p. 45)

Ondaatje presents Billy's violence in terms of the poetic image of energy: the energy necessary to both outlaw and artist. . . . Energy tightly controlled by form is one definition of a work of art; and in art the "one altered move" will result in the dissipation of energy, a bad poem. Or, when the energy of the work of art is directly expressive of violence, and when it is transmitted in a context where such artistic controls as irony are severely compromised, then the "one altered move" can be physically destructive beyond the aesthetic bounds. . . . Ondaatje's book depicts the shattering of the precarious control over the energy of Billy's violence, and the violence he evokes in those around him; the events then drive inexorably towards his death. (pp. 47-8)

If a writer's intentions can be most clearly seen in the places where he most drastically alters his source material, then Ondaatje's metamorphosis of the Chisums must be the very centre of his work. The impression that Ondaatje's book gives is that the Chisum ranch is a fairly small place, out in the desert miles from anywhere, inhabited only by Sallie and John, who is seen as a gentle, peace-loving man with little interest or influence in the world beyond his ranch. In fact, John Chisum was one of the largest and most influential landowners and cattlemen in the territory. . . . (p. 49)

The image presented in Ondaatje's book is, then, largely his own invention; and the pains he has taken to alter his source material indicate the importance he attaches to it. The Chisum ranch is the "still centre" of Billy's world. It is a place of peace, of affection, of comradeship. None of the apologists for Billy as a poor misunderstood child driven against his will to violence have ever provided him with such a beautiful and fully realized context for his "true nature": but Ondaatje succeeds in doing this without in the least sentimentalising Billy. (p. 50)

Ondaatje omits any account of Billy's early activities, such as his murders in the Lincoln County War, and presents him mainly in two contexts: the peace and beauty of the Chisum ranch, and the final chase and manhunt. In other words, Billy is seen almost entirely as victim. There are three extended accounts of killings in the book . . . and in every case the killer is Garrett. We never get any similar account of a killing by Billy. . . . In other words, Billy is a humane murderer. . . . Ondaatje stacks his deck. If the reader reacts in horror or disgust from the violence in the book, he is reacting mainly *against* Garrett. Although Ondaatje's Billy is far from a blameless character, there is a definite implication that the violence exists around him rather than in him. . . . (pp. 53-4)

Ondaatje's [Billy] is destroyed by something outside himself, something that itself remains calm and indestructible: and therefore, all the more terrifying. Garrett's character thus presents an interesting paredox: he is himself an embodiment of order, control; yet in contact with Billy he becomes the "altered move" which produces chaos.

Or is it chaos? It is violence, certainly, and death; but there is a kind of direction to it. Within the terms of the legend, it is an inexorable progress, and what it ends in is not Billy's death but Billy's apotheosis into legend: the creation, that is, of an aesthetic image. If Billy is one image of the artist, then surely Pat Garrett, even if his material is dead bodies, like his birds, is another? *The Collected Works of Billy the*

Kid is, after all, a tightly controlled book: Ondaatje is a careful artist, and the images of violence are never allowed to get out of hand in the book. The book is not chaos, the book is not manic. It is an attempt to comprehend the legend of Billy the Kid, to see him as one of the exemplary figures of modern consciousness, outlaw as artist, artist as outlaw. He is involved with violence, but the violence results from the conflict between himself and his society, it is a product of his symbiotic relationship with Pat Garrett. Ondaatje's final image of Billy sees him waking up after a bad night: the smell of smoke, the stain of violence, is still with him—but only in his shirt, which can be changed. We turn the page and find a photograph of a small boy smiling in a cowboy outfit: Billy's costume of violence turned into an image, a toy. That small boy is Michael Ondaatje, poet.

Ondaatje's Billy does not have the substantiality of history; his history is changed and fashioned into something else: legend, the aesthetic image in all its depth and detail, its vividness and force. (pp. 54-5)

Stephen Scobie, "Two Authors in Search of a Character," in Canadian Literature, *No. 54, Autumn, 1972, pp. 37-55.*

ANATOLE BROYARD

Based on the life of Buddy Bolden, one of the originators of New Orleans jazz, ["Coming Through Slaughter"] jumbles actual history, interviews with old jazzmen, snatches of local color, fictional reconstruction, three "sonographs" of dolphin sounds, primitive poetry and pretentious writing. Bolden's eventual insanity is romanticized, as if he blew himself beyond coherence on his horn. "Coming Through Slaughter" is written in several voices, none of them is satisfactory. Too many sentences float between cliché and bombast: "Swimming toward the sound of madness." "What he wanted was cruel, pure relationship." "The music was his dance in the auditorium of enemies." "In terror we lean in the direction that is most unlike us. Running past your own character into pain." "All suicides, all acts of privacy are romantic."

Now and then, when Mr. Ondaatje relaxes, "Coming Through Slaughter" warms up. The description of the mattress whores of New Orleans is properly appalling. Their beds on their backs, their ankles broken by the heavy sticks of monopolistic pimps, these ghosts of prostitutes ply their trade on the pavements, in the back alleys of shantytown. While the evocation of New Orleans is rather thin, an occasional image comes through.

Bolden finally went mad while leading a band through the streets in a parade. Mr. Ondaatje has embellished the occasion by introducing, among the people thronging the sidewalk, a girl who dances to Bolden's improvisations, mysteriously anticipating his every impulse. The scene is well done and not uninteresting, but it ultimately becomes self-conscious and arty. And whatever the relation between Bolden's lust for life, his music and his insanity, it is too pat to imply that he blew his mind over an unknown girl. . . .

A novel like "Coming Through Slaughter" [is] made up of shards of various techniques. . . . The author gives us all the broken pieces and leaves it to us to infer the final form. (p. 14)

Anatole Broyard, "New Woman, Old Jazz, Hemingway," in The New York Times Book Review *(© 1977 by The New York Times Company; reprinted by permission), April 24, 1977, pp. 14, 44.**

WILLIAM LOGAN

Compared to the creative mythologizing of Ondaatje's *The Collected Works of Billy the Kid . . .*, his selected poems [in *There's a Trick with a Knife I'm Learning To Do: Poems, 1963-1978*] are rather lusterless, straining even for their whimsical gestures. He assumes an amusing off-centerness—"The beautiful formed things caught at the wrong moment"—but having invented 31 similes for a child's unmusical voice, he has brought us no nearer that voice. His prosaic experience is implicitly contrasted with the lives of high purpose he is entranced by: Elizabeth I, Darwin, Philoctetes. Since the most affecting poems of his own life are responses to memory, perhaps only the past quickens this poet's imagination.

William Logan, "Poetry: 'There's a Trick with a Knife I'm Learning to Do: Poems, 1963-1978'," in Library Journal *(reprinted from* Library Journal, *April 1, 1979; published by R. R. Bowker Co. (a Xerox company); copyright © 1979 by Xerox Corporation), Vol. 104, No. 7, April 1, 1979, p. 833.*

G. E. MURRAY

Michael Ondaatje's poems in *There's a Trick With a Knife I'm Learning to Do* . . . use the lyric as a weapon. . . . [His] landscapes are populated by horrifying figures and events. It's a fashionable track, and any number of aspirants can turn out a glum swatch of verse given a dead animal or nightmare inspired by an anchovy pizza. Yet Ondaatje rises above the usual muck with an aggressively inventive, if sometimes offhanded, flourish. His freshness creates its own season of isolation in "the cell of civilized magic." (p. 578)

G. E. Murray, "Six Poets," in The Nation *(copyright 1979 by the Nation Associates, Inc.), Vol. 228, No. 19, May 19, 1979, pp. 578, 580.**

CHARLES MOLESWORTH

["There's a Trick with a Knife I'm Learning to Do: Poems 1963-1978" is] filled with odd angles of vision, but it lacks the kind of spectral music it seems to need. It's a poetry that mixes the bizarre and commonplace, but its accents are prosaic: "I have been seeing dragons again." And in another poem, "We are in a cell of civilized magic." There's a witty poem spoken through the persona of a young Queen Elizabeth I, and another about Henri Rousseau and the wealthy women who collect his paintings. But often there are juxtapositions that aren't sharp enough. . . .

[The] lack of a driving or lilting music and the barren punctuation create a disembodied effect.

This is a poetry that relies on a hushed approach, and on occasion its claims sound helpless and confused: "My mind is pouring chaos / in nets onto the page." But there is a yearning for wonder in this poetry, and a curiousity that informs the imaginative life of his poetry at its best. (p. 14)

Charles Molesworth, "Five Poets," in The New York Times Book Review *(© 1979 by The New York Times Company; reprinted by permission), September 2, 1979, pp. 8, 14.**

P

PERCY, Walker 1916-

Percy is an American novelist and essayist. His fictive concerns are serious and ambitious: in his work Percy seeks to reconcile the problem of faith in a secular world. He won the National Book Award in 1962 for his first novel, *The Moviegoer*. (See also *CLC*, Vols. 2, 3, 6, 8, and *Contemporary Authors*, Vols. 1-4, rev. ed.)

EDWARD J. CASHIN

Walker Percy's *Lancelot* reminds us of the novelist's role as conveyor of history. Although Percy is knowledgeable about the facts of Southern history, it is not factual history that he conveys. Rather it is that peculiar understanding of their own history which Southerners have that he reveals. (p. 875)

There is an indeterminate but very real point when a people's history becomes internalized. Myth becomes mores. When that happens to a tribe or to a nation, then the history as understood becomes more true than the history which historians seek to define. The novelist is a better historian of history-as-mores than the professional writer of history-as-it-happened. The novelist reaches deep into his psyche for his history, and he communicates readily to a wide audience because his readers recognize the same attitudes and perceptions within themselves. (pp. 875-76)

In *Lancelot,* Walker Percy writes about his perception of the South, and his perception is grounded in fact. The South came out of Virginia, and Lancelot Lamar Andrewes returns to Virginia to begin all over again. (p. 876)

Virginians did not confine their way of life to Virginia. When their available land began to give out, they migrated to Georgia and planted their dreams with their tobacco. . . . Because the South paused a moment in Georgia before rushing to the West, the newer states accord her the respect reserved for the oldest child. Walker Percy treats Georgia gently. Lance's first wife, Lucy Cobb, was a Georgia girl. Lance confesses that he was "ill at ease among the easy ingrown Georgians and Carolinians—where people seem to come and go, meet and part by agreed-upon but unspoken rules."

Something happened to the Virginian tradition in Georgia, and although Walker Percy does not refer to it, he sees its effects. The Virginia ethic merged with two other traditions. The oldest was the Charles Town (Charleston came later) way of life. . . . The Carolina planters were city folks, planting for the profit of it. They were merchants at heart and socializers by preference. They saw politics as another means of improving their fortune. (p. 877)

The other stream which met and intermingled with the Virginian as it flowed through Georgia was that curious kind of Puritanism growing out of the Great Awakening. (p. 878)

Percy readily recognizes the followers of the Great Awakening tradition as Southern. They are not *his* type of Southerner, but they deserve a certain respect. Lance characterizes one of them as "a good family man, believed in Jesus Christ, America, the Southern way of life, hated Communists and liberals, and was not altogether wrong on any count." Like most liberals who have regretted an earlier permissiveness, Percy is grateful to the Fundamentalists for clinging to their values. They were saved by their anti-intellectualism. They were right in trusting their emotions.

However, Walker Percy, in common with many others, fails to recognize the commercial tradition as genuinely Southern. He is angry at the New South for its pragmatism and crassness, unmindful of the Charles Town ethic. Nevertheless he perceives a type of Southerner who represents an amalgam of the Great Awakening and of Charles Town. "Do you want a portrait of the New Southerner? He is Billy Graham on Sunday and Richard Nixon the rest of the week. He calls on Jesus and steals, he's in business, he's in politics." In his scorn for the mercantile and the evangelical traditions, and in failing to recognize the blend as authentically Southern, Percy is left with the Virginia tradition. (pp. 878-79)

Percy distinguishes between the substance of what he would recapture and its shadow. He ridicules the Hollywood mimicking of externals. Lance's wife Margot restored him to her image of a Southern gentleman at the same time she restored their Belle Isle mansion. He was to be a composite of Ashley Wilkes, Leslie Howard, Jeff Davis, Gregory Peck, and a bit of Clark Gable. "I went along agreeably, amused by her extraordinary Texas notion that we aristocratic folk were somehow all of a piece. Of course we were not, not even aristocratic, and since I never felt much of a piece myself, I'd as soon dress the part." He began acting like Southern gentlemen do in the movies.

It is not that kind of play-acting which Percy identifies with Virginia. Rather it is the code of chivalry which the Virginian brought over from the disappearing feudal tradition in England. The code has become part of the Southern mores; it has become part of Percy. Of course, that is one very basic reason for his harking back to the chivalric values.

There is another reason. Percy tells us through Lance that the values of modern America are not worth living for. Much better to have died with Stonewall Jackson at Chancellorsville than to live with Johnny Carson in Burbank. Lance, or Percy, has had a craw full of the ethics of life adjustment. (pp. 879-80)

Lance Andrewes' great anguished cry is that he will not stand for this shallowness: "I can't stand the way things are. I cannot tolerate this age. What is more, I won't. That was my discovery: that I didn't have to." It is Percy's discovery that in his past there is an alternative life-style to that of the present. He will resurrect the values of an age which was scorned after Freud and forgotten after Dewey. . . . Lance's Third Revolution is to restore decency simply because decency is preferable to the absence of decency. He will return to Virginia to begin the reformation of society.

Walker Percy's novel illuminates history as mores and it does something more. It reminds us that there are other models for man than that of the computer or the conditioned reflex. They are models to be found in our past, when men dared to greatness because they saw themselves as only a little less than the angels. (p. 880)

Edward J. Cashin, "History As Mores: Walker Percy's 'Lancelot'," in The Georgia Review *(copyright, 1977, by the University of Georgia), Vol. XXXI, No. 4, Winter, 1977, pp. 875-80.*

THOMAS LeCLAIR

Percy's devil [Immelmann] is a modern avatar of the Faust and Don Juan myths so prominently alluded to in *Love in the Ruins,* but the details of Immelmann's appearance and method also owe much to the devil in Dostoyevsky's *The Brothers Karamazov,* a book which helped lead Percy into a systematic study of Existentialism. The ideas and terms that Percy borrows from Existential novelists like Dostoyevsky and Sartre and from the philosophers Kierkegaard, Heidegger, and Marcel give his fiction an interesting allusiveness and, at times, a real philosophical depth. . . . While *Love in the Ruins* is the work of a ranging intellect and observant eye, I think it is the least successful of Percy's four novels. Its weakness is a disturbing incongruity between intelligence and imagination. . . . I call this essay "Walker Percy's Devil" because Art Immelmann represents both Percy's philosophical allusiveness and the aesthetic inconsistency of the novel. Immelmann's temptation of [the protagonist] Tom More is the internal analogue of Percy's temptation by an old-fashioned art. Briefly put, Walker Percy's devil is Existential material in an un-Existential novel.

The primary terms in which Percy presents Tom More's psychological condition are angelism-bestialism—terms derived from Maritain's *The Dream of Descartes*. Tom More has both a Faustian abstractive pride and a Don Juanian absorption in carnality, and his fall issues from both. Immelmann promises a hedonistic life and encourages More to "'Develop your genius.'" While the latter can be read as a call to scientific pride, it is also more specifically an allusion to a Kierkegaardian essay, "Of the Difference Between a Genius and an Apostle," that Percy has said "was more responsible than anything else for my becoming a Catholic." . . . The Apostle, says Kierkegaard, has his authority from God; his message remains news because of its transcendent nature and authority. . . . For Kierkegaard the genius was born, not made, but anyone could make himself a Christian by exercising his freedom. Although the term "apostle" goes back to the beginnings of Christianity, Kierkegaard's emphasis on subjectivity and freedom gives the term an Existential quality.

Tom More introduces himself as a genius, a man who can "discern not this thing or that thing but rather the connection between the two." . . . [He] identifies himself in what Kierkegaard calls aesthetic terms and takes his authority from his intelligence rather than his faith. His lapsometer is the physical proof of his genius. Although it can diagnose the ills of post-modern man and can, with the attached ionizer, adjust people to their environment, the lapsometer is limited to the immanent. It cannot save—and might well help to damn—those it "cures." It almost damns the genius who has invented it and whose faith it nearly replaces.

Tensed between the call of genius and the meaning of faith, Tom More lives two half-lives—he orbits the world in abstraction and scampers its surface in carnality. In this condition he is ripe for the devil's temptation. . . . (pp. 3-6)

Immelmann's forebear is the devil in *The Brothers Karamazov* who describes himself as follows: "'Mephistopheles declared to Faust that he desired evil, but did only good. Well, he can say what he likes, it's quite the opposite with me. I am perhaps the one man in all creation who loves the truth and genuinely desires good.'" (p. 6)

[Through] this devil Dostoyevsky portrays an image of hellishness that Percy finds worth recalling, for in his discounting of spiritual issues Ivan's devil encourages both sin and an Existential inauthenticity. Although Dostoyevsky's devil and Percy's Immelmann do appeal to conventional pride, their call is not to rebellion but to spiritual amnesia and to an idea of happiness that is despair. By modeling his devil on Dostoyevsky's, Percy makes Immelmann both a traditional Christian tempter and an Existential "salaud." . . .

[The] actual dissolving of Art Immelmann comes through Tom More's mumbled prayer to his ancestor the saint. It is in the epilogue, five years later, that Percy develops his hero's recovery. Although some readers have complained about the sentimental patness of this section, it is consistent with the assumptions and progress of the book: if the novelist wants to put the devil in his novel and have his hero defeat him, then a storybook ending is not out of place. A passage from Kierkegaard's *Training in Christianity* summarizes the quality of life in the epilogue: "everyone for himself, in quiet inwardness before God, shall humble himself before what it is to be in the strictest sense a Christian, admit candidly before God how it stands with him, so that he might accept the grace which is offered to everyone who is imperfect, that is, to everyone. And then no further . . .". (p. 7)

Kierkegaard's understanding of what it is to be a Christian is essentially repeated in *Love in the Ruins* by the unlikely cleric Father Smith. "A gray stiff man," Smith is entirely unremarkable, a nearly anonymous man with an anonymous name. But Father Smith, like plain Father Boomer in *The Last Gentleman,* is the agent of God's news. Following Kierkegaard, Percy is illustrating that the knight of faith need be "no genius." . . . [If] Smith shows that genius is not required for faith, More evidences that genius, so long as it retains the capacity to wonder, does not preclude faith.

Genius, devil, and apostle—each of these central concepts has an Existential source. Yet the form Percy chooses for *Love in the Ruins* is disappointingly conventional and inconsistent with the Existentially-influenced aesthetic he has said he works from. A futuristic novel, *Love in the Ruins* is constructed like futuristic novels of the past. Characters are motivated and events are plotted. Time and space are quite conventionally handled. Although contemporary facts are amusingly distorted, the satire is neither very subtle nor imaginatively prophetic. The narrator shows signs of unreliability, but Percy does not choose to make More's befuddlement structurally central. . . . But Percy early in his career thought it necessary to change the structure of fiction to correspond with the changed nature of the world and his ways of thinking about it. . . . Yet despite his sense of radical social changes and radical philosophical needs, Percy does not extend his radicalism to literary form.

In several of his interviews Percy has stated some of the principles of the Existential novelist who will best respond to this new world. Basically, Percy explained to Carlton Cremeens, a novelist "should be concerned with what is the case in the world, the facts, the richness, the intricacy and the variety of the way things are." He begins with man in a situation: "I'm concerned with a certain quality of consciousness put down in a certain place and then seeing what kind of reaction takes place between a character and his environment and the people he meets." For the novelist exploring and discovering reality in his fiction, "telling a story and putting characters together so that something is going to happen" will be secondary. Percy further insisted that the novelist must avoid the "temptation to understand the [social] issues of the times in terms of sociology, in terms of abstractions." Without "writing in enigmas and acrostics," the novelist will make his philosophy "part and parcel of the novel, and there's no illustrating of theses." The novelist as phenomenologist of man in a concrete situation will tell the reader "something he already knows but which he doesn't quite know that he knows" in an indirect way and will, at all costs, avoid the edifying. If he successfully articulates the not quite known but shared condition of alienation, the result will be its reversal through the joy of naming. (pp. 8-10)

Although neither *The Moviegoer* nor *The Last Gentleman* is strictly experimental, Percy follows the principles quoted above rigorously and successfully in *The Moviegoer* and, with somewhat wider and looser application, in *The Last Gentleman. Love in the Ruins,* while suggesting, in its content, a greater apocalpytic urgency than do the first two books, is most distant from Percy's Existential aesthetic. *Love in the Ruins* begins with a familiar Percyean consciousness set down in a situation, the unwanted greening of America, that soon becomes a plot. As the novel progresses, More becomes less a meditative consciousness than a stimulus-response creature who tramps back and forth through the novel's four days. Action becomes plotted and predictable, and thus at odds with Percy's notion of fiction as exploration and discovery. The last half of the novel is dominated by dialogue and descriptions of action, action more externally exciting than internally revelatory. The novel's conventional cinematic quality diminishes the "richness, the intricacy and the variety of the way things are." There is an artificial intricacy of plot and a superficial variety of people without the parodic extremity. . . . The book is more dogmatic than *The Moviegoer* or *The Last Gentleman,* but the problem is not so much whether Percy has the authority to be edifying as whether his satire is equal to the complexity and artistic achievement of the comedy in his first two books. I don't think it is. . . . As an Existential exploration of a consciousness in a place, it is crowded with problem people rather than mysterious persons and things.

The malice from which Percy admittedly draws some of his creative energy combines with the book's emphasis upon action to simplify character. Minor characters in *The Moviegoer* and *The Last Gentleman* threaten to fold into caricatures. In *Love in the Ruins* many of the minor characters become the abstractions Percy warned himself against—exemplary figures of various social, political, philosophical, or scientific persuasions. (pp. 10-11)

Percy sees the novelist-novel-reader relation as an extension of the basic human language act of naming. In naming, a thing is symbolized not just for the namer but also, whether present or not, for the other person; it is an intersubjective process. . . . What Percy does stylistically in *Love in the Ruins* is to parody much of the bogus naming—scientific, mystical, and popular—that clamors in our ears. His devil speaks in the hoariest of clichés. But here again, so much of the linguistic thrust of the book is negative that the new positive naming is secondary. Despite recognizing the dangers of a used-up vocabulary, Percy's central terms, angelism-bestialism, are borrowed rather than invented. . . . The Apostle has the authority to pronounce the old words because they announce the same radical news. The novelist has to imagine new names. But between the parodic and the borrowed, there is little space in *Love in the Ruins* in which Percy's imagination can invent.

The problems *with* the novel are succinctly represented *in* the novel by the relation between Tom More and Art Immelmann. . . . Immelmann offers More fame, a chance to do good for others, and the conventionalized joy of "love in the ruins." Percy's artistic temptation closely parallels these three attractions, for in *Love in the Ruins* Percy tends toward popularity, edification, and conventionality of form. Percy's devil as a writer, then, is his betrayal of his own literary faith to a shopworn literary form, just as More's devil is his betrayal of his religious faith to a banal "love in the ruins," itself a literary cliché from Wells, Huxley, and Nathan that Percy identified in "The Man on the Train." The novel is thus a metafiction, a fiction about itself that hints at its weaknesses. The devil is old-fashioned Art/art.

Percy has made *Love in the Ruins* accessible to a large number of readers and has clarified his religious position, but at the expense of a philosophically and aesthetically consistent fiction. I have called Percy's tending toward popularity, edification, and conventionality of form his devil because these qualities correspond with Art Immelmann's temptation of Tom More and because they deprive us of the best in Percy—a philosophical rigor, subtle irony, precise wonder at the world, mixture of levels of discourse, a conception of the novel as a phenomenological exploration—qualities found most prominently in *The Moviegoer*. . . . Despite knowing more about language than other novelists, many of whom make it their subject, Percy has chosen to go on telling stories with ideas inside. In . . . *Lancelot,* Percy encases old materials from his essays in "Southern Gothic," yet *Lancelot* has about it a self-consciousness that suggests Percy may be examining—in something like a confession—some of his philosophical and literary temptations. The moviegoer, the last gentleman, the ranting genius-saint are all present in *Lancelot,* but form and language again disappoint. While *Love in the Ruins* and *Lancelot* are good stories and Percy one of our most thoughtful novelists, one comes to wish he had imagined through to a form that would have transmuted his enormous intelligence into some supreme verbal fiction. Perhaps one shouldn't complain about what he doesn't do, shouldn't look for devils. It's just that his essay, his interviews, and *The Moviegoer* make a promise that is unfulfilled or, more accurately, a promise not quite made, yet still somehow unkept. (pp. 11-13)

Thomas LeClair, "Walker Percy's Devil," in The Southern Literary Journal *(copyright 1977 by the Department of English, University of North Carolina at Chapel Hill), Vol. X, No. 1, Fall, 1977, pp. 3-13.*

ROBERT D. DANIEL

In an article published almost twenty years ago, Walker Percy talked of modern man's peculiar predicament, the result of secular man living under the protection of a tradition he ridicules and of religious man being unable to live the life his faith demands. Percy compares "our posture" to that of "the cat in the cartoon who ran off the cliff and found himself standing up in the air. Maybe he can get back to earth by backing up; on the other hand he might be in for a radical change of perspective." . . . After three novels showing the contortions of the cat in midair, Percy's new novel, *Lancelot,* is a dialogue between secular man and religious man on what the world may look like once the cat discovers that he is too far from the cliff to get back. (p. 186)

Lancelot clarifies his position through a mad black/white reduction of moral choices. Despite its limitations, such a reduction may be seductive to those of us tired of the complicated—and often fruitless—ironies of modern life. In questioning Lancelot's sanity, we are led to the central ethical question: How do we avoid the intolerance of false simplicity without slipping into the quagmire of relativism? Percy's answer seems to be that ethical questions ultimately have religious answers. Thus Percy uses Lancelot not only as a voice for satire, but also—and primarily—as an object of satire. Though Percy would agree that all the ills Lancelot rails against are deplorable, he suggests that these ills are best seen as symptoms of an even more serious disease than the moral decay which has existed in even the most religious societies. Lancelot's disease is full-fledged secularism, left unchecked by his refusal to accept the adulterated vaccine of contemporary religion. . . .

To adapt one of Percy's analogies, religious man and secular man agree that man finds himself on an island in space. There, for the purists on either side, the resemblance stops. To the religious, the island is not man's home; he is a castaway who has found himself washed ashore. For advice on returning home and on how best to treat his fellow islanders in the meantime, the religious man relies on messages that have been sent from across the sea. (p. 187)

To the secularists, bottle-watching is worthless since the contents of the bottles cannot be determined as true or false by any standards of island knowledge. But for Percy, the empirically verifiable/nonsense dichotomy drawn by the secularist begs the question. Instead Percy distinguishes three kinds of messages: (1) knowledge *sub specie aeternitatis*—knowledge that "can be arrived at anywhere by anyone and at any time," such as the discoveries of science and art; (2) island news—information relevant to our life at a particular moment on the island, such as being told that one's hut is burning; (3) news from across the sea—a message that speaks to our predicament as castaways. (p. 188)

[Lancelot] deceives himself because he assumes his lack of purpose—a sign of unacknowledged homesickness—can be cured by knowledge instead of news from across the sea. . . . In its most advanced stages, unacknowledged homesickness—alienation from one's self that results from an inability to accept alienation as man's natural state—causes man to need disaster to feel alive once he is jaded by pleasures.

Yet in his alcoholic stupor, Lancelot at least realizes the need to be watchful, to wait for news. However, the fact that he looks to the Ten O'Clock News for this important message concerning the individual's predicament indicates his misunderstanding of the nature of genuine news. . . . Lancelot's method [reveals] his desire to achieve certainty about human actions by reducing human complexities to physical events that can be recorded on film, thus eliminating the slipperiness of human thoughts and feelings that must be expressed in easily feigned words.

But there is madness in his method, though his madness is double-edged like Gulliver's. We find Lancelot's madness disturbing just as we are upset by Gulliver's preferring the horses in the stable to his family. Both rejections are difficult to accept even though we may feel that the reasons behind them are not that insane. Yet just as we reject Gulliver's uncompromising rationality as inhuman, the more we learn of Lancelot, the more we want a comfortable distance between ourselves and him. While we may sympathize with Lancelot's attack on the devaluation of language used to excuse sexual casualness, we sense a clinical element in his nature that scares us as sin touches his own life. Though keenly aware of his own feelings, Lancelot fails to acknowledge the limits of his moral position. . . . For Lancelot, without belief in God to provide a sense of transcendence, "loving a woman" becomes man's only absolute, gives man his only notion of infinity.

The problem with love, according to Lancelot himself, is that "ordinary sexual love" is the only love we can be sure exists. And unlike the nature of God, the sacredness of sexual love is a matter of perspective. . . . Lancelot has no perspective from which to judge the true view of sex.

Thus his desire to revenge Margot's unfaithfulness—like his anger at the promiscuity of his age—is groundless. (pp. 188-90)

Thus Lancelot attempts to re-establish an ethical order with even less foundation than Christian traditionalists. His only principle is negative, that he cannot tolerate the present age; instead he wants a simpler society. . . . Lancelot needs this reductive simplicity—life as the "simple scholastic syllogism" as he calls it elsewhere—because he has no means of dealing with the complexity of life when choices are not clear-cut, where women, for example, are too complex to be easily categorized as whores or ladies. Lancelot's insistence on *knowing* where one stands reduces human choices to a scientific problem.

For Percy, the failure of secular humanism is radical; stopgap measures eventually collapse when the chasm between the concrete person and the abstract theory becomes too wide. In pragmatic terms, there may be much to praise in the social and economic improvements fostered by secular humanism in its various forms. But in man's most crucial relationships with God and reality, secular humanism is bankrupt because it tells man nothing about himself as an individual, only about himself as an organism. If man accepts himself as merely an organism and the "ethical twilight of Christianity" becomes the dark "environment" of secularism, even murder becomes a trivial act: "Not even the knife at his throat seemed to make any difference. All it came down to was steel molecules entering skin molecules, artery molecules, blood cells." For Lancelot, it is an easy step from sex as molecules rubbing to murder as molecules separating. (p. 191)

Lancelot [is] a dialogue rather than a monologue: not just in the technical sense that Percival finally speaks at the very end, but in the sense that what he leaves unsaid—or finds unspeakable—is just as important to Percy's theme as Lancelot's raving. For *Lancelot* is as much a chronicle of the failure of contemporary religion as a satire on secularism. (p. 192)

While the most obvious satire is directed against conservative Christians, a quieter but equally damaging indictment is made against religious liberals like Percival. Percival's hipness, his role as a psychiatrist, cancels his effectiveness as a priest. As a radical solution to man's predicament, Christianity cannot come from the same roots as the problem; it cannot attempt to make man feel at home where he does not belong. Psychiatrists try to cure alienation, to make man feel adjusted, to teach him to lead a "meaningful" life in a secular city. The priest's duty is just the opposite, to insist man see himself as a castaway, as a being who should be alienated as long as he is estranged from God. (p. 193)

If one agrees with Percy that the growing darkness is not temporary, then *Lancelot* is, and this is highest praise, a timely novel. It has flaws: the irony is at times so heavy-handed that Percy's thumb gets in the picture; and with a few exceptions, the characters are too easily ignored because they are labeled so clearly. Still, there is much to admire in the powerful, hard-earned simplicity of Percy's style and his typically captivating opening and careful pacing. Most importantly, Walker Percy ranks with Swift as that rare accomplished acrobat, the novelist who can balance interesting fiction with serious ideas. (p. 194)

Robert D. Daniel, "Walker Percy's 'Lancelot': Secular Raving and Religious Silence" (copyright, 1978, by Robert D. Daniel), in The Southern Review, *Vol. 14, No. 1, January, 1978, pp. 186-94.*

ROBERT COLES

[For Percy, as indicated in his essay "Symbol as Need" (1954),] the inclination toward symbolization is not only a uniquely human one, but one in no way explained by reference to either evolution or biology. (p. 75)

"Symbolic transformation" for him is not a "need," but rather "a means of *knowing*." He wants not to put labels on people, but understand what they are doing. He believes that symbols enable us to acquire not "facts," but rather knowledge "in the Thomist and existential sense of identification of the knower with the object known." (p. 76)

[As] Percy puts it, "our common existence is validated" when one person learns from another that not only does a particular flower exist, and not only does it have a name, but it exists for each of them, and that state of existence can be jointly affirmed by two human beings through the use of words. (p. 77)

[Percy] has tried hard not to give up what he had once so exclusively believed in, the value of the scientific method, but instead [has tried] to add new ideas or values of his to old ones, and when necessary try to reconcile apparent incompatibilities. . . . Let man himself be the subject of "research" and we have what are sometimes called the "human sciences," and (in Percy's words) "certain notorious difficulties."

He examines them, and for a while anticipates himself as the novelist who can in a paragraph or two make his readers smile at the pretensions of various social scientists. (pp. 78-9)

[For] Percy it is indeed surprising, given the determinism of psychoanalytic theory, that a decision to seek "help" is ever made. How to account for the *decision,* the *choice,* the act of *will*?

Needless to say, those who want to regard themselves as scientists and nothing else don't take to words like those three: how does one quantify them, or for that matter fit them into an abstract, mechanistic scheme of forces and counterforces, drives and "defense mechanisms" designed to "push back" drives? . . . To existentialists the word [for the "unknowns" of science] is *mysteries,* and they are irreducible; that is, not ultimately objects of classification and reduction—to atoms or molecules, to "libido quanta," to a "mechanism of defense" or a unit or integer of some kind. Percy is quite comfortable with those mysteries; they lead, he knows, to other mysteries; and however unacknowledged, they persist in their obviousness and importance.

Especially important for Percy is what he and others drawn to existentialism have called intersubjectivity. It is a word hard to pin down, as are many words favored by existentialists. . . . The sphere of intersubjectivity is shared reflection: Marcel's *we are. Knowledge* and *meaning* are the mere beginnings of intersubjectivity—because both have to do with individuals directly or indirectly calling upon one another for assistance, and not least, rejoicing together when the mutual appeal is successful. (pp. 80-1)

"Symbolization is of its very essence an intersubjectivity." In other words, we don't only come to terms with the world by adapting to signals of various kinds (the province of behavioral psychologists to study); we also gain what Percy calls "possession" of the world by using symbols, and that second kind of knowledge is existential because what is comprehended has become part of ourselves, *is* in us—does

not require signals, however indirect or unobvious, but has been "made" by us, exactly as a poet comes up with his symbols, uses his words suggestively, so as to convey meaning. Percy believes such mental activity cannot be further reduced; it is what uniquely characterizes human beings—and it is what he calls a hermeneutic, a way of looking at and comprehending something, in this case the existential "facts" of our daily lives. (pp. 82-3)

[Percy] summarizes the existentialist's predicament: "This is a chair for you and me. That is a tree, everything is something, you are what you are, but *what am I*?" If the answer is elusive, or never really to be obtained, this side of heaven, the effort to find the answer goes on and on. Not only philosophers make such an attempt; we all do—and as he indicates how, Percy gets vivid. He speaks of "zones," a way, really, of getting specific about what gets called in the article "the-situation-in-which-we-find-ourselves." (pp. 83-4)

Percy, despite his interest in European existentialists, was clearly amused by the way a word like *alienation* had become absorbed into America's culture. He wrote ["The Man on the Train" (1956)] in order to redeem, as best he could, an interesting and valuable notion from its ironic fate: alienation as the norm. Taking on countless critics in his first sentence, he insists that "there is no such thing, strictly speaking, as a literature of alienation." When one is riding a train, he points out, and reading a book about a person who is alienated and riding a train, then one is not by any means the "alienated commuter," sitting on the train quietly and smugly, and quite untroubled by something called alienation. The word, the symbol, a whole so-called literature, have conspired to make a difference [in people's awareness]. . . . (p. 86)

For Percy the point is simply this: alienation is a "mode," a way of coming to terms with the world; it takes place when a commonly accepted world view, such as the "objective-empirical" one, no longer feels persuasive. Then the individual turns away from principles which have been previously held "true" if not sacred; indeed, discovers in them not a source of affirmation but the "root-source" of discontent. (p. 88)

As [Percy] tries to do justice to a whole philosophical literature, he feels compelled to become graphic, concrete; and increasingly, he does so by providing illustrative examples which, in essence, are brief but suggestive incidents, if not ideas for a short story. . . . (p. 91)

"The Message in the Bottle," was a parable rather than an analytic essay. Heidegger had once used the word *Geworfenheit* to describe man's existence. . . . (p. 127)

The essence of the castaway's situation or predicament is this: he is not at all aware of his origins or destiny, and he wants to know about both. He is not "objective" when he is doing so. (p. 129)

Christ's "good news" happens to be the "message in the bottle" which Percy happens to find most responsive to his situation. But he wrote the article not so much to indicate his own religious beliefs as to show through an extended image (the parable) what it is that separates the philosophers who have influenced him . . . from the assorted behaviorists, logical positivists, empiricists, semanticists, and philosophical idealists (from Kant on down) who have been so influential in recent Western history. Not for a moment does he want to forsake the "science" these latter value so highly. It is, quite simply, a matter of saying this: I have something to search for outside the laboratory or the seminar room, and without hard feelings I am going to do so. (pp. 132-33)

Philosophically the words [of Percy's essays] are the "existentialist's"; they are also the words of a man who had increasingly been drawn to the novel, with its concern for the particular, the man or woman who has a certain kind of character and meets up with others, with situations, and not least, with the hand of fate. (p. 143)

Percy wants to draw us close to Binx [protagonist and narrator of *The Moviegoer* (1961)], make us, it can be said, feel at home with him and his kind of living: oh, yes, the still young man who has a good job and a promising career, who is attractive and charming, a good catch for some lucky girl; he does at times seem a little strange, but that will go away, once he settles down, and anyway, one doesn't want someone *too* ordinary; this fellow has a touch of the mysterious to him, and that is always exciting.

The novel's tone is all-important. Binx speaks in a matter-of-fact way, and is only gently given to satire. . . . But he stops after a while, stops rubbing in his detachment, stops telling about all the ironies and absurdities of so-called civilized life. . . . Suddenly we are told: "The fact is I am quite happy in a movie, even a bad movie." Binx's despair is kept under wraps.

A good deal has been made by critics of the "meaning" of the movies, their "purpose" in this novel. They have been considered to be a reflection or "mirror" of "reality," a means of social observation and comment: what they "picture" is the dreams we have, or the kind of life we live, or would like to live—and on and on. Percy unquestionably uses the movies that way; they provide . . . an entry into the complexities of existentialist philosophy, a series of illustrations which make Kierkegaard and Heidegger become as familiar as—well, William Holden, John Wayne, or Orson Welles. But through the movies he also makes *Binx* familiar. . . . (pp. 147-48)

The movies enable Percy to let Binx reveal rather a lot about the condition of his soul, but to do so with a light, engaging touch. . . . [He] reminds us that we have all gone through similar experiences; the movies by now have become part of the "collective unconscious" of Americans. Yet, Binx is different: it is for others to have "a sweet and natural relationship, as they say in books," with a nice girl. . . . (pp. 148-49)

Once so freed [from "the everydayness of his own life"], he is able to start out on what he calls "the search." Negatively, the search is what "anyone would undertake," if he were able to get beyond the daily absorption in routines and habits. The search begins when for one reason or another a man "comes to," suddenly looks closely around, and notices just about everything—the "background" of life (in the form of persons, places, things) we all take for granted as we move along. . . . (pp. 149-50)

The articles Percy had been writing come to mind constantly as one goes through *The Moviegoer*. His philosophical preoccupations are enacted by Binx. There is Kierkegaard's "aesthetic stage"—not necessarily a sensual life, but one that moves along from "experience" to "experience." . . . However, some [people] move into quite another kind of life: "the ethical stage." Such people gain enough "title" to themselves, as Percy would put it, to be capable of sustained direction. . . . (pp. 151-52)

The man who is able to see and talk to himself as Binx does is in more jeopardy than he himself, or the reader, may realize. Binx has taken an implicit satisfaction in noticing others, keeping track of the foibles, the deception and pretense those others demonstrate, the thick web of illusions they spin for themselves. But the canny, knowing outsider, the aware observer, the ironist, the man who uses the "everydayness" of others as a means of getting a rotation or two himself, can also be the man who has nothing of his own. If others are blind, he has only the vision of their blindness. In a luminous moment Binx observes: "My exile in Gentilly has been the worst kind of self-deception." (p. 152)

At certain points in the novel Percy's didactic intentions appear, but never disruptively. The reader is free to glide through and beyond, simply enjoying a witty and charming Binx as he recalls his past or makes his clever appraisals. . . .

> I lived in my room as an Anyone living Anywhere and read fundamental books and only for diversion took walks around the neighborhood and saw an occasional movie. Certainly it did not matter to me where I was when I read such a book as *The Expanding Universe*. The greatest success of this enterprise, which I call my vertical search, came one night when I sat in a hotel room in Birmingham and read a book called *The Chemistry of Life*. When I finished it, it seemed to me that the main goals of my search were reached or were in principle reachable, whereupon I went out and saw a movie called *It Happened One Night* which was itself very good. A memorable night. The only difficulty was that though the universe had been disposed of, I myself was left over. There I lay in my hotel room with my search over, yet still obliged to draw one breath and then the next. But now I have undertaken a different kind of search, a horizontal search. As a consequence, what takes place in my room is less important. What is important is what I shall find when I leave my room and wander in the neighborhood. Before, I wandered as a diversion. Now I wander seriously and read as a diversion.

In that paragraph one finds allusions to Kierkegaard's life and "thinking"; a bit of self-representation on the part of the novelist; and a significant movement forward for the novel, all tucked into the charming flow of Binx's narrative voice: folksy, sly in its humor, serious as can be, but never portentous. (pp. 154-55)

Percy is no student of the film, but he knows what movies can become for a person, even as he uses them as an instrument in his principal character's "search." (p. 156)

[Binx struggles] throughout the novel to assume responsibility for [his fantasies—to] turn them to some account in life, rather than run from them or flirt with them intermittently. . . . [He is the] man who wanders, wonders, worries; who seems to slip away from any sustained involvement, yet be ever watchful of people. . . . (p. 157)

[Binx's] despair is the unwitting kind Kierkegaard mentioned—hence the quotation that precedes the novel ["The specific character of despair is precisely this: it is unaware of being despair."] (p. 158)

The tension in the novel is the tension in Binx's life, as he moves along on a search which at the same time he wants to undercut, or worse, size up all too exactly—and thereby thwart. (p. 161)

Bill Barrett [protagonist of *The Last Gentleman* (1966)] is not quite another Binx Bolling, but there are strong resemblances. Once again a young man seems to be adrift. . . . [Throughout the novel] he struggles with the same questions Binx could not avoid asking: there is a world out there, people and more people; I am curious about them, but why am I so disconnected from them? What to do—if anything?

Again we have as epigraph a brief familiar quotation from Kierkegaard: "If a man cannot forget, he will never amount to much." (p. 172)

And again, though now narrated in the third person, there is the quiet, brief, opening sentence—which can lead the reader anywhere: "One fine day in early summer a young man lay thinking in Central Park." Those first sentences mean more to Percy than they may to some writers; he labors over them at great length, and somehow they set the stage for the entire novel. . . . Beside Barrett in the park stands a symbol of his "condition," a large and expensive telescope. He uses it to scan the sky, to look at people. Percy's tone as a narrator draws the reader gradually toward Barrett; strange and eccentric, he nevertheless becomes a believable person who is not crazy, not bizarre, not a man who possesses a schizoid, voyeuristic "personality," not the grotesque become a moment's entertainment. He is thoroughly likable and interesting; and very important, he has a way of striking familiar chords: his moments of awkwardness or confusion remind us of similar experiences we've had. (p. 173)

Percy becomes quite satirical when he portrays the sophisticated world of the Northeast. He wants to show that the worries that bring others to psychiatrists, or prompt a whole range of fads, are not those that plague this "last gentleman" of his—who can face almost any disaster or threat that comes his way, who can shrug his shoulders at whatever "neurotic problem" he and his ever-so-serious psychoanalyst, Dr. Gamow, happen to examine, but who doesn't quite know how to face "the prospect of living through an ordinary Wednesday morning." (pp. 175-76)

Through Barrett's eyes (aided occasionally by the lens of his telescope), the obsessions and pretensions of mid-twentieth-century American secular society, as well as its earnest, decent side, get seen and heard. To a degree *The Last Gentleman* is the familiar novel of social observation: a character of broad sensibility, both serious and with a sense of humor, travels across a country; the various experiences he has, the accidents and incidents he encounters, enable the reader to glimpse what otherwise might go unnoticed. . . . And he has been granted by the author the gift of periodic release from the "everydayness" Binx Bolling fought so hard in *The Moviegoer*. . . .

Percy wants Barrett's sustained struggle to remind the rest of us of a moment or two we have had. (p. 178)

The Last Gentleman is a chronicle of ascent and descent: Barrett from the heights of his lofty (telescopic) vision toward the actual lives of others, among whom he finds himself increasingly located; Jamie toward the final, mysterious moment no one can comprehend in advance; Sutter from *his* heights—the loneliness of the man who uses abstract knowledge to keep himself removed from concrete involvement with others—and the rest of the Vaughts, whose humanity, in the tradition of existentialist thought, is evoked by Jamie's death.

The Last Gentleman is a continuation of Percy's ambitious effort to combine an interest in philosophical explication with the traditional requirements of the novel. (p. 181)

[In his philosophical writings Percy had] shown how the assertiveness of all too many scientists is itself derived from an illusion—. . . the illusion of certainty. And he had tried to indicate that the "existentialist" viewpoint . . . need not be opposed to the empirical or rational position. (pp. 183-84)

Barrett in the beginning of [*The Last Gentleman*] is the "man to whom all things seem possible and every course of action open." He is an exaggerated version of everyone. (p. 185)

Meanwhile Sutter is not inclined to abandon his freedom before any altar; Sutter is the existentialist who refuses the consolation of schools of thought, bodies of belief. He is himself, an individual—and if existentialists have anything in common . . . it is their insistence upon the extraordinary, almost defiant complexity of each individual. . . .

Existentialists are almost invariably obsessed with death: the ultimate choice anyone has—to end his life. . . . In *The Last Gentleman* Jamie's death at the end of the novel is an intense, powerfully rendered moment worthy of any nineteenth-century novelist. As the youth struggles vainly for life . . . Sutter stands nearby, ready to take his own life —an intention he has mentioned repeatedly in his notebooks, read all along by Barrett. On two accounts, then, the author has confronted Barrett with the presence of death, so much with us all through life: Jamie as a dying patient and Sutter as a likely suicide. As was the case with Binx in *The Moviegoer,* Percy's main character in *The Last Gentleman* is shaken to his foundations at the end of the novel. Sutter may yet end his life, but Barrett is now chasing him, wanting to talk. Barrett's spoken "wait" is enough to make Sutter stop his car. (p. 186)

With *The Last Gentleman* Percy consolidated himself as a writer who works on the borderline of philosophy, theology, and literature. *The Moviegoer* was proved not just an aberration, a one-time stroke of luck by a man who had been storing up ideas for a long time and needed a novel to add to the task of exposition he had set for himself. *The Last Gentleman* revealed a man of fiction who clearly enjoyed the old-fashioned virtues of the trade—storytelling, the amusement and edification of readers through the novelist's ability to use his imagination, conjure up all sorts of people, events, predicaments. But it was also the work of a man who had, perhaps, decided that if some things, as Rilke insisted, are unsayable (his *unsäglich*), a few important ideas can be given the flesh of life. . . .

[*Love in the Ruins*] has been repeatedly categorized as futuristic satire with the usual dose of dire prophecy, in the tradition of Orwell's *1984,* Huxley's *Brave New World* or Yevgeny Zamyatin's *We*. (p. 191)

[In this novel] Percy indicates how much whistling in the dark goes on, despite all the "enlightenment" we have managed to come up with: trips to the moon, computers for every turn of anyone's mind. And he has a hard time persuading himself, never mind his readers, that he is looking all that far into the future. He directs forceful satire at what he once referred to as "the Western democratic-technological humanistic view of man." In this novel, more than in the other two, he bears down hard on that "view," dissecting, clarifying, indicating soft spots, contradictions, ironies, or illusions, some of the last called "reality" or "scientific knowledge." We are not at all made to feel removed from Dr. More's so-called futuristic world, but rather kinsmen of his in the here-and-now. (p. 192)

There is no question that this novel offers Percy's most mordant and relentless critique of contemporary Western "culture" or "civilization." Nevertheless, the familiar Percy humor and sharp but compassionate eye for human foibles are present. There is, as usual, a plot that holds the reader, and quite enough action—all of which is to say that Percy continues to be a good novelist, whatever his other (polemical, critical) interests. Dr. Tom More tells the story —and again, despite Henry James's admonition, the first-person narrative form works out quite well. Percy's skill as a narrator is more developed than in his earlier novels. The sentences tend to be shorter, crisper, more pungent. In a few words he delivers not only good scenic description but pointed social and political sideswipes. As before, the first sentence does more than set the stage; a person is located, in all his and the world's dislocation, then set on the way to find whatever destiny seems, finally, to be his: "Now in these dread latter days of the old violent beloved U.S.A. and of the Christ-forgetting Christ-haunted death-dealing Western world I came to myself in a grove of young pines and the question came to me: has it happened at last?"

Has what happened? He is waiting for the world to end. The novel is in one sense no more "futuristic" than the Bible. . . . (p. 194)

When More intervenes to prevent a man's death at the hands of those who have taken upon themselves the right to decide such matters, he is in the kind of situation Heidegger spelled out as critical: a life-and-death situation in several senses of the word. At such moments we have a chance to find out a lot about ourselves. In every Percy novel there is a death; in this one Dr. More's daughter had died, precipitating one kind of crisis, and the question of what to do with the elderly patient—kill him "for the social good," or allow him his life and dignity—becomes for Dr. More a critical issue: to go along with others or find and assert unmistakably what he himself stands for.

The novel's ending has the familiar Percy ring: brief and undramatic. Dr. More has undergone no sudden and convincing conversion. (p. 205)

Every Percy novel ends on Marcel's theme of concreteness, Heidegger's "own most": the lapsometer and other such schemes, grand designs, brilliant projects or propositions are put aside in favor of a step toward a person and a specific kind of life (a beginning of it) with that person. No magical cure is wrought. A new kind of human being does not appear. We get no promise of a life hitherto undreamed of—which everyone will soon live. Nor does the plot suddenly generate a nicely coy and indirect message for the reader: try *this* and see how your life will go. (p. 207)

Dr. More strikes one as a middle-aged man who has long before tried just about all of Kierkegaard's "aesthetic" tricks, who has long before taken his ethical stand, only to find both himself and everyone else . . . hopelessly cynical, greedy, selfish, or thoughtless, regardless of social position or political persuasion. Perhaps the doctor's movement toward Ellen, so unpredictable, really, in terms of the novel, is meant to indicate that "leap of faith" Kierkegaard describes: the ethical man seems almost to reverse himself, go against his own hard-won ethical principles.

A man who wanted to know so much and save the whole world ends up tending to his lawn, his home, his wife. An abnegation of responsibility? The collapse of a "creative" man, just when he was on the brink of "self-realization"? Or a paradoxical "leap of faith" on the part of a tortured believer who once and for all has submitted himself to whatever design (including the attendant risks) that Divine Providence has in mind for him? The obligation to renounce pride, in all its varied and sometimes deceptive manifestations, is a lifelong one, More seems to have decided. He will never succeed in doing so. No man does. But he has put himself in a position to begin trying, something he had resisted doing for a long time. (pp. 207-08)

[The title character of Percy's *Lancelot* is] alive in the last quarter of the twentieth century. He is American, Southern, of "good" family: Lancelot Andrewes Lamar. The novel's plot is disarmingly simple, and suggestive. Lancelot is confined to a room in a place that is both a prison and a hospital. He is sick of mind, but has also committed a crime. . . .

[The novel] has him going back in time, recalling past events in his life, and reflecting upon what he and others near and far (we) have come to. He does so with his old friend Percival. . . . Only at the end does Percival say anything, and then one word at a time: "yes" or "no," spoken in response to a series of questions. *Lancelot* is a sustained reverie of yet another of Percy's seekers. . . . (p. 217)

[The] Lancelot of Percy's novel is reluctant to see himself as he was, to look candidly into his heart. He has suffered a lot, fallen by the way many times, but persisted in his search long enough to be at the point Percy has him—within sight of the Annunciation. If he could only see and comprehend fully what he has been about, his future will not be an endless repetition of outright misdeeds or moral evasions. (p. 219)

Lancelot, who comes up with existentialist ruminations that will not surprise Percy's fans, is a strongly sexual person, a sly and humorous observer, and, in the end, a murderer. His spells of amnesia and theological meditation yield with disarming ease to the imperatives of storytelling. This is Percy's shortest, most dramatic and sharply focused novel. Those who have basked in his extended cultural criticism and social satire will have to be content with brief moments here and there. (p. 220)

In an important moment of the novel, Lancelot tells his friend . . . : "How strange it is that a discovery like this, of evil, of a kinsman's dishonesty, a wife's infidelity, can shake you up, knock you out of your rut, be the occasion of a new way of looking at things." A little later on he connects his wife's sexual escapade to a momentous revelatory experience: "I discovered my own life."

The assertion of a man for whom a negative has a positive meaning. Lance had been drifting and without much sense of purpose. In fact, he had been in a daze. . . . (p. 226)

[Unfortunately,] Lance realizes that he did not discover anything "at the heart of evil." In fact, he discovered that "there was no 'secret' after all, no discovery. . . ." Except, perhaps, that there is hope. (p. 233)

In Percy's *Lancelot* the two knights have yet to reach the end of the journey. There are days ahead. They will continue to live, to ask questions, to find answers hard to come upon, to be, to be "in between." . . . "For us there is only the trying. The rest is not our business," T. S. Eliot said in a moment of renunciation as well as affirmation. It is a mixture this particular Lancelot, upon "discharge," will be struggling for. (p. 234)

In each of [Percy's] novels the central character, once freed to make his pilgrimage and continue his search, becomes almost impossible to write about any further. From that moment on the character is "living a life," a phrase Percy uses in such a way as to set up severe barriers to "analysis." . . . (p. 235)

Robert Coles, in his Walker Percy: An American Search *(copyright © 1978 by Robert Coles; reprinted by permission of Little, Brown and Co. in association with the Atlantic Monthly Press), Atlantic-Little, Brown, 1978, 250 p.*

* * *

PIERCY, Marge 1936-

Piercy, an American novelist and poet, is one of the most talented of the "activist writers." She has said that she "[doesn't] understand distinctions between private and social poetry," and the obliteration of that dichotomy—between "political" and "personal"—also distinguishes her fiction. (See also *CLC*, Vols. 3, 6, and *Contemporary Authors*, Vols. 5-8, rev. ed.)

CELIA BETSKY

Marge Piercy will leave a . . . lasting mark with . . . *Woman on the Edge of Time,* although it is not a perfect book. There is nothing like a suburban condition for Piercy; she tackles concepts as large as femininity and temporality, and her work functions in extremes, polarities which conflict and crash to the sound of unmitigated suffering. Those collisions are captured in highly personal and sympathetic human portraits. . . . (p. 38)

Although jarring at times, the oppositions Piercy sets up between present and future, rich and poor, urban squalor and scientific pastoralism, imprisonment and freedom, never produce caricatures. In fact, her utopia is more believable and moving than many renderings of contemporary reality. Like a latter-day D. H. Lawrence, she sees the future as a revival of tradition, eternal values and human ritual. . . . The organic is stronger than the synthetic, the real invalidates what is fake, and community thus becomes a state of mind.

Manipulating time in the context of a Kesey-esque mental hospital, Piercy projects the ambiguity of whether reality or imagination is at work; she penetrates the relationship between science fiction and delusion. *Woman on the Edge of Time* addresses the possibilities of actuality and hallucination. Unfortunately, this gives her almost too many ideas—she has really written two books, the story of [her protagonist's] victimization and a feminist handbook for the 22nd century. . . . (p. 39)

Woman on the Edge of Time, expanding on the political consciousness of Piercy's other novels and offering a future, resembling something like the 1960s gone right instead of wrong, integrates and internalizes rhetoric by making it the subject matter of plot itself. And Piercy's people, crazy or imagined, are worth caring for. (p. 40)

Celia Betsky, "Books Considered: 'Woman on the Edge of Time'," in The New Republic *(reprinted by permission of* The New Republic; *© 1970 The New Republic, Inc.), Vol. 175, No. 15, October 9, 1976, pp. 38-40.*

MARGARET ATWOOD

Marge Piercy now has eight books to her credit, four novels and four books of poetry. Her work has always had the courage both of her convictions and of its own (the difference between the two has occasionally been one of her problems), and [*Woman on the Edge of Time* and *Living in the Open*] are no exception. She is a serious writer who deserves the sort of considered attention which, too often, she does not get.

For instance, none of the reviews of *Woman on the Edge of Time* I've read to date even seems to have acknowledged its genre. . . .

Some reviewers treated [the] part of the book [when the protagonist is visited by a being from the future] as a regrettable daydream or even a hallucination caused by Connie's madness. Such an interpretation undercuts the entire book. . . . Other reviewers did not see Connie as insane but took Luciente and her troupe to be a pointless exercise in "science fiction," an exercise which should have no place in a piece of social realism. But Piercy is not that stupid. If she had intended a realistic novel she would have written one. *Woman on the Edge of Time* is a utopia, with all the virtues and shortcomings of the form, and many of the things reviewers found irksome are indigenous to the genre rather than the author. . . .

[It] is to Piercy's credit that she has given us a very human and rather grouchy traveler and a guide who sometimes loses her temper. (p. 601)

Piercy expends a good deal of energy trying to get every last detail *in,* to get it *right,* and to make rather too sure we get the point.

Numerous dangers await the author of a utopia. For one thing, inhabitants of utopias somehow cannot help coming across as slightly sanctimonious and preachy; they've been like that since More. And in addition all utopias suffer from the reader's secret conviction that a perfect world would be dull, so Piercy is careful to liven things up with festivals, ceremonies, nice clothes, and a hopeful description of untrammeled sexual interchange. . . .

This is a genre more at home in 19th-century England than in the America of the 1970s, where moral earnestness seems to have gone out of fashion. It's a daring thing for Piercy to have attempted, and it's entirely in keeping with her previous literary production that she should have done so. *Woman on the Edge of Time* is like a long inner dialogue in which Piercy answers her own questions about how a revised American society would work. The curious thing about serious utopias, as opposed to the satirical or entertainment variety, is that their authors never seem to write more than one of them; perhaps because they are products, finally, of the moral rather than the literary sense.

To turn from Piercy's utopia to her poetry is to turn from an imagined world to an imagination, from a sense to a sensibility. . . . I find the poetry more convincing. Piercy is committed to the search for honesty, however painful; to action, however futile; to getting it said and getting it done, however awkward the results may be. She's a feminist and a radical, but her poetry fleshes out these concepts in complex and sometimes startling ways, and she's no simple-minded sloganeer. "I ram on," she says of herself and her poetry; "I must make from this soft body some useful thing." . . .

Her poetry is "unfashionable," in that it is not flattish, understated, careful or bled. It reads as if she's never been in a creative writing class. The words crowd, lavish and lush, metaphors logjam, polemic rages, similes breed similes and sometimes unconscious puns, and its all part of Piercy's earthy aesthetic. . . . [Out] of all the surge and flux, the sometimes dutiful rhetoric, Piercy can build moments and sometimes whole poems that she would not have achieved with careful elegance. "People of the Shell," for instance, is superb, and it is not alone. Lines and aphorisms surface, flash and sink, poems transform themselves, words swirl. The literary ancestor here is not Dickinson but Whitman, and the vision is finally, despite the small ironies, a romantic one.

Like Whitman, Piercy must be read in chunks, not sips, and appreciated for her courage, gut energy and verbal fecundity, not for laconic polish. Dancing is hard and you may fall down, her poetry implies, but she is going to dance anyway. She rams on, and the reader can only applaud. (p. 602)

Margaret Atwood, "An Unfashionable Sensibility," in The Nation *(copyright 1976 by the Nation Associates, Inc.), Vol. 223, No. 19, December 4, 1976, pp. 601-02.*

ANATOLE BROYARD

I'd like to propose a program of civil rights for characters in novels. I don't think it is fair for authors to push them around or malign them just to make a point or put across a message. . . .

Marge Piercy's . . . novel, "The High Cost of Living," leads me to these reflections. In it she creates just one interesting character—and then destroys him. Not because the logic of his life or his circumstances demands it, because it is dramatically inevitable, but for reasons that I can only conjecture, and that, from all appearances, would seem to be polemical.

In "The High Cost of Living" Leslie, a young lesbian, and Bernie, a young male homosexual, struggle for the affections of Honor, a pretentious 17-year-old virgin. Although neither Leslie nor Bernie will admit it, Honor is so stultifyingly silly that they are more or less forced into an appreciation of each other. . . .

After some rather touching blundering, Leslie and Bernie make love. I found the scene appealing—not because they have "straightened out," but because their love-making develops out of a friendship that is strong enough to surmount difficulties. For a few hours, they are happy, which I am old-fashioned and sentimental enough to enjoy. Then Miss Piercy turns Bernie into an extremely unpleasant creature who is a contradiction of everything that has been happening to him. He becomes a tool for tightening the nuts and bolts of the author's sociology of sex. While Leslie is open to change, Bernie is the leopard, or leper, who cannot change his spots. When the three other men in the novel are exposed as compulsive lechers, one begins to sense a prejudice.

It would take a brave man, in the present social climate, to suggest that male homosexuals in novels tend to be wittier than female ones. Yet it does seem so emphatically true of Bernie and Leslie that I began to wonder whether Miss Piercy might not regard wit as a vice. . . .

Miss Piercy herself does not often condescend to wit, and the felicities of a decent prose style are inconsistent with her seriousness. . . .

At the end of the book, we leave Leslie, who has a black belt in karate, teaching militant women to defend themselves. Defend themselves against whom? I'm tempted to say against Miss Piercy.

Anatole Broyard, "One Critic's Fiction: 'The High Cost of Living'," in The New York Times Book Review *(© 1978 by The New York Times Company; reprinted by permission), January 22, 1978 p. 14.*

DEAN FLOWER

Marge Piercy's assumption about our modern confusions of identity seems to be that we hide in ill-fitting categories because they protect us from pain. . . . Piercy's singular achievement [in *The High Cost of Living*] is to make [a] prettily vulgar working-class girl [Honor] in Detroit attractive enough so that the other two [characters] are drawn to her. . . . Currently in a "French phase," [Honor] insists on such pronunciations as "Ber*nar,*" "Hono*rée*" and Frenchifying *sordid* into "sor'id." It all fits perfectly in the sor'id setting of Detroit's forgotten French names like Gratiot, Livernois, and the like. . . .

But Piercy's deeper concern lies with the cautiously-developed intimacy of Leslie and Bernard, which sends them each back into the past, questioning the anxieties and defenses of their sexual natures. . . . [The] mutual disappointments of Leslie and Bernard emerge almost palpably real. (p. 349)

Yet the novel isn't a test-tube for three characters who fail to resolve each other's problems, despite their final unhappy separateness. Its point of view belongs to Leslie: self-doubting yet fiercely self-disciplined, guilty if she doesn't work the Rape Hot Line or teach the womanly art of self-defense, but equally guilty if she doesn't slave for her Ph.D. in a male-dominated academic game where she also "must" succeed. Piercy captures her feminist anger in some of its predictable formulas ("she did not like the way men used bodies like hers to pin up on their walls and sell toothpaste and decorate glassware and magazines"), but we can't be consistently sure about the irony. Like her protagonist, Piercy it seems could go either way. Her loyalty to the Movement contests with a novelist's need for individual creative freedom, and that conflict riddles her novel with ambivalence. (p. 350)

Dean Flower, "The Way We Live Now," in The Hudson Review *(copyright © 1978 by The Hudson Review, Inc.; reprinted by permission), Vol. XXXI, No. 2, Summer, 1978, pp. 343-55.**

Divided into four sections named for the seasons, [*The Twelve-Spoked Wheel Flashing*] is rich in imagery, wit, and rhetoric; balanced in statement and detail. Piercy's writing is energetic, ranging from rage to passion to bitterness. She celebrates feminism, loving, nature; she condemns everything from war and sexism to pollution and food additives. She succeeds in what she sets out to do: to weld the personal with the political, the emotional with the intellectual.

"Notes on Current Books: 'The Twelve-Spoked Wheel Flashing'," in Virginia Quarterly Review *(copyright, 1978, by the* Virginia Quarterly Review, *The University of Virginia), Vol. 54, No. 4 (Autumn, 1978), p. 144.*

CHARLES MOLESWORTH

The spirit most felt in ["The Twelve-Spoked Wheel Flashing"] is generous love, but love combined with scrutiny and even humor. Arranged around the seasons, the book moves from city life to a Cape Cod retreat and back again; its concerns are the difficult balances that result when love, self-regard and moral concerns clash and reveal themselves. Like Adrienne Rich and Robert Lowell, but quite distinct from either, she turns her ego into the theater of operations. Politics, domestic tranquility and discord, supportive nature and nurturing art: all are plain-spokenly addressed, with an almost casual sense of form. As she says, "Like the Golem I am makeshift, lumbering." But the artistic ease is more than offset by the emotional drive: "You want only half / of me and I, / I want to be whole." Sometimes the figures go on a bit too long, and a metaphor begins to gasp, splitting its force between the clarity of feeling and the curve of beauty:

> a theme from Liszt
> I cannot have heard since
> I played it on the piano
> at age seven: the sensuous honey
> of melancholy veined
> smoky with lust.

But there are times when the excess comes right, especially in the funny passages, as this arrival scene at an airport shows:

> Either you are met by seven
> young Marxists who want to know
> at once What Is To Be Done
> or one professor who says, What?
> you have luggage. But I
> parked in the no
> parking zone.

The book spills over with a love of place, a restorative sense of home (perhaps its rarest quality), a need for growth and preservation. (p. 58)

Charles Molesworth, "Four Poets," in The New York Times Book Review *(© 1978 by The New York Times Company; reprinted by permission), November 26, 1978, pp. 58, 60.**

KEITH HARRISON

Marge Piercy's last book *Living in the Open* was an excellent one. [*The Twelve-Spoked Wheel Flashing*] extends some of the themes of the book—of being a woman, a roving poet, a gardener—but not always successfully. The last book was—as the title implied—"open." Here she imposes a seasonal scheme on the poems which does little for the book except to make it *look* more ordered.

What I often admire in Marge Piercy's work is her ability to give lyrical yet tough-minded exposés of difficult relationships. Often, the emotional courage of her work and her flowing rhythms work together—as a shock, then a healing salve. The danger is that she sometimes over-writes. She is very good when she is cryptic and fanciful at the same time, as here in "the meaningful exchange." The poem teeters on the edge of the surreal and the absurd, but succeeds in making its point very economically and disturbingly.

Elsewhere in the book I sensed the need for further editing. The proliferation of her often very powerful images sometimes works against her; some poems with wonderful passages are marred because they go on too long. Yet Marge Piercy is an important writer in a number of ways: she is charting a world, for men and women, which is often as uncomfortable as it is immediate and neglected. Her particular skill is to make us remember. If it sometimes hurts, it is not out of a desire to shock, but out of the conviction that an honest confrontation with ourselves is the only proper ground for joy. (p. 239)

Keith Harrison, "A Round of Poets," in The Carleton Miscellany *(copyright 1979 by Carleton College), Vol. XVII, Nos. 2 & 3, 1979, pp. 234-43.**

* * *

PLATH, Sylvia 1932-1963

Plath was an American poet, novelist, and short story writer. A leading member of the confessional school of poetry, Plath explores in her verse the horror and chaos that lurk beneath the appearance of sanity. Her violent, despairing poetic vision is presented in verse distinguished by technical control and brilliant imagery. Plath also published under the pseudonym Victoria Lucas. (See also *CLC*, Vols. 1, 2, 3, 5, 9, 11, and *Contemporary Authors*, Vols. 19-20; *Contemporary Authors Permanent Series*, Vol. 2.)

ARTHUR OBERG

[No] poet more than Sylvia Plath keeps reminding us of the terms and the ground of her writing. To say that she writes *in extremis* is not only an accurate statement of fact but a suggestion that more than aesthetic matters may be involved. (p. 127)

Ariel, Sylvia Plath's major posthumously published book of poems, begins and ends *in extremis.* "Morning Song," the opening poem, begins with the word "love." "Words," the concluding poem, ends on the word "life." The title of the last poem "Words," and the pun in the title of the opening poem "Morning Song" suggest the two other prominent centers here, art and death. Love and death, life and art—these are the extremities out of which the *Ariel* poems proceed. And Plath insisted upon them and returned to them for alignments of the most dangerous kind.

The *Ariel* poems reveal and often pursue a direction more nearly final than that found in Plath's earlier poetry or in her nonpoetic work. What surfaces in *Ariel* proves to be a love of extremity. It expresses itself in obsessive rhythm, in a momentum and an inventiveness of image, and in a defining vocabulary recognizable by what it is attracted to and by what it seeks: totality, finality, obduracy. In Plath's most central books of poetry, *The Colossus* and *Ariel,* the adjectives expose this range of thought and feeling. The attraction involves what is "sheer," "mere," "pure," "absolute," "necessary." Movement in the poems is toward what cannot be stopped or reversed, things "intractable" and "tireless." It is toward what lies beyond loving, human feeling, things "vast" and "immense." And toward what is unrepeatable, things "unique" and "perfect." Plath's recurrent use of the prefixes "in-," "un-," and "ir-" relates to this defining poetics. And her attempt at using words like "terrible," "awful," and "horrible" in their root sense further characterizes her poetry and its preferences. The vocabulary which she evolved in her poetry is never far from the limits her opening and concluding poems announced and made final as the proper centers among which her poems move. (p. 128)

The terms under which Plath chose to write her poems are unmistakably given, over and over. She sought to embrace nothing less than "everything." A procedure on this scale was bound to assume personal and historical, aesthetic and sexual dimensions. (pp. 128-29)

If ideally nothing escaped Plath, her tone when confronting what she called "atrocity" or "enormity" shifted between the mocking and the serious, the playful and the deadly. She could play child, adolescent, and adult, alternately, and at the same time. As a consequence, it sometimes is difficult to separate boast from threat or fear from wish in her readiness for the enormity of everything. . . . Predictably, the question of knowledge returned the poet to the smaller, but still large questions of love and death, life and art.

What can love manage. What is death's domain. What are the just concerns of life and of art. These involved Plath in the issue not only of poetic content but of poetic form as well.

At once inclusive and exclusive, the content of Sylvia Plath's poetry appropriated all provinces of knowledge. She not only accepted the extremity and enormity of history and personality but sought out the most outrageous facts and *facta* of life and art. Repeatedly, the impression she conveyed was that of a woman and poet to whom nothing was alien. In moving prose written after her death, Ted Hughes . . . attempted to detail this sense in her:

> The world of her poetry is one of emblematic visionary events, mathematical symmetries, clairvoyance, metamorphoses, and something resembling total biological and racial recall.

Hughes's last clause defines what readers coming to Plath's work even for the first time inevitably feel. (pp. 129-30)

What Sylvia Plath sought to manage as content, she also had to handle in and as form. The poetry she admitted admiring and the methods of composition attributed to her by people who knew her involved poems written "all-of-a-piece." Such poems are in evidence in the post-Romantic, organic verse she frequently succeeded in writing. . . .

If the word "organic" commonly has been turned into an almost meaningless term expressive of a quasi-mystical ideality which is present in a particular poem, for Plath's poetry it can be a critical term of the most descriptive and telling kind. The best poems in her first book, *The Colossus,* are organic in conception, in their management of matters as basic as stanza and line length and image. In the poem, "Man in Black," taken from the first book, Plath achieved a poem unmistakably "all-of-a-piece." . . . (p. 131)

What Plath accomplishes in "Man in Black" is nothing less than the achievement, wished for, willed, and executed, of the kind of organic, post-Romantic poem which she delighted in and which she aspired to write. . . .

The last line in "Man in Black"—"All of it, together"—succeeds impressively in underlining the impression that the poem has been or at least given the illusion of being "born all-of-a-piece." "Man in Black" concludes by becoming something like a completed miniature "Kubla Khan." The poem is there on the page, "all of it, together." In part, "Man in Black" is one more attempt at writing the final, Romantic poem in the English language. (p. 133)

The early poems, when seen in connection with the poems from the posthumous volumes, reveal a search on the part of the poet for objects or images adequate to whatever love or hate she wished to attach to them. In many of the late poems, she directed her relentless precision toward casting poems in the form of extended correlatives. In the first line of each poem, an interior state commonly is recorded toward which the rest of the movement of the poem is painstakingly devoted. . . . Each poem exposes a search for adequate image. Each exposes the wish to find whatever is in the vase or in the tree or behind the veil. In the course of each poem the poet steadily attempts [in Ted Hughes's words] "to locate just what it was that hurt." (p. 139)

Separately and as a group, ["Tulips," "The Swarm," and "A Birthday Present"] deal with problems of language, or, more specifically, with the adequacy of any image in the face of an extreme situation. They address the confrontation, immediate or potential, of something desired, yet also feared. And they address the problem of finding words able to express that confrontation. In each of these poems, the poet attempts to locate, by means of a run of images, what "it" is: in "Tulips," what "it" is that is in the vase and to what "it corresponds," a correspondence which signals sickness or health, life or death; in "The Swarm," what "it" is that is in the tree and, in the mind, so intriguing and threatening at the same time; in "A Birthday Present," what "it" is that can lie behind the veil and be the source of such comforting and horrible enormity. (pp. 142-43)

The need to locate what "it" is proves equally central to the movement and meanings of other poems of Plath's. In part, the mad and associational intensity of poems like "Lady Lazarus," "Daddy," and "The Applicant" becomes understandable in view of what the poet, there, is bent on relentlessly seeking out. . . . (p. 143)

"The Applicant," "Daddy," and "Lady Lazarus" reveal Plath centrally concerned with the universal habit of image-making, [but] this is not all. More important, in these poems she exhibits the extremes, personal and historical, to which image-making has been taken.

"Daddy" and "Lady Lazarus" extend and provide variations on the concerns of "The Applicant." In particular, they seek to locate what it was that hurt. These two poems radically confront Lear-like questions of man and his image, of what constitutes for him need and excess. "Is man no more than this? Consider him well," Lear mused. Both "Lady Lazarus" and "Daddy" raise issues as basic as image and as man. They seek to find images which will sufficiently body forth that man.

"Lady Lazarus" and "Daddy" are poems which seem written at the edge of sensibility and of imagistic technique. They both utilize an imagery of severe disintegration and dislocation. The public horrors of the Nazi concentration camps and the personal horrors of fragmented identities become interchangeable. Men are reduced to parts of bodies and to piles of things. The movement in each poem is at once historical and private; the confusion in these two spheres suggests the extent to which this century has often made it impossible to separate them. (p. 146)

The barkerlike tone of "Lady Lazarus" is not accidental. As in "Daddy," the persona strips herself before the reader . . . all the time utilizing a cool or slang idiom in order to disguise feeling. Sylvia Plath borrowed from a sideshow or vaudeville world the respect for virtuosity which the performer must acquire, for which the audience pays and never stops paying. Elsewhere in her work, she admired the virtuosity of the magician's unflinching girl or of the unshaking tattoo artist. Here, in "Lady Lazarus," it is the barker and the striptease artist who consume her attention. What the poet pursues in image and in rhyme (for example, the rhyming of "Jew" and "gobbledygoo") becomes part of the same process I observed in so many of her other poems, that attempt, brilliant and desperate, to locate what it was that hurt. (p. 147)

Sylvia Plath never stopped recording in her poetry the wish and need to clear a space for love. Yet she joined this to an inclination to see love as unreal, to accompanying fears of being unable to give and receive love, and to the eventual distortion and displacement of love in the verse. Loving completely or "wholly" she considered to be dangerous, from her earliest verse on.

Love was so much a part of her world that it often stood in her poetry for that world itself. When the world seemed unreal, so did love. In the early poetry, this sometimes approximated a secondhand, Romantic poetics. But the early poems also give evidence of some more profound sense of a loving unreality which the later poems turned into a more desperate, pathetic tableau of "valentine-faces" and candy or enamel-painted hearts.

Plath often wrote with humor and irony when she considered love. She could be the satirist alert to the sentiments of a Victorian or Edwardian age. She could be a shrewd psychologist of love's ambiguities. She could be sane and clairvoyant, joining writers as major as Shakespeare and Dostoyevsky in probing the darkness of the heart. But in what she wrote just before and at the time of *Ariel,* she began to establish a stance which I find problematic and dangerous. A progression is evident in her handling of love and the love poem that calls into question the loving of intentions which some of the first lines of poems announce, but which the tone of whole poems or the endings of poems commonly belie. (pp. 152-53)

In the important *Ariel* bee poems, her uncertainty issues in the fear of being hurt or fatally "stung" by love. It is the kind of bad joke or bad pun which comes to typify her late art. It expresses a situation so extreme and intolerable to her that only by such devices could she ever have hoped to manage her world. Lowell and Berryman use similar devices, but very often out of real strength. In Plath, however, the strategy commonly reduces to sheer helplessness.

The *Ariel* poems reveal a woman both too exposed and too unopen. The sexuality is relentless and overwhelming. The puns not only proliferate—"head," "queen," "screw," "cherry"—but succeed in words like "mail" (letter and "male") and "box" (sexual organ and coffin) in making explicit the meanings which are central to her work. (p. 154)

If Plath wished her poems to stand as love letters to the world, the perspective from which they proceed may, in the end, have made that wish impossible. Her metaphor for the world may very well have been a response to a loveless world. But it is here that the logic of the argument breaks down. For the poetry shows the controlling metaphor threatening to become the informing vision itself. By the time she wrote her last poems, there was less and less room for and patience with love. If the poems were once meant to create love, they came to stand for a world which had forgone or gone beyond some loving, human circumference.

The problem of artistic control which so many critics have addressed in Sylvia Plath I find less central and settleable than that of the controlling metaphor in her verse. Her best poems are incredibly controlled. But the issue of controlling metaphor lingers on long after a reader has decided whether the poems show control or "the look of control" or "controlled uncontrolledness."

The controlling metaphor affects much that happens in Plath's poetry. In the process of finding what to "do" with her love, she often concluded by inverting it. Poem by poem, not just in *Ariel,* she radically confused love and death, self and other. Images of love give way to images of incest ("Daddy," and the bee poems) and masturbation ("Suicide Off Egg Rock," "Ariel," "Death & Co.," "The Jailor," "Childless Woman"). Loveless images of madness, suicide, and solipsism—from the "I am, I am, I am" of "Suicide Off Egg Rock" to the "ich, ich, ich, ich" of "Daddy"—take on the force of leitmotifs for her work. And art, if capable of leading us back to loving, human contexts, here gives the impression of being one more inversion of love. It can be one more deception in this life.

In the late poems, something happens to language and to love and to the possibility of defining a self through love. Repeatedly, the health or breakdown of one is a reflection of the other. (pp. 156-57)

As a representative, twentieth-century writer, Plath lends to language as language a central place in her work. But in the implications and concluding achievement of this, she is entirely herself. In five very late poems, "Words," "Kindness," "Edge," "Contusion," and "The Fearful," she has no rival, perhaps fortunately so.

These poems, unlike "Lesbos" or "Stillborn" which show love and language breaking down but which discover no words or tone artful enough to manage that fact, succeed in what they attempt. They learn the art of leaving human love behind, but whether out of necessity or freedom it is not always clear.

The five poems share, aside from having been written during the last week of Plath's life, an assessment of a situation where love seems either absent or unreal, deceptive or unimportant. In all of them, there is a rightness in choice of phrase and word and a brilliance in the run of images in individual stanzas and in entire poems. (p. 158)

These poems all take an associational, imagistic technique to a point of deadly confusion and delusion where the poet can fold her poem-children back into her body simply by writing out the wish ("Edge") or where she is so uncomprehending of human, loving kindness that she cannot distinguish between children and roses ("Kindness").

What I am suggesting is that these late poems are not the mystically calm, orderly pieces which some critics have seen them to be. Instead, they are the terrible, terrifying creations of a woman who, near the end of a life, still could not do without love, even if she never learned what to do with it. As a result, the tone of the poems is something less than the matter-of-factness of the saint. (p. 160)

If love was never completely renounced by her, neither was it constant in her work. And the poems keep recording a journey and a movement as inevitable as death. Now that the poems which were written just before or at the same time as the *Ariel* poems have been collected and published in *Crossing the Water* and *Winter Trees,* we are afforded an even better means of charting and confirming larger movements and stages in her work. When Ted Hughes and other critics first wrote of an inevitable, conscious development in her poetry and when the titles of the posthumous books *Crossing the Water* and *Winter Trees* were first announced, I wondered how willful was the creation of that legendary development and reputation. But a consideration of the poems themselves and of her title, *The Colossus,* for her first book, helped to dispel such fears. In the same way, interpretations of her art after the fact of her suicide now strike me as less arbitrary and fallacious than they once did. That she eventually took her own life is important. It might be dangerous not to consider that fact seriously.

Plath's development from *The Colossus* to the poems of the later volumes is technical as much as it is psychic and spiritual. More particularly, that development concerns her use of image in connection with the possibilities for language and love. How that development implies and makes explicit a journey, her gathered work actualizes and clarifies.

By the title of her first volume, *The Colossus,* Plath signified what she would spend a lifetime trying to create. Sometimes she exchanged the colossus image for the image of an ark or a garden. But the intentions were always the same, to write words that would bear love and that would have life. The difficulty, however, was that, from the very beginning, her landscape risked turning into (to use images from her own poems) some nightmarish bestiary or wintering ship or burnt-out spa. The problem of what would be her controlling metaphor, then, was full upon her from her earliest work.

The poems she wrote after those included in *The Colossus* show her still involved in trying to put together saving, loving words. But the colossus which she feared would never get "put together entirely" and which she feared would be a ruin becomes more than a distant, playful fear. The opening and closing poems of *The Colossus*—"The Manor Garden" and "The Stones"—depend upon and establish the essential, ominous ambiguity that mark later poems like "Tulips." (pp. 161-62)

Now that *Crossing the Water* and *Winter Trees* have been published, there is the opportunity to observe the poet at every stage taking stock of her situation and development. *The Colossus* and *Ariel,* even before the other volumes appeared recently, showed her charting a course, or "getting there," as she put it; she assigned it as a title to one of her poems. If the exact nature of the journey or voyage or ride, all prominent metaphor in her verse, was often in doubt, its connection with love was not.

There are two major movements which the entire body of Plath's poetry suggests—toward the creation of love and toward some state beyond love. These movements are not strictly chronological any more than they are exclusive of one another. In part, they exist in and through the very last poems she wrote. But, as poems written in time, by a woman aware of time, they tend to build toward that point where the second movement, a state beyond human love, can be claimed, or at least volitionally prophesied. . . . Sometimes Plath depended upon the fierce repetitions of "would" or "shall" or "let us" in order to move toward and create that state beyond love. The syntax of poems like "A Birthday Present" and "Lady Lazarus" depend greatly upon such a volitional strategy. (pp. 162-63)

"Mystic" contains within it a countermovement toward a belief in earthly love.

The contradictory impression which "Mystic" succeeds in conveying not only is central to the meaning of that poem, but it also connects with a defining center in much of Plath's late verse. On the one hand, there is the woman who becomes a contemporary doubting Thomas, except that what she disbelieves are not Christ's wounds and resurrected presence but his love:

> How I would like to believe in tenderness.
> ("The Moon and the Yew Tree" . . .)

This moment is as desperate as any in modern poetry. It is as pathetic as Prufrock's musing on the mermaids, "I do not think that they will sing to me." (p. 165)

Marriage imagery is resplendent in Sylvia Plath's poetry. "Do" is recurrent and hypnotic as a word and as an action. At times the persona saying, "I do, I do," is a mechanical doll or a prisoner confessing to a crime. These senses of the word and phrase Plath commonly linked with the recital of the marriage vow. "Do" also is punned upon, especially in her poem, "Daddy." The German, familiar "du" or you ("do," "du," "you"—they even rhyme) of intimate address and love songs is recalled, almost as a reminder of the historical and personal perversions to which love and action can be subjected. (pp. 165-66)

The Colossus already revealed the poet's predilection for decadent unions between love and death, and art and life. If her browned gardenia and ghastly orchid recall *fin de siècle* botanical catalogues, it is in her taste in sounds, colors, jewels, music, painting, and literature that she shows herself to be a contemporary decadent. . . . In the poems that came after *The Colossus,* however, we are able to see how this incipient decadence is turned from something faintly literary into something closer to the poet's very self: "Pom! Pom! They would have killed me!" (pp. 166-67)

That Sylvia Plath wrote two last-words poems, one called just that ("Last Words") and another, "Words," I find significant. The major problem which I address in this chapter —to whom and to what do her poems finally belong—the two poems engage, although in the body of her poetry they are not unique in that concern. (p. 168)

"Last Words" is a very different kind of poem, closer in style to poems of intense desire like "Tulips," "A Birthday Present," or "The Arrival of the Bee Box." The poet in "Last Words" [in *Crossing the Water*] wants and volitionally unlooses herself from domestic things in order to achieve a state of utter mystic peace:

> It will be dark,
> And the shine of these small things sweeter than the
> face of Ishtar.

Ishtar, Babylonian and Assyrian goddess of love and fertility, is invoked. But it is the artful, statuary face of Ishtar which has importance for her in this poem. The state yearned for is death, not love. The word "sweeter" in this quotation goes back to a line earlier in the same poem, "I should sugar and preserve my days like fruit!" Sweetness commonly threatened loving deception for Plath. Here it carries equally dark connotations of preservation, but always at the unnatural expense of life. Sweetness proves costly, proves to be death.

As "Last Words" earns its authority, there emerges that tone, or "décor"—an important word for . . . Plath—which related to the matter of control and to whatever triumph or failure these final poems contain.

"Last Words" manages to indicate how the poet willed to move herself and her poetry toward love as much as it indicates how she could not handle the artful business she went about. "I can't stop it," she wrote in this poem. Here "It" meant not love or blood-hurt but the escape of spirit-breath or the release of images. (pp. 168-69)

"Last Words," like any of the major poems from *Ariel* or *Crossing the Water* or *Winter Trees,* does not dispose of the nagging sense that, in love as it may be with "a soldier repose than death's" (a phrase from an early poem, "The Sculptor"), in the end, it belongs to an art of elegy, less by choice than by some desperate, pathetic necessity. (p. 170)

If the late poems belong to anyone, they belong not to her father or husband or children or even to poetry (the sense of the poem as unloving love-child she never forgot). But to Death, Death the lover, Death the double. . . . (pp. 170-71)

What I have been tracing—the attempts of the poems to establish lyric and love and the countermovement toward elegy and to a deadly journey which could not be stopped—gain authority and intensity from the more recently released volumes. They never contradict but extend what the *Ariel* poems were about. The old faults prove to be the same; "love cannot come here," we again find.

The moving center of both books, *Crossing the Water* and *Winter Trees,* is that of a woman of sorrows. Recurrently,

Plath imagined herself as Mary and Christ. Ease, love, correspondence, and relationship all were yearned for and did not emerge. (p. 172)

If some important part of Sylvia Plath in her late poetry refused to accept a world of gigolos as the final version of the world, she never abandoned the doubt that she could recognize or accept love even were she able to manage it in her life and art. As a result, tone figures more and more prominently in the interpretation of the poems she left behind. Tone, its readiness and surety, dominates.

The posthumous poems expose discrepancies and failures of the most serious kind. The phoenix figure, prominent in various guises in her work, deserted her outside her poems. And the children-poems she imagined in the late poem, "Edge," folded back into her and taken out of this life, became painfully distinct from her in death—the two children fathered by Ted Hughes and left behind; the poems which were posthumous. And the Medea figure, once little more than a literary trapping in her early poem, "Aftermath," proved in the late poem, "Edge," only a pathetic wish denied to her outside of mythology. When she died, so did her long sought-after and invoked gods.

The confusions and delusions of art and life, wish fulfillment and reality, became exposed at her death. And they record a sad fact. But, beyond that and more important, they reach back to some sense of lovelessness or lack implicit in a major part of her poetry. The *Ariel* poems, looked at together with the poems from *Crossing the Water* and *Winter Trees,* now strike me as less in love's behalf than she would have liked them to be. Poems like "Daddy" and "Lady Lazarus" in the end may not be the triumphs which their momentum and inventiveness at times celebrate. Instead, and this is my sense of them, they belong more to elegy and to death, to the woman whose "loving associations" abandoned her as she sought to create images for them. (pp. 172-73)

Arthur Oberg, "Sylvia Plath: 'Love, Love, My Season'," in his Modern American Lyric: Lowell, Berryman, Creeley, and Plath *(copyright © 1978 by Rutgers, The State University of New Jersey; reprinted by permission of Rutgers University Press), Rutgers, 1978, pp. 127-73.*

ANTHONY THWAITE

That mystery and obfuscation, as well as pregnant misreading, have helped to create a Plath cult is undoubtedly true. That there *is* a cult-like interest in her life and work (the two often seen as inextricable) can't be denied. . . . (p. 40)

Re-reading all of her published poems, and reading or re-reading a mass of stuff written about her, I've been struck again and again by the dramatic *distancing* of so much of her work, the way in which she created poems which are precisely *not* cries from the heart, or from a sick mind, or from the edge of the precipice in an obtrusively narrow or personal way; and at the same time I've been struck by the way these poems are indeed quarrels with herself, dramatic debates between action and stillness, fulfilment and blankness, hope and despair, anger and love—not seen in those abstract shapes, of course, but translated into that dense and sprightly metaphorical discourse which is one of the languages of poetry and which was certainly her language.

Very often it is a pictorial language, the first level of metaphor, something seen: she has the attentive detail, the highlighted focus, of a *genre* painter. It comes out, for example, in the second part of her poem "Two Views of a Cadaver Room", in which that "little country, foolish, delicate" in the Brueghel painting is the frail and threatened place yearned for and sought—and sometimes found—in many Plath poems. Sometimes, in early poems and late ones, it is the country of Death, very still, very composed, very "accomplished"—to vary a word she used in one of the poems she wrote in the last week of her life, "Edge." Here the temptation is to read back into it one's retrospective knowledge. . . . But Sylvia Plath, like any good poet, didn't write poems as autobiographical or proleptic footnotes. (pp. 42-3)

The perfection, the accomplishment, the *necessity* of "Edge" have an inevitability which would, I think, seem just as inevitable if Sylvia Plath hadn't in fact killed herself within a week of writing it. The poem's stillness is a conscious weapon against distraction, and a stabilising one. The quarrel, for the moment, is over, resolved. That in a moment of desolation she miscalculated and pushed herself over the edge is . . . in a sense irrelevant. We need to remember this, so as not to magnify the manner of her death and thereby keep on reading it back into the poems. . . . Poems that survive . . .—survive and have currency—do so not because of legendary "circumstances" but because they are well-made things which extend us, enlarge us, and make us, too, survive and endure and enjoy. (pp. 43-4)

The notion of serious writers—especially, perhaps, serious women writers—playing with their obsessions, or joking about serious matters, is offensive to many people. The squeamishness of male critics confronted with the work of, say, Erica Jong has often been remarked. To justify or tidy up, such work is sterilised with the cosmetics of *black comedy, theatre of the absurd, sick humour,* etc. Sylvia Plath was a very controlled, very witty, and also very serious and ambitious writer, who had the bad luck to be born and brought up in a society which—at one and the same time—equated seriousness with solemnity and, in its more intellectual reaches, gave an odd and special status to what used to be called insanity. In a secular age, without belief but hungering for something transcendental, many felt like the natives in the Evelyn Waugh novel: "Very mad, very holy." . . .

What is unique about Sylvia Plath is not what happened to her and what she did to herself—the gas oven and the note to the doctor—but her control, her zest, her vitality *as a poet* up to that point. If we make her into a legend, we falsify and diminish her. (p. 44)

Anthony Thwaite, "Out of the Quarrel: On Sylvia Plath," in Encounter *(© 1979 by Encounter Ltd.), Vol. LIII, No. 2, August, 1979, pp. 40-4.*

CALVIN BEDIENT

Sylvia Plath was a romantic of the most self-cancelling kind. She reduced romanticism to a fever, a scream of defiance; but romantic she was, and exactly to the degree that she was alive and struggling. Her romanticism was her wish to live, if at times only in that touchingly qualified transcendence (located on no one's map of earth or heaven) where she could be born once again as her father's little girl. (p. 3)

Crushing, nearly Kafkaesque as this father worship was, it

is nonetheless moving. No embrace more longed for, more healing and validating than the father's. For so judgment gets a heart, distance takes us up and hugs us to the source of power. Plath is our scapegoat, the child who needed this blessing more, who would not give up asking for it until the effort killed her.

But her quest was by definition immature. And, except as the mote that provoked the splendid blindness of her poetry, what is its importance? Critics maunder about her vision, but as Irving Howe suggests, she had none. She saw neither the next world nor this one; she saw only her distance from each. What her husband called her "free and controlled access to depths formerly reserved to the primitive ecstatic priests" was at best a private clairvoyance, as her romanticism was a private "salvation."

It is true that her sense of the horror of Creation was up to the minute. But her relation to this commonplace was private and tandem. If she saw entropy as an animistic terror, a piranha religion drinking from live toes, it was not simply because the scientific view of things had once again been dipped into a child's and a poet's primitivism. It was specifically because her heart was under her father's foot, "sister of a stone." What her "vision" of the dripping "mercuric / Atoms that cripple" shows is not insight but an instinct for self-justification.

And if she drank dismay from history as we all do, she has nothing of interest to say about it. . . . Plath uses the historical and mythical as a vanity mirror. When she writes as if she were as abused as a Nazi victim she climbs to self-importance over the bodies of the dead. She enters a moral sphere that her amoral personal imagination cannot apprehend.

So her thought is not important. Nor, in a way, is her sensibility, for it was self-consumed in contradiction. Ambivalence afflicted her. For she did try to love life—how she tried. (pp. 4-5)

At worst, and often, her sensibility was "childish," overvulnerable: a chest pounding in terror, blood boiling blackly. . . . She was ever thus extreme. The whole strength of her sensibility lay in reaction, in the cry that, as Simone Weil says, is the innocence of the soul: "Why am I being hurt?" . . . Her imagination lacked justice. She used it as those backed against a wall use a knife, fingernails, anything.

Emotionally her work is a vicious circle of weakness and strength, the strength unstable because reactive. Her capacity for feeling injured and angry were equally awesome. Now she was a toadstool, her flesh falling apart at a nudge, now a lioness. Everything that enters her world seems either too strong to live with or too weak to live. How could she but disconcert us? Her sensibility has no horizon, no free space, no issue except extinction. Where Hughes in *Crow* flogs hackneyed horrors to get a sign of life from them, Plath had but to be herself to terrify.

Yet in a way her sensibility is useful, a monstrous dredging machine. Like the young woman in "The Tour" it addresses the maiden aunt in all of us and bids us look into our hearts. . . . Plath takes us down to where familial and other fears and resentments crawl; she exercises a dark-of-the-basement fascination. And we may come to see that it's only honest to admit our complicity in these petty and unreasonable and serious and pathetic passions. (pp. 5-6)

[Plath's] poetry is the inverse of the letters [found in *Letters Home*], their antimatter. This poet is not least curious in repudiating in her verse almost the whole of her daily consciousness, at any rate as her letters and reported conversations disclosed it. The letters mirror a lah-lahing Pollyanna whom the poetry, sneaking up behind, ruthlessly savages.

Plath *A*, the Plath people knew, not only struggled to "master" the fiction formulas of the slicks; she lived pulp dreams.

Husband, children, house, fame—she was to go after them as one pursues the Fully Desirable, the Approved. The frequent superlatives in her letters—the quarters and half-dollars of "amazing," "marvelous," "happiest"—were part of the dues she paid to the American dream.

Where in *Letters Home* are a poet's slatted observations, a poet's accents and reserves? Banality, banality; it never lets up. (p. 6)

Plath *B* saw through her—saw that she was thin air, the brilliance that bounces off mirrors. Plath *B* was Plath *A* when all the friendly mirrors were taken away. She was also a pointed retaliation against Plath *A*, against all that fulsome trust. (p. 7)

Plath *A*, Plath *B*, each acted on the post-Hegelian romantic belief that true being lies in intense feeling. No mute renunciation, no neutered acceptance, for her. If a rock crushes your toe, will you inquire into the law of gravity or do a dance of pain? Plath danced then kicked the rock.

She became our second queen (poor queen, mad queen) of subjectivity. The first of course was Emily Dickinson, an early influence. Both poets told "all the Truth," meaning all it would be pretty to leave out, but told it "slant," through the amusement rides, terror rides, of metaphor. Neither questioned the sufficiency or even the supremacy of her own intensity as a subject for art. Hence their terrific concentration. That both may have written partly to "fill the awful longitude" scored by a departed man also explains the peculiar urgency of some of their work, work that seems the outlet for a great vehemence. Both exemplify romantic passion, an infinitude of force imprisoned in a mortal personality. And the overcharged feeling in each produced a similar poetic of bolts. . . . To be sure, Plath is the more discursive even though she lacks Dickinson's deep (if gust-ruffled) power of reflection. She does not reflect, she reacts.

What is it to be a queen, as I have both mockingly and respectfully put it, of subjectivity? In Plath's case, writing against a nominally Christian culture (and against its backdrop), it is to have at best a macabre magnificence. The small demons attend Plath. Then, too, her self-pity is like an enormous underground labyrinth in which she wanders as if raging for her lost diadem—but the labyrinth itself is the only domain permitted to her, and her subjects have all gone away.

Yet how impressive she is as she wails, "Why am I being hurt?" How absolutely she commits herself to what Kierkegaard called "the moment of individuality," subjective being conceived as a unique, irreducible nexus of reality. And how much yearning her pain and anger express for the romantic experience of a lyrical harmony with others and with the world.

Yet to us Plath's subjectivity would be nothing without her objectifying dramatic values. Her astonishing force lies in the way she performs her emotions. She invents and speaks from within para-objective scenes that give body to her intensity without diminishing her subjectivity. If she attacks her feelings from outside, it is not to allay them but, with a director's aural and visual sort of dreaming, to delight in staging the person in her passions.

True, like all modern poets, she was handicapped for writing drama. When culture was sent to the boards by the increasing industrialization of society . . . , the poet lost a knowledge of other people and dramatic and narrative poetry fell away. What was left but to cultivate sensibility? Hence romantic lyricism. Yet, opposite though they tend to be, romanticism and drama share a common love: the blood-hot moment. It remained for the romantic poets—a Hopkins, a Yeats—to discover the dramatic values of the lyric itself.

Plath is one of the greatest of these inventors. It may be true that her only successful character creation was her imaginative exaggeration of her own. Still, how much drama this produced! Which of our other poets gives us so much of conflict, elliptical plot, eloquence under circumstantial stress? Plath is almost alone in the field. Her wounds forced her to her knees precisely at the center of all drama, what Karl Jaspers calls Communication, the struggle to love other persons. She could write only about herself, but she herself was the struggle of persons, she herself was drama.

To the intensity of her emotions Plath added the implicit intensity of fantasy, the piquancy of the peculiar, and turning-screw situations. The result was alarming, beautiful. And she was of it: her last poems could boast and wail with Captain Ahab, "A personality stands here." She was of it yet transformed. It was as if after a fateful sleep she had awakened fully herself but more concentrated, ignited by pressing circumstances, in a realm magic and terrible. (pp. 8-9)

Plath's fantasy, with its magnifications, macabre distortions, violence and magic and foreboding, exaggerates, but on behalf of subjective truth. It is a graph of affliction. (p. 9)

As if by a sudden access of dramatic impulse, [some] of the late poems combine momentum and momentousness—for instance, "Daddy," "Lady Lazarus," "Getting There," "Ariel," "Fever 103°." These poems simultaneously exhilarate and frighten by catching the moment just before, or just as, a tremendous tension peaks. Going over a hundred miles an hour and still on the road and getting there, Plath invents for the lyric a new urgency. (p. 10)

For the most part [Plath's style of monologue] is blocked in short sentences. Like tamps. And this sharp insistence of breath falls in with her visual startlingness. For she visualizes everything as if working from the very young child's assumption that to be at all is to be visible. Her whole content is shaped as for an appreciative and all but literal gaze; even the horrors enter as hypnotic objects of perception, as if winking light from a blade. . . . With theater at any rate the poems share a fascination with the espial of human behavior under stress. Plath seems to have wanted above all to see what she felt—not to understand it but to see it. . . . Nor in taking note of Plath's dramatic inventiveness can we avoid the impression that her poems unfold what is in some sense a tragedy. The poet had read classical tragedy at Cambridge, and its glamorous fatalism staggered her mind. . . . [Her] immersion in tragic literature may have caused her to emulate a destiny of passion and an unnatural yet crowning end.

Since nothing is more undramatic than a life, how to make a drama of it except by fabrication? Plath fabricated not after the Greek pattern (she was too anarchic to share its view of transgression) but after the simple model of a destroying passion. She went to where the flesh met the blade, omitting an explanatory world picture. (pp. 10-11)

Far from being a tragedy of will, like classical tragedy, Plath's is a tragedy of weakness, of a fatal vulnerability to the sense of injury. If there is heroism here, it talks of putting a stake in the fat black heart of a vampire; it talks like a pouting child. We feel pity and even terror before such sensitivity, but it has nothing to teach us. It looks like an accident in the scheme of things, a senseless failure.

Yet with its extremes of feeling, its spasms, barbarism, surprises, her tragedy has romantic power. Even as her fear and bitterness attack the quick of romanticism, numbing the nerve of love and life, her imagination startles her experience into drama. She wrote as if vividness itself could soothe suffering, as if she could escape pain by increasing its intensity.

To her dramatic imagination Plath brought a sense of language unceremoniously her own but still in the reverberant classical line: traditional grandeur sped up with a corresponding gain in mass. (pp. 14-15)

Her verbal and prosodic values blend with her dramatic values in being not only vivid in themselves but dramatic in their variety. From clauses as swift as Stevie Smith's to phrases as slow as Keats', dying into themselves of a swoon; from language tortuously lathed by lineation to sentences plopped down on the bartering counter of the line; from classical pentameter to the nude line "the nude" to spillaway lines of eighteen syllables; from a murmured chiming dialogue of vowels and consonants to vituperative repetitions; from slang to stunning metaphors—as a poet there was little she did not permit herself, and nothing she permitted herself to do that she did not do well.

She quickly burned through the elaborate prosody of her early poems. . . . She learned to get down into the foulness, to make foul itself fair. Her desperate force, her very ambition, made her drop her mouldy style and rush on 1961, 1962.

Romantic in its immediacy, her sharpened poetic was not quite typical of the sixties, and precisely to the extent that it was Poundian. Poundian in the first place as to eye. Her work unfolds perhaps for the first time the full dramatic potential of what T. E. Hulme called "the new visual art," an art depending "for its effect not on a kind of half sleep produced by meter, but on arresting the attention, so much so that the succession of visual images should exhaust one." . . . But though the new visual art set itself off from leisured traditional description by rapid-fire figuration, it was notorious for being static, limitedly pictorial. The instant fixing of a single impression, as by a jeweled pin, was its convention. Still, there was nothing to prevent its being thickcoming and developmental; it could be galvanized.

Or so Plath, more than any other, was to prove. She made images burst forth and succeed one another under acute psychological pressure, the dramatic crisis of the poem a generating furor. In violent import, color, solidity, and velocity her images are unsurpassed. Even when her spirit ebbs, her imagery ferments. In "Words," for instance, one metaphor instantly gives rise to two others, which are then elaborated in quick succession, each giving way and coming in again, but without any effect of haste. Proliferation has perhaps never been more subtle and vigorous, more constantly deepening.

But the most "delicate and difficult" part of the new art, so Hulme implies, is "fitting the rhythm" to the image—fitting *all* the sound, I might amend. And Plath's ear is no less gifted than her imaginative eye. For instance, she rivals Pound's hearkening ear for the calling back and forth and expressive rightness of sounds. Consider "And daylight lays its sameness on the wall," with its quasi-tedious fly-buzz of *a* and *s* and same-same meter, the slight staleness of the pentameter form precisely supporting the feeling. . . . In writing like this, the phrases are single beings made of rhythm and rhyme, inexhaustible to the emotional ear.

Her lineation sometimes shows the same headcocked quality. . . . The analogical imagination and a feeling for tensions at once spatial and dramatic contribute to this exquisite craft. Such lineation is gesture and architecture as well as rhythm; the tensions are to be seen as well as heard.

With Pound, Plath also shared the decidedly modern ear for what she called the "straight out" rhythms and words of prose and colloquial speech; like Pound, if less ambitiously and more evenly, she assimilated them into poetry, creating new verse rhythms. . . . The breathless doubling of a clause ("is it . . . is it . . . ?") is peculiarly Plathian. Although working free from meter Plath liked a rhyme or grammatical construction or beat that swung back even as it pounded on. She favored the piston rhythms of anxiety.

At times she may be too laboring in exposition, as in "Tulips" and "The Bee Meeting," though these poems have been much admired. . . . But no one will question her general authority in the colloquial range of the art. She was even more inventive at spoken than at written effects and worked them for an equal if different intensity. (pp. 15-17)

Plath's poetic, then, is Poundian—romantic. True, classical simplicity shows up in passages, and classical grace and proportion sometimes govern whole poems. Then, too, her persistent use of stanzas reflects the same orderly habit of mind that made her list each morning what she wanted to accomplish during the day. Undeniably, moreover, certain associations of the word "romantic" shrivel when held up to her flame. The shriek of her ego, the sound of a tense holding on to little, drove off every softness. She maximized horror as if she lived on menace. All the same, her poetic is full of romantic presence. No retreat, no passivity, can harbor in it; it is the aggressive poetic of one buried alive but not ready to die. (Even in expressing revulsion from reality she reached obsessively and inconsistently for visual analogy, a language of rapport.) What is her struggle against fear, pain, isolation, if not romantic? Perhaps we would deny her reasons for writing at all to think of it as anything else or anything less. (p. 18)

Calvin Bedient, "Sylvia Plath, Romantic . . . ," in Sylvia Plath: New Views on the Poetry, *edited by Gary Lane (copyright © 1979 by The Johns Hopkins University Press), The Johns Hopkins University Press, 1979, pp. 3-18.*

* * *

POTOK, Chaim 1929-

Potok's reputation as an American Jewish novelist was established with his first novel, *The Chosen*. In this as in all his fiction, his inspiration and focal concern has been traditional Judaism. (See also *CLC*, Vol. 7, and *Contemporary Authors*, Vols. 17-20, rev. ed.)

BARBARA AMIEL

To read Chaim Potok's *Wanderings*, a superbly written . . . history of the Jews, is to understand why [the] theme of vengeance is so much a part of Jewish history. It also serves to remind that, though the major event of Christianity celebrates birth and love, and Judaism the memory of slaughter and vengeance, both have often practised in each other's territory. . . .

[*Wanderings* is] the story of civilization—as it affects *his* people. Explains Potok: "Though I had studied history with great teachers in the Jewish Theological Seminary of America, I hesitated to move from the world of the imagination to the hard country of fact." His fears were unnecessary. As he traces the ancient exodus from Egypt of the "pitiful rabble, a mass of frightened, quarrelsome Asiatics wandering through the merciless sand and stone wilderness somewhere east of the Nile," Potok the novelist considers the great questions of imagination that historians may overlook. What, he asks, made Moses realize that slavery, an accepted custom, was wrong? "This is the point," answers Potok, "where the mind of man might turn a corner and come upon new and luminous awareness—an act of creation as mysterious as life itself."

Behind Potok's account of the Jewish struggle to stay alive through the vicissitudes of ancient and classical paganism, Islam and Christianity is Potok's own moral search: to understand how a people managed to survive both the seduction of comfort (the assimilation offered by some periods of Egypt, Greece and Spain) and the diabolical tortures of almost every other regime from ancient Rome to modern Russia, simply in order to remain Jews. It is, of course, an unanswerable question, but one he leaves unanswered with much scholarship and Jewish Style.

Barbara Amiel, "People from the School of Survival," in Maclean's Magazine *(© 1979 by* Maclean's Magazine; *reprinted by permission), Vol. 92, No. 1, January 1, 1979, p. 47.*

The 4000 years of Jewish history, life and culture captured between one set of covers would seem to be an impossibility—and is. But [*Wanderings*] comes as close to achieving the impossible as the present state of the literary and graphic arts can manage. Potok's combined talents as novelist and historian work well here in giving both narrative power and historical perspective to the wanderings of the Chosen people, their identification with the great cultures of the world—and their splendid contributions and enduring spirit.

"Books in Brief: 'Wanderings: Chaim Potok's History of the Jews'," in The Critic *(©* The Critic *1979; reprinted with the permission of the Thomas*

More Association, Chicago, Illinois), Vol. 37, No. 13, January 15, 1979, p. 7.

MICHAEL J. BANDLER

One cannot resist the temptation to observe without being facetious that as a historian, Potok solidifies his reputation as a fine novelist. Claiming no credentials as a historian, using hundreds of eminent sources and texts in several languages which he appreciatively acknowledges, he has fashioned an intelligent, thorough and credible one-volume chronicle [*Wanderings*] that breathes with a passion that is more common to fiction than to history.

It takes a writer with a flair for imagery, for example, to view the Jewish creative forces in Islamic-dominated 11th-century Spain as "nightingales in a sandstorm," and to describe the enthusiastic—though ominous—entry of Jews into the high culture of the 18th-century European Enlightenment as "whirling and pirouetting in a pagan danse macabre." And it takes a certain dramatic perception to shape two simple sentences—"Who was king? Who was not king?"—into ubiquitous signposts along the historical route of ascension, decline, revolution and resurgence. . . .

Fully aware that one cannot isolate a particular group's experiences from those of the rest of civilization, Potok treats carefully and fully the various religions and cultures —from ancient Sumer to 20th century America—that impinged on the saga of the Jews, and their political, social, cultsral and economic components as well as their dominant personalities. . . . He asks questions, poses possible answers based on archaeological or new historical data, and frequently relinquishes the issue unresolved. (p. B1)

It is not a book to be read in a concentrated period of time. . . . Rather, it should be savored, scene by provocative scene, mulled over and retained. No matter what one's faith, there are urgent lessons to be learned among the codes, covenants, triumphs and tragedies of the panoramic saga that continues dauntlessly along its unpredictable path. (p. B4)

Michael J. Bandler, "Faith's Long Journey," in The Christian Science Monitor *(reprinted by permission from* The Christian Science Monitor; *© 1979 The Christian Science Publishing Society; all rights reserved), February 12, 1979, pp. B1, B4.*

JACK RIEMER

Chaim Potok has not written a scholarly history of the Jews. No one person could possibly do that. . . . But what Potok has done [in *Wanderings*] is to dramatize all of Jewish history and bring it to life, as only a novelist could. He has done his homework well and has gone to the scholars. . . .

But after that, he has done something more, something they could not do, which is to make the bare bones of their scholarship come alive. He has made of Jewish history real theatre. He describes each period in dramatic terms as a conflict and a contrast between the Jewish people and the people whom they came in contact with, the ones who harbored and oppressed them. (p. 116)

There is a point to the subtitle of this book. It is indeed "Chaim Potok's History of the Jews," for the book is personal. In a way, it is as personal as his novels were. Just as there he really sought for his self in the guise of a story about a young man wrestling with modernity, so here he searches for his soul in the form of a confrontation with his roots and with his memories.

This is the story of a people that has endured much, that has endured almost as much as a people can. And yet, its last word is Yes: yes to life, yes to hope, yes to tomorrow. It is a story that all people who live in a frightening and fast-changing, broken and bewildering universe can read and take to heart, and Chaim Potok has told it well. (p. 117)

Jack Riemer, "Emerging Histories, Promising Pasts: 'Wanderings: Chaim Potok's History of the Jews'," in America *(© America Press, 1979; all rights reserved), Vol. 140, No. 6, February 17, 1979, pp. 116-17.*

* * *

PURDY, A(lfred) W(ellington) 1918-

One of Canada's most prominent poets, Purdy creates poetry noted for its vigor, humor, directness, and originality. (See also *CLC*, Vols. 3, 6, and *Contemporary Authors*, Vols. 81-84.)

MARGARET ATWOOD

As always, [in *Love in a burning building*] one has to swallow Purdy whole, take the horsing around and the hyperbole along with the painfully-arrived-at honesties and the moments of transcendently good poetry. Purdy writes like a cross between Shakespeare and a vaudeville comedian (so did Shakespeare) and that's not such a flip remark as it may seem: note those Shakespearean double "and"-linked adjectives ("my faint and yapping cry," "the sad and much emancipated world," "the unctuous and uneasy self I glimpse"), the way iambic pentameter keeps creeping in; and on the vaudeville end the patter acts, sad clown laughing at us laughing at him, telling awful jokes while knowing full well how awful they are. Purdy too is inherently dramatic; assumed by all his poems are a human speaking voice or voices and a responding audience, and his sense of timing is often superb. But these poems have been chosen according to subject—"sexual love and its mental counterpart," says Purdy—and it's matter rather than manner that deserves attention here. (p. 72)

[Purdy is] a semi-Romantic. He can hardly write Love without writing Death on the same page; his brand of immortality (see his introduction and "Archeology of Snow") is reminiscent of Shelley's; Byronic swashbuckle and Don Juanesque undercutting of one's own heroics, both are there. He's filled with yearnings for the ideal, the absolute, the eternal, with no unshakeable conviction they exist and with a consequent awareness of loss, transience and imperfection. What may have been meant is that Purdy's poems aren't pretty or foggy-eyed: the women in them are often, to Purdy's credit, solid flesh and blood, with a good deal of the latter. They do things the Blessed Damozel wouldn't: they sweat under the arms, menstruate, argue, sulk, have miscarriages, V.D., operations and orgasms (though not babies, oddly enough). They move in accurately observed surroundings full of what in a woman writer would be classed as typically female domestic imagery: Purdy is not above having insights in kitchens. . . . But Purdy has little trouble recognizing both his realism and his romanticism for what they are: "I can be two men if I have to," he says, and is.

Purdy's love poems demonstrate the self divided against itself to perhaps an even greater extent than do his poems on other subjects. Here the freedom-loving adventurer pulls against the husband, that "greyish drunkish largeish anguished man", and the female landscape (Purdy's metaphor) separates itself into corresponding territories of Others and Wife. From Wife-country, viewed sometimes as a prison and sometimes as a place of refuge, Purdy makes brief excursions into Otherland, alluring but also threatening. . . . Like Odysseus or a boomerang Purdy always returns, because Wife is where the action is and the action is not a tourist-trip but a battle.

It is this interaction which is central to the book, a constant unavoidable even when it is being denied and attacked. Like all crucial relationships it involves a number of emotions: Purdy, faced with the stubborn actuality of Wife, reacts with lust, anger, false pride, grudging admiration, claustrophobia, sadism, laughter, alienation, joy, fear of growing older and dying, and even a love "that can never be freedom exactly". But he doesn't make many guesses about the possible reciprocal feelings of Wife: either he doesn't know, thinks he can't know, or doesn't want to know. Thus the celebrated skirmish in "Home Made Beer"—"Whereupon my wife appeared from the bathroom / where she had been brooding for days / over the injustice of being a woman and / attacked me with a broom"—is made to seem both unprovoked (either being a woman isn't an injustice, or it is but why blame Purdy?) and funny, a sort of Edwardian seaside-postcard surly-wife gag; though an in-depth interview conducted on the other side of the bathroom door would doubtless have been revealing. Wife, however, except for occasional mutterings of "you bastard," remains silent, and is ultimately ungraspable, inscrutable, "neutral as nature". From this war-torn relationship emerge two of the consistently best poems in the book: "Love Poem", totally brutal and totally convincing, in which the poet identifies himself with the knife used to perform a painful and possibly fatal operation, and "Poem" [which is simple and so good]. (pp. 72-3)

It's also about as close as Purdy gets to tenderness, and it's perhaps noteworthy that it chronicles a sickness: Purdy is more likely to express this kind of love in connection with the woman's possible or fantasized death than in her here-and-now, awake and healthy presence. . . . His interest in sex tends to be metaphysical rather than sensual: sexual attraction may be a "comic disease" . . . , love may be "ambiguous" and sex "a bully", but still he can use it to convince himself he's alive and vital and (perhaps) to keep himself from dissolving into the cosmic soup, the flux of nature or the outer-space landscape that so repeatedly invades his bedrooms. Many times we find him recalling or memorializing old episodes and indulging in new ones in an attempt to banish his real enemies, pain, sorrow and—especially—time. . . . It is the fear of death and of vanishing, we realize, that underlies a lot of the Victory Burlesque joke-man routines . . . : as in war, the wisecracks sustain the illusion of sanity in the face of an otherwise intolerable anxiety. Purdy does indeed "take women serious", but he needs his laughter at times to keep himself from screaming.

Love in a burning building raises a lot of extra-poetic, even extra-Purdy questions. Is it possible for men and women to stop mythologizing, manipulating and attacking one another? Do all men divide women into Wife and Others, do they all share Purdy's tendency to think of women in terms of separate anatomical features . . . like cut-up chickens? Is Purdy's attitude towards women that of his sex, his country, his generation (in which case *Love* can be a handy guide for women who want to know what really goes on in the male skull, the Canadian male skull, etc.) or is it strictly personal?

Personal it certainly is. It may be more, but it's also one man's reflections, experiences and emotions, recorded so honestly that even the lies, the cruelties, the bathos and the trivialities are included. (pp. 73-4)

Margaret Atwood, "Love Is Ambiguous . . . Sex Is a Bully," in Canadian Literature, *No. 49, Summer, 1971, pp. 71-5.*

GEORGE WOODCOCK

[There] is no doubt of [Purdy's] deep intuitive grasp of the nature of the land, of the character of its history, though to claim him as purely a Canadian poet would be to do him an immense injustice. But Canada—and Loyalist Ontario in particular—is indeed the heart of his world. . . . (p. 8)

[The east-west] extremities of the land are the poles between which he suspends his vision of Canada, a vision that interprets geography and history as interpenetrating versions of each other. To further narrow his vision, it is essentially a rural one, which hardly recognizes a city except Vancouver (deurbanized by the penetrating sea), and it is based on the knowledge, which most Canadians are curiously anxious to avoid, that this is, even in human terms, an ancient and not a new land, a land already beginning to decay into maturity. (p. 9)

[What makes Purdy] a real rural poet, as distinct from a country sentimentalist, is his concreteness of view, an awareness of the brilliant surface of the earth as clear as that of an imagist, and yet at the same time a sense of depths and heights, of superreal dimensions, so that common things can suddenly become irradiated and the world swing into ecstasy.

But not too much into ecstasy for the existential relations to continue, and the vision of place to be poised between tradition and change, as in "Wilderness Gothic", one of his most completely successful poems, where he is watching a man across Roblin Lake repairing a church spire, working his way up towards its vanishing point, as if his faith pushed him beyond it. It is one of the poems in which Purdy deftly juxtaposes the different elements of his world, for as the man works at patching the edifice of a dying religion, the life of nature goes on in its old merciless way. (p. 10)

North, like West, is a cardinal direction for Purdy (as South over the border most certainly is not), and it is in some of his Arctic poems that he becomes most purely the poet of place, though even here it is often still the kind of dialogue between the man and his environment with its finned and feathered and flowered inhabitants, which is almost incessant at Roblin Lake, going on in other ways. (p. 11)

[Purdy] is not only wide in thought and subtle in vision, but also extremely versatile as a poetic craftsman who has worked his way through the forms and styles to his present open manner. . . . It is in the way he can manipulate the long line to create a variety of moods that Purdy has shown his growing power to fit the form exactly to the thought and thing, which is the sign of ultimate poetic craftsmanship. This is not to say that his poems are entirely linear in their overall structure, for often the juxtaposition of jarring or contrasting elements is an essential part of the effect he is seeking, and there are times when he uses the moderately short line very effectively to achieve a cumulative emotive effect. . . . But he is never one of your gasping, grunting, three-or-four-syllable-a-line men. No discursive, philosophic, historic, didactic poet—and Purdy is all these—ever can be.

Yet for all its didacticism, there is much in Purdy's poetry that has the effortless, gratuitous magic which has been the sign of a good poet in any age: lines like

> We live with death but it's life we die with
> in the blossoming earth where springs the rose . . .

or the whole of "Necropsy of Love", whose last lines have the kind of hypnotic midnight power of some of Keats or some Decadent poetry . . . :

> If death shall strip our bones of all but bones,
> then here's the flesh, and flesh that's drunken-sweet
> as wine cups in deceptive lunar light:
> reach up your hand and turn the moonlight off,
> and maybe it was never there at all,
> so never promise anything to me:
> but reach across the darkness with your hand,
> reach across the distance of tonight,
> and touch the moving moment once again
> before you fall asleep . . .

(pp. 13-14)

[There are] various poetic devices . . . which, having abandoned rhyme and ordinary metre, Purdy has recourse on the appropriate occasion: . . . [examples are] the use of alliteration and repetition, the presence at times of regular syllabic patterns, the occasional resort to galloping trochaic rhythms, and, as a matter of rhythm as well as language, a superb colloquial ear. . . .

[Purdy] is also the poet of comedy. . . . It is comedy that easily runs black, for it is based on a totally realistic sense of what individual man's fate is in a world where grandeur is a feat of the imagination; where man grows old though his lusts stay young; where his actions are contemptible though his thoughts are high; where his attempts to reconcile the animal and the human within him always end in comic absurdity. The decay and death that finally await him Purdy portrays with realistic horror, yet with compassion for the defeated, and with admiration for those who cry out in rage against [their] destiny. . . . (p. 14)

George Woodcock, "On the Poetry of Al Purdy," in Selected Poems *by Al Purdy (© 1972 by Al Purdy; reprinted by permission of The Canadian Publishers, McClelland and Stewart Limited, Toronto), McClelland, 1972, pp. 8-15.*

BARRY CAMERON

[*In Search of Owen Roblin* emerges] at a significant point in [Purdy's career and is] an epitome, a summing-up, of [his] thematic and rhetorical concerns. . . . Purdy's "country north of Belleville" is a country of the mind, Purdy's home as distinct from his environment, an emotionally and psychologically secure point in space and time from which to articulate and to attempt to define one's unique and generic being. . . . Purdy's *persona* is . . . in search of links with his ancestors in order to realize his place in the continuity of human life. . . . Purdy the poet's implicit search for an adequate language in the poem is a manifestation of the search for a psychic place that will yield meaning. Purdy long ago lapsed into what he calls the "original / sin of discursiveness," which was in my view actually a *felix culpa,* but *In Search of Owen Roblin* is unequivocally his most discursive poem, revealing his incessant need to talk, to articulate his feelings and attitudes in an effort to come to terms with them and to forestall the disappearance of the moment.

In Search of Owen Roblin is essentially a work about itself, and it crystallizes a theme that permeates all Purdy's work: man's motive for fiction in the root sense of the word (*fingere*—to make or shape), his need to structure his experiences in order to make sense of them, his need to mythologize the past and to "invent" memories. In a very significant way, we are all poets like Purdy, continuously creating and recreating our experiences, because our ordinary experiences—what we usually call life—in which everything fades immediately into the past, cannot provide a genuine sense of meaning. Fiction, in this fundamental sense, is really our only method of making life fully available, of preserving it as a present reality, and Purdy suggests in this poem and elsewhere that it is the only way in which the past and those who lived in the past continue to exist in the present. This motive for fiction accounts for the sense that a Purdy poem is only a fragment of some larger, incomplete poem that he is always writing and for his preoccupation with the artifacts of lost or disappearing civilizations . . . , for such artifacts are the result of man's attempt to preserve his experience and to give it human meaning. (p. 47)

This motive for fiction also accounts for the strong sense in Purdy's poems of the poet as a recorder and preserver of experience. . . . As poet, Purdy speaks for us, articulating our feelings and states of mind and, by so doing, helps us to speak for ourselves. The poet's task is an attempt to "register," to "screen," experience, to measure or fix it—to make it permanent in some way—but the attempt at fixity in Purdy's work is in continual tension with the open-endedness of his poems, which mimetically expresses the ultimate inability to structure permanently any experience, and with the sense of the Purdy poem as a meditative process. Consequently, *In Search of Owen Roblin* explores, as so many Purdy poems do, the ways in which past and present, fact and fiction, history and myth, constantly penetrate each other, reshaping and reinterpreting each other and, in so doing, reconstituting one's sense of reality.

Purdy is at his most interesting technically in the poem when he assumes the voice or mentality of a character different from his habitual *persona,* and if he has now completed his exploration of the poetic territory north of Belleville, this mode is certainly a technical area that could be explored further. (pp. 47-8)

A few poems in Purdy's . . . collection of poems, *Sex and Death* (which includes *Hiroshima Poems,* seven meditative poems on the moral-philosophical implications of Hiroshima for man, the last of which, "Remembering Hiroshima," is one of Purdy's most powerful philosophical poems), are in this mode. One of them, "In the Foothills", is the best in the collection. The *persona* is a primitive hunter who has identified with a prehistoric mammoth in its shrieking death (compare Purdy's identification with Albert, the prehistoric dinosaur, whose tail has been bitten in *On the Bearpaw Sea*) and who attempts to come to terms with himself and the meaning of the event by carving a mammoth on the stone of a mountain. In the hunter's cathartic need to objectify his feelings and to find meaning in life, a need we all share, Purdy has actually created a myth of the artist.

As in *In Search of Owen Roblin*, the *raison d'être* of *Sex and Death* is the motive for metaphor: the *persona* in all the poems is seeking understanding and existential realization. It is a collection of poems that reveals Purdy at the peak of his poetic performance. All the dimensions of the Purdy *persona* that we have come to expect are here, and his talent for energizing the trivial and commonplace, for making us see things that were there all along, has never been more efficacious. Despite the fact that his tonal virtuosity and genius with verbs have never been more evident, Purdy has perfected his poetic mode to the point where no technical device draws attention to itself. Purdy's work has now reached the stage of artless art, and this quality is charged with a rhetorical efficacy that makes the poems infinitely accessible. The sense in the poems here of one perception invariably and smoothly leading to another, emphasized by the sparing use of punctuation, establishes a sense of stylistic and ratiocinative continuity that, in turn, makes us aware of the meditative, explorative quality of the poems.

In Search of Owen Roblin is the fruition of the meditative mode that Purdy has been practicing ever since *Poems for All the Annettes*. . . . It is surely Purdy's best poem and his most important one for an understanding of all his work. . . . (p. 48)

Barry Cameron, "The Motive for Fiction," in The Canadian Forum, *Vol. LIV, No. 647, January, 1975, pp. 47-8.*

JOHN LYE

Al Purdy as poet is person and *persona;* there is no escaping the earthy cynical unselfconfident egotistical balding paunching middleaged man, deliberately common and secular. He is also by turns sensitive, boisterous, ironical, whimsical, sentimental, and sententious. . . . Despite the vivacity, the bluster, and the ironic mask, Purdy's essential stance is sentimental and conservative.

Purdy is a personal poet, and his style depends for its effectiveness on an apt use of the speaking voice. He who is speaking is often one of Purdy's three main *personae*—the common man, the boisterous man, or the sensitive man. The common-man *persona* is the base *persona,* the one on which his style stands. . . . The subjects of Purdy's poetry are common and ostensibly unpretentious—personal experiences, people he has known, domestic scenes. His poetic "place" is not a tower or a grove but a hand-built house out in nowhere. He has debarred himself from the role of "Poet", and we find him on his back under his old Pontiac (horny), grubbing around a ruined house (chased off), defecating near the Pole (savaged by dogs). His poetry when bad is just broken-lined prose, and the faults of his poetry otherwise—triviality, pretention, discursiveness, bathos, bad metaphors—similarly reflect the image of the common man. (p. 242)

The boisterous *persona,* lecherous, rowdy, drunken, accounts for some of his liveliest poetry (and most of his worst), and provides much of his humour. This persona is a blusterer and a great debunker, given to an amused deprecation of sensitive poets. . . . Through [the persona of the sensitive man] Purdy reaches some of the finest moments in his poetry; he reaches too "the still centre, / an involvement in silences" ("Winter Walking"), the religious centre of his world. . . . It is obvious that the boisterous *persona* does not hold the day, that regret, wistfulness, sensitivity creep back in. The opposition between these two roles represents a conflict basic to Purdy's poetry. The sensitive rather than the tough voice is the one that predominates. (pp. 242-43)

[His sentimentality, evident in poems like "Sculptors,"] this care for the hurt and the flawed, for "the inconsolable / walkers in the storm / cursing at the locked gates of fact" ("Nine Bean-Rows on the Moon"), is the ground of Purdy's stance.

Given the world, a stance such as this is open to defeat, and Purdy, in trying to deal with the world as "that sort of place", reacts against his own idealism and sentimentality. . . . Purdy cannot escape cynicism and doubt. . . . The reaction against sentimentality yields some fine and energetic poetry; but it remains a reaction. Whether by cynicism, retreat, or irony, it recognizes the pain of understanding that the world is a cruel place and that man is a flawed and a suffering thing.

The sense of man's impotence is accompanied by a sense of the transitory, of man's continual loss through time. . . . The sense of the transitory extends from the very personal to the elegiac, a sense of cultural loss closely associated with the individual's situation, found in poems such as "Country North of Belleville". Here, on abandoned farms, once the place of a simple but harsh life, "Old fences drift vaguely among trees" and "a pile of moss-covered stones / gathered for some ghost purpose / has lost meaning under the meaningless sky." (pp. 244-45)

Purdy does not, in lamenting man's state, rail against God. The "blind engineers of the universe" are merely figures of speech; in only a few poems does God appear, and in none of them does he exist. . . . Although for Purdy God does not exist, there is in his poetry a sensitivity to religious experience, an awareness of transcendence in the encounter with "silence", and a sense of loss and despair in the face of meaninglessness. The sense of this void, together with the care Purdy has for humanity, serve to strengthen a dependence upon the past and upon the continuity of human life. Not only do Purdy's poems continually implicate, appeal to, draw in the past, but they pose a theory of the continuum of history and a metaphysic of the continued existence of individuals. (pp. 246-47)

[A] sense of continuum is the basis of Purdy's humanist view of history. The continuum, history, has about it a certain stasis. Place is constant, time is not. Time does not move 'onward'; rather, it overlays itself, has depth. . . . It is important for Purdy that every individual retain his value through time; a continuity and a unity of human life results. (pp. 248-49)

It is important for an understanding of Purdy's approach and temper to note that [his] theories of history, time, and continuity of existence, are lodged in the most common experiences and situations. They are rarely elaborate expositions. When they are, they are placed in contexts which serve to de-emphasize the intellectual pretension of the material. . . . At the same time, he extends his poems through allusion to myth, to historical events, to far places, broadens the scope of the common, shows its full potential significance.

The way in which Purdy deals with social and political matters is consonant with and expressive of his sentimental and conservative stance. . . . Sometimes Purdy does protest civil injustice, but generally he accepts it as part of experience. He is concerned with the universal human condition and with the personal condition; these concerns are at once too broad and too narrow to yield much protest literature. (p. 250)

I have used the words "sensitive", "sympathetic", "caring", and "sentimental" rather freely in reference to Purdy's stance; I do not mean to intimate that he is a pantywaist, or that he is weak-willed (his poetry seems to fear this interpretation). About most of Purdy's poetry there is a fine vigour, generated not only by the self-protective boisterous voice, but also by the reaction against ideals which the harshness of the world stimulates, by the image of the common man caught in the midst of his (slightly ludicrous) situation, by an agile imagination, by the enormous energy of history which Purdy taps so often, and by a style of poetry rhetorical rather than reflective. The governing sensibility or disposition of Purdy's poetry, however, is humane and sympathetic. The emphasis is on the individual, on the meaning of his life and of his sorrows. The world with which the sensibility is faced is flawed, full of pain; God is apparently absent; meaning is precarious, hard to reach and hold. Sympathy and history are the two strongest sources of value; Purdy exercises and demands the first and creates a metaphysic which ensures the meaningfulness and the accessibility of the second. As history is accessible and provides value, and as the modern world apparently allows less value to the individual even than did past times, the poetry tends to be conservative and elegiac. As "The Country North of Belleville", one of his finest poems, has it, the land where value can best be contacted is also "the country of our defeat", to which we can return only with difficulty. (pp. 252-53)

John Lye, "The Road to Ameliasburg," in The Dalhousie Review, *Vol. 57, No. 2, Summer, 1977, pp. 242-53.*

ANTS REIGO

In the Purdy poem we are seldom aware of form, or even of verbal texture; we read for information, and once we have it, we feel disinclined to return to the verbal construct that delivered it to us. . . . The message or point of a Purdy poem is never very intimately related to its surface. The meaning of a line of Purdy's, for instance, hardly ever depends on our interpretation of a figure of speech; we never find any cross-qualification or refinement of meaning by the aural and visual qualities of the words themselves. . . . Purdy seems always to be less concerned with how he means than with what he means; he is quite willing to use the approximate word or image in an approximate way—indeed, he is forced to, in order to maintain the illusion of unpremeditated, casual speech. Understandably, we are apt on this basis to dismiss the whole question of form in Purdy's poetry, and to assume that in Purdy's case form is subservient to content. We say that it is "loose" or "open," meaning that it does not matter. But in fact, the Purdy poem does have a very definite, if not very restricting form.

Purdy's is not primarily a poetry of ideas; he writes about himself on the one hand, and about people and places on the other; and accordingly, his poetry ranges from self-disclosure to description. . . . But this range is deceptive. For whatever the subject, whatever the outward appearance, the pattern of the Purdy poem is the same. "Winter at Roblin Lake," for instance, is ostensibly an autobiographical document, lacking obvious structure and many of the trappings of poetry, whereas "Snow at Roblin Lake" is a more or less autonomous artefact, written in more or less traditional rhyming quatrains; the two poems seem similar only in the respect that their point and effect is gently humorous. On closer examination, however, we discover that both poems have the same plot: the speaker of the poem imagines the environment to be hostile and then articulates a response to it. We discover, moreover, that the humour of both poems relies on this plot and is, in effect, a transcendence of the imagined threat. We discover that these poems enact a drama of opposition, a dialectic. (p. 127)

[Upon] investigation, most of Purdy's poems turn out to be dialectical—greater or slighter oppositions between Purdy's self and the subject of the poem, followed by comic or pathetic reversals. . . .

In discovering the dialectic in the Purdy poem, however, we are not done with it. In the Purdy poem the dialectic is fleshed out in a certain way; there is a characteristic treatment of its terms. In Purdy's hands, the dialectic articulates a turning away from reality to the imagination, to fantasy. . . .

In ["Snow at Roblin Lake" and "Winter at Roblin Lake"], Purdy does not simply present us with a few miscellaneous details to contemplate as we will: he directs us through a progression of looks and glimpses, in which the environment is seen to increase in scale and power to fantastic, mythic proportions. This progression and escalation is effected by an increasingly figurative use of language within the poems: from denotation, to simile, to metaphor in "Winter at Roblin Lake"; and from denotation, to metaphor, to Biblical allusion in "Snow at Roblin Lake." The effect of the shifts in language and imagery is one of acceleration, of being first drawn, then swept away, as into a whirlpool. (p. 128)

[The] disinclination to dwell on the concrete or objectively real is revealed in his use of language. Purdy very rarely recreates the world in observed detail; instead, he refers and alludes to it. He delights neither in the sensuous qualities of words nor in his own senses. . . .

The people and things in Purdy's poetry are flat, denoted only by a name or, as in "Percy Lawson," by something like a "gold-toothed grin." . . . People and things . . . only exist in the flux of association, are registered in the poems as mental events rather than as substantial entities in their own right. Figurative language is used only in representing his own mental life, his response to his subject or occasion. (p. 129)

Purdy's whole attention is on the making of a poem. He is not interested in being fathful to his subject nor to himself. And it is to this that Purdy's tendency to turn from fact to fiction leads. For despite the trappings of sincerity, Purdy is not a confessional poet: he doesn't turn from the world in order to bare his soul, or to plumb his own depths; he is really remarkably reticent. . . . What we respond to is his art, his craftsmanship—when it succeeds, when Purdy's tendency to leave his occasion altogether behind is sufficiently resisted.

Purdy's poems, then, are artificial; they are verbal creations, products of wit, and our interest in them is the same as our interest in metaphysical poetry. We keep reading to see how he will justify the flight of fancy, the outrageous imagery, the historical and mythological allusions. Purdy merely uses larger and looser tropes than metaphor or analogy. (p. 130)

There is nothing restrictive about the form that Purdy has developed for himself. It is capable of much more than Purdy demands of it. And yet the picture we get of Purdy in his poems is of someone wearing blinkers, of someone labouring within unnecessary limitations. His intellectual and emotional range is narrower than it needs to be. Although Purdy sees and feels, he does neither with any intensity. . . . At the moments in Purdy's poems when we feel he is most open to the spiritual or mystical dimension, to any kind of transcendental or religious experience, he turns away, denying his poetry the kind of depth it most lacks. (p. 131)

Ants Reigo, "The Purdy Poem," in Canadian Literature, *No. 79, Winter, 1978, pp. 127-31.*

DOUG FETHERLING

There's an elemental lesson about Al Purdy's poetry to be learned by paging through the files of certain literary magazines of the past twenty-five years or so. In the earliest days of his career, Purdy gave his name, in all its Loyalist splendour, as Alfred Wellington Purdy. But he quickly condensed this to Alfred W. Purdy. Then came a long period of uncertainty and experiment when, with equal ease, he answered in print to both Alfred W. and A. W. Purdy. It's only been in the 1970s that his by-line has become completely stable in its least formal incarnation, just plain Al.

But that's not all. Concurrent with what otherwise would seem this simple exercise in marketing, another and more important form of ecdysis was taking place. As Purdy was reducing his name to its simplest and most appropriate form, he was undertaking to do the same to his poetry, freeing himself of some badly chosen early influences, a lot of unnatural speech, and various other foreign matter. To go back today and reread him, watching the reductive process by which he finds his distinctive style and rightful voice, is to experience a quiet, cumulative excitement. (p. 68)

[*Being Alive: Poems 1958-78* is] more than a fitting testament to his work up to now, but it's not just a pause for reflection at the age of sixty. It shows him in his present stride as a craftsman and a poetic personality, continuing the struggle to reach some sort of agreement with history.

A concern with how to find roots in an uprooted past, and what to do with them, seems to have always been central to many Canadian poets, and not simply to the obvious ones. With Purdy the question is nothing short of a daily obsession. (pp. 68-9)

One of the differences between him and other poets is that, in his case, environment has combined with his marvellous self-acquired education to produce a feeling for folklore. This is apparent in the anthropological turn he takes in many of his poems. . . . (p. 69)

[It's Purdy's comic] pose that allows [him] to comment on everyday misadventures and non-adventures. But even when writing about marital spats and the like, he's never very far from a serious purpose: married life, in Purdy's poems, is often an unconscious metaphor for the way history accumulates, the way things always go on but never remain the same. When he writes prose, which he does from time to time, Purdy tries using this same persona, but he's never as successful. His grammar is made to look dilapidated and the syntax always seems to have its shirttail hanging out. The problem is not that he lacks style; it's that he loses interest in writing which isn't poetry, which doesn't put his eye and his ear to working in unison.

To think of Purdy as a craftsman has never been very fashionable, but this just shows the folly of conventional wisdom. Many of his longer poems especially, such as "Hombre," his powerful obituary for Che Guevara, are marvellously put together, with jaggedness and mellifluousness played off against each other and repetition cleverly deployed. The result is the prose-like but hypnotic pace that's characteristic of his poems—a rhythm which, along with the particular use he makes of idiomatic language, could be called influential. (pp. 69-70)

If there's one conclusion to be drawn about Purdy from *Being Alive* it's that he's that rare creature in literary circles, a truly happy man—unmarked by rancour, living a well-considered life, trying basically to make sense of his past and his present. (p. 70)

Doug Fetherling, "Saturday Night Book Review Annual: Al Purdy's Obsessive Search for Roots," in Saturday Night *(copyright © 1978 by* Saturday Night*), Vol. 93, No. 9, November, 1978, pp. 68-70.*

BARBARA AMIEL

He is 60 years old and though he had started writing poetry in his early '20s it wasn't until he was over 40 that Al Purdy dented the Canadian poetry scene. From that point on he dented, good-naturedly, the ribs of a number of Canadian poets as well. A freight train rider in the Depression and a factory worker later on, at six-feet three-inches and still growing, Purdy seemed never to realize his own physical strength. . . . The same physical energy animates Purdy's poetry. If anyone, it is he who is Canada's working man's voice, enjoying our land with his fingertips as well as his mind. (pp. 49-50)

Sometimes he is accused of sentimentality in his outspoken love affair with Canada's sheer physical attraction. But Purdy is too wise, shrewd and good-humored for sentimentality. It takes rare reservoirs of rage, love and common sense to capture the contrasts and contradictions of a country as strong and weak, as ultramodern and prehistoric as Canada. (p. 50)

Barbara Amiel, "Capsule Comments on Canada," in Maclean's Magazine *(© 1979 by* Maclean's Magazine*; reprinted by permission), Vol. 92, No. 3, January 15, 1979, pp. 49-51.**

R

RAPHAEL, Frederic 1931-

Raphael is an American novelist, short story writer, critic, and dramatist for stage, screen, radio, and television. He has experimented with a variety of techniques in his novels to examine individuals within the English upper and middle classes. *Darling,* an original screenplay, won awards in England and America. Raphael resides in England. (See also *CLC,* Vol. 2, and *Contemporary Authors,* Vols. 1-4, rev. ed.)

ERIC MOON

[The opening scene of *Orchestra & Beginners* is a] country home in Sussex, where a typical upper-class British weekend house party is in progress. . . .

It is soon clear . . . that this scene, typical of Frederic Raphael's subtle method throughout, is set primarily for contrast and introduction. The autumn peacefulness of the Sussex weekend is deceptive; though it is scarcely alluded to, World War II has just begun. . . .

The Strausses, Leonard and Linda, alone seem aware that their lives are about to change fundamentally. But then, though they are in this old school group, they are not really of it. Leonard is a Jew, Linda an American. *Orchestra & Beginners* is the story of their marriage and its reshaping under the tensions of—among other things—the war. As the plot unfolds, the cracks in the apparently secure foundations of this "perfect" marriage are gradually revealed. (p. 43)

Orchestra & Beginners is a fascinating book with, on the one hand, the apparent expansiveness and leisured pace of the nineteenth-century novel but, on the other, a sophistication and glitter that are totally twentieth century. Essentially simple, the story is absorbing because of the intricacy of its construction; one is never quite sure in which direction it will move next.

Raphael has an incredibly intimate feel for place and atmosphere, which he creates with something of the delicate skill of the man who builds castles out of matchsticks, by carefully accumulating seemingly inconsequential details. Now and then, however, the technique is carried to excess, and he produces only one of those tiresome catalogues of trivia that clutter the later O'Hara novels. The dialogue exhibits the same contradictions: most of it is as charming and adroit as that in *Darling,* the excellent movie for which Raphael did the screenplay; but part of it is so slick and polished, notably in some of the emotional tussles between Leonard and Linda, as to seem contrived and stagey. The prose, again generally superb, can launch at intervals into purple passages. . . . (pp. 43-4)

The most telling flaw in the book, however, lies in the characterization of Leonard. Linda at one point observes that he has "the very look . . . of an official." It is Leonard's remoteness (there *is* the deadness of officialdom about him), not only from Linda but from the reader as well, that undermines the interest in the battle between Linda and her husband.

It is perhaps a tribute to the over-all strength of the plot and its construction that this book, despite faults and excesses, emerges as an intensely moving, charming, intelligent novel. . . . (p. 44)

Eric Moon, "Fierce Duel for Fulfillment," in Saturday Review *(© 1968 by Saturday Review, Inc.; reprinted with permission), Vol. LI, No. 12, March 23, 1968, pp. 43-4.*

The world [of *April, June and November*] in which Frederic Raphael's characters manoeuvre is populated by people who share dubious, though superficially attractive talents. They are all gifted, all civilized, all liberal, and all, without exception, excessively witty. Much of the narrative consists of dialogue which fairly dazzles with surface glitter: more neat epigrams to the paragraph than the script of a late-night chat show, and more deeply-felt opinions modestly hidden by sharp witticism than might fall from the lips of a graduate satirist running for political office.

The superficiality, of course, is not there to be despised; rather, it is the means by which the characters reveal their vulnerability, which ought, in turn, to elicit our sympathy while indicating that real depth is to be found beneath the banter. Before that can happen, though, it's essential that the reader should at least *begin* to believe in the people for whom he is supposed to feel—a difficult task, since the sheer speed and accuracy of their conversation is likely to make him conscious at once of the hours of careful composition taken to construct it. The assiduous, brilliant script each character seems to possess divorces him, as a stand-up comedian is divorced, from a world of real events and objects, so that when some mundane event *is* introduced it appears as misplaced as a workhouse in a fairy tale.

The impression is that characters scarcely ever stop talking unless it is to be speedily creative or trenchantly introspective; or to play football. . . .

"All Glitter," in The Times Literary Supplement *(© Times Newspapers Ltd. (London) 1972; reproduced from* The Times Literary Supplement *by permission), No. 3692, December 8, 1972, p. 1477.*

PETER ACKROYD

You might say, although it is heresy to do so, that character becomes a function of style in [*Richard's Things*]. For it is the style which dominates the book, and it is one of formality, distance and opaqueness. It has a singleness of tone which gathers all of the façades of reality into one space, and an emotion becomes just as much an object as a fruit-and-nut bar. I am becoming ponderous now, and I don't want to suggest that *Richard's Things* is a 'new novel' or anything approaching one. We will leave that to inferior novelists. What Mr Raphael has done is to make trivial events as touching and as credible as apparently 'significant' ones, and he has done so within an elliptic and ironical prose. He is not, however, just any old humourist and deep down, where it doesn't really matter, I found traces of good old-fashioned novelist's morality: "Nature is impersonal. Read it for meanings and it's absurd, callous, cruel, vindictive." Strong words, and it is fortunate that Mr. Raphael does not over-employ them. (p. 610)

Peter Ackroyd, "Defying the Conventions," in The Spectator *(© 1973 by* The Spectator; *reprinted by permission of* The Spectator*), Vol. 231, No. 7585, November 10, 1973, pp. 610-11.**

MARTIN LEVIN

Frederic Raphael, a writer who shifts psychological scenes with magical dexterity, depicts a broken triangle [in "Richard's Things"] that develops an unexpected kink when Richard's "things" fall in love with one another. . . . This is the kind of thing that could happen in a Colette novel, but Mr. Raphael is very much his own man. His style is wonderfully controlled; it abounds in original visions as it reveals more and more about . . . two women and their common bonds. It is full of unexpected horizons and interesting people—even to a burglar who makes a fleeting appearance. Not many novelists have so complete a mastery of their art.

Martin Levin, "Fiction and Poetry: 'Richard's Things'," in The New York Times Book Review *(© 1975 by The New York Times Company; reprinted by permission), October 26, 1975, p. 55.*

NEIL HEPBURN

It would be a great deal easier to like Frederic Raphael as a writer if his technical skill were less, or—since he is as scandalously accomplished as he is—if he felt less insecure about his readers' recognition of it. To puzzle over seven (or 17) types of ambiguity is pleasure of a high order; but to have them all pointed out, if not actually explained, with much nudging of bold type and winking of italics and puns significantly laid along the knows, is affronting: especially when, as in *California Time,* you find you cannot do without these artful aids.

'California time' is, its inventor says, 'a sequence of presents'—which in his book are given and received as well as lived through by people with [symbolically loaded] names. . . . *California Time,* on the other hand, is a sequence of paragraphs alternately printed in bold and light type, of which the bold seem to relate what happened in these ever-presents while the light comment upon the bold (no doubt itself a comment on the relationship of reality and writing), and simultaneously upon the structure of the book.

This kind of conjuring trick can be wearisome; but it cannot vitiate the conviction, which grows with reading, that what you have in your hands is a very remarkable book indeed. What its meaning is I should be hard put to it to say. . . . The themes of death and duality surface . . . , but the book does not seem to be 'about' them more than anything else.

Perhaps it is to do with American and European cultures in collision, with the death of the past and the new permanence of temporariness as a yardstick of values. And perhaps—perish the suspicion—it is merely about nothing more than Mr Raphael's skills. No doubt, it will take me some time to find out, since he is too clever for me on first reading, if not too clever by half; and I shall give the time willingly, not only because his book is strange and unsettling and demands close attention, but also because it is a striking compendium of wit, acute and bizarre imagery, and consummate style.

Neil Hepburn, "England in Hollywood," in The Listener *(© British Broadcasting Corp. 1975; reprinted by permission of Neil Hepburn), Vol. 94, No. 2431, November 6, 1975, p. 622.*

IVAN GOLD

"The ultimate Hollywood novel!" says Blurb, and for once he may be near the mark. . . . [In] Frederic Raphael's "California Time": Victor England, well-known director and ladies' man, returns to Hollywood to make a film. . . . [At times Raphael stops the action to drop numerous] helpful hints on how best to read a book called "California Time." (p. 33)

There are some remarkably funny scenes and exchanges in here [in addition to nearly a pun a page.] . . . [One] may imagine a benign purpose to the author's word-play, a determination, perhaps, that we be made constantly aware that we are *reading,* so as not to be hoodwinked by his skills into thinking we are already watching the movie of the book, or leafing through the book of the movie, or, worst of all, stuck up to our eyeballs in *life.*

In sum, there are some very happy moments in what Reviewer might call "this flawed, ambitious work," and the author of the screenplay for "Darling" can be indulged an ambitious flaw or two. (pp. 33-4)

Ivan Gold, "Fiction: 'California Time'," in The New York Times Book Review *(© 1976 by The New York Times Company; reprinted by permission), April 11, 1976, pp. 33-4.*

NICK TOTTON

Ten pages of *The Glittering Prizes* is highly entertaining; fifty pages begins to cloy with its unremitting sparkle; and after three hundred pages I was itching all over from the bite of witty gnats. Everyone in the book is witty, even the bit-parts; and the great bulk of the novel is dialogue, with the barest furnishing of characterisation and environment. It is, in fact, a conversion job from a television screenplay;

and makes one wonder why this convention of universal verbal brilliance is so much more acceptable on the screen (or stage) than in a novel. Part of the answer is that on the screen there is only one crack of the whip: if you miss something the first time round then it's gone for good. Wit cements a statement in our memory, much like rhyme in the oral epic. . . . [Here] too much wit is counterproductive, clogging rather than cementing.

Mr Raphael's goal is by no means pure entertainment. He is trying to describe and to criticise the Oxbridge process (still desultorily operating) by which intelligent young men and women adopt a convention of verbal agility, and viciousness, as a defence against a demanding environment—an armour inside which they may be stuck for the rest of their lives. Unfortunately, the analysis is embedded within the very convention it tries to analyse: a philosophical error which the linguistic analysts who loom over Mr Raphael's 'fifties Cambridge would be quick to attack. What it amounts to is kicking oneself for wearing steel-tipped shoes—painful and unedifying. The sheer small-time nastiness of most of the characters doesn't help, either. The accuracy with which Mr Raphael captures petty-intellectual cannibalism is not in doubt; but he captures only its surface, giving only a glossy celluloid illusion of its substance. First prize for glitter, then; but no prize for anything else. (p. 31)

Nick Totton, "Craftsmen," in The Spectator *(© 1976 by* The Spectator; *reprinted by permission of* The Spectator*), Vol. 237, No. 7744, November 27, 1976, pp. 30-1.**

JAMES BROCKWAY

As for Frederic Raphael's 'novel' version of his successful television series, *The Glittering Prizes,* it is not a novel but a script, ie, dialogue, cemented together with a few descriptive lines here and there. I am deeply grateful to Mr Raphael for this television series. . . . But isn't to present this book as a *novel* actually an offence under the Trades Description Act? . . . As a mirror held up to a society that glitters on the surface but has nothing underneath, these scripts are highly effective, but that was not, I believe, the idea. (p. 23)

James Brockway, "Going Down Bravely" (© copyright James Brockway 1977; reprinted with permission), in Books and Bookmen, *Vol. 22, No. 5, February, 1977, pp. 22-3.**

DEAN FLOWER

Adam Morris [protagonist of *The Glittering Prizes*] wants nothing more than to be smart and successful and win the glittering prizes of life. But he also wants to preserve his feisty, joking Jewish resilience, his artistic conscience, his happy marriage, his own identity, his distance. "If there's one boat I never want to be in," he says, "it's the same boat as everyone else." He finds himself thrown together with people at Cambridge University in the 1950's who want pretty much the same things—marriage, money, fame, comfortable accommodations to an imperfect society, nothing revolutionary. Over the next twenty years experience teaches them, some more harshly than others, the deceptions of their desires. Adam must confront, for example, the exploitative ugliness of his first career idea as a media man. (p. 346)

Raphael has learned something of his art from Forster: the satiric treatment of prejudice in *Passage to India,* the Cantabridgian vignettes of *The Longest Journey.* But Raphael works too much from dialogue alone, and characterization runs thin; it becomes only script and sometimes only soap opera. (p. 347)

Dean Flower, "The Way We Live Now," in The Hudson Review *(copyright © 1978 by The Hudson Review, Inc.; reprinted by permission), Vol. XXXI, No. 2, Summer, 1978, pp. 343-55.**

BLAKE MORRISON

Writers so consistently interested in social manners as Frederic Raphael are usually called 'class conscious'. What's special about Raphael is that he is conscious only of the middle class—in fact, only of the middle class couple. You need read no further than the opening sentences of Raphael's stories [in *Sleeps Six and Other Stories*] to discover that his abiding preoccupation is the coming together of the bourgeois he and she. . . .

Raphael has gone over this ground so often now, and with such assurance, that he's begun to look self-parodying. He was always indulgent towards his creations (his satirical jabs about as vicious as syrup), and now the saccharine has crept into his much-acclaimed wit: 'Frost still made mountainous birthday cakes out of molehills in the meadows.' There are good moments here in the title story and in two or three of the minimalist narratives where Raphael moves into unfamiliar territory. But at the end one is left feeling as empty as the unnamed subject of his story 'Benchmark': it all looks very accomplished, but a severe judgment would probably find that there's nothing much there.

Blake Morrison, "Making Tracks," in New Statesman *(© 1979 The Statesman & Nation Publishing Co. Ltd.), Vol. 98, No. 2523, July 27, 1979, p. 137.**

PATRICIA CRAIG

Adulteries in John Cheever's world are conducted, usually, with politeness and grace; in the stories of Frederic Raphael they are defined by a need in the participants altogether more brittle and grasping. The terms of the erotic arrangement are precise and precarious; not delicacy of spirit but deviousness may be responsible for this. Several of the stories [in *Sleeps Six and Other Stories*] are nothing but fragments, compressed to the point of insubstantiality. An ability to observe closely, with humour, hasn't saved the author from many lapses into smartness ('pregnant silences were followed by infantile noises'), and aphoristic gloss. As vignettes of modern life in a high-income zone these stories are occasionally impressive (the title story, for instance, begins to develop a kind of inner coherence), but one is left with a feeling of talents underused.

Patricia Craig, "Frederic Raphael's 'Sleeps Six and Other Stories'" (© copyright Patricia Craig, 1979; reprinted with permission), in Books and Bookmen, *Vol. 24, No. 11, August, 1979, p. 63.*

JOHN MELLORS

[In *Sleeps Six*] Frederic Raphael writes about the infidelities and other infelicities in middle-class marriages; typical titles are 'Acute Triangle', 'Similar Triangles', 'Upstairs, Downstairs' and 'Bridal Suite'. His characters are usually rich, randy, intelligent, unscrupulous and unhappy—the literary grandchildren of Scott Fitzgerald's beautiful and damned generation. Raphael would be a better writer if he did not try so hard to make every sentence wittier than the last. Too often the *soufflé* fails to rise and instead of an airy wit we have a soggy weight. . . . However, there is also much to admire in *Sleeps Six*, in particular Raphael's hip humour in his story of the wisecracking New York nympho and her maddeningly sedate psychiatrist. (p. 255)

John Mellors, "Psychic and Mental," in The Listener *(© British Broadcasting Corp. 1979; reprinted by permission of John Mellors), Vol. 102, No. 2625, August 23, 1979, pp. 254-55.**

* * *

RAVEN, Simon 1927-

Raven is a British novelist, playwright, screenwriter, essayist, and editor. A first-rate storyteller, he is known for his fast-paced social satires of the upper and upper-middle classes. Despite a simplistic approach to character and plot development, Raven's novels succeed as well-plotted entertainments, and have brought him a wide readership. (See also *Contemporary Authors*, Vols. 81-84.)

JAMES KENNAWAY

[If] you can plough through the first 130 pages [of *The Feathers of Death*], most of which are irrelevant, you will then be drawn into Mr. Raven's horrible world. As you lay down his book, you will bow in admiration to the clarity of his characterisation, the simplicity of his prose and the design of his plot. I greatly fear that he is a writer with a future, and I only hope I can discourage him.

His story is of a homosexual love affair (here we go again) between a god-like subaltern and an earth-child drummer. It is set against a background of peace-time soldiering in a troublesome colony where the regiment (which is neither cavalry nor infantry) is involved in some wog-suppression. It reaches an excellent climax in a sharp action against the natives, and the description of this battle . . . is masterly. There is no question at all that Mr Raven knows all the details of this sort of action and of other aspects of peace-time soldiering. There is also no question at all that he manages to present us with a totally false picture of British officers and men. A spell in the army and a spell in the classical sixth have produced not, as we might hope, a certain maturity of view, but an ugly case of astigmatism. . . .

Dismissing all the intolerable and repetitive table-talk (and looking back on his first novel it is this stuff, not the sodomy, that will, I hope, turn Mr Raven into a pillar of salt), I'd take issue with him on the behaviour of his troops. . . .

During the court-martial of Alastair Lynch, which forms the last section of the book, there are more brilliant moments, and at one point the hero almost changes from young god to young man. We can nearly put a face to him. It is more the pity, therefore, that Mr. Raven undoes his good in the last few pages by a single act (in itself too melodramatic for any heterosexual story) which serves to make his hero god again. It is his novel that he stabs in the back.

James Kennaway, "Old Harrovian," in New Statesman *(© 1959 The Statesman & Nation Publishing Co. Ltd.), Vol. LVII, No. 1455, January 31, 1959, p. 164.*

JOHN COLEMAN

Brother Cain is the oddest book I expect to read this year. Jacinth Crewe, after expulsion from school, premature departure from Cambridge, and enforced resignation from the Army, is taken on . . . by an international organisation bent on combating 'democratic excess and Communist exploitation.' . . . After a staggering indoctrination course, some tests and assorted sex, he ends up in Venice, confronting his assigned victims at a masked ball. With Jacinth's *character*, with his easy bisexuality, his Cambridge nostalgia and dreams, his peculiar concern with guarding his 'honour' (while fairly coolly going through with one of the nastiest acts imaginable), it would take an analyst to deal adequately. There are faint echoes of both Daisy Ashford and Ian Fleming in the chilly, jolly tone: 'after a busy evening spent buying cars and clothes, they had some dinner'—Mr. Raven frequently tells you what they had for dinner, and very nice too—but there is something that is Mr. Raven's own in the twists and turns down to a nightmare finale. Once past the early dream-sequences and organisational oratory, which I found elaborately dull, though ingenious, one is sucked along to the end. It is an unwholesome, caddish, talented book. (p. 559)

John Coleman, "The Facts of Fiction," in The Spectator *(© 1959 by* The Spectator; *reprinted by permission of* The Spectator*), Vol. 203, No. 6852, October 23, 1959, pp. 559-65.**

Mr. Simon Raven's odd and evidently serious book [*The English Gentleman*] sets out, it seems, to explain the history, traditions, state of mind and present decline of the gentleman in England, now, poor fellow, apparently much disregarded and thrown aside like an old glove. A gentleman's first qualification being a sense of *noblesse oblige,* Mr. Raven lets himself out at once, blandly claiming no sense of obligation and a taste for privilege without the inclination to go along with its responsibilities. Those are indeed fighting words, and Mr. Raven works hard at justifying them in the book's searching autobiographical passages, told with a curious combination of Ancient Mariner buttonholing zeal and the throb of True Romance. . . .

It is not too easy to decide, by the end, just what Mr. Raven thinks about the condition of the English gentleman, except that it is probably a dying one, or whether in fact he is suggesting that the Fellows of King's should take over government—no doubt in a friendly tone of voice.

"A Dying Race," in The Times Literary Supplement *(© Times Newspapers Ltd. (London) 1961; reproduced from* The Times Literary Supplement *by permission), No. 3120, December 15, 1961, p. 900.**

KERRY McSWEENEY

The very bulk of Raven's writing might suggest what a reading of his novels confirms: they are uneven in quality, occasionally repetitious and forced, and sometimes no more than entertaining. Only a few of them exhibit all of Raven's appreciable gifts as a novelist working together in harmony. These flaws should not, however, be allowed to obscure the fact that Raven is a serious and interesting novelist, whose works have yet to receive, at least in North America, the attention they deserve. (p. 106)

The action of Raven's novels all takes place within a world of privilege, leisure, and power, and it is his principal intention in them to describe, scrutinize, and judge the men who inhabit this world. The settings of major scenes are often described by Raven in careful and loving detail. . . . Raven is very good at rendering these settings and the activities they encompass. . . . Sometimes the function of these descriptions is purely decorative, but more often they are linked to the central themes and conflicts of the novels in such a way as to deepen and enrich them. When setting and theme are fully united the former become images of order, tradition, and seemliness (a favorite word of Raven's), or of their perversion. (p. 107)

What Raven anachronistically calls the "lower orders" seldom appear in his fiction except as private soldiers or servants. Another substantial portion of the human race who do not figure prominently in the fiction are women, for the enclaves of privilege about which Raven writes are almost exclusively male. . . . The inadequacy of his portrayal of women is one of the more serious shortcomings of Raven's fiction.

Raven's male characters tend to be completely worldly, untouched by anything that could be called Christian morality. For Raven, as for the classical Greeks he so admires, Christianity is folly. The only standard of conduct by which he is prepared to evaluate his characters is summed up in a comment made about a central figure in *Close of Play:* "no morals, only aesthetic preferences and personal loyalties". The core of personal loyalty is male friendship, a subject Raven treats with the greatest seriousness. . . . The love of friends may take the forms of worldly versions of *philia* and *agape,* but often in Raven's novels there is an admixture of *eros* as well. Homosexual love affairs dominate three of the novels, and are rendered with subtlety and skill. They are always handled from the point of view of the seducer, who develops an overwhelming passion for a beautiful young man. In each case the affair ends tragically. Together with the theme of betrayal, with which they are in each case closely linked, these affairs have for Raven an obsessive fascination, out of which have come some of the best and most compelling moments of his fiction. (pp. 107-08)

According to Raven, the main reason for the fragility of the code of personal loyalty is that the social ideals and sense of responsibility upon which such a code must be founded have largely disappeared from the modern world and become irrelevant to it. This is the subject explored in *The English Gentleman.* As a social analysis of twentieth-century Britain, this work leaves much to be desired (it is based almost entirely on the author's own experiences), and its main thesis doubtless strikes many readers as hopelessly reactionary or wilfully perverse. On the other hand, there seems to me to be a good deal of insight in *The English Gentleman,* a work which is of the first importance to an understanding of Raven's novels.

Its main argument is that there is no place in the modern world for the traditional qualities of the gentleman. . . . The modern age is characterized by a "preference, both popular and aristocratic, for what is spurious", and a "corresponding contempt for what is genuine". Decadent aristocrats and film stars are tolerated and even applauded by the public because their distinction is based solely on the accident of birth or personal appearance. But individuals possessing unusual personal qualities like intelligence, discipline, and self-respect—which are independent of possessions and not simply an accident of birth—tend to be ridiculed and held in contempt. Citizens of the welfare state are resentful of intrinsic superiority, for "merit is inalienable, an ever-present menace to the self-esteem of the mediocre." Standards based on character and honour have been replaced as models for emulation and admiration by worthless and tastelessly materialistic ones. (p. 108)

Raven's views on the current state of British fiction—outlined in "Reflections of a Middle-Aged Novelist", . . . closely echo the argument of *The English Gentleman.* The novelist's primary job, says Raven, is to maintain the interest of his reader. To do this he must build his work upon conflict and struggle. Because they lack these essentials, Raven admits to being dissatisfied and bored by the great majority of novels written by his younger British contemporaries. These writers know nothing of physical conflict, and in their work emotional conflict often fails to rise above "a state of masturbatory discontent". Being "progressive children of the age", they find moral conflict meaningless because of their absolute acceptance of welfare state notions of truth and justice. Novels founded on conflict inevitably suggest the unacceptable idea that, at least in some respects, some people are superior to the rest. In short, "what is destroying the quality of the novel, just as it is destroying the quality of life itself, is egalitarian dogma; for the chief fascination of novels, as of life, lies in the presentation, and the celebration, of human inequalities." (pp. 108-09)

None of [Raven's first four] novels is comparable to the best of the *Alms for Oblivion* series, though they all treat the two themes which dominate much of Raven's fiction: moral degeneration and the decline of personal loyalty. *Doctors Wear Scarlet* and *Brother Cain* are the least successful of the four because their thematic concerns are awkwardly and imperfectly embodied in the stories which contain them. (p. 109)

The principal trouble with *Doctors Wear Scarlet* is that until its final scenes [the two stories presented in the novel] are not properly united or effectively counterpointed. . . .

The faults of *Doctors Wear Scarlet* are also present in *Brother Cain,* with the addition of greater implausibility and of excessive didacticism—something most unusual in Raven. . . .

Brother Cain is basically an Ian Fleming-type adventure-fable, with an anti-hero rather than superman as protagonist. But there is a consistent theme running through the novel, although Raven is unable—as with the theme of moral degeneration in *Doctors Wear Scarlet*—to link this theme effectively with the narrative (p. 110)

In *The Feathers of Death* and *Close of Play,* the themes of moral degeneration and the decline of personal loyalty are handled in a more competent and convincing manner. *The Feathers of Death,* Raven's first published novel, is set in a British regiment stationed in a fictitious country that resembles Kenya. The events of the novel are wholly contained within the life of the regiment, whose activities and personalities are fully and convincingly rendered. This imparts to the novel a cohesiveness and a realism lacking in the novels discussed above and helps Raven keep his main thematic interest—the moral degeneration of Alastair Lynch—clearly in focus, and to maintain a mounting tension and a sense of impending disaster. (p. 111)

Close of Play is the last and best-constructed of the four early novels. Raven's touch is lighter and surer, and he has fully mastered his tendency to overwrite and to include too much irrelevant detail. The handling of the narrative is crisper and more assured, and for the first time Raven uses quick cuts from one character or group of characters to another, a technique that allows him to cover much ground in little time and to do more showing and less telling. . . . Also, although there are many changes in locale, the novel is dominated by one setting, a preparatory school in Kent and its cricket field. This setting becomes an emblem of the harmonious world of loyalty and responsibility which is threatened by those to whom these ideals are meaningless. Most importantly, in *Close of Play* theme and story are fully integrated. The study of honour and loyalty is carefully worked out through the contrast of two characters of similar background and occupation, who are both untouched by conventional morality, have the same superior aesthetic preferences, but differ completely in the matter of personal loyalty. In the novel's final scene, its sympathetic characters successfully conspire to murder the man whose disregard of the claims of honour and friendship has caused others much sorrow. In Raven's subsequent novels, however, it is not often that the forces of honour and probity can manage to maintain their standards or to cleanse even a small part of the Augean stables of modern life.

Since 1964, Raven has been at work on a series of novels, the scope and theme of which he has outlined:

> *Alms for Oblivion* will be a series of ten novels . . . to cover the English upper middle class scene since the war. The series is not planned as one long saga; each volume will present an independent story. The ten major characters are all loosely connected with one another by birth or upbringing. If there is one theme which will dominate the series it is that human effort and goodwill are persistently vulnerable to the malice of time, chance, and the rest of the human race.

This general description can be supplemented by means of a brief comparison with two other long and as yet uncompleted novel sequences by older contemporaries of Raven: Anthony Powell's [*A Dance to the Music of Time*] and C. P. Snow's *Strangers and Brothers*.

Like Powell, Raven centres his attention on a world of wealth and privilege. Both writers have small interest in morals, and Raven pays only slightly less attention than Powell to "aesthetic preferences". Male friendship, and the corrosion to which it is subject by time, is Powell's central preoccupation, as it is Raven's. But there is little of Powell's careful distancing, delicate patterning, or Proustian subtlety to be found in Raven, whose focus is much more squarely on the world as it is, rather than on its reflection in the mind of a cultivated and discriminating observer, obsessed by nuance. Like Snow's, Raven's novels are more loosely interconnected than Powell's, and more closely intervolved with political events and social change. Snow's fascination with power is matched by Raven's, and they both prefer to study it in closed and predominantly male worlds. Both use unadorned and workmanlike prose style, though here Raven is clearly superior to Snow, being by far the more lucid and articulate. Another advantage enjoyed by Raven is that his characters are free of the obsessive moral scruple—rooted in the hypersensitive conscience of the middle-class liberal—that tends to make Snow's characters rather colourless, pompous, and dull.

Although *Fielding Gray* (1967) was the fourth in the *Alms for Oblivion* series to be published, it is the first in point of the date of its action. It is Raven's finest and most powerful single novel, and the highpoint of his achievement to date. It tells a story of homosexual passion and the betrayal of friends, most effectively combining the themes of moral degeneration and the decline of personal loyalty. (pp. 111-13)

The Sabre Squadron (1966), set in Germany in 1952, is the next novel in the series, and is full, indeed too full, of colour and excitement. The main fault of the novel is that Raven has attempted to do too many things at once. A story of lonely scientific discovery is mixed with the study of a socialist conscience confronting the harsh realities of the Cold War in a way that is reminiscent of Snow's *The New Men*. The central action is a variation on the spy story *genre*. . . . In all of this, the familiar themes of male friendship and personal loyalty—though handled by Raven from a new and suggestive point of view—tend to become obscured, and though the novel is much superior to *Doctors Wear Scarlet* and *Brother Cain* it cannot be counted among Raven's genuine successes.

The Rich Pay Late (1964) and *Friends in Low Places* (1965) can be. These novels, set in 1956 and 1959 respectively, mark an expansion of Raven's powers as a novelist and a widening of his scope. In them Raven displays previously unsuspected talents, including a gift for comedy. Both novels offer a broad social panorama reflecting a wide range of upper-middle-class pursuits. Their settings are not restricted to school, college, and the army, but encompass the larger worlds of government and business. Raven handles most skilfully a large and variegated cast of characters and implicates them in the novels' main actions without becoming forced or contrived. Both novels are studies of corruption in high places and of the attainment and uses of power. The epigraph for both might well have been Shakespeare's lines from *Richard II:* "They well deserve to have That know the strong'st and surest way to get."

The action of each novel radiates outward from a central conflict: the struggle for control of an influential economic journal in *The Rich Pay Late,* and the contest for the Conservative nomination for a seat in Parliament in *Friends in Low Places*. In each case the ideals of personal honour and loyalty are embodied in Peter Morrison, the friend who had called Gray to account in *Fielding Gray*. In each conflict Morrison manages to retain his honour, but in both cases he loses power and influence, for the novels show with increasing clarity the impotence and irrelevance of the values Morrison embodies. (pp. 114-15)

[*The Judas Boy*] mixes together, in an adequate but less than fully satisfying manner, elements from the four previous novels. As in *The Rich Pay Late* and *Friends in Low Places* there is a central conflict—the attempt of powerful forces to stop a BBC producer from investigating American collusion in the Cypriot revolt against the British—the implications of which reach out to affect many of the same characters who appeared in the two earlier novels. The novel also includes much intrigue and adventure in the vein of *The Sabre Squadron,* in both of which novels the sinister American CIA agent, Earle Restarick, appears. Restarick is a paradigm of those qualities Raven most despises. As an American he is *de facto* "The enemy: he stood for change." A representative of the Americanized modern world, he exploits and betrays friendship in *The Sabre Squadron,* and in this novel—as a reviewer noted—he "coldly uses sexuality as a weapon against honour". (p. 115)

Places Where They Sing is the least satisfactory novel of the *Alms for Oblivion* series, although one would have thought its central situation a congenial one for Raven. Lancaster College must decide what to do with a large sum of money. Student radicals demand it be spent to provide new facilities for the maximum number of students, while the college fellows—in whose hands the decision rests—are divided between a limited and seemly version of this demand and the conservative suggestion that the money be spent to restore the College chapel and improve its famous choir. A confrontation ensues.

There are some good things in the novel, particularly its climactic scene in which an uncouth and sinister group of student revolutionaries . . . disrupt the singing of May madrigals and occupy the chapel. On the whole, however, despite its topicality, *Places Where They Sing* is not nearly so good as *The Masters* and *The Affair,* Snow's comparable novels set in a Cambridge college. Among the more annoying of its features is Raven's overindulgence of his tendency to characterize by sexual fetish. But its principal weakness is that Raven has not thought long or hard enough about the reasons for student unrest and its social causes. As a result, he is forced to rely on caricature and greatly oversimplified ideas.

It is too early to attempt any hard and fast judgements about the *Alms for Oblivion* series—there are four novels still to come—or even about Raven's achievement to date. Juding by past performance, it is not unlikely that Raven's fiction may develop in new and unexpected ways, and later novels may well force one to look at those already published in a different light. Raven's own evaluation of his work is disarmingly modest. Fielding Gray—latterly a novelist—clearly speaks for his creator in these comments on his craft: "I never said I was an artist. I am an entertainer . . . I arrange words in pleasing patterns in order to make money. I try to give good value—to see that my patterns are well-wrought—but I do not delude myself by inflating the nature of my function. I try to be neat, intelligent and lucid: let others be 'creative' or 'inspired'." But it is not necessary to inflate the value of what Simon Raven has so far produced in order to say that he is among the most entertaining, interesting, and talented of current British novelists. (p. 116)

Kerry McSweeney, "The Novels of Simon Raven," in Queen's Quarterly, *Vol. 72, No. 1, Spring, 1971, pp. 106-16.*

PETER STRAUB

Bring Forth the Body is the penultimate volume in Simon Raven's *Alms For Oblivion* series, but it stands quite easily on its own as a separate novel. In fact, there's maybe too much ease: Captain Detterling and Leonard Perceval conduct a quiet investigation into the causes of Somerset Lloyd-Jones's suicide, and the book is simply a series of false leads which finally wind around to revelation. The tone, in this roundup of characters from earlier novels, progressively darkens; and Raven invents an effortless stream of comic moments. . . .

Peter Straub, "Hot & Cold," in New Statesman *(© 1974 The Statesman & Nation Publishing Co. Ltd.), Vol. 88, No. 2276, November 1, 1974, p. 627.**

PETER ACKROYD

There are a great many novels concerned with political intrigue, but none of them have Mr Raven's peculiarly steely glint. He is a master craftsman, who can change scenes and characters without overt discomfort; his prose is always amusing, elegant, intelligent and never below the belt. Where else except in a Raven novel [*Bring Forth the Body*] could you find an old whore called Maisie who calls everyone "duckie" and paints her clients, as it were, in oils? Or a maid known as Dolly who is both honest and hardworking? A certain Peregrina Lloyd-James who is bored rather than tired, and a detective sergeant who looks like a "jacketed barrel"? Anglo-Saxon attitudes are alive and well and being ruthlessly sent up.

There are some odd moments, of course, but they are no more serious than the occasional cross-bat stroke. It is only in a night-club known as Annabel's (which must surely be a fictional creation) that matters go seriously wrong. It is here that an orgy is held, but unhappily it turns out to be an orgy of sentiments. There is a masque with a moral, and it is a moral which becomes all too painfully clear when Somerset Lloyd-James, the deceased party, is found to have been disturbed by religious doubts before his suicide: "God is not mocked" was his password to Hell, which only goes to show that the upper classes have forsaken their old virtues of self-reliance and stolidity, and have come to rely upon cheap sentiment. But, all in all, *Bring Forth The Body* is a British fiction of the most traditional and entertaining kind, and all the more solid for being self-consciously so.

Peter Ackroyd, "This England," in The Spectator *(© 1974 by* The Spectator; *reprinted by permission of* The Spectator*), Vol. 223, No. 7636, November 2, 1974, p. 573.**

JULIAN SYMONS

The Survivors is the tenth and last volume in Simon Raven's 'Alms For Oblivion' sequence, and the death of culture is somehow mixed up in it with the extinction of the English gentleman. 'Such gentlemen as survive, though honourable and decent men, can only be seen as futile anachronisms when once one properly appreciates the present conditions of society,' Mr Raven wrote 15 years ago. His view has hardened since then, and his gentlemen are no longer honourable and decent. . . .

The view of society put forward in these novels is not dissimilar to that found in the work of another Tory with a romantic view of the English gentleman, Evelyn Waugh. Both writers hankered to be 'gentlemen' themselves, and Raven in a semi-autobiographical book called *The English Gentleman* . . . writes amusingly about the vanity of his aspiration, which is perfectly expressed in the fact that a gentleman is never concerned with gentility. Both detest the spread of lower-middle-class morality that might be called Hooperism. In opposition to the various vulgarities of the modern world Raven invokes an ideal classicism, Waugh an ideal aristocracy. Both seem to believe that there are religious answers to the problems of the individual psyche. Both show a simple national patriotism ('British and proud of it,' as one Raven character says). The difference is that the abominable Waugh used his generally detestable or absurd ideas about society as material for considerable works of art, while the much more genial Raven has been able to produce only a collection of strip cartoons.

One should be clear about this. Simon Raven's talents are both inadequate and unsuited to his subject. The 'Alms For Oblivion' novels are consistently easy and amusing to read, but artistically they are negligible. Most of them contain scenes of political or sexual melodrama of the crudest kind, acted out by characters conceived in terms which are often ludicrous. Their most interesting attribute is an Ouida-like vigour, a sense that Mr. Raven is so enthralled by his own creations that he has come to believe in them himself. . . .

The Survivors [is] a book with less than its author's usual liveliness. The setting is Venice, and the underlying theme [is that] of a rotting rather than a botched civilisation. . . . There is less sexual action than usual, although not less talk. . . .

A strip cartoon may have the vicious power of caricature, but this one doesn't, because Simon Raven's talent is genial rather than corrosive. He has two veins of talent, one for melodrama and the other for wild lubricious comedy, but neither has been much help to him in dealing with a grand overall theme for which—as that English lady novelist might put it—he just hasn't the equipment.

Julian Symons, "Gentleman's Strip," in New Statesman *(© 1976 The Statesman and Nation Publishing Co. Ltd.), Vol. 91, No. 6, June 11, 1976, p. 778.*

MICHAEL BARBER

For all his worldly pagan sermonising, Simon Raven is as obsessed by sin and retribution as a hell-fire divine. This has been apparent from the very beginning of his *Alms for Oblivion* sequence, in the first volume of which the coarse-grained Jude Holbrook . . . is cruelly punished for his shystering by the death of his beloved young son. Since then all the protagonists, as well as a few more secondary players like Holbrook, have been weighed in the balance and found wanting. And while most of them have richly deserved their respective come-uppances, it's interesting that what has sometimes tipped the scales against them is a minor misdemeanour—minor, that is, by conventional standards but not, one supposes, by Mr Raven's. (p. 23)

[Beneath] their baroque trappings his books are as austere and symmetrical as a Doric temple, with every character oiling the wheels of a fine-meshed plot. . . .

[The] sequence as a whole [has] been an ambitious project because the author has tried to do three things at once: catch the flavour of that Upper and Upper-Middle Class world about which he is both contemptuous and affectionate; introduce and develop the nine or so loosely-connected characters who dominate the sequence; and at the same time present ten independent stories in such a way that each would entertain a reader new to the sequence. This is an awfully tall order, especially when you consider that there is no Lewis Eliot figure to hold it together.

So has he pulled it off?—Well, nearly, I think. The Raven charivari is as scandalously compelling as Evelyn Waugh's diaries. Vulgar, but not common (to borrow Waugh's phrase), it can accommodate a whore's parlour as readily as a smart cavalry mess. However, just as Waugh was eminently of the Twenties, so Raven is a Fifties' man. When it reflects events since then, as in *Places Where They Sing,* his mirror tends to blur or distort.

Judging from the blurb of *The Rich Pay Late,* it was Mr Raven's original intention to have ten characters appearing as the central consciousness of one whole story. In the event Fielding Gray hogs three books, while Peter Morrison, Daniel Mond and Detterling dominate one each. However, at various times during the four remaining volumes the author does go inside the other protagonists, so by the end of the sequence we do have some idea of what makes them all tick.

The above technique, allied to the fact that the sequence is not one long saga like *A Dance to the Music of Time,* certainly strengthens Mr Raven's hand in respect of the casual reader. But I'm sure I'm not alone in feeling that the exigencies of the roman-fleuve have determined that individually, not one volume of the decalogue has quite the pith of his first and fourth novels, *The Feathers of Death* . . . and *Close of Play*. Between them, these two books encapsulate the many mansions that make up Mr Raven's House of Fiction: public school; university; the Army; gambling; cricket (cricket fields are to Raven as hunting fields are to Trollope); classical scholarship; Aristotelian tragedy; homosexual love and heterosexual eroticism.

Both *The Feathers of Death* and *Close of Play* are elegiac. So too is *The Survivors,* but not simply because it concludes with the death and burial in Venice of poor Danny Mond. For when, as happens in the final pages, a largely honourable man like Peter Morrison can connive at the destruction of Venice by industrialists in order to retain his office as Minister of Commerce, the writing is on the wall: everything of value will soon be gone, so *carpe diem.* (p. 24)

Michael Barber, "The Last of the Wine" (© copyright Michael Barber 1977; reprinted with permission), in Books and Bookmen, *Vol. 22, No. 5, February, 1977, pp. 23-4.*

* * *

RECHY, John 1934-

Rechy is an American novelist. The appalling vision he presented in *City of Night* has been called morality transformed into nightmare. (See also *CLC*, Vol. 7, and *Contemporary Authors*, Vols. 5-8, rev. ed.)

STANTON HOFFMAN

In three important novels of the American literature of homosexuality—Gore Vidal's *The City and the Pillar,* Baldwin's *Giovanni's Room,* and John Rechy's *City of Night*—there is a changing relationship between the two poles of the "gay world" and the personal homosexual relationship, with the gay world as an emerging metaphor. The culmination of this emergence occurs, I think, in Rechy's novel, where the "gay world" and all its parts overwhelm not only the possibility of any relationship implying human involvement, but also the existence of the particular characters who would form this relationship if they could, and especially the existence of what is meant to be the center of focus in that novel, the narrator as character, and where it functions as a metaphor for a destructive and despair-ridden American reality. The America of these novels is the possibility of a vast hell always defining a smaller and intense personal hell.

That the "gay world" is seen literally as the threat to the individual homosexual trying to love and to define himself is understandable. . . . The feeling is that this world can explain both how hard it is to love in America and how necessary it is to love in America. In this last respect, the function of the "gay world" in these novels is in part rhetorical, serving to establish the necessity of love (not to love is to achieve this terrible world), and in part sociological, serving to establish causes for the failure of love.

The human beings who emerge, then, from these novels are beings who exist in a lonely, love-mad culture, and who seek to define themselves in the destructive context of that culture. (pp. 195-96)

The City and the Pillar, Giovanni's Room, and *City of Night* represent, I think, stages in the discovery and development of the possibilities of using a part of homosexual life as a metaphor for an American reality. . . . In *City of Night* the metaphor seems corrupt and out of control. (p. 197)

[The] hustler's world is almost the totality of the novel, for the novel's hero's relationship to this world is not one of attraction, but is one of complete entrance and submergence, so that he is always seen from within this world.

The presence then of the "I," the narrator, of this novel is rather implicit than explicit, and seems throughout to be overwhelmed by a large body of material which can only be held together in two respects—by the metaphorical implications of that material, and by the presentation on the literal level of plot of a fairly precise relationship between the individual homosexual and the hustler's world which he encounters. The particulars of the hustler's world, with its many parts, repetitions and variations, are intended to be related to an image of America in the novel which reveals that the hustler's world and the larger American context are analogous to each other, and that the male prostitute's world—really an extension of the "gay world"—is the metaphor for that larger context. The theme of Rechy's "I," in the guise of autobiography, beginning the novel with a remembrance of childhood, and ending the novel with a dialectic on love and a personal Ash Wednesday, is rarely felt in the body of this work, and then is brought in almost perfunctorily, as for instance in the novel's Los Angeles section. But it seems to be Rechy's intention to make each of the geographical sections of the novel mark a stage in the development of the "I." (p. 200)

That Rechy means his reader to make an identification between the hustler's world and the American reality, to see the one as representing the other, is perhaps clear from the relatively brief Chicago section of his novel. His image of Chicago is not a hustler's Chicago—rather it is a city seen in terms of various images of poverty, drunkeness, and loneliness. (p. 201)

And that Rechy means to see his male prostitute's world as mirroring in its specifics the specifics of the larger context of America is perhaps clear from an awareness that in the elaborateness and fullness of the presentation of the hustler's world there is some kind of vague scheme operating. For instance, the Los Angeles section has numerous parts and sub-sections—the stories of Miss Destiny, Chuck, Skipper, Lance, and Dean, and the married man the hero meets on the beach at Santa Monica. What one gets are the components of the hustler's world and the "gay world" which become the components of an American reality (and in this they become the components of the "I"). . . . The other major sections of the novel attempt to do the same thing. San Francisco extends the image of the "gay" hustling world to include boot fetishists, cultists, masochists, and sadists. It ends with a cry which seems central to the entire presentation of the "gay world," America, and the novel's hero. "'Oh, yes—but you know why I'm unhappy?' he repeated. 'Because—' he said, enunciating slowly, 'because—I wanna—wanna—lover. Yes! A Lover!'"

The failure of *City of Night* seems to me to lie in the unconvincing manner in which Rechy attempts to use a metaphor and to create a metaphorical level in his novel. Here there is the paradoxical situation of a failure to make the metaphor work coupled with an overconsciousness that it should be there working. Thus, in *City of Night* there exists a confused and inadequate literal level and an overabundance of reminders . . . that the novel is to have a metaphorical level. In this last respect, the novel's Chicago section seems especially crude.

The novel's literal level involves the encounter of the individual male prostitute and the world of male prostitution, meant to represent the encounter between the individual and the American reality in terms of the possibility of or destruction of love. That for the most part the novel's hero seems present implicitly—almost as if the self were obliterated in its encounter—might seem to represent the relationship between the individual and the reality which surrounds him and envelopes him. But in three places, Rechy makes his hero exist explicitly. And what Rechy does in these three places only confuses the relationship between the individual homosexual and the hustling world and seems to contradict what sections like the novel's Chicago section appear to assert. The relationship is never clear.

City of Night begins with a chapter of childhood remembrance. But one soon discovers there is no real character created here, despite the emphasis on an "I" which rarely appears elsewhere in the novel. This chapter is a chapter created around five or six incidents and images which will occasionally appear in various forms elsewhere, and which are too patently symbolic, and yet as symbols too fragile for the weight of the experiences and incidents of the novel. The past of the "I" seems too heavily manipulated, too artificial. (pp. 201-03)

[Throughout] the novel one does not know what this "I" really is. In the Jeremy section . . . Rechy's hero discovers that his desire to be loved and his refusal to give love in return is really a form of love. This, in part, is meant to explain his existence in the literal hustler's world. But this has little relationship to what is presented elsewhere of the encounter of the individual and the American reality—or what is presented elsewhere of Rechy's hero. It, in fact, is gratuitous, and does not seem at all meaningful. And in the very last section of his novel . . . , after an orgy of anonymous sex, and where Rechy's "I" encounters more and more voices which reveal the "ice age of the heart"; a resolution for the "I" is imposed upon the novel, as if the conclusion to a carefully created development of character. Rechy's hero undergoes a personal anguish, penitence, and desire for redemption. We are given then an image of the "I" hardly in keeping with any other image we have been given of the "I." The "I" is removed from the context of the other elements of the novel, and the novel's literal level is further confused.

This divorcing of elements can be seen in the way in which Rechy presents his hustler's world, despite the hint of a vague scheme controlling the materials of this world. The manner in which this world is presented seems to overwhelm its own metaphorical function, and thus to be separate from [other] parts of the novel. . . . For the multitude of details, the immensity of details concerning the hustler's world and the "gay world" are ultimately a part of a journalistic impulse, their justification no longer lying in an attempt to create a metaphor for an American reality and to present and cope with that reality, seeing it in terms of specific characteristics, describing and judging it. The real relationship between the "I" and the hustler's world is that of a tour guide to his homosexual travelogue.

What exists on this novel's literal level has little to do with what should exist on its literal level, if the terms of that literal level are to represent the terms of the novel's real theme—the individual confronting an American reality, and the individual unable to love in this reality. . . . In James Baldwin's *Giovanni's Room* the realization that a "gay" bar and the "gay world" are to represent the America from which David comes and the America that is within him is subtly suggested. In Vidal it is in one place stated. And in Rechy's novel, it is stated again and again. (pp. 203-04)

Stanton Hoffman, "The Cities of Night: John Rechy's 'City of Night' and the American Literature of Homosexuality," in Chicago Review *(reprinted by permission of* Chicago Review; *copyright © 1964 by* Chicago Review), *Vol. 17, Nos. 2 & 3, 1964, pp. 195-206.*

WARREN TALLMAN

Rechy's *City of Night* follows in its way much the same path that Kerouac traced in *On the Road*, eastside, westside and all around the country. And part of his desire—wild reaching of the writer's organism—is to swing this huge cityscape wordwise with a series of variations on the theme of the male hustlers' experiences in the homerotic world through which his narrator wanders. The novel is sure to be read as a confessional exposé documenting the night side of homosexual life. Which it is. But it seems to me that Rechy has a deeper than confessional interest in the nationwide sexual skid road he writes about. The determining factor there is not so much this, that or some other sexual inclination, but what is much worse, a starved male impotence so pervasive that any momentary recognition of sexual existence at all is the real dime some buddy may be persuaded to spare. That his narrator is searching for the sources of this impotence accounts for the at times strict, almost clinical aspects of the journey. But a deeper striving, some dream of the father, causes the writer to swing his huge city of dreadful male night at the strong wrist of what is at times a heroic writing nerve and style. (pp. 155-56)

Warren Tallman, "The Writing Life" (copyright © 1976 by Warren Tallman; reprinted by permission of the author), in Open Letter, *Third Series, No. 6, Winter, 1976-77, pp. 150-58.*

KEITH WALKER

[*The Sexual Outlaw* is a] fictionalized "non-fiction" account of a "true spectrum of the [homosexual] promiscuous experience", three days and nights in the life of Jim ("sometimes Jerry, sometimes John") alias John Rechy. . . .

By a quantitative measure, this sexual marathon seems to rate highly. And yet *The Sexual Outlaw* is not erotic, and is unlikely to excite anyone but a member of the Festival of Light. The "youngmen" (Rechy's own curious word) Jim, etc, encounters . . . are so lightly characterized as to be as enticing as a rubber model filled with warm water. . . .

The interest is in "Jim" alone, his body-building, his naive pride in his good looks . . . , and his obsession with "scoring". However the nakedness of the exposure of this obsession lends the book a certain raw energy, without which it would be intolerable. It is still a long way behind Rechy's first book, *City of Night,* which was published in 1964. This uncovered for many the world of the male hustler, and moved by its often powerful reticence and its ability to create memorably comic characters. *City of Night* was overwritten and pretentious, too, but since then Rechy has progressed to the dizzy height of a teacher of creative writing at the University of California at Los Angeles, and his novels have become more consciously arty. Thus *The Sexual Outlaw* begins with quotations from Camus and Melville, and ends with a satisfying nihilistic downbeat. . . . There is also what the blurb describes as "a stylized intermixture of forms and voices". These include such things as awful sub-Whitmanesque evocations of driving along the LA freeways, an interview with Rechy talking about himself as a writer, documents concerning the bizarre conduct of the LA police force, and lectures (some "imaginary", some apparently delivered) about Gay Liberation and The Homosexual Situation.

Since *The Sexual Outline* is, in the nature of things, unlikely to find many heterosexual readers, I will make little comment on these last parts except to say that I found the arguments very confused. The prohibition of "lewd acts in public places" in California as elsewhere applies to heterosexuals as well as homosexuals. That the police everywhere spend a disproportionate amount of their time harassing homosexuals is of course wrong, but there is a strong current of feeling in this book that Rechy, despite his protestations to the contrary, cherishes his status as an "outlaw", and would regret its passing. In the face of his passionate pleas for sexual liberation I find it odd that he disapproves so strongly of sadomasochistic practices, which with breathtaking innocence he seems to think are confined to homosexuals.

Keith Walker, "The Working Weekend," in The Times Literary Supplement *(© Times Newspapers Ltd. (London) 1978; reproduced from* The Times Literary Supplement *by permission), No. 3984, August 11, 1978, p. 908.*

* * *

RHYS, Jean 1894-1979

Rhys, an English novelist and short story writer, was born in the West Indies. *The Wide Sargasso Sea,* published in 1966 after a silence of twenty-seven years, led to a reprinting and reassessment of her earlier work. Her timeless narratives focus on lonely, passive, dependent women, whose lives parallel the author's in certain aspects. As a young woman, Rhys immigrated to England, was unsuccessful in a show business career, married but found herself abandoned in Europe, became a protégé of Ford Madox Ford, and disappeared from

the public eye after World War II, but was reintroduced when the BBC broadcast her *Good Morning, Midnight* in 1958. See also *CLC*, Vols. 2, 4, 6, and *Contemporary Authors*, Vols. 25-28, rev. ed.)

MICHAEL WOOD

The possibility of being substantially right in [one] way while being specifically wrong entails a stable world and a steady viewer. . . . Jean Rhys is many miles from such confidence, and her subdued, hesitating heroines live under something like the reverse [of this] rule. They and their tormentors can be specifically, superficially right a lot of the time, and still get the whole of the substance wrong; and Rhys herself is anxious not to claim too much for her own broken and threatened perceptions. . . .

[Jean Rhys's characters] have insights, but they have no means of sharing them. They can't find the right expression, and there is no one who will trust a word or a gesture *in spite* of its poverty. On the contrary, all communication is constantly entangled in a mass of misinterpretation. (p. 30)

There are no links in Rhys's fiction between a person's experience and the meaning that experience is likely to have for others. It's not that no two people see the world in the same way, although that is also true in her novels. It is (a narrower, more intense question) that no one else can see *me* the way I see myself. "The real secret," a girl thinks in another earlier story, might be "to be exactly like everybody else," for then the self as a separate, suffering entity would disappear. This is not a consummation to be wished, but it would bring a form of peace, and between this undesired peace and their chronic, beleaguered self-consciousness Jean Rhys's heroines live out their painful lives—most memorably in what are no doubt her three best works, *Voyage in the Dark, Good Morning, Midnight,* and *Wide Sargasso Sea.* In the other novels (*Quartet, After Leaving Mr. Mackenzie*) and volumes of stories (*The Left Bank, Tigers Are Better Looking*), these heroines are sometimes defined *only* by their fragility, and become something less than human, trapped birds beating against their cages, while the writer pleads too openly for our pity.

For her new book [*Sleep It Off, Lady*], Rhys has had the very good idea of putting sixteen stories together in such a way that their places and people correspond to the chronological order of her own life, with its childhood in the West Indies and its early adult Bohemian days in Europe; with its loves, illnesses, aging, and approaching death. . . . The result is neither a novel nor an autobiography—the characters change from story to story and none of them seems a simple self-portrait—but it is a record of a maturing, darkening mind, and the observant intelligence of Rhys's best fiction, the necessary counterpart to the unremitting vulnerability of her heroines, is well in evidence. . . .

The book dips every now and again into Rhys's particular form of sentimentality, a too simple view of lonely sensibility adrift in a heartless world ("Outside in the hostile street we got into the hateful bus") and a sense of life as just too predictably elusive ("was it perhaps only yesterday and everything that had happened since a strange dream?"). But mainly it holds up an urgent, quiet challenge to what Rhys in another book calls "life as it is." If we—men, culture, convention, respectability—have wasted, ruined, or ignored the real-life sisters of the women who appear in these pages, the loss is ours and a grievous one. To say nothing (because one can't say enough) of the loss to the women themselves.

Jean Rhys's women go under because they are imprisoned in their isolation and no one has the generosity to visit them there. (p. 31)

Michael Wood, "Endangered Species," in The New York Review of Books *(reprinted with permission from* The New York Review of Books; *copyright © 1976 Nyrev, Inc.), Vol. XXII, No. 18, November 11, 1976, pp. 30-2.**

ROBIE MACAULEY

Probably the most gratifying literary rediscovery of the 1960's was the revival of Jean Rhys. . . . And, thanks to that, we now have those fine, somber Rhys novels of the 1930's—largely about the lives of lonely women submerged in the depths of great cities. . . .

Sean O'Faolain once remarked . . . that the art of the modern short story lies half in not-telling. It is the good reader's art to supply the silent half, quickly and accurately, for himself. And this is the best clue to understanding the 16 new stories in "Sleep It Off, Lady." (p. 7)

[No] thumbnails of plot can transmit the particular tang of Jean Rhys's style or her splendid ability to choose what is said and to let the unsaid speak. The fact that the scenes themselves come from the West Indies or London Or Paris of decades past has no real bearing—these are very modern stories written with a quick, young sensibility. (p. 50)

Robie Macauley, "Things Unsaid and Said Too Often," in The New York Times Book Review *(© 1976 by The New York Times Company; reprinted by permission), November 21, 1976, pp. 7, 50.**

["Sleep It Off, Lady" contains] brief, nourishing stories about the ways in which people injure and comfort each other. . . . [No] matter where [her stories] are set, they all are gossipy, deceptively artless, and honest in an unusually subtle way about the meanderings of people's emotions. . . . [In] several stories ("Goodbye Marcus, Goodbye Rose," "The Chevalier of the Place Blanche," "Night Out 1925") Miss Rhys sniffs around the edges of sexual gamesmanship with the keenness of a dog on its favorite morning walk. It is probably the range of imagination that impresses one most: almost every story is filled with conversations that are so right in tone that one wonders how the author could have got under the skin of so many different sorts of people. And whether she is writing about seedy roués, aging spinsters, or hysterical secretaries, she manages to convey the quality of a whole life in a few pages. (p. 98)

"Books: 'Sleep It Off, Lady'," in The New Yorker *(© 1977 by The New Yorker Magazine, Inc.), Vol. LII, No. 47, January 10, 1977, pp. 98-9.*

PEGGY CRANE

Nearly all [Jean Rhys's] short stories and novels centre on a proud, sensitive woman, timidly putting out a hand for love and friendship and being continually rebuffed. For most the bottle becomes the only solace. The title story [of *Sleep It off, Lady*] starkly reflects this theme. Old Miss Verney, living alone in her country cottage could be Sasha Jensen of *Good Morning, Midnight* thirty years on. The vaguer fears of the younger woman are now concretised for Miss Verney into a large rat, real or imaginary, in the dilapidated garden shed. Forcing herself to replace a dustbin near the shed the old lady slips and cannot get up. A local girl leers at her, refusing her appeal for help. 'Sleep it off, Lady', she jeers, referring to the village gossip that Miss Verney drinks. Paralysed with fear, terrified of the rat, she is left alone in the dark. The postman finds her dead there next morning. The doctor says she died of shock and cold. He was treating her for a heart condition, he says.

This nightmarish quality of alienation—the difference between what one knows and feels and what others see and understand—permeates not only the other stories but all the author's work. Madness, guile, deceit, are never far away; yet at the heart of all her characters there is a core of innocence that prevents them from degenerating into sodden sluts or mean-minded maniacs. The world, she implies, is too ready to sneer, to think the worst of people, to hate those who, for whatever reason, be it birth or misfortune, do not conform. This, in Miss Rhys's canon, is particularly true of the English, never more so than when the person of their cold dislike is down and out. For lack of money is one of the great afflictions that runs through all her books, forcing girls to prostitution and men to greed. Yet, however impoverished they are, there is always the flicker of hope that tomorrow will be better. . . .

[Miss Rhys's] early novels, *Voyage in the Dark* and *Good Morning, Midnight,* written in the 1930's and reflecting some of that life, were ahead of their time in the free and laconic way they treated sex and love, in that order. Not surprisingly, these later stories are not of the same intensity, though several echo a similar theme. . . .

[*Wide Sargasso Sea*], inspired by Mr Rochester's mad Creole wife in *Jane Eyre,* brought together not only the suffering and alienation found in her other novels but a stunning evocation of West Indian life in the last century, with its smouldering hate left by the end of the slave trade and the collapse of the planter regime; its splendid beauty and hints of Negro 'obeah' or supernatural power creating an ambience both exotic and frightening. . . .

Even though her earliest works are so modern in style and content it is difficult to compare her with younger writers today. She etches in a wider canvas than Margaret Drabble, is equally sexually direct but less sentimental than Edna O'Brien, and is more self-centred than Nadine Gordimer. The laconic style of her first novels recalls some early Hemingway, except that no man could have written them. They are entirely feminine and few writers have depicted so honestly, without self-pity, a woman struggling alone to be herself.

Peggy Crane, "Writers in an Alien Land" (© copyright Peggy Crane 1977; reprinted with permission), in Books and Bookmen, *Vol. 22, No. 5, February, 1977, p. 60.*

GEORGE CORE

Jean Rhys is usually content to sketch the possibilities of her fictive situation, and the result is anecdote. . . . (p. ii)

My sense is that the work [in *Sleep It Off, Lady*] is not so much the material of short fiction as the fragments of several unfinished novels—one about childhood in the West Indies, another about adolescence and early maturity in finishing and dramatic schools, a third about night life in London (including the Battle of Britain), and the last about the rigors of old age.

One of the best of Miss Rhys's stories ("Insect World") contains this line: "Almost any book was better than life." Her characters tend to take that view of reality, and they have the feeling that they are play-acting in a strange world which will soon take on the actuality of their expectations. (p. iv)

George Core, "Wanton Life, Importunate Art," in The Sewanee Review *(reprinted by permission of the editor; © 1977 by The University of the South), Vol. LXXXV, No. 1, Winter, 1977, pp. ii-x.**

LOUIS JAMES

Although *Wide Sargasso Sea* was set almost entirely in the Caribbean, its first critics were more interested in its links with the Victorian classic, Charlotte Brontë's *Jane Eyre* (1847), for it told the story of Rochester's mad wife kept in the attic of Thornfield Hall. The point that Jean Rhys' book was a radical *revaluation* of *Jane Eyre* and its European attitudes from the perspective of a West Indian Creole was largely missed. (p. 111)

As Proust knew, memory can intensify and make clearer childhood experience, and it is no paradox that Jean Rhys' novel furthest in time from her Caribbean life should also be her most profoundly West Indian. The speech rhythms, the total imaginative context, from the sense impressions to the minutiae of social relationships, have an accuracy that give particular pleasure to those intimate with the Caribbean, and this is validated by the relevance of the themes to aspects of West Indian culture. Jean Rhys' vision is not that of Edward Brathwaite, although in important ways the two do overlap—notably both reject European materialism in favour of the vitality of the black folk culture. Yet Caribbean culture can never be narrowed to one perspective. (p. 112)

Jean Rhys' early writing about the Caribbean has a wide range. Some of it is vivid recreation—mixing cocktails for her father in the holiday house, or portraying an illiterate Roseau newspaper editor. Other pieces are short stories, Chekhovian in their depth and economy. "The Day they Burnt the Books" encapsulates not only a conflict between mulatto and European, but between two ways of life. (p. 113)

Imaginatively, perhaps the most remarkable achievement among her Caribbean stories is "Let them Call it Jazz". . . . In it, Jean Rhys writes—in dialect—from the point of view of a black girl from Martinique, living in Notting Hill, London. . . .

In its evocation of black emotional warmth and essential awareness of musical rhythm, the story has an unassuming relationship to the insights of *negritude*. (p. 114)

[*Voyage in the Dark*] was the first-written of all Jean Rhys' novels, and is still her favourite. It bears the same kind of relationship to *Wide Sargasso Sea* as Dickens' autobiographical *David Copperfield* bears to *Great Expectations*. Not only is one the mature reworking of the other, but what the earlier work lacks in symbolic objectivity, the first-written makes up in the freshness and poignancy of the personal element. *Voyage in the Dark* was composed from exercise-book diaries kept by the young Jean Rhys when living the desolate life of a chorus girl touring minor theatres in England. (p. 115)

[The book] is a delicate counterpoint of Anna's [sad and sordid] London experiences against her inner memories of the Caribbean. The skill with which this is done defeats analysis. . . . Ford Madox Ford accurately called it Rhys' "singular instinct for form." Each emotion and theme has to have its appropriate and unique rhythm. (p. 116)

It is [Rhys'] sensitivity of style that makes what may appear a simple contrast between England and the Caribbean so moving. Anna, on coming to England, writes: "It was as if a curtain had fallen, hiding everything I had ever known. It was almost like being born again. The colours were different, the smells were different, the feelings things gave you right down inside yourself [were] different. . . ." . . .

The difference not only in what is felt, but in the *ways* of feeling, is crucial to the effect of *Voyage in the Dark*. When Jean Rhys recreates the West Indian house with its verandah and latticed jalousies, dazed by the sun at noon, haunted by the moon at night, the prose itself becomes luminous. We see through the eyes of a child, reacting with responses of wonder and fear. . . . (p. 117)

By contrast, descriptions of England are lacking in these qualities. The fields are "squares like pocket-handkerchiefs; a small tidy look it had, everywhere fenced off from everywhere else." The few sensuous details of England express alienation: "The streets like smooth shut-in ravines and the dark houses frowning down." There is monotonous sameness. "There was always a little grey street leading to the stage-door of the theatre and another little grey street where your lodgings were, and rows of little houses with chimneys like funnels of dummy steamers and smoke the same colour as the sky." . . . In the Caribbean, even a cobweb was a significant detail. (p. 118)

Throughout *Voyage in the Dark,* the [black and white worlds] interweave, the imaginary remembered world more real than the actual present. (p. 119)

[There is an] imaginative interfusion of the Caribbean context with the personal themes [in] . . . Jean Rhys' books, and . . . a difference between *Voyage in the Dark* and *Wide Sargasso Sea* that is as important as the fact of poetic reworking of earlier themes: *Voyage in the Dark* ends with the silent agony of the ruined house. *Wide Sargasso Sea* ends with the fire. Fire is the ambivalent symbol of both destruction and passion. The young Anna suffers; the mature Antoinette *rebels* against the life-denying imprisonment of the English Rochester, and asserts her human need for colour, for passion, for love. And this development of theme not only shows Jean Rhys developing her treatment of the white-black dilemma in the West Indies; it also shows a deepening understanding of the West Indian predicament itself. (pp. 123-24)

Wide Sargasso Sea and *Voyage in the Dark* are interrelated. The movement from Anna to Antoinette is a progression in Jean Rhys' heroines from passive suffering to passionate strength, just as the exploration of the cold ruins of Anna's nightmare back to the burning of Coulibri is the deepening of her insight into West Indian history. The one novel lies at the beginning of her writing career; the other at its mature culmination. Yet the early book does not suffer in the comparison. *Voyage in the Dark* remains her most personal and evocative book. Not only does it capture a Caribbean childhood with delicacy; it also intensifies it within a powerful exploration of the experience of exile. And this is an experience known by many West Indians, both white and black. (p. 126)

Louis James, "Sun Fire—Painted Fire: Jean Rhys As a Caribbean Novelist," in Ariel *(copyright © 1977 The Board of Governors The University of Calgary), Vol. 8, No. 3, July, 1977, pp. 111-27.*

ELIZABETH ABEL

Although some articles on Rhys have appeared in popular magazines, she has received little critical attention, especially from women, despite her exceptional technical skill and the relevance of her subject matter to the women's movement. Is Rhys's relentless portrayal of passive, helpless heroines simply unpalatable to feminist critics? Or, perhaps more seriously, does Rhys's unremitting pessimism become an artistic failure that drives us to dismiss her vision despite her insight and control? Both questions, I believe, may be answered in the negative if we relinquish our expectation of a surface realism and adopt a psychological framework to explain the perversely self-destructive reactions of Rhys's heroines.

These reactions form the crux of Rhys's five novels, whose sparse and repetitive narratives are variations on the themes of failure and rejection. Although Rhys describes her heroines' progressive degeneration, often in excruciating detail, she fails to provide an adequate explanation for this process. A closer look at Rhys's recurrent heroine, however, reveals that in addition to her obvious passivity, she manifests several specific symptoms of schizophrenia: impoverished affect, apathy, obsessive thought and behavior coupled with the inability to take real initiative, a sense of the unreality of both the world and self, and a feeling of detachment from the body. Like schizophrenics, Rhys's heroines experience the world as a hostile environment and lead lives of isolation, detached from family and friends, unable to establish real contact with others. (pp. 155-56)

The particular approach to schizophrenia formulated by R. D. Laing is especially useful in analyzing the responses of Rhys's heroines. . . . Laing's insistence that schizophrenia is a legitimate and not uncommon response to certain interpersonal interactions provides a clue to understanding Rhys's heroines and thus the nucleus of Rhys's fiction. There is no question of influence here—Rhys wrote largely before Laing did—nor is the comparison directly demanded by the novels themselves. . . . Rather, Laing's account of the dynamics of schizophrenia provides a helpful framework for considering certain enigmatic features of Rhys's fiction. (p. 157)

[In *The Divided Self* Laing] describes the fundamental split that develops in the person lacking "ontological security," the sense that his or her identity is acceptable to others. Denied this basic security, a child may create a persona that conforms to parental desires and protects the "real" self from attacks on its identity. This division between a real internal self and a false external one that complies mechanically with the desires of others gradually intensifies. The real self becomes increasingly associated with the mind and the false self with the body. Because the real self attempts to remain unembodied in order to escape the threats to its identity, it tends to grow increasingly detached from concrete things. The split within the self thus leads to a secondary split between the real self and the external world, which is experienced in relation to the false self of the body and therefore as an empty and meaningless place. (pp. 157-58)

Laing's paradigm of the divided self is particularly useful in analyzing the behavior of Rhys's heroines in her middle novels, in which Rhys moves from the third-person narration of her first two novels to first-person narration by the heroines themselves, with a consequent new emphasis on the heroines' subjective lives. In *Voyage in the Dark* (1934) Rhys suggests that her heroine suffers from a sense of internal division between a responsive but covert inner self and a mechanical external one. This split is not identical to that which Laing describes: Anna Morgan's real self is the product of a happy childhood and not an escape from parental demands. Once this self is formed, however, Anna can find no way of confirming it in the England to which she moves, and it retreats within the mechanical being she becomes in response to her daily life. It is the relationship of these two selves within the person of Anna Morgan that constitutes the psychological interest of this novel, whose tale of unrequited love seems almost intentionally banal. (p. 158)

The conflict between Anna's two halves and the gradual loss of her more authentic self are mirrored in the novel's style. *Voyage in the Dark* is written in the first person, yet the tone is curiously flat and dry. When Anna remembers the past, however, the style changes in ways that suggest the qualities of her stifled inner life. At the most immediate level, these contrasts are obvious: the descriptions of the past are full of vivid adjectives, those of the present are comprised of sparse disjointed sentences that suggest both repetitiveness and lack of unity. But there are also more subtle stylistic differences, apparent in the opening pages of the novel, that help to shape our sense of Anna's different selves. The first two pages of the novel contrast Anna's recollection of her West Indian home with her impression of England. More important than the external contrast between the indistinguishably grey English towns and the varied smells and colors of the West Indies is Anna's manner of describing the two environments. When she remembers the West Indies, Anna speaks in the first person. . . . When she describes England, she speaks in the second person. . . . While the descriptions of both the West Indies and England contain long lists, these lists are subtly different. The smells that Anna recalls from the West Indies are linked associatively, such that each remembered smell recalls a different one, and the recollections blossom into a complete sensuous experience. The origin and center of the list is "what I thought about." The list describing England, on the other hand, does not originate with the self, but with the impersonal statement "There was," and each portion of the list begins with this statement understood. The list is a description not only of England, but also of Anna's experience of England, an experience comprised of discrete, repetitive units that never cohere into an organic unity and never blossom from herself. A few paragraphs later, Anna sums up her friend Maudie: "She was twenty-eight years old and all sorts of things had happened to her." . . . This is the English Anna's sense of what life is: time is additive, the self is passive, and there is no central, active "I" to unify experience. Anna's reaction to life is very much like her reaction to the book she is reading: "The print was very small, and the endless procession of words gave me a curious feeling—sad, excited and frightened. It wasn't what I was reading, it was the look of the dark, blurred words going on endlessly that gave me the feeling." . . . As Anna perceives these words deprived of any meaning that could give them shape or unity, she perceives her own experience as a list of fragments lacking any coherence. The book she is reading, appropriately enough, is *Nana,* a work that bears a clear relation to her own experience and whose title even echoes her name, but one whose author is removed from her by culture, time, and sex, and whose meaning eludes her through its endless lists of words. (pp. 159-60)

Using Laing's analysis of schizophrenia alerts us to aspects of Anna's conflicts that are buried in the narrative of her uneventful life. Perhaps Rhys's failure to develop these conflicts makes *Voyage in the Dark* one of her least engaging novels. In *Good Morning, Midnight,* Rhys probes beyond the experience of fragmentation she suggests in her earlier heroine. The progression from Anna's implicit feeling of division to the complex world of Sasha Jansen's psyche mirrors the development Laing portrays from the schizophrenic's initial sense of a divided self to the creation of a network of intrapsychic relationships that replace relationships with the external world. . . . The real action of *Good Morning, Midnight* occurs in Sasha's microcosmos, where the most important actors are Sasha's different selves and the other actors catalysts of her internal drama. (pp. 161-62)

[According to Laing] the detachment of the mental self from physical embodiment both protects it from and deprives it of contact with reality. By defining concrete interactions as the domain of the body, the mental self renounces the chance to "real-ize" itself through actual relationships. Inviolability initially offers advantages. Not constrained by the definitions imposed by concrete situations, the private self can obtain the illusion of omnipotence. In time, however, the original threat of a seemingly hostile reality is compounded by the fear that any real experience will compress the apparently transcendent self into a finite category. All action and perception must thus be experienced as belonging to the false self identified with the body: the real self can be comfortable only with the fantasies, thoughts, and memories that it creates and that consequently have no power to restrict its freedom. By remaining unembodied the inner self is safe, yet deeply impoverished. (p. 162)

Much of Sasha's inexplicably self-destructive behavior can be clarified in terms of Laing's description of the unembodied self. As threatened by affection as she is by animosity, Sasha rejects caresses as fiercely as the scraggy kitten with which she identifies. Greater than her need for human contact is her often mentioned need for a place in which to hide, the need to keep her inner self epart and undefined. . . . Paradoxically, Sasha's desire to preserve an undefined and private self alternates with her desire to assure herself of her existence, which she confirms by looking compulsively in numerous mirrors.

Sasha's attempt to preserve a self that is not identified with her body creates a dichotomous relationship with the outside world, a relationship underlined by Rhys's subtle suggestions of doubles throughout the novel: the bed for monsieur and the bed for madame, the old bald lady and her young companion, the optimistic Russian and his pessimistic counterpart, the cafe Pecanelli that becomes the Pig and Lily, the two American women and the pair of English girls, and most explicitly the painting Sasha buys of a double-headed, double-faced banjo player. To the extent that she withdraws into her unembodied self, Sasha experiences the world in terms of her own psychic state. Every aspect of the city then takes on some personal characteristic. Alternating with this flood of personal associations is a total absence of personal response, as if Sasha must dwell completely in her private mental world or be entirely subject to physical reality. (p. 163)

Rhys uses language in *Good Morning, Midnight* to emphasize Sasha's two modes of relating to reality. The basic style of the novel is paratactic: the short declarative sentences have few connective words to suggest relationships among the parts. The novel opens with a description of Sasha's hotel room in the present tense which, more than the voice of a speaker who has assimilated and ordered experience for deliberate narrative purposes, emphasizes the immediate presence of the separate objects. The description culminates significantly in the word "impasse." The next paragraph, containing Sasha's response to the scene she has described, begins with a first-person pronoun that jars against the impression of a cold objective world. But Sasha's response to her perception of her environment is to attempt to fit her life into a mechanical pattern analogous to the one she sees around her. (p. 164)

In contrast to this use of language to emphasize the fixity of physical reality, Rhys uses wordplay to characterize the subjective side of Sasha's experience. Sasha is susceptible to the suggestive power of words and at times constructs a verbal world of sounds detached from references. At these moments Sasha's thought incorporates language patterns similar to those used by schizophrenics. Although her speech is not as disorganized as the "word-salad" created by the schizophrenic's combination of words according to their personal associations, the tendency of her thoughts to develop through sounds as well as meanings recalls the "klang association," or association through sounds, that is often noted in schizophrenic speech. . . . Moreover, Sasha's language recalls that used by schizophrenics in its emphasis on the concrete nature of the words themselves. Words for Sasha occasionally take on physical reality, becoming the building blocks of an imaginary world that has its own dynamics. . . . Throughout *Good Morning, Midnight* phrases acquire an independent existence and recur in Sasha's mental world as autonomous entities which shape her thoughts as much as they are shaped by them. The fact that these phrases are often in French provides a linguistic correlative to Sasha's sense of fragmentation. (pp. 164-66)

The model of schizophrenia Laing presents in *The Divided Self* sensitizes us to nuances of Anna's and Sasha's mental processes. It does not, however, answer a fundamental question: what has reduced these heroines to such a helpless and divided state? To answer this question we must turn to a later work of Laing's, *Sanity, Madness, and the Family,* which he wrote with A. Esterson in 1964, and to Rhys's first two novels, *Quartet* (1928) and *After Leaving Mr. MacKenzie* (1931). Both sets of works are concerned primarily with the relation of the self to others rather than with the nature of the self in isolation.

In *Sanity, Madness, and the Family,* the compilation and interpretation of eleven intensive interviews with schizophrenic patients and their families, Laing and Esterson argue that the attitudes of their patients are intelligible responses to the failure of their parents to instill or support a sense of autonomy. This failure leads the child to question (or never to develop) an independent sense of self, to feel susceptible to the control of external forces, and to withdraw from the world in an attempt at self-preservation. (pp. 167-68)

All of [Laing and Esterson's] interviewees are women, yet despite the investigators' interest in the cultural determinants of schizophrenia, they fail to comment on this fact. The reader, however, may notice marked similarities between the attitudes conducive to schizophrenia in children and conventional expectations about female behavior. In each case they study, Laing and Esterson point out that the parents of their patients desired only that their daughters be passive and obedient, that they not assert themselves, and that they rely on others' authority—at most an exaggeration of cultural attitudes toward women. (p. 169)

What inferences may we draw from the apparent similarities between Laing's and Esterson's families and more pervasive attitudes? . . . [One] inference would be that there is a continuum between the general lack of confidence produced in women by cultural attitudes and the radical lack of sense of self characteristic of schizophrenia. Might it not be the case that the milder approximations of schizophrenia, or what Laing calls the schizoid state, are a more integral aspect of women's experience than of men's, are in fact an experience that many women recognize as an aspect of their lives for certain periods of time? Certainly, the recurrent themes of madness, defeat, and passivity that mark so much contemporary writing by women lends weight to the belief that women's most common experience can open almost imperceptibly into the pathological.

In this context Rhys's fiction appears less perversely pessimistic. Rhys paints an extreme picture of patriarchal society and of women's helplessness in it. This extremism is so pronounced that at times we may feel compelled to discount it as unrealistic and self-indulgent. The work of Laing and Esterson, however, may lead us to perceive that one value of this exaggeration is its revelation of the dangers implicit in the less overtly harmful facts of women's experience. (pp. 169-70)

Power is distributed unevenly in Rhys's world. The significant men in her novels have jobs, money, and consequently the power to appropriate women and discard them. The women, by contrast, are economically powerless, portrayed only as shop girls, chorus girls, or wives who buy security with subservience. For Rhys's women finding a man is a question of economic survival as well as of emotional fulfillment, and these interlocking needs reduce women to children for whom dependence is an obstacle to self-assertion. Men, who in Rhys's fiction are invariably older than the women they befriend, become parental figures through the authority accompanying economic strength. They define the values of their society, and women who question these values can find little support. The circle of women's experience that Rhys depicts is a vicious one: economic dependence induces psychological dependence and a consequent loss of confidence that reinforces the fundamental economic dependency.

Like the women interviewed by Laing and Esterson, Rhys's heroines are caught between their need for the support of parental figures and their need to preserve a sense of their identity. Rhys first explores this conflict through Marya Zelli, the young and impoverished heroine of *Quartet* befriended by the wealthy Heidlers. . . . (pp. 170-71)

Rhys explores the schizoid state more deeply in her middle novels. In her most recent novel, however, she elevates to an explicit theme the schizoid self perceptions that emerge in women's consciousness. Madness is the issue in *Wide Sargasso Sea,* Rhys's retelling of Bertha Antoinette Rochester's transformation from West Indian beauty and heiress to mad wife in the attic. The choice to make a heroine of Antoinette, who in *Jane Eyre* serves only as an obstacle to a desired marriage, is a loaded one, a reminder that behind the tale of female strength triumphant lies the parallel tale of female fragmentation. Antoinette becomes representative of women's disintegration, as Jane has been of their successful integration. Rhys endows Antoinette with symbolic resonance by focusing on her conflict with Rochester and by changing both characters from their Brontëan prototypes. Antoinette's madness may be overdetermined, but the component that derives from her relationship to Rochester is dramatized as part of an archetypal confrontation.

This confrontation, on the one hand, is a quintessential version of the male-female relationships Rhys has portrayed. Rochester . . . cannot tolerate emotional complexity in Antoinette and demands she fit his image of the proper English girl, which he constructs in part by changing her name to Bertha. Antoinette, like Rhys's other heroines, is necessarily split between the image thrust on her and her own knowledge of herself. . . . By identifying Rochester with attempted rationality and objectivity and Antoinette with intuition and subjectivity, Rhys dramatizes the interaction of two fundamentally different ways of ordering experience, and by subtly reinforcing Antoinette's perceptions, she forces us to re-examine our response to madness. Rochester may want to see things as black or white, but as Antoinette knows, a white person can be black, as she is a "white nigger." Things in *Wide Sargasso Sea* have contextual rather than absolute significance. (pp. 172-73)

In the final section of her novel, Rhys intensifies our conflict by encouraging us to believe in Antoinette's recovery while portraying her in actions that we know are "crazy" from *Jane Eyre*. (p. 174)

Why does Rhys work so hard to engage us emotionally in Antoinette's recovery of a sense of purpose? Primarily, I believe, to wedge the conflict of the novel into our own psyches, to force our intellectual and emotional responses into contradiction. Because we know objectively that Antoinette is mad, while we feel subjectively that she regains her sanity, we undergo the conflict that the novel dramatizes in its portrayal of the clashing points of view of Rochester and Antoinette, and we are forced to ask ourselves the question that the novel poses: how does one judge experience? Rhys provides no easy answer, yet she emphasizes the intuitive emotional responses traditionally considered "feminine" and associated in this novel with Antoinette and Christophine, and suggests that we may grant excessive authority to the supposedly "objective" intellectual response. (p. 175)

Rhys is a novelist, not a psychologist, and we cannot expect prescriptions about mental well-being. Nevertheless, her work suggests some pervasive attitudes about the inner conflicts of women. In both her earliest and most recent novels, Rhys suggests that the definition and reinforcement of values by men can drive women to deny their own experience, an act that lays the groundwork for a schizoid mental state. Conflict and fragmentation become increasingly explicit themes in Rhys's later fiction, reaching their most central role in *Good Morning, Midnight* and *Wide Sargasso Sea,* yet Rhys simultaneously comes to suggest some possibility of resolution. While the endings of *Quartet* and *After Leaving Mr. Mackenzie* are uniformly bleak, and that of *Voyage in the Dark* at best an ambiguous glimpse of hope for change, the endings of Rhys's last two novels leave their heroines with some feeling of wholeness, differently achieved, obviously incomplete, yet sufficiently substantial to afford some sense of resolution.

Concurrent with this partial leavening of Rhys's pessimism is her growing emphasis on women's relationships. A certain nostalgia for closeness with women marks all Rhys's novels, but it becomes more pronounced and is more often gratified in her later works. . . . The concurrence of Rhys's stress on female relationships with her willingness to imply the achievement of some personal unity may be more than coincidental. Although Rhys herself does not make this connection explicit, perhaps we can find buried in her bleak account at least a grain of hope that women's mutual affection could provide a supportive context in which experiences could be validated and denied emotions repossessed.

At best this is implicit in Rhys's stark narratives, yet it is an implication that should not be overlooked. Rhys's fiction seems grim because it describes unflinchingly a given social structure and its psychological consequences. Yet though Rhys offers no prospect of altering that structure, she does suggest some leeway in emotional responses. The spectrum of responses she portrays is a narrow one, but perhaps less narrow than a hasty reading indicates. Within her apparent determinism lie some subtle variations that a psychological framework can illuminate and clarify. Rhys's microscopic vision can shift, in the right perspective, to a microcosmic image of one aspect of women's mental lives. Rhys's scope may be small, but her perceptions are deep, and her pessimism not as final as it seems to be. To the now familiar topic of women and madness, Rhys contributes her detailed scrutiny of specific psychic mechanisms. Rhys's unremitting vision may anger or depress us, but it will illuminate us if we persevere. (pp. 175-77)

Elizabeth Abel, "Women and Schizophrenia: The Fiction of Jean Rhys," in Contemporary Literature *(© 1979 by the Board of Regents of the University of Wisconsin System), Vol. 20, No. 2, Spring, 1979, pp. 155-77.*

* * *

RICHARDS, I(vor) A(rmstrong) 1893-1979

Richards, an English critic, poet, playwright, editor, and semanticist, was one of the most influential figures in modern literary criticism. His theories uniting the principles of science and literature are fundamental precepts of formalist criticism. He also had a continuing interest in language and semantic theory which he explored in several books and essays. It was after a long career devoted to the exegesis of literature that Richards began to write poetry. His subtly rendered verse evidences his finely honed critical sense and his delight in the power and pleasure of the written word. (See

also *Contemporary Authors,* Vols. 41-44, rev. ed.; obituary, Vols. 89-92.)

ROBERT LOWELL

Goodbye Earth [Richards' first book of poetry] was begun when [he] was nearly sixty. It bristles with the difficulties of "mere mechanism," and is unique in not providing [an] exhibit of failure. . . .

Richards writing poetry is not much like the usual good critic. He doesn't wave a heavy baton, castigate the indulgences of the age, or try to build classical and exemplary models of rightness. He doesn't steel himself, entrench, and give an impression of unbelievable toils met. He is willing to be conventional, casual, and innocent, if he can be ingenious and himself. Though worlds apart from the slovenly, egotistical sprawl of the Bohemian, he glories in ingenuity. (p. 77)

[His poems] are prefaced by long, deep, and curious quotations; in the appendix, notes explain alternate meanings of words, and give more long, deep, and curious quotations. The poems themselves are loaded with steep reasoning, archaic words, technical terms, slang, special knowledges, and cunningly-exploded echoes from other literature. Often teacher, sage, idealist, and humorist huddle in one line—all elbowing and gouging for dominance. Fascinated by a poem's moments, one often has no idea what it means.

In perpetuity
Be here their prayer:
  May *may* become
  While *would* would waft
  Or let *let* be
Our sum our raft our quay.

On one level, these lines are the joyful light fingerwork of a puzzle; on another, they ache with the growing pains of apprenticeship. An almost impossibly forbidding fancy for a poem to make a prayer out of is given an almost impossibly difficult metrical hurdle. The repetitions bang, the three rhyme words in the last line have a blasé disjunctiveness, *waft* is coyly archaic, *let* seems to split into two contradictory and emotionally annihilating meanings. Even here, however, I feel an airy assurance and the amused, didactic modesty of authentic style.

About half of Richards' poems are very hard. He has a Welsh streak that loves to jangle words in the manner of Dylan Thomas and to give simple passions a dazzling crackle. Beyond this, his mind, brimming with semantics, philosophy, physics, and strange bits of information, is miraculously quick and subtle. He is perhaps the only poet since Empson who deserves to be difficult intellectually and is even forced to be. His harder poems are too jerky, twisted, and abstract to quite come off. They are pioneering drives, grappling with new, intractable material—now getting in a sure, devastating thrust, now rocking apart. Perhaps success and failure are irrelevant. What remains and matters is the gallantry and doggedness of the mind refusing to desert its customary tools and targets, its promise to stay standing in the arena of the impossible. . . .

He can put speculation, cosmic and grand enough for Lucretius, in a stanza that some late, rather Alexandrian troubadour might have invented as a problem of metrical acrobatics.

Balanced up somehow on a ball
    That spins
        And spirals
          As it plummets
Newton walked to Stourbridge Fair
   And bought his prism
That was to fell the founding wall
   Undo the
        All
   Renew the
        Fall!
        Bound through all limits
And far and here declare
   The mere abysm.

No other form could have encompassed this reasoning and given it the right tone of litheness and lightness and spellbinding daring and flat amusement. It is like attending a scientific experiment, one that can only be performed once. (p. 78)

Robert Lowell, "I. A. Richards As Poet," in Encounter *(© 1960 by Encounter Ltd.), Vol. XIV, No. 2, February, 1960, pp. 77-8.*

JAMES DICKEY

The poems [in *The Screens and Other Poems*] are about how the soul acts without appearing to, how it influences without seeming to, how it changes and doesn't change, how it makes us who we are without our ever knowing who we are. These are delicate themes, vastly complicated and perhaps impossible of solution, but Richards does very well by them, according his vast knowledge of semantics and the difficult interchanges between words, selves, and things to his subjects in poems which are really more like verse essays: speculative, logical, and refreshingly open-minded in the midst of their intelligent discourse-like approach. They are not by any means the work of a born poet, but rather the productions of a highly intelligent and dedicated bystander who has seen, late in life, that he holds a lifetime of poetic knowledge and information in his hands, and has wished to see what he could do with it on his own. This is understandable and commendable, and the difficult and modest successes of the poems are real successes. Nevertheless, I doubt that I shall give them the second and possibly other readings that they and their notes require, for Dr. Richards's verse is of a kind that I cannot for the life of me like very much. Its overingenuity seems to me just that, and this quality is, I strongly suspect, the main reason for the decline of the audience that Richards deplores in the long essay he appends to the poems. Too many potential readers think that it isn't worth all that trouble. The other few readers, those hardy ones who have their diplomas in the course, spend their time grimacing at each other like gymnasts, saying, "I can get more out of a poem than you can: more meanings, more possibilities of meaning, more extensions, more suggestions, more primary and secondary and tertiary ambiguities than you can." In answer, the poet says, "I can get more in, and some, even, that *none* of you can come at." I can't shake off the conviction that verse so written—verse like Richards's and Empson's—has done much to drive the audience underground, into the beatnik coffeehouses, with its specialized references, its recondite images from physics and semantics, its metaphors requiring knowledge of photons, tensors, and the malfunctioning of the pancreas in diabetes, all things that notes must be required to "fill the reader in" on and without which the meanings—even *one* of them—can't be grasped or even guessed at. It seems to me that the way to the audience Richards wants is through a poetry which makes available not endless subtleties to hash over in graduate seminars but poetry written with what Benn calls "primal vision": not many levels of meaning—though one can, from anything written in words, even advertisements, extract tangential connotations *ad infinitum*—but a single overwhelming one. . . . I don't want an intelligent, sensitive, and dedicated man like Richards to come down to the level of the man on the street, who is none of these things and couldn't care less. But I *am* saying that that man, who might conceivably have something to gain from poetry were he to come at it his own way through writers he could comprehend more or less quickly and then, if he wished, read later for their complexities, is likely to be and undoubtedly is repelled by an initial contact with the overrefinement of the intellect in verse, and by poetry written for only the super-intelligent, super-sensitive, and nuance-haunted audience which Richards posits, but which has not yet come into being. (pp. 180-82)

James Dickey, "I. A. Richards" (1962), in his Babel to Byzantium *(reprinted with the permission of Farrar, Straus & Giroux, Inc.; copyright © 1956, 1957, 1958, 1959, 1960, 1961, 1962, 1963, 1964, 1965, 1966, 1967, 1968 by James Dickey), Farrar, Straus, 1968, pp. 179-82.*

FRANK KERMODE

[*Internal Colloquies*] collects all Richards's verse. In one preface here reprinted he argues that there should be no discernible relation between a poet's practice and his critical theory; and although his poems (and their notes) do reflect some of his theoretical interests they are on the whole very unexpected in other ways. There is a dryness, a cerebral quality (often quite playful), which somehow lacks the tone of modernity as well as all sensuous appeal. The material is modern enough—meditations on grammar, on Wittgenstein—but the manner is Victorian. This is not simply a matter of archaism, though there's quite a lot of it. There's something about the solemn or mock-solemn teasing out of thoughts in bony, unsupple verses that takes one back a century. . . .

One of the best of these poems, 'Retort', speaks for itself as 'an empty Ought spinning itself its clew', and rather touchingly describes its mode of operation in the reader:

I sing, who nevertheless
  No accents have or breath.
I neither live nor die.
  But you, whom I possess . . .
    You, you know life and death
And throughly know; so I
What void I fill thereby.

Yet giving breath to these poems, or offering to be possessed by them, is an exhausting task. The notes, claiming to be helpful, are somewhat arbitrary. A not very important poem, 'Harvard Yard in April: April in Harvard Yard', has a commentary ten times the length of the text: others, though difficult, have no notes at all. Donnish allusions to other poems are unglossed, perhaps to avoid depriving dons of the easy pleasures of recognition. . . .

We're used to being reminded that the guides and commanders of this century's studies were nurtured in the civilisation that preceded it. Richards remembers, when he writes poetry, the great poets of his youth: he founds his verse on them as, in a sense, he founded his criticism on Coleridge and Arnold. He would be quick to point out that this does not constitute an adverse criticism: always adventurously modern, he distrusts easy modernism. His poetry, like his criticism—and perhaps his mountaineering, often celebrated in the poems—belongs to a continuous tradition, which does not exclude boldness and novelty, but will not accept them as good in themselves. Yet in stressing the 19th-century aspects of the poetry I suppose I am trying to find out why it leaves me unsatisfied (as do [his] plays, *Tomorrow Morning, Faustus!* and *Job's Comforting*). It's not that they take a bit of unravelling, nor that they lack interest. I think it must be that for all their sprightliness and the hard thinking that went into them they somehow lack genuine energy and authority—qualities we take for granted in the poet's prose. (p. 88)

Frank Kermode, "A Helping Word," in The Listener *(© British Broadcasting Corp. 1972; reprinted by permission of Frank Kermode), Vol. 88, No. 2260, July 20, 1972, pp. 87-8.*

RICHMOND LATTIMORE

I. A. Richards is a learned poet, a formal poet, a witty poet, and a philosophical poet. One thinks mechanically of "metaphysical," but I think Richards is more advanced in metaphysics (or at least epistemology, I have trouble telling which from which) than any metaphysical poet I can think of. His erudition ranges easily from the Bible and Plato through Shakespeare and Milton to Whitehead and Wittgenstein. His own philosophy and critical theory speak for themselves where he has expounded them in prose, but they live in the poetry, to which he came last. For he is the most distinguished of beginners (a published poet only since 1958) who makes many poets acclaimed as masters seem like beginners incompetent in their craft.

Technique, though vital, is not all, but it gives me a starting point. . . . If there is any such thing as "mere" technique (does Swinburne prove that there is?), there is more than that [in *Court of Appeal*]: the synoptic eye, the concentrated vividness of the snake, the texture of idea. There is much delight in word-play, for words themselves are magic pieces, and this poetry is anything but non-verbal; but the very pun-sequence can express a wry and witty pathos. . . . (pp. 303-04)

Such a chameleon nature of words accords with the whole fluid world of Richards. *Alaskan Meander,* written in elegant *terza rima,* enforces order on apparent wilful confusion; God or the world directs the wiggles. "How daunting is divine Autonomy" is how we end, echoing Milton. . . . But I find this optimism unusual. Sometimes it seems as if philosophy were nothing but a mess of cruxes, and the stuff of Richards' philosophy and of his poetry is one and the same. . . . Of his own poetry, Richards says: "Around every phrase—behind, on all sides, and ahead—there are other phrases: ready to compete or support, or recklessly bent on having their own way." Self and poetry alike are surrounded in a swarm of throwaways, discards, unwritten versions, unperformed acts and unthought thoughts, possibles, escaping dimensions. Yet the very constant dynamic failure to solve the insoluble is what generates the excitement of the quest and of the poetry. (pp. 304-06)

Richmond Lattimore, "Prospero," in I. A. Richards: Essays in His Honor, *edited by Reuben Brower, Helen Vendler, and John Hollander (copyright © 1973 by Oxford University Press, Inc.; reprinted by permission), Oxford University Press, New York, 1973, pp. 303-06.*

BERNARD F. DICK

That I. A. Richards was the progenitor of the New Criticism is now fairly well established; for the doubters [*Complementaries: Uncollected Essays*] will make it clear that as early as 1919, Richards thought of emotion as entering a work of art through a vehicle, a term that is now part of the critical vocabulary. These essays are important for another reason: they reveal an awesomely rational mind that is not afraid of schemata, equations or distinctions (art versus science, verifiable belief versus imaginative assent, the suggestion of poetry versus the coercion of prose). It is a mind much like Aristotle's, which also reveled in classifications and divisions . . . and as a result accomplished the primary task of criticism: elucidation.

The essays also include examples of practical criticism. When Richards explicates a text, he has few rivals. Serenely, he blots up all the ink that has been spilled over "Ode on a Grecian Urn" by reminding us that the urn was a burial urn and thus the poem is concerned with death and immortality. Hence the final verses, so often quoted and misinterpreted, depict Beauty and Truth as the end result of life, the culmination of Plato's ladder of ascent where Love and Knowledge become one. In a few paragraphs he solves the problem of belief in Dostoevsky by arguing that Dostoevsky had the *feelings* of religion without the corresponding *beliefs*, a tension that also recurs among his characters. . . .

Richards's critical ideas, . . . even in their inchoate form, bear the hallmark of genius.

Bernard F. Dick, "World Literature in Review: 'Complementaries: Uncollected Essays'," in World Literature Today *(copyright 1977 by the University of Oklahoma Press), Vol. 51, No. 3, Summer, 1977, p. 447.*

HELEN VENDLER

[I. A. Richards' poetry] is a poetry of speculation, taking as its subject states of mind and feeling experienced in the later years of a long life. Richards is gnomic, epigrammatic, and conclusively inconclusive: "What," "Whence," "Whither," and "Why" are the cardinal points of his compass of interrogation. "What do, what should, I want?" one poem inquires; "Why re-awaken?" asks another; "Whereto? Wherefrom?" echoes a third, thinking about Frost's two diverging roads. The persistence of questioning betrays Richards' conviction that query is still a viable form of thought. . . . One of Richards' best known "early" poems, reprinted [in *New and Selected Poems*], was called, in a very satisfying chiasmus, "Harvard Yard in April: April in Harvard Yard": it enunciates a firm, if tender, rejection of the shows of things in their classically appealing forms . . . for the "degrees of loneliness" of the thinker-spectator. The paradox of all of Richards' work in verse lies in his unshakable decision that life is a journey, with a direction, to a place, one of significance, in an hour, one of accomplishment. The mere fact that the hour does not declare itself, that the place remains indistinct, that the journey seems endless, that the results of the effort are problematic, does not in itself refute the model, but it does make the poems the work of a Tantalus. (pp. 49-50)

The new poems (1971-77) in [*New and Selected Poems*] do not depart notably from previous ones, whether in form or in concern: they maintain a metaphysical reflection on a number of subjects, ranging from an annual club dinner to political war in Ulster to a poem of W. B. Yeats. When a natural object appears—a goose here, an angler there, a fading letter on a desk—it is at once converted to emblematic use. (p. 50)

In his crabbed lines, Richards often resembles his master Hardy, ringing changes on the jests of the President of the Immortals: "*No right without a wrong . . . / No wrong without a right.*" Like Hardy, Richards engages in a defiant transvaluation of values, declaring "our dauntless Eve the original Saint" for her disobedience, and offering to canonize her. Richards' sturdy position-taking precludes a flexible verse: we do not possess for contrast any poetry from his youth, which he touchingly remembers as "my day-spring all bewilderment, so slow / Until noon toughened me to muddle through." Bewilderment and muddle alike have vanished from the uncompromisingly perplexed assertions of resistant will. (p. 51)

Competent testimony from the years after eighty is almost unheard of in literature. We may bridle at Richards' scolding of Yeats for saying "The intellect of man is forced to choose": Richards replies that the intellect is "no serf to force," and rebukes Yeats for self-pity. A poet, we think, may be allowed some self-pity; but Richards' stoic bravery forbids it, and his essentially sanguine temperament wakes, even in its ninth decade, to invent new exertions for itself:

Then re-dispose
Some lingering strength
To some old task;
Try to revive,
At length,
Some yet unshaken
Aim; regain
Or re-contrive
Some breath of morn
Reborn.

If the sense of task and aim is Miltonic, the phrases are reminiscent rather of Herbert, who, with the other metaphysicals, is echoed in these pages. . . . [The poetry his philosophy] produces arises not so much from a "new rhythm haunting the ear" (Hopkins) or "a vision" (Yeats) or a myth (Crane) or even from "a personal grudge" (Eliot) as from timeless, impersonal, and intellectually formulable questions (however deeply felt in private experience). A firm moral hope in the evolution of mind looks toward a human behavior less brutal than that now prevalent in the world, and keeps Richards' metaphysics warm. The life of the senses, when it enters the book, enters as a fleeting thing, subsumed in the strenuous or overshadowed by the life of the mind. "We, / Before the senses were / And after their despair, / Are what no eye can see." That assertive "are," independent of the senses, hangs in the invisible pre-existent Platonic life where these poems find their true home. (pp. 51-2)

Helen Vendler, "Still Journeying On," in Poetry *(© 1979 by The Modern Poetry Association; re-*

printed by permission of the Editor of Poetry), *Vol. CXXXIV, No. 1, April, 1979, pp. 49-52.*

D. ROGERS

I. A. Richards's poems are not easily read, but they repay reading. [*New and Selected Poems*] is his fourth book of poems and includes selections from the first three as well as a selection of recent work.

I do not think Richards has written better than in *Goodbye Earth* (1958). In "The Solitary Daffodil" the poet is beckoned from "committee doodled day" by "the cocktail roar." The flower welcomes him "And almost opened me a door / Through which I may still step to be / In Recollected Company." The "almost" prevents any identification with Wordsworth and underlines his modernity. To me "Lighting Fires in Snow" is a more perceptive comment on poetry than the recent "Ars Poetica." Fires are compared to poems. Both are most quickly killed by smothering. "Resign! Resign!" and "Conditional" are both from *The Screen and Other Poems* (1960). Both derive from experiences during mountain climbing. There is "no crest too tall / For our impertinence." What is gained? "The bootprint in the dust." But even that must be resigned. Climbing is a symbol for life, of which we are not bereft but which we must leave once we have lived. . . .

Richards's most recent work is, I think, too intellectually contrived to be good poetry. It lacks the spontaneity of the mountain poems.

D. Rogers, "World Literature in Review: 'New and Selected Poems'," in World Literature Today *(copyright 1979 by the University of Oklahoma Press), Vol. 53, No. 3, Summer, 1979, p. 512.*

* * *

ROBBE-GRILLET, Alain 1922-

Robbe-Grillet is a French novelist, essayist, screenwriter, and critic. In 1964 he published *Pour un nouveau roman,* a work which established the precepts of the New Novel movement. Rejecting traditional literary devices and theories as dishonest and misleading in their representation of the natural world, Robbe-Grillet proclaimed in his brilliant manifesto: "The world is neither significant nor absurd. It just is." He strives for complete objectivity in his writing and leaves the meaning intentionally ambiguous, for Robbe-Grillet wishes each reader to bring his own perceptive powers and life experiences to bear on his interpretation. Robbe-Grillet's theories and subsequent fictional works continue to be a center of controversy in literary circles. (See also *CLC,* Vols. 1, 2, 4, 6, 8, 10, and *Contemporary Authors,* Vols. 9-12, rev. ed.)

BRUCE MORRISSETTE

From the outset, the proliferation of game structures in the works of Alain Robbe-Grillet identifies this writer as a notable example of *artifex ludens.* Almost all the tendencies that were later to be termed "aspects ludiques" in his novels and films may be uncovered by careful scrutiny of his earliest productions. It is even possible to reduce the numerous game structures to a few basic models, such as the circular or winding path of individual *cases* or rectangles (like those usually found on board games played with dice), the maze or labyrinth, and the multiple-solution type of game, such as Clue, in which shuffling the cards representing characters and places allows each separate *partie,* although created out of identical elements, to lead to a totally different outcome.

The conception of a fundamentally game-like structure of the novel would make of specific games mentioned in the works, or played by the characters therein, examples of interior duplication, functioning with respect to the over-all structure in somewhat the same way as an "inner novel" (cf. *Jealousy*) or play (cf. *Last Year at Marienbad*) that duplicates, at the level of the characters, and within the fictional field, the general pattern of the novel or film. This integrative principle constitutes one type of "justification" of an actual game (as in *Marienbad*) as coherently incorporated into the esthetic structure. The literal game may be minimized, or may not appear at all; but the "metaphysical" aspect of general game structure cannot, since it is part of the novelistic technique, be avoided. It is in turn this metaphysical implication that protects the work from falling into the gratuity of a neo-Kantian "free play of the faculties" conception of fictional art which might, if pushed to the limit, reduce the creative process to a kind of esthetic billard game or acrobatic display. It is also evident that the problem of formalism in the use of game structures in novels and films has its parallels in painting (from abstract expressionism to Pop Art) and the other arts, especially contemporary music. (pp. 159-60)

In *The Erasers* (1953) Robbe-Grillet employs myth as hidden structure and establishes ingenious correspondences between myth and the semi-occult "game" of Tarot cards. Neither the myth (that of Oedipus) nor the Tarot cards are specifically mentioned in the text, and the general recognition now of their presence may be attributed to the publication of various critical essays, beginning with my own. It is now possible here to reinforce and extend my original findings, thanks to the unexpected and welcome collaboration of the distinguished surrealist critic Jacques Brunius. I had limited myself to studying more or less separately the systematic correspondences between the Oedipus myth and the plot of *The Erasers* (in which the protagonist seeks a murderer only to *become* that murderer in the end), reflected in references to an abandoned child, Thebes, the riddle of the Sphynx, Apollo's oracle, Laïus' chariot, and the like, and to parallels between traditional reading of certain Tarot cards and the fictional situations in which they occur (in hidden form) in the novel. (p. 162)

What Jacques Brunius has proposed to me . . . is the possibility of discerning in the novel certain cross-correspondences between the Oedipus Myth and the Tarot pack which would "bring out a troubling parallelism between the two perspectives on Destiny represented by Oedipus and the Tarot." The effect of these would be to further integrate the "game" aspect of the Tarot into the novel's total structure. . . . These findings do indeed create a new parallelism within the novel, and they demonstrate conclusively that the notion of game, in the sense of purely formal diversion, carries with it implications reaching all the way into the domains of archetypes and myths. True, the Tarot was rarely, if ever, played as a "pure" game, since it was used for fortune-telling and prophecy. Yet its structure and interpretative systems are game-like in their organization, and from its minor *arcanes* the pack of cards used in contemporary "empty" games has been derived.

While there are no outright or hidden references to games in *The Voyeur* (1955) and *Jealousy* (1957)—if we except such off-hand allusions as that to pin-ball machines in *The Voyeur* café scenes—, both novels show serial patternings with analogies to the general conception of game structure. . . . The entire series of 8-shaped objects and forms in *The Voyeur* is a case in point, as is the more subtle series of Y-shaped objects and designs which can be discerned in a minute reading of the text, and which are organized around the Y of the pubis and thus brought into the eroto-sadistic *gestalt* of the 8-shaped bonds, rings, and the like associated with Mathias' rape and murder of Jacqueline. Similarly, the V series of *Jealousy,* from the parquet floors to the accidental arrangement of logs waiting to be used on the footbridge, as well as the "spot" series (centipede, oil spot, grease spot at Franck's place at the table, defective spot in the window, and the like), may all be seen as an extension of a high-order game of "find the resemblance." Needless to say, this aspect of the novel is subordinated to less gamelike and more "serious" matters; but the games "that people play," like Mathias' burning of side-by-side holes with his cigarette, or like the husband's testing of the mathematical regularity of his trapezoidal banana fields, have easily recognizable psychic meanings, and find their place readily in novelistic structures that are far from constituting "mere" games.

It is *In the Labyrinth* (1959) which offers, for the first but not the last time in Robbe-Grillet's production, outright analogies with those board games that depend for their effect on multiple attempts, with advances and retreats, with side excursions into dead ends, with repeated efforts to find the "right" path to the center and win the game (in the case of the soldier in the novel, to deliver the box). The title of the work invites the comparison, and the paragraphs of the text itself often give the effect of a throw of the dice permitting no movement ("Non. Non.") or of frantic turnings from right to left (the scenes in the corridor), of arrivals in hopeless *impasses*. I have suggested that this whole pattern is metaphorical of the problem of writing this or any novel; in this view, the "game" aspect of randomness, multiplicity, and alternatives becomes allegorical of the creative process, somewhat in a Mallarméan sense. Every narrative effort is a throw of the dice, and will never abolish chance.

We now come to *Last Year at Marienbad* (1961), which could well serve as a model of game structure in novel and film. Readers will recall the world-wide reactions to this game, ranging from articles setting forth its basis in binary mathematics (or contesting this basis) to the distribution in movie houses, in New York and elsewhere, of booklets of matches with the rules of the game printed on the cover. Alain Resnais, the director, announced following the release of the film that the "Marienbad game" was a variant of the ancient "Chinese" game of Nim; it was also learned that Robbe-Grillet thought he had invented it, and that at least one angry French citizen, claiming to have both invented and patented the game, threatened to sue the producer, director, and scenarist. *Cinema 61* and *62* carried a learned debate on the mathematics of Nim. . . . Aside from the incidental interest of the game itself, the important point suggested by the existence of a mathematical theory is that Nim, both in reality and in the film, is not a "game" in the open sense, but the execution of a predetermined certainty by one familiar with its system. Obviously, only M, the husband figure, is privy to Nim's secrets in the film. . . . The antagonists X and M confront each other in two ways: in the struggle of passion to possess A, and in the duel of the mind to win at Nim (or at poker, dominos, etc.). A certain tonality of playing dice with the devil is sounded in these encounters at the gaming table. M always wins, but he "can lose," as he says, and in the end, he does; is it deliberately? (pp. 163-66)

All the games of the film, including the shooting gallery, reinforce the themes of contest domination, imposition of will upon another, even violence, that form the basis of the main action of *Marienbad*. Like the play on the château stage, the games of the film are forms of interior duplication, of *mise en abîme* in the Gidean sense, which serve not only to permit the characters themselves to take cognizance of their situations (as the statue does, for example), but to let the spectator or reader plunge deeper into the "vertical" significance of the work. (p. 166)

As for the other "games" of Robbe-Grillet's latest novel—the erotic sketches, the garden of statues, they are mostly examples of interior duplications linked in typically complicated ways to other elements in this, as well as previous works of the author.

Is the predilection for games and game structures evidence of excessive formalism in Robbe-Grillet? It would be possible to argue that . . . the creation of novels on game premises has given rise to certain tendencies in fiction leading away from the "serious" thematics (such as Sartrian *engagement,* the depiction of contemporary alienation, and the like) associated with the novel in the mind of the public. . . . [However,] game for Robbe-Grillet has come to mean structural freedom, absence of traditional rules of transition, viewpoint, chronology, and other parameters of previous fiction, and, on the constructive side, an invitation to create new models, to develop new combinations, to push ahead even further the aptly termed *nouveau roman.* (p. 167)

Bruce Morrissette, "Games and Game Structures in Robbe-Grillet," in Yale French Studies *(copyright ©* Yale French Studies *1968), No. 41, 1968, pp. 159-67.*

BEN STOLTZFUS

Robbe-Grillet, for all his disavowals, writes novels and films that are simultaneously useful and useless. Like the *Tel Quel* group, he rejects Sartre's insistence that the artist be committed to a cause beyond art. Art for the "nouveaux romanciers" is, in and of itself, a sufficient cause, and the artist, they feel, need not search for political or social involvement beyond his work. But unlike that of the "nouveaux nouveaux romanciers" Robbe-Grillet's art, even though it is reflexive and does explore the ramifications of the creative process, is, in spite of itself, rooted in reality. It is not a pure exercise in language or optics or structure. While the proponents of non-objective art may claim him, death and eroticism, as two of Robbe-Grillet's main themes, relate too strongly to the world (even though they may not be intended to mirror it), not to involve us in a relationship which postulates interaction. Robbe-Grillet's art occupies a middle ground somewhere between Sartre's extreme commitment of words to reality and the equally extreme linguistic hermeticism of the *Tel Quel* group. . . .

In *Le Voyeur* Robbe-Grillet imagines Mathias; Mathias imagines the seduction of Jacqueline. Robbe-Grillet imagines the doctor in *Dans le labyrinthe;* the doctor imagines the city maze of Reichenfels through which the soldier endlessly walks. Robbe-Grillet imagines Marienbad and his male lead invents a meeting "last year." Robbe-Grillet puts his characters on the Trans-Europ-Express where they invent their roles and adapt them to the continuously shifting demands of each hour, each new encounter, and each new complicating circumstance. Hence all the contradictions, which are not contradictions because everything is imaginary to begin with. *L'Homme que ment* is about a man who may or may not be telling the truth. It really does not matter and ultimately we do not care whether the things he says or imagines are true or not. What does interest us, if it interests us at all, is the process itself, since we are being asked to watch the imagination build its own reality and then destroy it. (p. 347)

Robbe-Grillet's novels of the 1950's, innovative as they were, evolved from a literary tradition which, for the most part, had gone unnoticed, and which only now, within the last decade, has been defining itself. Robbe-Grillet's work has obliged us to revalue earlier writers going as far back as Flaubert and Diderot's *Jacques le fataliste*. (p. 348)

The signs of *La Nausée, L'Étranger,* and *L'Emploi du temps* have familiar, identifiable, referents in the outside world. The signs of *Dans le labyrinthe* also seem to signify familiar things, but in doing so they serve only to entrap the wandering soldier. He becomes lost in a maze of familiar things which he expects to mean something, but which in fact are disorienting, as the author-protagonist explores one street after another, one dead-end after the next, opens doors that lead nowhere, ascends, descends staircases that, as in a Kafka novel, will never lead him to the place where he is supposed to meet the father. In spite of the fact that the messenger has forgotten the name of the street, the time of the rendezvous, and the name of the man he seeks, he walks compulsively in search of that elusive something that will provide him and the reader with some shred or thread of continuity out of the labyrinth of confusion. The soldier wanders through the city of Reichenfels in which necessary points of reference have vanished. Something is being signified, but the signifiers have disappeared. In due course the trapped soldier dies trying to deliver the enigmatic shoebox.

What has happened? It is as though the eternal minotaur has become the "connivence tragique" of language and things, a metaphoric alienation that would humanize an inhuman world in which objects and signs are merely "there" signifying nothing. The signs of this novel, therefore, have a double purpose and carry a double meaning. They refer the soldier and the reader to a seemingly familiar world of objects, streets, and places. However, when these are perceived as false, the novel turns back upon itself so that its conative, emotive, metalingual message . . . becomes reflexive, a structured internal meaning whose code orients the receiver, i.e., the reader, toward internal referents which seem to be either linguistic or affective. Language, says Robbe-Grillet, more specifically, metaphors which humanize and anthropomorphize our environment are responsible for its contamination and man's alienation.

In *Le Voyeur,* for example, the figure-eight imprint on the levy, in the center of which is the piton with its rusty excrescence, assumes significant sexual overtones for Mathias. He is fascinated with a crumpled blue cigarette wrapper floating on the water and the long detailed descriptions of its motions reveal the importance Mathias attributes to it. The wrapper—or more precisely cigarettes—is Mathias' image of violent sexual fantasy and desire. His eyes roam selectively and subjectively from the figure eight to the cigarette wrapper to sensual configurations of seaweed revealed when the water recedes from the rocks, back to the blue paper wrapper which emerges from the waves with the sound of a slap and is associated with the blue pack of cigarettes seen that morning in a bedroom of imagined violence. Figure eights are multiplied in their associations to include knots on doors, eyeglasses, cigarette holes in paper, the black holes of eyes, and presumably the burns on the genitalia of past, present and imaginary fictions. Robbe-Grillet has insisted that objects have no inherent symbolism, but he does not exclude their catalytic impact on an imagination that may precipitate actual or imagined crimes.

To say that waves "slap" against the rocks is an example of linguistic contamination, the type of tragic complicity Robbe-Grillet denounces. How then does he purify language, fumigate it, decontaminate it? Robbe-Grillet's ambiguous answer is to write novels like *Le Voyeur* and *La Jalousie* in which metaphor has been replaced by metonymy, novels in which language seems cleansed of metaphors, but is in fact as contaminated as ever, since contiguous descriptions of objects, in due course, begin to "ooze" violence or jealousy. . . . *Dans le labyrinthe* belongs to both worlds, the internal and the external, hence its hypnotic mood and extraordinary power. It can be read as a metaphysical allegory or as a self-reflexive novel.

In *La Maison de rendez-vous* the narrative voice moves back and forth in time: it remembers, imagines, observes, and most frequently, "plays" with different and contradictory possibilities. . . . Symbolic labyrinth or brothel, *La Maison de rendez-vous* is more than a place of encounter for clandestine relationships. It may be also the house of the author's imagination, or ours, or everybody's. It may well be the spot where objective and subjective reality meet, where illusion creates its own reality, where the play within the play's the thing. This novel is a house of encounter for many people and many things, not the least of which is the exploration of the artist's creative process.

Robbe-Grillet's exploration of the creative process reveals, as a corollary, a profound distrust of reality. Nor is it merely a reality that is in a constant state of flux. As a creator of fictions, he is asking his readers to believe in them, yet at the same time he negates the right to believe. He builds the reality of his fiction and then he destroys it. The unwary reader, like the soldier of *Dans le labyrinthe,* is now lost in the maze of the city. False streets, false doors, and false stairways are the labyrinth through which the creative process struggles to assert itself. But this game bears a strange resemblance to life because in the final analysis it is also a mirror of uncertainty, chaos, flux, and violence—those frequent reminders of the harsh world we are so well acquainted with. Any attempt to give Robbe-Grillet's art a solipsistic independence is bound to fail. Or perhaps it succeeds too well. Because if his art is only a game, a game which in spite of itself mirrors the sublimity of the absurd, or a game which the creator and his characters are free to play at will, and whose parts are interchangeable (as *Trans-Europ-Express* demonstrates so neatly), then language, words, or pictures are never only just what they are, but forever, in spite of "pure" intentions, will involve man in the world from which they claim to be autonomous.

Nevertheless, Robbe-Grillet's fiction casts doubt, not only

on the world which claims our attention, but also on itself as signifying something. In the second part of *Le Voyeur,* for example, Mathias "sur le double-circuit" spends most of his time trying to destroy the evidence of rape and murder that he has left behind. But in the third part Robbe-Grillet, the author, seems to be erasing the reality of the first two in order to focus our attention on the novel as pure creation—on the novel as object. If this is "the age of suspicion," as Nathalie Sarraute claims it is, then the only dimension of Robbe-Grillet's fiction that is not in doubt is the language itself. It is this indirect emphasis on the novelist's individual *parole* which, after *process,* makes the work of art reflexive, and in Robbe-Grillet's case, ultimately, poetic. (pp. 350-52)

[According to Roman Jakobson], in any work of literature, the discourse may move from topic to topic according to relationships of similarity, i.e., metaphor, or of contiguity, i.e., metonymy.

To reflect on the novel *La Jalousie* is to see it primarily in metonymic terms. Whenever the husband sees, imagines, or describes a centipede and its corollary, the stain, the reader, in due course, appropriately, substitutes the word or the feeling "jealousy." There is a signifier, *centipede,* and a signified concept, *jealousy:* this is its denotation. But since the word *centipede* or the descriptive paragraph identifying it has been substituted for the idea of *jealousy,* the relationship between the signifier and the signified can be defined as a *figure.* (p. 353)

Why do we have metonymy instead of metaphor? The answer depends on interpreting (i.e., providing the missing link) the contiguous metonymic signs: centipede-jealousy; sportscar-woman; driving-the sex act; car crashing into tree and bursting into flames-sexual climax, etc. . . . The protagonist's mind, his "temps mental," which is also the reader's "temps mental," filters all "reality" through the emotion of jealousy. Jealousy, then provides the *gestalt* for the sexual connotation of the images and the events described.

Everything that is seen, heard, imagined, and remembered is part of the poem which . . . meanders, stops, starts, retraces itself according to its own, invisible, yet for us clearly identifiable laws—laws of jealousy whose signs Robbe-Grillet has posted along the way: objects, descriptions, juxtapositions, associations that seem to define a process at work—the jealous mind objectified, rendered visible. The subjectivity of the mind has been exteriorized, as though a subconscious process had been identified and labeled. . . . The reader provides the missing links and, in so doing, recreates not only the jealous process which is the consciousness of the husband, but also the intention of the novelist himself. Once again the novel turns in upon itself and, like *Finnegans Wake,* has become reflexive. *La Jalousie* is a reflexive novel of process that is now also a poem.

As for the objects of *La Jalousie,* contrary to Robbe-Grillet's theoretical pronouncements, they have not been cleansed. The centipede, a blue piece of paper, a calendar on the wall, the sound of a car at night, like rusty pitons, blue cigarette wrappers, and slapping waves in *Le Voyeur,* act as catalysts to the husband's sensitized and susceptible mind. In this sense the husband, Mathias, Meursault, and Roquentin are kindred souls. . . . Where Sartre and Camus use metaphor to define tragic complicity ("la connivence tragique"), Robbe-Grillet uses metonymy. Nevertheless, like its predecessors, *La Jalousie* is a novel of process, only more so. Names disappear, faces disappear, characterization is even sketchier, and time circular. (pp. 353-54)

Robbe-Grillet's *parole,* the structure of *La Jalousie,* as in all his novels, focuses on its formal properties, away from referential significance. Nevertheless, the fascinating aspect of his work is that it can always be read on at least two levels. The descriptions are realistic . . . , but the novels themselves, in their total effect, call attention to their lack of realism, to their imaginary, self-willed dimension, to the fact that they signify the mind at work, the imagination, the creative process as pure invention, as poetry.

The meaning of Robbe-Grillet's books, and particularly his first, *Les Gommes,* is now much clearer than it used to be. All the contradictions of the novel: the detective who is a murderer; Wallas who has a double, named V. S.; the murder which is not a murder and which, although it apparently occurred at the beginning, occurs at the end; all the minute contradictions of reality—a reality which is at first constructed and then destroyed—are abolished by the creative process which effaces one possibility after another. Hypothetical possibilities also represent the artist's alternate choices. Since the work of art is, for the moment, the only admissible reality, many choices are possible, even contradictory ones. (p. 355)

According to Robbe-Grillet, every fiction is the story of a gamesman in a quicksand world who is continuously reinventing himself. Robbe-Grillet's art is, in fact, the mirror of constantly shifting and contradictory realities. The "man who lies" is therefore the main character and metaphor of such fiction. Not only is reality suspect, but all art as well, particularly that conventional art which is supposed to mirror a stable reality. But a novel which constructs itself and then questions its right to exist, abolishes itself, leaving us with the ontological void described in Sartre's *L'Etre et le néant.* (pp. 355-56)

It may be useful, finally, to distinguish between the traditional novel which depicts "life," the "nouveau roman" which pictures life and the novel itself, alternately, and the "nouveau nouveau roman" which is completely reflexive, picturing only itself. While Robbe-Grillet's novels may be self-reflexive, and like . . . non-objective paintings . . . be on the verge of abstraction, they always somehow, in spite of themselves, by virtue of their ambiguity, do finally signify more than themselves. Robbe-Grillet's *parole* is not purely formal and its referents are not exclusively within the work of art. . . . The silence of Robbe-Grillet's dreamlike constructions is, after all, our silence. The hesitant, circuitous patterns of his novels and of his protagonists' desires, lies, and imaginings are in large measure our own. The voyeurism of his early works and the sado-eroticism of his recent ones gives us a variety of "glissements progressifs du plaisir" between life and art, the real and the unreal, prose and poetry, bondage and freedom. Such is the ambiguity of Robbe-Grillet's Art as it objectifies itself while defining its essence, subjectively. (p. 356)

Ben Stoltzfus, "Alain Robbe-Grillet: The Reflexive Novel as Process and Poetry," in Symposium *(copyright © 1976 by Syracuse University Press), Vol. XXX, No. 4, Winter, 1976, pp. 343-57.*

ALWIN L. BAUM

In the fictional context of the *nouveau roman,* the problem of critical analysis is . . . compounded by the mediation of the object in language and its concomitant over-determination in the superimposed itineraries of narrative events, along with the necessity of demystifying the relation between subject and object, the signifier and the signified. . . .

Robbe-Grillet's first two novels, *Les Gommes* (1953) and *Le Voyeur* (1955), presented to the reading public a surface ambiguous enough to provide grounds for the most sardonic condemnations and the most elaborate apologetics. [Roland] Barthes was quick to recognize that the *nouveau roman* represented not merely a novel aesthetic, but that it attempted to revolutionize the hermeneutics of traditional fiction through its fidelity to the *ethos* of the world-as-object, a "degree zero" of extratextual signification. (p. 558)

That Robbe-Grillet had anticipated the value of a phenomenal *poétique,* even before the publication of his first novel, is evident in an essay on Beckett's *Waiting for Godot* [see *CLC,* Vol. 10], which he reads as a parable of Heideggerian *Dasein,* the dilemma of simply being there. And in his subsequent reflections on his own novels, Robbe-Grillet argues for a decontamination of the image from all psychological or cultural associations and for a consequent liberation of the text from critical expropriation. Those elements in his novels that shatter the window of interpretation may be swept under the carpet of the absurd, he observes, "but the world is neither significant nor absurd. It *is,* quite simply. . . . (p. 559)

Responding to critics who had condemned the anti-humanism implicit in the novels, particularly in *La Jalousie,* Robbe-Grillet admits that he may have gone "too fast"; that there existed no more than a "loose parallel" between his theories and the novels, after all; and that it was easier to indicate a new direction than to follow it, without an *échec*—a partial or even total impasse—constituting "a decisive, definitive proof of the error committed at the outset." (p. 560)

A narrative that records only what is seen and imagined by the narrator could scarcely avoid "complicity" with the object; indeed, the narrative objects and events could not exist without the mediating presence of his consciousness. *La Jalousie* constitutes a tour de force of Berkeley's cardinal axiom, *esse est percipi,* since there is nothing in the novel that may be presented to the reader without first being "seen" by the narrator-husband, and nothing he sees can remain uncontaminated by his consciousness.

Robbe-Grillet's fictional strategy may approximate Husserl's "eidetic reduction," or *epoché*—the bracketing of all presuppositions about existents and their conditional qualities—but it is bound to run into the same impasse that led Husserl to abandon the search for the thing-in-itself in favor of analyzing its *eidos,* its "essential" modes of being-in-consciousness. . . . [The] object may only "present itself" as a function of consciousness. This is, of course, the most familiar paradox in the metaphysical tradition, and the one from which phenomenology originally derived its rationale. . . . (p. 561)

If phenomenology has moved away from Hegel's elaboration of self-consciousness as a simulacrum of the universe, it had merely traced the arc of an infinitely long pendulum. . . . If the pendulum continued to . . . [move] back toward the fictional end of its arc, it would discover that narrative consciousness may only penetrate the "secret heart of things" at the risk of penetrating into itself, since the boundaries of the object are those of consciousness itself. It is from such a pendulum that Robbe-Grillet's heroes can be found dangling, most particularly because of the role played by the relativity of time and space in the collapse of Self and Other throughout the narratives and because of the role played by the relativity of language. If the whole of the fictional tradition has failed to scratch the surface of the object, it is because no object can appear in narrative without becoming *image,* and the *Dasein* of image can only be mapped-out by the omnipresence of consciousness at the crossroads of *eidos* and *logos.* It is the inherent duplicity of language, its overdetermination, that cuts into the secret heart of things in Robbe-Grillet's novels.

Even that most literal and objective scene in *La Jalousie*—the counting of the banana trees—could best be seen as a mirror image of the Berkeleyan forest which constitutes the husband's state of mind, its ellipses and retracings, its obsession to re-establish the continuity of an existence disrupted by jealousy, its hesitation and uncertainty over the suspicious evidence. The audit of the trees could, perhaps, constitute a mere distraction for the husband—a less disturbing sight, for example, than his recent vision of his wife in her bedroom reading her lover's letter—but it would be a *motivated* perception, even then, a reflection of his avoidance of pain. It is in this sense alone that the novel preserves a kind of narrative sequence, a chronology, but it is one governed purely by psychological resistance or association.

Of course, Robbe-Grillet deliberately avoids all conventional marks of transition from actuality to memory to fantasy, all verb tenses which would indicate the time of the episode, all qualifying adjectives and adverbs which would attest to the narrator's ubiquitous sentience and sentiment. There does seem to be a vacuum in the language of the text left by the absence of these *signes-du-narrateur,* but it is one which is essential to Robbe-Grillet's sense of an "actual" stream of consciousness as opposed to the "speaking consciousness" of Joyce's narrator, for example, whose language is full of the qualitative indices that signify a colloquy with the reader. The apparent artificiality of Robbe-Grillet's narrator derives from his nearly absolute silence, in his relation to the other characters and to the reader as well. It is a silence motivated in general, however, by the phenomenological assumption that any consciousness in progress would necessarily take its own presence and its own voice for granted. But that consciousness is never more in evidence than when it is absent. (pp. 561-62)

[The] space occupied by the surface of the text can only be the same space occupied by the intentional consciousness of the narrator—and the same *time.* . . . [The] actual development of scenes is juxtaposed with those the narrator "recalls, recreates, or even imagines." These two levels of action would seem to be only logical. The husband's jealousy would have to result from some actual set of events . . . [episodes which] would provide sufficient motivation, and one could assume they actually happened at some time, while the recurrent "distorted" versions of the same scenes could be attributed to the husband's growing jealousy.

The question is, when did they occur originally, and in what order? In the case of recurrent scenes, the solution is deceptively simple, since memory works in only one direction. Unless the husband is clairvoyant, only the first occurrence of each episode could constitute the actual event; all recurrent scenes would have to be considered memories, subject to the husband's fantasized elaborations. Consequently, the sequence of actual events would be relatively easy to reconstruct by mapping the first occurrences of each scene in chronological order. . . . But if [the itinerary thus determined] were the sequence of actual time, one would have to suppose that the husband's jealousy developed overnight, as it were, on the slightest pretext. (pp. 563-64)

[Any] of the repetitions could be taken for a similar occasion rather than a memory of a unique event. Naturally, Robbe-Grillet insures that each recurrence varies in some detail, and since most of them are routine activities, it is always ambiguous whether a particular episode constitutes another occasion or a memory. On the other hand, he makes sure that there are sufficiently identical details among those repeated scenes. I should say, identical *sentences,* since it is always a question of that subliminal presence of language, sequestered between the lines of *La Jalousie*. To assume that the same physical details could recur in the narrator's perception is one thing; it is another to assume that an identical phrase would be repeated, either in the fragments of "overheard" dialogue, or in the sentences of narrative description. The most ironic of these, of course, serves to mark at once the beginning and final scenes of the novel—*Maintenant l'ombre du pilier* ("Now the shadow of the column"). In essence, it is the sole pillar needed to support the chronological edifice of the text, since it marks time only in relation to the phenomenological cycle of narrative events. (pp. 564-65)

The ultimate Hegelian paradox in the novel is that what is true for the phenomena of the narrator's perception must also be true for the husband-as-object, his existence is equally dependent upon what he sees and what sees him. The itinerary of objects in the narrative can serve only as the mirror of his *conscience,* in the double sense; and the absolute rule of consciousness is that it has no opposite, one can never be un-conscious. The ellipses are all atemporal—they mark shifting trains of association. If the husband exists in "actuality," his life can last only as long as the events he describes. The narrative is as timeless as the *maintenant* with which it begins; it can be considered a single event, a phenomenon, in the literal sense. (p. 565)

Because the field of the husband's perception is confined only by the reach of his imagination, and because he is never unconscious, he can find himself only in a universe of his own making whose center is wherever he happens to be. And each perception is equally weighted with significance because its significance is constituted in its relation to all others—not merely the actual, but all of the possible moments of self-perception. The time of the narrative unfolds, consequently, on the metaphoric rather than the sequential plane. And what is true of time is equally true of space: it is significant only in its refusal to measure the distance between subject and object. (p. 566)

In the wake of several critical attempts to reappropriate a chrono-logic in *La Jalousie,* [Robbe-Grillet] admits that he had made such a reconstruction impossible. It was not a "whimsical shuffling of calendar time" in order to deceive *l'académie,* he reveals, but merely an attempt to demonstrate that the only order possible for the novel is that of its sentences: "the unfolding of a story which had no other reality than that of the narrative, a development which functioned nowhere else than in the mind of the invisible narrator, that is, of the writer, and of the reader."

It should be expected that this *poétique* merely exposes itself more insistently in *La Jalousie,* which has served as a crossroads in the development of the *nouveau roman*. It begins with Robbe-Grillet's first novel, *Les Gommes*. Here, the role of the column's shadow is played by the hero's watch. It stops, presumably at seven-thirty, when the action begins, and starts ticking again during the moment of the murder, the paradoxical denouement of the action. . . . As in *La Jalousie,* all of the episodes of the *histoire* are circumscribed by the same event and thus are compressed into the space of a split-second, the trajectory taken by the assassin's bullet. Of course, Robbe-Grillet deliberately confuses the identities of the victim, the assassin, and the detective in keeping with the ambiguity of time occupied by each of the murders at the perimeters of the novel. He thereby throws into question the actuality of all "intervening" events. But the interfusion of time and identity is no more arbitrary here than it is in *La Jalousie*—it functions to suggest that the only space where overlapping or mutually exclusive identities may coexist is that of a single consciousness. (pp. 567-68)

Indeed all the characters appear *de trop*. Dupont is at once victim and assassin, Albert Dupont as well as Daniel Dupont. Wallas is the special agent sent out to apprehend the assassin only to find himself become the victim, Dupont, or the murderer himself, depending upon the light in which one reads the final scene of the action. . . . Suddenly the skein of narrative journeys collapses, the identities staked out in each become superimposed. Like the paths traced by two cosmic worms eating their way through the einsteinian apple of the universe, those followed by Wallas and Dupont become one without ever having intersected until this moment. That intersection also collapses the *Dasein* of existences differentiated in time. Wallas, who has experienced flashbacks of a search for his father throughout the narrative, finds in the end that it is his own father (or himself at another time—in another *histoire*) whose essence is usurped by the confluence of their respective quests. (pp. 568-69)

That the quest for [the] eraser, which reappears in several of Robbe-Grillet's narratives, should be coterminous with Wallas' quest for his father's assassin is, of course, also a deliberate parody of the myth of narrative illusion. Like the indelible mark of the centipede in *La Jalousie,* the eraser becomes a talisman which reveals the narrative as a conjurer's trick, giving the illusion of linear progression through a "sequence" of simultaneously occurring alternatives of the action. . . . Like the photograph of the tableau in the window (a parody of mimesis remarkably similar to René Magritte's surrealist canvases), the eraser serves as a palimpsest upon which are brought into coexistence the past and the present, the mythical and the actual *histoires*. It cannot erase one or the other completely; traces of each remain, superimposed, as indeed they must in the reader's consciousness once the association has been made. A similar association of identities is occasioned in the surfacing of the eraser throughout the narrative, and in its wake trails again the question of narrative consciousness which finds metaphorical expression throughout this novel in the riddle of the sphynx. (p. 569)

As we might expect from any detective novel, it is the least suspicious consciousness that is invariably guilty of authoring the crime. In *Les Gommes* the role is fulfilled by *le patron* of the "Prologue." . . . It is *le patron,* in the double sense of "proprietor" and "pattern," who is again discovered in the "Epilogue," his massive body leaning on outspread arms, still staring with a twisted smile into the mirror-aquarium of his reflections, which are filled with floating images and spectres "from fifty years of badly digested existence." There can be little doubt that this flotsam serves doubly as the imagery of the text; that *le patron* is at once the editor and the author of the scenes of the novel; that the eraser best serves as the instrument of narrative choice—erasing now one episode, now another—always leaving behind the traces of each actuality and the anticipation of other possibilities; that the "time which sees all" of the prefatory note discovers, finally, the only possible solution to the riddle in the riddle itself.

It makes little difference that *le patron* is not completely alone in these scenes, that his actions are being observed by another narrator. Not until *La Jalousie* will the "efficient cause" and the "sufficient cause" of the narrative coincide in the sense of that *roman sur rien* dreamed of by Flaubert. It may be ironic, moreover, but it could scarcely be considered unfaithful to a genuine phenomenal poetics to present the author of the narrative *Dasein* with a mere walk-on role in it—dreams, films, and waking experience alike lend ample precedent to illustrate that the "subject" must be first the perceived. It is merely an illusion anyway since this is narrative, and the language of the entire text must reflect an image of a singly intentional consciousness, ubiquitous and omniscient behind all the protean disguises of his fictional discourse. The discrepancy between the proprietor and the "outside narrator" finds its rationale in the irony which obtains between the dreamer and the dreamed, the self-image of the perceiver as it plays across the mirrors of the "Other." It is the paradoxical discrepancy between consciousness and self-consciousness, the author and the text. (pp. 569-70)

This self-reflection, so obviously parodic, recurs in practically every line of the novel; even where it is not self-evident it exists between the lines, silhouetting the author's image in the interstices. It is Robbe-Grillet who arises from the tomb of the text, enshrouded in its *parole*. He is Wallas, playing the detective role worthy of Poe's Auguste Dupin, sequestering the solution to the riddle in the obvious by inverting the envelope of the text. In his search for the center of the city, which doubles for the center of the narrative, Wallas comes across a poster which he has seen throughout the country. . . . (p. 570)

This poster looks forward to the one which surfaces throughout the course of *Le Voyeur,* serving in its different guises to record the scene of the crime and the *scène-du-texte* . . . Along with the erasure of boundaries between hero, narrative, author, and reader, [Robbe-Grillet] erases those between his own novels, causing the fictional discourse to collapse in a confusion of intersecting images. "Trying to decipher the entanglement of curves and angles [in *Le Voyeur*], Mathias no longer recognizes anything—he is even incapable of establishing if there were actually two different superimposed images, or else a single image, or even a greater number." And when he steps back to get a better view of the whole, like the old man in *Les Gommes,* he finds merely a flux of representations changing and incomprehensible.

This *affiche* is indecipherable precisely because it is a simulacrum of the *paysage* of the narrative, a palimpsest of intertwining itineraries and overlapping images which call attention to the overdetermination of consciousness and to the endlessness of its modifications. As in all of Robbe-Grillet's novels, this is the narrative of a single consciousness. . . . If there exists a slight discrepancy between the narrator's point of view and that of Mathias, it cannot be considered grounds for a narrative duality, evidence for a distinction between the imaginary and the actual. The sole *voyeur* is the author—in actuality, the reader—who sees everything as it is, in itself. The sole time is that of the narration, the reading time, the six hours' itinerary through narrative consciousness which must double back upon itself like the figure-eight insignia of infinity that serves to structure the journey. The best metaphorical agent of authorial presence is Mathias as child, sitting at his desk looking out of the window at a seagull which he sketches. Aside from forming a convenient portrait of the artist, it collapses the space of time and identity separating Mathias and the child . . . and it serves at the same time to reveal the superimposition of the perceiver and the perceived. The child's collection of strings, coiled into figure-eights and kept in a box, is a model of the novelist's collection of narrative possibilities, the phenomena of the text.

The danger in this self-reflexive freeplay is that it might come full circle and seal the lid on its own tomb. Yet it could scarcely choose not to unmask itself as object. For the novel to pretend to be anything other than narrative would fictionalize the phenomenal interrelations of the consciousnesses which brings it into being. Robbe-Grillet thus attempts to dispel that pathetic fallacy which artificially differentiates the *histoire* within the text from the *histoire* of the text, and by implication, subject from object, the sign from its referent. The *nouveau roman* is thus obligated to record not only the narrator's visions but the author's revisions as well, since they are one and the same. (pp. 571-72)

If it was difficult to discern the *poétique* of self-actualization in Robbe-Grillet's early novels, the appearance of *Dans le labyrinthe* (1959) stripped away the last shreds of the veil from the metanovel. . . . *In the Labyrinth* merely uncovers the narrator, at his desk behind the velvet curtains that hide the window in front of him, at work on the novel which, describing the world "outside," comes into being as he writes. Yet here, too, the author must remain invisible. His presence is intuited only as the subliminal center of the infinite layers of association triggered in his perception of objects lying around him in his room. (pp. 573-74)

The novel . . . thrusts a mirror between the traditional semantic dualism of sign and referent—since the world signified by the fictional signifier is also fictional, it can admit no actuality outside itself. Robbe-Grillet goes a step further to argue that because it is the representative of all signs, language can have no signification outside itself, nothing is exterior to it. Following this logic, one would have to conclude with Robbe-Grillet that the narrative image is more real *because* it is imaginary; that is, because it demystifies the impasse between the imaginary and the real. Robbe-Grillet's invisible narrators are confronted everywhere with the problem of decoding a universe they have created. The implication of the texts is that there is no reality outside of the affabulation of consciousness, no truth which is not a fiction. (pp. 574-75)

Alwin L. Baum, "The Metanovel: Robbe-Grillet's Phenomenal 'Nouveau Roman'," in boundary 2 *(copyright ©* boundary 2, *1978), Vol. VI, No. 2, Winter, 1978, pp. 557-75.*

R. BARTKOWECH

In his first novel in almost seven years [*Topology of a Phantom City*], Alain Robbe-Grillet, spokesman and practitioner of the new novel (*nouveau roman*), conjures up the destroyed city of Vanadium. Using old and new tools "the city once more rears up . . ."—a city of both old and startlingly new forms. An archeologist (David G.? the narrator? the reader?) digs through abandoned rooms and endless corridors, "unrecognizable fragments of what were palatial homes, public buildings . . . houses of prostitution. . . ." (p. 11)

Topology begins with a section entitled "Incipit" (Latin, "It begins") and ends with a "Coda." Except for similar moves in *The Erasers* . . . , with its Prologue and Epilogue, and in *Jealousy* . . . , where, on the first page, we find "titles" for the eight sections, this is Robbe-Grillet's first novel whose text is stopped again and again with individually named chapters. Apropos of archeology, however, we are not given *chapters* but, instead, five "spaces." (pp. 11-12)

There are probably more V's in *Topology* than any single piece of writing to date. Most of the buildings we uncover are triangular—three V's at once! (One has to wonder why the author made no use of *vector*.) . . .

If Robbe-Grillet is digging through the rubble of his past work, what can be salvaged? What can be conjured up? Simply a topology of old structures? . . .

Some of the old tools we find here are the repetition of phrases and "confusions" (the "same" event happening again differently), impaled virgins, and general sadomasochistic episodes (women chained with iron bracelets, assassins dressed in black, gleaming stilettos plunged into white, supple breasts—all recalling earlier works, for example *La Maison de Rendezvous* and "The Secret Room"). . . .

Having a play performed within the action of the novel (here, "The Birth of David"), or employing stage-setting directives, is also a familiar technique, one he used in *Last Year at Marienbad* . . . , *La Maison, Project for a Revolution in New York,* and *Jealousy*. . . . In *Topology* we find cameras, pictures, drawings, and paintings, all described to set (and enact) scenes; we experience temporal reversals and overlaps (effected through his characteristic present tense grammar). Once again we are confronted with intentional "inaccuracies" and ambiguities." . . .

In a startling turn, he makes direct references to many of his past novels. Is Robbe-Grillet playing with his critics and/or his established reading audience? Perhaps he simply plans to "help us out"—with some *new* tools! . . .

The author's employment of language also marks a new turn in this work: the strange, illusive transitions of scenes; the addresses to and remarks about "the narrator," "the reader," "the dreamer," "the listener"; the looseness of his language resulting in sentence fragments, language rhythms. But what might be the two most striking contradictions to his past premises of the *nouveau roman* are his use of myth and poetic voice. Myth, one could safely argue, breeds depth, something Robbe-Grillet has come out strongly in opposition to.

Yet we find not only a myth related within the novel, but many scenes paralleling it. And it is difficult to see how poetic voice can yield anything *but* poetic vision—vision at least in most cases committed to a depth of things. . . .

Lest we think Robbe-Grillet out of control, he straightens us out: "We've had enough of outings into the country, voyages, adjectives, and metaphors. We tried that for fun; it wasn't much fun. We change." And later, the foliage of the vast, abandoned forest surrounding the impossibly large dwelling beats at the panes of the windows "like some sly sea alive with adjectives and metaphors, poised to swallow you up." Yet and still further on, in the "Coda," we are swimming once again in poetic voicings. Is Robbe-Grillet playing with us?

We might criticize this book in terms of the discrepancies it sets up between theory and practice. Speaking out against the metaphor in *For a New Novel* (essays on fiction), Robbe-Grillet states, "Metaphor is never an innocent figure of speech," and "metaphor is almost always a useless comparison which contributes nothing new to the description." In the same book we read, "*All* analogies are just as dangerous." Against myth and depth he says that "trying to define the direction of a still tentative development in the art of the novel, I described as a constant factor 'the destitution of the old myths of depth,'" and, "Drowned in the *depth* of things, man ultimately no longer perceives them. . . ." Against tragedy: "*Tragedy* may be defined, here, as an attempt to 'recover' the distance which exists between man and things as a new value. . . ." . . .

Even granting a difference between "recover" and "*un*cover" (as in archeology), there still remains this discrepancy: as an extra-novel maneuver a "tragic" uncovering is not problematic, for Vanadium is Robbe-Grillet's invented city (invented for the *first* time, and so we cannot have here the case of a *re*covery guised in an *un*covering)—yet internal to *Topology* the I-persona sacrifices non-illusion to the altar of tragedy, where myth, depth, poetic voice, and vision all reveal their jeweled stilletos, their black togas, their ambiguous intentions—he conjures up Vanadium. . . .

If Robbe-Grillet, in this latest novel, is digging through the rubble, why? For simply a topology of old structures? Sifting through visions conjured up, what does he find? If *Topology of a Phantom City* flaps like a fish out of water, it is only the water of prior critical jargon. Robbe-Grillet may be flapping not on the altar of his own sacrifice—but for the new novel, the new man. (p. 12)

R. Bartkowech, "Topology of a Phantom City: Alain Robbe-Grillet," in The American Book Review *(© 1978 by* The American Book Review*), Vol. 1, No. 2, April-May, 1978, pp. 11-12.*

JANE MILLER

It is possibly (a key word here) significant that Robbe-Grillet's phantom city [in *Topology of a Phantom City*] should have a topology and not a topography and that the reader should be required to accept the arbitrariness of the writer's perceptions and imaginings, while being expected to attend scrupulously to the single bar of a prison window which would be rectangular rather than spherical in cross-section. No doubt (another key phrase), we are wrong to rely on the author/voyeur, who may see variously or inaccurately, misunderstand what he sees, and wish, as well, to deceive us. . . . The invitation to participate in the construction and construing of the "text" may be genuine, but as soon as we accept it we find ourselves to be flailing amateurs, dangerously prone to confusing genres and predicting outcomes from internal evidence. The novel is certainly not, according to the famous Barthesian distinction, culpably *lisible*. What about *illisible*? . . .

As a technical exercise designed to demonstrate what a dodgy business reading is, especially if we've been schooled to depend on some notion of a writerly purpose, the novel is predictably (prediction, like expectation, being discouraged, of course) adroit. It is unlikely that the allusions to artefacts: painting, forms of script, mirror images, will be lost on the alert reader, whose wish that the Piranesi townscape might remain static long enough for its features to be examined will, of course, be frustrated. . . . Pity the obliging reader, dutifully attentive to clues to which all usefulness must be denied, conceding readily his crassness and limitations as a novel reader, and all for some only fairly tantalizing glimpses of artfully positioned and possibly bloodstained (it could in the end be melon juice) nighties and their temporary occupants.

Jane Miller, "Watching the Girls Go By," in The Times Literary Supplement *(© Times Newspapers Ltd (London) 1978; reproduced from* The Times Literary Supplement *by permission), No. 3982, July 28, 1978, p. 838.*

* * *

ROBERTS, Keith 1935-

Roberts is an English novelist, short story writer, editor, illustrator, and cartoonist. He is best known for his science fiction and fantasy, and has written under the pseudonyms of Alistair Bevan and David Stringer. (See also *Contemporary Authors*, Vols. 25-28, rev. ed.)

The Inner Wheel is one of those novels which begin with disembodied voices. . . . After some involvements and misunderstandings, and a last-minute halt to World War III, all ends predictably. This is school of Wyndham, without John Wyndham's smooth way with action—or his crisp enjoyment of English life turned upside down.

"Deadly Dials, Queer Quasars," in The Times Literary Supplement *(© Times Newspapers Ltd. (London) 1970; reproduced from* The Times Literary Supplement *by permission), No. 3567, July 9, 1970, p. 741.**

JONATHAN MEADES

As seems to be the all too frequent case with SF writers Keith Roberts is full of excellent and imaginative ideas yet executes his stories—which are, for the most part, nothing more than vehicles for them, or dramatic illustrations of them—with a singular lack of style and conviction. The first half of [*Machines and Men*] comprises pieces concerned with intrusions on the 'normal order'. These intrusions are natural—the basic elements of SF can be counted on the fingers of one (human) hand—of a temporal, technological and telepathic nature. Anxious to provide recognisable, safe and ordinary contemporary backdrops as a contrast to the phenomenal events depicted the author sets three stories in provincial English towns and peoples them with characters who might be best described as saloon bar oddballs. . . . These mostly unappealing characters find themselves involved in adventures of strange, bizarre, weird and totally predictable sorts. The best service the reviewer can render Roberts is to list his ideas, his initial premises, his really quite inspired fancies. They include murder by telepathy . . . , a form of cinematic representation which goes far beyond 3-D, the use of subliminal data in feature films and the delightful device for improving a car's performance employed by a shipwrecked navigator from outer space who lands in the Black Country. . . .

The stories in 'Man' are all set in future and distinctly dystopian societies. Roberts writes these pieces in the third person which is a welcome relief after his assumption of facile guises and his attempts to 'characterise' the various 'I's of the first half of the book. 'Therapy 2000', the most recently written, is quite the most engrossing of these fantasies, and not simply because its postulation is the easiest to entertain, to accept as probable. . . . In this story Roberts shows an uncharacteristic restraint and paints a detailed daub of a truly horrific, noisy, cramped environment and relates his tragicomic tale of a rather pathetic man with a deadpan sureness. Other futures he invents include a submarine village and an England where perpetual war is waged between drivers and pedestrians—an altogether conceivable contingency, as readers of 'Autocar' will appreciate. (p. 81)

In 'Yesterday's Tomorrows' which promised much but turned out to be little more than a catalogue Armitage tended to classify those who speculated on the future, somewhat arbitrarily it seemed, as 'optimistic' or 'pessimistic'—he thus ignored the *literary* qualities of the works he discussed and considered them as no more or less than blueprints. Now it occurs to me that maybe this is the way that SF writers consider that they should be judged, if judged they must be. Such matters as the fineness of the writing . . . , the magic of their devices, the harmony of conception and discharge, the subtlety of their characters and so on are of little importance compared to their 'originality', the newness of their stabs at what's to come. . . . In which case I suppose that this book is probably a lot better than I've given it credit for. (pp. 81-2)

Jonathan Meades, "Fiction: 'Machines and Men'" (© copyright Jonathan Meades 1973; reprinted with permission), in Books and Bookmen, *Vol. 18, No. 12, September, 1973, pp. 81-2.*

PETER ACKROYD

I have always thought that atomic desolation will hasten the advent of true Christianity, when the poor will inherit what is left of the earth, but now, according to Mr Roberts, so will the emotionally unstable. . . . [In *The Chalk Giants*] Mr Roberts sanctifies death and perversity with an ironic, apocalyptic grandeur. . . . Mr Roberts has seen the future, and it almost works. . . . [There is a moral] somewhere, but I am not going to stop and look. Indeed as Mr Roberts's narrative escalates, there seem to be a great many morals but unfortunately they remain at the stage of grim caricature.

It is not that the writing does not have its moments of pathos and subtlety; the life and eventual death of Stan is sad enough to be interesting, and Mr Roberts interweaves his death-throes with the no less painful lacerations of future shock. I suspected at first that the forward glimpses were fragments of Stan's leukaemic nightmare, but they become too unsubtle even for that. . . . [I am afraid that Mr Roberts world is] crude, and his narrative degenerates into stock historical fiction. . . .

Peter Ackroyd, "After the Holocaust," in The Spectator *(© 1974 by* The Spectator; *reprinted by permission of* The Spectator), *Vol. 232, No. 7599, February 16, 1974, p. 203.**

The beginning [of *The Chalk Giants*] is promising: fat middle-aged Potts is driving his Austin Champ westwards through Army roadblocks, trying to reach Corfe Castle where he and some ill-assorted acquaintances will set up an embattled community in the hopes of outliving some unspecified holocaust. But the book deteriorates rapidly thereafter. What was well written becomes overwritten, and the tense storyline becomes increasingly diffuse and impressionistic. The bulk of the narrative degenerates into dismal Celtic fantasy in the Moorcockian tradition, with Potts lying in bed and dreaming scenes which perhaps took place on the same site at previous crises in history. Rape, superstition and general pillage clutter the pages and negate the lingering hard reality of the beginning, with its late twentieth-century world of pillboxes and nuclear fallout. Potts may be dreaming of the past or foreseeing a primitive future; but by then it all seems too inconsequential to worry about.

"Science Fiction in Short," in The Times Literary Supplement *(© Times Newspapers Ltd. (London) 1974; reproduced from* The Times Literary Supplement *by permission), No. 3758, March 15, 1974, p. 269.**

GERALD JONAS

Yes, of course, ["The Chalk Giants"] . . . is too ambitious. How else can a reviewer describe a novel that attempts to chronicle the rise of a new, post-nuclear-holocaust civilization—wars, religion, politics, philosophy, literature and all—in less than two hundred pages? But having faulted Roberts for his lack of proportion, let me immediately add that "The Chalk Giants" is far more successful than it has any right to be.

The premise of the book is that the Bomb has wiped out all traces of civilization-as-we-know-it, leaving a handful of human survivors in a state of savagery. As these survivors begin the long climb upward, on an island that was once England, they unwittingly retrace the paths their forebears took. . . . Synopsized, it sounds too pat, too easy: a dollop of "The Golden Bough" here, a bit of "Morte d'Arthur" there, stir in some "Bullfinch's Mythology" and Biblical echoes, and serve with an air of wide-eyed discovery.

But Roberts avoids most of the pitfalls of this kind of S.F. myth-making, primarily because his narrative strategy is impeccable. Writing a sturdy, richly detailed third-person prose that wins our confidence without ever asking for it, he introduces us in each chapter to some ordinary people who are driven by circumstances to extraordinary acts of creation and destruction. In the following chapters, the people we have just met are spoken of as legends by other ordinary people, who are then stretched on the rack of history to become the legendary figures of succeeding chapters. . . .

What seemed on first reading to be a fable of man's unquenchable spirit comes, in retrospect, to stand for everything that precedes myths—all the false starts, the misguided efforts, the unsung exploits, the lucky and unlucky turns on which the fragile superstructure of civilization rests. (p. 22)

Gerald Jonas, "Of Things to Come," in The New York Times Book Review *(© 1975 by The New York Times Company; reprinted by permission), September 14, 1975, pp. 22, 26.**

ALGIS BUDRYS

Keith Roberts is the best English SF writer. He is not the best novelist—Arthur C. Clarke still is, I suppose, or David Compton when he's on—but by a measurable margin, Keith Roberts at anything less than novel length can do it all. *The Passing of The Dragons* [a collection of short stories] causes me to say all that.

There are apparently no limits to Roberts' range. (pp. 24-5)

Logic dictates that Roberts must in fact have limits to the range of themes he is willing to tackle, and observation shows that he has a tendency to underplay too much, which is sometimes to the detriment of a given piece of work. But it is going to take a full scale critical investigation to determine those limits, because Roberts does not let you see them, and there is never anything wrong with any given Roberts story that is so bad you expect anything less but the best from the next one.

And he has engaging recurrent attributes. The verisimilitude with which he describes obsolete or variant machinery —the steam road engines and semaphore station in *Pavane,* the canal lock mechanisms in "The Lake of Tuonela," the harvesters in "The Grain Kings"—is a delight to the mind. The sentence and paragraph rhythms with which he evokes the pulsebeat of an ocean in "The Deeps" or the emotions of Becky in "The White Boat," are a mature strength.

He has yet to learn how to bring all this to bear on a major theme over novel length. Perhaps this is because he can do so much in so few words that it will require a towering central statement before he writes a book he cannot exhaust before he completes it. But not everyone needs to be the novelist. That may be where the money is, but for some people it's not where the good work is. (p. 25)

Algis Budrys, "Books: 'The Passing of the Dragons'," in The Magazine of Fantasy and Science Fiction *(© 1977 by Mercury Press, Inc.; reprinted from* The Magazine of Fantasy and Science Fiction), *Vol. 54, No. 2, February, 1978, pp. 20-5.**

* * *

ROY, Gabrielle 1909-

A French-Canadian novelist, Roy was twice the winner of the Canadian Governor General's Award. Her fiction is nationalistic in character, treating themes such as the adverse effect of progress on Canada and its people. Although Roy writes in French, most of her novels have been translated into English. (See also *CLC*, Vol. 10, and *Contemporary Authors*, Vols. 53-56.)

HUGO McPHERSON

[The] nature of Gabrielle Roy's vision has . . . cut her off both from her fellow artists and from the popular audience. The typical heroes of Canadian fiction are intellectuals who search loquaciously for their own identity or Canada's, or "superior" observers who smile condescendingly at Canadian manners, or various sorts of crusaders, pioneers and rebels who face life boldly and bring it triumphantly to heel. Gabrielle Roy knows that such exceptional people do exist, but her whole concern is for the unnumbered thousands who "lead lives of quiet desperation"—the terrible meek. And she records their plight with a tolerance and compassion that rests not an patriotism, humanism or religiosity, but on a deep love of mankind. In the same way, though she shares the existential concern for the individual of such French contemporaries as Sartre, Camus, Malraux and De Beauvoir, she does not wield the scalpel of intellect with their clinical vigour. Gabrielle Roy *feels* rather than analyzes, and a sense of wonder and of mystery is always with her. She is a "witness" to the aches of her century and her culture rather than a reformer; and she believes that only *Love* can redeem the time.

Thus in her fiction Gabrielle Roy has held the mirror up to nature in the only way possible to her, but the image which she captures has been less and less a picture which Canadians understand or esteem. Her most popular book is *The Tin Flute* (*Bonheur d'occasion,* 1945), a story of Montreal slum dwellers. Its success, however, derives largely from its stunning documentary quality. Even in a decade enthralled by the *exposé* this book had a stinging authority. It arraigned the monster of big-city poverty with an accuracy that caught the last syllable of the market-vendor's cry and the tragic rhetoric of the Saint-Henri bum; and for English-speaking readers it revealed a backyard squalor which, though unpalatable at home, was vicariously exciting when spiced with *un zeste de Québec*. The works that followed, though welcomed by a few critics, lacked its topical appeal, and were proportionately less well received. *Where Nests the Water Hen* (*La Petite Poule d'Eau,* 1951) and *Street of Riches* (*Rue Deschambault,* 1957) were thought of as romantic retreats into a charmingly simple but irrecoverably *passé* frontier. And *The Cashier* (*Alexandre Chenevert,* 1955)—her most important work—was rejected as an altogether too painful case history. (pp. 47-8)

Gabrielle Roy's imaginative landscape, that is, big-city living, with its soot and noise, its mechanical routine and impersonality, suggests simultaneously both the pains of adulthood and the dislocations of this unhappy century. By contrast, the warm and simple life of the frontier and the provincial town is becoming a thing of the past—as dear, and as irrevocably lost as childhood or innocence.

This perception of the controlling pattern in Gabrielle Roy's work is essential to an understanding of her statement. The values of the garden, childhood, innocence, and the past, array themselves against the forces of the city, adulthood, "experience," and the present. . . . [However], Gabrielle Roy is unflinchingly aware that there is no real escape from the present. *Here* and *now* is where Everyman lives; and his greatest gifts in a world where both faith and justice have perished are his ability to endure and to love. The critics who have regarded *Street of Riches* and *Where Nests the Water Hen* as day-dreaming retreats from the present, then, are mistaken; these works are rediscoveries, deceptively gentle and subjective, of the meaning of valour, pain, aspiration and love. (p. 49)

If the garden and the past constantly draw her characters away from the cage—the grid-like pattern of the modern city—the prospect of the *future* constantly beckons to them and entices them. For the ingenuous Everyman, indeed, the future is a shining hope—a world of grandiose dream and fantasy in which suffering will magically end; and it is always just ahead. . . . The hope of the future is a greater consolation to Everyman than the dream of the past, but Gabrielle Roy's narrative makes it clear that both past and future are insecure anchors. The present is inescapable; it is *now;* the past and the future are delusions. (p. 50)

It is Everyman's character to hope and aspire; it is his fate, apparently, to learn that his power to achieve is tragically short of his ability to dream.

This is Gabrielle Roy's vision of life. It is far more significant, I think, than the vision of many novels which are more self-consciously "Canadian." . . .

Is the urbanized life which we are so busy creating totally dismal—a dark valley between the sunny hilltops of past and future—or can the cage of adult and urban life be made bearable? To answer this we must look searchingly at Gabrielle Roy's two novels of city life.

Since *The Tin Flute* was Gabrielle Roy's first major statement, we shall turn to it first. Its original title, *Bonheur d'occasion,* has no English equivalent. The blues singer might translate it freely as "Happiness is a some-time thing", for it implies "chance" happiness, "grab-bag" happiness and "bargain" happiness—a deceptive, fleeting joy. Its heroine is Florentine Lacasse, daughter of a poverty-stricken Montreal family who live precariously amid the factory whistles, railway crossings, slaughter-house smells and soot of the St. Henri quartier. Appropriately, the name Lacasse suggests a "box" or "locker," for these people are thwarted—caged—born into a world of ugliness and want which they are powerless to escape. But all of them, in individual ways, dream of a happier world. (p. 51)

The central situation of the story records Florentine's seduction by a ruthless young orphan, Jean Lévesque (Mr. "Bishop"), her desperation when she learns that she is pregnant and unwanted, and her reluctant marriage to Lévesque's shy friend Emmanuel Létourneau ("a starling"). It is in this situation, and in the excruciating history of Florentine's parents, Rose-Anna and Azarius, that Gabrielle Roy's irony reaches its deepest level. Jean Lévesque is a calculating young opportunist; and Florentine is a yearning, empty-headed little fool. Yet they both, finally, strike us as disarmingly pathetic, for neither the opportunist nor his victim is really in control of his destiny, and neither realizes that wealth, if it is not somehow warmed by compassion and love, can be as hideous as poverty. The novel's central perception and its chief irony is its depiction of the nature of poverty, the scourge which blinds its victims to all motives but acquisition. (p. 52)

Rose-Anna, we feel, is an image of the universal *mater dolorosa,* the infinitely loving mother whose "poverty of spirit" will inherit the earth. Yet her secret is not a conscious formula; it is simply a question of unpremeditated giving. In existentialist terms she is totally *engagé*—committed to a way of life in which the moment is all-important, and in which fortitude, compassion and love are the essential values.

But if these are the only values that can triumph over the squalor of St. Henri, *The Tin Flute* does not affirm that the world will accept them easily as a remedy for mankind's suffering. Rose-Anna ends her career in the same pose as her mother, a woman who has lived her life in the "garden" of a Quebec farmstead. . . . Even Emmanuel Létourneau, whose vision is close to Rose-Anna's, finds no confident solution to the enigma of the human situation. His wife, Florentine, is incapable of understanding a love devoid of ulterior motives. . . . "Emmanuel" is prepared to give his life to save his fellows, but he cannot be certain that his sacrifice will redeem the time.

The statement of *The Tin Flute* is veiled; Gabrielle Roy allowed "the look of things" to convey its own meaning without authorial comment. In *Street of Riches* and *Where Nests the Water Hen* she adopts a highly personal, subjective manner. These are works of "spiritual autobiography", but their insights are not essentially different from the documentary histories of the Lacasse family and Alexandre Chenevert. Gabrielle Roy's experience has taught her that life offers an endless series of storms and mischances. . . . (The image of the storm, indeed, is a leading motif in these novels.) In country places, however, we see life in its simplest form—stripped of the complexities of the city.

But if country life is a spring of revelation, there is no stopping the cycle of history from frontier to provincial town to big city—or from canoe to Titanic to space-ship. Rightly or wrongly, wisely or stupidly, man aspires. And hence a final question arises. Is the idea of progress an illusion? Is there no possibility of turning the cage into a blessed garden? Gabrielle Roy answers this ultimate question by describing the ordeal of Alexandre Chenevert, the Cashier.

It would be difficult to imagine a less promising subject for fiction than the career of Alexandre Chenevert, for he is a man to whom virtually *nothing* happens—a nonentity who breaks down under the pressures of city life, escapes briefly to the "earthly paradise" of Lac Vert, and returns home to die. Yet from the very first sentence he has an almost hypnotic fascination for us. . . . This little man, his mind awash in an endless tide of anxieties, is much more than a nameless Montreal clerk who suffers from insomnia and the aches of urban life; he is the neighbor across the street or the stranger who sits across from us in the cafeteria. Alexandre is *us*—Everyman. . . . Alexandre's malady is simply the human condition.

But Gabrielle Roy does not, as a number of her critics have argued, intend her story as a simple condemnation of urban living, for the cage of the bank (and the city) in which Alexandre passes his days is in its deepest sense the cage of adult life—of experience. Thus his trip to Lac Vert and the pristine beauty of nature is not a rejection of the abrasive facts of experience but an attempt to reassure himself that happiness and peace are genuine possibilities. (pp. 52-4)

[The electrified statue of Christ] is the most ironic image in all of Gabrielle Roy's work. In modern life, even the figure of Christ—the symbol of brotherhood and *love*—has become a towering mechanical monster. (p. 55)

[The very core of Gabrielle Roy's vision is that there] can be no return to the garden, but meekness and love can plant flowers in the cage and the wasteland. The poor in spirit—Mahatmas Gandhi, Alexandre Chenevert—have the secret. A final knowledge of Love's power comes to Alexandre as he lies in a hospital bed dying of cancer: the visits of his simple friends and clients reveal to him that his life has not been worthless or meaningless. In the face of his childlike helplessness, his friends abandon all past pettiness and rivalry. . . . The money-counting world takes small notice of his passing, and yet this humble sufferer whose name suggests both a conqueror and sturdy, growing tree, achieves a curious kind of immortality. (pp. 55-6)

I have omitted mention . . . of the wry and tender understatement of her humor; I have ignored her tendency towards episodic narrative, and the occasional awkwardness in chronology which breaks the unity of *Where Nests the Water Hen* and *Street of Riches*. I have also been unable to weigh the losses incurred in translation. . . . (p. 56)

At the moment these matters bulk large, because we are always in some degree the slaves of literary fashion. Our final judgment, however, will rest firmly on two things: has Gabrielle Roy had something significant to say? and has she said it well? She falls short, I think, of the panoramic sweep of our greatest novelists, and she lacks something of the intensity which enables a Katherine Mansfield to distill the meaning of a world in the microcosm of a moment. She has, however, given us a vision of ourselves which is immeasurably [powerful]. . . . (pp. 56-7)

Hugo McPherson, "The Garden and the Cage," in Canadian Literature, *No. 1, Summer, 1959, pp. 46-57.*

PHYLLIS GROSSKURTH

What in effect [Gabrielle Roy tells is] a fairy-tale. In a fairy tale all manner of misfortunes may befall the protagonists, but we know that they are protected by magic talismans. . . . Her characters are shielded from the encounter with the stalking familiar. They are treated as children not yet capable of venturing into the more sombre areas of existence.

Essentially Gabrielle Roy possesses a mother's-eye view of the world. The area of action in which her characters move is limited and conditioned both spatially and psychologically by the imposition such a focus places upon them. The predominant figure of her books is the earth-mother. In relation to her own characters, in her loving and protective concern Gabrielle Roy is an extension of this earth-mother. It is this *weltanschauung* which gives her novels their distinctively "feminine" quality.

The settings of her novels are Montreal, St. Boniface, and the wilds of northern Canada. An extensive arena, admittedly. But if one examines her novels closely, are her characters free to range within as wide a region as appears at first sight?

Montreal is the background for her first and third novels, *The Tin Flute* and *The Cashier*. A large, pulsating city throbs behind the action: but how does it function in the lives of the characters? The major point Gabrielle Roy is making about the Lacasse family is the inhibiting confinement of their lives. The riches and the excitement of Montreal might as well be on the moon so far as they are available to the slum-dwellers of Saint-Henri. (pp. 7-8)

In *The Tin Flute* poverty assumes a terrifying presence that conditions lives and shapes character. Zola described his characters as subject to the same forces as the stone on the road—that is, helpless objects crushed by vast impersonal forces over which they have no control. A similar strain of fatalism runs through *The Tin Flute*. There are constant references to the feeling of imprisonment experienced by the inhabitants of Saint-Henri. Their only outlet is helpless rage, distorted ambitions, foolish day-dreams, or grim resignation. (p. 8)

Like a steady, gentle flame, the figure of Rose-Anna glows at the heart of the Lacasse family. Her tenacious strength and devotion provide the little ones with the only security they know. Yet she too represents imprisonment. When Florentine reacts in horror to the realization that her mother is expecting her twelfth child, Rose-Anna murmurs, "One can only do one's best." . . . Florentine herself perpetuates the cycle and it is significant that at the end of the book she returns to share a home with her mother. (pp. 8-9)

The question is, does Gabrielle Roy understand these implications in Rose-Anna? She depicts her as a figure of fortitude, an earth-mother whose natural habitat is in the country with growing things. Fecund and vigorous, her natural role is to produce children, but she is thwarted in her need for happy fulfilment.

Gabrielle Roy seems to accept the traditional French-Canadian view of the mother as the strong centrifugal force in the home. Rose-Anna is planted firmly at the centre of the novel. (p. 9)

Now what is the situation in *The Cashier?* Alexandre Chenevert works in the heart of the heart of the city—the Savings Bank of the City and Island of Montreal. He feels completely trapped in his Kafka-like cell within the vault of a building into which a sudden shaft of sunlight arouses startled heads. On the streets and in the bus, he finds only further forms of imprisonment. He is incapable of handling a bewildering urban environment. Unable to sleep, he stands helplessly before the cold impersonality of the refrigerator: "Alexandre sensed his utter inferiority as a man, with all his little stomach troubles, his endless colds, his confused problems." He has never managed to function outside the protection of the womb. His continual self-pampering is an extension of the uterine embrace. In the dream-fantasy that finally sends him off to sleep, "A feeling of restfulness overwhelmed his soul as it found ease in the absence of all but vegetable life." Again, when he falls asleep at Lac Vert, the Freudian imagery is unmistakable:

> The intoxication of sinking between secret shores, more thickly green than the night! How ravishing the blue fronds which curled about his limbs and then slipped by! The quality of the silence in this muffled land! The unutterable absence of all life, except for the water's even and continuous murmur.

The memory of his strong-minded mother threads in and out of his thoughts. . . . Is it too much to speculate that in the robustly healthy Edmondine he finds the mother he had always craved? (pp. 9-10)

The two books set in the wide open spaces might seem exceptions to the theme of enclosure. The structure of *Where Nests the Water Hen*, however, is revealing. The first section, "Luzina Takes a Holiday," is an account of Luzina's annual pilgrimage from her lonely island to the comparative civilization of Sainte Rose du Lac to give birth to another addition to her enormous family. The next section, "The School on the Little Water Hen," is concerned with Luzina's attempts to bring learning to their isolation. The final section, "The Capuchin from Toutes Aides," while it centres on the activities of Father Joseph-Marie, is linked structurally and thematically to the earlier episodes.

The first section opens with a sense of remote isolation, of an immensity beyond the beyond. Yet note the pattern of development: we move progressively from open space to the inner island to our final destination, the enveloping warmth of the Tousignants' cabin. (p. 10)

The earth-mother is the centrifugal force, the centre of a loving radius, embracing all those whose lives she touches.

Incidentally, after the unrelieved bleakness of *The Tin Flute*, *Where Nests the Water Hen* exhibits a genuinely humourous vein. The type of humour is significant. Gabrielle Roy laughs affectionately at the child-like qualities of Luzina and Father Joseph-Marie. The laugh has the ring of a parent's indulgent tolerance of a child's solemnity.

The Hidden Mountain is one book by Gabrielle Roy in which we do not find the figure of the protective strong woman. Here she is concerned with man alone in the freest possible environment. But it is only through contact with other people that character can be revealed and developed. Even in novels in which the interior monologue technique is employed, the character reveals himself through his reactions to the external populated world. Pierre remains a cipher because there are no other characters on whom he can hone himself.

The last part of the book, the account of Pierre's life in Paris, is a lamentable failure. It is a disaster precisely because there has been no opportunity in the major part of the book for his character to be established. His friendship with the young artist Stanislas is inadequate artistically, entirely unconvincing emotionally, since it is simply hero-worship on the younger man's part.

Pierre is completely incapable of adapting himself to an urban environment. . . . In sum, there is a failure of nerve on his creator's part. She cannot trust him to launch out into the world with a complex personality and independent life of his own.

The two recollections of her childhood, *Street of Riches* and *The Road Past Altamont*, contain Gabrielle Roy's most overt treatment of dominant, protective motherhood. Although it is never named, one assumes that the town in the background is St. Boniface. Yet what a shadowy place it is! Christine's family live on the edge of town. In "The Move," one of the stories in *The Road Past Altamont*, Christine only on this single occasion passes through the town, but from the top of the cart it has the appearance of a mirage: "All the houses seemed to be still asleep, bathed in a curious and peaceful atmosphere of withdrawal. I had never seen our little town wearing this absent, gentle air of remoteness."

All the action radiates from the house on Rue Deschambault in which Maman plays the central role. In *The Road Past Altamont* Christine talks of breaking away to the wider world. In *Street of Riches* she moves only as far as Cardinal, but in *The Road Past Altamont* she speaks of having journeyed as far as Europe. However, we have never seen her leave and we have no idea what life on her own would be like. . . . In this book for the first time Gabrielle Roy faces the imprisoning noose of motherhood. In part she is endeavouring to understand and perhaps to forgive. Yet her attitude is ambiguous for home also means the security to which we all look back nostalgically from time to time. *The Road Past Altamont* is written in retrospect; we assume that Christine has already lived far away, yet the writing of the book is a pilgrimage to her past, to the roots that bind and cling.

There are other aspects of this circumscribed world which should be considered. Repeatedly Gabrielle Roy explores the illusion of individual freedom. Her characters are frequently torn between a longing for a more expansive existence and the undeniable circumstances which restrict them. This dichotomy is particularly true of Maman in the two St. Boniface books. Sometimes man is depicted as engaged in a struggle for existence which sets daily bounds on the opportunities available to him. Rose-Anna has mutely accepted the toil and the responsibility, the burdens that will accompany her as far as the grave. In *The Hidden Mountain* Pierre seems the freest of Gabrielle Roy's characters yet he is forced to accept the cruel fact that he must kill in order to survive.

In a sense Gabrielle Roy maintains the same loving yet firm control on her characters as her various earth-mothers exert over their offspring. The virtues which she extols are fortitude, endurance, concern for others; these are the negative virtues, those necessary in a world in which man is at the mercy of forces beyond his control. Her characters act intuitively; they do not engage in rational or irrational analysis; they are not torn by mental conflict; they are uninterested in ideas. We find obsession in Pierre's creative urge and in Maman's eagerness to embrace a life she has not yet comprehended. But we never see any of them devastated by sexual desire, exalted by religious ardour, excited by intellectual passion or stirred by the darker passions. Gabrielle Roy's is not an easy world for her characters; yet its challenges are comparatively straightforward. (pp. 11-13)

[They] are never faced with agonizing moral problems. . . . Her characters are lovable, gentle creatures, but they are simple and childlike. Gabrielle Roy totally ignores the darker spectres that inhabit men's souls; only occasionally . . . she allows her characters to experience one of those sudden revelations which unexpectedly opens a precipice at our feet. Alexandre Chenevert frets about the death of Gandhi; yet there is some justification for Eugénie's remonstrance, "After all, he was no relative of ours!"

It is for these limitations that we must deny her a place with the greatest novelists. . . .

One cannot say that Gabrielle Roy's is a vision of the world before the Fall, even in what critics have described as her "pastoral" novels. Man is not in a garden where all good things are simply within reach. Her characters have been banished from Eden, but the most important step in the process has been ignored. These childlike creatures have never tasted the forbidden fruit of the Knowledge of Good and Evil. They are bewildered, innocent exiles banished by a capricious God. (p. 13)

Phyllis Grosskurth, "Gabrielle Roy and the Silken Noose," in Canadian Literature, *No. 42, Autumn, 1969, pp. 6-13.*

JEANNETTE URBAS

In "Bonheur d'Occasion" poverty is not an incidental factor: it is basic to the situation of every character in the book. Poverty transcends the individual and becomes the problem of a whole district, of the whole world, when it is traced to its source, the Depression. (p. 69)

The smell of poverty, the grime of poverty, the deprivation of poverty permeate the whole book and the dream of an upward ascension in society is the dream of an escape from poverty. . . .

In "Bonheur d'Occasion" the working-people are individuals but they are also members of a working-class community. One has the sense of the existence of an industrial proletariat. Their lives and loves are closely interwoven with larger social forces which dominate and condition them—the Depression, the War. Their problems as individuals and their varied search for solutions cannot be separated from this larger framework. . . .

Unemployment has left its havoc in the wake of the lives of every character in "Bonheur d'Occasion" and the war becomes everyone's concern for selfish and other reasons. Every person in the book takes a stand and makes a decision with regard to the war, either directly or indirectly through the decisions of others. Love, personal emotions, personal problems intermesh intimately with large social forces. . . .

In Gabrielle Roy's books all the families are large, except for that of Alexandre Chenevert and of Elsa in "La Rivière sans repos". The very size of the family creates problems for the wife and mother, financial problems as well as those relating to personal fulfillment. On the positive side the large family helps to develop strong characters and warm hearts. . . . Mme Roy's mature women find their fullest expression, not as wives or individuals, but as mothers. (p. 70)

Mme Roy shows that sex which should be one of the mainsprings of married joy is an inhibiting factor in the marriage relationship. For the women it is something to avoid because it results in a rapid increase of their family. For the men it is something of a burden, given the wife's resistance and the attitudes of sin and secrecy that society associates with its performance. . . . Having endowed men with the desires of the flesh, it is nonetheless the saints that are revered, the men who abstain from such desires.

One wonders whether Mme Roy herself is not a little affected by this over-all climate of discomfort and restriction when one reads the description of the scene [in "Bonheur d'Occasion"] where Florentine is seduced by Jean. There are only bare indications of what takes place; none of these details are sensual in nature. In addition their love-making takes place under the accusing glances of the Madonna and the saints that adorn the room. . . .

[The] work of Gabrielle Roy abounds with various aspects of the "woman question". In "Rue Deschambault" the perceptive young Christine makes some penetrating observations concerning the social status of women. In the visit with Mme Nault she perceives how much more importance is attached to a woman who is married than to one who is not and she reflects on the injustice of this. . . . (p. 71)

The inequality between men and women is brought out in a different way in Eveline's comments to her son Robert when he encourages Christine's passion for flashy jewelry by giving her some money. She laments the fact that men stimulate the development of certain qualities in women, such as deception and cunning, and certain types of behaviour from which they are the first to suffer. It is a double standard which places a premium on ruse and scheming in a woman rather than frankness and a straight-forward simplicity. (pp. 71-2)

Mme Roy explores in a variety of ways the prestige bestowed on marriage as a state: the conflicts and double standards applied to the sexes, the problem of retaining and developing one's identity and aspirations within the framework of marriage. These questions cross language barriers and apply equally to French-Canadian and English-Canadian women. . . .

[One finds in general that Gabrielle Roy's] women are not only the stronger and more developed personalities, they are depicted with greater skill and a surer touch [than are the men]. (p. 72)

Mme Roy immerses us directly in the suffering of her characters: we feel, we think, we live with them. The appeal is directly to the heart. . . . One has the impression so often that Mme Roy's books are distillations of sorrow and human suffering made tolerable only by moments of joy and love that transcend them. (p. 73)

Jeannette Urbas, "Equations and Flutes," in Journal of Canadian Fiction *(reprinted by permission from* Journal of Canadian Fiction, *2050 Mackay St., Montreal, Quebec H3G 2J1, Canada), Vol. I, No. 2, 1972, pp. 69-73.**

PAUL SOCKEN

Gabrielle Roy's novels and collections of short stories, from her celebrated first novel *Bonheur d'occasion* (1945), to the present [*Garden in the Wind*], form a coherent body of thought and system of values. . . .

"A Tramp at the Door" is the story of a man who comes to the family's home posing as a relative from the East. His presence serves as a catalyst for the father's memories which flood to the surface. By the end of the tale the reader realizes that the stranger has become a member of the family, demonstrating once again the concept of the "family of man" that is at the heart of Gabrielle Roy's vision.

"Where Will You Go, Sam Lee Wong" recounts the life of a Chinese immigrant who sets up shop in a tiny Western town and lives there for twenty-five years. Like a number of Gabrielle Roy's characters in her other works, Sam Lee Wong is a man displaced both physically and spiritually yet never abandoning his hope to be at one with himself, "to reestablish contact between himself and his own reality."

The nearly mystical quality of "Hoodoo Valley," in which a group of Doukhobors find their "promised land," recalls the ideal land of peace and harmony in "The Old Man and the Child" (*The Road Past Altamont*).

The last story . . . , "Garden in the Wind," is quintessentially Gabrielle Roy. Images of gardens abound in Gabrielle Roy's works and represent the tenacious hope, amidst ostensibly insuperable odds, that man can live in harmony with his surroundings and with himself.

The link between these stories is the same one that connects all the volumes; people's lifelong struggle to understand the integrity of their own lives, to see their lives as a whole, and their need to create bridges of concern and understanding between themselves and others. The result is a dynamic tension between two different and yet fundamental aspects of the author's fictional world: the introspective and the outward looking. It is this very tension, and the success that she has demonstrated in dramatizing it, that makes Gabrielle Roy unique among Canadian writers.

Her writing is both Proustian, in its accent on self-discovery, and humanistic in the philosophical sense of that term. Everywhere there are roads, paths and, consequently, voyages, since all her characters are traveling the route of self-awareness. Those characters who finally become conscious of the reality of their own lives, like Alexandre Chenevert in *The Cashier,* are then in a position to understand their bonds with others.

Paul Socken, "Fellowship," in The Canadian Forum, *Vol. LVII, No. 678, February, 1978, p. 36.*

PAUL SCHLUETER

The very heterogeneity of Canadian prairie life is well illustrated by [the four tales in *Garden in the Wind*], two of which deal with Doukhobor and Ukrainian immigrants, one with a Chinese immigrant, and only one with French-Canadians. The title story deals tenderly with the plight of an aged Ukrainian couple wholly lost in the modern world, forgotten by their children, barely surviving on their minuscule farm. . . . The poignancy of the story is great, and Roy's tasteful handling of the subtle tensions between husband and wife is superb.

Somewhat the same kind of utopian hope is present in [the tale of] Sam Lee Wong. . . .

The other two stories, while effective, seem less significant, if for no other reason than the relative lack of plot; Roy's skill with atmosphere is as sharply realized as in the others. . . .

There is no doubt that Gabrielle Roy is consummately skilled in the craft of storytelling. These four tales at their best approach the work for which she is best known, but each one is a fine introduction to her skill as a writer.

Paul Schlueter, "Fiction: 'Garden in the Wind'," in Best Sellers *(copyright © 1978 Helen Dwight Reid Educational Foundation), Vol. 38, No. 5, August, 1978, p. 147.*

GEORGE WOODCOCK

There are books so poignant and so intense that it is hard to believe they do not spring out of personal experience, and one's problem is not to determine the ultimate source but to decide how directly actual events in the author's life are being presented. Gabrielle Roy's latest book, *Children of My Heart,* is—in my view—one of these rare works. I began to read it with apprehension, since the very subject—a young teacher's relationship with the children she taught—seemed at first fraught with all the perils of sentiment melting into sentimentality; I ended with the sense of surprised satisfaction one experiences when, in this cynical and knowing world of ours, a romantic vision is convincingly carried through into a work of art, when the real and the lyrical are effectively united.

Since it has a single uniting character, the anonymous young woman teacher who tells her own story, *Children of My Heart* can be regarded as a novel. . . . (p. 50)

[One] wonders how closely it resembles the kind of memoir Gabrielle Roy might have written of her own life in those years before she became a famous novelist, when she taught in the kinds of schools she describes. Perhaps it is the most notable sign of her artistry that we are not long concerned with this question, for it is the girl in the story as she stands in our mind's eye who holds our attention and not the writer whose persona she may and may not be. *Children of My Heart* stands, as all fiction should, on its own without the need to refer to its author's life. (p. 51)

The last and longest episode is the most complex, taking up more than a third of the book and telling of Médéric, a rebellious thirteen-year-old boy who is tamed, if that is the right term, by the teacher. . . . As the novel ends Médéric rides wildly beside her departing train and throws into the window a bouquet of prairie flowers, many of them rare ones. "It spoke of the young and fragile summer, barely born but it begins to die."

And this is the general feeling of *Children of My Heart,* the feeling of one of those lost summers of growing up when everything was seen and experienced with preternatural intensity and the world seemed to be divided as sharply into the dark and the luminous as the prairie village when the narrator first saw it, with its dingy houses of embittered old people in a setting of "desert spaces and the marvellous silence." There is an almost Wordsworthian progress from the light of innocence so clearly ignited in the younger children to the darkness of experience that Médéric begins to enter, and it is this knowledge that even love cannot wholly proof the spirit against adversity that makes so real the romanticism of *Children of My Heart*. Gabrielle Roy writes here at the height of her form. (p. 52)

George Woodcock, "Gabrielle Roy at the Height of Her Form," in Saturday Night *(copyright © 1979 by* Saturday Night*), Vol. 94, No. 4, May, 1979, pp. 50-2.*

JONATHAN M. WEISS

At first glance a reader might think that *Ces Enfants de ma vie* [*Children of My Heart*] is a collection of short stories, and indeed Roy does present us with six *nouvelles,* each of which could conceivably stand on its own. . . .

[Yet] each of the stories is a part of an organic whole, which finds its ultimate expression in the final and longest chapter. This is the story of the narrator's discreet and almost painful attachment for a fourteen-year-old pupil, Médéric. Médéric is the symbol of youth; he has within him most of the characteristics of the children in the other stories, and this overt symbolism makes the last chapter of the book less *vraisemblable* (though none the less effective for its dream-like quality) than the preceding chapters. . . . The bouquet of wildflowers thrown to the schoolmistress as the book closes comes to symbolize . . . [the] complex and painful period of life between adolescence and adulthood. . . .

Gabrielle Roy has given us a beautiful and delicate vision of the world of a woman entrusted with children not her own, and whom she loves in ways which are undefined and which can hardly even be admitted. This book further confirms Roy's stature as one of the most important of contemporary French Canadian authors. (p. 157)

Jonathan M. Weiss, "Creative Arts: 'Ces enfants de ma vie'," in The French Review *(copyright 1979 by the American Association of Teachers of French), Vol. 53, No. 1, October, 1979, pp. 156-57.*

* * *

RUDKIN, David 1936-

Rudkin is a British playwright and author of screenplays. His dramatic work is marked by seriousness of tone and a dense and complex artistic vision. (See also *Contemporary Authors,* Vols. 89-92.)

ANTHONY MASTERS

David Rudkin's *Ashes* . . . is a complex, confused play which it's difficult to deal with in a brief review and which one suspects the author didn't entirely sort out himself. For most of its length, it's concerned with charting the progress of an intelligent couple's attempts to overcome sterility; and a harrowing story it is, of endless, degrading sperm counts, ovary tests, detailed charts of their sex-life over a period of six months, and even demonstrations by condescending specialists of more efficient positions, illustrated by horrendous plastic models.

With a fruit-machine clunking and whirring on the soundtrack, they keep trying; she conceives, to a sarcastic *Veni Creator Spiritus,* miscarries (they were twins, cruelly) and has a hysterectomy as well; and finally they can't even adopt. But at this stage Colin, the husband, has to go home to Belfast for the funeral of his uncle, blown to pieces in the street, and in a long and graphic speech makes the connection with the sterility of Ireland's will to stop her own blood-letting. The trouble is that practically anything, including pollution and the energy crisis, can be, and is, put in terms of this one metaphor. . . .

Much of the intended poetic writing doesn't come off, but at its best it achieves a marvellous loamy richness and prodigality, typically Irish. . . .

Anthony Masters, "Theatre in the Community," (© copyright Anthony Masters 1974; reprinted with permission), in Plays and Players, *Vol. 21, No. 6, March, 1974, p. 47.*

JOHN ELSOM

Why is David Rudkin's *Ashes* . . . a sad, but not a tragic, play? What dimension does it lack? The brief reply, a kind of energy, begs more questions than it tentatively attempts to answer, for Rudkin's play bears all the signs of honest effort, which is energy of a kind. Its theme is as fundamental as that of Lorca's *Yerma,* which it resembles: childlessness, but seen from the angle of a couple, not just from a wife's. . . .

There is so much to respect about *Ashes* (not least, Rudkin's ambitiousness) that it goes against the grain to record that . . . [it] is a dreary, self-absorbed play. Rudkin has given himself a situation which he has not managed to develop into a story. From the tone of the opening scenes, we know that Anne and Colin will not have a child. Even when the urine tests prove positive (to the strains of triumphant music), an ominous piano rumble from the Erle King indicates that Death is not far behind. On one level, therefore, the situation cannot develop: it can only go from bad to worse. And so the final scenes of the play, and particularly Colin's long monologue about Ulster, are anticlimactic, leaving the feeling of one damn thing after another. . . .

[The] true failure of *Ashes* . . . is the lack of imaginative vitality. Rudkin knows what he wants to say, but he cannot find the dramatic means to do so.

John Elsom, "Ashes to Ashes," in The Listener *(© British Broadcasting Corp. 1975; reprinted by permission of John Elsom), Vol. 93, No. 2411, June 19, 1975, p. 817.*

JOHN COLEBY

Penda's Fen is a major television play, Expressionist in technique, making full use of the tricks available to the medium. It demonstrates how to compress and concentrate within the compass of the small screen the themes and images more fitted to larger locations. The awakening to manhood of the youth Stephen Franklin in the context of the ancient terrors presided over by Penda, the last pagan king in England, accompanied by Elgar's Dream of Gerontius . . . is treated imaginatively and sensitively; it is located firmly in the Malvern countryside and in the ways of its inhabitants. . . . The author occasionally gives the characters thoughts which do not arise from the context or would not be naturally reflected in the faces we are watching. Our attention shifts to what is being said, at the expense of the scene. A fast-moving narrative can be helped along in this way without breaking audience attention, but where ideas are being explored and worked out in terms of a static or slowly developing situation, it is a mixed blessing. Better, in drama, a 'voice under' supplied by the audience as the dramatist leaves them no choice.

John Coleby, "Plays in Print: 'Penda's Fen'," in Drama, *No. 120, Spring, 1976, p. 81.*

ERIKA MUNK

[*Ashes*] is astonishing—it affirms life without lying. The story is simple and ordinary, but touches on every major private and public concern; it is wonderfully written and structured with meticulous care, but its artfulness is never ornamental or self-serving. . . .

This is really Colin's play, about his fight against death. He loses his heritage and his inheritor; he no longer can place his hope for meaning either in past or future; the present is all that exists. [He] sums up his severance from the past by wryly transmuting a basic taunt: "Phoenix yerself!" That is: Rise up out of your own strength, be born of nothing. Of course the phoenix is the bird resurrected from ashes, but it has other senses, all appropriate: "Phoenix" means the blood-red one, according to Graves, "a title given to the moon as goddess of death-in-life," and Phoenix was the name of Achilles' tutor, blind and cursed with childlessness. *Ashes*'s grim themes of sterility, death, burning, futile knowledge, all are held paradoxically in a symbol which as a whole means resurrection. . . .

The language [is] at once strong and nuanced. . . . Much of the dialogue is natural, funny, and biting but understated, not evading emotion but choosing to be, well, British. Colin (who has been a writer) also uses a meditative tone, verging on the ironically intentional literary, to discuss the failure of his future and his rejection by the past ("the clan, from whose loins I come, had turned me out; to my own loins no child of tomorrow shall come: and I felt so—severed."). Anne, always more direct, narrates rather than meditates. No earth-mother cliché, she addresses her fetus, "Bloodbeast. Take over the graveyard in your own good time and your own right. If you see our values have failed us, cack on our graves."

Erika Munk, "Resurrection from the Ashes," in The Village Voice *(reprinted by permission of* The Village Voice; *copyright © The Village Voice, Inc., 1977), Vol. XXI, No. 1, January 3, 1977, p. 63.*

* * *

RUYSLINCK, Ward (pseudonym of Reimond Karel Maria de Belser) 1929-

Ruyslinck is a Dutch novelist and poet. Although considered one of the finest writers of the Netherlands, Ruyslinck is little known in the United States, largely because the bulk of his work has not appeared in translation.

ROGER GARFITT

The subtlety of *Golden Ophelia* . . . lies in its creating a picture of a 1984-like society that comes suspiciously to resemble the present. . . . The moral seems to be that it isn't only totalitarian regimes which reduce human values: they can reduce themselves quite informally, under conditions of material affluence. . . .

[The novel at first appears to be] a satirical parable from which the English reader, spared the experience of a totalitarian regime or an enemy occupation, can feel safely detached: but personal as well as social morality is at issue. Golden Ophelia is both a rose and [the protagonist's] name for the country girl who grew it and with whom he falls in love. To reveal the ending would be unfair: the shock is not that the worm should have found out the rose's bed of joy but that the rose should have been expecting him. What harrows the reader is to hear in the voice of Ophelia the tones of a moral vulgarity that he recognizes as in some measure his own, for he has foreseen her fall and Stefan [the protagonist] has not. Masterly in the development of its imagery and in the ironic echoing of phrases of dialogue, *Golden Ophelia* is a novel of great economy that ends in a controlled explosion.

Roger Garfitt, "Breaking Curfew," in The Times Literary Supplement *(© Times Newspapers Ltd. (London) 1975; reproduced from* The Times Literary Supplement *by permission), No. 3834, September 5, 1975, p. 998.*

VALENTINE CUNNINGHAM

What we want to hear we have translated promptly. Look how fast *Animal Farm* got about the world. So one assumes that Ward Ruyslinck's excitingly absurdist and grippingly disquieting meditation on our near-future has taken fourteen years to find an English publisher because it trades in the kind of dystopia we do not much care to relish. To be sure *The Reservation* casts—as do all gazings into brave new worlds—the obligatory cold eye on scientific inhumanism. But, and this distinguishes his bleakness from the frights of more popular visionaries, the god Ruyslinck sees failing is not Marxism but democracy. . . .

If [the] anti-capitalist plotting were all, though, *The Reser-*

vation would be impressive, but not nearly so impressive as in the event it is. . . . [What's] special about Ruyslinck's novel is that it shows people being denied the humanity they crave by "democratic" leaders who have gone in gleefully for brutism. . . . Ruyslinck's world has gone bestial. The novel builds a complex scaffolding of animal allusions. At best, beloveds are pets. At worst, men are predators, wolves and lions. People's names invoke animal connections: like Sim Ray the jazzman, and headmaster Whale. And of course Jonas [the protagonist] (or Jonah)—and it is only one of many nods towards Orwell—tumbles right inside the whale. "After all, why is your name Jonas?" Custodian of humane virtues, he is consigned, in the novel's most extraordinarily vivid touch, to an anthropological zoo, a collection of living freaks, types that social evolution is discarding. . . .

Even when he has turned from a living to an embalmed exhibit, though, Jonas has the last word. His is the accusation that explodes at the last. . . . "Of all living beings man is the most ferocious." It is an apt triumph, for Jonas had struggled for verbal truth against the slogan world of the masters who would turn all critics into commies and who made of the language of virtue a hypocritical façade. . . . [The] wisdoms of his diary, affirmations of the merits of Shakespeare and the pessimism of Graham Greene, had found their mark. As also, evidently, do the wisdoms of this novel: with its persisting echoes of Ionesco's nightmare. Bestiality on elephantine, rather than on mere rhinocerosian, scale; the gulled masses as stampeded elephant herds; unfunny elephant jokes abundant. It is just as Jonas reflected early on: "My generation had flung Ionesco's warning to the winds and . . . we had now got as far as elephant disease and that was no less disturbing."

Valentine Cunningham, "The Odd Elephant Out," in The Times Literary Supplement *(© Times Newspapers Ltd. (London) 1978; reproduced from* The Times Literary Supplement *by permission), No. 3982, July 28, 1978, p. 838.*

PETER BRUNING

Flemish writers, [Ruyslinck says,] should be concerned with European problems transcending Flemish parochialism. He has taken his own advice, and in scores of novels and short stories he uses a leitmotiv that is the antithesis of that Flemish gusto: the individual pitted against society and an unjust God. (p. 303)

The Depraved Sleepers (*De ontaarde slapers,* 1957) and *Golden Ophelia* (1966) . . . are permeated with postwar disenchantment: man is grotesquely ugly. He dreads aging, which ends in decay and death. Perceiving his animal nature as degrading, he fails in his love relationships. A perennial underdog, he loses his battle against a dehumanized society. A touch of black humor relieves the gloom: The protagonist in *The Depraved Sleepers* poses as a dignified mourner in a funeral procession to get a free ride. Behind black humor lurks black absurdity in *Golden Ophelia* when the hapless hero must properly petition to commit legal suicide. By distorting reality here to intensify his message, Ruyslinck has, unfortunately, weakened *Golden Ophelia* artistically.

On the whole, Ruyslinck's approach to his craft is conservative. Unlike his more experimental contemporaries, he continues a Flemish narrative tradition. A master of nuance, he manipulates language with virtuosity and relishes inventing new words. (pp. 303-04)

Peter Bruning, "World Literature in Review: 'The Depraved Sleepers' & 'Golden Ophelia'," in World Literature Today *(copyright 1979 by the University of Oklahoma Press), Vol. 53, No. 2, Spring, 1979, pp. 303-04.*

* * *

RYGA, George 1932-

A Canadian dramatist and novelist, Ryga also writes the music for the dancing or ballad singing which accompanies many of his plays. His protagonist is usually an underdog whose individuality is challenged by a repressive social system. Many critics have praised his accurate representation of dialogue and this talent is evident in his latest novel, *Night Desk*.

NEIL CARSON

In my opinion, [*The Ecstasy of Rita Joe*] establishes Ryga as the most exciting talent writing for the stage in Canada today. . . .

The Ecstasy of Rita Joe has been more widely seen and heard than many new Canadian plays and . . . is closely related to his published work, especially his novels *Hungry Hills* (1963) and *Ballad of a Stonepicker* (1966). . . . (p. 155)

If Ryga rejects romantic and physical love, he does not conclude that meaningful human relationships are impossible. On the contrary, he frequently shows a bond between individuals which he clearly believes to be more exalted than love in the usual sense. Ordinarily this is a relationship in a family (between brother and brother in "Indian", father and daughter in *Rita Joe,* boy and aunt in *Hungry Hills*). Occasionally, as in the father's grief over the loss of his horse in *Hungry Hills* and in the comic episode of Timothy and his ox in *Ballad of a Stonepicker,* the relationship may be between man and animal. . . . But in the world Ryga writes about there is little enough even of this second kind of love. It comes fleetingly, in moments of crisis, or in flashes of understanding, but is never indulged and often not even acknowledged. . . .

If Ryga's characters are partly tormented by their need for love in a world that denies it or corrupts its expression, many of them are even more profoundly troubled by existential longings. . . . (p. 158)

The sense of spiritual homelessness is common in Ryga's work and many of his characters define themselves by their relationship to a country they have lost or one they never find.

In his early work, this country seems to represent the lost time of youth, innocence, and happiness that is replaced by the cares of maturity and responsibility. The crisis is often a moment of choice which is precipitated by outside factors but which is faced by the protagonist with full awareness. . . . (p. 159)

[In *Ballad of a Stonepicker*] the protagonist no longer recognizes the crucial moment of decision and is caught instead in a process which he does not understand. The impression of passive suffering rather than deliberate action is conveyed further by the structure of the novel itself. Reminiscent of the ballad form, it consists of a number of apparently random memories told by an anonymous narrator.

The central character is essentially faceless, a symbol of the inarticulate victim. . . . (p. 160)

But if Ryga is suggesting that suffering is only partially explicable in terms of our own choices, and that many men are victims of a Fate they cannot control or comprehend, he does not seem to deny the possibility of meaning altogether. . . . Whether or not [the] twisted visions [of the narrator in *Ballad of a Stonepicker*] are the only visions possible is not made clear in the novel. Ryga himself seems temperamentally caught between the romanticism of hope and the romanticism of despair. But the intensity of his writing (in this novel at least) suggests that, although the stonepicker has lost his way, a way does nevertheless exist. . . . (pp. 160-61)

In structure, [*The Ecstasy of Rita Joe*] closely resembles *Ballad of a Stonepicker* or Arthur Miller's *After the Fall*, being a dramatization of memories and a search for identity. . . . (p. 161)

Ryga has that very rare gift for writing dialogue that has the sound of ordinary speech but the resonance of poetry. If he can master the technical and structural demands of the stage, we may yet have a Canadian play worthy to be mentioned in discussions of contemporary drama. (p. 162)

Neil Carson, "George Ryga and the Lost Country" (originally published in Canadian Literature, *Summer, 1970), in* Dramatists in Canada: Selected Essays, *edited by William H. New (copyright © 1972 by The University of British Columbia), The University of British Columbia Press, 1972, pp. 155-62.*

NEIL CARSON

[*Hungry Hills*] tells of the efforts of the young Snit Mandolin to find his roots and re-establish a home in the barren farmlands of northern Alberta, to which he returns after an absence of several years. The period covered is one hot, dry summer during which the protagonist discovers his incestuous origins and learns a kind of stoical integrity from his aunt, the one figure who seems to have survived the tortures of life in the hills with any dignity. . . . [The] novel shows Ryga's interest in the lives of the poor and oppressed as well as his preoccupation with problems of structure. One of the interesting features of Ryga's development as a writer has been his search for a form that would give him the flexibility he needs as an artist. His progress after the comparatively traditional realism of *Indian* and *Hungry Hills* has been in the direction of freer and freer forms—forms that in such later plays as *Sunrise on Sarah* and *Paracelsus* dispense almost altogether with conventional plot. The free-form structure of the plays (and of his second novel *Ballad of a Stonepicker*) allows Ryga to indulge to the full his tendency to alternate between the accurately delineated particular and the cloudy generalization which is a notable characteristic of his writing (and, some would say, his fatal weakness.)

On the face of it, *Hungry Hills* is a typical regional naturalistic novel with the strong emphasis on perversion and violence characteristic of the type. Certain parts of the novel also suggest a heavily didactic purpose (which may account for the work's "acclaim in the Soviet Union"). (p. 185)

One possible reading of the novel, then, is as a socialist tract in which Snit Mandolin is educated in the realities of economic oppression and the need for social action. (p. 186)

But there is much in the novel to discourage the kind of pious optimism implicit in such a reading. Ryga's vision of the hills is bleak, and his attitude towards social protest and grass roots political action is curiously ambivalent. Life in these hungry hills is no romantic idyll; it is nasty, poor, brutish and short. To survive in such an environment seems to require the inarticulate endurance of Aunt Matilda, the despairing superstition of Shnitka, or the ruthless outlawry of Johnny Swift. Snit's failure to change the society of the hills is bound up with his failure to find the home that he sought. For Snit remains alienated until the end. He rejects the criminal alternative and is reconciled with his indomitable aunt. But part of the wisdom he learns from the old woman is that one cannot find meaning for one's life in such traditional shibboleths as love or responsibility. . . . It is Ryga's refusal to present pat answers to the problems he raises that sets him above the kind of novelist that is suggested by the description of *Hungry Hills* on the cover of the recent edition as a "tragedy of depopulation of the rural countryside." What impresses in his work is not his social criticism, still less his portrayal of the agents of justice and bureaucracy, but his assertion of individual courage and dignity in the face of those most terrible oppressions—loneliness and death. (pp. 186-87)

Neil Carson, "Ryga Revisited," in Journal of Canadian Fiction *(reprinted by permission from* Journal of Canadian Fiction, *2050 MacKay St., Montreal, Quebec H3G, 2J1, Canada), Vol. IV, No. 4, 1976, pp. 185-87.*

W. H. ROCKETT

Romeo Kuchmir is a character who has found an author who has failed to find a proper place for Romeo. Kuchmir is literally all there is to George Ryga's new novel, *Night Desk*. He is not simply a narrator, as was Snit in Ryga's earlier *Hungry Hills*. Romeo is a soliloquist who has seized a stage no one else seems particularly interested in, and swells roundly enough to fill it with anecdote.

The stage he has seized is the strip of floor space before the clerk's desk of a third-rate hotel in a western city. The audience that goes with it is the night man, simply "kid" to Romeo and to us. (p. 83)

In his first play, *Indian*, Ryga's chief character pleads to the Indian agent: "I got no past . . . no future . . . nothing! . . . I dead! You get it? . . . I never been anybody. *I not just dead . . . I never live at all.*" Romeo is anxious to establish that he is the absolute antithesis of such a character: "I'm an outlaw, kid, a stallion. I'm goin' where I'm goin' an' no one asks me why." . . .

Romeo has tales, and no place to tell them except . . . before the night desk. There are no hungry hills here, no sense of dust and dirt and a place for such a character to strut his stuff about and be believed. We have not even a reasonable physical sense of Romeo: the kid [the novel's narrator] records words, not impressions. This man has only the body of the illustration on the book cover by Bill Featherston. What did Romeo or the kid, or Ryga for that matter, have to do with that?

And what sense does one make of the tales Romeo has to tell? He rejoices in the body, which is all well enough. He finds joy in twitting the order of things, pissing in the Winnipeg parking meters so they freeze up and are useless for a season. He talks rough, dropping his g's. He also talks too much poetry, thrown up against the roughness of original-ity. . . .

[Romeo] has made what Brian Parker has called a Ryga folk ballad. Words trigger other words, responses, new anecdotes, old ideas. Everything weaves back on senseless legs to the same loneliness; and the only fact clearly established is that the kid is only Romeo's second-best audience.

Romeo is his own best audience. He is probably the most interesting Ryga character since Rita Joe. What is amiss is that he is alone: soliloquizing before the night desk. He is a character in need of other characters as strong as he. He has to be seen.

Ryga has not given us in a novel the other eyes he could provide in a drama. Romeo [the prize fight promoter] is too alone, in the centre of the poster with small pictures of his stock all about. He desperately needs a play. (p. 84)

W. H. Rockett, "Ryga's Romeo: A Character in Search of a Book," in Saturday Night *(copyright © 1977 by* Saturday Night*), Vol. 92, No. 1, January/February, 1977, pp. 83-4.*

BRUCE BAILEY

Ploughmen of the Glacier is an undisguised, sometimes clumsy attempt to say something cosmic about what Ryga's stage directions call "the elemental loneliness of the protagonists." Most of the dialogue is between Lowery, a fly-by-night journalist, and Volcanic, a stereotypically crusty prospector. We can gather that these two are supposed to function as existential icons partly because we are told that their conversation unfolds in a setting which "is possibly surrealistic to suggest a mountainside, up and down which POOR BOY struggles in his eternal, groping quest." Poor Boy himself acts as the folksy Canadian equivalent of a Greek chorus chattering on about Life and Death. At the same time, he doggedly carries a leaky bucket of water up the mountain in order to fill a leaky trough.

In case we miss the significance of this, hard-bitten newspaperman Lowery steps out of character for a moment and draws an awkwardly literary parallel between Poor Boy's activity and the fruitless endeavour of Sisyphus. But there is an important difference between this home-grown Sisyphus and his counterpart as he appears in Camus' *The Myth of Sisyphus*. The philosopher's mythic model spites the gods by paradoxically rejoicing in his psychological freedom to appreciate the tragic beauty of a grand but pointless struggle. Poor Boy, on the other hand, concludes the drama with trite, simple-minded observations which are hardly worth the price of admission or the time spent watching the play. This might be acceptable if the play stood up as a visually and aurally exciting piece of work—but it does not. (p. 47)

Ploughmen of the Glacier is probably not Ryga's best work if judged for its sublety and theatricality. In any case, the brevity and the paucity of theatrical legerdemain . . . are not likely to leave an international audience satisfied. . . . (p. 48)

Bruce Bailey, "Existential Follies," in The Canadian Forum, *Vol. LVIII, No. 686, January-February, 1979, pp. 47-8.**

S

SACHS, Nelly 1891-1970

A German poet, playwright, and translator, Sachs left Germany for Swedish exile when the Nazis rose to power. Narrowly escaping the concentration camp, she chose to create in her work a monument to the sufferings of the Jews. Her poetry is lyrical and often psalm-like, drawing much of its inspiration from both Jewish and Christian mysticism. Death, redemption, and the human search for peace are important themes throughout her work, which Stephen Spender called "apocalyptic hymns rather than 'modern poetry'." Sachs was awarded the Nobel Prize in 1966. (See also *Contemporary Authors,* Vols. 25-28, rev. ed.; and *Contemporary Authors Permanent Series,* Vol. 2.)

STEPHEN SPENDER

One terrible aspect of our century is that fantasies horrible as the worst nightmares of writers like Baudelaire and Dostoevsky in the previous century have become literally true, realized in world wars, mass murder, genocide, concentration camps. They have come true in the minds of all of us, and in the lives and deaths of the victims. . . .

Nelly Sachs . . . escaped from the Germany of concentration camps into neutral Sweden in 1940. [She is] a poet who writes out of a life immersed in the horror of the actual nightmare, the deaths of those who were burned in ovens. Reading "O the Chimneys," one is there. One feels at once that here is a writer who does not make poetry out of material which she imagines from afar. Her poetry is the lived material itself.

Her poems have variety, but they might all be one poem, and each poem seems part of the suffering of her people in the camps, a death which in her imagination extraordinarily flows into the resurrection which is Israel. The idea of the Jewish people so prevails that the lives and the deaths seem aspects of the same consciousness. The history of destruction and rebuilding seems to happen at the same time, to be contained in a single moment of time, which is the concept of "my people."

In "Chorus of the Unborn," the unborn with their hope, the dead with their anguish, the murdered and the builders of new life, seem the same. . . . (p. 5)

One is scarcely aware, though, of the poet's sensibility as part of the contemporary literary scene. Her poetry is not at all about poetry, still less about the poet. It is, rather, a mouthpiece, the voice of her people, and has a personality only in that it so powerfully and exceptionally represents suffering. And the answer to the suffering is to see it in the light of the history of the Jews as the religious life.

In saying that Nelly Sachs creates religious apocalyptic hymns rather than "modern poetry," I don't mean either to denigrate that other poetry, or to suggest that she does not bring to her almost impersonal suffering great literary gifts, even ones from which literary poets might learn. She has great power and intelligence in exploiting certain aspects of real experience as symbols of metamorphosis. The smoke of the chimneys of the furnaces in which the Jews were burned by the Nazis becomes associated with dust, and dust with the dust on butterflies' wings, and with the sands of the desert. . . .

Nor is this poetry without a background in other literature, especially in Jewish mysticism. . . .

Sometimes indeed she reminds one faintly of contemporaries, especially in the play "Eli," which is a lyric rhapsody of voices of people in a Polish village "after the martyrdom," curiously similar to Dylan Thomas's "Under Milk Wood." Yet Thomas seems fanciful, imaginative, sympathetic; with Nelly Sachs these voices seem torn out of her. The mood is so different that the parallel with Thomas seems coincidental.

One can only enjoin the reader to read this book, because it teaches one to know what of all things in modern history we ought to know about—the nightmare and the rebirth. . . . Nelly Sachs being a poet of immensely powerful imagination conveys this suffering on another level of thought and experience identification. It is something that everyone capable of reading poetry should understand. (p. 34)

Stephen Spender, "Catastrophe and Redemption," in The New York Times Book Review *(© 1967 by The New York Times Company; reprinted by permission), October 8, 1967, pp. 5, 34.*

JOSEPH SLATER

[The publication of Nelly Sach's *O The Chimneys,* a selection of her work in translation,] enables the greatness of her spirit and her art to cross the frontier into English.

Her poetry seems almost designed for translation. It is formally and rhythmically free, concrete and sensuous, difficult in ellipsis and juxtaposition rather than in texture, startling in metaphor, often mysterious, but rarely ironic or ambiguous. Many lines can be rendered literally in English and yet remain poetic. . . .

Fantastic, expressionistic, Yeatsian (with Hassidic mysticism in place of Irish myth), Chagallian, [*Eli, a Mystery Play on the Sufferings of Israel*] is a drama of pursuit and retribution. At the end a Voice from above proclaims the "Last earthly moments of Israel," and its doctrine is simply stated in a phrase of her postscript: "No more trust in good on earth." It is the work through which, in radio and theatrical productions, Nelly Sachs became widely known in Germany, and it should have a place in the American theater. It ought to have been the prelude rather than the postlude to this book.

For the movement of her linked and interwoven poems and books is not from torment to despair, but from death to rebirth. The opening poems of her first book are lamentations. . . . But the great closing "choruses" of that book sing both the metamorphosis of tears into eternity and the rebirth of Israel itself in the mirror of its dying.

Her later works are variations and extensions of these themes, more inward and more subtly made, and elaborations of others: exile, language, love for the dead, the everlastingness of what has been, the slow evolution of man's knowledge of God. Ultimately, in the long sequence "Glowing Enigmas," two main themes emerge: sweet cravings for death and a turning through art back to life, "into the world again / with the haunting strength of letters." It is the second that dominates at the end. . . .

Heinrich Luebke, when he presented Nelly Sachs with the Friedenpreis in Frankfurt in 1965, said that her poems had been "works of forgiveness, of deliverance, of peace." They are. They are also rare examples of the power of art to metamorphose murder into beauty and death into life.

Joseph Slater, "From Death to Rebirth," in Saturday Review *(© 1967 by Saturday Review, Inc.; reprinted with permission), Vol. L, No. 44, November 4, 1967, p. 36.*

ALVIN H. ROSENFELD

Prior to the announcement of the Nobel Prize for Literature for 1966, Nelly Sachs, co-winner with S.Y. Agnon, was largely unknown, especially in this country. Almost nothing of her poetry had appeared in English translation; it was a rare article, whether scholarly or popular, that was devoted to her; and she was seldom referred to in books. Certainly there was no book in English *about* her. There still is none. In sum, she had virtually no audience here. (p. 356)

[It] was not easy for her to emerge from her general obscurity. She could claim no participation in the revival of a modern Jewish state or in its newly emerging literature. Her language was German, not Hebrew, or what is even more popular with an American audience, Yiddish. Her origins seemed somehow both archaic and anachronistic, in either case hard to sentimentalize; born in Berlin, the *old* Berlin, she was now living in Stockholm. Most distancing of all, perhaps, was that her art form was not only poetry but lyric poetry, and lyric poetry of an intensely personal, even private, kind—"glowing enigmas" as she herself called a large section of her work. She was not easily or naturally prepared for, but seemed, instead, suddenly to have materialized. What accounted for her?

The answer, of course, centered chiefly in her subject matter. She was a poet, *the* poet now of reputation, of the Holocaust, or, as she came to name it, of *das Leiden Israels*, "the sufferings of Israel." The titles of her books, by themselves, indicate her single, overriding concern: *In den Wohnungen des Todes* ("In the Dwellings of Death," 1947) was published immediately after the war and showed, from the start, that she had undertaken to commemorate the enormity of Jewish suffering in Europe. Her later work, collectively dedicated "to my dead brothers and sisters," continued and extended this same direction. . . . As these books make clear, Nelly Sachs was devoting her poetry and, with it, her life to remembering and ennobling the tragedy that had overtaken her time and her people. Hers was the most prodigious, the most consistently sustained, effort in poetry to record the Holocaust of European Jewry, and the Nobel Prize Committee, in honoring her, seemed also to be extending solemn honor to the millions who had gone to a silent, uncommemorated death. Through her voice, remarkably never highly impassioned, never outraged, they were given a chance to be heard. (pp. 356-57)

What can be said of [*O the Chimneys* and *The Seekers and Other Poems*]? First, one must be initially grateful for their appearance, inasmuch as they do now make available to American readers the work of an important but heretofore neglected poet. Second, although each volume is a collection of selected poems, the two together present almost the entirety of Miss Sach's mature poetry. (p. 358)

Miss Sachs's writings, persistent as they are in their remembrance and interpretation of the tragedy of the Holocaust, accumulate their effects most strongly in large groups of poems. Taken collectively, they comprise a moving body of poetry, but the fact is that in no single poem is Nelly Sachs as powerful as Paul Celan's *"Todesfuge,"* Jacob Glatstein's "Without Jews," "Smoke," or "Not the Dead Praise God," or Aaron Zeitlin's *"Ani Maamin."* This is not to deny the high value of her poetry, but only to begin to focus on where that value lies—not in any single masterpiece, but in coherent units of work. Miss Sachs was surely conscious of this quality in her poetry, and often, in her books, she took care to place particular poems in specific groupings, designating each of these by a separate title. . . . In each case, the poems in the sub-sections relate to and reinforce one another, and, in this fashion, they begin to accumulate a total effect of theme, mood, and general poetic value. This interrelatedness is basic to Nelly Sachs's poetry and, probably more than anything else, helps to direct and make meaningful the reader's response to it. To a remarkable degree Nelly Sachs's poetry all tends to move in the direction of a single, large poem, a pained but transcendent *kaddish* for the dead. This is its pathos, its beauty, its fullest achievement. (pp. 358-59)

I see no chance of Nelly Sachs winning a popular success with the Jewish reading public, or any other reading public, in this country, and essentially for one reason: she asks too much of us.

Nelly Sachs's poetry is a poetry of deep and even fearsome mood, so much so that one can enter into it only at the cost of rather severe detachment from the normal mood of one's daily life. There is a risk involved in reading such poetry, and the risk goes hand in hand with the kind of enrichment which the poetry can provide. A deepening of spirit can be gained only through an open release of spirit, through genuine engagement of the reader's imagination with the imagination of the poet. And Nelly Sachs's imagination, molded to such a great extent by her extreme empathy with the Jewish catastrophe in Europe, is often not far removed from silence and from the madness that waits within, and on the other side of, silence. . . . It is a poetry intimately familiar with despair—as it had to be, given its special task—and much of it records the torment and "lucid madness" that were both the accompanying pain and the possible victory of the poet's perceptions. (pp. 361-62)

"What now?" So many of Nelly Sachs's poems raise the question, and although various replies are given—ranging from rebirth in Israel, to silence, to madness, to death itself—the question finally remains unanswered. . . . Her poetry involves a continuous seeking-without-finding, a "wild craving after home" with the knowledge that, after Auschwitz, the world is homeless. . . . (p. 363)

"What now?" As one reads steadily in Nelly Sachs's poetry, one is beaten down by the persistence of that question, by the sheer tenaciousness of spirit that brought the poet to raise it again and again. She paid a high price for remaining faithful to this huge historic uncertainty which her terrible age foisted upon her and from which she refused any false release. The severe dislocations from normalcy, from common orientations to time and space, that characterize her poetry are part of this price. It is a poetry carved out of pain, a series of "dreams" evolved "out of wounds," as she again describes it in one of her late poems. Time, in her world, is *Herzenszeit,* and the heart, opened by a wound that will not close, counts off time by the heavy strokes of suffering and longing. Space is likewise abstracted from any framework of recognizable place and becomes, instead, *Schmerzenländer* ("lands of pain") and *Schweigen . . . ein neues Land* ("silence . . . a new land"). Life in this landscape of abstract and fragile dimensions is itself highly abstract and fragile, and is constituted principally of ephemeral and fading things: shadows, breath, trembling winds and nearly extinguished lights, an occasional sunbeam, sand and dust. There is not much permanence in such a world and certainly little comfort, yet it is an authentic world and honestly reflective of Nelly Sachs's experience. An exile herself, searching but never finding a true return to home, she finally lived a poet's existence in the sheer "language of breath." A finely articulated language of suffering, of all our suffering, became her home and her important legacy to us. I doubt that many will want to join her there. (pp. 363-64)

Alvin H. Rosenfeld, "The Poetry of Nelly Sachs," in Judaism *(copyright © 1971 by the American Jewish Congress), Vol. 20, No. 3, Summer, 1971, pp. 356-64.*

[The posthumous volume] *Teile dich Nacht* (the phrase comes . . . from one of Nelly Sachs's poems) is divided into four sections: the first contains poems written between 1962 and 1967, related for the most part to *Glühende Rätsel;* the second and third the beginnings of a new cycle which develops further the imagery and linguistic resources that went to the making of *Glühende Rätsel;* the fourth poems written in 1969, the last year of the author's life. Variants and fragments are not reprinted—these await the full critical edition which will surely become necessary in the near future.

Nelly Sachs conducts her "search for the living" out of a constant awareness of death and a possible spiritual attrition that is worse than death. The beloved, a "Du" addressed in many of these poems, has gone before into darkness, murdered by those who have killed humanity within themselves; reality and memory are filled with the presence of silent victims, human and animal, the hunted and their hunters. The "I" that addresses us or communes with itself speaks out of a physical sickness and weakness that threaten, constantly, to extinguish the envisioning spirit, close the eye that sees, silence the voice that still makes itself heard. Behind and within such awareness is the most terrible memory of all: that of a time in which the poet had been literally struck dumb by shock and suffering, had undergone an agony akin to death, mute as a fish. As omnipresent as the theme of death is that of homelessness: the feeling of being exiled from the country whose language is the poet's mother-tongue, of searching for communion among a people of alien speech.

It is not difficult to see what historical realities are reflected in these solemn poems, what persecutions and murders and drivings-out, what racial, national, ideological intolerance. Nelly Sachs offers her readers no easy consolation; she does not prettify or seek—as another German poet has so memorably said—to decorate the slaughterhouse with geraniums. The slaughterhouse is there, constantly present as immediate experience and indelible recollection. Yet terror and the experience of inhumanity are transmuted, through Nelly Sachs's characteristic alchemy, into fellow-feeling for all that lives; homelessness is transformed into a sympathetic "openness" which transcends limits and frontiers; alienation becomes a sense of nearness to other beings that feel strange and lost; hatred and bitterness are swallowed up in reverence and love.

These are not easy victories, and the poems that communicate them are not easy poems. Their rhythms are occasionally jagged and tortured, their leaps from image to image abrupt. They end, almost all of them, on the syntactical sign "—", the dash of aposiopesis, incompletion, receptiveness; they stand by themselves yet need also to be sustained and supplemented by each other, as men do. They are knit together by a recurrent imagery which looks back to a long poetic tradition yet grows in personal significance from poem to poem: sand and desert, the butterfly, the dumbly suffering fish, the circulating blood, the rolling planets; the figures of Deborah, Job, the Hebrew prophets; Leonardo da Vinci looking for a colour blacker than black to render the blackness of darkness; the mad, the sick and the old, the hunters and their victims. They are knit together, above all, by the need not to minimize the suffering of which the world is so full and yet to give that suffering a positive significance—so that one poet's transmutation of her pain and loss may increase the sum of humanity and understanding in the world to which she belongs. . . .

Loving openness to the unknown in the midst of pain and suffering: that is the keynote of Nelly Sachs's last poems. Here the urban, the intimately domestic, encounter the cosmic; personal concerns blend with the great searchings of mankind; the teachings of Jewish sages coexist easily with Christian symbolism and Germanic fairy-tale; what is still sayable merges into what can only be hinted at. Mystery and reality are conveyed together, through anaphora and aposiopesis; through a grave, sweet word-music that never becomes an empty swell but is caught up in short, spare lines in which the rhythm, the sound, the denotation and the connotation of each word receive their full weight. Nelly Sachs's voice is unmistakable in every one of her poems. . . . It is the voice of a major poet whose reputation this posthumous volume can only enhance and sustain. (p. 1265)

"Exile, Silence and Death," in The Times Literary Supplement *(© Times Newspapers Ltd. (London) 1971; reproduced from* The Times Literary Supplement *by permission), No. 3633, October 15, 1971, pp. 1265-66.*

* * *

SACKLER, Howard 1929-

Sackler is an American dramatist and screenwriter whose best-known play, *The Great White Hope,* explores race relations in a dramatization of the tragic but flamboyant career of America's first black heavyweight champion, Jack Johnson. Sackler won the Pulitzer Prize, the New York Drama Critics Circle Award, and a Tony Award for this play. (See also *Contemporary Authors,* Vols. 61-64.)

JULIUS NOVICK

Mr. Sackler has written a great sprawling chronicle in twenty scenes, laid between San Francisco and Budapest, as "Jack Jefferson" wanders the earth looking for a place where he can live in peace with his heavyweight title and his white mistress. Aristotle named "spectacle" as one of the parts of tragedy, and *The Great White Hope* is spectacular: it features a cakewalk, a prayer meeting, a voodoo ceremony, a funeral, and crowd scenes of all sorts. (p. 93)

Sackler's play is by no means one entire and perfect chrysolite. For one thing, it is far, far too long; I do not object to three-and-a-half-hour plays on principle, but this one repeats itself too many times. Furthermore, some of the important characters are unrealized in the writing; the champion's mistress, especially, is far too gracious, too faithful, and generally too perfect to be altogether persuasive. Even Jack Jefferson himself, until he is undermined by the persecutions he suffers, is somewhat too good to be true. For a wide array of additional reasons, a number of scenes fail to come off; the script "needs," as they say, "work."

But *The Great White Hope* matters very much all the same, just as it stands, because Sackler has gotten hold of a vitally significant piece of history, has realized just why it is significant, and has put that significance, in vivid human terms, on the stage. Jack Johnson/Jefferson, as Sackler depicts him, is not a well-behaved, serious-minded Negro like Booker T. Washington or Sidney Poitier; he mocks at white society, and he sleeps with a white woman. And this, in the land of the free and the home of the brave, is unendurable; America, Sackler suggests, absolutely cannot stand a "bad nigger."

For a while I sat watching the play and fighting its implications. I had it in mind to accuse Sackler of catering to the absurd, ugly and dangerous kind of Negro paranoia. . . . The play is by no means a calm and balanced assessment of the situation, but it seems clear to me that what Sackler implies is at least basically true; ours is still a racist society. But whatever conclusion we come to, the play demands of us, in urgently dramatic terms, that we examine the whole question and our stake in it. (pp. 93-4)

Julius Novick, "Tragic Cakewalk," in The Nation *(copyright 1968 by the Nation Associates, Inc.), Vol. 206, No. 3, January 15, 1968, pp. 93-4.*

RICHARD GILMAN

Howard Sackler's *The Great White Hope* is so pertinently addressed to our present concerns, makes such intelligent use of so many stage resources, possesses such fine energy in places and offers so many superior moments that I wish I could embrace it wholeheartedly and not feel, as I do, that something central hasn't been accomplished, something remains below the mark. The mark I have in mind is that line which nobody can or would want to fix with precision but that is there anyway, separating the plausible and welcome from the conclusive and inimitable. This play about the first Negro heavyweight champion, Jack Johnson, is distinguished, in other words, by everything except final authority, unassailable rightness.

Sackler has taken a history and a legend and animated one while revising the other. (p. 36)

In taking hold of [the events of Johnson's career as a fighter] Sackler moves throughout to establish a two-fold dramatic actuality: that of Johnson's own beleaguered, far from simple being and that of American racial consciousness and bad dream, for which he is both instigator and innocent occasion. The material calls unmistakably for some sort of "epic" treatment, but Sackler's choices aren't fully assured or in coherence with each other. Wavering among Brecht, topical revue and a sort of historical pageantry for his main structural lines, he has also to try to make space and atmosphere for his protagonist's private experiences. The failure quite to bring this off is responsible, I think, for the curious intermittent sagging of our interest, a curious thing because so much of the time we're being vigorously and adroitly solicited and because the raw stuff of the drama is so high in natural energy. . . .

Beyond this, there is the problem of Sackler's language. A case could be made for its doing the job, for its adequacy and general appropriateness. Yet if this is true, and I think it is, if Sackler seldom over-writes (a line like this is rare: "Time again to make us a big new wise proud dark man's world") it remains true, too, that he's done very little more than the job; he hasn't lifted this splendid material into any kind of irrefutable new statement. The point has nothing to do with a failure to be sufficiently "literary" but simply with Sackler's inhibitions (as I see them) in the face of history, which seems to demand restraint, a colloquialism designed to protect its "human" quality by adhering to the clichés and inadequacies of actual speech. But history is only ransomed by speech other than its own, by amazing utterance, and Sackler's gifts are clearly not for that. (p. 38)

Richard Gilman, "Not Quite Heavyweight," in The New Republic *(reprinted by permission of* The New Republic; *© 1968 The New Republic, Inc.), Vol. 159, No. 17, October 26, 1968, pp. 36, 38-9.*

JOHN SIMON

[*The Great White Hope*] generates considerable excitement. Generating excitement is not nearly so good as generating art, but, in these lean times, may have to do. How nice if Sackler, who had the good sense to use Shakespeare and Brecht as his models, had come up with something worthy of them; unfortunately, the writing is only hard-working, competent but overambitious middlebrow stuff. . . . (p. 707)

Nevertheless, the play has energy and variety. It knows when to hurtle and when to sashay forward, there is humor in it, and it does generate a growing sense of entrapment and doom. The Negro speech patterns are accurate and flavorous, and the protagonist, for one, does emerge a full and appealing human being. The other parts, even when they are no more than stereotypes, are at least swirlingly animated stereotypes. . . . Sackler has at any rate sketched in a historical play conceived in the grand style; some credit is due for the very boldness of his concept. (p. 709)

John Simon, "Chronicles: 'The Great White Hope'," in The Hudson Review *(copyright © 1969 by The Hudson Review, Inc.; reprinted by permission), Vol. XXI, No. 4, Winter, 1968-69, pp. 707-10.*

ROBERT KOTLOWITZ

Sackler has written a play [*The Great White Hope*] of caterwauling theatricality, in which all the surface techniques are distracting enough to nearly obscure the fact that almost nothing at all seems to be happening inside any of the characters. (p. 108)

And with it all goes an uncomfortable, nagging feeling that we have seen it before, nearly a quarter of a century ago, that it reminds us too much, in fact, of *Native Son,* that Jack Jefferson is Richard Wright's agonized hero, Bigger Thomas, swollen to celebrity size. But while *Native Son* was the direct, hot expression of uncontrollable black anger, *The Great White Hope,* written by a white man, seems in some of its aspects an act of nearly appalling self-hatred. It is populated by a huge cast of black angels (with one exception) and malevolent whites (with two exceptions), which allows us, the (mainly white) audience, to make a perfect cop-out: we can't identify with those whites onstage, it's not us up there, it's a race of other, vile Americans, whose guilt, however, we are perfectly willing to shoulder for the evening.

The Great White Hope has an enormous impact on audiences; and it is this impact, not the play itself, that is what people talk about. . . . (pp. 108-09)

Robert Kotlowitz, "Victims: Two Films and a Play," in Harper's *(copyright © 1968 by* Harper's Magazine; *all rights reserved; excerpted from the January, 1969 issue by special permission), Vol. 238, No. 1424, January, 1969, pp. 107-09.**

MARTIN GOTTFRIED

[*The Great White Hope*] was writing in the classic sense: rich *verbal* writing—verse, in fact, though few noticed that (which was as it should be if the verse is working and reading right). But it was also a production concept, a play of times, places, sounds, music, movement and shapes as well as of language, metaphor and humor.

The four plays in [*A Few Enquiries*] are very much the same sort, written with the stage in mind. . . . (p. iii)

What makes these plays—and Sackler—so unusual is that they are classical and poetic while being modern in their treatment of reality and their sense of the stage. They are literary, yet production-oriented. In short, Sackler is an artist, speaking in a unique voice without trying to fit into one school of playwrighting or another. His plays aren't naturalistic, but neither are they abstract. They work in the spaces of surrealism, where reality can be heightened or lowered, and so they must be read that way.

Sarah I find a play of great mystery, perhaps the most intriguing of the four. It is set backstage at a Victorian ballet theatre. There are terribly few playwrights who are interested in period, and even fewer who are capable of it. Yet, the theatre should be a place of pictures, of strange places. (pp. iii-iv)

The period of *Sarah* and, of course, its ballet setting, gives it a sense of Degas and that is how it should look—like one of the painter's gas-lit, frightened young ballerinas. The spookiness of the play—recurring, gory stage accidents; the dead dancer's stunned mother who had some (implied) relationship with the company owner—this spookiness is what the play is about. Looking for other meanings will only take you away from it.

There are some peculiar words in this play. Archaic dance terms like "pas de lyres," "congé" and "caracoles" aren't just indications of Sackler's research (though he is a formidable researcher). They are settings for othertimeliness and you will find others throughout the plays. (p. iv)

I find *The Nine O'Clock Mail* the weakest of these four and interestingly enough, it is the only contemporary one (that is, about fairly young people in a fairly familiar setting—a suburban home). It is the weakest, I think, because it is the only one primarily structured to make a point, because the point is not worth the effort, being too coy and pop-psych, and because the climax is contrived.

Mr. Welk and Jersey Jim is something else again. Now here is neat playwriting, a song and dance about words, a vaudeville turn in one act and a tragic one at that. . . .

Skippy is a mystery in three events. The events are the death of Harry's mother, the robbery of his store and the expiation of an old guilt. Its main thrust is the marital relationship that overcomes these events. (p. v)

Relationships run through all the plays: devoted, as in the Harry-Muriel marriage; suspended, as between Mrs. Webster and Mr. Bunn in *Sarah;* neurotic, as between Cynthia and Ted in *The Nine O'Clock Mail;* sadistic-masochistic, as between Mr. Welk and Jersey Jim. The plays have other things in common: the connection between love and vitality; fantasy; accidents that alter the course of a life; and ritualism.

The ritualism is striking. In *Sarah,* the young ballerina reenacts a death. In *The Nine O'Clock Mail,* a man cannot make love to his wife until he completes his obsessive mail ritual. In *Mr. Welk and Jersey Jim,* the rehearsal of a cross-examination becomes a macabre puppet performance for a half mad attorney and his victim-client. Finally, *Skippy* is about a man who needs one death to atone for another.

But it is Sackler's overall title, *A Few Enquiries,* that best ties the quartet together. The quote is from *Hamlet* (II, i), and is one most productions omit. It is Polonius speaking, asking Reynaldo to check in on Laertes in Paris. Like Polonius, Sackler's people are groping, with love and confusion, for contact—needing to know just what is going on with those they are close to and not being able to find out. . . . Upon *these* inquiries, Sackler himself is inquiring into the natures of these troubled lives—"how, and who; what means; and where they keep; what company, at what expense." At what expense—the question is crucial. What is given up for closeness?

To ask these questions, to make these inquiries, Sackler uses forms that are proportionate and diverse. Most consequentially—at least for the theatre—he uses the language with care, the structures with confidence, at a time when both language and structure are both suspect and rare. He is disciplined in a period of anarchy, writes for actors in a period of performers. He is his own man, as any artist must be. (pp. v-vi)

Martin Gottfried, in his introduction to A Few Enquiries *by Howard Sackler (copyright © 1970 by Howard Sackler; reprinted by permission of The Dial Press), Dial, 1970, pp. iii-vi.*

MEL GUSSOW

[In "Semmelweiss"] Howard Sackler has taken the life story of Ignaz Phillipp Semmelweiss . . . , the pioneer Hungarian physician, and transformed it into the spell-binding evening of theater.

On its very simplest level, Mr. Sackler's new play is a medical melodrama. . . . But given the playwright's talent . . . , "Semmelweiss" becomes something greater.

It is a classic story of conscience versus compromise, the individual combating convention. The play is not only about one courageous doctor, but also about all visionaries who have been brutalized for their ideas. Mr. Sackler's Semmelweiss is, in short, a legitimate hero and, finally, a martyr. . . .

Mr. Sackler is, of course, the author of "The Great White Hope." . . . In "Semmelweiss," Mr. Sackler uses a related approach. This is not a historical pageant, but a theatricalized interpretation. . . . [The drama] is developed in a tightly meshed long skein of encounters. There are three unrelenting acts, and an enormous cast which becomes a chorus of antagonism. Like Mr. Sackler's Jack Johnson, Semmelweiss is alone in a dilemma that rises in urgency. . . .

In the nine years since "The Great White Hope" it seemed that Mr. Sackler might be one of our many one-play American dramatists, who fail to equal their initial success. "Semmelweiss" makes it clear that Mr. Sackler is not only a playwright of stature, but an artist of maturity and vision. . . . It is a play that should endure.

Mel Gussow, "Masterly Drama in 'Semmelweiss'," in The New York Times, *Section III (© 1977 by The New York Times Company; reprinted by permission), November 24, 1977, p. 15.*

* * *

SARTON, (Eleanor) May 1912-

Sarton is a Belgian-born American poet and novelist. Her novels are distinguished by a fine sense of narrative technique and a simple, unadorned prose style. Critics acknowledge her skill in creating sensitive, revealing portraits of women. (See also *CLC*, Vol. 4, and *Contemporary Authors*, Vols. 1-4, rev. ed.)

DORIS GRUMBACH

May Sarton is very good, has always been very good, in suggesting personal bonds which hover on the edge of what we used to call "irregularity." Subtly placed and sketched in, they are often unknown to the persons themselves but for us they serve to deepen the understanding Sarton permits us of her characters' motivation. . . .

Although I persist in my feeling that "As We Are Now" (1973) is still May Sarton's best fiction, I find "Crucial Conversations" moving, in a way that few of her novels are. It is not without flaws, it is not prime Sarton, but then we are still waiting for what we have always expected she would some day do, and has not yet quite done. Her work gives us the sense of the perpetually promising; we look back over a just-read work with regret born of our recognition of her partial success. Here the structure is simple, almost too simple, direct without implication.

But as is usual with this poet-novelist who has never had quite the recognition her lifetime of work has deserved and has never achieved quite the full extent her talent seemed to portend, she offers us incidental insights. Howard Johnson's restaurants, she writes, "represent to those far away from home absolute security, the security that comes from knowing exactly what to expect in exactly what surroundings." And [in "Crucial Conversations"] when Poppy demands of Reed a generous settlement, Sarton wonders: "Was it really that almost no one was fully prepared to pay for his real life?"

May Sarton has always been fully prepared. Hers has been a long, fruitful, often valuable struggle with her muse, achieved amid the solitary terrors and pleasures of a single life. She has dealt with every aspect of the female existence, with every kind of love. In this latest novel she has taken another, new (for her) step forward, and suggested a radical solution to the human-bondage-in-marriage status. For her it is a daring leap.

Doris Grumbach, "Crucial Conversations," in The New York Times Book Review *(© 1975 by The New York Times Company; reprinted by permission), April 27, 1975, p. 4.*

JAMES MARTIN

May Sarton's poems [in *Collected Poems: 1930-1973*] enter and illuminate every natural corner of our lives. In twelve books of poems and fourteen novels, Ms. Sarton has, for more than forty years, made patient, enduring testament. The poems are not easy, nor were they meant to be, for the consciousness behind them seldom rests easy. She wanted "good violence to find organic form", and it almost always does. . . .

May Sarton's poems are so strong in their faith and in their positive response to the human condition that they will likely outlast much of the fashionable, cynical poetry of our era. One hopes that her passionate voice will continue restless and resolute for many years to come. (p. 115)

James Martin, "Questions of Style," in Poetry *(© 1975 by The Modern Poetry Association; reprinted by permission of the Editor of* Poetry*), Vol. CXXVI, No. 2, May, 1975, pp. 103-15.**

EDWARD WEEKS

Miss Sarton is usually best in her portraits of women, and

Poppy [the protagonist in *Crucial Conversations*], with her feelings of outrage and despair, is altogether believable. The interfering bachelor, Pip, has a feminine streak in him. The best scenes are when he is drawing out the twins, who applaud the divorce, or defending Poppy from the conventional criticism of her mother and mother-in-law. The desire of a woman who has been suffocated in her marriage to be true to herself in the last third of her life is very much of a reality and no longer considered a scandal in our society. The wonder is that Poppy waited so long. (p. 94)

Edward Weeks, "Life & Letters: 'Crucial Conversations'," in The Atlantic Monthly *(copyright © 1975 by the Atlantic Monthly Company, Boston, Mass.; reprinted with permission), Vol. 235, No. 6, June, 1975, pp. 93-4.*

MARJORIE PERLOFF

[Despite] the value she assigns to imagery in theory, Sarton's poems remain curiously disembodied. . . . [She] resorts to circumlocution, strained metaphor, abstract nouns, and constricting stanza forms. She sets up a wall between herself and her materials. (p. 273)

I think it is insufficient to dismiss her poetry, as have many reviewers, with the label "old-fashioned." "Old-fashioned" implies that Sarton is writing poetry perfectly adequate in itself but harking back to an earlier mode. . . . But Sarton doesn't quite bring off even those "old-fashioned" effects. Her lyrics are not reminiscent of Yeats or Hardy, two of her acknowledged influences; rather, there seems to be an unconscious split between what she wants to say—in this case, her insistence that one must be willing to take risks—and her technical apparatus. . . . Sarton longs, then, to "think in images" but resorts, all too often, to stock phrases and dogmatic assertion. There is insufficient distance between the poet as maker and the "I" as actor.

Occasionally, however, Sarton strikes a very different note. Two early poems, "'She Shall Be Called Woman'" and "My Sisters, O My Sisters" look ahead to the Feminist poetry of our own day. The theme of "'She Shall Be Called Woman'" is that Eve was happiest before she had anything to do with Adam. After the initial sex act ("the wound of desire"), she goes into the sea to cleanse herself, to recapture her own central being. She does not attain fulfillment until she realizes that she is sufficient unto herself: "I am the beginning, / the never-ending, / the perfect tree." Written in the early thirties in short free-verse lines, this poem expresses a sense of urgency wholly absent from Sarton's conventional love sonnets and meditations. "My Sisters, O My Sisters," written in the mid-forties, has a similar directness:

> Dorothy Wordsworth, dying, did not want to read,
> "I am too busy with my own feelings," she said.
>
> And all women who have wanted to break out
> Of the prison of consciousness to sing or shout
>
> Are strange monsters who renounce the treasure
> Of their silence for a curious devouring pleasure.
>
> Dickinson, Rossetti, Sappho—they all know it,
> Something is lost, strained, unforgiven in the poet.

These awkward couplets, written in a sort of Poulter's Measure with Ogden Nash rhymes, are not aesthetically pleasing, but "My Sisters" explores its theme with compelling honesty. The female poet's dilemma, Sarton posits, is "To come to the deep place where poet becomes woman," and she concludes: "And we shall never find ourselves again / Until we match men's greatness with our own." These lines could well serve as epigraph for a contemporary Feminist manifesto. Here, as in her strange novel *Mrs. Stevens Hears the Mermaids Singing,* Sarton was, in a sense, ahead of her time.

A prolific writer for five decades, Sarton has been driven to express herself in various literary forms. Perhaps if she had been born later, if she could have been more open with herself and with her readers about her homosexuality (carefully veiled in the poetry) and her real feelings about people, her verse would be less stilted, contrived, disembodied. She might have found a core of images that could express her vision—rather than the Acceptable Vision—of things. But I suspect that it is now too late. For even Sarton's most recent poems like "Letter to a Psychiatrist" turn personal suffering into hollow rhetoric:

> I watched the psychic surgeon,
> Stern, skilled, adroit,
> Cut deep into the heart
> And yet not hurt. . . .
> Old failures, old obsessions
> Cut away. . . .

Compare this to, say, Sylvia Plath's Bee Poems or "Fever 103°," and it is clear that Sarton is still erecting walls between herself and her experience. Yet "My Sisters" and the poem about Eve suggest that beneath the polite and stilted surfaces, the cloying rhymes and tedious iambic meters of Sarton's poetry, there is a rebellious self, struggling to break into speech. (pp. 274-76)

Marjorie Perloff, "Tradition and the Individual Talent," in The Southern Humanities Review *(copyright 1976 by Auburn University), Vol. 10, No. 3, Summer, 1976, pp. 269-76.**

JANE S. BAKERMAN

With the publication of *As We Are Now* (1973), May Sarton added another perspective to her continuing examination of two central and important themes. She treats in her novels two basic motifs from a variety of points of view, one of which is the driving need of each individual to "create" himself, to come to a deep and positive kind of self-understanding which will both liberate and discipline him so that he can live in the deepest and highest reaches. In the process of achieving that understanding, the individual must, also, come to understand others and his relations with them. The conflict that such a search generates is always identified in Sarton's works as the difficult and sometimes destructive thrust of each human to unite with others in friendship and love while he is dealing with an equally stronger urge to remain aloof and inward. . . .

In attempting to examine these motifs, Sarton has produced a series of novels in which various relations and points of view are explored, always striving to maintain in the works a cool and quiet tone which is designed to lend perspective and balance to what are crucially powerful patterns. That tone, a quality of perspective, is the focal point of both negative and positive critical comments. (p. 83)

While no reader is surprised to find contradictory evaluations among reviews and reviewers, one *is* surprised to find that little attention has been paid to the central themes. Too often, the analyses are limited to plot commentaries, without articulating the thematic unity of the various works. . . .

Not only are the themes themselves exciting, but the various stories into which Sarton embeds these explorations are fascinating—quite possibly a reason for critical preoccupation with the evaluation of plot and the confusion about Sarton's special, cool, clear, lucid tone. (p. 84)

The element that lends power and strength to Sarton's observations is her profound ability to deal with all kinds of love as valuable, strong, compelling. She sees the ability to handle love as central to the great energy and the deep wounds of the human condition, and she diminishes none of the manifestations of that love. Few contemporary writers have achieved that much. (p. 86)

One of her most brilliant achievements is to picture friendship as a redeeming, sustaining force; Sarton is one of the very few American writers to present a vivid picture of the importance and the nourishment of friendship between women. (pp. 89-90)

[Acceptance] of others and of one's self is close to the central purpose of human life, according to May Sarton. It is the aim of the creation of the self and the goal of all the kinds of friendship and all the kinds of love so vitally portrayed in her novels. That vitality is beautifully orchestrated by a cool, quiet tone: Sarton explores human emotions, never preaches about them, and her authorial voice is never strident. Sprig Wyeth complains in *The Birth of a Grandfather* that "People don't write enough about friendship"; the response is that "Perhaps they don't know very much about it." . . . May Sarton knows about it; she writes about friendship and love with an authority born of insight —the profit is, of course, the reader's. (p. 91)

Jane S. Bakerman, "'Kinds of Love': Love and Friendship in Novels of May Sarton," in Critique: Studies in Modern Fiction *(copyright © by James Dean Young 1978), Vol. XX, No. 2, 1978, pp. 83-91.*

JUDITH LEET

Entering into May Sarton's mind, through her [*The House by the Sea: A Journal*], is an agreeable and instructive experience. The small but telling events of her daily existence teach the reader, by example, how to reflect more keenly on one's own experiences.

Sarton's selected moments include a daily walk with her dog and cat through the woods, her feelings about aging, the visits of a close friend now almost senile, her efforts in her garden (she wishes visitors would observe it more attentively).

In her isolated home on the Maine coast, Sarton finds the utter solitude she needs for writing, and yet she does not escape periods of acute loneliness. She wrestles with the question: which is her greater need, Time for work or time for people? . . .

[Her] observations prove her theory of edging her way to the larger truths by dealing with smaller insights born of solitude. (p. 42)

Judith Leet, "On the Arts: 'The House by the Sea: A Journal'," in Ms. *(© 1978 Ms. Magazine Corp.), Vol. XII, No. 1, July, 1978, pp. 26-44.*

A Reckoning . . . is an unpretentious story deftly told. Though it turns on current themes [homosexuality], it is neither trendy nor strident. The book succeeds, unsurprisingly, as a refined and conventional piece of women's fiction.

"Life & Letters: 'A Reckoning'," in The Atlantic Monthly *(copyright © 1978 by The Atlantic Monthly Company, Boston, Mass.; reprinted with permission), Vol. 242, No. 6, December, 1978, p. 95.*

JAMES FINN COTTER

[In *Selected Poems of May Sarton*], the poems shift between established forms and free verse, the best being the least technically tight. When subject and technique converge, one discovers a work that is classic and contemporary, a "passion of the word." . . . Sarton has mastered the quality of timeless poetry, to observe and reflect at the same instant. She can look at herself objectively in "Gestalt at Sixty," examine her motives for seeking solitude, and accept age and death. Rilke's shadow falls on many poems, religious one like "Annunciation" and explicitly in "At Muzat." Sarton has an eye for the ridiculous in "Franz, a Goose" ("I am the goose of geese") and a sense of the tragic in poems on her father's death, the assassination of Martin Luther King, the Vietnam War. She favors feminine myths: Kali, Medusa, Athena, and Aphrodite, and she handles people better than nature in her poetry. (p. 121)

James Finn Cotter, "Familiar Poetry," in The Hudson Review *(copyright © 1979 by The Hudson Review, Inc.; reprinted by permission), Vol. XXXII, No. 1, Spring, 1979, pp. 109-22.**

LAURIE PROTHRO

Miss Sarton handles [the theme of *A Reckoning*] gracefully, absorbing the reader in [the turmoil of Laura, the protagonist] without depressing him. She touches on the indignities of dying, the cruelty of hospitals, the spirit trapped inside the body's broken shell, the fact that only the living can be healed by love—the dying must separate themselves from love. In *A Reckoning*, Laura is forced into these realizations; Miss Sarton already has come to terms with death's immediacy, as she reveals in her recently published *Selected Poems*. "Departure is the constant at this stage; / And all we know is that we cannot stop." But she does not dwell on death. Her poetry flows with the emotion of daily routines—smooth and calm, reassuring in its lack of extremes. Tableaux of life come alive in her poems; she records events and scenes with a painter's eye. She draws her metaphors from nature, whose cycle of creation and recreation she celebrates. If humanity could learn to let go "as trees let go / Their leaves, so casually," May Sarton convinces us, love would endure.

Laurie Prothro, "Books in Brief: 'A Reckoning' and 'Selected Poems of May Sarton'," in National Review *(© National Review, Inc., 1979; 150 East 35th St., New York, NY 10016), Vol. XXXI, No. 15, April 13, 1979, p. 498.*

* * *

SAYLES, John 1950-

Sayles is an American novelist and short story writer. His work is noted for its controlled prose style and its accurate

reflection of American dialects. (See also *CLC*, Vol. 7, 10, and *Contemporary Authors*, Vols. 57-60.)

VANCE BOURJAILY

Among the several literary careers that have started off strongly in the last five or six years, that of John Sayles is unusual and interesting. At a time when the general drift of American prose seems to be through baroque toward rococo, and the drift of narrative from psychopathological melodrama into fable and fantasy, Mr. Sayles is a revivalist of realism, old-time and unabashed.

This declaration could be supported comfortably on the evidence of Mr. Sayles' 1977 novel, "Union Dues." There will be some exceptions to it noted in describing ["The Anarchists' Convention"], a collection of short stories. . . .

The first of the 15 stories, "Home for Wayfarers," . . . is a slice-of-life piece, which displays a group of young women temporary office workers in Boston, as arbitrarily assorted as the members of a wartime infantry squad. . . . It's a display piece for a fine ear and deft control of characters. . . .

Though Mr. Sayles is generally more likely to spare his characters than condemn them, the third piece, "Schiffman's Ape," a well-imagined and well-researched account of a pair of field zoologists, is a little jarring in its hostility toward the scientists. In the fourth we are back again with blue-collar women, this time on a bowling night, and the directing of our sympathies in once more easy to take.

Then there is a *pas de deux* story called "The Cabinet Maker," in which readers of "Union Dues" will be reminded of Mr. Sayles' great relish for and knowledge of the details of particular kinds of work. . . . Throughout [the collection], the appetite for detail is both Mr. Sayles' strength and, occasionally, his weakness, for the detail is sometimes loaded on in a way that can't help but slow down the pace.

Section II of "The Anarchists' Convention" is a series of six stories that seem to have been saved from what may once have been intended as a picaresque novel about the education and travels of a high-school basketball player and drop-out named Brian McNeil. There are some good stories in the group, a little stylistic experimentation in vernacular in one or two that doesn't always work, some wit and some funny moments. (p. 15)

If John Sayles' kind of realism needs further definition, this collection suggests that it is not the protest naturalism and social despair of ancestors like Dreiser and Farrell. Society is after Mr. Sayles' characters, but they're a fast bunch, and know some good places to hide and some good people to hide with. The ancestry is more like the reportorial vigor of Jack London on one side and a little of the sweet impressionism of Stephen Crane on the other. (p. 33)

Vance Bourjaily, "A Revivalist of Realism," in The New York Times Book Review *(© 1979 by The New York Times Company; reprinted by permission), April 1, 1979, pp. 15, 33.*

EDWARD BUTSCHER

Union Dues firmly established John Sayles's gift for translating acute psychological insights into viable fiction, and [*The Anarchists' Convention*] indicates no lessening of that gift. Still, the author displays a disturbing tendency to dance at the brink of sentimentality, perhaps because he is so intent upon capturing lower-middle-class verities. Sayles's strongest virtues—his efficient plain style, his formal intelligence, his obvious compassion for his victimized characters—always prevent total aesthetic collapse, and several of the stories attain a perfect blend of manner and means. "I-80 Nebraska, m. 490—m. 205" maintains a fierce narrative pace that is almost surrealistic in its leaps from voice to voice along crackling CB waves as a rebel trucker, high on drugs and existential disgust with his culture, achieves mythic stature in his drive to destruction. . . . Despite an unabashedly romantic finale, the title story also defies the laws of literary gravity through its adoption of an ironic, self-mocking consciousness that will yield neither to the failure of the flesh nor the death of an ideal.

The Anarchists' Convention reaffirms Schopenhauer's vision of man as a creature in quest of a metaphysical reality, a reality that Sayles and his kind keep alive for us in this age of brute fact.

Edward Butscher, "Books in Brief: 'The Anarchists' Convention'," in Saturday Review *(© 1979 by Saturday Review Magazine Corp.; reprinted with permission), Vol. 6, No. 9, April 28, 1979, p. 46.*

GARRETT EPPS

[John Sayles] is described by his publisher as "a jack of all kinds of blue-collar trades." He is also, probably not coincidentally, one of our most exciting and accomplished young writers. His last novel, *Union Dues*, featured moving portraits of Americans at their jobs. . . . [*The Anarchists' Convention*] is also peopled by characters who leave the "music-masters" behind every morning; dishwashers, dog-breeders, cowboys, truck drivers, anthropologists in the field. Work does not just fill their time; it shapes their consciousness and gives form to their lives. . . .

Sayles has an unerring ear for American speech. . . . His characters, whether they are illegal aliens in California or office temps in Boston, speak with individuality and vividness. . . .

Keen powers of observation, of course, can serve as a crutch, leading the writer to produce journalistic fiction, the rendering of life without the leaven of imagination and the structure of art. "Golden State" suffers from this flaw, as do other stories in the book. . . .

Still others—the title story, and "Fission," an account of life in a midwestern bomb-shelter—are too satirical, too obviously pointed, to work as fiction. But the best stories bring together Sayles' eye, ear, and point of view to present a powerful view of America in the late '70s—a land of illegal aliens, Vietnamese refugees, sexually precocious teenagers, aging leftists and angry, restless women. At his best, Sayles has a tremendous gift for characterization—for rendering fictional people who are seen for themselves, without caricature but also without sentiment.

Two of the book's best stories—"Schiffman's Ape," about a pair of married anthropologists, and "Bad Dogs," about the sexual initiation of a high-school basketball star—present a view of human sexuality that suggests there is little difference between us and animals in this regard—that all our suffering and posturing in the name of love may be no more meaningful than the pluming and preening of our fellow-mammals during their own mating seasons. It is a measure of the compassion with which Sayles writes that this vision is neither depressing nor glib, but oddly reassuring. Such is the power of an artist who sees us as we are, at work and play.

Garrett Epps, "Tales of the Working Class," in Book World—The Washington Post *(© 1979, The Washington Post), April 29, 1979, p. M5.*

THOMAS LASK

It doesn't really require the 15 stories in John Sayles's collection ["The Anarchists' Convention"] to prove that Mr. Sayles has a winning way with the short story. In fact, any number of passages could be extracted from his two novels, "Pride of the Bimbos" and "Union Dues," to prove the point. (p. 425)

[The] six stories centering on Brian McNeil in ["The Anarchists' Convention"], if put between covers of a book, would make a substantial novella, and not only in bulk. For in their sequence, these tales constitute a rite of passage from the boy's adolescent fumbling with sex through his Western odyssey and arrival on the Coast, where the ominous portents of his future cast their shadows over him.

The collection also illustrates the author's approach to his material. A strong determinist strain runs through his work. (pp. 425-26)

Mr. Sayles's characters are end products of their environment. The heroic element is muted in his fiction. Most of the time, his people are acted upon. They do not so much suffer through life as endure it. But the harder they are hit, the less malleable they become. They become fixed, stolid, uncommunicative. That is why, in his fiction, the settings often have a richness that his people lack. . . .

Mr. Sayles is saved from the pessimistic bias of naturalism by a lyric language, a feel for the fantastic, best seen in "Pride of the Bimbos," and a sometimes hilarious sense of parody. Those ideological discussions in "Union Dues" are too good to be true. There is no Barth-like verbal prestidigitation, no cleverness or archness of a Donald Barthelme either.

Even at its most fantastic, there is a realistic underpinning to Mr. Sayles's fiction. A presupposed reality is considered the mark of reactionary esthetics, but that is to assume that everything has been said about the situations and characters Mr. Sayles writes about. . . . Rarified stages of consciousness or the extremes of sensibility are not the only stuff of fiction. (p. 426)

Thomas Lask, "'The Anarchists' Convention'," in The New York Times, *Section III (© 1979 by The New York Times Company; reprinted by permission), September 3, 1979 (and reprinted in* Books of the Times, *Vol. 11, No. 9, 1979, pp. 425-26).*

* * *

SHAFFER, Peter 1926-

Shaffer is an award-winning English dramatist, screenwriter, author of radio and television plays, literary critic, and novelist who writes psychological dramas depicting emotional complexities and conflicts. His 1973 play, *Equus,* was adapted for film in 1977. (See also *CLC,* Vol. 5, and *Contemporary Authors,* Vols. 25-28, rev. ed.)

JOHN RUSSELL TAYLOR

[The] most interesting quality of [Peter Shaffer's] work is its impersonality. His work has all the classic qualities of the traditional dramatist—cast-iron construction, a coherent and well-plotted story to tell, solid, realistic characterization, extreme fluency in the composition of lively, speakable, exactly placed dialogue—but ultimately he emerges in it as mysterious and impalpable as Walter, the central character of *Five Finger Exercise,* who, if he is the hero, must be one of the most chilly and enigmatic heroes on record. (p. 227)

[It] is unlikely that anyone would have predicted great things for him on the strength of these first two plays; the earlier, *Balance of Terror,* was a thriller about spies and counterspies tussling over an intercontinental ballistic missile, cunningly put together along conventional lines but nothing very out of the ordinary, and the later, *The Salt Lands,* was a patchily worked out though serious and well-constructed attempt to present a classical tragedy situation in terms of modern Israel.

All the more surprising, then, that his first performed stage play, *Five Finger Exercise,* should be so outstandingly successful on every level. For one thing, in it Shaffer invades that most dangerous of all territories for an English dramatist, the prosperous upper-middle-class drawing-room of a house in the Home Counties. Not only that, but his play is put together with the theatrical aplomb of a Pinero, well provided with dialogue of remarkable crispness and articulacy, and technically very much part of the mainstream tradition of British drama; it would have been written in much the same way (though perhaps it would not have found such ready backing) if John Osborne and the rest had never lived. (pp. 227-28)

[*Five Finger Exercise*] claims our attention not only for its traditional virtues, which are considerable, but because if we look at it more closely it turns out to be an unusually skilful and unexpected foray of new ideas and new perceptions into the fustiest stronghold of convention; having convinced the old-fashioned West End playgoer that it is 'all right'—not sordidly concerned with the kitchen sink, and certainly not in any way experimental, but just an ordinary play about people like you and me—it proceeds bit by bit to strip its characters and their way of life bare with as much ruthlessness as Ionesco sets about rather the same business in *The Bald Prima Donna.* Only here the weapon is psychological penetration: Shaffer takes the typical Dodie Smith-Esther McCracken family—fussy, scatterbrained mother, stolid, inarticulate father, bossy tomboy daughter, arty varsity-bound son—and instead of accepting them as the self-evident, indisputable *données* upon which a light comedy or drama can be based, he asks us to look at them, consider why they are as they are, and what would happen if suddenly something unexpected, from outside their normal experience, should intrude on the settled picture of complacent mediocrity.

The intruder in this instance is Walter, a strange, charming, mysteriously reserved young German tutor who acts as a catalyst for all sorts of violent and unexpected emotional reactions. Each member of the household sees him as a potential ally or lover: the mother dreams perhaps of a discreet affair with him or more probably of amorous proposals flatteringly pressed upon her and skilfully parried; the father finds he can talk to him in a way which is unthinkable with his own son; the level-headed daughter finds his lack of involvement disconcerting, and the son discovers in him at last the congenial companion he has been seeking (his mother in a bout of bitter fury at the end, when Walter has revealed that his feelings for her are infuriatingly filial, suggests that Clive's feelings for him are tinged with homosexuality, but there seems no real reason for us to believe her).

The originality of the observation, all the more potent for being disguised beneath an apparently conventional surface, is paralleled by the veiled originality of the form of expression used. Taken line by line there is nothing at all surprising or upsetting about Shaffer's style: it is just the usual pruned, heightened realism of traditional stage parlance. But if we look at the play as a whole it at once becomes apparent that the action does not progress, as one would expect, by way of conversations leading purposefully towards clear stages in the dramatic argument; instead, the play organizes itself into a series of splendid self-revealing tirades, usually directed at the passive, uninvolved head of Walter, who remains so mysterious (necessarily to his function in the play) precisely because he alone of the characters is not permitted to reveal himself in this way—the other characters reveal themselves to him just because he does not react sufficiently to spoil the imaginary pictures of him they are building up in their minds or step outside the role each has assigned him in his or her personal drama.

Five Finger Exercise is immensely clever, extremely well written, and completely theatrical in the best possible sense of the term; it is one of the most finished plays we have seen in the last five years. It is also quite impersonal, almost as though the author has felt it his duty to keep himself entirely out of the picture. This is not necessarily a bad thing . . . but it is disconcerting. (pp. 228-29)

John Russell Taylor, "Peter Shaffer," in his Anger and After: A Guide to the New British Drama *(© 1962 by John Russell Taylor; reprinted by permission of A D Peters & Co Ltd), Methuen and Co Ltd, 1962, pp. 227-30.*

RONALD HAYMAN

Almost nothing about Shaffer's future could have been predicted from *Five Finger Exercise,* which derives much of its basic plot from Turgenev's *A Month in the Country* but remains much more pedestrian, with nothing like the same sensitivity to atmosphere or the same penetration below the surface of character, though the adolescent son, with whom Shaffer can empathize most easily, emerges in greater depth than the others. Still, it is an impressively solid piece of theatrical craftsmanship, with cleverly contrived tensions, plentiful opportunities for the actors to engage the audience's emotions and effective build-ups to slightly melodramatic climaxes. . . .

The ambitious *Royal Hunt of the Sun* . . . was seriously overrated. Shaffer was trying to present the clash of two civilizations—the Incas and sixteenth-century Spain as represented by the Conquistadores. But the confrontation is mainly a verbal one between two men, Atahuallpa, the Sovereign Inca, and Pizarro, the conquistador who ends up as a convert to the Inca faith. . . .

[In *Royal Hunt of the Sun*] Shaffer fails to produce dialogue that suggests the sixteenth century. The Narrator's speeches are better written than the dialogue but generally the language is lustreless, tumbling into clichés and even pleonasms like 'trapped in time's cage' when nothing less than poetry would take the strain Shaffer is putting on it.

Of course his courage is admirable in jettisoning naturalism so wholeheartedly. . . . Time and place are treated equally unrealistically: the action sometimes embraces two scenes going on in different locales. He uses mime and he borrows certain tricks of stylization from the Oriental theatre. He is aiming at total theatre. . . . The trouble is that instead of unifying to contribute to the same effect, the various elements make their effects separately and some of them are superfluous and distracting. (p. 61)

Many of the ideas behind the play are interesting, particularly the suggestion of an inevitable link between evangelist Christianity and acquisitiveness, but the strenuously epic nature of the form, the crowding of the characters and the congestion of the story-line leave Shaffer with no elbow-room to develop his ideas. *The Battle of Shrivings* . . . is hardly less ambitious but it is naturalistic in conception and planned so that the explicit discussion of ideas should be central to the action. The basic conflict is between two Weltanschauungs and again it is worked out in terms of a conflict between two men—an apparently saintlike pacifist philosopher, modelled unmistakably on Bertrand Russell, and an anti-liberal, anti-traditionalist poet. The tension holds until the end of Act One, when war is declared between the two men. Theatrically the possibilities are enormous. They have agreed that the old philosopher will be the loser if he throws the vindictive poet out of his house before the week-end is over and his own pacifist principles prevent him from hitting back. It may have been reckless of Shaffer to commit himself to writing dialogue for two intellectuals of this calibre, but at least it ought to have been possible for him to evolve a theatrically effective battle between them and to develop both characters during the course of it. But again he fails to fuse the action and the debate, imposing a schematic development on both protagonists. The philosopher loses faith in humanism while the poet, like Pizarro in *The Royal Hunt of the Sun,* ends up unconvincingly as a convert to the beliefs of his victim. (p. 62)

Ronald Hayman, "Like a Woman They Keep Going Back To," in Drama, *No. 98, Autumn, 1970, pp. 60-2.**

JOHN RUSSELL TAYLOR

If one could complain about [*Five Finger Exercise*] (or express doubt at all) it would be on two counts. The first is perhaps largely temporary: the language of the younger characters is full of period slang which has got far enough back to sound dated without as yet taking on a period charm, and, worse, it is the superficial expression of a relationship which has too much heavy whimsy for comfort. . . . The other cause for complaint may also be rather subjective: it is that, in a period of unmistakably individual, personal drama, Shaffer seems to be resolutely impersonal. (p. 9)

[There] is one noticeable oddity the play has, from which, if we observed it, we might wonder whether Shaffer was more than he first appeared to be. That is the way that the play, while functioning (very well) within a tradition which sedulously avoided eloquence, which cultivated the understated, the matter-of-fact (or to put it in more acceptable terms, tended to depend rather heavily on Harold Pinter's second silence, when what is really happening between people is apparently unrelated, or very slightly related, to what they are actually saying), does suddenly burst out every so often into sizzling monologues in which the characters reveal themselves in quite a different way. (pp. 9-10)

All of these big speeches have one thing in common: they tell us something about the great preoccupation of drama during the decade of theatre of the Absurd and all that: communication, its possibilities and impossibilities. . . . Rarely do two characters succeed in communicating . . . , but if this is so, it is not so much because, as it was fashionable to say at the time, communication is impossible, but . . . because people who can and do communicate perfectly will often fear to communicate. (pp. 10-11)

But still, the playwright does not seem to be personally involved in his play to any significant degree. . . . This balance of sympathy in a dramatist is of course admirable, and makes for effective drama. But might one not be forgiven for wondering if a vital spark of passion was not missing? (p. 11)

[*The Royal Hunt of the Sun*] is at once a spectacular drama and a think-piece written in rather elaborate literary terms. As Shaffer himself summarized its theme . . . , it is 'a play about two men: one of them is an atheist, and the other is a god'.

[Shaffer also stated]:

> And the theme which lies behind their relationship is the search for God—the search for a definition of the idea of God. In fact, the play is an attempt to define the concept of God.

(p. 17)

Clearly Shaffer has progressed a long way in his dramatic thinking from the easy naturalism of *Five Finger Exercise. The Royal Hunt of the Sun* is a chronicle play covering a period of over four years and many thousands of miles journeying. It is, for all that, quite tightly organized, but evidently all the material could not be encompassed in a naturalistic drama—it can be done only by calling on all the resources of the theatre, deriving techniques partly from Kabuki, partly from Shakespeare's way with history, partly from Brechtian epic theatre. (p. 18)

The Royal Hunt of the Sun was a *tour de force,* to be followed . . . with another, in its own way perhaps even more extraordinary, *Black Comedy*. This is a piece of physical theatre at its most exhilaratingly virtuoso, based on an idea of dazzling simplicity. From seeing a Chinese theatre company in action, Shaffer had retained the image of actors creating the idea of darkness by miming it. And from this grew the idea of making a farce by simply reversing the normal light values. (p. 21)

As a piece of sheer theatrical machinery the play is impeccable, as brilliant as anything Shaffer has ever done. And almost indestructible: even in a far less than perfect production the structure carries the play. (p. 22)

The idea [in *The Battle of Shrivings*] is again, as in *The Royal Hunt of the Sun,* a head-on confrontation between two different ways of life, two opposing approaches to the business of living. But on this occasion the matter is talked out rather than acted out, and consequently the play seems to be lacking a dimension. . . . *The Battle of Shrivings* is a talk- and think-piece very much as many of Shaw's later plays are; it forces us to consider the ideas as ideas, and as such they tend to seem shallow and superficial. (p. 24)

[Though verbally *Equus*] is in places highly developed and breaks out into real eloquence, it is a piece which only fully exists in the theatre, in terms of the astonishing visual imaging of the action and the way the thought is precipitated into meaningful, unparaphrasable happening. . . .

The action of the play was inspired, Shaffer tells us in his note to the published text, by a real-life case of which he was once told the bare outlines—that a highly disturbed young man had inexplicably blinded a number of horses—and no more. This occurrence has been woven into a texture obviously suggested by (or at least heavily influenced by) R. D. Laing's idea that (to oversimplify drastically) conventional modern psychiatry has been unconsciously moulded by the Establishment into a tool for social manipulation, for preserving the 'norm'. (p. 27)

[What Shaffer] shows us, not really tells us—is the process of Alan Strang's gradual deviation from the respectable norm, into neurosis and a crime of cruelty to animals which is found universally shocking, inexplicable and prima facie evidence for his insanity and desperate need for psychiatric treatment which may be hoped to restore him to 'normality'. Linked with this in the play's loose-seeming yet taut and economical structure is a progressive demonstration of the hollowness and self-questioning of Dysart, the psychiatrist who is charged with this job of mental restoration. Shaffer does not make the elementary mistake, any more than R. D. Laing does, of romanticizing madness into a vision of the truth denied to the 'sane', but he does show us Alan's particular brand of insanity as a legitimate and valuable response to experience which brings its own benefits and has to be emasculated by society in the cause of self-preservation: Dysart, with his arid, uncommunicative relations with his wife, his academic devotion to his pet dream-world of classical Greek antiquity, comes eventually to a recognition that at the very least 'That boy has known a passion more ferocious than I have felt in any second of my life'. (pp. 28-9)

The questions [raised by the play] continue to vibrate after the play is over. But the fact that they do so is not so much because of Shaffer's verbal formulations, eloquent though they be. It is because in the play we ourselves have lived through Alan's experience with him, we have experienced vicariously some of his ecstasy in naked, pulsing contact with his god, we have made our own oblation to the dark gods of his dreams. The theatrical experience the play offers is mind-enlarging because it gets at our minds through our emotions, our instincts. It does not expound Laing's theories, it inexorably shows them worked out in practice, and silences argument. Its theatrical logic and power are unarguable, and if something of our instinctive response seeps into our intellect subliminally, that is probably no bad thing. (p. 31)

It is an extraordinary development, from the sober, old-fashioned, intelligent but scarcely profound formulations of *Five Finger Exercise* to the equally controlled yet in effect explosive expression of *Equus*. . . . [Shaffer's] gradual, unsparing exploration of the expressive possibilities of his chosen form, in which technical experiment has been accompanied by (necessitated by, no doubt, since as Shaffer says, the content dictates the form) an uncompromising rethinking of the material proper for drama, his own as well as anyone else's, has little by little established him as a major figure in world drama, a theatrical thinker who triumphantly escapes all narrow definitions and ends up a unique phenomenon, like nobody but himself. After *Five Finger Exercise* we might have agreed that the play was 'promising', and felt pretty certain that we knew exactly what it promised. After *Equus* there is just no guessing what he may do next, but it seems inevitable that it will be grand and glorious. (p. 32)

John Russell Taylor, in his Peter Shaffer *(© John Russell Taylor 1974; Longman Group Ltd., for the British Council), British Council, 1974, 34 p.*

DORIS M. DAY

[*White Liars*] explores the narrow gap between truth and reality, and how one eventually accepts fiction for fact. Set in a fortune-teller's booth, it shows three characters . . . the supposedly aristocratic clairvoyant, and two of her clients, twisting the truth to suit their wishes. I feel that it is more effective in presenting the harsh truth than was [the] original script in which a fourth character . . . intervened in the thought processes of the woman, and created confusion in the situation and development of the theme.

Truth is relative, but there is no doubt that in this play we see the work of a master playwright, someone who understands the medium of the theatre and the demands of a modern, intelligent audience. (p. 82)

Doris M. Day, "Theatre Bookshelf: 'White Liars'," in Drama, *No. 126, Autumn, 1977, pp. 80, 82.**

JOHN M. CLUM

Peter Shaffer's *Equus* [is] a play about the creation of a Dionysian religion in a highly rational world, a passionate worship that also reflects the Christian world's inability to integrate sexuality and religion. *Equus* is one of a number of plays by major contemporary playwrights that deal with the place of religion in a seemingly godless world. (p. 418)

Peter Shaffer has been, in his major work, . . . fascinated with the impulse toward faith. For him the adversary of the man of faith is not a cosmic void or universal chaos; it is rationality. For Shaffer, it is the cold, clinical, empirical man without faith who has created an orderly, materialistic world that has robbed man of those irrational qualities that can make life an intense experience. Shaffer is not as concerned with the eternal design as he is with the individual who has become a diminished thing. In his play, *The Royal Hunt of the Sun,* Shaffer pitted an historic conqueror of the New World, able to sail across uncharted seas, scale the loftiest mountains, and reduce a wealthy, glorious Inca culture to slavery, against an Inca prince who passionately, if irrationally, believes he is born of the gods of the sun. (p. 427)

What fascinated Shaffer in *The Royal Hunt of the Sun* is the sense that the dark Christian world offers man no joy, no ecstasy—that perhaps there are more fulfilling faiths. Again, Shaffer is not concerned with existence of a god: he is fascinated with man's need for religion, for transcendence, for passionate submission. Athahuallpa [the Inca prince] has a real, living faith. It does not matter that he is not, as he believes, immortal. It only matters that the faith sustains him throughout his life and makes his death bearable. Pizarro hoped he could worship a god. Ultimately he came to love a son, feel grief for a fellow mortal. Through that feeling, Pizarro's life was, for a few moments, affirmed.

At the center of all the spectacle that entranced one in *The Royal Hunt in the Sun* was the clash of ideas between two men; one middle aged and despairing, the other young and filled with faith. That same clash is at the core of *Equus,* but we are no longer in as overtly Christian a society. If Pizarro was the soldier servant of the Holy Catholic Church, killing and conquering so that Christ's kingdom could triumph on earth, Martin Dysart is the conqueror of the new religion of psychiatry, conquering minds in the name of normality and social efficiency. Dysart's nemesis is not the young son of the sun, king of his rich land, but a teenage boy who has created in his mind his own kingdom of god; a boy who has, in the middle of sterile, efficient contemporary society, created and lived a primal, passionate religion replete with ceremonies and sacrifices and total ecstasy.

Equus begins as something of a mystery story, "Why did the boy blind six horses with a metal spike?" but it becomes the clash between Dionysian passion and fluorescent comfort. (pp. 428-29)

Clearly Alan Strang is abnormal in a clinical sense. The job of a psychiatrist is to restore him, or bring him, to a normal state. But what does it mean to be normal? Our psychiatrist is not sure: "The Normal is the good smile in a child's eyes—all right. It is also the dead stare in a million adults. It both sustains and kills—like a God. It is the ordinary made beautiful: it is also the Average made lethal." . . . The exorcism necessary to make Alan Strang normal is the destruction of the religion which is the core of his life. . . . (p. 430)

Alan Strange will be cured. He will be sent back into the normal world. His worship of the horse-god will be exchanged for interest in a motorbike. He will no longer be impotent, but he will have lost the passion Dr. Martin Dysart so longs for.

Equus builds on the strange story of Alan Strang, but Dr. Martin Dysart is Shaffer's central character. . . . Dysart feels want that cannot be answered by the tangible things of this world. He is successful at his job, but he has gnawing doubts about the meaning of the normalcy for which he is molding people. He has a marriage and the money to live well and travel, but the marriage is now habit and the things do not satisfy. Dysart is missing the sense of transcendence that can come from a real worship. Speaking of himself as someone apart, he says: "What worship has he ever known? Real worship! Without worship you shrink, it's as brutal as that. . . . I shrank my *own* life." . . . What makes Dysart sense a diminution is his awareness that something very basic has been lost in our technological, pragmatic society, something intangible which must be regained if he is to live meaningfully: "I need—more desperately than my children need me—a way of seeing in the dark. What way is this? . . . *What dark is this?* . . . I cannot call it ordained of God: I can't get that far. I will however pay it so much homage." . . . (p. 431)

Shaffer gives us the temple of man's faith in scientific explanations and miracles but shows that there are basic needs of man that can never be met by efficiency. (p. 432)

John M. Clum, "Religion and Five Contemporary Plays: The Quest for God in a Godless World," in South Atlantic Quarterly *(reprinted by permission of the Publisher; copyright 1978 by Duke University Press, Durham, North Carolina), Vol. 77, No. 4, Autumn, 1978, pp. 418-32.**

* * *

SINCLAIR, Andrew 1935-

Sinclair, an English novelist, biographer, playwright, short story writer, screenwriter, and critic, is a versatile author who has written satire, comedy, travelogues, and social-historical dramas. His works reveal a combination of contemporary American and Gothic English influences. (See also *CLC*, Vol. 2, and *Contemporary Authors*, Vols. 9-12, rev. ed.)

LEE T. LEMON

Andrew Sinclair's *Magog,* sequel to *Gog,* might just be one of the best novels of the past few years. The earlier book was a stumbling romp through the history and mythology of the British Isles, conducted by Gog—in his contemporary incarnation an educated and wealthy but naive Englishman whose memories include those of his mythical and historical ancestors. British history, Celtic mythology, Blake's Prophetic Books, and the Anglo-Saxon and Norman invasions get jumbled together in the journey that Gog—who starts the novel as an amnesiac—makes from Northern England to London. But in *Gog,* Sinclair is in control of neither his materials nor his style, so what could have been a magnificently entertaining and wise fiction becomes a verbose exercise in overworked imagination.

But *Magog* is a different book. Magog, in this incarnation as in the myth the practical, conniving half-brother to Gog, is not hindered by his brother's ponderous memories. He is a kind of gadfly of meaningless change, moving from a relatively high government post through assorted positions of growing power and prestige. Despite the triteness of the theme, Sinclair does a fine job of showing the reader the peculiar anguish of the successful but hollow man. By the end of the novel, Magog the manipulator has learned that time brings new and shrewder manipulators, and that one does not have to manipulate for the things which give satisfaction.

Enough good things happen along the way to keep readers of quite diverse tastes turning the pages. Sinclair does a fine job of showing the intricacies of power and has a talent for the memorable turn of phrase. I'm not sure if *Magog* will hold up after several more readings; if it does, Sinclair has written probably the best English fiction since Durrell's *Alexandria Quartet.* (pp. 83-4)

Lee T. Lemon, "'Gog' and 'Magog'," in Prairie Schooner *(© 1974 by University of Nebraska Press; reprinted by permission from* Prairie Schooner*), Vol. XLVIII, No. 1, Spring, 1974, pp. 83-4.*

DONALD DAVIE

[In "Dylan Thomas: No Man More Magical"] Sinclair has written a much more responsible book than its format and its blurbs seem meant to suggest; and I imagine many a reader, seduced by the glossy photographs and, on the dust jacket, "the best lyric poet of his age . . . the greatest lyric poet of his age," will feel cheated by Sinclair's mostly sober and judicious narrative. He supplies no colorful roustabout anecdotes and delivers instead such chastening judgments as "he was a poet of the villa and the family," or, "if his role of the *enfant terrible* was essentially false, yet he played it to its death and his own." In fact, Sinclair is in some ways altogether too circumspect; because he sets his sights so consistently on Thomas as a private and domestic person, we are supposed to know for ourselves about Thomas's unparalleled fame—when it started, how it grew, who helped it along, who exploited it. Firmly insisting that in the end Thomas's self-destruction can be blamed on no one but Thomas himself, Sinclair rightly resists the sentimentalists who would have it that the poet was "a victim," yet he could still have named the names of those who connived at the self-destruction, accelerated it and made show biz money out of it. By not acknowledging how it was Thomas's fame that enabled him to destroy himself, Sinclair cannot deal with what, it seems to me, is the permanent lesson of Thomas's life story—that is to say, what it can mean nowadays for a poet to be famous and popular. . . .

If we ask what "lyric" means when Thomas is called, as he is by Sinclair, "the greatest lyric poet of his time" (in any language, apparently), the answer seems to be . . . : a lyric poet is one who is absolved from all civic responsibilities and all moral restraints on the strict understanding that by enacting his own self-destruction under the spotlights he shall vindicate his public in its resentful acquiescence to the restraints he is absolved from. Thomas would have followed out this logic easily enough; he was very sharp and unsparing in these matters, as we see whenever Sinclair quotes from his letters and reviews. Indeed, the horror is that Thomas almost certainly knew what was happening to him, even as he went along with it. Sinclair doesn't deny this, but he doesn't bring it out very forcibly.

Probably most people believe, as Andrew Sinclair seems to, that the squalid waste of the life is justified by the handful of poems which that life, and by implication that way of life, made possible. Reasonably enough, in what is a biography not a critical study, Sinclair takes it for granted that the artistic excellence of that handful of poems is universally admitted. It is not. Thomas's gifts were very great; but he used them to achieve effects which are, though powerful, artistically *coarse.* A taste for them is a taste that cannot respond to the subtleties and delicacies of the best of Thomas's forerunners and contemporaries. And there's evidence that Thomas knew that too. This much we can salute in him—he did not fool himself.

Donald Davie, "No One to Blame but Himself," in The New York Times Book Review *(© 1975 by The New York Times Company; reprinted by permission), November 9, 1975, p. 7.*

ROBERT FORREY

Jack [a biography of Jack London] is no dull, stuffily written biography; Sinclair combines the readability of a journalist with the erudition of an academic critic. If there is a serious fault with the book, it is that it lacks adequate focus or a consistently informing thesis. Mr. Sinclair tends to be rather eclectic in his intellectual approach—a Freudian insight or generality here, a pharmacological opinion there, a conventional literary judgment in another place. . . . [It] does lead—this admiration for London—to occasional weak positions, such as saying Joseph Noel's *Footloose in Arcadia* "is the source of nearly all of the scandal about Jack's life." This is the kind of view one might expect from a Jack London cultist but not from somebody of Mr. Sinclair's independence of mind. London himself, along with his second wife, had more than anybody been the source of much falsehood about London, as Sinclair elsewhere in the biography seems to acknowledge. In fact, on the same page as the Noel indictment, Sinclair admits, "Yet Jack had been his own mythologizer, and Charmian had aided and abetted his fond falsification of his own life." To say the least. (pp. 636-37)

Robert Forrey, "Recent Books on Modern Fiction: 'Jack'," in Modern Fiction Studies *(© copyright 1978 by Purdue Research Foundation, West Lafayette, Indiana), Vol. 24, No. 4, Winter, 1978-79, pp. 636-37.*

JAMES MONACO

[John Ford's] brash patriotism seems simplistic now—as do many of his films (still regarded by many as the height of Hollywood art). But the sentiments were deeply felt, and honest, and in the end informed by some compassionate values. Ford remains a very testy character: the sort of artist who requires an *apologia pro vita sua* rather than a straight biography.

Andrew Sinclair, novelist, historian and filmmaker, has provided just that in "John Ford." . . . The picture that emerges is problematic, as was the man, but in the end affectionate. Ford's life was writ large, and Mr. Sinclair rises to the challenge, spinning his yarn with less blarney than you might expect. (p. 20)

James Monaco, "Two Directors," in The New York Times Book Review *(© 1979 by The New York Times Company; reprinted by permission), March 4, 1979, pp. 20-1.**

BLAKE MORRISON

[There] can hardly have been a more demonic possession than that which afflicts Ernest Albert Pons, the central figure in Andrew Sinclair's new novel [*The Facts in the Case of E. A. Poe*]. Pons, a publisher's reader rather than an academic, has not only devoured every word written by Edgar Allan Poe, he believes in his more extreme moments that he actually is Poe—Poe, that is, reborn in the 20th century. . . .

Andrew Sinclair has always believed in the need to get close to his subjects or characters: when writing *Gog* he roughed it near Hadrian's Wall just as his protagonist had to; and in his 1977 study *Jack* he spoke of the 'passion' which Jack London had inspired in him. *The Facts in the Case of E. A. Poe* is part novel, part biography, but above all an investigation of the whole question of 'entering into' the lives of others. There are some narrative elements—Pons receiving a valentine, travelling, visiting a brother—but they are kept to a minimum. There are long passages which read simply as a life-history of Poe (even a bibliography is included). There is also a tricksy device at the end with Andrew Sinclair supplying 'editorial notes' purportedly given to him by Dupin, but in fact functioning as a kind of defence of the book's unconventional procedures. What are the differences between fiction, biography and autobiography? Where does the writer end and his subject begin? What is the relationship between the living and the dead, between present and past? These, Sinclair suggests, are the questions he had tried to set himself when starting out on his book.

An ambitious novel, then, but not one that readily endears itself. You can see how its faults follow automatically from its designs. The schizophrenic structure is inevitable given the disturbed central character, the interest in dual personalities, and the biography/fiction division. The meagre information about Pons's history and character reflects his subordination to his idol's history and character. But these allowances can't prevent it from seeming a mechanical working-out of a half-baked idea, and for anyone not fully conversant with Poe's life and work, this is a hard, unrewarding and at times painfully boring novel to have to read.

Blake Morrison, "Making Tracks," in New Statesman *(© 1979 The Statesman & Nation Publishing Co. Ltd.), Vol. 98, No. 2523, July 27, 1979, p. 137.**

PAUL ABLEMAN

[*The Facts in the Case of E. A. Poe*] is a rich and fascinating hybrid work—part fiction and part biography. Its hold on the reader stems, at least in part, from its use of one of the most successful of all literary formulae: the quest. . . .

The interplay of fact and fiction is complicated in itself but Mr Sinclair further complexifies a slight . . . book by making Pons a Brooklyn Jew, haunted by survivor's guilt at having escaped the holocaust in which most of his family perished. Mr Sinclair works hard to make this theme seem a natural extension of the material but the effort shows. The main strands of this book are really twisted together by intellectual force. . . .

The bulk of the book consists of Pons's reports to [his psychoanalyst] Dupin. In these, excellent, factual biographical sketches are juxtaposed with Pons's fictitious modern adventures.

Pons strives to recreate some of the poet's key experiences, usually with dismal results. . . .

These sections are excellent as are the 'link' passages where Pons reports back to Dupin. Sinclair skilfully catches the mocking repartee of New York analyst-patient exchanges, at least as they are usually represented in fiction. The question is: do the two parts fuse into a coherent work of literature? The answer is: not quite. Mr Sinclair cannot quite bring Pons and the modern Dupin into focus with the historical poet.

In the last resort, then, the book stands or falls as an idiosyncratic exercise in biography. Considered in this light, it has certain advantages over the productions of academics. Mr Sinclair's insights, credited to Pons, are those of a distinguished novelist. He intuitively perceives the relationship between Poe's life and work, anatomising it in witty and sometimes brilliant prose. He touches upon but fails to grapple deeply with the central and much-discussed paradox that Poe was idolized by the European symbolists, spearheaded by Baudelaire, and ignored, or downright despised, by American critics. . . .

Ernest Pons, in his capacity as vicarious biographer, does endow the old historian of the worm with a measure of universal significance.

It is no disparagement to say that this entertaining book belongs by right on the scholar's rather than the novel-reader's shelves.

Paul Ableman, "Questing," in The Spectator *(© 1979 by* The Spectator; *reprinted by permission of* The Spectator*), Vol. 243, No. 7881, July 28, 1979, p. 26.*

HERMIONE LEE

'No biographer can dare to describe Poe's state of mind better than he did himself. They can only hope to discern parts of their own identity in his.' Thus speaks 'Ernest Albert Pons,' the 'author' of Andrew Sinclair's ingenious and claustrophobic hybrid, part biography, part pastiche, part psychoanalysis [*The Facts in the Case of E. A. Poe*].

Pons's prose is as lush and frantic as Poe's, and he borrows freely from Poe's frenzied narrators: 'True!—nervous—very, very dreadfully nervous I have been and am; but why *will* you say that I am mad?' The unease which that tone of voice raises in all readers of Poe (who have, as it were, to go mad for the duration of the story) is cunningly re-evoked by 'Pons's' obsession with his *alter ego*. The novel sustains a clever play, along the lines of 'The Tell-Tale Heart' and 'Ligeia,' with our qualms about the narrator's sanity. . . .

Dupin's ambiguity (conscience, critic, shrink, assassin) and Pons's vacillations between clinical biographical deductions and irrational obsession are very close to Poe's methods. If, as Sinclair suggests, re-writing Poe is the only way to approach him, this is a sensitive and quite a gripping attempt to do so.

Other aspects of the book aren't as convincing. The underlying link between Poe's images of horror and the concentration camps is disquieting: the two subjects refuse to be thought about in the same breath. And there's a rather trite emphasis on America as a Waste Land. The main dissatisfaction, however, is more generally, with this sort of currently fashionable hybrid. The book falls dubiously between the facts in the imaginary case of Mr Pons, and the facts in the real case—so very much stranger than any fiction but his own—of Mr Poe.

Hermione Lee, "A Case of Possession," in The Observer *(reprinted by permission of The Observer Limited), No. 9805, July 29, 1979, p. 37.*

* * *

SLAVITT, David 1935-

Slavitt is an American poet, novelist, editor, translator, and critic. His poetry is rich in classical and historical allusion, and differs radically in character from his novels. These novels, written under the pseudonym of Henry Sutton, are admittedly produced by Slavitt for the income they guarantee and are calculated to exploit current taste in popular fiction. (See also *CLC*, Vol. 5, and *Contemporary Authors*, Vol. 21-24, rev. ed.)

Jerome Carpenter, male lead among the itinerant literati whose campus readings form a basis for the plot of *Anagrams*, is a poet: David Slavitt, try as he might, is not. From the moment we first encounter Carpenter a-quiver with 'plane phobia and poetic gestation en route to his first reading, it is clear that we are to get an episodic and all too fanciful view of the poetic process in full burgeon: or, at least, Mr. Slavitt's version of it. Worse, we are going to get the poem—in various stages of completion until, on the last page, we are presented with the finished article, a paradigm of the poet's emotional journey through the events in the novel, and approved by Carpenter, but in fact a tenth rate piece of work (and why not, it having been whipped up for no other reason than to lend credence to Carpenter's creativity?). This being so, it's well nigh impossible to think of Mr. Slavitt's bunch of writers as anything but Mr. Slavitt's version of a bunch of writers; the sexual hangups, the streams of consciousness, the timidities and the roaring boyishness—to say nothing of their impish word-games—seem like parts of a tailored script written for habitually type-cast actors. Carpenter's only human moment comes when the just-widowed wife of one of the group mistakes his poem for her husband's last work: he keeps quiet and surrenders the poem. The only flaw, here, is that it is presented as a selfless rather than selfish act.

"Lionized," in The Times Literary Supplement *(© Times Newspapers Ltd. (London) 1970; reproduced from* The Times Literary Supplement *by permission), No. 3584, November 6, 1970, p. 1291.*

HELEN VENDLER

[A] dreadful flatness and didacticism dooms all of Slavitt, whose tedious pentameters [in "Vital Signs"] offer no surprises, whose learning remains poetically inert, and whose new poems are, if anything, less interesting than his earlier ones. (p. 14)

Helen Vendler, "False Poets and Real Poets," in The New York Times Book Review *(© 1975 by The New York Times Company; reprinted by permission), September 7, 1975, pp. 6-14.**

VERNON YOUNG

[While many] poets have had to pluck up or come to terms with their grass roots before freely inhabiting a further subject, David Slavitt suffers from no such disability; child of the Eastern seaboard, and much more, he has no wilderness to exorcize. His ironic humanism is the beneficiary of three sources: his Hebraic ancestry, his education in the classical tongues and his New England residence. These divide fairly equally his interests as a poet; nearly all the contingent subjects in [*Vital Signs*, his] copious collection (186 poems, of which 83 are designated *New Poems*) are broadly accounted for by his triple inheritance. From it he has derived a sense of tragic futility in human pretensions, acquired poise, learned patience—and adopted cynicism enough to acknowledge, with Dr. Johnson, that "Nonsense we can live with is better than truth." (He never writes nonsense.) I don't know exactly what Joyce Carol Oates meant when she said, in praise, that "the near-ubiquitous voice of the era seems generally absent in Slavitt" (I'm not even sure how many poets speak with that voice!). Ubiquity is Slavitt's occupational hazard, more often his glory. He handles forensic issues as deftly as the private grief and there's scarcely a contemporary shibboleth (tourism, highjackers, Western movies, Plymouth Rock, the welfare state, militant women) at which he doesn't cast an eye: not a cold one; the labor he delights in physics cold. The contemporary mind, especially in the U.S.A., is unable to conceive that intellectual disenchantment is not synonymous with the absence of lively curiosity. The iniquities of history and the tiresome rebirth of True Believers need not affect our reconciliation with life, nor prevent our recognizing that all recovery is a necessary illusion. In the long run Slavitt agrees with Ortega: "To say that we live is the same as saying that we find ourselves in an atmosphere of definite possibilities." (Note especially "The Clearing" or the poem that supplies the title to this volume, where the poet stares into the "unpatched eye" of pain's "private face," "looking for company, for comfort, vital signs.").

If Slavitt would rather be a hammer than a nail, he knows how the nail feels but his compassion is restrained by the shrewd inference that few mortals deserve compassion. . . . He's his own man, as Miss Oates remarked, yet he speaks with divers tongues. . . . He inhabits history and the world of poetic forms as playfully as an otter its fluvial element; with no audible panting, he commands a diversity of stanzaic constructs and syllabic line-counts, tosses off ballads, sestinas, sonnets, *ottava rima,* dramatic monologues in unrhymed strophes of varying meters. Something like a duality, but not quite, offers itself to the intent reader: salvation as Odysseus or as Candide—the crafts of cutting loose or of cultivating one's garden, which amount to the same thing: art. . . . I don't know if anyone recognizes that in Slavitt Americans have their own Cavafy, their own Auden. That's much to have. . . . (pp. 595-97)

Vernon Young, "The Body of Man," in The Hudson Review *(copyright © 1975 by The Hudson Review, Inc.; reprinted by permission), Vol. XXVIII, No. 4, Winter, 1975-76, pp. 585-98.**

MARTIN LEVIN

What if—the donor in a heart transplant operation is the hospital's chief cardiologist? That's only one of the ironic What If's in ["King of Hearts,"] a novel that anatomizes the medical, legal and mythic consequences of a cardiac allograft. . . .

David Slavitt organizes . . . crises and conflicts into a reflective novel calculated to move the heart.

Martin Levin, "Fiction and Poetry: 'King of Hearts'," in The New York Times Book Review *(© 1977 by The New York Times Company; reprinted by permission), January 2, 1977, p. 18.*

ROBERT HOLLAND

Vital Signs is a selection of Slavitt's work from the last fifteen years, generous in size, in variety, and, most important, in spirit, the kind of book one should not just read, but live with.

Though he is no Yeats or Stevens, Slavitt speaks with his own quiet authority, from a relaxed, almost homely stance. And though he is not, to be sure, blazing new trails in American poetry, his poems have a classical quality which makes innovation seem merely irrelevant. Like [Marilyn] Hacker, he is fond of forms, but unlike her he does not use them as cages to restrain difficult and headstrong emotions; instead (what is more difficult) he simply lets them form themselves into the bodies of the thoughts and feelings they express. . . . [One] does not expect, from such modest instruments, the depth and range that the poet attains—from sarcastic satire (*Financial Statement*) to violent anecdote (*St. Ebba of Coldingham*) to anguished and chastened elegy. . . . (p. 294)

Learned as well as wise, Slavitt's omnivorous art devours not only his daily experience but the experience of ancient history and fable as well. I say *experience,* for the poet never uses the classics as pretentious window-dressing, but instead gives more than he takes, restoring to the artifacts the life that time, reverence, and library dust have stolen from them. This concern with retaining life—humor, spontaneity, warmth—in art, is a central theme throughout Slavitt's poetry, and a necessary principle of his aesthetic, for he sees very clearly what has happened to some of his forbears:

> Or they sing, hey-diddle, the cat and the fiddle—but
> even its nine lives prove to be finite,
> And after performing on lengths of its own gut,
> it dies and the music dies. There's a moral in it.

The moral in it, for Slavitt, is that one must turn to one's wit, and wits, one must take up "fooling around" to keep alive, taking chances with tone, form, and rhythm in order constantly to startle artifact into living art. (pp. 294-95)

Robert Holland, "Six or Seven Fools," in Poetry *(© 1977 by The Modern Poetry Association; reprinted by permission of the Editor of* Poetry*), Vol. CXXIX, No. 5, February, 1977, pp. 285-95.**

DOROTHY SINCLAIR

Despite David Slavitt's craftiness and insight, the life story of Jo Stern [in the novel *Jo Stern*] is so close to that of the late Jacqueline Susann as to cause this reader great discomfort. . . .

Slavitt, writing in first person, uses an intricate structure of flashbacks within flashbacks to narrate this pop novel which shouldn't have too much trouble taking off in a big way.

Dorothy Sinclair, "Books in Review: 'Jo Stern'," in West Coast Review of Books *(copyright 1978 by Rapport Publishing Co., Inc.), Vol. 4, No. 4, July, 1978, p. 36.*

JOCELYN PAYNE

A good horror story should make the reader's heart palpitate, make the shadows of the room seem threatening or at least make the breath quicken and the eyes, reluctantly fascinated, race over the page; *The Sacrifice* does none of these things. . . .

Though competently written in journeyman fashion the book lacks heart, a victim itself of eviscerating sacrifice. Author Henry Sutton is described as being a poet and classicist under his real name of David Slavitt. He should keep at it.

Jocelyn Payne, "Books in Review: The Sacrifice," in West Coast Review of Books *(copyright 1978 by Rapport Publishing Co., Inc.), Vol. 4, No. 6, November, 1978, p. 41.*

* * *

SLESSOR, Kenneth 1901-1971

Slessor was an Australian poet, journalist, and critic. His poetry is imaginative and lyrical, frequently showing evidence of his Australian heritage in its themes and imagery. Time, memory, and the sea are frequent themes in these poems, though often overcast with a sense of despair and melancholy.

Critics have cited Wilfred Owen as an important influence on Slessor's style. *Five Bells* is generally considered his most important work. (See also *Contemporary Authors*, obituary, Vols. 89-92.)

CHRIS WALLACE-CRABBE

The characteristic Australian poem is one in which there is just enough art to hold the job together: whether it gives voice to prophecy, belief or intimate emotion, it is unlikely to be remarkable for delicacy and precision.

In the midst of such a climate, Kenneth Slessor looks very much an odd man out. Reading his later poetry, in particular, one might easily believe that he had strayed to these shores from some more verbally sophisticated milieu, from the United States, say, or even New Zealand. And in surveying the full body of his work, as represented in *Poems* (1957), one could only be reinforced in such a judgement. For that collection charts the career of a man who acquired his artistic confidence first, and only slowly gained a measure of experience with which his art could be confronted. The verbal dandy appeared first: the poet followed after. (p. 342)

[In his early poetry Slessor] is already making of his diction a fine and flexible instrument which will be capable of transforming all manner of material into poetry. He is also, we might add, tightening his grasp on one thing he knows to be real, so that he may have some means of evaluating the ephemeral spectres of life. In the later poetry, one often feels that nothing but Slessor's verbal precision could salvage anything from the temporal flux.

Much of his early writing leaves an impression that we might define as painterly rather than poetic. In such poems as 'Pan at Lane Cove', 'Marco Polo' and even the more substantial 'Realities', the paraphrasable content is trivial and banal: Slessor's art here is found largely in his disposition of pictorial elements, of leaning statues, dark hedges, and formal pools touched by moonlight, or those remarkably intensified details which arrest the reader's attention in the first stanza of 'Pan at Lane Cove'. . . . Slessor is not interested in the respective values involved in the worlds of Pan and of Lane Cove; he is interested in the picturesque possibilities which their juxtaposition raises. (pp. 343-44)

Where the picturesque was his sole concern, Slessor's talents were undeniable. There is something of permanent value in the vividly patterned images of 'Nuremberg' and 'Next Turn', for all the remoteness of both lyrics. But where he sought to be explicit and give voice to an attitude, he merely revealed the crude simplifications of adolescent escapism. . . . (p. 344)

A much finer poem from this period is 'The Night-Ride'. It is successful *not* because Slessor has bluntly set out to find a viable analogy for his vision of life, but because it starts from a clear definition of local and specific perceptions. His magnificent verbal gifts are no longer wasted on the erection of pleasure domes in Neverneverland, but are devoted to recording the colours, shapes, surfaces of familiar things. (pp. 345-46)

We can account for the accelerating intensity of 'The Night-Ride' by regarding it as a sustained metaphorical account of Slessor's view of life as a process. His language focuses so hard on the train journey that the journey becomes the whole direction of a life. . . . And the direction is consistent with that which can be found in a great deal of Slessor's poetry: life is a rapid journey towards oblivion; other people and the bright surfaces of things are perceived through an intervening pane of glass; memorable experience consists of transient flashes amid a general obscurity of 'grey, rushing rivers of bush'.

The progression here, a progression from vivid perception towards a drugging sleep, is finally reversed—reversed, that is, without being negated—in one of Slessor's most brilliant late poems, that rhythmical and syntactical triumph, 'Sleep'. The swaying, evocative lines of this lyric carry the developing logic of three kinds of human situation. A voice speaks with soothing authority, . . . and in the course of the poem the voice seems not only Sleep addressing the sleeper, but also woman to lover and mother to foetus. In all three cases, the implied listener is held, enveloped, in a harmony of pulsing forces. And in each case these forces are protectively maternal, holding the listener back from the harsh facts which await him, and which are realized in the new, stark rhythm of the last stanza:

> Till daylight, the expulsion and awakening,
> The riving and the driving forth,
> Life with remorseless forceps beckoning—
> Pangs and betrayal of harsh birth.

Manifestly it is the best of all fates not to be born, not to be separated, not to wake up. In both these poems the most expressive passages reach towards the oblivion of the womb.

The threats of darkness and oblivion, transient phenomena and a baffled observer: from these preoccupations most of Slessor's poetry has been made, the flamboyant and the sardonic alike. The poems of his 'middle period', those first published in *Cuckooz Contrey* (1932), show little intellectual advance on the earlier work; they do however show that he has learned to use language with new precision and point. (pp. 346-47)

The unrealized fleshpots of yesteryear are giving way to wry monologues which eschew the excesses of Victorian Romanticism . . . without completely shedding its self indulgences. In 'Talbingo', 'Toilet of a Dandy', 'Metempsychosis' and particularly 'Elegy in a Botanic Gardens', the reader is aware of a familiar kind of alliance between weary disenchantment and a nervously alert wit. . . . The world of Tristan and the narratives of Courtly Love are no more than the faintest of echoes. A fine control of tone enables the poet not only to strike a balance between, but to fuse, his sense of emotional frustration and his unqualified delight in the objects of perception. . . . (pp. 347-48)

The finest thing in *Cuckooz Contrey* is also the most thoroughly original poem in that volume—'Five Visions of Captain Cook'. Here at last, especially in the magnificent fifth section, sharp observation and a fastidious fingering of words are involved in something of the first importance, because here at last Slessor's awareness of life has caught up with his mastery of language.

'Five Visions' is a concentrated drama of enterprise, action, memory, decay, and death. . . . [The] weight of the poem primarily reinforces our awareness of the flux and variety of life. (p. 348)

The poem ends with the memory of Cook's death and the image of Home's decline, for this is how life itself ends.

And in the poem at large, as in the old man's consciousness, the fulness of life is vividly displayed while the 'vague ancestral darknesses' exist no more than slenderly. Home lives in the past because this is to live with Cook's (and his own) vital exploits: and if he is now a fuddled old man, those exploits are still not cancelled out. The five visions are, as little in the early poetry was, visions of a world of experience; Cook's *Endeavour* is not 'a painted ship upon a painted ocean' but a familiar ground of human action.

The verse in part V has become a robust and flexible medium. Slessor is now capable of setting down a human situation in bold, concise outline. . . . Irony here is not a device to permit detachment; it represents a simple plea for human justice. Every detail . . . is completely functional.

Where the earlier gaudiness makes an appearance, it serves a new kind of purpose. . . . The brilliancies of Home's vision make a sharp contrast both with the tawdry inn and with the real Pacific Ocean. . . . The blind man's memory is throwing up wishful fantasies in which air, trees, water, birds, all are transformed into jewel-like emblems whose only life is a factitious one. Their very brilliance is a measure of the degree of escapism involved.

But this is not the whole story, for Home's sustaining memories are composed of facts as well as fantasies, of lived conflicts as well as halcyon days. Within a few lines we are caught up in a recapitualated narrative of violent physical action. The different quality of the old man's memory at this point is made clear by the rhythmical tightness that is achieved: there is in the verse a sense of flexed muscles and abrupt shocks. Half-line jolts against half-line, phrase against phrase, in the rush of events leading to Cook's death in the Sandwich Isles. Action is here presented without a rhetorical pattern or a false logic being superimposed. . . . [On] Cook's death, the memory fades and peace settles down once again, accompanied by the inexorable flow of the sea. (pp. 348-50)

Among the poems which Slessor published after 1933, there are four which can be said to mark the climax of his career. In these four poems, 'Sleep', 'South Country', 'Beach Burial', and 'Five Bells', the poet is completely at ease in the shaping of his experience. All the slack of his talent is taken up, his talent no longer dissipating itself in merely virtuoso effects.

It is surely no accident that these poems are among the last that Slessor wrote before falling silent. All four are marked at least by despair and frustration, perhaps by 'a faint ground-bass of disgust with life'. Two are elegies, one depicts life as a betrayal and the fourth ['South Country'], a masterpiece of expressionist landscape, ends with a strange, anthropomorphic vision. . . . 'Five Bells' is generally, and rightly, acknowledged to be Slessor's greatest achievement. After a few loose gestures in the first three stanzas, it is hard to find a flaw in the poem's shaping. The form is musical, organic, even to some extent cyclic; like a more famous poem that was perhaps being written at the same time, Eliot's *Four Quartets,* 'Five Bells' demonstrates the possibilities of this kind of form for metaphysical meditation. For the poem is far more than an elegy for a dead friend: it is an intensely dramatic meditation in which Slessor gathers up all his previous suggestions about time and flux and the value of life in a godless universe. (pp. 350-51)

The whole movement of the poem, its meditative undulation, embodies this vision of time, 'the flood that does not flow'.

It is the paradox of a 'flood that does not flow' which stands at the heart of 'Five Bells'. The structure is *both* progressive and cyclic; Joe both is and is not recalled from oblivion; life is both meaningful . . . and meaningless. On the one hand, Slessor creates meaning in the act of commemorating Joe's death; on the other, the elegy is saturated with premonitions of his own extinction. . . . Towards the end, empathy with Joe has become so complete that the poet's own fate comes to be the real concern of the poetry. . . . (pp. 351-52)

'Five Bells' is the final triumph of Sleesor's powers of language. He has made his world fully articulate and has thus set the seal upon his small but distinguished *oeuvre*. (p. 352)

Chris Wallace-Crabbe, "Kenneth Slessor and the Powers of Language," in The Literature of Australia, *edited by Geoffrey Dutton (copyright © Penguin Books Pty Ltd, 1964), Penguin Books, 1964, pp. 342-52.*

JUDITH WRIGHT

When we read the few poems Slessor has preserved from the ['twenties], certainly two conflicting impressions are left with us; the first of a . . . lustiness and decorative excess where image jostles image and texture is crusted with over-richness; but the second, which seems, as the poems succeed each other, to move nearer and nearer into the foreground, is an emptiness that underlies these feverish sensuosities, a lack of inner solidity, a perception of the abyss that increases gradually into terror.

It seems that in Slessor's poetry two conflicting forces meet —the Nietzchean cry that man must learn to suffice himself, must increase his capacities, must become physically and spiritually superior to himself; and the Nietzschean perception which underlay that demand, that when God is 'dead' nothing can protect man from the malice of the universe. (p. 140)

[In an address in 1931, Slessor] acknowledged his debt to Wilfred Owen and to Eliot, and stated his belief in 'experiment in rhythm . . . as a sort of hypnotic agent which will urge the mind to vibrate at a deeper level of consciousness than that of the superficial world'. He quotes his own experiments in rhythm changes and in 'analysed' rhyme and syllabic rhyme, 'The Country Ride', and 'Fixed Opinions' (a title altered in his latest collection to 'Fixed Ideas') to illustrate how he has attempted to carry on the experimentalism of Owen.

But experiment, he says, did not interest him for its own sake. In a radio talk . . . he said: 'The practical considerations that have guided me for many years have been those of form and experiment', form being defined as 'that shape of a work, whether in music, words or design, which seems most nearly to reflect the shape of the emotion which produced it.'

It is interesting that, in his choice of Owen as a master, Slessor took a path that English poetry, on the whole, during those years, rejected. . . . Clearly, in his admiration for Owen, Slessor's chief reason was that, in Owen's work as nowhere else, he saw the emotion behind the verse working to alter the shape and sound of the verse itself. 'The emotion of a poem', he says . . . , 'must make the experiment, not the experiment the poem.'

This interest in experiment not only provided a fresh channel for the verbal virtuosity of his early phase, but gave him a new impulse for his poetry. (p. 143)

['Five Visions of Captain Cook'] was the first of many later treatments of the theme of early sea-explorations. Other Australian poets took up the subject gladly, for its historical and rhetorical bearing on Australia's nationhood, but no one has treated it either with Slessor's inventive brilliance and lightness, or with his intrinsic melancholy. . . . The half-farcical, half-ironical note [upon which the poem ends] makes us recall Slessor's own disillusion and his denial of the city of humanity.

The note continues in Slessor's later poetry, growing in fact sharper, bitterer, more unendurable; as in 'The Castle of Glubbdubdrib', where the vision is of all the great minds of the past reduced to the status of mere slaves of the Glubbdubdribians, the cohorts of stupidity and greed. . . . (pp. 144-45)

[In 'Gulliver'] Slessor probably discovered the most precise and eloquent image of the plight of modern man that Australian poetry is ever likely to produce. Like his 'Stars', it is a pivotal poem. Where 'Stars' apparently marked the watershed between his earlier and middle phases of writing, 'Gulliver' seems to point forward to Slessor's last long poem, 'Five Bells', with its quieter acceptance of annihilation. (p. 145)

The crowding imagery, the coruscating phrases of Slessor's earlier poetry, seemed to dazzle like fireworks. . . . But behind the fireworks we are always conscious of dizzying and empty blackness, the 'cracks between the stars'. As his poetry matures, the veil of imagery thins, the darkness becomes more and more insistent. Darkness, isolated glittering lights, and emptiness—this is the background scenery of 'Five Bells'; the Harbour itself, the 'midnight water' that covers the bones of the dead men and is scarcely distinguishable from the air. And the darkness with its scattered lights seems also symbolic of the loneliness of men whose contacts are so transitory and far apart. This makes the final image of the harbour-buoys, 'tossing their fireballs wearily each to each', so obscurely moving—more moving than the bells themselves with their double reference, to time and to mortality.

This is a closely-linked and complete poem; and it is to all intents and purposes Slessor's last important communication. (p. 149)

Looking back over Slessor's poetic life, it seems as though silence was always in the background of all he has said, and has finally triumphed over his brilliant and feverish imagery. There is something about nearly all his poems that makes them seem skeletal—a construction of scintillating words, like a neon sky-advertisement against darkness. They have about them something rootless and desperate; even the increasing mastery of technique does not quite disguise their lack of content.

In the end, what Slessor tells us is that humanity is chaotically fragmented, isolated, unable to communicate with anything other than itself; (and communication between individuals is equally fragmentary and chaotic, subject to the whim of time and death). Lights spring up, glitter, seem to form a pattern, but blink out; we cannot say 'why you were here / Who now are gone'. This is not a poetry written for the sake of communication, but the desperate talk of a man who 'cannot escape those tunnels of nothingness, / The cracks in the spinning Cross'. The voice has now fallen silent. (p. 150)

[For] Slessor, it seems, activity is negated before it is undertaken. His poetry is essentially static in its nature; it is not stoic, . . . but epicurean. If human contacts are temporary and incomplete, if the glimpse of 'the moment's world' vanishes and 'the body dies and rots', what is left? Feeling certainly. . . .

But feeling too is momentary and chaotic, and may lead to cruelty, perversion, and disgust. . . . (p. 151)

[Nothing] is worth seeking, except perhaps a certain elegance in living. . . .

Perhaps this is the chief mark of Slessor's poetry—an elegance, a brilliance, that do not even seek to conceal the emptiness beneath, but describe their graceful figures as a skater does on ice.

In spite of his interest in technique and his twentieth-century despairs, Slessor is never an unconventional poet: that is, a poet who uses obscurity or jarring dissonance, or violence of rhythm or language, to express his personal distress. (pp. 151-52)

Yet the despair and the lack of direction beneath the poetry are authentically twentieth-century, and they stem, not from the Australian scene, but from European civilization and the rootlessness of the city. Pound's condemnation of 'the old bitch gone in the teeth', Eliot's 'Waste Land', find their echo in Slessor, though his preference for more traditional poetic methods and his lack of depth mask the immediate likeness. Slessor's is a poetry of the surface of life; what he cannot grasp by means of sense and intuition does not exist for him.

But this very lack of thought and emotion means that despair, when he discovers it is part of himself and of the world, is all the more irredeemable. He cannot . . . widen and deepen his world-view; he can experience, but he cannot interpret. There is a sense, indeed, in which Slessor's poetry is something very like inspired reportage. He does not seek for causes or solutions; he does not try to look into history or into the human soul. . . . (p. 152)

[Slessor] ended as the most nihilist of Australian writers—nihilist, as it were, in spite of himself and in spite of his rejection of the advance-guard of European writing, of the experimental work of Joyce, Pound and their followers. For the true nihilist is not the man who affirms the end of traditional modes of thought and feeling and the beginning of the reign of chaos; but the man for whom the meaning and significance of life are already negated by despair, no matter how elegant and technically accomplished its expression. And for Slessor, in the end, experience is rendered meaningless by its discontinuity, and communication between human beings is momentary, limited, and corrupted by time and death. Only 'the moment's world' can hold beauty and freedom and changelessness; and the moment is no more than a moment; it is not, as it is for Eliot, the guarantee of anything beyond itself. . . .

[In] Slessor's poetry the abyss is finally triumphant. (p. 153)

Judith Wright, "Kenneth Slessor–Romantic and Modern," in her Preoccupations in Australian

Poetry *(reprinted by permission of Oxford University Press, Inc.), Oxford University Press, Melbourne, 1965, pp. 140-53.*

T. INGLIS MOORE

Among Australian poets Kenneth Slessor emerges today as the finest craftsman of them all. He has mastered poetic form most completely, using it with the greatest brilliance and originality. In his skilful hands it moves like a gentled brumby, still vibrant with high mettle yet responsive to the light touch on the rein or the pressure of the knee. In his *Five Bells* each poem has its own individual shape and moves to its own distinctive rhythm. These fit the conception so closely that we feel the poem could have been written in this way only, and in no other. Subject and treatment have merged into the happiest of unions, integrated seamlessly, compelling us into conviction that the unity is indissoluble. (p. 113)

[Slessor enjoys] a variety of qualities. Gifted with an exceptional acuteness of the senses, he renders both inward feelings and outward objects with a nervous sensibility or intensity of perception akin to those of D. H. Lawrence. He gives even the inanimate chronometers of Captain Cook an almost Dickensian vitality by witty and vivid re-creations. As a satirist he can compass a Swift-like savagery. As a lyricist he modulates his rhythms to novel yet fitting effect, catches the tempo of colloquial speech, and launches his lines off with dynamic dactyls. He surprises with wholly original images, and delights with the sharp pungency of pictorial words. . . . Finally, we have Slessor the tragic poet of disillusionment, for ever pressing his face vainly against those earthly windows allowing him to see a reality of beauty which the glassy barriers prevent him from passing beyond to have and to hold. (pp. 113-14)

Slessor's poetry is most striking in its inherent sense of form. He is an architect building his constructions with a special genius for poetic design. This is only to be expected, perhaps, since no other Australian poet has concentrated on experimenting in form as continuously and effectively as Slessor has done throughout his poetic development, drawing on all the resources quarried by modern techniques. Certainly none has displayed such creative originality in constructing novel forms fitting their special functions so felicitously.

Here my conviction is deepened, too, by the absence in his best work of any birth-marks tokening the pangs of poetic travail. The poem arrives as if without labour, as if it were a Topsy that had not been born at all but 'just growed'. Each piece is idiosyncratic, bearing eyes, hair, and quirk of nose different from the features of other children sprung from the fertile marriage of Slessor's intellect and sensibility. Yet there is no doubt about their ancestry. Other influences have entered into their composition, as varied family strains enter into any child, but these have been absorbed. The poems are Slessor's own, stamped with his individual idiom. No other poet in this country—or elsewhere, for that matter—would have so worded, shaped, and cadenced such striking achievements as his 'Five Visions of Captain Cook', the superb evocation of 'Sleep', or that surprising and satisfying elegy, 'Five Bells'.

His genius for form shows itself undeniably, moreover, in the fact that he is always in the *Five Bells* collection the master, and not the servant, of his form. In the earlier *Earth-Visitors* and *Cuckooz Contrey* volumes he had often, like Browning, let the verse run away from him and cut its own pyrotechnic capers for the sheer fun of the fireworks. In these first and middle periods of development he makes the preoccupation with form too patent, and even when the subject is treated with robust exuberance one senses that the performance is dictated by the head, not the heart. The influences on the formal side, too, are noticeable. In these respects Slessor never attained the natural gusto combined with extraordinary originality of poetic design which made Browning unrivalled in all English poetry as the master of creative originality in verse form and treatment. Slessor borrowed, adapted, and combined until he finally wrought out his own constructions. Browning never had need to borrow, and invented his own verse patterns with a fecund singularity. Slessor worked his way towards a similar singularity, arriving at the highly individual patterns of the *Five Bells* pieces via the experiments in *Cuckooz Contrey*. In the later poems, his cometary rockets, his roman candles and catherine wheels, fly, whirl, and blaze in gallant display, but now he touches them off, not for their own brilliant sakes, but to use that brilliance to illuminate some subject in the most suitable fashion. Thus each piece is more than a brief burst of bravura flashing; it is also, and intrinsically, an illumination. It is a memorable revelation, with the form made one with the theme, whilst the earlier intellectual detachment has disappeared to give place to the quivering sensibility of passion and a deeply felt philosophy of tragedy. (pp. 114-15)

Five Bells clinched Slessor's claim to the front rank of Australian poets as a whole. The *One Hundred Poems* stands alongside R. D. FitzGerald's *Moonlight Acre:* these two volumes are the most important in our contemporary poetry. They show that FitzGerald and Slessor are the two practising poets in Australia today who have a calibre clearly higher than those of their contemporaries. (p. 115)

In reaching . . . maturity of thought and expression, Slessor went through three stages which displayed, along with separateness and progression, a common thread of continuity, so that we watch the unfolding of an active, experimental mind. (p. 116)

In the first (or *Earth-Visitors*) stage, the young poet of twenty-five years is largely romantic in theme and literary in diction. The luxuriance comes in his spirit and subject, however, rather than in treatment, since he displayed from the first a gift for craftsmanship and a disciplined sense of design. Indeed, the instinct for form creates effectiveness for pieces slight in content. The best poems here show traces of workmanship, but move easily and decisively, giving us the vivid painting of 'Rubens' Innocents', the skilful blending of single rhyme, double off-rhymes, and internal assonance. . . . (pp. 116-17)

If the strength of the *Earth-Visitors* stage lies in its form, the weakness is equally apparent in its content. As an intellectual Slessor is in revolt against Georgian romanticism; his dramatic poem 'The Man of Sentiment' uses the figure of Laurence Sterne to flay sentimentalism. He indicates his alternative when the singing girl Catherine tells Sterne she will leave him for lustier lads who will clip her with hotter lips. Thus sentimentalism is rejected for sensualism, and this first stage of Slessor is a sensual one, with stress on the erotic. (p. 117)

Far more significant in *Earth-Visitors* are the verses revealing Slessor as the modern artist, the first gleanings of the lode which was to pay most richly in later workings. Even at this first voluptuous feast in the halls of *Vision* the poet was deeply conscious of the skull grinning mouthlessly on the banqueting table, and this grim *memento mori* is the constant element in all his work, giving it an undercurrent of bitter continuity. The images of death—the skull, bones, and ghosts—are favourite motifs reappearing at every stage of his progress until they culminate in *Five Bells*. (pp. 117-18)

In his second stage, represented by *Cuckooz Contrey* and covering the years 1927-32, Slessor is essentially the intellectualist, and the satiric note grows stronger to stress the constant theme of frustration. Instead of McCrae and Lindsay, the influences have become those of Swift in regard to outlook and of Ezra Pound and T. S. Eliot in respect to form. (p. 118)

In the section of *Cuckooz Contrey* called 'The Old Play' Slessor uses a favourite image of the world as a theatre and life as a stale farce in the spirit of cynical sophistication used by Pound and the earlier Eliot. Every now and then, however, the real Slessor bursts into this nonchalance and smashes its brittle elegance with a passionate cry of despair. Thus the unity of this section is cleft by the incongruity between attitudes fundamentally contradictory—the flippant cynicism which is a negation of feeling in its treatment of life as a sorry jest of frustration and the deeper disillusionment which utters a vibrant Swift-like protest at its sorriness. (pp. 118-19)

Easily the best poems of *Cuckooz Contrey,* to my mind, are those in the Captain Cook series, 'Captain Dobbin', and such realistic pieces as 'Country Towns'. Here Slessor tackles life at first hand, although the romantic element enters in with stories of an adventurous past in exploration of perilous seas and strange shores. Here, in a highly flexible free or blank verse, romance and realism are blended to make a new and potent draught. Here the old frustration, cynicism, and bitterness are gone; instead a fresh, strong wind of healthy purpose and hard-won achievement blows through these tales of hardy mariners. . . .

If the varied themes and forms of *Cuckooz Contrey* denote a Slessor still trying out his powers, in *Five Bells* he sails into his home port triumphantly bearing his own idiom. In his first stage he was partly derivative, despite his good craftsmanship, while there was weakness in subject matter; in his second he was brilliant but artificial, frankly experimental, responsive to influences until he charted his own passage in the Cook series of poems; in the third stage he is completely himself, rich with assurance in his subjects and master of his medium. The two trends . . . are seen in their fulfilment: realism of theme and incisiveness of treatment. (p. 119)

Five Bells represents a culmination of previous work: the climax of a varied but gradual development. It hardly contains a poem which does not have affinities in idea or form with previous poems. . . .

This last volume shows Slessor as two poets with two dominant moods and themes, both developed from earlier work in a natural continuity. One is the sensualist, translating sense impressions into words with a fierce intensity and a delicate precision. But this time the perceptions are realistic excerpts from experience instead of excursions into imaginary worlds. Now he writes of William Street, local trams, and Sydney Harbour instead of Tartary courts and Cuckooz Contrey. The other poet is the intellectualist who has matured into a grim philosopher of time and death. The macabre touch, always present, has become stronger. The sense of desolation, again, is sharpened by the fact that it is aroused by actualities. The philosophy is not only asserted, but felt and expressed in amazingly concrete terms; the hard clarity of the intellect works in images and sense-words burning with emotional heat.

If *Five Bells* is notable as a continuation which is also a progression, it is even more striking in the felicity and originality of the forms employed. Each of the verses is forceful with its own freshness of form. . . . (p. 120)

[Slessor possesses] the easy command of a wide variety of forms, modernist and traditional alike, and the technique used to such effectiveness in 'Last Trams', 'Sensuality', and the poem to McCrae. However dazzling its virtuosity, each technique is always ancillary to the poem's purpose, convincing us that the formal dress is the only right wear for the thought. Equally striking is the assurance of the rhythms, expanding and contracting, curved or cubed at the stress of the emotional intonation, compassing a strength and flexibility beyond those of any other Australian poet. This rhythm is dynamic and sinewy, often launching off with explosive dactyls, shunning the conventional anapaest like the plague, avoiding both the metrical sing-song of romantic verse and the rhetorical roll cultivated by Wilmot and Baylebridge. In nothing is Slessor more contemporary, too, than in the colloquial character of his later rhythms, since many of the later poems are not songs but colloquies—dramatic monologues charged with Browningesque ease and liveliness. Since rhythm derives from emotion, moreover, Slessor's rhythmic vitality is an undeniable testament of his sincerity of feeling. . . .

Another quality of Slessor is his continuous and admirable concreteness of language, rich in colour sense, highly pictorial, tinged with sensuous imagery. Like Blake, he abhors the abstract in Spectre or Emanation; he practises the belief of Benedetto Croce that 'Art is Life within the four corners of an image'. (p. 122)

Finally, turning from those elements of style and form in which Slessor so excels, we come to his philosophy and find that his work reveals, first, an acute relish of life with its beauty and love, and second, a sense of frustration which passes into resentment, and finally an angry despair at the victory over life won by time and death, a victory which reduces reality to an irrevocable nothingness. Each of his three main volumes ends in pessimism: *Earth-Visitors,* after all the roistering and wenching, closes with frustration, the dissolution of life, and the passing of the bells of Music; *Cuckooz Contrey* finishes with a desolate appeal to the man-made gods not to leave us 'crying in emptiness'. . . .

[The] pursuit of death is Ken Slessor's main preoccupation as a poet; it ends in nescience, and he emerges as a grim nihilist. . . . [He] is essentially a tragic poet, beset by doom, and his finest poem is the elegy, *Five Bells,* where the tension so finely maintained throughout is clenched at last on predestined emptiness. . . . [Slessor] finds no comforting defiance or immortality in his night of disillusionment and despair; there is only the tortured bitterness of a realistic, clear-eyed acceptance of the annihilating dooms wrought on man by time and death. (p. 123)

T. Inglis Moore, "Kenneth Slessor," in Critical Essays on Kenneth Slessor, *edited by A. K. Thomson, The Jacaranda Press, 1968, pp. 113-23.*

A. C. W. MITCHELL

Close examination shows that Slessor's poetry is in fact characterized by . . . the grotesque, an element which appears in the early poems . . . as a garish and superficial ornamentation, a precious style, and a deliberate search for the unconventional, but which he learns to control and utilize with considerable effectiveness about the time he writes 'Captain Dobbin'.

A likely origin of this grotesque element can be found in Slessor's association with the 'Vision' school, despite the fact that he himself discounts the significance of this association. His poetry shows the influence of this school in a number of ways. One of the dominant influences on the group was the art of Peter Rubens . . . , and it becomes evident that Slessor's imagery is in part a conscious imitation of the grotesque as it appears in Rubens's paintings and consequently in [works by Slessor's associates]. (p. 131)

[Much] of Slessor's imagery can be understood as a poetic rendering of the grotesque, not in any concern with a play on conventional imagery, although there are examples of this, but in the incongruous combination of 'unlikely elements'. And while the following discussion tends to concentrate on Slessor's imagery, his themes can also be considered in the light of the grotesque. In his imagery we can see this effect operating in two distinct ways. The profusion or agglomeration of images characteristic of his early poetry is in many cases grotesque, but more significantly many of the individual images are grotesque in themselves, either from the association of incongruous ideas as metaphors, or from the combination of such ideas in a symbol. Of course it might be argued that this use of imagery is in fact the use of conceits. But the point is that Slessor's conceits . . . are conceits with a difference. There is something in their content, in the way they are used, that is peculiar to Slessor. Although he is attempting to be ingenious, he is not so much concerned with being fantastic; with him this is not, ultimately an affectation.

Many of the early poems, such as 'Thieves' Kitchen', 'The Ghost', and several of the series entitled 'Music', seem to exist only as a profusion of images without much coherent intellectual content, apart from that imposed somewhat desultorily in the final line or two. Of all the early poems it may be said that they exist primarily in so far as they express through their imagery that peculiar animated gaiety associated with the 'Vision' school. . . . Even Slessor's later, maturer poems, such as 'North Country', 'Last Trams', 'William Street', and especially 'To the Poetry of Hugh McCrae', rely heavily on the sudden fusion of unusual components in the images for their effectiveness.

At its worst, his poetry is a succession of images with little connection other than that of a robustious animalism. 'Earth-visitors' is one such poem. Princes, barons, kings of old Tartary, archdukes, and postboys; viols, gold vapours, crusted stones, cambric, cloth of gold, gold rain, and warm guineas of love—the profusion is facile. The element of grotesqueness is introduced when this proliferation begins to be felt as a surfeit, an excess of richness. . . . In this particular poem the images are conducive to 'a confusion of sharp dreams', which is the point of the first four stanzas, and which is inconclusively related to the following lines where a luminous Venus comes 'knocking in the night', something like an adult version of Wee Willie Winkie.

In 'The Ghost' we are confronted with the grotesque achieved in much the same way as Rubens achieved his effects. The six quatrains present a number of images of luxuriousness and pleasure in the act of living, just as Rubens fills his canvas with crowds of lively courtesans and gallants, and ornaments denoting richness. Slessor builds up his effects with a number of images conjuring up a world of wild revels: old Spanish wine, pasties in pyramids, flagons with silver lids, fuming platters, and dim chambers, maidens in dark passages, wenches with tousled silk, and beds of milk under carved canopies. . . . There is something strikingly effective in the contrast between the sumptuousness and moist luxuriousness of the dining and wenching, and the ghost's spareness and dryness as conveyed by the simile: 'Like a white leaf'. One can possibly account for this by the inversion of light—the scene within being emphasized as dim so that the stark whiteness of the ghost's face against the dark pane stands out in a most startling way—and perhaps also by the underlying hollowness of the situations each side of the glass. The effect of this is to create an undercurrent of irony in the transition between the two situations; the actual grotesqueness stems from the suddenness of the transition from the tumbling of wenches to the motionless, lifeless face of the ghost at the window. Moreover, it depends heavily on the concentration of close contrasts between the two situations. They are almost an exact inverse of each other. (pp. 133-35)

[Venus appears as] an emblem of physical desirability rather than a symbol of beauty (considered as an abstraction), and consequently when she occurs in an image we get a peculiar tension set up between the physical and the ideal, which in effect is that characteristic of Slessor's imagery we have been calling the grotesque. This tension can be seen in the following lines from 'Earth-Visitors':

> She is there suddenly, lit by no torch or moon,
> But by the shining of her naked body.
> Her breasts are berries broken in snow; her hair
> Blows in a gold rain over and over them
> She flings her kisses like warm guineas of love. . . .

Some of these images come dangerously near to being ridiculous, but if we accept Victor Hugo's contention that 'La grotesque est le germe de la comedie', this serves only to support the thesis that much of Slessor's imagery is to be understood in terms of the grotesque.

It should be emphasized that the grotesque is not necessarily repulsive, nor is it necessarily ludicrous, although traces of these qualities are often detected in it. It is not in the least unsuccessful art. . . . Its particular value to the poet is that it 'startles into new awareness', and when Slessor uses the grotesque to advantage, he transcends the merely surprising or startling to give fresh insights into the experience he is presenting. . . . (pp. 136-37)

It is noticeable that the recurrent Venus-image becomes less persistent in the later poems, though it by no means dies out. in his maturer phase, Slessor began to exploit two symbols that had intrigued him from his earliest poems, namely stone and the window. . . . Both carry implications of death: stone as either a gravestone or the emblem of fixity, sterility, and therefore a spiritual of living death; and the window (as we have seen in 'The Ghost') as the 'pygmy strait' between life and death. . . . The point to be made here is that the individual image becomes vivid and poignant only when the symbolic interpretation is combined with the literal statement, and this is startling or grotesque in the way we have defined it only because the symbols are somewhat grotesque in themselves (though this is truer of the window than it is of the stone). We are reminded time and again of 'the world of dead men staring out of glass', so that the insistence on glass in 'Captain Dobbin', as windows, flasks, bottles, and his reading-glass, takes on special overtones not only of exclusion or remoteness from a full and active life, but also of the brittleness of life itself. (p. 137)

Slessor advances from the mere exploitation of the grotesque for its own sake in his imagery, to a mature and considered exploration of its usefulness as a technique for startling us into new awareness, into fresh perceptions of the experience he presents to us. One may feel that this imagery, 'written with such perplexity', reveals a concern for the merely spectacular and sensational which leads to a fundamental shallowness in his themes. . . . But Slessor's 'considered breaking of the rules', his 'experiments in anarchy', seem to be vindicated by such poems as 'Five Bells' and 'Beach Burial'. (p. 138)

A. C. W. Mitchell, "Kenneth Slessor and the Grotesque," in Critical Essays on Kenneth Slessor, *edited by A. K. Thomson, The Jacaranda Press, 1968, pp. 131-38.*

* * *

SORRENTINO, Gilbert 1929-

Sorrentino, an American poet, novelist, and critic, and an editor of Grove Press, values, for his own work, "a verse dense in its particulars, but flexible in its total structure." (See also *CLC*, Vol. 7, and *Contemporary Authors*, Vols. 77-80.)

SHARON FAWCETT [THESEN]

Gilbert Sorrentino's *Splendide-Hôtel* is a splendid book. The Splendide-Hôtel ('built in a chaos of glaciers and the polar night'), invented by Arthur Rimbaud and reinvented by Sorrentino is a place in the country of a poet's mind where people and poems come to stay for a while, perhaps forever. Sorrentino's heart rests there a spell to render alphabetically the Splendide-Hôtel and its guests and its pests (so many rats as to take over the whole world.) The alphabeticalness is important because it's simple and because the words a poet writes are things made of alphabet elements where vowels are the sounding spaces.

Splendide-Hôtel is altogether a 'radiant gist' and Sorrentino pays homage in this book to Williams and Rimbaud whose spinnings of art into the matter of the quotidian—and here my dictionary tells me with astonishing accuracy to this content, that the 'quotidian' is anything that returns every day; a fever whose paroxysms return every day—whose spinnings are perhaps mentioned by the academics drinking vodka highballs in the lounge of the Splendide-Hôtel. The alphabet is the Splendide-Hôtel, an act of the imagination. The realm of 'Letters.' . . . [Those] who love the Alchemy of the Word are 'left finally with its essence to be set against the world.' Against those Men of Letters, no matter how snazzy, whose language is that of 'instruction booklets on the installation of air conditioners' Sorrentino turns his invective, there reminding me most of Williams who would declare that all writing but Poetry is a lie. And in this real respect, *Splendide-Hôtel* is a defense of Poetry, radically so, in that it returns to the primary construct of words to get at primary meanings, images. (pp. 97-8)

The gulfs of darkness residing in the mundane both [Williams and Rimbaud] revelled in become Sorrentino's puzzlements over a selfdestructing America: 'I don't know why. One week they were playing shuffleboard at Jack's Inn, drinking Schenley and Falstaff, and the next they were at home, searching for a vein.' H. Heroin. Hydrogen Bomb. Hotel. Home. 'Sa porte est ouverte à la misère.' Today there are poets boarding the bus marked *L'ENFER* and taking it to Prince George, B.C. via Paterson, New Jersey.

The correspondences, Sorrentino says, are easy to pinpoint and by now you can probably see where some of them lie. I love this book called *Splendide-Hôtel*. (p. 99)

Sharon Fawcett [Thesen], "Colors" (copyright © 1976 by Sharon Fawcett [Thesen]; reprinted by permission of the author), in Open Letter, *Third Series, No. 5, Summer, 1976, pp. 97-9.*

GERALD GREALISH

The Orangery, a collection of 84 liberally formed sonnets, each containing a variation of the word "orange," is not about orange. True enough, though, as Sorrentino says in one of these poems, "These oranges hold it all."

Non sequiturs as sequiturs, sequiturs as non sequiturs, are here "absolute logic." You are, when you read this, entering a world where experience is what it is. Not yours. Yet you are invited in even when you are not "invited" in. "Nothing is the thing that rhymes with orange," the poet tells us—and don't look for reason either. (p. 327)

Here you arrive at a place, places, as indefinite as those places which, in William Blakes world, synthesize into geographic-imaginative-spiritual locations. And the method too is not dissimilar; there is a network of words which are repeated in different contexts, which do not mean, when they recur, the same thing in any strict sense, yet carry with them, in some accumulative sense, a constancy. Many are colors other than orange. Many are not colors. These "symbols" make themselves. Appearing, as they do, in the strangest of juxtapositions, often it is their incongruity that establishes them. . . .

But as random as orange and so many other colors, images, and adjectives, are, they create the texture for what is a very emotive work. The connections through it all to the mother who died, and for whom is held the most loving of memories, resonate again and again.

The elusive "Madame Mystere," antagonist and synthesis of "woman" for the male voice here, engenders the confusion of mother, sensuous woman, confidante, and untouchable. "Orange" is the access to her mystery, yet remains itself, and can only hint through indirection, misdirection even. . . .

Need I say it? This is a beautiful book. (p. 328)

Gerald Grealish, "Non-Fiction: 'The Orangery',"

in Best Sellers *(copyright © 1979 Helen Dwight Reid Educational Foundation), Vol. 38, No. 10, January, 1979, pp. 327-28.*

VALERIE TRUEBLOOD

In 1971 Gilbert Sorrentino published a novel about poets, *Imaginative Qualities of Actual Things*, a savage book full of judgments his acquintances must have prayed would not be thought to refer to them. ("Free! Free! Irremediably poor. Such work is irremediable because it has no working parts. It is a great chunk of, say, Liederkranz." . . .) I mention this book because it is very good, still awaiting its public, at least on my coast, and because Sorrentino has both gifts, fictional and poetic, in a measure I don't think we've seen since Williams.

These poems dazzle at first with their intense colors, and inside them like a bee is enough spite to scare the browser. . . . Immediately you hear Stevens, and Rimbaud at his bitterest. "Note the bitterness and wanton/patterns of assault," Sorrentino urges.

He doubts his readers, offers his cruel poems and his tender ones with a faint sneer. He is offering a great deal. With color in *The Orangery* he makes a street from the past (his, America's) to the nerves of his reader. . . .

The Orangery is a series . . . in an elegiac key, in which anger is the treble to a bass of grief and memory. . . . It is a life-story told in a few scenes barely limned—or invented. . . . It is also a portrait, in vignettes, colors, ditties, of an invented Texas (Sorrentino is a New Yorker), a sleazy brilliantly-colored place inhabited by Mexicali Rose and Mr. America among others; outside this Texas are an equally chromatic Florida: a real (though past, and softened) New Jersey; the fields of Kansas; Brooklyn and Queens; Joliet, Mobile. I think this is the best poem-of-America (taking it as one poem in many parts) in years. Sorrentino's sense of strain is not the popular anxiety, but the strain, as Williams experienced it, of being American, being an artist in America, trying to see without repudiating the whole, to repudiate without losing sentience.

Valerie Trueblood, "Books: 'The Orangery'," in The American Poetry Review *(copyright © 1979 by World Poetry, Inc.; reprinted by permission of Valerie Trueblood), Vol. 8, No. 1, January-February, 1979, p. 29.*

JOHN LEONARD

There is a very real question as to whether avant-garde fiction can survive Gilbert Sorrentino's new novel ["Mulligan Stew"]. There is also a question as to whether the New York publishing community can survive it too, although that, of course, is much less interesting. "Mulligan Stew," instead of consisting of meat and vegetables, consists entirely of literature, of parody and complaint and paranoia and pop-absurdism. It is as if Buck Mulligan was a hero or had written "Ulysses," instead of Stephen Dedalus and James Joyce. But Mr. Sorrentino contains, and reviles, them all.

"Mulligan Stew" is full of Joyce, too much so; and of Nabokov, Flaubert, Proust, Gogol, Flann O'Brien, D. H. Lawrence, Edmund (Bunny) Wilson, Norman Mailer, Henry James, Bernard Malamud, the Marquis de Sade, Thomas Dekker, Sylvia Plath, John Updike, Anaïs Nin, Zane Grey, Erica Jong, William H. Gass, various Latin Americans, everybody else I haven't mentioned, plus the rest of us—the entire service class of careerist bookchat. It is as if all of Lionel Trilling's bad dreams about the teaching of modernism had been stuffed inside a single typewriter. (p. 244)

Among the many literary artifacts that "Mulligan Stew" parodies are the mystery novel, the pornographic novel, the western, the 17th-century masque, the 20th-century publisher's catalogue, female erotic poetry, book reviews, art criticism, writers' notebooks, monographs on mathematics, baseball scorecards and astrology charts. The masque, as one might expect, owes a lot to "Ulysses" in "Nighttown" and goes on too long. Most of the parodies, in fact, go on too long, but they are so funny that I can't imagine how to cut them, and neither could Mr. Sorrentino. One exception is the brief parody of erotic poetry, which is such liberated rubbish that it made me cry. Mr. Sorrentino has been accused, and accuses one of his characters, of misogyny. The charge should have been good taste. (pp. 244-45)

To summarize the action in "Mulligan Stew" is to make a fool of oneself in public. So what else is new? Lamont, an experimental novelist of the obscure school, seldom reviewed and never read, is writing a "new wave" murder mystery. This means that he deposits several characters borrowed from F. Scott Fitzgerald into a twilight zone invented, perhaps, by Alain Robbe-Grillet, and makes them talk like Dashiell Hammett. . . .

Add faith, inauthenticity, flashback, interior harangue, identity crisis, paranoia, dream, fracture, puns, sex, bile, death and footnotes—"Mulligan Stew" is a combination of incest and cannibalism. It shows up for cocktails, in the library, dressed like the Death of the Novel, a suicide-kit of modernism. I found it hilarious. It is also full of rage.

It rages against the packagers and merchandisers and pedagogues of the sensibility as a commodity. Mr. Sorrentino, a novelist and poet of extreme and alarming seriousness, is just as angry as he is clever. (p. 245)

John Leonard, "'Mulligan Stew'," in The New York Times, *Section III (© 1979 by The New York Times Company; reprinted by permission), May 24, 1979 (and reprinted in* Books of the Times, *Vol. II, No. 5, 1979, pp. 244-45).*

ERNEST LARSEN

Billed as a "new wave murder mystery" whose subject is really "the comic possibilities of modern literary history," *Mulligan Stew* appears to be Sorrentino's lunge for the main chance. . . .

While *Mulligan Stew* could use a little of the mystery's rigor, it fits far more comfortably in the avant-garde's cracked but commodious crockpot. The avant-garde tradition may be temporarily exhausted, but it has produced some notable messes. Would that the overstocked *Mulligan Stew* were one of them.

This particular melange, too clever to bother with the mechanics of mystery, deliberately (so deliberately) exploits the most vapid cliche the avant-garde has to offer. You've got one sentence to guess it. Right, the novel about the writer writing a novel. . . .

One section is pretty funny. Before the novel proper begins —before even the title page—Sorrentino parodies a number of publishers' and editors' (mostly reject) letters about the novel. . . .

Apart from the humor, there's a noticeable defensive and even contemptuous undertone in beginning a book this way. This is not ameliorated by the triple-play epigraph that soon follows. . . .

[The quality of the writing in the "novel within the novel"] is so deliberately, so unrelievedly awful that it's hard to imagine what pleasure Sorrentino got out of the considerable effort. The picture he gives of the act of writing is one of unmitigated misery, and he pushes the punishment so far as to give three equally lame versions of the first chapter.

Each of these pieces of driftwood from the inside novel is followed by fragments from [other writings] . . . , all apparently intended to provide opportunities for Sorrentino to dazzle us with his virtuoso parodic talents. It would all float like so much effluvia between the chapters of bombast were it not for two threads Sorrentino thoughtfully throws out to keep the reader from succumbing to total despair.

The first is the ludicrous melodrama of Lamont's burgeoning paranoia. . . .

The other thread he provides is the whimsical device of giving his characters Beaumont and Halpin existence outside Lamont's novel about them. . . . Sorrentino's platonic notion that all fictional characters are created from a pool of preexistent fictional possibilities helps to explain and excuse his systematic "comic" abuse of them. . . .

The layers of irony, literary gamesmanship, and self-protection are so thick in this novel that one searches in vain for a single moment of authenticity. Sorrentino's sophistication and verbal ability (he has to be writing this bad on purpose) preclude the possibility that he doesn't know what he's doing in perpetrating this hoax. . . .

Denying us both intellectual and natural sustenance, Sorrentino imperiously starves his readers by offering an inedible mock-up of a novel, mere decoration instead of the real thing.

Ernest Larsen, "Colonel Mustard in the Study with the Smith-Corona," in The Village Voice *(copyright © 1979; reprinted by permission), Vol. XXIV, No. 22, May 28, 1979, p. 81.*

MARTIN BOOTH

[Gilbert Sorrentino's] work takes in the form and tradition of such writers as Rakosi, Bronk and, in emotive stance, Bly.

His diction is terse but not sparse [in *The Orangery*] and he has the observant knowledge of the authoritarian poet, and the ability to expand simple action or sight into a vast panorama of feeling and pathos, much of it implied, and here lies the skill.

No light verse, the work needs concentrated reading, which is what English poetry readers lack. It is time such extraterritorial offerings were accepted.

Martin Booth, "The Dated, the Demanding, the Daunting," in Tribune *(reprinted by permission of* Tribune, *London), Vol. 43, No. 23, June 8, 1979, p. 7.**

MICHAEL DIRDA

Let's begin with the essentials. *Mulligan Stew* is utterly dazzling. Its pedigree goes back, not to the well-made novel, but rather to the "anatomy"—those extravaganzas that sprawl across world literature, offering encyclopedic, and usually comic, views of life and its foibles. Like *Gargantua and Pantagruel* or *Tristram Shandy, Mulligan Stew* sustains a display of linguistic virtuosity that takes your breath away. It contains some of the best parodies since S. J. Perelman at his most manic, and perhaps the most corrosive satire of the literary scene since early Aldous Huxley. This is a novel with all the stops pulled out, Gilbert Sorrentino's masterpiece. . . .

A mulligan stew can contain anything—and Sorrentino has said that he wanted to be able to put anything into his book. He has. Part of its pleasure is in its variety: there are morsels for every literary taste. Essentially, the book parodies—with enormous gusto—the degraded language of cheap fiction, bad poetry, academic criticism. To control, if only gingerly, a chaos of language, Sorrentino employs three interconnected, yet distinct, stories. The narrative lines may seem complicated in summary, but each is clearly labeled and a reader will have no trouble keeping things straight. (p. C1)

Among the tastiest morsels of *Mulligan Stew* is an interview with a Nabokov look-alike named Thomas McCoy. "One wishes to create characters," says McCoy when questioned about his novelistic intent, "who will speak directly to the minds of comparative literature professors and intelligent book reviewers." Sorrentino, in his own way of course, does just this: the better read you are, the more jokes you get. . . .

Like Perelman, Sorrentino also relishes mixing metaphors and changing allusions in the middle of a sentence. . . . At times he comes out with home truths perfect in their perverse logic. . . .

The dual highpoints of *Mulligan Stew* are *Flawless Play Restored: The Masque of Fungo* and the orgy scene at the Club Zap. The first is a Joycean phantasmagoria—comparable to the Bloom in Nighttown section of *Ulysses*—with a cast of thousands, among whom are Susan B. Anthony and Barnacle Bill. . . . The whole thing is a carnival of off-color jokes, puns and burlesques, including a takeoff on Robert Herrick: "When as in scanties Betsy goes."

As should be clear by now, Sorrentino possesses a Rabelaisian bawdiness—some of his funniest jokes are not quotable here. . . .

One should bear in mind that all of these puns and witticisms are happening "with the rapidity of speed itself"—they never let up. Still, the scenes are sufficiently paced so that the various stylistic acrobatics seldom pall—for example, a parodically dry paper on mathematical proofs thoughtfully prepares the reader for the luxurious orgy scene. Much of Sorrentino's brilliance and humor depend too on the gradual building of a situation and a language maniacally appropriate to it. . . .

One hopes that this brilliant tour de force will bring [Gilbert Sorrentino] the recognition he deserves. . . . (p. C6)

Michael Dirda, "The Far Side of Parodies," in Book World—The Washington Post *(© 1979,* The Washington Post*), June 17, 1979, pp. C1, C6.*

THOMAS R. EDWARDS

Mulligan Stew is a quite wonderful book of literary joking and parody—if there had been no Joyce, no Gide or Sterne or Borges or Robbe-Grillet or Nabokov or Perelman, I'm almost convinced that Sorrentino could have invented them. Since he didn't, his book could be called derivative, but it plays with its great originals with such lively intelligence, understanding, and affection as to make obscure the distinction between creative and critical imagination. . . .

[The fussy woodenness of the dialogue of the novel within this novel suggests] the puzzles we get into by trying to use language, *any* language, at all. The novelist who tries, and fails, to make sense with words, the characters who struggle to get out of one book only to find themselves in another, even less congenial one, are in a way our representatives, since the "real" world is as incurably verbal as any fictional one.

The nice thing about Sorrentino is that he finds this predicament a funny one, as Joyce did too—the thing to do is not to philosophize about it but to bring in as many more words, of whatever kind, as one can think of. . . . *Mulligan Stew* will not, I'm afraid, be widely read, but I recommend trying it out on anyone whose literacy and sense of humor may need testing. (p. 42)

Thomas R. Edwards, "Feeding on Fantasy," in The New York Review of Books *(reprinted with permission from* The New York Review of Books; *copyright © 1979 Nyrev, Inc.), Vol. XXVI, No. 12, July 19, 1979, pp. 41-2.**

ALLEN LACY

A work of true comic genius, [*Mulligan Stew*] not only entertains and engages the intelligent reader, but also manages to shed light on the processes of literary creation, on the making of bad novels as well as good ones.

Mulligan Stew may prove to be the literary curiosity of the year, perhaps the decade. . . .

[It's] easy to see why some editors were reluctant to take the book on. *Mulligan Stew* is long (and to my mind could still stand a good pruning). It fits into no standard literary genre. . . . Abounding in puns both delicious and terrible and in allusions to a vast range of other literature, *Mulligan Stew* requires readers with well-furnished minds and a taste for verbal pyrotechnics. . . .

To appreciate *Mulligan Stew* properly, the reader must realize Sorrentino's strategy: to fashion a wonderful literary concoction out of ingredients in themselves often quite horrible and unpalatable. The book *is* a fine stew that transcends its own ingredients—or perhaps a kaleidoscope that uses mirrors to transform scraps of torn paper into patterns that dazzle the eye. . . .

Mulligan Stew is a leisurely book, sometimes slow, but with many delights along the way. Sorrentino's imagination is playful and droll, especially in his lists and catalogues. . . .

Mulligan Stew is chock full . . . of delicious stuff. It may even be, as one of those editors who turned it down said, a commercial risk—and yet "a great book, perhaps . . . a masterpiece."

Allen Lacy, "Take One Rejection Slip, Add Water, and Stir," in Books & Arts *(copyright © 1979 by The Chronicle of Higher Education, Inc.), Vol. XVIII, No. 20, July 23, 1979, p. R4.*

MALCOLM BRADBURY

Since all literature is susceptible to parody, why not, then make parody literature? Gilbert Sorrentino has, with impressive results. "Mulligan Stew" has given me as much pleasure and intellectual joy as I have had from a novel in a long time.

"Mulligan Stew" is a work of contemporary experiment, and there are those who will classify it under the new, somewhat sagging banner of post-modernism, a movement ripe for redevelopment. But it is experiment raised to such a level of comedy—Flann O'Brien, whose influence pervades this novel, calls it "hilaritas," and it is a true esthetic principle—that it often risks all intellectual conviction in giving enjoyment (though it often forfeits enjoyment for the sake of intellectual conviction). . . .

No reader should be put off by the news that this is a book about writing. . . .

The book's pleasure lies in its conviction that anything—and nothing—may be done with words. Plots are absurd but they grow; characters are paper but they live; the story stays busy, and even refuses to stop when we do. (p. 9)

[Mr. Sorrentino] revels in the wordy tomb of the times, in the sheer range of its offerings. . . . He also wishes to show the nature of our verbal prisons. "Mulligan Stew"—the title hints it—is a neo-Joycean concoction, spawning invention, delighting in lists, inventing languages, animating the endlessly comic fact that every sentence we write may generate its opposite, every structure of significance we create risks being parodied to the point of insignificance, every generative element in any story can move in an infinitude of directions. "Mulligan Stew" mocks the act of creation. It also thrives on it, turning itself into an abundant and extravagantly decorated display of the pleasures of the imagination. (p. 18)

Malcolm Bradbury, "Writing Mocking Writing," in The New York Times Book Review *(© 1979 by The New York Times Company; reprinted by permission), August 26, 1979, pp. 9, 18.*

* * *

SOUSTER, (Holmes) Raymond 1921-

A Canadian poet and editor, Souster is a "poet of Toronto" and celebrates that city and its people in unsophisticated, epigrammatic verse. There is a compassionate tone in much of Souster's poetry, and his focus is often on social concerns: the despair of the underprivileged and the problems of political systems and urban society. His work bears the influence of the Imagist school of poetry, particularly the work of William Carlos Williams. Souster has also written two novels under the pseudonyms of John Holmes and Raymond Holmes. (See also *CLC*, Vol. 5, and *Contemporary Authors*, Vols. 13-16, rev. ed.)

LOUIS DUDEK

[The] permanent ground of Souster's poetry is human deprivation and loss. Unlike other poets who find their dream of happiness and fulfilment in the future, or even in the present, he looks backward to the past. . . . Happiness is "a lost but recovered joy"; and all are "groping for something lost they will never find / in the drab of the street, in the dirt, in the smoke, in the noise." The imagery of youth usually conveys this meaning of loss in Souster's poetry, as in "Young Girls", where it is also an image of sexual promise; or in the poem remembering boyhood—

> It's nothing but desire to live again, fresh from
> the beginning like a child.

Some of his most moving and beautiful poems turn on this theme. . . . [Joy] is often the achieved reward of Souster's patient realistic vision, so that retrospective nostalgia is only a more defeated direction in an idealism that ends in measure and acceptance.

The sense of loss and deprivation, the erosion of time, the cruel impersonality and brutality of the city are nevertheless the groundwork of these poems. Nor is it a private and personal condition limited to the poet. The bulk of Souster's poetry deals with other people—the people of the city —and these are truly observed, not faceless democratic symbols as for example in Carl Sandburg. They are actual individuals (not that characterization is any aim in poetry); their pain is real, and their "wasted bitter years" are specific as their deaths and entrances. A personal predicament is projected outward in this human landscape, and at the same time a truth about the general life is revealed (since the individual is our source of knowledge about the universal, the mass, and a single imagination, if it has poetic scope, sympathy, the gift of extension, becomes representative for mankind). (pp. 201-02)

Souster's verdict on modern life is not very cheerful. Whether there is truth in [his] picture of waste, vanity, frustration, poverty and desperation, we may allow the reader to judge. The poetry is not a sociological survey filled with ideological jargon, nor is it a political language about power or prestige or money; Souster's depiction of modern life is humble, human, and close to the satisfactions and discomforts of the average man. He shows people in their intimate real moments of despair, love, and pleasure. And the first of these is the ground-tone of his canvas of life.

Images of escape, liberation, total self-realization on a plane of pure fantasy, will be found in Souster's poetry. These are important, but they should not distract us from the main direction of his development. . . . Souster never takes the risk of total abandon, he merely observes and participates by observation, in a wishful fantasy. . . . (pp. 202-03)

To accept the limitations of actuality, however, is Souster's primary road of poetic development. Here the fact—at its worst—must be attested in the face of human loss and failure—"It must be like this"—so that we can go on and endure. . . . In contrast to Souster's early poems, which expressed their disillusion by means of invective, [his] middle poems are often starkly objective and non-committal. Since they, too, turn on a conflict between the actual and something lost, irony and ripe humour often come into play; in fact, if the balance falls heavily on the side of harsh reality, cynicism results inevitably. . . . (p. 204)

Reconciliation with life—with boredom, with suffering, with defeat and death—is his sad and constant achievement. . . . (p. 205)

Souster is surprised on occasion with the gift of inexplicable joy. Renunciation and acceptance of inevitable tragedy set the stage for a burst of song such as could only be equalled or surpassed by the first promise with which life began. Souster repeatedly discovers poetic ecstasy at the end of renunciation and suffering: as this pattern is perceived, the brief poems at the end of [his collection *The Colour of the Times*] readily yield up their honey. . . . There is a delicacy of arrangement in *The Colour of the Times* that may be missed by the unwary reader. Again and again poems interpret one another and add nuances of meaning by their placing. (p. 206)

[This] is poetry of the highest order. Apparently casual and even haphazard at times, it has a sureness of touch and scope of vision that will amaze and delight futurity. The best description of it, with the larger implications of the theme we have followed, appears in a single brief poem, "I Watched a Bird," which is one of Souster's finest pieces, and one in which again the bird speaks for the poet (perhaps unawares) yet conveys everything:

> I watched a bird blown in the sky
> like some poor thing without control,
> dipping and swerving here and there
> with wings spread wide and motionless.
>
> I watched a bird tossed down the wind
> that never fought or uttered cry,
> surrendered to that boundless air,
> caught up in that great mystery.

(pp. 207-08)

Louis Dudek, "Groundhog among the Stars: The Poetry of Raymond Souster" (originally published in a slightly different version in Canadian Literature, *No. 22, Autumn, 1964), in his* Selected Essays and Criticism *(© Louis Dudek and The Tecumseh Press Limited 1978), Tecumseh Press, 1978, pp. 193-208.*

HAYDEN CARRUTH

The evidence of Souster's spontaneous writing method is on every page of [*The Colour of the Times*]. In fact it goes a good deal further than that. Poets who refuse to revise their work, on the ground that revision always sullies the spotlessness of the original poetic impulse, are common nowadays, but most are willing to correct errors in grammar or slips of the pen; at least they are in those cases where the errors are simply stupid and meaningless. Not Souster. Either he is not willing, or he refuses, for whatever reason, to look at the printer's proofs. How else can you account for the poem in which he speaks of the 'socketless eyes' of dead people when what he means is 'eyeless sockets'? In a poem called 'The Lovers' he mixes up the cases of his pronouns; in another poem he says 'sever' where he means 'impale', he writes 'I can't decide which will outlive each other' when what he really can't decide is which idiomatic expression he intends to use, and elsewhere 'trace' as a verb is confused with 'print', 'ands' and 'buts' are used indiscriminately, a man splits rock with an axe (maybe that's possible in Ontario, but not in Vermont), streams are 'offshoots' (not tributaries, in-shoots) of rivers, and so on.

Souster has the answer to all this, of course. Word-polishing. 'It makes me want to laugh,' he says, and elsewhere: 'O let nothing matter if not beautiful . . . as that singing water.' In other words, a poem that has any life in it will sustain itself in spite of these imperfections. Maybe so; I have been choosing, quite consciously, the picayune defects to harp on. But the point is that the life of a poem, like any life, can be killed if it is mishandled, and short of that it can be crippled, distorted, enfeebled. Is it a thing worth taking some trouble over, or isn't it? Because Souster's book is crowded with much larger defects that really do destroy the beauty and vigour of the poems in which they occur. And these larger defects, I believe, are of the same order as the smaller ones: the result of carelessness and a refusal to give thought. (pp. 82-3)

What is the problem here? Is it that Souster's sensibility, responding freely, too often gives back only a spate of puerile nonsense? Sometimes that seems to be the case. In other cases the poems or parts of poems that are cast in worn-out diction appear to have been manufactured by the poet as a matter of duty. His sensibility has responded vaguely, in no language at all, or has given him only a fragment of a metaphor, a hint, a titillation. He is loath to let the occasion pass, and in consequence he grinds out, as best he can, in a kind of autosuggestive aesthetic euphoria, anything that sounds 'poetic'. At any rate that's the impression afforded by a good many poems in the book. In all these cases the defects are so evident that one simply cannot believe they are unrecognizable to the poet himself, all the more since he shows himself to be, time and again, a man of skill, sensitivity, and judgement.

I believe the only thing wrong with Souster is the literary philosophy to which he has committed himself. And let me say explicitly that this has nothing to do with being a rebel, nothing to do with writing in free forms (his rhymed and metred poems are awful and he shouldn't attempt them), nothing to do with being any particular order of poet at all. It has to do with his responsibilities to his poem, his language, and his people; and these responsibilities, curtly defined, are: to make the poem live, or at least to have the courtesy to refrain from killing it; to 'purify the language of the tribe'; and to propagate the example of being's integrity. . . . [Many of the poems] declare that the responsibilities may be discharged merely by assuming the mantle of poet, i.e. by responding, by giving free rein to sensibility; spontaneously, automatically. It can't be done. Responsibility means work and thought. Work and thought mean craft.

The first of the larger defects in Souster's poems was a defect of diction. The second is a defect of metric. (pp. 84-5)

[We] know from his best work that he can manage the poetic line with delicacy and intelligence. But many too many poems move in [a] thumping gait, resulting in a complete loss of tension and of the line-value as the fundamental unit of the poem. [In this case] the poem dies. A question of prosodic distrophy.

Sousters' third defect is sentimentality. (pp. 86-7)

Now at last I shall mention a few of the good things I have observed in Souster's writing—only a few because there isn't space for more. . . . [His] poetry reminds me in some respects of Villon's. The most important similarity is the way each poet conveys the presence of his city, Paris and Toronto; more than that, it is the way each poet writes as if he were the first urban poet, as if no-one had done it before. Souster's Toronto is not so much vivid as it is simply, palpably there: the great northern city, bare, cold, ugly, windswept, yet full of life, indispensable to that life. And this is the freshness that Souster brings to much of his writing. For instance, his poems of love-sorrow written in terms of an empty bed. . . . To write in these true, simple terms, these folk terms, and to do so without on the one hand the least artifice or condescension, or on the other the slightest trace of slobbery, is a high accomplishment. At his best Souster does it. And at his best also—this is why I have been so unabashed in my criticisms—he demolishes his own faults; forcefully, naturally, entirely.

Here is a poem called 'Easter Sunday':

> The day begins
> too well. The wind
> summer's, out
> of season,
> the sun, shy
> behind clouds,
> surely will burst through
> in brilliance
> soon.
>
> But rain with thunder
> before evening.
> Behind the stone
> rolled away
> another and another
> without end.

(pp. 91-2)

In 'Easter Sunday' the second part is a genuine part, it resolves the poem, it derives naturally from the first part; the poem is *realized.* Notice the diction. Not one word too many (only one adjective in the entire poem), not one word out of place; no word that does not stretch in the expansiveness of its own content. Notice the metric. The line is used, not cast away; it is various, taut, close to the poet's feeling. In the first part the ragged movement, going in and out, is exactly the arhythmic chiaroscuro of an April day; and the second part, heavier, more regular, is precisely what it should be—not portentous, not solemn, not settled, not weary, not pitying, yet a little of all these, and more. The ending is, in fact, as beautiful a memorialization of Easter's pathetic triumph as I can recall. Notice that the poem has no imitativeness, no sentimentality. None? That would be impossible, and poetry-readers will be able to adduce other instances of religious thunder, including some famous ones. But the thunder here is original, I'm sure. This happened; somewhere, somehow it was enacted before the poet's consciousness. And the last line, which some might call hackneyed, cannot be that now; not after the other fourteen lines. Its echo of the liturgy, so slight, is a case of marvelous poetic tact. 'Easter Sunday' is small, probably too small to support much weight of enthusiasm or long study, but I think it is perfect of its kind. . . . It may be Souster's best poem. (p. 92)

Souster's major theme [is] the cruelty of a commercial nation. The recurrent figures in his poems are bums, drunks, cripples, soldiers, whores, the children of the poor, old ladies, Negroes, and the poet himself as a companion to all these. Through the collected poems runs too a thread of allusion, more or less covert, to heroin and the needle, intensifying the Villonesque intimations of the underworld. Here, in these poems written out of a radical concern, Souster again runs the risk, quite an extreme one, of tawdriness and sentimentality, throwing us back into the world of the Thirties; Daddy Warbucks on the one hand, and solidarity forever on the other. Usually he avoids it, but not always. (p. 93)

[Yet] there are many fine passages, enough to show what

Souster can do when he exerts his capacities for feeling and thought, declining the easy temptations of sensibility. . . . Sometimes it is difficult to believe that the same person who wrote the poems of the city also wrote the suburban poems about putting up storm windows and chasing a skunk from under the porch. The question now seems to be: where does Souster go from here? What can he, and Canada, realize from the beginning—fine in parts but fragmentary and muddled—that he has made? (p. 94)

Hayden Carruth, "To Souster from Vermont," in The Tamarack Review, *No. 34, Winter, 1965, pp. 81-95.*

GEORGE JONAS

The surface values of Raymond Souster's poetry are easily discernible and have been pointed out many times. He is gentle and humane. He frequently writes about small events and common people. He observes with affection the streets and characters of his native Toronto. He seems to like cats, baseball players, and newspaper vendors. His poems are simple and direct.

The Years . . . supports and reinforces this view of Souster, perhaps with something of a vengeance. . . .

Souster has [the capacity to feel others' misfortunes deeply], and it could make his poetry grotesquely sentimental and ultimately very bad. It is hard to say why it doesn't, but it is probably for two reasons. First, he means it. Second, he is a poet and not a pretender. (p. 35)

The Years includes a well-known poem ["Death Chant for Mr. Johnson's America"] which, to my mind, represents Souster at his didactic worst. . . . [While] he may be a master of the simple-minded love song, the simple-minded hate song is not Souster's speed. He is capable of making the sickliest sentiments about blind newspaper vendors ring true, but his curse on Imperial America sounds forced, faddish and phoney. This is bad, because Souster's main asset as a poet is not inventiveness of form or profundity of thought, but emotional honesty and integrity. Normally he is not trying to be clever, current or fashionable; he means what he says and makes the reader believe him. (pp. 35-6)

Souster is neither a pedant nor a performer, and his world is not of the classroom or the circus. No don or demon, he doesn't lecture ex cathedra or strum his guitar from beyond the grave. His world, in fact, is the world of most men and women who work for a living in ordinary jobs, ride the subway, watch television, and kill a few bottles of beer in the evening. Souster shares their lifestyle and, on a different level of awareness, their inner lives: if they were in the habit of writing poetry it is Souster's kind of poetry that they would write. They are the people, and they certainly outnumber, possibly outweigh, and frequently survive professors and clowns. (p. 36)

George Jonas, "It Is Hard Not to Be Affected by His Spell," in Saturday Night *(copyright © 1971 by* Saturday Night*), Vol. 86, No. 12, December, 1971, pp. 35-6.*

F. W. WATT

[In *Change-Up: New Poems* Souster] gives us one of the freshest and best books he has ever written. There is nothing radically new, only modest developments, in technique and subject-matter. But the vignettes of city and domestic life are clearer and more vivid, the language still more transparent, with fewer of those occasional verbal blotches that make us uncomfortably conscious there is someone between us and the experience trying to influence our feelings. Above all, the candour and sincerity are more undeniable than ever. Souster refuses to become slick and glib. If his pitying hand slips too easily into his pocket to bribe a beggar's outstretched palm, Souster himself is the first to notice it and feel ashamed. There is, I think, a more somber view of reality than ever, yet never histrionic, always embodied in the facts of life closest to the poet's experience. Only he could put his strangled cat Minou and the body of Mussolini hanging upside down in the same poem, a lucid, fiercely exact poem, and make us feel with anguish that indeed "There is no escape / no other place to go / the murderers are everywhere."

Only Souster, too, could undress his wife in front of us, celebrate conjugal love as if it were as "hot and good" as any affair, startle, disturb, embarrass, and touch us with his awkward intimate revelations and finally win the day—leave us moved by a new sense of the possibilities of human tenderness and fidelity and sincerity. (p. 41)

F. W. Watt, "Why Poetry? Eleven Answers," in The Canadian Forum, *Vol. LV, No. 651, June, 1975, pp. 40-1.**

ROBERT FULFORD

The reason Raymond Souster hasn't changed much as a poet in the last three decades or so—hasn't Developed, hasn't Extended His Range, hasn't Re-Assessed His Position—is that he started off in the 1940s doing what he wanted to do and has never stopped wanting to do it. What he's been doing, all these years, is writing hymns of praise to the Toronto he loves and to the professionals he admires. Souster is the most Torontocentric of Canadian poets. (pp. 75, 77)

In his new book, *Extra Innings,* there's a poem called "Old Woman on Yonge Street" in which the poet simply observes an old woman and marvels at her resilience. It could have been written by Souster in 1955—which is not to take anything away from its purely Sousterian beauty or from its abiding respect for its subject. There are poems that refer to the old Ford Hotel, the Trillium ferryboat going to Toronto Island, the Isaacs Gallery. Souster is Toronto's own sweet singer, the Whitman of the repressed old city that is slowly giving way to the new cosmopolitan metropolis. (p. 77)

Souster's other theme through all these years has been professionalism, particularly as demonstrated in sports, poetry, and jazz. . . . His tendency to celebrate his fellow poets has increased in recent years—his subjects in this book range from Rilke to Charles Olson, from Archibald Lampman to W.W.E. Ross, the much neglected figure who brought modern poetry to Canada. (pp. 77, 79)

Extra Innings does show one new tendency: Souster has been brooding about modern history, and there are fourteen highly ironic poems about historical events and historical figures, distributed through the book but all given the heading "Pictures of a Long-Lost World." . . . These are all neatly put together, but often they come dangerously close to journalism; parts of them also owe something to the Found Poems of John Robert Colombo, whom Souster acknowledges in one dedication. They aren't the best poems in the book, by a long way, but they're probably just a temporary aberration, a minor diversion from Souster's main occupation—celebrating the city he loves so much that he almost forgives it for what it is. (p. 79)

Robert Fulford, "A Certain Love for Toronto," in Saturday Night *(copyright © 1977 by* Saturday Night*), Vol. 92, No. 6, July, 1977, pp. 75, 77, 79.*

DAVID JACKEL

Although *Extra Innings* is sub-titled "New Poems," the reader familiar with Souster's work will not find in this collection much that is "new" in subject-matter and in style. Few, however, will be disappointed by this. Souster's greatest strength is his ability to go on finding, in his own life and in the ordinary life around him, materials for poetry. This unforced consistency deserves our respect, as does Souster's obvious sympathy for the victims of cruelty and misfortune and, most particularly, of the pervasive indifference that marks urban life. Concern and compassion are as evident in this collection as they have been in his previous volumes, and are, as usual, plainly and directly expressed.

While Souster's sense of values is impressive, many of his poems are not. The materials drawn from ordinary life are often trivial, the directly-stated feelings are seldom examined, and the colloquial style sinks at times to flatness and cliché. (p. 37)

Souster is assuming, of course, that many readers, having had similar experiences in their own lives, will not find it difficult to associate themselves with the poet's emotional response. Easy emotional commitments are nearly always suspect, however, even in poetry. . . .

And when Souster, in "Waiting for the Poem to Come Through," makes an analogy between writing a poem and hitting a curve ball, serious baseball fans with a serious interest in poetry and literary criticism may find the analogy forced and unconvincing, because it depends too much on the poet's own set of associations, and on a view of poetry which the poem itself does not describe, much less defend. . . .

At his best . . . , Souster's method is not the associational one. In "The Day of the Small Winds," "The Week of the Small Leaves," and "The Season of the Small, Small Spider" (except for its inflated final line), we are given not private enthusiasms but close observations of nature, rendered in language for the most part both precise and evocative. (p. 38)

David Jackel, "Private Enthusiasms," in The Canadian Forum, *Vol. LVII, No. 673, August, 1977, pp. 37-8.*

* * *

SOYINKA, Wole (Akinwande Oluwole Soyinka) 1934-

Soyinka, a Nigerian dramatist, director, poet, and novelist, is considered one of the most important contemporary African dramatists writing in English. Underlying all his work is African folklore, with its relevance to social and political elements. Critics agree that his two-year political imprisonment in Nigeria had a tremendous effect on his writing, changing his once hopeful outlook to one of growing despair and pessimism. (See also *CLC*, Vols. 3, 5, and *Contemporary Authors*, Vols. 13-16, rev. ed.)

ALAN BRIEN

Mr. Soyinka is a fluent, funny and angry West African, but he has not yet begun to understand how to work out a verse or to organise a play. . . .

Mr. Soyinka's verse was mainly in the cata-Logue manner with clumsy pamphleteering phrases ('untransmuted emotion,' 'venery,' 'chillun worse than their sires') leading into unusual and unprecise images ('the moon bounds like a fried egg in oil'). The humour was occasionally attractively raw and tough. . . . The farther away from the Chelsea street-poet he went the more natural and affecting Mr. Soyinka became. His play, *The Invention,* revealed his limitations even more embarrassingly. The original idea was quite sharp and provocative. . . . But now the idea has been kicked off, it must be passed from player to player until it smacks the goal. Mr. Soyinka has no way out of the narrative dilemmas he has set himself. Eventually he tries to abolish them all with a version of the Emperor's-New-Clothes device. The humours and the horrors of the situation are both too easy. (p. 629)

Alan Brien, "Where Spades Are Trumps," in The Spectator *(© 1959 by* The Spectator; *reprinted by permission of* The Spectator*), Vol. 203, No. 6854, November 6, 1959, pp. 629-30.**

MARTIN ESSLIN

[Drama] deals with the basic human emotions and predicaments in a social context, both in the interaction of several characters on the stage, and in the even more important interaction between the stage and the audience. The basic human emotions are still involved, but they are expressed through social conventions which may be totally different from one society to another. (p. 33)

This is not to say that universal, or almost universal, drama is wholly impossible. There may, after all, be social conventions that are shared by very large sections of humanity, if not by all mankind. . . . It is only occasionally that the very strangeness of the social context is a factor *in favour* of an imported play which allows it to cash in on its *exoticisms*. But, alas, experience shows that delight in exoticism almost invariably fastens on superficial, external factors (like the bare bosoms of African dance companies) and therefore tends to favour the most shallow importations which concentrate on such surface elements. (p. 34)

[But, it might be argued, the work of Wole Soyinka] should be largely exempt from these considerations; for, after all, [he is] writing in English. Far from being an advantage, in my opinion, this is a further handicap. Not that [Soyinka is] in any way at a disadvantage in using the English language. On the contrary: [he is a real master] of all its nuances and [is, indeed, a very considerable artist]. . . . Here again the problem arises from the nature of drama itself. . . . We are here presented with African peasants, African fishermen, African labourers expressing themselves in impeccable English. Of course in reality they speak their own languages equally impeccably and the [playwright has] merely *translated* what they would have said is those languages into the equivalent English. Precisely! Which is to say that these original plays labour under the universal handicap of all translated drama. . . . Realistic plays in non-Standard idioms are *untranslatable*. Only highly stylised *poetic drama* has a chance in translation. And that surely is the reason why . . . Wole Soyinka's prose (which only occasionally is heightened to verse) . . . remains on a strictly formalised, stylised level. (pp. 34-5)

Wole Soyinka is of a . . . romantic turn of mind: he revels in variety and diversity, alternating between farce (*The Trials of Brother Jero*), tragedy (*The Strong Breed*) and romantic mythology (*A Dance of the Forests*), changing from prose to verse within one play and employing the full panoply of the great African tradition of dance and mime. . . . [The plays] are firmly set in the present—a very recognisable independent Nigeria with its corrupting town-life set against superstition and backwardness in the countryside (e.g. *The Swamp Dwellers, The Lion and the Jewel*) and ambitious members of Parliament falling for the career prospects held out to them by fraudulent sectarian cultists (*Brother Jero*).

Undoubtedly the most ambitious of Soyinka's plays is *A Dance of the Forests,* a kind of African *Midsummer Night's Dream,* in which a group of three guilty people is lured into the woods by a group of nature gods and spirits and confronted with their own guilt, which at the same time, is shown to be identical with the guilt of previous incarnations of the same human beings in one of the great golden ages of the African past that have in recent years been rediscovered to such good purpose. . . . Chastened by the recognition of their true natures, but unpunished, the three guilty human beings return from the forest. This is only one, if in my opinion, the principal, strand in a many-layered poetic texture which the author handles with consummate skill.

The Lion and the Jewel, in a much lighter mood, again contrasts the present and the past; the forward looking moderns and the upholders of past traditions. Here it is a beautiful girl, Sidi, the village *belle* of Ilujinle, who stands between the two warring worlds. . . . This is a gay, lighthearted play, with much mime and dance. But it surely also has an allegorical meaning. Is Sidi the Nigerian people who might believe in the impotence of the past but will nevertheless experience its power? Wole Soyinka seems indeed a romantic! (p. 38)

Wole Soyinka is a highly accomplished playwright. My only criticism of his dramatic technique concerns his somewhat overfree, and somewhat confusing, use of flash-back scenes. In practice the flashback (which is largely a cinematic technique) does not work very effectively on the stage which does not possess the subtle fade-outs of the screen, so that flashbacks as a rule involve clumsy scene shifting in the dark, loss of continuity and easy flow of the action etc. This is not to say that the flashback should not be used, merely, that it should be used with caution and be introduced with the utmost degree of clarity. . . .

But this is a minor technical criticism of Soyinka's work. I have no doubt whatever that he is a master-craftsman of the theatre and a major dramatic poet. (p. 39)

Martin Esslin, "Two African Playwrights," in Black Orpheus *(© Mbari Ibadan 1966; reprinted by permission of the author), No. 19, March, 1966, pp. 33-9.**

JOHN F. POVEY

[The] connection between traditional drama and religious ritual has led some commentators to note a similarity between the origins of African and Greek drama. Both arise from public celebration of local festival that approaches religious rite. Soyinka's own *A Dance of the Forests* is developed from the Yoruba Egungun Festival. Probably the point is theoretically valid, but I doubt whether we are helped to proper evaluation of this drama if we have the sublime power of Greek tragedy echoing in our memory.

Some new African dramatists aim at the conventionally European structure. They simply take over the format of the British "well made play." Only the fact that the characters are African and that the set is located in Africa supply any local element. . . . Other dramatists experiment boldly and extend the area available to drama by merging the European structure with specifically Nigerian aspects to begin the creation of a distinctively national Nigerian drama.

The writer who has achieved most for this new drama is Wole Soyinka. . . . Though an impressive poet—his renowned *Telephone Conversation* is one of the few writings that see the agony of colour prejudice as a subject for sardonic humour—he is, above all, a man of the theater. Soyinka is equally gifted as writer, director, producer and actor. The theater is the single focus of all his artistic activity. (pp. 129-130)

So much of recent interest in drama in Africa stems from Soyinka's determined and brilliant explorations. . . . Soyinka's plays and productions have made Nigerian drama closely approximate to the totality of African drama. (p. 130)

[*The Swamp Dwellers* and *The Lion and the Jewel*] exemplify two tones of Soyinka's dramatic writing. His theme is always some aspect of Africa struggling with the social and religious problems arising from the transition from tradition to modernity. Sometimes his tone is cheerfully comic, at others the situation becomes a vehicle for high tragedy.

The Lion and the Jewel is a joyous comedy with a touch of serious social comment. . . . *The Lion and the Jewel* speaks of progress and the bride price, the conflict between western concepts of progress and traditional African custom. By making the conservative patriarch a figure of leonic proportions and by putting the arguments for progress in the mouth of the snivelling and ludicrous school teacher, Soyinka prevents us from judging the alternatives in the usual stereotyped way. (p. 131)

Soyinka sought deliberately to initiate a new drama which would utilize the resources of the English language but would draw its emotional sustenance, not from abroad, but from the continuing cultural tradition of his own country. (pp. 132-33)

[*A Dance of the Forests* is a play] linked more closely than any other to the folk tradition of Nigeria. Soyinka borrows his theme from this source while adapting it to make a specifically modern statement. The play, with scarcely disguised symbolism, concerns a human community on the occasion of the most important "gathering of the tribes." They appeal to the gods to allow some of their noble ancestors to return from the dead to join the tribe in the ceremonies of this august moment. . . . The whole concept ridicules the African viewpoint that glorifies the past at the expense of the present. The sentimentalized glamour of the past is exposed so that the same absurdities may not be reenacted in the future. This constitutes a bold assertion to an audience awaiting an easy appeal to racial heroics. . . .

The dramatic power of the surging forest dance [in the play] carries its own visual conviction. It is this that shows Soyinka to be a man of the theater not simply a writer who might air his concerns equally effectively in the pages of a novel. (p. 133)

To find the universal in the particular, the world truth in the African situation is what Soyinka achieves. His Africa is not separated from the world but united to it by Soyinka's dramatic vision. . . . Soyinka is succeeding in becoming an African dramatist and the measure of his achievement is apparent in that we must stress equally both of those terms. (pp. 134-35)

John F. Povey, "Wole Soyinka and the Nigerian Drama," in Tri-Quarterly *(© 1966 by* Tri-Quarterly*), No. 5, Fall, 1966, pp. 129-35.*

MARGARET LAURENCE

Wole Soyinka's writing often seems like a juggling act. He can keep any number of plates—and valuable plates, at that—spinning in the air all at the same time. He is able to handle many themes simultaneously without ever endangering the reality of his characters. His people are never ciphers or symbols, always persons speaking in their own voices. He is a volatile writer, and he achieves in his work an almost unbelievable amount of vitality. He is well known as a poet, and he has written one novel, but it is as a playwright that he has done his major work so far. (p. 11)

In his work Soyinka enriches and gives dramatic emphasis to modern themes by drawing upon the religion, the mythology and the poetry of the African past. Yoruba gods inhabit his plays, and he uses the Yoruba drums, including the talking drums, as they have been used for centuries to heighten and define rituals. He also makes use of the dance and mask idiom which are an integral part of traditional Yoruba drama. He combines these elements with contemporary settings and with themes which are universal, and the results are sometimes electrifying. . . .

Generally speaking, Soyinka's plays contain everything necessary to understand his references to Yoruba gods or cults. Nevertheless, because Soyinka's background is so wide, and includes influences both from the European theatre (Brecht, Dürrenmatt and Arden have all been said to have influenced him) and from African traditional drama, and because his frame of reference includes a double mythology, Yoruba and Christian, it is necessary to . . . realise that his writing, both in form and content, owes as much to African sources as it does to European. (p. 12)

The Yoruba festival which has the closest bearing on the work of Soyinka is the Festival of Ogun, which is still celebrated each year. Ogun is the Yoruba god of war and of iron. He is the protector god of hunters and carvers and all who work with iron. . . .

In the plays of Soyinka, Ogun takes on new dimensions and acquires meanings which are psychological and symbolic, but it is important to remember that for many of Soyinka's characters, . . . Ogun is believed in literally. (p. 15)

Traditional religious masquerade is not the only form of Yoruba drama which has had an influence on the plays of Wole Soyinka. A popular theatre, with plays performed in Yoruba, had its origins in the Christian Church, and particularly with such sects as the Apostolic Church and the Seraphim and Cherubim. These sects, some thirty years ago, began to produce biblical plays which can be compared with the European medieval passion plays and morality plays, strong-lined and simply motivated. (p. 16)

Wole Soyinka's inheritance and background [includes] the mask dramas of *Egungun,* the Yoruba pantheon of gods, the praise-songs and the rituals of the festivals, the ever-present drums which convey both words and emotions, the Yoruba mythology and proverbs, the folk opera with its chanted songs and its quick-paced and often violent action. He has drawn material from all these sources, transforming it into something rich and strange and new, and adding to it his own ability to create individual character and his own way of seeing.

Irony, in [*The Lion and the Jewel*], is used with a delicate touch. The manners and customs of both the old Africa and the new are satirised, but lightly, never with the bitter vigour that marks Soyinka's social commentaries in his later plays. All the protagonists in this play are treated affectionately. (pp. 18-19)

[*The Trials of Brother Jero,* a] short comedy, is a take-off or send-up of the many evangelists, prophets and other religious curiosities who flourish and milk money from the gullible along the beaches of Lagos. It has the simplest structure of all Soyinka's plays, and in fact the entire plot hangs on the well-worn device of concealed identity. (p. 22)

There are strands of both traditional religion and Christianity in [*The Strong Breed*]. The elders and priest, the sacred grove, the carrying of the year's evils to the river—these are drawn from African religions. But the whole play in a sense is a parallel with the Christian passion story—the man who must ultimately act the role demanded of him as his father's son, the temptation to evade the role, the final facing of the role of redeemer who takes upon himself the sins of all, the death on the cross (the sacred tree).

Soyinka is exploring the nature both of human sacrifice, where the victim is unwilling, and of a type of martyrdom where the victim offers himself. . . . And in his death there are various elements—a desire to serve, a desire to give meaning to his own life, and finally a desire to die.

The Strong Breed is an exceedingly compact play. In a relatively short space, Soyinka has managed to convey and contrast concepts relating to figures found in many societies and many religions. . . .

A Dance of the Forests is Soyinka's most intricate play. Among many other things, it contains some extremely vitriolic comments on corrupt politicians and a number of pointed warnings about the dangers which face a newly independent country. . . . The play has been criticised for its obscurity, and it is true that parts of it are difficult and open to more than one interpretation. . . . The action is rapid—sometimes almost too rapid; the themes are never dealt with singly but always more than one at a time; the idiom is frequently unfamiliar; the poetic imagery is sometimes bewildering. Nevertheless, a great deal does come across, even on a first contact with this play. (pp. 27-9)

In terms of social themes, Soyinka seeks to establish a relationship with the past which will neither stifle and dominate man nor sever him from his roots. In terms of psychological or spiritual themes, Soyinka seeks to make us look at those aspects of ourselves which we would rather not see, to induce us to examine them and at least admit their existence. (pp. 44-5)

There are some parts of *A Dance of the Forests* which seem overloaded. There are moments when the multiplicity of themes creates the feeling that there are a few too many plates spinning in the air—some of them speed by without being properly seen, and some crash down. But these are minor flaws in a work of enormous richness. . . . The use of the mask and dance idiom reinforces the splendid vividness of the play and heightens the sense of mystery which is essential to the 'welcoming of the dead'. Humour and poetry exist side by side in this play in ways that might be disastrous but never are.

A Dance of the Forests is pertinent not only to Africa and to newly independent countries there, but also to any and every man's relationship with his past, with his gods and with the concealed parts of his own heart. (pp. 45-6)

Unlike *A Dance of the Forests,* in *The Road* the maskers are never used for any broad spectacular effects. A group of masked dancers enters once, in a flashback which takes us to the Festival of Ogun. But chiefly, the use of masks is limited to one particularly significant mask, and in this play the whole concept of possession by the spirit of the mask is explored minutely, in both religious and psychological terms. (p. 47)

Soyinka's portrayal of character in [*The Road*]. . . is of a very high order. They are all observably and movingly alive. And yet his exploration of the state of possession, his use of masks and drums, his inclusion of dirges—all these serve to make of the play an elaborate dance of death. (p. 63)

The Road is Soyinka's most mature work so far. Its form shows greater control over his medium than is shown in *A Dance of the Forests*. He displays in *The Road* his usual ability to create living characters, but here they are more diverse and more deeply explored than anything he has previously attempted. The play gives a picture of some aspects of contemporary Nigeria, and it also looks searchingly at a theme which has no boundaries, the fact that man is the only animal who knows he must die. Man can bear to die, but not to die with a total lack of meaning. So we invent meanings, and believe in them even if they fall to pieces as we look at them. (p. 64)

Soyinka's first novel [*The Interpreters*] is a work in which moments of pure comedy are skilfully blended with a scrutinising irony. The bizarre and the beautiful coexist in passages of description of forest and sea and city. Above all, living people inhabit the novel's pages. The interpreters are a group of young intellectuals, men who went to university together in Nigeria and then went away to England or America for further studies. Now they are back home and can meet together as a group once more, comparing reactions and opinions, testing themselves against the eyes and feelings of the others, protecting each other when they can and giving their affection or grief when they cannot. They are interpreting their society, but they are interpreting themselves as well, and each man's view turns both outward and inward. (pp. 64-5)

The themes of messianic desire, the nature of death, the portion of death born into every soul, do not emerge as tellingly in this novel as they do in *The Road,* and yet in a sense the characters who act as protagonists in this ritual fencing with death are more sinister than their counterparts in *The Road*. Both Professor and Murano [of *The Road*] are characters with whom we can feel contact and sympathy. Noah and Lazarus [in *The Interpreters*]—although they are admittedly less fully drawn characters—are altogether more ominous and frightening. Perhaps that was the intention. Perhaps Professor's ornate oratory and laughter-cloaked oddity are too appealing. Perhaps the dark side of the moon is not shown, in *The Road,* to be half dark enough. (p. 73)

As in nearly everything that Soyinka has written, this novel combines social and psychological themes. The picture of Nigerian university life is lively and often searingly funny, akin in its iconoclastic humour to the early novels of Kingsley Amis in England and to Saul Bellow or Bernard Malamud in America.

What comes across best in this novel is the picture Soyinka draws of the interpreters themselves. . . . Each man steps from the printed page with all the paradox and conflict and warmth of a living man. To have done this with five closely associated characters, and to have maintained unfailingly the uniqueness of each, is a remarkable achievement.

A few themes recur again and again, in varying forms, throughout all of Soyinka's work. One of these is the reinstatement of the old gods, especially Ogun, both in a traditional and a contemporary way—that is, as gods revealing themselves to men directly, and in a symbolic way as facets of the human personality which cannot be expressed in anything other than this essentially poetic manner.

In Soyinka's presentation of the conflict between the values of the old society and the new, he constantly attacks both and also constantly sees the value of both. He can offer a withering assessment of the ancient king, Mata Kharibu, in *A Dance of the Forests,* and he can point out the fallacies of the old religion, as he does in *The Swamp Dwellers.* In contrast, there is his affectionate treatment of Baroka, the old Bale, in *The Lion and the Jewel,* or the integrity of the Warrior in *A Dance of the Forests.* As far as the present is concerned, what appears in his work as a continuing anger is his dislike of the limited and stultified mission-school outlook, his hatred of corrupt politics, and his sardonic attitude towards the prim status-seeking within the universities. On the other hand, he provides a sympathetic and subtle characterisation of the present generation of intellectuals in *The Interpreters.* To Soyinka, the artist cannot be with-drawn or isolated—he is part of his society and may have to try to change it, but never easily, never without a deep and possibly self-protective scepticism.

Psychological or spiritual themes are as important to Soyinka as social ones. He explores the question of human sacrifice in much of his writing. *The Road* expresses the culmination, so far, of this exploration, in the way in which Professor wants his rejects of the road to live as potential and willing sacrifices to The Road, which is Ogun himself. The same theme appears in *The Strong Breed,* where Eman is drawn to offer himself, and the main enquiry of this play is into the differences between scapegoat and redeemer. In *A Dance of the Forests,* Oremole the apprentice does not actually want to die, but to some extent his act in mocking Demoke until the master-carver flings him from the treetop to his death is not only a human act of spite but also a religious one of fervour, performed on behalf of his god Oro.

The theme of sacrifice leads into the theme of martyrdom, which for Soyinka means the *chosen* death. It can be seen in *A Dance of the Forests,* in Demoke's death wish, the one aspect of himself which he is unable fully to face, and which is symbolically expressed by the Half Child, the *abiku,* the child born with death in its soul. The same theme can be seen in *The Road,* with Professor's desire to know his own death without dying, and his inevitable death caused by his determination to know beyond the limits of human knowledge. Again, in *The Strong Breed,* Eman not only fulfills his destiny and duty, but also is drawn to a death which he himself has chosen and yielded to. Noah, in *The Interpreters,* is a man nudged falsely into the role of saintly martyr by his master Lazarus, who has messianic tendencies himself but who is compelled to fulfil them through his manipulation of someone else's life. What comes out, again and again, in all these works, is the concept of a man *giving* his own death—giving his death in order to learn its nature, in order to defeat it and in order to prove stronger than the finality.

Surrounding this central desire to control death, there are other important characteristics exhibited by Soyinka's people in their dramatic ballet-like encounters with death, encounters which are as delicately precise and as ritualistic as a bull-fight. They wish not only to conquer death by somehow anticipating it and learning it. They also desire to impose a meaning on it, a meaning which may not intrinsically be there at all. The murderer and the martyred messiah interest Soyinka for exactly the same reason—both are drawn magnetically towards death, both are fascinated with its nature, both may desire their own deaths more than anything else, even though one appears only to want to kill and the other appears only to want to save.

The murderer, the scapegoat, the messiah—none of these, in Soyinka's writing, are seen as *them.* They are, undeniably, ourselves. If there is a core to his work, it is certainly this.

Soyinka's writing is life-filled, overflowing with energy, capable of realising human personalities and catching the sound of one particular voice, at times intensely comic, coloured with rhythm and dance, with drums and masquerade. But underneath, there is a concern with the inner territory of the spirit, a painful appraisal of the usually hidden parts of the mind. This strong undercurrent in his writing places him, ultimately, among the chroniclers of the areas of darkness within us all. (pp. 73-6)

Margaret Laurence, "Voices of Life, Dance of Death: Wole Soyinka," in her Long Drums and Cannons: Nigerian Dramatists and Novelists *(© 1968 by Margaret Laurence; reprinted by permission of Holt, Rinehart and Winston; in Canada by Macmillan, London and Basingstoke), Frederick A. Praeger, Publishers, 1969, pp. 11-76.*

The news that Wole Soyinka was following up his recent spate of activity in drama, poetry and polemical prose with a second novel must have stirred expectations of another work as complex and richly textured as *The Interpreters. Season of Anomy* is not that book; it belongs, rather, with his other post-prison writings in its narrower margin of hope, its determination to face and master the dragon of terror, its more direct use of allegory and representative character. These qualities associate it in particular with his last play, *Madmen and Specialists.* The system of *The Interpreters* was a kind of mythologized realism, which offered characters highly individuated in their daily aspects, yet drawn towards a universal harmony through the divine, eternal aspects which they shared with the gods. In *Season of Anomy* the treatment of both character and incident is allegorical throughout. The characters hardly take on individual life and there are none of the metaphysical subtleties which made his earlier novel so difficult, yet so rewarding. The rewards of *Season of Anomy* are of a kind we have come recently to expect from Mr Soyinka—an unrelenting determination to count the cost of Nigeria's tragic years, to show us how near the human spirit came to extinction or despair. The generalized power of his allegory is all the greater because it is not precisely located in time; it has elements of the situation before, during and after the civil war.

To this purpose his new fictional method, with its relatively cool prose, is well suited. Soyinka's favourite themes of seed-time, harvest and all that threatens them are handled with a controlled and lyrical grace. There can be no doubt of his meaning, or of the painful relevance of events in his fictional African country. . . .

Since the principal actors of this novel are really functions, alternative modes of action and being in a desperate time, the best writing is often found in description. And what is described, as in much of Mr Soyinka's recent writing, is almost obsessively horrifying. He is determined to rub his countrymen's faces in the deeds now officially forgotten or denied. It is a thankless service, though perhaps a necessary one, and it is to be hoped that his own creative impulse can now move beyond it. The last line of the novel—"In the forests, life began to stir"—suggests that it might.

"Dragon Slayer," in The Times Literary Supplement *(© Times Newspapers Ltd. (London) 1973; reproduced from* The Times Literary Supplement *by permission), No. 3745, December 14, 1973, p. 1529.*

JOHN UPDIKE

[Soyinka] is remembered in Nigeria with awe, both for a political boldness that landed him in prison and for a commanding intellect that is manifest in every genre he tackles. "Myth, Literature and the African World" . . . displays him as a critic and lecturer. . . . Soyinka discusses material —Yoruba myths and ritual dramas, plays by Afro-Brazilians as well as by Nigerians, postwar African novels and poetry good and bad—not within the usual province of the educated Westerner; but he does so with ample cross-references to Greek drama, Nietzschean aesthetics, Jungian philosophy, and Sartrean opinionizing, and in an accent uncompromisingly, if not even mordantly, lofty. . . .

Soyinka's long, fibrous sentences, not easy to pry apart, generally contain some meat, or milk. (p. 147)

We are best situated to appreciate his brilliance when it focusses on matters close to us. . . . Though his language bristles with the full armory of European critical methodology, Soyinka resists domination by extolling the profundities of African art and by giving some sacred figures of Western modernism rough treatment. Beckett—whose plays would seem exactly to fill Soyinka's prescription for ritual theatre as "a paradigm for the cosmic human condition"—is dismissed to "the lunatic fringe," and "the dotty excursions of W. B. Yeats into a private never-never land" are marvelled at for being taken seriously. African literature is commended for is refusal "to respond to the blandishment of literary ideology-manifesto art, and an imaginary representative of Cartesian civilization is finally addressed as "one-who-thinks, white-creature-in-pith-helmet-in-African-jungle-who-thinks and, finally, white-man-who-has-problems-believing-in-his-own-existence."

Yet so intent is Mr. Soyinka's will to see into the heart of his own culture that his recourse to points of invidious reference within ours arouses no disposition to argue. . . . [He] impresses us as being an analyst first, a propagandist second. Even at his most haughtily wordy, he has the voice of a true critic, who wishes not to praise or blame but to comprehend and explicate. (p. 148)

John Updike, "Books: 'Myth, Literature and the African World'," in The New Yorker *(© 1977 by The New Yorker Magazine, Inc.), Vol. LIII, No. 13, May 16, 1977, pp. 147-48.*

* * *

SPACKS, Barry 1931-

Spacks is an American poet and novelist. (See also *Contemporary Authors,* Vols. 29-32, rev. ed.)

ALAN WILLIAMSON

Barry Spacks is a conservative poet who is also vivacious, likeable, and skilled. He inclines to strict meters and ostentatious rhyme-schemes, which he handles with a deftness reminiscent of Wilbur, or, at bitterer moments, of Snodgrass. . . . Most of Spacks's best poems are essentially epigrams; he also has the rarer gift of writing good nonsense on serious subjects (*The World as a Vision of the Unity in Flesh, Homage to Henry James*). His character portraits—the "shoe clerk's bride", a whole taxonomy of students and professors—are two dimensional, but often so precisely observed as to induce delighted recognition. His painterly eye for landscape is also exact. On the other hand, when he tries to express emotion, or, worse, existential pondering, directly, he often becomes vague and maudlin: "if he'd take one step he'd come into / her love, that waits for him, a summer field."

Spacks's practice thus bears out the anti-Romantic credo expressed in his title poem: the poet does best to diminish his view of himself, and concentrate on pure technique, in order to pass from unorganized inspiration ("the company of children") to some higher analogue. The program is reminiscent of an earlier poetic generation overshadowed by New Critical formalism; and I often feel that Spacks's good poems could as easily have been written fifteen years ago as now. This is a little depressing, since the poet's own time is overflowing with innovations and schools, while the mode he hearkens back to seemed so cagy and restricting that most of its best practitioners have since abandoned it, or else lapsed into relative silence. But *The Company of Children* is itself a most undepressing book, and perhaps should not be weighed in such ponderous cultural-historical terms. (pp. 282-83)

Alan Williamson, "Beginners and Renewers," in Poetry *(© 1970 by The Modern Poetry Association; reprinted by permission of the Editor of* Poetry*), Vol. CXV, No. 4, January, 1970, pp. 281-85.**

GREG KUZMA

[Barry Spacks's] poems are about things the readers of this journal are themselves familiar with: students, jury duty, washing windows, books, poetry. Not only are the poems about these things, they are faithful to them. Spacks rarely tries to force the natural range of his subjects into uncomfortable reaches toward soul or essence. So these poems confirm the validity of Spacks's common but difficult life.

There is a good deal of structure to the poems, but instead of lending the poems an artificial quality the structure gives the poems additional grace. They are refreshing in times when much young American poetry delights in secret principles of organization, mysterious "deep images," confusion of line length and the abolishment of meaningful stanzaic patterning. One could say that Mr. Spacks is a gentleman; he will never leave the reader uncomfortable or embarrassed or clutching for orientation. He is consistent, solid, and responsible.

Nevertheless, the impression which Mr. Spacks has and makes of the world, that of a quaint and dusty, if sometimes chaotic, workshop, suggests perhaps a casualness too specialized for some of the profoundly awful events of modern life. In places he sounds like Frost; he has Frost's soundness and optimism—but not much of his other sides. One's initial response is that Spacks needs to deepen, perhaps to have something happen to him that pulls at the tightness of his vision. At times one is even tempted to revive the old instinct and brand the poems "academic." (p. 359)

Generally, [the poems in *The Company of Children*] are lightly muscled, polite. They have the grace of good swimmers. The ease with which they cover their distances may suggest that the difficult wrestling we admire our larger poets for is not yet part of this poet's commitment. Spacks is conservative; he never strains himself on anything too large for him. And one might regret this too sensible behavior; there is a monotony to all these medium-sized triumphs.

At the same time one comes to admire Spacks for speaking of what he knows, and writing from the strength of what he can handle. Until he stumbles into darkness, if he happens to, and out again, or chooses to makes his poems there, these entertaining and well made poems serve as a kind of good advice. (p. 360)

Greg Kuzma, "Poet in the Academy," in Prairie Schooner *(© 1971 by University of Nebraska Press; reprinted by permission from* Prairie Schooner*), Vol. XLIV, No. 4, Winter, 1970-71, pp. 358-60.*

ROGER DICKINSON-BROWN

Barry Spacks's *Teaching the Penguins to Fly* is a . . . sophisticated and professional book, at least in the superficial senses of the words. . . . [Here one finds] the tender clutter, the good beer and coffee quotidian of anybody's life, no further shaped nor understood.

Far too often Spacks has no subject. . . . But this most valuable and difficult poetry requires a special emotional and intellectual comprehension, and Spacks rarely achieves it. (pp. 379-80)

Although he usually writes in none, Spacks sometimes uses one of several forms, and sometimes well. In "Comparing X-Rays" the iambic rhythms are the plodding, dull movements, imagined by people who have not read Momaday, Elizabeth Daryush, Frost, Cunningham, Stevens, Tate,

Ransom, and Winters, to be inherent in a twentieth-century accentual-syllabic line; and the fourth line falls apart in an uninteresting way, perhaps in the struggle for rhyme. . . . (p. 380)

Most of the best poems occur in the final section of the book. These are often simultaneously curious and unpretentious poems, written in what at least approaches real prosody—often in the new unrhymed four-stress podic line ("Foolfish"). Several of these poems successfully personify animals, plants, or abstractions. . . .

These poems skirt the danger of excessive allusiveness or, alternatively, irrelevant circumstance—a common problem in modern art which causes it to age poorly. "After the 'I Ching'," although damaged by several of these faults, also musters Spacks's virtues: a real subject, a counterpoint of grammatical phrase against verse line, and enough verse measure and rhyme to permit the poem to amount to something more than a striking fragment. It is the best in the book. . . . (p. 381)

Roger Dickinson-Brown, "The Second Godine Poetry Chapbook Series" (copyright, 1978, by Roger Dickinson-Brown), in The Southern Review, *Vol. 14, No. 2, April, 1978, pp. 375-89.**

[Most of the poems in *Imagining a Unicorn* are in Barry Spacks's] favorite métier: a witty or serious reflection on some comic event or person in everyday living. . . . Although the poet is unsparingly honest, humor, sympathy, and tenderness are more characteristic than such a vitriolic, though deserved, outburst of scorn as "Malediction." "Hand of the mind" and "Gerard" are unforgettable for lyrical simplicity and dramatic transformation of the past, respectively. Noteworthy are the character portraits of Emily Dickinson, Pablo Neruda, and Timothy Holm. But it is the title poem that best represents the author's capacity for combining symbolism, poetic language, rhythm, and deep insight. By comparison with it, many of the other poems seem slight and undeveloped. Interesting and observant as they are, they depend too often on conversational tone and diction, leaving the reader hungry for music, form, and vision.

"Language and Literature: 'Imagining a Unicorn'," in Choice *(copyright © 1978 by American Library Association), Vol. 15, No. 10, December, 1978, p. 1374.*

JAMES FINN COTTER

[Barry Spacks] shows more religious spirit in his title poem, "Imagining a Unicorn," than in acres of [William] Everson. The poem depicts the Cloister tapestries in its separate scenes, the climax coming with the Unicorn in Captivity panel. . . . Spacks transforms a familiar art work into a personal poem, weaving words into scenery, mixing medieval and modern sensibilities. His style in other poems combines conversational slang with an academically precise syntax and tone. . . . I enjoyed "Seeing Pablo Neruda," a poem about spotting the poet at Harvard Square—or was it Octavio Paz? Spacks will never be sure and his poetry mimics his insecurity. He writes humorously about having a street named after him, nastily about litterbugs, and emotionally about his dead mother and a student killed in a gliding accident. We learn a lot about the poet from his writing, and the news is intelligent and good. (p. 117)

James Finn Cotter, "Familiar Poetry," in The Hudson Review *(copyright © 1979 by The Hudson Review, Inc.; reprinted by permission), Vol. XXXII, No. 1, Spring, 1979, pp. 109-22.**

DAVE SMITH

Barry Spacks is not one of those writers one hears about at the literary watering holes, though he is the author of two novels and, now, a fourth book of poems, *Imagining a Unicorn*. His method of handling a poem is generally to tame it to a traditional form, to rhyme, to statement, to petite jokes and multiple ironies. . . . [A poem such as "I Will"] might as easily have been written by Wilbur, Nemerov, or Ciardi. . . . If we are too prone to write off such decorous virtues as symmetry, wit, sensibility, it may be that our sense of an actual life is abused by such paper-scratching.

Yet we have need of court jesters as well as priests and we do ourselves a disservice to junk humor and intelligence, craft and music. If we still derive, as I argue, pleasure from memorable sounding words (the testament of history is still comfortably on the side of the angels of verse), then Spacks is often as good as those I have lumped him with. Sometimes better. I know of few more beautiful poems of desperation than his "Who Then Is Crazy" (in *Teaching The Penguins To Fly*). Spacks is, *sui generis,* a poet of the cityscape, of manner and style. . . . He is feisty, too, as stylists usually are. But Spacks is also capable of a wild and sudden glare directly into the heart of things and he is talented enough to make the art serve his seeing. "The Pale Ones," for example, is a fine poem about "basic creatures" we dream back to us. My favorite poem in this book pits what Spacks, as artist, represents against a student committed to passion and his own way, a student killed hang-gliding. . . . [It is a] loving elegy. . . . If, in Spacks, we get less of the Jamesian "full fact" than we desire, if we do not get heaven itself, he provides us with some splendid waystations for which we should give a proper thanks. (p. 32)

Dave Smith, "Dancing through Life among Others: Some Recent Poetry from Younger American Poets," in The American Poetry Review *(copyright © 1979 by World Poetry, Inc.; reprinted by permission of Dave Smith), Vol. 8, No. 3, May-June, 1979, pp. 29-33.**

* * *

STEWART, J(ohn) I(nnes) M(ackintosh) 1906-

Stewart is a British novelist, critic, and short story writer. As Michael Innes, he has written crime novels centering on academic and aristocratic characters involved in remarkably intricate plots. In the fiction appearing under his own name, he often considers the artist in society. (See also *CLC*, Vol. 7, and *Contemporary Authors*, Vols. 85-88.)

JULIAN SYMONS

[Michael Innes certainly gave his books a thick] coating of urbane literary conversation, rather in the manner of Peacock strained through or distorted by Aldous Huxley. The Innes books were immediately acclaimed as something new in detective fiction from the publication in 1935 of *Death at the President's Lodging,* a title with misleading implications for the United States, where it was rather tamely renamed *Seven Suspects.* The *Times Literary Supplement* said that he was a newcomer who at once took his place in the front rank and, with the publication of *Hamlet, Revenge!* (1936), called him "in a class by himself among writers of detective fiction."

There was actually nothing very new about Innes's approach. J. C. Masterman, in *An Oxford Tragedy* (1933), had produced very much the same kind of "don's delight" book, marked by the same sort of urbanity. But Innes is the finest of the Farceurs, a writer who turns the detective story into an overcivilized joke, by a frivolity which makes it a literary conversation piece with some detection taking place on the side. There is no greater quotation spotter or capper in crime literature than Inspector (later Sir John) Appleby, and few Innes characters of this period will flinch at playing a parlor game which involves remembering quotations about bells in Shakespeare. Appleby, when confronted by the "fourteen bulky volumes of the Argentorati Athenaeus," murmurs: "The Deipnosophists . . . Schweighauser's edition . . . takes up a lot of room. . . . Dindorf's compacter . . . and there he is." Appleby shows off, not out of sheer pretentiousness like Wimsey or Vance, but from genuine high spirits. The Innes stories cannot compare as puzzles with the work of Van Dine or Queen. Their strength is in their flippant gaiety, and perhaps the best of them all is *Stop Press* (1939), in which he dispenses with the almost obligatory murder, and keeps the story balanced on little jets of unfailingly amusing talk. (pp. 126-27)

Julian Symons, "The Golden Age: The Thirties," in his Mortal Consequences: A History—From the Detective Story to the Crime Novel *(copyright © 1972 by Julian Symons; reprinted by permission of Harper & Row, Publishers, Inc.; in Canada by Curtis Brown Ltd), Harper, 1972, pp. 118-32.**

AGATE NESAULE KROUSE and MARGOT PETERS

The outrageous punning on Professor Pluckrose's death (*The Weight of the Evidence,* 1944), the flamboyant and likable professorial forger of *The Long Farewell* (1958), and the amusing escapades of the Patriarchs at Oxford (*A Family Affair,* 1969) testify to Innes's essential reverence for university tradition and innocence. He takes it for granted that his professors' learning is vast, their integrity almost unchallengeable, and their flaws not serious enough to discredit their calling.

A late Innes story seems to reveal a change of attitude. In *An Awkward Lie* (1971), Innes follows Bobby Appleby, son of the famous quotation-capping detective Sir John, back to his old prep school on the track of a murdered mathematics teacher. . . . Nostalgia takes over . . . as Bobby finds the carved desks, muddy football boots, and crumpled candy wrappings unchanged since his school days. When we discover that Overcombe houses a beautiful and good golden girl, an eccentric but sporting old art teacher, two precocious empire-builders named Walcot and Breadon, and finally the world's greatest cryptographer . . . , we realize that for Innes order, tradition, and British salvation still rest with academe. (pp. 372-73)

Agate Nesaule Krouse and Margot Peters, "Murder in Academe," in Southwest Review *(© 1977 by Southern Methodist University Press), Vol. 62, No. 4, Autumn, 1977, pp. 372-73.**

NEWGATE CALLENDAR

["Honeybath's Haven"] is a leisurely, traditional British mystery in which page after page is spent establishing character. Not until more than halfway through is there, finally, a murder. There are the required eccentrics and Dickensian types. . . . The prose is stately and Victorian. . . . It's all very civilized and, unfortunately, also a bit labored.

Newgate Callendar, "Crime: 'Honeybath's Haven'," in The New York Times Book Review *(© 1978 by The New York Times Company; reprinted by permission), June 11, 1978, p. 35.*

JEREMY TREGLOWN

Full Term is the last of Stewart's five Oxford novels, and the closing chapters are full of poignant narrative knottings. Like most of his fiction, it's extremely well-constructed and contains some genuinely funny characters. . . .

What makes it hard to take, especially in the early pages before you get acclimatised, is the ponderous archaism of the style. Pattullo, the narrator, is supposed to be a temporary Fellow, imported only a year ago from his London life as a successful dramatist. But this is a dramatist who thinks stage electricians still talk about rheostats, who refers to people nearby as being 'within bow-shot', whose friends say things like 'This is a damned rum place, Pattullo', and who has a conversation with an undergraduate that goes, 'Junkin is a frightfully good producer, isn't he?'—'He may become one. He's no end enthusiastic.' He even calls Britain, 'The kingdom'. But if you can get past all that, he's a likeable, gallant, unselfish, romantic kind of chap with a good eye for a yarn. . . .

Jeremy Treglown, "Snob Story," in New Statesman *(© 1978 The Statesman & Nation Publishing Co. Ltd.), Vol. 96, No. 2468, July 7, 1978, p. 27.**

SUSAN KENNEDY

[On the whole, *Full Term*] does not contain as many intricate side plots and proliferating confusions as [Stewart's] earlier novels, but the dramatic high points, when they come, are devastating in their effect: Ranald McKechnie, the remote classical don married to the woman Pattullo once loved, at last struck down by his mechanical leaf-gathering and scrub cutting monster; Fiona, with whom Pattullo has been conducting a muffled and elusive affair, finally rejecting his tentative proposal in an enraged outburst of masterly irony.

To someone new to the series [Stewart's Oxford novels]—and there cannot be many at this late stage—this volume will not be particularly accessible. There are few new faces, and much delving into Pattullo's complicated past. . . .

Full Term is largely concerned with tying up the loose ends of Pattullo's life so far (we find him at the end enjoying vicarious parenthood, so we can be sure he will be carried on into the future), and some lighter threads are left undone. A short visit to Otby finds the three Mumfords, whose disreputable goings on have excited much alarm throughout the series, under siege from Pattullo's discarded wife Penny. Particularly distressing is a glimpse of Cedric reduced to senile amatory ravings. But we are not told how things turn out.

The series has been stretched as far as it can comfortably go: so choked with past incident is it that forward progression has become very difficult. . . . There is consequently a slight sense of strain throughout *Full Term,* but none the less it brings *A Staircase in Surrey* to a satisfactory conclusion, completing what amounts to a celebration of Oxford, unequal in its parts perhaps, but always providing great entertainment, not least in its gallery of eccentric dons and dons' wives. One of the real pleasures for the reader has been in observing the way a character such as Arnold Lempriere (whose memorial service closes the series) has been subtly built up from book to book. The novels have been informative, too—it would almost be possible to extract from the whole work an invaluable guide entitled "Stewart on Oxford Parties", ranging from five-year-olds' birthday celebrations to sherry with the Provost to the full formality of a Gaudy dinner.

Susan Kennedy, "Donnish Delights," in The Times Literary Supplement *(© Times Newspapers Ltd. (London) 1978; reproduced from* The Times Literary Supplement *by permission), No. 3979, July 7, 1978, p. 757.*

JEREMY TAMBLING

J.I.M. Stewart's compilation of stories, *Our England is a Garden,* . . . charts the loss of certain English values the author clearly prizes. . . . Stewart seems unwilling to face the present: when we are told, in the second story (about a don invited to write his autobiography), that 'the best English memoirs, after all, had been written long ago, and he had read pretty well every one of them while still an undergraduate', the implicit attitude is that Culture belongs to the past. No wonder Stewart's Professor Mannering notices that 'a tremendous amount of nonsense is written about literature, even more than is written about history'. We know what literature is, dammit: you read it when you're an undergraduate, and it's not good form to question standards or values. Such attitudes predominate in Stewart's fiction—attitudes too conventional and received to really begin to test your own thinking and prejudices.

Jeremy Tambling, "Nature Study," in New Statesman *(© 1979 The Statesman Publishing Co. Ltd.), Vol. 98, No. 2525, August 10, 1979, p. 208.**

HERMIONE LEE

[To turn] to the prim, crusty, Ciceronian rectitude of J.I.M. Stewart's four long stories [in 'Our England Is a Garden'] is to seem to travel sharply backwards in time and downwards in temperature. So jocularly urbane is the archaic narrative, so blandly resting on Edwardian class assumptions, that at times it seems almost to be parodying itself.

Mr Stewart is ironic at the expense of those who live in the past, and his stories—about the downfall of a stately home, the humiliation of elderly academics—show the inevitable enfeebling of traditions. But he has not himself given up to what he calls 'classlessness.'

The stories have, as is to be expected, efficient amusing twists, and they 'do' the vanishing classes expertly: aristocratic landowners (being replaced by cooks' sons), real scholars (being replaced by 'the miserable race of periodical reviewers.') But they are chilling and disdainful pieces, not greatly interested in human beings. As one of his characters remarks: 'All this about *feelings* remains an intellectual conception.'

Hermione Lee, "Backwoods Messiah," in The Observer *(reprinted by permission of The Observer Limited), No. 9808, August 19, 1979, p. 36.**

STUART, (Hilton) Jesse 1907-

Stuart, an American novelist, short story writer, and poet, writes primarily about the poor people of Appalachia. Much of his fiction has a distinct oral character, replete with the mountain dialect and mannerisms of its narrator. He is a master of the short story and his best work is distinguished by its well-drawn characters and strong narrative flow. Although he is sometimes accused of being unselectively prolific, many critics believe that his work is underrated by the critical community as a whole. (See also *CLC*, Vols. 1, 8, 11, and *Contemporary Authors*, Vols. 5-8, rev. ed.)

DAYTON KOHLER

[Good] regional writing is always made at home. Jesse Stuart has written five books without going far beyond the borders of W-Hollow in his native Greenup County. Ten or twelve families live in the hollow, and he has written poems and stories about all of them. These real people behind his stories would make an interesting article in themselves. (p. 524)

Stuart came into literature in 1934 with an amazing collection of 703 sonnets, *Man with a Bull-Tongue Plow.* Many of these poems were pure description, a re-creation in lyric language and mood of the Kentucky landscape in all weathers and seasons. Others told with innocent frankness of the adventures, loves, and dreams of Jesse Stuart, poet and plowman of the hills. Then in the third section the book came roaringly to life when the writer resurrected more than two hundred dead in Plum Grove churchyard to tell the stories of their humble lives. The method suggested *Spoon River Anthology,* but these stories—grim, humorous, profane—had nothing in common with Edgar Lee Masters' studies in pessimism and defeat. The poetry was often trite and prosy and crude. It was also as native as a whippoorwill and as full of provincial flavor as a persimmon. Critics, viewing Stuart's book with mixed feelings, tried to account for his earthy vigor by calling him a Kentucky Robert Burns. The true explanation of his talent, I believe, lies closer home. These poems and the prose which followed show us something of the pioneer experience as it has survived on a ruined frontier. In everything he has written we can find evidence of a tradition which goes back beyond the Sut Lovingood papers and Augustus Longstreet's *Georgia Scenes* to the anonymous story-tellers of the frontier. (pp. 524-25)

Folklore and fantasy appeared at every halt on the westward march, and the best hunters and rail-splitters passed into legend. . . . These stories had a geography, a mythology, and a lingo of their own. Some were streaked with ballad sentiment. Others crackled with bawdy humor. But mostly these tales were comic elaborations of character or drawling reminiscence in which the frontiersman dramatized himself with shrewd appraisal and salty enjoyment. (p. 525)

Behind all this is an awareness of the beauty of river and forest which gives our literature its most authentic theme. It is the brief, westering American dream in the language of the people who lived it.

In his short stories Jesse Stuart has caught the echoes of this frontier world. *Head o' W-Hollow* and *Men of the Mountains* are filled with pioneer tags of realism and rough humor. (pp. 525-26)

He has a frontiersman's delight in tall talk and tall deeds. "The Blue Tick Pig" has weird overtones of the Paul Bunyan legends in its account of a runt that learned to milk cows. There is genuine folk fantasy in the story of a quiet tramp, a champion worker in the cornfields, who is finally arrested for stealing all the brass in the neighborhood. Grandpa Grayhouse asked his family to keep his body salted down in the house for six months while they held a party every week in his memory. These doings become the scandal of the countryside. "Huey, the Engineer" and "Uncle Jeff" belong to the John Henry tradition, stories of strong mountain men beaten in the end by the machine. These tales have the tall-story blend of sharp, dry realism and fantastic invention.

Jesse Stuart tells his stories without apology or comment. Whether grimly realistic or wildly humorous, they bear the manner of tales that have been common for a long time. Part of this effect comes, I think, from his use of the present tense and a first-person narrator through whom the experience is presented. These stylistic devices make it plain that he thinks of the short story as a narrative told, for on the printed page they approximate the tones of voice, the pauses, the decisive accents of speech. His colloquial language adds also to the oral manner that we find in frontier yarns. Sometimes this style makes for vivid reporting. . . . Less expertly handled, it falls into the flat, declarative rhythm of meager prose. (pp. 526-27)

In *Beyond Dark Hills* he tells of his own life on the arrested frontier. A provincial innocence and cocksureness touches the chapters on his hardy ancestors and his boyhood, and the account of his struggles to get an education reveals a provincial distrust of cities; but his pictures of mountain life are written with great feeling and sincerity. . . . Stuart's autobiography is pure regional writing, simple in finish and tone, and more effective than his novel in showing us the piety and violence of his people. *Trees of Heaven* presents another phase of the frontier experience, the old grudge fight between the settler and the squatter. . . . At times the novel reads like a parody of all the hillbilly fiction ever written. Its faults are obvious. The plot is sentimental and trivial, its dialogue extravagant, its social problem unresolved. Stuart's imagination is free and vivid, but sustained-passage work between the scenes of his novel is impossible for him. *Trees of Heaven* lives only in single episodes. . . . (pp. 527-28)

After five books his writing remains a frontier talent for anecdote and character drawing, and the chief impression from his work is one of much power poorly controlled. He is by turn a reporter, an atmosphere man, a poet, and a racy fabulist. He has the mixed strains of pioneer fatalism and broad humor which produced the lonesome ditties and tall stories. He also has the pioneer's morbid concern for death, a subject which he treats either with sentimentality or with the cruelty of casual humor. At his best he seems to know instinctively the meaning of life in terms of a people and a place, and he can describe the look and feel and smell of things with joyous certainty. But as an artist he is without discipline—perhaps incapable of it. The truth may be that he is not temperamentally a writer at all but a conversationalist with a quick eye and ear and a lively gift of expression. As such, he stands at the end of a tradition in American story-telling rather than at the beginning of a new one. (p. 528)

Dayton Kohler, "Jesse Stuart and James Still: Moutain Regionalists," in College English *(copyright © 1942 by the National Council of Teachers of English), Vol. 3, No. 6, March, 1942. pp. 523-33.**

FRANK H. LEAVELL

[In *Trees of Heaven,* Tarvin Bushman] is the ideal youngster with no faults and few complexities. Created simply, he is free to observe and make his own judgments. He has the adolescent qualities of wanting to find a mate and to establish his own identity independent of his parents. But throughout the story he thinks and reacts more as an adult than as an adolescent.

Although Stuart's younger brother James is the physical model for Tarvin, many parallels might be drawn between Tarvin and the author. . . . Never is an ironic gap created between Stuart and Tarvin. Tarvin has the author's complete sympathy and is never proven wrong in any judgment or action. The observations of this study, therefore, are based on the assumption that Tarvin's opinions are identical with Stuart's.

The most fundamental theme in all of Stuart's life and writing is man's dependence upon the land. While the theme may reflect some influence from Emerson, its roots are certainly in Stuart's own experience. The theme is this: A man draws his strength and nourishment from the land. Its produce feeds his body as its poetry feeds his soul. He thrives when he is close to the soil; he withers when he forsakes it and sojourns in the city. His prime duty is to respect and care for the land just as the land provides his needs. In death his body is returned to the soil. And through his communion with the land he finds a mystic communion with God. Yet this view of the land stops short of pantheism. Nature remains inanimate; God remains transcendent.

Beneath their differences, the love for the land is the constant that unites [Tarvin's father, Anse Bushman, and Boliver] Tussie. The two share a sense of territorial possession and stand ready to fight for their territories. Both are farmers who see the land as a wilderness to be tamed and cultivated. Both draw their strength from the land and hold themselves superior to the city people who have forsaken it. Both enjoy the beauty of the land and spend time abroad absorbing its poetry.

But a dualism is created in the presentation of two different concepts of owning the land—one by legal deed of ownership and the other by natural right of occupancy. The conflict between Anse and Boliver merely reflects a larger social conflict. In the microcosm of the book, society has tried to make laws of ownership in terms of deeds and cash purchase. But these man-made laws are insufficient to overcome the individual's natural right to possess the land on which he lives. (pp. 55-6)

[Anse Bushman's] right to his farm, both by legal ownership and by natural possession, is never questioned. Although he is seventy, he still has a young man's dreams of the future. Unfortunately, however, his dreams are not limited to his own farm. He has always been driven by a mania to own more land. When he buys the Sexton Land Tract, his concept of ownership does not provide for those squatters who live on the land without a deed. His first action upon buying the new land is to have the squatters removed.

But the squatters hold a different view in this dualism of territorial possession. These people [the Tussies] have lived on the Sexton Land Tract for generations, cutting timber and farming little plots of ground. They believe that their right to live on the land by natural possession is stronger than any legal deed, and many stand ready to kill any man who tries to dispossess them. (pp. 56-7)

If Bushman's legal ownership of the land is symbolized by a deed, the Tussies' natural possession of the land is symbolized by the Tussie cemetery shaded by the trees of heaven, which give the novel its title. Here lie the ancestors of the squatters in the soil from which the trees grow. The ailanthus trees—or trees of heaven—are a quaint symbol. Despite the romantic treatment they are given in the novel, ailanthus trees are generally considered weed trees, good for nothing, growing rapidly over alley fences, and producing unsightly flowers with a foul odor. They are hard to get rid of and often grow where not much else will. Perhaps they are ironically a better symbol for the squatters than Stuart intended.

This dualism in the conception of land ownership leads naturally to a set of social distinctions. While the Bushman family are the only characters of their class to play an important part in this story, they represent the establishment in the community. (pp. 57-8)

The squatters, on the other hand, comprise a distinctly inferior social class. . . . They may be compared with Faulkner's Snopeses or indeed any immigrant minority group moving into an established society. . . .

[Their] mutual distrust is not hard to fathom. Indeed the drama is played out almost everywhere that two different social classes become a threat to each other. (p. 58)

[Both Anse Bushman and Boliver Tussie] are good farmers who see the new land as wilderness to be tamed into fields of corn and tobacco. Since Anse is more ambitious for wider dominion and more profit, he is proportionately less concerned for the wild creatures. Burning the hill [to clear it] is a quick way to exploit the land. Although Boliver never opposes the project and is later enthusiastic about getting his seeds into the new fields, he is less greedy for profit and proportionately more sympathetic for the creatures. Left to himself, he would probably have cleared the land with hoe and ax, which Anse estimates would have taken two years.

Whichever approach is right, the burning hill is compared to hell. Although the metaphor rests on the visual image rather than on any theological implications, the scene could suggest the sinfulness of greed and the wanton exploitation of the land at the expense of the wild creatures. (p. 59)

The different relationships Bushman and Tussie have with the land give rise to a dualism in attitudes toward work and play. Bushman's motivation to own more land and to raise a better crop than anybody else reflects his pride. His ambition has driven him into a fanatic dedication to the work ethic to the exclusion of all other values. . . . But inwardly it has left him self-righteous, blind to the feelings and rights of others, and unsatisfied with his own achievements. . . . [His] prevailing attitude is that play is sinful because it distracts from work.

But his family have suffered most from his work ethic. Except for Tarvin, his children have been completely alienated by his austerity. (p. 60)

While the Tussies undergo little growth in the novel, Tarvin's growing appreciation of them results in an evolving portrayal of the family. Tarvin's early contempt gradually becomes admiration, while he comes to reject his father's work ethic and accept the Tussie life-style. Tarvin's views leave little doubt where Jesse Stuart's values lie in relation to the dualism of work and play. (p. 61)

The sin of Anse, then, is not only in his extreme dedication to hard work, but in the brutal imposition of his code on his family and the Tussies. The two opposing values are reconciled when he allows the Tussies to return to their home. This reconciliation takes an interesting twist. Throughout the book, Boliver makes little if any change. . . . The concessions and reforms are all on the part of Anse. This means that in the conflicts of work habits and life-styles the victory belongs entirely to Boliver.

As portrayed in this novel and in many of Stuart's works, the hill people are often fiercely independent and take a dim view of the laws of government on any level. To them the higher law is the moral right of the individual to remain on his own land, to pursue his own harmless interests, and to fight his own battles. This tradition initiates the dualism of the law versus the individual.

Stuart portrays the law as unfair and inhumane. (pp. 61-2)

Stuart portrays the law as corrupt. Failing in other ways to evict Boliver from his land, Anse brings him to court in a lawsuit. While this courtroom scene is a brilliant display of humor and local color, it also carries a bitter indictment of the legal process. In an introductory paragraph written in italics, his only intrusion into the story, Stuart condemns this courtroom as a perversion of American ideals. (pp. 62-3)

Stuart carries his attack on the corruption of the law further in his portrayal of its officials. . . . These are caricatures, to be sure, but their use emphasizes Stuart's ridicule of the corruption of the law.

Finally, Stuart portrays the law as ineffectual. The hill people are too self-sufficient to let the corrupt process of law settle their quarrels. (p. 63)

This dualism between the law and the individual comes to focus in Anse, whose moral decline can be traced in his manipulation of the law. At first he is pictured as an upright and law-abiding citizen. In the context of the story, his first step toward degradation occurs when he buys the Sexton land, thus alienating himself from the community of hill people who are opposing the sale of the tract. Next he uses the law—the sheriff—to remove the squatters, retaining only Boliver's family, whom he intends to manipulate for his own profit. His later eviction of Boliver, based on personal rather than business charges, is obviously motivated by his greed to claim the Tussie crop for himself. . . . [He] finds that he is unable to fight his own battle as he had boasted he would do, for the Tussies are too many for him. Thus he resorts to the lawsuit. At this point Tarvin confesses that Subrinea is going to have his baby. Afraid that the union will hurt his chances in the lawsuit, and blind to the love between the young people, Anse proposes: "I can git you out'n it, Tarvin. . . . I can git four men to swear they monkeyed with her. That will make her a whore. The Law won't do nothin to you." . . . The once law-abiding and independent Bushman is now ready to manipulate the law by false witness to destroy the character of Subrinea and achieve his own ends.

Like the law, religion in *Trees of Heaven* is a significant theme, and it can be observed in terms of a dualism between this world and the hereafter. These balancing perspectives can be traced through Anse's two experiences of rebirth, and reconciliations of some of the dualisms already described can be discerned here.

His first rebirth, which is entirely of this world, occurs as Anse walks abroad all night in a spring thunderstorm. Significantly, this scene follows the hill burning, which may symbolize his transgression against the land. Although his rebirth does not solve the problem of man and the land, it does override it with a cleansing and fresh start traditionally associated with the rebirth of spring. (pp. 63-4)

This storm, the resurrection of spring, is his baptism. He is washed clean in body and mind, and he is reborn to his identity with the land. But as magnificent as this resurrection scene may be, it results in no moral or spiritual change in him.

His second rebirth is his spiritual conversion as a result of his nearly fatal accident. He is struck in the head by a falling limb at the time of his lowest moral ebb—after he has evicted the Tussies and is greedily trying to harvest their crop for himself. For three days (significantly) he lies in a coma. When he awakens, he tells Fronnie of his conversion. This spiritual conversion comes in the form of a vision, or token. It is in two parts—a vision of a worship service in Plum Grove Church and a vision of hell. This second rebirth is far more effective than the first in making a new man of Anse, for he renounces his old habits and attitudes as well as reversing his treatment of the Tussies. . . .

In the conversion of Anse are reconciled many of the dualisms of the book. The problems of territorial possession and class distinctions are reconciled as Anse invites Boliver to return to his home and crops. . . .

The final dualism to be considered is the difference between marriage by God's laws and marriage by man's laws. In the union of Tarvin and Subrinea, most of the conflicts of the novel are brought into focus and reconciled.

The love story between the children of opposing families follows the traditional Romeo-Juliet pattern. Their love is consummated on the coldest night of the year in the sheep shanty adjacent to the barn, on the same bed with the newborn lambs (symbolizing innocence) which Subrinea has rescued from freezing. From that time on, both Tarvin and Subrinea consider themselves married by natural law. (p. 66)

Stuart's endorsement of this natural union is emphatic enough. Clearly both Tarvin and Subrinea are virgins, and their union is the consummation of the deepest and purest love. The scene in the lambing shanty must rank high among the most beautiful in all of Stuart's canon. Although explicit descriptions of sexual activity are rare indeed for Stuart, he handles this scene with immaculate taste. . . .

As the protagonist, Tarvin is faced with the crucial decisions in the novel, making his choices and evaluations in the context of the larger conflicts. In choosing Subrinea as his mate, he puts his evaluations to the test, for all of his decisions are associated with her. And through these decisions his growth from adolescence to manhood can be traced. (p. 67)

Although Subrinea is a far more colorful character than Tarvin, she serves the story only as his love partner. She has no major decisions to face. In choosing Tarvin, she has everything to gain and nothing to lose. . . . A hard worker and faithful lover, she has all the virtues: untainted purity, laughter and joy, resourceful ingenuity, and most of all a warm heart. Devoid of faults, she transcends humanity to become an earth goddess. . . . It is not hard to see that Tarvin's natural union with her is symbolic of man's marriage to the land.

But is she a convincing character? It is true that as the daughter of Crissie, who is not of the Tussie-Beaver clan, she has escaped the blight of incest. But how has she escaped the Tussie social training? As beautiful and radiantly sexual as she is, how has she retained her purity in the face of her family customs, the advances of the lumberjacks, and even the encouragement of her father? While such a character would be absurd in the hands of deterministic naturalists like Dreiser or Crane, she is certainly consistent with Stuart's belief in freedom of choice and self-reliance. Indeed, *The Thread That Runs So True* and many other stories are crowded with such noble characters, and even Stuart's own self-image is one of a man rising above environmental obstacles by his own will to attain nobility. Another dualism, environment versus free will, is reconciled in Subrinea.

Thus in the natural marriage of Tarvin and Subrinea, all of the other dualisms are reconciled. The feuding Bushman and Tussie families, with all their opposing values and social differences, are united. Work and play are brought into balance. The laws of men and the laws of God are merged. And man, at last, has wed the land. (pp. 68-9)

Frank H. Leavell, "Dualism in Stuart's 'Trees of Heaven'," in Jesse Stuart: Essays on His Work, *edited by J. R. Le Master and Mary Washington Clarke (copyright © 1977 by The University Press of Kentucky), University Press of Kentucky, 1977, pp. 54-69.*

KENNETH CLARKE

Stuart uses authentic regional dialect, faithfully rendering his time and place, combining his knowledge of life with imagination to create a unique literary expression. . . . Most of his characters are drawn from direct observation, sometimes lacking even the mask of a fictional name, and their speech is the speech Stuart has heard and used all his life. Although the reader who is unfamiliar with authentic Kentucky hill speech may feel that a rendition is exaggerated, careful examination suggests that Stuart's recollection and rendition are reliable, and that exaggeration, where it does occur, is a device employed for dramatic or comic purposes. In any case, he has usually avoided the gross errors of "eye" dialect characterized by misspelling and overworked archaisms that flawed the work of many earlier regional writers. . . . [He is] one of his own principal characters, many of the others being his family and neighbors. Their folklife is his, as he recalls it and lives it. Where he does describe the expressions and antics of a "low-down trashy set" is in the light of the values and judgments of a regional culture rather than in the mode of condescending gentility. The wisdom and worth of some of his relatively uneducated hill people is not diminished by their use of folk speech; similarly, the shoddy character of some of his better-educated townsmen is not concealed by their use of "standard" English.

Stuart's use of brief traditional formulas is a significant aid in characterization as well as a means of reinforcing a sense of a time and a place. Some of these are sayings or expressions of traditional wisdom upon which characters act or upon which they judge an event. Stuart uses the expressions as they occur in actual oral tradition instead of correcting them to make them conform to scriptures or other literary sources. (p. 119)

Omens, or tokens, as many folk call them, are similarly functional in that they faithfully portray traditional beliefs about foreknowledge. In addition, they may establish tension, tone, and foreshadowing. . . .

Birdlore, dreamlore, and similar ancient devices for folk prognostication survive as an active element in the folk community, and they sometimes surface in the context of the oral tale, another kind of folklore Stuart uses freely. His use of the folktale is a rewarding subject for the investigating folklorist. Here one finds a range from direct use of an identifiable local legend to so skillful a fabrication that it sends the investigator to his library in a futile effort to document it. Some contemporary folklorists find it useful to distinguish between transcriptive folklore and functional folklore in a writer's works. They label transcriptive the tale, song, or other expression which is entertaining or instructive on its own merits and appears, therefore, virtually unchanged as it exists in oral tradition. The writer merely creates a situation in which it can be presented. The flimsy frame of an old man answering the questions of a little boy in the works of Joel Chandler Harris is an example of this device, and the reworked folktales the old man tells illustrate the transcriptive use of folklore.

Functional use of folklore is more subtle. Here the folkloric expression or the allusion to it is subordinated to a specific literary requirement such as the development of character or setting. The tale-telling bent of two fictional characters [Op Akers in *The Good Spirit* and Grandpa Tussie in *Taps for Private Tussie*] reveals how functional the folktale is in Stuart's writing. (p. 120)

Although Op tells several kinds of tales, the ghost tale is most useful in this novel because it ties in with a mysterious "ghost" on Laurel Ridge—which finally turns out to be a living person. Old Op reports on so many beliefs, practices, and local happenings that one is inclined to think of him as a kind of Appalachian Uncle Remus, a fictional creation used for presentation of transcriptive folklore. The book is a novel, however, and it does have a plot. Examination of its folklore and folklife content shows that it is largely functional in the sense that it serves to enhance characterization, make vivid the setting, and advance the plot.

Stuart injects a subtle ambiguity into his presentation of Op Akers as a naïve backwoodsman who is completely comfortable with his belief in ghosts. Old Op drives off city intruders who claim they are not superstitious by telling them hair-raising tales about snakes and ghosts. It is never quite clear whether he is being merely ingenuous or crafty, in the time-honored American tradition of the countryman getting the best of "sophisticated" urbanites. In any case, the situation is traditional in both oral and written literature. . . . (p. 122)

Whether the tales Op Akers and Grandpa Tussie tell in their respective novels are identifiable as traditional oral narratives or are creations of the author does not alter their folkloric role. The fact is that Stuart, intimately familiar with long, windy yarns, first-person hunting and fishing whoppers, legends, and scary ghost stories in oral tradition, has created two believable folk types, each one presented as a raconteur. The distinctive functional aspect of their renditions is that their narrations help to maintain tone and theme as well as to extend characterization. Old Op is a gentle recluse, a healer and believer. His tales, even if gross exaggerations, are presented in a positive way, reflecting the author's approval of his creation. Grandpa Tussie's repertoire gives more emphasis to tall tales rendered in keeping with an entirely different kind of characterization and in a very different kind of novel. *The Good Spirit* is a gentle romance; *Taps* is a "Dogpatch" style caricature of the welfare syndrome, a comedy containing a considerable element of satire. . . .

[Stuart] freely combines a rich heritage of folklore with his literary education in a variety of creative moods, and that he rarely makes a conscious effort to use folklore as a special focus. He does, however, use a good tale or custom as a springboard for a composition. (p. 123)

"Rain on Tanyard Hollow" is Stuart's adaptation of a tale type widely known in oral tradition. Essentially, the tale concerns a man who buys or prays for a change of weather and gets more than he bargained for. Maritime versions of the tale involve the superstitious belief that a becalmed sailor can buy wind by tossing a coin overboard. This act usually brings on a storm rather than a beneficial breeze, whereupon the sailor observes that a smaller purchase would have been in order. A dry-land version has the farmer pray for rain, get a gullywasher, then observe that a more modest prayer would have been better. Stuart uses this theme, having Pappie get down on his knees in the dried-up strawberry patch and utter a mighty prayer for rain. Because his wife has taunted him about his faith, he overreaches, praying for a storm. (pp. 123-24)

Pappie gets exactly what he prays for. Lightning splits big oak trees and chickens go to roost in the midday gloom. The resulting flood washes away the corn crop and sends mud and rocks into the house. . . . [A] flock of visiting relatives who have been eating Pappie out of house and home pray for relief and promise the Lord they will leave Tanyard Hollow and never return if they survive. (p. 124)

Folklore here includes the folktale itself, regional speech, beliefs, regional life-style, and the hillman's ambiguous involvement with fundamentalist religion and superstition. The folktale itself, sometimes only a paragraph-length anecdote with a punch line such as "A quarter's worth would have been enough," is just one element of the mixture that bears Stuart's hallmark for humorous effect—exaggeration and incongruity. (pp. 124-25)

Folklore in Stuart's fiction cannot be fully evaluated by merely cataloging the songs, tales, beliefs, regional lexicon, or other specific elements. Cataloging can be an instructive exercise for an undergraduate student learning to use the library tools of folklore research, but merely to label a song fragment by a Child number or to tag a narrative passage with a Thompson motif number is a classroom exercise rather than an evaluation. A knowledge of field-collected folklore materials is, of course, essential, just as biographical knowledge of Stuart will reveal his authentic "insider" view of the culture. Equally important, his mode of comic exaggeration must be taken into account, so that the critic can avoid the error of assuming that there really is or was a frog-trouncing day in Greenup County.

Beyond those elements of folklore that can be cataloged, however, there is a matrix that holds them together which is fully as traditional as a folksong or a folktale, yet too diffuse to be neatly abstracted and verified on a checklist. This omnipresent element is the collective folkways that produce stereotyped values, attitudes, and responses. Some of the best folklore in Stuart's writing is his evocation of the matrix rather than specific bits of folklore embedded in it. (pp. 125-26)

The general matrix of folklife forms a kind of backdrop in ["Uncle Casper,"] a mildly satiric story about politics at the grassroots level. Embedded in the rambling recollections are elements of two traveling anecdotes about snakes. The fact that snake tales turn up regularly in conversations of country people seems inevitable in a state having a large population of timber rattlesnakes and copperheads. (p. 128)

The mortally dangerous constricting power of a nonpoisonous snake in Kentucky exists only in folk imagination. The motif occurs in oral narratives in various contexts, one of which has the snake get under the long skirts of a woman and coil about her waist. This titillating version then presents a dilemma for a black servant. Dare he lift his mistress's skirts to save her life? Stuart used the basic folk motif of the potentially lethal constrictor in a highly original piece of creative writing, a capsule example of his multilevel adaptation of folklore for literary purposes.

This sampling of folkloric elements in Stuart's works reveals the variety of both the folklore and the ways in which it serves the author's literary purposes. It reveals also the naturalness of the use of traditional materials by an "insider" in the culture. Certainly Stuart is not condescendingly genteel, and he is not on an intellectual slumming tour. He is, rather, the kind of American author some nineteenth-century critics, especially Emerson and Whitman, were calling for when they stressed the American experience in terms of strongly local, natural language rather than effete borrowing from cultivated European expression. They extolled the American workman close to the soil or the frontier rather than the aristocrat insulated from grassroots experience and expression. Development of authentic American literature, they felt, must come from the vigor of the folk experience, necessarily local, idiomatic, and relatively independent of refined antecedent models. Such writing is enhanced by accurate use of regional folklore. Partly as a result of his familiarity with the folklore and folklife of his region, Stuart has added a strong, original voice to the main thrust of American literature. (p. 129)

Kenneth Clarke, "Jesse Stuart's Use of Folklore," in Jesse Stuart: Essays on His Work, *edited by J. R. Le Master and Mary Washington Clarke (copyright © 1977 by The University Press of Kentucky), University Press of Kentucky, 1977, pp. 117-29.*

* * *

SWENSON, May 1919-

An American poet, playwright, critic, editor, and translator, Swenson is noted for her verbally sophisticated, tactile poetry. Howard Moss has said of her work: "Her surfaces are wonderfully painted and lead to surprising and mysterious depths. In the best of [her] poems, inner and outer vision meet." (See also *CLC*, Vol. 4, *Contemporary Authors*, Vols. 5-8, rev. ed., and *Something about the Author*, Vol. 15.)

WILLIAM STAFFORD

No one today is more deft and lucky in discovering a poem than May Swenson. Her work [in *Half Sun Half Sleep*] often appears to be proceeding calmly, just descriptive and accurate; but then suddenly it opens into something that looms beyond the material, something that impends and implies. . . .

So graceful is the progression in her poems that they launch confidently into any form, carrying through it to easy, apt variations. Often her way is to define things, but the definitions have a stealthy trend: what she chooses and the way she progresses heap upon the reader a consistent, incremental effect. (p. 184)

In the continuing work of Miss Swenson the question becomes: will her luck provide worthy encounters? Will she become distracted by this poking so interestedly in a dilettantish way into stray things? Sometimes, as in *The Secret in the Cat,* you think that she is just clever, apt with diction, able to maintain a chosen topic and to rev it up. But that same cleverness often leads into wilder and more interesting regions, as in *A Bird's Life.* Some of the cleverest poems, just through their intense unity, succeed in becoming greater things, as in the heart poem mentioned earlier, or in *Sleeping Overnight on the Shore,* or in a wonderful poem about *The Watch.* Partly, the most successful poems succeed through the ambition, the scope of the curiosity, of the writer; she pursues remote things, how the universe started, what will happen when . . . if. . . . (pp. 184-85)

William Stafford, "A Five-Book Shelf," in Poetry *(© 1967 by The Modern Poetry Association; reprinted by permission of the Editor of* Poetry*), Vol. CXI, No. 3, December, 1967, pp. 184-88.**

ALICIA OSTRIKER

Most humanists show very little curiosity about the physical world outside the self, and usually a positive antipathy to the mental processes we call scientific. . . . Science will not go away because poets ignore it, and in fact we ignore any great human enterprise at our peril. Yet few poets presently venture beyond dread or annoyance toward the works and ways of physics, chemistry, biology, and fewer bring back more than a gimcrack souvenir or two. . . .

[May Swenson] is known as a nature poet, "one of the few good poets who write good poems about nature . . . not just comparing it to states of mind or society," as Elizabeth Bishop has remarked. You can easily cull a bestiary from her work . . . and always with a wondering, curious eye, an intense concern about the structure and texture of her subject, an extraordinary tactility. . . . She watches things over long periods, and tracks her metaphors through itineraries of implications, with pleasure.

But beyond the naturalist's patient observation lies something else. What critics have called Swenson's "calculated naivete" or her ability to become "a child, but a highly sophisticated child," is actually that childlike ability to envision something freshly, to ask incessant questions and always be prepared for unexpected answers—required of the creative scientist. "What things really are we would like to know," she murmurs, and what else is the motive of the speculative intellect? Swenson's poetry asks as many questions as a four-year-old, and she wants to know not only how things are made and what they resemble, but where they are going and how we fit in. (p. 35)

While Swenson does not write on feminist themes most of the time, she does so occasionally, with electrifying results. . . . Most often, she blends, she balances. Science, technology, the mental life of observation, speculation: she has invaded these traditionally "masculine" territories. Yet her consistent intimacy with her world, which contains no trace of the archetypal "masculine" will to conquer or control it, seems archetypally "feminine." So does the way she lets herself be precise yet tentative and vulnerable about her observations . . . , and her affinity for the small-scale object, like Emily Dickinson's, also reads like a feminine characteristic. . . .

To Swenson, everything in the world speaks body language. . . . If anatomy is destiny, Swenson is at home (and humorous) with that, knowing we share that fate, finding no discrepancy whatever between what some would call a woman's body and a man's mind. . . .

Swenson has always had an individual style, though bearing traces here and there of Cummings, Marianne Moore, and especially Emily Dickinson. She has always been committed to formal experimentation, and she has often played with the shapes of poems. I would like to dwell here on one book, *Iconographs,* in which the composition of shaped poems has become systematic, in order to show how, apart from producing some beautiful things to look at, the method extends an observer's eyebeam to a new dimension.

Iconographs consists of 46 poems, each of which plays a typographical game. Each has been given a unique shape or frame. Verticals, angles and curves, quirky spacings and capitalizations have all been used. The intention, Swenson suggests in a note, has been "to cause an instant object-to-eye encounter with each poem even before it is read word-for-word. To have simultaneity as well as sequence. To make an existence in space, as well as time, for the poem." The title, she further remarks, can imply:

> *icon* "a symbol hardly distinguished from the object symbolized"
> *icono-* from the Greek eikonos meaning "image" or "likeness"
> *graph* "diagram" or "system of connections or interrelations"
> *-graph* from the Greek graphe meaning "carve" . . . "indicating the instrument as well as the written product of the instrument."

But such descriptions scarcely prepare us for the power of the opening poem, *Bleeding*. . . . [Beyond the effectively poetic] language, the most frightening thing in the poem is that visible slash down the page, that speaks, that takes the breath away. (p. 36)

"Bleeding" and "Feel Me" have in common, technically, a white line cutting the text. This happens often in *Iconographs,* and I will not belabor the possibility that "inner space" may be available as actual substance to a woman poet. The point is that in both poems, space *is* substantial. It stands in the verbal rhythm for hesitation, a gap the voice must leap in every line. It slows the tempo, enforces stillness, makes room for meditation. Visually it "means" separation, as if, between the knife and the cut, between the living and the dying, between experience and the ability to comprehend experience, falls this white shadow. Emotionally, the space expresses that sadness, appropriately wordless, which we feel in the face of all disunity we wish to heal but—so far, so ill—recognize we cannot. . . .

Williams suggested, as a formula for the poetic process, "in the particular to discover the universal." ["Feel Me"] stands as a major enactment of that idea. It is particularly touching that the naturalist's habits of patient attention, and the scientific imperative of hypothesizing as many explanations as possible for any mystery, ready to accept each, yet fixing on none, have been applied so perfectly to the depths of the human condition.

Much of the power here, as well as the intelligence, derives from a cross-cut play of rhyming sounds and assonances, either reinforcing or counterpointing meaning. (p. 37)

[Her poem "Fire Island"] illustrates the fact that the shapes in *Iconographs* are commonly agreeable to look at, but never because of a mechanical symmetry. Order shapes these poems, but so do pinches of disorder and randomness. If one margin of a poem forms a straight line or a simple curve, another is ragged. If sentences are simple, line-breaks cut their syntax unexpectedly. Where rhyme occurs it does so irregularly, or if the rhyme and meter are regular, then the pattern imposed breaks up and disguises them. In other words, Swenson has taken care to make her poems by the same principles—mixing Law and Chance—which we believe nature itself employs to make all of its objects, from DNA molecules to clusters of galaxies. . . .

Some final points about the method of *Iconographs*. If all poetry approaches metaphor insofar as it creates verbal equivalents for non-verbal experience, then consciously shaped poetry is a sort of P^{28}poetry raised by one power. First the experience or perception, then the text necessary to state the experience and all its implications truly, then a visual shape related to both. Swenson distinguishes her method of composition from that of concrete poetry by insisting that the text of each poem comes first, and can be considered complete and self-sufficient before the shapes are found. Shape then becomes a metaphor, enriching language as language enriches experience. But where concrete poems typically, and deliberately, have no interest separable from the visual, the technique in *Iconographs* maintains distinctions. Perhaps we should call it an art of simile rather than metaphor. Word and picture do not fuse, any more than the special sensation offered by our ear and eye can ever become one sensation, or any more than the external world we behold and the internal world which beholds it can ever become one. Connection exists instead of identity, tantalizing and delighting. . . .

The formal fragmentation of "free verse" necessarily reflects not only social and political incoherence, but a failure of the belief that nature offers us models of significant form. . . . We may at this moment be coming around to a rediscovery, and a finer perception, of natural laws and natural freedoms, and our position within them.

Swenson does not theorize on the subject, but her work

shows some ways to express our relation to the natural world as we comprehend it. The shapes in *Iconographs* are shapes of speculation, balanced between the patterned and the random—for so we presently guess Nature to be—and attempting to capture both the ways we fit into the world and the ways we cannot fit. They are playful, quirky, eccentric, and imply that these are qualities intrinsic to the world as well as ourselves. But Swenson is modest as well as mentally fearless, and will not let us pretend that our model-building is more than that. (p. 38)

Alicia Ostriker, "May Swenson and the Shapes of Speculation," in The American Poetry Review *(copyright © 1978 by World Poetry, Inc.; reprinted by permission of Alicia Ostriker), Vol. 7, No. 2, March-April, 1978, pp. 35-8.*

ROSEMARY JOHNSON

These poems [in *New and Selected Things Taking Place*] mutter in the passive voice: "it is observed"; "it happens." The event, the text, stands out even as our guide to it steps back so as not to block the view. May Swenson indeed camouflages herself marvelously, and her protective coloration conveys respect. So we see "The World" clarified but glean only hints of "her world." For the poetry has no heroine and no heroics. . . .

Transparency of self can allow the meaning to shine through, yet it also may merely thin down the work. Often subjects beg for the author's presence, for an opinion to be voiced to add a bit of depth. In her more public roles Swenson needs to outfit herself more for the occasion. Camouflage, it turns out, is not always suitable.

Nor is knowledge without inspiration. Swenson does not exactly suffer from "ambition without understanding" but she comes close. She will try her hand at explaining the universe in brief. "Models of the Universe" sums up the expansion and contraction of everything that has been, is, or will be in twenty-seven lines. . . .

Space exploration fascinates Swenson and she brings to the subject the involved detachment of a good on-the-spot reporter. (p. 47)

Swenson searches heaven and earth for a vantage point. The problem is, none exists. The meanings of God's spangled heavens have long since spilt out into the Einsteinian universe. Matter is motion. Fixed viewpoints swirl away and Swenson so much needs a firm footing and a clear view at first hand of things taking place. The sun, moon, and earth spinning in space are for her, and nearly everybody else, news—acceptable hearsay—third-hand reports. Remote.

New and Selected Things Taking Place also offers many Town and Country poems describing the tasteful, civilized life. . . . In most of these her outline is blotted out. We get superb journalism with flair, somewhat like a non-Byronic Byron.

The citified tends to pale Swenson into urbane anonymity. She needs to separate herself from the criss-crossing of men for her negative capability to work. Then she is not forced into a role but may adopt a stance reminiscent of a certain sort of Victorian who toyed seriously with science and letters. . . . Some may say curiosity does not always constitute learning, but it's a fair substitute. May Swenson, for one, possesses an eye for detail and thrills at something felt to be observed for the first time. (p. 48)

May Swenson derives her prime inspiration not from Mother Nature but from nature; she is too empirical to be classified as a "nature-poet." Her close, first-hand observation of the external world, coupled with scrupulous attention to the particular, labels her, wittingly or unwittingly, as a "naturalist." She is also a poet and may lay claim as such to a literary tradition and to her own particular forebears (e.e. cummings and Emily Dickinson for sure, probably Blake and Herbert, Apollinaire perhaps), but she covers her trail well. The book contains, I believe, no direct references to literature and in her particular field of inquiry, the outside or the outdoors, she blithely slips away from the formal, well worn path of the pastoral . . . in order to plunge into new territory. She follows odd byways, stalking to catch the local fauna unawares. (pp. 49-50)

Swenson tinctures her city with nacreous hues and dolly dyes, stains it with rust and dirt. The controlling image is of oil and water, the attraction and repulsion of the city's heart which deliquesces into the crooning, spinning, purling pigeons. (p. 51)

May Swenson can fairly be described as gun-shy. *Homo sapiens* makes her nervous. If she cannot declass man a notch or two, fur and feather him as it were, objectify him, she nerves herself and resorts to anthropomorphizing, as she does in the brilliant pot-calling-the-kettle-black, male-female dialogue of "Bleeding," with its text slashed diagonally by a white ribbon of alienation. Generally May Swenson fumbles whenever she has human preoccupations—sporting, social, whatever—on her mind. The voiced-interaction poems drum along, their cross-cutting repetition of words monotonous and mind-numbing, like a mantra. (p. 52)

May Swenson is palpably a poet in search of disciplines—a methodology. She assembles the work *ad hoc* on the page, from scratch each time, with little traditional foundation, and must perforce handcraft the structures on which to tack her themes. (pp. 53-4)

Diagrammatic poetry occurs after the fact. It converts the past. Descriptive verse labors to bring the fact, things gone, into the focus of the present. Description is telescopic and sighted into the past; it conveys the past. May Swenson searches out things that are the results of former activity, souvenirs pressed in between the pages of the then and now. Such momentoes are usually, for her, prints in which she sets mental time-exposures, forages for tracks, traces, casts, imprints, footprints—all left-overs. She translates the evidence of the happening into words, transposes the words into a format, and fixes it all for the record: on the page, set in the present. . . .

Swenson is not interested so much in reproducing process but in salvaging from it, in fishing things from the stream of time and placing them in the province of space. Space is more important than time in this sort of poetry. (p. 54)

[She] takes incredible leaps across time and space. Sometimes we are carried along, sometimes we hang back unable to suspend our disbelief. "Almanac" works. "A moon flinched into being," and the crescent on her nail, hit by a hammer, "waxed yellow, waned to a sliver that now sets white, here at the rim I cut tonight." And during the time it took to grow out, events wildly out of scale, widely separated by space and time, take place believably:

In the dark
quarter-inch of this moon before it arrived
at my nail's tip, an unmanned airship
dived 200 miles to the hem of space, and
vanished.

(p. 58)

Oddly enough Swenson does not speak body language in the usual sense of measuring things by what one's five senses reveal; she avoids seeing things from the human point of view. From choice she peers out at the world through the eyes of the thing under scrutiny. Also, perhaps because she is wont to fashion her verse to fit her subject, she has no sense of scale, not even the primary adult yardstick of height that egocentrically deems all things greater or lesser than oneself. The idea that "The DNA Molecule is The Nude Descending a Staircase" baffles the understanding and beggars the imagination. The poet does better in her outrageous "Forest" with its "pines, aggressive as erect tails of cats."

May Swenson lives on the Eastern seaboard, writes with a Western accent, and sees with a certain amused, clear-sighted naiveté. One has the impression most poetry written by women still is an interior matter and is set within four walls. Although she is not oblivious to the problems of being female, May Swenson is not indoors enough, let alone enough in her own skin, to accommodate herself to the woman poet's present persona. She does not want to "make waves" in the sense of stirring up trouble. She leaves the problem of gender pretty much alone, if only because it could be messy (cf. "Bleeding"). She edges away from the subjective, yet she holds with Romanticism, by which I mean an interest in the particular over the general, the single over the recurring. In selecting events, animals, men, scenery, topics, she is drawn to the non-nondescript, the unique occasion: a moon-landing, the strange animal (bison not cow), the odd man out (a blind man), the picturesque canyons, lakes, or into the gothic and the magical.

But when she is put on her mettle and forced to catch the meaning of the antithetically banal or the flux and flurry of water and snow, wind and weather, then she gives us poems such as "Working on Wall Street" and "Looking Uptown" and her *Iconographs*. Then she shines. (p. 59)

Rosemary Johnson, "All Things Bright and Beautiful," in Parnassus: Poetry in Review *(copyright © Poetry in Review Foundation), Vol. 7, No. 1, Fall-Winter, 1978, pp. 47-59.*

ANNE STEVENSON

[To describe her poems as clever and skeptical] is not to say that Miss Swenson has no heart, but that she keeps it strictly under the discipline of her brain. "New & Selected Things Taking Place" is a title that in itself demonstrates a certain skepticism about poetry. Her poems are not poems, but "things taking place." They take place in a number of shapes and are subject to a few too many tricks for my taste, and yet there is no doubt that underneath the verbal fireworks lies a sophisticated seriousness. Poems about her mother and father, their lives, their deaths, eschew the self-preoccupation of their genre and manage to be witty and moving at the same time. Miss Swenson is also a fine ornithologist; her birds and landscapes are distinct enough to make an exile weak with homesickness. . . . [She] is something of a philosopher, though her point of view is not mystical but analytical and detached. She takes a refreshing delight in the metaphysically absurd and is, in particular, a mistress of the poetic conceit. Writing of surfaces, of things, of ideas, she prefers to observe them rather than explore more obscure layers of their meaning. So in a poem, "Colors Without Objects," she writes:

I wait for a few
iridium specks of idea to thrive
in the culture of my eye.

To the culture of her eye she is devoted, and between eye and mind she takes in a great deal: DNA molecules, moon walks, seas, tides, cities, snows, people. Without at all meaning to be disparaging, May Swenson seems to be the ideal New Yorker poet—amusing, perceptive, expert with metaphor and unabashedly concerned with incidentals. (p. 13)

Anne Stevenson, "With Head and Heart," in The New York Times Book Review *(© 1979 by The New York Times Company; reprinted by permission), February 11, 1979, pp. 12-13.**

VICTOR HOWES

May Swenson's poems [in *New and Selected Things Taking Place*] aspire to the condition of jewels. At their crystalline best they are hard and bright, glinting of green, stargold and topaz.

Not to be confused with diamonds in the rough, Swenson's poems are polished to within an inch of their lives, and they live, from image to image, in tiny darts of frosty fire. . . .

Swenson's subjects range from zoo animals to moon landings, from butterflies "in sequin coat / peacock bright" to Georgia O'Keeffe's paintings, "Cerulean is solid. Clouds are tiles, or floats of ice / a cobalt spa melts." . . .

One comes to feel that nothing is lost that is visible, that there is nothing the poet's eye cannot see and describe. But May Swenson is a poet of light, not shadow. In this generous, retrospective sampling of her work, her eye is caught by surfaces, contours, textures. Again and again her images will take your breath away, but rarely will she trouble your thoughts or touch your heart.

Swenson is a poet who can say with Joseph Conrad, "I want to make you see." But Conrad could make us see into the heart of darkness. It is in that direction that Swenson must move as a poet if she wishes to press beyond surfaces, however jewelled, however exotic, however green, stargold or topaz.

Victor Howes, "Poems with Polish," in The Christian Science Monitor *(reprinted by permission from* The Christian Science Monitor; *© 1979 The Christian Science Publishing Society; all rights reserved), February 12, 1979, p. B11.*

JASCHA KESSLER

[May Swenson's *New and Selected Things Taking Place*] is obviously meant to stand as a capstone to her career as a poet. Sixty poems come from the years since 1970, but the larger part of the book is a selection from five previous books of poems. We can thus, with *New and Selected Things Taking Place,* come to a full appreciation of her poetic goals and methods.

I think I might call May Swenson a meditative poet. However, it is the character of her meditations that ought to be distinguished here, however briefly. To do that, it may be useful to place her in the history of a certain kind of poetry during the 20th Century; that is, a kind of poetry [Imagism] that claimed attention during the first thirty years of this century. . . . The Imagist poets aimed at simplifying syntax, eliminating verbiage and thus getting rid of a whole accumulated weight of centuries of social ideas, conventions, sentiments and ways of taking the world and emotions for granted. To do this, they concentrated on objects, on the way things appeared, on elementary sensations, sight and sound and touch.

The classic Imagist anthology is full of severe and simple poems; but the movement soon developed in other ways. Swenson may be said to derive from Marianne Moore's poetry. And Moore made complex, prose-rhythmic structures, mostly descriptive and tightly intellectual in their forms and formulations. Moore furthermore hid her own emotions away completely: her passion is to be found in a kind of moralizing of the world of things, a strong ethical meaning that all her poems convey. Not religious or social ethics, but the ethics of a stoical individualism, of the disciplined mind's contemplation of subjects for poetry. Swenson reduces Moore's coloration of the world by means of her ethics to a form of seeing or hearing. She makes many kinds of verbal structures; she is playful and varied; and she is very impersonal. She says she thinks of her poems as "things"—as objects meant to occupy a place on a page. She says, "No thing is like any other, while everything resembles many another. This conundrum applies to all phenomena, in nature and experience. The new made thing turns out to be both unique and familiar."

As a result we have an intense concentration on descriptions of landscapes, or on actions set in landscapes. There is a sense that the poet has been a tourist to several parts of the world, and written her poems as forms of snapshots and memorabilia. Of course her [perspective] takes in far more than the camera, and indeed she often manages to place herself in the landscape too, and in such ways that one soon realizes that her emotions are at work in very odd and sometimes ecstatic ways, so that we find a constant attempt to identify with the world of things as they are in the world. . . . [The] result is a somewhat mystical vision. I call it mystical simply because it is imaginative and not scientifically objective . . . we are talking about a poet, not a scientist, after all, who must measure his things, to begin with. Nor are we talking about a philosopher either, who must account for the ways things take place. . . . [The] poet's task comes before either scientist or philosopher, for it describes the things that take place, and even, to speak more truly, puts them there for us, on the page. . . .

[One] might say that there is and always has been, through Swenson's ruthless suppression of surface emotions and ideas and personality a sort of coldness, a detached eye, amused however, and indifferent. . . .

Jascha Kessler, "May Swenson's 'New and Selected Things Taking Place'," in his radio broadcast on KUSC-FM–Los Angeles, CA, April 11, 1979.

CHARLES SAUNDERS

The verse in May Swenson's "Snow in New York" which draws the speaker's reverie to its climax is the statement "Snow in New York is like poetry, or clothes made of roses." . . . It shocks in its combination of the ordinary and the unexpected: snow has been one of the surface subjects of the poem continuously, but "clothes made of roses" seems a sudden leap of the imagination. Of course, the poignance of the latter phrase strikes us as right because it extends the train of paradoxical or contrasting images Swenson has set in motion from the beginning of the poem. . . . And naturally, "clothes made of roses," by their seeming sheer impracticality, would fit right in with poetry as something one does not, ostensibly, "need," cannot "build" with, and probably would not use to "feed."

However, this same phrase possibly contains an allusion which not only serves to show that the "clothes" are necessary and useful but also binds the poem together, helps to characterize the speaker, and clarify Swenson's ironic point. I submit that "clothes made of roses" may leap unconsciously from the speaker's imagination as a remembrance of the famous dancer Nijinsky (1890-1950), the buried subject of the poem's second stanza. Specifically, the reference may be to one of the most memorable parts Nijinsky assumed with the Ballets Russes, that of the rose in the 1911 production of *Le Spectre de la Rose*. It was in this ballet that Nijinsky, according to his lifelong friend Anatole Bourman, seemed to have become "a rose petal carried on a breath of wind through an open window in a graceful parabola of crimson and green" and to have "transcended human limitations and danced into the heart of poesy." . . . (p. 41)

If we permit this allusion to function in the poem, then obviously we see that the unexpected has actually been foreshadowed, and in a manner psychologically appropriate to the speaker. For the speaker, . . . despondent over the place of poetry in a "real" world, fails to recognize the parallel between the frozen life-giving element and the later-paralyzed dancer and his clothes made of roses. As the snow will eventually become water, so the subconscious memory becomes "necessary" to the speaker: it feeds presently . . . , and literally as much as figuratively builds the train of perceptions that are the poem—albeit unwittingly to its speaker if not to Swenson the poet. Swenson's ironic point is complete. (pp. 41-2)

Charles Saunders, "Swenson's 'Snow in New York'," in The Explicator *(copyright © 1979 by Helen Dwight Reid Educational Foundation), Vol. 38, No. 1, Fall, 1979, pp. 41-2.*

* * *

SYMONS, Julian 1912-

Symons is a British mystery novelist, critic, biographer, poet, short story writer, editor, and playwright. His work portrays the corruption and moral decay of contemporary society, often using the crime novel as a vehicle for examining, in Symon's words, "the violence behind respectable faces." Critics have cited the influence of W. H. Auden and of surrealism on his poetry. (See also *CLC*, Vol. 2, and *Contemporary Authors*, Vols. 49-52.)

CHRISTOPHER PYM

It is difficult to fault [*The Progress of a Crime,* a] shrewd, sardonic account of how, in our time, murder quite easily gets done; how a case is handled in the cells and in the courts; what life is like on a local newspaper; and what a newspaper peer sounds like at the Fleet Street end of a telephone. Among the cynical go-getters, the brutal and the wayward, a young reporter and his girl keep a flag or so flying without being at all sentimentalised over. This is one of the truest and most sensible (and, because of the spare, brisk writing, one of the most compellingly readable) English crime novels for years.

Christopher Pym, "It's a Crime," in The Spectator; *reprinted by permission of* The Spectator), *Vol. 205, No. 6892, July 29, 1960, p. 192.**

ANTHONY BOUCHER

Julian Symons seems to be deliberately trying, in ["The Belting Inheritance"], . . . to see to what extent a first-rate professional can animate such moldy stencils as the will-changing old lady and the long-lost claimant who may be an impostor. His success is astonishing, especially in view of the fact that he sets himself the further problem of writing from an 18-year-old viewpoint. This exercise in virtuosity (especially brilliant in its scenes of a young man's discovery of Paris) is far removed from the serious novels of character and society which we have come to expect from Symons—but it is highly enjoyable on its own terms.

Anthony Boucher, "Criminals at Large," in The New York Times Book Review *(© 1965 by The New York Times Company; reprinted by permission), July 21, 1965, p. 12.**

PATRICK COSGRAVE

[*A three pipe Problem*] is historically based . . . in a contemporary sense: the action takes place today. But the detective is Sherlock Holmes! Rather, he is an actor named Sheridan Haynes who is playing the great detective in a long-running TV series, and occupies a flat in Baker St provided by the television company as part of their publicity drive. Haynes is, too, a Holmes connoisseur: he knows the books intimately, and he treasures the values they represent, as well as the skills of the great detective. In many passages of fine and ambiguous writing Mr Symons almost makes Haynes over into Holmes. Finally, jeered at by his colleagues, and mocked by his unfaithful wife, Haynes turns detective, and applies the methods of Holmes to the solution of a mysterious series of murders. There are many fine things in the book—including meditations on the changed condition of London, which are especially beautifully done—but perhaps the finest is the way Mr Symons maintains the balance between Haynes's rather dotty ambition, which could so easily have toppled over into farce, the real seriousness of the crime, and the application of the actor's considerable intelligence to its solution. The book is a *tour de force* of a most uncommon kind; and the best thing Mr Symons has done.

Patrick Cosgrave, "New Developments," in The Spectator *(© 1975 by* The Spectator; *reprinted by permission of* The Spectator), *Vol. 234, No. 7656, March 22, 1975, p. 345.**

As his title ["A Three-Pipe Problem"] so nicely suggests, Mr. Symons entertains us here with a neo-Sherlock Holmes adventure. There is a series of apparently related killings in London—today's London—and an enterprising reporter elicits from a television actor starring in a Sherlock Holmes show the observation that Holmes would have been easily able to solve the case. The ensuing newspaper jeers drive the actor to play his role offstage. The result is a most enjoyable confusion that sees the Holmesian method pitted against both the elusive murderer and the scornful technicians of Scotland Yard. Mr. Symons also obliges us during the crucial climactic hours of his story by producing a fine, anachronistic pea-soup fog.

"Books: 'A Three-Pipe Problem'," in The New Yorker *(© 1975 by The New Yorker Magazine, Inc.), Vol. LI, No. 15, June 2, 1975, p. 112.*

ALLEN J. HUBIN

Julian Symons does not repeat himself: each novel stands alone on its own credentials, which are usually impressive. Thus *The Blackheath Poisonings* . . . , "A Victorian Murder Mystery." So effectively does Symons conjure up the Blackheath suburb of London, with Albert House and Victoria Villa and the family that lived and died—of arsenic—there in the 1890's, that the join between fiction and history is seamless. (pp. 11-12)

Allen J. Hubin, "AJH Reviews: 'The Blackheath Poisonings'," in The Armchair Detective *(copyright © 1979 by* The Armchair Detective), *Vol. 12, No. 1, January, 1979, pp. 11-12.*

STEVEN R. CARTER

Julian Symons has helped to increase the range and worth of crime fiction in many ways. For example, his crime novels, like Ross Macdonald's, combine ingenious plotting with psychological and social probing. In addition, he has a gift, like Nicolas Freeling, for wry humor and satire. However, the variety of his forms and techniques goes beyond that of any other crime writer. He has written conventional detective novels (*Bland Beginning, Bogue's Fortune, The Belting Inheritance*), a detective fiction parody (*The Immaterial Murder Case*), a political thriller (*The Broken Penny*), several psychological crime novels (*The Man Who Killed Himself, The Man Whose Dreams Came True*, etc.), some nightmarish portrayals of modern society (*The Thirty-First of February, The Players and the Game*, etc.), some acute social satires (*The Plain Man, The End of Solomon Grundy*), and a humorous novel about a contemporary incarnation of Sherlock Holmes (*A Three-Pipe Problem*). The success of many of his experiments in the form has shown that the mystery need not constrain a talented writer either technically or thematically. His main contribution to the crime novel is that he has proven how flexible a vehicle it is for presenting a personal vision of the stresses of modern western civilization. . . .

Symons is disturbed most by the narrowing of personality through western civilization's excessive emphases on order, respectability, mechanical routine, and material "success"; by lack of communication stemming from inhibitions of narrowed personalities, from efforts to maintain respectable images, and from fears of facing difficult and unpleasant issues; by society's moralistic attempt to eliminate relatively harmless games (sexual and otherwise) which offer an "unsuitable" release from social tensions; and by the lack of sufficient alternatives to the stresses of civilization. All of these serious concerns, appropriate for mainstream fiction, are treated in depth in Symons' crime novels. . . .

In Symons' eyes, the preference for money and social status over such things as spontaneity, creativity, meaningful work, etc., is a destructive one. A large part of the horror at the end of *The Narrowing Circle* comes from the reader's awareness that Dave Nelson is killing an essential part of himself by his decision to accept the sleazy material success which an ulcer-ridden entrepreneur offers him. (p. 57)

One other major way in which personalities are narrowed in Symons' crime novels is through submitting to routine. . . . In a symbolic scene in *The Thirty-First of February,* "a small regiment of black Homburg hats marched down Bezyl Street." The scene leaves little doubt that the men beneath the hats are cogs in a machine. Significantly, Anderson wears a hat while he is attached to the agency, but misplaces and eventually loses it when he is jogged out of his mechanical life into chaos and irrational terror. It is also noteworthy that Inspector Cresse, who is described as unimaginative, always keeps a firm hold on his bowler hat. (p. 58)

One of the most intriguing and unusual aspects of Symons' work is his stress on games. . . .

In Symons' eyes, games often serve as safety valves which enable people to endure the various pressures which civilization places on them and to cope with their insecurities. This function is extremely important since, as the company psychologist in *The Players and the Game* argues, "anything that causes insecurity is a breeding ground for crime" and "the 'bad elements' in our society are the ones on whom the greatest pressures have been applied." (p. 59)

Symons has implied often that anyone might become a criminal by being subjected to too much pressure, by having insufficient outlets for release from pressure, or by surrendering to his fantasies. . . .

Next to *The Players and the Game,* the universal vulnerability to forces from within and without is suggested most strongly in *The Man Who Lost His Wife*. For example, in the scene in which the young hitchhiker David confronts the obnoxious Jerry Painter on a lonely stretch of road and points a gun at him, he laments that "it's so damned easy [to murder]. They shouldn't make it so easy." Except for his temper, David seems a decent person, but he is sorely tempted to kill Painter because of his abuse and his sudden hate-filled decision to leave David and his girlfriend stranded. It couldn't have been a touchier situation; at that point, it would have taken little to make David pull the trigger. (p. 60)

Symons places little emphasis on heroism in any form since he believes that all men contain a mixture of strengths and weaknesses and can be broken under too heavy a strain. He does, however, display a limited respect for the "heroic" labors of groups, provided that each individual shares in the responsibility and can make significant contributions to the final result. (p. 61)

Steven R. Carter, "Julian Symons and Civilization's Discontents," in The Armchair Detective *(copyright © 1979 by* The Armchair Detective*), Vol. 12, No. 1, January, 1979, pp. 57-61.*

As the title ["The Blackheath Poisonings"] suggests and the subtitle ["A Victorian Murder Mystery"] proclaims, [this novel] is a period piece, but it is a period piece so thoroughly yet unobtrusively of its intended period that it would seem to be the work of a contemporary hand. The setting is the villagey London suburb of Blackheath in 1890, and the story involves a large middle-class family living amiably on two neighboring estates. . . . All are comfortably supported by the family business, a toy manufactory, and the lives of all appear to be uneventfully serene. Then the son-in-law dies of a suspiciously acute indigestion, but the family physician (a definitive dodderer) signs a natural-cause death certificate. Then the matriarch rises in pain from the supper table, and dies unequivocally of arsenic poisoning. Here, most emphatically, is a book to relish. (pp. 66-7)

"Books: 'The Blackheath Poisonings'," in The New Yorker *(© 1979 by The New Yorker Magazine, Inc.), Vol. LIV, No. 46, January 1, 1979, pp. 66-7.*

JACK SULLIVAN

In "Mortal Consequences," his distinguished study of detective fiction, Julian Symons states that the best Victorian mysteries were those that assumed memorable characters and stories to be as important as ingenious puzzles. "The Blackheath Poisonings," Mr. Symons' own attempt at a Victorian mystery, makes the same assumption, with delightful results.

Mr. Symons' 1890's setting is described in intricate detail but also with a sense of fun and wit. . . .

Obviously, a considerable amount of research has gone into "The Blackheath Poisonings." . . . But the book never seems pedantic: with 17 novels to his credit, Mr. Symons does not need to show off. His period details—especially the marvelous quips about Wilde, Shaw and other members of the Victorian avant-garde—are always used to enhance a scene or advance the plot. Eschewing the clichés of historical novels, Mr. Symons manages to create a convincing Victorian ambience without a single pretentious epigraph or wordy history lesson. . . .

Indeed, every aspect of "The Blackheath Poisonings" is graced with intelligence and restraint. The style is an admirable compromise between Victorian leisureliness and modern conciseness: without pretending to be Victorian, it reproduces the feel, and occasionally the syntax, of the period. The characters are sharply drawn, especially young Paul Vandervent, whose journal entries on death and loneliness are surprisingly poignant, and whose humanity keeps the novel's complex ratiocination from lapsing into mechanical trickery. The minor grotesques—including a bumbling, self-serving doctor and a pious teetotaling vegetarian—are also a treat. Most satisfying of all is Mr. Symons' ability to tell a story and sustain suspense.

Jack Sullivan, "Grotesques and Villains," in The New York Times Book Review *(© 1979 by The New York Times Company; reprinted by permission), February 4, 1979, p. 14.**

T

TANIZAKI, Jun'ichirō 1886-1965

A Japanese novelist, short story writer, and dramatist, Tanizaki wrote in a detached, analytical style about sexual obsession and perversion. While often morbid, Tanizaki never descended to the sordid or the sensational, for it was not his intention to exploit his sexual themes but to reveal the compelling and mysterious nature of sexuality and its relation to cruelty and violence. (See also *CLC*, Vol. 8, and *Contemporary Authors*, obituary, Vols. 25-28, rev. ed.)

WAYNE FALKE

Faced with Tanizaki's *Sasame Yuki* (*The Makioka Sisters*), popular criticism has tried to find Western analogues for the techniques and themes of this major Japanese novel. Because it deals with bourgeois life and with humdrum events of human existence, because it finally results in a seemingly broad view of society, it is called a naturalistic novel. (pp. 19-20)

[While] *Sasame Yuki* does have characteristics in common with a French tradition, these are minor and it is Murasaki's *Tale of Genji,* a courtly romance, that is the immediate model for *Sasame Yuki.* The fact that Tanizaki interrupted work on a modern translation of *Genji* to write a chronicle of the Makiokas is significant, particularly when several of his novels are compared. It becomes clear that Tanizaki's quest is not for a duplication of reality, in the Zola manner, but it is a quest for ideal beauty, embodied in ancient traditions and artistically expressed in the Japanese female.

What popular critics have in mind when they say Tanizaki is a naturalistic writer seems to be, first, that he is a chronicler of a society rather than of a single individual; second, that he uses detail to place characters in an observable reality; third, he as author-artist maintains detachment from his characters; and fourth, the animal functions (teeth brushing, using bedpans) are permissible parts of a work of art. The single largest danger of judgment is to assume that these are qualities of naturalism. While they certainly may appear in the naturalistic novel, the use of them does not necessarily produce naturalism, nor does the failure to use them preclude it. The essence of naturalism lies deeper in the purpose and overall effect of the novel. In this respect Tanizaki's works (except *Kagi* [*The Key*] which stands apart from his other novels . . .) bear little relation to the Zolaesque tradition.

The title of the translation is partially to blame for the misunderstanding of *Sasame Yuki.* The Japanese title means "delicate snow" and is a poetic symbol of transitory beauty, whereas *The Makioka Sisters* gives the impression that the book is truly a chronicle of domestic life. The subject matter, however, is closer to a poetic vision (something Zola denounces with vehemence) of the essential beauty of an older way of life in contrast with the harshness of Japan's westernization, symbolized by Tokyo.

Structurally, *Sasame Yuki* owes nothing to Zola. Murasaki—and indeed all traditional Japanese writers—compose episodically, with no obvious emphasis given to certain actions as guides to further development. Interest is concentrated on the individual scene and development is accomplished only by demonstrating change from scene to scene. This differs from Western episodic treatment which generally means only that the same characters are present in a series of separate actions, and in the totality there is no development either of action or of character. Murasaki utilizes, by oblique reference, each episode to show a growing complexity in Genji's character and to record his growth from rascally young prince, to honored court official, to mature man. What is principally lacking in Japanese fiction that is present in Western is a deliberate cause and effect delineation. The Japanese writer deals with effects and causation is only hinted at, if mentioned at all.

Tanizaki did not need Zola to teach him the use of detail either. The *Tale of Genji* is highly sensuous (akin to French chivalric romance) in its details, and it is this use of detail that Tanizaki follows, rather than the detailed sketching in of physical environment. Tanizaki never describes a room in detail, unless it is used functionally to tell his reader how much better life was in the old days or to impress upon him how degraded and degenerate the present is. The point is that Tanizaki works upon the reader, and not necessarily only upon the character.

The large interest of Murasaki, and of Tanizaki in *Sasame Yuki,* is the fleeting beauty of nature and of life itself. Time, then, is not perceived clearly chronologically, but in large blocks at the return of an annual event or with the realization that years have passed. (pp. 20-1)

[Tanizaki] does not place faith in a scientific method which will lead men to near-godhead, to control over nature; rather, he asserts that an aesthetic tradition of the remote past has value, and that modern materialism suppresses it. Social stability is to be achieved by re-evaluating Western and Eastern ideas to see that the Western importations, are, after all, foreign borrowings rather than a logical development of a native tradition. . . . Tanizaki is a writer attempting to hold back the waves of Westernism that have obscured the native culture.

Unlike Zola's works, however, Tanizaki's novels give little sense that large forces are at work upon the individual. In a novel by Zola, destiny or at least powers affecting the lives of millions in the present and untold generations in the future are consciously felt. In Tanizaki's novels, the cultural conflict is not a massive force, but merely a nagging uneasiness felt by his characters, but hardly ever verbalized. (p. 22)

Another romantic aspect of Tanizaki's work is related to the theme of his quest for the ideal woman who becomes the embodiment of Japan's aesthetic tradition. (She is an anachronism as much as the Western chaste maiden in the ivory tower of Medieval romance would be in modern America.) This quest in consistently developed through Tanizaki's works since 1929 and the publication of *Tade Kuu Mushi*. Tanizaki pinpoints Kaname's marital difficulties: "You really should have stayed single—all woman-worshippers should be single. They never find the woman who answers all the requirements." (p. 23)

It is not surprising, then, to find a major character in *Sasame Yuki* who is something of an anachronism. Yukiko, the third of the Makioka sisters, is unmarriageable because she is the ideal woman who recurs throughout Tanizaki's novels. (pp. 23-4)

Tanizaki's distaste for the methods of the naturalistic novel (the explicit statement) is clear when his last novel, *Kagi*, is placed in the line of his development as a novelist. The theme of the quest for the ideal woman (symbol of a better tradition) is present, but *Kagi* demonstrates Tanizaki's embitterment with literary as well as social matters in contemporary Japan. He concedes in this novel that the forces of the West have won, and he laments that old Japanese tradition is lost. This novel is deliberately naturalistic, and form and content are denunciatory of all that Tanizaki dislikes about the West. In anger, Tanizaki floods his literary world with light, and the resulting ugliness is a call for the aesthetic world of shadows.

In his essay, "In Praise of Shadows" (1934), Tanizaki asserts that beauty is an insubstantial phenomenon which thrives only in shadows. He longs for the old houses, with deep eaves, which were always half dark, for, among other reasons, lacquerware, which is gaudy in sunlight, is a thing of subtle beauty in shadow. Similarly, geishas with their blackened teeth and green lipstick seen by candlelight, as he remembers them from his youth, were ephemerally beautiful. (p. 24)

Kagi can best be understood as a deliberate violation of this aesthetic dictum—as a demonstration of the ugliness bright light (the full statement) reveals. In the harsh glare of a fluorescent light, the husband searches his wife's nude body for its hidden beauty. Toshiko is stretched out, half-anaesthetized with brandy, as if she were on a clinical dissection table. He tries to record her beauty with a camera, symbol of realism, the destroyer of beauty. The novel is a study in the degradation of Japanese tradition by modern technology, for Toshiko is a Kyoto woman, and she should embody the virtues of Japan before the Western invasion. Like Toshiko, Japan has given up its traditional modes of conduct, and the result is a garish nightmare of unrewarding frenzy, for the husband dies without having found either aesthetic or sexual satisfaction.

If Tanizaki can be credited with a philosophy, it is that aesthetic experience—the theatre, calligraphy, the dance, music, poetry, moon-viewing, cherry blossom viewing—is significant and has eternal value. The concept, reminiscent of both French and English romanticism, is anathema to Zola, who would flatly deny that Montsou miners would be better off enjoying the transitory glory of cherry blossoms. (pp. 24-5)

Wayne Falke, "Tanizaki: Opponent of Naturalism," in Critique: Studies in Modern Fiction *(copyright © by* Critique, *1966), Vol. VIII, No. 3, 1966, pp. 19-25.*

ARTHUR G. KIMBALL

[In *Diary of a Mad Old Man* Tanizaki's symbolic eroticism] is earthy, realistic, clinically detailed. (p. 109)

The efforts of Tanizaki's old man [Tokusuke] are not so much a quest for identity as an attempt to preserve the image he understands well and more or less accepts. He tries to extract the last bit of life-juice from the shriveled facts of his existence, affirming through diary and desire the significance of who he is. (pp. 109-10)

But he is hardly crazy. The title's assertion, that he is a mad old man (*futen rojin*), is surely ironic. For one thing, his diary account is lucid. When he looks at the record of a year before, he realizes he is getting forgetful and acknowledges it. His analysis of his own motives is perceptive. (p. 110)

The madness, rather, is the madness of life itself, the lunacy of a world where the creative drive is shackled to a decaying frame identified by pulsebeats, urine analysis, and doses of medicine—and described in complicated medical jargon. . . . Old Tokusuke's existence comes increasingly to be defined by such clinical facts of life. On the comic level —and there is a good deal of comedy—Tanizaki satirizes the Japanese in particular and modern man in general. On the more serious level, Tokusuke's fate suggests a society which has developed analysis of the physical functions to a remarkable degree, but shows myopia in comprehension of the spirit. I'm trying to put the *id* back in Yid, says the Jewish narrator in Philip Roth's *Portnoy's Complaint*. Tanizaki's mad old man only needs the bed restored to bedlam, a redress of the imbalance in a society in danger of dedicating itself to the quantitative instead of qualitative measure of man. (pp. 111-12)

Tokusuke creatively affirms himself not only in his diary and his sexual fancies, but in the artistry by which he engages in the "game" both he and Satsuko understand, and of course by the skill with which he teases the reader to the same expectations he enjoys. . . . The *Diary* is a happy book, and, as far as the reader knows, Tokusuke's last act is affirmative. There is in fact a touch of that archetypal figure, the Trickster, in Tanizaki's mad old man. One sees it in his mischievous delight in stirring up family friction, in his sexual urges, and most of all in his creative spirit which, one likes to think, transcends the inevitable. Erasmus would have liked Tokusuke; he would have seen in him an excellent likeness of his second class of "folly." . . . The mad old man's identity is worth pondering. (pp. 113-14)

Arthur G. Kimball, "The Last Extremity," in his Crisis in Identity and Contemporary Japanese Novels *(copyright © 1973 by Charles E. Tuttle Co., Inc.), Charles E. Tuttle Company, 1973, pp. 94-114.**

SUMIE JONES

Tanizaki Junichirō's works are often described as "sensuous," "dazzling," "exquisite," "devilish," or "sick." One associates his name with the exquisite beauty of a firefly seen through the sleeve of a silk kimono, or the perverse sexuality of a man exhausted by the nightly pleasure of being tortured by his wife. It seems that he writes in order to see what an artist can do with a theme or image that happens to capture his creative ambition. The "germ" of his fiction is sensual and aesthetic, rather than ideological. . . .

Each of Tanizaki's works has one or two central images or themes which are so uncommon as to haunt the reader. *Diary of a Mad Old Man* offers as theme an old man's tremendous desire for certain parts of the body of his daughter-in-law, and as image, the beautiful young woman's footprints engraved on the old man's tombstone. In theme, *The Key* concentrates on two diaries, each written with the knowledge of the other person reading it; and its controlling image is a necklace on the naked body of the wife which excites the husband to death. In his famous dispute with Akutagawa Ryūnosuke, Tanizaki declared that he does not feel like writing or reading a work about ordinary facts, and that only lies and fantasies can stimulate him to write. (p. 321)

The result of Tanizaki's untiring labor over words is an appearance of easy and unbroken composition. Thus, most of his works are accounts in simple words of a self-contained and somewhat twisted reality, in which accepted logical patterns are ignored. Describing the extraordinary in a nonchalant tone, as if reporting an ordinary event in familiar, flowing language, has the effect of stripping the reader of his demand for normal logic, as we see in the case of Kafka.

A second aspect, which critics have mostly ignored and occasionally considered a flaw, is the structure of his narrative. That is his secret trick. In his essay on *Story of Shunkin,* Tanizaki discusses what he considers the most important thing in fiction and how it can be achieved. In his mind, to make the reader feel that the events in the work are all real is far more important than to impress him with the author's artistry. The more artistic the work, the more false it appears. Thus, he recommends that a fiction have the appearance of someone *narrating* a summary of events rather than of an author *describing* details. He says that in writing *Story of Shunkin* his utmost concern was "what kind of form would give the impression of actuality," and that he arrived "at the sneakiest and easiest way an author can think of." He does not tell us exactly what is the "sneaky and easy way."

In *Story of Shunkin* Tanizaki effectively practices his theory of narration and summary. The sneaky part of it is the way he puts together the "summaries" and "narrations." This novella germinates from the image of an incredibly beautiful woman to whom sight is denied: if the woman is a perfect beauty otherwise, and if she must depend only on touch and hearing, how would her blindness affect her psychology, behavior and life-style, and particularly, what effect would it have on her love-life? This captivating idea is developed through the use of layered screens of narration. Besides a narrator, there are documentary and verbal reports. The author pretends to put a distance between the reader and the incidents by warning him of the unreliability of the narrator's sources of information, while at the same time drawing him into the points of view of the narrator, of the old lady, and finally of Sasuke, the lover.

The narrator is quite uncertain of his role. . . . [As the narrative voice shifts] the reader feels that this narrator, or even the author, does not know what he is doing, while his curiosity is increased by a fear that he may not be told all he wants to know. Later, as the narrator moves back and forth in a seemingly disordered fashion between quotations and narrations, he is carried away by his own imagination. The result is a fusion of accounts of the narrator's own experience, unedited quotations from a written document or an informant, and the narrator's objective comments, mingled with his fantasies. (pp. 321-23)

Toward the end of the story, Sasuke's biography, Teru's observations, and the narrator's fantasies mingle into one voice. The reader gives up, without realizing it, his attempt to separate the three views from one another, and facts from illusions. . . . By obscuring memory, and by creating distance, [Tanizaki] builds beautiful illusions "totally different from the actual," and by the screen of narration over facts he renders his images "more and more vivid." (p. 323)

Only a small number of Tanizaki's shorter stories are written in what he calls "regular fiction form:" objective third-person narrative with dialogues in direct quotation. Most of them are written as memoirs, diaries, letters, essays, and other kinds of documents, singly or in combination. And in the more successful works, the unreliable narrator plays an important role. . . . *The Floating Bridge of Dreams,* one of Tanizaki's last works, is the summation of his skills in dealing with uncertain memories as a theme and device. Here a father consciously prevents a child from distinguishing between his dead mother and stepmother, so that the boy creates throughout his life an idealized image of a mother, mothers, or the essence of mother. (pp. 323-24)

Beginning with the use of uncertain memory in *The Boy* and *The Magician,* Tanizaki develops through his career, more and more complex structures of narration and subtler kinds of unreliability.

Among Tanizaki's works, when the narrator of an extraordinary event is unquestionably reliable, the reader is not disarmed. *A Crippen Case in Japan,* in documentary essay form, keeps the reader detached from the masochist's experience. It conveys the author's view that such sexual behavior is a common phenomenon to be viewed matter-of-factly. In *Story of Tomoda and Matsunaga,* the reliable narrator and trustworthy correspondent seem to be the reason why this Jekyll-and-Hyde story fails to involve the reader in the strangeness of the situation.

The device most frequently used by Tanizaki is a first-person narrative of which the center is a recounting of a narration by another person, or a long account of, or quotation from, a document. In most of these, his trick operates in the same way as in *Story of Shunkin*. First, the reader is captured by curiosity about a peculiar fact because of the narrator's uncertainty. On the one hand, his detective instinct is stirred. On the other, he is ready to hang on to any fragmentary information he can get. Then he is vaguely convinced by the narrator's credibility, because he seems at least sincere. . . . And when a shift from objectivity to subjectivity is made through multiple views, it is more likely to pass undetected than is one single view which changes its perspective. In this process, there is no firm ground of judgment and belief as between author and reader. The reader is tossed to and fro between one uncertainty and another, until he slides into the slot provided by the author. (p. 325)

Sumie Jones, "How Tanizaki Disarms the Intellectual Reader," in Literature East and West *(© Literature East and West Inc.), Vol. XVIII, Nos. 2-4, June-December, 1974, pp. 321-29.*

* * *

TATE, (John Orley) Allen 1899-1979

Tate was an American poet, critic, novelist, and man of letters. A member of the "Fugitive Group" of artists, Tate created poetry that reflected the concerns of his fellow Fugitives: the life and landscape of the agrarian South inform all of his work. Tate's best poetry presents a world where the mythical and historical past serve allegorically to illuminate simple, personal experience. (See also *CLC*, Vols, 2, 4, 6, 9, 11, and *Contemporary Authors*, Vols. 5-8, rev. ed.; obituary, Vols. 85-88.)

ALAN WILLIAMSON

To speak of Allen Tate and the personal epic—that peculiarly modern form which views historical material entirely through the glass of a private sensibility, fragmenting it into the elements of a series of lyrics rather than presenting it whole, as narrative—is to find oneself in difficulties at the start. Tate as critic has questioned the validity of the genre in Ezra Pound's *Cantos* and has rejected it in Hart Crane's *The Bridge*. . . . Yet Tate has followed his own advice only as a prose writer. In poetry, he has made his deepest, most artistically complex judgments on the past and the present, and has reached out toward the long poem in "Seasons of the Soul" and the unfinished terzinas, through exactly that lyric concentration on the self which, in theory, he questions.

The paradox deepens when one grasps the importance of action and narrative in Tate's philosophy, as set forth in the central essays "The Symbolic Imagination: The Mirrors of Dante" and "The Angelic Imagination: Poe as God." Following Jacques Maritain, Tate argues that the crucial fault of post-Cartesian thought is "angelism"—the aspiration to a direct, nonsensory knowledge of the essences of things—which Thomistic philosophy reserves to the angels. (p. 714)

"The Angelic Imagination" which Tate sees in modern science, and in the romanticism of Poe and Crane, creates "hypertrophies" of feeling, will, and intellect, by claiming to deal with essences. The hypertrophy of the intellect is its claim to complete objectivity, "whereby it declares itself independent of the human situation in the quest of essential knowledge." A hypertrophy of the will is implicit for Tate, both in scientific control over nature and in the *alchimie du verbe* of the symbolists. . . . Tate's later philosophy preserves Eliot's idea of the dissociation of sensibility, but makes it the symptom of a still deeper disorder, angelism. Neurotic-romantic man, of whom we are all in some degree incarnations, is both more conscious and more prey to the unconscious than his classical and healthy counterpart; his disconnected thought and his fantasies, concomitantly enlarged, threaten his ability to act in terms of reality. (pp. 715-16)

Upon [the] opposition of the symbolic and the angelic rests Tate's dislike of the modern world, his tendency—like Pound and Eliot—to make utopias of the more active, less individualistic cultures of the past. But Tate's utopia is a more ambiguous one than Pound's, because it is also his personal past. . . . It is Tate's curse—but perhaps ultimately his blessing—that idealization of the past does not free him from his central moral anxiety, but brings it back to him with redoubled force. In writing of the heroic past in a personal, postsymbolist mode, Tate acknowledges his double consciousness as an "angelic" man in love with the vision of a world where his own conflicts are transcended. But unable to experience such a world, outwardly or inwardly, he is therefore not utterly certain that it exists.

Tate has, of course, tried to draw the distinction between past and present with a more impersonal assurance, notably in the early poems "Retroduction to American History" and "Causerie." But these poems seem unsatisfyingly simplistic, even arrogant, when compared with those in which Tate feels detached from what he condemns. When Tate uses Eliot's method of ironic parallelism through literary allusion, the allusion often becomes a mere token of the goodness of the old days; unlike Eliot, Tate does not allow the moral problems and complexities of the earlier work to become part of his own poem. (pp. 716-17)

[If] one is looking for a great poetry of history, the most dangerous result of . . . polemical adulation of the past is that it tends to reduce the stature of the moral issues that the past struggled, and mostly failed, to resolve—as when Tate asserts, in his "Retroduction," that the problems of the *Oresteia* are "less subtle than you think," and important mainly as a contrast to the present—"Heredity / / Proposes love, love exacts language, and we lack / / Language."

In the "Ode to the Confederate Dead," by contrast, an open self-preoccupation leads to a more complex and troubled view of the past. Tate has written, in "Narcissus as Narcissus," that the poem is about "solipsism," which he defines as "a . . . doctrine which says that we create the world in the act of perceiving it"; but "solipsism," in the poem, seems to expand to include any thought or feeling that cannot lead, or be related, to outward action. The speaker wishes to celebrate the Confederate Dead, but he can *do* nothing but stand still outside a gate and reflect. For the future author of "The Angelic Imagination," such a situation is not only, as it was for Matthew Arnold, artistically dubious; it is paradoxically explosive and fraught with psychic peril. (pp. 717-18)

On an emotional level, ["Ode to the Confederate Dead"] reveals a double attitude toward the past: it is too remote yet devouringly close, adored but subliminally resented. And even intellectually, the poem expresses unwilling doubts about the past: to be "hurried beyond decision" seems enviable to one trapped in "mute speculation," but it cannot solve the most ultimate human problems the poem touches on, those of free will and justification. (p. 720)

In Tate's earlier poems we observe a progression from a satire bitterly confident in past ideals to a fear that all history is chaotic, irredeemable. World War II seems to have confirmed Tate in this more inclusive pessimism; like Robert Lowell, he condemned both sides, and the atmosphere of hatred, propaganda, and overwhelming military technology seemed to him the triumph of abstract experience over particular humaneness. In "Seasons of the Soul" and the related "Winter Mask," the sense of historical entrapment thus becomes more inclusive, but the real area of conflict, fear, and hope becomes more personal: "Why it is man hates / His own salvation, / Prefers the way to hell." (p. 721)

The three sections Tate has published from his unfinished poem in terza rima—though only "The Swimmers" is directly historical—are both a recapitulation and a profound resolution of the problems underlying Tate's poetry of history. They are a kind of personal *Divine Comedy,* in the sense that a religious experience has allowed Tate to journey wholly into the feared realm of dreams, traumas, twilight half-hallucinations, as Dante journeyed into hell, without the fear of being trapped there, unable to return to the outside world. They also follow the Dante described in "The Symbolic Imagination," who brings with him all the levels of his own experience, in particular the sexual, to be incorporated and reinterpreted even in his highest moments of religious insight.

The dominant symbols of the sequence are light and darkness, and water. Water . . . is an ambivalent element, powerful to save, but also to destroy those distorted or in error. Light, as in "The Symbolic Imagination," is the invisible power of God that makes itself known to us only in making known external reality.

The concluding passage of "The Maimed Man" declares the theme: in the "small half-hell" of "love disordered" and of a childhood haunted by familial "shades," the speaker has dangerously "played swimmer of night"—night being defined as the dream, the Platonic cave, and, for the first time explicitly, as the Freudian wish to return to the womb. He now prays to be admitted to the higher, or regenerative, meaning of water. . . . It is hard not to associate [his] infinite regression of dreams with terrifying images of solipsism in Tate's earlier work. Yet the journey ends in a reconciliation of water with "noonday," and of the "shadowy womb" with a transcendent Mother. (pp. 725-26)

Though ["The Swimmers"] describes a lynching, it is not a political poem in any ordinary sense; the lynching becomes a generalized symbol of original sin, of the evil lurking in communal, as well as individual, dreams. (p. 727)

The antithesis of light and sound used in "The Maimed Man" and, with beautiful unobtrusiveness, in "The Swimmers," [is in "The Buried Lake"] made clear: while light places man in the outward world, sound (music and poetry) springs from the pulse, man's deepest sense of inner being, and projects it outward. Here lies the dreaded solipsism; yet Tate now affirms that the two senses can correspond, like the Way and the way back. For dreams and the power to tell them are both operations of the light upon unconsciousness—the "buried lake" not perceivable by the senses ("not seen even by me") until they themeselves act upon it—therefore, the dream is said to be dreamt at Santa Lucia's "command." . . .

If this reading is correct, the "secret plan" that saves the dreamer from anxiety is an appropriate one; in the compartmentalized realm of art, he asserts his masculine control, and impregnates. . . . What is at issue . . . goes beyond the psychoanalytic; it is the romantic idea of the emanation, the idea that the artist's self-sufficient imagination produces an ideal image, at once beloved object of knowledge, and regenerated world, which he can then find or create in reality. (p. 728)

["The Buried Lake"] ends with an assessment of the claims, personal and artistic, to be made for the dreamer's experience. There is still a hint of the darkening shadow of history: in an "off season," the poet's "leaf" has yet to unfold the "formal cherry," whether that means a finished masterpiece, a wholehearted religious conversion, or happiness in life. Tate's invocation of "Cape jasmine, wild azalea, eglantine" reminds one of Eliot's nostalgia for the "bent goldenrod" at the end of *Ash-Wednesday.* But where Eliot held that the renewal of the love of life on a purely generative level should be seen as the enemy of further spiritual progress, Tate sticks with his interior flora. He insists on the completeness and order of the experience within its natural embodiments, and on the necessary onward movement of life, hesitant, earthly, and unpredictable. . . . Yet he stresses, too, the reality of the "invisible . . . mass" of implications that the natural experience throws off, caught in a mirror world of art or religion but not, therefore, angelic. If the ending makes Tate's religious conversion somewhat less complete than Eliot's, it does not lessen his sense of fulfillment as a human being: "I knew that I had known enduring love."

Tate's poetry of history is concerned throughout with the relation of an individual to an idealized past and to a present that, in his view, shares his defects without recognizing them as such. The stance of much of the prose and poetry is that the individual is deeply unworthy, and should desire only to bring himself closer, as in "Emblems," to the destiny and the standards of the ancestors. But in some poems —"Mother and Son," perhaps the "Ode," and certainly the second part of "Seasons of the Soul"—there is an undercurrent of contrary feeling: a bitter suspicion that the domination of the past, rather than the deficiencies of modern thought, is responsible for the sense of suffocation and unreality in present experience. The essays, for all their traditionalism, surely express a similar impulse in stressing the need to accept the body and the actual, living world. Given this obsessive ambivalent concern with the problem of tradition and individuation, it is hardly surprising that regressive ideas come up so frequently in the psychoanalytic overtones of the poetry. The two contexts of feeling are so profoundly related that any argument as to which was the symbol, which the primary psychic concern, would be most useless and academic.

These problems, when all is said, are universal human ones, not invented by the special concerns of the defeated South, or the Spengler-haunted 1920s. I would suggest that Allen Tate has come to treat them more universally in the process of treating them more personally; and has, thus, come to envision resolutions which, being psychological and religious, are largely independent of history. One result, understandably, is a less idealistic view of the southern past: its elements of morbid romanticism and destructiveness are fully acknowledged in the terzinas. At the same time, the modern perspective of psychoanalysis, which would once have been satirized, is partially incorporated—in particular, its idea of the conscious reliving of early and traumatic experience as a way of release from the solipsism of neurotic repetition. Yet the terzinas, more than any of Tate's earlier work, demonstrate the guiding and expansive possibilities of tradition. Not only does a conversion to Catholicism "reduce the toll" of self-exploration, but the poems are literally and intentionally imitative: Dante provides not only a few symbols (as in "Seasons of the Soul"), but the form itself and many of the most striking qualities of diction. In his late and best period, by committing himself to a personal epic written in homage to a dramatic one, Tate converts his Furies into Eumenides; he draws sustenance from both sides of an ambivalence which, at the time of the "Ode," seemed virtually paralytic. (pp. 731-32)

Alan Williamson, "Allen Tate and the Personal Epic," in The Southern Review *(copyright, 1976, by Alan Williamson), Vol. 12, No. 4, October, 1976, pp. 714-32.*

HILTON KRAMER

For readers of a certain age—I have in mind those who, like myself, first came to modern poetry (and to the criticism written to defend and elucidate it) in the years just after the Second World War—the publication of Allen Tate's "Collected poems 1919-1976" . . . is an event that stirs a good many memories and associations. . . . [In the] first years after the war Mr. Tate already seemed a venerable survivor of several lost worlds. The Nashville of the Fugitives, the New York of the young Malcolm Cowley and Kenneth Burke and E. E. Cummings, like the Paris of Gertrude Stein and Ford Madox Ford, had receded into the mists of literary legend. . . .

[Today] the battles of the New Criticism and the literary and political divisions they engendered are as distant from us as the Nashville of the Fugitives. They too evoke yet another lost world. . . .

Throughout [the complex history of the New Criticism], Mr. Tate was never a writer easy to take hold of. For the New Criticism enjoined us to concentrate our attention on the poem itself—when it ventured into discussions of fiction or drama, it seemed to treat them too as poetic structures—and not to be bemused by the distractions of literary history, or indeed history of any sort. It was on the *text,* and not the context, that the New Criticism directed all intelligence, and yet the critical imperatives that focused so narrowly on the isolated literary object—isolated, that is, from the world that had produced it—seemed to carry with them a distinct but unacknowledged context of their own. (p. 3)

The odd thing about all this, so far as Mr. Tate's own writings were concerned, was that he had been all along a writer—as poet, critic, novelist and biographer—deeply immersed in the materials of history, and there could never be any question of separating *his* literary achievements from their attachment to the historical imagination. Only by means of a certain pedagogical magic and a classroom atmosphere of extreme casuistry could the author of "Ode to the Confederate Dead," of that fine novel "The Fathers" . . . and "Reactionary Essays on Poetry and Ideas" be separated from the iron grip of history. It was done, of course, but the result, I think, was to blur his distinction, especially his distinction as a poet. The New Criticism may have enhanced our appreciation of his powers of literary artifice, but it diminished our understanding of the vision that such artifice was designed to serve. In this respect, the most blatant of Mr. Tate's political and historical essays often prove a better guide to the poetry than the most accomplished explications of his language and structure. (pp. 3, 36)

Returning to the poetry again on the occasion of this new "Collected Poems," one is indeed keenly aware that "time and history" is its central concern and "man's attachment to the past" its major theme, but it is a particular history that so impresses itself on our imagination—the history of a lost world carried in the mind of a Southerner, a classicist and an artist exiled to a Northern culture in which the imperatives of industrialism, philistinism and bourgeois capitalism reinforce a sense of irretrievable defeat.

The tragic dimension of Mr. Tate's poetry, which we feel most profoundly in the poems written in memory of friends—especially in "Seasons of the Soul," written in memory of John Peale Bishop, and "The Eye," written for E. E. Cummings—as well as in the better-known "Ode to the Confederate Dead," the irony of which is in its not being an ode at all, is to be found precisely in this consciousness of exile from a history that holds the poet in its power. All that can be retrieved from this history, and from the sense of defeat that is inseparable from it and which in the end is indistinguishable from the scenario of existence itself, is what the artist makes of it. Is this, perhaps, why the poems written in memory of friends who were also poets seem to carry a special power?

It is, in any case, in this sense of history—the most encompassing of Mr. Tate's lost worlds—that we find the source of both the politics that may appall us and the poetry that moves and instructs us. . . . This is a poetry that is formal, elegant, "metaphysical"; and coming to it today from an immersion in the newer, looser, more solipsistic modes of contemporary verse, it too conjures up a lost world—a world of flawless, well-made structures and meters that flatter and educate the ear. But it is also a poetry of knowledge, a poetry confident in its assumption that poetry has something to tell us about our experience, about history, that only poetry can tell us. Mr. Tate's very long and distinguished career is, in its way, a kind of parable on the poet's vocation, for his poetry is often wise as well as beautiful in ways that his prose is not. It is the poetry that will live. (pp. 36-7)

Hilton Kramer, "Allen Tate: Lost Worlds," in The New York Times Book Review *(© 1978 by The New York Times Company; reprinted by permission), January 8, 1978, pp. 3, 36-7.*

J. A. BRYANT, JR.

Most readers have long known that Tate has produced some of the finest poetry of his generation. This is true even of unsympathetic readers inclined to complain that the corpus is uneven in quality (as it is) and unfulfilled in promise (as it is not). Most consider the single novel [*The Fathers*] a distinguished achievement, though few have recognized that it constitutes the great watershed in Tate's life as an artist, bringing into significant conjunction the insights, tendencies, and techniques of his early work and anticipating the masterworks that began to appear after 1940. As for criticism, no one—at least no one since the appearance of *Essays of Four Decades* in 1969—has doubted that in an age of critics Tate stands with the half dozen best and most influential. Now it is possible to regard the whole as a series of forays into the knowledge essential to our self-awareness as latter-day heirs of western civilization. Tate, we see, was never more than incidentally Fugitive, Agrarian, or even southern but was from first to last the colonial European, incidentally sired in Clark County, Kentucky, and doomed to live with the frustration of somehow having been born a legitimate spiritual child of Aristotle in a world dominated by children of Plato and Descartes.

Nevertheless the fact of Tate's southernness has often raised unwarranted expectations about his work, even in the minds of some who ought to have known better. This is especially true of *The Fathers,* a major novel. . . . [The] world which Allen Tate describes is the perennial world of humankind, characterized by order and the appearance of stability on the one hand and by a restless dynamism on the other, both of which aspects seek to prevail as well as to exist in the face of a vast uncharacterized abyss which John Milton in another context called "the womb of nature and perhaps her grave." (pp. 274-75)

[The] numinous tends to intrude whenever an author repeatedly projects himself in his work, and Tate has frequently tended to do that. This should now be clear to anyone who looks carefully at the new version of the collected poems [*Collected Poems 1919-1976*] and mentally supplements the progression presented there with the progression that has always been more or less apparent in the prose. It could not have been otherwise. For anyone convinced as Tate is that he and his contemporaries (to say nothing of forebears for several generations) have been victims of a dualism that has inhibited communion between human beings, poisoned their natural relationship with the rest of creation, and tended to leave intellectual man stranded in a solipsistic trap, writing exclusively about impersonal subjects would have constituted inconsistency if not dishonesty. Early in his practice as a poet Tate began to let the creation of poetry serve as a strategy for exploring this complicated predicament, perhaps with the hope of finding some way out of it; and to judge by the poems from about 1925 on he soon came to see that the same set of problems had tended to become critical in western thought whenever Platonism got the upper hand. . . . [A] moving presentation of [the consequences of the triumph of Platonism], and one tied to southern history, is the one in the final version (1937) of "Ode to the Confederate Dead." There the man by the gate, concerned to honor the fallen soldiers, learns to his despair that mortality is certain and that human identity, whether glorious or inglorious, is probably doomed to be irretrievably lost in the abyss that counts us all. The "Ode" itself presents no resolution, of course; but writing it was certainly part of the process whereby Tate approached the resolution that came close to being explicit in the joint action of George Posey and Lacy Buchan in *The Fathers*. Both men were prisoners of their own minds—"Plato's Christians in the cave," to use a phrase from one of the later poems; both were trapped in social systems that had atrophied into sets of formal gestures. Their hope of deliverance came when genuine human love began to break through the walls of the cave to make possible the renewal of genuine social communion. (pp. 281-82)

Tate defined the role of the man of letters in one of his finest essays as that of the supervisor of the culture of language, "to which the rest of culture is subordinate," but he defined the function of culture as "communion in time through love, which is beyond time." This is the context for the major poetry that he wrote and published after 1940.

By common consent that major achievement also includes "More Sonnets at Christmas," "Seasons of the Soul," and the three poems in terza rima that Tate published early in the 1950s. Again personal chronology is relevant. The sonnets bring to the surface a personal need that Tate was later to meet by entering the Catholic church in 1950; and "Seasons of the Soul" taken as a whole is a recollection of a life converted into a prayer preliminary to confession. Commentators have discerned in its four sections concentration successively upon political man, solipsistic man, sexual man, and religious man; but these divisions should not be taken as absolute. The whole man, in all his aspects and contradictions, is present in each of the four; and the conclusion consists of a plea to confess, which is a final and presumably successful attempt to break out of the cave after other measures, including the recourse to sex, have failed. Consistent throughout is the presence, shadowy at first and then explicit, of the female complement to the speaker's persona. The mother of silences has been identified with St. Monica, with the mother of an earlier "Mother and Son," and with the Old South. She may well be all of these, but she is none of them precisely. It is more useful to call her Tate's dimly realized Beatrice, and it is hardly accident that for his projected longer poem, which became in the end a long short poem in three parts, Tate used Dante's terza rima with its suggestions of the scope of the *Commedia* and of the woman who symbolized for much of the poem the motive power of its action. (pp. 283-84)

With Tate . . . the love of God is never separable from the love of neighbor, male or female; and it is appropriate that part 3 of *Collected Poems* (the last two parts consist of translations and early poems) should conclude with two recent pieces addressed to his wife and children. In some collections poems like these would be disregarded by reviewers as being personal and not properly amenable to criticism; but all of Tate's work is inseparable from Tate's life, and this review is not criticism of the usual kind. When Tate writes to his wife in "Farewell Rehearsed," "love of you was all the air I breathed," he is writing of the "enduring love" that still had not found incarnation when he wrote "Buried Lake," of the love that bound Lacy Buchan to George Posey and led Aeneas on his westward quest, and of the love that brought Augustine to his knees and Dante from Hell to Heaven. It might appear that the cure for solipsism presented here is simply to find some "other" to touch, acknowledge, and know; but Tate leaves undeclared the specifics of a solution as well as the ultimate responsibility for man's isolation. . . .

T. S. Eliot wrote on Tate's sixtieth birthday that his several literary achievements, considerable as they are separately, are greater than the sum of their parts. He also declared Tate a sage. Perhaps it is allowable now to observe that the parts of Tate's life as a whole, considerable as they are, are also greater in sum than they are separately. It is certainly mandatory to note that with *Collected Poems 1919-1976* we have before us something extremely rare in the modern world, a man of letters, full and entire, in grace, in wisdom, and in charity. It is possible that he is a sage, though Tate would probably reject that role. It is clear that he has kept bright the instrument of language in our time and that he has made it illuminate as well as shine. (p. 285)

J. A. Bryant, Jr., "Allen Tate: The Man of Letters in the Modern World," in The Sewanee Review *(reprinted by permission of the editor; © 1978 by The University of the South), Vol. LXXXVI, No. 2, Spring, 1978, pp. 274-85.*

ROY FULLER

In the thirties (and it did not end with the thirties) I greatly admired Tate for the sonorous and noble effects in much of his poetry, which I wanted to make a part of my own. Moreover, certain rhythms or, perhaps more accurately, turns of phrase seemed to me so finely and inevitably poetic that all that could be done was to try to echo them. . . . (p. 234)

The following is what I started by saying when I [reviewed Tate's *Poems 1920-1945: A Selection* (published in England) in 1948] (I had just quoted the end of Ransom's "Survey of Literature"—"God have mercy on the sinner / Who must write with . . . Only consonants and vowels"):

> We should be obtuse indeed if we despised mere consonants and vowels. The pre-eminent virtue of Allen Tate's poetry seems to me to be precisely the consistent integrity of its language. I can think of no other living poet (and I include Mr. Eliot) who has made fewer concessions to the easy, the rehearsed or the slipshod methods of writing verse. . . . I'm aware, I think, of all the objections which can be made to Tate's poetry. It is often very obscure—sometimes needlessly obscure: it is often very thick—like metaphysical poetry without the tropes: occasionally it is rather irritatingly illogical. And many poems have for an end or a climax instead of a shot to the bull's-eye a piece of ambiguity which lays too heavy a task on the reader's imagination or powers of interpretation. But then again it seems to me that even these faults add up to a kind of virtue—although it is perhaps only an historical virtue. Tate's poetry is very much a part of dissident art—confused, perhaps, but unconsciously as well as deliberately probing at the contradictions of modern existence and seeking redeeming integrations.

I hope these ancient words, so naïvely presumptuous about the road and duty of the poet, have nonetheless been worth resuscitating. To me they are interesting as showing that thirty years ago Tate seemed pre-eminently part of the obscurer end of the "Modern Movement," whereas now any obscurity would be taken more or less for granted. (pp. 235-36)

[The] section of "Early Poems" [from *Collected Poems 1919-1976*] consists of forty-six pieces, none of them labeled later than "1924."

The juvenilia of few poets could stand such an exhumation. But there is little here of merely morbid interest: on the contrary, much to astound and delight. A whole vestibule, as it were, has been added to the edifice of Tate's poetry—and thereby light is let in and perspectives meaningfully lengthened. Many of these early poems remind us of the strange epoch of poetic difficulty and even non-meaning they come from—so strange as often to disarm us by the effects produced:

> We made a silence, for teacups, once
> After cosmic gall had bittered a lidless night,
> Then touched the dizzy apples of Acrasia, once,—
> Once we were shattered with a storm of light.

The linguistic and musical splendor of the mature Tate is often thus prefigured. But the section is far more than a version of a poetry that was going to improve in finish, unity, and authority; in its quite compact extent it indicates Tate's origins as a poet and also a number of "ways not taken." (p. 238)

As a young man Tate was a poet full of fancy, energy, cleverness, and cockiness. A poem like "Resurgam," where Ransom and Eliot have largely replaced earlier influences, is in no sense an exercise and survives as something with a phrase-making and rhythmic power illuminating and even going beyond its inspirers:

> Life stood on the top stair a moment
> Waved her last gray slander down the stair,
> I will not forget her absent eyes
> Her other smile like one rose
> Falling, falling everywhere.

(p. 239)

[We] must greatly regret that in Tate the obligation to Eliotesque solemnity left so little room for Eliotesque frivolity. Although the "Two Conceits" from his later years is not, truth to say, a really successful bit of fun, the man himself is humorous and ironic, fertile in informal judgments of humans and art, and born at a later time (when "light" verse came to acquire more sanction) could surely have more often laid aside the bardic robes. (p. 240)

Tate is especially a poet needing to be read aloud. I have perhaps gone on too much about his obscurity (and may touch on it again) but there is no doubt that poems that seem daunting to the eye, both prosodically and semantically, immediately surrender more of themselves if spoken.

"Trapped in a burly house" one reads in an early poem and can't help smiling at the epithet—so unexpected, so nearly undescriptive, so poetic, so Tatean. Of course, the mature poetry is full of such felicities and they were part of Tate's initial appeal to me, are part of his perennial appeal, of his essential poetic creativity. But we are bound to ask ourselves, particularly in view of the troubled times during which his poems have been available, if his humanity, his message, his reaction to those times have adequately matched his ingenious interest in language and culture, in poetry *qua* poetry. (p. 242)

Tate's flowering was in the nihilism of the post-1914-1918 Western world. The futility of urban life and the sterility of thought (very Rickwordian) may be seen in poems like "Retroduction to American History." Rickword emerged from all that as a Marxist; Crane committed suicide. Tate embraced Roman Catholicism but I think only at rare moments (possibly most notably in "The Eagle") can he be regarded as a religious poet. . . . That he was so firmly fixed in his formative period (which this book now gives so much more extended a view of) is surely a reason for the comparative exiguousness of his later poetry.

Yet despite its sparseness there is no falling off, rather, notable accretions. In the 1943 "Ode to Our Young Proconsuls of the Air" (which more and more I come to think of as a very remarkable poem indeed) Tate's conservatism is even more ambiguous than in earlier times, the irony poured out in doubles, not singles. And it could be argued that not until 1944, in "Seasons of the Soul" (which must be one of the best modern poems), does Tate's humanity fully reveal itself. . . . (pp. 242-43)

One has a twinge of regret that when, later, Tate set off on a long autobiographical poem (still unfinished) he chose that form so apt in English to lead to trouble—*terza rima*. Despite the many marvels in the three sections we have of it, we can't help wanting more of this response to "experience," even if of a less grand and ingenious kind. . . .

But I must not . . . depreciate the beauties and mysteries—essentially verbal but more than verbal—of Tate's poetry at every stage of his career. In a real sense they are its justification and seem inexhaustible. . . . (p. 243)

Tate has survived his times and mere contemporaneities, not by ignoring them or being irrelevant to them but by sticking to his highest aspirations and exercising his talents so far as possible always at their best. Who will ever feel that he had plumbed this poetry or that it holds for him no further meanings or astonishments? As will be clear, I myself have eliminated over the years almost all of the grudging element in my reading of this poet whose reputation I believe can only ever be threatened by temporary trendiness among critics and readers. (p. 244)

Roy Fuller, "Tate Full Length" (copyright, 1978, by Roy Fuller), in The Southern Review, *Vol. 14, No. 2, April, 1978, pp. 233-44.*

LOUIS D. RUBIN, JR.

[The body of Allen Tate's poetry] is slim—as slim as Eliot's and Ransom's. He published one novel, *The Fathers* (1938). A remarkable work, it was never widely popular; but like Allen's best poetry, it remains in print, and I think it is destined to last.

Why did one so greatly and variously gifted write and publish so little? What he said of his friend John Ransom was not, I think true of him: that he set out deliberately to be a Minor Poet. . . . My observation is that as an imaginative writer Allen had a gift that was highly and intricately autobiographical. This may seem odd, in that his poetics placed a premium upon achieved anonymity, classical restraint, the primacy of craftsmanship over subject—the antithesis of the romantic subjective artist whose work is the fervent unmediated outpouring of his own sensibilities. "As a poet I have no experience," he once remarked. Yet—and perhaps the paradox is the key—almost all that Allen wrote is drawn either directly from his own situation or from that of his immediate forebears. He used to speak of himself as having conducted his education in public, and if by that statement he meant that his writings consisted of his openly enunciated response to his own experience, it is quite appropriate.

As poet and critic Allen had impeccable taste. His literary coat-of-arms might well have borne the motto *nil admirari* —to be astonished at and by nothing. So fastidious was his literary sensibility that he could not tolerate blemish or imperfection, and this habit of mind no doubt served to lessen, or at any rate to restrict, his response to much work that was flawed but powerful. . . . I believe that this fastidiousness was what inhibited him from publishing or even continuing to work for very long on anything of his own that did not seem absolutely right to him. His sensibility and his taste were whole and unified; had it been otherwise, he might have written more. Again, though, he would not have been Allen Tate. What he did write is not merely distinguished: it is unique in its distinction. (p. 270)

As a literary critic Allen, like many other poets, was active and assertive. "I never knew what I thought about anything until I had written about it," he once wrote. "To write an essay was to find out what I thought; for I did not know at the beginning how or where it would end." Clearly this is not quite true: there is too much consistency in Allen's critical judgement to be accounted for by any such haphazard procedure. It would be more accurate, perhaps, to say that he wrote his criticism to identify and formulate what he felt —that, like Wordsworth, Coleridge, and his master Eliot, he wrote about literature, and sometimes edited it for publication, in order to instruct his audience in how to read the literature which he admired and championed, including his own. My own belief is that he possessed the most brilliantly conceptual mind of his generation of poet-critics, and that, had he elected to do so, he could have produced a body of critical work such as no other critic in the English language, not even Johnson, Coleridge, or Brooks, ever evolved. (p. 272)

We shall not be able to replace Allen Tate. We have the poetry, the novel, the essays; but, as he declared of another poet, "he who dribbled couplets like a snake / Coiled to a lithe precision in the sun / Is missing." (pp. 272-73)

Louis D. Rubin, Jr., "Allen Tate 1899-1979," in The Sewanee Review *(reprinted by permission of the editor; © 1979 by The University of the South), Vol. LXXXVII, No. 2, Spring, 1979, pp. 267-73.*

* * *

TAYLOR, Robert Lewis 1912-

Taylor is an American novelist, biographer, journalist, humorist, and author of short stories. Best known for his adventure stories, Taylor won the 1959 Pulitzer Prize in Fiction for his novel *The Travels of Jaimie McPheeters*. This picaresque novel, generally considered his most successful, is distinguished by its lively narrative, vivid dialogue, and imaginative characterizations. Taylor wrote *New Yorker* profiles from 1939-48, many of which were later collected in book form. He has also written full-length biographies of figures such as Winston Churchill, W. C. Fields, and Carry Nation. (See also *Contemporary Authors*, Vols. 1-4, rev. ed., and *Something about the Author*, Vol. 10.)

LEWIS NORDYKE

["The Travels of Jaimie McPheeters" is] a top-quality tale of the trail to California's gold fields and grassy valleys in 1819. (p. 40)

This novel is as authentic as any story any man could have told after making the trip. It is based largely on the journal of an adventurer who did make it—Dr. Joseph Middleton.

In addition to this on-the-scene report, many other authentic narratives and documents contributed to the story.

Mr. Taylor . . . is a versatile writer. In the main, he tells this story in the first-person, out of the mouth of a 14-year-old lad, Jaimie McPheeters—but the heart of it is related in the letters and journals of Jaimie's father, Dr. Sardius McPheeters. Mr. Taylor pivots nimbly and convincingly from the words of an unusually bright lad . . . to those of a rather blustery, but lovable, man.

This is a tremendously exciting novel, and it has the added zest of being in sharp focus historically. Some of the incidents of violence will curl the hair of many a reader. (p. 41)

Lewis Nordyke, "Western Odyssey," in The New York Times Book Review *(© 1958 by The New York Times Company; reprinted by permission), March 16, 1958, pp. 40-1.*

WINTHROP SARGEANT

"The Travels of Jaimie McPheeters" is full of thoroughly researched minutiae about wagon trains, Indian ways, gold mining, life in the San Francisco of the time, and such, and is delivered in a cheerful, funny, and headlong prose that makes its unabashed theatricality a total delight.

Winthrop Sargeant, "Books: 'The Travels of Jaimie McPheeters'," in The New York Times Book Review *(© 1958 by The New York Times Company; reprinted by permission), March 22, 1958, p. 154.*

OLIVER La FARGE

Let not the size of ["The Travels of Jaimie McPheeters"] dismay you. It is a small-scale "Anthony Adverse" of the California gold rush with touches of "Huckleberry Finn," a lively, often funny, picaresque tale that conveys a real feel of what it must have been like on the immigrant trails and in the gold fields, and only occasionally does the story become too long. The publisher's blurb stresses the author's "meticulously researched facts," and he himself appends a bibliography of nigh on to 150 titles, but he is too good a novelist to let mere facts stand in the way of a good story.

Considering the enjoyment this reviewer had from the book, he should not carp at minor faults, but a few comments must be made. On the score of "meticulous research," it is odd to find Algonkian words in the mouths of Caddoan-speaking Pawnees, or an Indian Maiden whom the Algonkian Cheyennes of Minnesota called by a New Mexico Tewa name.

Yes indeed, there is an Indian Maiden. One of the charms of this book is its unabashed use exclusively of stock characters. There are Bad Indians who are cowardly, do not wash, and stink. There are Good Indians, who are brave, generous and well scrubbed. Jaimie's father is that old standby, the brilliant, highly educated, charming ne'er-do-well, whose weaknesses keep himself and his son in the state of motion necessary to maintain the story while he enables the author to make comments of which Jamie himself would be incapable. (pp. 23, 42)

[Jaimie's] tale, written with what is intended to be artless candor and unconscious humor (some of which is delicious, some obvious, some contrived), is broken at intervals by his father's flowery journal and letters. This provides nice contrast, and must have been fun for the author.

Jaimie is a good-hearted bad boy, owing much to Huck Finn, full of naïve, sharp observations, innocence, and common sense. Sometimes he is the adult looking back on boyhood, at others he is nearer ten than fourteen years of age. . . .

Near the end of the book he experiences a passage right out of Krafft-Ebing with an elderly prostitute, which has the effect of awakening in him a healthy interest in the Indian Maiden, who becomes the Future Bride. In fact, characterization of the book's hero is subordinated to the point-to-point needs of the story or to the author's wish to play for a laugh or a shock.

The book is fun to read: It has verve; locale and period are well captured. Sober criticisms, then, become captious. (p. 42)

Oliver La Farge, "Fourteen in '49," in The Saturday Review *(entire issue copyright 1958 by Saturday Review Associates, Inc.; reprinted with permission), Vol. XCI, No. 16, April 19, 1958, pp. 23, 42.*

MICHAEL MEWSHAW

"A Roaring in the Wind," Robert Lewis Taylor's 14th book, is described on its cover as a novel as well as a "History of Alder Gulch, Montana." But unfortunately it falls far short in both categories. At best it is a fitfully interesting miscellany of vignettes and facts about frontier life. . . .

Taylor, with a weakness for mere cataloguing, does little to shape his material or to pace the accumulation of incidents. It takes more than 100 pages for him just to reach Alder Gulch and by the time he gets there, he seems to have forgotten why he made the trip. Perhaps he, like this reader, was distracted by the lackluster style of the historical journals and diaries from which he incessantly quotes. (p. 32)

One can't avoid noticing that the journals appear to have infected Taylor's own prose. To cite several examples among hundreds: "News of the arrest rolled like a prairie fire"; "Time, even a short time, is the only real healer"; "The miners cried like babies."

To compensate for lines like these, it would take a story of rare strength or characters of preternatural interest. But "A Roaring in the Wind" lacks both. (pp. 32-3)

In the American West, with its acres of emptiness and dinning silences, pioneers often lost their sense of time and direction. Robert Lewis Taylor . . . seems to have suffered the same fate, staggering through barren spaces, wandering in circles, never realizing that he has lost his way and his reader. (p. 33)

Michael Mewshaw, "Three Novels," in The New York Times Book Review *(© 1978 by The New York Times Company; reprinted by permission), February 5, 1978, pp. 32-3.**

KRIS SCHUSLER

Having loved novels dealing with the early West, when one comes along that so captures the essence of that time, the book becomes a treasured piece to share among friends. . . . [*A Roaring in the Wind*] captures that essence of the nostalgia and romance of the American frontier. . . . It is with the introduction of the vigilance committees, the Vigilantes, that Taylor's knowledge of the early West comes into play. In the process he weaves a tale that is both fascinating and humorous.

Kris Schusler, "Books in Review: 'A Roaring in the Wind'," in West Coast Review of Books *(copyright 1978 by Rapport Publishing Co., Inc.), Vol 4, No. 2, March, 1978, p. 26.*

RANDY SHIPP

Historical fiction buffs may find ["A Roaring in the Wind"] somewhat of a disappointment. Taylor's description of life in frontier gold rush towns is lively and entertaining, but his plot and character development leave something to be desired. . . .

Looking for adventure, a young man . . . finds himself a part of the rough mining towns of preterritorial Montana. His description of the people and places he encounters reads like a cross between the rollicking humor of Mark Twain's "Roughing It" and the poignancy of Bret Harte's short stories.

The novel's authenticity is enhanced by the quotes from diaries and newspaper accounts of events of the era. In this respect, it is similar to Taylor's Pulitzer Prize winning "The Travels of Jaimie McPheeters." Unfortunately, though, the character and plot development of "A Roaring in the Wind" aren't nearly as strong. The result is pages and pages of local color through which shadowy characters wander, following a tenuous plot line.

Randy Shipp, "Taylor's New Novel Set in Frontier Mining Towns," in The Christian Science Monitor *(reprinted by permission from* The Christian Science Monitor; *© 1978 The Christian Science Publishing Society; all rights reserved), March 1, 1978, p. 26.*

PAUL SCHLUETER

A Roaring in the Wind, one more work about the Old West, with all the usual clichés and overworked situations and characters, simply didn't seem very promising.

But Taylor has done a good job. The extensive bibliography merely suggests that he has done his homework (or at least looked up book titles); the novel itself suggests that he has been able to transform the deadness of facts into the life of fiction in a manner that may well win him the same acclaim that his *The Travels of Jaimie McPheeters* did some two decades ago. In fact, there is an echo of that earlier work. . . .

Taylor has an undistinguished style, and the "footnotes" included by Ross, the narrator of the account given to us in the novel, are pretentious and obtrusive. Yet the book comes alive for the reader, and its humor, authenticity, occasional bawdiness, and conflict make for an adventurous reading experience.

Paul Schlueter, "Fiction: 'A Roaring in the Wind'," in Best Sellers *(copyright © 1978 Helen Dwight Reid Educational Foundation), Vol. 38, No. 2, May, 1978, p. 40.*

* * *

TREVOR, William (pseudonym of William Trevor Cox) 1928-

Trevor is an Irish-born novelist, short story writer, dramatist, and screenwriter now living in England. His writings are peopled with the unfortunates of society. Trevor depicts them, in his subtle and economical prose, with ironic detachment. (See also *CLC*, Vols. 7, 9, and *Contemporary Authors*, Vols. 9-12, rev. ed.)

WALTER SULLIVAN

[The] story of an evil child is venerable and [William Trevor] brings to his handling of it few approaches that are new. But he does his work with dignity and gives us the best fruits of his talent until almost the end of *The Children of Dynmouth.* He fashions a character out of the dubious clichés of the age, puts breath in his lungs and blood in his veins, and moulds him into the monstrous Timothy Gedge, abandoned by his father, ignored by his mother and older sister, virtually companionless except for the television set that he watches continually. Timothy hatches a plan to lift himself above his ordinary existence. (p. 321)

Flannery O'Connor said that we are accustomed to the face of evil, and this is largely true, I think, but Gedge is an exception. He horrifies us by his youthful competence in the art of destroying human felicity, by his imperviousness to advice or insult, by his indifference to the goodwill of others. . . . It seems proper that the rector of the village church should be one of the principals who bring an end to Gedge's reign of terror. Good and evil square off in classic enmity, but then the Reverend Featherston—and Trevor too, I assume, since the treatment is in no way ironic—loses the courage of his convictions.

Mrs. Featherston stands firm for the notion of evil in the world—malevolent forces at work within and among us. But, of course, educated people can hardly countenance such medieval misconceptions. Our realities are physical, our morals and metaphysics subjective and relative; our most cruelly perpetrated depredations are cries for help, evidence of our own need for understanding and pity. The greater pity in my judgment is that a novel so finely conceived, so well furnished with good characters, and so successful in endowing old images and devices with freshness should flounder and sink so badly at its conclusion. To imply that sooner or later the shrinks and the socialists will put an end to evil is to drag out an old chestnut indeed—and to negate the fine performance which leads up to this foolishness. (p. 322)

Walter Sullivan, "Documents from the Ice Age: Recent British Novels," in The Sewanee Review *(reprinted by permission of the editor; © 1978 by The University of the South), Vol. LXXXVI, No. 2, Spring, 1978, pp. 320-25.**

ZAHIR JAMAL

[In *Lovers of Their Time*] Trevor's open, persevering sympathies go out to the unrecognised characters of time; ordinary lives shaped through silt and scythe and then forsaken or betrayed by failures of not-so-common understanding. But though his people look back over the England and Ireland of the last 40 years, there's no moistness about the steady eyes which look at them. It's the unimaginative interruption of continuing time's own alterations to which these chronicles draw attention. History for intelligent conservatives, perhaps; but no bad vacation exercise for silly radicals either.

For Trevor caters to no settled taste for accusation. No slickly adumbrated malignity defeats the progress of his characters' lives; only the uncomprehending entrenchments of the everlasting dull. (p. 380)

Only the most practised art could give [the] barely perceptible forsakings [of his characters] their characteristically unforced yet painful movement. Trevor manages the thing in nearly every case; in charting how across the harsh years of the last war, a young girl's fresh attachments slowly twist into an adult cruelty; in catching the meaning behind the absence at Christmas of a family's long-standing friend; in following a neglected child's gradual retreat into a permanent fantasy. Through all such knots and breaks of time a rare aptitude for patience is the unassuming form of Trevor's irreplaceable imagination. (pp. 380-81)

Zahir Jamal, "Silt and Scythe," in New Statesman *(© 1978 The Statesman & Nation Publishing Co. Ltd.), Vol. 96, No. 2479, September 22, 1978, pp. 380-81.**

TOM PAULIN

William Trevor is one of the acknowledged masters of the short story. He is an Anglo-Irish writer who now lives in Devon and so he is an exiled member of a disappearing social class. . . . This is Trevor's heritage and it is at once his strength and his weakness. It enables him [in *Lovers of Their Time*] to present with the most accurate sympathy that desperately principled Irish intransigence which in "Another Christmas" makes an otherwise gentle Irish exile destroy a long-standing friendship. . . . Trevor tells the story with that impartial economy which is one of the most remarkable features of his writing.

Often Trevor returns to that notoriously Irish condition of being trapped by racial memories and historical bitterness. Usually he treats this subject with a resigned detachment which is effective and appealing, but sometimes the contradictions that underlie his detachment make him the passive victim of a nostalgia for vanished decencies. In a trilogy of stories called "Matilda's Endland" he describes an Englishwoman who hates the present and who believes that "there's nothing wrong with living in the past." Here, Trevor appears to be justly critical of that national nostalgia which keeps *The Country Diary of an Edwardian Lady* at the top of the bestseller lists—he seems, in other words, to be investigating an English fixation with the past. And yet the three stories are suffused with loving memories of lost summers and lush pastures. . . . For Trevor, an obsession with the past is a kind of madness—Matilda's nostalgia eventually drives her mad—and yet there is a deep dislike of contemporary reality in his stories.

In "Broken Homes", for example, the delinquent children who desecrate old Mrs Malby's flat assume a parabolic significance. . . . No opinion should interfere with an appreciation of the unforced artistry and superb economy of this brilliant story. The children's violation of the old woman's decent privacy is registered with such accuracy that one can only admire its narrative perfection. (pp. 50-1)

"Torridge", like "Broken Homes", is a masterpiece, and yet there is a quality in Trevor's prose and characterisation which is curiously processed and ersatz: the characters speak in the clipped twittering accents of British films of the 1940s (a grocer asks, "What can I entice you to, sir?"). Many of the characters—the Reverend Throataway, for example—are as flat as the butcher, the baker, the candlestick maker in the card game of Happy Families, and the prose style somehow manages to possess both a spare simplicity and a superannuated drabness. Norman Britt and Marie in the title-story are more like meek Edwardians than lovers in the 1960s. All too often Trevor settles for a decent, tolerant, middle-brow obviousness, a kind of synthetic mustiness. . . . The oddly dated atmosphere of Trevor's stories is the main obstacle to a more complete—and more generous—appreciation of his talent. (p. 52)

Tom Paulin, "Abandoned Prefabs," in Encounter *(© 1979 by Encounter Ltd.), Vol. LII, No. 1, January, 1979, pp. 49-55.**

V. S. PRITCHETT

[William Trevor] is one of the finest short story writers at present writing in the Anglo-Irish modes. His people are those who, in the course of their lives, are so humdrum in their ordinariness, so removed from the power of expressing themselves that he has to efface himself in order to speak for them. They appear to be confused by experience and in moral judgment, but they live by an obscure dignity and pride which they are either too shy or too unskilled to reveal at once: his art is to show they have their part in an exceptional destiny and even in a history beyond the private. Impartially he will justify them. . . .

In nearly all Trevor's stories [in *Lovers of Their Time and Other Stories*] we are led on at first by plain unpretending words about things done to prosaic people; then comes this explosion of conscience, the assertion of will which in some cases may lead to hallucination and madness. In that disordered state the victim has his or her victory; these people are not oddities but figures crucified by the continuity of evil and cruelty in human history, particularly the violent history of, say, the wars and cruelties of the last sixty years of this century. Theirs is a private moral revolt. The point is important, for Trevor has sometimes been thought of as the quiet recorder of "out of date" lives living tamely on memories of memories, as times change.

Tragically (comically too) he is aware of the seismic shock that history, even the ignorance of it, has prepared for the dumb or the successful. The obvious ironies are not laughed off; he goes deeper and more ruthlessly than that. The Irish in him—one would guess—faces the horrors, the English the plain dismays of having to accept circumstance by putting on the best face available. . . .

The most powerful story in this collection is "Attracta"; it is set in today's Northern Ireland and after the usual quiet beginning, assaults us with the tale of two terrible political murders. . . . [The protagonist] discovers one of the perpetrators is now a harmless old man. Quietly she stands in her schoolroom and insists on telling the children about the soldier's murder and how the killers sent his head to his wife. . . .

The sickened children are Protestants—they are stupefied by her attempt to stir a moral reflection. The outraged parents demand that the old teacher shall be retired. What is more remarkable even than the tale is that it conveys what is going on in the backs of the minds of all the people in the town, of whatever faction: of how all, except one or two bigots, are helplessly trying to evade or forget the evils that entangle them. As his master Chekhov did, William Trevor simply, patiently, truthfully allows life to present itself, without preaching; he is the master of the small movements of conscience that worry away at the human imagination and our passions.

V. S. Pritchett, "Explosions of Conscience," in The New York Review of Books *(reprinted with permission from* The New York Review of Books; *copyright © 1979 Nyrev, Inc.), Vol. XXVI, No. 6, April 19, 1979, p. 8.*

BENJAMIN DeMOTT

[Some British authors] abide by conventions of brevity, control, and traditional form without ever sounding like under-reachers. Perhaps the best of these is William Trevor, represented this season by *Lovers of Their Time*. . . . One sequence of tales in this book aims at nothing less than a recreation of the stunting impact of two world wars on the mind of a rural village. Two stories grapple, at the level of facts of feeling, with the Ulster anguish as endured by Protestants in the South and by Irish Catholics in England. And the book begins by walking unblinkingly up to the Conflict of Generations (an elderly woman and a gang of cosseted louts from a Comprehensive School) and charging it with genuinely fresh meaning. . . .

[Trevor] has a quiet voice—modest, reserved, delicately inflected. The recurring gesture in this collection is a smoothing of folds—a movement of mind continually asking recognition of our power (blessed and deluding) of assimilating, domesticating—finally of hiding—the strangeness of human deeds and days. And the most striking achievement is the title story, an almost indescribable romance that's partly about the Beatles, partly about the mystique of Abroad, partly about the discovery in the sixties that everybody is a wild and crazy guy for whom life really ought to be Fun. In twenty calm pages "Lovers of Their Time" aspires to—and reaches—the condition of music, history, zany domestic comedy, and lyric poetry. . . . But the same low-keyed yet exhilarating sense of fictional possibility that animates this story breathes throughout the book. It's bold, original, energetically ambitious work, marvelously assured; it's also British to the core. (p. 92)

Benjamin DeMott, "British to the Core," in The Atlantic Monthly *(copyright © 1979 by The Atlantic Monthly Company, Boston, Mass.; reprinted with permission), Vol. 243, No. 5, May, 1979, pp. 89-92.**

JOSH RUBINS

Can a short story do it all? Can it close in on an intense moment of feeling and dig down to illuminate the psychological whys and wherefores and reach out to touch on themes that lie far beyond the strictly personal? And can it do all this while seeming as spontaneous as gossip, as uncomfortably convincing as an overheard confession on a crosstown bus?

The answer is a resounding, grateful yes—as long as William Trevor is doing the storytelling, and then only sometimes. . . . [*Lovers of Their Time* deserves] the broadest of audiences, especially since over half of [the collection] offers William Trevor at his many-layered best.

Not that Trevor's slightly less ambitious tales are unsuccessful. Far from it. "Flights of Fancy" calls on the familiar figure of the plain, virginal, and self-sufficient middle-aged spinster—a mainstay of sensitive British fiction—but casts her in an odd and unnerving role: recipient of an unwanted, timid pass (at a company Christmas party) from a pretty yet coarse young lesbian. . . . And, in "Torridge," the savagery of English public school homosexual intrigues—scrupulously forgotten when those senior-boy "protectors" and junior-boy "*bijous*" grow up and marry—is flung in the faces of three aging Old Boys in the presence of their edgy wives and vulnerable offspring.

In these probings of hypocrisy, sexual and otherwise, Trevor is never less than compassionate; but he quietly sees through pose after pose, implying a whole sheaf of psychological work-ups with nips of dialogue and surprising, oddly perfect bits of detail.

Still, it's when Trevor projects his self-exposing characters into grander schemes that he really soars. The vagaries of time. The cruelty of war. The madness of mob hatred. The decline of decency. Commonplace themes all, but rarely have they been invoked with such compact eloquence, and rarely have they found themselves in such three-dimensional company. . . .

["Matilda's England" is] a three-part, three-decade memoir that begins with nine-year-old Matilda in the Indian summer of 1939. Her father is dead in the war by 1941, and when her brother follows suit soon after, Matilda ties up all her pain in a single equation, blaming the second casualty on her widowed mother's imperfect state of mourning: "I said that in a war against the Germans you couldn't afford to take chances, you couldn't go kissing a man when your husband had been killed." And by the 1960s all that cruelty has been internalized—turned against a well-meaning husband, turned inward in isolation as England decays around her. "There are casualties in war . . . thousands of miles from where the fighting is." In less sure fiction, such explicit soundings might be there to keep us from missing the point. In "Matilda's England," the intonations of the theme are more like lines in a powerful liturgy, an inescapable responsive reading.

Similarly, the other full-scale triumphs here go after big fish with plot hooks that avoid both sentimentality and showily antisentimental irony. (p. 44)

Josh Rubins, "Doing It All," in Saturday Review *(© 1979 by Saturday Review Magazine Corp.; reprinted with permission), Vol. 6, No. 10, May 12, 1979, pp. 44-5.*

* * *

TUTUOLA, Amos 1920-

Tutuola is a Nigerian novelist and short story writer best known for his first book, *The Palm-Wine Drinkard.* This novel, considered his best, is noted for its epic theme, vernacular prose, and use of myth, fairy tale, and the extravagant exaggeration characteristic of the tall story. Although Tutuola is a highly imaginative, original writer, his subsequent works have met with a cool critical reception. (See also *CLC,* Vol. 5, and *Contemporary Authors,* Vols. 9-12, rev. ed.)

JOHN V. MURRA

In 1952 the United Society for Christian Literature in London received for publication a manuscript from Lagos, Nigeria, whose author was Amos Tutuola, a messenger in a government office. It was not the kind of material they usually handled; still, they were willing to pass it on. Soon afterward Faber and Faber brought out "The Palm-Wine

Drinkard" to considerable critical acclaim. . . . The work received no such welcome from West African readers. Babasola Johnson, in the weekly *West Africa,* went so far as to say that it "should not have been published at all."

[Like his first, Mr. Tutuola's second book, "My Life in the Bush of Ghosts,"] uses elements and tales of traditional Yoruba folklore; a seven-year-old boy escapes from his village during a slave raid and wanders through the off-limits forest of the Ghosts for twenty-four hair-raising years. His adventures include transformations into a cow that cannot eat grass and into a chief judge in the Ghosts' Assize Court who is a graduate of a Ghost Methodist School; he is sentenced at least twice to be sacrificed and for a while is elevated to godhood and in turn receives sacrifices; he marries two ghost women, one of them a super-lady, who live in Nameless Town. . . .

The images from Western technology which so delighted the literary critics in the "Drinkard" are still here. . . . There are fewer pleasant experiences; the good life occasionally found by the Drinkard as he searches for his palm-wine tapster is almost absent in the "Bush." Christianity and God with a capital G, unmentioned in the first work, provide us here with a striking example of syncretism, the intimate blend of two cultural traditions. (p. 261)

Like any first-class teller of folk tales, Mr. Tutuola has modified and projected while retelling his traditional material. A second reinterpretation took place when he chose to write in English, not Yoruba; the reader who discovers African literature here does so through Tutuola's wonderfully terse, graphic, and personal use of what Dylan Thomas called his "young English." . . . Turns of phrase which so charm the Western reader are frequently literal translations from the Yoruba. He does not hesitate to coin words: the Drinkard was not a drunk—he just drank palm-wine in a serious and purposeful manner; Deads' Town may be a literal translation, but it also seems poetically more appropriate than Town of the Dead.

It is just this poetic use of the English language that facilitates the rejection of Tutuola's work by many West African readers. They are shocked by its crudities, the lack of inhibition, the occasional obscurities; it seems "a long tale in a language we did not understand." To a reader whose excellent English or French is gained at the cost of neglecting his own tongue, mostly in mission schools with their distrust of the pupil's spontaneity and imagination—Shakespeare and the Governor's Annual Report are the proffered models in matters of style—all this recognition for "translating Yoruba ideas in almost the same sequence as they occur to his mind" must indeed be a puzzle and a shock. To clarify the author's "Unreturnable Heaven's Land," one reader proposes "the undiscover'd country from whose bourn no traveler returns."

The rejection, actually, goes deeper than the matter of language. . . . Tutuola's obvious immersion in the mythological past, with its gods, ghosts, wars, sacrifices, and submerged terrors, seems a preoccupation which delays progress; the genre shows "no marks of possible future development" into a modern West African literature. They end by wondering at the reasons why Tutuola's books so delight the outsider. (pp. 261-62)

Here the effects of colonial status on intellectual attitudes can easily be seen. Unfamiliar, because of a colonial education, with the creative role of folklore in the development of [other] literatures, the West African middle class rejects, we hope temporarily, its own rich oral tradition and sees in Tutuola's success only the European's preference for an Africa where savagery is the dominant theme. (p. 262)

John V. Murra, "The Unconscious of a Race," in The Nation *(copyright 1954 by the Nation Associates, Inc.), Vol. 179, No. 13, September 25, 1954, pp. 261-62.*

MARGARET LAURENCE

Amos Tutuola's strangely poetic writing was quick to gain recognition in England and America, but in his own country it was at first widely criticised because of its bizarre use of English and because Tutuola was dealing with a past which many people were trying to forget, a past associated with the old gods and the spirits of forest and village, an ancestral past whose traditions for many of the present generation had lost their powers of reassurance while still retaining some powers of fear and threat. Nowadays Tutuola's work is recognised and admired by a whole generation of more sophisticated Nigerian writers, who no longer feel the need to deny their roots, but Tutuola has little in common with these young intellectuals either. His writing does not belong to any mainstream. It is neither contemporary nor traditional. It is, really, quite timeless and quite individual, although Tutuola has been greatly influenced by his Yoruba background. (p. 126)

He is in a sense an epic poet who as a man belongs nowhere, and this isolation is both his tragedy and his artistic strength. . . .

The Yoruba culture is rich in folk tales, stories of gods and spirits, talking animals, magic charms and powers, people who are transformed into gazelles or fish or birds. Tutuola draws deeply upon the folk tales and myths of his own people, using this material in a way that is strictly his own, sometimes taking snatches of Yoruba tales or characters from Yoruba mythology and recreating them in his own fantastic manner, sometimes combining past and present in such creatures as the Television-Handed Ghostess. He is able to use the Yoruba tales in a variety of ways because they are genuinely his, and often he does not seem to be using them consciously at all. They are simply his frame of reference, the terms in which he naturally tends to think. The tone of Tutuola's writing also resembles that of many Yoruba tales, for it is both humorous and poetic, and it fluctuates between a portrayal of beauty and lightness and a portrayal of grotesque ugliness. . . .

[Whatever] his sources, in his best work Tutuola makes something new from his material. He writes very much out of himself, and his writing stands alone, unrelated to any other Nigerian writing in English. There is a tremendous courage about the man, for he has been able to go on alone, remaining true to an inner sight which perceives both the dazzling multicoloured areas of dream and the appalling forests of nightmare.

Tutuola's first book [*The Palm-Wine Drinkard*] is his masterpiece. It takes the form of an odyssey, a journey into the underworld which the hero undertakes in order to prove himself. It is really a journey of the spirit, in which the hero meets the monster-creations of his own mind, suffers torments, wins victories and finally returns to his own country, able now to rule it because of the wisdom his experiences have given him and because of the power he has gained through the terrors he has overcome. It is, of course, a classic journey, found in the mythologies of all cultures. It has been compared to Orpheus in the underworld, to Bunyan's *Pilgrim's Progress,* to Dante, to the journey of Odysseus. (pp. 127-28)

[*My Life in the Bush of Ghosts*] approaches and in some ways even surpasses *The Palm-Wine Drinkard* in the grotesque quality of its visions, although the work as a whole is not as powerful as the first. 'Bush', to a West African, means the rain-forest or what Europeans and Americans might call the jungle. 'Ghosts' in this book are not the spirits of dead persons, but rather spirits who have never lived as people but have always inhabited their own spirit world which coexists with ours.

The hero is lost from his home and enters the Bush of Ghosts as a boy of seven. He emerges as a man many years later. [The critic] Gerald Moore sees the story as a kind of *rite de passage,* an initiation, and undoubtedly this is so. As well, however, the story is a journey into the depths of the subconscious. Tutuola may not have intended it to be this; indeed, if he had intended it, it probably would not have worked out that way, for this type of exploration has to be done out of necessity, not calculation. The book appears to be a painful setting down of the publicly suppressed areas of the mind. In this fictional guise, the forbidden can be looked at, and the horrifying or appalling side of the self can be brought into the open. The 'self' in this sense means all our selves, for although the forest looks (and is) different to every pair of eyes, it is there in varying shapes and forms for us all. Few are brave enough to look at it, and fewer still to record it.

It is a grim world we are shown here. There is an obsession with pain, flogging, humiliation, torture, excreta. The torments of the hero are feared but also masochistically sought. The image of the mother is an interesting and ambiguous one, for the boy keeps thinking of his own mother with warmth and affection, yet he encounters such repulsive mother-types as the Flash-Eyed Mother, whose entire attention, significantly enough, is taken up with the snarling and evil-looking infant heads which are sprouting all over her body, and who therefore neglects all her other ghost children, including the hero, who has been taken into the community as one of her family. (pp. 132-33)

The deep split in the mind between the old gods and the new is expressed poetically and with great power. Tutuola never in this book actually names the old Yoruba gods—in fact, he hardly ever refers to them as gods at all. The old gods inhabit his writing in the form of spirits and ghosts, and most of these are frightening. . . . The hero of the story fears all these ghosts very much indeed, yet he repeatedly seeks their company. He cannot get away from them. The attitudes to Christianity, as they appear in this book, are mixed, to say the least. The conflicts which are laid bare here are the same conflicts as those described by Achebe in *Things Fall Apart* and *Arrow of God,* but in the work of Tutuola the clash between religions is not being described as such and is perhaps not even recognised as such. It is brought out in quite a different way, in terms of the main character's suffering, a suffering which only if it is viewed very superficially can be believed in as being merely external adventure. The hero puts a yearning faith in the Christian God. He is always saying 'as God is so good—'. At one point he discovers his long-dead cousin in the tenth Town of Ghosts, and finds that the cousin has set up a mission. The mission sign—humorously and yet in a way almost heartbreakingly—reads, THE METHODIST CHURCH OF THE BUSH OF GHOSTS. Rarely has dichotomy been expressed in so few words.

The unacknowledged resentment against Christianity comes out almost with a sense of relief and release, like someone speaking a long-forbidden obscenity in order to break its haunting power. This resentment is perhaps not so very difficult to grasp, for it is directed against the religion which severed several generations of Africans from their own past. It appears in odd forms—sometimes by taking Christian rituals and turning them inside out or upside down. (pp. 133-34)

The old religions of Africa have combined with Christianity in some peculiar ways. The two have also clashed—and clashed tragically—within the individual minds of men. The whole story of this conflict is only now beginning to emerge clearly. A writer such as Achebe deals with it by trying to understand it and perceive it, by re-creating it within the personalities of his characters, characters who are not himself but who exist as themselves. This is the method of the novelist. Tutuola's method is poetic and intuitive. Here we get the conflict raw. Whether or not he means it to be there, it *is* there. (p. 135)

The ending is enigmatic. 'This is what hatred did.' This conclusion does not seem to make sense in the external context, but it has specific meaning if it is viewed as another direct and indeed tragic statement from the inner world. *My Life in the Bush of Ghosts* is the work of someone who has walked in the pit of hell, and who has been courageous enough to open his eyes while he was there. . . .

[*Simbi and the Satyr of the Dark Jungle*] concerns the learning of wisdom through ordeal. It is not as strong a story as either *The Palm-Wine Drinkard* or *My Life in the Bush of Ghosts,* but much of it is written in a sprightly manner which is partly produced by the appearance of more conversation than the previous books contained.

Simbi is Tutuola's only book not written in the first person. He succeeds best with a first-person narration, as though he were able in this way to get inside the personality of the central character and to write with the unfailingly true sound of a human voice.

Simbi is the daughter of a wealthy woman. She is an only child and has been brought up in luxury. She is also naturally gifted, being a lovely girl and having a fine singing voice. But Simbi grows weary of her pleasant life, and longs to experience '. . . the "Poverty" and the "Punishment"'. She prays to know the meaning of poverty and punishment, and her dangerous prayer is quickly answered. (p. 136)

As with so much of Tutuola's work, under the lightness and humour, under the descriptions of enchanted places [in *Simbi*], there lies the continuing theme of pain, dreaded and yet sought. (p. 138)

[*The Brave African Huntress*] is something of a disappointment. It is altogether thinner in texture, not so richly imaginative as his first three books, although there are flashes of the old style—for example, in chapter headings such as The

Animal That Died But His Eyes Still Alive (the heroine prudently salvages the animal's skull with its glowing eyes and uses it as a night light), or in beautifully expressive phrases such as 'Whisperly the king spoke—'. (pp. 138-39)

[Despite] the frequently humorous tone of the surface, the main underlying theme [of *Feather Woman of the Jungle*] is a masochistic one. For the story's hero the goal is to be achieved only through pain and humiliation, suffering which he is compelled to seek, not really for its own sake but in order that the enduring of it may permit the gates to be opened to the desired end. (pp. 145-46)

Amos Tutuola has a way of combining the macabre and the beautiful, the horrifying and the humorous, the familiar and the mysterious. One of the most impressive things about him when he is at his best is the vitality of his writing and the completely unstudied and casual way in which he makes his dramatic effects. (p. 146)

Essentially, however, the themes are dark ones, themes which can in no sense be said to exclude any one of us. . . . [The] magic is never a mock-up, never a sham—it is always the real thing. But if Tutuola's books are for children [as some critics suggest], it is only in the same way that *Gulliver's Travels* was once thought to be.

Tutuola's books are not really novels. They are episodic and they follow the classical lines of the sagas found in all cultures. He writes best when most intuitively and most intensely inward. His forests are certainly and in detail the outer ones but they are, as well, the forests of the mind, where the individual meets and grapples with the creatures of his own imagination. These creatures are aspects of himself, aspects of his response to the world into which he was born, the world to which he must continue to return if he is to live as a man. (pp. 146-47)

Margaret Laurence, "A Twofold Forest: Amos Tutuola," in her Long Drums and Cannons: Nigerian Dramatists and Novelists *(© 1968 by Margaret Laurence; reprinted by permission of Holt, Rinehart and Winston; in Canada by Macmillan, London and Basingstoke), Frederick A. Praeger, Publishers, 1969, pp. 126-47.*

PAUL EDWARDS

[*The Palm-Wine Drinkard*] is more commonly admired for its free-running fancy than for anything that could be called its structure, and apart from its archetypal form of the quest, there might appear to be little evidence of patterning. . . . Indeed, what seems to be a clear instance of the absence of form is the introduction of the tale of the quarrel between earth and heaven into the novel's closing pages. But I suggest that it might be less arbitrary than it appears, and that the episode is given its peculiar prominence as the culmination of a central and repeated image. . . .

I propose to begin my case by referring to Northrop Frye's *Anatomy of Criticism*, particularly to his description of opposed apocalyptic and demonic worlds, imaged characteristically as farm or garden on the one hand, wilderness on the other. (p. 57)

It is clear that these opposed worlds resemble those of the Drinkard. At the start of the tale we learn that he is a kind of farmer, but living complacently in a world of false fertility. . . . Death suddenly enters this false Paradise when first his generous father, and then his skilled tapster die, the two men on whom he has been dependent; nature too now demands her fee, the farm goes to waste; and the Drinkard's vulnerability is defined in social terms as his fair-weather friends desert him. So he enters the wilderness in which he is to stray, searching for Deads' Town, and his journey is to be characterized by a rhythmic movement between, on the one hand, states of terror and distress, and, on the other periods in temporary Edens associated with farming, trees, and another recurrent image of harmony, music and dance.

The Drinkard's powers of endurance and his ability to deal with suffering begin to emerge in his adventures in Death's house and the underworld of the skulls where he wins his wife. (p. 58)

Whether good or evil, the creatures of the bush are unable to move from their own places, but the Drinkard is established as the one who can, indeed must, keep moving. To farm is delightful, but the Drinkard has entered upon the journey of the imagination and must pursue it to its end. (p. 60)

The tale ends with the reconciliation of Heaven and Earth by Water, the three elements . . . into which Drum, Song, and Dance vanished. There does seem to be a shaping imagination at work here of a more complex kind than is usually associated with this tale. The Drinkard has grown, through experience and vision, from a layabout to a man of spiritual powers. Through his vision and knowledge, he is able to serve the land and the men who work it, men like his seven diligent brothers. He has passed through various sufferings without which he could never have experienced the harmonious farm-and-dance life of Wraith-Island, the tree-dance of Faithful-Mother, or the universal dance of Drum, Song, and Dance. In each case, the harmony of song and dance is associated with vegetable life, either in the image of the farm, or that of the tree. And he brings back with him from Deads' Town another image of creation, the egg. Fallen mankind destroys the egg, but the Drinkard's knowledge remains, and it is he who knows how the gods are to be propitiated, and his people ultimately saved.

That something like the pattern described exists in the tale is, I think, unquestionable. . . . [What is striking] is the similarity of so many elements of this work to those of European and Oriental myth, and the discovery which we need to make over and over again, it seems, that in spite of surface differences, men continue to bring up remarkably similar things from the mental underworld. (p. 64)

Paul Edwards, "The Farm and the Wilderness in Tutuola's 'The Palm-Wine Drinkard'" (copyright Paul Edwards; by permission of Hans Zell (Publishers) Limited), in Journal of Commonwealth Literature, *Vol. IX, No. 1, August, 1974, pp. 57-65.*

DAVID ARNASON

The Palm Wine Drinkard burst onto the world literary scene in 1952, and was an immediate and smashing success. This was balanced by Tutuola's cool reception by Nigerian critics, who felt that the quaintness of Tutuola's style was the chief appeal to outsiders, and that he was read with condescension. Most western critics deny that they treat Tutuola condescendingly, and attempt to prove their point by treating Nigerian critics with condescension, mocking their aspirations towards progress and culture.

There is right on both sides. *The Palm Wine Drinkard* is an excellent book and the style is refreshing and interesting. At the same time, it is also a very limited style, and the Nigerians are quite right in pointing out that it is not a model to be held up for young Nigerians to emulate. Nigerians are very sensitive about language. They live in a country in which dozens of languages are spoken and wisely or not, they have chosen English as their official language. This in itself creates other problems. Each speaker brings to bear upon English the stress, rhythm, intonation, sounds and structure of his native tongue. . . . Thus certain features of Tutuola's language, his conversion of adjectives into verbs ("I would jealous him"), the strange time sense created by his adverbial uses of "there", and his special use of conjunctives are not so much inventive as they are natural forms to him. This is not to deny inventiveness to Tutuola, but to point out that some of the criticism raised by his countrymen is not merely unreasonable. . . .

The objection of Tutuola's style is not so much a criticism of *The Palm Wine Drinkard* as a thing in itself, but a criticism of it as a model, and this is an important distinction. It would be a mistake to suggest that the verve and dynamism of Tutuola's style are purely the felicitous result of a marriage of Yoruba and English. If this were so, any partly educated Yoruba writing in English could be expected to produce an equally captivating style, and this is clearly not the case. There is a great deal of inventiveness and intuitive awareness of the possibilities of English in Tutuola's work. . . .

Tutuola is an impressive stylist. . . .

In fact, the elements which lend dynamism and power to Tutuola's style are the same elements which make for power in any more conventional style: a terse economy of means, vivid and concrete language, sure and descriptive detail, and original and imaginative imagery. (p. 56)

[However,] Tutuola succeeds not because of his idiosyncratic English, but in spite of it.

It cannot be denied, of course, that at various points Tutuola's blending of Yoruba sentence structure and English vocabulary produces strikingly powerful and original effects. These are, however, felicitous accidents and should not be used as a gauge of Tutuola's capacity to handle language. His use of the word "drinkard" may indeed be an inspired blending of the English "drinker" and "drunkard" to create a new concept of the man who drinks too much, but to whom may not be applied the pejorative connotations of the world "drunkard". More likely though, it is simply an error resulting from the fact that in spoken Yoruba the vowel sound "u" as in "drunkard" does not exist. Nor are all his singular usages so fortunate. His use of the word "patentee" to refer to those who treat patients in a hospital is unclear and confusing.

The second point on which Western and Nigerian critics tend to disagree is on the nature of Tutuola's talent. At the extremes, some Western critics find a totally inventive talent, creatively discovering universal themes. They draw parallels between Tutuola and such writers as Dante, Spencer, and Bunyan and marvel at such untutored genius. The extreme position of his detractors is that Tutuola has no talent; that his work is for the most part a slavish imitation of [D. O.] Fagunwa, or else a bad retelling of Yoruba folk tales, full of error and unwelcome innovation. . . .

Tutuola did read *Pilgrim's Progress* in 1948, just two years before he wrote *The Palm Wine Drinkard,* and the similarities between the two may thus be presumed less than coincidental. . . . [As] the evidence gathers, it appears that all of the incidents in *The Palm Wine Drinkard* are based on folk tales and myths. . . .

The truth of the matter, I think, lies somewhere in the middle. Tutuola is neither a great and inspired original creator nor a dull and slavish imitator. His is what Joseph Campbell calls a syncretic imagination. It reconciles opposites and creates syntheses. His method is eclectic, drawing from all sources and merging wildly disparate elements into a wholly believable unity. The syncretic imagination functions at every level of Tutuola's art. It is, first of all, apparent in the style. With no apparent difficulty Tutuola combines imagery drawn from a pre-industrial, animistic and magic-based cultural sensibility with imagery drawn from an industrial, monotheistic, and scientific cultural sensibility. . . . [The] pattern of imagery reaches its ultimate point in Tutuola's second book *My Life in The Bush of Ghosts* in which appears a wonderful monster, The Television Handed Ghostess.

The syncretic imagination functions at the level of narrative as well. Dozens of dualities are reconciled in the sweep of the story. The spiritual world and the human world are merged. The hero of the book is a mortal, but he is also "Father of Gods". (p. 57)

At the deepest level operates what Joseph Campbell in *The Masks of God* calls "syncretic monotheism". The monsters, spirits and gods of the bush operate without apparent conflict in a universe in which the Christian God is also apparently present and operative; though by no means to be presumed to have more power than any of the other gods. For example, when the spirits of Unreturnable Heavens Town leave the hero and his wife buried to their necks and prey to the evil whims of children, the Christian God intervenes to save them. . . .

It is Tutuola's ability to synthesize all elements of the African experience into a cohesive form that is his chief claim to genius. *The Palm Wine Drinkard* is not a kind of gothic novel which requires suspension of disbelief so that we can vicariously experience nameless terrors. It creates a believable world in which terror is functional, and in which the monsters are infused with the human elements that make them terrible.

It remains, finally, to discuss the form of the book. It is called a novel, though that seems inappropriate. The story exists outside of the societal web, and most of the judgements we customarily make about novels are simply irrelevant. Judgements about characterization, setting, thematic unity and social relevance are of little importance in discussion of *The Palm Wine Drinkard*. . . .

In fact, *The Palm Wine Drinkard* is a saga. When any preliterate, oral society becomes literate and begins to write out of its own experience, its attempts to transmit the material from the old oral tradition into the new literary mode produce an heroic form that may be broadly called the saga. Roughly equivalent forms have occurred in most cultures that have managed to emerge to the literate level on their own or have managed to escape being completely overwhelmed by another dominating culture.

A comparison of *The Palm Wine Drinkard* with the early Icelandic sagas provides a great number of interesting similarities. The early Icelandic sagas are based on the folk tales and myths of an earlier oral culture, as is *The Palm Wine Drinkard*. The Icelandic saga-writer did not create essentially new material, but transformed the stories of the bardic tradition, giving them his individual shape. It would appear that Tutuola has done just this; like the saga-writer he has relied on a story telling tradition, but has given his own particular treatment to the traditional material. The sagas are picaresque, episodic works, in which the supernatural is operative, and in which the heroes often have magical powers themselves. All of this can be said equally of *The Palm Wine Drinkard*. The heroes of the sagas often encounter dreadful monsters with whom they do battle. . . . The basic pattern of most of the sagas is the form of the quest, and that is the form that Tutuola employs. . . .

The chief difference between *The Palm Wine Drinkard* and other sagas is that they are written in the vernacular languages, while *The Palm Wine Drinkard* is written in the language of the dominant culture. This is a significant fact. . . .

As it is, Tutuola's work remains a fascinating example of the natural evolution of a literature. In other circumstances it might have been the key to a developing literature. Under present circumstances it appears to be a dead end. Tutuola's English has not the resources to serve as a stylistic model for younger writers. His saga form and his folk tale material are unlikely to be used again in anything like the form he uses them. Nigeria is rapidly becoming a modern, industrialized state, and new gods are in the ascendant. (p. 58)

David Arnason, "Amos Tutuola's 'The Palm Wine Drinkard': The Nature of Tutuola's Achievement," in Journal of Canadian Fiction *(reprinted by permission from* Journal of Canadian Fiction, *2050 Mackay St., Montreal, Quebec H3G 2J1, Canada), Vol. III, No. 4, 1975, pp. 56-9.*

CHIKWENYE OKONJO OGUNYEMI

[In *Feather Woman of the Jungle*] Tutuola's raconteur, in accordance with African tradition, is an old man, the typical sage who passes on his experiences and wisdom to the younger generation. He casts a spell on his audience with his palm wine and stories as a "baba alawo" would with his concoctions and incantations. Each story-telling session is preceded by dancing and drinking to help establish a spirit of togetherness. They form part of the ritual. There is the need in the raconteur to be in control, to be in authority, to have power, a need that has driven him to be somewhat repetitive. However, his skill earns him respect and love from his subjects and admiration from the neighboring villages. (p. 20)

In keeping with the oral tradition, Tutuola's hero is a romantic with romantic stories to tell. There are elements of exaggeration in the tales, with characters that are flat rather than rounded. The work is necessarily episodic, limited by the mode of narration and the constraints of a live audience who cannot go on listening indefinitely. To keep interest from flagging, the raconteur has to be inventive. . . . There is also the tendency to be repetitive, to retain the speaking voice. Incorporated into this is the need for the extraordinary in story telling, the need for the uncanny, linking not only man with man, man with nature, but also man with his gods and the unseen world. The spirit that informs *Feather Woman* is thus one of mysticism. (pp. 25-6)

[In] African folk tales, the "good" and the persevering are rewarded while the bad are punished. . . . [In *Feather Woman of the Jungle*] the outer plot is cleverly linked with the inner plot through many reverberations. Consequently, for his fearlessness as a young man in the inner story, Tutuola's hero is rewarded by making material gains and realizing his ambitions in his quest. His career culminates in his inheritance of his village as a kingdom. Again as reward for his skill as a story teller, his reputation spreads to other kingdoms simultaneously with his consolidation of power at home. The evil-doers are appropriately punished with death in the instances of the Feather Woman and the treacherous Queen in the Bush of Quietness. (p. 28)

The African mode of story telling is flexible. . . . [*Feather Woman of the Jungle* can be considered a series of short stories or as a sustained work in the folk novel genre.] But what happens to our appreciation of these stories meant to have been heard but instead read? Reading with the possibility of rereading makes us more critical; it makes the stories sound like larger-than-life fictions. Fortunately the novel is flexible enough to accommodate diverse materials; we can therefore consider . . . [Tutuola's novel as an unconscious experimentation, as an African contribution to the evolving genre of the novel. The strength of the work] is in the African element which imbues the raconteur with an inscrutable power that is not completely submerged by European influence; this power gives the raconteur a hypnotic force so that he can control his audience, with his juju, his goopher, the power of the word. For, in the final analysis, it is the strangeness of Tutuola's English . . . [which distinguishes his novel, and which emphasises his oral quality, his Africanness]. (pp. 28-9)

Chikwenye Okonjo Ogunyemi, "The Africaness of 'The Conjure Woman' and 'Feather Woman of the Jungle'," in Ariel *(copyright © 1977 The Board of Governors The University of Calgary), Vol. 8, No. 2, April, 1977, pp. 17-30.**

V

VITTORINI, Elio 1908-1966

Vittorini was an Italian editor, short story writer, novelist, and critic whose anti-Fascism colored much of his fiction. In *Conversation in Sicily,* however, he transcended the limitations of political fiction to produce his finest work. Vittorini was stylistically influenced by American ficiton; his dialogue, narrative pace, characterizations, and settings reflect a strong indebtedness to Hemingway. (See also *CLC,* Vol. 6, 9, and *Contemporary Authors,* obituary, Vols. 25-28, rev. ed.)

SERGIO J. PACIFICI

[*Diario in pubblico*] is easily another indisputable proof of the vitality, intelligence and range of one of the foremost contemporary Italian men of letters. . . . It is a prime document to understand in depth the socio-political scene of today's Italy, as well as Vittorini's own poetics. In a larger sense, too, it is a history full of valuable observations on the cultural torment endured by a whole generation of Italians brought up under fascism. (p. 95)

These pages . . . contribute substantially to presenting a sharper image than the other, woefully neglected side of this artist's complex personality: that of the critic, the vigorous social and political polemicist, the passionate and sharp raisonneur who comments upon a multitude of crucial issues of his, and any other modern generation. . . .

Diario in pubblico is a kind of spiritual and intellectual autobiography, written without the usual concessions, retractions, revelations of a sensitive artist (say, Gide) who is writing his life for posterity. . . . Vittorini dislikes skirting an issue, no matter how unpopular his point of view may be. He is interested, rather, in presenting a documented history of his growth, as a man and an artist, and I believe it fulfills this task even when it presents views that may seem puzzling or contradictory. (p. 96)

[The] book does have a certain coherence in that the image that emerges out of its pages is that of a man deeply committed to dramatize man's "situation" in our century but also to analyze in the historical (or, as Vittorini would say, the "cultural") context the problems of the world in which he lives. . . . To understand the spirit that dictated *Diario in pubblico* we must go back to something Vittorini wrote in the early thirties: "We must think with our body." And he added, as a corollary: "Intellectualism means to think only with our mind." (p. 97)

From the early stage, Vittorini became increasingly concerned with those issues that obsess him even today: personal freedom, both political and artistic; the relation between life and literature; the impact of society and the ruling régime on man. As in a vast and complex symphony, these are the recurring themes, always clarified, enlarged, considered from a different vantage point. Gradually, as Vittorini has matured, his concepts have become more lucid and his perceptive intellect has eloquently stated that art may never be conceived of as a means to edify the masses, or an instrument to propagandize a particular "political" view of society. (pp. 97-8)

The essays, notes, observations and reflections that are the very flesh and bones of *Diario in pubblico* seem to me to represent a kind of summa of what Vittorini is, ideologically and critically, today; but they are also the "other" means to communicate with his fellow men, to experiment with ideas, to test the validity of certain assumptions and eventually reach a better understanding of at least a measure of that Truth toward which every human being aspires. As one reaches the end of the volume one has the definite feeling that he has traveled all along in the company of a sensitive, "liberal" individual, who knows that while his goal may never be achieved because it lies beyond the possibilities of finite man, he must nevertheless continue—for his sake and for that of mankind. The journey is replete with obstacles of all sorts, and disappointments; and frustrations and enigmas. But it is a thrilling one, well worth our time and effort. (p. 98)

Sergio J. Pacifici, "Understanding Vittorini 'Whole'," in Italian Quarterly *(copyright © 1958 by* Italian Quarterly*), Vol. 1, No. 4, Winter, 1958, pp. 95-8.*

GLAUCO CAMBON

The informed reader who, years hence, in perusing *In Sicily* may bluepencil the obvious derivations in an iterative prose that shows the lesson of Hemingway, of Gertrude Stein, of Sherwood Anderson, of William Saroyan, will easily resist the temptation of dismissing the book as an Americanese pastiche—if he has a fine ear. He will, furthermore, recognize the creaking emphasis in some of the dialogue, in many of the situations, in the painfully constructed allegory; but he will see right away that this clumsiness is honest, that it does not mark just a climactic moment in Italian literary fashions (i.e., the American style after the Paris vogue): that it represents, in short, a significant gesture. The gesture belongs more to ethical and political history than it does to poetry, to be sure. . . . [But in] protesting oppression, organized violence and obscurantism at the outset of World War II Vittorini was speaking as the poet he is, whatever doctrine may have inspired him at the time; and the stratagem of allegory, meant to elude the prying eyes of censors, was not a mere piece of convenient machinery.

For it was, yes, surface doubletalk with a hidden political purpose, a cunning weapon for an *engagé* writer in times of distress; but more than that, and almost in spite of its intrinsic aim, it had something to do with that innocent doubletalk which is the ambiguity of fable. Vittorini may be dear to many, signally those who were his partners in the Italian Underground, because of his commitment to a Marxist ideology which played a basic role in the years of struggle against tyranny, and which he subsequently evolved into a democratic version of socialism precisely with a view to reasserting his opposition to tyranny. . . . Vittorini, however, matters more to us as a fabulist. (pp. 20-1)

The dialectic of conspicuous wealth and pressing poverty, which underlies the motley pageant of politics in twentieth-century Italy, makes for ideological documentarism, *littérature engagée,* that favorite commentary on the dogmas of the Marxist Church Militant. Then literature becomes didactic, a matter of stories with a moral; *In Sicily* largely fits this category. Literature as action, that is. Literature as fable, valid in itself as an act of imaginative knowledge, is what Vittorini gives us at his best. (p. 21)

[Perhaps the counterpoint of dream and the most destitute reality] is a perennial motif of fable, whether sprung anonymously from the humus of folklore or consciously reshaped and even invented by a sophisticated Andersen. In . . . most European fairytales, we have the story of the poor man who finds a treasure by magical means, of the poor boy who marries a princess, of the destitute hero who becomes king, of Cinderella who rises from abject servitude in a spellbound night. Magic, that shortcut to success, is dream, and dream is the riches of the poor. In Vittorini's stories, the poor enter the Kingdom of Heaven, without leaving Mother Earth. This happens because they keep dreaming, and their dream is their innocence, retained or maybe strengthened through the harrowing experience of need. At the same time, the dream is not a flight from reality; the starved family gathered around their dissatisfying supper table in a hovel on the outskirts of Milan, in *The Twilight of the Elephant,* can dream of the wealth of life in the universe while concentrating on an anchovy which would require a second coming of Christ to be rewardingly partaken among so many hungers, and their dying visitor opens their eyes to the value of life as they, *even* they or perhaps *they* above all, have it here and now. Erica, in *The Dark and the Light* . . . , keeps dreaming of "things as they are" as well as of what they might be, and the result is an innocent gratefulness for their existence, for having a world no matter what; the world may mean ownership, competition or oppression beyond the sphere of her astonished innocence, but to her it is miracle. . . . In her poverty, then, she is richer than whoever owns, controls and warps the world around her. Fable is more than mere delusion, in her case; it is a weird revelation of what reality is in its primal, incorrupt state, before men start distorting it with their divisions and appropriations; the utopia some adults revert to in their dreams, or in their conscious efforts to change society for the better.

Abandoned by her parents with her younger brothers, Erica becomes a prostitute, and thus solves the problem of earning a living for all of them. What might have degenerated into the tear-jerking cliché of some nineteenth-century literature becomes, in Vittorini's expert hands, a focused mystery, unsentimentally narrated. . . . [She] keeps her innocence, in a world which denies it. Poverty has deprived her of her parents, of decency, of virginity, but basically it has not degraded her. The writer has no business telling us whether she will keep innocent as she is in the first stage of her new life; he is not interested in giving us the sad story of the soiled lily, nor does he try to copy Dostoevsky's mystical whores. And, while his social implications are unmistakable, since he never resigns to the injustice Erica herself has to accept without understanding it, he keeps the focus on her inner experience, rather than use her for moral purposes of denunciation. The poet, of course, carries the day over the committed ideologist, . . . even if we are aware of the implicit "lesson" that, as long as the many Ericas of the world are allowed to suffer like this, we all share a guilt not even her innocence can atone for. At the same time, as long as there are Ericas in the world at large despite what we do or do not do in their regard, hope remains possible.

Evangelical rhetoric is definitely avoided by Vittorini when, in stressing the self-giving nature of Erica's behavior, he makes it a paradoxical fulfillment. . . . One can read the uncynically cruel fable in the Marxist light of alienation as the conversion of all social and human reality into "wares." One can see in it the existential paradox of innocence *through* experience. One can, finally, remember that both Vittorini's cult of the life force as embodied in the various "elephants" or "garibaldine" or disenchanted "mothers," Lawrentian as it is, and his theme of purity versus and through corruption, of poverty versus "wealth," tend to refine themselves into a dialectic which is Franciscan no less than Marxist. His personal discovery of America, itself a dimension of his dream as it was and is for so many Italian proletarians, itself a fable as he says it is for Saroyan, has fortified him in the poetical exploration of the elemental. Unlike some passages of his other work, the prose I have been sampling from the beginning and the end of *The Dark and the Light* sounds like himself, not like retranslated Hemingway or Faulkner. He owes this to his inner "wealth," stimulated by the earlier shared poverty. (pp. 22-4)

Glauco Cambon, "Elio Vittorini: Between Poverty and Wealth," in Wisconsin Studies in Contemporary Literature *(© 1962,* Wisconsin Studies in Contemporary Literature*), Vol. 3, No. 1, Winter, 1962, pp. 20-4.*

BRUCE MERRY

The surface impression of [*Conversazione in Sicilia*] . . . is a transparently simple plot, with a pervasive air of fable and persistently paradoxical use of language. It was immediately acclaimed a classic and is still considered the purest literary distillation of the anti-fascist experience in Italy. It holds an oblique fascination for Italian writers and intellectuals as a cardinal point which must be accounted for in any attempt to grasp the intellectual directions of modern Italian writing. But is it sufficient to take the book as a political denunciation? And if so, why was it written at such a level of poetic abstraction? The purpose of the present essay is to try to answer these questions by defining the novel as a "polyvalent" text (a technical term borrowed from serial music) and hence to set out four possible "values" which the variables in the text may correspond to, and argue that since no single interpretation can account for the complexities of Vittorini's style, they all merge ultimately in the fourth, which is the level where language is pure literary play. In fact, the "polyvalence" of the plot finds a precise analogue in the multiple (or "polysemous") resources of the style, because the latter refuses to be harnessed to a single meaning, continuously constraining grammar and word-order into unorthodox patterns. (p. 108)

It is true of no modern Italian novel so much as *Conversazione* that the written page presents a continuous "discussion of its own poetics," for the individual effect achieved by a particular episode always tends to be a self-conscious exaggeration of its literary possibilities. Where a page is by intention narrative, it has a marked inclination towards narrative in the grand manner. Descriptive pages present the symptoms of the set piece or the purple passage, and where there is symbolism, Vittorini deploys many of the devices of classical rhetoric to accentuate and pinpoint the lower surfaces of meaning. Thus, the writing in *Conversazione* always follows the logic of its intent and may strike the reader as unrelieved across individual episodes, in spite of its manifest over-all economy. As the sum of a wide range of disparate parts, it recalls a doctrine propounded by the Russian theorist V. Sklovskij on style: "The quality of a style consists in its ability to express the greatest possible number of ideas with the least possible number of words." If a written text achieves its effects by self-conscious striving, that is to say by following the logic of its intent in individual passages rigorously, then it is most likely to expose this intent at every turn of the narrative. This is especially true of *Conversazione*. . . . *Conversazione* [can be accepted] as a traditional descriptive story, since the surface level of the text clearly presents a sensitive evocation of Sicily. At every point in the narrative, Vittorini offers vignettes and sketches of the island, although he was at pains, in the epilogue of the book . . . , to profess a complete lack of authorial concern for the geographical coordinates of his ostensible subject. The style is, in fact, admirably fitted to a straight sequential narrative spaced out with descriptive glimpses of the character's environment: Vittorini employs a matter-of-fact Italian prose built out of nouns and verbs, actions and their agents, with a limpid and transparent syntax that can be mastered so easily that the reader transfers his concentration to the choice of words. The main line train "sped clattering between orange groves and the sea;" the country train "entered a rocky gorge and then a wood of prickly-pear trees." A boy yells out at "the scampering train, and the sun blazed down on his cries, the red flags, and the station-masters' red caps." (pp. 109-10)

Above all, it can be said that Vittorini's descriptions serve to convey a special sense of the privileged childhood landscape, which is an aesthetic temptation for all novelists and consists in recalling a particular scene so acutely that all other scenes seem momentarily irrelevant. . . . However, the primary task of the novelist is to make what he describes seem exceptional at deeper levels than that of the privileged landscape, so that Vittorini is immediately faced by the task of transforming a mass of purely descriptive material into a narrative of universal significance.

The solution is by way of symbols, by turning the actions and images of his characters into symbols of recurring actions and recurring characters, and the identification of this process of universal symbolism in *Conversazione* offers the second main line of approach to the text. . . . [It] is made clear in the text itself that there is a simultaneous co-existence of different layers of significance in the narrative body of *Conversazione*. . . . (p. 111)

A different way of looking at *Conversazione* altogether is to isolate the voices and dialogue which make up so large a part of the book. In this way, they suggest a series of formal choral settings in which the various anti-fascist messages seem to fall into a fugue pattern throughout the narrative, for it is true that the weight of spoken material offers the strongest ground for a straight political reading of the text. (p. 113)

Towards the end of a fugue, the entries often overlap one another and are drawn together in a device called *stretto*, by which the voices tend to sing on top of each other as a means of intensifying excitement. Thus, the last three chapters of *Conversazione* . . . see the five voices of the novel singing their cumulative anti-fascist subject in *stretto* around the fascist war memorial, until the returning first voice of the hero breaks down and weeps with mingled grief and drunkenness. In this way the "abstract furies" of the Fugue Subject receive their concluding contrapuntal expression and the enduring impression of the novel is a chorally constructed political protest.

And yet the salient feature of experimental literary work is often a built-in resistance to the commonsense view that the text must develop its ideas in a coherent way. Ambiguity of intention may well be the factor which produces plurality of effect, so that the pure element of mystification in *Conversazione* can be both serious and gratuitous at once. The plot of the novel may be interpreted as combinative play, and its language as polysemous and unresolved; so that there is, in fact, no particular *signifié*, other than the incantatory power of words. . . . (p. 114)

[The reader] may well wonder if [what appear to be innuendos and] symbols are there consciously at all. If so, do they carry a political or anti-fascist message, and, more important, are they placed among a set of like tools and instruments in order to distract the reader, or to make him wonder whether he is being deliberately distracted?

The actual events of the plot can be examined in the same kind of way, and invite us to form a similar conclusion. The work becomes a "polyvalent" text, in that it acquires a spread of possible meanings, possibly contradictory but no one of them to the exclusion of any other. The juxtaposition of one incident with another may be designed to produce a joke, or a frustrated expectation in the reader, rather than a link in the narrative chain. . . . In this kind of narrative, where a combined motive seems to carry more weight than a psychological reason, the justification for an event is the event itself. The reason need not be plausible or true, but it may be anything from gratuitous and trivial to intentionally misleading. (p. 115)

In sum, language and plot move on two parallel lines in *Conversazione*, polysemous and polyvalent in partnership.

Neither line can be coerced inside any one of the various interpretations which have been outlined above. However, to adopt the fourth and view Vittorini's masterpiece as an extended combinatory *jeu,* a novel in which form completely dominates content, is the interpretation which the text has been seen to insinuate as the key to itself. Beyond its realistic and political dimensions, Vittorini's novel is also a gratuitous literary act inside literature, and with the characteristic paradox of experimental writing presents itself as an anti-novel disguised within the tradition of novel. (pp. 115-16)

Bruce Merry, "Vittorini's Multiple Resources of Style: 'Conversazione in Sicilia'," in MOSAIC: A Journal for the Comparative Study of Literature and Ideas *(copyright © 1972 by the University of Manitoba Press; acknowledgment of previous publication is herewith made), Vol. 5, No. 3 (Spring, 1972), pp. 107-16.*

MARIANNE SHAPIRO

The journey of Silvestro in Vittorini's *Conversazione in Sicilia* follows the lineaments of heroic myth. Its sequence of quest, discovery, and rebirth has been associated with the lives of a string of heroes—Ulysses, Parsifal, Aeneas, Theseus—and may be justly considered to have escaped the narrow confines of topical Italian neorealism. Yet an aspect of the myth relates specifically and poignantly to Italian literature as a whole: this is the general lack of one powerful father-figure as a dynamic element in the plot. . . . [The] persona of the Gran Lombardo in Vittorini's novel . . . [functions] as a crucial link between Silvestro and a transient series of father-figures; and between Vittorini and Dante. (p. 70)

Silvestro's fatherlessness is paralleled by the plight of a society that must be rebegotten. . . . Vittorini stretches an arc from Silvestro to his ancestor (the maternal grandfather), thereby recreating the father. The effect is to trace his matrilineal descent, but also to emphasize the capital value of the Gran Lombardo, who adumbrates this development. Much of the value of *Conversazione in Sicilia* is to be found in its paratactic structure, furthered by a litany of repetitions that challenges the reader to heightened responsibilities. . . . Within the book the Gran Lombardo points past the figure of the insignificant and inadequate father back to a mythicized grandfather. Like the Gran Lombardo, Silvestro's grandfather was of overpowering stature, had three fine daughters . . . , and was the best rider in the countryside. . . . Silvestro wonders if his own father had ever resembled him at all. . . . He seems familiar, yet legendary; Silvestro names him the Gran Lombardo, and other characters take a place subordinate to his and become assimilated to their land and origins. . . . Only the Gran Lombardo's outstanding physical and moral presence . . . can provide an initial definition of individual potentiality or the full powers of a man. (pp. 71-2)

The character of the Gran Lombardo as well as his name points beyond Silvestro's grandfather to the mythicized figure and heroic age of Cacciaguida in Dante's *Paradiso* (XV-XVII), which accords great importance to the theme of paternity. It will be useful for us to examine the striking image whereby Dante in *Par.* XVII 1-3 places himself on a par with an antique figure by comparing himself to Phaeton. The poet chooses the moment of the legend when young Phaeton, having boasted that the Sun was his father, against the taunts of Epaphus went to his mother to demand proof of his parentage. . . . (p. 72)

It is the emotional state which Dante and Phaeton share that forms the basis of comparison. Although mentioned twice in three lines, Phaeton is not called by his name, but is identified first in reference to his mother and then to his father. Not only does Dante feel himself to be both apprehensive and proud in the presence of his glorious ancestor Cacciaguida, like Phaeton when he approched Clymene, but he is perceived to be so by both Beatrice and Cacciaguida. Their perception of him in the role of proud yet questioning son implies that they see themselves as his spiritual parents, with Beatrice forming a parallel to Phaeton's mother. Insofar as she acts as guide and initiator, Beatrice can be said to be a spiritual mother to the pilgrim. In fact, later in the *Paradiso* (*Par.* XXII 1-7) she is explicitly assigned this role.

Dante's question about his place in this spiritual family is answered even before he asks it. However, like Phaeton, Dante seeks proof. He wants to know precisely and definitely how his own life will reflect or test the qualities he has inherited. He therefore asks Cacciaguida to gloss the book of his future, and the response Cacciaguida gives is that of Dante's exile and lonely journey. He will undergo a metaphorical fall, but in his exile he will find the patronage of the *gran Lombardo.*

There is no historicity within the *Paradiso,* and therefore no anomaly exists in the metaphorical union of Cacciaguida and Beatrice. Dante's restructuring of the myth of Phaeton here corresponds to the transformative experience of conversion—a change from one course to another. Through Beatrice's intervention dictated from above Dante abandons the way that leads to death and follows the way that leads to life. This is the pattern of Christian conversion.

We have reason to question the prevalence of Christian forms in *Conversazione in Sicilia.* Yet Silvestro's return to his mother, temporary as indeed Dante's was, brings him too to a longer journey of far-reaching significance which continues past her tutelage. Concezione effects a "spiritual" union with Silvestro's grandfather. And Vittorini's paronomastic title unmistakably points to a conversion whereby *astratti furori* akin to *acedia* are replaced by infused virtues within a context that is both rooted in history and profoundly metahistorical. (pp. 72-3)

The implications of Dante's exile find parallels in Silvestro's: each is, in the words of Curtius on Dante, "the personal corroboration of a disorder in the life of the world." For Silvestro is physically as well as spiritually exiled. . . . (p. 73)

Vittorini preserves the exhortative function of Dante's Cacciaguida and transfers it to the Gran Lombardo. The man of Cacciaguida's prophecy looms in the pilgrim's future, just as Silvestro's grandfather does in the past. We may thus descry two pairs of father-figures: that of Cacciaguida and the *gran Lombardo,* and of Vittorini's *Gran Lombardo* and the mother's father. In both instances, then, the idea of the *Gran Lombardo* is closely linked to another prominent grandfather and compensates for the father's absence. While the spirit of Cacciaguida will give way to the strength of a living man, we might argue that Vittorini's *gran Lombardo* adumbrates a shade. Yet in each case the guiding father-function passes on into a series of figures—in

Dante's *Comedy,* to saints; in *Conversazione in Sicilia,* to Porfirio and Ezechiele, whose allusive names and speech supersede the mother and conclude Silvestro's enlightenment. Three times Silvestro attempts to touch his brother, whose ghost appears to him at its end; three times we are reminded of Dante's presence in the book. Vittorini continues to the end to raise the problem of the boundaries of his novel, which the reader is thereby instructed to conceive multidimensionally through an insistent implication of a community of minds creating it. Both the mythic and the historic dimensions of *Conversazione in Sicilia* are defined by its distant kinship to the *Comedy*. Silvestro's conversation takes place for a specific time in a certain spatial context but reveals itself simultanteously as "a moment in an age-old exchange of talk," compelling an awareness of its unbounded historical potential. Allusive naming is but one means whereby the fundamental link with Dante is established. The character and function of the Gran Lombardo/*nonno* speak directly to their historical antecedents. (pp. 75-6)

Both [Dante's and Vittorini's] pairs of benefactors (one speaking, one silent) confirm the ritual and exemplary value of the journey and give sanction to its quest. And both ultimately make possible the writing of the poem.

Vittorini left evidence that for him Dante provided a revelation of unalterable truths. The composite of Gran Lombardo/*nonno* represents a statement, inside and outside of the book as object, that links it to a defined historical reality. Beyond this statement the connection establishes a suspension between history and myth. Each member evokes an heroic Italy in a stable age linked ultimately through Dante to Fiesole and Rome, an Italic past where arms and letters exist in indissoluble accord. (pp. 76-7)

Marianne Shapiro, "The 'Gran Lombardo': Vittorini and Dante," in Italica, *Vol. 52, No. 1, Spring, 1975, pp. 70-7.*

ISABEL QUIGLY

It has taken twenty-six years for Elio Vittorini's central work [*Women of Messina*] to reach us in translation; years that have turned a tract for the post-war times into a document of historical interest, and have confirmed its predictions, justified its ironies, fulfilled at least some of its economic and social prophecies. Yet it keeps much of its power and even a certain glory. Its interest is now more aesthetic, less social, than it was in its early days; its qualities appear in its structure and nature as a novel rather than in its political message; its utopianism has been, if not silenced, at least softened with time, disappointment and clear-sightedness. Vittorini himself, when he died nine years ago, a luminous figure on the Italian literary scene rather than a great name outside it, had lost much of the ardour with which he first wrote it. Indeed, for years he kept returning to the original, correcting and rewriting it. . . .

In the original, *Women of Messina* is difficult for an outsider, being full, like most of Vittorini's writing, of nicknames and elisions, and of the ruminative, repetitive confusion of Italian speech when used by simple people in a choral, back-and-forth sort of way. Wave-like and incantatory, it repeats itself, shifts into patterns and moves collectively in certain directions, orchestrated by sympathy or antipathy, using words to say something beyond their usual meaning, and mood to express emotion. . . .

The inner life of people without much verbal facility but with a powerful ability to communicate emotionally, to establish contacts in what seems an almost magnetic fashion with like-minded—or rather, like-spirited—others, is something Vittorini tried passionately to put across. But in spite of moments of intuition, sudden flashes that reveal a man, a moment or a feeling with almost painful exactness, his effects are really cumulative. As *Women of Messina* goes ahead it becomes denser, the sporadic talk becomes clearer, and its parts are drawn together to make a statement—Vittorini's own. . . .

Vittorini's political utopianism may seem a long way from us now but his broad economic ideas, in their simplicity and even in what now seems their workability, are much closer. What would he have made of the present cult of self-sufficiency, of woodsmoke in place of bottled gas and pan pipes instead of juke-box boogiewoogie? Things have, in a sense, swung his way but one cannot tell if this sense would be his, were he still here to tell us.

Isabel Quigly, "Simple Solutions," in The Times Literary Supplement *(© Times Newspapers Ltd. (London) 1975; reproduced from* The Times Literary Supplement *by permission), No. 3827, July 18, 1975, p. 793.*

NEIL HEPBURN

Women of Messina is [a] fascinating oddity. . . . It is a strange book to appear in 1975, written in a style, all too faithfully rendered in the English, based closely on the prewar Hemingway whom Elio Vittorini so much admired.

This makes it quite difficult to read even if, as one is assured, it authentically expresses the inarticulacies of Italian peasant communication. But it is also a curiously appropriate tract for our times, for it recounts the trials and vicissitudes of a commune dedicated to, or at least based on, self-sufficiency and mutual support. . . .

[The] outside world intrudes: the scorn of the city-dwellers for the peasant community's lack of information and modern comforts is enough to foment discontent and, soon, decay. These days, the temptations are all the other way; but that does not invalidate the message, or diminish the solid if rather low-key satisfaction to be had from the book.

Neil Hepburn, "Poisoned Man," in The Listener *(© British Broadcasting Corp. 1975; reprinted by permission of Neil Hepburn), Vol. 94, No. 2420, August 21, 1975, p. 254.**

W

WALCOTT, Derek 1930-

Walcott is a West Indian poet and playwright. With the publication in 1962 of *In a Green Night,* he was hailed as the first outstanding Caribbean poet. A recurring theme in Walcott's verse is the isolation of man, and in particular the isolation of the artist. (See also *CLC,* Vols. 2, 4, 9, and *Contemporary Authors,* Vols. 89-92.)

JAMES DICKEY

Derek Walcott is a Negro from the Caribbean, and most of his poems are related to this fact. . . . Mr. Walcott's Africa obsesses him, and in several fine poems [in "Selected Poems"] it undergoes a powerful and painful transmutation into symbolic ground, the better known for having never been seen. "How can I turn from Africa and live?" the poet asks, but live he does, walking through his Antillean world and speaking with anger and imagination of what he sees.

One is left, finally, with a complex, troubling sense of the Caribbean Islands, their reality and unreality, their "filth and foam," their curious and fateful role as the ex-slave's place of dislocation and now, strangely—and often wonderfully—his spectacular home ground. And Mr. Walcott's book, doubly welcome in a time of timidity and correctness, is very much there as well.

James Dickey, "Different Voices, Different Tones," in The New York Times Book Review *(© 1964 by The New York Times Company; reprinted by permission), September 13, 1964, p. 44.**

WILLIAM LOGAN

"That sail which leans on light, / tired of islands, / a schooner beating up the Caribbean // for home" [from *Sea Grapes*] indicates the extraordinary acuity of vision under Derek Walcott's control, an acuity that combines terrifying precision with fresh metaphorical invention. . . . Sight, our frailest sense, most easily detects the decay of the world. . . . To confront us with the seen, Walcott reveals the numinous force of the tawdry, the cheap, the broken-down. Everywhere his metaphors pull the world to themselves: "Desolate lemons, hold / tight, in your bowl of earth, / the light to your bitter flesh". Only things seen exactly, not in the right light or the wrong light, but in a manner that quickens them, can rise from the page, neither mirage nor miracle. Walcott, ever interested in the intimate dependency of things, outlines the local gravity that arranges objects about an object:

> The chapel, as the pivot of this valley,
> round which whatever is rooted loosely turns—
> men, women, ditches, the revolving fields
> of bananas, the secondary roads—
> draws all to it, to the altar
> and the massive altarpiece . . .

It should not surprise that visual and religious power are related; all our religions are based on optical transactions, the supernatural made natural, and seen.

Walcott's locus, though he strays to New York's Chelsea Hotel, and flies to Los Angeles, is the Caribbean. . . . When he writes of poets and poetry, it is with a vigor and freshness that overcome their limitations as subjects—usually we find them choices of self-indulgence or narrowness of view. (pp. 228-29)

So many of his metaphors are of light, it is no wonder that Walcott's torture is Promethean ("we were all netted to one rock / by vines of iron, our livers / picked by corbeaux and condors / in the New World"). Titanic talent embitters, because it can perceive its limitations. It is just that embittered note, that arrogance that flaws the music of these poems, that recovers from the classical and the beautiful the profoundly human. There is no poem here that does not repay re-reading. An ear as perfectly tuned to language as Walcott's is uncommon. His occasional rhyme is muted; it exerts only a slight pull at the lines, and controls their tides. . . . [If] there is magic in language, it is in such poems as these, which wed intense feeling, in both elegy and self-dissection, to complex tone and sound. Walcott is one of a dozen or so poets writing in English who deserve constant and informed attention. (p. 229)

William Logan, "Language against Fear," in Poetry *(© 1977 by The Modern Poetry Association; reprinted by permission of the Editor of* Poetry*), Vol. CXXX, No. 4, July, 1977, pp. 221-29.**

VALERIE TRUEBLOOD

The West Indian poet Derek Walcott published his first book of poetry in 1949, when he was still in his teens. His second, *In a Green Night,* came out in 1962, and since that time he has given us five more (as well as numerous plays) and a world. "World" has lost its punch from being applied to the districts of too many writers; I wish it could be reclaimed for Walcott's poetry, which keeps an axis and has size, and sometimes has a grand, planetary movement carrying the movement on its surface. When I read *The Gulf* I thought of the three-year-old next door who called the white end-papers of his book "sky". This very largeness, of subject and of feeling, has seemed a flaw to some critics, and it is true that Walcott's poems run the risk of the impersonal and the rhetorical. It seems to me they defeat these enemies and in doing so many of them move up and away from the common run of poems and close to the best ones.

Of course, affinity with the best can be seen as a flaw, when much poetry is code, or tender hallooing to the self. Walcott is a balanced, meditative poet; he regards, thinks, looks for resolution, blames angrily but specifically, and does not single himself out as the last sane man in bedlam, nor yet as the most burdened, the prisoner or the victim. First and last he praises. He makes his reader work, but what we find out is something more than how complex he is. . . .

[When Walcott] looks at Nature it doesn't come apart into components, it enlarges, and includes him. The heat of the "unsubtle, unequivocal sun" comes down on all confusion and sometimes "the wind smells of salt / and a certain breeze lifts / the sprigs of the coralita / as if, like us, / lifting our heads, at our happiest, / it too smells the freshness of life." In "Sainte Lucie", the long poem at the center of *Sea Grapes,* the secret "for which the dolphins kept diving / that should have rounded the day" seems to be reality, the "something always being missed" that eludes him until he finds it by means of the poem.

Sea Grapes starts on an island and goes everywhere, always coming back, as Walcott has done, to islands. Many of his themes sound in the title poem . . . the wanderer, home, "the ancient war between obsession and responsibility", the possible consolation of art. . . .

He has absorbed so many influences that picking them out of his poetry is like saying aha, baking powder! when you taste a cake. If the image of people as harvest in "The Bright Field" "derives" from Auden's "As I Walked out one Evening" it also derives from the Bible and from collective perception. . . . His alternating anger and pacifism have their roots in Caribbean life and in the traits and gifts that make him a poet. His struggle with his history and circumstances is part of the struggle to be truthful as well as to be ready for signal moments like the one in "The Bright Field", of release from history. (p. 7)

His political poems are notable for their lack of satisfaction and their sense of responsibility. There is no poet sitting in them with all the right ideas. Still, some of them have such authority that it seems there must be self-righteousness too, lurking somewhere; there isn't. . . .

Walcott has been criticized at home for not making the break with the great tradition of English literature and writing in "the language of the tribe". He has written and talked about this subject; he knows the times "a bush would turn in the wind / with a toothless giggle, / and certain roots refused English". His way is to find what we didn't know was there is English, while keeping its excellences. Because his mood is often one of deep chagrin, even despair, it may be his readers have been waiting for the mood to turn to rage, and for the language to become un-beautiful. The rage was there all along for the looking; it is tougher now, in poems like "The Lost Federation" and "Parades, Parades", and the language has been pared down but it still has its abundance. . . .

The long autobiographical poem *Another Life* followed the lonely, fiery work of *The Gulf,* and in it Walcott explored his past and his culture, trying to "begin again, from what we have always known, nothing". That "nothing" is humble indeed, coming at the end of a book that has longed so hard to know, and known so much. . . . The distance between Walcott and the child and youth of *Another Life* is implied in the title, yet he is re-established (on another island, Trinidad) in the world he left, and a sense of the power he has drawn from his home pervades his work. . . .

The wryness of Naipaul, the stinging, comical irony of Lamming, say, describing the war coming to Barbados in his childhood, are missing from this poem, which attempts something different, the evocation of a paradise. But all is not sweetness: the child's innocence is mixed with presentiments of treachery, and his street in paradise contains an "alphabet of the emaciated." . . . (p. 8)

Walcott is known as a poet of finish and control, one so controlled that he can dispense with the convention for understatement. Yet one of the interesting things about his poetry is its occasional abandon, when he is suddenly speaking up very emotionally or with a particular guileless susceptibility. You don't expect, after the first ten pages of *Sea Grapes,* to arrive at "The Cloud", which is about Eden. In it a cloud is passing over the first couple after their lovemaking, and the last line is "and, as it moved, he named it Tenderness". This kind of line, with its capital letter and its woozy hopefulness, is an example of the passivity that can sometimes come over Walcott. It has a funny charm. There are examples of it throughout his work, and sometimes a whole poem is conducted in this mood—a kind of innocence. . . .

"Oddjob, a Bull Terrier" might not have been allowed in by a younger poet. It is in a special English tradition of animal poems. . . . "Oddjob" is an elegy. The dog's silence is one of its mysteries—and its death that leaves more silence. The poet looks for a reason for his disproportionate grief and finds only that "You prepare for one sorrow / but another comes", and that love can't be put anywhere safe from this silence: "it is the one love, it is the same, / and it is blest / deepest by loss".

Walcott's poems are inhabited by birds, which are what snow was for Delmore Schwartz. When they appear everything pauses. Pigeons, hawks, geese, herons, crows, pelicans—large homely birds without much song that do one thing, fly. When they fly over we should look down, at what they are leaving. Sometimes they officiate, blessing something going on below, or they compensate, rising to counteract the earthward pull of the human events, or . . . they simply lift off and fly and that is their comment. . . .

His pleasure in the emblematic results in one odd kind of personal poem: the shy one. He likes to show a feeling or an idea for a minute and then move it out of the way before we're tired of it, sometimes before we're sure what it is. "The Fist" and "Endings" in *Sea Grapes* do this. . . .

He is not always lyrical. Sometimes he sees in "some grey monochrome, much like this metre". Or the lyrical must be fought down: "Haven't you sworn off such poems for this year, / and no more on the moon?" . . . He is prey to melancholy. . . . (p. 9)

His descriptive language is sometimes an old one. "The wind, wave-muscled, kept its steady mowing" could come out of Virgil, but "so there are little wires of music / some marron up in the hills, by Aux Lyons, / some christening" could only have come from this island poet, with "candelabra of cocoa" and "the lost, lost valleys / of sugar, the bus-rides", and "when the morning sunlight / shivered with malaria, / and the night sea grew tepid / with weeds, like a bush-bath". . . . Just when you are thinking a particular poem is the best you reread the elegy "The Wind in the Dooryard", or the age-poems, or "The Bridge", or the deceptively slumbrous "Midsummer, England." . . . (pp. 9-10)

When you come to the end of "Sainte Lucie", the central poem of *Sea Grapes,* you turn back to the beginning to see how you arrived at the feeling of grace that closes it. . . . [This] is Walcott's Eden, where the snake may be heavenly too, and the faith spoken of is nearly pantheism, close in spirit to Whitman's "And will never be any more perfection than there is now". (p. 10)

Valerie Trueblood, "On Derek Walcott," in The American Poetry Review *(copyright © 1978 by World Poetry, Inc.; reprinted by permission of Valerie Trueblood), Vol. 7, No. 3, June, 1978, pp. 7-10.*

BENJAMIN DeMOTT

Derek Walcott's superb new collection ["The Star-Apple Kingdom"] is described by its publishers as an "odyssey," and justly. The book opens with a long narrative about a poor mulatto sailor in flight northward from Trinidad, closes with the title poem, which dramatizes revolutionary movements of mind and feeling in Jamaica, and includes several shorter pieces set in island villages in St. Croix and elsewhere. The only items remote from the Caribbean circuit are a salute to Joseph Brodsky and a memorial to Robert Lowell.

The chief preoccupation, though, isn't peregrination, but power—or rather power and its undoings, actual and imagined, temporary and permanent. And contemporary political realities—the developed nations versus the third world —are frequently in sight. . . .

The exploitative masters who populate these poems are a various lot—slave-ship captains and kingpin admirals, as well as capitalist tycoons and representatives of the classic 19th-century imperialist cultures. . . . And the causes of the masters' undoings are as various as the characters themselves. (p. 11)

[Throughout] "The Star-Apple Kingdom," the impression is of a subject known to its marrow, explored in microcosm and macrocosm, past and present, both for its political bearings and for the light it casts on the moral development of our kind. . . .

It is scripture nowadays that political poetry is almost invariably smutched by highmindedness, phony commitment and detachable sentiment. But "The Star-Apple Kingdom" seems to me utterly free of such pollutions. In skies this high, with contexts of thought and feeling this rich, self-righteousness is a flea—it wouldn't be noticed if it were there. Nor does the poet's embattlement ever come across as a matter of contentious opinion; it is first of all a charge on the language, a stirring muscularity in the verse. Walcott's struggle with the dominating mad masters who pack it in in these poems packs his line with fury. A ceaseless energy conversion is in process, seemingly—larger-than-life physical force becoming verbal force and producing in the end verse which, while densely particularized and personally accented, is also spacious as a tide, irresistible, Elizabethan.

And, far more important than any of this, the poet's conception of himself as spokesman is accompanied by an ability to imagine believably comprehensive voices, tuned to bottom dog and visionary alike. . . .

"The Star-Apple Kingdom" marks . . . the return, after an absence, of a moving public speech to poetry in English. And that places it with the headiest and rarest kinds of poetic experience—fruitful to people who practice the art and to all the rest of us, too. (p. 30)

Benjamin DeMott, "Poems of Caribbean Wounds," in The New York Times Book Review *(© 1979 by The New York Times Company; reprinted by permission), May 13, 1979, pp. 11, 30.*

G. E. MURRAY

In the past decade, Derek Walcott has established himself as one of the very best English poets. *The Star-Apple Kingdom* enhances that reputation.

Walcott's special strength . . . is in the narrative, which depends on an accumulation of effects. Shifting from island patois to burlap idiom to eloquent statement, Walcott follows the miracles of the Caribbean and other "forlorn stations," achieving a respect for and harmony with nature. Even when he means to be strident, as with his description of a mysterious woman as "a black umbrella blown inside out / by the wind of revolution," he assumes a classical stance, Elizabethan airs. Not that archaism or direct influence are involved. Rather a particular skill and emotion has survived the centuries and found in Walcott an exceptional modern-day host.

G. E. Murray, "Six Poets," in The Nation *(copyright 1979 by the Nation Associates, Inc.), Vol. 228, No. 19, May 19, 1979, pp. 578, 580.**

JOHN SIMON

[*Remembrance*] is typical poet's theater. Using the hoary framing device of the interview, it has A. P. Jordan, an aging schoolteacher, relive episodes from his past. Most of these focus on two set-pieces (probably short stories by Walcott) about an untalented painter son and an interracial romance of Jordan's. . . . Despite an occasional felicitous turn of phrase, this is all choppy, fragmented going, lacking character development or true propulsive energy—it would do as well or better as declamation from a dais. . . . This is a play that only buffs of poetry readings could love. (p. 78)

John Simon, "Folie à deux," in New York *Magazine (copyright © 1979 by News Group Publications, Inc.; reprinted with the permission of* New York *Magazine), Vol. 12, No. 21, May 21, 1979, pp. 76-8.**

EDITH OLIVER

A retired Trinidadian teacher, Albert Jordan, in Port of Spain, is the hero of Derek Walcott's "Remembrance." . . . He is a sardonic, humorous old man, bored and fed up, an "anachronism" in independent Trinidad, his head (and heart) crammed with English poetry, and still grief-stricken at the death of his elder son in a riot years before, when a British policeman's gun went off accidentally. A black man unable to feel a part of the black world, Jordan is yet too wise to feel at home in the British tradition. (p. 105)

"Remembrance" is a loosely constructed play (and none the worse for that), slowing and darkening as it proceeds. Its chief pleasures lie in its details and its lines. Mr. Walcott is a poet, and his writing is of a quality we seldom hear in the theatre. (p. 106)

Edith Oliver, "Displaced Person," in The New Yorker *(© 1979 by The New Yorker Magazine, Inc.), Vol. LV, No. 14, May 21, 1979, pp. 105-06.*

SELDEN RODMAN

Since the death of Robert Lowell, there has been no poet writing in English who combines vernacular and the grand manner so successfully as Derek Walcott. . . . What Shakespeare did without any strain, modern poets like Lowell, Walcott, and Neruda do with heroic effort, and the resulting styles are not always as easy to follow as these poets with a passion to communicate must have hoped. In the first and longest of the poems in [*The Star-Apple Kingdom*], for example, Walcott uses a device that doesn't work—speaking through the tongue of a protagonist whose bad grammar (in dialect) is a jarring counterpoint to his high-flown rhetoric. . . . [In] the rest of the poems there is no such tonal switching, no gap between brutal content and stylistic sublimity, as Walcott unfurls his anti-colonialist flag. . . .

Selden Rodman, "Books in Brief: 'The Star-Apple Kingdom'," in National Review *(© National Review, Inc., 1979; 150 East 35th St., New York, NY 10016), Vol. XXXI, No. 21, May 25, 1979, p. 694.*

ROBERT MAZZOCCO

Derek Walcott has both a seafarer's resourcefulness, appropriate to a West Indian, and a moralist's eye for character and commitment. In this powerful new book [*The Star-Apple Kingdom*] he mediates again the "ancient war between obsession and responsibility" or reflects on the current of history as it afflicts the forfeited beauty of his troubled Antillean world. "The sea is History," he says in one poem, and presents a panoply of Genesis and Exodus and Babylonian Captivity through images of the ocean continually "turning blank pages / looking for History."

And in *The Star-Apple Kingdom* that search for history remains a constant theme. . . .

Dislocation, both emotional and historical, is of course a natural part of the Walcott strategy. And no more so than in one of the new book's most successful pieces, the long opening poem, "The Schooner *Flight*," a threnody of conflict and survival during a bedeviled Caribbean voyage, set in the idiom of a knockabout Trinidadian sailor. . . . A dramatic monologue in bold iambs, it is unique, I think, to contemporary verse, reminiscent of some of the tales of Conrad, *Youth* and *Typhoon*, in particular, and of Peter Matthiessen's *Far Tortuga*—and here and there on a par with them. The sailor's voice, despite occasional awkwardness in colloquial expression, is nevertheless strikingly modulated, alternately roughened and grand, unassuming in its ironies, its appraisal of "the white man" and "the nigger":

> The first chain my hands and apologize, "History";
> the next said I wasn't black enough for their pride. . . .

Conrad is the memorialist of the colonial experience, sees in its triumph its own defeat; this gives his work its magnificent "sense of finality." . . .

Walcott's position as a "Third World" poet, an exemplar of the neocolonial experience, is culturally more difficult—hence more ambiguous. He learned the drama of his situation early enough, defining himself as both the artist educated in the "English tongue I love," . . . and as the native who is mute, whose tale he will tell. But most of *In a Green Night: Poems 1948-60* seemed potent largely as travelogue, even the vatic or visionary strains in bondage to the guile of local color. It was only much later, when he was perhaps following the example of Lowell, opening himself to existential or confessional motifs, the quarrels of public and private life, the burning of the city of Castries or the Biafran invasion, that his negotiations with reality began—first with *The Gulf* in 1970, then continuing through the autobiographical *Another Life* of 1973 and *Sea Grapes* of 1976. In these works, Walcott's own frustrated sense of tribal culture, the lure of the primitive, his debates with Sartrean concepts of "bourgeois culture" or "revolutionary culture," created poems of great individual merit—"Frederiksted Nights," "Sainte Lucie," "Negatives." Yet others were somehow beset with a fugitive or assaultive air.

What's notable, though, about much of *The Star-Apple Kingdom* is its ecumenical balance. Speech is still touchstone, but no longer so declamatory, no longer seduced by the epical. The old nagging, inventive anger has become the simpler, blunter "anger of love." . . .

Walcott has found an almost spontaneous way of speaking about History or "the pain of history words contain," as if it were the hero or anti-hero of his world. Often he seems less a witness to the times, a chronicler of upheavals and renewals, than to the landscapes and seascapes themselves over which emerge the faces of generations, or reveries of childhood in his "star-apple kingdom" that is now "a tree of grenades," or the travail of the sea that can bring its own sort of balm. . . .

Of course throughout his career Walcott's leitmotif has always been the natural embrace of adversity—that, and a certain nobility of spirit or elevation of tone. It is not for nothing that the flights of birds—the pelicans and men-o'-war and buzzards—form a familiar presence in his panoramas. I did not much care for his early work. Then the "nobility" seemed too ceremonious or portentous, ultimately an affectation. But happily Walcott is no longer a *grand seigneur* of the tropics. Most of the poems are buoyant with fact, grim with experience; yet also salutary, I think even celebratory in the older Walcott's sardonic way. He is a poet who is now in his late forties, and even in what he elsewhere calls "the bleak modesty of middle age" there is every reason to believe he is at the threshold of his best work.

Robert Mazzocco, "Embracing Adversity," in The New York Review of Books *(reprinted with permission from* The New York Review of Books; *copyright © 1979 Nyrev, Inc.), Vol. XXVI, No. 9, May 31, 1979, p. 34.*

* * *

WALKER, David Harry 1911-

Walker is a Scottish-born Canadian novelist, short story writer, and author of children's books. A versatile and prolific writer, he is best known for adventure novels with fast-paced plots. Walker has drawn from his diverse personal experience, setting his novels in Scotland, Germany, India, and Canada. His novel *The Pillar* is based on the five years he spent in a German prison camp during World War II. (See also *Contemporary Authors,* Vols. 1-4, rev. ed., and *Something about the Author,* Vol. 8.)

MARTIN LEVIN

The instrument of annihilation in this doomsday novel ["The Lord's Pink Ocean"] is no longer the Bomb but the Ecology. David Walker fancies a blight of pink algae smothering the planet Earth, save for spots in Greenland, Siberia and a few isolated hideouts.

One of these oases is a Canadian valley giving shelter to a black and a white family, imperfectly integrated, but ready to join forces against any intruder who threatens their noble savagery. This calls for the rubbing out of stray missionaries or potential world leaders who happen to stop by and it even leads to a bit of parricide. Mr. Walker is anti-technology, pro-state-of-nature and an engaging storyteller.

Martin Levin, "Fiction: 'The Lord's Pink Ocean'," in The New York Times Book Review *(© 1972 by The New York Times Company; reprinted by permission), August 20, 1972, p. 26.*

NEIL MILLAR

"Black Dougal" announces itself as "a novel that proves crime pays." It proves nothing of the sort—although it may help, in a small way, to increase the crime rate.

But it does show how the corset of popularity can limit a genuine talent. Mr. Walker could give us far better things than this.

The writing is discreet, the touch light, the tension sustained. The story moves along. But it's a yarn for mature-age schoolboys who ought to know better. The plot is so loose that the author's talent falls right through it.

Nevertheless, the talent is still visible, like a stored garden bulb. All it needs is a better plot to flower it.

Neil Millar, "Nature," in The Christian Science Monitor *(reprinted by permission from* The Christian Science Monitor; *© 1974 The Christian Science Publishing Society; all rights reserved), February 13, 1974, p. F5.*

ALLAN MASSIE

Mr Walker brings the adventure novel back to private life [with *Ash*]. It is good to find that it is not necessary to shoot presidents or topple governments, ravage Africa, rob Fort Knox or lay negresses to generate excitement: that a simple chase in which man is both quarry and hunter is enough. The device of the parallel plot of Ash's novel might seem out of place, rather too literary; the more so as his involvement in that book intertwines with and acts upon the course of events. It does not come out like that, however, because it is well handled; proving once again that you can get away with what you can bring off.

Allan Massie, "A Bonny Fighter," in The Times Literary Supplement *(© Times Newspapers Ltd. (London) 1976; reproduced from* The Times Literary Supplement *by permission), No. 3,869, May 7, 1976, p. 561.*

MARTIN LEVIN

Nigel Ash is a hot tempered ex-flier, ex-smuggler, ex-black sheep—holed up in the North Woods to get in touch with himself. This is the kind of ruminative but venturesome hero whom David Walker knows how to put into action exceedingly well. In a log cabin owned by his banker brother, Ash tries to exorcise his past by transmuting it into a novel, but reality keeps interfering with regeneration. . . . An encounter with a couple of vicious poachers leads to violence and to a chase in which Mr. Walker gets everything together, past and present, in the fortifying atmosphere of the great outdoors.

Martin Levin, "Fiction: 'Ash'," in The New York Times Book Review *(© 1976 by The New York Times Company; reprinted by permission), June 20, 1976, p. 32.*

ROBIN WINKS

Walker was a good Canadian regional writer, and his Maritime Provinces were always convincing. Ever since *Winter of Madness* and *Cab-Intersec,* Walker has been writing like a parody of Ian Fleming crossed with Eric Ambler, and the latest, *Ash,* is a parody of himself. Almost literally so, in that Nigel Ash, "a traveler alone," a man who is driven "to defy the conventions and laws of society" (to be fair, these oldies but goodies are part of the dust jacket copy, and Walker may never have been given a chance to veto them), is writing a novel about a man who, having killed, is pursued through the Scottish Highlands, precisely the subject of Walker's own first novel, *The Storm and the Silence.* Now Ash is also pursued, in New Brunswick. If all of this also sounds like a pastiche from John Buchan, Walker leaves no doubt, for crucial action takes place at Huntingtower. The problem is, the book is crowded with conversation, and Buchan's perception that fear arises best from an empty and silent landscape seems to be lacking. (pp. 29-30)

Robin Winks, "Robin Winks on Mysteries," in The New Republic *(reprinted by permission of* The New Republic; *© 1976 The New Republic, Inc.), Vol. 174, No. 26, June 26, 1976, pp. 29-30.**

* * *

WARNER, Francis 1937-

Warner, a British poet, dramatist, and editor, writes traditional English verse, incorporating into his work standard elements of style as used by Shakespeare, Swinburne, and Spenser. (See also *Contemporary Authors,* Vols. 53-56.)

[Few] will trouble to work out the symbolism because, in [*Lying Figures* and *Maguettes*], Mr Warner shows himself to be without even the most basic dramatic gifts. He has almost invented a new genre—the Theatre of the Unspeakable. Gonad, for example, is not only the male reproductive system, but also, to judge from this sentence, a German refugee: "What age do you think is my wife?" Other unsayable lines include, "Well! I too can play games, and with who better than his boss. Guppy." And this: "Like used soap in an uncleaned out hotel." And this: "Flattery succeeds, not because we are taken in, but while disclaiming it as implausible with our minds, we welcome it with our emotions." Neatly put that. . . . And, finally, this: "You have left me high and dry when I most needed you, you, despicable coward!" Thunder outside the French windows.

"Clashing Symbols," in The Times Literary Supplement *(©Times Newspapers Ltd. (London) 1973; reproduced from* The Times Literary Supplement *by permission), No. 3708, March 30, 1973, p. 354.*

[*Meeting Ends: a Play*] is selfconsciously modern, poetically overweight, heavily and obscurely symbolic, and studded with remote literary allusions; but at the same time it is full of banalities, coarse—as well as recondite—puns, gossipy anecdotes, eroticism, and nudity. The characters seem mostly to declaim to the audience in paradoxes and Wildean inverted aphorisms, now and then reaching a climax in long, ranting monologues. . . .

"Language and Literature: 'Meeting Ends: A Play'," in Choice *(copyright © 1975 by American Library Association), Vol. 12, No. 2, April, 1975, p. 225.*

JOHN COLEBY

Francis Warner's *Killing Time* is the final part of his *Requiem* trilogy. This expensive paperback is covered with quotes which pre-empt critical cliché; this I deplore not just because I am now obliged to describe the work in plain language but also because complex hyperbole is more likely to frighten off potential readers than to attract them. If . . . they can overcome the shock of the price and the horror of the pseudsy blurb they will find that a clever man with a fertile imagination has created a theatrical and impressionist work about why we fight and what happens when we do. He has set it in the human brain with ingenious parallels and references—including calling characters Squaloid, Phagocyte and Quark. He writes rather fancy dialogue which swings from the poetic via some awful jokes to the pompous. The play is above all written for performance; clever it may be, and difficult it would be to stage, but it should reward the effort. Nevertheless it is not for faint-hearts or the squeamish. . . . Those who would commit themselves to a serious, absorbing and original piece of theatre could do worse than consider this one. (p. 70)

John Coleby, "Plays in Print: 'Killing Time'," in Drama, *No. 123, Winter, 1976, pp. 70-3.*

* * *

WEISS, Theodore 1916-

Weiss is an American poet, critic, and editor. In opposition to the current popularity of the loose confessional style of poetry, Weiss has primarily written long, carefully constructed narrative poems. He is most noted for his "Gunsight," a narrative poem described by some critics as the best long poem since William Carlos Williams's "Paterson." (See also *CLC*, Vols. 3, 8, and *Contemporary Authors*, Vols. 9-12, rev. ed.)

REGINALD GIBBONS

[Weiss's long poems should alert us] to the narrowness of range of many of the short poems of our time. Weiss's own shorter poems (very few of them under thirty lines) have always presented an uncommon combination of dense texture and subtle, sometimes elusive, substance. The texture of these poems often turns out to *be* the substance, and the time-bound experience of reading his poems is, more than with most poets, the apprehension of a meaning which can rarely be ordered into structural, spatial schemas after it has impressed itself on the reader. The poems are of a supremely articulate emotional and perceptual progress.

Technically, Weiss's work began in *The Catch* as a manipulation of rhymes, strung like beads on the characteristically long thread of his sentence. His poems were occasions formalized less according to rule than in accord with the poet's ear, which hears echoes and half-rhymes nearly everywhere (punning is simply one instance of this). At times the reader had the sense of standing inside a carillon as the bells resounded with harmonics of each other's pitches. . . . But Weiss's range also extended to a less self-conscious sort of language, appropriate to more occasions, which offered the reader a music based on a kind of hovering metric never fully established. . . . (pp. 18-19)

Further, there was something of William Carlos Williams' casual artfulness and eye for the tableau. . . . [However, the poems] do their work over the span of the whole, not in the aggregate of the parts; they give precedence to music and syntax over image.

Weiss's range of tone is employed from the beginning to capture not so much a wide range of experience as his sense of the plenitude of each experience. . . . And the presentation of perception and emotional flux—that oblique articulation of emotion, as perception takes hold and unveils what it has already grasped—gives the poems their characteristic texture.

From his first poems to *Fireweeds* . . . Weiss's method has been consistent: His distinct sense of language produces the conflation of perception and emotion. . . . [For] example, the outspoken musings of Caliban in "Caliban Remembers" (1968) amaze in the way Caliban's capabilities—in Shakespeare little more than robust Elizabethan grunting and complaint—prove greater than Shakespeare (or Browning) took them to be. What seems a speech of limited grasp and what is certainly a mind of limited scope are granted nonetheless a vivid immediacy of perception which in fact *springs from* Caliban's strange language (not, after all, native to his tongue, which was originally dumb). The emotional range of the forsaken monster lies in the very possibilities of this language.

The characteristic voice of Weiss's mature work is not so thickly textured as Caliban's, however. There is a richness not so much of metaphor as of close-packed, simpler figures, often linked by apposition, to which a symbolic significance cannot always readily be assigned. The plenitude of experience fascinates on its own, and Weiss's quick succession of perceptions continues to govern his syntax. By stretching out and harnessing a whole team of energetic figures, this syntax gives at once an inimitable sense of time passing as we read, and of the simultaneity of diverse emotions and recognitions. It is a technique which is Weiss's signature. . . . (pp. 19-21)

[If] Weiss is a poet interested in complex perceptions, this is not for him a question of bizarre correspondences, or deep images only an eyeblink from inarticulateness. On the contrary, his impulse has been to stare long. As if his varied line-indentations were a slight shifting of the head, to gain perspective as a painter or a heron might, he has filled many of his poems with probing, tentative, reflective catalogues. By registering the way things look, these catalogues construct a progress of emotion through stages toward [congealment]. . . .

In [*Fireweeds*] this method is at work more consistently and more successfully than it was in any previous volume. Still glossing the "great catch" of experience, the poems insist on the irreducibility of the life of man, the marvel that—at times—it is. This insistence on plenitude (even the plenitude of sorrow) comes also from a struggle against the most reductive, obsessive, and modern of the seven deadly sins, despair. Even at his most somber, as in "The Polish Question," . . . Weiss can maintain a sad jauntiness, although in doing so he does not rely too heavily on conveying his own personality to the reader. The self-consciousness of language is still there, but it is no more a reflection of the poet's *self* than a singer's voice thrown from stage to audience is a measure of his ego. (p. 23)

It has been objected on occasion that Weiss's poems are difficult, and it is usually . . . close harmony (which in longer poems breaks chords into arpeggios) and the involved syntax that strike some readers as calling too much attention to themselves to allow the whole poem to take shape. But Weiss's poems are meant to be read *through;* they are events in time. Their method is rarely one of isolated brilliancies; instead of the presentation of an emotional complex in an instant of time, they give the reader the time-bound unfolding of an emotional progress. In addition, the urge behind this sort of difficulty—if it is difficulty—seems to me to arise primarily out of our culture. Frederic Jameson, in discussing music and literary style, establishes that the modern writer has striven—must strive—to create works which resist the drive of the culture to turn them into commodities. (pp. 25-6)

[Every] writer must agree with Jameson that "real thought demands a descent into the materiality of language and a consent to time itself in the form of the sentence. . . . It is enough to evoke the fad for rapid reading and the habitual conscious or unconscious skimming of newspaper and advertising slogans, for us to understand the deeper social reasons for the stubborn insistence of modern poetry on the materiality and density of language, on words felt not as transparency but rather as things themselves." . . . This is the clue to Weiss's work, especially when we consider the aspect of timing in his poetry. He *does* ramble; rambling is the heart of his method. It is an encompassing, through tentative stages, through ceaseless apposition and parenthesis, of the sinewy, back-tracking syntax of thought, of the shifting kaleidoscope of perception, until one reaches revelation. Whether this revelation is of the strange or of the familiar it is always a product of passionate feeling, which, as Pound said, "causes patterns to arise in the mind."

But Weiss is not simply interested in the pattern—he wants the prodigality of things themselves which, as they form and reform in patterns, retain their own unpatterned bounty. . . . (p. 26)

[If] not clarity, then cohesion is the watchword of Weiss's use of language. This cohesion is especially present in the way he telescopes his syntax by deleting relative pronouns. Thus the compressed, knotty quality of the phrase: "satisfied that no voice lives [that] can sever it from itself." . . . (p. 27)

But can one simply record, with a kind of stunned pleasure, the very excesses not only of natural beauty when we are lucky, and of human contact when we are vitally alive, but also of brutality, waste, fear, and the multitudinous sufferings we inflict on each other? In fact, Weiss seems to say that the very capability of seeing the many, the richness of the proliferation of evil itself, fascinates even as it horrifies. (pp. 27-8)

Odysseus and Penelope have been constant presences in Weiss's work, leading him on yet remaining out of reach, instructing him in love as well as in loneliness and wandering. In "The Storeroom," Penelope steps forth as the center of Weiss's interest (which in a way makes him an imagining Odysseus). In and out of the storeroom where Odysseus' bow lies waiting for what is inevitable, Penelope goes back over this story, which Weiss so loves that he catalogues not only what the storeroom holds but also what Penelope has managed to make of her life without her husband. The mood throughout is of a sort masked anticipation, as the mere mention of items in the storeroom promises the fury and resolution of Odysseus' return. (pp. 29-30)

[Weiss never shies] away from the reference to high culture, and its assumption of familiarity with the literary classics and with painting. Each allusion serves to slow the progress, so that the savor may intensify. Nor is the allusiveness confined to explicit references to art, music, books. There are also technical resources which themselves allude to Weiss's concord with the rhythmic energy of Robert Browning and Gerard Manley Hopkins. All this is both a common ground for the poems, and their burden. The pacing of the poems, which we have placed at the center of their particular method, is a kind of further experimentation with the elliptical quality of Browning's monologues and the highly self-conscious rhythmic artifice of Hopkins' poems.

But adopting neither Browning's fascination with the odd and the perverse, nor Hopkins' fitfulness of emotion as it is reflected in his rhythms, Weiss prefers a more even-keeled, yet at the same time, more oblique method. He inspects the ordinary but places it in an odd light; he maintains a tension between an artificial syntax and the speech rhythms on which it is based. As a result both these rhythms and the aspect of the ordinary are heightened as the reader sees each in the slow-motion sequence of the poem. This poetic strategy, so consistent throughout Weiss's work, necessarily leads to larger questions, the most important of which develops precisely out of the presence in his work of these pronounced emblems of high culture: what is the link between the artist's way of history-making and the overwhelming history that has been, and is being, made around him? Weiss's response is "The Polish Question."

Not things as they are but as they ought to be, was what poetry presented over and above history, according to Aristotle. This implies that poetry, even better than history, can make sure of its interpretation, and "The Polish Question" addresses this problem. As if the poem were speaking in a voice of its own, it expresses the wish that poems and paintings could so seal themselves up, with their own attendant light and shadow, that there would never be any doubt in the reader or spectator about what was meant, and when it was meant, and where. But to achieve this, the poem must then suggest, even as it begins, that the reader will inevitably—necessarily—supply some details himself. The hope of utter completion, of faithful representation to anything that *was,* must be abandoned even as it is mentioned. The reader's own individual history will enable him to add to the poem his own [variation]. . . . As if to emphasize the variability of the individual's response, Weiss's sort of verisimilitude makes it impossible to rush through this poem. Each reader has to turn it in his hands in the hope that, from some angle, the lines of the table, as in Cézanne's still-lifes, will seem to meet each other in an imagined center, behind the living solidity of apples and pears. But like Cézanne's tables, these poems will not resolve themselves into the view from a single perspective. They want to hold the reader in that moment of active perception. As the mind struggles to form the whole out of the progress of the parts, it finds that the struggle *is* the whole. It is a process in time. Not "Make it new," but "Make it last." (pp. 31-3)

Reginald Gibbons, "The Cure: Theodore Weiss's Poetry," in Modern Poetry Studies *(copyright 1978, by Media Study, Inc.), Vol. IX, No. 1, Spring, 1978, pp. 18-33.*

JOHN MOLE

[*Views & Spectacles*] should serve to introduce new English readers to an urbane, spikily intelligent writer for whom the making of poetry is a delighted idiosyncratic conversation shaped around parentheses, hesitations and qualifications, breaking out at intervals into sheer affirmation. Often seeming a little awkward (even wilfully mannered) at first reading, these are poems which demand careful attention until their voice is assimilated and the necessary balance of mind achieved in one's response. Not that they are obscure but, both in their syntax and in a habit of shooting off at ruminative tangents from what appears to be a direct narrative line, they are surprising and often refreshingly unpredictable. A number of them begin, deceptively, as anecdotes but then the event dissolves into the larger questions it has raised or . . . is peremptorily dismissed. . . .

[Despite] the ironic checks and balances which dictate the style and pace of his work, [Weiss is] a celebrator, a yessayer, a kind of upper-case e. e. cummings for whom every last is a first. . . .

[Like William Carlos Williams], his work is that of a complex, restless optimist. . . . For Williams it was "no ideas but in things". For Professor Weiss it is "at once to see / nation, no poetry. The spectacles he asks for, in the selection's title poem, are "a pair . . . apt / to spot at least two times / at once . . . or at least dismiss / the blur and tenses between what's / in what's out". They become emblematic of the emphasis he places on the significance of small particulars closely observed and precisely arranged to make sense of the world ("parts / that must harmonise into something / that rewards them for being, rewards / with what they are") and views become more or less spectacular depending upon the intensity with which they are absorbed. . . . We notice what we can, and the bits that Professor Weiss is able to use become his quirky celebrations, fragments cohering into distinctive, sharp-minded poems. Less successful are those occasions when his habitual accentuation of the positive becomes banal statement—"Somewhere in all this / I have a sense of what it is to be really / alive"—and although in a poem such as "A Letter from the Pigmies" *Dear Whoever-You-Are-That-You-Are* is addressed with a whimsically engaging intimacy, an embarrassing note of cock-eyed optimism inflates things to a pitch of sentimental rhetoric which verges on the back-slapping cheerfulness of a Rodgers and Hammerstein chorus. . . .

Despite these lapses, though, *Views & Spectacles* contains many good poems and a handful of outstanding ones. . . .

John Mole, "Celebrating the Crumbs," in The Times Literary Supplement *(© Times Newspapers Ltd. (London) 1978; reproduced from* The Times Literary Supplement *by permission), No. 3994, October 20, 1978, p. 1215.*

ROBERT STOCK

Theodore Weiss' poetry is among the most demanding (which is not necessarily to say obscure) currently being written, not because it is erudite, far-ranging, uncompromising, and oblique, as it certainly is, but by virtue of the poet's *modus operandi* of reconciling fragments through the fashioning of multi-faceted wholes. His rich thematic diversity, various but specific characterization (for his work abounds in real people), and accelerated interplay between objects and notions, all combine to keep the reader in an intensely mobile state, as befits a poetry of the "demeanors of the mind."

Although I propose to indicate a number of Weiss' recurrent motifs, one, fragmentation, must be mentioned at once; for much of his poetic method, as well as his obliquity, stems from this theme. More than a theme, it is the underlying structure, the form and sign, by which passion may be brought to equal hope. (pp. 1-2)

Ideal phenomenalism, in its zeal to reduce material to patterns made up of sensa and the gaps between, has left the physical world in fragments. . . . The problem faced by Weiss, and perhaps faced more critically by him than by any other of our contemporary American poets, is: how to reconstruct a world in shambles in such a way as to fill in the gaps in sense patterns, so that pterodactyls and antarctic rock, never seen by man, may nevertheless exist? What is the continuant that constitutes the world whole? Weiss, whose approach is similar to phenomenology's, recommends the intent examination of immediate experience. . . . The *intention* (in the phenomenological sense of the word) to follow such a course is, in fact, the sought-after continuant. (p. 2)

Now Weiss, in thought and language radically opposed to his only world in ruins, must notwithstanding present the appearance of fragmentation, for the texture of object-gap-object-gap is the result of centuries of a false metaphysics of perception, . . . and that is how his readers behold reality. . . . [Fragmentation] has to be presented only to be made whole and continuous once more. Consequently his very language must find the tropes and syntax to enact the twin drama of destruction and reconstruction, wounding and healing, division and integrity. Weiss addresses several strategies to this end.

One such strategy is prolepsis, the figure of anticipation, whose building blocks look random but fit securely and handsomely. Others are dislocation and disassociation. It is tmesis, however, that provides Weiss with his most dramatic and persistent means of division and re-integration. Tmesis: welding together fragments; a cutting. A familiar example is Hopkins' "brim, in a flash, full," constructed from *brimful in a flash*. Tmesis admits of a texture as tightly woven as Pindar's Greek or Horace's Latin, and permits syntactic elements to avoid or combine with whatever other elements the poet finds significant, a property not common to the rigidity of English grammar. Moreover, and more importantly, tmesis divides insofar as it introjects a middle between parts of a conventional phrase (as in the example from Hopkins) or word (as in "ungoddamned-dependable"). Its division is purely formal; its re-integration is meaningfully formal. (pp. 2-3)

A mattersome property of tmesis is its two-fold directional mobility. Its poles, although stretched apart by the intruded matter, exert pressure against both sides of the middle: the stretching can bind or alienate the terms; the pressure can be a grave threat or a subtle caress. It behooves the craftsman either to maintain the terms in tension or to control the degree of stretch and pressure according to what is appropriate to form and content. Weiss is past-master of this aspect of his art, and his utilization of it is ubiquitous; it is everywhere in lines and phrases, but can extend to embrace total poems. Dramatic enjambment is its preferred linear means, comma and dash its characteristic punctuation. Dashes set Weiss' world between something more intimate than parentheses, more binding than brackets, more present than the blank spaces of a Dickey. Dashes circumscribe Weiss' phrases with the zero phonetic value of silence; reading them is like tiptoeing over mined ground, confronted at every moment with the threat of fragmentation. But it must be remembered that dashes, if disjunctive, are also conjunctive. (p. 3)

Tmesis, then, the characteristic mode of Weiss, is simultaneous fragmentation and unification, a passion equal to hope. (p. 4)

[At] the age of 35, Weiss, already a mature poet widely published in literary magazines, decides that it is time to issue a first book. Thus it is not surprising that so many of his techniques, themes, and central symbols are already established in *The Catch*. Nor will his future work be one of radical changes that give the impression of false starts; rather he will develop, broaden, deepen, consolidate. And he will meet earlier selves in later poems, like Shelley meeting himself in the garden.

To make a catch you need a hook, so Weiss at the outset provides us with "The Hook." Here we are immediately plunged into his sea of the imagination. . . . It is a paeon to hope, a fusion of passion and hope. But all the while the artist is refining his craft of juxtaposition and tmesis, deftly transforming scenes from cafeteria to quarry to sea, from inner to outer: a revelation of order within the seemingly fragmentary. Every future triumph will be such a catch. . . . [The] poles of Weiss' language are the Swan of Avon and the Passaic Goose, Shakespeare and William Carlos Williams, and the effort at fusion is here—and in his most recent book, *Fireweeds,*—in progress. More than two disparate ways of speaking are at stake, however; here are two epochs (with many more between), two worlds, two sets of moral values. Sometimes Weiss' syntax buckles under the stress and urgency (as in the first stanza of his marvelous "The Dance Called David"), but almost never his diction. . . . Weiss has the delightful temerity to load his puns with meaning till they groan more obstreperously than any irreverent reader possibly could. . . . "Shades of Caesar" is the most ambitious poem in *The Catch*. Weiss' erudition is enormous, and he is not too timid or squint-eyed to employ it, here or in any other appropriate place. "Shades of Caesar" avails itself of this erudition to view the city's desecration from the vantage of the academic community. While observing the loves of Caesar-Cleopatra and Odysseus-Calypso merge in the troubled waters of the Nile and "the lordly Hudson" (I believe Weiss' use of the adjective precedes Paul Goodman's), the reader experiences the collapse of the heroic dimension. Seeds of Weiss' masterpiece, "Caliban Remembers," are to be found embedded in this poem.

Despite the breath-taking successes of this first book, his second, *Outlanders,* is clearly an advance. Symbols and lemmas are developed not only within each poem but also from poem to poem in a more deliberate manner than in the earlier book; there is a greater cohesiveness and unity achieved. One such lemma is "the state of weeds," and, by means of poetry's reflexive nature, here turned explicit, the state of poems. In the singable opening poem, the book's title is defined as weeds, their persistence and pride in lowliness. . . . "The Greater Music" is attended by a delicate train of inner- and off-rhymes, as befits orphic song. As though he were saying it for the greatest music, the wholly integrated occasion, Weiss rarely indulges our ears with rhyme. This omission, since it implies that his other efforts are secondary, not "the greater," seems to me a basic defect: the poet has sacrificed his most reverberating string to a hierarchy of value judgments that is, after all, putative and only argumentative. . . . The stoicism that Weiss associates with Odysseus recommends that over-integration be resisted with courage. Stoicism, it should be indicated, is in itself a major Weissean theme, and usually appears accompanied by joy. Except for Richard Wilbur and the Spanish Jorge Guillén, Weiss is perhaps the most joyous poet now celebrating in America. But the stoical attitude requires courage, too, and a stance of bear-the-world-and-it-will-bear-you. (pp. 4-6)

In the opulent scene-painting of "An Egyptian Passage" he describes two disparate worlds, and, by a thrilling change in point of view, the poet "sitting on a polar star," recomposes the world in a visual-spatial epiphany. Weiss' version of St. Francis occurs in "Descent," and characteristically he is "pining to compose the world." But primarily this poem is a lament for loss of belief in a golden Orphic Age. Because love can partially restore this age, self-consolation does not cheapen sentiment. Richard Howard, in many respects an astute commentator on Weiss, woefully and implacably undervalues him as a love poet, whether that love be domestic or an aspect of agape. (p. 7)

Nothing in [Weiss'] work thus far had prepared his audience for such magnitude, complexity, and ambition [as emerged with the publication of *Gunsight* in 1962]. Nor had the poet overreached himself. The protagonist (or, better, the center of consciousness) of "Gunsight" is a young soldier who is experiencing (the only proper word for his complex of reactions) surgery under ether. Into his consciousness, clouded and distorted by the anesthetic, throngs a phantasmagoria of voices, distinct and typographically signaled, that are simultaneously the same and the other ("the same is the other," Weiss has written elsewhere), or, as he wrote in still another connection, "all things communicate invisibly, exchanging their fluids and messages." Thus are the Weissean themes continuant throughout the fabric of his work.

There is another voice, too, auctorial, a narrator's or the poet's, a voice dist nctly Shakespearean, whereas the phantasmagoria usually sounds like the Passaic goose. But even in the auctorial voice, even in the lines that serve as introduction, penetration into the wounded consciousness is profound and pervasive, for the poet will make no false and self-limiting claims to objectivity. So adroit is Weiss' handling of this polyphony of voices that the need for tmesis is obviated, and it is so coherent and dramatically textured that mere isolation of a word or phase (sometimes repeated from pages earlier) can return situations and notions to us without confusion, blending them into new situations and notions.

As the poem is built on particular voices, it also displays a scheme of varying temporal levels: the operating table is both past and present. Memory hearkens back to a childhood hunting expedition which blurs with soldiering episodes and exploits, his wound, and the operation itself, all accomplished through polyphonous (rather than syntactic) tmesis and multi-referent syntax and diction. . . . Throughout [this poem's] phantasmagoria of voicings and temporal levels the struggle between consciousness and anesthetic possesses moral overtones of the stoic theme, and provides, literally and figuratively, a feat of endurance. (pp. 7-8)

Amazingly, Richard Howard considers "Gunsight" to be without literary and classical references. This is so far from being true that the poem's crisis is a grand, commanding *katabasis* closely modeled on those of Homer and Vergil, and outdistancing Eliot's, Pound's, and even Crane's, in significance and ordinary, everyday application. In it the narrator-poet is transformed into a Tiresias-like figure, a boding tension. . . . And, indeed, this section bristles and sparkles with references to Homer, Vergil, Dante, and, if my reading is correct, the tragedies of Shakespeare. (pp. 8-9)

One feature of "Gunsight" is that it can be profitably read in different ways, each providing new perspectives. Experiment with reading only the wounded soldier's lines, then add the various voices in italics, and, finally, the narrator-poet's lines. It is instructive to confront the success of Weiss' voicings with the failure of James Dickey, in *The Zodiac,* to give voice to his Marsman's drunken speeches. . . . Weiss' moral force is evident in every word.

Weiss' next book, *The Medium,* elaborates on what the poet is able to redeem through art and love. . . . The most ambitious poem in *The Medium* is "Two for Heinrich Bleucher." Here Weiss returns to the ideas, so often twinned in his mind, of exile and the university as a viable community of scholars. . . . [The] poem leaves me just a trifle uneasy. I would blame the complication of roles inherent in the teacher-scholar-exile tmesis, and possibly the introduction of Socrates stretches the poem further out of shape and debilitates ideas as well as landscape. The poem's nobility remains intact, despite my quibbles.

The Last Day and the First (1968) seems to me Weiss' most accomplished book so far, and one among its poems, "Caliban Remembers," his crowning achievement. The realism of "Gunsight" is that of the play of intersubjectivity, whose true hero is the many, not the one. "Caliban Remembers" is the precise opposite insofar as it isolates and compresses realism into a single consciousness. If there is a multi-consciousness in any way operative, it derives from a quartet composed of Weiss and the poem's three great predecessors, Shakespeare, Browning, and Auden. Richard Howard sees the debt to Shakespeare and Auden, but only "permanent dispossessions" from Browning. I am not altogether certain I know what Mr. Howard means; I am certain I do not agree with what I think he means. Weiss conceives of Caliban as a composite which he must break down without dispossessing any of the resulting fragments. In fact, Weiss' language in this poem is a tribute to and a contemporary preservation of Browning's. The modern poet alters the Victorian's world view, nothing more, nothing less. "The Tempest" is an extraordinary tmesis whose poles are the newly forged myth of Ariel and Caliban; "Caliban Remembers" is a mythic tmesis, similarly extraordinary, whose poles are Caliban's consciousness and his bodysense, with the world in between at full stretch and pull. . . . As Prospero abandoned his wand, Caliban, now part Ariel, renounces possessive magic and the prevalent powers in order to immerse himself in the flux of efts and ooze, like William Carlos Williams baptized in the filthy Passaic. This work, the finest long poem in decades and entirely *sui generis,* is haunted by tutelary spirits. It is a pity that Weiss has not fully come to grips with the complementary figure of Ariel, though there are traces of him in the poet's gardeners of soil and university, as well as in Caliban. (pp. 9-11)

After the triumphs of *The Last Day and the First,* his next volume, *The World Before Us* (1970), marks time. The poet sits way back, invites his soul, experiments tried themes in new combinations, and performs the satisfying feats of reworking the fire-words and fishing symbols in the recollected light of "Caliban Remembers." (p. 11)

With *Fireweeds* (1976) . . . relaxation is over, tmesis returns, and the scholar-poet, perhaps reinvigorated upon completion of a long study of Shakespeare's early comedies and history plays, rides the crest of his intellect. In this book Weiss has need for all his courage and wit, for here he most specifically and forthrightly confronts our times and our evils; and yet there are high—I almost wrote lavish—praises given, too. All in all, *Fireweeds* does not contain his best poems, perhaps, but it is his ripest book. The title conjoins two ubiquitous Weissean symbols: the sparks and fire of words, i.e. the Word as pentecostal sacrament, and the weeds that must not be lost. It might be argued that the contents of this book tend to be wisdom-poems, not quests for wisdom, and at least two of them, "The Storeroom" and "A Charm Against the Toothache," approach his major work.

"The Storeroom" and "Another and Another and . . ." continue, augment and consolidate the Odyssean adventure in the stoic mind of the poems, while "As You Like It" contradicts Auden's contention that people are indifferent to the great event. (pp. 11-12)

[In poem after poem in *Fireweeds,* Weiss shows] no falling off, no embers, a burning house rather than a flaring up (though, like Marianne Moore, he must be permitted his modesty), weeds and flowers still carefully tended, swan and goose luxuriating together, a sacrament of words. This is "the passion equal to all hope," not merely to hope, and, no matter how his surroundings fragment, it shows no sign of weakening. (p. 12)

Robert Stock, "A Passion Equal to All Hope: Theodore Weiss," in The Hollins Critic *(copyright 1979 by Hollins College), Vol. XVI, No. 2, April, 1979, pp. 1-12.*

* * *

WELCH, James 1940-

Welch is an American Indian poet and novelist. He draws most of the material for his fiction from the experiences of his youth on an Indian reservation in Montana. The emotional power of Welch's writing is partly a result of his dual abilities to address the topical problems of Indians in contemporary America and to explore the universal complexities of the human condition. (See also *CLC,* Vol. 6, and *Contemporary Authors,* Vols. 85-88.)

ROGER SALE

The writing [in *Winter in the Blood*] is constantly fending off easy attitudes and conclusions with a flat, brooding precision. The reader keeps wanting to be able to make something of it all, to be clear how these people are Indians, how being an Indian makes a difference. Welch himself is a Montanan, Blackfoot and Gros Ventre, and in *Winter in the Blood* one may find out what it is like to be an Indian, this Indian, but just what that means is never once offered us for summary or conclusion. It is an unnervingly beautiful book. (p. 20)

As one might imagine, there are fine conversations in bars, and they have just the right quality of aimlessness and direction of life being lived and not lived. (p. 21)

Writing as flat and quiet as this, in a novel that is mostly dialogue, tempts one to think of Hemingway, to praise its tact and understatement. But *Winter in the Blood* has no such Hemingway sense of style or life; it states everything fully, seeks no sense that these people are responding "gracefully under pressure," because there is no pressure. But that does not lead Welch either to absurdist acceptance or to despair, but to a careful page-by-page measurement of the precise value of however little there is to these lives. Of course in a book like this there is bound to be a problem with plot, because one is inevitably attitudinizing if one uses a plot to give the lives shape or if one refuses to use plot to refuse to give them shape. Here too Welch's instinct seems to me just right. Beyond the first excitement of finding a book so carefully done, one can begin to get twitchy and ask where it is all going, restless with the possibility that Welch will try to get away with saying it is going nowhere. (pp. 21-2)

James Welch in this first novel is only a truth-teller, and *Winter in the Blood* may be the only one he can write because writers this sternly devoted to telling the truth often don't have many more than one or two tales to tell. We must hope not. *Winter in the Blood* is short, done almost before one feels well begun with it, but I felt very much in its presence long after I had finished. (p. 22)

Roger Sale, "Winter's Tales," in The New York Review of Books *(reprinted with permission from* The New York Review of Books; *copyright © 1974 Nyrev, Inc.), Vol. XXI, No. 20, December 12, 1974, pp. 18-22.**

JOHN R. MILTON

[James Welch] is the best American Indian poet in terms of techniques, production, attitudes, and what must be called competence. One argument advanced against this opinion is that his forms and style are not peculiarly Indian, that he writes good poetry but not Indian poetry. It is true that Welch's poems are not syntactically complicated by his oral language traditions; they are at least partially indicative of his college training. Yet, what is characteristic of Indian poetry is not primarily a left-over dependence on nonwritten native language patterns. . . . More importantly, the Indian writer has a close personal relationship with the earth and its creatures. . . . He writes in quite simple rhythms, as though they are dictated by the rhythms of the natural world. And his imagery is often oriental . . . in its complex simplicity. Finally, of course, it is the poet's experiences as an Indian which determine the subject matter of the poems.

Welch, like many Indian poets, has said that he wants to be known as a poet, not as an Indian poet. That is both right and understandable. Nevertheless, it is inevitable that many of his poems deal with reservation life in Montana, with inferior economic conditions, and with protests against the Washington bureaus responsible for Indian welfare, in addition to the more personal matters of family, tradition, and religion. Some of Welch's poems are sharply satiric; others are softly suggestive, as in this line from "Snow Country Weavers":

say in my mind
I saw your spiders weaving
threads
to bandage up the day

(p. 83)

John R. Milton, "New American Indian Writers," in The Contemporary Literary Scene 1973, *edited by Frank N. Magill (copyright © 1974 by Frank N. Magill), Salem Press, Inc., 1974, pp. 82-6.**

BLANCHE H. GELFANT

James Welch's fine novel, *Winter in the Blood,* the story of a 32-year-old Indian on a Montana reservation, depends upon understatement, requires it, would be impossible to tell without its restraint. For the story of Indian dispossession is stark and terrible, and, unlike science fiction, true. . . . The story implicates victor and vanquished in a shared guilt, the white man for having aggressed, the red man for having succumbed. Whatever the reasons or the excuses, the consequences remain inexcusable. The consequences are here in the book, in the narrator's bruised body and defeated spirit, and in the writer's grace. James Welch is not his protagonist, and that must remain a sole and important consolation. The novel begins with an image of dilapidation, the Earthboy place in shambles. . . . We are accustomed to speak of alienation as the pervasive theme of twentieth-century American fiction, but the alienation of the middle-class white man seems a whining, self-pitying pose beside the experience of the American Indian, separated as he is from his land, his traditions, his people, his customs, his past; separated from himself. All of the narrator's memories are of loss. . . . The narrator does nothing but wander through bars and unfamiliar bedrooms, drunk, beaten, dazed, pursuing a girl, or the dream of a girl, who holds the only promise of something better, "the promise of warm things." . . . His hope, not only for salvation but for life itself, lies in the possibility of awakened desire. Wanting nothing, caring for no one, feeling only loss, he will die —broken, tamed, and trapped. . . . Welch's narrator anaesthetizes himself in order to endure the pain of his total dispossession; but apathy, like winter in the blood, is not transcendence, but death. . . . *Winter in the Blood* is quiet, straightforward, and unflinching, a simple and striking story about death—the death of a people, a tradition, a land, a river, a promise. We must read it to our despair. (pp. 311-12)

Blanche H. Gelfant, "Fiction Chronicle: 'Winter in the Blood'," in The Hudson Review *(copyright © 1975 by The Hudson Review, Inc.; reprinted by permission), Vol. XXVIII, No. 2, Summer, 1975, pp. 311-12.*

SYED AMANUDDIN

Nature and Native American poetry are not merely related by alliteration; they also have a spiritual bond which is a result of hundreds of years of contact and togetherness. Social protest, subjective explorations of existence and other themes are present in Native American poetry as in other American minority poetry. But the affinity between nature and the Native Americans is natural and spiritual and is conspicuously absent in contemporary poetry by other ethnic groups. . . . The strange cosmic perspective that haunts the Indian mind does not lose itself in its pursuit of the transitory and the superficial, although it does not totally ignore current social realities.

James Welch's poetry has all these characteristics. . . . (p. 142)

Welch is not always serious. The old man in "Grandma's Man" paints the cry of a goose so long that it floats off the canvas into thin air. Similar humor is seen in "Never Give A Bum An Even Break." But his best poems are serious and philosophical, and nature dominates much of his poetry. (p. 143)

Syed Amanuddin, "World Literature in Review: 'Riding the Earthboy 40'," in World Literature Today *(copyright 1977 by the University of Oklahoma Press), Vol. 51, No. 1, Winter, 1977, pp. 142-43.*

ROBERT HOLLAND

In *Riding the Earthboy 40,* . . . [James Welch] would give us something of the material and spiritual poverty of the American Indian reservation, or rather, and more significantly, of the no-man's-land of small towns at their fringes where the two cultures meet, usually unhappily. . . . Welch has lived this, and knows the territory, not only the degradation of this passage, but the other side as well, the attempts to resist assimilation, preserve the native culture and resurrect its significance in the face of colonial conditions. Recent popular treatments of the situation have, inevitably, reduced it to cliché, and so one hopes, reading this book, that the poetry will come to the rescue. But Welch's language is not equal to the task. As the two cultures mingle uneasily, so two kinds of diction mix in the poems, but seldom do they produce the chemistry needed to precipitate poetry. A soft, "elemental" diction (clouds, dreams, sky, snow, bones, blood), aimed apparently at drawing on archetypal energies, produces only vagueness (as in the worst of Merwin) and is incongruous with Welch's other characteristic diction, a racy slang. . . . Also mixed into this unfortunate brew are a couple of staple ingredients from the contemporary poetic kitchen—a colorful but tasteless essence of synesthesia ("Shawls color the rainbow a new odor") and that indispensable monosodium glutamate of our time, inane surrealism: "Elephants are whispering in backyards." Occasionally an image will strike a spark, cutting to the heart of a dilemma ("These Indians once imitated life") or rendering a landscape ("sky so blue / the eagles spoke in foreign tongues"), but for the most part the poems are a jumble of competing tones and confused impressions.

Part of the reason, I suspect, that Welch does not sharpen his diction and clarify his tone is an underlying fear of sentimentality. He speaks in more than one poem about "sentimental crap", and given the potential bathos of his subject, his fear is understandable. . . . But in his attempts to evade sentimentality, Welch ends up evading feeling as well, and the real issues. . . . Either way, the poet, along with his persona, remains "distant / as the cloud I came in on", and Welch does l1ttle service either to poetry or to the American Indian. (pp. 287-89)

Robert Holland, "Six or Seven Fools," in Poetry *(© 1977 by The Modern Poetry Association; reprinted by permission of the Editor of* Poetry*), Vol. CXXIX, No. 5, February, 1977, pp. 285-95.**

DON KUNZ

Winter in the Blood . . . is a novel in which the nameless protagonist's search for an authentic and meaningful sense of being in the world is structured around various distances. Distance is articulated in essentially three forms—physical, emotional, and aesthetic. The physical (including temporal) distance at which his family and others are held partly causes their emotional remoteness from or coolness toward the protagonist, and he temporarily loses sight of who he is. His emotional distance, in turn, makes him a wanderer, leading him to establish an even greater distance from these others in an accelerating process until the principal action of homecoming is torture. For most of the novel the protagonist is variously lost in a steadily increasing distance: he is directionless, beaten, absorbed, and uncomprehending. Paradoxically, only when he flees from himself and from the ignorant grasping of others and relives his painful winter memories does he attain that positive quality inherent in distance which we call perspective and so truly finds himself, having come home. The acquisition of a knowable and valued self at the conclusion is affirmed by the act of telling his story through techniques which involve the aesthetic application of distance—actions perceived symbolically, images which gradually cluster like stars into constellations of meaning, and especially the objective correlative, which transmutes emotion into action which evokes emotion in others and so by an act of imagination diminishes the distances among us all. (pp. 98-9)

Don Kunz, "Lost in the Distance of Winter: James Welch's 'Winter in the Blood'," in Critique: Studies in Modern Fiction *(copyright © by James Dean Young 1978), Vol. XX, No. 1, 1978, pp. 93-9.*

ANDREW HORTON

There are few laughs in *Winter in the Blood* . . . even though the narrator shares characteristics of a trickster, joker, and fool. . . . [The] narrator is a mediator and thus an ambiguous and equivocal character. The polar terms he attempts to mediate or reconcile are the fundamental ones of life and death, past and present, winter and summer, Indian and white cultures, the nature of men and women, sex and love, self and others. But unlike the tricksters of his Indian heritage, Welch's narrator is *human* and so must pay the psychological and spiritual price for existing between extremes, unreconciled to either of them. . . . [He] is his own man discontent with his present, haunted by his past . . . , and uncertain of his future. His isolation is all the more bitter as we realize how important a sense of belonging and a spirit of community were for tribal Indians. The comic spirit of traditional harmony becomes the bitter humor of separation in Welch's novel.

The humor in *Winter in the Blood* arises from the dialogue and from the descriptive passages, that is, both from the narrator's actions and from his thoughts. In both cases the humor is bitter because it is never distanced far enough from pain and absurdity to be truly comic. . . . This humor does not invite hearty laughter. We may chuckle (grandmother as murderer) or snicker (the death of the oatmeal man) but we are always aware that the narrator's humor reflects the seriousness of his condition.

The novel is filled with such ironic encounters and discoveries. Given different circumstances, much of the humor, even the black humor, would be much funnier. But in the context of Welch's book, the jokes, ironies, and absurd situations become a series of bitter happenings that enable the narrator to cushion himself from his personal difficulties, without providing him or us with the healing balm of true laughter. (pp. 132-33)

The least funny moments occur in town. As he drinks, fights, and copulates, the narrator is part of a sleezy white man's world of neon signs, cheap beer, fast women, slow country music, rundown hotels, and battered cars. The humor in these scenes is barroom humor, the kind of hard-nosed crude joking one expects to find in a 'B' detective movie of the 1940's and 50's. But even in such movies we usually laugh at tough-guy talk despite the seedy background because we recognize the lingo as the stuff of the detective *genre*. . . . [The] narrator jokes with us, himself, and others only because he means business, because he is serious about his life.

There is a progression of the bitter humor in the "town" scenes of the book toward even more absurd and thus humorless circumstances. (pp. 133-34)

Welch's ironic humor is finally used as a self-protecting mechanism. As events become more serious—beginning with the death of his grandmother—the narrator increases his use of humor. . . .

The death of the narrator's grandmother also leads him back to Yellow Calf and a discovery of his true grandfather. He begins the encounter with a poor joke about the bottle of "Vin Rose" he has brought being a French wine made from roses. But the conversation soon leads to the moment of realization (Yellow Calf is the narrator's grandfather) and thus comic liberation as the narrator briefly breaks into open laughter: "I began to laugh, at first quietly, with neither bitterness nor humor. It was the laughter of one who understands a moment in his life, of one who has been let in on the secret through luck and circumstance: 'You . . . you're the one.' I laughed, as the secret unfolded itself. 'The only one . . . you, her hunter . . .' And the way behind my eyes broke." . . . (p. 136)

The pure comic nature of this epiphany is made all the more significant because it is set off by Bird's fart. The narrator had heard Yellow Calf's story and has begun to ponder its meaning. Yet only after this unexpected "comic relief" is the narrator jolted, through the crudest of all humor, into a clear insight. Furthermore, the narrator ponders that Bird's "one instant of corruption" as he terms the fart, is a metaphor for the sudden truth he has learned. The foul air of the narrator's past has finally burst out bringing relief and laughter.

In this brief moment the narrator's bitterness and ironic joking fall away as he experiences the healing power of the kind of laughter the Indian comic ceremony dramas evoked. He realizes that it is not only winter he feels in his blood (the sense of death and distance) but also his grandfather's silent laughter. And yet even this moment is directly the result of supposedly "low" comedy as Bird's humorous trumpeting closely unites Bird, the narrator, and Yellow Calf in an instant of shared communion. In one flash of recognition Welch succeeds in touching the extremes of experience and fusing them as one moment of truth through pure laughter. Without the fart the narrator's insight may have been yet another painful discovery. With Bird's unwitting help such knowledge is transformed into a sense of liberation. (pp. 136-37)

From the time they dig the grave until the time the grandmother is buried, [the narrator] also includes his final interview with Yellow Calf, the death of Bird, and his own serious thoughts about his life. Or, more correctly, the narrator has chosen to record enough farcical humor to keep himself and his narrative from being overwhelmed by his troubles even though he is unable to bring that humor to its full comic fruition because of the winter he feels in his blood. (p. 138)

During the funeral, there is a hint that the narrator may be beginning to transcend his condition. In the "Epilogue" he carefully explains what clothing everyone wore to the funeral. When he comes to his grandmother, he states: "The old lady wore a shiny orange coffin with flecks of black ingrained beneath the surface. It had been sealed up in Harlem, so we never did find out what kind of makeup job the undertaker had done on her." . . . Describing the old lady as "wearing" a coffin suggests she continues to exist even if she no longer lives. This is a "joke," but it is also in keeping with the Indian concept of death as a continuation of life.

If this moment is a transcendent one, it is also highly ambiguous. The narrator's comment about his grandmother wearing a shiny coffin and his final action of tossing her pouch into the open grave, suggest an affirmation of the old lady's spirit, a kind of communication: he knows how important the pouch was to her, thus she would want to have it with her. But not enough is said for us to feel easy about such transcendence. In fact, he may simply be closing off the past by tossing in the pouch. Either way, the ambiquity adds to the final bitterness of the humor and thus our impression of the novel.

No clear catharsis has taken place. There has been the moment of illumination with Yellow Calf, but no convincing evidence of a significant change in the narrator as a result. The wise fool is wise enough to see some humor in his winter moods, but not enough a fool to be able, like Lame Bull, to drink a healthy toast to life after his grandmother's death. As an artist-trickster he has manipulated his experiences into words and those words into passages presented in a certain order to create the narrative we read. But he cannot "trick" himself into happiness or fulfillment or satisfaction. Humor thus remains an indication of his perceptiveness, a reminder of his ability to partially control and protect his life. And yet it is ultimately a bitter humor because he has not closed the distance within himself and between himself and others enough to see the punch lines. (pp. 138-39)

Andrew Horton, "The Bitter Humor of 'Winter in the Blood'," in American Indian Quarterly *(copyright © Society for American Indian Studies & Research 1978), Vol. 4, No. 2, May, 1978, pp. 131-39.*

ALAN R. VELIE

Winter in the Blood is in no way a protest novel. Not only is it far more complex, it really is neither bitter nor angry. In fact, although it is powerful and moving in places, it is primarily comic.

Once one abandons the idea that all Indian novels must be angry, it is not surprising to find that *Winter in the Blood* has a strong comic undercurrent. The comic novel is becoming the dominant genre in fiction today. . . . And Welch, although he is isolated geographically in Montana, is a writer who is well aware of literary trends. Much of his poetry evinces the influence of the surrealism which Robert Bly and James Wright have imported from South America. In his fiction he employs his own variation of the black humor used by Reed, Pynchon, et al. (p. 142)

Welch's humor varies from raucous farce to subtle satire, and it informs every corner of the novel. (pp. 143-44)

Most of the humor is verbal, however. Welch makes masterful use of ironic diction to undercut the dignity of his characters. (p. 144)

However long a list we make of funny things in *Winter in the Blood,* two questions arise: How much humor is enough to make a novel comic, and what happens if in addition to the humor there is a good deal of pathos? It is impossible to give a quantitative answer to the first question, but both questions can be answered at once if we say that in a comic novel the author plays most key situations for laughs rather than pathos. . . . There is some genuine pathos in *Winter in the Blood,* the most obvious example being the death of Mose. But in the most important scenes, the epiphany in which the hero recognizes his roots, and the funeral, Welch deliberately opts for comedy. (pp. 144-45)

Perhaps the best, funniest, and most successful scene in the novel is the ending. Normally funerals are not the stuff of comedy since death is not something people usually laugh about. If treated properly however, anything, even death, can be a source of humor, and Welch succeeds in making the funeral comic. (p. 146)

Lame Bull's eulogy for the old woman is a highly comic masterpiece of left-handed praise: "Here lies a simple woman . . . who devoted her life to . . . rocking . . . and not a bad word about anybody. . . . Not the best mother in the world . . . but a good mother, notwithstanding . . . who could take it and dish it out . . . who never gave anybody any crap." . . . As counterpoint to Lame Bull's speech, we have the random thoughts of the hero, who is not sufficiently interested in the proceedings to keep his mind on them. . . . Obviously Welch is not taking his hero seriously here, nor treating the funeral as a serious occasion. Quite clearly he is presenting the situation comically so that it will amuse the reader.

Winter in the Blood starts and ends on a comic note. In between the tone varies from pathos . . . to farce. . . . It never approaches the stridency and bitterness of a protest novel. Throughout most of the book and certainly in most of the key scenes, the tone is richly comic. (pp. 146-47)

Alan R. Velie, "'Winter in the Blood' as Comic Novel," in American Indian Quarterly *(copyright © Society for American Indian Studies & Research 1978), Vol. 4, No. 2, May, 1978, pp. 141-47.*

* * *

WELTY, Eudora 1909-

Welty, an American novelist, short story writer, and nonfiction and juvenile writer, is considered a Southern regionalist and is frequently compared to William Faulkner, Katherine Anne Porter, and Caroline Gordon. Her stories revolve around the relationships within families, focusing on the emotional complexities which face the individual. (See also *CLC*, Vols. 1, 2, 5, and *Contemporary Authors*, Vols. 9-12, rev. ed.)

GRANVILLE HICKS

[Miss Welty has not] sought to create a region of her own, as Faulkner has done with his Yoknapatawpha County, and to that extent she is a less self-conscious regionalist than he. She has merely taken her material where she found it—i.e., not far from home. . . .

When *A Curtain of Green* appeared, in 1941, some reviewers quickly concluded that the author was one more Southern realist with a penchant for squalor. . . .

But if one reads carefully, it is apparent that Miss Welty is not preoccupied with violence and horror, in the way that Erskine Caldwell so often is and not even to the extent that William Faulkner sometimes is. The meaning of the story is never in the violence, nor is the abnormality of the characters their important quality. (p. 70)

Squalor, violence, and decadence have in themselves no importance for Miss Welty. They are merely facts, and facts, whether pleasant or unpleasant, are no more than means to an end. What matters in her stories is never the thing that happens but the effect of the thing on human beings. Her concern, in other words, is with states of mind, and her emphasis falls upon those emotional states that cannot be easily articulated. (p. 71)

Miss Welty knows how, if ever an author did, to let facts speak for themselves, but she does not systematically refrain, in the Hemingway manner, from the direct account of emotional states. Although her later work is never so explicit as "Death of a Traveling Salesman," she does not hesitate to tell us what is going on within the mind of a character when it serves her purpose to do so. With beautiful adroitness, of which only a deliberate analyst can be conscious, she slips from the objective to the subjective, at just the moment to achieve the maximum of revelation. . . . So far as technique is concerned, her characteristic quality is [to maintain a] perfect balance between the objective and the subjective.

In another sense her work is remarkably objective. . . . Each story is an excursion of her imagination into the minds of others, and one finds in the two collections an extraordinary variety of subject matter. . . . [Her] emotional range stretches from the poignant to the overwhelming, and from humor to the blackest tragedy. Nor do her stories always conform to the patterns that have been discussed. There is, for example, "Powerhouse," an enigmatic story of a Negro orchestra leader with a strong, wild rhythm in it, or there is "The Wide Net," with its fine colloquial style and country humor. Miss Welty's versatility baffles the pigeonholers.

Yet in all this variety there are, of course, persistent themes. The first is the mystery of personality, which Miss Welty perceives in two forms—the mystery of others and the mystery of self. The failure of human beings to understand one another, one of the perennial themes of literature, she treats often as tragedy and sometimes, as in "A Piece of News" and "The Wide Net," as comedy, though always with serious overtones. The mystery of identity, central in such a story as "Old Mr. Marblehall," figures in some degree in almost every one of her tales.

Closely related to this first theme is her second, the problem of what brings people together and what holds them apart. (p. 72)

The flat, poker-faced narrative [of *The Robber Bridegroom*] is enriched by a dry humor that delights in the absurdities that are being described, and it is interrupted by descriptive and meditative passages of great beauty and by colorfully fantastic episodes in which historical and legendary figures . . . take part. . . .

The Robber Bridegroom has its excellences, but it was in *Delta Wedding* (1946) that Miss Welty was to show what she could do with the novel. The book is a triumph of sensitivity: the atmosphere of the Delta in September; the excitement and commotion of a household preparing for a wedding; the feeling of a crowded house; the feeling of a house full of children; the special quality of a particular and unusual family. . . . It is a technical triumph, too: the constant, subtle shifting of the point of view to render the most that can be rendered. (p. 73)

If *Delta Wedding* is one of the finest novels of recent years, it is because Miss Welty's sensibility is equal to the burden she has imposed upon it, the burden of a sustained narrative. . . . It is held up from beginning to end by unfailing insight into the subtle and complicated emotions of its characters and by a matchless gift for making us feel what they feel.

In *The Golden Apples* (1949) Miss Welty did not attempt that kind of sustained effort. The same characters figure in various episodes, and of some of them we have a cumulative revelation, but each episode stands by itself. It is, in part, a book about small-town life, and the quality of its understanding of small-town ways reminds one of Anderson and Faulkner. In another, more important aspect it is concerned with the mystery of personality. (p. 74)

In *The Robber Bridegroom* and a couple of short stories [Miss Welty] has deliberately created legends of her own, but these are less important than the tales in which the ordinary events of life in contemporary Mississippi take on the purity and—to use a reckless word—the universality of legend. . . .

Her work has often been compared with that of Virginia Woolf and Katherine Mansfield, but the resemblances seem to me superficial. In the beginning, I suspect, she learned a good deal from Katherine Anne Porter, about both the shaping of a story and the manipulation of words, but she has followed her own path of development, so that today the individuality of her prose is as obvious as it is quietly asserted. (p. 75)

Miss Welty is, to be sure, a Southern writer, in the sense that the South is her subject matter, just as it is Faulkner's. Furthermore, again like Faulkner, she lives in the midst of the life she writes about. She is a writer with roots, a fact significantly reflected in all her work. But if she shares in the heritage of the South, she also shares in the literary tradition of Western civilization, and shares at least as fully and deeply as the most up-to-date New York intellectual. And not only that: she proves, as the good regionalists have always proved, that the deeper one goes into the heart of a region, the more one transcends its geographical boundaries. (p. 76)

Granville Hicks, "Eudora Welty," in College English *(copyright © 1952 by the National Council of Teachers of English), Vol. 14, No. 2, November, 1952, pp. 69-76.*

ROBERT PENN WARREN

[The] stories of *The Wide Net* represent a specializing, an intensifying, of one of the many strains which were present in *A Curtain of Green*. All of the stories in *A Curtain of Green* bear the impress of Miss Welty's individual talent, but there is a great variety among them in subject matter and method and, more particularly, mood. . . . The material of many of the stories was sad, or violent, or warped, and even the comedy and wit were not straight, but if read from one point of view, if read as a performance, the book was exhilarating, even gay, as though the author were innocently delighted not only with the variety of the world but with the variety of ways in which one could look at the world and the variety of things that stories could be and still be stories. Behind the innocent delight of the craftsman, and of the admirer of the world, there was also a seriousness, a philosophical cast of mind, which gave coherence to the book, but on the surface there was the variety, the succession of surprises. In *The Wide Net* we do not find the surprises. The stories are more nearly cut to one pattern. (pp. 156-57)

[On] the first page, with the first sentence, we enter a special world: "Whatever happened, it happened in extraordinary times, in a season of dreams . . ." And that is the world in which we are going to live until we reach the last sentence of the last story. "Whatever happened," the first sentence begins, as though the author cannot be quite sure what did happen, cannot quite undertake to resolve the meaning of the recorded event, cannot, in fact, be too sure of recording all of the event. This is coyness, of course; or a way of warning the reader that he cannot expect quite the ordinary direct light on the event. . . . [The] faces and gestures and events often have something of the grave retardation, the gnomic intensity, the portentous suggestiveness of dreams. The logic of things here is not quite the logic by which we live, or think we live, our ordinary daylight lives. (p. 157)

[Usually] the wrenching of logic is not in terms of events themselves, though "The Purple Hat" is a fantasy, and "Asphodel" moves in the direction of fantasy. Usually the events as events might be given a perfectly realistic treatment. . . . But in these cases where the events and their ordering are "natural" and not supernatural or fantastic, the stories themselves finally belong to the "season of dreams" because of the special tone and mood, the special perspective, the special sensibility with which they are rendered. (p. 158)

There is [as critics have charged] a good deal of the falsely poetic in Miss Welty's present style, metaphors that simply pretend to an underlying logic, and metaphors (and descriptions) that, though good themselves, are irrelevant to the business in hand. And sometimes Miss Welty's refusal to play up the objective action—her attempt to define and refine the response rather than to present the stimulus—does result in a blurred effect. (p. 159)

[We may see in "A Still Moment"] a theme which seems to underlie the stories. For convenience, though at the risk of incompleteness, or even distortion, we may call it Innocence and Experience. . . .

Let us look at this theme in relation to other stories. (p. 162)

"A Memory" presents the moment of the discovery of the two poles—the dream and the world; the idea and nature; innocence and experience; individuality and the anonymous, devouring life-flux; meaning and force; love and knowledge. It presents the contrast in terms of horror (as do "The Petrified Man" and "Why I Live at the P. O." when taken in the context of Miss Welty's work), and with the issue left in suspension, but other stories present it with different emphases and tonalities.

For instance, when William Wallace, in "The Wide Net," goes out to dredge the river, he is presumably driven by the fear that his wife has jumped in, but the fear is absorbed into the world of the river, and in a saturnalian revel he prances about with a great catfish hung on his belt, like a river-god laughing and leaping. (pp. 163-64)

[We] recall that Hazel, the wife who is supposed to have committed suicide by drowning, is pregnant: she had sunk herself in the devouring life-flux, has lost her individuality there, just as the men hunting for the body have lost the meaning of their mission. For the river is simply force, which does not have its own definition. . . . Man has the definition, the dream, but when he plunges into the river he runs the risk of having it washed away. But it is important to notice that in this story, there is not horror at the basic contrast, but a kind of gay acceptance of the issue: when William Wallace gets home he finds that his wife had fooled him, and spanks her, and then she lies smiling in the crook of his arm. "It was the same as any other chase in the end." (pp. 164-65)

It is not that there is a standard resolution for the contrasts which is repeated from story to story; rather, the contrasts, being basic, are not susceptible of a single standard resolution, and there is an implicit irony in Miss Welty's work. But if we once realize this, we can recognize that the contrasts are understood not in mechanical but in vital terms: the contrasts provide the terms of human effort, for the dream must be carried to, submitted to, the world, innocence to experience, love to knowledge, knowledge to the fact, individuality to communion. What resolution is possible is, if I read the stories with understanding, in terms of the vital effort. The effort is a "mystery," because it is in terms of the effort, doomed to failure but essential, that the human manifests itself as human. (p. 167)

I do not mean to imply that her stories should be read as allegories, with a neat point-to-point equating of image and idea. It is true that a few of her stories, such as "The Wide Net," do approach the limit of allegory, but even in such cases we find rather than the system of allegory a tissue of symbols which emerge from, and disappear into, a world of scene and action which, once we discount the author's special perspective, is recognizable in realistic terms. The method is similar to the method of much modern poetry, and to that of much modern fiction and drama, but at the same time it is a method as old as fable, myth, and parable. It is a method by which the items of fiction (scene, action, character, etc.) are presented not as document but as comment, not as a report but as a thing made, not as history but as idea. Even in the most realistic and reportorial fiction, the social picture, the psychological analysis, and the pattern of action do not rest at the level of mere report; they finally operate as expressive symbols as well. (pp. 167-68)

[There] remains a sense of the vividness of the actual world. . . . In fact, it may be said that when the vividness of the actual world is best maintained, when we get the sense of one picture superimposed upon another, different and yet somehow the same, the stories are most successful.

The stories which fail are stories like "The Purple Hat" and "Asphodel" in which the material seems to be manipulated in terms of an idea, in which the relation between the image and the vision has become mechanical, in which there is a strain. (p. 168)

I do not feel that [*The Wide Net,* as charged,] is obscure. If anything, the dream-like effect in many of the stories seems to result from the author's undertaking to squeeze meaning from the item which, in ordinary realistic fiction, would be passed over with a casual glance. Hence the portentousness, the retardation, the otherworldliness. . . . [Miss Welty] wants us to get [the] smallest gesture, to participate in her vision of things as intensely meaningful. And so there is almost always a gloss to the fable. . . .

It is quite possible that Miss Welty has pushed her method to its most extreme limit. It is also possible that the method, if pursued much farther, would lead to monotony and self-imitation and merely decorative elaboration. Perhaps we shall get a fuller drama when her vision is submitted more daringly to the fact, when the definition is plunged into the devouring river. But meanwhile Miss Welty has given us several stories of brilliance and intensity; and as for the future, Miss Welty is a writer of great resourcefulness, sensitivity, and intelligence, and can probably fend for herself. (p. 169)

Robert Penn Warren, "Love and Separateness in

Eudora Welty" (originally published as "The Love and the Separateness in Miss Welty," in a different version in The Kenyon Review, *Vol. VI, No. 2, Spring, 1944), in his* Selected Essays of Robert Penn Warren *(copyright © 1958 by Robert Penn Warren; reprinted by permission of Random House, Inc.), Random House, 1958, pp. 156-69.*

GUY DAVENPORT

The optimist of Eudora Welty's *The Optimist's Daughter* is a Mississippi judge named McKelva, and his optimism is hearty enough, foolish enough, generous enough, to lead him to marry in his old age a young wife, a woman from Texas whom he had met at a Bar Association convention. Wanda Fay Chisom is her name. Had she come to the attention of Faulkner, her name would be Snopes, and if Flannery O'Connor had created her, she would be named Shiflet. She is, in the pecking order of the South, white trash.

Miss Welty has been fascinated before by these rapacious, weak-witted, pathologically selfish daughters of the dispossessed, and likes to bring them into sharp contrast (as in *The Ponder Heart*) with the decrepit chivalry and good manners of the Mississippi gentry. The result, however complex and sensitive Miss Welty's handling of the misalliance, is always a wail of grief that an older generation is being replaced by barbarians.

Miss Welty's art modulates finely between satire and tragedy. She relishes the absurd and the incongruous, and has the canny gift of being able to translate them into tragic understanding. The power behind this rare ability is a firm moral sense of human conduct. Miss Welty's values might seem at first inspection to be Christian and Humanist, but they are yet broader in a curious sense. They are *archaic*. They are as old as civilization itself.

The brilliant, meticulously rendered surfaces of Miss Welty's fiction are always transparencies through which we can see the ancient stories told and retold thousands of times. In Laurel, the Judge's daughter, we can see the figure of Psyche (her husband-to-be was named Phil, that is, *philos*, Love) and thus the one-dimensional Wanda Fay becomes a concentrate of Psyche's nasty, hateful sister. There is nothing mechanical (or simple-minded) in these symbolic gestures of Miss Welty. Myths must be retold to stay fresh. Miss Welty has told the myth of Cupid and Psyche many times, blending it mysteriously with kindred myths of loss and redemption, evoking its details with charm and wit. (Cupid, for instance, appears in the story "June Recital" as a half-naked sailor running with his shirt—his wings—flying from his shoulders.)

Miss Welty keeps returning to one central myth, that of Persephone, whose regenerate virginity formed the old Greek understanding of the death and growth of perennial nature. Persephone alive is the natural order, or cosmos; Persephone in Hades, or dead, is raw matter (rock, dirt, spiritless disorder). Thus Laurel (matter shaped by light as a tree) is the living Persephone in this brilliant little novel, and Wanda Fay (*wand*, a dead stick; *fay*, a spirit from underground) is the dead Persephone. How do we say this otherwise? That the spirit is dying in our time? That we live in a spiritual hell rather than a natural order?

Miss Welty is a deep (and unexplored) writer. Her masterpiece is the long novel *Losing Battles* (an Orpheus and Eurydice so intricately retold that it seems upside down: Eurydice reclaims Orpheus!) which befuddled the critics, some of whom made the awful mistake of thinking Miss Welty a regional writer, a local colorist. If she is, so was Ovid.

In *The Optimist's Daughter* Miss Welty returns to her early (and well-known) story, "Petrified Man." Here she wrote her severest vision of conduct without morals or values, which have been replaced by greed in all its forms (vanity, pride, selfishness, the full devastation of the sins). The moral condemnation in that powerful story grows from a concern for life as archaic as the myths which it alludes to.

The Optimist's Daughter must therefore be read with imagination and open eyes. Note how carefully it flows against a frieze of flowers, as if all the action were a ritual of spring. The people are all rootless (the Texas Chisoms live in cars instead of houses) or withering. The vision is chilling and tragic, and yet it implies a cyclical pattern, and redemption is always a miracle. (p. 697)

Guy Davenport, "Primal Visions," in National Review *(© National Review, Inc., 1972; 150 East 35th St., New York, NY 10016), Vol. XXIV, No. 24, June 23, 1972, pp. 697-98.**

JOHN A. ALLEN

The characters in Eudora Welty's fiction are fortunate indeed, for they are conceived in kindness, justice and compassion by the imagination that creates them. In Miss Welty's work, the strong and the weak, the magnanimous and the mean alike, in every circumstance retain their human dignity. "I don't have an ounce of revenge in my body," Edna Earle Ponder assures her auditor, and the words may aptly be applied to the author of "The Ponder Heart." The reader, too, enjoys Miss Welty's evenhanded bounty. On every page she tacitly gives him credit for being adequately prepared to face the shock of truth, sufficiently enamored of the real to relish its unexpected faces, rational enough to know that reason yields in the end to mystery. Her view of life is not idealized, nor is it tough in the sense of denying mortal existence its proper and inalienable graces. We are safe, in reading a Welty novel, from being dinned at, scolded, hoodwinked, lectured, flattered or condescended to. Secure from malice, anger or contempt, we enjoy a vision of the world depicted with an objectivity which is enriched by warmth and charity. If Eudora Welty has a bias, it springs from affection for the human race. (p. 605)

For Eudora Welty, showing the action of a novel through a woman's eyes is not an act of aggression but of illumination.

To be sure, Miss Welty delights her readers with the heroic antics of certain male characters: Uncle Daniel, Mike Fink, Jamie Lockhart, Jack Renfro, Curly Stovall, Major Bullock. However, . . . the suggestion here is not that male heroes are inherently ridiculous but that these characters are not, at least initially, true heroes at all. Criteria for genuine heroism as Miss Welty sees it can be found obliquely conveyed throughout her fiction. The work of demolition—to call it that—which she performs upon the conventional image of the male hero has the effect not of attacking the male sex and its image of itself but of clearing the way for a conception of heroic action which does fuller justice to the actual potentialities for heroism in men and women alike.

The tendency of Eudora Welty's fiction is indeed antiheroic; that is, it makes legitimate fun of the posturing male hero-adventurer whose main objective, to paraphrase Uncle Curtis in "Losing Battles," is to butt the world like a billy goat and make it pay him heed. An appropriate emblem of this species of hero is the Perseus of Greek myth; appropriate, that is, when Perseus' heroics are taken at face value: he averts his eyes, swings the magic sword, and lo!, with upraised arm he displays his trophy—the snaky severed head of the Medusa. Thereafter, he can use the Medusa-power as his own, striking his pose again and again with the gory trophy held on high to turn his enemies to stone. (pp. 605-06)

The interpretation of the Perseus myth in "The Golden Apples" is put forward by Miss Welty through the thoughts of that book's hero, Virgie Rainey, . . . [as she recalls a picture of] Perseus with the head of Medusa. "The vaunting was what she remembered, that uplifted arm." Yet it is not the image of the hero triumphant that has become a permanent part of her mind but the stroke of the sword he wielded. "Cutting off the Medusa's head," she thinks,

> was the heroic act, perhaps, that made visible a horror in life, that was at once the horror in love . . .—the separateness.

The stroke of Perseus is not, in itself, a triumph of any kind. So far from ridding the world of a horror, it reveals one. It is not an act of liberation, not even an assertion of the sovereign will. The important thing, for Virgie, is not what Perseus has done to Medusa; it is what the deed, like a stroke of fate, has done to him. . . . In the first moment of the heroic stroke, the hero wields the sword; in the second moment, he becomes the victim of that stroke. In the third moment, he achieves some measure of gain in understanding which leads on to self-renewal. (pp. 607-09)

Although, in the eyes of the world, Virgie Rainey has achieved nothing noteworthy, she is, in her context in "The Golden Apples," a type of the true hero. Her heroism does not derive from what is usually thought of as heroic action but from her capacity to feel and, through feeling, to know. (p. 609)

John A. Allen, "Eudora Welty: The Three Moments," in Virginia Quarterly Review *(copyright, 1975, by the* Virginia Quarterly Review, *The University of Virginia), Vol. 51, No. 4 (Autumn, 1975), pp. 605-27.*

CAROLE COOK

The introduction to her snapshot album of depression-era Mississippi, *One Time, One Place,* helps explain why [Welty's] home state has been her locale. No professional photographer, no outsider, could ever have captured the naturalness of her subjects, but she was "part of it, born into it, taken for granted." From this unique vantage point, unseen as the fly upon the wall, Welty has been able to write about all that is neither typical nor taken for granted in the life of the South. Originality of both subject and technique has been her one constant.

So we look to [*The Eye of the Story,* a] collection of essays, reviews, and personal pieces . . . to see what it reveals about her artistic creed and affinities. And lo, in addition to her canny insight into the work of her peers and masters and her great gift for pinpointing a writer's inspiration for coming to writing at all, many of these studies seem to be as much about Eudora Welty as about anything else. (pp. 37-8)

[If the essays on her favorite authors] were all there was to this volume—a series of touchstones for understanding Welty's stories—it would be quite enough. But as it happens, there is also a second dimension, another and more splendid gift from Welty to her readers. For in her studies of individual writers and in the more abstract section "On Writing"—which includes her defense of regional writing ("Place in Fiction") and of Faulkner, "the white Mississippian" ("Must the Novelist Crusade?")—she has made that dry art of criticism into a human, even moving practice. As critic, Welty is not lawgiver but friend and teacher. The words "feeling," "passion," "life," "communication," occur again and again in her attempts to lead her reader by the hand up to the books that have meant so much to her.

She explains at one point—referring most probably to the discovery of her own vocation—that "it's when reading begins to impress on us what degrees . . . of communication are possible between novelists and ourselves as readers that we surmise what it has meant, can mean, to write novels." *What it can mean to write novels.* This, it seems to me, is the real and very impassioned message behind all of Eudora Welty's criticism, and one that very few writers are in a position to transmit, because as she herself notes, story writing and critical analysis are entirely separate gifts, "like spelling and playing the flute."

The problem of criticism is that the meaning of writing is inseparable from the act of writing. There can never be a translation of a whole story into a commentary on its parts in which the story does not suffer. Welty's solution to this paradox is to treat the story as an intimate communication of feeling between just two persons—the writer and the reader, each bound to the other for the duration of the story by the moral responsibility the intimacy implies.

But whether she is writing fiction or criticism, Welty never forgets to be entertaining. She's as lively and engaging a critic as ever lived, and this is just another mark of her shrewdness. (p. 38)

Carole Cook, "Critic, Friend, and Teacher," in Saturday Review *(© 1978 by Saturday Review Magazine Corp.; reprinted with permission), Vol. 5, No. 15, April 29, 1978, pp. 37-8.*

VICTORIA GLENDINNING

In this invigorating selection of her reviews and essays ["The Eye of the Story"], Eudora Welty constantly touches the painful place where literary critic and creative writer meet. They are, she seems to suggest, essentially at cross-purposes. . . . The writer does not seek to solve the "mystery of language" but rather to take advantage of it. Criticism tries to solve the mystery, by translating fiction into another language. . . .

The pieces in this book about the climate of the fiction writer's mind should be prescribed reading for all literary critics. Also included here are some essays of reminiscence, from her childhood on. . . . She believes—and as a Southern writer this is something on which she has been challenged—that novelists should not be political crusaders. . . .

A long section is given over to book reviews, and here Miss Welty, given her views on academic criticism, stands in the eye not only of the story but of the storm. She stands calmly, because she is sure of her ground. She writes not so much as a critic as a sensitive reader. She makes the relationship between reading and writing extraordinarily close. The literary critic is in a way a code-breaker, and therefore an antagonist; Miss Welty is all receptiveness. She uses the words "pleasure" and "sweetness" without embarrassment or sentiment.

Not that she is without her moments of asperity. She picks out for castigation two modern trends. . . . The first is the "bad novel" of today that is "unhappily like the tale told to the analyst. It is not communication, it is confession—often of nothing more than some mild weakness. It is self-absorbed, self-indulgent, too often self-pitying. And it's dull." Her second target is the sort of long literary biography . . . that is "one whole compilation of details from outside. . . . One original insight would have equalled the force of a dozen of these pages." (p. 7)

[It] is in writing of those authors she most admires that the difficulty in finding a "language" for criticism, or for appreciation, becomes apparent. "I could say that [Green's] 'Concluding' is like Venus on a clear evening going down over water, and if you agreed—still worse if you disagreed—where are we now?" So she poses the problem herself. Faulkner's prose is "intolerantly and intolerably unanalyzable." In good fiction "the shapes the work takes are marvelous . . . it is hard to speak further of them." Words fail. Words fail because the work itself stands, and she is not prepared to diminish it "in other words."

Miss Welty leads one back to the books themselves. (p. 43)

Victoria Glendinning, "Eudora Welty in Type and Person," in The New York Times Book Review *(© 1978 by The New York Times Company; reprinted by permission), May 7, 1978, pp. 7, 43.*

ROBERT B. SHAW

When a novelist can articulate what he knows by feel, he calls criticism down out of its self-generated clouds. This is the welcome service rendered by Eudora Welty's selection of essays and reviews, *The Eye of the Story*. It could as justly have been called *The Eye of the Storyteller*. In criticism as in fiction, Miss Welty's observations are blessed with a dazzling accuracy; her sight penetrates to the point of insight. . . .

Miss Welty's appreciations [essays on her favorite writers] prove that a sympathy with the subject need not blur the critic's discernment, and may in fact focus it on what is central to the achievement under study. . . .

The book reviews are in many cases as keenly perceptive as the longer essays, and in all cases but one they are as positive in their judgments. The exception is Arthur Mizener's biography of Ford Madox Ford, which Miss Welty finds hard to forgive. Characteristically, she identifies the biographer's chief problem as a settled incompatibility with his subject, a bias as damaging to the book as its "coarse-grained prose." (p. 765)

I must admit that I found myself perversely wishing, especially in the book review section, that Miss Welty had allowed herself such astringency more often. It would have provided this part of the collection with a not unwelcome variety of tone and texture. But I gather that her usual policy has been to let bad books sink of their own weight—a practice bespeaking good sense as much as forbearance.

If her essays on writers are celebrations of craftsmanship, of what admired predecessors have done, her essays on writing celebrate craft itself. These theoretical pieces have more than sufficient interest for the general reader; but for the apprentice writer they should be assigned reading. Allowing for some lacunae, they comprise in less than 80 pages a sort of basic writer's manual, everywhere lucid and concise, nowhere oversimplified. Perhaps the most valuable piece is "Place in Fiction," already well-known since its separate appearance. It is impossible after reading it to think any longer in clichés about "regional literature." That this discussion should come from Eudora Welty, whom many now think of as our greatest living regional writer, seems a pleasant irony. In this and in the surrounding essays her theorizing grounds itself in concrete examples sensitively chosen. (pp. 765-66)

If there is any defect to be found in Miss Welty's critical pieces, it would be that, for all their brilliance, they labor in places under a tone of unleavened solemnity. One occasionally notices just enough constraint or wariness of manner to be reminded that for this author such writing is the work of the left hand.

This is a minor objection, and it does not apply in any way to the concluding section of personal memoirs and sketches. Here Miss Welty comes nearest to her own fictive art, in which comedy and deep feeling are so effectively interwoven. The memories of childhood in Jackson, Miss. or of a "pageant of birds" witnessed in a black church in the 1940s, are touching, funny and sad all at once. . . .

In the last piece in the volume, which appeared as preface to a collection of snapshots she took while working for the WPA in Mississippi in the depression, Miss Welty writes of how her camera began to teach her "a storywriter's truth: the thing to wait on, to reach there in time for, is the moment in which people reveal themselves." This led her to determine early on that her aim in art "would be not to point the finger in judgment but to part a curtain, that invisible shadow that falls between people, the veil of indifference to each other's presence, each other's wonder, each other's human plight." I closed this book thinking that in it, as in her fiction, the job had been well done, the moments of revelation, after the patient, necessary waiting, captured in order to be generously shared. (p. 766)

Robert B. Shaw, "A Storyteller's Appreciations," in The Nation *(copyright 1978 by the Nation Associates, Inc.), Vol. 226, No. 24, June 24, 1978, pp. 765-66.*

ROSS FELD

Welty, I think, offers [in *The Eye of the Story*] a truer, more adroit vision of fiction than either that of a language-functionary like Gass, whose protocols are ensured against outside tampering, or that of a lifelikeness-affirmer like Gardner, who, frustrated by the intransigent surprise of the world, disgustedly spits in the soup because it's already too thin.

"Great fiction shows us not how to conduct our behavior but how to feel." As simple—and enormous—as that. Also a statement not to be taken too lightly: it only *looks* mild. Right hopes and goals, right speech, fine—but where and what is right sensation? Welty knows—and her fiction knows more deeply—that by setting them out on a loose leash, the lenient novelist riskily allows his characters the harsh freedom to land themselves in their own particular holes, to suffer the same discrepancies, inconveniences, even unbearable situations—unsolved by either language or good intentions—that we do. Like us, they "find out and keep hold of who they are, often by feeling where it hurts or how it pinches." They can be flummoxed, slipped-up, even dead wrong. Yet there's a difference, *the* big one: unlike our own, the errors and shortcomings of fictional characters tremble always with "the possibility that they may indeed reveal everything."

Which is why "we come looking in fiction with more longing than in any experience save love." *Everything* may suddenly—on the very next page—be made clear. And the writer waits apprehensively along with us, providing "performance"—ideally something fine, fervent, and accurate—but knowing all along that it's finally going to be "magic" that will step in and crown art's moment. Fiction's special "magic"—a matrix of inspired stumblings, accidental splendors—ensures that the human imperfection of performance will itself seem the most dazzling gift, that in the spilled drop, not the saved one, will "the whole shimmering fabric" be reflected. Each one of Welty's essays patiently demonstrates either how vain or how coldly, needlessly ascetic it is to argue for more . . . [or] bargain for less. (pp. 92-3)

Ross Feld, "Motives for Metaphor," in Harper's *(copyright © 1978; all rights reserved; excerpted from the October, 1978 issue of* Harper's Magazine*), Vol. 257, No. 1541, October, 1978, pp. 89-93.**

LEWIS A. LAWSON

To hear Eudora Welty tell it [in *Eye of the Story*] she was born to read. . . .

Miss Welty has never gotten her fill of fiction. In a beautiful image she describes the effect of fiction on her life: as a child she was taken into the darkness of Kentucky's Mammoth Cave; when the guide struck a light she was dazzled by all the splendor of the rock formations that had been around her all along. So fiction lights up the experience that would otherwise slip by us unnoticed. That is to say, Miss Welty regards fiction as an exploration of reality, each new fiction "some fresh approximation of human truth." She would not dismiss that reality consisting solely of material objects, a view of the world so entrancing these days, but she clearly thinks that a superior reality derives from the morality which resides in human relationships. That reality is most clearly revealed to us by fiction, which can intensify our personal response by suffusing it with the accumulated insight of the race.

"Making reality real is art's responsibility," Miss Welty asserts in her famous "Place in Fiction," and she has held fiction—for her the most realistic of art's forms—severely to account. But if she has had high expectations for fiction, she has been quick to praise when her expectations have been met. (p. 215)

Eudora Welty early discovered that, as instructive to her soul as another's fiction might be (and this is the testimony in each of her essays about other writers), it ultimately remained that person's province. At that point she knew that either she could be thankful for, or at least content with, a world defined by others or she could attempt to craft her own, even though the labor would consume her life. (pp. 215-16)

Miss Welty's fictions testify that she is blessed with a profound insight—there are times when she conveys life's fragility with a pain that hurts like an autumn day. But the plentitude of her fictions and the brilliance of her essays "On Writing" declare that she has not let brilliance keep her from working at her craft.

These essays on her tools, especially "Place in Fiction" and "Some Notes on Time in Fiction," reveal a craftsmanship that is filled with pride, in the sense that Miss Welty sees pride in Katherine Anne Porter's prose, that is, "pride in the language, pride in using the language to search out human meanings, pride in making a good piece of work." Miss Welty's work (and that word cannot be too much stressed) reveals self-respect and satisfaction in effort spent, those meanings of "pride" she detects in Miss Porter's work. (p. 216)

For more than forty years Eudora Welty has, in her urgency, made magnificent use of her tools. For too many of those years she was that other writer from Mississippi or one of that wondrous generation of Southern women writers. Even yet there is not a body of criticism commensurate to her achievement—too often she suffers when the generalizations about Southern literature or about any one of her fellow practitioners are applied to her.

But with the colligation here of her own best pieces of criticism there can no longer be any excuse for mistreating her. Her critical perceptions about other writers are like boomerangs: they fly straight to their mark, but if that target should be removed, they speed directly back to her. There they join the body of comment that she has made about (her own) technique. All in all, what the comments say is that Eudora Welty must know more about loneliness than ever Robinson Crusoe did. Loneliness here is not understood as social isolation, but that vision which has, if only for a moment, glimpsed the flimsiness of all those social constructions that advertise communion. Miss Welty's characters are obsessed to talk, and sometimes the complaint is heard that nothing happens except talk in a Welty novel. That is precisely the point: nothing happens—and would happen more if we did not talk. . . . In her own Mammoth Cave, Eudora Welty has been lighting candles against time and death all these years. (pp. 216-17)

Lewis A. Lawson, "Lighting Candles," in Modern Age *(copyright © 1979 by the Intercollegiate Studies Institute, Inc.), Vol. 23, No. 2, Spring, 1979, pp. 215-17.*

* * *

WEST, Paul 1930-

A novelist, critic, poet, teacher, essayist, and short story writer, West is an Englishman now living in America. He became known for the zany inventiveness of the Alley Jaggers novels; but it is *Words for a Deaf Daughter* that reveals his essential optimism. (See also *CLC*, Vol. 7, and *Contemporary Authors*, Vols. 13-16, rev. ed.)

CARL SAGAN

Paul West's *Gala* . . . is a kind of sequel to his much acclaimed and extraordinarily sensitive *Words for a Deaf Daughter,* a nonfiction work about his brain-injured child. *Gala* is a kind of wish fulfillment of a hoped-for but unrealized summer visit by his daughter. It is notable for many reasons, one of which is its rich use of scientific facts and metaphor in the development of the story. Major ideas in astronomy and in the genetic code are woven skillfully into the text both overtly and subtly. . . . (p. 28)

Carl Sagan, "Carl Sagan on Science," in The New Republic *(reprinted by permission of* The New Republic; *© 1976 The New Republic, Inc.), Vol. 175, No. 21, November 20, 1976, pp. 26-30.*

WALTON BEACHAM

Paul West is probably tired of being called an "intelligent writer," and finding himself compared to Anthony Burgess and Vladimir Nabokov book after book. . . . Worse, Paul West is probably tired of being categorized as an English writer and set in the tradition of those he admires: D. H. Lawrence, Virginia Woolf, E. M. Forster. . . .

Paul West is a complicated man—his books almost as complex—full of enormous energy which he has somehow never managed to unleash, although his works are impressive and the list of them nearly as long as those of the writers he admires. . . .

[If] we, as readers, are ever to understand and appreciate West, as we finally learned to appreciate Burgess and Nabokov after so many embarrassing misperceptions, then we must establish how he uses the mind, through metaphor, to impose order on a disordered universe.

In his critical essays, West says that metaphor is the means by which the mind can search for relationships which will settle the heart, and he proposes an intriguing premise for art. Modern man's inclination, West says, is to ask, "why is there chaos in life?" when the question should be, "why is there any order at all?" . . . West offers as a working axiom that we cannot assume order as a means of questioning disorder, except as the mind is capable of imposing metaphor, and it is the mind that so troubles West and haunts his books.

In *Words for a Deaf Daughter,* one of the most difficult matters for West to accept is that Mandy is not only stone deaf but that she may also be brain damaged. For years the parents sustain hope that Mandy's difficulties with life are a result of her hearing defect, and much of the sympathy and emotion of Mandy's story comes when the parents, having finally learned that their daughter does not possess normal intelligence, are able to allow Mandy her own world and to accept it as if it were theirs. (p. 21)

In all his imaginative books from *The Snow Leopard* (poems), to the trilogy, to *Colonel Mint* (novel), West establishes a world in which the competition between structure and disorder drives man deeper into himself, so that if he ever emerges, it is as a creature who is frantic to control those forces larger than himself. He cries against the cosmos in defiance of his subservience, and struggles to establish order over the chaos as proof of his autonomy.

No wonder, then, that with all this behind him West feels compelled to try to release himself from his daughter by exploring the universe with her. He is like a god, who having formed an imperfect creation must diminish his responsibility by giving his creature his own powers and freedom. *Gala,* says West in the preface, is a kind of wish fulfillment, by which he means that he can establish through imagination a relationship with his daughter that is impossible in real life. *Gala* is a "fictional sequel" to *Words for a Deaf Daughter*—it is Mandy come home at age 14 from her special school in England for a two-week reunion with her father. "Gala" means celebration; it means Galatea; it means galaxy, but it is much more. The novel attempts to impose order on two lives by reducing the universe to Mandy's level of understanding and making her its master. (pp. 21-2)

Mandy's fictional name is Milk (from Michaela); the father's is Deulius. He is Daedalus designing wings so that Icarus can escape the labyrinth, but this time the progeny will fly to the depths of outer space—to the Milky Way, and ride its mythical constellations as if they were bucking broncos. In the basement of their . . . house, Deulius, Milk and Deulius's mistress, Pi, paint, drill and wire an electric universe, and the progress which the trio makes toward completing the project coincides with the time when Milk must return to her systematized life in England. These two weeks with Deulius represent her flight, and quite literally Milk loves to soar. The novel is full of planes, kites and all types of modern alchemy which cast their spell and tint an impossible escape with magic. Deulius is a Pygmalion who, through a passion for his creation, brings Galatea alive and imbues her with a spirit of his own. But West, unlike Pygmalion, understands that he does not want to possess what he has created, no more than Daedalus can command Icarus not to fly to the sun.

Given wings, who wouldn't fly as high as the Milky Way? Only Daedalus and Paul West, for West recognizes the metaphor of labyrinths and the paradox of controlling the intellect so masterfully that Daedalus can design an ordered system complex enough that even he cannot escape it. (p. 22)

With this kind of texture to his stories, West would expect to be called an "intelligent writer" and to be compared to his countrymen. What else can you say about a writer who possesses superior intellect, education, craft and a heart consumed by the black hole of emotion? Critics want to praise West because they sense the potential energy which all his works contain, and because they don't quite understand how he comes so close to making his stories explode in our faces, only to defuse them at the last moment. American critics would like to say of *Gala,* as they have said in a flair of controversy about his other books, that West has not freed himself from himself; that he is chained to the confines of the mind, and that as long as this prevails, he will never quite convey the heights and depths of the human heart in conflict with itself. And West, of course, would say to these romanticists that the range of the mind is so much greater than the puny spirit of the heart.

Evaluating the merits of Paul West's books is a difficult matter for all of us who are trying to decide whether readers and critics make any difference to art as it exists for its own sake and ours, and I suspect that West will continue to be called "intelligent" long after his readers finally come to see that Burgess and Greene are not intelligent writers in the same sense. But maybe not. West has earned all the adjectives his critics use in praise of him—"triumphant, masterful, brilliant. . . ." *Words* is a sympathetic book for anyone who feels responsible for anyone else, afflicted or not, and West's use of the intellect in that book may be the only way he can deal with such an intensely emotional and pathetic situation which, as the critics have said, "is not gloomy sad, but world sad." Certainly, *Gala* is the inevitable sequel to it, and West's impressive variety of books establishes clearly that he is a gifted man. And yet . . . and yet. . . .

In *Words for a Deaf Daughter,* West develops a maxim which defines Mandy's world and his own as father of a damaged child: "you discover what you discover because you have lost what you've lost." What West discovers at the end of *Gala* is that he, not Milk, has flown beyond the sun and like Pi must travel to infinity before he can close the open end of an indefinite number. *Gala* convinces us of that, and in doing so turns the story into Deulius's, not Milk's. And yet it is Milk who speaks for us all metaphorically, and West knows this even if he can't write the story without making it his own.

At the very end of the novel, after Milk has been returned to school, Deulius visits his mother who lives in England, and she asks if Milk has been good during her visit in Florida. "Good?" says Deulius. "She was perfect. Know what she did? Aired my pajamas for me on the second day by draping them over the folding chair on the balcony. Aired my pajamas even though they weren't damp."

What else can a critic say? Milk has made a metaphor for the metaphor of love, if only West's body would sweat a little. (pp. 22-3)

Walton Beacham, "Without Perspiration," in The Nation *(copyright 1977 by the Nation Associates, Inc.), Vol. 224, No. 1, January 1-8, 1977, pp. 21-3.*

J. D. O'HARA

A gala is a festive celebration, an abnormal interruption in life's routine. *Gala* is also Greek for milk, and thence the source of those astronomical splashes the galaxies, especially our own Milky Way. Milk is also linked to our infancy and hence our origins, genetic and familial. Linked so to life at its personal origin and its widest impersonal extension, milk is too valuable to treat lightly, yet we must not cry over it spilt.

Such observations are brought home to our business and bosom by [*Gala*]. Its narrator is the father of a 14-year-old girl nicknamed Milk. . . . Milk is exuberant, amusing, and lovely. . . .

Milk is also hopelessly retarded, brain-damaged from birth, and almost completely deaf. . . . [In] this fictional sequel to his biographical *Words for a Deaf Daughter* novelist and father Paul West engages in a heroic endeavor to come to terms with the fact of Milk's flawed existence. His attempt encompasses a wide range of extravagant colors, sights, and events with which he fills up Milk's mind. It also includes his survey of a universe of abnormalities, a totality of surds in which our reasonable normality looks no less deviant than the grotesque facts of physical existence. . . .

[We] are put continually in Milk's charming, frightening, heartrending presence; we are reminded of the continuous strain of caring for a loved and potentially explosive mind . . . ; we are always aware, even during the story's most amusing and intriguing moments, that "part of the story of this book's story is the acid-on-the-nerves of writing it at all."

Luckily there is no way to compare pains, no way to know if Milk's predicament is worse even than her father's. We can never know how she feels; but we can all imagine how he feels, imagine what it is to be linked by love to such sorrow and affliction. And West spares us and himself nothing except self-pity. His narrator faces all the nightmares, even that of the police state in which the deformed are punished, even that ultimate pain in which the permanently maimed child is imagined as her perfected self, whole, witty, learned, and articulate. *("I know, I know, you've been waiting all your life for this conversation.")*

At the visit's end the narrator is exhausted. You will be, too. But the getting there, in all its sadness, obsession, hysteria, eloquence, and even boredom, will have justified the fuss we make about the arts. This is a beautiful novel. Beauty is difficult.

J. D. O'Hara, "The Focus of a Flawed Universe," in Book World—The Washington Post *(© 1977,* The Washington Post*), January 2, 1977, p. G3.*

EDMUND WHITE

"Eloquence is variety," a character says toward the end of "Gala," and if the equation is true then this autobiographical novel is wildly eloquent. Paul West . . . has a style as full of exotic ingredients as God's bouillabaisse and, in its references to nature, as comprehensive as Noah's inventory. . . .

[If] these pages were printed in stanzas and with quirky line-breaks, they could easily pass for verse of a very high order. . . .

Paul West [invents] . . . startling, dazzling meditations. His mind traveling in a comet's path, he intersects the fixed orbits of other people's preoccupations. He muses on history, biology, philosophy, literature, music, love, London, New York (which he describes as "tonic, lush, optional"), religion, divorce, anthropology. He has thrown a mental party for his readers—a gala, a festivity that links two human beings to the constellations.

Edmund White, "God's Bouillabaisse," in The New York Times Book Review *(© 1977 by The New York Times Company; reprinted by permission), July 3, 1977, p. 13.*

JAY L. HALIO

Centered mostly on a minuscule geographical area . . . and for a finite period of time, *Gala* succeeds in establishing the enormous perspective of man in the universe—perspective, that is, not place, although place helps provide the perspective, of course. Deulius constantly raises questions, often evoked by trying to make sense out of his daughter's congenital birth defect. Bowled over by his first good look at the Milky Way, and repeatedly amazed by it afterward, "What," he asks, "am I to make of that chunk of the universe in the context of Milk herself?" He can find no answer, and probably there is none, yet he continues to engage in "interrogative speculation." "Bold questions, yet somehow always askew or ill defined, come and go in my mind like sharks which cannot stop." Still the reunion is an unexpected success, far better than he dared hope. And the end is managed with lightness, humor, and poignancy. The interrogative speculation will continue, as the short epilogue indicates; much is learned, more is left to learn. (pp. 254-55)

Jay L. Halio, "Persons Placed and Displaced," in The Southern Review *(copyright, 1979, by Jay L. Halio), Vol. 15, No. 1, January, 1979, pp. 250-56.**

* * *

WHEELOCK, John Hall 1886-1978

Wheelock was an American poet, editor, critic, and translator. Wheelock's poetry, traditional in form, expresses delight in natural beauty. His first published poetry appeared in 1905 in *Verses of Two Undergraduates,* a collaborative effort of Wheelock and his friend and Harvard classmate, Van Wyck Brooks. (See also *Contemporary Authors,* Vols. 13-16, rev. ed.; obituary, Vols. 77-80.)

HENRY TAYLOR

Wheelock's development has been slow and sometimes painful; in his determination not to succumb to the whims of fashion, he has sometimes seemed to move backward instead of forward. But in his later years he finally wrote a number of poems which are worth all the trouble, and which are not diminished by the lesser poems [*By Daylight and In Dream: New and Selected Poems*]. . . .

[This volume] contains, in roughly chronological order, all the poems which Wheelock wishes to preserve. The collection is weighted in favor of relatively recent work. . . . (p. 460)

But even though vast numbers of early poems have been left behind, those which remain are enough to suggest the difficulties which plagued the young poet. He wrote, for one thing, with incredible haste—he published sizeable collections in 1911, 1912, 1913, 1919, 1922, 1927, and 1936—and so must often have failed to see how little of this verse was his own, and how much of it was a pastiche of early favorites such as Henley, Whitman, and Wordsworth. There are whole poems here which seem to have been written by the ghost of an anonymous nineteenth-century voice. . . . (pp. 460-61)

But even as Wheelock continued to pour out volumes of this kind of work, he gradually increased his command over formal and structural elements, so that even bad poems began to reveal arresting musical and rhythmical details, as in this final stanza from "Translation":

> Now, as you read these verses—from afar,
> This very moment, from this printed rhyme,
> I cry to you out of the wheels of Time,
> I call to you across the morning-star.

The arrangement of stresses and vowel-sounds is more artfully controlled here, and arouses some pleasure, still too slight to overcome the sentimental and derivative phrases; but the control and the pleasure are there, and are the foundation for the good poems Wheelock came to write in his late sixties. (p. 461)

Whatever the reasons, there is no doubt that Wheelock's later work is a great improvement over the earlier; the improvement is especially remarkable when we realize that no radical shift occurred in thematic or formal preoccupations. The later poems grow naturally out of the earlier ones, pursuing the same themes of love, death, and the tragic nature of life; they move in the same traditional forms. But their voice is distinctively Wheelock's own. (pp. 461-62)

The profound change in Wheelock's poetry has been wrought by comparatively slight adjustments in the earlier style. Some phrases here still border on triteness, but they have been absorbed into a distinctive, controlled, and dateless voice. Old ideas restated with a minimum of idiosyncrasy are hard to work into poems, but Wheelock manages to do so regularly and memorably. . . .

Among the best of [the poems presented is] the title poem of this collection ["By Daylight and In Dream"]. . . . In three long sections of blank verse, the speaker confronts his impending death, made more poignant by the remnants of his past, which lie all around him. Wheelock has wisely avoided trying to resolve the vast questions which suggest themselves in the course of his meditation. At certain moments, he looks toward the possibility of eternal life, and at other moments he accepts the finality of death, celebrating the holiness of earth, "the graveyard of the self-effacing dead". The poem concludes with a dream in which various voices offer various answers to the question of what follows death; but the speaker is still living at the end of the poem, and there is a strong suggestion that the importance of the future still lies this side of the grave. A small formal detail underscores this notion; the blank-verse line is broken between the end of one section and the beginning of another, and the third section ends with a short line. It has not been filled out, which hints that there is more to come, not of this poem, but of the stuff of which it is made.

Wheelock has at last written his share of fine poems, and they are all here; and there is extra pleasure to be gained from respect for [his] perseverance . . . and from the realization that Wheelock, at eighty-five, continues to contemplate his future work. (p. 463)

Henry Taylor, "The Collected Poems of John Hall Wheelock," in The Sewanee Review *(reprinted by permission of the editor; © 1971 by The University of the South), Vol. LXXIX, No. 3, Summer, 1971, pp. 460-63.*

JAY B. HUBBELL

For fifty years [John Hall Wheelock] has been regularly listed among the living American poets, but far too many critics have been content with merely labeling him as "traditional," "conservative," and sometimes even "reactionary." He was not among the poets whose reputations owed so much to the backing of Louis Untermeyer, Amy Lowell, and Ezra Pound; and he is not the favorite of those literary journalists in our time who are more interested in a poet's political and social opinions than in the quality of his poetry. Wheelock is no propagandist, and he is not a literary rebel or an alienated American artist. He is more deeply concerned about the quality of his poetry than about his reputation. He is as intelligent, as well-informed, and in the best sense as "sophisticated" as any of his critics or any living poet. (pp. 295-96)

Wheelock sees himself, in his own words, not as an "end" or a "beginning," but as a "link in the long chain of tradition, each link of which is different from any other." He is, as I see him, in the mainstream of the Anglo-American literary tradition, which in large part derives from the literatures of ancient Greece, Rome, and Palestine. He has studied the *Iliad,* the *Divine Comedy, Faust,* and other supreme masterpieces, and he has seen that they survive "because of a special vitality inherent in them"; and he believes that they in turn "will generate, throughout time, by their creative energy and influence, the succession of works that constitute the continuing body of literature." Like a symphony of Beethoven or a painting by Rembrandt, a great poem serves to remind us of our common humanity; and it links the past with the present and the future.

Wheelock would no doubt acknowledge his kinship with our older American writers. Like Emerson and Whitman, he is always conscious of the unity of all life. Like Melville and Hawthorne, he sees that from the human point of view the nature of things is tragic. Like Poe, he is a musician forever searching for the magical words which will bring us, in Allen Tate's memorable phrase, "knowledge carried to the heart." (pp. 296-97)

Wheelock has a keen sense of humor, which is best seen in a group of poems entitled "Scherzo." They vary from fun and nonsense to satire and burlesque. "The Plumber as the Missing Letter" parodies the style of Wallace Stevens. "Please Turn Off the Moonlight" satirizes poems that are visual, analytic, obscure, or devoid of emotion. (p. 306)

Wheelock's attitude toward his reputation is like that of Herman Melville, who in old age remarked to Titus Munson Coan: "My books will speak for themselves, and all the better if I avoid the rattling egotism by which so many win a certain vogue for a certain time." "The final arbiter" of fame, as Wheelock wrote in *What Is Poetry?,* "will not be the audience in space, the mass audience at any given moment, but the audience in time, the qualified reader throughout the ages." (p. 307)

Wheelock's place in our literature is secure. He is, in the words of Allen Tate, "one of the best poets in English." What he has to say lacks a certain fashionable novelty, but it will ring as true in the year 2000 as it does today. What he has done—and he has done it better than most of his English and American contemporaries—is to make us feel anew the wonder, the mystery, the sadness, the joy, and the unity of life. Wheelock is a major American poet. (p. 310)

Jay B. Hubbell, "A Major American Poet: John Hall Wheelock," in South Atlantic Quarterly *(reprinted by permission of the Publisher; copyright 1973 by Duke University Press, Durham, North Carolina), Vol. 72, No. 2, Spring, 1973, pp. 295-310.*

JAMES DICKEY

[Wheelock] was a classicist, and his poems came from the conviction that poetry releases human emotion when it is most compressed by the medium of form. One of his best poems, dedicated to his father and titled "The Gardener," passionately and quietly emphasizes that his father took the way of the artist and laid his gardens out according to strict order, so that the beauty of vegetable foliage would be related to the human mind:

Truly, your labors have not been in vain;
These woods, these walks, these gardens—everywhere
I look, the glories of your love remain.
Therefore, for you, now beyond praise or prayer,
Before the night falls that shall make us one,
In which neither of us will know or care,
This kiss, father, from him who was your son.

It is a wonderful poem, written in terza rima, the great rhythm of Dante, and is an inspired example of the relationship that John Hall Wheelock held between himself, his craft, his world and his father. (pp. 14, 56)

[Wheelock] began with his large, innocent heart as a rather shameless sentimentalist. The early work is good, the kind of thing that one can accede to after a couple of beers. The rhythms are somewhat in the manner of Swinburne, and there is a heavy cast of the fin de siècle over these early poems. . . . In these lush and almost mawkish verses, an unerring sense of timing is evident, which is, even though employed in such sentimental and period-ridden themes, unusual and interesting. . . . Wheelock, though his lyricism deepened over the years, became increasingly moving, in the manner of a man no longer interested in Swinburnian Romanticism but involved far more profoundly in the meaning of his own existence: his past, his family, the landscapes that had surrounded him over the years of his long life, and a very noble coming-to-terms with the intolerable burden of memory. . . .

Anyone who cares for the human imagination should read the beautifully cadenced poems of this compassionate, talented and peacefully creative man. We should be privileged to join him, in his own words, "in the wilderness of heaven." (p. 56)

James Dickey, "Compassionate Classicist," in The New York Times Book Review *(© 1978 by The New York Times Company; reprinted by permission), December 10, 1978, pp. 14, 56.*

JAMES FINN COTTER

The present world seems far removed from the poetry of John Hall Wheelock. His posthumous book [*This Blessèd Earth, New and Selected Poems, 1927-1977*] contains his last and selected poems, a short but important summing-up. The nineteenth-century air things wear in these poems seems appropriate and true in old age, and the advice in "Self-Counsel in Age" suitable to any poet: "Sing for your own delight—though there be none / To hear you out." Wheelock, like Whitman, remembers a thrush singing to young lovers and he describes the suffering existence itself knows within us. Wisdom and thanksgiving shine through his lines, and his old-fashioned fervor makes "Address to Existence" and "Affirmation" lyrical in their didacticism. Similar themes occur in the selected poems: philosophical acceptance in "The Holy Earth," love of nature in "The Fish-Hawk," and oneness with the dead in "Dear Men and Women." Admiration is the only response for a poet so solicitous of his audience. (pp. 121-22)

James Finn Cotter, "Familiar Poetry," in The Hudson Review *(copyright © 1979 by The Hudson Review, Inc.; reprinted by permission), Vol. XXXII, No. 1, Spring, 1979, pp. 109-22.**

CALVIN BEDIENT

Wheelock published his first poem in 1900, and his longevity, coupled with what James Dickey called "his large, innocent heart" [see excerpt above] and his career as an editor, are almost enough to melt the point of a critic's pen. But to praise Wheelock is to confuse the end of literature with sentiments. His poems [collected in *This Blessèd Earth*] go on and on being moved. . . . His softened melancholy and his gratitude for existence vie for control of his tone. Laid on thick and thick, the honey sickens. (p. 296)

To praise Wheelock is also to praise pastiche, mostly of Wordsworth. It's to rout the moderns from Yeats to Lowell, who distrusted the consolations not only of sentiment but of a time-slickened style. To be high-soundingly high-souled, as Wheelock is, to use "lonely" as he does in "Now the high lonely stars of night come on" or write any part of "the tender / High fortitude of the spirit shining through," is to murmur unconsciously from the Sleeper's Den, outside modernity and outside what Eliot called the intolerable wrestle with words and meanings. (p. 297)

Calvin Bedient, "Poetry Comfortable and Uncomfortable," in The Sewanee Review *(reprinted by permission of the editor; © 1979 by The University of the South), Vol. LXXXVII, No. 2, Spring, 1979, pp. 296-304.**

* * *

WIEBE, Rudy 1934-

Wiebe is a Canadian novelist, short story writer, and critic. His devout belief in the Mennonite religion informs all of his work, and serves to illuminate Wiebe's concept of modern man. Although his work has been criticized as overly didactic, Wiebe addresses the complex problems of belief in a direct and forceful manner. (See also *CLC*, Vols. 6, 11, and *Contemporary Authors*, Vols. 37-40, rev. ed.)

HILDEGARD E. TIESSEN

Rudy Wiebe's *Peace Shall Destroy Many* (1962) and *The Blue Mountains of China* (1970) function within the Canadian literary context not only as works of Prairie fiction, but also as documents that illuminate Mennonitism, a peculiar religious and ethnic orientation which has impressed itself upon the Prairie landscape for the past 100 years. In each novel the material used is Mennonite, and the thematic framework in which it is cast is a theological one, tempered primarily by the author's own interpretation of Anabaptist teaching. . . . Wiebe already alludes to what later becomes a major motif in *The Blue Mountains of China:* "they were a religious nation without a country. They were driven from Switzerland to America, from Holland and northern Germany to Prussia, then Russia, finally to North and South America." . . .

The story Wiebe tells of the Mennonites in *The Blue Mountains of China*—although the details make it a mixture of what he would choose to call "layers of fact" and "prisms of fiction"—is a genuine physical and spiritual history of these people [as they fled from Russia in the 1920s]. . . .

Wiebe's first and third novels are contemporary explorations of the Mennonite way of life. . . . The early Anabaptist fathers had stressed in their teachings a literal application of Jesus's concept of the brotherhood of man. In his fiction Wiebe attempts to demonstrate that the man who would seriously wish to express that principle of brotherhood, and so live at peace with his neighbour, must first find peace within his own soul. . . . Wiebe's theology, as he provides it in *Peace Shall Destroy Many* and *The Blue Mountains of China,* is concerned above all with a definition of this inner peace and with a fictional exploration of some men's discovery of it. . . . (p. 71)

Apparently somewhat embarrassed by Wiebe's explicitly religious themes, reviewers failed generally to receive [*Peace Shall Destroy Many*] on its own terms—as a serious attempt to deal aesthetically with a way of life dogmatically sustained by the non-resistant Mennonite prairie settlers—and acknowledged the work simply as a token of a new author's "promise." Numerous influential members of the Mennonite community itself were unable to approach the book from a detached perspective, and so further obscured the merits of the work with heated and prolonged controversy.

Critical consideration of *Peace Shall Destroy Many* remains confined to the contexts of the early reviews, in which the novel is perceived frequently as being flawed by undue moralizing. Those reviewers who have criticized the novel for what appears to them to be a disproportionate religious vision, and those who have chosen to ignore its religious thrust altogether, have remained oblivious to the presence in the novel of young Hal Wiens, who is, both thematically and structurally, a central figure in the book. *Peace Shall Destroy Many* is not primarily his story, yet Hal . . . represents the positive force which is sustained throughout the novel and which finally points toward a renewal of the life of the community. . . .

It is through the character of Hal that Wiebe delicately sustains a positive vision in the novel. Unlike the adults in the community, Hal is not caught in a perpetual self-defeating struggle with his environment. . . . Wiebe expresses his hope in the possibility of a community of people who, like the simple child, will learn to live at peace with themselves, and others. (p. 72)

[*The Blue Mountains of China*] is concerned with the practical experience of [inner] peace in man's life. Central to an understanding of the theology of both novels are Joseph Dueck's lengthy comments on the several meanings of the term peace, comments making up a treatise rather too awkwardly presented within the context of *Peace Shall Destroy Many,* in the form of a letter from Dueck to Thom Wiens. Wiebe will not be misunderstood here. (p. 73)

Apathy and retreat had become for the Mennonites a vulgarized expression of the concept of social and political passivity which had been adopted by the Anabaptists during and after their many years of persecution. Although they had originated as the forceful left wing of the Reformation, the Mennonites, driven relentlessly by their pursuers into the far corners of the continent, were early forced to withdraw from all forms of public life. They came to be known, and to regard themselves, as "die Stille im Lande;" that is, "the quiet in the land." Their passivity was most obviously demonstrated in their doctrine of non-resistance, a belief initially respected by the governments of the countries in which they chose to settle. Dueck insists that the Mennonites must begin to express their pacifism not by turning away from the hatred and warfare in the world, but by combatting it with positive action, an idea more violently reiterated by the inwardly tormented Samuel U. Reimer. . . . (pp. 73-4)

Sam Reimer stands somewhere between those characters whom Wiebe presents as people able to more forward positively, enthusiastically embracing an existence to which a faith in God has given meaning, and those in whom irrepressible guilt has brought about a complete rejection of life. Beside Sam on the one hand is David Epp, "reckless of anything save his reckless faith." . . .

The prose passage which expresses David's emotions when he arrives in Russia, after crossing back alone over the blue mountains of China, contains one of the most explicit allusions to the title of the novel and illuminates the thematic significance of the title within the context of the work. The phrase, "the blue line . . . of the mountains," is interrupted by a significant short interior monologue—a narrative mode which, throughout the novel, renders the most personal responses of a character to his immediate condition—"*over every hilltop is peace now every treetop moves through you: every breath cease the nestlings hush in the wood now only wait you too will soon have peace*." . . .

The only peace which David Epp can finally experience—the peace that was denied Sam Reimer—is the peace of God documented by Joseph Dueck in *Peace Shall Destroy Many:* "the peace of reconciliation with God and therefore the peace of conscious fellowship with God through God in Christ." As he sits in his deserted Russian home David sees the mountains again, but recognizing the irony inherent in what the blue mountains of China had actually come to represent to him, he sees them in a significantly new light: "he thought he could see the blue line . . . of the mountains far away, beautiful as they had ever been from there. But he knew now that was only his imagination. Or romantic nostalgia." (p. 74)

The most prominent theme of *The Blue Mountains of China* is that Mennonites are New Testament Christians whose promised land "isn't anywhere on earth." Their role, according to Wiebe, is not to seek the peace which they variously and erroneously have interpreted as quiescence, good order, or public tranquility. Peace, Wiebe insists, is an inner state. Nor are they to become passive and apathetic at home, as Sam Reimer says, accusingly, "growing fat off the land." According to Wiebe's theology, Jesus came not to bring man *Gemütlichkeit,* but, as John Reimer says, He came "to lead a revolution." . . .

Of all Wiebe's mature characters—that is, those who have passed beyond the time of childhood innocence and the accompanying "peacefulness" demonstrated by Hal Wiens in *Peace Shall Destroy Many*—it is Frieda Friesen who stands out as the one who expresses most completely that perfect state of being. (p. 75)

Frieda, in her "true quiet faith," is satisfied that her life is in God's hands. In her gentle first-person narratives, which are effectively interspersed throughout *The Blue Mountains of China,* she emphasizes in her quiet way the value of her own experiences, and by implication, the ultimately coherent, meaningful nature of experience in general. (pp. 75-6)

Wiebe is able to use her life as a fictional exploration of what it might mean for a human being to experience peace, such as the world cannot give, trust in God that allows him to accept both the easy and the hard of life with goodwill and enthusiasm. Wiebe has created in Frieda a completely believable and engaging character living out an ideal freedom from that inner tension which has come to be called the existential *angst* and thriving as a spiritual being regardless of the nature of external circumstances. Simply to affirm the truth of a promise of God is for many of Wiebe's characters the most significant gesture of their lives. To be able to live day by day in quiet faith, with the conscious knowledge of being at peace because, in the words of Frieda Friesen, "some things in this world only God has to understand," is the promise realized. (p. 76)

Hildegard E. Tiessen, "A Mighty Inner River: 'Peace' in the Fiction of Rudy Wiebe," in The Canadian Forum, *Vol. II, No. 4, Fall, 1973, pp. 71-6.*

W. J. KEITH

Sir Walter Scott employed the historical novel to analyze the process of history; Tolstoy used it to illustrate his own philosophy of history. Rudy Wiebe (and I should state here that I consider him thoroughly capable of sustaining these lofty comparisons) is more interested in using his art to explore the enigmas of history and to recreate the experience of living at a time of historical crisis. All his characters are authentic, and he occupies a territory closer than any of his novelist-predecessors to that of the professional historians. His creative faculty is to be found in the convincing motivations he provides for his protagonists and the artistic balance that he achieves in his selection of available incident. . . .

[*The Scorched-Wood People*] is Wiebe's first novel to rely upon a single first-person perspective, and the strain sometimes shows. He asks his reader to accept an unusual authorial convention; an effort of both imagination and sympathy is necessary. But if the reader is prepared to make this effort, the rewards are considerable.

The Scorched-Wood People is best approached as a series of imaginative tableaux. It lacks the gradual development to which we are accustomed in a traditional novel. Each section relates to the next not by any necessary plot-connection, but because it adds yet another facet to the ultimate understanding of Riel's life. . . . The spirit rather than the letter of history is presented. . . . Until now, he has avoided presenting the act of love, but his unforgettable portrayal of a sexual encounter between Riel and Marguerite is evidence of the astonishing emotional range that he can now encompass. . . .

Pierre Falcon, the tough, ribald yet devout Métis poet, blends with Rudy Wiebe, the most visionary of our novelists, to recreate Riel's crusade which, we are told, "became more religious than political." And the power of their combined vision transcends what the unimaginative might consider the limitations of a historical reconstruction. . . .

The Scorched-Wood People may not even be a novel in the strictest sense, but it is magnificent.

W. J. Keith, "Riel's Great Vision," in The Canadian Forum, *Vol. LVII, No. 677, December-January, 1977-78, p. 34.*

FRANCIS MANSBRIDGE

Most contemporary Canadian novelists are writing within an urban context. To be more precise, their concerns are generally those of our society in its more "highly developed" state—the problem of alienation, a sense of personal guilt, the search for basic values, the healing power of love

—all are concerns which modern Canadian novelists explore, often with great skill and sensitivity. The nature of these concerns is often shaped by a vision of the world in which the traditional feelings of community have broken down; the individual finds himself in existential isolation, charting his own fate with no exterior guide on which he can rely, and no possibility of any return to a state in which the individual can strengthen himself on the values of those with whom he shares his life.

If not entirely opposed to this mainstream of the contemporary Canadian novel, Rudy Wiebe's interests are certainly divergent. Throughout Wiebe's work is a strong sense of community—a sense of man as part of a larger context, even though his protagonists often spend much of their time trying to establish their identity either within or in opposition to their community. His earlier work draws on his Mennonite background as a correlative through which to express this sense of community. Often, as in his first novel *Peace Shall Destroy Many,* the negative elements of repression exerted by the community are portrayed vividly. But even here the feeling emerges that the community is good and will, in some form or another, survive. It is logical that Wiebe should turn in his more recent writing to re-create the history of Big Bear and his times. Like the Mennonite society, the Indian society of this time possessed a strong sense of community, although, in Wiebe's version at least, a greater sense of the spiritual content of life. His novel *The Temptations of Big Bear* is the most detailed evocation of this society, but later writing has continued to reveal Wiebe's fascination with this time. . . . (p. 42)

Peace Shall Destroy Many describes the attempts of Wapiti, a Mennonite community in northern Saskatchewan, to isolate itself from the changing world of 1944. More particularly, it relates the growth of Thomas Wiens to manhood, and his consequent struggle for freedom in a community whose repressiveness allows little room for original thinking or acting. The formidable figure of Peter Block, (aptly named, for he blocks Thom's growth), is the major obstacle to Thom's achievement of independence. Block, the founder and unquestioned head of the community, is the autocratic father-figure whom Thom must confront to gain the power to release his own character.

The structure of the novel reveals considerable control in the hands of the young novelist. Oppositions between the old and the new, between youth and age, and between instinct and rationality, are effectively presented. Frequent changes of pace and the ability to express feelings associated with domestic scenes or bitter elemental conflicts help give the novel variety and interest. Wiebe's main problem in this novel appears to be assimilating a wide range of thoughts and ideas into a sufficiently refined form. The structure is sturdy, but roughhewn. There are too many passages . . . in which Wiebe indulges in long discussions of issues. While they have considerable merit these might have been presented more effectively either symbolically or through action. (p. 43)

Wiebe is not a great prose stylist; he is living proof of the strange fact that a writer may be a considerable novelist while having a very indifferent command of the English language. . . .

Wiebe's frequently awkward and ponderous style recalls that of [Frederick Grove]. Mordecai Richler has said of Grove that "the plain fact is he couldn't write very well." True, yet he is a formidable novelist, and so is Wiebe. But Wiebe's prose does have its difficult moments. (p. 44)

Similarities in characterization exist between Grove and Wiebe. Each has an ability to create impressive pioneer figures, but a similar faltering when attempting more "modern" character types. While Razia Tantamount and Hank Unger, in *Peace Shall Destroy Many,* are the least convincing characters in this novel, the Mennonite characters have a deeply realized vitality. And Wiebe is capable of a naturalness and humour with his characters, as in the scenes in the Wiens' household, that Grove rarely achieves.

Yet if Wiebe sometimes writes awkwardly, there are also happier times, as in the preludes to each of the four sections of which the novel is composed. They are both structurally and stylistically accomplished. . . . (p. 45)

Rudy Wiebe's later novels are generally more accomplished as works of art, but *Peace Shall Destroy Many* has an unusual appeal. While he was born a Mennonite, it is neither possible nor relevant to know the extent to which this novel might be based on recollections of his early life. It is relevant, though, that the novel has a burning urgency not shared by his later works to the same extent. *Peace Shall Destroy Many* is a rough work. The style is often awkward, the characterization uneven, and the didactic elements often obtrusive. But it is borne onward by a rare driving passion. Wiebe conveys the feeling that he cares very much about his characters and what happens to them.

As a form which from its origins has been closely associated with the middle class, the novel has always had the old puritan problem of "how to live" closer to its heart than has any other literary genre. Yet an intense moralistic concern, as expressed in *Peace Shall Destroy Many,* became less fashionable by mid-century, as novelists tended to veil their concern beneath layers of coolness and sophistication. Perhaps Wiebe's stronger sense of community enables him to keep the problem of "how to live" closer to the forefront of his work. . . . [Wiebe] is not afraid of committing himself—not even at the risk of appearing a fool. And sometimes the results are, indeed, strange, as in his second novel *First and Vital Candle.* But this ability to let go can also create an impressive splendour which shines through in such accomplishments as *The Temptations of Big Bear* or *Peace Shall Destroy Many.* His willingness to try the unusual makes him one of the most individual novelists writing in Canada today. (pp. 48-9)

Francis Mansbridge, "Wiebe's Sense of Community," in Canadian Literature, *No. 77, Summer, 1978, pp. 42-9.*

R. P. BILAN

[*The Blue Mountains of China*] is an impressive achievement. Although the problem of didacticism and the "syntactical awkwardness" in Wiebe's style—which leads to some very murky writing in places—are . . . obtrusive weaknesses . . . , they are more than offset by the novel's strengths. In *The Blue Mountains of China* Rudy Wiebe not only vividly recounts the history of a segment of the Mennonite people, but, more importantly, he presents a complex judgment of the Mennonites and the modern world, and compellingly dramatizes his own radically Christian vision. (p. 50)

For Rudy Wiebe, and the Mennonites he presents in his novel, the "kinds of things that we struggle with" are primarily questions of religious belief. However, the struggle for faith and a truly Christian way of life is beset by many difficulties: the suffering in life, the attractions of the secular materialistic world, and, particularly for the Mennonites, the temptation to isolate themselves from the rest of the world.

Wiebe tells the Mennonites' history and explores his central themes in a book with a very unusual and complex structure. Many of the thirteen chapters of the novel read as almost self-contained stories, but Wiebe connects them in part by an intricate series of cross-references that help explain previous chapters and look forward to the ensuing ones. . . . The primary source of unity and continuity in the novel, however, is provided by the four chapters narrated by Frieda Friesen. (pp. 50-1)

[Frieda's temptation] scene has a crucial structural and thematic significance in the novel. Frieda's faith is strengthened here, and, of equal importance, the nature of her temptation is deliberately left ambiguous, for what is being emphasized is her resistance to *any* temptation. But in much of the rest of the novel Wiebe examines the experience of Mennonites who succumb to various "temptations." The main structural principle of the first half of the book, in fact, is to alternate the presentation of Frieda's faith with a chapter showing a Mennonite struggling with the confines of the religious tradition.

Jakob Friesen IV is in many ways a contrasting figure to Frieda. . . . Jakob never recovers from the guilt of abandoning his son and comes, unlike Frieda, to doubt God's justice. (p. 52)

Wiebe's attitude towards the Mennonites and the modern world is complex, and can't be ascertained from any single chapter. "The Well," which is in certain ways complementary to "Over the Red Line," examining the same issues, presents a different picture. . . . The trip made to the well by Anna Friesen, Frieda's daughter, dramatizes the choice between two kinds of life. And now for the first time Wiebe criticizes the conservatism of the Mennonites who have come to South America. The Indian women they encounter have a freedom and naturalness that the Mennonites distrust. (pp. 55-6)

It is not, however, primarily the Indians that cause the conservative Kanadier to worry, but the Russlander Mennonites—those who have become "modern" and those who, like Jakob Friesen, had stayed in Russia until 1929. . . . (p. 56)

The ultimate temptation that confronts a Mennonite, however, is to lose faith because of personal suffering. Jakob Friesen IV . . . in chapter eight, "The Cloister of the Lilies," as a prisoner in Siberia in 1932, is unable to accept his suffering without misgiving. As Jakob and another prisoner are being moved they stumble onto a cloister; within they discover a picture of a row of lilies hidden beneath the grime on a wall. This seems to symbolize Jakob's own relation to his faith; it is buried, hidden, indeed almost lost. As they wait out the blizzard a man arrives with his wife, who is dying, and they are desperately trying to reach home. . . . The woman is raped by the guards, yet she and her husband endure, and his advice to Jakob is "Survive." . . . Unlike Jakob, the man not only accepts his suffering but is able to affirm that "God is good." Jakob is at the point of losing his faith entirely, or at least doubting it; at the end of the novel he claims he "believes nothing." Yet Jakob is obsessed with the man's ambiguous statement: "Whatever the man had said . . . seemed for an instant to blaze with a kind of holy wisdom that was." Jakob's attempts to understand the statement show that he is still struggling with his faith, and it is because of this struggle that later, as an old man, he is attracted to John Reimer.

Having examined various Mennonites in conflict with their faith, Wiebe begins to emphasize more directly, in the second half of the novel, the kind of Christian response he himself admires. David Epp . . . in chapter nine, "Drink Ye All of It," represents the ethical ideal in Wiebe's religious vision. David and his family, with a group of Mennonites, escape from Russia into China, but David fears that the Mennonites left behind may be punished for their act. He decides, therefore, that he must leave his family and return to Russia to see if he can possibly exonerate the other Mennonites. He is giving up his freedom, and probably his life, in what may be a quixotic gesture. But the heroic nature of his act reverberates throughout the rest of the novel in the lives of those who come after him. . . . In his radical concern for others and in his willingness to sacrifice himself, David Epp shows himself to be a true follower of Christ. (pp. 57-8)

The problem of the lack of religious faith in the modern world is confronted directly by Wiebe in the last two chapters of the novel. Here he examines the radical responses of two men appalled both by the materialism of modern life *and* by the insularity of other Mennonites. "The Vietnam Call of Samuel V. Reimer" is accurately described by W. J. Keith as a "biblical parallel-cum-parody (I Samuel 3) which succeeds in being both humorous and serious at the same time." Samuel is called by God to go and proclaim peace in Vietnam. Wiebe apparently wants us to believe in the authenticity of Samuel's voice, but, in any case, in showing the resistance to Samuel and his mission, Wiebe presents his critique of the modern world. There is a total lack of faith and an inability to believe in the very possibility that God would still speak directly to man. . . . Samuel Reimer achieves a sense of what, in Wiebe's view, a truly fully Christian life involves, but the opposition to his plan proves too much for him; unlike David Epp, he fails to act on his belief. He gives in to despair and dies, and the story ends on an ironic note with the triumph of the material values he abhorred. (pp. 59-60)

[In the last chapter] John puts forth a view of Christianity which radically challenges the basic assumptions of the conservative Mennonites—and of many other Christians as well. He insists that a wide social concern is of the essence of Christianity. . . . John is especially critical of the position taken by the Mennonite church, for he argues that Jesus didn't intend to achieve his revolution "by setting up a church that can never change no matter where on earth or in what century it is." He redefines what the real church should be: "No! The church Jesus began is us *living, everywhere,* a new *society* that sets all the old ideas of man living with other men on its head." The new society is built by our "thinking different" about everything.

In articulating this view of Christianity John is quite obviously a spokesman for Wiebe himself. . . . [As] Wiebe is largely using John to assert his own view, rather than fully dramatizing it, the novel comes close to being overtly didactic at this point. . . . In the final section, however, where John attempts to explain his views to Jakob Friesen, the professed unbeliever, Wiebe is more successful at dramatizing his religious beliefs. (pp. 61-2)

[The novel's] title comes from the appearance of the Greater Khingan Mountains of China which David Epp [saw] as he led his people out of Russia. . . . The blue mountains symbolize the hope of the Mennonites that somewhere they will find a place where they will be able to lead their lives and religion in total peace and freedom. But the blue is "mocking" because the goal is unattainable, and, in the eyes of John Reimer—and Rudy Wiebe—it is finally undesirable. The Mennonites' dream of isolating and insulating themselves from the world involves a failure of true Christian responsibility, which is shown by being involved *in* the world. (p. 62)

R. P. Bilan, "Wiebe and Religious Struggle," in Canadian Literature, *No. 77, Summer, 1978, pp. 50-63.*

* * *

WILBUR, Richard 1921-

Wilbur is an American poet, critic, translator, and editor. The formal wit and elegance of his poetry have elicited comparison with the metaphysical poets. He received the Pulitzer Prize in Poetry for 1957. (See also *CLC*, Vols. 3, 6, 9, and *Contemporary Authors*, Vols. 1-4, rev. ed.)

JOHN CIARDI

Wilbur's first book, "The Beautiful Changes" (1947), marked him immediately as something special. A trace of indebtedness to Yeats and a clear line of descent from Marianne Moore were visible as signs that his talent was still emergent, but of the existence of that talent there could be no doubt. The poems, richly worded and strictly formal, nevertheless moved within their strictures with an ease and assurance that marked Wilbur as the possessor of as fine an ear for the smooth-flowing line and the self-rounding stanza rhythm as could be claimed by any man now writing in English. He had, moreover, achieved a metaphoric sense undeniably his own. Consider for example this description of a ballet dancer fresh from the formal perfections of her dance and now slumped into the shapelessness of human fatigue:

> So she will turn and walk through metal halls
> To where some ancient woman will unmesh
> Her small strict shape, and yawns will turn her face
> Into a little wilderness of flesh.

And rich as are the immediate physical sensations of such a description, it is the nature of Wilbur's talent that these physical punctualities are precisely *that which is thought with*. . . . The passage is not only a description of a particular tired dancer, but of the boundary between life and artifice, a boundary crossed and recrossed in Wilbur's poems, always with the central driving intention of finding that artifice which will most include the most of life. For Wilbur is a poet at mortal play, an artificer. Even the title of his first book ("changes" must be read both as a noun and as a verb) attest how carefully he plans his double meanings.

This theme of artifice—I am tempted almost to call it the theology and humanism of artifice—rose free of the earlier indebtednesses and emerged deepened and enriched in "Ceremony and Other Poems" (1950). And here, too, it became apparent both immediately and by hindsight that Wilbur was emerging as a master of a subtle, urbane, and self-convincing diction that was peculiarly his own, the mark of his own way of seeing and saying. (p. 18)

[With] "Things of This World," his enormous gifts grown into their mature assurance, Wilbur certainly emerges as our serenest, urbanest, and most melodic poet. To say Wilbur has matured is not to imply that he will not accomplish finer things yet, and I would suggest for instance that in his search for a serene diction he might place less reliance on such adjectives as "clear," "pure," "calm," and "graceful." It is exactly the qualities labeled by these adjectives that best describe the best Wilbur poems, but it is very much to the point, I believe, that in those best poems the clarity, purity, calm and grace emerge thing-wise and self-living, not by adjectival assertion. Minor qualifications aside (and Wilbur's successes would sustain far greater flaws than these) there is a kind of unmistakable inevitability in a typical Wilbur passage. There is nothing flashy about; in fact, Wilbur makes it look so easy that one might almost overlook how good it really is. Consider these lines for example, a passage following a reference to children at play:

> Above their heads the maples with a stiff
> Compliance entertain the air
> In abrupt gusts, losing the look of trees
> In rushed and cloudy metamorphoses,
> Their shadows all a brilliant disrepair.

The self-rounding of the total stanza rhythm is one Wilbur signature. The quality of the metaphor, physically suggestive yet alive with idea, is another. So are the play and paradox of "stiff compliance." And there is a fourth, to me even more impressive quality, and that is exactly the one most readers would most likely overlook, and that is the Latin root-sense that shines through so much of Wilbur's diction. "Compliance" means in current usage "to yield to" but at root it means either (the derivation may be disputed either may) "to fold up" or "to be filled up with." And whether one hears the root as *plicare* or *plere* the root does function. So, even more clearly in "entertain" (from the roots *inter* and *tenir*, "to hold between"). The aptness of those root suggestions when applied to wind-blown trees and when juxtaposed to "stiff" (itself—and this joyously derived from Latin *stipes* meaning "a tree trunk or vegetable stalk") will illustrate how richly Wilbur works his diction in depth. One may slide over the surfaces paying no attention to these riches and find reward enough. Wilbur certainly is not the man to slug the reader into noticing his excellences. But they are there to be found. Nor is there any more valuable function the poet can perform than to reawaken the root sense of the language, to keep it a living instrument in the mouth of his people. (pp. 18-19)

Instead of cognate-snapping, as the academic dullards invariably do, [in his translation of Moliere's "The Misanthrope"] Wilbur has found English equivalents for the turn and nuance of the French, and the fact that he has managed to do so in rhymed couplets that not only respect themselves as English poetry but that allow the play to be staged . . . with great success is testament enough. . . .

There are also to consider Wilbur's stunning translations of lyrics by Baudelaire, Valéry, Jammes, and Philippe de Thaun, the last two of which are included in both "Things of This World" and "A Bestiary." . . . Wilbur has managed to take four sweetly tuned lyrics and to convey them, despite a heavy freight of rhyme, into English lyrics as sweetly tuned as the originals in a serene and urbane act of imagination and devotion. A rare miracle, Wilbur has caught it four times in these renderings. (p. 19)

John Ciardi, "Our Most Melodic Poet," in The Saturday Review *(entire issue copyright 1956 by Saturday Review Associates, Inc.; reprinted with permission), Vol. XXXIX, No. 33, August 18, 1956, pp. 18-19.*

M. L. ROSENTHAL

[In] *Things of This World* Richard Wilbur seems beset by a sort of ennui, the result of a conceptual dependence which bedevils him with an especially treasonous subtlety. Though he is still one of our better poets, the things his poetry says and lives by are so much of the essence of the modern Anglo-American heritage that others have already preëmpted the original and audacious modes of expression he might otherwise use. Compare his "An Event" with Stevens' "Thirteen Ways of Looking at a Blackbird," for instance. The younger poet has been almost forced into a blander, more discursive tack, for which even his highly developed grace and skill of rhetoric cannot fully compensate. Rhetoric, incidentally, is put to sharper use in the one political piece here: "Speech for the Repeal of the McCarran Act." Genuine poetic energy and concreteness quicken the effect of this piece, which augurs the revival of a genre recently much neglected. But this poet's main chance does not lie in a political direction.

Wilbur's own medicine for his disease is, for him, a good one: translation, and a turn of emphasis toward French sources that goes with it. His dominating vision has always been the aesthetic-secular one of the post-Romantic tradition:

> I take this world for better or for worse,
> But seeing rose carafes conceive the sun
> My thirst conceives a fierier universe.

Still, Wilbur finds it difficult, in his usual voice, to present this vision as truth; he rather argues for it as an ideal. Everything changes, however, when he takes on a different voice or mask by translating from the French. Then, particularly in rendering Baudelaire's "*L'Invitation au Voyage*" and Valéry's "Helen," he is at once far within the vision. Again, with Jammes' "A Prayer to Go to Paradise with the Donkeys," he is from the start at a pitch of pure elation for which he strives in vain elsewhere. Moreover, of the successful poems here that are *not* translations, the best are those most closely approaching the dream-atmosphere of the French Symbolist tradition (as opposed to the Emersonian or morally melioristic streak in contemporary American Poetry, which has at times overborne Wilbur's sense of himself). (p. 372)

M. L. Rosenthal, "Tradition and Transition," in The Nation *(copyright 1956 by the Nation Associates, Inc.), Vol. 183, No. 18, November 3, 1956, pp. 372-74.**

WILLIAM DICKEY

Richard Wilbur, in [*Walking to Sleep*] shows again the ability of the shape-changer, the capacity to move from form to form, or even from voice to voice, depending on the particular requirements made of him by the development of a given poem. In a period when the identity of the poet is often associated with the singularity of his voice (Marianne Moore, Wallace Stevens), Wilbur's ability to mute the insistence of personality may make the level of his accomplishment less immediately evident, because the accomplishment is expressed in so many different ways. Wilbur is both a translator and a theatre-poet: situations in which one must speak another's words, or hear another voice speaking one's own.

The title of Wilbur's second book was *Ceremony,* and that word still expresses, I think, much of his most central approach to the poem. To Wilbur . . . it seems to me that form is a means of understanding, the shape of the poem one of the most serious comments on the meaning of the poem. And it seems also that form functions as a kind of charm: ceremony is the way in which the tissue of events is not only understood, but made moral and substantial. The long title poem of this book, "Walking to Sleep," is an exercise in how to control and formalize language to a given purpose. . . . The poem is a magic by which to go to sleep; it is also a comment on the way such magics work: they permit us to achieve an agreement with the world of which we are a part. That agreement is not a submission, or even necessarily a reconciliation, but it is an awareness of an order. . . . (pp. 363-64)

An intelligent affection, and an intelligent remorse; a sense of event in a long and various context: these are the qualities that seem most central here. They will not allow a poetry of extremes: the howl of absolute emotion or the arid geometries of absolute intellection. Aware both of people and their contexts, they celebrate that difficult thing: the simultaneous tenuousness and necessity of civilization. (p. 364)

William Dickey, "A Place in the Country," in The Hudson Review *(copyright © 1969 by The Hudson Review, Inc.; reprinted by permission), Vol. 22, No. 2, Summer, 1969, pp. 347-64.**

PAUL RAMSEY

Richard Wilbur does what he does well and gladly, learns new ways and enjoys them too. The charges against him are mostly compliments. Yes, he has mastered the iambic line and some other meters; yes, he wears his grace with ease; yes, his poems respond to his control. But these virtues do not set him necessary limits. The counter-evidence is too much present in his work for anyone truly to claim, "Here in a well-lit salon you must of need stay, the crystal polished, the corners cleared." The counterevidence is the pure loveliness becoming, sometimes against his protestations, in its very purity transcendent; lies in the many fine and memorable phrasings; and must include, among poems published in books prior to 1976, "Two Voices in a Meadow" and the longer poem *Walking to Sleep*. (p. 294)

[I speak] as an early and continuing admirer, and speak in approval. And yet? And yet. The counterevidence does need to be carefully selected. Wilbur has seldom published a bad poem, and seldom a poem from which one does not derive some genuine pleasure; yet the really first-rate poems, the poems that illumine the secret places and to which one returns with a deeper gratitude, are fewer than I would wish. Theodore Roethke, as quoted on the dust-jacket of *The Mind-Reader,* found in Wilbur not a "graceful mind" but a "mind of grace." Well, both; almost always the former; sometimes, blessedly, the latter.

Wilbur himself makes the point in "On My Own Work" in his critical collection, *Responses*. . . . (pp. 294-95)

Responses is . . . occasional criticism. The title means responses to occasions and hence is less relativistic and impressionistic than it may sound. Wilbur is not saying that all responses are equal or that the essays are merely responses, but he is not very far from the comfort of that fastness. His criticism could hardly be called bellicose, nor is it much engaged in finding true grounds for its being. He is, though, to his credit, not antitheoretical, for at times he accepts and defends John Crowe Ransom's view of poetry as world-bodying, as opposed to the Shelleyan or transcendant view. . . .

As a reader of the poetry would expect, Wilbur's prose often pleases: apt unpredicted metaphors, frisky asides, pungent balancings. Yet an idle copy-editor named (pseudonymously, since I am inventing her) Darleen Longhans has failed him in her task of bashing out verbosely indirect constructions. . . .

One also expects—and receives—astute respondings. Wilbur is at his best "one on one," reading poems he likes of poets he likes, such as Poe, Frost, and, in the first-rate essay "'Sumptuous Destitution,'" Emily Dickinson. "Poetry's Debt to Poetry" is a very good study of the necessity and dangers of literary emulation. . . . (p. 295)

The Mind-Reader contains some excellent light verse, including "Piccola Commedia," with its unexpected household of characters and its closing chill. The calm precision of touch, the middle-distanced eye, the self-awareness of technique, which make for a comfortably joyful light verse, tend to undercut more serious occasions. . . . In most of the poems in the book, skillful as they are, the self-consciousness of control does not vanish or utterly transmute. The arrivals too often arrive too easily, content with their pleasing home.

The title poem is a larger event, one of his best poems. The speaker of their dramatic monologue is a crafty, drunken, yet genuinely gifted mind-reader, sitting at a "corner café table." The auditor seems to be any listener until the ending plays a double joke: "Ah, you have read my mind. One more, perhaps . . . [ellipsis Wilbur's] / A mezzo-litro. Grazie, professore."

The first joke is funny because easy, an alcoholic's self-spoof; no major powers of telepathy are required to tell that the drinker wants another drink. The other joke is on us: the auditor being thanked is identified only by the last word in the poem. Why a "professore" and what kind? A college professor, the primary meaning in Italian, seems the most likely, so one guesses—we aren't told—a college professor relevantly attentive, doing psychical research on telepathy. If so, then surely the professor is receiving something more and something less than the whole truth from a man who has admitted to "Trumpery" and "cheat[ings]." Yet the authority of the narrator is only shadowed. The joke is a joke, not a dissolving of the poem's being. (pp. 295-96)

The blank verse is extremely good. Much of the poem is well within the rules of even strict traditional iambics, and the departures are not extreme for twentieth-century poetry. (p. 296)

The verse moves, with no large huffing of transition, among the conversational ("They found, when I was little, / That I"), the lyrically descriptive ("Through mica shimmer to a moss of pines"), the perturbedly descriptive ("It is as when a pipe-wrench, catapulted / From the jounced back of a pick-up truck, dives headlong"), the scornful ("fashionable folk, / Mocking and ravenously credulous"), and among what the mind-reader and the poet will have of richly exact imagery and perceiving meditation.

The mind-reader is not, and does not in any direct way symbolize, a poet, but some analogies are present, not overthumped. The mind-reader is a fascinating man in his own right (and wrong), and his skepticism turns about, as when he speaks of "skeptics bent on proving me a fraud / For fear that some small wonder, unexplained, / Should leave a fissure in the world, and all / Saint Michael's host come flapping back." Near the end of the poem the mind-reader opens a door for a sad look and listen, wondering whether he has missed a "resonance," God's "huge attention" offering true regard; and yet nearer the end of the poem he turns from "drinking studiously" (to lower the blind on concern) to a hunger for a place reminiscent of *The Tempest:* "Where the wrench beds in mud, the sun-hat hangs / In densest branches, and the book is drowned."

To question and to hunger are not yet to arrive, and, as in so very much poetry of our time, themes hint their vanishing. The hunger for hope (God's "attention," "sweetness") and for pure escape to silence strangely merge in the mind-reader's mind (as Wilbur reads that mind).

Yet, even in the vanishing (wrench, sun-hat, book), the sense of affirmation is strong, the poem's reality fulfilled. For which, our thanks. Grazie, poeta. (pp. 296-97)

Paul Ramsey, "Grazie," in The Sewanee Review *(reprinted by permission of the editor; © 1978 by The University of the South), Vol. LXXXVI, No. 2, Spring, 1978, pp. 294-97.*

ANNE WILLIAMS

Richard Wilbur's "Beasts" expresses nostalgia for a lost Eden, not of childhood, but of unconscious animal existence. Evil is man's alone, created by recognition of suffering and intensified by human efforts to resolve or lessen it. Thus the animals dwell in "major freedom." Wilbur's survey of the chain of being progresses from beasts to man by way of the halfway creature, the werewolf. (One remembers that in traditional descriptions of the chain, man occupies this position.) Reason is now the substitute for transcendent divinity, but it brings with it disintegrating harmony: "major" to "minor"; "concordance" to discord; peace to war; "slumber" to waking, present contentment to unsatisfied yearning.

"Beasts" is unified by pervasive musical imagery. Phrases that first appear to be a series of playful, localized metaphors gradually emerge by the end of the second stanza as a unifying motif and then as a symbolic reminder of the traditional *discordia concors* metaphor, an explanation for the usefulness of evil in the harmony of the whole creation. The first two stanzas portray the animal world "where though all things differ, all agree." This world is suffused with harmony, a completeness and interdependence between the beasts and nature. . . . [The] creatures are neither alien nor fearful, even of death.

The continuous presence of the moon guides the reader through this survey of creation. The beasts' responses to its light also illustrate the loss of harmony which accompanies developing consciousness. Among the animals, the moon is an active participant, a member of the company. . . . But among men, its light leads to harm and darkness. Wholly passive, observed rather than observing, its results are baleful.

The werewolf provides a modulation between the two modes of being, the "major" and minor freedom. (p. 27)

The werewolf's painful reversion is accomplished as other men, "far from thicket and pad-fall," also watch the moon. These observers find its beauty "painful" and their response illustrates the felt intervention of consciousness. Man, the scholar, at his most conscious and remote from nature, "construes" the "lucid mood" and the "risen hunter." The moon moves him, but the very adjectives are the attributions of his perception. Like the werewolf's windowglass, the lens of man's consciousness separates him from nature. Man reads the book of nature rather than experiencing it as the gull does. He construes—interprets, analyzes, in an attempt to discover the structure and sense. (pp. 27-8)

Wilbur distinguishes between "beasts" and "monsters"; all beasts belong to nature (man included), but man alone brings "monsters into the cities, crows on the public statues." The city symbolizes civilization, the height of man's conscious ordering, but also his alienation and fall from nature. . . .

"Beasts" ironically reverses the spiral structure of poems like "The Ancient Mariner" which also deal with the relation of human consciousness to nature. We end in the "dark unbridled waters," . . . in a darkness of ignorance and perverted potential. . . . Such darkness is unknown to the animals that cannot strive or seek, betray and fail. The poem suggests a grim reversal of the Faust myth enacted in a universe without transcendence: man's striving intellect, imperfect and thus continually failing, leads him to damnation. (p. 28)

Anne Williams, "Wilbur's 'Beasts'," in The Explicator *(copyright © 1979 by Helen Dwight Reid Educational Foundation), Vol. 37, No. 4, Summer, 1979, pp. 27-8.*

BRUCE MICHELSON

When it came out in 1976, *The Mind-Reader* didn't change any minds. As Richard Wilbur's latest collection of poems, the book was reviewed about eighteen times in predictable ways: people who had understood and liked his work before had more nice things to say (William Pritchard, for example, in the *Hudson Review*), and people who were stuck on the old idea that Wilbur is a safe soul, somebody to be arch about, did their usual dance. Wilbur has spent thirty years sharpening our sense of irony and showing us that wit and passionate intensity can have everything to do with each other. That is the kind of cause that divides people for good—and so it is no surprise that some of *The Mind-Reader*'s readers found there the same old Wilbur they expected.

There are, however, some new sides to the Wilbur who shows himself here. One thing that is new is the book's defiant surfaces. The poems are as witty and elegant and deadly serious as ever, but the collection, taken altogether, seems to stand up against every kind of poet-chic, as if Wilbur meant to strut around for a moment, with an angry glint in his eye, wearing the "bourgeois" mask which his detractors hang on him. (p. 763)

We get a marriage toast that celebrates marriage, we get riddles and jokes, tour de force translations of Villon, Du Bellay, Vosnesensky, and others, poems about Johnny Appleseed and his apples, the Fourth of July, milkweed, mushrooms, shallots, all of them graceful, well-mannered and outwardly tranquil celebrations of love, light, life. But the readers who are usually irked by that sort of thing will be especially upset with "Cottage Street, 1953," which seems to have irreverent things to say about Sylvia Plath.

"Cottage Street" is, according to Wilbur, a "composite" recollection of the young woman Wilbur actually knew. The setting is the Wellesley home of Edna Ward, Wilbur's mother-in-law and a friend of "frightened Mrs. Plath," who is here for tea with her "pale, slumped daughter" recovering from a suicide attempt. But there is nothing snide about the poem. It is meant to recall the powerlessness that Wilbur felt (and must still feel), with his hard-won faith in the order of things, to speak of that faith to such abject despair. . . . (p. 764)

The poem ends by contrasting the death of Edna Ward, at eighty-eight, with Sylvia's suicide; and these are the lines which anger people. Mrs. Ward dies,

> The thin hand reaching out, the last word *love,*
>
> Outliving Sylvia who, condemned to live,
> Shall study for a decade, as she must,
> To state at last her brilliant negative
> In poems free and helpless and unjust.

The bluntness is surprising, but no poet writing in this language has ever chosen his words more carefully than Wilbur, and "unjust" is exactly what he means. His sympathy for the desperate, brilliant young woman runs deep, but finally he states his positive, as *he* must, his faith in an obscure but fundamental goodness in life. He turns away from a vision which is ontologically "unjust," meaning faithless as well as unfair. This is the first occasion when Wilbur in any of his poems has spoken directly about a fellow poet, and it seems to me as gentle and just an observation as anyone who believes can make about anyone who doesn't. . . .

Close reading is what Wilbur still requires, not because his poems have grown more obscure and idiosyncratic. The rich surfaces have grown rougher and wilder, the resolutions are down deeper and take a steadier gaze to find. But the poems still work like Wyeth's paintings: we enter into familiar worlds full of light and fresh air—and then we find that there are tigers aprowl in the tall grass and that the safe artist who dreams these safe landscapes has been farther out on the edge than most of the sword-dancers we have heard about. The life-and-death business is still the struggle of the imagination to make sense of the world's turbulence; the difference is that the turbulence is more intense. (p. 765)

The best use of this new roughness turns up in the mushroom poem, "Children of Darkness," a lyric about those rootless, nasty-looking things that grow in the deep shade, feeding on death and rot. Wilbur has written about ugly things before, dead dogs and vultures; but he has never been this lurid before. . . . (p. 766)

The beauty in all this horror is that these ugly things break death down so that life can rise up again; they keep nature new and fresh, and a steady, serious look at them can do the same thing for us. . . .

There is one perfect, classic haiku in the book, "Sleepless at Crown Point," which catches Wilbur's whole struggle in twelve words:

All night, this headland
Lunges into the rumpling
Capework of the wind.

For three decades Wilbur's head-land, that wakeful, witty sensibility of his, has been lunging into dark, vaporous, disheveled places. Everything takes place on the border between light and shadow; it is no good if you go to sleep at your crown point and never go sleepless into the dark; it is no good if you go out there and never come back again. Sometimes the escape from the darkness is a narrow one. The collection's title poem is a dramatic monologue (the first long one that Wilbur has published), from the kind of sensibility that Wilbur's almost is—that is, one that hasn't found its way back. (p. 767)

[The] man on the front of the dust jacket [of the volume], the silhouette at the café table, has Wilbur's shape, as he should; for this mind worn down with detail and misfortune and all those perceptions which can break anyone who seeks the "resonance in all their fretting" *is* Wilbur, the other side of the man—not simply the visionary that he struggles against becoming, but the visionary that, for all controlled surfaces, he always is. . . .

[There] are poems here which, unfolding as they do with each new reading, are going to be hard to get rid of. If I am a little uneasy it is for one unfair reason: I find myself wishing that this astounding poet would put out something big or flashy enough to turn more heads and absolutely stop all this talk about safety and propriety. The biggest surprise in the book is that dramatic monologue, and if it turns out to be a direction that Wilbur will follow, I may get my foolish wish. But what we have from him already is poetry to be very grateful for, poetry that we cannot be permitted to forget. (p. 768)

Bruce Michelson, "Richard Wilbur's 'The Mind Reader'," in The Southern Review *(copyright, 1979, by Bruce Michelson), Vol. 15, No. 3, July, 1979, pp. 763-68.*

* * *

WILD, Peter 1940-

Wild is an American poet. He creates poetry marked by surreal images and exuberant energy, reflecting his sensitivity to the physical world, especially his love for the natural beauty of the southwestern United States. (See also *Contemporary Authors*, Vols. 5-8, rev. ed.)

WILLIAM PITT ROOT

[Peter Wild] is little known except to the readers of little literary magazines. This is too bad, because he is one of the better surrealist poets at a time when surrealism suffers in more public hands.

What is good about Wild's work is its lucence, vitality, and respect for mysteries. Image by image, it is clear, and often enough I finish reading a poem certain of the internal dynamic of coherence but unable to exhaust it by any description, contenting myself to experience what I cannot explain. Wild is weak in his tendency to indulge his eye or his ear even when they are receiving nothing worth making record of and when he overworks his imagination and comes up with a trifle from the shallows, such as the section entitled "God Is A Helicopter With A Big Searchlight" in *3 Poems*.

His *forte* is the dreamstate in which what happens is clear, feels inevitable, and yet has as its frame of reference a kind of wonder. . . . (p. 51)

[The] title poem [of *Fat Man Poems*] defines both Wild's gifts and the rather limiting use he can put them to. "He walks through seas of himself, / always deeper; horizons fade", and it is as though he dissolves and is reassembled into a new strange form by the sea; then

he draws
his clustered world behind him;
happily waves his arms,
and the birds fly,
then settle on his head . . .

becoming his own universe, he sits
watching the far-off girls
thin as beaten gold.

If I am somewhat charmed by the picture, I am somewhat more disappointed, finally, to recognize this gesture as a surreal equivalent of Yeats's failed yearning for an Innisfree. Again, Stevens, among others, is relevant to remember here for his warning against the surrealist's special temptation to invent rather than discover, to indulge fantasy rather than employ it. Peter Wild is most interesting when he's ashore. (p. 52)

William Pitt Root, "Anything but Over," in Poetry *(© 1973 by The Modern Poetry Association; reprinted by permission of the Editor of* Poetry*), Vol. CXXIII, No. 1, October, 1973, pp. 34-56.**

The reasons for [Wild's popularity] are clear. The poetry is set in the Southwest, the garden of Eden for this season's younger generation. Added to this immediately attractive, if confining, sense of locale is a diction marked by unexpected turns of phrase and tricky end linked lines that suggest the significance of statement so hard won by poets like Wright and Haines. Wild's best work is probably in "Mica Mountain Poems." In poems like "Rattlesnake" language and meaning create excitement and vitality. This achievement and promise is already a little diminished in "Love Poems" where the love affair is more with language than with sense. . . . "Wild's Magical Book of Cranial Effusions" and the more comprehensive, "New and Selected Poems" confirm a debilitating preoccupation with inventiveness at the expense of quiet comprehension. There are excellent lines, even splendid poems like "Kite Man," but the work as a whole turns back on itself at maniac speed. The present collection ["Cochise"] is full of restless energy. The uses of rhyme seem never to have occurred to this poet. All of the poems rest upon an upsetting and unconfined encounter with the physical world—weather, landscape, or people. These collisions end by being as baffling to the poet as they are to us. Possibilities skyrocket into fantasy. "My whole life is a trance, I hope to break from," he writes. But surely this fancy cat dance around any effort at integration with reality is the key to his success. That kind of thinking has been popular for a long time; it is particularly beguiling here.

"Notes on Current Books: 'Cochise'," in Virginia Quarterly Review *(copyright, 1974, by the* Virginia Quarterly Review, *The University of Virginia), Vol. 50, No. 3 (Summer, 1974), p. lxxxiv.*

JOHN R. CARPENTER

The attitudes expressed in [*Cochise*] are agreeable: romantic love of Indians (without much information or contact), of wild animals, of nature. Wild's favorite images are flames, saints, streams of blood, mouths, claws, slaughter, and lightning; however, his poems are generally peaceful and benign. These recurring images have an independent existence in the poet's mind: they are not related to what he sees, but he likes them and they are part of his permanent repertory. The poet declares his independence from the prosaic world of everyday reality and enters a strange, whimsical world where there is neither the pungency and vivid sensations of the physical world, nor the obsessions and deep feelings of the subconscious. Curious lines crop up like "the cathedrals of his nostrils," "a fireplace big enough for a man roast," "lightning drips from beneath her ribs", "a cheek married to the ditch grass", "baked potatoes burst from heat / from the ears of secretaries". These are imaginative, although often hard to visualize. Many poems are set pieces, such as ["Climbers," "The Poor," "Sailors," "The Indians," and "The Hobo"]. In a realistic sense they have almost nothing to do with the people mentioned in the titles, but they do not try to describe archetypes either, nor are they after the bigger game of psychological processes, feelings, or meanings. Many poems are enigmatic and contain interesting novelties, but it would be a mistake to search for meaning behind them. Wild seems to want to escape from both meaning and sharp feelings; he says that his poetry is "regional, seasoned by the surreal", and his poems often resemble automatic writing which fails to make contact with the subconscious. (p. 167)

John R. Carpenter, "The Big Machine," in Poetry *(© 1974 by The Modern Poetry Association; reprinted by permission of the Editor of* Poetry*), Vol. CXXV, No. 3, December, 1974, pp. 166-73.**

PETER COOLEY

The Cloning shows Wild's feeling for forces in the natural world with a vitality close to Lawrence's yet more surreal. This poet experiences life through the body yet works for a transcendence in many poems. (p. 478)

Cloning is a voyage into different parts of America, but the journey is not progressive, and it never pretends to be conclusive. We gather the momentum instead from single poem after single poem presented not as perceptions of one egocentric "I" but as vision itself looking at experience. (p. 479)

Again and again the contrast between vision and actuality in the past and present is Wild's concern. . . . Seemingly arbitrary connections often juxtapose both realms, too, in relationships not clear till we experience the total design of the poem. . . .

Wild is one of our most prolific and most talented poets, his poems appearing in every conceivable sort of publication. . . . He is a young poet not to watch for, but to read now. (p. 480)

Peter Cooley, "Visions and Revisions: Four Poets," in Michigan Quarterly Review *(copyright © The University of Michigan, 1976), Vol. XV, No. 4, Fall, 1976, pp. 473-80.*

* * *

WILLIAMS, Thomas 1926-

Although his books are varied in plot and setting, throughout Williams's fiction runs his central themes of the responsibility of man to nature and the greater responsibility of man, and especially of the artist, to other humans. *The Hair of Harold Roux,* which is distinguished by its artful use of the novel within a novel device, won the 1976 National Book Award for fiction. (See also *Contemporary Authors,* Vols. 1-4, rev. ed.)

MARTIN LEVIN

["Town Burning"] gives new life to an old theme: the native's return, and reinforces [Thomas Williams's] unusual status as an elegist of small-town America. . . .

With a perspective that is both dour and sympathetic, Mr. Williams sketches [protagonist] Cotter's circle of friends and enemies. . . . The centerpiece of the novel is its protagonist's precarious relationship with his mother, father and brother, a beautifully stated arrangement of inhibited love and subtly shaded hostility. A forest fire simplifies these compacts and acts as a crucible for new alignments. Symbolically, the novel begins and ends in a graveyard, which frames the novelist's regard for all there is in life.

Martin Levin, "Reader's Report," in The New York Times Book Review *(© 1970 by The New York Times Company; reprinted by permission), March 29, 1970, p. 25.*

R. V. CASSILL

In periods of social equilibrium it may suffice the artist to be the "antenna of the race," as Pound called those who register the substance and force of realities ignored by the complacent sensibility. Now, in the fissioning of legal, political, moral, academic and semantic anarchy the artist—specifically the novelist—becomes by default also the conservator of the self-destructing community in which he finds himself. This is Williams's implied theme. It is the principle on which he has constructed a credible hero—the last truly responsible man.

Aaron Benham the novelist sits, in the beginning, among his own written contributions to the blithering universe exploding away from his study. Even in his own room the "one firm label in this area seems to be 'miscellaneous.'" Responsibility begins with the recognition that his finished books and stories have become fragments of the general chaos on the instant of their completion. The order, meaning and celebration to which he is committed as a writer lie in the work to be done, in fictionalizing the dreams and circumstances of his middle age. . . .

Benham is also a fully married man. His novel in hand is a commitment to reconciling his present marriage with the pathos of the college love affair he is writing about. So he must fictionalize the sacrifice of "Mary Tolliver" to balance his moral and emotional accounts with the living mother of his children. And since Mary is one of the sweetest victims since Iphigenia's throat was cut, the guilt of her sacrifice must be paid again in the coin of recreated grief. . . .

The device of a novel within a novel is something of a commonplace and has to be commended here for the authority of its usage rather than for its ingenuity. The reader will find Benham's recreated past even more poignant than the present episodes. In the iris of twice-fictional Mary's eye there is "the smallest shard of green, like a splinter of jade," and this charming physical aberration is not more precisely rendered than her speech, her religio-sexual conflicts and her gallantry. She is a creature worthy of adoration—therefore worthy of ravishment—and her reckless young lover can't separate his impulses toward both. . . .

The story of "Mary," "Allard" and their college fellows could certainly stand alone, poignant and profound. It is the account of a young man's discovery that his friends and enemies "were all larger continents than he had suspected, dangerous and enveloping." But they are larger yet because their figures and passions reappear in the other cords of the net where the novelist holds time and experience secure from senseless vanishings. Largeness, indeed, is the very signature of Williams's book. None of the multitudinous characters is miniaturized. All the scenes are fully wrought, not merely exploited for chance lines, contrasts, or quick effects. Everywhere the language flows from the purest vernacular to the elevations demanded by distilled perception. Our largest sympathies are roused, tormented and consoled.

R. V. Cassill, "The Last Responsible Man," in Book World—The Washington Post *(© 1974,* The Washington Post*), May 19, 1974, p. 7.*

ROBERT BUCKLER

[Since *The Hair of Harold Roux*] is about an academic in an ivory tower who is *also* a would-be novelist with writer's block, I ought to have found it the dreariest novel I had ever read. But I didn't. It is full of surprises. Aaron Benham, professor of English, married and moderately successful, has reached the run-in to middle age, and finds his life sterile. His escapes are tonning around on his Honda and remembering his youth, about which he plans a novel. He has the title—'The Hair of Harold Roux'—but cannot find the words.

And so he simply dreams about it. . . . Why are [his] memories so crucial? Well, because he had potential: with its beckoning future, so much cosier than exposed maturity! But potential to do what? Even in his youth, there is an essential hollowness about Aaron. And here is the novel's flaw. Unlike . . . [other novels] which set this syndrome against a larger world outside, Thomas Williams's novel proves to be private, esoteric and hypochondriac, after all. (p.350)

Robert Buckler, "Anguished Americans," in The Listener *(© British Broadcasting Corp. 1975; reprinted by permission of Robert Buckler), Vol. 94, No. 2423, September 11, 1975, pp. 349-50.**

JOHN GARDNER

Williams has always been more a preacher and entertainer than a serious novelist. If he deals with weighty matters, he does not deal with them weightily: He goes for Hollywood images, Hollywood sentiments and Hollywood's notion of "serious thought." I don't mind such things in novels for adults, though I don't exactly love them. In novels for children, sentimentality and preaching make me cross. "Tsuga's Children" is both: The publisher calls it a novel that "will be read with enchantment by adults and young people alike." (p. 13)

[The] language, emotions and surprising heroics recall Bomba, Boy of the Jungle, Raggedy Ann and the Hardy boys. The good, of course, are very very good, as mushy language insists. . . .

The bad, on the other hand, are outrageously bad, though as in all schlock children's fiction they can be converted from bad to good, if the author feels like it, just like that. And as in all deeply sentimental pseudo-art (as Jung pointed out), mindless, gooey sweetness comes hand in hand with sadism. . . .

Williams's themes, the oneness of all Nature and human responsibility here on this planet, are themes as noble as the mind can think up. But however it's disguised—as drama for adults or as drama for children—melodramatic, mushy writing is an offense against the spirit. In several mildly hysterical passages, Williams makes children the hope of the world. I agree, up to a point, that children are each new generation's hope. But, despite his good intentions, Williams writes, as did Eugene Field, work that leads children in both wrong directions—toward soft-minded goody-goodyness and toward the sadist's delight in pain. (p. 44)

John Gardner, "Children Good and Bad," in The New York Times Book Review *(© 1977 by* The New York Times *Company; reprinted by permission), May 15, 1977, pp. 13, 44.*

LINDA KUEHL

Tsuga's Children begins: "Once there was a family named Hemlock who lived, in another time, near the base of Cascom Mountain . . .". Into the Hemlock family's timeless environs—the distilled setting for Thomas Williams's allegorical tale—comes an ancient, dark personage who does not use her tongue to speak or her eyes to see. She moves into the Hemlocks' humble home and lures the children, Arn and Jen, to the valley of a dark mountain inhabited by an immortal race called Old People. There they become spiritual children of the legendary Tsuga. . . . Through initiation and trial by fire, Arn and Jen attain ultimate knowledge of that which is beyond the utterable and the visually verifiable.

Surely the universality of such a theme and the simplicity of the storytelling should not offend one. Yet this reader was put off by the author's indulging himself in lofty themes that students of literature fondly embrace as mirror evidence of their own superior sensibilities and noble natures. The same preciousness is found in Williams's prior novel, *The Hair of Harry Roux*. . . . Both *Roux* and *Tsuga* are bathed in self-congratulatory virtue. While in *Tsuga* the implication of myth is manifestly present, it cannot work its intended spell, for magic and wonder do not illuminate or attend it.

Linda Kuehl, "Books in Brief: 'Tsuga's Children'," in Saturday Review *(© 1977 by Saturday Review Magazine Corp.; reprinted with permission), Vol. 4, No. 20, July 9, 1977, p. 36.*

JEROME KLINKOWITZ

Thomas Williams is the kind of novelist you keep calling "a young writer." He won a National Book Award for "The Hair of Harold Roux," and "Town Burning" and "Whipple's Castle" added to his reputation. Then you realize he's 52 years old, a distinguished college professor publishing his eighth book, and well on his way to being "remembered."

Most authors have to die, or stop writing, to make that grade. But every so often a novelist comes along who can win immortality with one foot still planted in the day-to-day world. Williams is trying to do that now, and with "The Followed Man" he comes closer to success than most other popular writers with such high literary hopes. . . .

In this book, people with good stories to tell are allowed to tell them, and Thomas Williams keeps it all under firm control. His novel is written out of the accumulated wisdom of a modern lit professor, and occasionally he risks showing off how much Frost, Faulkner, Cheever and Updike he knows. But Williams also knows when to stand back and let life play itself out and form its own rules.

The book's only totally hopeless character is, appropriately, an English prof who hasn't learned this lesson. A writer himself, this poor soul is utterly forgettable. But Thomas Williams deserves to be remembered, while being blessed with many years to write more novels as good as this one.

Jerome Klinkowitz, "A Man Alone—Alone with Death," in The Chicago Sun-Times *(reprinted with permission of* The Chicago Sun-Times; and the author*), October 1, 1978, p. 11.*

The attentive, detail-laden prose of this somber tale [*The Followed Man*] shares many of the virtues of [the protagonist's] hand-built cabin: it is sturdy, attractive, and provides warmth in a chilly environment. But faults in the construction—frequent coincidences, occurrences that lead nowhere—point out the ordinariness of a plot full of sex and violence, and despite the cast of cowed and snarling characters, it is never quite possible to believe in Luke's paranoia. Disappointingly, *The Followed Man* lacks the depth as well as the complexity of Williams's award-winning *The Hair of Harold Roux*.

"Life & Letters: 'The Followed Man'," in The Atlantic Monthly *(copyright © 1978 by The Atlantic Monthly Company, Boston, Mass.; reprinted with permission), Vol. 242, No. 6, December, 1978, p. 94.*

DONALD HALL

The Followed Man is Williams' best novel, strong, beautiful, and harrowing. . . . [It] contains less distraction from Williams' harsh vision of things. Williams seems to have grown into acceptance of his vision, and to acknowledge it for the first time. On the one hand he continues to describe a natural world of great beauty—especially rural New England, outdoors, with its associated virtues of self-reliance, durability, and fortitude. But Thomas Williams is not making novels that resemble calendar New England, for on the other hand the strongest emotions in his novels—*The Followed Man* in particular—are human pain and guilt. (p. 107)

The plot . . . may seem as arbitrary as life itself, tilted entirely to the side of blackness. But that is not all that there is in this novel. Through everything, Carr maintains his decency, as we see him struggle to make square corners, solid walls, and a roof with the right pitch—invoking order and sanity by carpentering, much as Hemingway's fisherman fights madness by meticulous fishing. Carr is a hero in his resolute will to endure, even if endurance necessitates removal and solitude. The society he removes himself from is depraved—the society that follows him, even in the country. He struggles to avoid the guilt of complicity. (pp. 108-09)

Donald Hall, "The Best Unknown," in National Review *(© National Review, Inc., 1979; 150 East 35th St., New York, N.Y. 10016), Vol. XXXI, No. 3, January 19, 1979, pp. 107-09.*

* * *

WILSON, Colin 1931-

Wilson is a British novelist, essayist, and playwright. Essentially a phenomenologist, he has pursued the "sources of human energy" into the dark corners of witchcraft and the occult in his many books of fiction and nonfiction. (See also *CLC*, Vol. 3, *Contemporary Authors*, Vols. 1-4, rev. ed.)

MARTHA ECKMAN

My contention is that *The Outsider* contains the key idea to understanding the twentieth century, and that it contains all the seminal ideas of Wilson's later works, though I would agree quickly that Wilson was probably unaware at that time of the direction his theories would take. The initial premise in *The Outsider* is that since about 1800, with the development of the Romantic Movement in art, literature, and philosophy, a group of outstanding individuals has developed who are no longer satisfied with the dead-end streets of scientific or existential thought. They insist upon breaking out of their "prisons" of the mind in search of ultimate reality, whatever that may be. . . . In defending his outsider concept, Wilson has surveyed the works of a staggering number of writers, artists, and philosophers. (p. 63)

Wilson has said that, for the sake of convenience, his starting point lies in William James's essay "The Energies of Man." Add to the James essay Shaw's evolutionary concepts of the philosopher-scholar, as found in the rarely performed "Don Juan in Hell" from *Man and Superman,* plus Husserl's concept of intentionality (as Wilson uses it to extend the borders of existential thought), and you have the bare bones of Wilson's recurrent themes. He has expounded these themes in science fiction, sex novels, and some really good detective-spy fiction. In his *The Occult: A History,* he relates the outsider theme to major figures in the occult. Maintaining an objective distance from the flamboyance involved in reports of magic, telepathy, precognition, clairvoyance, water-witching, mind-altering drugs, the *I Ching,* the Kabbalah, and the tarot cards, he states:

> Faculty X is simply that latent power that human beings possess to reach beyond the present. . . . It would be a mistake to think of Faculty X as an "occult" faculty. It is not; it is the power to grasp reality, and it unites the two halves of man's mind, conscious and subconscious. . . . Faculty X is not a "sixth sense," but an ordinary poten-

> tiality of consciousness . . . it is the key not only to so-called occult experience, but to the whole future evolution of the human race.

"Faculty X" is probably the key term in Wilson's *The Occult,* and it is quite as serviceable as other terms being used these days for forces in the human mind we have not explained. It relates to the outsider concept in that many, perhaps all, outsiders possessed it to one degree or another and were, through its use, able to extend their creativity. (p. 64)

In most Wilson novels, the hero begins to suspect that there is more to life than appears on the surface. Through an exercise of the will, "Faculty X" is mobilized. . . .

In *Voyage to a Beginning,* Wilson states additional convictions found repeatedly in his novels: (1) that consciousness needs to be expanded by an act of *will*—not through hallucinogens and not through the trance state achieved by a number of religious groups—and (2) that there is *meaning* in the evolving world, as opposed to the popular existential view that planet Earth is a meaningless, accidental, and absurb fiasco. (p. 65)

Wilson claims to be thoroughly existentialist. He denies Sartre's belief that "there is no essential you," nevertheless, and finds Sartre's negative attitude phenomenologically unsound because it distorts *intentionality.* He emphasizes the limitless possibilities for his own "new existentialism," maintaining that its optimism is a more valid stance than Sartre's pessimistic "nausea" because he (Wilson) has taken Maslow's "peak experiences," Frankl's "will to meaning," and Husserl's "need to know" (intentionality) into consideration. . . . Wilson suggests that someday—through evolution, the collective unconscious, even DNA coding—humankind will be able to use "Faculty X" quite as easily as it uses any of the five physical senses today. (pp. 65-6)

I feel fairly strongly that Wilson has not developed any clear understanding of mysticism as distinguished from or related to the occult. All his novels and nonfiction so far seem to indicate that he is not particularly interested in spiritual development nor in implications of consciousness expansion in a social context. His chief interest seems to be simply in individual mind control *per se.* (p. 68)

I would like to leave my nagging concern about social consequences for the nonce, then, and look briefly at what happens to the *individual* with an expanded consciousness, who has made use of his "Faculty X." In *God of the Labyrinth,* Wilson creates a hero who decides that "nothing is worth possessing except intensity of consciousness." Soon after coming to this decision, the hero finds himself capable of giving an exhibition in sexual athletics which might boggle the pedestrian mind. . . . What Wilson does in the particular novel . . . [mentioned] is, simply, to apply the old occult ideas to a twentieth century fictional context. (pp. 69-70)

The most fascinating aspect of the book to me personally, and presumably to Wilson also, was the possiblility that two personalities might exist in the same body. While the hero searches physically and psychically for the author of an eighteenth century sex journal, he gradually permits the personality of the dead author to "return" from the dead and inhabit his (the hero's) very alive body. . . . What Colin Wilson does not bother to tell the uninitiated reader is that this development would be called, in occultist circles, "possession." Not reincarnation, mind you. And Possession is *not* a desirable state of affairs, witness *The Three Faces of Eve* as its nearest psychological analogy. In *God of the Labyrinth,* then, mind control has traveled full circle to become mind domination. (p. 70)

Martha Eckman, "Colin Wilson and the Occult" (originally an address delivered at the Third National Meeting of the Popular Culture Association), in The Contemporary Literary Scene 1973, *edited by Frank N. Magill (copyright © 1974 by Frank N. Magill), Salem Press, Inc., 1974, pp. 62-74.*

HELEN McNEIL

In *Mysteries,* Colin Wilson reveals that the germ of his subjective compendium of psychology and the occult began when he was trying to write over 3,000 words a day for a compendium of crime. Wilson kept waking up in the night with a terrible sense of anxiety. Standing back from this tale, it seems to be about the consequences of trying to write too much dreck too fast, but for Wilson his 'panic effect' came from a weaker personality and required a supranatural cure, which he calls 'the school-mistress effect'. The rest of his 667-page book is a similar mélange of willed over-reading and gullible summary. Kabbalism, hermeticism, gnosticism and alchemy are relatively unsympathetically treated, probably because they are related to major religions and so aren't entirely prey to the whims of the post-rational mind. . . .

Modern occultism of the sort enthusiastically described by Colin Wilson is not about knowledge, however non-scientific, but about not knowing. Again and again its structure is that of horror: the small lit room reminding one of the dark limitless space beyond and beneath.

Helen McNeil, "A Severed Head," in New Statesman *(© 1978 The Statesman & Nation Publishing Co. Ltd.), Vol. 96, Nos. 2492 & 2493, December 22 & 29, 1978, p. 885.**

CHRISTOPHER BIRD

[In *Mysteries*] Colin Wilson addresses the same theme that has consistently threaded its way through all of his books, beginning with *The Outsider,* which brought him world attention in his early twenties—that so-called "conscious" human beings are pygmies, mere fragments of their true selves.

But, he avers, "human beings will one day recognize, beyond all possibility of doubt, that consciousness *is* freedom. . . .

Part of Wilson's hopeful conclusion is directly based on his personal confrontation with a series of what he calls "panic anxiety attacks" which lasted several months and brought him to the edge of a nervous breakdown. . . .

Wilson's account of how he finally overcame these attacks is a courageous example of how it is possible to deal with oppressive problems through introspection. . . .

Wilson lays a large share of the blame for this state of affairs on our incessant search for security. He maintains that while freedom from risk and doubt is essential to human experience, to overemphasize it slows down the learning experience we have come upon this planet to acquire. . . .

The unfortunate truth is that humans, in the present stage of their evolution, appear all too ready to accept lack of meaning, just as animals accept physical suffering. Wilson believes that only shock or crisis can release them from a state of suffocation and bring them to a realization of higher purpose and a feeling of being totally alive. . . .

Readers of *Mysteries* will be called upon . . . to adjust their thinking to worlds beyond the bleakly materialist and limited version of the cosmos presently expounded by mainstream science. In so doing, they will be introduced to an encyclopedic panoply of marvels and worthwhile philosophical insights, all of which are as entertaining as they are disturbing.

Christopher Bird, "The Robot within Us," in Book World—The Washington Post *(© 1978,* The Washington Post*), December 24, 1978, p. E3.*

ALAN HULL WALTON

[*Mysteries*] marks a new 'high' in Wilson's prodigious output, placing him in the top rank of serious contemporary investigators of the paranormal.

The detail and wide range of the book (well documented) defies analysis in these few pages. But each and every example and subject is described, probed and weighed-up with such an eagle-eye that the volume immediately becomes 'definitive'. Moreover, the flow of writing is so natural and unaffected that nothing could be easier to read. There is, I think, only a single word which adequately sums up the qualities of this enormous opus of over 260,000 words—already a 'classic' in its own right—and that word is *superlative*. I might add that, after many years of study of such works, my opinion is a carefully considered one. And it is a volume one 'simply can't put down', but must go on reading, and reading . . . and re-reading. (p. 41)

[Wilson] writes in a style which any intelligent man or woman can grasp quite simply. Indeed his lengthy examples and explanations have all the compulsion and thrill of a masterly *who-done-it?* . . .

I have suggested . . . that some of the best and more perceptive scientists . . . are already beginning to accept 'the unusual' and paranormal, and to investigate them. . . . [But] the vast mass of scientists still remain unwilling to leave their comfortable cubby-holes or take off their blinkers. Which is one more reason why this book is so important. It will give all such individuals a severe jolt—and cause them to think again. . . . (p. 42)

[If] the reader will turn to Wilson's *Magnum Opus,* I think he will agree with me that it reflects an almost superhuman amount of research and magically ruminative thought, both of which belong to that quality defined as 'genius'. (p. 43)

Alan Hull Walton, "Colin Wilson's 'Magnum Opus'" (© copyright Alan Hull Walton 1979; reprinted with permission), in Books and Bookmen, *Vol. 24, No. 6, March, 1979, pp. 41-3.*

PAUL T. HORNAK

[*Mysteries*] is an encyclopedic treatment of the supernatural that begins with the assumption that seers, UFO watchers, dowsers, and people haunted by ghosts are not kidding. They honestly believe they've seen something, Wilson maintains, and on this basis he recites case after spooky case of happenings that seem to defy explanation. If he had stopped at storytelling, *Mysteries* could be written off as an unfortunate triumph of gullibility over good sense. But Wilson goes three reckless steps further. He tells why people have seen whatever they've seen, how someday we all will be able to see, and why the ability is a good thing. . . . As proof of his bizarre theory, Wilson offers the testimony of persons widely regarded as cranks. He puts inordinate trust in hunches: he praises one source for putting across a "feeling of revelation." Trying to validate the unknown by invoking the unknown, he calls upon the "unconscious," the "subconscious," "higher levels" of thought. When these devices fail, the weapon of last resort is emotion. "This vast computer we call the brain was *meant* to operate at a far higher level of efficiency." Wilson, in search of otherworldly meaning, argues with simple earthly shouting. (pp. 1448, 1451)

Paul T. Hornak, "Books in Brief: 'Mysteries'," in National Review *(© National Review, Inc., 1979; 150 East 35th St., New York, NY 10016), Vol. XXXI, No. 45, November 9, 1979, pp. 1448, 1451.*

CLIFFORD P. BENDAU

Colin Wilson is not an academic. Not tied to a specific discipline, he concerns himself with the entire spectrum of the humanities. His case-book studies of the human condition are written with a sense of urgency, often ignoring the formal guidelines of academic writing. As a result, he has been criticized as self-righteous in expression, and unsound in analysis. In some respects, the critics are right. When subjected to analysis, his arguments often fall short. Isolated from the whole, individual works may appear to be hasty generalizations. But logical analysis and isolated dissection, while valid for criticism, do not justify a complete rejection of Wilson's ideas. These are not the only criteria available.

Wilson is concerned with the truth of the world "out there," not with formal logic. His writings are the response of an individual to the problems of existence. When he says that his beliefs are true, the justification is grounded in their usefulness in dealing with the practical problems of existence. Wilson is not a spectator. Unlike the scientist or mathematician, he is not interested in discovering universal theoretical truths. He is interested in the particulars of existence, here and now. He is oriented practically to the way reality could and should be. . . .

Confidence in his own genius, coupled with an unquestioning belief in his significance as a writer, enabled Wilson to draw heavily from his own experiences. His first book *The Outsider,* was largely a recapitulation of his personal journal entries. after the initial critical reaction, Wilson's subjective approach was not well received. Yet he has never tried to conceal the personal nature of his work. On the contrary, his aims and motives were clearly established in his autobiography as the attempt to investigate facts and relate those facts to his own experience. (p. 5)

Although his work at first glance seems diverse and unconnected, there are consistent and unifying themes that permeate the whole. These themes, embryonic in his first book, develop with Wilson's maturation as a writer. The first seven books, the Outsider Cycle, were written as a reexamination of modern philosophy. The cycle provided a foundation for a new existentialism that would go beyond the impasse created by the old existentialism. Wilson contends that certain European existentialists, due to narrow vision and improper methodological tools, failed to transcend the apparent negativity of life; consequently, by mid-century philosophy was stuck in the dead end of pessimism. Likewise, the Logical Positivist approach failed. Logical and linguistic analysis are fine on paper, but do not, claims Wilson, affect life in the real world. Modern philosophy has failed to reveal the underlying meaning to be found in human existence.

The new existentialism is an attempt to take over where the old existentialism failed. Wilson's thematic development progresses toward this goal. He asserts that the nihilism of modern philosophy is a result of a distortion of thought. It is imperative that man find a new philosophy to "prevent these distortions and reestablish a more direct contact with existence." Through the tool of phenomenology, the philosopher can combat the distortions imposed by the mind on thought itself. . . . To focus on the boredom, the meaninglessness, the incapacity for freedom while overlooking the moments of broadened perception is philosophically myopic [Wilson says]. The momentary "glimpse of meaning" that is occasionally perceived through the clouds of despair is in itself enough to disclaim the meaning of nihilism. These "glimpses of meaning" are the key issue in Wilson's writings on the imagination. . . .

Wilson approaches the problem of freedom through the concept of the outsider. The outsider is an evolutionary type of person confronted by a specific problem. He, more sensitive than the ordinary man, sees beyond the facade of meaning erected by society to conceal the chaos of life. He stands outside institutionalized values because "he alone knows he is sick, in a civilization that does not know it is sick." Without the values of society and without values of his own, the outsider witnesses his life with a sense of futility—he is not free, but is born into the bondage of a world policed by ordinary men who neither see the triviality of their concerns, nor recognize the horrors and contingency lurking behind the facade of order. (p. 6)

If existentialism was a "philosophy of freedom," then its greatest oversight was its concern with the freedom of "ordinary everyday consciousness." Wilson sees another aspect to human freedom, an extraordinary consciousness that strives for the more objective and positive evolutionary values, those values that reside outside of man. . . .

It is the problem of contingency, claims Wilson, that is the major obstacle for the new existentialism. By using the word "contingency," Wilson is referring to the uncertain, unpredictable, and insecure nature of the universe. . . .

In rejecting the notion of contingency, Wilson contends that meaning and values reside in the world. The real problem is that man, due to the narrowness of ordinary consciousness, does not see them. Belief in life's contingency naturally flows out of "the fallacy of passive perception." Wilson contends that the mistaken belief that human consciousness is passive, coupled with the narrowness of consciousness, is the cause of the inability to grasp the meaning present in the world. (p. 8)

The Logical Positivist claims that it is meaningless to ask questions about the meaning of life. The Existentialist claims that it is existence itself that is meaningless. Wilson, in declaring that meaning is revealed in moments of intensity, claims "to have produced the only acceptable alternative." The poetic, mystic, and religious experience are moments that seem to deny the contingency of life. They give insight into meaning, deny the accidental quality of existence, and go beyond the distortions man imposes on his own consciousness. They can no longer be regarded as abnormal. (pp. 9-10)

Aligning himself with William James, Wilson believes that these experiences are not supernatural, but merely extensions of the ordinary everyday consciousness. Unlike James, Wilson does not feel the need to suspend judgment; the answer to the problem of meaning is found in the structure of consciousness. . . .

Wilson asserts that an act of will boosts perception, that perception can be intensified by an effort of concentration. In short, evolution can be seen as the product of the will to purpose. (p. 10)

Through his concept of the evolutionary will, Wilson brings us back to the problem of the outsider. The outsider is the harbinger of evolutionary change. He, more sensitive than the average human being, is prone to insight experiences that reveal man's higher destiny. Because he is different, because language fails him, because ordinary life among ordinary man bores him, he steps outside of society. (p. 11)

Although it is true that Wilson frequently deals with the mystic-religious experience, it would be misleading to label him a mystic. His books often deal with individuals described as mystics or visionaries, but throughout all of his writings he does not make a strong personal claim to mystic experience. (p. 14)

To Wilson's mind, man, through a heroic effort, and by learning how to discipline the mind, can experience the world in an entirely different way. The human being, like no other animal, has the ability to choose what and how he perceives. Because of his imagination, because of his ability to see further, because he can choose to evolve toward greatness or fall by the way of triviality, man is responsible for his own destiny. He must learn the subtleties of thinking. When he masters the process of rationality and recognizes that the reality of the moment of vision is a better alternative than everyday reality, he will occupy the realm of mind. It is the imagination, claims Wilson, that will bring us closer to this realm of mind. (p. 16)

The Age of Defeat is a continued search for the heroic. Dealing with not only literature, but also dabbling in sociology and economics, Wilson attempts to show that the absence of the hero in literature is a reflection of the modern writer's perception of reality. As such, it is not a mere literary problem. He sees "defeatism" as an interdisciplinary problem, and calls on the combined forces of literature and philosophy to overcome it. . . .

If there is no true portrait of the hero in modern literature, then what, one might ask, is a "true" hero? . . . [In] *The Introduction to the New Existentialism,* Wilson carefully defines the "existential hero" as one who "has glimpses of joy that are beyond anything possible to the born coward: the ecstacy of power and freedom." Wilson explains that this awareness is coupled with the knowledge of the human condition with all of its existential pain and misery. Although the existential hero is aware of the negative qualities, he does not believe in them as ultimate reality. His reality is permeated with a belief in "freedom as absolute power." He is strong in his ability to overcome human frailties. He believes that even "human contingency will prove to be an illusion in the light of absolute freedom." In short, Wilson concludes, the hero "is totally the optimist and adventurer," one who does not recognize the legitimacy of "insurmountable obstacles." The existential hero may be destroyed, but never defeated. This definition is one that, if somewhat implausible, certainly cannot be criticized as lacking in ambition. Considered in the overall framework of Wilson's philosophical system, it reveals a developmental consistency.

Wilson's concept of the "existential hero" draws together his philosophical ideas concerning freedom, will, and evolution. As a part of his philosophy, it reflects his belief in the positive nature of reality, as well as his theoretical positions on the nature and function of imagination. Thus, it is also a part of his literary theory. (p. 18)

If the function of the creative writer is to help restore man's sense of purpose, and, in turn, man's sense of significance, then literature, claims Wilson, must be value-laden. The imagination, literature, and values are all tightly interwoven. Any attempt to separate them is purposeless. . . . Within the writer's material there is always a subtle and implicit value claim. Meaning, in the sense of the purpose of human existence, is a prerequisite for the writer. (p. 19)

An author employs existential realism *only* if he goes beyond the narrowly perceived reality of everyday consciousness. He must investigate reality phenomenologically, and present the reader with an undistorted vision that goes beyond the "natural standpoint." It is here that the reader actively involves himself in the writer's picture of reality. The novel, for this reason, must be somewhat didactic. The writer's vision must be communicated to, and accepted by, the reader. This dynamic interchange between the writer and the reader is the element most often criticized in Wilson's own fictional works, in addition to his evident self-confidence and attitude of supreme self-righteousness. Whether justified or not in the eyes of his critics, Wilson not only stood fast to his literary theory, but proceeded to establish new grounds for evaluating literature. These grounds, concerned with existential human values, would be the cornerstone of "Existential Criticism." (p. 21)

[Existential] criticism "is an attempt to judge works of art by the contribution they make to the science of living, to judge them by standards of *meaning* as well as impact." The two types of criticism are necessarily related. Existential criticism and literary criticism are complimentary. One deals with the interpretation of the technical "facts" of creative writing. The other deals with the interpretation of the existential "facts" of the writer's reality. Both tacitly recognize that "facts" do not live apart from their interpretation. (p. 22)

[Wilson's] work has been unfairly scrutinized. . . . Many of the critical challenges have been supported by fallacious reasoning, unfair generalization, attacks to the person, and irrelevant conclusions. . . .

Some critics, directly or indirectly, have attacked Wilson's work on the basis of a "low-level intellectual quality." They seem to have been preoccupied with his lack of formal education. Ironically, Wilson's success as a literary "working class hero" was an outgrowth of the same factor. What was originally described as the "luminous intelligence" of a twenty-four-year-old writer soon became the fraudulent outpourings of a "British type, lower middle class, self-educated bohemian." The same qualities that critics used to support the belief that Colin Wilson was a genius were used to denounce him as a "scrambled egghead." (p. 27)

The critics were not altogether wrong. Wilson's early books were in many ways the works of a young and inexperienced writer. His urgency for expression often betrayed his intent. At twenty-four he felt confident that his ideas were important. Where many writers derive their "authority" and confidence from their advanced degrees, Wilson's confidence evolved from his extensive reading and life experiences. He viewed himself as having no less authority because of his lack of formal education. Unlike more humble writers, he never alluded to his authority sheepishly. He proclaimed it. In this light it is understandable why his person was the primary target of attack. . . . There was, in spite of an early toxic reaction to success, an urgency in Wilson's concerns. His search for truth seems honest and sincere, even at this early date.

Wilson's holistic approach to his subject matter has been another point of critical attack. His positions often exemplified as well as justified connecting and interrelated elements in literature, philosophy, music, art, psychology and history. In short, Wilson was a pioneer in the interdisciplinary approach to problem solving; he could never justify the separation of philosophy from art or literature. (p. 28)

The Outsider [1956] is one of the trenchant argumentative statements of the middle-Fifties. Considered within the placid mood of the times, the torrential outpourings of the previously unknown Colin Wilson were challenging not only to the literary establishment, but also to the popular market as well.

Whether Wilson set out deliberately to dazzle or perplex his readership is uncertain. The text of *The Outsider* is far from self-explanatory; one can search frustratingly for a specific theme. Yet Wilson displays an obvious erudition that, in this case, does not dazzle for its own sake. . . . Wilson studies those individuals, in fact and fiction, who fit his concept of outsider types; those who search for a way out, pursuing truth at all costs, striving to be free from the banality of ordinary existence. (p. 30)

In many ways, the ideas in *The Outsider* represent an embryonic stage in Wilson's search for a "religious" answer to the problem of alienation. A special type of religiosity will begin to develop, and continues to develop, throughout the remainder of his work. (pp. 30-1)

If the success of *The Outsider* was phenomenal, the failure of his next book [*Religion and the Rebel* (1957)] was equally so. (p. 31)

[George Bernard Shaw's] idea of the life force is clearly seen in *Religion and the Rebel* [where] the outsider is an evolutionary development of the life force in man. This Shavian life-force is, in times of crisis, capable of creating a higher, more developed form of life. Wilson, like . . . Shaw, is anti-Darwinian and anti-determinist. Human beings and animals change through evolution because they want to change. Change is not an accident. It is a function of the evolutionary will. The outsider is the noble knight who meets the crisis of the Western world.

It is, to some degree, true that Wilson's "megalomania" does reveal itself in *Religion and the Rebel.* However, one must recognize the urgency of his concerns. If there are "inconsistencies" and "wild thrashings about," these come from a self-appointed mission to deliver a message. (pp. 31-2)

Shorter, but no less controversial, than his previous books, [*The Age of Defeat* (1959)] takes issue with the overwhelming attitude of defeat and disaster present in contemporary literature. Here, Wilson hypothesizes that literature is merely a reflection of the world of its creators, and that it is modern society in general that suffers from the "fallacy of insignificance." This malady must be cured if man is to evolve to his proper stature. . . .

The Age of Defeat prompted some criticism from those who felt that Wilson did not generate any ideas of his own. This may be true, but, for all of the palaver and nit-picking, Wilson here takes on a rather difficult task: the restructuring of literature. His approach builds upon casebook examples from life and literature, and is not intended merely to display creative insights. His studies are methodical and empirical, yet no less creative than those of the mathematician or scientist. (p. 32)

Wilson's first novel [*Ritual in the Dark* (1960)] is a study that aims at a different sensibility in the reader. Focusing on the inevitable frustrations that arise out of the conflict between self and society, this existential tale puts literary theory into practice through the lives of several outsiders. As evidenced by the title, the story deals with the mythic appeal of both sex and violence, and lends itself to a questioning of both human motives and actions.

The novel chronicles the slowly-awakening consciousness of Gerard Sorme. This is a "novel of initiation," and, like any initiation rite, there is a painful encounter that leads to growth and an added dimension of insight. (pp. 32-3)

By portraying two outsider types in conjunction with each other, Wilson develops conflicting interpretations of certain events. Set against the semi-misanthropic Gerard Sorme is an outsider of a different sort. Austin Nunne is wealthy and knowledgeable, a refined dilettante writer who has a penchant for Nijinsky and sadistic murder. The interactions between Sorme and Nunne create most of the tension in the story. (p. 33)

Sorme represents the outsider who is able to integrate creative energies into his search for the positive aspects of freedom, while Nunne represents the outsider who is unable to deal with these forces. In Nunne we see the destruction of both self and society. . . .

Wilson's fiction is didactic. It is the nature of his style to make fiction and non-fiction complementary as instructional devices; an unusual, but not illegitimate technique aimed concurrently at different sensibilities in the reader. At times, however, Wilson goes too far: his characters not only preach Wilson's ideas, but often resemble that man himself. In the case of *Ritual,* this resemblance is a minor flaw, and the book remains an extraordinary first novel. (p. 34)

In *The Strength to Dream: Literature and the Imagination* [1962], Wilson continues to expand his earlier statements on literary theory as set out in *Age of Defeat.*

Strength is a chronicle of the "inaccuracies of imagination" that are considered to be literature. Wilson, because he is intent on finding an underlying order or pattern to the general laws of imagination, carefully evaluates literary history. Although the book is ostensibly about literature, this fourth volume in the outsider cycle is really a study "with a view to defining the concept of reality." (p. 35)

The World of Violence [1963] is the third novel dealing with the underlying theme of "initiation." Its basic premise is the "conflict between the world of the intellect and the world of physical violence." . . .

Wilson intends to involve the reader in the conflict. Thus, the violence and low-key sexuality are never meant for sensationalist purposes, but to create a tension between the reader and the characters. Whether Wilson succeeds is questionable. (p. 36)

Considered within the framework of the creation of an evolutionary hero, *The World of Violence,* like *Ritual in the Dark* and *Adrift in Soho,* is a positive step in the right direction. At this point, Wilson is still at an experimental stage in his fiction. What is apparent in *The World of Violence* is that Wilson is making progress. The maturation of the hero is displayed through a new ability to make positive value choices and to act upon those choices. (pp. 36-7)

Roughly, the theory of symbolic response [in *Origins of the Sexual Impulse* (1963)] states that the origins of the sexual impulse are not found within the Freudian libido. Sexual activity is a response to symbols, and symbols are invested with meaning from a separate source. In human sexuality the symbol is given meaning by a curious aspect of the inner self that is continually searching for purpose from within. In other words, the imagination invests a particular object with sexual meaning. The source of meaning is found within man rather than without.

If the source of sexual meaning is found within the individual, then, according to the theory, ideas of "normal" sex and "perversion" fall apart. The standard is subjective rather than objective. Meaning is now seen as the projection of inner meaning upon the world. This projection of meaning or, as Wilson calls it, intentionality, is the origin of the sexual impulse.

The book received a cool response from the critics, who considered the book to be an excuse to write luridly about sexual matters. Others felt that Wilson was living up to his reputation for putting forth incomprehensible studies that were nothing more than a "hodgepodge." (p. 37)

Whether or not Wilson is qualified to develop a theory of sexual psychology is a legitimate question. But whether Wilson had ever intended to formulate a grand theory of sexuality for its own sake is doubtful. What is most important to Wilson's overall thesis is the idea of the intentionality of consciousness. In this light, *Origins of the Sexual Impulse* is closely aligned with his writings on the evolutionary purposiveness of life.

Wilson's novels often illustrate the ideas of his philosophical works. In *Man Without a Shadow* [1963], he unabashedly demonstrates that the ideas discussed in *Origins of the Sexual Impulse* can be approached from the fictional angle. (pp. 37-8)

Wilson's most obvious concern is with the demonstration of the points made in *Origin of the Sexual Impulse:* the apparent interrelationship between the sexual drive, criminality, and the imagination, or, more specifically, the role sex plays in man's total being.

Wilson's heroes, up to this point, have been thinking men prone to philosophizing and intellectualizing. As they slowly become aware of the passion and intensity of life, the limitless potential of freedom, and the virtual "powerhouse" within them, they experience a broadening perception of their own consciousness. Wilson's heroes have evolved, and after the fourth novel continue to evolve. [Next,] . . . Wilson "moves into new forms which plunge their heroes from thought into action, from understanding into being." (p. 38)

[*Necessary Doubt* (1964) is] a step in Wilson's evolutionary development as a writer. Although on the level of intellectual thriller it is a little overstated, it still remains an engaging story. What keeps the reader involved through the intellectual digressions is the enthusiasm of the presentation, and Wilson himself. (p. 39)

[Wilson's] fiction consistently strives to meet the stringent demands of existential realism, and the philosophy found within is constructed situationally throughout the narratives. The characters in Wilson's novels live in a world that abounds with negativity, yet are able to see beyond their squalid surroundings. In their inner dialogue, as well as in their conversations, they expound the new existentialism. In the past Wilson had, on occasion, been a bit too enthusiastic about the new philosophy; many of the novels suffer from didacticism. However, most of his recent fiction has been more subtle. . . . (p. 42)

Murder is of interest to Wilson because "it is the most extreme form of denial of this human potential." His approach, in *The Casebook of Murder* [1969], is to splash his readers in the face with enough cold water to rouse them from their passivity, and generate an active interest in their own freedom. Looking for homicidal patterns, Wilson surveys violent crimes of the last few centuries. In doing so he is making an attempt to establish the "changing fashions in murder," and gathering evidence to support his thesis that these crimes are crimes of freedom.

Voyage to a Beginning: A Preliminary Autobiography [1969], criticized as resembling the "miracle promising ads" often found "in the back of sex magazines," is Wilson's attempt to present his life and ideas in a straightforward narrative. In general, the critics seemed to be affronted by an autobiography from someone so young. But the book, in spite of the caustic comments it received, is recommended for anyone interested in the "aims and motives" of Wilson's work up to 1969. Its value is in the insight it gives the reader into Colin Wilson's version of his own story. (pp. 45-6)

[*Strindberg* (1970)] is a psychological drama that portrays one night in the life of August Strindberg. Unlike the politically controversial work of the late sixties, Wilson's play is concerned with the matter of the individual. The individual, August Strindberg, is struggling with the internal and external conflicts of his own personality. The play, through techniques of dream dramatization and the juxtaposition of conscious and unconscious realities, questions what is genuinely real.

The overt question of *Strindberg* is that of sanity. Wilson presents his audience with a macabre situation replete with incongruous incidents. Strindberg, whether awake or asleep, is confronted by his past through the accusations of various influential participants. In a surrealistic trial the man and his work are "tried" and defended. The covert question of *Strindberg* is the question of reality. Through "experimental" dramatic techniques Wilson divests the stage of its linear quality. He offers his audience a new kind of dramatic space in which to perceive differently. He gives his audience different perceptual realities that obscure the fundamentalist notion of what is real. *Strindberg* is a penetrating, almost voyeuristic, glimpse into the artist's inner conflict as he is confronted by "his own existence." (p. 49)

Wilson's earlier documentations of murder and violent crime were the first two parts of a murder trilogy completed in 1972 with publication of *The Order of Assassins.* Whereas *An Encyclopedia of Murder* was a reference book, and *A Casebook of Murder* was a social history of homicide, *The Order of Assassins* is about the psychology of murder. It is the most readable of the series, and is concerned with a special type of murder. Assassination is "murder committed for its own sake." The assassin, one who has a personal concern with the insidious act, commits murder as a "means of self-fulfillment, a creative act." This is similar to what is presented in the novel *Lingard.*

Through an analysis of "high I.Q." murders, the book presents the reader with an interesting twist to the outsider theory. The word "assassin" goes back to an early Moslem religious sect whose members killed out of personal conviction or obedience to orders. There is an almost "demonic" quality associated with this type of murder, a "need for violence," "an indifference" to the victim. When outsiders become killers they are prone to become assassins. They are highly or at least moderately intelligent; they are rebellious by nature; they are seething with excess energy. These men are similar to, yet different from, the artistic outsider. Like the artist, the criminal knows he is not ordinary, he tends to defy social tradition, and he releases outbursts of psychic energy in his acts. Unlike the artist, the criminal's acts are violent crimes. The artist commits acts that have the effect of integrating him into society; the "assassin always walks alone." The assassin, unable to release energy in a positive way, suffers from "frustration of the will-drive." (pp. 53-4)

[*The Order of Assassins*] is interwoven with actual literary characters and criminals, and with differing psychological theories. It is well integrated and documented. Its major fault lies in the repetition of subject matter. But this is true, of course, for the entire spectrum of Wilson's work. (p. 54)

The Space Vampires (1976) is Wilson at his best. His writing always works well when he chooses subjects that can carry his philosophical weight, when he builds on philosophical foundations that galvanize his fiction with the nonfiction. Written with a simplicity of style and language, *Vampires* is a compelling and thought-provoking fictional work. This is Wilson's third science-fiction novel, and it is a further adaption of the mind parasites theme. Focusing on ideas of will and human potential, he takes his metaphor one step into the future. The space vampire, like the mind parasite, is an invading force that drains its human host of all vitality and will. Like its Draculan counterpart, it controls the minds of its victims but unlike its historical predecessor, the space vampire sucks out, not the blood, but the life force of its unfortunate prey.

The Space Vampires is more pointedly science-fictional than any of Wilson's earlier attempts. (p. 57)

Although much of the format seems to parallel Wilson's earlier novels, there are several clear differences in *Vampires*. In many of his other books Wilson falls into philosophical rambling and didacticism. What keeps the reader interested in *The Space Vampires* is the rapid-fire quality to the development of plot and story. And where some of the earlier fictions reveal the mystery or solution too early in the story, *Vampires* is quite different. Throughout the tale the reader is aware of a progression of events. The hero develops and awakens to an understanding of the problem in logical fashion, the plot is reasonably clear cut, and the resolution is anticipated in advance. The major difference between this most recent book and the earlier ones is to be found in Wilson's reversals. The last ten or twenty pages change the reader's understanding of the story through a rapid series of sudden changes. (pp. 58-9)

Wilson's basic underlying themes of the strength of the human will to resist invasion, the laziness and self-obsessed stupidity of most human beings, the second-hand nature of what man calls knowledge, and the recognition of the glimpse of meaning available when consciousness is fully used, are all present in this story. *The Space Vampires* remains one of Wilson's most successful creations, philosophical without being dull, a thoroughly entertaining fiction in every respect. (p. 59)

All persons, according to Wilson, have creative potentiality that remains untapped. The ability to tap into this potential depends upon positive, rather than negative, energy. Human boredom, resulting from the overefficiency of human habit systems, the robot-like response to daily life, and the resultant narrowing of perceptions, generates negative energy. Negative energy tends to obscure meaning, and this in turn slackens the will, making positive assertion difficult if not impossible.

The essence of Wilson's position is that man can and must expand the present modes of consciousness. His casebook studies are meant to give people an idea of what can be developed. The phenomenon of man's resignation to littleness is used to show the reader that man is perceptually aware of very little; but moreover, that man is conscious or unconsciously *choosing* not to be aware. If this is not changed, if man fails to concentrate on the assertion of will, he will ultimately forget how to be aware. (p. 60)

Clifford P. Bendau, in his Colin Wilson: The Outsider and Beyond *(copyright © 1979 by Clifford P. Bendau), The Borgo Press, 1979, 63 p.*

* * *

WILSON, Lanford 1937-

Wilson is an award-winning American playwright associated with off-Broadway and off-off-Broadway theater. He is best known as the author of the popular play *The Hot l Baltimore*. (See also *CLC*, Vol. 7, and *Contemporary Authors*, Vols. 17-20, rev. ed.)

CATHARINE HUGHES

Coming immediately after *The Hot L Baltimore*, which won the 1973 Drama Critics Circle 'best play' award, Lanford Wilson's *The Mound Builders* was . . . a disappointment, not to mention a considerable bore.

Seemingly, [the play's plot] would contain ample opportunities to explore each character's nature and attitudes, their approaches to life and their ideas concerning Man's destiny. Seemingly, it would also offer the occasion for major conflicts and confrontations among this diverse group of people. Sadly, it does not, for they are not people but insufficiently explored, inadequately motivated puppets in the playwright's hands. Only the sister, and, fleetingly, the young man intent on turning the property, his property, into a lucrative site for highways, dams and motels, thus obliterating forever the lost civilisation, come alive. Only at the end does the conflict between two approaches to civilisation—and life—come into focus. Before that, there is endless rumination, endless padding, endless pseudo-profundity.

In *Hot L Baltimore*, the decline of the once illustrious hotel became a strikingly effective metaphor for the decline and disillusion of the dreams of the inhabitants. The 'mound builders' metaphor never becomes an even remotely effective one. Man—the archaeologists—may seek to build their own scholarly monuments and others—the young Chad—his in the form of motels and fortunes, but a play must have more life, more living figures, to make such a metaphor resonant and dramatically viable. It must reach considerably farther beneath the surface, not settle for the superficial characterisation and amateur psychology of *The Mound Builders*, . . . if it is to have anything truly worth saying about ourselves or our past. (p. 34)

Catharine Hughes, "New York" (© copyright Catharine Hughes 1975; reprinted with permission), in Plays and Players, *Vol. 22, No. 8, May, 1975, pp. 34-5.*

RICHARD EDER

You cannot build a serviceable bridge out of flowers unless you are an ant; and Lanford Wilson's vocabulary of freaks, sensitive and even charming as it may be, is not the right material to construct the history of a decade. . . .

["The Fifth of July"] attempts to reflect upon what the 70's have made of the 60's. What is left, the question goes and not for the first time, of the impassioned spirit of the marches and the flower-children.

Mr. Wilson's talent is for the frail oddities of life, for waifs who gather in a haze of intersecting fantasies. The intersections are often pretty and whimsical; they have a humor and wryness that can compensate for the fact that the melancholy that goes with it is rather vapid and loose. . . .

Mr. Wilson has assembled a stageful of luminous freaks. Some of them are tiresome and familiar, but several have a delicate sharpness and some real force.

Not enough, though, to bear a whole message about our times. Their curlicues are pressed flat by the need to signify, and at climactic moments they carry trayfuls of symbols stacked so high as to quite obliterate the faces of their bearers. . . .

The play's essence, however, is a complex and gaudy series of serious games that the characters play with each other and with themselves.

The talk is extravagant, funny and often piercing, but its function is to build up the extremities represented by each of the characters rather than to take them in any particular direction.

Each, carried by the times, has in some way spoiled the hopes of his or her youth. It is not a dramatic spoiling; none was more than a vessel of the times, and when the times changed so did each of them, helplessly.

Richard Eder, "Theater: '5th of July' Is Staged," in The New York Times *(© 1978 by The New York Times Company; reprinted by permission), April 28, 1978, p. C3.*

EDITH OLIVER

The action [of "The 5th of July"] just seems to drift along. There are monologues—indeed, the play at times could be considered an amalgam of these arias which arise out of not much of anything—there are sessions of reminiscence of the old days at Berkeley . . . ; there are dustups and reconciliations; and there are a few passages of genuine comedy. Yet beneath all the apparently random activity there are feelings, most of them sexual, and a story, of sorts, is being told. The evening ends with a burst of violence, a revelation, and a resolution, also of sorts.

"The 5th of July" is Mr. Wilson's most ambitious play so far, and, regrettably, it is his most verbose, seeming at times to be almost smothered in words; those monologues become very trying. There is no doubt, though, that he is a writer, in a profession crowded with non-writers. (But only Chekhov can write Chekhov's plays.) The four principal characters are the Berkeley classmates, remnants of the nineteen-sixties treading water in the nineteen-seventies, and they are on-and-off believable and on-and-off synthetic.

Edith Oliver, "The Theatre: 'The 5th of July'," in The New Yorker *(© 1978 by The New Yorker Magazine, Inc.), Vol. LIV, No. 12, May 8, 1978, p. 90.*

JOHN SIMON

Lanford Wilson's *The 5th of July* is a pretty good Chekhovian play written too late. . . .

Wilson's Chekhov does not out-Chekhov the originals; it is merely out of place in its anachronistic garb, like people in nineteenth-century attire in a Danish-modern living room. . . .

[With the] unlikely plot device . . . needed to keep the characters spinning in the semblance of a non-vacuum . . . you have a clash of remembrances, recriminations, interests, and expectations. What you do not have, however, is dramatic development: a forward movement of a significant sort, a true change of human dynamics, despite not one but two switcheroos thrown in at the end. There are small conflicts, less than shattering revelations, and, mostly, people persisting in their old semi-impotent, semi-resigned ways.

All that is very Chekhovian—this sense of *plus ça change,* these people loving and hating one another to a stalemate, this blasé and cunning chatter that cannot keep the wolf of reality from the door, this getting nowhere even when one is most on the go, the very business of selling a house (*Cherry Orchard*) or planting for the future (*Uncle Vanya*) or yearning for other places (*Three Sisters*). But it doesn't work, for two reasons. It looks, sounds, and feels like a copy, however witty, wistful, and exquisite; and all that aimlessness, frustration, and failure does not have a compelling substratum of loss. In Chekhov's Russia, there were intimations of a collapsing empire, of a social order headed for bloody extinction; in Wilson's world, there is only the sense of the departed sixties, with their feeble political and sexual protests coming to an end. That is the implied fifth of July: the post-activist, post-coital, post-holiday depression.

Within this somewhat less than weighty framework, the individual moonings and moanings are also, unsurprisingly, trivial. But Wilson writes intelligent, amusing, racy dialogue, and is able to create lively albeit minuscule confrontations. The play is never uninteresting; it is merely, in the most profound sense, unsatisfying. (p. 77)

John Simon, "Likable but Unlikely Transplant," in New York *Magazine (copyright © 1978 by News Group Publications, Inc.; reprinted with the permission of* New York *Magazine), Vol. 11, No. 20, May 15, 1978, pp. 77-8.**

ERIKA MUNK

From the beginning it's obvious that *The 5th of July* is a deliberate variation on the theme of *Cherry Orchard.* It's equally clear by the end that melancholy comic naturalism has become a hollow structure, which, though it can still enclose a core of affectionate humaneness, has decayed toward soap opera and the quiet but unambiguous happy ending. . . .

There are many tender, tart, and funny moments and clever sections of contrapuntally overlapped dialogue. It is also a relief to see gay relationships taken for granted. But the central metaphorical anecdote (about dying from hunger through fear of eating something contaminated) is heavy-handed, Ken's Vietnam memories are cliched and unconvincing, and two of the women characters are treated very nastily. . . . The message is, I suppose, upbeat: Life can be warm and rooted, even for a legless homosexual, a lonely single mother, a 67-year-old widow with a mild stroke, a 13-year-old with a newly discovered rotten father . . . all you need is a radiantly beautiful farmhouse and the gumption not to let the city slickers buy you out. Perhaps if I lived in [such a set], I'd believe in happy endings, too.

Erika Munk, "Home Rule," in The Village Voice *(reprinted by permission of* The Village Voice; *copyright © The Village Voice, Inc., 1978), Vol. XXIII, No. 20, May 15, 1978, p. 99.**

EDITH OLIVER

["Talley's Folly"] is set in a boathouse—very gingerbready in design—during an evening in 1944 when Sally Talley, aged thirty-one, a spinster with leftish leanings, is courted and won by Matt Friedman, aged forty-two, an accountant from St. Louis. . . . All the action is the difficult, ultimately successful attempt by each of them to pin the other down. Matt, teasing, devious, and jokey, eventually talks of his family's being on the run from country to country in Europe during his childhood, and Sally, proud and private, eventually tells of her engagement as a young girl to a local boy—an engagement that was terminated when she became ill with tuberculosis—and when they have finished we are aware that the reason that neither of them has married before is exactly the reason that they should marry now. (pp. 84, 86)

The ninety-four minutes [of the play] . . . are rather short on content, but Mr. Wilson has become so skillful a craftsman and writer that he can catch and hold an audience's attention. The playful mood that he establishes and its serious undertone are right, and the show is always at least diverting. (p. 86)

Edith Oliver, "At the Boathouse," in The New Yorker *(© 1979 by The New Yorker Magazine, Inc.), Vol. LV, No. 13, May 14, 1979, pp. 84, 86.**

JULIUS NOVICK

For years Mr. Wilson's work did not interest me much; *The Hot l Baltimore,* his big hit, struck me as rather tired in its conventionality. But with *5th of July* last year, . . . it seemed to me that Mr. Wilson was on to something: there was a new vividness, a new vigor. . . .

Mr. Wilson's new vigor, if not his new vividness, has ebbed noticeably in *Talley's Folly,* however, and the old sentimentality has resurged.

On this occasion Mr. Wilson is quite up front about being sentimental; in an opening monologue, Matt tells us that we are in for a "valentine," a "waltz." . . .

Matt is the Jewish stereotype in its most idealized form: warm, wise, witty, well-read, gentle, bespectacled and shaped by suffering. But I am here to tell you that there still are warm, wise, witty, well-read, gentle, bespectacled, Jewish men around, and even the suffering seems right for 1944. Matt is much *nicer* than any Jew that a Jewish writer would dream of creating, but, that granted, Mr. Wilson has written him impeccably. Not only are the cadences of Yiddish-inspired English rendered with authenticity and grace; the thinking and the experience behind them seem Jewish too. . . .

Sally also belongs to a type, somewhat less defined in her case: the young woman too spunky and intelligent for the mean-minded small town she lives in. . . .

Talley's Folly is funny and charming. . . . I don't even mind its sentimentality as such, much. Matt Friedman believes that people have "Humpty-Dumpty complexes": they think they're eggs, and are afraid to let other people get through their shells, and so lose out on life. A truth—and the play demonstrates, quite touchingly at moments, what good things can happen when people leave their Humpty-Dumpty complexes behind.

What got me down about *Talley's Folly* was the damned predictability and repetitiousness of it—not the inevitability of the happy ending, but the way nothing happens on the way to the happy ending that wasn't obviously going to happen.

Julius Novick, "Sentimental Journey," in The Village Voice *(copyright © 1979; reprinted by permission), Vol. XXIV, No. 19, May 14, 1979, p. 95.**

JOHN SIMON

[*Talley's Folly*] is a duologue between Matt and Sally, from sundown through moonrise and thence to the start of three decades of married happiness. . . . Matt and Sally can play out their duet of pursuit and evasion, hopefulness and disillusion, until revelations of their pasts to each other bring better understanding, absolution through mutual compassion, and final tremulous affirmation of love. It is a curious love that slowly emerges from a protective husk of banter, teasing, even pugnacity. Once out, however, it can match the moon in its zenith—hold its own even under the coming scrutiny of long sunlight.

Gradually, with the double assurance of a master of psychology and dramaturgy, Wilson unfolds not so much a series of events as a conversation that will last two joint lifetimes. . . . Wilson has written some of the most tender, wisely funny, chargedly understated dialogue I have heard from a stage in many a moon, dialogue fraught with the essence of the greatest drama on earth: that of two pitiful yet glorious human beings clumsily and splendidly staggering toward each other.

It is dialogue that, like most exalted stage dialogue, skirts the ridiculous only to stumble triumphantly onto the sublime. Says Matt: "We are so much alike to be so different, aren't we?" It sounds almost like nonsense, yet its seeming awkwardness stems only from its pressing through to the limits of the articulable; it is about that strange paradox that can make two people with identical needs and yearnings the most skittishly skirmishing antagonists. After explaining his undue tarrying by the emptiness of his car's gas tank, Matt finally confesses: "The car isn't out of gas." "What is it out of?" "Hope. The car is out of hope." The statement neither anthropomorphizes a machine nor reifies the human beings implied by the image; it simply suggests that the whole world, from a dumb engine to an overcomplicated psyche, requires the same spiritual essence to move forward. . . .

Lanford Wilson understands the interplay of the absurd and the miraculous—indeed, their very identity—and how it sustains life. (p. 76)

Wilson is the only American playwright I can think of who is steadily growing, improving, paring himself down to essentials. *Talley's Folly* is—in range, mood, scope—a minor work, although a broad social background is suggestively sketched in; but the fineness of its details makes up in penetrancy and pervasiveness for what it may lack in weight and impact. Its small, insistent truths, like sand in a beach house, seep into every cranny of our awareness. (pp. 76-7)

John Simon, "Folie a deux," in New York *Magazine (copyright © 1979 by News Group Publications, Inc.; reprinted with the permission of* New York *Magazine), Vol. 12, No. 21, May 21, 1979, pp. 76-8.**

HAROLD CLURMAN

Years ago . . . *Talley's Folly* . . . would not have been considered a play. . . . The piece contains almost no plot in the ordinary sense of that term. Nevertheless, we are charmed. . . .

Talley's Folly is sustained by the engaging humor of its writing. . . . [Wilson] is a prolific playwright and his plays . . . vary in large degree in form and content. But their keynote is a tenderness subdued and masked by quizzical objectivity. Wilson harbors a special sympathy for oddballs of every sort, but this is usually held in check in an effort to avoid outright sentimentality.

Harold Clurman, "Theater: 'Talley's Folly'," in The Nation *(copyright 1979 by the Nation Associates, Inc.), Vol. 228, No. 20, May 26, 1979, p. 609.*

STANLEY KAUFFMANN

[*Talley's Folly*] is another piece of Lanford Wilson's front-porch knitting about the South Central states, full of the click-clack of theatrical needles that obviously brings joy to critical hearts nostalgic for old fashions. The play is a two character hokum-jokum—a self-styled "waltz." . . . The way in which the man of the pair addresses the audience at the beginning and end; the ungainliness and self-doubt of the woman; the loneliness of two wounded people; the seedy elegance of the setting; the inclusion of inserted jokes —these are all Tennessee Williams derivatives. The difference from the best Williams is that no authentic mood or character or feeling is ever generated, just a series of facsimiles that lead to revelations whose only point is to justify the series of facsimiles that led to these revelations whose only point etc. . . .

[The] glibly summoned nostalgia, the distant band music, the southern summer evenings, are just further deployments of familiar theatrical devices.

Yet the huzzahs range across the (alleged) spectrum of critics. And intelligent "civilians"—people not specifically engaged in the theater—go to *Talley's Folly*, and other plays that could be cited, then leave with their heads shaking: in wonderment at the praise and in despair about going back to the theater.

Stanley Kauffmann, "Stages of Discussion" (© 1979 The New Republic, Inc.; reprinted by permission of Brandt & Brandt Literary Agents, Inc.), in The New Republic, *Vol. 180. No. 23, June 9, 1979, p. 24.*

* * *

WOLF, Christa 1929-

Wolf is an East German novelist, short story writer, and essayist. Realistic and often autobiographical, her work reflects the political pressures and turbulence she has witnessed in her country. Because of its inherent criticism and analysis, some of her fiction has suffered censorship from the East German government. (See also *Contemporary Authors*, Vols. 85-88.)

JACK D. ZIPES

The theme of alienation in contemporary East German novels is most pronounced in Christa Wolf's *The Quest for Christa T.* Here, a young woman, as narrator, tries to piece together the life of her friend Christa T., who died of leukemia at the age of thirty-five. (p. 13)

In outline form, the story seems trivial. There is nothing outstanding or remarkable about Christa T. But, that is exactly the point. Christa Wolf writes about an average woman in East Germany, and she wants to understand why this woman is "drained" of her exuberance for life. In this respect, a disease, leukemia, is used metaphorically, as Solzhenitsyn uses it in *Cancer Ward:* Christa T. is suffering from a social sickness, which emanates from pathological conditions in her society. The narrator of the story feels compelled to analyze this sickness because she, too, may become "infected," and hence, seeks a cure.

As in Kant's *Die Aula*, there is a dialectical relationship established between the narrator and her material. The past life and development of Christa T. are critically examined in the present so that the future may be changed. Using notes and diaries bequeathed her by Christa T., the narrator reconstructs the picture of a woman who had great hopes about contributing as a teacher to socialist development in the German Democratic Republic. However, these hopes were dampened by the hypocrisy and rigidity of petty bureaucrats. As a woman, she felt manipulated, and the result is that Christa T. withdrew into herself, reluctantly, in order to escape being reified by the social system. However, Christa T. never gives up hope for the socialist revolution, as one of her last dreams reveals. She is only overcome by the "disease," and the cure for this disease is partially suggested in the telling of Christa's story. . . . (pp. 13-14)

[It] becomes clear that the narrator has written about Christa's growing alienation in order to question the conditions which led to her withdrawal and death. This life of an average young woman in East Germany must be made known *now*, because the narrator, as a woman and citizen of the German Democratic Republic, shares the alienation of Christa T. and conveys it continually in her narrative. In this respect the narrative is more of a struggle than a quest, a struggle against the insidious disease which cuts man off from both himself and the rest of mankind. (p. 14)

Jack D. Zipes, "Growing Pains in the Contemporary German Novel–East and West," in MOSAIC: A Journal for the Comparative Study of Literature and Ideas *(copyright © 1972 by the University of Manitoba Press; acknowledgment of previous publication is herewith made), Vol. 5, No. 3 (Spring, 1972), pp. 1-17.**

ERNESTINE SCHLANT

[*Moskauer Novelle*] is constructed around the pattern: German woman falls in love with Russian man, yet both renounce this love. In this first publication, Christa Wolf has already found the theme that will occupy her exclusively: human, personal relations in juxtaposition to the demands of a socialist society. *Der geteilte Himmel* repeats this theme, this time applied to the two Germanies. The novel centers on the separation of Rita, who remains in the East, from her boy friend Manfred, who leaves for the West. After a break-down, Rita relives in the hospital her time with Manfred, their discussions, their decisions. Convalescence indicates not just a physical recovery but a spiritual process, an affirmation of life in the GDR. Christa Wolf tries to show how such a decision is not motivated by considerations of imperialism and capitalism versus communism, but that it is first and foremost a profoundly human decision that involves two individuals. East German critics immediately attacked the novel for insufficient ideological conviction and decadent subjectivism and found much fault with the fact that Manfred, the intellectual, leaves East Germany while Rita makes her decision on the basis of feelings and cannot even give ideologically convincing reasons for her actions. Reviews of this novel in East and West Germany may again serve as yardsticks for the entirely different points of view on either side of the "divided skies." While East German critics objected to the personal and subjectivist position of the author and the lack of ideological conviction, their West German colleagues, before turning to the novel itself, attacked East German criticism for dealing with the novel as if it were an essay, a report, or any other written statement whose sole significance lies in the ideological content and not in any artistic achievement. Then they proceeded to decimate the novel as a literary work. (p. 151)

[In] 1969, Christa Wolf presented her next book, *Nachdenken über Christa T.*, which was immediately hailed by critics in West Germany as one of the most significant novels written in East Germany, whereas East German reviews were variously negative. The novel reconstructs (through diaries, literary sketches, unfinished letters, which were handed over to a former friend of Christa T.) the life and death of a "stranger," a young woman, wife, and mother who alienates herself from society, rejects the new world of those who no longer have any imagination, any depth, who are routine people. Yet, in the death of Christa T., Christa Wolf also criticizes those who cannot adjust to the new society. Life, the future, and progress belong to those who affirm the reality in which they live and to which they contribute.

GDR-reality intrudes into this novel only to the extent to which Christa T. must live with it—and she barely takes notice of it. The wide panorama of the novels of socialist realism is abandoned. (pp. 151-52)

Ernestine Schlant, "Fiction in the German Democratic Republic during the Past," in Modern Fiction Studies *(© copyright 1975 by Purdue Research Foundation, West Lafayette, Indiana), Vol. 21, No. 2, Summer, 1975, pp. 139-55.**

W. V. BLOMSTER

The reconstruction of developmental years lived in the arena dominated by National Socialism once again proves itself a valid literary undertaking. The success of Wolf's [*Kindheitsmuster*] . . . affirms the durability of this thematic material.

The narrative-time structure of this work . . . is as complex as it is successful. The focal point is a two-day visit by narrator and family to the small town of her birth—now in Poland—in July 1971. This brief span of hours retrospectively becomes the threshold from which the narrator reenters her early life at that point in 1932 when, at the age of three, she consciously used the word "I" for the first time. . . . [The] growth of the narrative is painstakingly dated through contrapuntal references to events in Vietnam and Chile and to such dissimilar persons as General Pinochet and Daniel Ellsberg. The account gains further tension through a fourth time dimension, centered upon the narrator's teen-age daughter, in whose eyes are reflected events of which she has no direct experience.

This careful study of the past results in a panorama of historical universality; the review of these events from an adult perspective places central emphasis upon the nature and function of the individual within this context. The major question, "How did we become what we are?" is confronted by the disturbing inquiry: "Can every human being be turned into a beast?"

The overall success of the work lies in Wolf's fresh view upon the crisis of expression. She assumes that, in an ideal case, total correspondence between the structures of experience and those of narration would be possible; this would permit the "precision of imagination" which she seeks. Such a technique, she concludes, cannot exist, for life is a dynamic process which continues beyond and thus invalidates even the most sophisticated narrative structure. Faced by this dilemma, only two choices seem indicated: "To remain speechless or to live in the third person." In her quest for expression, however, Wolf finds a third possibility in a variation upon the Wittgensteinian theme: "About that of which one cannot speak, one must gradually cease being silent." Resignation before this task is not permissible: "We shall never succeed in explaining why things have gone the way they have and not differently; nonetheless, we must not hesitate to undertake at least the preliminaries for future explanations." The writer, through the exercise of "moral memory," mediates between past and present.

Only a hint of the grandiose dimensions of this work and the achievement involved can be given here. It is regrettable that Wolf has chosen to alloy such narrative gold with the propagandistic dross of repeated references to American political machinations. Unjust as the deeds mentioned may have been, the manner in which Wolf has employed them cheapens her work. On the other side of the coin, her mention of events in Czechoslovakia in 1968 is almost unrecognizable behind the melodramatic slag with which it is veiled. (pp. 611-12)

W. V. Blomster, "World Literature in Review: 'Kindheitsmuster'," in Books Abroad *(copyright 1977 by the University of Oklahoma Press), Vol. 51, No. 4, Autumn, 1977, pp. 611-12.*

B. M. KANE

Christa Wolf's latest work *Kindheitsmuster* (1976) is her first attempt to give a comprehensive account of the exceptional and traumatic social upheavals which accompanied the crucial formative years of her childhood. . . . For Christa Wolf who is anxious not merely to document and give shape to its influence on her own early years, but also to clarify the lingering, ill-defined effects on the present, there also arises the difficulty of narrative method. . . . The narrative structure devised for *Kindheitsmuster* offers a complex and ingenious answer to these problems. The novel moves over three different time spans. . . . Christa Wolf moves effortlessly back and forth between these different time levels, weaving them into a web of association and implication between past and present to produce a novel which is about memory, about journeys actual and metaphorical, about the tantalising pursuit of formative childhood experiences and the influences which have made her and her generation what they are. (pp. 19-20)

For Christa Wolf . . . the true feel and significance of the years spent under National Socialism cannot be rendered through the organisation of factual historical detail about the period. . . . Christa Wolf sees the task . . . of the literary imagination not only to speculate about the range of emotions which lay beneath the surface appearance [of socio-political events] but, more importantly, to cancel the treacheries of memory and to correct the falsification of the image of the childhood self which comes as a natural part of growing up. . . . (pp. 20-1)

It is an integral part of this process and of the technique of the novel that the act of sifting and reflecting upon the past is never hidden from the reader. Sharing, as it were, the exasperation at coffee stains on the finished manuscript, the act of writing is constantly before us. We participate in the circumstances which accompany Christa Wolf as she writes; the effect on her of current political events, or the response to public readings of completed chapters are all incorporated into the progressing work. This makes *Kindheitsmuster* a radically different proposition from other meticulously researched and lightly fictionalised Nazi childhoods. (p. 21)

To single out isolated aspects of the novel . . . is to give only a partial impression of a scope and complexity which have their source in the juxtaposition of marvellously authentic images of the past with the reflectiveness of a fertile intelligence which is able to expand those images into new and often sombre contexts. One graphic instance of this is provided by the passages dealing with Nelly's confrontation, as her family treks westwards before the advancing Russian armies, with the human legacy of the concentration camps. This episode sparks observations on the psychological consequences of the survival syndrome. . . .

It is excursions such as this, and the ability to focus on the lingering implications for the present of Germany's recent past which produces the dense and challenging text of *Kindheitsmuster,* one of the most accomplished pieces of fiction to emerge from Germany—West or East—in recent years. (pp. 22-3)

B. M. Kane, "In Search of the Past: Christa Wolf's 'Kindheitsmuster'," in Modern Languages, *Vol. LIX, No. 1, March, 1978, pp. 19-23.*

PETER GRAVES

It is no coincidence that the contemporary German novelists most readily associated with the theme of war-guilt are all from West Germany. . . .

The literature of East Germany [has focused] . . . overwhelmingly on the present and future, the building-up of socialism and the bright hope it represents. . . .

It is against this background that the measure of Christa Wolf's achievement in her new work, *Kindheitsmuster,* must be judged. "What is past is not dead", she begins provocatively, "It is not even past. We separate ourselves from it and pretend to be strangers." The past that she then proceeds to evoke is her own, those years from 1932 to 1946 when, between the ages of three and seventeen, the "patterns of childhood" to which the title refers were formed. . . .

[The narrative of the fictional-autobiographical family], however, occupies barely half of the book, for parallel with it runs an account of a two-day visit in July 1971, by Christa Wolf, her husband, her brother, and Lenka, her fourteen-year-old daughter, back to Landsberg, which now lies in Poland and is called Gorzów Wielkopolski. But this is no sentimental journey: it is a reckoning with a past that still haunts and, with the presence of Lenka, an attempt to explain to a contemporary teenager how these things could have happened. The confrontation of two epochs in the form of mother and daughter is one of the book's greatest strengths. Not only does it demonstrate the organic and emotional ties that link past and present, but it also shows the delusion of putting a neat full-stop after 1945 in the fond hope that the blame and all the emotional repercussions could be channelled conveniently westwards. *Kindheitsmuster* is a plea to remember and learn from the past and at the same time an appeal for vigilance and sensitivity in the present.

But there is more, for on top of this dual perspective we are also given a detailed and soul-searching account of the actual process of writing, with interwoven reflections on the problems of narrative form. . . .

Thus we have a running commentary on the genesis and progress of the book, with disquisitions on the technical problems and the writer's own misgivings before the task she has set herself. All very interesting, painstakingly honest even, but it becomes a little wearisome that the reader should constantly have his own judgment preempted and that Christa Wolf should seek so persistently to undermine her own achievement. Her writing is sufficiently powerful to be allowed to speak for itself, and although a certain amount of formal scaffolding can be illuminating, here it sometimes runs the risk of obscuring the edifice within.

However, the continual shifting between levels of narration is in fact handled very smoothly, and, despite its excess baggage, *Kindheitsmuster* . . . never completely loses its momentum. It is a courageous book that breaks taboos and, as we have come to expect from Christa Wolf, it is infused with an integrity and a deep moral concern that raise it far above the narrow and selfconscious partisanship of much GDR literature. It speaks equally to East and West Germany—itself a daring accomplishment for an East German author—but also, with its atmospheric depiction of a fateful era and its patent and compelling truthfulness, to wider audiences beyond.

Peter Graves, "Reckoning with the Past," in The Times Literary Supplement *(© Times Newspapers Ltd. (London) 1978; reproduced from* The Times Literary Supplement *by permission), No. 3966, April 7, 1978, p. 396.*

* * *

WRIGHT, Richard 1908-1960

An American short story writer and novelist, Wright was praised for his early realistic portraits of the experiences, fears, and frustrations of southern blacks. Wright was a spokesman for black rights and beliefs, and his early work depicts a southern society that exhibits few outside influences. His later work, of which *Native Son* is an example, shows both broader scope and the author's philosophical movement from political naiveté to Marxist belief, and finally to an anti-Marxist attitude. (See also *CLC,* Vols. 1, 3, 4, 9.)

JUNE JORDAN

Richard Wright was a Black man born on a white, Mississippi plantation, and carried, by fits and starts, from one white, southern town to the next. In short, he was born into the antagonistic context of hostile whites wielding power against him. In this, his background mirrors our majority Black experience. And so, we readily accept the validity of *Native Son*/Bigger Thomas, who pits himself against overwhelming, white force. Moreover, *Native Son* (undoubtedly Wright's most influential book) conforms to white standards we have swallowed regarding literary weight: It is apparently symbolic (rather than realistic), "serious" (unrelievedly grim), socio-political (rather than "personal") in its scale, and not so much "emotional" as impassioned in its deliberate execution.

Given the antagonistic premise of *Native Son*/the personal beginnings of Richard Wright, a Black man on enemy turf, it follows that his novel should pull you forward with its furious imagination, saturate the reader with varieties of hatred, deal horror, climax in violence, and ram hard—ram hard—against a destiny of doom. But suppose the premise is a different one? (pp. 5-6)

June Jordan, "On Richard Wright and Zora Neale Hurston: Notes toward a Balancing of Love and Hatred" (copyright © 1974 June Jordan), in Black World, *Vol. XXIII, No. 10, August, 1974, pp. 4-8.**

WILLIAM PEDEN

Wright's stories of helpless or long-suffering Blacks victimized by societal and individual White brutality mark the beginning of a new era in Black fiction and even his least important pieces contain unforgettable scenes and characters that burn their way into the reader's consciousness; characteristic is the savage sequence of events of "Big Boy Leaves Home," climaxed by a lynching which leaves the protagonist completely lost, alienated from life, a victim of meaningless and unjustified racial hatred and bigotry. But for all his talent, Wright's people—misunderstood, exploited, vilely misused by Whites—tend to be almost as one-dimensional as many of the stereotypes of the proletarian short fiction of the thirties. As a sad and moving testimonial to the evil of racism and its effect upon a gifted and bitterly disillusioned human being, *Uncle Tom's Children* and *Eight Men* constitute a disturbing and towering and permanent landmark in the literary history of Black-White relations, and their influence upon the younger generation of Black writers was and continues to be profound. (pp. 233-34)

William Peden, "The Black Explosion," in Studies in Short Fiction *(copyright 1975 by Newberry College), Vol. XII, No. 3, Summer, 1975, pp. 231-41.**

ROBERT F. MOSS

With the rise of black studies programs throughout the country, an omnibus collection of Wright's work was inevitable. The author's widow, Ellen Wright, and Michel Fabre . . . have assembled a broad sampling of Wright's work. . . . Although the [*Richard Wright Reader*] is weighted toward Wright's fiction, there are representative selections from his correspondence, his poetry, his political and literary essays, and his travel writing. (p. 46)

Surveying its scope, we see that a man's past is never really dead. For Wright, the formative experiences were his mother's religious fanaticism (she was a Seventh-day Adventist), with its crippling repressions and proscriptions, and the virulent racism that confronted him at nearly every stage of his determined search for self-realization. Brutalized and misunderstood by both his family and his society, Wright developed personal characteristics that were reflected in most of his writing: rebelliousness, introversion, a quest for selfhood, a longing for stable and meaningful values, an appetite for violence.

The editors lead off with a segment from *Black Boy* that depicts Wright's adolescent struggle to educate himself beyond his station with forbidden library books. . . . He had already outgrown the one-dimensional identity whites had designed for him and was learning to hate instead of fear them. "It was probably a mere accident that I never killed," he comments offhandedly. It is no surprise, then, to move on to Wright's short journalistic piece, "Joe Louis Uncovers Dynamite," one of the author's earliest publications, and find Wright exulting over Louis's defeat of Max Baer in their 1935 bout. Racial antagonism and violence come together again in "Long Black Song" and "Fire and Cloud," a couple of rather crude stories from *Uncle Tom's Children*. These two strains culminate in *Native Son*, in which Wright's account of the black American's caged misery is so convincing that we accept murder as an understandable (if not excusable) response.

Freedom, an especially sacred word in the black vocabulary, meant more than just political liberty to Wright. The search for an authentic self consumed the novelist from one end of his career to the other as he shed successive identities supplied by his religion-obsessed mother, by the southern bigots he fled, and by the northern Communists he joined. But *The Outsider* shows that Wright, for all his intelligence and willpower, could not remake himself. The existentialism he embraced so fervently was only another religion, replacing both Christianity and communism, whereas the novel's spiritual thrashings, rhetorical afflatus, and relentless pedantry are more reminiscent of the tabernacle than of the French cafés Wright frequented at that time.

Many of these same conclusions can be drawn from *American Hunger*, a slender, autobiographical work that was detached from the original manuscript of *Black Boy* and that has now been published in its entirety for the first time. Here, writing of Chicago in the 1930s, Wright is at his naturalistic best. He offers spare and telling sketches of racial abuse and condescension, of working conditions at the time, of poisonous factionalism and ideological rigidity among the Communists, of his groping emergence as an artist. Like all of Wright's memorable work, it makes creative use of his past rather than turning away from it in self-defeating gestures of renunciation. As in *Native Son* and *Black Boy*, he brings an unusual combination of intelligence and candor to the subject of race relations and teaches blacks what to be proud of in their heritage—and whites what to be ashamed of in theirs. (pp. 46-7)

Robert F. Moss, "Caged Misery," in Saturday Review *(© 1978 by Saturday Review Magazine Corp.; reprinted with permission), Vol. 5, No. 8, January 21, 1978, pp. 45-7.*

JOHN WIDEMAN

The principal value of any reader is that it can present in a single volume a broad sampling of a master's work. The publication of the "Richard Wright Reader" is to be applauded on this account, because the range of subject matter and technique Mr. Wright commanded have been lost to the audience that knows him only as the "angry" author of "Native Son" and "Black Boy." Without disparaging either novel, one can acknowledge that they offer a limited portrait of the artist at a distinct time and place in his career; the selections in this book remind us that Mr. Wright's career spanned 22 productive years.

It is not difficult to find reasons for the fascination Mr. Wright's life and work continue to have for black writers. As Mr. Fabre [the co-editor] often indicates in his notes, Mr. Wright was a conscious artist, a writer who learned from his reading of other masters, who employed inventive literary techniques to dramatize his knowledge of black language and culture. The pattern of Mr. Wright's early life mirrored the mass migration of blacks from South to North, from rural areas to the cities, from communal folk life to urban alienation. In "Black Boy," "Lawd Today" and "Native Son" the promise and bitter disappointment of these historic movements are captured. Mr. Wright's later years reflect the intellectual odyssey of black people in the second half of the 20th century. He examined the legacy of the African past; he documented the rise of the emerging nations and analyzed the political consequences of this redistribution of power for all oppressed people. Although Mr. Wright temporarily embraced various *isms*—communism, black nationalism, existentialism—he regarded each system as valid only so long as it freed him to grapple on his own terms with the vast, unclassifiable welter of experience. Always at the center of Mr. Wright's work is his insistence on the sanctity of the individual imagination, but this insistence is tempered by his vision of black people's collective destiny. In "Blueprint for Negro Writing" he has left us his example, his challenge: "The Negro writer . . . has a serious responsibility. In order to do justice to his subject matter, in order to depict Negro life in all of its manifold and intricate relationships, a deep, informed, and complex consciousness is necessary: a consciousness which draws for its strength upon the fluid lore of a great people, and molds this lore with the concepts that move and direct the forces of history today." (p. 32)

John Wideman, "Native Son," in The New York Times Book Review *(© 1978 by The New York Times Company; reprinted by permission), March 5, 1978, pp. 11, 32.*

EVELYN GROSS AVERY

Uncle Tom and Sambo have disappeared from contemporary black literature. The black rebel, driven to assert himself, often violently, has replaced the acquiescent victim. . . . The writer most frequently credited with making the Negro "visible" is Richard Wright. . . . Offering historical and sociological, as well as psychological insights into the American character, Wright examines the rebel, his behavior and motivations, his background. Products of a lower-class black environment, Wright's rebels are well acquainted with hunger, disease, poverty. They learn quickly from frightened mothers and beaten fathers not to expect much from America. Their dreams of power are undercut by the reality of Jim Crow and more subtle discrimination. Ambition is discouraged; impotency reinforced. All entrances and exits are blocked. Trapped, Wright's black man may choose to suffer his fate passively; he may reluctantly accept his status as a victim. But not for long. Wright's victims are generally minor characters or else they evolve into sullen rebels. (pp. 4-5)

Wright's rebels [are] lonely, alienated individuals [who] seek affirmation in action. Passion, impulsiveness, and often violence characterize many of Wright's protagonists. Most are nonreflective and unable to articulate their agony. Driven by explosive emotions, they seek escape in alcohol, sex, and brutal encounters. Some leave the repressive South for the "promised land." Movement from town to city, job to job is common. Family and friends disperse; new alliances are formed but inevitably nothing changes. Disenchantment grows, finally erupting in violence. Meaning is found not in the past, but in the present. The rebel's identity depends on action. . . . Wright's rebels feel most exhilarated, most alive when they have taken life. (p. 6)

Wright's strongest fiction, written before he left the United States, deals with the problems of lower class Southern and Northern Negroes. (p. 7)

For most of Wright's protagonists the only alternative is violent rebellion if they are to replace self-contempt with self-respect. Persecuted for years, they become powder kegs of rage waiting to be ignited. The pattern is established in *Uncle Tom's Children,* Southern tales depicting the development of Negro victim into black rebel. The seeds of Northern defiance are planted in the South where a gentle minister helplessly watches his congregation starve; a Negro woman is beaten while trying to protect her son; a hard working farmer discovers that his wife is "fair game" for whites; and a Negro youth witnesses his friends' brutal murder and mutilation. Two of the stories—"Fire and Cloud" and "Bright and Morning Star"—written during Wright's communist period, suggest radical political action as a possible solution for the Negro's troubles, but they are not representative of the collection, which pits individual blacks against villainous whites. (p. 18)

Native Son serves as Wright's warning to white America to recognize her invisible sons before they ruthlessly judge and condemn their country. With nothing to live for, his characters are willing to die for freedom. The more intelligent and sensitive they are, the more they threaten society, as Cross Damon proves when a sense of powerlessness drives him to play God in *The Outsider.* Despite Wright's insistence that race is only incidental to the novel, evidence indicates otherwise. "Damon's crimes were part and parcel of the everyday life of man, most particularly Black men." What distinguishes Damon from Wright's other black rebels is his philosophical temperament, his tendency to analyze his actions. In other respects he fits the tradition of Wright's persecuted protagonists. Though well educated, he is frustrated and . . . locked into a monotonous, demeaning post office job and an unhappy marriage. . . . Although he lies and kills, he is able to deceive the Communists and Eva, his white girlfriend, by acting naive and innocent. In fact, the whole novel focuses on his role playing, his attempt to take advantage of a train wreck and assume a new identity in New York. But Cross can no more change his behavior and escape his problem than Bigger can.

Intended as an existential hero of any race, he is really a "vicious, angry . . . intellectual version of [the primitive] Bigger Thomas." Both manipulate people in order to feel powerful. (pp. 21-2)

Wright's black Christianity emphasizes humility, submission, and other worldliness—all of which consign Negroes to living deaths. In *Black Boy, Native Son,* and "The Man Who Lived Underground," autocratic churches, self-serving preachers, and hysterical congregations exude death and darkness. Protagonists like Bigger Thomas and Fred Daniels find little in religion to guide them and much to make them rebel. (p. 32)

In *Black Power* Wright examined Christianity's destructive impact on Africans and Afro-Americans. Both British imperialists and American slave masters, he believed, used the church to tame "the savages." Unknowingly missionaries contributed to white supremacy with unfortunate consequences for the blacks. Africans were treated as pagan children unable to govern themselves. Their traditions were labelled barbarous; their high priests and medicine men were stripped of authority, and the natives were made dependent on whites. Severe psychological problems developed. Like American Negroes, Africans "lived uneasily and frustratedly in two worlds . . . believing in neither of them." . . . (p. 33)

In the autobiographical *Black Boy,* the author identifies Negro religion with white repression. Both foster unwarranted shame and guilt. Church emphasis on original sin reinforces guilt about skin color. In both cases the Negro is marked from birth and made to feel guilty over that which he cannot control. Whites equate black with evil; the church stresses man's innate wickedness. Together they convince Negroes of their inferiority. Understandably, then, Wright depicts his grandmother as the most oppressive, powerful figure in the family. Nearly white and fanatically religious, she represents the conspiracy of white society and black church to restrain Negroes. Rigid, humorless, and harshly disciplinarian, Granny struggles to prove her purity, her whiteness by cleansing the sinners around her. . . . Cleanliness of soul, mind, and body are stressed constantly. But baths and prayers cannot change reality: Richard is black; his mother and brother are black; and Granny with her few drops of Negro blood is black. Ultimately they have to face the fact that white society and the black church make salvation possible only in the next life. Some, especially Wright's women, accept such precepts and redouble their efforts to gain entry into heaven. Others, particularly his young male protagonists, remain skeptical about a religion which values death more than life. They require answers but receive lectures or sermons. (p. 41)

[The] atmosphere in Wright's churches is claustrophobic and death-like. For Wright and other black writers most Negro churches were indifferent to life. In *Black Boy* "terrifyingly sweet hymns" . . . , joyous outbursts, and powerful sermons praise death which will free suffering Negroes from this world. The faithful will be rewarded in heaven, but darkness, fire, and brimstone await nonbelievers like Wright. (p. 47)

Clearly, Wright's myopic church . . . cannot guide the lost. Its promise of salvation is empty; its baptismal water is dirty, and incapable of purifying desperate black men. In fact, water, like fire, is used as a symbol of death by Wright. In one surrealistic scene [in *Eight Men*] Daniels, trying to cleanse himself physically and spiritually, imagines the faucet water turning into blood. In another scene he dreams of himself as Christ walking on water and attempting to save a drowning woman and baby. But Daniels (and by extension Christianity) fails: the sea turns rough, pulling all three into its swirling depths. The sequence foreshadows Daniels's actual death. Rejected by the church, he surrenders to the police who shoot him as he leads them to his hideaway. The last image is one of Daniels's swallowing "thick, bitter water" . . . which becomes his soggy grave. . . . [In *Native Son*] Bigger becomes the target of [police] hoses and is overwhelmed by rushing streams of freezing water. Later in prison, when he recalls the icy water, Bigger is visited by the Reverend Hammond who preaches to him about Christ's mercy and prays that the "Lawd [will] wash [his sins] as white snow." . . . The scene underscores the church's delusions, and the inappropriateness of white Christianity's symbols and rituals for suffering Negroes.

Understandably then, most of Wright's protagonists, like their author, reject the church. They are unable to reconcile Christ's saintly crucifix with the K.K.K.'s fiery cross. To embrace the former, as their submissive mothers do, may prolong their lives, but they rebel and are unwilling to pay the price—emasculation and death of the spirit. Like Wright, they "cannot feel weak and lost in a cosmic manner . . . [and they are revolted by how] His creatures serve Him." . . . Grovelling before whites is reprehensible but may be necessary; grovelling before God is contemptible. Furthermore, they cannot believe in their mothers' insatiable God who demands complete obedience and sacrifice of all earthly pleasures. Such a God, Wright believed, worsened the Negroes' plight, depriving them of dignity and initiative. (pp. 49-50)

In *Twelve Million Black Voices* Wright recorded the "complex movement of a debased feudal folk toward a twentieth century urbanization." . . . Described in *Black Boy* and several recent biographies, Wright's life reflects a migratory pattern which began in rural Mississippi and ended in cosmopolitan Paris. ba desire to escape persecution and humiliation caused him first to leave the South and later the nation. The decision was not easy, for it is apparent that he thought of himself as an American and also missed the South whose beauty and folk culture he describes in *Black Boy, Uncle Tom's Children,* and *The Long Dream*. . . . Although the "nightmarish landscape" haunts the author with its scenes of degradations, castrations, and lynchings, there is another attractive, almost seductive side to the South, a world of "morning dew . . . , wet, green garden paths . . . , dreamy Mississippi waters . . . , of wild geese and sugar cane," and hovering over all "the blood-red glare of the sun's afterglow." . . . It was the South's lushness which nurtured Wright and which he was forced to leave but never forgot, as his fiction repeatedly illustrates. (p. 79)

Some of Wright's southern folk endure in a way that his other characters do not. They are the real heroes of his fiction. In "The Man Who Saw The Flood" a black peasant family return to their water soaked land after a ravaging flood. A certain stoicism prevails as the family gives thanks that a few possessions [were spared]. . . . It is as if the people and the land are one in their determination to persevere, to recover, and sustain life. . . . Those who remain in the rural South sometimes perish, but their lives are marked by a courage and commitment which Wright's northern characters lack. (pp. 86-7)

As they leave their land, Wright's characters become corrupted. Thus, in *The Long Dream* Tyree Tucker enriches himself at the expense of poor blacks. Since the tale is set in the rural South, he attempts to fulfill his familial responsibility but he lacks the Old Testament dignity which Wright's peasants exhibit. As a member of the black bourgeoisie, he has lost touch with nature and his people. Instead of tilling the land, he exploits helpless Negroes and cooperates with crooked whites to maintain his power. But the latter betray him, and in the end he dies without dignity, like most of Wright's northern protagonists. (p. 87)

Professionally Wright . . . found himself dependent on Jewish liberals. . . . Jews offered money, personal and literary advice, protection against racism, and love, all of which Wright needed and appreciated. But such assistance also emphasized his helplessness and dependency.

Not surprisingly, Wright's ambivalence about Jews appears in his writing. . . . According to *Black Boy,* black anti-Semitism originated in the church and home. Parents "generally approved" of it; the fundamentalists encouraged it. "Antagonism towards Jews," Wright observed, "was bred in

[Negroes] from childhood; it was not merely racial prejudice, it was part of their cultural heritage." . . . Like Baldwin, Wright realized that Jews occupied a precarious position in America and therefore provided safe targets for Negro frustration. . . . Both Southern Negroes and Jews found it easier to turn on each other than on white Christians.

The complexity of Negro-Jewish relations increased as Wright travelled North. In the more subtly racist North blacks entered a "no man's land" in human relations, never knowing precisely what to expect from whites and especially from Jews. (pp. 95-7)

Wright's ambivalence towards Jews is developed most fully in *Native Son*. Bigger Thomas resents the Jews who own so many businesses in Chicago's Black Belt, but he values his Jewish lawyer's assistance. For the first time in his life, he meets a white who seems concerned about him. Yet the relationship also unsettles Bigger who becomes vulnerable after he learns to trust Max. Helpless, he "felt that he was sitting and holding his life . . . in his hands, waiting for Max to tell him what to do with it; and it made him hate himself." . . . By breaking down Bigger's defenses, his hatred of whites, by encouraging him to analyze racism and to communicate his feelings, Max acquires tremendous power over his black client. Not only is he responsible for his defense but for his soul as well. One wrong glance or word can shatter Bigger's confidence and faith. Unfortunately Max . . . cannot truly empathize with blacks. Culturally and morally on "another planet" . . . , he is horrified by Bigger's rationalization of murder. . . . [He] is blind to the black rebel's unique sensibility. (p. 98)

Evelyn Gross Avery, in her Rebels and Victims: The Fiction of Richard Wright and Bernard Malamud *(copyright © 1979 by Kennikat Press Corp.; reprinted by permission of Kennikat Press Corp.), Kennikat, 1979, 116 p.*

Appendix

THE EXCERPTS IN CLC, VOLUME 14 WERE REPRINTED FROM THE FOLLOWING PERIODICALS:

America
The American Book Review
American Indian Quarterly
The American Poetry Review
The American Scandinavian Review
The American Scholar
The Antioch Review
Ariel
Arizona Quarterly
The Armchair Detective
Arts Magazine
The Atlantic Monthly
The Bell
Best Sellers
Black Orpheus
Black World
Book Forum
Book Week—New York Herald Tribune
Book World—The Washington Post
Booklist
Books Abroad
Books and Art
Books and Bookmen
boundary 2
The Canadian Forum
Canadian Literature
The Carleton Miscellany
Chicago Review
The Chicago Sun-Times
Choice
The Christian Century
The Christian Science Monitor
College English
Commentary
Commonweal
Comparative Drama
Contemporary Literature
The Criterion
The Critic
Critical Quarterly
Critique: Studies in Modern Fiction
The Dalhousie Review
Drama
Éire-Ireland
Encounter
Esquire
Essays in Criticism
The Explicator
Extrapolation
Forum for Modern Language Studies
The French Review
The Georgia Review
German Life & Letters
Harper's
Hispanic Review
The Hollins Critic
The Hudson Review
Irish University Review: A Journal of Irish Studies
Italian Quarterly
Italica
Journal of American Studies
Journal of Canadian Fiction
Journal of Commonwealth Literature
The Journal of Irish Literature
The Journal of Narrative Technique
Journal of Popular Culture
Judaism
The Kenyon Review
Kirkus Reviews
Library Journal
The Listener
Literary Criterion
Literary Half-Yearly
Literature and Psychology
Literature East and West
London Magazine
Maclean's Magazine
The Magazine of Fantasy and Science Fiction
The Massachusetts Review
Michigan Quarterly Review
The Midwest Quarterly
The Minnesota Review
Modern Age
Modern Drama
Modern Fiction Studies
The Modern Language Review
Modern Languages
Modern Poetry Studies
Moons and Lion Tailes
MOSAIC: A Journal for the Comparative Study of Literature and Ideas
Mother Jones
Ms.
The Nation
National Review
The New England Quarterly
The New Leader
The New Republic
The New Review
New Statesman
New York Magazine
The New York Review of Books
The New York Times
The New York Times Book Review
The New Yorker
The Observer
The Ontario Review

THE EXCERPTS IN CLC, VOLUME 14, WERE REPRINTED FROM THE FOLLOWING BOOKS:

Adams, Robert Martin, AfterJoyce: Studies in Fiction After "Ulysses," *Oxford University Press, 1977.*

Armstrong, William A., ed., Experimental Drama, *Bell and Sons, 1963.*

Beck, Warren, Faulkner: Essays, *University of Wisconsin Press, 1976.*

Bigsby, C.W.E., Confrontation and Commitment: A Study of Contemporary American Drama, 1959-66, *University of Missouri Press, 1968.*

Braudy, Leo, ed., Norman Mailer: A Collection of Critical Essays, *Prentice-Hall, 1972.*

Brée, Germaine, ed., Camus: A Collection of Critical Essays, *Prentice-Hall, 1962.*

Brower, Reuben, Vendler, Helen, and Hollander, John, eds., I. A. Richards: Essays in His Honor, *Oxford University Press, 1973.*

Coles, Robert, Walker Percy: An American Search, *Atlantic-Little, Brown, 1978.*

Conron, Brandon, ed., Morley Callaghan, *McGraw-Hill Ryerson, 1975.*

Corrigan, Robert W., ed., The New Theatre of Europe, *Dell, 1962.*

Curtius, E. R., Essays on European Literature: Kritische Essays zur europäischen Literatur, *trans. by Michael Kowal, Princeton University Press, 1973.*

Debicki, Andrew P., Dámaso Alonso, *Twayne, 1970.*

Dickey, James, Babel to Byzantium, *Farrar, Straus, 1968.*

Dodsworth, Martin, ed., The Survival of Poetry: A Contemporary Survey, *Faber and Faber, 1970.*

Dudek, Louis, Selected Essays and Criticism, *Tecumseh Press, 1978.*

Dutton, Geoffrey, ed., The Literature of Australia, *Penguin Books, 1964.*

Falk, Doris V., Lillian Hellman, *Ungar, 1978.*

French, Warren, ed., The Fifties: Fiction, Poetry, Drama, *Everett/Edwards, 1970.*

Friedman, Melvin J., ed., Samuel Beckett Now, *University of Chicago Press, 1970.*

Ginsberg, Allen, Allen Verbatim: Lectures on Poetry, Politics, Consciousness, *ed. by Gordon Ball, McGraw-Hill, 1974.*

Gossett, Louise Y., Violence in Recent Southern Fiction, *Duke University Press, 1965.*

Gray, Richard, The Literature of Memory: Modern Writers of the American South, *Johns Hopkins University Press, 1977.*

Grossvogel, David I., Four Playwrights and a Postscript, *Cornell University Press, 1962.*

Heilburn, Carolyn G., Christopher Isherwood, *Columbia University Press, 1970.*

Kerr, Elizabeth M., William Faulkner's Gothic Domain, *Kennikat Press, 1979.*

Kimball, Arthur G., Crisis in Identity and Contemporary Japanese Novels, *Charles E. Tuttle, 1973.*

Knight, Damon, In Search of Wonder: Essays on Modern Science Fiction, ***revised edition, Advent, 1967.***

Laurence, Margaret, Long Drums and Cannons: Nigerian Dramatists and Novelists, *Frederick A. Praeger, 1969.*

Lazere, Donald, The Unique Creation of Albert Camus, *Yale University Press, 1973.*

Le Master, J. R. and Clarke, Mary Washington, eds., Jesse Stuart: Essays on His Work, *University Press of Kentucky, 1977.*

Levertov, Denise, The Poet in the World, *New Directions, 1973.*

Madden, David, ed., Proletarian Writers of the Thirties, *Southern Illinois University Press, 1968.*

Mathews, Richard, Aldiss Unbound: The Science Fiction of Brian W. Aldiss, *Borgo Press, 1977.*

Matthews, James H., Frank O'Connor, *Bucknell University Press, 1976.*

McCormick, E. H., New Zealand Literature: A Survey, *Oxford University Press, 1959.*

Magill, Frank N., ed., The Contemporary Literary Scene 1973, *Salem Press, 1974.*

New, William H., ed., Dramatists in Canada: Selected Essays, *University of British Columbia Press, 1972.*

Nott, Kathleen, The Emperor's Clothes, *William Heinemann, 1953.*

Oberg, Arthur, Modern American Lyric: Lowell, Berryman, Creeley, and Plath, *Rutgers University Press, 1978.*

Olander, Joseph D. and Greenberg, Martin Harry, eds., Robert A. Heinlein, *Taplinger, 1978.*

Pronko, Leonard Cabell, Theater East and West: Perspectives toward a Total Theater, *University of California Press, 1967.*

Sartre, Jean-Paul, Literary and Philosophical Essays of Jean-Paul Sartre, *trans. by Annette Michelson, Criterion Books, 1955.*

Sheehy, Maurice, ed., Michael/Frank: Studies on Frank O'Connor, *Knopf, 1969.*

Spencer, Sharon, Collage of Dreams: The Writings of Anaïs Nin, *Swallow, 1977.*

Symons, Julian, Mortal Consequences: A History—From the Detective Story to the Crime Novel, *Harper, 1972.*

Taylor, John Russell, Anger and After: A Guide to the New British Drama, *Methuen, 1962.*

Taylor, John Russell, Peter Shaffer, *British Council, 1974.*

Thomson, A. K., ed., Critical Essays on Kenneth Slessor, *Jacaranda Press, 1968.*

Vidal, Gore, Matters of Fact and of Fiction: Essays 1973-1976, *Random House, 1977.*

Warren, Robert Penn, Selected Essays of Robert Penn Warren, *Random House, 1958.*

Wolfe, Peter, Dreamers Who Live Their Dreams: The World of Ross Macdonald's Novels, *Popular Press, 1976.*

Wright, Judith, Preoccupations in Australian Poetry, *Oxford University Press, 1965.*

Cumulative Index to Critics

CRITIC INDEX

CRITIC INDEX

CRITIC INDEX

CRITIC INDEX

CRITIC INDEX

CRITIC INDEX

CRITIC INDEX

CRITIC INDEX

CRITIC INDEX

CRITIC INDEX

CRITIC INDEX

CRITIC INDEX

CRITIC INDEX

CRITIC INDEX

CRITIC INDEX

CRITIC INDEX

CRITIC INDEX

CRITIC INDEX

CRITIC INDEX

CRITIC INDEX

CRITIC INDEX

CRITIC INDEX

CRITIC INDEX

CRITIC INDEX

CRITIC INDEX

CRITIC INDEX

CRITIC INDEX

CRITIC INDEX

CRITIC INDEX

CRITIC INDEX

CRITIC INDEX

CRITIC INDEX

CRITIC INDEX

CRITIC INDEX

CRITIC INDEX

CRITIC INDEX

CRITIC INDEX

CRITIC INDEX

CRITIC INDEX

CRITIC INDEX

CRITIC INDEX

CRITIC INDEX

CRITIC INDEX

CRITIC INDEX

CRITIC INDEX

CRITIC INDEX

CRITIC INDEX

CRITIC INDEX

CRITIC INDEX

CRITIC INDEX

Cumulative Index to Authors

AUTHOR INDEX

AUTHOR INDEX

AUTHOR INDEX

AUTHOR INDEX